Pas d'armes and Late Medieval Chivalry

A Casebook

THE LIVERPOOL HISTORICAL CASEBOOKS SERIES

Series Editors: Kelly DeVries and Michael Livingston

Pas d'armes and Late Medieval Chivalry

A Casebook

edited by
Rosalind Brown-Grant
and
Mario Damen

LIVERPOOL UNIVERSITY PRESS

First published in 2025 by
Liverpool University Press
4 Cambridge Street
Liverpool
L69 7ZU

British Library Cataloguing-in-Publication data
A British Library CIP record is available

ISBN 978-1-83553-766-4

Typeset by Carnegie Book Production, Lancaster
Printed and bound by TJ International Ltd, Padstow, Cornwall, PL28 8RW

Contents

Part II: Essays

Foreword and Acknowledgements

This Casebook on *pas d'armes* is the fruit of an international, interdisciplinary research network funded by the UK's Arts and Humanities Research Council (AHRC) and entitled 'The Joust as Performance: *Pas d'armes* and Late Medieval Chivalry'. Led by Rosalind Brown-Grant (University of Leeds) and Mario Damen (University of Amsterdam) and comprising fifteen art historians, historians, literary scholars and material culture scholars, the network ran from 1 October 2020 to 30 September 2023. During the first eighteen months of the project, which were impacted by the COVID-19 pandemic, the group held a series of nine online workshops at which it discussed methodology, analysed selected primary sources and planned public engagement activities (principally, a virtual exhibition and an online talk at the Royal Armouries Museum in Leeds). It also discussed research papers presented by its members at a three-day conference held in Leeds in early July 2022, followed by a Round Table at the International Medieval Congress that showcased the network's various research and public engagement outputs.

In addition to consulting the Sources, Essays and other research tools provided in the Casebook itself, scholars interested in *pas d'armes* are invited to avail themselves of the online resources that have also resulted from the group's work. With the exception of some extra translations (termed 'Supplementary Sources') of narrative accounts that could not be fitted into the Casebook, and which can be found at Liverpool University Press Digital Collaboration Hub (https://liverpooluniversitypress.manifoldapp.org/projects/pas-d-armes-casebook), these are all hosted on the network website (www.pasdarmes.org) and are aimed at both specialist and non-specialist audiences. For the specialist, the website features an innovative relational database containing details of the settings, weapons and personnel involved in all the *pas d'armes* that were organised *c.*1420–*c.*1520. For the non-specialist, the website provides a brief overview of these chivalric events and a virtual exhibition fully illustrated with images from manuscript accounts of *pas d'armes* and other texts, as well as photographs of arms and armour of the period that are held in museum collections in the UK. This exhibition explains the full life-cycle of a *pas d'armes*: what had to be organised prior to one of these tournaments, what then took place at it and how it was commemorated thereafter.

The network's primary debt of gratitude is to the AHRC for funding the project. It is equally indebted to a number of other institutions for their help and support: the School of Languages, Cultures and Societies (University of Leeds), Drury University, Northwestern University and the University of Neuchâtel for their financial assistance towards the costs of making the Casebook available via Open Access; the Fondation pour la Protection du Patrimoine Culturel, Historique et Artisanal (Switzerland), also for their financial assistance towards meeting these Open Access costs; and the National Library of

Russia (St Petersburg) for granting permission to reproduce miniatures from their unique manuscript of the *Relation du Pas de Saumur* in both the Casebook and the virtual exhibition.

Grateful thanks are also due to particular individuals: Jacob Deacon, for his work as administrative assistant to the research network; Clare Litt, for her advice and support as commissioning editor at Liverpool University Press; Margaret Scott, for her invaluable expertise on aspects of medieval clothing and textiles; Graeme Small, for his help on late medieval moneys of account and coins; Craig Taylor, for sharing his rediscovery of a manuscript hitherto thought lost of Guillaume Leseur's *Histoire de Gaston IV, comte de Foix*, an important source for a number of *pas d'armes* held in Anjou; and Marina Viallon, for sharing her knowledge of a little-known Spanish manuscript containing an account of two Parisian *pas d'armes* that took place in 1484 following the coronation of King Charles VIII.

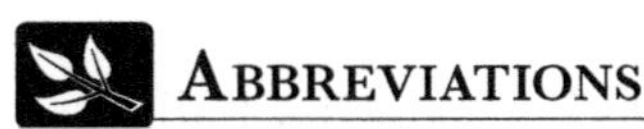

Abbreviations

ADN B — Lille, Archives départementales du Nord, Série B

AGHNF — P. Louis Lainé, *Archives généalogiques et historiques de la noblesse de France …*, 11 vols (Paris: Chez l'auteur, 1828–50)

AGSM — Feliciano Rámirez de Arellano, José Sancho Rayón and Francisco de Zabálburu, eds, 'Crónica de Don Juan II de Castilla por Álvar García de Santa María (1420–1434). Conclusion (1428 a 1434)', in *Colección de documentos inéditos para la historia de España*, 100 (Madrid: R. Marco y Viñas, 1891), pp. 3–410

ANADS — Éloi-Amédée de Foras, *Armorial et nobiliaire de l'ancien duché de Savoie*, 5 vols (Grenoble: Edouard Allier, 1863–1938)

AR — Brussels, Algemeen Rijksarchief, Archieven van de Rekenkamers, Registers

ARCT — Auguste Dufour, ed., 'Adrianeo: récit des cérémonies, tournois et autres réjouissances qui ont eu lieu à Ivrée à l'occasion du baptême du prince Adrien de Savoie (1522)', *Mémoires et documents publiés par la Société savoisienne d'histoire et d'archéologie*, 9 (1865), 251–437

Arsenal — Bibliothèque de l'Arsenal

BL — British Library

BM — Bibliothèque Municipale

BnF — Bibliothèque nationale de France

BP — Bernard Prost, ed., *Traités du duel judiciaire: relations de pas d'armes et tournois* (Paris: L. Willem, 1872)

BU — Bibliothèque Universitaire

CdF — Cour de France

CdV — Louis Prosper Gachard, ed., *Collection des voyages des souverains des Pays-Bas*, 4 vols (Brussels: F. Hayez, 1876), vol. 1

CL — Rosalind Brown-Grant and Mario Damen, trans., *A Chivalric Life: The Book of the Deeds of Messire Jacques de Lalaing* (Woodbridge: Boydell Press, 2022)

COTO — Raphaël De Smedt, ed., *Les chevaliers de l'Ordre de la Toison d'or au XVe siècle. Notices bio-bibliographiques*, 2nd revised edition (Frankfurt am Main: Peter Lang, 2000)

CPM — Henri Stein, '*Chanson du Pas de Marsannay* (1443)', *Bibliothèque de l'École des Chartes*, 82 (1921), 330–7

CRC	Marta López Izquierdo and Lola Pons Rodríguez, eds, *Coronación del rey Carlos VIII de Francia y fiestas que se hicieron (1484): Edición del ms. e-IV-5 de la Biblioteca de San Lorenzo de El Escorial*, nouvelle édition [en ligne] (Paris: e-Spania Books, 2015)
DBE	*Diccionario biográfico electrónico* of the Real Academia de la Historia
DBF	J. Balteau *et al.*, *Dictionnaire de biographie française* (Paris: Letouzey et Ané, 1933)
DBI	*Dizionario biografico degli Italiani* (Rome: Istituto della Enciclopedia Italiana, 1960–)
DEC	Aureliano Sánchez Martín, ed., *Crónica de Enrique IV, de Diego Enríquez del Castillo* (Valladolid: Universidad de Valladolid. Secretariado de Publicaciones, 1994)
DHS	Dictionnaire historique de la Suisse
DMF	Dictionnaire du Moyen Français (1330–1500)
DN	François-Alexandre Aubert de La Chenaye-Desbois, *Dictionnaire de la noblesse* …, 3rd edition, 19 vols (Paris: Schlesinger, 1866–76)
ECMR	Albert Lecoy de la Marche, ed., *Extraits des comptes et mémoriaux du roi René, pour servir à l'histoire des arts au XVe siècle, publiés d'après les originaux des Archives nationales* (Paris: Société de l'École des Chartes, 1873)
EdM	Louis Douët-d'Arcq, ed., *La chronique d'Enguerran de Monstrelet, en deux livres, avec pièces justificatives 1400–1444*, Société de l'Histoire de France, 6 vols (Paris: Renouard, 1857–62)
EMDT	Gale Owen-Crocker, Elizabeth Coatsworth and Maria Hayward, eds, *Encyclopedia of Medieval Dress and Textiles of the British Isles c. 450–1450* (Leiden: Brill, 2012)
FPG	Lorenzo Galindez de Carvajal, ed., *Crónica del señor rey Don Juan II compilado por Fernando Pérez de Guzmán* (Valencia: Monfort, 1779)
GC	M. le baron Kervyn de Lettenhove, ed., *Oeuvres de Georges Chastellain*, 8 vols (Brussels: F. Heussner, 1863–66)
GCC	Jean-Claude Delclos, ed., *Georges Chastellain, Chronique: les fragments du livre IV révélés par l'Additional Manuscript 54156 de la British Library* (Geneva: Droz, 1991)
GCM	Gilbert Chanveau (Montjoie King of Arms), *L'ordre des joustes faictes à Paris à l'entrée de la royne* (Paris: no known publisher, 1514)
GDH	Louis Moréri, *Le Grand Dictionnaire historique* …, 10 vols (Paris: Jacques Vincent, 1759)
GvdS	Robert Scholten, ed., *Clevische Chronik nach der Originalhandschrift des Gert van der Schüren nebst Vorgeschichte und Zusätzen von Turck* (Cleves: Boss, 1884)
HB	Henri Courteault, Léonce Cellier and Marie-Henriette Jullien, eds, *Les chroniques du roi Charles VII par Gilles le Bouvier dit le Héraut Berry* (Paris: C. Klincksieck, 1979)
HBB	Samuel Guichenon, *Histoire de Bresse et de Bugey, justifiée par chartes, titres, chroniques* … (Lyon: Huguenon et Ravaud, 1650)

HCMLI Juan de Mata Carriazo y Arroquia, ed., *Hechos del Condestable don Miguel Lucas de Iranzo (crónica del siglo XV)* (Madrid: Espasa-Calpe, 1940), pp. 58–9

HCS Robert Lindsay of Pitscottie, *The History and Chronicles of Scotland Written and Collected by Robert Lindesay of Pitscottie*, ed. by Aeneas J. G. Mackay, 3 vols (Edinburgh: Scottish Text Society, 1899–1911), vol. 1, pp. 231–2

HGF Henri Courteault, ed., *Histoire de Gaston IV de Foix, par Guillaume Leseur. Chronique française inédite du XVe siècle*, 2 vols (Paris: H. Laurens, 1893–96)

HGFMO Henri Courteault, ed., 'Le manuscrit original de l'*Histoire de Gaston IV, comte de Foix*, par Guillaume Leseur. Additions et corrections à l'édition de cette chronique', *Annuaire-bulletin de la Société de l'histoire de France*, 43 (1906), 180–212

HKB Adriaan Justus Enschede, ed., 'Huwelijksplechtigheden van Karel van Bourgondië en Margaretha van York', in *Kronijk van het Historisch Genootschap gevestigd te Utrecht*, 22 (1866), 17–71

HMF Le Père Anselme de Sainte-Marie, *Histoire généalogique et chronologique de la maison royale de France et … des grands officiers de la Couronne*, 9 vols (Paris: La Compagnie des Libraires, 1726–30)

JdA René de Maulde La Clavière, ed., *Chroniques de Louis XII par Jean d'Auton*, 4 vols (Paris: Librairie Renouard, 1889–95)

JdC Frédéric, baron de Reiffenberg, ed., *Mémoires de J. du Clercq*, 4 vols (Brussels: Arnold Lacrosse, 1823)

JDH R. H. G. Chalon, ed., *Les mémoires de Messire Jean, seigneur de Haynin et de Louvegnies, chevalier (1465–1477)*, 2 vols (Mons: Em. Hoyois, 1842)

JDI M. le baron J. B. M. C. Kervyn de Lettenhove, 'II. La joute de la Dame Inconnue à Bruxelles. – La joute du sire de Commines et du sire de Jonvelle à Bruges', *Compte-rendu des séances de la Commission royale d'Histoire*, 2me Série 11 (1878), 473–86

JLBS John Leslie, *The Historie of Scotland Written … by Jhone Leslie Bishop of Rosse*, ed. by E. G. Cody, 2 vols (Edinburgh: Scottish Text Society, 1888–95), vol. 2, p. 128

JLdSR François Morand, ed., *Chronique de Jean le Fèvre, seigneur de Saint-Remy*, 2 vols (Paris: Renouard, 1876)

JLdSR – Ép. François Morand, ed., 'Épître de Jean le Fèvre, seigneur de Saint-Remy', *Annuaire-bulletin de la Société de l'histoire de France*, 21 (1884), 177–240

JM Georges Doutrepont and Omer Jodogne, eds, *Chroniques de Jean Molinet*, Collection des anciens auteurs belges, 3 vols (Brussels: Palais des Académies, 1935)

KBR Koninklijke Bibliotheek/Bibliothèque royale

LB Juan de Mata Carriazo y Arroquia, ed., *Refundición de la crónica del halconero por el obispo Don Lope Barrientos (hasta ahora inédita)*, Colección de crónicas españolas, 9 (Madrid: Espasa-Calpe, 1946)

LF Emmy Springer, '*Les Fais de Messire Jacques de Lalain* de Jean Lefèvre de Saint-Rémy' (unpublished PhD dissertation, Université de Paris III – Sorbonne Nouvelle, 1982)

LPH	Fernando Arroyo Ilera and Juan de Pineda, eds, *Libro del Passo Honroso defendido por el excelente caballero Suero de Quiñones*, Textos Medievales, 38 (Valencia: Editorial Anubar, 1970)
MdE	Gaston du Fresne de Beaucourt, ed., *Chronique de Mathieu d'Escouchy*, Société de l'Histoire de France, 3 vols (Paris: Mme Veuve Jules Renouard, 1863–64)
MmM	Hans Cools, *Mannen met macht. Edellieden en de moderne staat in de Bourgondisch-Habsburgse landen (1475–1530)* (Zutphen: Walburg, 2001)
MT	Ralph Moffat, 'The Medieval Tournament: Chivalry, Heraldry and Reality. An Edition and Analysis of Three Fifteenth-Century Tournament Manuscripts' (unpublished PhD dissertation, University of Leeds, 2010)
NLR	National Library of Russia
OHDB	Valérie Bessey, Jean-Marie Cauchies and Werner Paravicini, eds, *Les ordonnances de l'hôtel des ducs de Bourgogne, vol. 3: Marie de Bourgogne, Maximilien d'Autriche et Philippe le Beau 1477–1506* (Berlin: Peter Lang, 2019)
OdLM	Henri Beaune and Jules d'Arbaumont, eds, *Mémoires d'Olivier de La Marche, maître d'hôtel et capitaine des gardes de Charles le Téméraire*, 4 vols (Paris: Librairie Renouard, 1883–84)
PAB	Georges Adrien Crapelet, ed., *Le pas d'armes de la bergère maintenu au tournoi de Tarascon* (Paris: Crapelet, 1828)
PB	Harry F. Williams, '*Le Pas de la Bergère.* A Critical Edition', *Fifteenth Century Studies*, 17 (1990), 485–513
PC	'Tournoi fait à Carignan par le duc Philibert le Beau', in Samuel Guichenon, *Histoire généalogique de la royale Maison de Savoie*, 2nd edition, 5 vols (Turin: J. M. Briolo, 1778), vol. 4/2, pp. 469–77
PCB	Prosopographia Curiae Burgundicae
PCEEB	*Publication du Centre Européen d'Études Bourguignonnes*
PCH	Juan de Mata Carriazo y Arroquia, ed., *Crónica del halconero de Juan II, Pedro Carrillo de Huete (hasta ahora inédita)*, Colección de crónicas españolas, 8 (Madrid: Espasa-Calpe, 1946)
PH	Pero Rodríguez de Lena, *El Passo Honroso de Suero de Quiñones (1434)* (selected passages), in *Jousting in Medieval and Renaissance Iberia*, Noel Fallows (Woodbridge: Boydell Press, 2010), pp. 399–501
PPF	Chloé Horn, Anne Rochebouet and Michelle Szkilnik, eds, *Le Pas du Perron Fée (Édition des manuscrits Paris, BnF fr 5739 et Lille BU 104* (Paris: Champion, 2013)
PPR	René de Maulde La Clavière, *Procédures politiques du règne de Louis XII* (Paris: Imprimerie nationale, 1885)
PS	Marie-Claude de Crécy, ed., *Le Roman de Ponthus et Sidoine* (Geneva: Droz, 1997)
PSr	Natalia Elagina *et al.*, eds, *Das Turnierbuch für René d'Anjou (Le Pas de Saumur): Vollständige Faksimile-Ausgabe im Originalformat der Handschrift Codex Fr. F. XIV Nr. 4 der Russischen Nationalbibliothek in St. Petersburg* (Graz: Akademische Druck und Verlagsanstalt, 1998)

PSt	Auguste Vayssière, ed., *Le Pas des armes de Sandricourt. Relation d'un Tournoi donné en 1493 au château de ce nom, publié d'après un manuscrit de la Bibliothèque de l'Arsenal et l'imprimé du temps* (Paris: Léon Willem, 1874)
SH	Marc de Vulson [given as Wlson] de la Colombière, *La Science heroique, traitant de la noblesse, de l'origine des armes de leurs blasons, & symboles, des tymbres, bourlets, couronnes, cimiers, lambrequins, supports, & tenans, & autres ornements de l'escu; de la deuise, & du cry de guerre, de l'escu pendant & des pas & emprises des anciens cheualiers, des formes differentes de leurs tombeaux; et des marques exterieures de l'escu de nos roys, des reynes, & enfans de France, & des officiers de la couronne, et de la maison du roy*, 2nd edition (Paris: Sebastien Mabre-Cramoisy, 1669)
TA	T. Dickson and James Balfour Paul, eds, *Accounts of the Lord High Treasurer of Scotland*, 12 vols (Edinburgh: Scottish Text Society, 1877–1916)
TG	A. Fourtier, 'Un tournoi à Genève en 1498', *Revue nobiliaire, héraldique et biographique*, 8 (1873), 373–7
VdF	Marie-Thérèse Caron, *Les voeux du Faisan, noblesse en fête, esprit de croisade: le manuscrit français 11594 de la Bibliothèque Nationale de France*, Burgundica 7 (Turnhout: Brepols, 2003)
VdN	Évelyne Van den Neste, *Tournois, joutes, pas d'armes dans les villes de Flandre à la fin du Moyen Âge (1300–1486)* (Paris: École des Chartes, 1996)
VT	Marc de Vulson [given as Wlson] de la Colombière, *Le vray theatre de l'honneur de la chevalerie, ou le Miroir de la noblesse, contenant les combats ou jeux sacrez des Grecs et des Romains, les triomphes, les tournois, les joustes, les pas, les emprises ou entreprises, les armes, les combats à la barriere, les carrosels, les courses de bague et de la quintaine, les machines, les chariots de triomphe, les cartels, les devises, les prix, les voeux, les sermens, les ceremonies, les statuts, les ordres et autres magnificences et exercices des anciens nobles durant la paix* (Paris: A. Courbé, 1648)

Contributors

Catherine Blunk is Associate Professor of French at Drury University in Springfield, Missouri. She has a BA in French and International Studies as well as a Masters and PhD in French from the University of Wisconsin-Madison, where she wrote her dissertation on the poetics of the tournament in late medieval chronicle and romance. She continues to research tournaments and has published on the *pas d'armes*.

Thalia Brero is Assistant Professor at the University of Neuchâtel, where she teaches History of the Middle Ages and of the Renaissance. She studied at the University of Lausanne, was a visiting scholar at Université Paris-Est Créteil and at Ghent University and a research and teaching fellow at the University of Geneva. She works on ceremonies and rituals in late medieval courts (especially Savoy), dynastic strategies, princely meetings and Renaissance printed news reports.

Rosalind Brown-Grant is Emerita Professor of Late Medieval French Literature at the University of Leeds. She has a BA in Modern Languages (French and Italian) and a PhD from the University of Manchester. She has published numerous books and articles on Christine de Pizan's works in defence of women, late medieval romance, late medieval historiographical writing and text/image relations in medieval manuscripts, and has also edited and translated several medieval French texts.

Mario Damen is Associate Professor of Medieval History at the University of Amsterdam. He studied History at the University of Leiden and in Santiago de Compostela and subsequently gained his PhD at the Vrije Universiteit Amsterdam with the award of *cum laude*. He has published widely on the cultural and socio-political history of the late medieval Low Countries in general, and on the nobility and tournaments in particular.

Anne D. Hedeman is Distinguished Professor Emerita of Art History at the University of Kansas. She has published extensively on the relationships between text and image in vernacular late medieval French manuscripts. Her research pays particular attention to the means by which illustrations of historical, classical or contemporary texts originating in non-French cultures employ illumination to communicate effectively with late medieval French readers.

Ralph Moffat is Curator of European Arms and Armour at Glasgow Museums. He has an MA (Hons) in Scottish Historical Studies and an MSc in Medieval Studies from the University of Edinburgh. His doctorate from the University of Leeds involved a study of an original fifteenth-century manuscript on tournaments in the Royal Armouries Library. He has published several articles and a book on arms and armour with a particular focus on the Middle Ages.

Alan V. Murray is Professor of Medieval European History at the University of Leeds. He studied History, German Language and Literature and Folk Studies at the Universities of St Andrews, Salzburg and Freiburg. He has published extensively on the crusades, warfare and chivalry. His work on tournaments includes several essays on tourneys and jousting in the German-speaking countries, with a particular focus on the Styrian nobleman Ulrich von Liechtenstein.

Christina Normore is Associate Professor of Art History at Northwestern University. She received her BA in Art History and Religion from Oberlin College and her doctorate in Art History from the University of Chicago. She has published on the aesthetic and social priorities of late medieval court banquets in north-western Europe, particularly the Valois Burgundian court, and is currently focusing on the role of the arts in promoting and questioning militarism during the Hundred Years War and on the implications of the current 'global turn' in Medieval Studies.

Klaus Oschema is Director of the Institut Historique Allemand in Paris and Professor of Late Medieval History at the Ruhr-University Bochum. Having studied History, Philosophy and English at the Universities of Bamberg and Paris X-Nanterre, he was awarded his PhD by the Technical University Dresden and the École Pratique des Hautes Études (Paris). He has taught at Berne (Switzerland), Heidelberg and Frankfurt. His research focuses on late medieval nobility and courtly society (Burgundy, Savoy), astrology in the late Middle Ages and conceptions of geographical and cultural world order in the medieval period.

Justin M. Sturgeon is Assistant Professor of Art History at the University of Western Florida. His work centres on illuminated medieval manuscripts and the interaction between text, image and material culture in order to address questions about chivalric identity and status. His most recent research examines these issues within the context of René of Anjou's *Livre des tournois*, a fifteenth-century treatise that describes and visualises the author's idealised form of a late medieval tournament.

Michelle Szkilnik is Emerita Professor of French Medieval Literature at the University of Sorbonne Nouvelle (Paris) and has a doctorate from this institution. A specialist of narrative literature, she has published numerous articles and books about medieval French romances from the twelfth to the fifteenth centuries and has also edited and translated several medieval French texts.

Marina Viallon is an art historian specialising in arms and armour, equestrian equipment and knightly court festivals. She studied art history at the École du Louvre in Paris before getting a Masters in Museum Studies and an MA in Medieval Studies at the University of Leeds; her PhD at the École Pratique des Hautes Études in Paris was on French Renaissance courtly tournaments. She has worked at the Musée de l'Armée in Paris and the Metropolitan Museum of Art in New York and has published numerous articles in books and exhibition catalogues on her fields of expertise.

Illustrations

Maps

Tables

Figures

Rosalind Brown-Grant, Mario Damen and Catherine Blunk

Introduction: *Pas d'armes* and Late Medieval Chivalry

In the early fifteenth century, a new type of tournament appeared in Western Europe: the *pas d'armes* (English: 'passage of arms').[1] This highly ritualised form of chivalric competition and elite entertainment probably originated in the Iberian Peninsula and soon became popular, spreading to Anjou, the Burgundian lands and France, and even reaching Savoy and Scotland. It involved a knight (or group of knights) issuing a challenge to all comers, provided they were of noble birth, who wished to fight him (or them) using lances, swords or pollaxes. These combats, which were usually fought between individuals, on foot or on horseback, but sometimes between groups of knights, took place within a theatrical framework incorporating literary and historical motifs drawn from chivalric and courtly literature. In turn, these actual *pas d'armes* could also inspire fictional narratives that often included such events in their accounts of a hero's ascent from promising young squire to experienced knight who performed marvellous feats of arms, both in the tilting yard and on the field of battle.

Although *pas d'armes* are familiar to historians of chivalry, there is no specialist publication in English that discusses this type of chivalric event in depth, apart from a chapter in a general book on jousts and tournaments by Richard Barber and Juliet Barker.[2] Moreover, even when the primary sources (whether narrative accounts or administrative documents) that recount these tournaments have been published, they are generally only available in their original language and in nineteenth-century editions that lack a modern scholarly apparatus. This Casebook on the *pas d'armes* thus has two main aims: on the one hand, it seeks to provide greater access to many of the narrative, financial and pictorial sources concerning such events; on the other, it attempts to demonstrate how these sources can be used to develop scholarly debates on the *pas d'armes* in new directions. Before outlining the structure of this volume and the various research tools offered by the scholarly project of which it is a part, it is first necessary to give a definition of the *pas d'armes*, to identify its origins, to establish the narrative and administrative sources available for these chivalric events and to explain how scholars from different disciplines have previously approached this kind of tournament.

---

[1] In many of the narrative accounts of these events, this term is often shortened to *pas*, particularly in their titles, such as the *Pas du Perron Fée* (Bruges, 1463); however, the longer formulation *pas des armes* is also found in some late fifteenth- and early sixteenth-century French examples, such as the *Pas des armes de Sandricourt* (1493).

[2] Richard Barber and Juliet Barker, *Tournaments: Jousts, Chivalry and Pageants in the Middle Ages* (Woodbridge: Boydell Press, 1989), pp. 107–38.

DEFINING THE *PAS D'ARMES*

In order to situate the *pas d'armes* as a particular type of knightly combat within the broader context of late medieval chivalric culture, some definitions of more general terms relating to this field are indispensable. Thus, 'tournament' is used here to mean the overarching class of martial and chivalric events organised and performed by the noble elites of Europe in the late Middle Ages, just as the expression *fait d'armes* (feat of arms) was employed by contemporaries as an umbrella term that could refer to several different types of combat. More specifically, the original '*mêlée*-tournament', from the late eleventh century onwards, was, in the words of David Crouch, 'a mock battle involving hundreds and sometimes thousands of knights fighting over a very large area', whereas jousts were 'individual fights on horseback in a confined space'.[3]

A *pas d'armes* was understood by contemporary audiences and participants to be a specific form of *emprise*: that is, a chivalric exploit undertaken by a knight or squire who was therefore deemed to be its *entrepreneur*. An *emprise* involved committing oneself to performing different types of combat, either mounted, such as jousting with lances on horseback, or on foot using weapons such as swords or pollaxes, against one or more opponents. At the same time, the term *emprise* could also be used to refer to a physical object such as a bracelet, cuff or shackle — often presented as a token of the *entrepreneur*'s devotion to his lady — which he wore and which challengers had to touch as a sign of their wish to do combat with him; the final removal of this object literally and figuratively released the *entrepreneur* from his *emprise*.[4] Before the *pas* was held, the *entrepreneur* would issue a set of rules governing the way in which his *emprise* was to be fought, which were often referred to as *articles* or *chapitres* (chapters of arms). These rules specified the type of harness and saddle to be used, the kinds of weapon permitted (sharpened or rebated), the number of courses with the lance to be run or blows with swords or pollaxes to be exchanged, etc. The rules were then publicised by heralds within one or several territories, whilst the *entrepreneur* would travel from court to court in search of knights and squires who would take up his challenge.

If a *pas d'armes* is an *emprise* in the general sense given above, an *emprise* is not always a *pas d'armes*. One particular feature of the *pas* is that the *entrepreneur* sets himself up as the defender of a specific place and so his challengers travel to fight him. The term *pas* thus specifically refers to a 'passage', such as a crossroads or a river crossing, or a symbolic object such as a *perron* (often in the form of a large stone or a column), which was to be defended against all comers. Such 'passages' could be located in the countryside, outside a castle or in an urban market square.

Another important feature of a *pas d'armes* that characterises it as such is its fictional underpinning. This was often described in detail in a letter of challenge or declaration in which the *entrepreneur*, who could be referred to by his real name or by an incognito (for example, the 'Wild Knight' or the 'Knight of the Golden Tree'), explained his reasons for organising the *pas*, which could be his devotion to a particular lady or his commitment to some specific cause, such as defending the Church. The literary associations of the *pas* could also be accentuated by its physical setting, which, in addition to a set of lists for the combats and stands for the judges and high-ranking spectators, could also include an

---

[3] David Crouch, *Tournament* (London: Hambledon, 2006), p. 1. See also below, p. 4, and the Glossary.

[4] For a contemporary example of the expression 'touching the *emprise*', see MT, pp. 32–3.

elaborate ephemeral architecture and *mise en scène*. Thus, objects such as an arch, a *perron* or a tree might have coloured shields hanging from them so as to indicate the different types of combat to be fought and which competitors, or heralds acting on their behalf, had to touch to show their acceptance of the challenge. These objects, and/or a pavilion or a fountain often adorned with statues, might be guarded by an officer of arms, a dwarf, a giant or a 'Wild Man', by artificial beasts, such as griffins, or even by real animals, such as lions.

Whilst some *pas d'armes* were staged as part of a much larger programme of festivities in celebration of a particular occasion, such as a wedding, a baptism or a Joyous Entry, even those held as standalone events often featured elaborate dinners and were accompanied by dramatised entertainments known as *entremets*, both between and after the combats. Finally, although some *entrepreneurs* of *pas d'armes* faced their challengers alone, others were aided in combat by another knight or squire or were effectively the captains of whole teams of defenders.

When and where did this ritualised form of tournament originate and why did it prove to be so appealing, with nearly forty such events having been attested in late medieval Europe?

Origins of the *Pas d'Armes*

The antecedents of the *pas* were both literary and historical. The term *pas* may have come from a legend attached to the Third Crusade (1189–92) about how the French king, Philippe Auguste, with a group of twelve knights that included the English king, Richard I, succeeded in defending a narrow passage or *pas* near Jerusalem against the great Muslim leader, Saladin. This legend was written up in a thirteenth-century text called the *Pas Saladin*.[5] That this text was familiar to audiences in later medieval France can be seen from Jean Froissart's account of the Joyous Entry of Queen Isabeau of Bavaria into Paris in 1389, in which the chronicler describes the battle of the *Pas* being recreated as an 'esbatement' (entertainment) along the procession route that the queen would follow.[6]

Arthurian romances, such as those composed by the late twelfth-century writer Chrétien de Troyes and his thirteenth-century continuators, which featured knights such as Lancelot fighting at a bridge, also inspired historical *pas d'armes*, as did non-Arthurian romances whose heroes were pseudo-historical figures such as the late fourteenth- or early fifteenth-century Galician knight Ponthus, who defends a fountain.[7] Other popular literary motifs on which historical *pas d'armes* drew for inspiration include the shepherds and shepherdesses of the pastoral genre and the gods and goddesses of the allegorical genre, with the latter being particularly influential in the early sixteenth century.[8] In

[5] See Anna Maria Finoli, '*Le Pas Saladin*: de Jaffa aux côtes de l'Angleterre', in *Quant l'ung amy pour l'autre veille: Mélanges de moyen français offerts à Claude Thiry*, ed. by Tania Van Hemelryck and Maria Colombo Timelli (Turnhout: Brepols, 2008), pp. 113–21; and Sébastien Nadot, *Le Spectacle des joutes: Sport et courtoisie à la fin du Moyen Âge* (Rennes: Presses Universitaires de Rennes, 2012), pp. 12–14.

[6] See the Online Froissart <https://www.dhi.ac.uk/onlinefroissart> [accessed 6 June 2024] (following London, BL, Harley 4379–4380, fol. 6r).

[7] See PS; and for a translation of this text, see Source 1.

[8] Whilst the Angevin *Pas de la Bergère* (Tarascon, 1449) exemplifies the former genre (see Source 6), the Savoyard *Pas* of Carignano (1504) exemplifies the latter (see Source 15).

turn, texts such as Antoine de La Sale's *Jean de Saintré* (1456), which present their heroes organising a *pas*, modelled themselves closely on the way actual *pas d'armes* wrote up the different phases before, during and after the combats, and so added further to this stock of literary examples.[9]

In terms of historical antecedents, if the heyday of the *pas d'armes* was undoubtedly the mid- to late fifteenth century, it nonetheless evolved out of pre-existing forms of medieval tournament. The first tournaments held in the twelfth century consisted of a *mêlée* or pitched battle fought between teams, which might be preceded by an hour or two of preliminary jousts. *Mêlées* were conducted over a large area, such as a field without any enclosures, using a range of weapons that included sharpened swords, lances, maces and knives, with knights fighting on horseback or on foot as they would in times of war.[10]

It was not until the second decade of the thirteenth century that jousting became more popular than the *mêlée*,[11] which led to a new form of tournament known as a Round Table. First appearing in Cyprus but spreading to Austria, England and France by 1240,[12] Round Tables consisted solely of jousting, usually with rebated weapons. Being somewhat safer than *mêlées*, they were not generally subject to religious or royal prohibitions against tournaments. An individual knight in a joust or a one-to-one combat was much simpler to identify than one who was involved in a distant *mêlée*, thus making it easier to recognise individual prowess, especially as heraldic markers such as personalised coats of arms and crests were becoming more commonplace in this period.[13] Entertainments outside the lists, such as singing and dancing, also featured at these events.

As their name suggests, a particular hallmark of Round Tables was that their participants often adopted the identity and coats of arms of Arthurian knights, as was the case at the tournaments held in Le Hem (1278) and Chauvency (1285) in northern France.[14] Whilst *pas d'armes* would likewise be inspired by Arthurian literary motifs and would adopt the Round Table's model of a tree or a *perron* to which the shields of the combatants were attached, they differ from the Round Table, whose competitors could select both the role they wished to play — that of defender or challenger — and the number of courses they wanted to run during the jousts. Moreover, unlike the *pas d'armes*, the emphasis during the Round Table was on the combatants' performance as teams rather than as individuals.[15] Whilst the role-playing and pageantry typical of Round Tables became a prominent characteristic of English tournaments by the middle of the fourteenth century,[16] the

---

[9] See Michelle Szkilnik, *Jean de Saintré: une carrière chevaleresque au XVe siècle* (Geneva: Droz, 2003).

[10] Crouch, *Tournament*, pp. 78–9.

[11] *Ibid.*, p. 116.

[12] *Ibid.*, p. 117.

[13] *Ibid.*, pp. 119–20.

[14] See Nigel Bryant, trans., *The Tournaments at Le Hem and Chauvency. Sarrasin, The Romance of Le Hem, Jacques Bretel, The Tournament at Chauvency* (Woodbridge: Boydell Press, 2020).

[15] Malcolm Vale, 'Le tournoi dans la France du Nord, l'Angleterre et les Pays-Bas (1280–1440)', in *Théâtre et spectacles hier et aujourd'hui: Moyen âge et Renaissance. Actes du 115e Congrès National des Sociétés Savantes (Avignon, 1990). Section d'histoire médiévale et de philologie* (Paris: Éditions du CTHS, 1991), pp. 263–71 (p. 267); Torsten Hiltmann, 'Un État de noblesse et de chevalerie sans pareilles? Tournois et hérauts d'armes à la cour des ducs de Bourgogne', in *La cour de Bourgogne et l'Europe: le rayonnement et les limites d'un modèle culturel*, ed. by Werner Paravicini, Torsten Hiltmann and Frank Viltart (Ostfildern: Jan Thorbecke Verlag, 2013), pp. 253–88 (pp. 260–1).

[16] Barber and Barker, *Tournaments*, pp. 30–50.

nobility stopped holding (and attending) Round Tables when they began to be organised by urban authorities in places such as Paris and Tournai, as they no longer served to highlight the nobility's distinctiveness as the imitators of noble literary models.[17]

An example of another type of precursor of the *pas d'armes* organised by members of the nobility is the tournament held at the abbey of Saint-Inglevert situated between Boulogne-sur-Mer and Calais in March and April 1390. Publicised by three French knights — Jean II Le Meingre, known as Boucicaut, Renaud de Roye and Jean de Sempy — this event saw these three men defend the lists against all comers. Whilst Richard Barber and Juliet Barker have described this tournament, which took place during a period of truce between the English and the French, as featuring 'the most famous jousts of the fourteenth century', of which six different accounts have come down to us,[18] there is some debate amongst scholars as to whether Saint-Inglevert should in fact be classified as a *pas d'armes*. Some elements of these jousts can indeed be found in the later *pas*: letters of challenge were circulated in advance in which the types of weapon (rebated or sharp-tipped lances) and shield, number of courses run and rules of engagement were outlined; challengers were explicitly invited to touch a shield (either of peace or of war) of one of the defenders in order to indicate their willingness to engage in combat; the event itself was heavily sponsored by a patron (King Charles VI of France); and the organisers donated their arms to a church in Boulogne-sur-Mer, an action that was also often performed by some of their fifteenth-century counterparts in *pas d'armes*. Nevertheless, the chief commentator on this event, Froissart, described Saint-Inglevert not as a *pas* but rather as either 'armes' (arms) or a 'jeu' (game) and the activity involved as being 'jouster' (jousting). Furthermore, not only did it take place on a military frontier, which was in effect a real rather than a symbolic passage,[19] but no theatrical *mise en scène* or fictive scenario seems to have been part of the way in which the event was set up (see below).

The first tournaments to which the French term *pas d'armes* — or, more accurately, its Castilian equivalent, *paso de armas* — was explicitly applied were held in the early fifteenth century in the Iberian Peninsula. Some of these events stipulated jousting with rebated lances, whereas others featured combats on horseback and on foot with sharpened weapons. Some even included tourneys, which were similar to *mêlées* in being fought in pairs or teams, albeit on a smaller scale.[20] The fanciful jousts of Round Tables also found new expression at these events, in that festive theatrics could exist alongside this variety of combat forms and weapons. From there the *pas d'armes* spread to the ducal courts in Anjou and the Burgundian lands and to the royal court in France, where they would take on their most lavish and spectacular form yet. Unlike Round Tables, which had been adopted by urban elites, proof of noble ancestry, usually on both the paternal and the maternal side, was required for participation in these events, thus making the *paso* or *pas*

[17] VdN, p. 53.

[18] Barber and Barker, *Tournaments*, p. 43; Steven Muhlberger, *Deeds of Arms: Formal Combats in the Late Fourteenth Century* (Highland Village, TX: Chivalry Bookshelf, 2005), pp. 70, 198–9.

[19] See the Online Froissart <https://www.dhi.ac.uk/onlinefroissart> (following London, BL, Harley 4379–4380, fols 43r–60v). See also Élisabeth Gaucher, 'Les joutes de Saint-Inglevert: perception et écriture d'un événement historique pendant la Guerre de Cent Ans', *Le Moyen Âge*, 102 (1996), 229–43 (pp. 233–5), who argues in favour of calling this event a *pas*.

[20] Noel Fallows, *Jousting in Medieval and Renaissance Iberia* (Woodbridge: Boydell Press, 2010), p. 3. No *pas d'armes* ever consisted of just a *mêlée*, however.

an important instrument of distinction for the higher nobility.[21] Finally, in the sixteenth century, as chivalric contests grew ever more stage-managed and choreographed, the term *pas d'armes*, in the French context in particular, became used almost interchangeably with the more general term *tournoy* (tournament).[22] If, then, the *pas* lost much of its earlier, specific flavour in this later period, this was not before leaving a lasting legacy in terms of the sheer number of events of this type that were organised and of which evidence has come down to us.

Sources for the *pas d'armes*

Although often spectacular, a *pas* was by its very nature an ephemeral event, with the competitors' armorial shields and parts of the architectural décor often being taken away at the end to be displayed in a local castle, church or hospital.[23] By far the most durable form of commemoration of a *pas d'armes* was therefore the written text. The vast majority of the narrative accounts of these events are written in prose, but verse was also used for composing such texts in the Angevin milieu, where it was a highly popular medium for courtly and chivalric literature.[24] In addition, numerous administrative documents also provide us with details of how a *pas* was staged.

Many of the authors of the narrative accounts of *pas d'armes* were the heralds who had been involved in publicising the event, such as Orléans Herald, who names himself as the author of the northern French *Pas des armes de Sandricourt* (1493), the chief *entrepreneur* of which was Louis de Hédouville.[25] Other authors who do not give their names but were likely to have been heralds include the person responsible for commemorating the Burgundian *Pas du Perron Fée* (Bruges, 1463), organised by Philippe de Lalaing.[26] This should not surprise us, as heralds were traditionally very heavily involved in the staging of tournaments. They not only proclaimed and publicised the event beforehand but helped the judges evaluate the performance of the tourneyers during it and took care of the record-keeping afterwards. Indeed, from the early beginnings of the tournament it was heralds who produced written reports with short descriptions of the participants, their coats of arms and the prize winners: these descriptions, which were also very popular among those knights who had not participated in the tournament itself, were the sources of the first armorials.[27]

Heralds were probably involved in the writing of other forms of narrative too, such as the chivalric biography known as the *Livre des faits de messire Jacques de Lalaing* (early

[21] Malcolm Vale, *War and Chivalry: Warfare and Aristocratic Culture in England, France and Burgundy* (London: Duckworth and Co., 1981), pp. 96–7.

[22] See Essay 4, p. 431.

[23] At two Burgundian events, for example, shields were removed from the *Pas de l'Arbre Charlemagne* (Marsannay-la-Côte, 1443) and parts of the décor were removed from the *Pas de la Fontaine des Pleurs* (Chalon-sur-Saône, 1449–50): see Sources 4 and 7, respectively.

[24] See Florence Bouchet, ed., *René d'Anjou, écrivain et mécène (1409–1480)* (Turnhout: Brepols, 2011).

[25] See PSt, and Source 13.

[26] See PPF, and Sources 11a and 11b.

[27] Crouch, *Tournament*, p. 225. Armorials are manuscripts containing collections of coats of arms, drawn or painted, in a specific order — geographically, institutionally or heraldically — with or without a text to identify the escutcheons. A collection of coats of arms recorded at a specific battle or tournament, for example, is normally called an occasional armorial or roll of arms. Michel Pastoureau, *Les armoiries* (Turnhout: Brepols, 1976), p. 39.

1470s), which includes an account of the Burgundian *Pas de la Fontaine des Pleurs* (Chalon-sur-Saône, 1449–50) that was organised by its eponymous hero.[28] Heralds' reports of *pas d'armes* could also serve as the basis for chroniclers' versions of these events. For instance, Olivier de La Marche, the prolific historiographer of many Burgundian tournaments, freely acknowledges his debt to heralds in his account of the *Pas de l'Arbre Charlemagne* (Marsannay-la-Côte, 1443) held by Pierre de Bauffremont, lord of Charny.[29]

Although most of the narrative accounts of *pas d'armes* were produced by heralds and chroniclers, there were nonetheless other types of author too. For example, the poem recounting the *Pas de la Bergère* (Tarascon, 1449) organised by Philippe de Lenoncourt and Philibert de Laigue was written by Louis de Beauvau, a knight from Anjou who had himself jousted at the event.[30] The account commemorating the famous Angevin *Pas de la Joyeuse Garde/Pas de Saumur* (1446), held by Duke René of Anjou, was composed by a cleric who reveals his ecclesiastical status without divulging his name.[31] A fragmentary and incomplete description of the *Pas* of Brussels (1503), staged by the nobleman Antoine de Lalaing, was written up by the *entrepreneur* himself in his chronicle account of the journey to Spain of his lord, Archduke Philip the Fair.[32]

In addition to recording who had participated in these events, another key focus of the authors of *pas d'armes* narratives was on how their account could provide a means of teaching their readers about chivalry through retelling the competitors' martial deeds. Their accounts were therefore meant to be not just commemorative but also prescriptive, offering their readers good examples to follow in their own lives whilst also indicating the bad examples to be avoided. Of particular interest to many of these writers was also the spectacle of the *pas*. They therefore pay a lot of attention to how each competitor entered the lists, which high-ranking figures accompanied him, how lavishly he — and his horse — were dressed (in silk, satin, velvet, cloth of gold, and with jewels or gold ornaments, etc.), what the crest on top of his helm was made of (egret feathers, gemstones, expensive veils, etc.) and even how many times an *entrepreneur* changed his outfits in the course of a multi-day event.

The pre-circulated articles or chapters of arms outlining the rules of engagement for these events could also be preserved by chroniclers or heralds, either on their own or as part of a longer narrative. In the latter case, when they were not reproduced verbatim but rather were incorporated into the narrative, this could involve an awkward transposition of verb tenses, as these chapters were designed to stipulate in the future or conditional tense what *would* happen at a *pas d'armes*, whereas the narrative account itself was written in the past tense in order to record what *did* happen.[33]

As well as these various forms of historiographical narrative recounting the *pas d'armes*, a second but much less well-known textual source of information about these events is the surviving financial records. These can be found either in the administrative accounts of the towns that part-subsidised an *entrepreneur*'s organisation of such an event or in the records of the princely households with which the *entrepreneur* and/or the competitors on

[28] See CL, pp. 210–17, 219–51.
[29] See OdLM, vol. 1, pp. 283–7, 290–324, 324–35.
[30] See PB, and Source 6.
[31] See PSr, and Source 7.
[32] See CdV, pp. xiv–xv, 123; and Source 14.
[33] See, for example, Sources 4 and 12.

his team were connected. From the urban accounts, which often detail payments made to carpenters and labourers, it is possible to calculate the costs involved in preparing a suitable playing surface for combat, in building lists and pavilions for the competitors, in erecting stands for judges, heralds and high-ranking guests and even in creating pieces of ephemeral architecture such as a huge column or a castle associated with the fictional scenario of a particular *pas*.[34] These accounts could also include the sums paid to the owners of private houses that were rented as temporary residences by high-ranking guests or as vantage points from which to witness events and could specify the gifts, either in kind or in money, that were granted to competitors.[35] Princely financial accounts of a particular lord or lady could likewise list payments made directly to the organisers of these events,[36] or to the armourers, cloth merchants, jewellers and tailors who provided the arms, armour and clothing worn by participants and their horses, as well as the materials used for the post-combat festivities.[37]

Apart from these written records, another important way in which the memory of these chivalric events was preserved was through the illustrations that accompanied the narrative accounts of a number of *pas* that were held in Anjou, the Burgundian lands and France. In the manuscripts of standalone texts devoted to recounting a specific tournament, these images could range from a single frontispiece, as for the *Pas de la Bergère*, to a cycle of around ten miniatures, as for the *Pas des armes de Sandricourt*, and even to a uniquely lavish ninety images for the *Pas de la Joyeuse Garde/Pas de Saumur*.[38] In the case of one record of a *pas* that is included in a much longer narrative, namely the chivalric biography of Jacques de Lalaing, three out of a cycle of eighteen miniatures in total in three different illustrated manuscripts of this text are devoted to this event, one to the fictional setting and two to some of the combats featured at it.[39] Although a certain amount of artistic licence has to be allowed for in these miniatures as pictorial sources, which interpret as much as they record the event through the use of iconographical convention, they nonetheless abound in meticulously detailed coats of arms, crests and clothing that do in fact often tally with the descriptions of these items in the narrative texts and with the mentions of them in financial accounts.[40] Again, as for the producers of many of the written accounts of *pas d'armes*, the names of the artists involved in creating these image cycles are usually unknown to us, being referred to only by a sobriquet such as the 'Master of the Getty Lalaing'; it is very rare that these images can be attributed to a particular named artist, as in the case of Simon Bening in this same manuscript.[41]

---

[34] For the *Pas du Perron Fée* and the *Pas* of Brussels, see Sources 11b and 14, respectively.

[35] For the *Pas du Perron Fée*, see Source 11b.

[36] For the *Pas de la Bergère*, see Source 6.

[37] For the *Pas* of Carignano, see Source 15.

[38] For the *Pas de la Bergère*, see Source 6; for the *Pas des armes de Sandricourt*, see Source 13 and Essay 4; for the *Pas de la Joyeuse Garde/Pas de Saumur*, see Source 5 and Essays 2 and 7.

[39] See Essay 6, pp. 489–90, 493–4.

[40] See Source 6.

[41] In the case of the Lalaing biography preserved in Los Angeles, J. Paul Getty Museum, 114, Simon Bening produced the elaborate frontispiece featuring the supposed author of the text dressed as the King of Arms of the Burgundian Order of the Golden Fleece, whereas the Master of the Getty Lalaing painted the other seventeen miniatures depicting scenes from the narrative.

Whilst armorials have survived as the pictorial records of some late medieval tournaments, none are known to exist for any specific *pas d'armes*. The only *pas d'armes* manuscript that incorporates a series of heraldic depictions that comes closest to an armorial roll is El Escorial, Real Biblioteca del Monasterio de San Lorenzo, e-IV-5 (fols 59v–63r): here, the armorial shields of thirty-one competitors at Claude de Vaudrey's *Pas du Chevalier au Souci* (near Paris, 1484) are depicted alongside the narrative recounting their names. This manuscript has an account of both this event and the *Pas* of Paris that immediately preceded it, the two tournaments forming part of the festivities that followed Charles VIII's coronation in Reims (May 1484) and his Royal Entry into Paris (July 1484).[42]

The importance of heraldry as a visual source for these events is also evident in the narrative and administrative accounts. These records go into great detail on the coats of arms that were depicted on the banners, pennons and horse trappers of the *entrepreneur* and the other competitors, worn in the form of coat armour, or painted on their shields or on the ephemeral architecture of the *pas*, even if, unfortunately, none of these actual items now survives. Such heraldic display not only served to show the identity of the individual tourneyers but also allowed the nobility as a social group to put itself on display in a public space. In this way, heraldry served both to exclude non-nobles from competing in these events and to highlight what was distinctive about the highest-ranking echelons of late medieval society.[43]

Finally, the actual weapons used at *pas d'armes* are likewise a key source for scholars, even if it is impossible to link any actual examples of arms and armour currently preserved in museum collections to those used at these particular tournaments. Nevertheless, what the narrative accounts of *pas d'armes* say about the size and shape of these items and the fighting techniques employed to wield these weapons clearly underlines the fact that the contestants at these events were engaged in serious and dangerous combats where the risk of injury was high. The material culture of the *pas* can thus be studied by using other sources (administrative, narrative and pictorial) to put these weapons into context and to assess their martial, economic and symbolic significance.

Scholarly approaches to the *pas d'armes*

The *pas d'armes* has received two main forms of attention from scholars over the past few hundred years, each of which has yielded valuable results: the first is the publication of editions of primary sources; the second is the analytical study of this type of tournament. The former began much earlier than the latter: for instance, in the seventeenth century antiquarians such as Marc Vulson de la Colombière enthusiastically collected and transcribed all sorts of materials relating to courtly and chivalric culture, including narratives of *pas*.[44] In the

42 CRC, paragraphs 73–81 (*Pas* of Paris), paragraphs 82–126 (*Pas du Chevalier au Souci*). See <https://rbme.patrimonionacional.es/s/rbme/item/13537#?xywh=-486%2C-91%2C3310%2C1804> [accessed 6 June 2024] for the images of these coats of arms. For a translation of the narrative account of these two *pas d'armes*, see Supplementary Source 2, Liverpool University Press Digital Collaboration Hub <https://liverpooluniversitypress.manifoldapp.org/projects/pas-d-armes-casebook> [accessed 1 November 2024].

43 Vale, *War and Chivalry*, pp. 95–9.

44 See VT and SH. On the *Pas* of Carignano (1504), see PC, the work of the Savoyard antiquarian Samuel Guichenon.

nineteenth century, Belgian and French aristocratic scholars, such as Henri Beaune and Jules d'Arbaucourt, Henri Courteault, Gaston du Fresne de Beaucourt, Félix Brassart, Louis Douët-d'Arcq and Joseph Kervyn de Lettenhove, sought to publish an authoritative body of medieval texts to promote the study of this period; their publications include numerous editions of chapters of arms and of surviving narrative accounts of *pas d'armes*.[45]

Although much of the information contained in these nineteenth-century editions remains of value, the modern scholar can often be frustrated by their editors' lack of precision concerning the particular manuscript sources that they used to compile their texts,[46] as well as by the absence of a proper scholarly apparatus providing, for instance, information about the people who participated in these events. By contrast, although the nineteenth-century editions of financial accounts that contain entries about the *pas d'armes* are often more systematic in what they cover and more reliable in their transcriptions than those of the narrative sources, they are nonetheless frustratingly rare, being largely confined to the ducal court of Anjou and to some of the towns in the Burgundian lands.[47] More information of this type may, however, remain to be discovered in the archives.

In the late twentieth and early twenty-first centuries, researchers such as G. A. Lester and Ralph Moffat have produced modern scholarly editions of medieval tournament books that are collections of miscellaneous narrative accounts in both English and French of chivalric events; these books have included a number of *pas d'armes*.[48] Several modern editions have also been produced of narratives devoted to a particular *pas*, although these vary greatly in the quality of their critical apparatus. For example, Natalia Elagina *et al.*'s edition of the *Relation du Pas de Saumur* (as the poem devoted to this event is known) and the edition by Chloé Horne, Anne Rochebouet and Michelle Szkilnik of the different manuscript versions of the *Pas du Perron Fée* offer meticulous transcriptions of the original texts and provide full notes on the biographies of the participants at these events, thus facilitating scholarly engagement with these works.[49] Less useful is Harry F. Williams's edition of the poem recounting the *Pas de la Bergère*, which is marred by an unreliable glossary on the arms, armour and clothing terms appearing in it.[50]

As the examples cited above indicate, the bulk of the editorial work on sources for *pas d'armes* has focused on Middle French texts commemorating tournaments held in Anjou, the Burgundian lands and France, which is where the greatest concentration of such events is undoubtedly to be found. Where editions of the various chronicles in which Castilian *pasos* are mentioned have been published, they are more rigorous than many of

---

[45] On editions produced by Beaune and d'Arbaumont, see OdLM; by Beaucourt, see MdE; by Brassart, see *Le Pas du Perron Fée, tenu à Bruges, en 1463, par le chevalier Philippe de Lalaing* (Douai: L. Crépin, 1874); by Douët-d'Arcq, see EdM; by Kervyn de Lettenhove, see GC and JDI.

[46] This is especially true of Auguste Vayssière's edition of the *Pas des armes de Sandricourt* (1493): see PSt.

[47] See, for example, Albert Lecoy de la Marche's edition of René of Anjou's household accounts in ECMR, and Louis Gilliodts-van Severen's partial edition of the town account of 1463 of Bruges concerning the *Pas du Perron Fée* in his *Inventaire des archives de la ville de Bruges. Section première: Inventaire des chartes. Première série: treizième au seizième siècle*, 9 vols (Bruges: Gailliard, 1871–85), vol. 5, pp. 533–5.

[48] Godfrey Allen Lester, *Sir John Paston's Grete Boke: A Descriptive Index with an Introduction of British Library MS. Lansdowne 285* (Woodbridge: Boydell & Brewer, 1984); and MT.

[49] See PSr and PPF, respectively.

[50] See PB.

the nineteenth-century works on the Burgundian and French *pas*,[51] but these chronicles tend to contain much shorter accounts of these *pasos* in the first place. By contrast, where a much lengthier narrative exists, as for the most famous Castilian event, the *Paso Honroso* (Órbigo Bridge, near León, 1434), the edition of it produced by Noel Fallows in his broader study of jousting in Iberia preserves only part of the original text.[52]

Moreover, those editions of the narrative and administrative sources for *pas d'armes* that have appeared in print have usually been published in their original language (Medieval Castilian, Middle Dutch, Middle French, etc.) which can thus present a considerable linguistic challenge to scholars unfamiliar with these languages. Translations of these works into modern English are few and far between: Anthony Annunziata's compilation of translated extracts from a range of *pas* offers a useful taster of the available sources;[53] Fallows' partial edition of the *Paso Honroso* includes a facing-page translation of these sections;[54] Andrew Brown and Graeme Small's study of court and civic society translates excerpts from Olivier de La Marche's account of the *Pas de l'Arbre d'or* (Bruges, 1468);[55] and, most recently, Rosalind Brown-Grant and Mario Damen's complete translation of the Lalaing biography includes its account of the *Fontaine des Pleurs*.[56]

As for the illuminated manuscripts of *pas d'armes*, whilst a number of these have been digitised and can now be consulted online, this is sadly not true of the unique manuscripts of either the *Pas de la Bergère* (Paris, BnF, fr. 1974) or the *Pas de la Joyeuse Garde/Pas de Saumur* (St Petersburg, NLR, fr. F. p. XIV, 4).[57]

If the first approach to the *pas d'armes* has been to make the sources for these events available in print, the second approach, one taken by scholars from a variety of disciplinary perspectives — cultural, social and political history, literary studies, material culture, gender studies and art history — has been more analytical in nature. One of the earliest scholars to make use of the nineteenth-century editions in order to analyse the *pas* was the

---

[51] See AGSM; FPG; HCMLI; LB; PCH.

[52] See PH. At the time of his death in 2022, Fallows was working on a full edition of this text with facing-page English translation; it is hoped that this work may be brought to completion in the near future by a team of collaborators.

[53] Anthony Annunziata, 'Teaching the *pas d'armes*', in *The Study of Chivalry: Resources and Approaches*, ed. by Howell Chickering and Thomas H. Seiler (Kalamazoo, MI: Medieval Institute Publications, 1988), pp. 556–82.

[54] See PH.

[55] Andrew Brown and Graeme Small, eds., *Court and Civic Society in the Burgundian Low Countries c. 1420–1530* (Manchester: Manchester University Press, 2007), pp. 54–85. For the only description in Middle Dutch of a *pas d'armes*, see the report written on the same event by the Bruges rhetorician Anthonis de Roovere in HKB.

[56] See CL.

[57] For digitised manuscripts and early printed editions of the *Pas des armes de Sandricourt*, see Paris, BnF Arsenal, 3958 Réserve: ark:/12148/btv1b550057254; Paris, BnF, fr. 1436 (*Armoriaux de la Table Ronde*, including 'Le Pas des armes de Sandricourt' and 'Description des tournois faits l'an 1519 à Chambly et Bailleul'): ark:/12148/btv1b10525465m; Paris, BnF, Vélins 1033: ark:/12148/bpt6k15241119; and BnF, Vélins 1034: http://catalogue.bnf.fr/ark:/12148/cb36283971x. For digitised manuscripts of the *Livre des faits de messire Jacques de Lalaing*, see Paris, BnF, fr. 16830: ark:/12148/btv1b10537591f; and Los Angeles, J. Paul Getty Museum, 114: <https://www.getty.edu/art/collection/object/109M32> [accessed 6 June 2024].

Dutch cultural historian Johan Huizinga, whose ground-breaking *Herfsttij der middeleeuwen* (1919)[58] laid much of the foundation for future study of this phenomenon. Identifying seven *pas d'armes* by name, Huizinga argues that the knight (i.e. *entrepreneur*) who organises the *pas* is often modelled on the anonymous or 'unknown' knights of Arthurian romance, something he likens to the 'childlike imaginings of the fairy tale'. Yet, Huizinga also stresses the 'erotic character' of *pas* and their 'bloody violence', and sees the knights who competed at these tournaments as expressing their love for their ladies in the sublimated form of chivalric service to them, given that women formed a key part of the audiences at such events. Finally, Huizinga emphasises the dramatic and emotional impact that the *pas d'armes* would have produced on both those who fought in them and those who spectated at them, this impact being heightened by the use of ephemeral architecture, props, role-playing characters and heraldic symbolism and colours.[59]

Following Huizinga's work in both this foundational study and his own later *Homo Ludens* (1938), where he argues for seeing the *pas d'armes* and other forms of tournament as examples of 'play', in the sense of voluntary acts that could involve disguise and were bound by certain rules with the capacity to create social bonds between participants,[60] much of the debate on the topic has been dominated by the issue of whether it should be regarded more properly as a type of sport or a form of theatre than as real fighting. Those scholars who have argued that the *pas* should be classified as a kind of sport include Sébastien Nadot, who sees these events as being comparable to present-day sporting encounters, in that those who competed at them had to not only observe certain rules and regulations (chapters of arms) but also undergo intensive physical training and become expert in the use of specialised equipment (especially for mounted combat) so as to avoid injury.[61] Similarly, Noel Fallows describes the joust, a key element of many *pas*, as 'the greatest sport of the medieval age',[62] and regards rule-based tournaments such as *pas d'armes* as contributing to 'the overall development of a sporting ethos', especially when it came to winning prizes, a characteristic element of most sports today.[63]

Those who have interpreted the *pas d'armes* not as a sport but rather as a form of theatre, given its origins in the highly dramatised tournament form of the Round Table, include Alice Planche. Directly comparing the material and social infrastructure of the

---

[58] Johan Huizinga, *Herfsttij der middeleeuwen. Studie over levens- en gedachtenvormen der veertiende en vijftiende eeuw in Frankrijk en de Nederlanden* (Haarlem: H. D. Tjeenk Willink & Zoon, 1919).

[59] Johan Huizinga, *Autumntide of the Middle Ages: A Study of Forms of Life and Thought of the Fourteenth and Fifteenth Centuries in France and the Low Countries*, ed. by Anton van der Lem and Graeme Small, trans. by Diane Webb (Leiden: Leiden University Press, 2020), pp. 117, 121.

[60] Johan Huizinga, *Homo ludens: A Study of the Play-Element in Culture* (Boston, MA: Beacon Press, 1955), pp. 13, 122–31. See also Andrew Brown, 'Huizinga's Autumn. The Burgundian Court at Play', in *Rereading Huizinga: Autumn of the Middle Ages, a Century Later*, ed. by Peter Arnade, Martha C. Howell and Anton van der Lem (Amsterdam: Amsterdam University Press, 2019), pp. 25–40 (pp. 29–31, 35).

[61] Nadot, *Le Spectacle*, pp. 25–8, 35–6, 327.

[62] Noel Fallows, 'Rules and Order', in *A Cultural History of Sport in the Medieval Age*, ed. by Noel Fallows (London: Bloomsbury, 2022), pp. 113–40 (p. 118).

[63] Noel Fallows, 'Introduction', in *ibid.*, pp. 1–34 (p. 15). Compare Gert Melville, 'Der Held in Szene gesetzt: einige Bilder und Gedanken zu Jacques de Lalaing und seinem Pas d'armes de la Fontaine des Pleurs', in *'Aufführung' und 'Schrift' in Mittelalter und früher Neuzeit*, ed. by Jan-Dirk Müller (Stuttgart: Metzler, 1996), pp. 253–86 (p. 275), who argues that all the competitors in a *pas* were winners since the only thing that was at stake was honour.

pas with that of the medieval theatre, she suggests that, while the noble competitors at these chivalric events may have been of a different social class from the town-dwellers who staged medieval plays, there were nonetheless striking similarities between these two types of event, even if the outcomes in theatre were pre-ordained by a script whereas those of a *pas* were unpredictable. Both involved extensive advance planning and organisation, both featured a purpose-built architectural infrastructure for the participants, spectators and judges, and both stimulated a certain level of participation in the event from the audience watching.[64] Jean-Pierre Jourdan likewise emphasises the inherent theatricality of the *pas*, with the lists constituting an enclosed space, the presence of symbolic objects such as a tree, a column, a bridge or a gate contributing to the 'mystery' of the *pas*, and the setting of the whole event on either a real or a symbolic border or in an urban market square, creating a symbolic ritual space.[65] This theatrical aspect of *pas d'armes*, which is underlined by the inclusion of elaborate dramatic interludes (*entremets*) and dances, can thus be seen as a precursor of sixteenth-century chivalric events that, as William Henry Jackson argues, incorporated 'artistic forms of renaissance and baroque theatre, ballet and opera, forms which flourished at the same princely courts as and drew some of their features from the tournament'.[66] Many scholars would, however, now be happy to accept that the *pas d'armes* incorporated elements of both sport and theatre. As Malcolm Vale puts it, the *pas* is a 'later medieval *Gesamtkunstwerk* binding the arts of war and peace, and employing allegory, poetry, ceremonial and music to achieve its dramatic effects'.[67]

Vale's view that the *pas* brought together the arts of war and peace points to a second area of debate, namely whether these events were purely a form of chivalric entertainment or also served as preparation for actual warfare. Sydney Anglo and Noel Fallows have both adopted the first position, arguing that jousting was increasingly 'irrelevant to contemporary warfare' and that 'the activity was an end unto itself, with the result that jousters trained above all to be good jousters.'[68] By contrast, for Vale and other historians such as Helen Watanabe-O'Kelly, the fact that these chivalric encounters involved a wide variety of combat techniques, both on foot and on horseback, meant that they were able to retain a military relevance well into the seventeenth century.[69]

---

[64] Alice Planche, 'Du tournoi au théâtre en Bourgogne. Le Pas de la Fontaine des Pleurs à Chalon-sur-Saône, 1449–1450', *Le Moyen Âge*, 81 (1975), 97–128 (pp. 126–8).

[65] Jean-Pierre Jourdan, 'Le thème du pas d'armes dans le royaume de France (Bourgogne, Anjou) à la fin du Moyen Âge: aspects d'un théâtre de chevalerie', in *Théâtre et spectacles hier et aujourd'hui: Moyen âge et Renaissance. Actes du 115e Congrès National des Sociétés Savantes (Avignon, 1990). Section d'histoire médiévale et de philologie* (Paris: Éditions du CTHS, 1991), pp. 285–304 (pp. 286–90).

[66] William Henry Jackson, 'The Tournament and Chivalry in German Tournament Books of the Sixteenth Century and in the Literary Works of Emperor Maximilian I', in *The Ideals and Practice of Medieval Knighthood*, ed. by Ruth Harvey and Christopher Harper-Bill (Woodbridge: Boydell Press, 1986), pp. 49–73 (p. 73).

[67] Vale, *War and Chivalry*, p. 68.

[68] Sydney Anglo, 'The Tournament at Binche', in *Charles V, Prince Philip, and the Politics of Succession. Imperial Festivities in Mons and Hainault, 1549*, ed. by Margaret McGowan and Margaret Shewring (Turnhout: Brepols, 2020), pp. 223–41 (p. 238); Fallows, *Jousting*, pp. 240–1, 292.

[69] Vale, *War and Chivalry*, pp. 70, 78–80; Helen Watanabe-O'Kelly, 'Tournaments and their Relevance for Warfare in the Early Modern Period', *European History Quarterly*, 20 (1990), 451–63. See also Mario Damen, 'Tournaments and the Integration of the Nobility in the Habsburg Composite State', *Renaissance Quarterly*, 76.2 (2023), 497–541.

This latter view of *pas d'armes* has been bolstered by those scholars writing from a material cultural perspective, including Richard Barber and Juliet Barker, who, along with Vale, have produced detailed studies of the weaponry and armour used at this type of tournament.[70] In their opinion, new military techniques adopted by both cavalry and infantry had an impact not only on the way in which battles (and also the mock battles of the *pas*) were waged in the later Middle Ages but also on the materials knights used to protect themselves and attack their opponents. These included the development of plate armour and new types of helmet, such as the sallet, as well as the appearance of the lance-rest to facilitate the balancing of the heavy lance across the body and to enhance the impact of the blow when the two jousters encountered.

Given that the arms and armour used in the *pas* were often identical to those used in actual armed conflict, such tournaments did clearly hone the knight's chivalric prowess in times of peace and provide him with a training for times of war. Indeed, more recent scholars, such as Tobias Capwell and Ralph Moffat, have developed this approach further by studying surviving examples of arms and armour — albeit ones that cannot be definitively linked to particular *pas d'armes* — in conjunction with the narrative and pictorial sources relating to these events so as to gauge more precisely how competitors might have used them.[71]

In addition to debates about whether the *pas d'armes* was a form of sport or theatre and whether or not it was a type of preparation for war, a third, complementary area of study has been developed by scholars such as Jean-Pierre Jourdan, who have focused rather on the socio-political aspect of these events. In his view, the point of the *pas* was to create bonds between noble competitors rather than to break them, hence the need to provide proof of one's nobility so as to forge social and political alliances. For Jourdan, this also explains why 'foreigners' were sometimes excluded from participating in these events, this being to reduce the likelihood of political conflict arising from the combats, and why opponents usually made a gesture of reconciliation, such as touching hands, after competing against each other.[72] Similarly, Éric Bousmar has highlighted the ways in which the *pas* helped to foster diplomatic relations between an international brotherhood of knights and their princes and to promote cohesion between knights belonging to the same polity, particularly in the Burgundian lands.[73] Andries Van den Abeele has also focused

---

70 Vale, *War and Chivalry*, pp. 100–28; Barber and Barker, *Tournaments*, pp. 98–102, 107–38.

71 Tobias Capwell, *Arms and Armour of the Medieval Joust* (Leeds: Royal Armouries Museum, 2018); *idem*, 'Armor, Weapons, and Combat in the Getty Lalaing', in *A Knight for the Ages: Jacques de Lalaing and the Art of Chivalry*, ed. by Elizabeth Morrison (Los Angeles: The J. Paul Getty Museum, 2018), pp. 151–64; and MT.

72 See Jourdan, 'Le thème du pas d'armes', pp. 301–3; *idem*, 'Le symbolisme politique du pas dans le royaume de France (Bourgogne et Anjou) à la fin du moyen âge', *Journal of Medieval History*, 18 (1992), 161–81; *idem*, 'Le thème du Pas et de l'Emprise. Espaces symboliques et rituels d'alliance en France à la fin du Moyen Âge', *Éthnologie française*, 22.2 (1992), 172–84.

73 Éric Bousmar, 'Pasos de armas, justas y torneos en la corte de Borgoña (siglo XV y principios del XVI). Imaginario caballeresco, rituales e implicaciones socio-políticas', in *El legado de Borgoña: Fiesta y ceremonia cortesana en la Europa de los Austrias (1454–1648)*, ed. by Krista De Jonge, Bernardo J. García García and Alicia Esteban Estríngana (Madrid: Fundación Carlos de Amberes/Marcial Pons Ediciones de Historia, 2010), pp. 561–605; *idem*, 'Jousting at the Court of Burgundy. The "Pas d'armes": Shifts in Scenario, Location and Recruitment', in *Staging the Court of Burgundy: Proceedings of the Conference 'The Splendour of Burgundy'*, ed. by Wim Blockmans *et al.* (Turnhout/London: Brepols/Harvey Miller, 2013), pp. 75–84.

on the relations between the participants at a *pas* — as well as the underlying tensions that these bonds could belie — in his analysis of the divergent agendas being pursued by the *entrepreneur* and the various defenders and challengers at the *Pas du Perron Fée*.[74]

A further area of socio-political debate on the *pas d'armes* has been the extent to which these events were exclusively courtly in nature or were also influenced by the non-courtly, urban environment in which many of them took place. For example, historians such as Nadot, Barber and Barker have tended to derive their conclusions about the overwhelmingly courtly aspect of these tournaments from their reading of contemporary commentators on the *pas d'armes* such as the Burgundian chroniclers.[75] These accounts naturally stress the involvement of courtiers, and even the occasional presence or participation of the prince in these *pas*, not to mention the astonishing display of luxury clothes, horse trappers, armour, armorial banners and pennons that took place at them. However, at the same time as describing all these items in detail, in order to emphasise the dazzling visual spectacle offered by these events, the chroniclers systematically downplay — or do not even mention — the general urban setting of many of these events.

Challenging this view of the *pas d'armes* as uniquely courtly based on the surviving narrative sources, other historians such as Élodie Lecuppre-Desjardin have argued that the organisation of these events in the middle of a town not only had a notable impact on urban space, converting the open marketplace into a 'closed universe', but also allowed them to serve as an 'instrument of pacification' in the hands of the prince and the nobility vis-à-vis the urban population.[76] By contrast, Évelyne Van den Neste and Mario Damen have stressed the fact that *pas d'armes*, in spite of being noble, chivalric entertainments, could actually help to bring together both the urban and courtly milieus of the Burgundian Low Countries, not surprisingly perhaps, given that a lively jousting culture was often already present in these towns.[77] In Bruges, for example, a jousting society known as the 'Witte Beer' (White Bear) was active from the late fourteenth century onwards, staging an annual jousting event. The presence of a prosperous and organised urban elite who owned horses and armour was certainly a great stimulus for the organisation of chivalric activities not only in Flemish towns such as Bruges and Lille but also in other urban centres of Brabant, Hainaut and Artois. Furthermore, as Juliet Vale and Robert Stein have shown, the holding of such events was not simply an attempt to imitate an aristocratic lifestyle but rather had its own dynamic, stemming mainly from socio-political developments in the towns whereby jousts, much like archery and crossbow competitions, evolved into

---

[74] Andries Van den Abeele, 'De Wapenpas van de Betoverde Burcht, voorbode van de machtsgreep door Karel de Stoute', *Handelingen van het Genootschap voor Geschiedenis te Brugge*, 146 (2009), 93–139. For a similar approach in the context of later Habsburg chivalric events, see Damen, 'Tournaments'.

[75] Barber and Barker, *Tournaments*, pp. 110–25; and Nadot, *Le Spectacle*, pp. 273–81.

[76] Élodie Lecuppre-Desjardin, *La ville des cérémonies: Essai sur la communication politique dans les anciens Pays-Bas bourguignons* (Turnhout: Brepols, 2004), pp. 205–10.

[77] VdN; Mario Damen, 'The Town as a Stage? Urban Space and Tournaments in Late Medieval Brussels', *Urban History*, 43.1 (2016), 47–71. Although no *pas* are known to have taken place in the Holy Roman Empire, other types of tournament may have served a similar socio-political function there: see Thomas Zotz, 'Adel, Burgertum und Turniere in Deutschen Stadten', in *Das ritterliche Turnier im Mittelalter: Beiträge zu einer vergleichenden Formen- und Verhaltensgeschichte des Rittertums*, ed. by Josef Fleckenstein (Göttingen: Vandenhoeck & Ruprecht, 1985), pp. 450–99 (pp. 473–85); and Klaus Militzer, 'Turniere in Köln', *Jahrbuch des Kölnischen Geschichtsvereins*, 64.1 (2015), 37–60.

inter-urban contests in which the honour of the towns and their ruling lineages was at stake.[78] That not only the local nobility but sometimes even the duke and members of his household took part in them indicates that these events enjoyed considerable prestige. However, as Andrew Brown has demonstrated, towards the end of the fifteenth century political and economic problems made it increasingly difficult for the urban elites of Bruges and Lille to participate in, let alone organise, these annual jousting events.[79] Whilst the highly exclusive *pas d'armes*, in which competitors had to prove that they were of noble birth on all four sides, survived this decline, its main stage and audience were no longer predominantly urban by the first quarter of the sixteenth century.

Still on the socio-political dimensions of the *pas*, but from a different perspective, is the approach taken by scholars who have focused on the role of gender. Ruth Mazo Karras, for example, has argued that medieval tournaments, including *pas d'armes*, promoted a form of aristocratic masculine identity that was both homosocial, in terms of the bonds they fostered between competing knights, and heterosexual, in positioning ladies as admiring and appreciative spectators of these knights' feats of arms and as amorous inspirers of chivalric prowess.[80] Whilst Karras herself suggests that women's actual agency in these two capacities was somewhat limited, other scholars, such as Bousmar, have seen their roles as more active and influential than Karras's analysis would allow.[81]

So far, then, the approaches to the *pas d'armes* set out above have emphasised using the surviving primary sources as a means by which to situate it in cultural, martial and socio-political contexts. However, an alternative line of enquiry has been to take these sources themselves as an object of study in their own right and to examine the reciprocal influence of literature on actual practice, and vice versa, as pioneered by Armand Strubel, Annette Lindner and particularly Michel Stanesco.[82] In Stanesco's view, *pas d'armes* are examples of what he terms the *enromancement* (romanticisation) of medieval chivalric culture, whereby knights of the period strove consciously to imitate literary models in order to prove their own worthiness of being commemorated for their military deeds, whether on the field of battle or the tilting yard.[83] Following in their footsteps, other scholars, such as

---

[78] Juliet Vale, *Edward III and Chivalry: Chivalric Society and its Context, 1270–1350* (Woodbridge: Boydell Press, 1982), pp. 25–41; Robert Stein, 'An Urban Network in the Medieval Low Countries. A Cultural Approach', in *Networks, Regions and Nations: Shaping Identities in the Low Countries, 1300–1650*, ed. by Robert Stein and Judith Pollmann (Leiden: Brill, 2010), pp. 43–71 (pp. 48–54).

[79] Andrew Brown, 'Urban Jousts in the Later Middle Ages: The White Bear of Bruges', *Revue Belge de Philologie et d'Histoire*, 78 (2000), 315–30.

[80] Ruth Mazo Karras, *From Boys to Men: Formations of Masculinity in Late Medieval Europe* (Philadelphia: University of Pennsylvania Press, 2003).

[81] Éric Bousmar, 'La place des hommes et des femmes dans les fêtes de cour bourguignonnes (Philippe le Bon–Charles le Hardi)', *PCEEB*, 34 (1994), 123–43. See also Nadot, *Le Spectacle*, pp. 179–87; Audrey Pennel, 'Des hourds aux lices: la place des dames dans les enluminures des tournois et Pas d'armes aux XIVe et XVe siècle', *Francia. Forschungen zur westeuropäischen Geschichte*, 46 (2019), 431–42.

[82] Armand Strubel, 'Le *pas d'armes*: le tournoi entre le romanesque et le théâtral', in *Théâtre et spectacles hier et aujourd'hui: Moyen âge et Renaissance. Actes du 115e Congrès National des Sociétés Savantes (Avignon, 1990). Section d'histoire médiévale et de philologie* (Paris: Éditions du CTHS, 1991), pp. 273–84; Annette Lindner, 'L'influence du roman chevaleresque français sur le pas d'armes', *PCEEB*, 31 (1991), 67–78; Michel Stanesco, *Jeux d'errance du chevalier médiéval: aspects ludiques de la fonction guerrière dans la littérature du Moyen Âge flamboyant* (Leiden: Brill, 1988), p. 23.

[83] Stanesco, *Jeux d'errance*, p. 23.

Catherine Blunk, Rosalind Brown-Grant, Michelle Szkilnik and Jane H. M. Taylor, have highlighted the degree of cross-fertilisation between the accounts of *pas d'armes* contained in works of chivalric and courtly fiction, such as La Sale's *Jean de Saintré* and other less well-known examples from the Angevin, Burgundian and French courts, and those which describe actual *pas*.[84]

Scholars studying the illuminated texts commemorating actual *pas* have often attempted to reconstruct the conditions under which they were brought into being and to determine the reasons behind their commissioning, as is the case of Christian de Mérindol in his analysis of the heavily illustrated *Pas de Saumur* manuscript. Others have focused instead on text/image relations in these works, particularly the degree to which text and image can differ in their presentation and interpretation of both the combats and the post-combat festivities at *pas d'armes*.[85] Noting the relative scarcity of images of *pas* in general, Guillaume Bureaux has argued that the vividness of the textual descriptions of these events can help compensate for the lack of direct pictorialisation in many cases.[86]

To sum up this survey of the two main strands of scholarship on the *pas d'armes*, those wishing to study this chivalric phenomenon now have at their disposal a wealth of primary sources about particular events, especially those held in Anjou and the Burgundian lands, thanks to the richness of the written and pictorial records that survive for them. However, information for other geographical areas, such as Castile, is harder to come by and scholarly access is not helped by a continuing lack of material in translation. Moreover, valuable though much of the existing interpretive scholarship is on the *pas d'armes*, many questions not only remain unanswered but would also benefit from being tackled in a multi-disciplinary fashion. The Sources and Essays offered here in this Casebook thus attempt to address these two significant shortcomings.

---

84 Catherine Blunk, 'La vois des hiraus: the Poetics of Tournament in Late Medieval Chronicle and Romance' (unpublished PhD dissertation, University of Wisconsin-Madison, 2008); *eadem*, 'Faux pas in the Chronicles. What is a *pas d'armes*?', in *The Medieval Chronicle 11*, ed. by Erik Kooper and Sjoerd Levelt (Turnhout: Brepols, 2018), pp. 87–107; *eadem*, 'Between Sport and Theatre: How Spectacular was the *Pas d'armes*?', in *The Medieval Tournament as Spectacle: Tourneys, Jousts and Pas d'Armes, 1100–1600*, ed. by Alan V. Murray and Karen Watts (Woodbridge: Boydell Press, 2020), pp. 120–38; Rosalind Brown-Grant, 'Art Imitating Life Imitating Art? Representations of the *Pas d'armes* in Burgundian Prose Romance: The Case of *Jehan d'Avennes*', in *The Medieval Tournament as Spectacle: Tourneys, Jousts and Pas d'Armes, 1100–1600*, ed. by Alan V. Murray and Karen Watts (Woodbridge: Boydell Press, 2020), pp. 139–54; Michelle Szkilnik, 'Que lisaient les chevaliers du XVe siècle? Le témoignage du *Pas du Perron Fée*', *Le Moyen Français*, 68 (2011), 103–14; Jane H. M. Taylor, '"Une gente pastourelle": René d'Anjou, Louis de Beauvau et le Pas d'armes de la bergère', in *René d'Anjou, écrivain et mécène (1409–1480)*, ed. by Florence Bouchet (Turnhout: Brepols, 2011), pp. 197–208; *eadem*, 'La fête comme performance, le livre comme document: le Pas de Saumur', in *Les arts et les lettres en Provence au temps du roi René*, ed. by Chantal Connochie-Bourgne and Valérie Gontero-Lauze (Aix-en-Provence: Presses Universitaires de Provence, 2013), pp. 233–41.

85 Élisabeth Gaucher, '*Le Livre des Fais de Jacques de Lalain*: Texte et image', *Le Moyen Âge*, 95 (1989), 503–18; and Michelle Szkilnik, 'Mise en mots, mise en images: *Le Livre des Faits du bon chevalier Jacques de Lalain*', *Ateliers (Cahiers de la Maison de Recherche, Université Charles de Gaulle–Lille 3)*, 30 (2003), 75–87.

86 Christian de Mérindol, *Les fêtes de chevalerie à la cour du roi René. Emblématique, art et histoire (les joutes de Nancy, le Pas de Saumur et le Pas de Tarascon)* (Paris: Éditions du CTHS, 1993); Guillaume Bureaux, 'Pas d'armes et vide iconographique: quand le texte doit remplacer l'image (XVe siècle)', *Perspectives médiévales*, 38 (2017) <https://journals.openedition.org/peme/12792> [accessed 6 June 2024].

Structure and aims of the present volume

In order to facilitate scholars' engagement with both the narrative and financial sources for the *pas d'armes* and the surviving pictorial evidence for them, the texts translated in Part I of this volume include narrative works by a range of different authors — chroniclers, memoirists, heralds, knights and clerics — who were active across nearly a century of writing in at least five different territories, the order in which they appear here being chronological. These texts represent the full range of primary materials available to scholars, which run from the pleasingly complete to the tantalisingly fragmentary. Given that modern editions of narratives relating to fictional *pas* are generally easier to access than those which record historical *pas*, only one such example has been included, albeit an influential early one: this is Source 1, on the romance of *Ponthus et Sidoine* (discussed in Essay 6), which also includes three miniatures of scenes depicting the eponymous hero's *emprise* taken from a particularly beautiful manuscript version of the text.

For a small number of the historical *pas*, both a complete narrative account, with an accompanying image, and multiple entries in financial accounts exist. In these exceptional instances, juxtaposition of the different sources enables scholars to obtain a fuller understanding of how these events were actually staged than when just one type of account is analysed in isolation from the others. With all three kinds of material being present in Source 6 on the poem recounting the *Pas de la Bergère*, it is thus possible to see how an event of this nature was experienced by those who competed at it, how it was financed and how it was commemorated for posterity both textually and visually. For other events of which a complete narrative record survives (as opposed to just chapters of arms), this too has been rendered in full wherever possible, as in Source 7 on La Marche's account of the *Fontaine des Pleurs* (discussed in Essay 6), Source 9 on Georges Chastelain's account of the *Pas du Compagnon à la Larme Blanche* (Le Quesnoy, 1458), and Source 13 on Orléans Herald's account of the *Pas des armes de Sandricourt* (discussed in Essay 4). Put into dialogue with each other, what these accounts of two Burgundian and one northern French *pas* reveal is the range of different attitudes adopted towards these events by the authors who wrote them up, in particular the contrast between the ultra-enthusiastic La Marche, the more restrained Chastelain and the self-effacing but heavily invested herald.

For those historical events where the narrative account is too long to be translated in full, representative extracts have been chosen to cover different aspects or phases of them. Hence, for example, in Source 5, on the poem recounting the *Pas* held at Saumur (discussed in Essays 2 and 7), the selected extract of the first fifty-eight stanzas narrates the whole of the opening sequence that explains how this *pas* came to be organised and how the first in a long series of jousts was conducted at it. This is also the case in Source 15, which is an account of a *pas d'armes*, hitherto not identified as such, that took place at Carignano (1504) in the duchy of Savoy (discussed in Essays 1 and 6). The excerpts from it illustrate the motivation behind the organisation of this *pas*, which was to celebrate the wedding of one of the Savoyard duke's most important courtiers, as well as the nature of the festivities that followed the combats over the course of the event. This source, which is also accompanied by extracts from a financial document relating to the tournament, is important not only for putting Savoy firmly on the map as a court that staged *pas d'armes* but also for revealing the role that women, most notably the duchess of Savoy, Margaret of Austria, could play in staging these entertainments. Similarly, in Source 11a, extracts from two different narrative accounts of the *Pas du Perron Fée* (discussed in Essay 3) have been chosen to demonstrate the contrasting ways in which the treatment of the declaration of the event, its setting and its closing sequences could be handled by two different authors. This is complemented by Source 11b, which features extracts relating to the same event from both urban and court financial accounts that are available only in archival form; here, the accounts in Middle Dutch and Middle French, respectively, are both transcribed in the original language and given a facing-page translation. What these two sources show with particular clarity is the range of actors involved in the organisation of these events and the different priorities of those who subsidised them and those who commissioned manuscript versions of them.

A representative selection of narrative accounts that preserve only the chapters of arms has also been included in this first part of the volume, thus illustrating the conventions governing the writing of these texts and the degree to which they could vary in terms of their literary style and tone. Of course, whilst these chapters of arms were probably written up by heralds, they would have done so at the behest of the particular *entrepreneur* whose stamp would also thereby be imprinted on them. These examples are as follows: Source 4 features the chapters of the *Pas de l'Arbre Charlemagne* preserved in Enguerrand de Monstrelet's chronicle that would have been written up for Pierre de Bauffremont, lord of Charny; Source 12 contains the chapters of the *Pas de l'Arbre d'or* that were composed on behalf of Antoine, the Great Bastard of Burgundy; and Source 16 consists of the chapters governing the *Emprise of the Wild Knight of the Black Lady* (Edinburgh, 1507 and 1508) that were written up in Middle French by Marchmont Herald, probably at the command of King James IV of Scotland (discussed in Essay 5). This latter important document concerning a Scottish tournament that probably took place in two consecutive years and which has not previously been seen as a *pas*, is derived from the material preserved in the antiquarian collection of Vulson de la Colombière.

A final set of sources comprises those concerning *pas* in Castile and the Low Countries for which we have only brief mentions in much longer narratives — mostly chronicles, but also one chivalric biography[87] — and/or administrative sources. Thus, Source 2 is on the *Paso de la Fuerte Ventura* (Valladolid, 1428), staged by Enrique of Aragon; Source 3 covers the *Paso de Valladolid* (1440), organised by Ruy Díaz de Mendoza; Source 8 concerns the *Paso de El Pardo* (1459), held by Beltrán de la Cueva; Source 10 features the *Paso de Jaén* (1462), arranged by Fernán Mexía; and Source 14 presents a *pas* managed by Antoine de Lalaing (Brussels, 1503) (the first and the last of these are discussed in Essay 1). What these examples demonstrate is the need for scholars of *pas d'armes* to base their studies on all the available types of source material, including financial accounts, which, in some cases, enable the identification of an historical *pas* that has otherwise not been recognised as such. For instance, in the case of Source 14, the evidence amassed on the event organised by Antoine de Lalaing has not hitherto been included in scholarly discussions of *pas d'armes* but this material clearly shows him following in the footsteps of the earlier Jacques and Philippe de Lalaing, thus revealing how different generations of the same family could be heavily invested in these tournaments as a way of enhancing not only their individual prestige but also the renown of their entire lineage.

---

[87] Sources 2, 3, 8 and 14 are extracted from chronicles, whereas Source 10 is from a chivalric biography.

In order to facilitate the reader's access to these translated materials, each Source is accompanied by a short introductory essay setting out where the *pas d'armes* was held, who organised it, how it related to its particular cultural milieu, what its combats consisted of and who wrote it up; a select bibliography is also provided for each Source.

The seven essays contained in Part II of this Casebook address the second main aim of this volume: namely, to develop some of the existing avenues of enquiry on the *pas d'armes* whilst also taking scholarly debate on this topic in new directions. These essays not only draw extensively on many of the Sources from Part I but also demonstrate the importance of exploiting the full range of available narrative, financial and pictorial materials in order to examine these tournaments in as complete a fashion as possible and to bring fresh perspectives to bear on them. A key issue addressed by a number of these essays is that of cultural transmission: that is, how and why *pas d'armes* came to be adopted in certain milieus and not others. Essay 1, by Thalia Brero, Mario Damen and Klaus Oschema, thus seeks to explain why *pas d'armes* originated in Castile, why they spread thence to the Burgundian lands and to the ducal court of Savoy — which has not previously been identified as the location of such events — and, conversely, why they never took off in German-speaking courts such as those of Cleves and Habsburg. On this question of the geographical spread of *pas d'armes*, Essay 5 by Alan V. Murray reveals that, unlike in England, which was never a milieu favouring the organisation of this type of tournament, the court of James IV of Scotland does seem to have welcomed them, holding a particularly spectacular example — or probably two of them under the same name — in Edinburgh in 1507 and 1508. Essay 4 by Marina Viallon examines the influence exerted on early sixteenth-century tournaments in France by probably the most elaborate of all French *pas d'armes*, that held at Sandricourt (1493). Her focus here is on the innovative form of combat that was devised at this event, whereby the defenders and challengers fought each other not only as teams in the lists but also individually 'in the manner of Arthurian knights-errant' as they wandered through an evocatively named 'Labyrinthine Forest'.

A second strand of essays in the volume interrogates two particularly famous *pas d'armes* — one from Anjou and the other from the Burgundian Low Countries — from different critical angles but with a shared focus on the manuscript traditions of the narratives recounting these events. Essay 2, by Anne D. Hedeman and Justin Sturgeon, reassesses the St Petersburg manuscript that preserves the sole narrative account of the *Pas de la Joyeuse Garde/Pas de Saumur* (1446). Their study of text/image relations, heraldry and memorialisation within the manuscript allows them to make a new argument about who commissioned this famous illuminated codex and why they did so. Essay 3, by Mario Damen and Michelle Szkilnik, concentrates on the *Pas du Perron Fée* (Bruges, 1463), which they examine in terms of the personal motivations of the *entrepreneur*, Philippe de Lalaing, the complex urban/court relations revealed by juxtaposing the narrative and financial accounts pertaining to it, and the role played by the different manuscript versions of the narrative in the construction of family memory.

A final pair of essays seeks to deepen our understanding of the gender and power relations inherent in the *pas* in terms of how these events involved the expression of both homosocial and heterosexual masculine identity. Essay 6, by Rosalind Brown-Grant, looks at two important issues governing the construction of chivalric masculinity at these events: ethics, in terms of rule-making and rule-breaking in their combats, as seen in various Castilian and Burgundian examples; and erotics, in terms of women's influence on how the male competitors at them were perceived, as seen in both Burgundian and Savoyard examples. Essay 7, by Christina Normore, which is devoted to the St Petersburg manuscript of the poem recounting the *Pas* at Saumur, also focuses on questions of gender but this time from a more corporeal perspective. Her analysis of the manuscript's representations of both chivalric and non-chivalric bodies — that is, of the men who competed at the event, of the various ladies who participated in it, and of the dwarf who stage-managed it — complicates any simplistic reading of the power dynamics involved in this *pas* concerning who was there to be looked at and who did the looking and how this affects the reader/viewer's interpretation of the tournament.

In addition to the Sources and the Essays presented here, a number of other research tools have been included in this Casebook. A Map and a Table of *pas d'armes* are provided below and a Note to the Translations explaining the editorial principles adopted for the Sources has been supplied immediately after this introduction. At the end of the volume is a Glossary defining the most important terms of arms, armour and clothing featured in both the Sources and the Essays; those items included in this glossary have been asterisked on their first mention in each particular Source/Essay. The Bibliography that follows the Glossary lists all the archival, manuscript and printed primary sources, secondary sources and web-based sources cited in the volume.

Naturally, the views offered in this Casebook do not constitute the last word on the *pas*. A number of questions undoubtedly await further investigation. For instance, can more *pas d'armes* be identified in as-yet-unedited archival or financial sources? For what reasons did the rulers of other territories, which possessed their own chivalric cultures and had extensive cultural and political links to many of the courts discussed here, not adopt the *pas d'armes* as a significant chivalric event? The example of England springs to mind, as does that of Italy — aside from the parts belonging to the duchy of Savoy — and even further afield in Eastern Europe, particularly Poland and Hungary, given their lively chivalric cultures. Even on French territory, the greater interest in *pas d'armes* shown at the ducal court of René of Anjou than at the royal court of King Charles VII would repay closer study, as would the fact that Charles VIII's support for *pas d'armes* such as those held at Paris (1484) and Sandricourt (1493) was largely limited to allowing noble *entrepreneurs* such as Louis, duke of Orléans, Claude de Vaudrey and Louis de Hédouville to organise them.[88] Given the emphasis placed by many scholars on the socio-political functions of the *pas*, does comparison of different narrative accounts of the same event reveal the divergent political agendas of their respective authors? Finally, what might analysis of other non-chivalric bodies in *pas d'armes*, such as those of giants and Wild Men/Women, reveal about the gender and power issues raised by these figures who exerted such a pull on the medieval imagination? The authors and translators of the Sources and Essays presented in this volume, who are also the creators of the additional resources provided online, will have more than achieved their aims if this Casebook succeeds in stimulating further research on this fascinating aspect of late medieval chivalric culture.

* * * * * * * * * *

[88] See Philippe Contamine, 'Les tournois en France à la fin du Moyen Âge', in *Das ritterliche Turnier im Mittelalter: Beiträge zu einer vergleichenden Formen und Verhaltensgeschichte des Ritterturms*, ed. by Josef Fleckenstein (Göttingen: Vandenhoeck and Ruprecht, 1985), pp. 425–49 (pp. 446–7).

Locations of *pas d'armes*, *c.*1420–*c.*1520
SCOTLAND
Edinburgh
North Sea
Ghent
BRABANT
Bruges
FLANDERS
Mechelen
Lille
Saint Omer
Brussels
ARTOIS
Le Quesnoy
HAINAUT
Rhine
Moselle
Seine
Sandricourt
Marne
Châlons-sur-Marne
Paris
Meuse
Nancy
Yonne
LORRAINE
ANJOU
Loire
Launay
Marsannay-la-Côte
FRANCHE-COMTÉ
Saône
Atlantic Ocean
Saumur
Chinon
Bourges
BERRY
BURGUNDY
Nozeroy
Chalon-sur-Saône
Vincelles
Bourg
Geneva
SAVOY
Ivrea
FRANCE
Turin
Carignano
Rhône
Garonne
Tarascon
PROVENCE
Puente del Órbigo
Valladolid
Duero
Ebro
ARAGON
Barcelona
CASTILE
Tajo
El Pardo
Mediterranean Sea
Guadiana
Guadalquivir
Jaén
N
0
km
250
UvA-K 0423

Table of pas d'armes

Because it has not been an easy task to produce the Map and Table, a few words are necessary to explain how and why they were compiled. All depends on, first, the amount of detail that the actual primary sources provide, and, second, how strictly one applies the definition of a *pas* as set out above in the Introduction to the data distilled from these sources. Third, future research on late medieval manuscripts and archival sources will doubtless uncover new events that can be classified as *pas d'armes*. For these reasons, the list of events illustrated on the Map and presented in the Table is not intended to be seen as exhaustive — far from it.

For pragmatic reasons, both of these research tools cover events starting from the 1420s. Most scholars agree that one of the first *pas* was the *Paso de la Fuerte Ventura* in 1428 in Valladolid, but, as is argued in this volume, other similar chivalric events in the Iberian Peninsula, which were in turn influenced by knightly traffic to and from France and the Burgundian Low Countries, may well have preceded it.[89] The chronological timespan of this book as a whole is one century; hence the end point in the Map and Table is around 1520. Whilst this opens up the possibility of exploring the (dis)continuities of the *pas* in the last quarter of the fifteenth century and the first quarter of the sixteenth century, especially outside Anjou and the Burgundian lands, it also takes account of the fact that the term *pas d'armes* (or even *pas des armes*) in the French context in particular, became almost interchangeable with the more general term *tournoy* (tournament) after this point.

As the Table shows, the period 1428–63 marked a high point in the numbers of *pas d'armes* that were staged: over a period of thirty-five years no fewer than twenty-one events were organised, comprising 54 per cent of the thirty-nine *pas* that have been identified here. Most of these events took place under the aegis of three princes: Juan II, king of Castile (three events), René, duke of Anjou (four events) and Philip the Good, duke of Burgundy (six events), albeit the Angevin duke was the only one who was directly involved in the organisation of some *pas* (in which he also competed), whereas Juan and Philip simply facilitated and/or contributed financially to the *pas* held in their lands.[90] If it is not a coincidence that contacts between these three courts were extensive in this period, the personalities of these three princes must also have played an important role in this particular flowering of the *pas*. All of them also had to deal with noble rivals from different regions within their territories who were eager to perform feats of arms so as to mark themselves out from others in order to obtain princely favours or positions, to contract advantageous marriages or to increase their status. The three princes in question likewise tried to neutralise possible threats from their nobles by integrating them into knightly orders intended to promote chivalric behaviour, to foster cooperation between them and even to unify the nobility.[91] Finally, the literary culture at these three courts may have had a hand in the promotion of *pas d'armes*, as the inventories of the libraries of these princes and their highest-ranking nobles reveal a vivid interest in the chivalric literature

[89] See Essay 1.

[90] Bertrand Schnerb, *L'État bourguignon: 1363–1477* (Paris: Perrin, 2006), p. 332; Bousmar, 'Pasos', p. 552.

[91] D'Arcy Jonathan Dacre Boulton, *The Knights of the Crown: the Monarchical Orders of Knighthood in Later Medieval Europe 1325–1520* (Woodbridge: Boydell Press, 1987), pp. 13–14, 496–8.

of the past.[92] Nevertheless, it would be wrong to focus solely on princes and their courts as instigators of *pas d'armes*, as it was largely their noble subjects themselves who took the initiative to stage and to participate in these chivalric competitions where noble values could be displayed, by which they could differentiate themselves from their peers and the rest of late medieval society.

The information provided by the Table includes the name of the *pas*, the year in which it was held, the place where it was staged, the name of the *entrepreneur(s)*,[93] the name of the prince who authorised it, the primary source(s) containing the narrative and/or administrative accounts of it and the number of the Source that translates it here and/or of the Essay in which it is discussed. The names of the *pas* are derived directly from the primary sources and are also rendered in English translation. In cases where no 'official' name exists, the *pas* has been named after the town in which it was held (e.g. Brussels, Carignano). More details about all of these events (e.g., exact dates, names of challengers, composition of the teams, type of combats, theatrical scenario, ephemeral architecture, guests and spectators etc.) can be found in the Sources and Essays in this volume as well as in the online database that has been provided on the project website (www.pasdarmes.org). The events have been listed in chronological order rather than simply by geographical area, as has hitherto tended to be the case in scholarship on the *pas*; instead, the distribution of these events across Western Europe is illustrated in the Map. Being based on research by the authors of the Sources and Essays presented in this volume, the chronological and geographical coverage of the Map and Table is rather broader than that of earlier studies of the *pas d'armes*. Thus, although the Table includes all of the *pas* listed by Barber and Barker, by Nadot and by Torsten Hiltmann, it also includes a number of other such events, in particular those held in the duchy of Savoy and the kingdom of Scotland, which are discussed here.[94]

---

[92] On this aspect, see Essay 1.

[93] Where a primary source has supplied insufficient information to allow for full identification of an *entrepreneur*, his name has been cited in inverted commas in the Table, e.g. 'Ferriez'.

[94] Barber and Barker, *Tournaments*, pp. 98–102, 107–38; Nadot, *Le Spectacle*, pp. 335–7; Hiltmann, 'Un État', pp. 258–9, 262–4. However, the table excludes some of the events listed for the period 1443–1549 in Guillaume Bureaux, 'Union et désunion de la noblesse en parade. Le rôle des Pas d'armes dans l'entretien des rivalités chevaleresques entre cours princières occidentales, XVe–XVIe siècles (Anjou, Bourgogne, France, Saint-Empire)' (unpublished PhD dissertation, Normandie Université, 2018), pp. 34–5, 45–6, 50, 64; these are the *Pas du Camp du Drap d'or* (Field of Cloth of Gold) (1520) and the *Pas de Worms*, which took place in 1495 but which he erroneously dates to 1514. For a discussion of this latter tournament, see Essay 1.

Thanks are due to Klaus Oschema and S. H. Rigby for their comments on an earlier version of this introduction.

Table of *pas d'armes* organised in Europe, *c*.1420–*c*.1520

Name	Year	Place	*Entrepreneur(s)*	Authorised by	Primary sources	Source	Essay
Paso de la Fuerte Ventura (*Paso* of the Daunting Adventure)	1428	Kingdom of Castile, Valladolid, Plaza Mayor	Enrique of Aragon	Juan II, king of Castile	AGSM, p. 16; FPG, p. 250; LB, pp. 59–62; PCH, pp. 20–2	2	1
Paso Honroso (*Paso* of Honour)	1434	Kingdom of Castile, Órbigo Bridge (now Hospital de Órbigo) near León	Suero de Quiñones	Juan II, king of Castile	LPH; PH		1, 6
Paso de Valladolid (*Paso* of Valladolid)	1440	Kingdom of Castile, Valladolid, Plaza Mayor?	Ruy Díaz de Mendoza	Juan II, king of Castile	FPG, pp. 411–12	3	6
Pas de l'Arbre Charlemagne (*Pas* of the Tree of Charlemagne)	1443	Duchy of Burgundy, Marsannay-la-Côte, by an elm tree (near Dijon)	Pierre de Bauffremont	Philip the Good, duke of Burgundy	EdM, vol. 6, pp. 68–73; OdLM, vol. 1, pp. 283–7, 290–335; CPM, pp. 330–7	4	1, 6
Pas de Nancy (*Pas* of Nancy)	1445	Duchy of Lorraine, Nancy, Place de la Carrière	René of Anjou, duke of Anjou; Louis de Luxembourg, count of Saint-Pol; Ferry II de Vaudémont-Lorraine; Pierre II de Brézé; Philippe de Lenoncourt (HGF); Charles of Anjou, count of Maine; Louis de Luxembourg, count of Saint-Pol replaced by Jacques de Lalaing (LF)	René of Anjou, duke of Anjou (with Charles VII?)	HB, pp. 269–72; HGF, vol. 1, pp. 129–70; LF, pp. 72–118; MdE, vol. 1, pp. 40–2; OdLM, vol. 2, pp. 59–61; Paris, BnF, fr. 5054, fols 128r–129v		

Name	Year	Place	*Entrepreneur(s)*	Authorised by	Primary sources	Source	Essay
Pas (?) de Châlons-sur-Marne (*Pas* of Châlons-sur-Marne)	1445	Kingdom of France, Châlons-en-Champagne, Place du Marché	Jean de Vaudémont-Lorraine; Louis de Beauvau, lord of Beauvau; Jean de Hangest, lord of Genlis; L'Ardenois[95]	Charles VII, king of France?	Berlin, Ham. 606, fols 62v–74r; HB, pp. 272–3; HGF, vol. 1, pp. 170–94; HGFMO, pp. 191–2; LF, p. 118; MdE, vol. 1, pp. 42–51; OdLM, vol. 2, pp. 54–9		
Pas du Géant à la Blanche Dame du Pavillon (*Pas* of the Giant and the White Lady of the Pavilion)	1446	Duchy of Anjou, Launay, at the country manor of René of Anjou	René of Anjou, duke of Anjou; Ferry II de Vaudémont-Lorraine; Philippe de Lenoncourt; Jean de Fénétrange, lord of Fénétrange; Louis de Beauvau, lord of Beauvau	René of Anjou, duke of Anjou	Berlin, Ham. 606, fols 131v–140r; HGFMO, pp. 201–2		
Pas de la Gueule du Dragon/ *Pas du Rocher Périlleux* (*Pas* of the Dragon's Mouth/*Pas* of the Perilous Rock)	1446	Kingdom of France, between Chinon and Razilly[96]	Gaston IV, count of Foix; Guillaume d'Harcourt, count of Tancarville; Claude de Châteauneuf; Guillaume de Courcelles	Charles VII, king of France?	Berlin, Ham. 606, fols 98v–129v; HGF, vol. 1, pp. 194–5; PSr, pp. 68–9	5	2

95 This is probably Jean de Barbençon, lord of Donstiennes in Hainaut; many of his lineage were called 'L'Ardenois' (i.e. presumably L'Ardennais), including his father, Guy. Ernest Matthieu, 'La reconnaissance par les États de Hainaut de Charles le Téméraire comme héritier du comté en 1465', *Bulletin de la Commission royale d'Histoire*, 55.13 (1886), 225–42 (p. 238).

96 The distance between these two castles is around 7 km; whilst Chinon is also now a commune (dép. Indre-et-Loire, rég. Centre-Val de Loire), Razilly exists only as a castle.

Name	Year	Place	*Entrepreneur(s)*	Authorised by	Primary sources	Source	Essay
Pas de la Joyeuse Garde/Pas de Saumur (*Pas* of the Joyous Guard/*Pas* of Saumur)	1446	Duchy of Anjou, Saumur, at the castle	René of Anjou, duke of Anjou, and a large team of defenders too numerous to list here	René of Anjou, duke of Anjou	Berlin, Ham. 606, fols 76r–96v; MdE, vol. 1, pp. 107–8; PSr	5	2, 7
Pas du Chevalier Aventureux (*Pas* of the Adventurous Knight)	1447	Duchy of Berry, Bourges	Guillaume d'Harcourt, count of Tancarville	Not stated	Berlin, Ham. 606, fols 164r–169r; HGFMO, pp. 193–7		
Pas de la Belle Pèlerine (*Pas* of the Beautiful Pilgrim)	1449	County of Artois, Saint-Martin-lez-Tatinghem, on the road between Calais and Saint-Omer	Jean de Luxembourg, bastard of Saint-Pol	Philip the Good, duke of Burgundy	MdE, vol. 1, pp. 244–63; OdLM, vol. 2, pp. 118–23, 129–35		6
Pas de la Bergère (*Pas* of the Shepherdess)	1449	County of Provence, Tarascon, in or near the castle and by the Rhône	Philippe de Lenoncourt; Philibert de Laigue	René of Anjou, duke of Anjou (and count of Provence)	ECMR; PAB; PB	6	6
Pas de la Fontaine des Pleurs (*Pas* of the Fountain of Tears)	1449 –50	Duchy of Burgundy, Chalon-sur-Saône, the island of Saint-Laurent in the River Saône	Jacques de Lalaing	Philip the Good, duke of Burgundy	GC, vol. 8, pp. 188–247; JLdSR – Ép., pp. 206–38; LF, pp. 311–404; MdE, vol. 1, pp. 264–73; OdLM, vol. 2, pp. 142–205	7	1, 3, 6

Name	Year	Place	*Entrepreneur(s)*	Authorised by	Primary sources	Source	Essay
Pas du Chevalier au Cygne (*Pas* of the Swan Knight)	1454	County of Flanders, Lille, exact location unclear	Adolf of Cleves, lord of Ravenstein	Not stated	Marie-Thérèse Caron, *La noblesse dans le Duché de Bourgogne 1315–1477* (Lille: Presses Universitaires de Lille, 1987), pp. 109–13; JdC, vol. 2, pp. 195–9; MdE, vol. 2, pp. 118–30; OdLM, vol. 2, pp. 340–50		1, 3
Pas du Pin aux Pommes d'Or (*Pas* of the Pine Tree with the Golden Apples)	1455	Kingdom of Aragon, Barcelona, Passeig del Born	Gaston IV, count of Foix	Not stated	HGF, vol. 2, pp. 44–59; Félix Pasquier and Henri Courteault, eds, *Chroniques romanes des comtes de Foix* (Foix: Gadrat Ainé, 1895), p. 77		
Pas du Compagnon à la Larme Blanche (*Pas* of the Companion of the White Teardrop)	1458	County of Hainaut, Le Quesnoy, exact location unclear	Guillaume de Moullon	Philip the Good, duke of Burgundy	GC, vol. 3, pp. 462–6; GCC, pp. 127–39	9	1
Paso de El Pardo (*Paso* of El Pardo)	1459	Kingdom of Castile, El Pardo, near the royal hunting lodge	Beltrán de la Cueva	Enrique IV, king of Castile	DEC, pp. 168–70	8	6
Paso de Jaén (*Paso* of Jaén)	1461	Kingdom of Castile, Jaén, Plaza del Arrabal	Fernán Mexía	Miguel Lucas de Iranzo	HCMLI, pp. 58–9	10	

Name	Year	Place	*Entrepreneur(s)*	Authorised by	Primary sources	Source	Essay
Pas de Lille (*Pas* of Lille)	1461	County of Flanders, Lille, Place du Marché	Antoine, the Great Bastard of Burgundy		VdN, pp. 322–5		3
Pas du Perron Fée (*Pas* of the Enchanted Column)	1463	County of Flanders, Bruges, Markt	Philippe de Lalaing	Philip the Good, duke of Burgundy	AR 32515, fols 36r, 40r, 46r–47r, 52v–53v; PPF	11	1, 3
Pas de la Dame Inconnue (*Pas* of the Unknown Lady)[97]	1463	County of Flanders, Bruges	Antoine, the Great Bastard of Burgundy; Philippe de Crève-coeur; Pedro Vásquez de Saavedra	Philip the Good, duke of Burgundy	JDI		1, 3
Pas de l'Arbre d'or (*Pas* of the Golden Tree)	1468	County of Flanders, Bruges, Markt	Antoine, the Great Bastard of Burgundy	Charles the Bold, duke of Burgundy	HKB; JDH, vol. 1, pp. 113–32; MT, pp. 106–12; OdLM, vol. 3, pp. 123–201; OdLM, vol. 4, pp. 95–144	12	1, 6
Pas de la Dame Sauvage (*Pas* of the Wild Lady)	1470	County of Flanders, Ghent, Vismarkt	Claude de Vaudrey	Charles the Bold, duke of Burgundy	BP, pp. 55–95		6
Pas of Paris	1484	Kingdom of France, Paris, Rue Saint-Antoine	Louis, duke of Orléans, the future King Louis XII	Charles VIII, king of France	CRC, paragraphs 73–81		

97 This *pas* never in fact took place as no challengers showed up for it. For more details, see Essay 3.

Name	Year	Place	*Entrepreneur(s)*	Authorised by	Primary sources	Source	Essay
Pas du Chevalier au Souci (*Pas* of the Knight of the Marigold/ Knight of Sorrow)	1484	Kingdom of France, outside Paris towards the Bois de Vincennes	Claude de Vaudrey	Charles VIII, king of France	CRC, paragraphs 82–126		
Pas of Mechelen	1491	Duchy of Brabant, Mechelen, Grote Markt	Claude de Salins	Philip the Fair, son of Maximilian, archduke of Austria	JM, vol. 2, pp. 225–8		1
Pas des armes de Sandricourt (*Pas* of Sandricourt)	1493	Kingdom of France, Sandricourt, three locations around the castle	Louis de Hédouville	Charles VIII, king of France	PSt	13	4
Fait d'armes in Geneva (Feat of Arms in Geneva)	1498	Geneva, exact location unknown	Unknown, but possibly one of the four defenders (Philibert de Challant; Bertrand de Lucinge; 'Ferriez';[98] Ognas[99])	Philibert II, duke of Savoy	TG		1
Grosses joustes in Geneva (Grand jousts in Geneva)	1501	Geneva, exact location unknown	Philibert II, duke of Savoy	Philibert II, duke of Savoy and the city of Geneva	JM, pp. 495–6		1
Armes in Bourg (Feat of arms in Bourg)	1503	Duchy of Savoy, Bourg	François de Chevron-Villette	Philibert II, duke of Savoy	CdV, pp. 287–9		1

[98] This person has not been identified, hence his name has been left in inverted commas.

[99] This is Jean d'Aydie, known as Ognas, who was a *maître d'hôtel* of King Charles VIII (1497). CdF, no. 2406.

Name	Year	Place	*Entrepreneur(s)*	Authorised by	Primary sources	Source	Essay
Pas of Brussels	1503	Duchy of Brabant, Brussels, Grote Markt	Antoine de Lalaing	Philip the Fair, archduke of Austria	AR 30949, fols 184r–185r; CdV, pp. 335–40	14	1
Pas of Carignano	1504	Duchy of Savoy, the castle of Carignano	Philibert II, duke of Savoy	Philibert II, duke of Savoy	PC; Max Bruchet, *Marguerite d'Autriche, duchesse de Savoie* (Lille: Danel, 1927), pp. 323–4	15	1, 6
Emprise of the Wild Knight of the Black Lady (1)	1507	Kingdom of Scotland, Edinburgh, Palace of Holyroodhouse	James IV, king of Scotland	James IV, king of Scotland	JLBS, vol. 2, p. 128; SH, pp. 491–5; TA, vol. 3, pp. 258–60, 365–94	16	5
Emprise of the Wild Knight of the Black Lady (2)	1508	Kingdom of Scotland, Edinburgh, Palace of Holyroodhouse	James IV, king of Scotland	James IV, king of Scotland	HCS, vol. 1, pp. 242–4; TA, vol. 4, pp. 13–27, 117–29	16	5
Pas de Vincelles (*Pas* of Vincelles)	1512	County of Franche-Comté, Vincelles, in the courtyard of the castle	Claude de Salins	Charles, archduke of Austria	BP, pp. 223–33		1
Pas des armes de l'Arc triomphal (*Pas* of the Triumphal Arch)	1514	Paris, near the Hôtel des Tournelles	François, duke of Valois	Louis XII, king of France	GCM, n.p		4
Pas de Nozeroy (*Pas* of Nozeroy)	1519	County of Franche-Comté, Nozeroy, in the courtyard and great hall of the castle	Philibert de Chalon	Not stated	BP, pp. 235–59		1

Name	Year	Place	*Entrepreneur(s)*	Authorised by	Primary sources	Source	Essay
Chevaliers Errants aux Tournois de Chambly et Bailleul (Knights-Errant at the Tournaments of Chambly and Bailleul)	1519	Kingdom of France, various castles (Chambly, Bailleul, Esches, Montagny, L'Isle-Adam and Méry)	Tanguy de La Motte; the lord of La Concy and Montagny[100]	Not stated	René Botto, *L'Isle-Adam et sa région au temps des tournois, 1493 et 1519* (L'Isle-Adam: Les amis de l'Isle-Adam, 2007), pp. 62–85		4
Pas of Ivrea	1522	Duchy of Savoy, Piedmont, Ivrea	Charles II, duke of Savoy	Charles II, duke of Savoy	ARCT, pp. 251–437		1

[100] This may be Jacques de Fouilleuse (d. before 1544), lord of La Concy, Flavacourt, Montagny and Bazincourt, whose family had a residence in the town of Gisors. Étienne Hamon, *Un chantier flamboyant et son rayonnement: Gisors et les églises du Vexin français* (Besançon: Presses Universitaires de Franche-Comté/Société des Antiquaires de Normandie, 2008), pp. 80–1.

Note to the translations

Outlined here below is the rationale behind certain stylistic and editorial practices adopted in the translations of the narrative and administrative materials presented here in the Casebook.

The style of many of the medieval Castilian and Middle French prose narrative accounts cited is characterised by the use of long Latinate sentences with multiple sub-clauses, strings of near-synonyms of nouns and verbs, pseudo-legalistic formulae such as *ledit/le dessusdit/el dicho* (the said/the above-mentioned) and narratorial interventions such as *comme vous oyez/assés avez oÿ* (as you can hear/as you have heard at length), etc. Whilst it is important to convey something of the flavour of the original text in a translation, it would be wrong to do so to the point of weariness given that our modern literary sensibilities are rather different from those of these texts' original audience. For this reason, sentences have been shortened where possible and causal links between clauses made more explicit; extra phrasing in square brackets has also been added at times to make better grammatical sense in the English translation. Phrases such as *the said/above-mentioned* have been retained in only a few cases where they help to explicate a sentence with multiple subject or object pronouns or if they are an integral part of the formal style employed in a written document such as chapters of arms. Translations of the two verse narrative accounts, those recounting the *Pas de la Joyeuse Garde/Pas de Saumur* and the *Pas de la Bergère*, are in blank verse because of the almost impossible challenge of trying to respect their original complex rhyming schemes whilst rendering the sense of the text in the target language. However, these verse translations attempt, as far as possible, to render the sense of the original line by line whilst obviously having to make some allowances at times for the differences between Middle French and modern English syntax.

In dealing with the names of people and places mentioned in both the narrative and the administrative accounts, the aim has been to reconcile a number of different imperatives: to respect the author's own usage where possible; to help the reader of the translation navigate easily between the text, footnotes and index; and to adopt standardised forms that facilitate cross-referencing between the text, modern histories of the countries in which these *pas d'armes* took place and works by other medieval writers. First names of all historical figures originating from predominantly French-speaking lands have been given in modern French with a standardised spelling (e.g. Antoine, Hervé, Jacques, Jean). The same also applies to most of their family names (e.g. Louis de Hédouville, Jacques de Lalaing), except for those of people belonging to the highest social ranks, for whom a conventional anglicised form exists (e.g. Margaret of Austria). Those figures hailing from the Dutch-speaking parts of the Burgundian lands, whose names are commonly approximated in French form in both narrative and administrative sources, have been referred to in these texts by the French version of their name (e.g. Jean de Halluin) since this is what the author uses, but the Dutch name has been included in the relevant footnotes (e.g. Jan van Halewijn). Where Dutch names have been used in the text itself, these have been standardised to a modern form (e.g. Jan de Leeuw). The names of those persons from other parts of Europe have been rendered in a modern spelling appropriate to the language of their country of origin (e.g. Adolf of Cleves, Suero de Quiñones, Pedro Vásquez de Saavedra). All titles have been anglicised, such as lord/lady, count/countess, duke/duchess, king/queen etc. However, Messire and Mademoiselle, etc., for which there are no satisfactory English equivalents, have been kept as they are when part of a person's title (e.g. Messire Jacques de Lalaing, Mademoiselle de Saint-Cyr).

For well-known places where there is a conventional anglicised version, this has been used (e.g. Aragon, Bruges, Brussels, Castile, Ghent, Lombardy, River Scheldt) and for those places that are readily understandable to an English-language readership or for which there is no English equivalent, the name in the text has either been modernised (e.g. Chalon-sur-Saône, Marsannay-la-Côte) or reproduced as it is used in the specific European country (e.g. Jaén). The map of *pas d'armes* provided likewise renders the names of places according to these three principles.

The original version (with any significant variant spellings) of the names of people and places mentioned in the narrative and administrative accounts is given in square brackets at the start of the footnote that supplies basic information on them. These footnotes have been provided for all figures, events and key places mentioned in these accounts, for relevant literary conventions and allusions, for corrections and clarification of passages in the texts that pose particular problems of interpretation and for important technical terms such as those relating to aspects of chivalric custom, dress, jousting and warfare. More general information on these technical terms can be found in the Glossary.

These translations are intended principally to appeal to a general readership interested in finding out more about medieval chivalry and the feats performed by some of its most illustrious exponents at these *pas d'armes*. However, they are also designed to help more specialised readers, such as students and scholars of medieval literature or history, to access these narrative and administrative accounts in their original edited or manuscript versions. For this reason, page or folio numbers to the original accounts in prose have been systematically provided in parentheses in all translations for ease of reference; likewise, the translations of the two verse narratives use the same stanza numbering as that found in the editions used.

In creating an edition of the financial accounts in Middle Dutch (Sources 11b and 14), the guidelines of the Koninklijk Nederlands Historisch Genootschap (Royal Dutch Historical Society) have been followed in order to render the text more readable for the non-specialist: abbreviations have been expanded (except in the different moneys of account and in cases where more than one expansion of the abbreviation is possible, such as in *voirs.* (i.e 'said'), which can be expanded to either *voirseid* or *voirscreven*); accents and punctuation have been added; upper- and lower-case letters have been normalised (e.g. in names or at the beginning of a sentence); spaces between words have been added where needed; and Roman numerals have been transcribed into Arabic numerals. Certain letters (i, ii, u, uu) are transcribed as they are actually used in the word (i can be i or j, ii can be ii or ij, u can be u or v, uu can be uu, uv, vu or w).

Finally, the default currency unit referred to in both the Sources and the Essays is the *livre* (pound) of forty Flemish *gros* (groats), the standard silver coinage that formed the basis of most of the accounts across the Burgundian composite state that were consulted for this book. The pound as a money of account (i.e. a denomination of money used in reckoning accounts, and so on, but not issued as actual coins or paper money) consisted of twenty *sous* (shillings, abbreviated as s.) and every *sou* consisted of twelve *deniers* (pennies, abbreviated as d.). When a different money of account is used in the sources (e.g. the pound *parisis* or the pound *tournois*, both normally reckoned in twenty groats, the Brabantine pound of 160 groats, or the Flemish pound *gros* of 240 groats) this is specifically indicated. When actual coins (e.g. *écus*, *francs*, *rijnsgulden*) are referred to in the sources, they are indicated with their value in groats so as to give the reader an idea of their relative value.

Part I: Sources

Rosalind Brown-Grant and Christina Normore

Source 1

Le Roman de Ponthus et Sidoine (*The Romance of Ponthus and Sidoine*)

This source consists of a discussion of the manuscript and illustrative tradition of this romance and a translation of the episode concerning the eponymous hero's *emprise* that is a *pas d'armes* in all but name.

Author: unknown

Language: Middle French

Edition used: Marie-Claude de Crécy, ed., *Le Roman de Ponthus et Sidoine* (Geneva: Droz, 1997), pp. 52–76 (= PS)

Select bibliography:

Blunk, Catherine, 'Je cuidoie avoir bien fait: Saintré and the Rules of the Game', *Medieval Feminist Forum: A Journal of Gender and Sexuality*, 52.2 (2017), 102–50

Brown-Grant, Rosalind, 'Art Imitating Life Imitating Art? Representations of the *pas d'armes* in Burgundian Prose Romance: The Case of *Jehan d'Avennes*', in *The Medieval Tournament as Spectacle*, ed. by Alan V. Murray and Karen Watts (Woodbridge: Boydell, 2020), pp. 139–54

——, *French Romance of the Later Middle Ages: Gender, Morality, and Desire* (Oxford: Oxford University Press, 2008), pp. 31–6

Fresco, Karen and Anne D. Hedeman, eds, *Collections in Context: The Organization of Knowledge and Community in Europe* (Columbus: The Ohio State University Press, 2020)

Reynolds, Catherine, 'The Shrewsbury Book, British Library, Royal MS 15 E.VI', in *Medieval Art, Architecture and Archaeology at Rouen*, ed. by Jenny Stratford (Leeds: The British Archaeological Association, 1993), pp. 109–16

Szkilnik, Michelle, *Jean de Saintré: une carrière chevaleresque au XVe siècle* (Geneva: Droz, 2003)

Taylor, Jane H. M., 'Image as Reception: Antoine de la Sale's *Le petit Jehan de Saintré*', in *Literary Aspects of Courtly Culture*, ed. by Donald Maddox and Sara Sturm-Maddox (Cambridge: D. S. Brewer, 1994), pp. 265–79

Introduction

This chivalric romance written in prose probably originates from Anjou and can be dated to after 1390 and before 1424.[1] The eponymous hero is a young knight, the son of the king

[1] PS, pp. xcviii–cv.

of Galicia, who has gone into exile following the occupation of his country by the Saracens and finds a home at the court of the king of Brittany. His great feats of prowess both in tournaments and on the battlefield earn him the love of the king's daughter, Sidoine, with whom he conducts a chaste and discreet relationship that goes on for a number of years. After many adventures in which the lovers are separated as much due to jealous interference from a disloyal erstwhile companion of Ponthus's as to the hero's various military commitments, he eventually reconquers Galicia from the Saracens, marries Sidoine and becomes king over both his own country of origin and Brittany. The text was extremely popular in the fifteenth and sixteenth centuries, being extant in twenty-eight manuscripts and ten early printed editions; it gained a wide readership in Anjou, the Burgundian lands, England, France, Savoy and Spain and was translated into several other European languages (Dutch, English and German).[2]

The romance is 'realist' insofar as the action takes place in actual cities of France, England and Iberia, and many of the characters, though fictional, bear names that are reminiscent of actual Breton and Angevin families, such as La Tour and Lusignan. However, the text also contains elements that are distinctly Arthurian, being drawn from earlier verse romance models such as Chrétien de Troyes's late twelfth-century *Yvain*, also known as the *Chevalier au lion*. These elements feature prominently in the episode which is of interest here, namely Ponthus's organisation of 'an *emprise* that would involve feats of arms', an event that takes place on every Tuesday for a year. For example, the general setting of Ponthus's *emprise** is none other than the famous forest of Broceliande, in which many an Arthurian knight-errant finds adventure; more particularly, the location he elects to defend is the Fountain of Barenton, which is linked in many Arthurian tales with Merlin.[3] The hero initiates each of the jousts at his *emprise* by pouring water from the fountain over a stone, causing it to raise a brief but violent storm, in a direct borrowing from Chrétien's *Yvain* (lines 380–448). His chief herald and helper at this event is another staple of Arthurian romance, an ugly but extremely competent and faithful dwarf. Finally, the *emprise* culminates in a lavish prize-giving ceremony held in the forest at Pentecost, a time of year when, in Arthurian tales, a king typically holds open court and gathers all his knights around him.

Significantly, that this whole episode is the only part of this otherwise 'realist' narrative to have this Arthurian colouration flags up the fact that the hero is self-reflexively play-acting in his chivalric *emprise*. Whilst these theatrical elements also inscribe Ponthus's *pas* firmly in the tradition of actual thirteenth- and fourteenth-century tournaments, such as those at Le Hem (1278) and Chauvency (1285),[4] which likewise drew heavily on Arthurian themes, they anticipate many of the later historical *pas d'armes*, particularly those in the Angevin and Burgundian spheres, thus making the hero's undertaking a precursor of this type of event. For instance, as *entrepreneur** and defender of the *emprise*, Ponthus produces a written set of rules stipulating that each joust should involve three courses with the lance followed by foot combat with rebated swords until one of the two competitors surrenders; he sends

---

2 *Ibid.*, pp. vii–xxxvi.

3 This fountain still exists in the forest of Broceliande. On Broceliande itself, see Alan Lupack, *Oxford Guide to Arthurian Literature and Legend* (Oxford: Oxford University Press, 2005), p. 437.

4 Nigel Bryant, trans., *The Tournaments at Le Hem and Chauvency: Sarrasin, The Romance of Le Hem, Jacques Bretel, The Tournament at Chauvency* (Woodbridge: Boydell Press, 2020).

his dwarf out across Europe to invite challengers to come from far and wide; he adopts chivalric incognito for the duration of the event, calling himself the 'Chevalier Noir aux Armes Blanches' (Black Knight of the White Arms); he puts his shield with his coat of arms up in a tree, along with a horn that his dwarf blows to signal the start of each day's jousting; and, at the end of the *emprise*, he offers prizes to the best jouster and to the one who fights hardest and most skilfully with the sword. The role given in this event to his lady, Sidoine, is that all those defeated in the combats have to surrender themselves to her as her 'prisoners', albeit they are treated with great hospitality by her and her father and are soon 'released' so that they can watch the rest of the jousts back in Broceliande.

This year-long *emprise* in which Ponthus is the sole defender is followed by a much shorter event after he has resumed his rightful place at the king's court: it too can be regarded as anticipating actual historical *pas d'armes*, which often included shorter and/ or different forms of combat following the main undertaking.[5] Here, abandoning the Arthurian backdrop of his *emprise*, Ponthus takes on the identity of the 'Chevalier Blanc à la Rose Vermeille' (White Knight of the Red Rose) and, along with five of his companions, holds a two-day joust in Rennes for many of those knights who had already competed against him in the earlier event; Sidoine, elected the most beautiful lady at Rennes, distributes lavish prizes from among her own riches.

The long *emprise* episode in *Ponthus et Sidoine* would itself prove influential on later prose romances, particularly *Cleriadus et Meliadice* (*c.*1440) where the eponymous hero, for love of his lady Meliadice, disguises himself as the 'Chevalier Vert' (Green Knight) and holds a joust every day for a month at a setting in a forest that he dubs the 'Joyeuse Maison' (Joyous House).[6] Whilst neither *Ponthus et Sidoine* nor *Cleriadus et Meliadice* uses the term *pas d'armes* to describe these events, it *is* explicitly used in two other late medieval prose romances, Antoine de La Sale's *Jean de Saintré* (1456)[7] and *Jehan d'Avennes* (written between 1460 and 1467 by an unnamed author),[8] perhaps because by then these two latter works, which hail from the Angevin and Burgundian cultural milieus respectively, had been fully opened up to the influence of actual historical *pas d'armes*. Thus, echoing Ponthus's *emprise*, Jean de Saintré (who refrains from hiding his identity), is encouraged by his lady-love, the Dame des Belles Cousines, to hold a *pas* for three days a week in May between Gravelines and Calais in order to attract English competitors,[9] whilst Jehan d'Avennes, seeking to impress his aloof beloved, the countess of Artois, disguises himself as the 'Chevalier Blanc' (White Knight) and also pits himself against English knights for

---

[5] As, for example, at the *Pas de l'Arbre Charlemagne* (Marsannay-la-Côte, 1443), the *Pas de la Fontaine des Pleurs* (Chalon-sur-Saône, 1449–50) and the *Pas de l'Arbre d'or* (Bruges, 1468): see Sources 4, 7 and 12, respectively.

[6] Gaston Zink, ed., *Cleriadus et Meliadice: roman en prose du XVe siècle* (Geneva: Droz, 1984), pp. 211–69 (no English translation available).

[7] Antoine de La Sale, *Jehan de Saintré*, ed. by Joël Blanchard and trans. by Michel Quereuil (Paris: Livre de Poche, 1995); and *idem*, *Jean de Saintré: A Late Medieval Education in Love and Chivalry*, trans. by Roberta Krueger and Jane H. M. Taylor (Philadelphia: University of Pennsylvania Press, 2014), pp. 116–21.

[8] Danielle Quéruel, ed., *L'istoire de tres vaillans princez monseigneur Jehan d'Avennes* (Villeneuve d'Ascq: Presses Universitaires du Septentrion, 1997), pp. 74–98 (no English translation available).

[9] Catherine Blunk, 'Je cuidoie avoir bien fait: Saintré and the Rules of the Game', *Medieval Feminist Forum: A Journal of Gender and Sexuality*, 52.2 (2017), 102–50.

the first fortnight in April in a forest near Bordeaux, close to the border of the territory occupied by English forces.[10]

A further element that all four of these romances have in common is that they lent themselves readily to being illuminated, with miniatures being devoted specifically to the *emprise/pas d'armes* episodes in each: *Ponthus et Sidoine*, London, BL, Royal 15 E VI, also known as the Shrewsbury Book, has three out of thirty-five miniatures (see below);[11] *Cleriadus et Meliadice*, London, BL, Royal 20 C II, has three out of twenty-eight miniatures;[12] *Jean de Saintré*, Brussels, KBR, 9547, has one out of seventy-seven miniatures,[13] whilst the version contained in London, BL, Cotton Nero D IX, which has ten miniatures, is missing a folio where the description of the start of Saintré's *pas* is located and so may also have had an illumination devoted to this event;[14] *Jehan d'Avennes*, Paris, BnF, fr. 12572, has three out of seventeen miniatures.[15] Finally, Ponthus's fame as a fictional *entrepreneur* would also seem to have influenced the way in which one particular historical *entrepreneur*, Jacques de Lalaing, was perceived by some spectators to have conducted his *Pas de la Fontaine des Pleurs* (1449–50), with the ladies who attended this event at Chalon-sur-Saône dubbing him a 'new Ponthus', according to Olivier de La Marche.[16] In the translation of the *emprise* sequence from *Ponthus et Sidoine* that follows the discussion of the illuminations in one particular manuscript of the text, page numbers in parentheses have been provided for ease of reference to De Crécy's edition.

IMAGES

The three miniatures reproduced here come from a fifteenth-century compendium once owned by the British royal family and now housed by the British Library as Royal 15 E VI.[17] Popularly known as the Shrewsbury Book, this manuscript was commissioned by John Talbot, first earl of Shrewsbury (*c*.1387–1453), as a gift for Margaret of Anjou (1430–82) on her marriage to King Henry VI of England in 1445. The daughter of René of Anjou and Isabelle of Lorraine, Margaret had been raised in an Angevin court deeply invested in tournament and chivalry. Margaret was also a close relative of the French king Charles VII, and her marriage was part of a larger set of negotiations that brought about a temporary lull in the hostilities of the Hundred Years War — and a concomitant

---

[10] Rosalind Brown-Grant, 'Art Imitating Life Imitating Art? Representations of the *Pas d'armes* in Burgundian Prose Romance: The Case of *Jehan d'Avennes*', in *The Medieval Tournament as Spectacle: Tourneys, Jousts and Pas d'Armes, 1100–1600*, ed. by Alan V. Murray and Karen Watts (Woodbridge: Boydell Press, 2020), pp. 139–54.

[11] Fols 213r, 213v, 215r.

[12] Fols 56v, 64r, 66v.

[13] Fol. 109v.

[14] Fol. 63r, as indicated by the darker foliation numbers visible.

[15] Fols 34r, 37v, 42v. See Brown-Grant, 'Art Imitating Life Imitating Art?'

[16] See Essay 6, p. 496.

[17] A full reproduction of the manuscript and preliminary bibliography can be found at https://www.bl.uk/manuscripts/FullDisplay.aspx?ref=Royal_MS_15_e_vi [accessed 30 September 2023]. For an overview of its visual programme and codicology, see Anne D. Hedeman, 'Collecting Images: The Role of the Visual in the Shrewsbury Book (BL Ms. Royal 15 E. vi)', in *Collections in Context: The Organization of Knowledge and Community in Europe*, ed. by Karen Fresco and Anne D. Hedeman (Columbus: The Ohio State University Press, 2020), pp. 99–104.

increase in tournament activity — in the late 1440s. Talbot was a prominent English military commander whose death while attempting a cavalry charge against artillery at the Battle of Castillon (1457) is sometimes mythologised as the end of the age of chivalry. The Shrewsbury Book speaks to their joint interest in chivalric materials both imaginary and practical, drawing together fifteen texts in French that range from the fictional adventures of *Ponthus et Sidoine* and the Alexander Romance to the non-fictional war manual *L'Arbre des batailles* of Honorat Bovet (1387) and Statutes of the Garter.

While scholars sometimes refer to the currently anonymous painters who executed the manuscript's 144 miniatures by the single sobriquet of the Talbot Master, several artists were in fact involved.[18] Such joint production practice was common in the period and greatly increased the speed at which a massive manuscript such as this one could be completed. At 440 folios (880 modern pages), the Shrewsbury Book was a substantial undertaking under any conditions, but it was also probably a hurried production given the historical circumstances of its commission and gifting.[19] The Shrewsbury Book's artists are believed to have lived in the English stronghold of Rouen; a continental base of production would have allowed Talbot to easily offer the manuscript to Margaret of Anjou when he served as her official escort from France to meet her royal fiancé.

The Shrewsbury Book is copiously but selectively illuminated: while some texts received only one miniature, others were given extended image cycles. Particular attention was given to *Ponthus et Sidoine*, which, at thirty-five miniatures, is the second most heavily illuminated section of the manuscript (it is exceeded only by the far better-known and frequently illustrated Alexander Romance).[20] Since illumination is often a sign of value in medieval manuscripts, this suggests that the text either appealed strongly to Talbot himself or he believed it would be of special interest to Margaret. The visual prominence of *Ponthus et Sidoine* in the Shrewsbury Book is especially notable given the fact that the romance was rarely illuminated: of the twenty-eight known manuscripts catalogued by Marie-Claude de Crécy, only three (including the Shrewsbury Book) contain illuminations.[21] The other two cycles are smaller: Paris, BnF, naf. 10169 includes nineteen miniatures whilst Cambridge, Cambridge University Library, Hh.3.16 contains only five.[22] The *pas d'armes* is illuminated in all three extant cycles, signalling its importance for fifteenth-century readers.

---

[18] Catherine Reynolds, 'The Shrewsbury Book, British Library, Royal MS 15 E.VI', in *Medieval Art, Architecture and Archaeology at Rouen*, ed. by Jenny Stratford (Leeds: The British Archaeological Association, 1993), pp. 109–16, has identified four styles in the manuscript; even the large number of illuminations in the Talbot Master style are the work of multiple hands, according to Hedeman, 'Collecting', pp. 100–2.

[19] Reynolds, 'The Shrewsbury Book', pp. 110–11.

[20] As also noted in Karen Fresco, 'Christine de Pizan's *Livre des fais d'armes et de chevalerie* and the Coherence of BL Ms. Royal 15 E. vi', in *Collections in Context: The Organization of Knowledge and Community in Europe*, ed. by Karen Fresco and Anne D. Hedeman (Columbus: The Ohio State University Press, 2020), pp. 151–88 (pp. 157–8).

[21] PS, pp. vii–xxxvi.

[22] The Paris manuscript, of which fols 145r–210v are dedicated to *Ponthus et Sidoine*, devotes five images to the hero's *emprise*, those on fols 164v, 165v, 166v and 169r. The Cambridge manuscript, which contains just this text, devotes two images to it, those on fols 27r (formerly 28r before fol. 20 was removed from the manuscript) and 35v (formerly 36v): see Montague Rhodes James, 'Unpublished Description by M. R. James of Cambridge, University Library, MS Hh.3.16 (*Ponthus et Sidoine*)' <https://doi.org/10.17863/CAM.67883> [accessed 18 June 2024].

Figure 1. Arrival of the challengers for the *emprise*. *Ponthus et Sidoine* in the *Shrewsbury Book*. London, BL, Royal 15 E VI, fol. 213r. Photo: BL.

As was common, the three miniatures reproduced here appeared at the head of individual chapters above a rubric that indicated the chapter topic: the textual source used for this translation places chapter breaks at slightly different points, but the reader should know that the placement would have seemed more logically consistent in the original manuscript context. Together, they offer a summary of three main stages of a classic *pas d'armes*: the journey and arrival of challengers (Figure 1); the bout between the defender and a challenger (here Ponthus and Bernard de La Roche) (Figure 2); and the celebration that followed the conclusion of the combats (Figure 3). The depiction of the fight on folio 213v (Figure 2) — like the combats shown in the later *Relation du Pas de Saumur* manuscript discussed elsewhere in the present volume[23] — interestingly avoid the traditional tournament imagery in which viewers are placed in stands. Instead, the relatively typical romance scene of single combat has been moved into the middle ground, leaving the foreground to a mixed-sex group of standing spectators whose animated hand gestures indicate that they are engaged in lively conversation about the bout. The importance of the audience's reaction to the fighters' display is equally highlighted in the celebration scene in folio 215r (Figure 3), where the king of Brittany and his court (including Princess Sidoine) repeatedly point towards Ponthus as they heap praise upon him, a public recognition that appears to slightly overwhelm him as he raises his hand to his forehead.

[23] See Source 5 and Essays 2 and 7.

Figure 2. Ponthus jousts with Bernard de La Roche. *Ponthus et Sidoine* in the *Shrewsbury Book*. London, BL, Royal 15 E VI, fol. 213v. Photo: BL.

Figure 3. Festivities following the conclusion of the *emprise*. *Ponthus et Sidoine* in the *Shrewsbury Book*. London, BL, Royal 15 E VI, fol. 215r. Photo: BL.

TRANSLATION

[Context: Earlier in this chapter, Guenelet, one of Ponthus's thirteen companions who had come with him on his exile from Galicia, becomes envious of the love between the hero and Sidoine, the king's daughter, and so causes trouble between them by spreading the rumour that Ponthus loves another lady more than he does Sidoine. Shocked at hearing this news, Sidoine becomes cold towards the hero, causing him to leave her father's court for a year, during which time he decides to organise his chivalric undertaking.]

(52) **Chapter V**

And so Ponthus thought that he would perform an *emprise* that would involve feats of arms. He therefore wrote out a set of rules and sent for a dwarf whom he dressed up very finely and handsomely in a silken gown and gave him a valet and horses as well as a letter containing this formal set of rules which read as follows:

'The Black Knight of the White Arms lets it be known to the best knights of every country that every Tuesday for a year at the hour of prime,[24] they will find at the Fountain of Adventures[25] a black pavilion with white arms. They will see a tree with a shield hanging in it as well as a horn that a dwarf will blow; once it has been blown, an elderly damsel with a circlet of gold will emerge from the pavilion, accompanied by a hermit. She will tell the knights what to do and will take them to the meadow (53) where the Black Knight can be found, fully armed in his harness, who will run three courses with the lance. After the joust, he will fight *à outrance** with a sharp-edged sword* without a thrusting point. The knight whom he defeats will ask all those knights present who, in good faith, is the most beautiful maiden in the whole of Brittany. He will then surrender himself to her as her prisoner, on behalf of the Sorrowing Black Knight of the White Arms, to do with as she sees fit. And let it be known that all those who have done combat with him will gather at Pentecost a year later in this very forest where a feast will be held.[26] The one who has jousted the best will receive the lance and the gonfanon[27] as well as a circlet of gold with *marguerites*[28] on it; the one who has struck the heaviest blow with the sword and fought the best with it will receive the sword with the golden baldrick as well as a gold crown. And, if it should so happen that someone vanquishes the Black Knight, he may send him as a prisoner to whichever lady or damsel he pleases.'

After Ponthus had given the letters to the dwarf, he ordered him to journey round all the courts of France where he knew that there would be gatherings, feasts and jousts going on, and to spread news of his event far and wide. The dwarf, who was a very eloquent speaker, travelled all over the country announcing the event. They marvelled at this knight who wanted to undertake this contest for which he wished to select the best knights from every land. Many of them made themselves ready to go, saying that it would be a great

[24] Prime is the first canonical hour and takes place at six o'clock in the morning.

[25] Also referred to in the text as the Fountain of Marvels and the Fountain of Barenton (see above, n. 3).

[26] See above, Introduction, p. 40.

[27] A type of heraldic flag or banner. DMF.

[28] A *marguerite* is a type of pearl and also the French word for a daisy. DMF. The gold crown mentioned here is later described (see below, p. 56) as being 'decorated with large daisies made of pearls and precious stones'.

honour for whoever won the sword or the lance and even more so for whoever was able to defeat him.

(54) It was not long before a good number of them made their way from Brittany and other lands. Ponthus had had his followers, the prior and the hermit, swear not to give his identity away. He sent off to Rennes, which was formerly known as Ville Rouge, for all that he needed. He also sent for an elderly damsel who was in his confidence and had her dressed in a tunic and a silken mantle with a large circlet of gold on her grey head; he also had her wear a veil in the German style[29] on her face so as to keep her identity a secret. Ponthus then disguised himself as a hermit with white hair and white beard and put a mask on his face; in his hand he held a letter containing the set of rules.

It so happened that that Tuesday morning a whole host of knights arrived who were hoping to undertake a feat of arms against the Black Knight. This was at the Fountain of Marvels, which some refer to as the Fountain of Barenton. There they saw a great tent and pavilion. It was not long before a dwarf, who was very ugly and had a pug-like face, emerged from the pavilion and went up to a large tree from which hung a large horn and the black shield with white arms. He took the horn and gave a very loud blast on it. Then, after the dwarf had blown the horn, out from the pavilion came the damsel and the hermit who led her horse by a golden bridle. The two of them went up to the shield and had it announced by the dwarf that those knights from every country who wished to do battle with the Black Knight should hang up their shields in the large tree. Around the tree were lances with iron hooks on them where everyone could hang up his shield. (55) Each man who was there duly did so. When they were all in place, the dwarf said: 'My damsel here instructs me to tell you that her wish is to select four shields from amongst all of yours by shooting at them with an arrow with gold fletchings*. The one whose shield she hits first should go and arm himself for this Tuesday; the second one whose shield she hits should ready himself for the following Tuesday; the third one should be prepared for the third Tuesday, and the fourth one for the fourth Tuesday. At the end of the month she will shoot another four arrows into another four shields. She will do the same each month for a year starting from now such that fifty-two knights in all will have their challenge taken up, these being the best and the most renowned that my damsel will pick as she sees fit. This will happen for the whole year or until one is found who can defeat the Black Knight in combat.'

After the dwarf had finished speaking, he rode into the pavilion and brought out a wonderfully wrought Turkish bow* and four gilt arrows with gold fletchings. The damsel and the hermit then started to go round the tree and inspect the shields. When they had had a very close look at all of them, the hermit advised the damsel as to which of them she should shoot at. She then drew four arrows and shot them into four shields. The first

[29] Whilst French aristocratic female headdresses tended to expose their wearers' faces in the period of composition of this tale, women in an arc of countries around France to the north and east liked fluted veils with frilled edges, worn at varying distances from the face; this is probably what is being referred to here as a 'veil in the German style', particularly since the garment in question is meant to cover up part of the elderly damsel's face. See Margaret Scott, *Medieval Dress and Fashion* (London: British Library, 2007), pp. 118, fig. 72, 120. See also Jules Guiffrey, ed., *Inventaires de Jean duc de Berry (1401–1416)*, 2 vols (Paris: Ernest Leroux, 1894), vol. 1, p. 272, no. 1012, which lists fabric purchased 'à atourner dames, à la manière d'Alemaigne' (for making ladies' headdresses, in the German style).

of these belonged to Bernard de La Roche, who was held (56) to be the best knight in Brittany. The second one belonged to Geoffroi de Lusignan, thought to be the best in Poitou. The third one belonged to Landry de La Tour, deemed the best of the Angevins and those from the Hurepois.[30] The fourth one belonged to the count of Mortain, seen as the best of the Normans who were there.[31] Once she had completed her four shots, the hermit took her back to the great tent which was black with white arms. Straight afterwards, he dismounted and put on all his armour before coming out of the tent. He had his shield around his neck, his lance in his hand, and was seated on a large black horse that was all covered in a black siglaton[32] with white arms that was very finely made indeed. The knight was tall with long legs and looked very fearsome. Many of those present cast admiring glances at him and they marvelled at who he might be, for the rumour was that Ponthus had gone to the kingdom of Poland and Hungary to take part in a war being waged there,[33] which is why nobody thought that it could be him.

It was not long before Bernard de La Roche, whose shield had been shot at with an arrow, came nobly armed with a great host of horns and buisines[34] playing so loud that the air resounded with the noise. The knight took a golden cup, dipped it into the fountain and poured it over the stone. As the water spread out, it began to thunder and hail and the weather grew wild,[35] but only for a short time. Those who were strangers to the place were amazed at this marvellous fountain. Each time before the joust began, Ponthus poured the water in this way. He then remounted his horse, with his helm* on his head, took up his lance and spurred his mount towards Bernard, with Bernard charging likewise towards him. They dealt each other such great blows that they pierced their shields before they passed each other, turned round and struck one another with the result that Bernard and his horse were brought to the ground. But (57) Bernard leapt back up onto his feet. When the Black Knight saw that he was on foot, he got off his horse and ran towards him with his sword of polished steel and dealt him a series of heavy blows wherever he could land them. Bernard defended himself as best he could, but Ponthus rained down such mighty blows that he broke through everything his sword touched, striking one particular blow that tore off the helm's face-plate with breathing holes* as well as the [decorative] circular band atop it and wounding him slightly in the face. Bernard raised his sword and struck at Ponthus, but Ponthus thrust his shield in front of him so that the blow fell upon it. The sword went a good six inches into it and

---

30 The Hurepois is a region to the south of the Île de France, situated between the Seine and the Loire.

31 Ponthus was already familiar with many of these knights, as they had fought with him against Karadas, the son of the sultan of Babylon who had attacked Brittany in an earlier episode; on defeating him in a final confrontation on board a Saracen ship, Ponthus wins various precious items that he later gives as prizes at his *emprise*. PS, ch. III.

32 Siglaton (also spelt ciclaton) was a very rich silk fabric, possibly originally from Byzantium, often described as incorporating areas of pattern worked in metal thread; here it refers to a trapper* made of this fabric. See <http://lexissearch.arts.manchester.ac.uk/entry.aspx?word=ciclatoun> [accessed 7 June 2024].

33 The text implies here that the kingdoms of Poland and Hungary were united: this was indeed the case from 1370 to 1382, when they were ruled in a personal union by Louis I of Hungary, also known as Louis the Great (1326–82). PS, p. civ.

34 A type of long, straight, metal trumpet that was used mainly for ceremonial and military purposes. DMF.

35 See above, Introduction, p. 40.

became stuck there; Bernard was unable to retrieve it, so firmly embedded had it become. On seeing what had happened, Ponthus pulled his shield with such force that it and the sword itself shot towards him. When Bernard found himself without his sword, he was dismayed. Ponthus then said to him: 'Sir knight, it is time that you surrendered yourself to the mercy of the most beautiful maiden in the realm.' Bernard said nothing in reply, like one who is angry and displeased. So Ponthus said to him: 'Sir knight never, may it so please God, would I attack you when you have no means with which to defend yourself.' Bernard then came forward, thinking to use his fists against him but Ponthus, who was tall and strong, approached him, took his man by the helm and pulled him towards him so violently that he made him fall to the ground on his hands. He then stood over him and said: 'I will let you go and join the prison of the most beautiful lady whom you should greet on behalf of the Black Knight.'

As Ponthus stepped back, Bernard saw clearly just how gracious this knight was. He therefore prized him even more highly and went up to the knights who had been watching the combat, saying to them: 'My good lords, I have found my master. Never before did (58) I find a knight who was as fearsome, courteous and strong as he. I therefore request that you tell me who is the most beautiful lady in the realm.'

They were of the opinion that this was the king's daughter, whose name was Sidoine; this opinion was shared by all. Bernard then departed and went off to Vannes.[36]

I will leave off speaking about Bernard and come back to Ponthus.

(59) **Chapter VI**

Ponthus got on his horse and rode into the forest, his mount making a loud noise as it ran galloping along. He took certain paths with which he was very familiar in order that no one might know where he had gone. He arrived at the priory, went inside and shut the gate behind him before dismounting from his horse and having his armour taken off him. The damsel, the dwarf and all the others in masks stayed in their pavilions until nightfall and only made their way there once everyone else had gone to bed.

I will leave off speaking about them and will return to Sidoine and Bernard de La Roche.

(60) **Chapter VII**

Day and night Sidoine was in a state of sorrow and distress ever since Elios, her damsel, had told her that Ponthus had said to her that he would be absent from the country for a while; she thought that it was because of the frosty welcome she had given him.[37] She repented bitterly of her conduct, lamenting long and hard and saying: 'Alas! What a wretch I am! I have now lost him because of my great folly! Cursed be he who first brought me that piece of news for I can clearly see that, if it wasn't for the fear on his part that he was out of favour with me, he would not have left the country. It was great foolishness on my part to have any doubt that his gentle heart was not more loyal than that of any other.'

[36] Vannes at this time was the capital of the kingdom of Brittany. PS, p. 385.

[37] See context above. Guenelet's name aptly evokes that of the traitor Ganelon in the famous late eleventh-century epic, the *Chanson de Roland*.

She wept and sorrowed in her heart and was full of regret, fear and sadness at having lost him. Thus did she lament both night and day. Ponthus was also greatly missed by those at court. The king himself could not stay quiet about it, as he missed him enormously; so did Ponthus's cousin[38] and all his other companions, as well as many others both high- and low-born. The whole court was saddened.

It was not long before Bernard made his way there. He asked for the beautiful Sidoine in order to tell her that he was her prisoner. The king sent for her and she came along with a great company of ladies and damsels. The knights and all manner of other people then gathered to hear Bernard, lord of La Roche, speak. When Sidoine (61) came into the great hall, Bernard went down on his knees before her and, in a loud voice so that all could hear him, said: 'My lady, I am sent to you by the Black Knight of the White Arms who, through his prowess, has defeated me in combat and told me to surrender myself as a prisoner to the most beautiful maiden in the kingdom. I asked all the knights and squires who were present to tell me who was the most beautiful, and you were the one whom they all named. I therefore put myself in your prison as your knight to do with as you please. Moreover, he asked me to greet you on his behalf.'

Sidoine blushed in her embarrassment at being described as the most beautiful one. 'In truth', she said, 'I thank them for it but they have spoken about me rather frivolously. Nonetheless, I thank the knight who sent you here. Tell me now if you know who he is.' 'Indeed, my lady,' said he, 'I know nothing.' 'What?' said the king, 'Is it not possible to find out who he is?' 'Truly, it is not,' said Bernard, 'But I can tell you that he is the most handsome knight in arms that I ever saw, and the one who knows best how to strike with lance and sword. I would say that he is a little taller than Ponthus, whom he resembles a good deal, but it cannot be him as the word is that he is in the kingdom of Poland or Hungary where a war is going on.'

Much was then said about the Black Knight and how, the following Tuesday, he would fight against Geoffroi de Lusignan and, the Tuesday after that, against Landry de La Tour, and then the count of Mortain.

The king and the ladies gave a very warm welcome to the lord of La Roche and all ate together in the great hall in the king's company. Sidoine teased Bernard, saying: 'I'm very pleased to have acquired such a prisoner as the lord of La Roche. You must be very fearful about what (62) kind of prison you will have to endure.' Bernard broke into a smile and said: 'My lady, if you do not throw me into a worse prison than this one, I will endure it very well. And you should know that, in my opinion, before this year is out, you will have a far greater number of prisoners to deal with and I will not be on my own.'

After they had eaten, dances and carols[39] started up. But Sidoine scarcely danced at all and would have refrained completely if she hadn't been worried that someone might notice how distressed she was.

I will leave off talking about them and the court and will come back to the second Tuesday.

---

[38] This cousin, Ponthus's closest companion and most faithful friend, is named Polidès.

[39] A lively medieval dance where the dancers sing as they move around in a circle. DMF.

(63) **Chapter VIII**

It was a lovely, clear day. The lord of Lusignan, who was an extremely fine knight, put on all his armour and went up to the fountain. The Black Knight came out of the pavilions with his lance in his hand and his shield around his neck. Once they caught sight of each other, they let their mounts run and met to exchange great blows, with the result that the horses fell to the ground on their rumps and the two men nearly came off as well. They gathered themselves once more and took up fresh lances that were strong and heavy with sharp tips. The two knights then retreated before riding at each other a second time as fast as they could in order to throw their bodies and their horses at one another. They struck such tremendous blows on their buckled-on shields that they all collapsed, both horses and riders. The impact was so great that Geoffroi de Lusignan's mount fell on top of his body, with its head underneath him. Neither knight nor animal could move as Geoffroi's leg and thigh were crushed under the horse and had been badly damaged by it. Ponthus's mount got back on its feet with him on top of it, and he was very ashamed at having been brought down. When he saw that his opponent was unable to move from under his horse, he dismounted and went over to the (64) knight, helping to pull him out from underneath his mount. Geoffroi's foot was dislocated at the ankle and he could only stand on one leg but, nonetheless, he put his hand to his sword, like one who is full of great courage and boldness. However, when Ponthus saw that he could only stand on one foot, he had no wish to strike him but let him deal a blow or two before saying to him: 'Sir knight, I can see you are in such poor shape that it would be shameful of me to attack you.' 'Why?' said Geoffroi, 'I do not consider myself beaten as long as I can wield my sword.'

And as he made as if to strike Ponthus, he hit his foot against a stone and fell over. Ponthus helped him to his feet, saying: 'Sir, if you were fully able, I would run at you, but I can see that you are in a bad way. You will not surrender yourself to me but rather to the most beautiful damsel in the whole of Brittany who will show you mercy and whom you will greet on behalf of the Black Knight. I beg you, therefore, let us not do any more than we have already done, for I know full well that, if you were completely well, you would not have left me as intact as you have, as I have long been aware of your prowess.' When Geoffroi saw how gracious the knight was, he valued him even more highly and said to him: 'Sir, I will go where it pleases you to tell me to. Furthermore, if I thought that it would not displease you, I would ask you your name.' 'Sir, neither you nor anyone else will know that for the time being,' came the reply, so Geoffroi gave up trying to ask anything more about it.

Ponthus then took his leave of him and went back into the forest along the secret paths that he had taken the previous time. Those who had watched the combat were full of amazement, saying: 'The Black Knight is very merciful and courteous. Did you not see how (65) gracious he was in not wanting to touch the other knight when he saw the extent of his injuries and in helping him up twice to his feet?' Much was made of the knight and they praised him greatly. They went up to Geoffroi de Lusignan who was unable to move and who said to Landry: 'My dear companion, I will wait until next Tuesday in order to keep you company on your way to see the fair Sidoine if you are not able to give a better account of yourself than I did.' 'Sir,' said Landry, 'In combats no one can tell what will happen as they are so unpredictable, and you are not responsible for what befell you as it was due to your horse collapsing on top of you, which no one can guard against. But I think that no shame will come to me if I follow in the example of knights like you and Bernard de La Roche.' They then spoke about other matters. As gently as could be, he was carried to Montfort[40] and treated so that he could ride with his leg resting on a suspended wooden board.[41]

The following Tuesday when the day was bright and clear, it so happened that various people arrived from all parts to see the combat. At the hour of prime, the Black Knight of the White Arms came out of the pavilions, along with his damsel and dwarf; from the other side came Landry de La Tour. They tucked their lances under their elbows with the gonfanons hanging down and charged at each other at high speed but without encountering. They therefore passed on and turned round very fast with the result that they struck each other's shields and broke their lances. They then ran at each with their steel swords, dealing one another great blows wherever and whenever they could manage to land them. They remained for a long time (66) on horseback. And yet Ponthus stood tall in his stirrups and struck Landry with all his might, leaving him completely stunned. After having dealt this blow, Ponthus saw his opponent sway and so he grabbed him by the helm, pulled him as hard as he could and threw him to the ground in a dazed state. Still Landry managed to get back on his feet as soon as he was able to. Seeing his opponent on foot, Ponthus said to himself that he would not attack him whilst he was mounted and the other not, as it would not redound to his honour. He therefore got off his horse, put his shield out in front of him and held his sword in his hand, before going over to attack him. Landry did his best to defend himself, knowing full well that he was dealing with no mere novice. Ponthus came at him and dealt him a blow that caused his sword to slip and hit the shield such that it chopped off about a quarter of it. Landry fought back with great blows wherever he could hit home and gave a very good account of defending himself, like a knight who was wonderfully strong. He kept this up for some time, with Ponthus striking him hard wherever he was able to land his blows. He was amazed at how long his opponent could hold out against him. Their shields and helms were cut to pieces and, shortly afterwards, they began to tire and had to stop and catch their breath, with each one leaning on his sword. Landry spoke up first, saying: 'Sir knight, I do not know who you are but I can safely say that I did not expect to find such strength and valour in you as I have done at this time of the morning. However, before you defeat me in combat, you will have even more of your work cut out for you than you already have done!' 'Not so,' replied Ponthus, 'By holy faith, you will surrender yourself to the most beautiful damsel or (67) my heart is lying to me. You will make a gift to her of this sword!'

He then raised his sword and struck him, like one who is deeply ashamed that his opponent has held out so long against him. The fight then became even fiercer, with blood flowing down to their feet. After Ponthus landed one blow on his man, Landry gave him one on his temple, causing severe damage to his helm. Ponthus then turned his shield round, took his sword in both hands and struck Landry such a heavy blow that he left him stunned and no wonder, for the battle between the two of them had gone on so long that they could barely keep themselves upright. Ponthus dealt blow after blow until he could see that Landry was tiring and left reeling from all the punishment that he had given and received. And so Ponthus harried his man more and more, up to the point where

[40] Montfort (arr. Rennes, dép. Ille-et-Vilaine).

[41] This way of riding, with legs out horizontally on a suspended board (*pallecte/pallette*) was apparently a very ancient one, often used by women. PS, p. 336.

he could see that he was starting to sway. He then went up to him and pushed him with all his might, with the result that he knocked him down and he too fell to the ground. Yet Ponthus landed on top of him so that Landry was unable to get back up, and he said to him: 'Sir knight, yield!' Landry didn't utter a word and held out with great difficulty, being greatly dismayed at having to surrender. Thereupon Ponthus, like one possessed of extraordinary courtesy, said to him: 'Sir knight, surrender to the fair damsel, I entreat you; let there be no further quarrel between us for we have striven long enough against each other.' It was then that Landry de La Tour saw just how courteous the knight was that he had fought against, and so said to him: 'Sir, I willingly surrender to her, since that is your pleasure.' 'That is good enough for me,' replied Ponthus.

(68) He then stood up feeling very tired and drained from the heavy blows that he had given and received during this great battle that had lasted so long. With some difficulty, he went over to his horse, mounted it and headed off into the forest at great speed towards where the trees were thicker and he was soon lost to view. Geoffroi de Lusignan and various others went over to Landry de La Tour and asked him how he fared. He told them he fared well, considering how hard the fight had been, but that he had met his master. 'Ha!' said Geoffroi, 'You and I will go to the most beautiful lady and throw ourselves on her mercy.' 'Sir,' said Landry, 'I will certainly keep you company because it is not right that you should go without me.' Thus did the two companions tease each other. Landry was disarmed and found that he had a lot of injuries, but he was not worried about it as none of them was so great as to stop him from getting on horseback.

Three days later, then, they went off to surrender to the fair Sidoine. The king bade them a very warm and joyful welcome as to two of the best knights that could be found in any land and ones so highly renowned for their fine deeds of chivalry. They went up to Sidoine and threw themselves on her mercy. She, being very wise and courteous, received them with much pleasure, entertaining and honouring them greatly; she also gave them silk mantles lined with grey fur as well as some rich and beautiful belts, from each of which hung a very lovely *aumoniere*.[42] The two knights thanked her and told her that they were very content with their prison, since such imprisonment was not hard to bear. 'My lords,' she said, 'I don't know who the knight is who has sent you to me but both he and you honour me without good cause, for there are plenty of ladies who are far more beautiful and becoming in this kingdom, whoever took the trouble to look for and find them.' 'My lady,' they replied, 'General opinion must be believed because all chose you as the most beautiful.' They then exchanged many a teasing word on (69) various subjects. They were there for two days, one of them with the king and the other with Sidoine, before they were given permission to take their leave.

They therefore set off to see the combat with the count of Mortain, who was a very fine knight. The elderly damsel and the dwarf came out with the Turkish bow and the four arrows, as you have heard before, and the hermit in the mask held her horse by the golden bridle and pointed out to her which four shields she should shoot at for that month. The elderly lady shot first at the shield of Thibaut de Blois, who was highly renowned as a great knight; the second was shot at that of the count of Dammartin; the third at the shield of Henri de Montmorency; and the fourth at the shield of Robert de Roussillon.

---

[42] A kind of pouch carried at the waist as a purse, typically used for holding coins intended to be given as alms. DMF.

These were the four knights with the highest reputation for chivalry whose shields were hung on that day, for Ponthus had his spies who enquired about the best knights whose shields had been put up and what their coats of arms were. For this reason, he could not fail, just as those present said that the elderly lady had not failed to choose the best ones. Once she had shot all four arrows, she withdrew into the pavilions.

It was not long before the Black Knight emerged, fully armed from head to toe, his shield around his neck and his lance in his hand. From the other side came the count of Mortain, very richly equipped and accompanied by a great host of trumpets, horns and flutes. No sooner did they see each other than they let their horses run and struck heavy blows at one another. Ponthus sent the (70) count reeling backwards and narrowly missed knocking him off his horse. They put their hands to their swords and ran at each other with great ferocity. Yet Ponthus dealt such strong and heavy blows that he cut into whatever he touched. The count defended himself as best he could, so the fight lasted for a long time. But Ponthus, who was marvellously tall and strong, took his man by the helm and pulled him to him with such vigour that he tore it off him and threw it to the ground, leaving the count in just his mail coif*. Ponthus then landed a tremendous blow upon him with the sword, but not with the blade of his weapon, telling him to yield. The count held out longer but had to surrender in the end, whether he liked it or not. Ponthus thereupon told his opponent to give himself up to the most beautiful damsel in Brittany before he went off into the forest as was his custom. The count went to surrender himself to the beautiful Sidoine, just as the others had done. Both she and her father, the king, showered him with honours.

The following Tuesday, Ponthus fought against Thibaut de Blois and then against all the others up to the end of the month, but it is not possible to recount all the fights and bouts that each of them fought both that month and the others, for there were so many fine jousts, tough contests and noble feats of arms that it would take far too long to describe them for those who would like to hear about all of them. Yet, in the end, each and every one of Ponthus's opponents was defeated in battle and sent to the beautiful Sidoine's prison. These were the fifty-two best knights that could be found in any land since, in order to acquire honour, all those who heard about the fine knights going to test themselves and about the defender who was choosing only the very best to perform feats of arms with him were keen to be of their number and to measure themselves against him. Word of this spread throughout (71) France and Germany and all other countries such that everyone was making their way there and hanging up their shields. Many a one came from France and from other realms and lands. Ponthus always chose the best of them and only fought against one from each land in order that his reputation might spread as far as possible. Among the fifty-two knights were the duke of Austria, the duke of Lorraine, the duke of Bar, the count of Montbéliart, the count of Montfort as well as many other counts and dukes, and also Messire Guillaume des Barres, Messire Ernout de Hainaut, the count of Savoy and other fine knights. I will refrain from naming them all as it would take far too long to do so. I will therefore return to my story to keep things short. Eventually it came to Pentecost at the end of the year when all the prisoners came to surrender themselves, as they had been ordered to do.

(72) **Chapter IX**

Ponthus had a great hall decked out with leaves and greenery next to the Fountain of Marvels, also known as the Fountain of Barenton, and he sent for meats and all manner of wines and other provisions. He sent a message to the king that said: 'To the good king of Brittany: the Black Knight of the White Arms greets you in all friendship and respect. He humbly begs that it be your pleasure to come at the feast of Pentecost to the forest of Broceliande and to the Fountain of Marvels, accompanied by the most beautiful ladies and damsels of your kingdom, not forgetting your daughter so that she may advise who should receive the prize, judging by who has jousted the best and who has put up the strongest and finest fight of all the fifty-two knights on the Tuesdays of the past year.'

When the king saw the content of the message, he was overjoyed; he said that the Black Knight showed him great honour and that he would be there. He sent for his daughter and told her the news, entrusting her with the task of finding the most beautiful ladies and damsels in the kingdom to come with her at Pentecost. 'And (73), dear daughter,' said the king, 'This you must do since the Black Knight has done you a great honour in using his sword to send you prisoners from among so many fine knights and great lords, thereby bringing great renown to both you and our kingdom. For this reason, I regard myself as most beholden to him.' The fair Sidoine went down on her knees and said: 'Since it is your pleasure, I will do as you command.' She then had letters written to all the great ladies of Brittany, telling them to join her at Ploërmel[43] two days before Pentecost and to bring in their entourage the most beautiful ladies and damsels that they could find. Delighted, the ladies who received Sidoine's order made themselves ready and came on the appointed day.

The gathering was very full. On the day of Pentecost itself, they came and brought tents and pavilions which they had put up everywhere, such that it would have seemed to you like a great army. Ponthus came before the king and had sent altogether thirteen sets of splendid garments to his thirteen companions as well as one to Herlant, the seneschal, having sent for them the day before in order that they might keep him company. Let it not be asked if his close cousin Polidès and his companions were overjoyed at the glory that God had shown him! They all went up before the king. When the king realised that it was Ponthus who had performed so many feats of arms, there is no question that he was filled with joy and showered him with every honour and made much of him, being unable to restrain himself from hugging and kissing him. The king then said to Ponthus: 'You have kept yourself hidden from us for quite some time. It was said that you were in Hungary or Poland where a war was going on, but, in good faith, my heart told me (74) that it was you performing these marvels.' Ponthus blushed and said nothing, for he was embarrassed at receiving such praise from the king.

After this, he went over to Sidoine who was there with a very fine company of beautiful ladies and damsels. Ponthus bowed to her and greeted her, and she returned his greeting like one whose heart was more full of joy than it could possibly imagine. And yet she said to him with a smile: 'So, Ponthus, you have been hiding from us for a long while in this forest! I am wondering if you haven't become a Wild Man.' 'Ah, my lady,' he said, 'Begging your grace, I would be easy to tame.' He then left her side, like one who is overcome at being in his lady's presence, given that it had been so long since he had last seen her. He therefore went to greet the ladies who had bedecked themselves with foliage and chaplets,[44] saying to them: 'My ladies, I pray to God that each of you may have whatever her heart desires for, in good faith, it is a glorious thing to behold such a beautiful company.' The

---

43 Ploërmel (arr. Vannes, dép. Morbihan).

44 Chaplet here means a circlet or a wreath of flowers. DMF.

ladies returned his greeting and were full of joy at seeing him, for they truly loved him above all other knights and said to one another: 'It's Ponthus, the good and handsome knight! Blessed be God for the great honour that He has shown him and may He keep him safe on our behalf as the best knight in the world.'

So many fine words were said about him both far and near. To the fountain came the king and the ladies in great joyfulness, and there they dismounted. From the other side came all the knights who had travelled from afar. The king and the ladies greeted them most warmly. There was a tremendous sound of musical instruments (75) of many kinds, such that the whole forest rang and resounded with it. Both the king and Ponthus did great honour to the dukes and the lords, including the dukes of Austria, Lorraine and Bar, as well as the counts of Dammartin, Savoy and Montbéliart, and other high-ranking lords. They went to hear Mass sung by the bishop of Rennes before coming into the great hall. There the king, the ladies and Sidoine all sat on the high dais, with the others each taking their place according to their station.

The feast was magnificent and the great hall was immense. On one side hung the shields of all fifty-two knights who had been defeated. The *entremets** was very charming and original, consisting of armed children play-fighting together, along with other entertainments. Six of the most beautiful ladies, six damsels, six of the oldest and best knights and six squires were asked to stand up. Some of them brought in the lance and the black gonfanon with white arms, decorated with large *marguerites* and pearls from the Orient, as well as a magnificent gold circlet encrusted with pearls and fine gemstones. The others brought in a glorious sword whose pommel was made of gold with a silk baldrick embellished with rich jewels and beautiful *marguerites* from the Orient, as well as a superb gold crown decorated with large daisies made of pearls and precious stones. It was a delight to see such riches that Ponthus had won from the ship belonging to the sultan's son![45] He said to himself that he could not put them to better use than to bring them out before so many princes as all his deeds would then be most honourably displayed. The ladies and the knights walked round and round the room, singing as they went, as if they were unsure to whom these prizes should be awarded. They finally came up to the lord of Lusignan and presented to him the lance with the gonfanon; they also placed the rich gold circlet on his head as befitting the best (76) jouster. Afterwards, they went over to Landry de La Tour and presented him with the magnificent sword, placing on his head the fine crown, whether he liked it or not, for he tried to excuse himself and refuse the prize, saying that though they did him honour he had not earned it as there were several others who had deserved it more; he blushed and was embarrassed. But Ponthus had ordered that this should be so for he said, in good faith, that Landry had given him the most to do on a single day and that Geoffroi had also jousted extremely well. Minstrels then began to strike up all manner of instruments and heralds to shout out, such that one would not have heard God's thunder; so loud was the noise that it filled the woods and the enclosures! Ponthus laid on many different types of meat and good wines and gave generous gifts to the heralds and minstrels.

---

[45] See above, n. 31.

Thanks are due to Margaret Scott for her invaluable help in deciphering and translating some of the references to clothing and textiles in this text.

Mario Damen

Source 2

The *Paso de la Fuerte Ventura* (*Paso* of the Daunting Adventure), Valladolid, 1428

This source consists of a translation of a narrative account of this event.

Author: Pedro Carrillo de Huete

Language: Medieval Castilian

Manuscript source: Madrid, Biblioteca Nacional, 9945

Edition used: Juan de Mata Carriazo y Arroquia, ed., *Crónica del halconero de Juan II, Pedro Carrillo de Huete (hasta ahora inédita)*, Colección de crónicas españolas, 8 (Madrid: Espasa-Calpe, 1946), pp. 20–2 (= PCH)

Select bibliography:

Barber, Richard, and Juliet Barker, *Tournaments: Jousts, Chivalry and Pageants in the Middle Ages* (New York: Weidenfeld & Nicolson, 1989), p. 98

Fernández de Córdova Miralles, Álvaro, 'L'impact de la Bourgogne sur la cour castillane des Trastamare', in *La cour de Bourgogne et l'Europe: le rayonnement et les limites d'un modèle culturel; actes du colloque international tenu à Paris les 9, 10 et 11 octobre 2007*, ed. by Werner Paravicini, Torsten Hiltmann and Frank Viltart (Ostfildern: Jan Thorbecke Verlag, 2013), pp. 593–630 (pp. 607–8)

Nadot, Sébastien, *Le Spectacle des joutes: Sport et courtoisie à la fin du Moyen Âge* (Rennes: Presses Universitaires de Rennes, 2012), pp. 19, 134, 195–6, 284

Riquer, Martín de, *Vida caballeresca en la España del siglo XV* (Madrid: Gráficas Marina, 1965), p. 67

Ruiz, Teofilo F., *A King Travels: Festive Traditions in Late Medieval and Early Modern Spain* (Princeton, NJ: Princeton University Press, 2012), pp. 231–3, 335–8

Introduction

The *Paso de la Fuerte Ventura* is one of the first *pas d'armes* that we know of and was celebrated on the Plaza Mayor of Valladolid on Tuesday 18 May 1428 under the aegis of the court of King Juan II of Castile (1405–54). The *entrepreneur** or organiser of the *Paso* was the Infante Enrique of Aragon (1400–45), third son of King Fernando I of Aragon (1380–1416), who had acted as regent of Castile in the years 1406–15.[1] Enrique became one of the most prominent noblemen of Castile when he inherited the Castilian possessions of his father in

[1] DBE, lemma 'Enrique de Aragon'.

1416.[2] Valladolid was an important centre for the kings of Castile: King Juan II was born (and would later be temporarily buried) there and he usually resided in the palace of San Pablo, constructed in the grounds of the convent of the same name. Hence it became not only a major administrative centre, where the *cortes* (the assembly of the representatives of the three Estates of the realm) were often convened, but also a place where many courtly celebrations were held.[3] This *paso* was even embedded in a series of chivalric events during the months of May and June of 1428,[4] which were organised by the main political protagonists of the Castilian court, each of whom did so in turn.[5] The second event was the actual *Paso de la Fuerte Ventura* of Enrique of Aragon. Most authors relate this as a one-day event, although one royal chronicler, Álvar García de Santa María, who gave a brief account of it (see below) mentions that the feast lasted for six days.[6]

The organiser of the *paso*, Enrique of Aragon, competed with a team consisting of five defenders. Their challenge was taken up by the kings of Castile and Navarre, accompanied by teams consisting of twenty-four and twelve knights, respectively, as well as by other knights who competed individually rather than as part of a team. The event seems to have been rather 'closed' in nature, although one chronicler mentions the presence of some 'caballeros extrangeros' (foreign knights) but without providing any further information about them.[7] In any case, there is no evidence that chapters of arms (if there were any) or invitations were sent across the Iberian Peninsula and beyond. The bouts consisted of both individual and collective jousts, but this is not spelled out in detail in the account that preserves it. The fighting was so intense that the *entrepreneur* had an unfortunate fall from which he almost died and one of his team members was seriously injured by his opponent and did subsequently die from the wound that he had received. The atmosphere of political rivalry pervading the Castilian court in this period may have played a role in this, but casualties seem to be the rule rather than the exception in Castilian chivalric events, such as the *Paso Honroso* (Órbigo Bridge, near León, 1434), where one competitor suffered a particularly gruesome death from a lance tip that penetrated his skull.[8] Another distinctive element of the Castilian *paso* was the structure of the so-called 'passage' itself, which was either an arch, as at this event and the *Paso de El Pardo* (1459),[9] or a bridge, as at the *Paso Honroso* and the *Paso de Jaén* (1461).[10] Little information is available about the exact theatrical scenario governing the *Paso de la Fuerte Ventura*, at least when compared to the more elaborate descriptions of the Angevin and Burgundian *pas*, such as the *Pas de la Bergère* (Tarascon, 1449) and the *Pas*

---

[2] Sébastien Nadot, *Le Spectacle des joutes: Sport et courtoisie à la fin du Moyen Âge* (Rennes: Presses Universitaires de Rennes, 2012), p. 284; Teofilo F. Ruiz, *A King Travels: Festive Traditions in Late Medieval and Early Modern Spain* (Princeton, NJ: Princeton University Press, 2012), pp. 231–2.

[3] Francisco de Paula Cañas Gálves, *El itinerario de la corte de Juan II de Castilla (1418–1454)* (Madrid: Silex Ediciones, 2007), p. 149.

[4] For more details on the five chivalric events of May and June and on the political strife in the 1420s between the two competing noble factions of Castile, see Essay 1.

[5] See PCH, pp. 19–27; LB, pp. 59–66; and the summary in Ruiz, *A King Travels*, pp. 335–8.

[6] AGSM, p. 16.

[7] FPG, p. 250.

[8] Noel Fallows, *Jousting in Medieval and Renaissance Iberia* (Woodbridge: Boydell Press, 2010), pp. 482–3; on the level of violence at this event, see also Essay 6.

[9] See Source 8.

[10] See Source 10.

du Perron Fée (Bruges, 1463), respectively.[11] Nevertheless, the *entremets**, the inscriptions of the texts that were painted on the ephemeral architecture and the dialogue between the herald and the challengers all point to an event involving a scenario of some kind and a fixed set of rules, which unfortunately have not come down to us.[12]

The *Paso de la Fuerte Ventura* is described in four different chronicles, which were all written under the patronage of the Castilian kings, another characteristic feature of most *pasos* celebrated in this kingdom.[13] The first and most extensive report was written by King Juan's falconer, Pedro Carrillo de Huete (*c.*1380–*c.*1448), who was knighted in 1407 and held office at the Castilian court until 1455. Carillo was an eyewitness of the event since he acted as one of the judges at the *paso*. Interestingly, he refers to himself in the text in the third-person voice in this judging role, which may be a kind of humility device whereby the author avoids drawing attention to himself.[14] The narrative forms part of his chronicle on the Castilian court under Juan II between 1420 and 1450. The transmission of the text, however, is somewhat complicated. The original manuscript is lost and the version that is preserved — a sixteenth-century copy of a fifteenth-century copy — is incomplete.[15] However, despite its convoluted provenance, this version serves as the basis of the translation given here, as it is the most elaborate description of this *paso* and was itself based on the original account of Carrillo. Lope de Barrientos, Juan's confessor, made another copy of the lost original chronicle of Carrillo de Huete, now known as the 'Refundición', which was also lost but has come down to us in a sixteenth-century copy.[16] This second version very much resembles the first report of the *paso* in style, length and content, but has some small additions and variations, which will be indicated in the footnotes to the translation. Fernán Pérez de Guzmán (*c.*1378–1460), of a noble family from Toledo, wrote a third, shorter account in his chronicle of Juan II which tends to be biased towards Álvaro de Luna, the king's favourite.[17] The fourth and shortest report was composed by Álvar García de Santa María (*c.*1380–1460), from Burgos, who occupied a local administrative office for several decades. He was officially installed as royal chronicler in 1406, a post which he held until 1434.[18]

[11] See Sources 6 and 11a.

[12] Álvaro Fernández de Córdova Miralles, 'L'impact de la Bourgogne sur la cour castillane des Trastamare', in *La cour de Bourgogne et l'Europe: le rayonnement et les limites d'un modèle culturel; actes du colloque international tenu à Paris les 9, 10 et 11 octobre 2007*, ed. by Werner Paravicini, Torsten Hiltmann and Frank Viltart (Ostfildern: Jan Thorbecke Verlag, 2013), pp. 593–630 (p. 608).

[13] Whilst this is the case of the *Paso de Valladolid* (1440) (see Source 3) and that of El Pardo, the narrative account of the *Paso de Jaén* is preserved in a chivalric biography, rather than a royal chronicle.

[14] See also Source 14, where Antoine de Lalaing uses the third-person voice to recount the *Pas* of Brussels which he himself organised.

[15] DBE, lemma 'Pero Carrillo de Huete'; PCH, pp. ix–xv. PCH is an edition of Madrid, Biblioteca Nacional, 9945.

[16] LB, pp. ix–xix. LB is an edition of El Escorial, Real Biblioteca del Monasterio de San Lorenzo, X-II-13.

[17] See FPG, p. 250; and DBE, lemma 'Fernán Pérez de Guzmán'. Luna, constable of Castile, the most senior army and household officer of the king, organised the first chivalric event of the series held in Valladolid on 2 May. DBE, lemma 'Álvaro de Luna'.

[18] See AGSM, p. 16; and DBE, lemma 'Álvar García de Santa María'. AGSM is an edition based on the following manuscript: El Escorial, Real Biblioteca del Monasterio de San Lorenzo, X-II-2.

In the translation that follows, page numbers in parentheses have been inserted for ease of reference to Carriazo y Arroquia's edition.

TRANSLATION

(20) About the festivity that the Infante Don Enrique organised in Valladolid

On Tuesday, the eighteenth day of May in the year of Our Lord 1428, the Infante Don Enrique[19] organised a very notable[20] festivity in the following manner: on the square of the said town[21] at the corner of the street[22] that connects the Puerta del Campo with the square, he constructed a fortress of wood and cloth.[23] It was built in the following way: a very high tower was crowned with four turrets; there was a belfry on top of the tower and a bell placed inside it. A column, fashioned in the same way as the tower so as to look like [it was made of] stone, was placed on top of the belfry. On the column stood a gilded griffin which held a very large white and red standard in its front paws. On each of the four turrets of the tower was a smaller standard of the same kind as the large one.

The tower was surrounded by a very high fence with four turrets and an outer fence which was a little lower than it and had a further twelve turrets. On each of these turrets stood a well-dressed lady.[24] The ground floor of the (21) fortress contained dressing rooms for the infante, as well as stables and mangers for the horses.

A tilt* made of canes[25] was placed between the fortress and a gated arch[26] with two more towers through which all the knight-adventurers had to pass. On this arch was the following inscription: 'This is the Arch of the Dangerous Passage of the Daunting Adventure'. On top of each of the two towers stood a man with a horn. The fortress and the towers were made to look as if they were made of bricks. On a scaffold [built into]

---

[19] [el ynfante don Enrrique]. Enrique of Aragon (1400–45), infante of Aragon, marqués of Villena and count of Alburquerque, was the brother of King Alfonso V of Aragon and brother-in-law of King Juan II of Castile (see below, n. 37); he was also Grandmaster of the Order of Santiago (1409–45). DBE, lemma 'Enrique de Aragon'.

[20] Note that the chronicler already describes the *paso* in a way that distinguishes it from the other chivalric events that both preceded and followed it in the series. See above, p. 58, and Essay 1.

[21] That is, the Plaza Mayor of Valladolid.

[22] That is, the Calle de Santiago.

[23] García de Santa María describes this structure as a wooden 'Alcázar', the Arabic word used for a fortified palace where the king resides. AGSM, p. 16.

[24] It is not clear whether there were ladies standing only on the twelve turrets of the outer fence or on all sixteen turrets.

[25] The usual word for tilt in Castilian is *tela*, which literally means cloth and may refer to the material that the earliest tilts were made of, these in fact being a Castilian invention. See Richard Barber and Juliet Barker, *Tournaments: Jousts, Chivalry and Pageants in the Middle Ages* (New York: Weidenfeld & Nicolson, 1989), pp. 98, 196; Tobias Capwell, *Arms and Armour of the Medieval Joust* (Leeds: Royal Armouries Museum, 2018), p. 81.

[26] LB, p. 60, has the lesson 'varco' instead of 'arco', meaning boat. See also Martín de Riquer, *Vida caballeresca en la España del siglo XV* (Madrid: Gráficas Marina, 1965), p. 67.

the fence next to the tower was a very large gilded wheel; this was called 'The Wheel of Fortune'.[27] At the foot of the wheel was a very elaborate seat.

When all of this had been made to his specifications, the said lord infante defended [the passage] in royal harness* with five[28] other knights who were accompanying him; these were: Juan Manrique,[29] son of García Fernández Manrique,[30] *Frey* Gutierre de Cárdenas,[31] Lope de Rojas,[32] Álvaro de Sandoval,[33] and Diego de Tejeda.[34] Before he armed himself, the infante went to the foot of the fortress with many noblemen from his household and danced there awhile right in front of the building. Afterwards they freed from the fortress many hens, goats and rams that were living there before the infante then mounted his horse and rode off to his lodgings.

He staged an *entremés** in the following manner: eight very finely dressed damsels came riding on gentle coursers*, all with their trappers*. They were followed by a goddess on a cart who was accompanied by twelve damsels, all of whom were singing, as well as many minstrels.[35] They accommodated the goddess in the seat that stood at the foot of the wheel, with the other damsels [clustered] around her. On the towers of the gate stood many noblemen wearing coat armours* laden with *argentaría** in the livery that the lord infante had given them.

The infante and his knights then armed themselves in his fortress. (22) As various knights came up to the Arch of the Daunting Adventure, those who were standing

---

[27] LB, p. 60, has the lesson 'rueda de la ventura' instead of 'rueda de la aventura', in line with the name of the arch.

[28] Pérez de Guzmán mentions six knights. FPG, p. 250.

[29] [Jhoan Manrrique]. Juan Fernández Manrique (d. 1498), son of García (see below, n. 30), was count of Castañeda after the death of his father (1436) and chancellor of Castile (from 1437). Luis de Salazar y Castro, *Historia genealogica de la casa de Lara* (Madrid: Llanos y Guzman, 1696), pp. 506–24.

[30] [Garçia Fernández Manrrique]. García Fernández Manrique (d. 1436); from 1414, he was in the service of Enrique of Aragon as *mayordomo* (the equivalent of a French *maître d'hôtel*) and, thanks to the intervention of the latter, King Juan II gave him the lordship of Castañeda in Asturias with the title of count. In the 1420s, he chose the side of King Juan II against the Aragonese faction and even fought against his former master Enrique in 1429. DBE, lemma 'García Fernández Manrique'.

[31] The word *frey* used here is an indication that he was a member of a military order, probably that of Santiago. Gutierre died in 1450 at the siege of the castle of Torija. He was the son of García López de Cárdenas, *comendador mayor* of the Order of Santiago, and brother to Alonso, who later became Grand-master of the same Order. Not to be confused with his namesake, Gutierre de Cárdenas (1440–1503), who played a major political role in Castile in the last decades of the fifteenth century. DBE, lemma 'García López de Cárdenas'.

[32] This lesson has been taken from LB, p. 60. PCH, p. 21, has the lesson 'Lope de Foyos'. It is not clear who this person is.

[33] [Albaro de Sandobal]. It is not clear who this person is. Pérez de Guzmán (FPG, p. 250) notes that he is the nephew of the count of Castro (abbreviated from Castrojeriz, near Burgos), a title held from 1426 onwards by Diego Gómez de Sandoval y Rojas, a firm supporter of the Infante Enrique (which caused him to lose his titles and lordships in Castile after 1429); from 1411, he was also governor of Castile. DBE, lemma 'Diego Sandoval y Rojas'.

[34] [Diego de Texeda]. Diego de Tejeda was considered by Juan II to be a supporter of Enrique of Aragon and hence, from January 1430, was seen as a traitor. PCH, p. 49.

[35] LB, p. 60, adds that 'the cart was pulled by two horses and twenty foot soldiers dressed in white and red livery'.

on the towers blew their horns and a lady rang the fortress bell.[36] At this, a lady on a hackney* came out of the fortress accompanied by a herald and said: 'Knights, what fate has brought you to this dangerous passage which is called that of the Daunting Adventure? You would do better to turn round because you cannot pass through without jousting!' Their reply then came that they were prepared to do just this. The lord king of Castile[37] stepped forward with twenty-four knights, all dressed in gowns of dagged* green cloth whilst the lord king's gown was laden with gilded *argentaría*, trimmed with precious ermine filled with down, and [decorated with] diadems [in the shape] of butterflies.[38] The lord king broke two heavy lances and he jousted in such a knightly fashion that no one could equal him. After that, the king of Navarre[39] ran courses with [a company consisting of] twelve knights, all with crests of windmills. The lord king of Navarre broke one lance.

Gonzalo de Quadros[40] fought a bout with the lord infante as a defender and broke one heavy lance. As a consequence, the infante fell against the tilt with such force that they thought he had died. Then followed another combat between a squire of the lord infante, who was one of his fellow defenders, and Ruy Díaz de Mendoza,[41] *mayordomo* of the lord king of Castile. This squire received such a severe wound to his body that he died within two hours; his name was Álvaro de Sandoval.[42]

After night had fallen, the kings, the queen and the infantes all went to dinner with the infante at the house of Don Alfonso Enríquez,[43] admiral of Castile, where they all

---

[36] According to Pérez de Guzmán, the challengers rang the bell to indicate the number of courses that they wanted to run. FPG, p. 250.

[37] Juan II (1405–54), king of Castile and Leon (r. 1406–54), son of Enrique III and Catherine of Lancaster, was married to 1. María of Aragon (1403–45), sister of King Alfonso V, King Juan II the Great of Aragon and Enrique of Aragon, and 2. Isabel of Portugal (1428–96, not to be confused with her namesake, the wife of the Burgundian duke, Philip the Good). DBE, lemma 'Juan II de Castilla'.

[38] LB, p. 61, adds here that as 'the king entered the lists in this manner, the queen, the infantas and the other ladies [were] seated in the stands watching the joust'.

[39] Juan II the Great of Aragon (1398–1479), king of Navarre (r. 1425–79) as well as king of Aragon and Sicily (r. 1458–79), son of Fernando I and Leonor of Alburquerque, brother of Alfonso V and Enrique of Aragon, was married to 1. Blanca I of Navarre, queen of Navarre (r. 1425–41), and 2. Juana Enríquez.

[40] [Gonzalo de Cuadros]. Gonzalo de Quadros (d. 1461), son of Diego, was a knight and poet from the town of Seville, where he occupied different functions in the town administration. He was one of the Castilian noblemen who were partisans of the Infante Enrique until 1430, when he changed sides and supported Álvaro de Luna. In another contemporary chronicle he is described as one of the most outstanding jousters of the king's household. Antonio Chas Aguión, 'Gonzalo de Quadros. Hidalgo, justador y poeta de cancionero', *Revista de poética medieval*, 28 (2014), 35–55 (pp. 41, 49–52); Fallows, *Jousting*, p. 93.

[41] [Ruy Díaz de Mendoça]. Ruy Díaz de Mendoza (d. 1477). In 1426, he succeeded his father, Juan Hurtado de Mendoza, as *mayordomo* of King Juan II of Castile. In the 1430s and 1440s, he fought in several military campaigns for the king under the leadership of Álvaro de Luna. DBE, lemma 'Ruy Díaz de Mendoza de Arrellano'. In 1440, he would himself organise a *paso* in Valladolid: see Source 3.

[42] Sandoval is earlier referred to as a knight, which is also the lesson of LB, p. 61.

[43] [don Alfonso Enrriques]. Alonso or Alfonso Enríquez (1354–1429), illegitimate son of Fadrique Alfonso and hence a grandson of King Alfonso XI of Castile, was admiral of Castile from 1405 and was succeeded in this office after his death in 1429 by his son Fadrique. Esteban Ortega Gato, 'Los Enríquez, almirantes de Castilla', *Publicaciones de la Institución Tello Téllez de Meneses*, 70 (1999), 23–65.

spent the night.[44] The judges at this joust were Diego de Ribera, governor of Andalucía,[45] Rodrigo de Perea, governor of Cazorla,[46] Pedro Carrillo de Huete, the king's head falconer,[47] and Juan Carrillo de Toledo.[48]

---

[44] Pérez de Gúzman mentions that, on this occasion, Enrique donated many gifts not only to the knights and nobles from his own household but also to minstrels, trumpeters and foreign knights. FPG, p. 250. García de Santa María specifically says that the gifts for his men concerned forty or fifty 'crochas' all covered in *argentaría*: this is probably a mistranscription by the editor of the word *clochas* (French: *cloches*; English: cloaks), i.e. garments sometimes used for riding that could be ankle-length, were likely to be of a circular cut, and could require a great deal of fabric, thus providing ample scope for displaying a lot of silver jewellery, as seems to be the case here. AGSM, p. 16. See also Francisco Bautista, 'La segunda parte de la *Crónica de Juan II*: borradores y texto definitivo', *Cahiers d'études hispaniques médiévales*, 37.1 (2014), 105–38; Victor Gay, *Glossaire archéologique du Moyen Âge et de la Renaissance*, 2 vols (Paris: Librairie de la Société Bibliographique, 1887), vol. 1, pp. 396–7 (entry on *cloches*). Thanks are due to Margaret Scott for her help in identifying this garment.

[45] Diego Gómez de Ribera (d. 1434, at the siege of Álora), son of Per Afán de Ribera, succeeded his father as *adelantado* (governor) of Andalucía in 1416. Ribera was a brother-in-law by marriage of Álvaro de Luna, who acted as a protector of his son's interests after his death. DBE, lemma 'Diego (Gómez) de Ribera'.

[46] Rodrigo Pera (d. 1438, at the battle of Baza) was governor of Cazorla until his death. PCH, p. 200.

[47] See above, p. 59.

[48] [Jhoan Carrillo de Toledo]. LB, p. 62, refers to him as mayor of Toledo. Juan Carrillo de Toledo did indeed fulfil this role until 1438, when he was appointed by King Juan II as governor of Cazorla. He was a *protégé* of Álvaro de Luna, on whose side he fought in various battles for more than twenty years. DBE, lemma 'Juan Carillo de Toledo'.

Thanks are due to Catherine Blunk and Rosalind Brown-Grant for their insightful comments on an earlier version of this translation.

Mario Damen

Source 3

The *Paso de Valladolid* (*Paso* of Valladolid), 1440

This source consists of a translation of a narrative account of this event.

Author: Fernán Pérez de Guzmán

Language: Medieval Castilian

Edition used: Lorenzo Galindez de Carvajal, ed., *Crónica del señor rey Don Juan II compilado por Fernando Pérez de Guzmán* (Valencia: Monfort, 1779), pp. 411–12 (= FPG)

Select bibliography:

Barber, Richard, and Juliet Barker, *Tournaments: Jousts, Chivalry and Pageants in the Middle Ages* (New York: Weidenfeld & Nicolson, 1989), p. 101

Fernández de Córdova, Álvaro, 'L'impact de la Bourgogne sur la cour castillane des Trastamare', in *La cour de Bourgogne et l'Europe: le rayonnement et les limites d'un modèle culturel; actes du colloque international tenu à Paris les 9, 10 et 11 octobre 2007*, ed. by Werner Paravicini, Torsten Hiltmann and Frank Viltart (Ostfildern: Jan Thorbecke Verlag, 2013), pp. 593–630 (pp. 607–8)

Nadot, Sébastien, *Le Spectacle des joutes: Sport et courtoisie à la fin du Moyen Âge* (Rennes: Presses Universitaires de Rennes, 2012), pp. 131, 245, 275, 335

Riquer, Martín de, *Vida caballeresca en la España del siglo XV* (Madrid: Gráficas Marina, 1965), pp. 54–6

Torre y Franco-Romero, Lucas de, 'Mosén Diego de Valera. Su vida y sus obras', *Boletín de la Real Academia de Historia*, 64 (1914), 50–83 (pp. 71–6)

Introduction

This *paso de armas* took place in the third week of September 1440 in Valladolid. Ruy Díaz de Mendoza, *mayordomo* (equivalent to the French *maître d'hôtel*) of King Juan II of Castile organised the event, which was staged to mark the occasion of the marriage of Enrique, the eldest son and heir of the Castilian king, to Blanca II, the eldest surviving daughter of King Juan II the Great of Aragon, king of Navarre. The relatively short account of this *paso*, written by the chronicler Fernán Pérez de Guzmán (see below), does not reveal many details. For example, the exact date of the event can be deduced only from the fact that it probably took place between 15 September, the day of the wedding, and 21 September, the day that Pedro Manrique, the *adelantado* (governor) of the kingdom of León, died, which is specifically mentioned by the chronicler after the description of the *paso*.[1] Secondly, the

[1] FPG, p. 412; DBE, lemma 'Pedro Manrique'.

precise location is unclear. Valladolid was an important administrative and ceremonial centre for the kings of Castile, and the event was probably held either on the Plaza Mayor, the main town square where the *Paso de la Fuerte Ventura* had previously taken place in 1428,[2] or on the Plaza de San Pablo, where the royal palace, the venue of the wedding, was located.[3] Finally, no information is given that corresponds to the conventional elements of a *pas d'armes*, namely the chapters of arms, the material form of the *paso* (the passage, such as a bridge or a gate, as in other Castilian *pasos*), the fictional scenario or any specially built ephemeral architecture.[4]

Nevertheless, the chronicler does elaborate on the level of violence that occurred during the *paso* and which led to at least two deaths and two serious casualties among the combatants. This was sufficient reason for the king to end the event early, even though the *entrepreneur** Díaz de Mendoza had declared that it would last for forty days. The high number of victims could have been caused by the only rule mentioned in the account: that is, that competitors should run courses on horseback until they had broken four lances with sharpened tips. By contrast, in Burgundian *pas d'armes* of the 1440s, a set number of courses with lances was usually stipulated, such as twelve in the *Pas de l'Arbre Charlemagne* (Marsannay-la-Côte, 1443), or even twenty-five in the *Pas de la Fontaine des Pleurs* (1449–50), but not the number of lances that had to be broken.[5] Whilst this rule may have encouraged the competitors to take more risks than normal during the combats, another factor that may have contributed to the high number of casualties was the tense atmosphere at the Castilian court caused by the factional strife between supporters of the infantes of Aragon and those of King Juan II.[6]

Paradoxically, the *Paso de Valladolid* should be viewed against the backdrop of the reconciliation of King Juan II with the infantes of Aragon after the treaties of Toledo of September 1436 and that of Castronuño of November 1439. One of the consequences of these treaties was the union of the royal houses of Castile and Navarre through the marriage of Enrique and Blanca II, as mentioned above. This wedding took place in the presence of the kings and their respective wives, María of Aragon, sister of Juan II the Great, and Blanca I of Navarre, as well as many high-ranking nobles from Castile and Navarre.[7] Unlike the *Paso de la Fuerte Ventura*, in which both kings participated in Valladolid alongside the organiser, Enrique of Aragon, no members of the royal families of the Iberian kingdoms were involved in the actual *Paso de Valladolid*, other than in their

---

2 See Source 2.

3 On this same square, Jacques de Lalaing, a knight from Hainaut who was the future *entrepreneur* of the *Pas de la Fontaine des Pleurs* (Chalon-sur-Saône, 1449–50), would fight a bout in February 1448 against Diego de Gúzman, a Castilian nobleman who had been given permission by Juan II, king of Castile, to touch an *emprise* that Lalaing was wearing during his travels around Europe. On this episode recounted in Lalaing's biography, see CL, pp. 157–8; see also Source 7.

4 For a more detailed discussion of the characteristics of a *pas d'armes*, see the Introduction and Essay 1. For the material form that the 'passage' could take in other Castilian *pasos*, see Sources 2 (*Paso de la Fuerte Ventura*), 8 (*Paso de El Pardo*) and 10 (*Paso de Jaén*).

5 See Sources 4 and 7, respectively.

6 For further details on these rivalries at the Castilian court, see Source 2 and Essay 1.

7 DBE, lemmata 'Blanca II de Navarra' and 'Enrique IV'. The rapprochement of Juan II with the infantes of Aragon coincided with the (second) exile of Álvaro de Luna, the king of Castile's favourite, from the court in 1440. DBE, lemma 'Álvaro de Luna'. On this figure, see also Source 2, p. 59.

role as spectators. Nor is there any overlap between the participants at these two events, apart from one person: the *entrepreneur*, Ruy Díaz de Mendoza. Díaz de Mendoza was certainly one of the king's favourites, having fought several military campaigns for him in the 1430s, and being one of the three tutors of the crown prince Enrique from 1436.[8] The king thus entrusted his courtier with the organisation of this particular event, which may have been intended to serve as an example of chivalric behaviour for his son.

Whereas these two Castilian *pasos* held in Valladolid at different dates seem to be unrelated, there is, however, a link between the second one, under discussion here, and the first *pas d'armes* that would be staged three years later in July/August 1443 in the Burgundian lands, this being the *Pas de l'Arbre Charlemagne.* Immediately after describing the *Paso de Valladolid*, Pérez de Guzmán mentions the arrival at the court of King Juan II of Castile of the Burgundian herald, Châteaubelin, who had come to announce the chapters of arms pertaining to this chivalric event organised by Pierre de Bauffremont, lord of Charny.[9] These chapters of arms, which the herald was allowed to read out loud at court, were probably translated from French into Castilian. Although they have not survived, a copy of the Catalan version of them has been preserved, meaning that Châteaubelin or another herald also visited the Aragonese court around the same time.[10] As these chapters were issued only on 8 March 1442, Châteaubelin must have arrived in Valladolid after that date, which suggests that the chronicler inserted this information at this particular point in his account precisely in order to make the connection between the *Paso de Valladolid* and its Burgundian counterpart.[11]

As mentioned above, the narrative account of this *paso* comes from a chronicle on the reign of King Juan II of Castile written by Fernán Pérez de Guzmán (*c.*1378–1460). There is some debate about the authorship of this chronicle as Álvar García de Santa María, the royal chronicler appointed in 1406, started working on it but stopped in 1434.[12] It was then taken up by another royal chronicler, Pedro Carrillo de Huete.[13] In the 1450s, Pérez de Guzmán compiled, edited and completed a manuscript covering the entire reign of Juan II. This manuscript of Pérez de Guzmán, which is no longer extant, was for years kept in the private chambers of Isabella I of Castile (1451–1504), the eldest

[8] DBE, lemma 'Ruy Díaz de Mendoza y Arrellano'.

[9] See Source 4; and OdLM, vol. 1, pp. 283–7, 290–324, 324–35. For a short poem on this event by an unknown author, see CPM.

[10] For the Catalan version, see Martín de Riquer, *Lletres de batalla: cartells de deseiximents i capítols de passos d'armes*, Els nostres clàssics, 3 vols (Barcelona: Barcino, 1963–68), vol. 3, pp. 5–18, and *idem*, *Vida caballeresca en la España del siglo XV* (Madrid: Gráficas Marina, 1965), p. 54. No Catalan or Aragonese knights actually competed in the *Pas de l'Arbre Charlemagne*, however.

[11] See Lucas de Torre y Franco-Romero, 'Mosén Diego de Valera. Su vida y sus obras', *Boletín de la Real Academia de Historia*, 64 (1914), 50–83 (p. 74); and Álvaro Fernández de Córdova Miralles, 'L'impact de la Bourgogne et la cour castillane des Trastamare', in *La cour de Bourgogne et l'Europe. Le rayonnement et les limites d'un modèle culturel; actes du colloque international tenu à Paris les 9, 10 et 11 octobre 2007*, ed. by Werner Paravicini, Torsten Hiltmann and Franck Viltart (Ostfildern: Jan Thorbecke Verlag, 2013), pp. 593–630 (p. 609), who both propose 1442 as the date of the herald's arrival at the Castilian court. See also Sébastien Nadot, *Le Spectacle des joutes: Sport et courtoisie à la fin du Moyen Âge* (Rennes: Presses Universitaires de Rennes, 2012), p. 157.

[12] DBE, lemma 'Álvar García de Santa María'. See also Source 2.

[13] DBE, lemma 'Álvaro de Luna'.

daughter of Juan II and Isabel of Portugal. It formed the basis of the first printed edition of 1517, which was dedicated to the new king of Castile, Charles V (1500–58).[14]

Guzmán came from a noble family of Toledo, being the son of Pedro Suárez de Guzmán and Elvira de Ayala. At a young age he had already inherited his father's lordship of Batres, 45 km to the north of Toledo, when his father died at the siege of Lisbon in 1384. He was introduced at the Castilian court in the 1390s by his uncle, the chancellor Pero López de Ayala, whom he accompanied on several diplomatic missions. It was in the last years of the fourteenth century that he wrote his first poems as compiled in the *Cancionero de Baena*. Although in the early 1420s he defended the cause of the infantes of Aragon, he passed over to the side of King Juan II in 1425 and even participated in a military expedition against Aragon in 1429. In the 1430s, he became more alienated from the court and retired to his residence in Batres. Whereas in the 1430s and 1440s he mainly wrote poetry, in the 1450s he dedicated himself to the writing of biographies, the two most important ones being those of King Juan II and Álvaro de Luna, composed around 1455 when both of these men had already died.[15]

In the translation that follows, page numbers in parentheses have been inserted for ease of reference to Galindez de Carvajal's edition.

TRANSLATION

(411) **Chapter 16**
On the *paso* held by Ruy Díaz de Mendoza[16] in Valladolid at the wedding[17] of the prince Don Enrique[18] and Doña Blanca,[19] and on those who were killed and injured during this *paso*

During the wedding of the prince Don Enrique and the princess Doña Blanca, Ruy Díaz de Mendoza accomplished a singular feat of arms in the following manner: he held a *paso* in this town of Valladolid[20] for forty days[21] with nineteen knights and nobles of his

[14] FPG, p. 20. For this edition, see Lorenzo Galindez de Carvajal, ed., *Crónica del serenísimo rey don Juan el segundo* (Logroño: Arnaldo Guillén de Brocar, 1517).

[15] DBE, lemma 'Fernán Pérez de Guzmán'.

[16] Ruy Díaz de Mendoza (d. 1477), succeeded his father, Juan Hurtado de Mendoza, in 1426 as *mayordomo* of King Juan II of Castile. In 1428, he participated in the *Paso de la Fuerte Ventura* (see Source 2). He received the title of count of Castrojeriz in 1476. DBE, lemma 'Ruy Díaz de Mendoza y Arrellano'.

[17] This wedding took place on 15 September 1440 in the palace of San Pablo in Valladolid, as is mentioned in the preceding chapter of the chronicle. FPG, p. 410.

[18] Enrique IV of Castile (1425–74) was, at that time, the only son of King Juan II and María of Aragon.

[19] Blanca II of Navarre (1424–64) was the daughter of Juan II of Aragon and Blanca I of Navarre, both of whom were present at her marriage to Enrique IV of Castile (see above, n. 18). Their marriage was eventually annulled in 1453 on the grounds that it had not been 'consummated'. José-Luis Martín, *Enrique IV de Castilla: Rey de Navarra, Príncipe de Cataluña* (Hondarribia: Nerea, 2003), pp. 33–5.

[20] On its location, see above, p. 65.

[21] It is not clear how many days the *paso* actually lasted, as the event was stopped by the king. The duration of forty days may have biblical connotations and other *pas d'armes*, such as the *Pas de l'Arbre Charlemagne*, are also said to have been this length (see Source 4, p. 72).

household [being pitted] against all knights and noblemen, both from Castile and from abroad, who wanted to accept this challenge. Against each one who came, the said Ruy Díaz, or anyone from his company, had to run as many courses in the lists in jousting harness* as were necessary until he had broken four lances with sharpened tips. Many knights and noblemen presented themselves at these combats but it was not possible for all of them to take part as the king called a halt to them because they were so dangerous that a knight from Toro,[22] called Pedro Portocarrero,[23] died after being wounded in the face by a nobleman named Lope de Lazcano,[24] one of the defenders of the *paso*. Another nobleman, called Juan de Salazar,[25] a household officer of Gómez Carrillo de Acuña,[26] was so badly hurt in the right arm by Rodrigo de Ulloa,[27] that he died three days after their fight. Likewise Diego de Sandoval,[28] a nephew of the count of Castro,[29] was very dangerously injured when he was struck on the bevor* by Juan de Zornoza,[30] thus causing him to fall slowly from the saddle, although it was Our Lord's wish that he miraculously survive this encounter. Don Enrique,[31] brother of the admiral,[32] was hurt in the left arm and broke a shinbone; yet, despite this, he bravely carried on fighting to the end of his bout without attending to his wounds. This was the reason why so many who had presented themselves as challengers could not complete their feats of arms.

---

[22] This town is situated some 65 km to the west of Valladolid.

[23] It is not clear who this is. He is not to be confused with his namesake, Pedro Portocarrero (d. 1429), lord of Moguer, who was a brother-in-law of Álvaro de Luna. FPG, p. 176; LP, p. 104.

[24] Juan López de Lazcano belonged to a noble dynasty from Gipuzkoa in the Basque Country.

[25] No information is available about him.

[26] Gómez Carrillo de Acuña (d. 1446), who came from an illegitimate line of the royal house of Castile, was married to María of Castile; he was an ally of Álvaro de Luna and held high-ranking offices in the households of both Juan II and Enrique IV when he was crown prince. DBE, lemma 'Gómez Carrillo de Acuña'.

[27] [Rodrigo de Olloa]. It is not clear who his parents were, but in the description of the *Paso Honroso* (1434) it is mentioned that he was a nephew of Pero Yañez (aka Periañez) de Ulloa, first notary of King Juan II, and that he belonged to the household of Ruy Díaz de Mendoza. Furthermore, before his participation in the *Paso Honroso* he asked to be dubbed a knight by its *entrepreneur*, Suero de Quiñones. After this was done, he ran seven courses against Lope de Aller, one of Quiñones' fellow defenders, in which they broke three lances. LPH, pp. 23–4. He should not be confused with his namesake Rodrigo de Ulloa (d. 1496), son of Pero, who was a diplomat and financial administrator in the service of Isabella I of Castile. DBE, lemma 'Rodrigo de Ulloa'.

[28] No information is available about him, but he may have been related to Álvaro de Sandoval, who died at the *Paso de la Fuerte Ventura* (see Source 2, p. 62). Pérez de Guzmán (FPG, p. 250) also remarks that Álvaro was the nephew of the count of Castro.

[29] This title was held from 1426 by Diego Gómez de Sandoval y Rojas, a fervent supporter of the Infante Enrique (which caused him to lose both his titles and lordships in Castile after 1429); he was also governor of Castile from 1411. DBE, lemma 'Diego Sandoval y Rojas'.

[30] No information is available about him, but his surname refers to a family from Biscay in the Basque Country.

[31] Enrique Enríquez (d. 1480), son of Alfonso, was a great-grandson of King Alfonso XI of Castile. DBE, lemma 'Enrique de Mendoza'.

[32] Fadrique Enríquez (1390–1473), son of Alfonso, was a great-grandson of King Alfonso XI of Castile; he was admiral of Castile from 1429, succeeding his father in this office. Together with Beatriz of Portugal, he was a godparent at the wedding of Enrique and Blanca II of Navarre. Esteban Ortega Gato, 'Los Enríquez, almirantes de Castilla', *Publicaciones de la Institución Tello Téllez de Meneses*, 70 (1999), 23–65; FPG, p. 410.

Chapter 18
On how a herald of Duke Philippe of Burgundy[33] came to the king's court and, with his permission, published the chapters of certain [feats of] arms that my lord Pierre de Bauffremont, lord of Charny,[34] wanted to stage near the town of Dijon in Burgundy between two castles, one called Perrigny[35] and the other Marsannay[36]

At that time, a herald of Duke Philippe of Burgundy, named Châteaubelin,[37] came to the court of King Don Juan. In the great hall,[38] in the presence of the kings of Castile and Navarre, the prince Don Enrique and the Infante Don Enrique,[39] and all the other counts and knights of the king's household, he asked for permission from the king on behalf of my lord Pierre de Bauffremont, lord of Charny, to publish the chapters of certain [feats of] arms which the said lord of Charny planned to stage according to certain stipulations in the month of August of the coming year [14]41,[40] near a town called Dijon in Burgundy,[41] between two castles, one called Perrigny and the other Marsannay. The king granted [him permission to] read the said chapters out loud. After they had been read, there were many [men present] who declared their willingness to go and perform [at] the said [feat of] arms, but this is something that this historical account will only speak

---

33 [Felipo de Borgoña]. That is, Philip the Good, duke of Burgundy.

34 [Pierres de Brefemonte, Señor de Charni]. Pierre de Bauffremont (*c*.1397–1472), lord of Charny, was made a member of the Order of the Golden Fleece when it was founded (1430); he was a chamberlain (1426/7, 1433–58) then councillor-chamberlain (1454) of Philip the Good and later a *chevalier d'honneur* of Margaret of York (1468). In August 1435, he had fought a feat of arms against the Castilian nobleman Juan de Merlo at the conclusion of the Congress of Arras, and was the *entrepreneur* of the *Pas de l'Arbre Charlemagne* (1443). COTO, pp. 45–7; PCB no. 321; Riquer, *Vida*, pp. 36–9. See also Source 4.

35 [Parñi]. Perrigny-lès-Dijon, near Dijon. This castle was owned by Mathieu Regnault, receiver-general of the duchy of Burgundy, and it was the place where Bauffremont and his companions were lodged during this *pas*. OdLM, vol. 1, p. 294; PCB no. 4861.

36 [Marcenay]. Marsannay-la-Côte, near Dijon. This castle was owned by the Benedictine abbey situated there. OdLM, vol. 1, p. 294.

37 [Xateobelin]. Châteaubelin was a herald in the service of Philip the Good from 1442. In that year, he is mentioned as a member of Philip's retinue in Dijon on 30 April. PCB no. 1011. This means that he must have travelled to Valladolid probably after that date, as the chapters of arms of the *Arbre Charlemagne* were only published on 8 March 1442. See Source 4, p. 79. In 1449, this herald would also publicise the chapters of arms of Jean de Luxembourg's *Pas de la Belle Pèlerine* in Iberia. Riquer, *Vida*, p. 54.

38 On the palace of San Pablo, see above, p. 65.

39 Enrique of Aragon (1400–45), Infante of Aragon, *marqués* of Villena and count of Alburquerque, was the brother of King Alfonso V of Aragon and brother-in-law of King Juan II. He was the *entrepreneur* of the *Paso de la Fuerte Ventura* (see Source 2). DBE, lemma 'Enrique de Aragon'. He is not specifically mentioned in the context of the *Paso de Valladolid*. However, when all the wedding festivities were over, around mid-October 1440, he did organise his own feat of arms in Valladolid, a 'justa muy grande' (very grand joust) in royal harness*, in which six defenders, all members of his household, were pitted against twenty-five noble challengers. The event took place without any casualties and was witnessed by the royals of Castile and Navarre. FPG, p. 413.

40 This date is problematic because the chapters of arms of the *Pas de l'Arbre Charlemagne* were only published on 8 March 1442. See also above, n. 37.

41 That is, the duchy of Burgundy.

about later.[42] At that time, the king ordered my lord Diego de Valera,[43] his *doncel*,[44] to go on his behalf and visit the queen of Dacia,[45] his aunt and sister of the queen Doña Catalina,[46] the king of England[47] and the duke of Burgundy, and commanded that Asturias, his herald and marshal of arms,[48] go with him. My lord Diego humbly asked the king to give him permission to participate in the *pas* held by the lord of Charny and also to wear an *emprise** [denoting] certain [feats of] arms that he planned to carry out on his journey on his own initiative. The king graciously gave him leave to do so and provided him with a very large amount of supplies (412) for the duration of a year which is how long the said journey might take, as well as gifts of tailor-made clothes made of blue velour velvet lined with marten, and a very good horse. In this manner my lord Diego departed, made his way [to the *pas*] and there very honourably performed both the [feats of] arms of the *pas*[49] and those that he had requested; those [pertaining to] the *pas* were against Thibaut de Rougemont, lord of Ruffey and Molinot,[50] and those of his *emprise* were against Jacques de Challant, lord of Aymavilles.[51] When these [feats of] arms were finished, the duke [of Burgundy] sent him[52] twelve cups and two platters of fifty marks of silver[53] and he accomplished all

---

[42] In fact, the chronicle later only mentions the participation of Diego de Valera in the *Arbre Charlemagne* and not that of other Castilian noblemen who also took part in it, such as Pedro Vásquez de Saavedra. On this figure, see Essay 1; and Riquer, *Vida*, pp. 54–7.

[43] Diego de Valera (1412–*c.*1488), born in Cuenca, came into the service of King Juan II (1427) who appointed him as *doncel* (see below, n. 44) of the crown prince Enrique two years later. He was knighted at the siege of Huelma (1435). In 1437–38, he had already undertaken a diplomatic mission for the king to France and Bohemia. Valera was a prolific chronicler and author of various treatises, including one on the nature of 'true' nobility. DBE, lemma 'Diego de Valera'.

[44] This office at the Castilian court, at the rank of page, was initially held by young members of noble families who were not yet knighted. *Damoiseau* is the French equivalent of this Castilian title.

[45] Dacia refers here to Denmark, which, at that time, was part of the Kalmar union; up to 1439, it was ruled by Eric of Pomerania. He was married to Philippa of England, who was remotely related to King Juan II through his mother, Catalina. However, she had already died in 1430 and was buried in Linköping in Sweden. Torre y Franco-Romero, 'Mosén Diego', pp. 72–3.

[46] Catalina of Lancaster (1373–1418), the daughter of John of Gaunt and Constanza of Castile, was married to Enrique III of Castile; hence she was the mother of King Juan II.

[47] Henry VI (1421–71), king of England.

[48] No further information is available about this herald. In 1445, he received a gift of 12lb. from Philip the Good when he was in Ghent, probably at the time of the Chapter of the Golden Fleece that was celebrated in December in the town. ADN B 1988, fol. 196r.

[49] Valera arrived in Marsannay-la-Côte around 11 July 1443. OdLM, pp. 297, 305.

[50] [Tibaut de Rogemont, Señor de Rufi y de Molinot]. Thibaut de Rougemont (d. after 1473), squire, was lord of Rougemont and of Ruffey-sur-l'Ognon, Tilchâtel and Augey. HMF, vol. 7, p. 37, para. B; OdLM, vol. 1, p. 306. Although the Castilian chronicler also mentions Molinot here, this lordship was in fact owned by Pierre de Bauffremont, not Rougemont.

[51] [Jaques de Xalau, Señor de Amavila]. Jacques de Challant (d. 1459), lord of Aymavilles, Châtillon, Ussel, Verrès, Issogne and Greines, was a native of Savoy but held lands in the county of Burgundy (Franche-Comté); he was a member of the Savoyard Order of the Collar (1440) and a chamberlain of Duke Louis I of Savoy. He was also a challenger at the *Arbre Charlemagne*. OdLM, vol. 1, p. 320; François Capre, *Catalogue des chevaliers de l'Ordre du Collier de Savoye* (Turin: Barthélémy Zavatte, 1654), fols 70v–71r.

[52] That is, Diego de Valera.

[53] The silver mark in late medieval Castile consisted of eight ounces, weighing approximately 230 grams.

that the king had ordered him to do. Although the queen of Dacia, the king's aunt, had died on his arrival, he managed to go to a town called Lubic[54] where she was buried, [this being] a very notable place; from there my lord Diego returned to Castile.

[54] It is not clear which town this refers to: it may be Linköping in Sweden (see above, n. 45) but is more likely to be Lübeck, which was an important Hanseatic town whose name is closer phonetically to Lubic.

Thanks are due to Catherine Blunk and Rosalind Brown-Grant for their comments on an earlier version of this translation.

Rosalind Brown-Grant

Source 4

The *Pas de l'Arbre Charlemagne* (*Pas* of the Tree of Charlemagne), Marsannay-la-Côte, 1443

This source consists of a translation of the letter of challenge and chapters of arms for this event.

Author: Enguerrand de Monstrelet

Language: Middle French

Edition used: Louis Douët-d'Arcq, ed., *La chronique d'Enguerran de Monstrelet, en deux livres, avec pièces justificatives 1400–1444*, Société de l'Histoire de France, 6 vols (Paris: Renouard, 1857), vol. 6, pp. 68–73 (= EdM). For a narrative account of the actual event itself, see OdLM, vol. 1, pp. 283–7, 290–324, 324–35. For a short poem by an unknown author, see CPM.

Select bibliography:

Blunk, Catherine, 'Faux pas in the Chronicles. What is a *Pas d'armes*?', in *The Medieval Chronicle 11*, ed. by Erik Kooper and Sjoerd Levelt (Turnhout: Brepols, 2018), pp. 87–107

Brown-Grant, Rosalind, 'Narrative Style in Burgundian Chronicles of the Later Middle Ages', *Viator*, 42.2 (2011), 233–82

Vaughan, Richard, *Philip the Good: The Apogee of Burgundy* (London/New York: Longman, 1970)

Whitbread, Rachael E., 'Tournaments, Jousts and Duels: Formal Combats in England and France, circa 1380–1440' (unpublished PhD dissertation, University of York, 2013)

Introduction

This *pas d'armes*, the first to take place in the Burgundian composite state, was held at Marsannay-la-Côte, near Dijon; it lasted for forty days from 1 July to 8 August 1443 (excluding Sundays and feast days). The chapters of arms as preserved in the chronicle of Enguerrand de Monstrelet (*c.*1390–1453), which are translated here below, state that the event was to be held at the end of a section of paved road that ran from Dijon to Auxonne near to a large tree known as the Hermits' Tree. In fact, as is explained in the narrative account of the event contained in the memoirs of Olivier de La Marche (*c.*1425–1502), the *pas* was moved to the so-called Tree of Charlemagne (an elm) that grew a mile outside Dijon on the road to Nuits-St-Georges.[1]

[1] See Richard Vaughan, *Philip the Good: The Apogee of Burgundy* (London/New York: Longman, 1970), p. 147; and OdLM, vol. 1, p. 290. For a discussion and useful map of the setting as constructed from

The *entrepreneur* of the *Pas de l'Arbre Charlemagne*, Pierre de Bauffremont, lord and count of Charny, was an eminent figure in the household of the Burgundian duke Philip the Good. He was also a jouster of some renown who had already distinguished himself in a single combat on horseback and on foot with a Castilian knight, Juan de Merlo; this fight was held over two days at the Congress of Arras in 1435 against the backdrop of complex peace negotiations between Burgundy, England and France as part of the Hundred Years War.[2] At the *pas*, Bauffremont led a team of twelve other Burgundian knights, this choice of number being doubtless intended to evoke the number of knights traditionally associated with King Arthur's Round Table, which, itself, is an allusion to the twelve apostles.[3]

Challengers at this *pas* had the choice of striking either a black shield painted with golden tears, which entitled them to joust against one of the defenders for up to twelve courses with the lance, or a violet shield painted with black tears, which allowed them to undertake a foot combat with one of the defenders with either pollaxes or swords for up to fifteen strokes. Challenges were accepted only from knights and squires who were from lands outside those held by either the king of France or the duke of Burgundy. This stipulation may have been because the *entrepreneur* not only wished to attract a more international set of competitors but was under explicit instruction from his lord, Philip the Good, not to pit men against each other who were affiliated to either the French king or the duke himself, the better to avoid inflaming Franco-Burgundian tensions at this time.[4]

This exclusionary strategy seems to have paid off, as the event attracted numerous challengers from foreign parts, including two illustrious knights from Castile. The first of these was Pedro Vásquez de Saavedra, who had already fought at a tournament in Cologne that was witnessed by various Burgundian courtiers and in a single combat against Sir Richard de Wydville in Westminster on 26 November 1440.[5] The second was Diego de Valera, who was also a chronicler and author of various treatises, including one on the nature of 'true' nobility.[6] Each of these Castilians made a favourable impression on the high-ranking Burgundian spectators, including the duke himself, who judged several of the combats in this event: whilst Saavedra was made a chamberlain shortly afterwards in the ducal household at the request of Bauffremont, the *entrepreneur*, Valera was given permission by Philip the Good to hold a separate combat based on his personal *emprise* that

La Marche's account, see Sébastien Nadot, *Le Spectacle des joutes: Sport et courtoisie à la fin du Moyen Âge* (Rennes: Presses Universitaires de Rennes, 2012), pp. 191–3.

2 The combats are recounted in EdM, vol. 5, pp. 138–43. See also Vaughan, *Philip the Good*, pp. 98–107, for the Congress of Arras, and p. 146, for the Bauffremont/Merlo combats; Rachael E. Whitbread, 'Tournaments, Jousts and Duels: Formal Combats in England and France, circa 1380–1440' (unpublished PhD dissertation, University of York, 2013), pp. 96–9, for the combats; and Essay 1, p. 333.

3 See Laura Hibbard Loomis, 'Arthur's Round Table', *Proceedings of the Modern Language Association*, 41.4 (1926), 771–84.

4 On Franco-Burgundian relations in the decade or so following the Congress of Arras, see Vaughan, *Philip the Good*, pp. 98–126.

5 See William E. Baumgaertner, *Squires, Knights, Barons, Kings: War and Politics in Fifteenth Century England* (Bloomington, IN: Trafford Publishing, 2010), no page nos.

6 See Florence Serrano, 'La ficcionalización de Diego de Valera en la literatura borgoñona', in *Mosén Diego de Valera: Entre las armas y las letras*, ed. by Cristina Moya García (Woodbridge: Tamesis, 2014), pp. 53–62.

Jacques de Challant, one of the defenders of the *pas*, was allowed to touch in acceptance of the Castilian's challenge.[7]

Also present was a large contingent of less well-known knights and squires from the ducal court of Louis I of Savoy, a duchy with which Philip the Good had sought to foster good relations through truces from 1423 onwards.[8] Whilst most of these Savoyard contestants acquitted themselves very well, one in particular, a certain Martin Ballart from Piedmont, rather disgraced themself by boasting of his accomplishments beforehand and then failing to make good on these claims, according to La Marche's account of this event.[9] In addition, there was an Italian from the court of Milan (Jacopo dei Vischi, count of San Martino Canavese), a squire from English-held Gascony (Bernard de Vostin) and at least two squires from the Dauphiné (Henri de Gouvignon and Louis de La Basine, with a third, Jacques de Montagu, also possibly hailing from there or from Savoy).

The setting of the event employed a certain degree of symbolism (tears, a fountain, a tree and so on), as is evident from the chapters of arms, but La Marche adds that the *entrepreneur* built up the fountain that was already there at the foot of the Tree of Charlemagne and added a column with statues of God, the Virgin Mary and St Anne on top and the thirteen coats of arms of the defenders inscribed along its length; Bauffremont also had a large stone cross with a statue of himself kneeling and fully armed next to it erected a short distance away on the road back towards Dijon.[10] This *pas* therefore lacked an obvious fictional scenario featuring an earthly female chivalric muse, perhaps because it was the first such event to be held in the Burgundian lands. Later *pas d'armes* organised by knights attached to this ducal court certainly made up for it by devising their own very elaborate scenarios, such as Philippe de Lalaing's *Pas du Perron Fée* (Bruges, 1463).[11]

Whilst the actual combats at the *Pas de l'Arbre Charlemagne* were written up in great detail and with evident enthusiasm by La Marche, who explains that this was the first tournament he ever witnessed (he would not yet have been twenty years old at the time),[12] the chapters of arms are preserved only in the chronicle of Enguerrand de Monstrelet. That Monstrelet should simply reproduce the chapters of arms is in line with his usual practice, as his narrative style is not only much less voluble than that of La Marche, as a general rule, but he tends not to give his own account of an event if he did not witness it at firsthand, preferring instead to reproduce a factual document that presents the bare bones of it, such as the text of a peace treaty or a marriage contract, for example.[13]

Unlike some later *pas d'armes* narratives, such as that of the *Pas des armes de Sandricourt* (1493), which attempt, often somewhat awkwardly, to transpose into the past tense those

---

[7] *Ibid.* See also CPM, which shows how this short poem focuses as much on the fight between Challant and Valera as it does on the *pas* itself.

[8] On Franco-Savoyard relations, see Vaughan, *Philip the Good*, pp. 7–8.

[9] On this incident, see Essay 6, pp. 486–7.

[10] OdLM, vol. 1, pp. 292–3.

[11] See Source 11a.

[12] See Alistair Millar, 'Olivier de La Marche and the Court of Burgundy, *c.*1425–1502' (unpublished PhD dissertation, University of Edinburgh, 1996) <https://era.ed.ac.uk/handle/1842/1540> [accessed 18 June 2024]; and Catherine Emerson, *Olivier de La Marche and the Rhetoric of Fifteenth-Century Historiography* (Woodbridge: Boydell Press, 2004).

[13] See Rosalind Brown-Grant, 'Narrative Style in Burgundian Chronicles of the Later Middle Ages', *Viator*, 42.2 (2011), 233–82.

verbs in the future tense contained in the chapters of arms, which, after all, were meant to serve as advance publicity for an event that was yet to happen,[14] Monstrelet's chronicle reproduces the information that they contain practically verbatim. For this reason, the translation that follows also respects Monstrelet's factual style in another related way: that is, by preserving more of the legalistic phrases *ledit* and *le dessusdit* (the said, the afore-mentioned)[15] than in the narrative accounts of the combats in other *pas d'armes* sources translated in the present volume, where they have been minimised to avoid taxing the patience of the modern reader. In this translation, page numbers in parentheses have been provided for ease of reference to volume 6 of Douët-d'Arcq's edition of Monstrelet's chronicle.

Translation

(68) Chapter CCLXXII. How certain knights and gentlemen of the court of the duke of Burgundy undertook a feat of arms in the manner described hereafter

Item, at that same time, the duke of Burgundy being present in his Burgundian lands, a number of gentlemen of his household and his realm — for his pleasure and with his permission — had it published and announced in various marches and lands of Burgundy that if there were any noblemen who wished to do combat and obtain honour, they would be received by them in order to perform certain feats of arms that they had undertaken to do. The names of these gentlemen will be given hereafter, as will the substance of the chapters regarding this matter that were sent out to the above-mentioned lands by Messire Pierre de Bauffremont, lord of Charny,[16] who was the chief instigator of this undertaking.

Chapter CCLXXIII. Copy of the aforesaid announcement and the names of those who were due to perform this feat of arms

'In honour of Our Lord and his most glorious mother, my lady St Anne and my lord St George,[17] I, Pierre de Bauffremont, lord of Charny, Molinot and Montfort, knight, councillor and chamberlain to the most high, most powerful and most excellent prince, my most redoubtable and sovereign lord, (69) my lord the duke of Burgundy, let it be known to all princes, barons, knights and squires without reproach — except for those of the kingdom of France and of lands that are allied or subject to my abovesaid

---

[14] See Source 13.

[15] See Michelle Szkilnik, *Jean de Saintré: une carrière chevaleresque au XVe siècle* (Geneva: Droz, 2003), p. 74.

[16] [Pierre de Buisemont/Baufremont, seigneur de Chargni, de Monlyet et de Montfort]. Pierre de Bauffremont (*c.*1397–1472), lord of Charny, was made a member of the Order of the Golden Fleece when it was founded (1430); he was a chamberlain (1426/7, 1433–58) then councillor-chamberlain (1454) of Philip the Good and later a *chevalier d'honneur* of Margaret of York (1468). COTO, pp. 45–7; PCB no. 321; OdLM, vol. 1, pp. 291–5.

[17] Later Burgundian *pas d'armes* often have this dedication to God, the Virgin, her mother St Anne and St George; the last of these was the patron saint of chivalry. See Jacques de Lalaing's *Pas de la Fontaine des Pleurs* (1449–50) in LF, p. 312; CL, p. 211, which also adds St James, the *entrepreneur*'s own patron saint (James = Jacques).

sovereign lord — that in order to augment and enhance the most noble profession and pursuit of arms, my wish and intention are that, with twelve knights and squires who are of gentle* birth on all four sides,[18] whose names follow on hereafter — that is to say, Thibaut, lord of Rougemont and Mussy,[19] Messire Guillaume de Bauffremont, lord of Scey-sur-Saône and Sombernon,[20] Guillaume de Vienne, lord of Montbis and Gilley,[21] Jean, lord of Valangin,[22] Jean, lord of Rupt and Autricourt,[23] Guillaume de Champdivers, lord of Chevigny,[24] Jean de Cicon, lord of Rantechaux,[25] Antoine de Vaudrey, lord of L'Aigle,[26] Guillaume de Vaudrey, lord of Courlaoux,[27] Jacques de Challant, lord

[18] This means that the competitors' grandparents on both the paternal and maternal sides had to be of noble birth.

[19] [Thiébault, seigneur de Rougemont et de Mussy]. Thibaut de Rougemont (d. after 1473), squire, was lord of Rougemont and of Ruffey-sur-l'Ognon, Tilchâtel and Augey; his sister, Alix de Rougemont, was married to Jean de Vergy, lord of Champuant. HMF, vol. 7, p. 37, para. B; OdLM, vol. 1, p. 306. The reference to the lordship of Mussy here is incorrect and may be an authorial, scribal or editorial misreading of Ruffey.

[20] [Guillaume de Brefremont, seigneur de Sees et de Souvegnon]. Guillaume de Bauffremont (d. 1474), lord of Scey-sur-Saône and Sombernon, as well as Remilly, Trembloy, Ruffey, Clervaux, Malain and Grosbois, was a chamberlain of Philip the Good (1426/7–58). HMF, vol. 1, p. 559, para. E; PCB no. 296; OdLM, vol. 1, p. 317.

[21] [Guillaume de Viane, seigneur de Monbis et Gilly]. Guillaume de Vienne (before 1438?–71), squire, was lord of Montbis, Arc-en-Barrois, Chaigny, Bonencontre, Gilley (now Gilly-lès-Cîteaux; dép. Côte-d'Or, eastern France), Flaigy, Marnay and Persan. GDH, vol. 6, pp. 91–2; HMF, vol. 7, p. 809, para. D; OdLM, vol. 1, p. 311.

[22] [Jehan, seigneur de Walengen]. Jean III de Neuchâtel-Valangin (*c.*1410–97), was lord of Aarberg and Valangin; his link with the Neuchâtel family is through his wife, Mahaut de Neuchâtel. HMF, vol. 8, p. 349, para. B; Georges-Auguste Matile, *Histoire de la seigneurie de Valangin jusqu'à sa réunion à la Directe en 1592* (Neuchâtel: Imprimerie de James Attinger, 1852), pp. 126–200; OdLM, vol. 1, p. 318.

[23] [Jehan, seigneur de Rap et de Ciricourt]. This may be Jean de Goux, lord of Rupt and Autricourt, who was a chamberlain of Charles the Bold (1474). PCB no. 2875.

[24] [Guillaume de Champdivers, seigneur de Cheingni]. This is probably the son of Guillaume de Champdivers (d. *c.*1439), who was bailiff of Aval (1414–19) in Philip the Good's great council. Alphonse Rousset, *Dictionnaire géographique, historique et statistique des communes de la Franche-Comté et des hameaux qui en dépendent, classés par département: Tome premier, département du Jura* (Besançon: Bintot Imprimeur-Libraire, 1853), p. 438. The Guillaume who competed at the *Arbre Charlemagne* fought for Philip in the Ghent war and was knighted before the battle of Gavere (1453). La Marche refers to this person as the 'lord of Champdivers' in his accounts of both this event (OdLM, vol. 1, pp. 313–14) and the *Pas de la Fontaine des Pleurs* (Chalon-sur-Saône, 1449–50), where Guillaume accompanied a challenger, Jean de Villeneuve, into the lists for his fight with Jacques de Lalaing (OdLM, vol. 2, p. 193). The lords of Champdivers were also lords of Chevigny (dép. Jura, rég. Bourgogne-Franche-Comté) in the fifteenth century, hence this title given here in Monstrelet's text. Henri Passier, 'Dictionnaire de la noblesse de Franche-Comté de Bourgogne', *Revue historique nobiliaire et biographique*, nouvelle série, 6 (1870–71), 75–89 (p. 86).

[25] [Jehan de Chiron, seigneur de Ranchevières]. Jean de Cicon (d. 1454/5?), lord of Rantechaux (dép. Doubs, rég. Bourgogne-Franche-Comté), was a member of this very old and venerable family from the county of Burgundy. DN, vol. 5, p. 735; OdLM, vol. 1, p. 314.

[26] [Anthoine de Vaudray, seigneur de Laigle]. Antoine de Vaudrey, lord of L'Aigle, was a cupbearer (1431/2–49) and then a chamberlain (1449–58) of Philip the Good. PCB no. 532; OdLM, vol. 1, p. 310.

[27] [Guillaume de Vauldray, seigneur de Collaon]. Guillaume de Vaudrey, lord of Courlaoux, was a pantler* (1438–45) and then a chamberlain (1449) of Philip the Good. PCB no. 607; OdLM, vol. 1, p. 307.

of Aymavilles,[28] Messire Aimé, lord of Espiry,[29] and Jean de Chaumergy[30] — to guard and defend a *pas* situated on the main route from Dijon to Auxonne, at the end of the paved road coming from the said town of Auxonne and [near] a large tree known as the Hermits' Tree. All this will be in the form and manner as follows:

First: there are two shields, one of which is black, strewn with golden tears, and the other is violet, strewn with black tears.[31] These shields will be hung up on the Hermits' Tree and their stipulation will be that all those who have the black shield with golden tears touched by a King of Arms, herald or pursuivant, will be obliged to do combat on horseback with me or one of my aforesaid knights or squires, up to a total of twelve courses of the lance with sharpened lance-heads.[32]

Item, in performing the (70) said combat, if one of us is brought down to the ground by a lance struck in a clean attaint* on the harness*, he who has fallen to the ground in this manner will give the companion* who brought him down a diamond of his choice.

Item, each of them will be armed in a harness of his own choosing, whether double* or single*, one regularly used for jousting and without any illegal devices on it. It is expected that the lance-rest* affixed to the breastplate will confer no advantage, other than being of the kind worn in war.

Item, every man will bring his own lance-fittings and lance-heads, with the proviso that the vamplate* which sits in front of the hand will be no more than four inches wide. Item: the lances will all be of the same length measured from the tip to the rest; this length will be stipulated by me.

Item, in order to perform and accomplish these feats of arms on horseback, I will provide lances for everybody that are ready for use inside the lists; these will be identical to those used by me and my companions.

Item, these feats of arms will take place at the tilt*, which will be six feet high.'

---

[28] [Jaques de Chalant, seigneur d'Ameville]. Jacques de Challant (d. 1459), lord of Aymavilles, Châtillon, Ussel, Verrès, Issogne and Greines, was a native of Savoy but held lands in the county of Burgundy (Franche-Comté); he was a member of the Savoyard Order of the Collar (1440) and a chamberlain of Duke Louis I of Savoy. OdLM, vol. 1, p. 320; François Capre, *Catalogue des chevaliers de l'Ordre du Collier de Savoye* (Turin: Barthélémy Zavatte, 1654), fols 70v–71r.

[29] [Amé, seigneur de Espirey]. Aimé de Rabutin (d. 1472), lord of Espiry and Balorre, was bailiff of Charolais; famed in his time for his skill at tournaments, such as at the *Pas de la Fontaine des Pleurs* (1449–50), he was also a loyal soldier and died at the siege of Beauvais during Charles the Bold's conflict with Louis XI. GDH, vol. 5, p. 426.

[30] [Jehan de Chaingny]. Jean de Chaumergy (d. 1455) was a squire of the stables of Philip the Good (1438–49). PCB no. 417.

[31] The colour black was closely associated with Philip the Good, but it was his son, Charles the Bold, when he was still count of Charolais, who particularly favoured the combination of black and violet. See Sophie Jolivet, 'La construction d'une image: Philippe le Bon et le noir (1419–1467)', in *Se vêtir à la cour en Europe, 1400–1815*, ed. by Isabelle Paresys and Natacha Coquery (Villeneuve d'Ascq: Institut de recherches historiques du Septentrion, 2011), pp. 27–42. Jacques de Lalaing at his later *pas* followed Bauffremont's lead in having black and violet shields decorated with tears but also added a third shield, painted white. LF, p. 317; CL, p. 213.

[32] This mention of sharpened lance-heads indicates the serious nature of these jousts as a martial and chivalric exercise.

Here follow the articles on the foot combat

'Afterwards, those princes, barons, knights and squires of the aforesaid condition,[33] who would prefer to do combat on foot, will be obliged, as above, to touch the violet shield with the black tears and to fight with either pollaxes* or swords*, whichever is their preference, for up to fifteen strokes.

Item, in the course of this combat, if one of them touches the ground with his hands or his knees, (71) he who has done so will be obliged to give the other man a ruby of whatever value he chooses.

Item, each man will be armed in a harness of the kind regularly used for fighting in the lists.

Item, if one of them is without a pollaxe or a sword, I will supply him with one that is sufficient and identical to those used by me and my companions. On these pollaxes and swords there will be nothing that should not rightfully be there, whether hooks or some other illegal device.

Item, [as for] he who is intent on fighting a foot combat with me, if one of us falls with his whole body to the ground, he will be obliged to surrender himself wherever the *hostelant*[34] orders him [to go].

Item, he who is taken prisoner in this way will be obliged to pay a ransom for his deliverance of over 500 *écus* to whomsoever, male or female, the *ostelent* decides to specify.

Item, those of the aforesaid foreigners[35] need not request me or my companions for they will find someone to do combat with them at all hours, as stipulated and prescribed in this document.

Item, the above-mentioned foreigners will only be allowed to fight either me or my companions once, that is to say, once on horseback and once on foot; they cannot ask for more than this from either me or my said companions for the duration of the present competition.

Item, the said combats on horseback and on foot will take place in the following fashion: that is to say, those on horseback will be held on Monday, Tuesday and Wednesday, and those on foot will be held on Thursday, Friday and Saturday.

Item, the said *pas* will thus begin on the first day of July in the year (72) 1443; it will last for forty days, discounting Sundays and any feast days as are held in the city of Rome.

Item, none of the aforesaid princes, barons, knights or squires may be allowed to pass within a quarter of a league[36] of the *pas* without either performing or accomplishing the said feats of arms or without leaving a pledge [to do so], that is to say his sword or his spurs, whichever he chooses.

---

[33] See above, n. 18.

[34] Monstrelet appears to be the only person to use this word, with the alternative spelling of *ostelent* in the next sentence, the etymology of which is obscure: the editor of his text (EdM, p. 71 n. 1) suggests that it designates the person who breaks up the fight, the *oste-lance*, i.e. the one who takes the lance away. Alternatively, it may be derived from the term *hoste* (army). Either way, the meaning is clear enough here from the context and so the word has been left untranslated.

[35] 'Foreigners' here means the challengers coming from lands outside those belonging to either the king of France or the duke of Burgundy.

[36] A French league (*lieue commune de France*) is normally 4444 metres. H. de Schrijver, *De oude landmaten in Vlaanderen* (Brussels: Simon Stevin, 1968), p. 26.

Item, in order to perform and accomplish the said combats, whether on horseback or on foot, in the manner and order outlined above, I have humbly beseeched and requested my aforesaid sovereign lord that, by his grace, he grant me leave to undertake them. He, desirous of their being completed, has graciously allowed me to do so. In order to hold them, he hereby gives and has given me as a judge the most high and powerful prince, my redoutable lord and sovereign, my lord the count of Nevers and Rethel,[37] or, in his absence, my lord the marshal, the count of Freiburg and Neuchâtel.[38]

In order that it be clear that these present chapters proceed from my own will and intention, given my desire to accomplish them in the aforesaid manner, I have had them sealed with my seal and signed by my hand, this eighth day of March, 1442.[39]

Item, I beg all the above princes, barons, knights and squires not to imagine that there is any ill intention behind this. I am doing this solely in order to enhance the noble profession and pursuit of arms and to make the acquaintance through combat of the well-renowned and valiant princes and nobles described above who (73) might wish to participate.

Item, those nobles coming from foreign parts will be loyally assured of a valid and trustworthy safe-conduct[40] from my said sovereign lord or, in his absence, from his marshal.'

[37] Charles of Burgundy (1414–64), also known as Charles I, was count of Nevers and Rethel. PCB no. 533. On his death he was succeeded as count of Nevers and Rethel by his brother, Jean of Burgundy (1415–91), count of Étampes. PCB no. 664. See OdLM, vol. 1, p. 298, where this person playing the role of judge is erroneously referred to as 'Monseigneur Loys de Bourgoingne'.

[38] [le conte de Fribourg et de Noefchastel]. Jean, count of Freiburg and lord of Neuchâtel (d. 1458), was marshal of Burgundy (1440–43) and a councillor-chamberlain of Philip the Good (1433–49). PCB no. 568; OdLM, vol. 1, p. 311.

[39] Throughout the Burgundian lands, as well as in many other European countries, the Easter cycle determined the start of a new year in the later Middle Ages. In the year 1443, Easter Sunday was celebrated on 21 April, so all dates between 1 January and 20 April would be noted as '1442'.

[40] See above, n. 4, on the generally tense situation between France, England and Burgundy in this period and thus the need for would-be challengers at these events to be able to travel freely and in safety.

Thanks are due to Mario Damen and Ralph Moffat for their helpful comments on various aspects of this translation.

Catherine Blunk and Rosalind Brown-Grant

Source 5

The *Pas de la Joyeuse Garde*/*Pas de Saumur* (*Pas* of the Joyous Guard/*Pas* of Saumur), 1446

This source consists of a selected extract from a narrative account of this *pas d'armes* that covers the opening stages of the event.

Author: A cleric, identity unknown

Language: Middle French

Edition used: Natalia Elagina *et al.*, eds, *Das Turnierbuch für René d'Anjou (Le Pas de Saumur): Vollständige Faksimile-Ausgabe im Originalformat der Handschrift Codex Fr. F. XIV Nr. 4 der Russischen National-bibliothek in St. Petersburg* (Graz: Akademische Druck und Verlagsanstalt, 1998), pp. 67–113 (= PSr)

Select bibliography:

Bianciotto, Gabriel, 'Le pas d'armes de Saumur (1446) et la vie chevaleresque à la cour de René d'Anjou', in *Le Roi René: René, duc d'Anjou, de Bar et de Lorraine, roi de Sicile et de Jerusalem, roi d'Aragon, comte de Provence, 1409–1480: actes du colloque international, Avignon, 13, 14, 15 juin 1981*, ed. by Gabriel Bianciotto ([Avignon]: Annales Universitaires d'Avignon, 1986), pp. 1–16

Ferré, Rose-Marie, 'Les ecclésiastiques et les fêtes profanes à la cour de René d'Anjou: l'exemple du Pas de Saumur', in *L'artiste et le clerc: Commandes artistiques des grands ecclésiastiques à la fin du Moyen Âge (XIVe–XVIe siècles)*, ed. by Fabienne Joubert, Cultures et civilisations médiévales, 35 (Paris: Presses de l'Université de Paris-Sorbonne, 2006), pp. 351–70

Mérindol, Christian de, *Les fêtes de chevalerie à la cour du roi René: Emblématique, art et histoire (les joutes de Nancy, le Pas de Saumur et le Pas de Tarascon)* (Paris: Éditions du CTHS, 1993)

Introduction

This *pas d'armes* organised by René, king of Naples and duke of Anjou, a fervent devotee of tournaments as well as a noted patron of the arts,[1] took place over a forty-day period between 26 June and 7 August 1446. Held at the castle of Saumur, one of René of Anjou's favourite residences, which is located near the town of the same name on the River Loire, it followed shortly after another tournament in which he also participated that was staged between Chinon and Razilly in May 1446. This event, known as either the *Pas de la Gueule*

[1] Albert Lecoy de la Marche, *Le roi René: sa vie, son administration, ses travaux artistiques et littéraires*, 2 vols (Paris: Librairie de Firmin-Didot frères, fils et cie, 1875).

du Dragon or the *Pas du Rocher Périlleux*, was organised by four noblemen closely connected to King Charles VII of France, who may also have financed it.[2] As *entrepreneur** at Saumur, René was aided by a team of between twenty-three and forty other defenders, all of whom were closely aligned with his court. They were challenged by eighty visiting knights and squires who were mostly linked to the court of Charles VII. Many of these figures, whether defenders or challengers on this particular occasion at Saumur, had also competed in the earlier event at Chinon/Razilly as well as in other tournaments often referred to as *pas d'armes* that took place either in the kingdom of France, as at Châlons-sur-Marne (1445), or in the Angevin sphere, as at Nancy (1445), Launay (1446) and Bourges (1447).[3]

Consisting solely of jousts fought with rebated lances, the event began with an opening procession during which a lady ceremoniously placed a shield on a *perron**, a marble column that each challenger had to strike upon arrival into the lists. A meal followed, after which the jousting began. The end of the *pas* was marked by a closing procession, an awards ceremony and the removal of the shield from the column. According to Rose-Marie Ferré, this event at Saumur was clearly the largest festive production of René's early reign, and one that cost an enormous sum of money.[4] For example, the canon Guillaume Tourneville, whom René tasked with organising the *pas*, received the extraordinary sum of 1200 *livres tournois* for his role in making the preparations, although the exact extent of these is unknown.

Information on this tournament, which is often referred to by various different names, is contained in four different sources. The first of these is an administrative source, a *quittance générale* (receipt) from René's household accounts dated 1455, which alludes to the event as both the '*pas du Perron*' and the '*pas de Saumur*'.[5] The second is a chronicle by the Burgundian writer Mathieu d'Escouchy (1420–82), who includes a very short narrative account of this *pas* but without attributing a precise title to it.[6] The third, also a chronicle, is by the southern French author Guillaume Leseur, who calls it the *Pas du Perron* in his *Histoire de Gaston IV, comte de Foix* (*c*.1477–8).[7] The fourth and by far the most extensive narrative record of this *pas*

---

[2] These are: Gaston IV, count of Foix; Guillaume d'Harcourt, count of Tancarville (see below, n. 78); Claude de Châteauneuf, a squire of the stables of the king; and Guillaume de Courcelles, the king's first *valet de chambre*. This information comes from Berlin, Staatsbibliothek, Preußischer Kulturbesitz, Ham. 606 (fol. 98v), a recently rediscovered manuscript of Guillaume Leseur's *Histoire de Gaston IV, comte de Foix*, which thus supplements the material in HGF and HGFMO. For a translation of Leseur's narrative account of this event, those mentioned in n. 3 below and the *Pas de Saumur* itself, see Supplementary Source 1, Liverpool University Press Digital Collaboration Hub <https://liverpooluniversitypress.manifoldapp.org/projects/pas-d-armes-casebook> [accessed 1 November 2021].

[3] Lecoy de la Marche, *Le roi René*; Berlin, Ham. 606. The tournaments at Launay and Bourges are known as the *Pas du Géant à la Blanche Dame du Pavillon* and the *Pas du Chevalier Aventureux*, respectively. For an overview of all these tournaments, see the Table of *pas d'armes*, pp. 25–6.

[4] Rose-Marie Ferré, 'Les ecclésiastiques et les fêtes profanes à la cour de René d'Anjou: l'exemple du Pas de Saumur', in *L'artiste et le clerc: Commandes artistiques des grands ecclésiastiques à la fin du Moyen Âge (XIVe–XVIe siècles)*, ed. by Fabienne Joubert, Cultures et civilisations médiévales, 35 (Paris: Presses de l'Université de Paris-Sorbonne, 2006), pp. 351–70 (pp. 355–8).

[5] *Ibid.*, p. 365.

[6] MdE, vol. 1, pp. 107–8. For a detailed analysis of his description of the event, see Essay 7.

[7] HGF, pp. 171, 195–6 (p. 195); HGFMO; and Berlin, Ham. 606 (fols 76r–96v). The list of the jousters and the days on which the jousts took place vary considerably in this source. The count of Foix competed at Saumur as a challenger and at Bourges (1447), and was purportedly one of the *entrepreneurs* at Chinon/Razilly (see above, n. 2).

is written in verse and preserved in a richly illuminated manuscript: St Petersburg, National Library of Russia, fr. F. p. XIV, 4. This account goes into quite some detail on the literary inspiration of the event, which draws on the episode of Lancelot and the Joyous Guard from Arthurian romance,[8] hence giving rise to the title of the *Pas de la Joyeuse Garde* by which the tournament at Saumur is also sometimes known. Gabriel Bianciotto dates the composition of this poem, referred to by its modern editors as the *Relation du Pas de Saumur*, to between August 1446 and February 1447: that is, shortly after the event itself took place.[9]

The *Relation* as preserved in the St Petersburg codex is far and away the most heavily illuminated extant manuscript of any *pas d'armes* narrative, containing ninety-one images, mostly of jousts, illustrating 247 stanzas of verse.[10] Each stanza consists of sixteen octosyllabic verses with an *aaab aaab bbbc bbbc* rhyme scheme. Only two other *pas* accounts are written in verse, one a short poem by an unknown author commemorating the Burgundian *Pas de l'Arbre Charlemagne* (Marsannay-la-Côte, 1443) that was organised by Pierre de Bauffremont, lord of Charny,[11] and the other recording the *Pas de la Bergère* (Tarascon, 1449),[12] organised by Philippe de Lenoncourt and Philibert de Laigue, both of whom served at René of Anjou's court and had earlier competed at Saumur.[13]

Whilst it is already unusual for a *pas d'armes* account that the author of the *Pas de la Bergère*, Louis de Beauvau, was a nobleman and a highly experienced knight, being the most frequent jouster at Saumur and a challenger at Tarascon,[14] it is even more unusual that the author of the *Relation* was neither a herald,[15] nor a chronicler[16] or an ex-competitor like Beauvau, but rather a cleric, one who confesses to having a lack of experience in matters of arms.[17] Moreover, as the *Relation* poet explains, he was not in attendance at Saumur for the whole event and so had to rely on the testimony of others — probably the heralds and scribes who were there to assist the judges — for further information on it and for clarification of particular points. At times, too, the poet alludes to the written documents, such as a letter or declaration of challenge and chapters of arms that would have been circulated by René's heralds prior to the event but which have not come down to us.[18] He also makes somewhat obscure reference to elements of the staging of the *pas*, such as a hermit and a

---

[8] On this Arthurian context, see Essay 7.

[9] Gabriel Bianciotto, 'Le pas d'armes de Saumur (1446) et la vie chevaleresque à la cour de René d'Anjou', in *Le Roi René: René, duc d'Anjou, de Bar et de Lorraine, roi de Sicile et de Jerusalem, roi d'Aragon, comte de Provence, 1409–1480: actes du colloque international, Avignon, 13, 14, 15 juin 1981*, ed. by Gabriel Bianciotto ([Avignon]: Annales Universitaires d'Avignon, 1986), pp. 1–16 (p. 11).

[10] For a detailed discussion of this manuscript, see Essays 2 and 7.

[11] For an edition of this poem, see CPM.

[12] See Source 6.

[13] On these two figures, see below, nn. 43 and 51, respectively.

[14] On this figure, see below, n. 37.

[15] Whilst the author of the *Pas des armes de Sandricourt* (1493) explicitly names himself as Orléans Herald, it is highly likely that those who wrote up the narrative accounts of the *Pas du Perron Fée* (Bruges, 1463) and the *Pas* of Carignano (1504) were also heralds. See Sources 13, 11a and 15, respectively.

[16] The most prolific and enthusiastic recorder of *pas d'armes* is undoubtedly the Burgundian historiographer Olivier de La Marche (*c.*1425–1502), who describes several of these events at length in his *Mémoires*. For example, see Source 7 (*Pas de la Fontaine des Pleurs*).

[17] On the author's clerical status, see Ferré, 'Les ecclésiastiques', pp. 360–3.

[18] Leseur also mentions 'les articles et chappitres' of the jousts but explicitly states that he has excluded them so as to keep his account brief. Berlin, Ham. 606, fols 76v–77r.

hermitage, and to the awarding of a ruby and a diamond as prizes, which he presumably gleaned from these documents.

The translated extract from the *Relation* that follows consists of the first fifty-eight stanzas, in which the author briefly recounts what happened at the *Pas de la Gueule du Dragon/Pas du Rocher Périlleux* at Chinon/Razilly by way of a preamble to the event at Saumur and describes the motivation for holding this second *pas* (the desire to please the ladies and to stave off idleness among the nobility, both of which are classic tropes for this kind of event), the opening procession, the dinner that followed and the first joust that was contested at it. The rest of the poem recounts the entries of each competitor into the lists and their ensuing combat: these descriptions of jousts have the repetitive, formulaic quality characteristic of many *pas* narratives, despite being written in verse. The end of the *Relation* includes descriptions of the closing procession, the awards ceremony and the removal of the shield from the column. Throughout the text, the poet refers to himself in the first-person voice in order to comment self-reflexively on the process of how he wrote up the event. In keeping with a mode of writing that was very popular in Angevin circles and which René himself cultivated,[19] the poet also uses allegorical allusion to frame this *pas* as being one governed by personifications such as Fortune, Honour, Largesse, Loyalty, Prowess and Renown.

The translation that follows is in blank verse which, for ease of reference to the original as contained in the edition by Elagina *et al.*, uses the same stanza numbering; it also attempts, as far as possible, to render the sense of the original line by line whilst obviously having to make some allowances at times for the differences between Middle French and modern English syntax.

TRANSLATION

1.

Out of loyal will owed,
With neither dishonest intention
Nor any other interested thought,
To your high excellency and
Happy, royal majesty,
Prosperous and cordial,
Merciful, benevolent and loyal,
Prince of most worthy clemency
And of redoubtable magnificence:
I presume to bring into your presence
This account, created out of ignorance,
Of the *Pas* and the column, situated near
The castle, which was filled with pleasure,
Arms, honour, and valour,
As ordered by your authority
In the year 1446.

---

19 See the studies in Florence Bouchet, ed., *René d'Anjou, écrivain et mécène (1409–1480)* (Turnhout: Brepols, 2011).

2.

It was undertaken for a lady
Out of a love kept secret from all,[20]
As I understand it — and, by my soul,
One could not choose another more beautiful than she.
All burning with an amorous flame
With neither ignoble thoughts nor other form of dishonour,
Were many shields and blades dented
By those about whom you can read hereafter,
As I intend to commit to writing
As well — or at least not too badly —
As I am able to recount or say,
With the help of experienced people
Who know plenty about arms.
Though you may despise my shortcomings,
I turn to the ladies who awarded the prize
To make amends for it.

3.

In order to give an account of it
So that it is preserved in memory,
Honour, holding assembly
In his high and royal domain —
A glorious castle situated on the Loire — ,
Ordered it to be set up as a place
That would be worthy for all time
For those who would like to see
Exploits, bravery, and skill.
If Nobility does her duty
It will be clearly seen
That the bravest who was ever born
Has wished this to be executed
And to let it be known far and wide
So that noblemen will be moved
To aspire to being crowned with the prize.

4.

And because one finds it written
In ancient tales, where one reads
That pain and pleasure were to be had
When, at the Dolorous Guard,

---

[20] This trope of a tournament being undertaken for the secret love of a lady is a common one in *pas d'armes* accounts but is underlined here by the reference to Lancelot in stanza 4. René of Anjou's reputation as a courtly lover as hinted at here was cultivated through many of his own later writings, such as the allegorical narrative poem the *Livre du Coeur d'Amour épris* (1457).

Lancelot overcame the giant
But, out of annoyance, dropped his shield
In front of the dwarf, who picked it up
And placed it in the pavilion for safe keeping,
Then named it the Joyous Guard,
So this is also the case, for whoever looks carefully,
Of this *pas*, because, even if it takes a while,
I intend so to render it to the best of my ability,
May it please God; even if I take my time in doing so,
No Turkish, Lombard,
Or French fashion[21] will constrain me:
Purely my limited wits will.

5.

Rather than asking the permission of all noble hearts
Who have intelligence, knowledge and worth,
I wish to give pre-eminence to the honour
Of the ladies in this undertaking,
In whom there is such sweetness,
Cleverness, joy,
Beauty and radiance,
More than either eye or heart could tell.
Next, I wish to describe the appearance
And setting of the castle and of the *emprise**[22] itself,
All in the order in which it was organised,
How everyone was seated and where the lions were placed.
If I should fail, by God let me know,
Because in this matter reproach would be called for.
First, I will give an account and testimony
Of the kings, dukes, counts and barons.

6.

For I wish to tell a pleasing tale
Of the lady, how she was dressed,
And how she would come out of the castle and go back in,
And of the Saracens in the tower
Where the large standard was,
So that the expert does
Not find me to be a liar.
I also wish to tell how the defender would leave

---

[21] This reference to Turkish, Lombard and French fashion (in what may be either a sartorial or a literary sense) is very obscure: whilst the Turks and the Lombards did not always enjoy a positive reputation in late medieval France, the last of these perhaps alludes punningly to something about French (i.e. Parisian?) culture that was negatively viewed at the Angevin court.

[22] This term is to be understood here as a synonym for *pas*.

The castle and come here to the place
Where the dwarf and the lion were;[23]
How he would pick up the shield
When the challenger knocked it down,
And to speak of the place where they would give out
The prize[s] and how they proclaimed
The results that were awarded
Until the setting of the sun.

7.

Using the reports of the senators[24] —
Those judging the *pas*, the experts — ,
Who do not lie about these things,
I intend to recount all of this,
[Whilst also drawing on the views of] former knights and honourable
Authorities and witnesses
About these valiant jousters,
Each according to his worth.
Without favour or fiction
I will relate to you the actions of these worthy men
To the very best of my ability,
According to their rank;
I cannot do so quite yet
Because I lack access to
The written account and the stipulations,[25]
And the time has not yet come
When I might be able to say all that I wish to.

8.

But to see, hear and learn
Is why I came to Saumur
On the third day of August, and to gain
A clear grasp of these events,
So that my feeble understanding
Could be faithfully expanded

---

[23] The term *liepart* (literally, 'leopard') used in this stanza, probably to make the rhyme with *estandart* (standard) and *part* (place), could also refer to a heraldic lion. DMF. However, the earlier description and the manuscript illustrations make it clear that the animals attached to the column are lions, not leopards.

[24] This term is employed metaphorically here as a kind of classical allusion to Roman senators so as to laud the probity of the judges of the *Pas*.

[25] The poet here is referring explicitly to the fact that he had seen neither the original letter or declaration of challenge nor the chapters of arms regulating this *pas* when he wrote his account of it, even though he does later allude to various elements that were presumably included in them, such as a hermit (stanza 24) and a hermitage (stanza 50), as well as prizes consisting of a ruby (stanza 24) and a diamond (stanza 53).

To write the truth, without making mistakes,
According to the true judgement
Of those who saw the beginning
And the culmination [of the *Pas*],
Which they speak about like experts,
Being wise and noble in judgement.
They have written about this truthfully
So that it will long be remembered
In the very highest honour.

9.

In the year after the disruption
Of the wars[26] was brought to an end,
When Charles VII[27] ruled as king
And Louis, the only son of France,[28] was flourishing,
— By divine right heir,
An illustrious prince and fountain of justice — ,
What happened, to the best of my ability,
I wish to preserve for posterity.
This is in loyal obedience
To the high prince full of valour
Whom I acknowledge in this poem:
René of Anjou, king of Sicily,
Duke of Bar, count of Provence
And of Lorraine by providence,[29]
Who organised the *Pas*
About which I wish to speak for the common good.

10.

For in this season,
Between Razilly and Chinon,
In front of the Dragon's Mouth
No lady nor damsel could pass by
Unaccompanied by a noble man of renown
Who, through arms, had made a name for himself,
Without having a glove or a chin knot[30]

---

[26] A truce between England and France called at Tours on 28 May 1444, during the course of the Hundred Years War, was reinforced by the marriage of René's daughter, Margaret of Anjou, with Henry VI of England (23 April 1445), an event celebrated by a *pas de joustes* at Nancy; the truce lasted until 1449. Graeme Small, *Late Medieval France* (Basingstoke: Palgrave Macmillan, 2009), pp. 151, 162–3.

[27] Charles VII (1403–61) was king of France from 1422 to his death.

[28] Louis XI (1423–83), son of Charles VII, was *dauphin* at the time of the *Pas* and became king of France on his father's death in 1461.

[29] René of Anjou (1409–80), duke of Anjou and count of Provence (1434–80), also reigned as king of Naples (1435–42) before being deposed as the preceding dynasty was restored to power.

[30] This probably refers to the ribbon that ties a hood under a lady's chin.

Taken from her as a challenge
By four noblemen who devised it
As a new *emprise* of arms, one
By which no joyful, beautiful,
Good, loyal, or faithful woman
Could pass by without her beloved
Breaking two lances for her
Against his courtly enemy.

11.

To this place, many men of worth
Who were in thrall to love
And wished to seek the prize of honour
Went to deposit the tokens
That they had taken from their ladies.
Committing to break two lances,
The first one to be taken [hostage]
Would take pledges in the form of gold rings
And put a stop to the outrages
Performed by those brutal Wild Men
Who came out of their dens
To grab the ladies by their [horses'] bridles,
Even though they should not be manhandled in this way.
Many high-born [men] went there,
[Ones] valiant and worthy, prudent and wise,
To be their ladies' escorts.

12.

When word reached His Highness,
The wise, worthy and generous
King René, who is full of prowess,
Resplendent in fruit and flower,[31]
And ever successful in arms,
He humbly requested his lady
To allow him to liberate her from
The Wild Men that day;
Out of loyalty and true love,
He would uphold her honour.
She promptly replied
That she had another who would liberate her.
Thus, full of suffering, he left her,
[Wracked with] distress, anguish and languor,
Doubting that he would ever again be well.

---

[31] To be read metaphorically: bearing both fruit and flowers, René is like a fertile, productive tree and full of virtues.

13.
But Fortune, who makes the brave man
Happy through boldness,
And lays low the doubtful,
Very gently commanded
This most chivalrous prince
To be neither pensive[32] nor fearful.
Through the countess of Évreux[33]
She very gently requested him —
Despite his having suffered a cruel rejection — ,
Not to be dismayed in any way
But to joust in a joyful manner,
Whoever asked him kindly to do so.
He was armed mysteriously, all in black,
As was his horse's trapper*,
And he performed so many feats of arms
That they sent him the prize.

14.
The day soon came when
Into the lists, looking darker than a blackberry,[34]
Rode the prince for whom I labour,
Who liberated his lady in fine style.
The heart, which weeps tears of blood
And knows no joy to savour,
Did not waste a single hour
Before winning the prize from them all.
Long did he joust that day for the one
Who had rejected and rebuffed him.
Never did any lady doubt him so much!
For this reason must he be remembered,
Just as afterwards he governed
The *pas d'armes*, which began
In June, just gone,
With the shield on the marble column.

15.
This whole shield with pansy flowers
Was strewn; they were thickly clustered

---

[32] A pun is being made here on the adjective *pansis* (pensive/thoughtful) and the flower which René goes on to adopt as his emblem at the *Pas* in Saumur, i.e. the pansy (*pensee*), which also means 'thought'.

[33] Jeanne du Bec-Crespin (b. before 1425) was countess of Évreux through her marriage to Pierre de Brézé, count of Évreux. PSr, p. 146.

[34] The St Petersburg manuscript of the *Relation* devotes one miniature (fol. 3r) to the *Pas de la Gueule du Dragon/Pas du Rocher Périlleux*, which depicts both René and his horse in a completely black harness that accurately matches this textual description of him: see Essay 2 and Figure 18 reproduced on p. 385.

On the vermilion field and had been gathered
By Honour and Largesse,
And enhanced by Prowess.
These three Ladies, well versed
In counsel, came together
To put this *pas* into motion.
Loyalty too, the mistress,
Who never once ceases
To keep company with Nobility,
Was there on that Sunday morning,
Dressed like a princess.
No sooner had everyone heard Mass,
Than the shield, all covered in red satin,
Was carried over by its strap.

16.

Next to this column,
On each side, was a lion.
A dwarf in a pavilion
Guarded the shield which hung there;
If anyone approached it,
Be he a king, duke, count or baron,
And a man of arms, noble in name,
To ask anything about the shield,
[The dwarf] let it be known immediately.
A lady or a damsel would come out,
Bringing with her
A man of arms from among those on the inside* team.
The pansies were by no means neglected
But rather covered his vermilion trappings;
There he would run six courses
Against the one who stood in the lists.

17.

It is not hard for me to recount,
To every loyal heart that is clean and pure,
How they processed from the castle of Saumur
Which is so noble, magnificent and splendid;
To keep it quiet would be unfortunate,
Given that many Greeks, Hungarians and Turks,
Many foreigners, full of delight,
Came from formidable countries
To see this knightly
Emprise, joyous above all others,
This glorious festivity
[Organised by] that most excellent and noble prince,
His happy nobles

And all their lordly company.
My life would be most unfortunate
If I were slow to name them.

18.

There, at the said castle situated above the
Happy and prosperous town of Saumur,
Were,[35] with the king of Sicily:
Ferry, my lord of Lorraine;[36]
The lord of Beauvau,[37] a most useful man
Of arms and highly skilled,
Loyal and valiant among a thousand;
Guy de Laval, baron of Maine
And lord of the domain of Loué;[38]
Jean de Beauvau[39] took great pains there,
As did that fine captain
Named Geoffroy de Saint-Belin.[40]
All of them did as much, out of good intentions,[41]
On every day of the week,

---

[35] Unless otherwise stated, all the men named in this and the following stanzas were defenders at Saumur who fought on René's team.

[36] Ferry II de Vaudémont-Lorraine (d. 1470), the husband of Yolande of Anjou, daughter of René of Anjou and Isabelle of Lorraine, was a member of René's Order of the Crescent (1448). He was one of the five defenders at Nancy (1445) and also jousted at Châlons-sur-Marne (1445), Chinon/Razilly (1446), Launay (1446) and the *Pas de la Bergère* at Tarascon (1449); he was judged the best defender at Saumur and also won the grand prize at Tarascon. Christian de Mérindol, *Les fêtes de chevalerie à la cour du roi René: Emblématique, art et histoire (les joutes de Nancy, le Pas de Saumur et le Pas de Tarascon)* (Paris: Éditions du CTHS, 1993), pp. 183–5; PSr, p. 130.

[37] Louis I de Beauvau (*c.*1418–62/3), lord of Beauvau and Sermaise in Anjou, was a councillor-chamberlain of René, a member of the Order of the Crescent (1448) and seneschal of Anjou (*c.*1458). He competed on Charles VII's teams at Nancy and Châlons-sur-Marne, both in 1445, but fought on René's side at Saumur and Launay (1446), and competed at Chinon/Razilly (1446). Not only was he the author of the poem commemorating the *Pas de la Bergère*, but the *Roman de Troyle et Criseida* (*c.*1453–55), a translation of Giovanni Boccaccio's *Il Filostrato*, is also attributed to him. Mérindol, *Les fêtes*, pp. 126–8; PSr, p. 125; HGFMO, p. 201.

[38] [baron ou Mayne]. Guy de Laval (d. 1484), count of Laval (from 1414) and lord of Loué, was a member of the Order of the Crescent (1448), a councillor-chamberlain of René, a councillor of King Charles VII (1446–47) and seneschal of Anjou (1474). He jousted at Châlons-sur-Marne (1445) and Launay (1446) where he substituted for René of Anjou as a defender, and at Tarascon (1449). Mérindol, *Les fêtes*, pp. 168–9; PSr, p. 128.

[39] [Jehan de Beauvau]. Jean de Beauvau (1421–69), younger brother of Louis de Beauvau, was a member of the Order of the Crescent (1452), seneschal of Anjou (1458) and a chamberlain of René. PSr, p. 125.

[40] [Geuffroy de Saint Belin]. Geoffroy de Saint-Belin (d. 1465), baron of Saxefontaine, was bailiff and captain of Chaumont (1448) and a squire of the stables of Charles VII (1450). He jousted at Châlons-sur-Marne (1445). Mérindol, *Les fêtes*, p. 179; PSr, p. 129.

[41] The original reads 'de pensee sayne': another pun on the double meaning of *pensee* as both 'pansy' and 'thought'.

As Jason did for Helen.[42]
Lenoncourt,[43] Guerry,[44] Crespin[45]...

19.

... And the ever-composed Jean Cossa,[46]
As well as 'Le Bègue' Duplessis,[47]
Broke many large, heavy and solid
Lances through their valour.
And more than six other nobles,
Whose names are mentioned hereafter
Are identified by order and according
To the days that were appointed
For these arms* of courtesy which were not *à outrance**,
And were fought with lances that were all the same
In length, with no difference between them,
But not in width.
All of this was done in the hope
Of giving pleasure to the ladies
Who were there in person
In their lovely stand.

20.

Because human death brings an end to[48]
Earthly love, since it undoes

---

[42] The poet has muddled up his mythology here, probably for the sake of the rhyme (*sayne/sepmaine/Helayne*): Jason was the lover of Medea and Paris was the lover of Helen. The only link between Jason and Helen is that her two brothers, Castor and Polydeuces, were members of the Argonauts who sailed with Jason on his quest to find the Golden Fleece. Oskar Seyffert, *The Dictionary of Classical Mythology, Religion, Literature and Art* (New York: Gramercy Books, 1995), pp. 61–3.

[43] Philippe de Lenoncourt (1400–83), lord of Lenoncourt, Gondrecourt, Serres and Frouard, was a member of the Order of the Crescent (1452), a squire of the stables of René (1451–53) and later his Master of the Horse (1470), governor of the duchy of Bar (1470) and a councillor-chamberlain of Louis XI. He was one of the five defenders at Nancy (1445), he jousted and won a prize at Châlons-sur-Marne (1445) and fought at Launay (1446) as a defender; he was one of the two *entrepreneurs* at Tarascon (1449). Mérindol, *Les fêtes*, p. 170; PSr, p. 128; HGFMO, p. 201.

[44] Guerry de Charno was a retainer of René; he also jousted at Tarascon (1449). Mérindol, *Les fêtes*, p. 140.

[45] [Crepin]. Jean Crespin was a squire of the stables of René (1451). PSr, p. 146.

[46] [Jehan Cosse]. Jean (Giovanni) Cossa (*c.*1400–76), baron of Grimaud and count of Troya, was a member of the Order of the Crescent (1448), a councillor-chamberlain of René, lieutenant-general of Sicily (1446) and grand seneschal of Provence (1470); he also jousted at Launay (1446) and Tarascon (1449). Mérindol, *Les fêtes*, pp. 143–4; PSr, p. 126.

[47] [le Becgue du Plessis]. Jean Duplessis (known as 'Le Bègue', meaning 'the Stutterer') was a member of the order of the Crescent (after 1452), a squire of the stables in René's household (1454) and a councillor of René (1469–70). PSr, p. 127.

[48] The complex rhyme scheme of this stanza is based almost entirely on verbs such as *acorder/concorder/discorder/recorder*, etc. that are cognates of *corder* (to tie) and which play on the Latin words *chorda*, relating both to rope (Fr. *corde*) and musical chords/harmony (Fr. *accord*) and *cor/cordis*, meaning the heart (Fr.

Those who are united by a common purpose
And adore singing in unison,
Each one must bind himself to entreating God
To receive his soul and to wrap it up
In His sweet mercy.
He is the One whom we must remember in our hearts
For being willing to agree to,
Accommodate and assent to
Our actions, and to give His blessing
To our feats of arms, which we preserve in memory.
Indeed, who would not hold fast
To that which should unite us?
The hood should not fail to be untied[49]
By a knight who is both valiant and wise.

21.

Let us return to those in the castle
And speak of other things,
Leaving behind that which is not fine
Or in harmony with nature.
It is far more pleasant to speak
Of arms, lances and blades.
Love does not fear a mortal blow
Whilst Courage triumphs over misfortune
And is sustenance for the valiant.
Honour has never succumbed to
Corruption, but rather to rectitude.
What treasure could be greater than
Playing one's role, forging one's build,
Conducting oneself well, standing tall,
As all noble creatures should aspire to do?
[This is worth] one hundred thousand times more than gold.

22.

Varennes[50] and Laigue,[51] following the path,
Came out joyously behind
The dwarf who emerged first, with his mace,

---

coeur). These verbs have thus been translated here using various metaphors of tying/uniting, of being in harmony/agreement/assent and of remembering (the heart being the seat of memory in medieval thought).

[49] This final image, that of the hood being untied, may also be a link back to the pun of the chin knot in stanza 10 above.

[50] [Varennez]. Jean de Varennes was *maître d'hôtel* in René's household (1451). PSr, p. 130.

[51] [Laygue]. Philibert de Laigue, of a family from Bourges, was a squire and councillor-chamberlain of René (probably after 1451) and seneschal of Bar (1480); he was also one of the two *entrepreneurs* at Tarascon (1449). Mérindol, *Les fêtes*, p. 165; PSr, p. 128.

To put the shield back up on the column,
For it had been knocked down
By a challenger who had allowed no time
For the dwarf to threaten
Him into putting it back up again.
Before long, you would have seen him advance
And go right up to the castle
To seek the assistance of the lady,
To sound the cymbals in the belfry
And the trumpets and clarions without end,
And to lower the bridge for help.
I could not describe for you
All the noise, clamour and commotion!

23.

To keep things brief,
La Jaille,[52] Bourmont,[53] Seraucourt,[54]
And many others from this court —
All high-born men of great worth
To whom Nobility is no stranger,
And from whom she does not turn away — ,
Promptly made their way to defend this *pas*
In a manner that was both fine and pleasing:
This I saw, and so know for myself.
All was made possible by the noble means
Of King René, their earthly
Prince and natural lord,
Who spared no honours —
His wealth was not for him alone to keep — ;[55]
Upon my soul, I regard him — without blaming
Anyone else — as the very best.

24.

At present, I am no longer sure of the names
Of those on the inside team, but I resolve
To name the rest in the order in which
They fought on the days of the jousts.

---

[52] Philibert de La Jaille (d. before 1459?), was a *valet tranchant* of René (1451) who may have jousted at Nancy (1445) and definitely did joust at Tarascon (1449). Mérindol, *Les fêtes*, p. 164; PSr, p. 128.

[53] [Bromont]. Gilles de Bourmont was a chamberlain of René (1444). PSr, p. 126.

[54] [Seraucort]. Jean de Seraucourt was captain of the castle of Tarascon (1447), a *valet tranchant* (1469–70) and then a squire of the stables (1477) in René's household. PSr, p. 129.

[55] This is a way of lauding René's largesse as a prince and his awareness of needing to spend his wealth on others so as to bind them to him.

From reading[56] about how the combats were to be run,
Foreigners came in great numbers
To the secluded place
Where the hermit lived and gave them instructions.[57]
He told them about the *emprise*
Of the *Pas* and counselled each one
On how to conduct himself,
In order to win the prize and the ruby[58]
From the lady who would lead out
The one from the inside team and bring him
Into the lists, where they would joust
Joyously, with crest, helm* and trapper.

25.

From out of the noble castle, to defend it against outsiders,
Armed and glorious as an angel,
Came my lord Jean de Fénétrange,[59]
As did Honorat de Berre;[60]
Guillaume de Moullon[61] too was of their company.
All of them had fringed trappers,
Vermilion in colour. Whoever put himself forward
Will be mentioned here,
As will all the days that were appointed [for the jousts].
Whoever was granted favour or mercy,
Should not be troubled or dismayed,
For everything will be noted, by the grace of God.
Guillaume Desbans,[62] Chevigny,[63]
Godefroy:[64] none of these were daunted,

---

56 This is another explicit reference by the poet to the letter or declaration of challenge and/or the chapters of arms that would have circulated prior to the event as advance publicity for it.

57 On this detail which is only alluded to in the poem but would have been outlined in the documents publicising the event, see above, introduction, p. 82.

58 See previous note.

59 [Jehan de Fenestrange]. Jean de Fénétrange (d. 1467), a member of the Order of the Crescent (1452), jousted at Launay (1446). PSr, p. 127.

60 [Honnouret de Barre]. Honorat de Berre (d. after 1483), lord of Entrevennes, was a squire (1448, 1451), councillor-chamberlain (1469–70) and *grand maître d'hôtel* (after 1472) in René's household; he also jousted at Tarascon (1449). Mérindol, *Les fêtes*, pp. 129–30; PSr, p. 125.

61 [Guillaume de Mullon]. Guillaume de Moullon was a member of the Order of the Crescent (1448). Mérindol, *Les fêtes*, p. 176. As a guest of Duke Philip the Good of Burgundy, he was the *entrepreneur* of the *Pas du Compagnon à la Larme Blanche* held at Le Quesnoy (1458): see Source 9.

62 [Guillaume des Banx]. Guillaume Desbans was a servant of René (1453). Mérindol, *Les fêtes*, pp. 148–9.

63 [Chyvigny]. Guillaume de Chevigny (d. 1479), was associated with the house of Anjou and was a chamberlain of René's younger brother, Charles of Anjou, count of Maine. PSr, p. 126.

64 [Goddeffroy]. Godefroy de Jupeleu (d. 1467), was associated with the household of Anjou according to the accounts for 1451. PSr, p. 128.

And Carrion[65] committed himself to the hilt,
Each of them according to his rank and place.[66]

26.

With that I leave this matter,
Which remains complete,
To tell you about the judges of the *pas*
And their scribes.
Quite rightly, they did not demand too high a price
But rather, most willingly and goodheartedly,
Judged everything to the full
As experts and worthy men,
[Who are] visibly generous and honourable,
With no taint of corruption.
Their judgement did not falter,
And was proclaimed by the King of Arms,[67]
Whose speech was wholly in line with it,
Dressed as he was in his garments of vermilion;
If their ruling was not in someone's favour,
This was in line with what had occurred.

27.

But in order that by both voice and sight
The feats of arms could best be judged,
The judges were selected in the
Manner stated below:
Two knights of very high rank,
Two joyful and knowledgeable squires
Who were prudent, experienced and not too old,
And had in the past amassed
Much honour and wisdom.
One of these was the lord of Tucé,[68]

---

65 [Quarrion]. François Carrion, lord of La Grise, was a cupbearer of René. He fought as a challenger at Saumur. Mérindol, *Les fêtes*, p. 139.

66 By the end of this stanza, the *Relation* poet names all but two defenders of the *Pas* as well as one challenger, François Carrion. One of the defenders he does not name here is Messire Auvregnays (Auvregnas Champron or Chapron) who, according to Mathieu d'Escouchy, was killed during his joust with Antoine de Prie (MdE, vol. 1, p. 108). The poet refuses to say much about this, and the joust is one of three that remain unillustrated: see Essay 7, pp. 506–7. The other defender whom he does not mention in this early part of the *Relation* is Surléon Spinola de Spinolis (d. 1460), who jousted with Charles de Grolée.

67 Macé de Houssay (d. before 1467), lord of Houssay, was a councillor of René and herald of the Order of the Crescent under the name 'Los', meaning 'renown' or 'praise' (DMF). PSr, p. 124.

68 [seigneur de Tussé]. Beaudoin de Champagne, lord of Tucé, was a councillor of Charles VII (1429–38) and treasurer of Anjou (1445). PSr, p. 123.

The other, the lord of Martigné;[69]
Antoine de La Sale[70] was also there.
Harduin Fresneau[71] did not stop
Until he had also roped in
Guillaume Bernard[72] and Sablé[73]
To write about this event.

28.

All seven[74] were in the stand,
Seated together at the very top,
So as to see what was good and what less so,
And to judge it all fairly.
If the judging is not too heated,
It is good to show who is most worthy,
Since one must be fair to all
In order to eschew blame.
Many dukes, counts and barons,
Many noblemen of high lineage,
Were at the *Pas* on this occasion
To acquire honour through deeds of arms
And to rid themselves, without fail,
Of that amorous poison
Of which no one is ever cured
Without humbly entreating a lady.

29.

Thus was this *emprise* accomplished,
Conducted and carried out by prudence;
And whoever hears the rest

---

[69] [seigneur de Marthigné]. Guillaume de La Jumelière (d. before 1465), lord of Martigné-Briant, was a member of the Order of the Crescent. PSr, p. 123; Mérindol, *Les fêtes*, p. 166.

[70] [Anthoine de la Sale]. Antoine de La Sale (*c.*1386–1460), who served at the courts of Louis II and Louis III of Anjou and was the tutor of René's son, Jean of Calabria (1426–70), wrote *Jean de Saintré* (1456), a prose romance in which he describes the imagined *emprises* of his protagonist, which include a *pas d'armes*, and the *Traité des anciens et des nouveaux tournois* (1459). He attended tournaments at Nancy, Ghent and Brussels. PSr, p. 123; Antoine de La Sale, *Jehan de Saintré*, ed. by Joël Blanchard and Michel Quéreuil (Paris: Livre de Poche, 1995); *idem*, *Jean de Saintré: A Late Medieval Education in Love and Chivalry*, trans. by Roberta Krueger and Jane H. M. Taylor (Philadelphia: University of Pennsylvania Press, 2014); Michelle Szkilnik, *Jean de Saintré: une carrière chevaleresque au XVe siècle* (Geneva: Droz, 2003); and Sylvie Lefèvre, *Antoine de la Sale: la fabrique de l'œuvre et de l'écrivain. Suivi de l'édition critique du Traité des anciens et des nouveaux tournois* (Geneva: Droz, 2006).

[71] [Hardoin Fresneau]. Harduin Fresneau (d. 1448), lord of Fenolières, was a councillor of René as well as captain of the castles of Angers and Montfaucon (1448). PSr, p. 123.

[72] [Guillaume Bernart]. Guillaume Bernard was a secretary of René (1451). PSr, p. 124.

[73] [Sable]. Guillaume Gauquelin, known as Sablé (d. 1464), was a secretary of René and later head of the court of auditors for Anjou. PSr, p. 124.

[74] That is, the four judges, their two scribes and the King of Arms.

Will understand its meaning.
For a moral purpose was it conceived,
By the person who brought to fruition
This *pas* that was undertaken
As sporting entertainment.
I have written this for you rapidly
And sketchily in sections,
But afterwards you will hear about
The lady bringing out the shield,
The procession and the opening
Of the *Pas*, as well as its completion
And the honourable way in which it ended,
With the shield being taken down from the column.

30.

I beg all those who are prudent and wise,
As well as noble of heart and lineage,
To look deep into themselves
As they endure my badly written verses —
My words which lack all eloquence
And have been put together in this leafy place,
A solitary, wild spot,
Such unpolished, ignorant, and imperfect words
In sentences so badly put together — ,
And to consider that I am creating
This poem [in order to recount] the noble deeds,
The prizes awarded according to the judgement
Of those noble, perfect judges
Who were entrusted with the task and the role
Of rewarding the noble deeds performed,
The beginning of which now follows.

31.

One Sunday morning, before breakfast,
On the twenty-sixth day of June
When both nobles and commoners were present,
From out of the magnificent castle
Of Saumur, as everyone knows,
On the side towards Loudon,
And half as close again as
Half a bowshot from this castle
Which is beautiful, lavish, noble, delightful and propitious,
The shield was taken to the lists,
To be hung on the column for the purpose
Of performing feats of arms. This procession
Was extraordinary and flawless,
Being full of splendour, brilliantly organised,

Honourable, joyous and ceremonious;
Never was its like experienced before.

32.

It was a beautiful day on that morning,
For the sun was shining in a cloudless sky:
The weather was good that year,
Which made everybody happy.
Good fortune smiled down
On him who saw the orderly procession
From the castle, which was more elaborate
That anything anyone had ever seen before.
The skies were blue,
And all the elements[75] were such
That one could not have wished for better:
Everything was given over to pleasure.
First out were two old, tall,
Gruesome Saracens
Leading two ferocious lions;
Each of them held a club in his hand.

33.

Next came a squire
Mounted on a trappered destrier*,
Riding along very well in the stirrups,
And carrying a large standard.
The many heralds and minstrels,
Who are often apt to kill boredom
And keen to laud someone's honour,
Each of them with his coat armour* on,
Were a glorious sight to behold!
After them, it was not long before
There emerged from the castle
The two scribes of the judges of the *Pas*;
Each of them held in his hand
The paper on which he would write down
The deeds of arms that would be performed
On the days appointed for this purpose.

34.

Then, out from inside came
The four presiding judges —

---

[75] The four elements that were thought in the medieval period to make up all physical matter below the heavens were imagined as concentric circles, with the earth in the middle surrounded by water, air and fire, respectively. DMF.

All of them noble, knowledgeable, virtuous and prudent — ,
In very honourable and fine array,
As I mentioned previously in the
Corresponding chapters
On this matter, for they knew well
How to make a glorious start
To this joyous and incomparable *pas*.
A long and distinguished garment of vermilion
Was worn by each of them,
And each held a white baton in his hand.[76]
Their judgements were deemed very trustworthy
Once arrived at, and very reasonable;
They favoured no one,
Except when it was appropriate to do so.

35.

Next came trumpets and clarions:
Through the castle, down to the river, up to the hills and mountains
Their sounds rang out,
So sweet was their melody.
[They were] followed by counts and barons,
[On] destriers spurred greatly on
Through these gates and over these bridges;
Never was such immense joy
Ever seen, no matter what one says.
No one came out in confusion,
But rather all took great care
To sally forth in good order.
If I am mistaken, may whoever saw it
And thinks I have misspoken
Dare to contradict me on this point,
For I never saw such a thing in France.

36.

At the sound of these clarions made all of metal,[77]
A dwarf, dressed in cloth of gold,
Came out, wearing a turban on his head like a Moor.
He was mounted on a beautiful hackney*
And held his mace in his hand; what's more,

---

[76] The white baton signalled the judges' authority at these events.

[77] The text specifies that these instruments were 'sans cor' (without horn), i.e. of metal alone, hence the translation; this choice of material may have been because the all-metal instrument was louder than one partly made of horn. It may also serve to make a distinction between these instruments and the horn which the dwarf himself uses to signal to the defenders in the castle that a challenge has been made. On this aspect of the dwarf, see Essay 2, p. 379, and Figure 16 reproduced on p. 381, for an image of him performing this action; on the dwarf more generally, see Essay 7.

He cut a swath through those who were the finest
In honour and arms because
He had [with him] the lovely damsel,
The maiden who was young, wise and high-born,
A noble and joyful young girl,
Who, as she sat in the saddle, held in her arms
The shield to be put on the column,
One strewn with that freshly blooming flower
That is known as the pansy.
She was dressed in this livery
That was apt for the season of the *Pas*.

37.

Ferry, the worthy and the valiant in arms,
Who conducted himself most honourably
In defending the *pas* in a loyal and steadfast fashion,
Was armed in his full harness*.
Tancarville[78] did not shed a tear
But rather was most joyful, and was put into
His harness by those closest to him.
He was a gentle*, agreeable and courteous count,
— Such is how I have known him for some time — ,
And was on the outside* team on this occasion.
That first day of the jousts and of this tournament
Was opened by these two.
Beauvau and Jean Cossa, I saw,
And Ferry, first of all; these three truly,
Along with King René, upheld the mission
Of the *Pas* with great honour.

38.

Richly dressed
Was the damsel, and riding
On a white hackney
With a great [horse-]harness* [laden with] *orfèvrerie**;
She sat her mount well and was finely turned out
With a very noble company.
She was led that day by [her horse's] bridle
That was held by a large and noble body of squires of the stable;
After her came a large gathering

[78] Guillaume d'Harcourt, count of Tancarville, was viscount of Melun, constable and hereditary chamberlain of Normandy and a royal councillor (1436–51); he was also minister of waters and forests in France (1452–61) and seneschal of Anjou (1473). He was a challenger at Saumur and at Launay (1446), a defender at Chinon/Razilly (1446) and sole defender at Bourges (1447). His daughter, Jeanne d'Harcourt, married René's grandson, René II. PSr, p. 144; Mérindol, *Les fêtes*, pp. 162–3; HGFMO, p. 201.

Of ladies and knights;
Nobility was truly there in force.
She made a circuit of the lists,
Then, with a joyful expression, placed the shield
On the column, with the dwarf's help.
She commanded him to guard it
With his life, both day and night.

39.

The agitated lions
Were attached to the column;
Two Saracens were ensconced nearby
As experts charged with guarding them,
For they sometimes stood up and other times lay down.
They were not released from there
Nor unleashed from their chains
Until the shield was taken away.
In addition, the dwarf was sent back
To the pavilion which had been promised him.
His eyes did not shut
As he watched over everything with great care,
Fearing that his enemies
Would create trouble;
He had been ordered to do this
By Mademoiselle de Blâmont.[79]

40.

Then, without another word, you would have witnessed
Trumpets and clarions sounding as they
Called everyone to return,
In the same fashion as that in which they had come,
Back to the castle for dinner.
In the belfry, the standard was given
To the Saracens, who were ordered to
Place it right on top in the wind
As a signal to everyone, both high and low,
That if anyone came to the lists
Armed and not unequipped
In order to touch the shield on the column,
Those in the belfry were to
Sound the horn until

---

[79] [ma damoiselle de Blancmont]. This probably refers to Isabelle de Blâmont, daughter of Thiébaut II de Blâmont (d. 1431), and his wife, Marguerite de Lorraine, sister of Antoine de Vaudémont; Isabelle later married Jean de La Haye, lord of Passavant and Mortaigne (1449). PSr, p. 146; <http://www.blamont.info/textes482.html> [accessed 18 June 2024].

One of the best of the inside team was brought out
To defend the shield.

41.

Into the castle returned His Highness,
King René, with his nobles.
A most lavish dinner was made ready
And brought in with great ceremony.
There was the noble princess,
Queen Isabelle,[80] the only pathway
Towards honour without end,
Ever eager to offer a kind welcome,
Being beautiful and virtuous, noble and joyful;
In that great spacious hall,
That was full of her splendid family,
She received people with great charm
And no presumptuousness.
Her manner was not in the least unpleasant,
And her speech was most gracious,
As all those present attested.

42.

The castle abounded in great joy
And in cries of 'Largesse!'; the very pinnacle
Of honour held sway there
Over all other worldly pleasures.
I believe that never did I hear
Such demonstrations of joy,
Nor have I heard the high nobility so joyful,
As I am asserting with great confidence here.
Ladies were there in abundance,
Whom I did not know,
Except for the very flower of France:
[This is] my lady of Beauvau,[81] who is so-called
By high edict and authority;
She is [so] marvellously full of virtue,
That all live in hope
Of her receiving the foretold grace [of God].

---

80 [Ysabeau, royne]. Isabelle of Lorraine (1400/10–53), daughter of Charles II, duke of Lorraine, and Margaret of Bavaria, married René of Anjou (1420); she was also duchess of Bar (1420–28, and again 1445–58), duchess of Lorraine (1431–53) and queen of Naples (1435–53). She is mentioned as being in attendance at Tarascon (1449). PSr, pp. 145–6.

81 Marguerite de Chambley (d. 1456), lady of Beauvau, was the wife of Louis de Beauvau, a defender at Saumur and author of the poem recounting the *Pas de la Bergère* (see above, n. 37). PSr, p. 146.

43.

In this castle where true love
Was reputed [to reside] without any vile outcry,
Discontent, disagreement, or other rumour,
[Dwelt] these high-born ladies
And damsels of great honour,
[Who were] beautiful, virtuous and worthy,
With neither reproach nor other folly,
[Being] noble, joyful, untarnished by any faults;
Such prudent and loyal women
That, if I had one hundred thousand souls,
For their love I would set them all ablaze
With the bitter fires of burning desire
So as to shame all those disgraceful people,
Who are gossipmongers full of slanders,
Murderers of honour, renown and reputation,
Who take pleasure in speaking badly [of others].

44.

Loyal Lady Renown,
Who has such goodness in her, is so loved by her own,
And is considered by everyone else
To be very humble, compassionate and wise,
Endowed with reason,
Acclaimed as most charitable,
Famed for her generosity,
Gentle and eloquent in speech
In accordance with wise teaching
And unwavering in reply,
Of fine appearance and decorous conduct
In both words and deeds:
She was present at this *pas*
From the first to the fortieth day,
For that was how long it lasted, as I understand it,
Except for every Friday.

45.

My lady Yolande[82] was there,
Daughter of this excellent prince
Who, with no reluctance whatsoever,
Was chief *entrepreneur* of the *Pas*.

---

[82] [ma dame Yollant]. Yolande of Anjou (1428–84), lady of Vaudémont, the eldest daughter of René of Anjou and Isabelle of Lorraine, was married to Ferry II de Vaudémont-Lorraine, the grand prizewinner at Saumur (1445). She inherited the duchy of Lorraine after the death of René's grandson, Nicolas of Anjou, and ceded it to her son, René II of Lorraine. PSr, p. 146.

To tell the truth,
Many noblemen were not slow
To accomplish their goals there
And to partake of this dish of honour.
It did not disappoint as a *pardon d'armes*,[83]
Because never at Saint-Jacques du Haut Pas[84]
Where from Paris one goes at a leisurely pace,
Was there ever so much worldly joy
Or refined pleasure to be had
As at this event,
Where no one died
In a fit of madness or sudden rage.

46.
At the dinner, the benediction
Was given by the bishop
Of Orange[85] with great solemnity,
In honour and fear of God.
The poor, reduced to begging,
Whom one could see were in adversity,
Were provided for
By the king without stinting.
With many rich tapestries
The hall was decorated and adorned;
Magnificent tableware made of
Gold and silver was displayed on those high daises.
Many ballads and laments —
Some in solace, some in sorrow — ,
Were composed there without constraint,
As well as rondeaux[86] and satirical songs.

47.
At the doors stood the officers
Of arms and others
Whose role was to bear arms or uphold justice,

---

83 It is not clear why the term *pardon d'armes* is used here instead of *pas d'armes*, but it is also found in Antoine de La Sale's *Traité des anciens et des nouveaux tournois*; it seems to have the connotation of a festivity where an indulgence could be obtained. Lefèvre, *Antoine de la Sale*, p. 336.

84 A church in Paris on the rue Saint-Jacques, which was on the pilgrimage route to Santiago de Compostela.

85 [l'evesque … d'Orenge]. Antonio Bretone (Ferrier) (d. 1450) was bishop of Sant'Agata de' Goti, Italy (1437), archbishop of Sorrento (1440), archbishop of Orange, France (1442), and bishop of Orange, France. He belonged to René and Isabelle's circle of confidants and was chaplain of the Order of the Crescent (1451). PSr, p. 146.

86 A poem of ten or thirteen lines with only two rhymes throughout and with the opening words used twice as a refrain.

Chamberlains and butlers,
Noble barons and knights,
High-ranking squires of the stables,
Cupbearers too, and pantlers*,
Each according to his rank; as well as
All those who best know how to run a court.
All were happy and joyful,
And ready to give service wherever needed.
There was great joy and celebration
On this day that did not disappoint;
The pleasures it afforded were such
That I do not think, here below the heavens,
Such delights can be found today on earth.

48.

At the dinner, grandly and honourably seated,
Were the king
And the queen,
As well as others, as was only fitting.
The household officers took every care
To serve in a fine and proper manner
The large quantities of wines and meats;
Every person there felt themselves content.
The royal estate was maintained,
As honour demanded,
And upheld with great magnificence
In that spacious hall
That befitted a great king.
He gave of his wealth to everybody,
But his all to the nobility in particular,
With a joyful and happy countenance.

49.

When the dinner was over, out came
Many beautiful ladies,
And many noble knights, as I recall,
Over to their stands which were set up and enclosed
With the judges of the *Pas* who
Had been entrusted with ending disputes
And reaching agreements concerning it.
All around at the top of the stands
Was drapery well attached by nails,
But which was open on the side where the jousters were
And could close again behind them.
On this day that the *Pas* opened,
No destriers would be given any rest,
And no lances would remain unused!

Many worthy men, mark my words,
Amassed great honour there.

50.

I very much want to tell you
The names of those
Who came to the *Pas* to joust
Against those who were there to defend it, and to tell how
Feared they were for their strength and might,
And all so deserving of mention.
I will recount, without abasing one or exalting another,
But rather according to the days on which they fought,
How the challengers came out of the hermitage[87]
Where they put on their armour,
When they wanted to strike the shield
To make those from inside the castle come out;
Which helm, which crest they wore,
Which lance, which trapper they bore,
Which destrier they rode on that day:
It is writing that makes memory last.

51.

From the place arranged outside the town
Came the count of Tancarville,
He who awakens all pleasure:
He wore a splendid harness
And rode a large destrier from Seville.
This mount was very agile and able,
And wore an appropriate trapper,
The colour of which I cannot state
For indeed, I could not find out, but before long
I will make enquiries to do so,
And will supply this information later.
Merrily he came into the lists,
Accompanied in marvellous style.
There he did not waste much time,
As he quickly found his purpose.

52.

He came to attack the shield and
Knocked it off, turning it upside down.
The lions snorted like bears
And the dwarf began to make a lot of noise.

[87] On this detail, which is only alluded to in the poem but would have been outlined in the documents publicising the event, see above, introduction, p. 82.

The outcry from the towers was immense,
With the trumpets and drums
Never ceasing to sound out,
For they seemed very agitated,
And the noise in the castle would not die down.
It was not long at all before
A young, lovely and courtly
Lady, joyfully dressed in rich attire
All in the French style,
Stated her view of this outrageous behaviour
As she went over to the dwarf to make her complaint
And demand that this affront be avenged.

53.

Then you would have seen the dwarf
Ride up to the gates of the castle and call out
Bravely, without fear,
To humbly request that the lady
Quickly avenge the shield
That she had attached to the column.
A strange warrior had knocked it
Right down to the ground
And headed out to the lists alone.
For this reason he had come to find her
To ask for immediate help.
He could not keep this news to himself
And said that if he didn't die from it before long,
He would win great honour [for the lady],
Or a diamond,[88] for the trouble.

54.

At this sound, my lord Ferry,
Who was full of joy and not at all dismayed,
Said: 'This news just makes me laugh!
I must serve the pansy flowers
And the ladies who have nurtured me.
May my will never falter
For I would rather rot in hell
Than that they not be picked up,
Whoever it was that knocked them down.'
They were not left long on the ground
Before he picked them up.
His destrier was covered in vermilion,

[88] On this detail, which is only alluded to in the poem but would have been outlined in the documents publicising the event, see above, introduction, p. 82.

This being the livery of the *Pas*,[89]
With flowers scattered on the shield, as described above,
That shone in the sunlight.

55.

Inside the castle, mounted
On a white hackney
Decorated with rich *orfèvrerie*,
On that day, was Mademoiselle
De Blâmont; she was well turned out,
Being dressed in the vermilion livery
Of the *Pas*, with a fresh and joyful air.
Below her breast was a fine cord
By which the noble lady, who was both pleasing and beautiful,
Held my lord Ferry at her side.
He, on his destrier, armed and ready
With helm and crest, was already in the saddle,
His lance in his hand, about to fight
For the pansy flowers that she wore
On behalf of King René.

56.

Then the gates were opened,
The bridges lowered by experts
And all the paths cleared,
From the way out of the royal castle.
Clarions called out with great fervour
So that the feats of arms might be acknowledged,
These being crowned with honour,
Free will and generosity.
Next, out came the dwarf on his horse
Who headed downhill
Along a particular path;
This was in front of the lady who was leading
Her special champion,
Ferry de Lorraine, who,
Loyally and whole-heartedly, defended the *Pas*
Against the challengers in the lists.

57.

On that day, these two adventurers,
Mounted and armed in the lists
And accompanied by their kinsmen,

---

[89] The defenders of the *Pas* all wore the same motif on their and their horses' bodies — that is, pansies on a vermilion field — but they wore their own family crests on their helms.

Let their destriers run.
Ferry represented those from the inside team
And Tancarville those from the outside.
The lady and the dwarf waited
To see who would come out on top.
You would have seen lances strike hard
And break at every charge,
As help was nobly given to defending the flowers.
The lady then humbly came forth,
As the courses finished, to ask
That the judges reward
The one who had acquired honour
In the most gracious fashion.

58.

It was ordered by the judges
Appointed by King René,
That the prize be given
To the one who had performed most valiantly.
The damsel, with great joy, brought
Her champion crowned with glory
Back to the castle, to the sound
Of the clarions.
Accompanying her back to the castle
Was the dwarf, who rode before her
And was richly dressed in cloth of gold.
In the belfry there was immense agitation
Far more than from the blows of a hammer!

Thanks are due to Michelle Szkilnik for her assistance with deciphering and translating parts of this narrative account, and to Craig Taylor for helping to supply biographical information on the competitors at this event.

Rosalind Brown-Grant and Christina Normore

Source 6

The *Pas de la Bergère* (*Pas* of the Shepherdess), Tarascon, 1449

This source consists of a discussion of the frontispiece of the unique manuscript in which the verse narrative account of this *pas* is preserved and a translation of both this poem and extracts from a financial account related to the event.

Author: (1) of the narrative account: Louis de Beauvau; (2) of the financial account: unknown

Language: Middle French, for both the narrative and financial accounts

Editions used:

(1) for the narrative account: Harry F. Williams, '*Le Pas de la Bergère.* A Critical Edition', *Fifteenth Century Studies*, 17 (1990), 485–513 (= PB); see also Georges Adrien Crapelet, ed., *Le pas d'armes de la bergère maintenu au tournoi de Tarascon* (Paris: Crapelet, 1828) (= PAB).

(2) for the financial account: Albert Lecoy de la Marche, ed., *Extraits des comptes et mémoriaux du roi René, pour servir à l'histoire des arts au XVe siècle, publiés d'après les originaux des Archives nationales* (Paris: Société de l'École des Chartes, 1873), pp. 324–7 (= ECMR).

Select bibliography:

Avril, François, and Nicole Reynaud, eds, *Les manuscrits à peintures en France 1440–1520* (Paris: Bibliothèque nationale, 1993)

Bianciotto, Gabriel, ed., *Le Roman de Troyle*, 2 vols (Rouen: Publications de l'Université de Rouen, 1994), vol. 1

Hüe, Denis, 'La Bergère et le tournoyeur, coutumes et costumes des parades amoureuses à la cour d'Anjou-Provence', in *Les arts et les lettres en Provence au temps du Roi René*, ed. by Chantal Connochie-Bourgne and Valérie Gontero-Lauze (Aix-en-Provence: Presses Universitaires de Provence, 2013), pp. 243–59

Launet, Charles de, 'Un curieux tournoi: le pas d'armes de la Bergère tenu au tournoi de Tarascon', *Hidalguia*, 35 (1987), 193–203

Lecoy de la Marche, Albert, *Le roi René: sa vie, son administration, ses travaux artistiques et littéraires*, 2 vols (Paris: Librairie de Firmin-Didot frères, fils et cie, 1875)

Mérindol, Christian de, *Les fêtes de chevalerie à la cour du roi René. Emblématique, art et histoire (les joutes de Nancy, le Pas de Saumur et le Pas de Tarascon)* (Paris: Éditions du CTHS, 1993)

Taylor, Jane H. M., '"Une gente pastourelle": René d'Anjou, Louis de Beauvau et le Pas d'armes de la bergère', in *René d'Anjou, écrivain et mécène (1409–1480)*, ed. by Florence Bouchet (Turnhout: Brepols, 2011), pp. 197–208

INTRODUCTION

This *pas d'armes* took place either in or near to the castle of Tarascon, which was located in the centre of the town of the same name and next to the River Rhône, about 22 km south of Avignon (Provence). The jousts were held over three days on 3–8 June 1449, with a rest day between each one. The *entrepreneurs* of the event were Philippe de Lenoncourt and Philibert de Laigue, both of whom were high-ranking nobles at the court of René of Anjou, who was at that time count of Provence. The two *entrepreneurs* took it in turns to joust against the eighteen challengers, all of whom were closely connected to the Angevin court and around half of whom had already competed at the *Pas de la Joyeuse Garde/Pas de Saumur* that René had organised near the castle of Saumur in 1446.[1] Many of them had also competed at other tournaments, often referred to as *pas d'armes*, that took place either in the Angevin sphere, as at Nancy (1445) and Launay (1446), or in the kingdom of France, as at Châlons-sur Marne (1445), Chinon/Razilly (1446) and Bourges (1447).[2] As happened at Saumur, the outright winner of the jousts at the *Pas de la Bergère* was judged to be Ferry II de Vaudémont-Lorraine, René's son-in-law.

Unlike the majority of *pas d'armes*, which are loosely based on motifs and/or characters from Arthurian or chivalric romances, this particular tournament draws on the pastoral tradition, which could take both dramatic form, as in Adam de la Halle's late thirteenth-century play *Le Jeu de Robin et Marion*, and lyric form, as in the many *pastourelle* poems, dating from the same century, that were written by *trouvères* such as Thibaut de Champagne and Jacques de Cambrai.[3] Central to this pastoral tradition is the idea of a rural idyll, one inhabited by shepherds and shepherdesses who sing and dance together, which is disturbed when a knight comes across an attractive shepherdess in the fields and makes advances to her. The shepherdess either rebuffs the knight with her witty remarks and/or threats to set her fellow shepherds (including her own lover) on him, lets herself be seduced by him or even suffers rape at his hands; once the knight has gone on his way, the shepherds resume their merry-making. The *Bergère* retains only a few elements from this tradition: the lady in whose defence the *pas* is being fought is presented as a shepherdess; the two defenders, Lenoncourt and Laigue, are disguised as shepherds, and all the challengers are either knights or squires. Whilst the shepherdess in this *pas* is still, arguably, a kind of sexual bait

---

1 PSr; and Christian de Mérindol, *Les fêtes de chevalerie à la cour du roi René. Emblématique, art et histoire (les joutes de Nancy, le Pas de Saumur et le Pas de Tarascon)* (Paris: Éditions du CTHS, 1993).

2 Albert Lecoy de la Marche, *Le roi René: sa vie, son administration, ses travaux artistiques et littéraires*, 2 vols (Paris: Librairie de Firmin-Didot frères, fils et cie, 1875); and Berlin, Staatsbibliothek, Preußischer Kulturbesitz, Ham. 606, a recently rediscovered manuscript of Guillaume Leseur's *Histoire de Gaston IV, comte de Foix*, which thus supplements the material in HGF and HGFMO. The tournament at Launay is known as the *Pas du Géant à la Blanche Dame du Pavillon*, that held between Chinon and Razilly as the *Pas de la Gueule du Dragon/Pas du Rocher Périlleux*, and that at Bourges as the *Pas du Chevalier Aventureux*. For an overview of these events, see the Table of *pas d'armes*, pp. 25–7. For a translation of the narrative accounts of the various *pas d'armes* covered in Leseur's manuscript, see Supplementary Source 1, Liverpool University Press Digital Collaboration Hub <https://liverpooluniversitypress.manifoldapp.org/projects/pas-d-armes-casebook> [accessed 1 November 2024].

3 Joël Blanchard, *La pastorale en France aux XIVe et XVe siècles: Recherches sur les structures de l'imaginaire médiéval* (Paris: Honoré Champion, 1983); William Paden, *The Medieval Pastourelle* (New York: Garland, 1987); Geri L. Smith, *The Medieval French Pastourelle Tradition: Poetic Motivations and Generic Transformations* (Gainesville: University Press of Florida, 2009).

for knights, as she rewards the victorious challengers' efforts in the joust with a gold ring, a bouquet of flowers and a kiss, this aspect of the pastoral tradition is nonetheless treated in a very adulterated and courtly fashion, it being made very clear that all of the people playing these roles belong to the nobility, not to the lower classes.

The narrative account of this *pas* is also highly unusual in having been written up not by a herald or a chronicler who witnessed it at firsthand but rather by a nobleman, an illustrious jouster in his own right who competed in it and presumably composed his account shortly afterwards. This is Louis de Beauvau, seneschal of Anjou, who was also the author of the *Roman de Troyle et Criseida* (*c.*1453–55), a translation of Giovanni Boccaccio's *Il Filostrato.*[4] He addressed the work to Louis de Luxembourg, count of Saint-Pol, for reasons that must remain speculative. For example, Beauvau's dedication (lines 1–24) links the *Bergère* to earlier events such as that at Saumur through the supposed questions asked by Luxembourg, who, despite having a very strong reputation as a jouster such as at Nancy (1445) where he was a defender, fought at neither Saumur nor Tarascon and may therefore have wished to be kept informed of how these Angevin tournaments had been conducted; Luxembourg himself was an ally of René of Anjou, his daughter Isabelle de Luxembourg having married Charles of Anjou, René's brother, in 1444.

Like the narrative account of the *Joyeuse Garde/Saumur* and much of the courtly literature that came out of the Angevin court, the text commemorating this event is written in verse; in this instance, ninety *douzains* (twelve-line stanzas) of decasyllabic verse that use an *abab bccd dede* rhyme scheme. Beauvau, being both a jouster and a man of proven literary abilities, may have used this rather unusual rhyme scheme and lyric form, which are not generally attested in narrative works before 1450, to associate symbolically this story of combat with the world of courtliness that the lyric tradition both celebrates and embodies.[5] Furthermore, whilst the text's focus on the challengers' appearance as they enter the lists, the number of lances broken and the prizes awarded is otherwise fairly typical of *pas d'armes* narratives, it also differs from them in one key aspect of its literary style which it borrows from the pastoral tradition: namely, the somewhat precious use of diminutives (*chosettes*, *doucettement*, etc.) to describe the shepherdess and her accoutrements.

The text is preserved in a single manuscript containing one illumination (see below) and may be an autograph by the author.[6] The translation of it that follows after the discussion of the manuscript and illustrative tradition of the text is in blank verse, which, for ease of reference to the original as contained in Williams' edition, uses the same stanza and line numbering; it also attempts, as far as possible, to render the sense of the original line by line whilst obviously having to make some allowances at times for the differences between Middle French and modern English syntax.

This translation of the narrative account is followed by that of payments recorded in René of Anjou's financial accounts for 3–13 June 1449 which shed important light on the actual organisation of the *Bergère*. These payments concern services rendered by musicians and heralds at the event as well as items produced by various artisans such as armourers

[4] Gabriel Bianciotto, ed., *Le Roman de Troyle*, 2 vols (Rouen: Publications de l'Université de Rouen, 1994), vol. 1.

[5] Denis Hüe, 'La Bergère et le tournoyeur, coutumes et costumes des parades amoureuses à la cour d'Anjou-Provence', in *Les arts et les lettres en Provence au temps du Roi René*, ed. by Chantal Connochie-Bourgne and Valérie Gontero-Lauze (Aix-en-Provence: Presses Universitaires de Provence, 2013), pp. 243–59.

[6] Paris, BnF, fr. 1974, vellum, twenty-four fols (forty-eight modern pages).

and tailors that were gifted by René to some of the high-ranking people and their servants who took part in it. In particular, the fabrics mentioned in these accounts show, somewhat paradoxically, that no expense was spared in the making of the outfits of those characters of supposedly humble origin, such as the two shepherd-defenders of the *Pas* and the eponymous shepherdess herself. Moreover, the entry for 11 June 1449 concerning the expensive grey damask used for the 'shepherdess's gown' reveals that it was Isabelle de Lenoncourt — probably a sister or daughter of Philippe de Lenoncourt — who played this key role in the event, even though she is not named in the poem.[7] This information gives the lie to the idea sometimes held by scholars that the shepherdess was played by Jeanne de Laval (1433–98), René of Anjou's mistress, who later became his second wife (1454) after the death of his first wife, Isabelle of Lorraine (1453).[8]

Above all, perhaps, these accounts attest to René's generous sponsorship of this *pas d'armes*, even if Louis de Beauvau in his narrative refers to him only as 'the king' and gives no indication that he was the inspiration for this event, Lenoncourt and Laigue being explicitly named as the two *entrepreneurs*. In the context of this specific *pas d'armes*, René's involvement can be seen to be comparable to that of the Burgundian duke Philip the Good, who, despite not being identified in either the narrative or financial records as an *entrepreneur* of particular events such as Jacques de Lalaing's *Pas de la Fontaine des Pleurs* (Chalon-sur-Saône, 1449–50) was nonetheless a very active and enthusiastic supporter of them.[9] For ease of reference in this translation of the financial accounts, page numbers have been given in parentheses to Lecoy de la Marche's edition; numbers in bold are those he gives to the entries in the account.

IMAGE

Paris, BnF, fr. 1974, the sole manuscript of Louis de Beauvau's poetic recounting of the *Pas de la Bergère*, the first page of which is reproduced here (Figure 4), was probably written shortly after the event. At twenty-four folios, it is short for a luxury manuscript of the period and contains only the poem and a single initial miniature (fol. 1r). Despite its limited length, the physical details of the manuscript indicate that the text was considered important by its creators and that the manuscript was intended as a gift from the author Louis de Beauvau to Louis de Luxembourg, count of Saint-Pol, a fellow noble and tournament aficionado.[10]

The manuscript shows signs of both thoughtful planning and execution. The twenty-four folios are divided into three quires each containing eight sheets of vellum: the first and last page each have a single stanza, while all other pages contain two stanzas. The

[7] ECMR, p. 324 n. 2.

[8] PAB, p. 41. This suggestion about Jeanne de Laval is influenced by a text written between 1454 and 1461 recounting the love between a shepherd and shepherdess entitled *Regnault et Jehanneton* that is sometimes attributed to René, who supposedly dedicated it to her, an attribution confirmed in the most recent edition of it: see Gilles Roussineau, ed. and trans., *Regnault et Jeanneton*, Textes littéraires français, 610 (Geneva: Droz, 2012). A final piece of evidence that militates against seeing Jeanne as the shepherdess at this *pas* is that René's first wife, Isabelle, is explicitly mentioned at the end of the poem as attending the post-combat feast (line 1050).

[9] Lecoy de la Marche, *Le roi René*.

[10] Sylvie Lefèvre, *Antoine de la Sale: la fabrique de l'œuvre et de l'écrivain. Suivi de l'édition critique du Traité des anciens et des nouveaux tournois* (Geneva: Droz, 2006), pp. 242–3.

Figure 4. Miniature of the Shepherdess with her flock and the black and white shields struck to summon the defenders; additional marginal illumination and decorated initials with insignia of Louis de Beauvau and Louis de Luxembourg. *Pas de la Bergère*. Paris, BnF, fr. 1974, fol. 1r. Photo: BnF.

handwritten letters are highly regular throughout (a difficult feat for an untrained scribe) and the text contains minimal abbreviations and errors. Although only one page was decorated, these more prosaic elements indicate the care that was put into the planning of the object as a whole.

The only illustrated page performs a great deal of work within the span of a space measuring a mere 19.7 x 14.28 cm. Both the large miniature at the top of the text block and the elaborate marginal decorations are attributed to Barthélemy d'Eyck, one of the most important painters working at the court of René, duke of Anjou.[11] As his surname suggests, Barthélemy was probably born in modern Belgium and his artistic approach is closely aligned with that of artists such as Jan van Eyck, who were predominantly based in the Burgundian Netherlands. Much of his extant work is found in manuscripts and is characterised not only by his naturalism but also by a close connection between compositional details and text. In keeping with this general approach, the miniature here depicting the *Pas*'s titular shepherdess aligns with the descriptions given of the setting of the joust by Louis de Beauvau. As in the narrative and administrative accounts, the 'shepherdess' wears an upscale version of traditional shepherdess garb, including a dark-coloured dress (here of meticulously rendered patterned damask), embroidered side pouch and hood. In a court culture where the quality of cloth was a key marker of social hierarchy, the actress's aristocratic status is suggested both by the quality of her garments and the luxurious pillows on which she sits. She is shown crafting the bouquets that she will give to the winners of the competition, an activity mentioned in the accompanying poem (line 123) that echoes the frequent visual depictions of shepherdesses handling or crafting garlands in manuscripts from the first half of the fifteenth century.[12] At the right stands the tree with the black and white shields that challengers would use to summon the two knights. In an extra-textual detail, the flock of sheep penned in the background are likewise shown as black and white.

In addition to setting the scene for the competition that will be described below, the first folio also visually signals the fact that this manuscript was meant to be a gift, an object that created a bond between the giver and receiver. Just as the participants in tournaments often wore costumes that featured their heraldry and personal emblems, Louis de Beauvau and Louis de Luxembourg are represented through a series of heraldic and para-heraldic signs in this manuscript.[13] Some of these signs would have been instantly legible at the time, others were obscure even then and would have required more intimate knowledge of the two men to be understood. The noble status and lineage of the two men was most clearly indicated by their coats of arms, both of which appear here. Louis de Beauvau's arms are prominently placed at the centre of the bottom margin, a location where the coats of arms of a patron or owner often appear on manuscripts of all types in this period. Louis de Luxembourg's coat of arms appears in the first letter of the text, another common location for an owner's arms or portrait. While this shield is smaller than that of Beauvau, other signs signal Louis de Luxembourg's significance. Although now dark and difficult

---

[11] François Avril and Nicole Reynaud, eds, *Les manuscrits à peintures en France 1440–1520* (Paris: Bibliothèque nationale, 1993), pp. 224–37; Nicole Reynaud, 'Barthélemy d'Eyck avant 1450', *Revue de l'Art*, 84 (1989), 22–43.

[12] Leslie C. Jones and Jonathan J. G. Alexander, 'The Annunciation to the Shepherdess', *Studies in Iconography*, 24 (2003), 165–98 (pp. 166–74).

[13] Avril and Reynaud, *Les manuscrits à peintures*, p. 231.

to decipher as a result of the degradation of the pigments used, the central lion rampant would have once been a vibrant red that stood out clearly against the cooler surrounding colours. The use of blue and gold to frame the arms would also have pointed to their prestige. These expensive pigments were commonly used to highlight the importance of a word or phrase: the names of the most significant holidays in the calendars of the most luxurious Books of Hours, for instance, might be written in either blue or gold.[14] Here, the blue and gold C is the first letter of the word *comte* (count), which is both the first word of the poem and Louis de Luxembourg's title.

This official heraldic symbolism was paired with additional common forms of courtly self-representation that were more difficult to understand. The widespread use of personal colours, emblems/devices and mottoes in late medieval courts was a crucial means by which nobles expressed their individuality, often in enigmatic terms that could be deciphered only if the observer already knew the individual well. This intimate knowledge and personal attention were seen as signs of allegiance, making emblems a powerful way for nobles to connect with each other.[15] For example, Louis de Beauvau's arms are here accompanied by his personal motto *Sans departir*, a grammatically awkward phrase that suggests he is loyal (never leaving or renouncing) but leaves unspoken to whom or to what he is devoted: their identity could only have been known by Beauvau's close confidants. Similarly, Louis de Luxembourg is represented through one of his personal emblems in the highly naturalistic images of blue and black tassels that fill the margins, a symbol whose precise meaning is now lost.

Translation (1): Narrative account

1.

Gentle* count and most noble lord
Louis de Luxembourg,[16] to whom by reason
Power and honour are attributed:
From Lusignan,[17] that ancient house,
You are extracted, and from which
Also came emperors of Germany,
Many kings of Cyprus and many kings of Bohemia.
By nobility, by prowess and by valour,

---

[14] For an example of this in the manuscript of a Book of Hours owned by René of Anjou and partially illuminated by Barthélemy d'Eyck, see London, BL, Egerton 1070, fols 6r–11v.

[15] Susan Crane, *Performance of the Self* (Philadelphia: University of Pennsylvania Press, 2002), pp. 15–20.

[16] [Loÿs de Lucembourc]. Louis de Luxembourg (1418–75), count of Saint-Pol, Ligny and Conversan, was a councillor of King Charles VII and was knighted by the dauphin, Louis, after the siege of Dieppe (1443); he jousted at both Nancy and Châlons-sur-Marne (1445). PAB, p. 109; Mérindol, *Les fêtes*, p. 165. He was also a councillor-chamberlain of Philip the Good (1438–49) and, although he refused membership of the Order of the Golden Fleece (1445), he played an active role in Philip's army in the Ghent war (1451–53) and made his vow at the Feast of the Pheasant (1454); he also participated in the Burgundian *Pas du Perron Fée* (Bruges, 1463). PCB no. 697; VdF no. 138.

[17] The Lusignans were a noble family of Poitou (a province of western France) that provided numerous crusaders and kings of Jerusalem, Cyprus and Lesser Armenia.

Among the knights of France
By your very person you show yourself
Whether in feast, in joust or in arms *à outrance**,
To be skilled and expert, worthy of praise and honour.

2.

All fine and glorious exploits you relish
Hearing about, as well as great undertakings,
And this I know, because you asked me once
About the *Pas* and the wonderful combats
That at Saumur were so brilliantly undertaken[18]
And performed by many a nobleman
Who valiantly fought in the jousts,
By the grace of the Almighty Creator.
I, who am all yours and your servant in all things,
Louis de Beauvau, seneschal of Anjou,[19]
Send you herewith a work written by a minor author,[20]
Though I scarcely know where [to].[21]

3.

For I have long been a servant to Love
And to all ladies in Love's name,
Without making any great complaint or lament
And without suffering too much in this pursuit.
My pleasure has tended to this end,
As you well know, and also to the actions
That in this matter have been performed by me.
True it is that by the most pleasant delight
Of a happy hour when I sprang out of bed,
Which well and truly took possession of me,
A sudden desire seized me
Which I was then beholden to fulfil.

4.

Just as joyfulness of spirit
Leads gentle hearts where it pleases

---

[18] On the *Pas de la Joyeuse Garde/Pas de Saumur*, see the Table of *pas d'armes*, p. 27, Essays 2 and 7, and Source 5.

[19] [Loÿs]. Louis I de Beauvau (*c.*1418–62/3), lord of Beauvau and Sermaise in Anjou, was a councillor-chamberlain of René of Anjou, a member of René's Order of the Crescent (1448) and seneschal of Anjou (*c.*1458). He competed for King Charles VII's team at Nancy (1445) and was a defender at Châlons-sur-Marne (1445), but jousted for René's team at Saumur (1446) and was a defender at Launay (1446); he also fought at Chinon/Razilly (1446). Mérindol, *Les fêtes*, pp. 126–8; PSr, p. 125.

[20] The author here refers to himself self-deprecatingly, using a classic humility topos, as he also does at the end of the poem (see below, lines 1077–80).

[21] The precise meaning of this line is somewhat obscure.

But yet no good intention is lost,
I managed to persuade Ferry, my lord of Lorraine,[22]
With great delight
And without any ill intention, trouble or dismay,
To announce a combat for the first of May
Just gone, a joust for all comers
Which was so appealing to some
That various little urges to emulate their example arose[23]
In two gentle and pleasant squires
Who went on to perform such lovely little deeds.

5.

On that Mayday in fine harnesses* of war
We jousted most sweetly;
As for our feats, for those who might wish to know,
I make no other mention of them here.
Rather, it was on the first of June in fact
That Philippe de Lenoncourt[24]
And Philibert de Laigue,[25] without demur,
Had the *Pas* of the Shepherdess announced,
This being no greatly strange event
To see, if you had witnessed it;
For indeed, it was most sweet, pleasing and light-hearted,
As anyone who wrote about it would have said.

6.

These two men had the jousts proclaimed
Around all parts in order to achieve their purpose,

---

[22] [Ferri, mon seigneur de Lorainne]. Ferry II de Vaudémont-Lorraine (d. 1470), count of Vaudémont and lord of Joinville, married Yolande, daughter of René of Anjou (1445), joined René's Order of the Crescent (1448) and became governor of the duchy of Bar (1456) and lieutenant-general of the kingdom of Sicily (1459). He jousted as a defender at Nancy (1445), as a challenger at Châlons-sur-Marne (1445), fought on René's team at Saumur (1446), where he was ultimately pronounced the winner, and at Launay (1446) and Chinon/Razilly (1446). Mérindol, *Les fêtes*, pp. 183–5; PSr, p. 130.

[23] The original text uses the term *enviettes*, but Hüe, 'La Bergère', p. 246, sees this as being about the desire to emulate rather than strictly envy or jealousy on the defenders' part, an interpretation adopted here.

[24] [Phelippe de Lenoncourt]. Philippe de Lenoncourt (1400–83), lord of Lenoncourt, Gondrecourt, Serres and Frouard, was a member of the Order of the Crescent (1452), squire of the stables of René of Anjou (1451–53) and later his Master of the Horse (1470), as well as governor of the duchy of Bar (1470); he was also a councillor-chamberlain of Louis XI. He jousted as a defender at Nancy (1445), as a challenger at Châlons-sur-Marne (1445), where he was named as winner of the attacking team, as a defender at Launay (1446) and on René's team at Saumur (1446). Mérindol, *Les fêtes*, p. 170; PSr, p. 128.

[25] [Philebert de l'Aigue]. Philibert de Laigue, of a family from Bourges, was a squire and councillor-chamberlain (probably after 1451) of René of Anjou and seneschal of Bar (1480). Mérindol, *Les fêtes*, p. 165; PSr, p. 128.

Having them cried in all suitable places
By Romarin,[26] who, during his lifetime,
Was for a long while a pursuivant
Of my most redoubtable lord and master,
The king of Sicily,[27] who undertook
Most willingly to watch over the jousts
And to ensure that everyone's rights were upheld,
For he took great pleasure and delight in this,
As you can clearly see, without delay,
In the chapters whose contents are as follows:

7.

'We let it be known to all generally,
Both knights and gentle squires,
That on the forthcoming first of June
All those who are intent on jousting
Will find, in Tarascon, in a most fitting place,
A set of lists for jousting
Set up for these pleasant entertainments.
And at one end, as everyone will see,
There will be a gentle shepherdess[28]
Guarding her little sheep under a tree;
As is right and proper, she will have
All the charming little things she needs.

8.

Two shields for jousting will be attached to the tree:
One white, signifying happiness,
Which will be untouched by any other colour;
The other black, signifying sadness.
These two shields will be there by virtue
Of two gentle shepherd-squires,[29]
Acting in the manner of loyal servants
In order to gain the favour of the shepherdess.
For those who wish to know more,

[26] [Rommarin]. According to Christian de Mérindol, 'Rois d'armes et poursuivants à la cour d'Anjou au temps du roi René', *Revue du Nord*, 88 (2006), 617–30 (p. 619), this figure, (attested 1446–53) served René of Anjou and was often entrusted with carrying letters on important matters.

[27] René of Anjou (1409–80), duke of Anjou and count of Provence (1434–80), also reigned as king of Naples (1435–42) before being deposed as the preceding dynasty was restored to power. He was an important patron of the arts and tournament enthusiast who wrote numerous works including the *Traité de la forme et devis d'un tournoi* (between 1444 and 1450) and the *Livre du Coeur d'Amour épris* (1457) and organised tournaments at Nancy (1445) and Saumur (1446). Lecoy de La Marche, *Le roi René*.

[28] This part was played by Isabelle de Lenoncourt: see above, introduction, p. 114; and below, entry 733 in the financial account.

[29] These roles are played by the two *entrepreneurs*, Lenoncourt and Laigue.

The white shield is for those who are happy in love,
The black for those who are not; let him not strike
Either of the shields who does not understand the game.

9.

Whocver wishcs to joust with thc shcphcrds
And is contented with both Love and his lady
May go up to the black shield without fear,
Being one who calls himself a true servant,
And touch it with a weapon without incurring blame.
He who is discontented must touch the white shield;
He will have time to couch his lance
But no sooner will he have made his entrance
Than a shepherd will come out to meet him.
Whoever is the first to break three lances
Will win the prize, as is stipulated
In the chapters of the present jousts.

10.

If the shepherd breaks three lances
Before the one who is on the outside team*,
As will be decided by the judges,
If he so wishes, he will order him
Through an officer of arms, as he sees fit,
For up to twenty leagues around, no less,
To take a gold ring, no matter what,
For presenting to a lady or a damsel
Who will be chosen by him. And if it so happens
That the one on the outside team is the winner,
He may there kiss the shepherdess,
Provided that he first takes off his helm.

11.

This honour will he indeed receive from her
In front of everyone and, what is more, she will give him
A lovely bouquet of flowers, delicately composed
And held by a fine gold ring.
There they will joust with elegant shields* of horn,
And if one of the two is brought down to the ground
Horse and all, or wounded or, as he executes his run
By chance or mishap
Is either unable or unwilling to break three lances,
He will lose a ring; to this there is no remedy.
But he who wounds a horse does all in vain,
For he has no hope of winning the prize.

12.

To him, come from outside, who has broken his three lances
With the greatest skill,
The most valour and in the smallest number of courses —
As determined by the decision and judgement
Of both a knight and a King of Arms,
Whose role it is to assess and to uphold
All the cases that might arise —
The said shepherdess will send
Up to twenty leagues away, wherever he may be,
A diamond worth a hundred *écus*
Or thereabouts, and there it will be taken
By a herald as soon as the pronouncement has been made.

13.

In jousting helms* and harness
It is understood that everyone shall fight;
With saddles* for war, also, without a doubt,
And coronals* too as they see fit.
On the other hand, if needs be, they may
Change their destriers* at any time and their armour,
Whilst the lances measured in the lists,
Are all to be the same length and weight.
The *Pas* will last for three days in total,
From at least one hour after midday
To six o'clock, and, for greater comfort,
There will be a day of rest between each one.

14.

The said shepherds will only
Meet to do battle with those coming from outside
The once, in order that no one
In this matter will be disappointed.
Furthermore, it is also foreseen
That if there are those who take it upon themselves
To touch the shields together,
The shepherds will still only receive them
One at a time. Let it be known
That in a case like this the order will be determined
Such that he who comes first will be served first,
So as to avoid any discontent arising.'

15.

There now remains little of substance
To say about the chapters of the *Pas*,
Which, on an elegant board,
Were written up in the lists in proper fashion.

He who composed them certainly did not forget
Also to include the story behind them,
This being well expressed, the better to attract attention.
But hereafter must follow the sequence of events
According to how it actually took place;
As for the entry into the lists
That was also written up by the judges.
The two were, in my opinion, broadly in agreement.

16.

When the appointed day and hour came round,
Which was supposed to be at midday,
And everyone was ready and happy
To make his entrance according to his turn,
He who performed the best was he who best knew
How to conduct himself at this *pas*.
He who arrived first could witness
The minstrels in very fine array,
The trumpeters making a great sound,
With such a large number of heralds
In attendance that, without a doubt,
It is hard to recount here just how many of them there were.

17.

And then came a gentle pursuivant
Also wearing his coat armour*,
Who was following close behind them,
Carrying the two shepherds' shields.
God knows that the rest of them
Followed on in fine order!
There you would have seen the shepherdess,
The knight, first judge on her right,
The king of arms, the other, on her left,
They being the ones to assess the combats.
The sheep followed on closely
So as not to stray far from her side.

18.

Each man was mounted on a fine horse,
Except for two who led the sheep;
All this in the order in which I have told it.
He who strove to be the best dressed
Had made every effort to parade his finery.
The shepherdess was mounted on a hackney*
That was very nobly arrayed
In a rich cloth of gold patterned in crimson.
The horse which she rode was held

By the bridle by two young men
Walking on foot, who were also gentlemen
But well disguised in shepherds' clothing.

19.

Next came the two shepherd-jousters
On two destriers covered in trappers*;
It was hard to mistake them for shepherds or herders
As their clothing was so unlike theirs.[30]
They were not wearing their helms
And their shields were doubtless being carried by another,
But of their armour and harness for the joust
There was not the slightest piece missing.
If one had been there, one would not
Soon have tired of gazing at them, as well as the great host
Of servants who were likewise not on foot,
If any of them were intent on serving properly.

20.

When they came in order into the lists
Everyone knew where he was meant to go
As their pavilions were in different places.
There you would have seen the two shepherds withdraw
With their servants accompanying them
Into a lovely lodge next to the enclosed area.
And, the better to organise and welcome everyone,
The shepherdess had her own appointed space,
Which was as prettily done up as anything
With trees, flowers and soft verdure
As finely wrought as it could be;
There she sat waiting for the adventure to begin.

21.

The pursuivant hung up the two shields
In a tree next to the shepherdess,
And stayed in that position as he waited
Without moving from the door of his little tower
In order to pass on to the shepherds the news
About the challengers who would come that way.
But they had to wait a very long time
For the jousters from outside to appear:
So keen at that moment

[30] See below, entry 733 in the financial account, which details the much more expensive grey cloth 'made in Lille' used for the *entrepreneurs*' outfits compared with the cheaper cloth 'made in Béziers' used for their servants' jackets.

Were all those heralds, minstrels and trumpeters
To have them enter one by one, with the intention
Of seeing them thrown beyond the boundary of the lists.

22.

The shepherdess was wearing a garment
That fitted her body very well,
And was very elegantly laced up at the side;
It was made of a patterned damask[31]
Of a lovely grey colour that was not too dark,[32]
And was very well lined and edged around
With miniver. Yet no other headdress did she wear
Than a pretty townswoman's hood[33]
Pink in colour, which, howsoever she wore it,
Suited her well, in many people's opinion;
Her shepherd's staff, about six feet high,
Had a crook on it made of fine silver.

23.

She also had a small silver gourd
By her side, with which to refresh her little mouth.
A pouch too she carried with her,
Along with her other things, which was really dainty;
She truly did resemble a gentle shepherdess,
Judging by her manner and her bearing
Which gave rise to many a gracious remark.
The trapper of the shepherds mentioned above
Was wholly grey in colour,[34]
Embroidered in gold; gourds and staffs
Were very prettily depicted on it,
Along with pouches, flints, flutes and little bagpipes.[35]

---

[31] Williams' edition here reads 'dames' (ladies) when it should read 'damas' (damask): this has been corrected in the translation using Crapelet's edition, p. 72.

[32] On the fabric of this dress, see above, introduction, p. 114; and below, entry 733 in the financial account.

[33] See below, entry 734 in the financial account and n. 100, on the fine woollen fabric that this hood was made from, which is termed *escarlate* (scarlet). See also Julia Kalbfleisch, ed. *Le Triumphe des Dames von Olivier de La Marche. Ausgabe nach den Handschriften* (Rostock: Adlers Erben, 1901), p. 82, stanza 145, where the poet notes that ladies' hats are made of velvet, damask or satin whereas those of townswomen are more properly made of *escarlate.*

[34] Like the shepherd-defenders's outfits, these trappers were of the same expensive grey cloth 'made in Lille': see below, entry 733 in the financial account.

[35] These objects embroidered in gold all refer to the typical accoutrements of shepherds according to the pastoral tradition of the period.

24.

The lower edges of this grey trapper were dagged*.[36]
Purple in colour were their crests
Of ostrich plumes done up in a most elegant fashion,
Which sat on top of their long, tall helms:
They were truly very handsome.
Also adding to their finery
Was a lovely, long veil[37]
That hung off the rumps of their horses.
One of them was constantly waiting in attendance,
One by the white shield, the other by the black;
At the first encounter that called them into action,
One of the two leapt out of his lodge.

25.

The first day of June was in fact
The day of Pentecost itself,
And, since it rained so heavily,
With the toll that everyone knows this takes,
The jousts didn't start on that day;
Rather, all were readily of the opinion
That it should begin on the third day of the month.
It was thus postponed until the Tuesday,
With the entry into the lists at midday
Of the shepherds and the shepherdess.
This was how that day, the Sunday, ended,
For both the two of them and for her.

26.

Around one hour after midday
When it was foreseen that someone would shortly come and start to joust
Against one of the two shepherds,
No matter what it may cost him,
There came to strike the white shield without hesitation
A squire very finely arrayed.

---

[36] On the text's use of the term *frape/frappe* to refer to this type of decoration, known as dagging, see below, n. 58.

[37] The text here specifies that this is a *couvrechief* (headcovering) *de plaisance*, a term that also appears in lines 346, 402, 451–2, 697, 747, 806, 835. The precise meaning of *plaisance* is obscure (a gauzy silk that comes from Piacenza, Italy?), but, whatever its origin, sources such as René of Anjou's *Livre des Tournois* (Paris, BnF, fr. 2696, fols 79v and 101v) suggest that a *couvrechief de plaisance* was indeed a delicate, transparent headcovering used by women that could be given as a prize to the winner or used to wrap up a prize. For this reason it has been translated here as 'veil'. Where the text simply uses the term *couvrechief*, as in lines 321, 430, 504, 576 (see below), this has been translated as a 'headcovering', i.e. without quite the same connotations of gauzy luxury.

This was in fact Pierre Carrion,[38]
Who was on a grey destrier,
A horse that was good for running very fast and very boldly.
One or two turns of the lists he made,
His lance in his hand and his foot in the stirrup;
When he had completed his circuit, he suddenly turned round.

27.

As usual, his trapper was red in colour,
All bestrewn with golden letters
And bordered with a good quantity of pearls;
Even though it was very large and wide
And covered with a gauzy layer of very fine linen,[39]
It had a band of miniver all around it,
With his shield done up the same way.
His helm was richly decorated
With a very large and ample headcovering
Of the kind usually worn by damsels at court.
Eager to do battle with him, out came
The shepherd, Philippe de Lenoncourt.

28.

This shepherd had a bay destrier
Which charged straight out into the lists
As he sallied forth to engage his man, as he should.
They crossed on the first run
With their two lances. On the second, indisputably,
They broke both of them with force,
One of them against the shield, and the other the same way;
On the third run also both were broken.
But Carrion shattered his against the shield
While the shepherd's hit powerfully against the helm,
A good part of which was damaged,
Thus did he cleanly break his lance.

29.

Not long after, Louis de Montberon[40]
Came up on a bay destrier without hesitation,
Delicately spurring his mount

---

[38] Pierre Carrion was squire to Jean, duke of Calabria, René of Anjou's eldest son and heir, and *valet tranchant* of René (1451). Mérindol, *Les fêtes*, p. 139.

[39] This fabric is specified in the text as *linomple* and paraphrased here as 'very fine linen' from the definition in the DMF; see also line 529, where it appears again.

[40] [Loÿs de Monberon]. Louis de Montberon (1420–1501), lord of Fontaine and Cholandrai, from an illustrious family of the Angoumois, was the grandson of a marshal of France and a servant of King Charles VII. PAB, p. 111; Mérindol, *Les fêtes*, p. 174.

In order to make a clean strike at the black shield,
And not staying there long thereafter.
As he had chosen to have his colours *parti*,
His trapper and his shield were half-tan and half-blue.
In these same colours he wore
A fine crest of ostrich plumes
Topped with a lovely veil
That hung down behind; he held himself well
In his harness, giving an impression of strength.

30.

To fight him, in defence of the black shield, came
Philibert de Laigue, one of the shepherds,
Riding a bay destrier; without further ado
He broke two lances in as many runs,
Striking the shield; little recourse
On these two runs could Montberon take
Against the shepherd, apart from one blow that pleased him.
On the third run, he broke his lance
On the upper part of the shield, though this blow was not taken lightly
By the shepherd
Who, for his part, made such a fearsome charge
That he broke his third lance easily by aiming at the lower part of the shield.

31.

Next came another young squire,
Whose name, for a fact, was Coaraze,[41]
Riding a black destrier; never could he
Possibly be bored on such an occasion.
He touched the black shield with joy.
His shield and his trapper were both of black,
As was the crest of plumes atop
His helm, which was very ample.
Philibert saw that he was ready to pay up
But nonetheless he had not yet won the day.
If the joust between these two was a fine one,
Neither of them spared the other a thing.

32.

Coaraze on the first run
Took a very heavy blow to the helm,
While the shepherd escaped being hit at all, hence
Neither of them broke his lance.

[41] [Couraze]. Ramon-Arnalt Coaraze, a lord from an old noble family of Béarn, was a chamberlain of King Charles VII (1426) and his councillor (1443); he was still alive in 1456. Mérindol, *Les fêtes*, p. 143.

On the second run, Coaraze it was
Who disarmed the shepherd of his pauldron*,
Breaking nothing but the part that he had struck
As Coaraze himself escaped being hit.
On the third run, each of them was struck
So cleanly that their two lances broke
On their shields; which of them took the heavier blow
None could tell other than those who were there to see it.

33.

On the fourth run, Coaraze dealt such a fine blow
With his lance on the shield, and the fact
That it was with a coronal matters not a jot,
As the shepherd acknowledged the quality of the hit.
On the fifth run, so true was the aim of each
That on their shields, with valour,
Their two lances broke; and Coaraze once again
Was delighted at how these things had gone.
Soon up came Philibert de La Jaille,[42]
A squire hopeful of finding favour,
Mounted boldly on a roan destrier
In order to strike a joyous blow on the white shield.

34.

His trapper was all of miniver,
As was his shield;
On his helm there was indeed a crest
All made of white ostrich plumes.
Atop that he was well decked out
In a fine long veil
That billowed out as it hung down behind.
He did his duty by touching the white shield;
Keen to fight against him
Was the shepherd Lenoncourt, who made his move
In order to see what he might be able to achieve,
For the fight between them was only very short.

35.

They each in fine style broke two lances,
Hitting them on the shields at the first pass.
On the second run, the shepherd accomplished little;
La Jaille's lance went home

[42] [Philebert]. Philibert de La Jaille (d. before 1459?) was a *valet tranchant* of René of Anjou (1451). He may have jousted at Nancy (1445) and definitely jousted for René's team at Saumur (1446). Mérindol, *Les fêtes*, p. 164; PSr, p. 128.

On the shepherd's shield, breaking cleanly.
On the third run, it also struck firm upon the shield,
Thus bringing that day's jousting to a close.
The shepherdess was escorted back
To the lodge appointed to her
In the same manner as had been done before.
So, in this fashion, did the day go by,
Full of immense pleasure and great joy.

36.

On the Thursday, as God is my witness,
Came a squire named Guillaume d'Yve,[43]
Also known as Willemart,
On a roan destrier that took well
To the spur on arriving in the lists.
A white trapper was then his preference,
Which was bestrewn with the foliage of a tree;
Red letters and other smaller ones of white
He had chosen for his pleasure to have depicted;
From his helm a headcovering hung down
Behind him; and, in accordance with the chapters
On the white shield, he was ready for action.

37.

To fight him came the shepherd Philibert,
And both of them soon broke their lances
On their shields; equally clean too
Was the second blow that each man struck in this encounter.
On the third pass, Willemart's lance
Crossed over between the two of them and Philibert's
Lance was then broken. Then up rode I,
After that, to strike the black shield,
Since winning or holding firm
Were without a doubt my sole intention;
Hence I didn't stay there long
As I was so full of ardour.

38.

I was mounted on a fine bay destrier
And was well armed, I can assure you;
Indeed, red was the colour of my whole harness:
Lances, shield, trapper and helm.
Even the great ostrich plumes that I wore on top
Were coloured red; and behind my head

[43] Guillaume d'Yve, known as Willemart, was a retainer of René of Anjou. Mérindol, *Les fêtes*, p. 186.

Hung down a beautiful long white veil
That really looked the part.
My shield bore an inscription
Written in gold letters, a motto composed by me
Because it went so well with my apparel,
It was: 'The reddest jousters take it!'[44]

39.

Three lances and three red standards
Of taffeta I had, in truth,
Which were long and wide in dimension,
My thought being that I had plenty to achieve.
To fight me came Philibert without delay,
And we broke our two lances cleanly
On the first encounter, on the very uppermost part
Of our shields. On the second run, fearlessly,
I disarmed him of his pauldron straightaway,
Neatly too I removed his gaignepain*,
Without breaking my lance I managed to hold firm
Such that nothing could he do, his aim being all in vain.

40.

On the third encounter, the shepherd did indeed
Break his lance high up on my shield.
I achieved nothing as I crossed my lance
Such that my blow was rendered worthless.
On the fourth run, I attacked him
With such force that my lance did break,
His own strike being no less good than mine.
The fifth time round, I swung my lance around so well
That into two it shattered and flew off
While his lance crossed and failed to touch me.
The ring and the bouquet were mine, in short,
As was the kiss which I treasured greatly.

41.

If one should not really talk about oneself
Nor praise one's own deeds too highly,
And if I have spoken about myself too favourably,
I think that I may be forgiven for it,
For I cannot sacrifice the truth
By writing fibs or lies.
Whoever might take this for a fable or a dream,

[44] The original text reads 'Les plus rouges y sont prins', meaning that those clad all in red, like Beauvau himself, are bent on achieving victory.

That is not the case here; doubt not that what I have written
About this *pas* is the whole truth,
Something on which I pride myself.
As you well know, I put myself about in every place
Like a sow rooting in a field of flax.

42.

After me came Tanguy Duchâtel,[45]
A squire of joyous disposition,
Mounted on a fine grey horse both handsome and good-natured,
Who acquitted himself well in all he undertook.
He had adopted a trapper of black and tan,
Bestrewn with many a golden letter.
A noble damsel named
The lady of Cabanes was there.[46]
Behind him she came, gaily carrying
His helm that had a damsel's headdress on it,
Along with a letter 'I' of gold,[47] that was delicately crowned
With a beautiful headcovering.

43.

On the shaffron* of his horse stood
Three ostrich plumes: one black,
Another blue, and the third was
Gold in colour. To fight him, in truth,
Came Lenoncourt, as mentioned above.
From the first encounter their two lances
Broke on their shields, without hesitation.
On the second and third strikes, Lenoncourt
Did not miss his aim. To keep my narrative short,
Thus did he break three lances;
But thereafter came one of the leaders of the court
Who achieved all that he wanted to.

44.

For next came Ferry, my lord of Lorraine,[48]
Mounted as a squire on his grey destrier.
He was pleasingly arrayed in all his trappings,

---

[45] [du Chastel]. Tanguy IV Duchâtel (1419–74), from Brittany, was grand seneschal of Provence for René of Anjou (1439–50), a councillor-chamberlain and Master of the Horse of Charles VII of France, and then Louis XI. He jousted at Chinon/Razilly (1446) and for the king at Saumur (1446). Mérindol, *Les fêtes*, p. 150; PSr, p. 137.

[46] This probably refers to the lady of Cabanes, Jacquette Budé (1425–65), wife of Antoine de Pontevès, lord of Cabanes (see below, n. 62).

[47] This letter 'I' may well represent the initial 'J' of Jacquette.

[48] See above, n. 22.

As is only right and proper,
The better to honour his house in full.
Of black velvet was the trapper of his destrier,
With appliqué of white and green
Cut in the shape of a horse-harness*;[49]
His shield was decorated likewise.
On his helm stood a great ostrich plume:
Looked at from toe to top or top to toe,
He was armed like a [true] man of the realm.[50]

45.

Made of very fine linen,[51] he bore on his right arm
A lovely sleeve from a chemise;
It must have been brocaded with gold thread,[52]
And was finely bestrewn with leaves of green
That were very prettily and delicately done.
As was only right, on his shaffron
Stood three large ostrich plumes.
From all four of his lances a standard hung,
One made of taffeta that was flowing, wide and long,
And coloured black, white and green with silver letters;
One by one, and in their entirety,
They were cleanly broken to many spectators' delight.

46.

Up to touch the white shield went he,
And soon came Lenoncourt the shepherd,
Who, verily, couched his lance
To fight him without taking long about it.
Yet I know for a fact that that day
My lord Ferry achieved so much that, to tell the truth,
It should suffice for a single event.
On the first pass, their lances crossed,

---

49 The original text in lines 523–4 reads: 'Et loqueté tant de blanc que de vert/En la façon de harnois de cheval'. The verb *loqueter* (literally, 'to cut into strips', DMF) is used here to refer to the cutting out of shapes from white and green fabrics to be appliquéed onto black velvet in order to make this trapper for Ferry II de Vaudémont-Lorraine's horse. Entry 734 in the financial account (see below), which records the payment made to a dressmaker for this work, matches these details exactly but uses the verb *deffrapper* instead to describe this process. See also line 627, where the term *loqueté* is likewise used to describe white fabric shapes that have been appliquéed onto a grey trapper, this time for Robert Dufay's horse.

50 Albeit slightly obscurely phrased, this description was presumably meant to flatter Ferry as it reflects the fact that he was René of Anjou's son-in-law.

51 Specified in the text as *linomple*: see above, n. 39.

52 Brocading is a technique whereby the threads that create a pattern are confined to the area where they are required to make the pattern, rather than being used throughout the fabric. See Gale R. Owen-Crocker, 'Brocading', in EMDT, pp. 97–8.

But they didn't hold back thereafter;
On the second run, the shepherd hit him.
I don't know what they were planning in their hearts
But his shattered lance told it plain enough.

47.

My lord Ferry did little then
On that run, but on the third, as I well know,
He executed a far greater one, in truth,
Such that he broke his lance, which the other man failed to do.
Yet for the fourth run, everyone was full of praise;
The wood fell in pieces to the ground.
On the fifth run too, everything was smashed with great force,
Neither man omitting to strike the other.
But, on the sixth, my lord attacked
The shepherd, hitting him so hard
That his lance flew off into splinters;
One after the other, four lances in all were broken.[53]

48.

When he received his bouquet, his ring
And his kiss, he took off his trapper
And sent it without the least delay
Over to the shepherdess. Afterwards, I assure you,
Strode gaily up with great confidence
Gaspard Cossa,[54] a very gentle squire,
On a roan that did not misbehave.
His trapper was of an English cloth
Of the most unusual workmanship that one could ever see.
On his helm stood a fine crest of lilies
With the prettiest flowers to be found on earth,
And a hanging headcovering of the choicest kind.

49.

He went up to strike the black shield
And Philibert came forward to defend.
They fought so well together
That they broke their lances straightaway.
The second pass was of no less quality

---

[53] The fact that Ferry broke four lances rather than just the stipulated three, as well as being the most socially eminent jouster at the event, probably explains why he was given the grand prize at the end of this *pas*.

[54] [Gaspart Cosse]. Gaspard Cossa, son of Jean (Giovanni) Cossa (see below, n. 63) was a pantler* of René of Anjou (1451) and joined the Order of the Croissant between 1462 and 1480; he was one of the less experienced competitors at this event. PAB, p. 112; Bianciotto, ed., *Le Roman*, vol. 1, p. 173; Mérindol, *Les fêtes*, p. 144.

For in two runs they broke four lances.
Yet on the third pass, they did not do likewise,
For the shepherd Philibert did so well
That his lance touched cleanly and firmly
Against Gaspard, flying into pieces.
I firmly believe that, through the openings of his helm,
He could hear full well the sound of the clash he made.[55]

50.

The king himself served Gaspard Cossa,[56]
As he did several others, truth be told;
At the very least, when he saw a young man
Who was not experienced in the joust
He graciously came down
From his stand to render him a service,
Bringing him afterwards into the lists
A lance, by way of making a small gesture to him.
This gave several of them the courage
To conduct themselves valiantly in the joust;
He showed them honour and favour
By behaving in this fashion in the lists.

51.

Then came Philibert de Stainville,[57]
A squire who rode a bay destrier
And carried himself well, like one in a thousand;
With a grey trapper deeply dagged,[58] as I observed,
And a shield likewise fitting and gay
That was bestrewn with small blue flowers.
On top of all these things described above
Were ostrich plumes, also blue and grey,
Gathered into a crest upon his helm;
Two taller white plumes rose above it.

---

[55] The author here is emphasising the sheer power of this blow as, normally, a jouster would not hear through his helm the sound of the strike he made due to the amount of padding within it.

[56] See above, n. 54, on this competitor's relative youth and lack of experience.

[57] [Philebert]. Philibert, lord of Stainville, from an illustrious family of Lorraine, was a squire and pantler (1458) of René of Anjou, bailiff of Bar and Bassigny and René's lieutenant in Sicily, as well as *viguier* (magistrate) of Arles and Tarascon. PAB, pp. 112–13; Mérindol, *Les fêtes*, p. 181.

[58] The original text here reads 'Housse de gris de frappe': PAB, p. 102, glosses *gris* as meaning an expensive type of fur, whilst Williams' edition also glosses *frappe* as meaning fur. This has been corrected in the translation so that *gris* refers to the colour of the trapper and the term *frappe* refers to dagging, which has some overlap with the literal meaning of the verb *loqueter*. The same expression, *frape/frappe/de frappe*, is also used for trappers of horses belonging to the two shepherd-defenders (see above, line 277) and of Robert Dufay and Guy de Laval (see below, lines 627 and 800, respectively). For an image of horses' trappers dagged in this fashion, see René of Anjou, *Livre des tournois*, Paris, BnF, fr. 2696, fol. 28r. See also Gale R. Owen-Crocker, 'Dagging', in EMDT, p. 167.

In this manner did he ride straight up
To the white shield, exuding strength and power.

52.

To fight him came Philibert the shepherd,
And Stainville damaged his gaignepain
Without breaking his lance on that occasion;
Yet the shepherd did break
His at that point, as it so happened.
However, on the second, third and fourth runs,
Stainville broke his lance into four pieces,
As he struck the shepherd.
Thus did Stainville conduct himself extremely well,
On that day; let there be no doubt about this
For truly, even at the risk of losing his life,
He had no fear of putting his strength to the test.

53.

Then up came Robert Dufay,[59]
On a grey destrier in a trapper of grey[60]
With an appliqué pattern of white and deep dagging[61]
Done so well that more finely wrought
It could not have been, nor garnered more praise.
His shield too was all of white but for
The little black tears that it had in profusion,
As well as two fine black letters.
On his helm was also draped
A blue banderole, by my faith,
Which bore more letters, white in colour,
Two of which were J and M.

54.

He went up to strike the black shield;
But it was Lenoncourt the shepherd and he
Who from the outset, in fact, fought that round,
Such that both of them shattered their lances;
And, as lots of spectators could see, the shepherd
Broke the shield of Robert Dufay

---

[59] [du Faÿ]. Robert Dufay, a squire of René of Anjou, may have been from an illustrious Burgundian family of this name based near Langres (nowadays dép. Haute-Marne, rég. Grand-Est, France) that then made advantageous connections to various families in Lorraine, such as Duchâtel, Ville and Haussonville. PAB, p. 113; Mérindol, *Les fêtes*, p. 151.

[60] See below, entry 731 in the financial account, for the money Dufay received from René to help pay for his trapper in the *Pas*.

[61] The original text reads 'De *loqueté* et *frappe* entrevint/De blanc' (emphasis added): on these terms, see above, nn. 36 and 49.

Right across, to everyone's amazement.
On the second run, each man broke his lance,
But, on the third, the shepherd charged forward with such force
That he smashed his weapon whilst his opponent did not:
Sometimes it is not always the handsomest [fighters] who have the pleasure
Of receiving honour and renown.

55.

And so was Thursday thus concluded,
For that day only seven men came to fight.
On the Sunday, I tell you truly,
They showed how they went from strength to strength;
For on this third day, each man encountered the other so well
That some thought they would be brought down to the ground.
At the appointed hour, came in great haste
Antoine de Pontevès who, indeed,
Is known as the lord of Cabanes;[62]
He was finely mounted on a bay destrier.
Without stopping, he rode up to the white shield
In the manner that you will shortly hear.

56.

White were both his shield and his trapper,
Each bordered with a lovely band of miniver,
And bestrewn with a good number of golden letters
Which matched his whole apparel very well.
His helm was elegantly decorated
With a very finely done crest
That had a long pennon attached behind.
There was also a banderole atop the crest
Which, as was only fitting,
Was of blue and white plumes,
As was the banderole which,
Like the trapper and the shield, were not those of a novice.

57.

Indeed, on the shaffron of his destrier
Two plumes in the above-named colours
Were fixed; and then came, in short,
Philibert, one of the two aforesaid shepherds
To fight him; their hearts were so given over
To the idea of striking well that the said shepherd
Broke his lance on the shield in a fine, clean blow.

---

[62] [Anthoyne de Ponteves]. Antoine de Pontevès (1420–92), lord of Cabanes, from an illustrious Provençal family, was a retainer of René of Anjou. PAB, p. 113.

Yet Cabanes, who was not there in vain,
Disarmed him of his gaignepain
Without breaking his lance at all.
On the second pass, it was clear that their two lances
Were plainly broken on their shields.

58.

And if, on the third pass, the shepherd strove well,
His opponent, for his part, failed to strike him;
Then afterwards it was Jean Cossa who took over,[63]
A squire who would give a good account of himself,
As he thought, in this challenging game.
On a bay destrier, Jean Cossa's choice of
Trapper was in the same pattern
As that of the king: grey, white, and black, no less.
On his helm he had, come what may,
Three large well-chosen ostrich plumes,
And a handsome bourrelet*, for good measure;
All were in the afore-mentioned colours.

59.

In place of a veil
He had a cleaning cloth[64] on his right arm
As well as a horse's comb, in fact.
He went up to strike the white shield.
Philibert, who knew what he was about,
Broke his lance cleanly on his helm
On the first run, and Jean Cossa did likewise on his shield.
They crossed on the second pass,
And then, on the third and fourth runs, without fail
They smashed four lances on their shields,
Thus making a good tally of broken weapons,
Considering all the fine blows that each had dealt.

---

[63] [Jehan Cosse]. Jean (Giovanni) Cossa (*c.*1400–76), baron of Grimaud and count of Troya, was a member of the Order of the Crescent (1448), a councillor-chamberlain of René of Anjou, lieutenant-general of Sicily (1466) and grand seneschal of Provence (1470). He jousted at Launay (1446) and as a defender at Saumur (1446). Mérindol, *Les fêtes*, pp. 143–4; PSr, p. 126.

[64] The word used in the original text, *espoussette*, can also mean 'sack', but, coupled with the comb that Cossa is wearing on his armour, it seems more logical that both these items refer to the grooming of horses. This divergence from the more courtly norm of having a veil hanging from one's harness may suggest a slightly jocular side to Cossa or it could be seen as his paying tribute to all the work done by the horses in these competitions. For similar instances of divergence from these norms governing the competitors' courtly appearance, see the chapters of arms related to the tournaments of *The Wild Knight of the Black Lady* (Edinburgh, 1507–08) in Source 16; see also Essay 5.

60.

Jean Cossa, on the fifth run, broke his lance
On the shield, and the shepherd his on the helm,
Such that he put Jean Cossa out of the lists
And he had to go off into a quiet corner.
Then came the turn of Guerry de Charno,[65]
A squire, in order to strike the white shield.
For those who want to know how he was arrayed,
He was mounted on a bay destrier,
With, as I well know, a trapper, shield and lance
And a banderole mounted on his helm,
All of them in black. There he put himself to the test
Against the shepherd ready to meet his challenge.

61.

Out came Lenoncourt and, by way of welcome,
Each man broke his lance neatly on the shield
During this first pass. On the second,
Guerry once again, as I remember well,
Broke his next lance, but then unwilling
Became his destrier to proceed in the lists,
Such that neither could strike the other for some time.
Guerry, in truth, retreated at this point
Saddened and upset, as they had failed to break
Their three lances. The lord of Mison[66]
Came next, who was certainly well equipped,
And we'll speak now about how well he performed.

62.

This man is Messire Foulques d'Agoult,
In all respects a gentle knight,
And in the joust very experienced and well-versed.
He was on a white destrier
With everything he needed to do his duty.
His trapper was of a fine white taffeta
With foliage of gold that jingled a good deal;
He also carried a great staff
On which, for his amusement,
Was written in letters of gold 'L. is worth more'.[67]

---

[65] [Guerri]. Guerry de Charno was a retainer of René of Anjou who jousted on his team at Saumur (1446). Mérindol, *Les fêtes*, p. 140.

[66] [Fouques d'Agaut]. Foulques d'Agoult, lord of Mison, was a member of the Order of the Crescent (1449). Mérindol, *Les fêtes*, p. 118.

[67] This 'L' is probably a pun either on '*Elle*', as in '*She* is worth more', or a lady's name that begins with this letter.

To tell the truth in full,
His appearance was elegant on every count.

63.

He had on his helm a great crest
Of ostrich plumes, and also out behind it
A veil hung down.
In this fashion he made his entrance,
Going up in a joyful manner
To strike the black shield in determined style.
To fight him, with vigour, came
Philibert the shepherd, as noted above.
Without dispute, they both broke
Their lances on the first pass.
Philippe then smashed another into pieces
Whilst Mison crossed his very high.

64.

But on the third run the shepherd struck
His helm above the sight*
So hard that his lance was broken.
If Mison had to suffer this setback,
He also found that his own lance met its mark,
On the uppermost part of the shield, but failed to break.
Each one has to take what he can get:
Such is the way and custom of war.
After Mison came Honorat de Berre,[68]
A squire on a roan horse;
One can ask at length about his qualities,
But in the joust he is a force to be reckoned with.

65.

On his helm was a crest of ostrich plumes
Coloured black and white and nicely done;
I believe that between here and Prussia
Its like cannot be found by anyone.
I do not know whence came the motto
That was written out in plain upon his shield,
Saying: 'By God's belly, there is no
Other one like her; no, by God's blood!'

---

[68] Honorat de Berre (d. after 1483), lord of Entrevennes, was a squire (1448, 1451), a councillor-chamberlain (1469–70) and a *grand maître d'hôtel* (after 1472) of René of Anjou; he jousted on René's team at Saumur (1446). Mérindol, *Les fêtes*, pp. 129–30; PSr, p. 125. On the possibility that Honorat may have died in 1495, see Elsa Espin, 'Résolution d'une énigme héraldique: Honorat de Berre et l'Adoration de l'Enfant', *Revue française d'héraldique et de sigillographie – Études en ligne* (2020) <http://sfhs-rfhs.fr/wp-content/PDF/articles/RFHS_W_2020_001.pdf> [accessed 19 June 2024].

This inscription in white, right in the middle
Of his shield, was deliberately placed
Such that, in truth, it was just where it should be;
His trapper and his shield were both of black.

66.

Straight up he went to strike the white shield,
And Philibert, as the defender due to fight him,
Came forth without delay, his right to uphold.
On the helm at which he made his aim
He soon broke his lance with no hesitation,
While Honorat broke his on the upper part of the shield.
On the second run they charged at each other
And once more valiantly broke
Their two lances; on the third run, likewise,
The shepherd truly did not miss his aim
And, though Honorat crossed, he still
Managed to break his, but it was not worth a penny.

67.

Messire Guy, knight of Laval
And lord of Loué, in truth,[69]
Came after him on a bay destrier,
Riding gaily towards the black shield.
Trapper, shield and all his equipment
Were in white, red and blue
Parti in thirds, as was his choice,
And dagged; in addition he had
A great crest as lovely as can be.
As for holding oneself well,
He certainly knew how to do it,
As I can safely say about him.

68.

His crest was in three colours,
With four long veils
Hanging down behind, and one also on his right arm.
He was there in all his might;
Moreover, his appearance was by no means lessened
By the three good-sized plumes

---

[69] Guy de Laval (d. 1484), count of Laval (from 1414) and lord of Loué, was a member of the Order of the Crescent (1448), a councillor-chamberlain of René of Anjou, a councillor of King Charles VII (1446–47) and seneschal of Anjou (1474). He jousted at Châlons-sur-Marne (1445), Launay (1446) where he substituted for René of Anjou as a defender, and on Charles VII's team at Saumur (1446) against René. Mérindol, *Les fêtes*, pp. 168–9; PSr, p. 128.

Perched on the shaffron in the aforesaid colours.
In this manner was his challenge taken up
Most gladly by the shepherd Lenoncourt.
There, straight off, they crossed;
But the following run was not a quiet one,
For each broke his lance against the shield.

69.

The third run garnered ample praise
As each man joyfully broke his lance.
When it came to the fourth one, my lord of Loué
Performed no less well for, truth to tell,
He broke his lance into pieces from a high blow
Struck on the above-named shepherd's shield,
Such that the honour was unquestionably
Due him from the shepherdess.
After him came, as I hereby assure you,
Jean Bézelin, also known as Jarret,[70]
A squire who performed his duty very well
Without demur and straightaway.

70.

He was well mounted on a fine-natured grey destrier
For giving and receiving blows;
He gave little thought, in truth, to worldly honours
Other than to striking well with the coronal of his lance.
His trapper was red and had lovely speckles
Of white strewn all over it; the only decoration
That he had atop his helm
Was a veil; in this manner he went up
To strike the white shield and, after that,
Out came Lenoncourt, the gentle shepherd,
With whom Jarret fought so well
That he brought the *Pas* to a truly fine end.

71.

First off, in only two runs,
Were all four lances broken, in fact.
Thus neither of them was holding back the least;
Aiming really well to hit each other cleanly,
They won great praise from many who were there.
In the end, neither one gave the other any quarter
Until the third lance was broken

---

[70] [Jehan]. Jean Bézelin, known as Jarret, was a squire of the stables of René of Anjou. Mérindol, *Les fêtes*, p. 130.

By Jean Bézelin, which brought the *Pas* to a close.
The whole time many a gracious dinner
Was held there, with no one feeling melancholy
Since it was not the done thing
To attend an event like this without making merry.

72.

My goodness! God knows if there were more than six strikes
That were held to be of little account
And which, even if the lances did not break, were so well couched
That the strongest and most daunting
Without doubt inspired the most fear!
Some there were whose blows were soft,
Prettily done, but their aim was true,
Which were scarcely remarked upon,
And so were not put down in writing.
These were seen as spoilt runs;
Yet nonetheless one could still prize them in one's heart,
Some more, in fact, than many a lance that broke.

73.

Of the way and manner
In which the judgement was reached,
And how the *Pas* of the Shepherdess was concluded,
I will now go on to tell you,
In order to give those reading about it
The fullest possible account.
No sooner did six o'clock come round, in truth,
Than the pursuivant on horseback
Went up right before
The judges' stand, and said to them:
'Come down directly and approach,
For the shepherdess sends for you to do so right away.'

74.

Immediately the judges came down
From their stand without asking the reason
Why, and set off on their way,
Both of them on horseback. When in her presence,
The aforesaid shepherdess immediately
Commanded them to come and speak to the king.
They went off in fine state
Towards his stand and, once in his presence,
Requested him for permission, in her name,
To announce the end of the above-named *Pas*;
She, kneeling and making great reverence,
Went before the king in supplication.

75.

And when the king had given his consent,
The judges went back; and, since
She had clearly heard the king's permission,
They found her there standing tall
In her stand. Though she had already
Heard it, their gracious and clear report
Was listened to, whereupon the pursuivant
Was called over most graciously by her,
Before she gave him the command
To go over to the tree where the two shields were hanging,
And, without further ado, to fetch
The two shepherds and hand them back the shields.

76.

When the pursuivant had executed her order,
With trumpets and clarions playing merrily,
They came to her fully armed,
Their shields around their necks and their helms on their heads,
Showing, as ever, their readiness to
Bow down before her when they came into her presence;
This they duly did, in a manner most elegant.
She bade them, through the King of Arms, to cease
Henceforth from wishing to
Joust any more, either there or anywhere else,
In order to keep the said *Pas* going;
This was done in the following words:

77.

'Most charming and honourable squires,
Who have upheld the truly delightful challenge
Like noble and gentle shepherds
Of the most gracious shepherdess,
I have been ordered by her —
And God forbid I fail her in any way! —
To prohibit you now from jousting.
Accept this, and hear my plea,
For she regards her *pas* as now complete,
According to all the chapters that governed it,
In a most valiant manner, such that never will she
Fail to remember all your gracious deeds.

78.

For this reason, I forbid you to continue the joust,
But, once more, I give you the command
That here and now you must, in sum,
Take off forthwith your helms.

It has been your great pleasure
To serve her with such humility,
Hence she wishes now to thank you
For the trouble you have taken on her behalf
By giving you a kiss, so take note of this
Like her good and loyal servants that you are.'
Thus, all according to her wishes,
Did the two shepherds take off their helms.

79.

After she had kissed them most sweetly,
The King of Arms sent the pursuivant
To each end of the lists and he, in a loud
Voice, announced the end, as he had been commanded,
Of the *Pas* held on her behalf which had attracted
Nobles in such fine numbers.
The pursuivant forthwith,
Being very well schooled in such matters,
And mindful of the honour, pleasure and delight that it involved,
Proclaimed the end, but this was done
In the following manner and form,
With him first saying 'Now hear ye!' three times in a row.

80.

'To all noble and gentle knights
And squires who, in order to take pleasure
When fighting, treasure the performance of fine feats of arms,
Or strive to do their duty,
It is hereby announced
That the *Pas* of the noble shepherdess
That was earlier organised on her behalf,
And which was due to last three days
For five hours after midday,
By two shepherds against all comers,
One after the other, must now come to an end
For everything is henceforth accomplished.

81.

Furthermore, I declare to you
That, after supper at the castle, without fail,
In the king's presence, I tell you truthfully,
And before the queen,[71] where the dance will be held

[71] Isabelle of Lorraine (1400/10–53), daughter of Charles II, duke of Lorraine, and Margaret of Bavaria, married René of Anjou (1420); she was also duchess of Bar (1420–28, and again 1445–58), duchess of Lorraine (1431–53) and queen of Sicily (1435–53). PSr, pp. 145–6.

In a most noble company with an abundance
Of honours and festivities,
The grand prize will be given and awarded
To him who has deserved it the most.'
Once the pursuivant had fulfilled his duty,
The shepherdess, as she had done
On the other occasions, went off, I saw, on horseback;
Never could one tire of gazing after her.

82.

Judges, shepherds, minstrels and trumpeters,
And she too, with all her company,
Performed two circuits within the boundaries
Of the lists, making merry as they went,
Before she went off, she and her followers,
Straight to the castle where she led her gay existence.
The two shields were no longer being carried
By the pursuivant, but rather by the shepherds;
Several heralds who were well-versed in the matter,
Along with five or six pursuivants,
Amused themselves as they departed,
Crying 'Lenoncourt! Laigue!' at the top of their voices.

83.

After supper, the said shepherdess
Emerged joyfully from her chamber,
In her outfit, and was escorted
In the same fashion and order as had been used
On the Thursday and the Tuesday,
But for the fact that she was not on horseback.
Daintly on foot towards the dancing
She made her way in the following manner:
The minstrels and trumpeters went first,
With the pursuivant behind them, carrying the grand prize
Aloft in front of her,
She came behind as she had been taught to do.

84.

The pursuivant held a white baton
In his other hand, being dressed then
In his coat armour, as was only proper;
All the heralds were sporting
Theirs too; and, bolstered by them all
The two judges to the right and to the left
Of her took their place, as was only fitting.
There you would have heard trumpets sounding,
And, besides, other instruments playing loud.

Everything was so very delightfully arranged
That they couldn't have been more in tune with each other;
Thus did they arrive before the king.

85.

When they were all assembled in his presence
And had gone down on their knees as they beheld his face,
The King of Arms most reverently
Uttered to him the following words in a measured fashion:
'Sire, your good pleasure
And permission having previously been granted,
The shepherdess has now come before you
In order to award the grand prize forthwith
To the one who, without a doubt, has earned it,
Being the one from outside who has most claim to it
Since, truly, she would not wish to do anything
That was not just or fair to all concerned.'

86.

On hearing the king's kind permission given in response,
Which was both courteous and gracious,
The whole company was overcome with joy,
And went over, with grand delight,
Towards Ferry, my lord of Lorraine.
The King of Arms, when he approached him,
Took from the hand of the pursuivant himself
The jewel, and delivered it straightaway
To her as she took it over directly
To the said lord; no one thereupon held back
From taking delight once more
In shouting out loud: 'Lorraine takes it!'

87.

The shepherdess was escorted by the judges
To the lord's side, so that she might dance with him.
When the dance was over and done,
All the heralds, the better to while away the time,
Went back, as everyone can well imagine,
To the said lord in an outpouring of joy and merriment
So as to thank him for the great generosity he had shown,
Crying out loud: 'Largesse to the shepherds!'
They then led these faithful servants
Into their mistress's chamber and, it seems to me,
That meat and wine were there in plenty
Such that together they made a merry feast of it.

88.

The shepherdess having withdrawn at this point,
The king had wine and spices served;
Then, when these refreshments had been taken,
You would have seen the charming conduct
Of the ladies who wished to assemble
In front of the king and the queen
So as to take their leave of them. All from the surrounding lands
Were the many ladies and damsels,
Young and noble, gracious and lovely,
Who were pained at having to make their departure.
You should know that some there present were disobedient enough
To want to accompany them home wherever they went.

89.

To Avignon, Arles and Carpentras,
The following day off they went together,
With some saying delightful silly things,
Some, for their part, amusing themselves,
And yet others talking about little love affairs.
So many were there from Salon, Aye and Marseille
That it was truly a wonder;
Even from Venice a great number had come,
And from Languedoc, which I didn't mention before,
From Montpellier too, and from Nîmes,
Such that later, indeed, arrived at court
Many a well-turned verse, in rhymes both rich and simple.

90.

Many a sweet regret and an elegant sigh
You would have heard pouring forth from these tender hearts
At being made to leave behind and abandon
Such pleasure; and I saw trembling
One in particular who thought her heart would break
From having to say farewell, so sorrowful and upset was she.
I beg your pardon if there is anything to criticise
In this little book that I am sending you herewith;
If I had been able to do it better, you would have found it better.
My dear lord, I am but a modest writer,
But I have done it as I know how to —
With the help of a servant of mine.

TRANSLATION (2): FINANCIAL ACCOUNT

(324) **731.** 3 June 1449.

To Robert Dufay,[72] squire, on the third day of the said month, 8 *florins*,[73] which the aforesaid lord[74] gave him so that he could have a trapper made for jousting at the *Pas* of the Shepherdess; as attested by certification from Jean Cossa, lord of Grimaud,[75] and by receipt from the said Dufay; total: 8 fl.

To Romarin, pursuivant, and on his behalf,[76] Viennois the (325) herald, Nicole the trumpeter[77] and others, on the same day, 15 *florins*, given to them by order of the aforesaid lord as largesse[78] relating to the festivities at the *Pas* of the Shepherdess; total, by certification from my above-mentioned lord, the seneschal,[79] and by receipt from the said Romarin: 15 fl.

To Jean Regnault[80] and others with cymbals and tambourines, on the same day, 1 *florin*, as a gift to them for having played their instruments at the said festivities, as certified by the aforesaid seneschal; total: 1 fl.

732. 10 June 1449.

To Viennois,[81] herald of my lord the dauphin, on the tenth day of the said month — in 10 *écus* worth 21 *gros* 2 *patacs*[82] apiece, — 17 *florins* 8 *gros* 4 *patacs*[83] as a gift given to him by the said lord in consideration of his having stayed and resided in Tarascon for ten whole days in order to watch the aforesaid *Pas*, by order of my lord, the above-mentioned dauphin, as attested by certification from Philippe de Lenoncourt; total: 17 fl. 8 gr. 4 p.

To Mermet du Perry,[84] armourer, on the same day, 1 *florin* owed to him for having polished

---

72 [Robert du Fay]. See above, lines 625–48 in the narrative account.

73 A *florin* was a gold coin minted originally in Florence but also in other places in the later Middle Ages. DMF.

74 Throughout these account entries, 'the said' or 'the aforesaid' lord refers to René of Anjou, except for one entry where it is ambiguous (see below, n. 85).

75 [Jehan Cosse, seigneur de Grimault]. See above, lines 687– 712 in the narrative account.

76 The implication here is that Romarin is in charge of redistributing these moneys to the others mentioned in this entry.

77 On trumpets being played at this *pas*, see above, lines 189, 250, 902, 973, 993, 1004 in the narrative account.

78 Largesse here refers to the extra money given by the lord, René of Anjou, to these heralds, who would be expected to make it known publicly that he had shown such generosity towards them on top of their normal wages. For comparison, see above, line 1040 in the narrative account, for the heralds fêting the largesse of the two shepherd-defenders.

79 This refers to Louis de Beauvau, author of the narrative account of the *Pas de la Bergère*, who was seneschal of Anjou.

80 [Jehan Regnault]. He was a musician, as the context of the entry makes clear. On instruments (other than trumpets) being sounded at this *pas*, see above, line 1005 in the narrative account.

81 No information is available about who the person holding this office was in 1449.

82 An *écu* is a gold or silver French coin of varying value that featured the arms of the lord who had it minted; the *gros* is a silver coin also of varying value; a *patac* is a Provençal coin worth three *deniers locaux* in Avignon. DMF.

83 These currencies are recalculated here into *florins* to enable accounting: hence, ten *écus* = 210 *gros*, twenty *patacs*, which is converted here into seventeen *florins* eight *gros* four *patacs*, meaning that one *florin* = twelve *gros*, and one *gros* = eight *patacs*.

84 This person also appears in other entries in these accounts: ECMR, nos 586, 591, 592.

a legharness for the above lord[85] as well as one of his helms; cost, by certification from my lord of Mallelièvre,[86] squire of the stables, etc.: 1 fl.

733. 11 June 1449.

To Robinet the Frenchman,[87] dulcimer player, the eleventh day of the said month, 6 *florins*, which the said lord gave him in consideration of the fact that for several days he played this instrument in front of him, the queen and others during the said *Pas*. Total, by certification from the said seneschal: 6 fl.

To Perret Guiot,[88] hose maker, the eleventh day of the said month, for the items described hereafter, 65 *florins* 6 *gros* 4 *patacs*, that is to say: for 7 *cannes* and 2½ *paumes*[89] of grey cloth made in Lille given by the said lord to Philippe de Lenoncourt and Philibert de Laigue, squires, to make the coverings and trappers for (326) their destriers, the lower part of their jackets and other things that they need for holding the *Pas* of the Shepherdess, to the value of 5 *florins* 6 *gros* per *canne*, which comes to 39 *florins* 10 *gros* 4 *patacs*; also owed to him[90] for another piece of grey cloth made in Béziers, amounting to 11 *cannes*, in order to make the jackets for their servants at the joust, to the value of 2 *florins* 4 *gros* per *canne*, which comes to 25 *florins* 8 *gros*; the total of which is 65 *florins* 6 *gros* 4 *patacs*, by certification from the said lord of Mallelièvre, and by receipt, etc.: 65 fl. 6 gr. 4 p.

To the said Perret, on the same day, 17 *florins* 6 *gros*, which sum is owed to him for 5 *cannes* of white and green cloth for cutting out and making into the shape of a horse's harness to be appliquéed onto a trapper of black velvet that was given by the afore-named lord to Monseigneur Ferry[91] for jousting at the said *Pas* of the Shepherdess, to make a *giornea*[92] with dagging hanging from its shoulders[93] as well as jackets for those serving at the joust, to the value of 3 *florins* and 6 *gros* per *canne* for each of them; as attested by certification from Philippe de Lenoncourt and by receipt, etc.: 17 fl. 6 gr.

---

85 Logically, this must refer here to armour belonging to Philippe de Lenoncourt rather than to René, since the latter did not compete at this event.

86 Bertrand de La Haye (*c*.1425–after 1458), lord of Mallelièvre, was the brother of Jean de La Haye, lord of Passavant and Mortaigne, and a member of René of Anjou's Order of the Crescent (1449) who fought at the *Joyeuse Garde/Saumur* (1446). Mérindol, *Les fêtes*, p. 164. Bertrand is attested in March 1458 as having borrowed a book about Julius Caesar from the library of the abbot of Saint-Florent near Saumur; hence his death must have occurred after this date. 'VII. Canton de Mortagne. Emprunt par le seigneur de la Mallièvre du roman de Julius César, en 1458', *Société de l'émulation de la Vendée pour le développment de l'agriculture, des sciences, lettres et arts: Annuaire départemental*, quatrième année (1857), 237–9. Bertrand also appears in other entries in these accounts: see ECMR, nos 598, 635.

87 [Robert le Francoys]. This musician also appears in another entry in these accounts: ECMR, no. 744.

88 [Perret/Pieret Guiot]. No information is available about this person, who appears only in this entry in the accounts.

89 A *canne* is a unit of measure approximating to about a metre; a *paume* is a smaller unit of measure, approximating to about 20 cm. DMF.

90 That is, Perret Guiot.

91 Ferry II de Vaudémont-Lorraine: see above, lines 40–3, 517–68 of the narrative account.

92 This is 'a short, open-sided cape-like garment'. Margaret Scott, *Medieval Dress and Fashion* (London: British Library, 2007), p. 123, caption to Fig. 75.

93 The term used in the original text is *alles* (wings), but has been translated here as 'dagging', given that the *giornea* was a garment with open sides that were often dagged.

[Next follow two entries regarding items purchased for the tournament at Launay]

To Romarin,[94] the pursuivant, on the same day, 4 *florins*, for the purchase of 400 [leaves of] gold mixed with silver which he bought in Avignon in order to paint the standards on the lances of the said Monseigneur Ferry for when he jousted. Total, by certification from Philippe de Lenoncourt and by receipt from Romarin: 4 fl.

To Ozias de Nyons,[95] a merchant of Avignon, on the above-mentioned day, 40 *florins* for the purchase of 4 *cannes* of grey damask, given by the said lord to Isabelle de Lenoncourt[96] to make her shepherdess's gown, this being to the value of 10 *florins* per *canne*. Total, by (327) certification from my lord, the aforesaid seneschal, and by receipt, etc.: 40 fl.

734. 13 June 1449.

To Noël Boutault,[97] tailor, on the thirteenth day of the said month, for the fabric and the making up of a pourpoint in green damask for the said lord for the first day of the above-mentioned *Pas*, 3 *florins* 6 *gros*, and for an Italian *giornea* of black velvet for the same lord, 1 *florin* 9 *gros*.

To the said Noël, on the same day mentioned above, for the making up of a harness[98] in black velvet decorated with a gold fringe for the said lord for the first day of May at a cost of 2 *florins*; for the making up of a horse trapper in black velvet for jousting, with green and white cloth appliqué that was given to the said Monseigneur Ferry,[99] 2 *florins* 6 *gros*; for the making up of an Italian *giornea* in black velvet also with appliqué in these same colours, for wearing over the harness at a cost of 1 *florin*; for 4 *paumes* of scarlet[100] for making the shepherdess's hood,[101] to the value of 23 *florins* per *canne*; total: 11 *florins* 6 *gros*.

---

[94] See above, line 64 of the narrative account.

[95] This person, also known as Ozias de Mons, also appears in other entries in these accounts: ECMR, nos 349, 475, 606, 618, 620, 658, 680, 681, 747.

[96] [Ysabeau de Lenoncourt]. See introduction, p. 114.

[97] This person also appears in other entries in these accounts: ECMR, nos 749, 751.

[98] This seems to refer to an item of clothing made to look like a harness, as it was intended to be worn underneath a *giornea*.

[99] For these same details in the narrative account, see above, lines 522–4.

[100] Scarlet here refers to 'a high-priced luxury woollen broadcloth' that was not necessarily red but was usually brightly coloured. John Munro, 'Scarlet', in EMDT, pp. 477–81.

[101] The hood itself is described in the narrative account as being 'pink in colour': see above, lines 260–1.

Thanks are due to Margaret Scott for her invaluable help in deciphering, translating and documenting many of the references to clothing and textiles in both the narrative and financial accounts for this *pas d'armes*, and to Craig Taylor for helping to supply biographical information on the competitors at this event.

Rosalind Brown-Grant

Source 7

The *Pas de la Fontaine des Pleurs* (*Pas* of the Fountain of Tears), Chalon-sur-Saône, 1449–50

This source consists of a translation of a complete narrative account of this event.

Author: Olivier de La Marche

Language: Middle French

Edition used: Henri Beaune and Jules d'Arbaumont, eds, *Mémoires d'Olivier de La Marche, maître d'hôtel et capitaine des gardes de Charles le Téméraire*, 4 vols (Paris: Librairie Renouard, 1883–84), vol. 2, pp. 141–204 (= OdLM). Another narrative account of this *pas d'armes* is contained in the chivalric biography known as the *Livre des faits de messire Jacques de Lalaing*: see LF, pp. 311–26 (chapters of arms) and 331–404 (event); CL, pp. 210–17 (chapters of arms) and 219–51 (event).

Select bibliography:

Devaux, Jean, 'Le culte du héros chevaleresque dans les *Mémoires* d'Olivier de la Marche', *PCEEB*, 41 (2001), 53–66

Emerson, Catherine, *Olivier de La Marche and the Rhetoric of Fifteenth-Century Historiography* (Woodbridge: Boydell Press, 2004)

Forster, Loïs, 'Les pas d'armes et emprises d'armes dans la formation chevaleresque au XVe siècle: L'exemple de Jacques de Lalaing', in *La construction du militaire, Volume 2: Cultures et identités combattantes en Europe de la guerre de Cent Ans à l'entre-deux guerres*, ed. by Benjamin Deruelle and Arnaud Guinier (Paris: Éditions de la Sorbonne, 2017), pp. 93–116

Gaucher, Élisabeth, '*Le Livre des Fais de Jacques de Lalain*: Texte et image', *Le Moyen Âge*, 95 (1989), 503–18

Millar, Alistair, 'Olivier de La Marche and the Court of Burgundy, *c.*1425–1502' (unpublished PhD dissertation, University of Edinburgh, 1996) <https://era.ed.ac.uk/handle/1842/1540>

Nadot, Sébastien, *Le Spectacle des joutes: Sport et courtoisie à la fin du Moyen Âge* (Rennes: Presses Universitaires de Rennes, 2012)

Szkilnik, Michelle, 'Mise en mots, mise en images: *Le Livre des Faits du bon chevalier Jacques de Lalain*', *Ateliers (Cahiers de la Maison de Recherche, Université Charles de Gaulle–Lille 3)*, 30 (2003), 75–87

INTRODUCTION

This *pas d'armes* was held on the island of Saint-Laurent, which divides the River Saône into two large channels at the town of Chalon-sur-Saône in the duchy of Burgundy.[1] It lasted for a year from the start of November 1449 to the end of October 1450,[2] a pavilion being erected at the beginning of each month so as to receive challengers and then taken down again after the fights for that period had finished. The bouts themselves mostly took place on Saturdays, except for the combats against the final six challengers (out of a total of ten), which all had to be fitted into the last month of the *Pas*. The *entrepreneur** of the event, Jacques de Lalaing (*c.*1421–53), was a renowned knight in the household of the Burgundian duke, Philip the Good (1396–1467).[3] Lalaing had already distinguished himself as a competitor in the lists by this date, having fought in a tournament at Nancy (1445) against various opponents, taken up the challenge of an *emprise** worn by the Sicilian/Aragonese knight, Jean de Boniface, at Ghent in the same year and organised his own *emprise* in 1447, which took him across Europe and culminated in a combat at Valladolid against a Castilian knight, Diego de Guzmán (1448).[4] Lalaing had also competed in another event organised on his own initiative at Stirling against Master James Douglas (1449), this latter tournament also simultaneously pitting his uncle, Simon de Lalaing, and a Breton squire, Hervé de Mériadec, against two Scottish opponents.[5]

Lalaing was the sole defender at his *pas d'armes* and challengers at this event had the choice of striking one of three shields, all of which were painted with tears, this being a key symbol of the *Fontaine des Pleurs*: the white shield stipulated fighting with pollaxes for as many strokes as the challenger wished; the violet shield stipulated fighting with swords, likewise for as many strokes as the challenger wished; and the black shield stipulated

---

[1] Chalon-sur-Saône is nowadays situated in France (dép. Saône-et-Loire, rég. Bourgogne-Franche-Comté) and Saint-Laurent is a suburb of the town. For the precise location of the *pas* itself, see Sébastien Nadot, *Le Spectacle des joutes: Sport et courtoisie à la fin du Moyen Âge* (Rennes: Presses Universitaires de Rennes, 2012), p. 194, fig. 5.

[2] See CL, p. 218 n. 425, and below, n. 29, for corroboration of these dates as given in the Lalaing biography by the accounts of the receiver-general of the duchy of Burgundy; however, see also below, n. 18, for the discrepancy between the biographer's and La Marche's datings of the event.

[3] For the key events of Lalaing's life, see CL, introduction, pp. 1–42.

[4] Lalaing's *emprise* of 1447–48, which had its own chapters of arms, consisted of his wearing a golden bracelet to which a headcovering was attached which challengers were invited to touch in order to do combat with him. He initially travelled through England, France, Iberia and Scotland (and later Italy) hoping to attract challengers, but the only foreign court where permission was given him to undertake a fight was in Castile against Guzmán. On home territory, Philip the Good permitted Lalaing to fight against an English squire, Thomas Keith, at Bruges in 1449, this person having had to make his way over to the Burgundian lands as the English king, Henry VI, had refused to allow him to touch Lalaing's *emprise* when he was in London earlier that year. See LF, pp. 160–3, CL, pp. 144–6 (chapters of arms of the *emprise*); LF, pp. 184–92, pp. 217–38, CL, pp. 154–9, 169–78 (Valladolid); LF, pp. 300–10, CL, pp. 105–10 (Bruges). See also OdLM, vol. 2, pp. 110–11, 123–9 (Bruges); and Loïs Forster, 'Les pas d'armes et emprises d'armes dans la formation chevaleresque au XVe siècle: L'exemple de Jacques de Lalaing', in *La construction du militaire, Volume 2: Cultures et identités combattantes en Europe de la guerre de Cent Ans à l'entre-deux guerres*, ed. by Benjamin Deruelle and Arnaud Guinier (Paris: Éditions de la Sorbonne, 2017), pp. 93–116.

[5] Although Lalaing initially intended this combat at Stirling to be part of his *emprise*, James Douglas requested different rules so that it was not just a single combat between the two men. See LF, pp. 272–96; CL, pp. 191–205. See also OdLM, vol. 2, pp. 105–9.

fighting twenty-five courses with lances. All of the weapons used in the combats were unrebated; hence the dangers involved were very real and thus accrued greatly to the contestants' honour. Challenges were accepted from any knights and squires of sufficiently noble birth, including those who were from lands held by the duke of Burgundy.[6] Most of the ten challengers who came were indeed from Burgundian lands, the exceptions being Jean de Boniface, against whom Lalaing had fought some years before, and a squire from Savoy, one Jacques d'Avanchy.

The setting of Jacques de Lalaing's *pas* was heavily symbolic but, unlike other contemporary Burgundian or Angevin events, such as the *Pas de la Belle Pèlerine* (Saint-Omer, 1449) or the *Pas de la Bergère* (Tarascon, 1449), it did not feature an earthly female chivalric muse. Rather, it seems to have been an expression of the *entrepreneur*'s deep piety, which involved particular devotion to the Virgin Mary and his own crusading ambitions,[7] being based on the idea of inviting challengers to come to the aid of a 'Lady of Tears', a symbol of the beset Church. This figure, probably in the form of a statue, was placed in front of a pavilion weeping into a fountain that collected her tears, next to which stood the representation of a unicorn bearing the three shields of challenge. Lalaing's pavilion itself, in which he armed himself ready for his combats, was decorated with a representation of the Virgin and Child. On guard at the pavilion was Charolais Herald, the main officer of arms at this event, who received the heralds and pursuivants who came to touch the shields on behalf of the knights and squires wishing to take up Lalaing's challenge. Moreover, the event itself was timed to coincide with a Jubilee or Holy year, when pilgrims who went to Rome would receive a plenary indulgence (i.e. complete remission of their sins), and was thus intended to attract knights and squires passing through the region on their way to see the pope; Lalaing himself made this journey to Rome after his *Pas* had finished.

The combats at the *Fontaine des Pleurs* were written up in great detail and with evident relish by the Burgundian historiographer Olivier de La Marche (*c.*1425–1502) in his *Mémoires* that he composed piecemeal over nearly fifty years. Although La Marche claims to have witnessed this tournament at firsthand[8] — whether or not he was there for the whole year is hard to determine[9] — he is also likely to have drawn on other sources, such as heralds' reports, for some of its details.[10] Not only does he explicitly acknowledge having used materials of this kind at earlier events, such as the *Pas de l'Arbre Charlemagne* (Marsannay-la-Côte, 1443),[11] but he also refers directly from time to time in his own account of the *Fontaine des Pleurs* to pieces of information gleaned from others, either

---

[6] See below, p. 156, for La Marche's comment on this aspect of Lalaing's event.

[7] CL, introduction, pp. 25–6.

[8] See below, for example, where he refers explicitly to his recollections of what happened when Lalaing fought at this event against particular opponents such as Pierre de Chandio (p. 162), Gérard de Roussillon (p. 168), Jacques d'Avanchy (p. 176), Jean de Villeneuve, known as Pasquoy (p. 179), and Gaspart de Dourtan (p. 180).

[9] See Alistair Millar, 'Olivier de La Marche and the Court of Burgundy, c.1425–1502' (unpublished PhD dissertation, University of Edinburgh, 1996) <https://era.ed.ac.uk/handle/1842/1540> [accessed 19 June 2024], p. 14, who notes the memoirist's early links with Chalon-sur-Saône through his mother who owned property there.

[10] See below, for example, in the cases of Pierre de Chandio (p. 162), Jean de Boniface (p. 163) and Gérard de Roussillon (pp. 167–8).

[11] OdLM, vol. 1, p. 291.

orally or in writing.[12] Moreover, La Marche was already well acquainted with Lalaing by this time, having seen him compete at the events in Nancy, Ghent and Bruges that he recorded in his *Mémoires*;[13] indeed, this knight was something of a chivalric hero to the historiographer.[14] He was also clearly familiar with the chapters of arms for Lalaing's *pas*, as he occasionally alludes to them in his account of the event,[15] but he does not include them in his own narrative. This is not out of line with his practice elsewhere, as they are similarly omitted in his account of the *Arbre Charlemagne*.

These chapters *are*, however, included in the chivalric biography known as the *Livre des faits de messire Jacques de Lalaing* (early 1470s), which also offers a full narrative account of the *Fontaine des Pleurs*. Compiled from various sources, probably by a Burgundian herald, this text bases its account of the *Pas* on the epistle written by Toison d'or, the Burgundian King of Arms, a role performed at that time by Jean Lefèvre de Saint-Rémy, who was also the judge for much of Lalaing's event in Chalon-sur-Saône.[16] This epistle was written up by Lefèvre de Saint-Rémy shortly after Jacques's death in July 1453, when he was fighting for Philip the Good in the Ghent war of 1451–53, and sent to his father, Guillaume de Lalaing.

These two narrative sources for Lalaing's *pas d'armes* have much in common but do differ in some areas, placing emphasis on very different aspects of it at times.[17] For example, they do not always tally in terms of either dates[18] or the order in which the combats were fought.[19] The Lalaing biography is also much more punctilious in recording the coats of arms wore by the various challengers and goes into far more detail on the post-combat festivities.[20] La Marche, by contrast, seems much more interested in delving into the backstory of certain competitors so as to explain their motivations and/or particular circumstances,[21] in analysing the precise fighting techniques employed by the combatants, and in describing the exact specifications of the weapons used (particularly the pollaxes and swords). Whilst some of these latter details may have been gleaned from other sources, La Marche's expertise in these technical aspects of combat, which is also in evidence in

---

[12] See below, for example, on the Boniface joust (p. 165). On the use La Marche made in the writing up of his memoirs of others' contemporaneous notes of events, see Claude Gaier, 'Technique des combats singuliers d'après les auteurs "bourguignons" du XVe siècle', *Le Moyen Âge*, 91 (1985), 415–57 (pp. 421–2), and *Le Moyen Âge*, 92 (1986), 5–40.

[13] OdLM, vol. 2, pp. 60 (Nancy); 81–2, 96–104 (Ghent); 105–9 (Stirling); 110–11, 123–9 (Bruges).

[14] Catherine Emerson, '"Tel estat que peust faire le filz aisné légitime de Bourgoingne": Antoine, Great Bastard of Burgundy and Olivier de La Marche', *PCEEB*, 41 (2001), 77–87; Jean Devaux, 'Le culte du héros chevaleresque dans les *Mémoires* d'Olivier de la Marche', *PCEEB*, 41 (2001), 53–66.

[15] For example, see below regarding Pedro Vásquez de Saavedra (p. 157) and Boniface (pp. 163–4).

[16] JLdSR – Ép.

[17] Catherine Emerson, *Olivier de La Marche and the Rhetoric of Fifteenth-Century Historiography* (Woodbridge: Boydell Press, 2004), pp. 172–3, 193–4, 195–6, 202–3, 208–9.

[18] For example, see below, p. 169, where La Marche claims that the *Pas* ran for a year from September 1449, whereas the Lalaing biographer states that it lasted from the beginning of November 1449 to the end of October 1450.

[19] See below, n. 104.

[20] Élisabeth Gaucher, '*Le Livre des Fais de Jacques de Lalain*: Texte et image', *Le Moyen Âge*, 95 (1989), 503–18; Michelle Szkilnik, 'Mise en mots, mise en images: *Le Livre des Faits du bon chevalier Jacques de Lalain*', *Ateliers (Cahiers de la Maison de Recherche, Université Charles de Gaulle–Lille 3)*, 30 (2003), 75–87.

[21] For example, see below his accounts of the squire Gérard de Roussillon (p. 167), the lord of Espiry, Aimé de Rabutin (p. 170), and the lord of Saint-Bonnet, Claude Pitois (pp. 172–3).

his account of the *Arbre Charlemagne*, if to a slightly lesser degree, is not surprising; he was, after all, in Claude Gaier's words, an 'homme de guerre par excellence' (a consummate man of war), being captain of Charles the Bold's guards and a prisoner at the battle of Nancy in 1477 when the Burgundian duke himself was killed.[22]

In this translation of La Marche's complete text — except for two short passages that are not directly related to Lalaing's *Pas* — page numbers in parentheses have been provided for ease of reference to volume 2 of Beaune and d'Arbaumont's edition.

TRANSLATION

(141) **Chapter XXI**
[...] **how the lord of Lalaing[23] held the *Pas* of the Fountain of Tears in Chalon-sur-Saône**

[...] (142) Thus the year [14]48[24] went by without further incident, as did part of the year 1449. The duke made merry and held great festivities in his good towns where he was much loved and gladly seen. Now we come to recounting the noble *pas* that the good and virtuous Messire Jacques de Lalaing held for a whole year in the land of Burgundy, as well as the fine feats of arms that he performed and the different noblemen against whom he fought. However, first it is important that I answer a question that (143) could be asked about this matter, which is as follows: why did Messire Jacques hold his *pas* in Burgundy,[25] a land that was subject to his sovereign lord and prince, and yet did not exclude his prince's subjects from [participating in] it?[26] Also, why did he organise his *pas* during a Jubilee period and at that particular time? To this I make the following response by citing Messire Jacques's own words to me, for I was sufficiently closely acquainted with him to be privy to his secrets compared to anybody else of my age in the Burgundian household. He said that he went to Burgundy for two reasons: the first was because in that land there were many fine noblemen and people who wished to display their nobility and bravery; the second was because the area was situated at the crossroads between France, England, Spain and Scotland for the purpose of travelling to Rome, given that the holy pardons and Jubilee of the year 1450 were imminent. It therefore seemed to him that, for these two reasons, more noblemen would be aware of his *emprise*[27] and more of them would be more likely to come

---

[22] Gaier, 'Technique', pp. 420–1. See also below, pp. 176–8 (Jacques d'Avanchy bout) where La Marche parades his intimate knowledge of arms, armour and fighting techniques.

[23] Jacques de Lalaing was not actually the lord of Lalaing at this time; this was his father, Guillaume de Lalaing (d. 1475). CL, introduction, pp. 2–7.

[24] Written 'l'an quarante-huit' (the year forty-eight).

[25] 'Burgundy' here means the duchy of Burgundy within the kingdom of France, which gave the ducal dynasty its name, but Lalaing himself was from Hainaut rather than from this part of the Burgundian composite state, hence the reference to him later on in La Marche's account as a 'foreigner' (see below, p. 160). CL, introduction, pp. 7–13.

[26] La Marche would seem to be drawing a contrast here between Lalaing's inclusion of knights and squires who were loyal to the Burgundian duke at this event and the exclusion of such competitors from the earliest Burgundian *pas d'armes*, the *Arbre Charlemagne*, as stipulated in its chapters of arms: see Source 4, p. 75.

[27] *Emprise* here refers to the chapters of arms relating to this *pas d'armes* and the shields that were to be touched by challengers who came to the event; it is not to be confused with Lalaing's earlier *emprise*,

to his *pas* and touch his *emprise*. This was all the more reason for his second consideration, which is that it was his wish — if it so pleased God — to have presented his coat of arms or to have presented himself in person in closed lists in order to fight thirty challengers before he reached thirty years of age. Indeed, it is true to say that, at the time when he came to Burgundy to hold his *pas*, he was already twenty-nine years old, by about a month or seven weeks.[28] For these two closely related reasons, (144) Messire Jacques held his *pas* in Burgundy at the above-mentioned date. This event proceeded in the following manner.

Messire Jacques de Lalaing took up residence in Chalon-sur-Saône, a town in the duchy of Burgundy, and was accompanied by Pedro Vásquez de Saavedra,[29] a very gentle* knight of whom mention was made above, that is to say where the account was given of the *Pas*[30] held by the lord of Charny.[31] This Messire Pedro was an experienced man, one sound in both body and counsel. It is my belief that if Messire Jacques had suffered any illness or other mishap, it was his intention to have (145) himself replaced by Messire Pedro; as his chapters made clear, he was not obliged to fight in person.[32] Several noblemen were with him and he was there in great estate, being fully and richly accompanied. Moreover, the duke of Burgundy sent Toison d'or, King of Arms,[33] to be the judge in his absence. Having taken up residence, Messire Jacques de Lalaing prepared his *pas* and all that pertained to it according to his plans and wishes. It is important to understand, as noted above, that the town and city[34] of Chalon are situated in the duchy of Burgundy and that the Saône, together with the Doubs, is the frontier between the county and the duchy of Burgundy.

---

which involved his travelling to foreign courts to seek out challengers who were invited to touch his bracelet with the attached headcovering.

28 On the vexed issue of Lalaing's age, see CL, introduction, pp. 12–13. If this is August 1449, La Marche would seem to be suggesting that Lalaing was born in September/October 1420.

29 [Pietre Vasque]. Pedro Vásquez de Saavedra (*c.*1410–77), originally from Castile, was a chamberlain of Philip the Good (1443–59); he was in London and Cologne before participating in the *Arbre Charlemagne* (1443) and took part in a naval expedition under the command of Waleran de Wavrin (also known as Waleran de Berlettes) to Constantinople and the Black Sea that was directed against the Ottoman Turks (1444). He also fought in the Ghent war (1451–53) and made his vow at the Feast of the Pheasant in Lille (1454). PCB no. 1056; VdF no. 208. See also OdLM, vol. 2, p. 144 n. 2, where the editors cite the account of the receiver-general of the duchy of Burgundy in Dijon, Archives de la Côte-d'Or, B 1717, fol. 60r, which details the sum paid on 18 October 1449 to Pedro Vásquez for the expenses that he would incur at the *Pas* in his capacity as Lalaing's helper; this account thus confirms the start of November as the date on which the event opened.

30 For La Marche's narrative account of the *Arbre Charlemagne*, see OdLM, vol. 1, pp. 283–7, 290–324, 324–51.

31 Pierre de Bauffremont (*c.*1397–1472), lord of Charny, a member of the Order of the Golden Fleece from its inception (1430), was a chamberlain (1426/7, 1433–58) then councillor-chamberlain (1454) of Philip the Good and later a *chevalier d'honneur* of Margaret of York (1468). COTO, pp. 45–7; PCB no. 321.

32 The seventeenth chapter of arms explicitly states that if the *entrepreneur* of the *Pas* was unable to fight for a legitimate reason, such as having suffered an injury, he would be within his rights to appoint a replacement. LF, p. 321; CL, p. 215.

33 [Thoison d'or]. Jean Lefèvre de Saint-Rémy (*c.*1396–1468) was King of Arms of the Golden Fleece (1431–68) and also a chronicler in his own right. PCB no. 545; Alexandre Grosjean, *Toison d'or et sa plume: La Chronique de Jean Lefèvre de Saint-Rémy*, Burgundica, 25 (Turnhout: Brepols, 2017).

34 The text makes a distinction between the city, meaning the oldest, central part of Chalon-sur-Saône, and the town, meaning what has grown around this centre over time. The term *faubourg*, used

These two rivers pass under a great bridge, at one end of which is a large *faubourg* known as Saint-Laurent. This *faubourg* is surrounded by the river, as if it were an island.[35] On this island is a very lovely plain, like a meadow, where there is now a church belonging to the order of the Cordeliers,[36] which was built after that time. It is on this island that the *entrepreneur* had the lists put up as well as the cloth barrier* for jousting on horseback. The surface was very well prepared with sand and everything else that was needed. Likewise, a stand was built for the judge and for the lords. Then, on the first Saturday in September in the year 1449,[37] a pavilion was erected at the end of the great bridge (146) on the Saint-Laurent side, the domain of the duke of Burgundy by virtue of his being the viscount of Auxonne.[38] This pavilion was very finely palissaded and no one could approach it without the permission of Charolais Herald,[39] a herald of great note who was an officer of arms to Charles, count of Charolais.[40] He wore his coat armour* and held a white baton in his hand; his role was to guard the images[41] that had been ordered for the *entrepreneur*'s *emprise.* The first of these, at the highest point of the back of the pavilion, was a painting of the glorious Virgin Mary, with the Redeemer of the World, her son and lord, held in her arms. Further down, to the right-hand side of this image was the representation of a lady in very decorous and costly dress. She wore a simple headcovering and was depicted weeping in such a manner that her tears fell down and ran onto the left-hand side [of the image] where there was a fountain with a unicorn placed next to it in such a fashion that it held up the three shields, these being meant to signify the three different types of combat that the *entrepreneur* wished to undertake in his *emprise.* The first of these was white, for combat with the pollaxe; the second was violet, for combat with the sword; the third, which was set underneath the other two in this triple display, was black, for combat with lances. All three shields were strewn with blue tears; it is for this reason (147) that the lady was named the Lady of Tears and the fountain was called the Fountain of Tears.

Now have I described how this noble *pas* was undertaken and the arrangements that were made for it: these things were seen as novel and unusual in that place and they attracted a great deal of attention from many different people. On that same day, a herald

---

in the next sentence to refer to the island of Saint-Laurent, means a surrounding area or district that has gradually been incorporated into the town; hence it has been left untranslated here.

35 There was in fact a bridge linking the island of Saint-Laurent to Chalon-sur-Saône, but crossing the river each time in a boat meant that Lalaing would be clearly seen by the inhabitants of the town, thus heightening the theatrical sense of his undertaking a journey in order to defend his *pas.* Nadot, *Le Spectacle*, p. 194.

36 This church, belonging to Franciscan friars, was constructed with the support of Philip the Good in the period 1451–60. Emerson, *Olivier de La Marche*, p. 172.

37 That is, on 6 September 1449.

38 Auxonne is nowadays situated in France (arr. Dijon, dép. Côte-d'Or, rég. Bourgogne-Franche-Comté).

39 [Charrolois le herault]. No information is available about who served in this role in 1449. PCB no. 547. Jean Lefèvre de Saint-Rémy was Charolais Herald until he became King of Arms of the Golden Fleece (1431). Grosjean, *Toison d'or*, pp. 73–4.

40 [Charles de Charrollois]. Charles, count of Charolais (1433–77), the future duke Charles the Bold, was the son of Philip the Good and Isabel of Portugal; he was married to 1. Catherine of France, 2. Isabel of Bourbon, 3. Margaret of York. PCB no. 612; COTO no. 34.

41 On the discrepancies between the form and placement of these various images in the accounts of La Marche and the Lalaing biographer, see Gaucher, '*Le Livre des Fais*' and Szkilnik, 'Mise en mots'.

by the name of Toulongeon[42] came to the palissade and called over the herald who was guarding the pavilion, saying to him: 'Noble herald, I request permission to enter and touch one of the three shields that have been entrusted to your care, both for and in the name of a noble squire called Pierre de Chandio.'[43] The herald received him very joyfully, telling him that he was most welcome and giving him permission to enter. Toulongeon, like the experienced officer he was, knelt down before the Virgin Mary, greeted (148) the Lady of Tears and then touched the white shield, saying: 'I am touching the white shield both for and in the name of the squire Pierre de Chandio. I confirm in truthful words that, on the day that is allotted to him, he will be here in person to perform the feats of arms stipulated and regulated by the said shield and in accordance with the chapters of arms of the noble *entrepreneur*, if God should keep him from harm and save him from [having to fulfil] a legitimate commitment.' With that, he took his leave and left the palissade. The pavilion was guarded and left up until midday when Charolais finished his duties and gave his report of that day's adventure to the good knight, Messire Jacques de Lalaing, saying how Pierre de Chandio had had the white shield touched. Messire Jacques was very pleased and welcomed Toulongeon Herald who had brought this good news, giving him a gift and setting him an imminent date for the combat, which was to be on the following Saturday.

On that date, which was the thirteenth day of September,[44] the lists were prepared, the judge's stand was put up and the pavilions erected for the two champions. Messire Jacques's pavilion was made of white satin strewn with blue tears; that of Chandio was of red satin, emblazoned with his coat of arms on the pavilion's decorative textile trimmings.[45] The judge took his place, accompanied by Guillaume, lord of Sercey,[46] who was at that time bailiff of Chalon, by Master Pierre, lord of Goux,[47] an important man in the duke's great council who was subsequently made chancellor, and by various other councillors and noblemen who were experienced in the pursuit of arms. Once they had taken their seats, Messire (149) Jacques left the Carmelite church[48] situated near the town gate and in the

---

[42] No information is available about who served in this role in 1449.

[43] [Pierre de Chandios]. Pierre de Chandio, from a noble family of Franche-Comté, was the son of Jean and Jeanne de Bauffremont; he is not known to have had any connection to the Burgundian ducal household.

[44] This date is probably incorrect, as Lalaing was away defending the town of Gravelines until 13 September. CL, pp. 29 and 218.

[45] The text uses the term *goutieres* (DMF: 'parement de passementerie'); the definition given in the translation above is from Gina Barrett, 'Passementerie', in EMDT, pp. 403–6.

[46] [Guillaume, seigneur de Sercy]. Guillaume de Sercey, lord of Champalement and Igornay, was owner of the castle of Sercey (1427–64). Louis de Contenson, 'Le château de Sercy', *Bulletin Monumental*, 73 (1909), 98–126. See also below, n. 80.

[47] Pierre de Goux (1408–71), a jurist by training (hence his title of Master) was originally from a non-noble family but was knighted by Philip the Good at the battle of Gavere (1453); he became Philip's *maître des requêtes* (master of requests) (1451), one of his chamberlains (1458), and chancellor (1465), in which capacity he also served Charles the Bold. PCB no. 2024; Richard Vaughan, *Charles the Bold: The Last Valois Duke of Burgundy* (London/New York: Longman, 1973), pp. 8, 74.

[48] This church was founded as part of a Carmelite convent in 1317; only a chapel of it survives today as a reading room in the modern Bibliothèque Municipale <https://www.lejsl.com/edition-de-chalon/2019/08/26/a-chalon-une-excursion-dans-le-passe-de-la-bibliotheque-municipale> [accessed 19 June 2024]. The map provided in Nadot, *Le Spectacle*, p. 194, locates this church in the north-eastern

faubourg of the gate of Saint-Jean du Maizel.[49] After having devoutly heard three Masses, he stepped into a covered boat, accompanied by Messire Pedro Vásquez and several other noblemen of his household, for he was there in high estate. Moreover, he met up when he was in the duchy with two noblemen who were brothers, the elder being Messire Claude de Toulongeon, lord of La Bastie,[50] and the younger Tristan de Toulongeon, lord of Soucy;[51] these two were the sons of Messire Antoine de Toulongeon,[52] the former marshal of Burgundy, the one under whose command the battle of Bar[53] was won and the duke, René of Lorraine,[54] taken prisoner. These two lords from the household of the duke of Burgundy were worthy and courageous men and, because Messire Jacques was a foreigner in that land, they kept company with him and never left his side for the whole duration of the *Pas*.[55] In this manner the knight crossed the River Saône, moored up on the island where he was to undertake combat and stepped out of his boat; he was dressed in a long robe of grey cloth of gold lined with marten fur. In his hand he held a banderole, adorned with images of the objects of his veneration;[56] he made the sign of the cross with this banderole as he did so, and very nicely too. He came into the lists and presented himself

---

corner of the town, but in fact it is north-west of the island of Saint-Laurent, just across the other side of the River Saône, as can be seen on a town map of 1575.

[49] This area was north-west of the island of Saint-Laurent.

[50] Claude de Toulongeon (1421–1503), lord of La Bastie-sur-Cerdon, was dubbed a knight at the battle of Gavere (1453), made his vow at the Feast of the Pheasant (1454) and was a councillor-chamberlain of Philip the Good (1454–75). He participated in the *Pas de l'Arbre d'or* in Bruges (1468) and was a member of the Order of the Golden Fleece (1481). PCB no. 1736; COTO no. 93; VdF no. 202.

[51] Tristan de Toulongeon, lord of Soucy, was a squire of the stables and later chamberlain in the households of both Philip the Good and Charles the Bold (1453–75). PCB no. 1795.

[52] [Anthoine de Toulongeon]. Antoine de Toulongeon (d. 1432), was a chamberlain of Philip the Good (1426) and marshal of Burgundy (1430–32). PCB no. 229.

[53] Better known as the battle of Bulgnéville (2 July 1431), this was fought between two cousins, Antoine of Lorraine, count of Vaudémont, and René of Anjou, duke of Bar, over the succession of the duchy of Lorraine; René lost and was taken prisoner in Dijon by Duke Philip the Good. Richard Vaughan, *Philip the Good: The Apogee of Burgundy* (London/New York: Longman, 1970), pp. 26–7; Bertrand Schnerb, *Bulgnéville (1431): L'état bourguignon prend pied en Lorraine* (Paris: Economica, 1993).

[54] [Regnier de Lorraine]. René (1409–80), duke of Anjou and count of Provence (1434–80), also reigned as king of Naples (1435–42) before being deposed as the preceding dynasty was restored to power; the form of his name as given in La Marche's account underlines his claim to the duchy of Lorraine: see previous note. René was an important patron of the arts and tournament enthusiast who wrote numerous works, including the *Traité de la forme et devis d'un tournoi* (more commonly known as the *Livre des tournois*) (between 1444 and 1450) and the *Livre du Coeur d'Amour épris* (1457); he also organised tournaments that are often referred to by both contemporary sources and modern scholars as *pas d'armes* at Nancy (1445) and Launay (1446), as well as the famous *Pas de la Joyeuse Garde/Pas de Saumur* (1446); he was also in attendance at the *Pas de la Bergère* (Tarascon, 1449) that was organised by two noblemen from the Angevin court. Albert Lecoy de La Marche, *Le roi René: sa vie, son administration, ses travaux artistiques et littéraires*, 2 vols (Paris: Firmin Didot, 1875). See Sources 5 (*Joyeuse Garde/Saumur*) and 6 (*Bergère*).

[55] La Marche is alluding here to the custom of a knight-*entrepreneur* (whether of an *emprise* or a *pas d'armes*) who was competing at an event held outside his home territory being given counsellors by the local lord so as to ensure that he was aware of local customs and practices; in Jacques de Lalaing's case, this also happened when he took his *emprise* to Iberia and was given counsellors from the area to advise him in his combat against Diego de Guzmán in Valladolid (1448). LF, p. 220; CL, p. 170.

[56] This banderole may have had an image of the Virgin Mary on it, given that she is a key figure in the whole setting of the *Pas*, but La Marche does not make this explicit.

before the judge, saying in his (150) own words: 'Noble King of Arms of the Golden Fleece, appointed to be my judge in this contest by my most redoubtable and sovereign lord, my lord the duke of Burgundy and count of Hainaut,[57] I come before you to hold and defend the *emprise* of this *pas*, and to play my part in delivering and accomplishing the feats of arms requested and undertaken by Pierre de Chandio, in accordance with the content of the chapters written for this purpose.' The judge, dressed in the coat armour of the duke of Burgundy and holding a white baton in his hand, received and welcomed him most honourably before the *entrepreneur* withdrew to his pavilion.

It was not long before Pierre de Chandio made his appearance as he came over from the great bridge of Chalon.[58] He was on horseback, fully armed in his harness* with a basinet* on his head and his coat armour on. In truth, he was one of the tallest and most powerful squires to be found in all of Burgundy or the Nivernais;[59] he would have been around thirty-one years old. He was accompanied by the lords of Mirebeau,[60] Charny[61] and Scey-sur-Saône,[62] his uncles, as well as by so many of the lords and nobles of Burgundy that I estimate his entourage (151) to have comprised more than four hundred noblemen. Chandio entered the lists on a horse emblazoned with his coat of arms and then dismounted. The lord of Charny was at his side as he went over to the judge, and it was he who spoke up and said: 'Noble King of Arms of the Golden Fleece, appointed as judge in this contest by my most redoubtable and sovereign lord, the duke and count of Burgundy, behold Pierre de Chandio, my nephew, who stands before you this day in order to deliver and accomplish — with the help of God — the feats of arms requested by him to be undertaken against the *entrepreneur* of this noble *pas*, in accordance with the chapters of arms and as stipulated by the white shield that he has had touched.' The King of Arms welcomed and received him as was his due, and he went back to his pavilion. At this, everyone withdrew from the lists and the usual announcements were made. During this time, a close cousin of mine named Antoine de La Marche, lord of Sandon,[63] who had been appointed as marshal of the lists, went over to Chandio by order of the judge in order to ask him how many blows with the pollaxe he wished to request for (152) performing and delivering this feat of arms; Chandio's preference was for seventeen blows. The marshal then went over first to the judge to inform him of the number of blows and then to Messire Jacques de Lalaing to let him know his opponent's wishes and to ask him for the pollaxes that it was his duty to provide in order to undertake

[57] This reference to Philip the Good as count of Hainaut flags up the link with Jacques de Lalaing's home territory. CL, introduction, pp. 7–13.

[58] This reference to a bridge makes the point that it is Jacques de Lalaing's prerogative to arrive at the lists by boat, and thus make a more dramatic entrance, whereas all his challengers presumably took the bridge. See above, n. 35.

[59] [Nivernois]. The Nivernais is a province of France, around the city of Nevers, which forms the modern dép. Nièvre; it roughly coincides with the former duchy of Nevers.

[60] [Myrebeaud]. Jean de Bauffremont (d. 1462), lord of Mirebeau, was married to Marguerite de Chalon. HMF, vol. 8, p. 425, para. A.

[61] Pierre de Bauffremont: see above, n. 31.

[62] [seigneur de Seyl]. Guillaume de Bauffremont, lord of Scey-sur-Saône and Sombernon, as well as Remilly, Trembloy, Ruffey, Clervaux, Malain and Grosbois, was a chamberlain of Philip the Good (1426/7–58). HMF, vol. 1, p. 559, para. E; PCB no. 296. He was one of the defenders at the *Arbre Charlemagne*, alongside his brother, Pierre, *entrepreneur* of this event. OdLM, vol. 1, p. 317.

[63] [Anthoine de La Marche]. No further information is available about him.

the combat. The two pollaxes given and delivered to him were long and heavy: the hammers and heads of these weapons were of the *bec de faucon** type, with a large and heavy spike on both the topside and the underside [of the head]; they were fitted [to the wooden shaft on either side of this head] with a flat, iron plate[64] that was riveted with three large [but] short diamond-shaped nail-heads in a somewhat similar way to that which lance-heads for jousting in war are, that is without a coronal*. These pollaxes were taken over to Chandio to make his choice, with the one left being brought to the *entrepreneur.* It was not long before Pierre de Chandio emerged from his pavilion, with his coat armour on, his basinet on his head and his visor down; he made the sign of the cross with his banderole. His uncle, the lord of Charny, then handed him his pollaxe and accompanied him right up to the entrance to the lists. From the other side came Messire Jacques de Lalaing: he was wearing his harness and, instead of a coat armour, he was dressed in a paltock*, the sleeves of which were made of white satin strewn with blue tears in the colour of the shield that his opponent had touched. He wore a small, round sallet* with the visor covering his face and was armed with a little hounskull* (153) of steel mail. Then, after using his banderole to commend himself to God, he was handed his pollaxe by Messire Pedro Vásquez. Next, the two champions strode up confidently to face each other and met just in front of the judge. At first, they were wary of each other but it was not long before they started to run at one another, exchanging very hard and heavy blows that were both dealt and received most valiantly. I recollect that Lalaing, who knew that the pollaxes he had provided and distributed were not equipped with a [nearly strong enough] spike or tip on the underside [of the head] with which to damage his opponent's armour or injure him, performed a tremendous manoeuvre by turning his pollaxe round and taking the spike's hammer head in his left hand, thus making the top part of the pollaxe into the tail* and the tail into the hammer. He then advanced with a mighty thrust and struck Chandio with the spike of his pollaxe on the visor of his basinet, dealing him such a powerful blow that he broke the tip of the spike on the visor. Yet Chandio, who was tall, strong, powerful and brave, didn't retreat one step. Instead, the fight between them resumed even more fiercely and harshly than before, and they attacked each other with such vigour that the seventeen blows Chandio had requested were very soon accomplished. At this point, Toison d'or threw down his baton and the two men were separated by the men-at-arms who had been ordered to serve as guards and officials, as is customary in these matters. When they had been taken before the judge, they touched hands and each man went back to where he had started from. These feats (154) of arms were completed on a Saturday, the eighteenth day of September in the year 1449.[65]

September, October, November and December then went by and it was not until the second Saturday in January[66] that Messire Jean de Boniface,[67] an Aragonese knight who

[64] This plate is now known as a languet*.

[65] Earlier, La Marche stated that this bout took place on Saturday 13 September, which is a correct date; however, 18 September 1449, as he recalls it here, did not fall on a Saturday. The dates he gives as Saturdays for 4, 11 and 18 October 1449 are all correct.

[66] That is, on 10 January 1450 (modern style): see below, n. 76, on when the new year officially started in the Burgundian composite state.

[67] [Jehan de Bonniface]. The origins of this knight are not entirely clear, which is why the French version of his name has been kept here. His surname may refer to Bonifacio, a town situated on the

had previously fought against Messire Jacques in Ghent as recounted above,[68] arrived at the pavilion. This pavilion was put up on every Saturday for a year, in accordance with the content of the chapters of arms.[69] Boniface had made his way there from the county of Burgundy and, when he saw the pavilion with its images and allegorical setting, as well as the herald dressed in his coat armour who was guarding the palissade, he dismounted from his horse, greeted the herald and entreated him to explain the origin and meaning of the pavilion and of the allegory behind it. The herald, who knew what he was about, explained to him how a knight, the *entrepreneur* in this contest, whose name he did not reveal, had ordered him to guard the Fountain of Tears every Saturday for a year, in order to allow any nobleman who wished to touch one or more of the three shields that were hanging above the fountain. He told Boniface what each of the three shields signified and described as fully as he could what the *emprise* consisted of, offering to give him a copy of the chapters of arms in writing. The knight, who was overjoyed to have come across such an adventure, asked for permission to enter, which was duly granted him. With his own hand he touched the white (155) and the black shields whilst the herald noted down his name and asked him where his lodgings were; he replied that it was at the [sign of] the *Âne Rayé*[70] near [the church of] Saint-Georges, inside the town of Chalon.

Returning to Messire Jacques, the herald gave his report, explaining that Messire Jean de Boniface had touched both the black and the white shields. Messire Jacques then sent two noblemen to see [the knight], and they presented him, on the *entrepreneur*'s behalf, with a horse and a harness and everything that he would need to perform the feat of arms. He was allotted Friday, the twenty-fourth day of the month, as the date on which to fight on horseback, and the following day, the twenty-fifth, for the foot combat.[71] This he accepted and thus were the dates fixed for these two combats to be held.

On the Friday, the twenty-fourth day of the month, as noted above, the lists were made ready and the cloth barrier put up for the joust, as was right and proper. Messire Jean de Boniface then duly presented himself fully armed. His horse was decked out in his colours and he had it announced to the King of Arms of (156) the Golden Fleece, the judge in this contest as mentioned before, that he had come across the pavilion by a lucky chance. He had seen the image of the Lady of Tears together with the three shields hanging over the fountain and had heard about various noble chapters of arms announcing the *emprise*

---

southern tip of the island of Corsica, which was in the possession of King Alfonso V of Aragon between 1420 and 1453, hence La Marche's referring to him as Aragonese here even if he is not consistent across his *Mémoires* in doing so: see below, n. 68. By contrast, in the Lalaing biography (chapters LXVIII and LXXXVI) there are several references to Boniface as having Lombard connections (LF, pp. 343, 400; CL, pp. 225, 249) but he is more usually called 'le chevalier sicilien' (the Sicilian knight).

[68] Jacques de Lalaing was allowed by Duke Philip the Good to touch Jean de Boniface's *emprise* when he came to Antwerp in 1445, prior to their actual fight in Ghent. In La Marche's narrative account of this event, to which he alludes here (OdLM, vol. 2, pp. 81–2, 96–104), he refers to him as 'ung chevalier du royaume de Castile, serviteur du duc de Millan' (a knight from the kingdom of Castile, servant of the duke of Milan), that is, Filippo Maria Visconti (r. 1412–47), rather than stressing his connections with Aragon.

[69] The chapters of arms are in fact less specific than this, stipulating that a pavilion was to be put up on the first few days of every month for a year and that an officer of arms would be there on the first day of each of these months. LF, p. 313; CL, p. 211.

[70] This is presumably an inn, the name of which means 'the Striped Donkey'.

[71] The correct dates for this year were in fact Friday 23 January and Saturday 24 January.

and the intentions of the noble knight-*entrepreneur* of this honourable *pas* — whose name was not disclosed in the chapters of arms — and so he was presenting himself that day to perform the twenty-five courses with the lance stipulated in the chapters to be run against the *entrepreneur*, whoever he might be. He accepted these terms as if he was unaware that it was in fact Messire Jacques de Lalaing against whom he had fought in the town of Ghent — or at least he was pretending to be unaware of this. After he had presented himself, he went back to the end of the barrier and ran his horse, as he had been allowed to do. A few moments later, the *entrepreneur*, who had come from the Carmelite [church] and had crossed the river in his boat, presented himself before the judge. He was dressed in a long robe of black velvet and was very honourably accompanied by the lords and noblemen of Burgundy whom he had already won over by his virtuous conduct; they had conceived such affection and esteem for him that they all sought him out, loved and prized him, including Pierre de Chandio, his companion*, who had already competed against him and was there with his family and friends. Jacques then went back to his pavilion, which was done out like a little tent made of black silk and strewn with blue tears. Once he had put on his harness, he emerged from the tent, appropriately armed and mounted on his horse which was decked out in black velvet strewn with blue tears. The lances, which were equipped and armed as required, were handed over to Antoine de La Marche, marshal of the lists. (157) The announcements were made and two lances were brought out, with Messire Jean de Boniface having his choice of them. On the first run, they failed to hit each other. On the second, they both struck home. On the third, they both hit each other in the area between the four points* and Boniface broke his lance. On the fourth run, Messire Jacques struck Boniface in the space below his pauldron-reinforce*, piercing his harness and breaking his lance. For his part, Boniface on the same run struck a very heavy blow on Messire Jacques's armet* and wrapper*. On the sixth run, both men failed to strike each other. On the seventh, Boniface broke his lance on Messire Jacques's pauldron-reinforce whilst he hit Boniface in the area between the four points, in a clean attaint*. It so happened during this run that Messire Jacques's lance was split from the tip right down to the butt but was not otherwise broken. It was therefore the case that two new lances were brought out, with the challenger from outside* having his choice of them. Boniface took one of them but those who were serving him did not want the other lance to be taken over to the *entrepreneur*, saying that the one he had just used was unbroken even though it was split and, according to the chapters of arms, each (158) man had to run with the same lance until it was broken. Messire Jacques was happy to do so, but those in his entourage would not allow it. The debate thus continued on both sides with the judge not knowing quite how to adjudicate or what to decide since, on the *entrepreneur*'s side, they were saying that the lance was split and splintered from a clean attaint and that he would not accept dealing a blow with it that would be of so little worth; on the other side, they were asking the judge to abide by the chapters of arms, saying that the lance was neither broken nor shortened. The judge was very perplexed and did not know what to order them to do. At this point, the marshal of the lists,[72] who was a very experienced man, picked up a stick and pushed it through the split in the lance. He then carried it over to Messire Jean de

[72] Although La Marche recounts, perhaps for reasons of family pride, that it was his relative, Antoine de La Marche, who intervened in the dispute, the Lalaing biographer states that it was Pedro Vásquez de Saavedra, the *entrepreneur*'s aide, who performed this task: see CL, p. 227.

Boniface and said to him: 'My lord knight, do you really wish your opponent to run at you with this lance which can do you absolutely no harm whatsoever?' The knight looked at the lance, which was very badly damaged, and told him to have it taken away; he had no wish to run against an opponent bearing a broken weapon. A new lance was therefore given to Messire Jacques for the eighth run, on which they both missed each other. On the ninth, Messire Jean de Boniface struck (159) the tip of his lance on his companion's armet whilst Messire Jacques hit him under the pauldron-reinforce close to where he had previously struck him, pierced Boniface's harness and broke his lance. On the tenth run, Boniface dealt a very hard blow whereas Messire Jacques failed to strike him. On the eleventh run, Boniface missed and Messire Jacques hit him close to where he had earlier struck him twice, damaging his opponent's harness badly as well as his own lance. On the twelfth run, both men landed heavy blows on each other. On the thirteenth, they each hit home but Messire Jacques once again found the spot that he had previously struck and through which he had caused such damage to his opponent's harness. Some said that Boniface had had his harness tempered in some kind of water that protected it so well that a lance-head couldn't get through it. It is true to say that he was wearing such a light harness of war that, without some kind of device or artifice, it was impossible for it to withstand the blows that Messire Jacques had landed on it. However, the minutes and hours of the event were marching on and so it happened that, on the fourteenth run, Messire Jacques hit his man close to where all the other blows had landed and pierced the harness through and through: if his lance-rest* had not broken when he dealt this blow, the tip would have gone into the knight's body. When those in Boniface's company saw his harness was so badly damaged that he could not safely continue fighting, as also did those lords and noblemen present, they called to the judge. For this reason the knight was sent over to Toison d'or, who told him that he was not sufficiently (160) well armed to keep such a gentle knight as himself safe; he would not be acting as a fair judge should if he allowed him to carry on risking himself before him. For this reason, Toison d'or begged Boniface either to put on a more protective harness or to be satisfied with what he had achieved in this bout; fourteen courses had been well and truly completed such that the remaining eleven courses, that made up the total of twenty-five as stipulated by the black shield that he had touched, could be dispensed with. Moreover, he was due to fight on foot with pollaxes the following day and had asked for twenty-one blows with that weapon to be exchanged. Thus was this feat of arms brought to a close.

The next day, which was a Saturday,[73] the pavilions were put up: Boniface's little pavilion was made of white cloth emblazoned with his coat of arms; he made his presentation dressed in a black robe and went off to arm himself in his pavilion. From the other side, Messire Jacques de Lalaing made his appearance. The announcements were made, the ceremonies performed and the two pollaxes delivered and distributed, with each man receiving his. Once everything was prepared, Boniface emerged from his pavilion; he was fully armed and wore a coat armour and an Italian armet on his head that was topped with a cluster of black plumes. He marched with great boldness and courage, brandishing his pollaxe in his hands and shouting, in his Aragonese tongue:[74]

---

[73] That is, Saturday 24 January.

[74] La Marche frequently comments on the different languages spoken by foreign knights at the tournaments that he witnessed: see, for example, his comment on the rather hapless Savoyard squire Martin

(161) 'Come forth, knight! Whoever has a beautiful lady should guard her well!' Messire Jacques advanced from the other side; he was wearing a hounskull and a sallet and was dressed in the same harness and clothing that he had worn in his fight with Pierre de Chandio. He too walked boldly up to face his companion. As they met, Boniface raised his pollaxe to attack Messire Jacques but the blow was parried and they went at each other most valiantly. To tell the truth, Boniface's head was not well protected for foot combat and two or three times Messire Jacques came at him from the side and dealt him several heavy blows with the hammer of his pollaxe but without harming him. Once Messire Jacques realised that he couldn't shake his man by raining blows down on him, he went in close against his weapon using the tail of his own pollaxe in a reverse move. Having created this opening for himself, he grabbed the knight's crest in his right hand and pulled down on it with all his might in a very powerful manoeuvre. This enabled him to bring his opponent down to the ground with his face in the sand. Having achieved this, Messire Jacques went over towards the judge. The knight was helped to his feet by the guards and officials and taken over to the judge who told him that he was satisfied with what the knight had done and said that he had acquitted himself well in taking up arms against Messire Jacques de Lalaing. When the knight heard Messire Jacques named as his companion and recognised him, he greeted him with great honour and pleasure; they embraced each other and thus were their deeds of arms concluded. (162) From that month of February onwards, no other noblemen came to touch the shields until the following August.[75] During that time, Messire Jacques was at court for a while, where he was very warmly received by everyone.

Thus 1449 came to an end[76] and 1450 began, this being the holy and salvific Jubilee year in which the great general pardon would be held in Rome. From all parts pilgrims both male and female would be making their way to Rome, passing through the land of Burgundy and elsewhere in such great numbers that it was a most noble, holy and devout thing to witness. It is incumbent upon me to [carry on] speaking about the *Pas* and the *emprise* begun by that good knight, Messire Jacques de Lalaing, as described above, and to relate the many and various chivalrous feats of arms executed at that event by this knight and his companions. Indeed, it would be a great loss and shame if they were not preserved for posterity and I would regard myself as lazy and recreant in my labours if I did not employ my pen and my small talent to the best of my ability in order to write about these noble deeds that I myself witnessed.

The first Saturday of the month of May in the year 1450,[77] the pavilion was set up as usual and, as always, continued to be put up every Saturday of the year for the duration of the *emprise*. To the pavilion came (163) a young squire from Burgundy named Gérard de Roussillon;[78] he was a fine competitor, being tall, straight-backed and with a good

Ballart speaking 'en son Piemontois' (in his Piedmontese tongue) at the *Arbre Charlemagne*: OdLM, vol. 1, p. 322. On this figure, see also Essay 6.

[75] See OdLM, vol. 2, p. 162 nn. 1 and 2, where the editors point out that La Marche contradicts himself here, having earlier said that the fights with Boniface took place in January (p. 154), not February, and going on to explain that the next challenger comes along in May (p. 162), not August.

[76] Throughout the Burgundian composite state, as well as in many other European countries, the Easter cycle determined the start of a new year in the later Middle Ages.

[77] That is, 2 May 1450.

[78] [Gerard de Rossillon]. Gérard de Rochebaron, known as Roussillon, was the son of Antoine de

build. This squire addressed himself to Charolais Herald, asking for his leave to enter as he wished to touch the white shield with the intention of engaging the knight-*entrepreneur* in combat with the pollaxe for a total of twenty-five blows. The herald allowed him to enter and Gérard touched the shield. After this, it was reported to Messire Jacques de Lalaing, who soon sent him word to fix a date. However, Gérard had failed to obtain either consent or counsel from his father, family or friends; he was also very young, being just a squire, was poorly accompanied with neither father nor friends present and was badly equipped, since he did not have a proper harness, clothing or anything else that was needed. Messire Jacques, by contrast, was a renowned knight who was very experienced, skilled and expert in the pursuit of arms. For these reasons, the combat was postponed to the twenty-eighth day of that month of May, on which date many lords and noblemen from Burgundy came to keep company with Gérard, for he did have some good and notable friends, as well as others who were there to watch the fighting. (164) Because Toison d'or was away travelling on a mission for his prince at that time,[79] the duke of Burgundy gave the order that he would be replaced as judge of the event by Guillaume, lord of Sercey. This Guillaume was a squire, a very fine, wise and renowned man who was first squire of the stables to the good duke,[80] as has been noted above.

So, on the twenty-eighth day, as mentioned before, the lists were made ready and the marshal of the lists for that day was Guillaume Rolin, lord of Beauchamp.[81] The knight-*entrepreneur* presented himself in his customary manner whilst Gérard, coming from the other side, made his appearance in fine company. He was tall, armed with a basinet on his head and his visor raised. He was dressed in his coat armour and his horse was adorned with a matching trapper*; he was preceded by a banner bearing his full coat of arms. This gave rise to some discussion, as some said (165) that the lord of Clomot,[82] his father, had never

---

Rochebaron, lord of Berzé, and Philippote of Burgundy, a bastard daughter of John the Fearless, duke of Burgundy. From 1452 onwards, he was a cupbearer and a squire of the stables in the service of Philip the Good, Charles of Charolais, Isabel of Bourbon and Isabel of Portugal. He participated in the *Pas du Chevalier au Cygne* (Lille, 1454), fighting against Adolf of Cleves, lord of Ravenstein, and made his vow at the Feast of the Pheasant at the same time. PCB nos 184, 237; Nadot, *Le spectacle*, p. 336; Monique Sommé, *Isabelle de Portugal, duchesse de Bourgogne: une femme au pouvoir au XVe siècle*, Histoire et civilisations (Villeneuve d'Ascq: Presses Universitaires du Septentrion, 1998), p. 286; VdF nos 178bis, 190. This squire has a very evocative name, being that of the eponymous hero of a famous epic and later romance that were greatly prized by the duke of Burgundy for their depiction of a ninth-century Burgundian knight who rebelled against the king of France.

[79] In fact, on 27 March Toison d'or was already present in the duke's household in Brussels. Between 6 May and 21 July 1450, he made a trip to see the king of France in Rouen in Normandy, together with Jean de Croÿ and other councillors and ambassadors, concerning French pirates who had been capturing the boats of Flemish citizens. ADN B 2008 fols 96v, 104v–105r; PCB no. 545; Grosjean, *Toison d'or*, pp. 313–14.

[80] Active in the household of Philip the Good from 1420, Guillaume de Sercey was first squire of the stables (1438–58). PCB no. 168.

[81] [seigneur de Beauchemin]. Guillaume Rolin, lord of Beauchamp, was a son of Nicolas Rolin, the famous chancellor of Philip the Good. Guillaume served both Philip and Charles the Bold, briefly defecting to King Louis XI of France (1470) after a falling out with Charles, but he returned to serve in his army (1471) and became captain of Dijon (1475). Vaughan, *Charles the Bold*, pp. 257–8.

[82] Antoine de Rochebaron, lord of Clomot and Berzé, was an *écuyer tranchant* of Philip, count of Charolais (the future Philip the Good) (1426/7), and then a chamberlain (1426/7–33) and councillor-chamberlain

called himself a banneret, and others said that he was from Châtillon-en-Bazois,[83] which in the Nivernais is held to be the first banner. In the end, Gérard had his banner carried [in] without further debate and he presented himself before the judge, to whom he spoke in a very confident manner. He then went back to his pavilion, which was blue in colour, as I recall; he was led by Philibert de Vaudrey[84] who was of great assistance to him on that day in all his affairs. The announcements were made and the ceremonies performed, the pollaxes were given out according to the rules, and the two men emerged from their pavilions. Because Gérard had been informed that Messire Jacques generally fought in a sallet with a hounskull, he had himself provided with a round sallet and similar head and neck defence which he put on. The two men advanced towards one another, Gérard with great composure for he had been advised, on account of his young age, not to get heated up. The *entrepreneur*, for his part, marched in a very orderly fashion, being a man of great experience, one well accustomed and attuned to the daunting and intimidating discipline of fighting in closed lists. As they approached each other in front of the judge, the *entrepreneur* ran at Gérard with great ferocity but the latter coolly absorbed these (166) first blows. He then courageously parried Messire Jacques de Lalaing's strokes and bold attacks with a great deal of self-assurance. Having valiantly seen off this first assault made on him, he then attacked his companion in turn, proving himself to be strong, fierce and powerful in the fight. Various blows were given and received on both sides before Messire Jacques attempted to strike Gérard with the hammer of his pollaxe. Yet Gérard, by making a sideways move, parried the blow and carried his parry through so that he struck the *entrepreneur* on the edge of his sallet on the right-hand side, with the knight then receiving this blow on his shoulder. However, it did him little harm and when the knight saw just how cool-headed and bold the squire was, he reached out with his left hand towards his companion's weapon and grabbed hold of it. With his right hand, he raised the head of his own pollaxe which he held tight in his hand and struck at his opponent's face. The squire threw his own right hand forward but received a blow on the right cheek, albeit one that gave him little cause for concern. The *entrepreneur* repeated this manoeuvre several times but without gaining any further advantage. The baton was thus thrown down on this occasion and the two champions separated, each to great honour and acclaim. This Gérard de Roussillon was the first person ever to fight against Messire Jacques without wearing a visor.

[Next follows a short description of a fight between Jean Rasoir,[85] *a squire in Jacques de Lalaing's household, and a Burgundian squire named Michaut de Certaines,*[86] *that took place outside the context of the* pas *proper, as well as an explanation of how Duke Charles of Orléans and his wife, Marie of Cleves, came to Chalon-sur-Saône to watch the combats.]*

(1438–58) of his. PCB no. 237. Clomot nowadays is a commune (arr. Beaune, dép. Côte-d'Or, rég. Bourgogne-Franche-Comté).

[83] Châtillon-en-Bazois nowadays is a commune (arr. Château-Chinon, dép. Nièvre, rég. Bourgogne-Franche-Comté).

[84] [Philibert de Vauldrey]. Philibert de Vaudrey, a member of a family that produced several generations of excellent jousters, was later a pantler* of Charles the Bold (1474). PCB no. 3387.

[85] No further information is available about him.

[86] See below, n. 116.

(172) *[...]* the duke of Orléans[87] was in residence for a long time in Lyon on the River Rhône, with the duchess[88] at his side. On his way home, he took a route via Chalon, at the same time as the *Pas* was being held. It was a real boon for the knight-*enterpreneur* to have so many nobles expressly present to watch and bear witness to the great solemnity of his *emprise*, and especially such a high, noble prince and a lovely, virtuous princess. He entertained them most royally, even at the pavilion in front of the Fountain of Tears.

On a Saturday when the pavilion had been put up as was the usual custom, the duke of Orléans, the duchess and Mademoiselle d'Arguel,[89] the duke's niece who (173) was at that time widely acknowledged throughout the land to be the very epitome of beauty, good sense and virtue, were all there with a large company of ladies and damsels, knights and nobles to see how the shields were guarded by the herald mentioned above. The good knight of Lalaing thought that some of these foreigners, who were French, Italians, Provençals and others, some of whom were very fine, elegant and upstanding personages at the court of the duke of Orléans, might take pity on the image of the Lady of Tears and touch one of his shields. However, this was not to be, nor did anything else happen during that month or indeed until the month of September when the year-long term of the *emprise* was due to expire. That September saw some very honourable and chivalrous feats, as you will shortly hear. The duke and the duchess only passed through Burgundy on their way back to their own lands.

[Next follows a very short section in which La Marche recounts how he first met François, son and heir of the count of Étampes[90] and brother of Mademoiselle d'Arguel, who later became duke of Brittany.]

Time passed by over these months, as noted above, until the first Saturday of September, the last month of the *pas*.[91] This Saturday fell on the (174) second or third day of the month[92] and, because it was apparent that several people were coming to touch the shields of the *emprise*, a great number of nobles and other people gathered in Chalon and made their way to where the pavilion was set up. The first one to touch a shield was Claude de

---

[87] Charles I of Orléans (1394–1465), duke of Orléans, count of Blois and Soissons, was the son of Louis I of Orléans and Valentine Visconti; he was married to 1. Isabelle of France, 2. Bonne of Armagnac, 3. Marie of Cleves. He was imprisoned by the English after the battle of Agincourt (1415) and released only in 1440, the year in which he contracted his third marriage and became a member of the Order of the Golden Fleece; he was also a famous poet of the era. COTO no. 37.

[88] Marie of Cleves (1426–87), daughter of Adolf, duke of Cleves and Marie of Burgundy, sister of Philip the Good, was married to Charles, duke of Orléans; she was a guest in the household of Philip the Good and Isabel of Portugal (1439–40). PCB no. 4320. According to the Lalaing biography, Marie of Cleves witnessed Lalaing's exploits in the tournament at Nancy (1445) and regarded him as her courtly servant; as to whether or not Lalaing himself harboured amorous feelings for her, as some modern scholars have claimed, see CL, pp. 17, 32, 45, 104–6, 144–5 n. 228.

[89] Although, confusingly, La Marche twice refers to this person as if she was unmarried, it is in fact Catherine of Brittany (d. 1476), daughter of Richard, count of Étampes, and Marguerite of Orléans (sister of Duke Charles I); in 1438, she married Guillaume VII de Chalon (1415–75), lord of Arguel, a councillor of Philip the Good (1426) and guest in his household (1442). PCB no. 1045.

[90] François II, eldest son of Richard d'Étampes and Marguerite of Orléans, became duke of Brittany in 1458. OdLM, vol. 2, p. 173 n. 2.

[91] See above, n. 29, on La Marche's incorrect dating of the year spanned by this *pas*.

[92] In fact, the first Saturday fell on 5 September in 1450, whereas 3 October 1450 was a Saturday, hence La Marche's possible confusion.

Sainte-Hélène, known as Pitois, lord of Saint-Bonnet;[93] he had the white shield touched. The second was a knight who went by the name of the 'Unknown Knight'; this was Messire Aimé de Rabutin, lord of Espiry.[94] The reason why he had adopted this name is because he had been present at the *Pas* to watch the knight-*entrepreneur* perform his feats of arms and combats, in spite of the fact that, according to the chapters of arms, those who had watched the fights and bouts at the *Pas* should not and could not then compete against the *entrepreneur* afterwards.[95] The knight was afraid that his wish to fight would not be granted and yet he really wanted to be allowed in. He touched the shield, mindful that the month was nearly over, calling himself by a disguised name in order that, if he was not able to take part, there would at least be less noise made about it. He wrote (175) some gracious letters to Messire Jacques de Lalaing, the *entrepreneur*, confessing to him that he had already watched him fight several times in the *Pas* and had been so struck by Lalaing's chivalrous conduct, skill, strength and knightly virtue with which he, the *entrepreneur*, had so greatly exalted and enhanced the high reputation of the *Pas* that he, the lord of Espiry, wished above all else that he could possibly desire to bring succour to the Lady of Tears and to be counted among the very fortunate number of competitors in this *emprise*. He longed to test himself against Lalaing, who was known and reputed far and wide to be a knight full of valour, virtue and grace, and so he humbly beseeched him to grant him permission to participate in this undertaking. This request was couched in very fine and elegant terms of which the knight had plenty at his disposal, for he was held in his day to be one of the most valiant, wise, agreeable and courtly knights of Burgundy, or indeed to be known anywhere. He was one of the thirteen who had defended the *Pas* of the Tree of Charlemagne alongside the lord of Charny, as I wrote in the first book [of my memoirs].[96] To cut to the chase, the good knight of Lalaing (176) was overjoyed and granted him his request and gave him leave, on his behalf, to make the same concession to six other noblemen, if he was asked to do so.[97]

After the Unknown Knight had touched the white shield as the previous man had done, Savoy Herald[98] came up to the pavilion dressed in his coat armour; he told Charolais

---

[93] [Claude de Saincte Helene, dit Pietois, seigneur de Sainct Bonnot]. Claude Pitois, lord of Saint-Bonnet, was the son of Guyot Pitois and Catherine de Saint-Bonnet. In the 1430s, his parents had to mortgage their goods to pay his ransom when he was imprisoned by the French king. On 24 February 1450 — that is, during the *Pas* — he sold the lordship of Mimande but this was bought back by his cousin, Jean Pitois (see below, n. 103), a year later. Antoine Marie d'Hozier de Sérigny, *Armorial général ou registres de la noblesse de France*, 3 vols (Paris: Pierre Prault, 1752), vol. 3, p. 6; Marie-Thérèse Caron, *La noblesse dans le Duché de Bourgogne 1315–1477* (Lille: Presses Universitaires de Lille, 1987), p. 303.

[94] [Amé Rabutin]. Aimé de Rabutin (d. 1472), lord of Espiry and Balorre, was bailiff of Charolais; famed in his time for his skill at tournaments, such as the *Arbre Charlemagne* as well as Lalaing's *pas*, he was also a loyal soldier and died at the siege of Beauvais during Charles the Bold's conflict with King Louis XI of France. GDH, vol. 5, p. 426.

[95] For this stipulation, see LF, pp. 315–16; CL, pp. 212–13. On this incident which is explicated much more fully in La Marche's account than in the Lalaing biography, see Essay 6.

[96] OdLM, vol. 1, pp. 314–15.

[97] La Marche seems to suggest here, somewhat oddly, that Lalaing granted the lord of Espiry not only the right to fight him but also the prerogative of giving six other knights permission to do so, thus serving as a kind of intermediary to Lalaing in attracting challengers to the *Pas*. This detail is lacking in the Lalaing biography.

[98] In LF, p. 355; CL, p. 232, this person is referred to as Piedmont Herald, who was in the service

that he had been sent there by a nobleman who had ordered him to touch all three shields since it was his wish to come in person and undertake the adventure of the three shields in order to bring help to the Lady of Tears. His wish was granted and the herald gave his master's name in this matter as that of Jacques d'Avanchy,[99] a most gentle squire from the duchy of Savoy. The fourth one was Guillaume Basam,[100] a squire from Burgundy, who had the black shield touched. The fifth was Jean de Villeneuve, known as Pasquoy,[101] also a squire from Burgundy, a powerful and skilful man, who had the white shield touched. The sixth was Gaspart de Dourtan,[102] likewise a squire from Burgundy, who at that time was renowned for being a powerful and formidable figure; he had the white shield touched. The seventh, also a squire from Burgundy, was called Jean Pitois,[103] a tall and strong man, who similarly had the white shield touched. The names of all seven men were taken over to Messire Jacques de Lalaing and recorded in the order in which they had had the shields touched.[104] The combats then took place as follows.

(177) The first one to present himself that month to perform a feat of arms was Messire Claude de Sainte-Hélène, known as Pitois, lord of Saint-Bonnet, who had been the first to touch the white shield, as mentioned above. The others were likewise dealt with in order, in accordance with the contents of the chapters of arms. I recall that it was on a Friday[105] that this knight presented himself to Toison d'or who had returned from his travels and was accompanied by knights and squires from the duke's council, all wise and discerning men and clerics[106] of high renown. The lord of La Queuille[107] accompanied Messire Claude as his kinsman, as well as various other noblemen. He presented himself

---

of Louis of Savoy, duke of Savoy (1434–65). No information is available about who served in this role in 1449.

[99] [Jaques d'Avanchies]. Jacques d'Avanchy (nowadays Vanchy, cant. Bellegarde-sur-Valserine, dép. Ain), from a Savoyard family, was a page in the household of Duke Amédée VII of Savoy in his capacity as bishop of Geneva. Guido Castelnuovo, 'Le veneur d'Espagne. Noblesse seigneuriale et cour princière en Savoie au XVe siècle', in *Mémoires de cours: Études offertes à Agostino Paravicini Bagliani par ses collègues et élèves de l'Université de Lausanne*, ed. by Bernard Andenmatten *et al.* (Lausanne: Cahiers lausannois d'histoire médiévale, 2008), pp. 257–74.

[100] [Guillaume Basam/Bassam]. This squire, who is referred to in the Lalaing biography as Guillaume d'Amange (LF, pp. 355, 382; CL, pp. 233, 243), may have been from Amange, a village in Franche-Comté (arr. Dole, dép. Jura).

[101] [Jehan de Villeneufve]. No information is available about this person.

[102] [Gaspart de Dourtain]. Gaspart de Dourtan, mentioned in the household of Charles the Bold from 1469, was a squire of the stables (1472–75). PCB no. 2697.

[103] [Jehan Pietois]. Jean Pitois, lord of La Creuze, son of Jean. On 20 February 1451, he bought the lordship of Mimande which his cousin Claude (see above, n. 93) had put up for sale. Hozier de Sérigny, *Armorial général*, vol. 3, p. 8.

[104] See LF, pp. 354–5; CL, pp. 232–3, for the slightly different order in which the Lalaing biographer says these figures came to make their challenges: Claude Pitois, the lord of Espiry, Jean de Villeneuve, Gaspart de Dourtan, Jacques d'Avanchy, Guillaume d'Amange, Jean Pitois.

[105] This would be Friday 11 September.

[106] This is likely to be a reference to Jean Chevrot (d. 1460), bishop of Tournai and president of the ducal council (1433–54) (PCB no. 736); and to Jean Germain, bishop of Chalon-sur-Saône (see below, n. 134).

[107] This may be Charles, lord of La Queuille (1435–68), son of Jacques, lord of La Queuille and Chateauneuf (1400–42) <https://www.ancestry.co.uk/genealogy/records/charles-seigneur-de-la-queuille-24-1cdcbhp> [accessed 19 June 2024].

without his armour and dressed in a long robe before withdrawing to his pavilion. From the other side, Messire Jacques de Lalaing presented himself in his usual fashion. Let it not be forgotten that the judge sent the marshal of the lists over to Claude Pitois to find out how many blows with the pollaxe he wished [to exchange]. The knight's response was that it was his understanding they were due to fight with pollaxes for as long as it took for one of them to be brought to the ground or to drop his weapon; it was for this reason that he had touched the white shield. This was relayed back to the judge and the *entrepreneur.* Whilst the latter declared that he was happy with this, the judge said that, in fact, he only had authority (178) from his prince to oversee the combats fought in accordance with the contents of the chapters of arms as signed and sealed by Messire Jacques de Lalaing. These stated that the challenger from the outside had to request a set number of blows; he as judge was authorised to supervise and adjudicate combats consisting of a fixed number of blows and not otherwise. This was communicated to Pitois but he persisted in his earlier request, for which he was reproached by his friends and family who told him that it was arrogant not to proceed according to the chapters of arms and not to do as the others had done. Even the judge insisted that he would not supervise a feat of arms over which he had no authority. Once Pitois realised this, he asked for forty-one blows with the pollaxe and so the matter was decided. After the weapons had been presented and the announcements made, Pitois emerged from his pavilion. He was young, of medium build, strong and squarely set, and had one of the best physiques in the whole of Burgundy. He was dressed in his coat armour and wore a sallet with a *barbuta**. From the other side came Messire Jacques de Lalaing, accompanied on that day by the lord of Charny. Those who had already done combat with him were also present, as was Messire Pedro Vásquez who never left his side, being the person in whose assistance and counsel he placed great trust and who was ready to take his place as defender should the need arise. The two men marched up to face each other before the judge. Pitois (179) strode along very boldly and straightaway thought to strike the *entrepreneur* in the face with the lower part of his pollaxe. Lalaing very coolly parried this blow. Pitois then brought his weapon close in to his own body and used all his might to throw it between his opponent's legs in the aim — so it would appear — of trying either to stop him from walking or to lift and raise him up from between his legs, thus putting him at a disadvantage. Yet the *entrepreneur* put his right hand on his companion's pollaxe and thwarted his plan with great self-assurance, using his blow to bring his arm down on his companion's neck. Pitois then grabbed tight hold of him and his weapon round the upper part of his body. The two men were locked together and gave every appearance of fighting like mortal enemies. Messire Jacques twice strove to bring his man down to the ground by tripping him up, but Pitois held out for a long time against his companion's strength and skill, thereby demonstrating what a talented, brave and resilient knight he was. As Messire Jacques was harrying and testing him in this way, he reached his left hand through to the spike on the pollaxe which he was holding close to his companion's head and pulled against his face; the latter could not get him to relax or release his hold without abandoning his own position, which did not look likely to be to his advantage. All he could do was to twist his head underneath Messire Jacques's arm which meant that he was held in a grip known as the *cornemuse.*[108] Feeling himself to have

[108] *Cornemuse* means 'bagpipes': the image of Lalaing holding his opponent's head under his arm thus recalls the way this musical instrument is played by holding the bag underneath one's armpit.

been put at such a disadvantage, he soon tried with all his might to (180) break out of this hold and to push Messire Jacques away. Yet Lalaing kept a firm grip on him and, in one move, pulled him with such force that the two of them dropped down one on top of the other. Indeed, Pitois never once let go and so the two knights fell in such a way that Pitois landed with his back on the sand whilst Messire Jacques landed on all fours; only his body was therefore in contact with Pitois and he could not work himself free because Pitois held him so fast. Messire Jacques lay on top of his companion, with his pollaxe crossed underneath him on his stomach, and made no further movement. At this point, Toison d'or threw down his baton and the two men were taken and lifted up together by the guards. Pitois retained his grip on Lalaing until the two of them were back on their feet. They were then led over to the judge who made them touch hands. Because of what had happened, Messire Jacques wanted to send Pitois the [forfeit of the] bracelet that was stipulated in his chapters of arms,[109] but the latter countered this by saying that he would send one [in turn] to Messire Jacques since the two of them had both fallen full-length to the ground. In the end, their friends on both sides intervened and (181) nothing more was said about the bracelet. Afterwards, they became firm friends and Pitois accompanied Messire Jacques de Lalaing as far as the kingdom of Naples in order to join him in combat, if needs be.[110]

Thus was Friday spent. The next day,[111] at about ten o'clock in the morning, the *entrepreneur* presented himself and, from the other side, came Messire Aimé de Rabutin, lord of Espiry, the knight who had called himself the Unknown Knight. Because the way in which he conducted himself appears to me to offer a good and honourable example for those listening,[112] it has been my wish to describe him and his actions in some detail. So it was that he was accompanied by a large number of noblemen who were his family and friends, and he was flanked by Messire Antoine de Montagu, lord of Couches,[113] and the lord of La Queuille, mentioned above, both of whom were great lords of Burgundy and of good repute in all aspects that a knight should be. This knight was preceded by two officers of arms, both dressed in his coat of arms, who led his horse by the bridle. He was mounted on a white hackney with a large horse-harness* that had three hangings of crimson velvet; above this the horse had a trapper that was a delicate veil, so fine (182) that

---

[109] This is stipulated in the fourth chapter of arms: LF, p. 318; CL, p. 213. The same forfeit was imposed on Jean de Boniface, who accepted it graciously, but this is recounted only in the Lalaing biography (LF, p. 348; CL, p. 229). On this incident, see Forster, 'Les pas d'armes', and Essay 6.

[110] This would be Saturday 12 September.

[111] This detail supplied by La Marche about Claude Pitois becoming Lalaing's travelling companion on his journey to Naples after the end of the *Pas* is not present in the Lalaing biography. On Lalaing's desire to continue wearing his original *emprise* for foreign knights to touch and accept his challenge whilst he was on his travels through Italy, see below, p. 183.

[112] The lord of Espiry is one of several knights, including Jacques de Lalaing, who are held up as chivalric paragons by La Marche. Devaux, 'Le culte'.

[113] [Anthoine de Montagu]. Claude de Montagu, lord of Couches (whom La Marche incorrectly calls Antoine) (1406–71, at the battle of Buxy), was married to Louise de la Tour d'Auvergne and was considered to be one of the richest nobles of the duchy of Burgundy; he was a member of the Order of the Golden Fleece (1468). COTO no. 70; Florian Grollimund, 'Un puissant seigneur bourguignon au château de Couches: Claude de Montagu', in *Chastels et maisons fortes en Bourgogne, IV: Actes des journées de castellologie de Bourgogne, 2010–2012*, ed. by Hervé Mouillebouche and Brigitte Colas (Chagny: Centre de Castellologie de Bourgogne, 2014), pp. 273–88.

one could see both the horse and horse-harness beneath. The trapper came down as far as the ground and was held up in place at each corner by a young squire of around twelve or thirteen years of age. Two of them were children of the house of Blaisy,[114] the lord of Couches's nephews, and the other two were sons of the lord of Espiry.[115] All four children were dressed in long robes of white damask cloth and wore scarlet bourrelet-chaperons* with green liripipes*. The knight himself was wearing the exact same garb as he sat on his white hackney, as noted before, and thus did he make his way on horseback into the lists, his banderole of devotion in his hand. He presented himself in person with great self-assurance and then went back to his pavilion, which took the form of a little tent of white satin decorated and embellished as you will shortly hear.

The knight requested fifty-five blows with the pollaxe and the weapons were handed to Michaut de Certaines,[116] who was serving as marshal of the lists on that day. The pollaxes were taken over to the lord of Espiry for him to have first choice, as was the custom. These long, heavy weapons were equipped with steeled spikes at both ends and were (183) the first ones with underside-spikes that the *entrepreneur* had used at this *pas*. The knight made his choice with little ado or testing [of the weapons], taking the first one that came to hand.

The announcements were made, the ceremonies performed and the guards and officials given their orders. Out from his pavilion came the *entrepreneur*, Messire Jacques, in a very measured fashion. He was accompanied by Messire Pedro Vásquez, as noted before, together with all those who had already fought with him in the lists. I need to return now to the matter of how the lord of Espiry requested the judge to let his four 'counsellors'[117] — that is the four above-mentioned young squires — remain in the lists, a request that was duly granted. The knight's pavilion was then opened up: it was draped inside with an expensive black cloth of gold that not only covered a large chair but also served as a floor covering throughout the entire tent and even spread outside it for a distance of more than two yards.[118] The knight himself was seated on the chair, fully armed in his harness, with his coat armour on, a sallet with visor on his head and a short wrapper; he was holding a banderole in his hand and was finishing up a prayer that he had started to recite. His legs were crossed and, to tell the truth, he looked just like a Caesar or one of the Worthies[119] seated in triumph. Clustered here and there around him were the four children, his counsellors, and no one else. Once he had finished his prayer, the knight

---

[114] [Blesey]. These boys were Claude II and Guillaume de Blaisy. Colette Beaune, trans., '*Le Livre des faits du bon chevalier messire Jacques de Lalaing*', in *Splendeurs de la cour de Bourgogne: récits et chroniques*, ed. by Danielle Régnier-Bohler (Paris: Laffont, 1995), pp. 1193–410 (p. 1337 n. 1).

[115] These boys were Hugues and Cyprien de Rabutin. *Ibid.*, p. 1337 n. 2.

[116] [Michault de Certaines]. This figure seems to have been from a family based in the Nivernais whose origins went back to the fourteenth century. Henri Beaune and Jules d'Arbaumont, eds, *La noblesse aux états de Bourgogne, de 1350 à 1789* (Dijon: Lamarche Libraire-Éditeur, 1864), p. 146.

[117] This rather jocular reference to the young boys as the combatant's 'counsellors' nonetheless alludes to the custom of each competitor having men assigned to him to advise him in the lists. See above, n. 55.

[118] The unit of measure given in the text is the *aune*: this equates to 1.18 metres (DMF), so here comes to just over two yards.

[119] This is a reference to the motif of the Nine Worthies (three biblical, three Roman and three medieval) to whom knights of the Middle Ages were often compared. Craig Taylor, *Chivalry and the Ideals of Knighthood in France during the Hundred Years War* (Cambridge: Cambridge University Press, 2013), p. 10.

stood up, made the sign of the cross with his banderole and walked out of his pavilion. He then crossed himself once more and handed his banderole (184) to the two young squires who were flanking him on his left-hand side; the two on his right-hand side handed him his pollaxe. This ceremony was much more swiftly and elegantly performed than I have managed to convey in writing. The good knight of Lalaing watched him from the front of his pavilion: he was armed in his usual fashion with his pollaxe held in his hand and was waiting to see if [his opponent] was ready to set off; the impression given him by this person was that he was a confident knight who was very sure of what he was about. The two knights then walked up to face each other. After taking roughly six paces, the lord of Espiry stopped and ripped off the visor from his sallet with his right hand, throwing it some distance behind him. This left his face fully exposed, the reason for it being that he was a short-sighted man and wanted his vision to be unobstructed. The two knights lined up very boldly against each other and the battle between them soon heated up on both sides as they made rapid thrusts at one another's faces. They parried and withstood several blows of the pollaxe, with each of them being struck by the other before they finally accomplished the agreed number of fifty-five blows in valiant style. The guards took hold of them even as the two men carried on wielding their weapons so as to continue fighting and attacking each other. The two of them were certainly held in such esteem and affection that their friends, servants and wellwishers on both sides fervently wished for the fight to be over without either of them suffering any violence or mishap, as was (185) indeed the case. The two of them were thus led over to the judge and from there took their leave of one another as brothers and good friends.

At that time, in that particular week, Messire Jean, lord of Créquy,[120] returned home from a trip to Jerusalem via Rome where he had obtained the holy pardon; he was a most noble and virtuous knight about whom I wrote in the first book of my memoirs.[121] This lord of Créquy was Messire Jacques de Lalaing's uncle, his mother's brother.[122] Even though he had been abroad for over a year, at great expense and on important missions, since he had a large company of knights and noblemen with him, the love he bore his nephew led him to make a stop at Chalon, which thus added greatly to the noble company that was with him. In fact, truth to tell, because of his well-renowned virtues, Messire Jacques had become so beloved by all the noblemen of Burgundy that those fellow countrymen who were the last ones to fight against him were hard pressed to find anyone willing to accompany them when they lined up against Messire Jacques, except from among their

---

[120] [Jehan, seigneur de Crequy]. Jean V de Créquy (*c.*1400–72), lord of Créquy (1411), Fressin and Canaples, was a councillor-chamberlain of Philip the Good (1426–58), *chevalier d'honneur* of Isabel of Bourbon (1458) and a member of the Order of the Golden Fleece (1430). He organised and defended the jousts in Saint-Omer (1439) on the occasion of the marriage of Charles of Charolais (i.e. the future Charles the Bold) to Catherine of France and made his vow at the Feast of the Pheasant (1454). PCB no. 392; VdF no. 47; COTO no. 23.

[121] La Marche mentions Jean V de Créquy as an illustrious member of Philip the Good's entourage in Besançon (1442) in preparation for a visit from Frederick III, king of the Romans (OdLM, vol. 1, p. 272), and also as a participant in the *Pas de la Belle Pèlerine* (Saint-Omer, 1449) when he accompanied the *entrepreneur*, Jean de Haubourdin, bastard of Saint-Pol, into the lists (OdLM, vol. 2, p. 133).

[122] Jeanne de Créquy (d. 1495?), Jean V de Créquy's sister, was married for a very short time to Robert VIII de Wavrin (d. 1415, at the battle of Agincourt) and then, a few months later, to Guillaume de Lalaing.

closest friends who could not in all honour abandon them. As a consequence of the lord of Créquy's arrival, Messire Jacques accelerated the pace at which he fought his bouts in that final month, managing to perform nine combats in fourteen days, sometimes even two in one day, as you will hear.

On the following Monday[123] came Jacques d'Avanchy (186), the Savoyard squire who had touched all three shields, as noted above, in order to compete in the foot combat according to the conditions stipulated by the white shield. The squire presented himself dressed in a long robe before heading back to his pavilion. After the knight-*entrepreneur* had presented himself, the squire asked for seventeen blows with the pollaxe. The weapons were brought over, the announcements made and ceremonies performed. Out came the squire from his pavilion, wearing his coat armour and with a sallet and visor on his head; his neck was covered and protected in a simple mail gorget* and his face was exposed. As for Messire Jacques de Lalaing, he wore his usual harness except for the fact that he had removed the gauntlet from his right hand.[124] Concerning the weapons that the *entrepreneur* had had brought over, these pollaxes were long and heavy with large steeled spikes on both the topside and the underside of the head; ever since the combat that had taken place between him and the lord of Espiry, he always used pollaxes with an underside-spike, which he had not done before, as noted above. The two champions then walked out with their weapons in their hands in order to square up to each other. The squire, who was a man of small and slender build, lined up valiantly and with his [very] first blow went for his companion's left hand with the hammer of his pollaxe. However, the knight calmly parried this blow and, on the second blow, the squire raised his weapon up in his arms in the hope of striking him higher on the body. The knight parried this blow too very forcibly with the lower part of his pollaxe, causing (187) the squire to make a half-spin away. With this same move, the knight countered by using the underside-spike in order to strike his man right on his gorget, causing the squire to retreat two paces from him. When the squire, who was fierce and confident, saw that he was at the mercy of the knight's weapon and realised that the further he stood away from him the less use his weapon was to him, he screwed up his courage and strode forward, his pollaxe in his hand, right up to Messire Jacques and placed his right hand on the knight's weapon. He then swiftly moved his left hand and abandoned his own pollaxe in order to get a firmer grip on that of his companion. As I recall, the squire's pollaxe was then kept pressed against Messire Jacques's body. However, the knight took two or three paces backwards, pulling the squire who was holding onto his pollaxe with all his might; this manoeuvre caused the squire's weapon to drop down onto the sand. Yet, the squire still didn't relax his grip and when the judge saw that he had no weapon of his own, he threw down his baton. The two of them were then grabbed by the guards, with Jacques d'Avanchy having lost his pollaxe but holding on to Messire Jacques's weapon with both hands so as to block him. I was so close to them that I heard Messire Jacques say to him after the guards had seized them: 'Let go of my pollaxe, for you shall not have it!', at which point the squire did let go. The two of them went up before the judge but did not touch hands at that point, because the other

[123] That is, Monday 14 September 1450.

[124] Lalaing's gradual removal of various pieces of armour is an indication of his desire to test himself to the full in his *pas*.

two combats that d'Avanchy had asked for by touching the black and violet shields had not yet been fought between the two men.

(188) The following Wednesday,[125] the two men made their appearance at around eight o'clock in the morning, with Messire Jacques de Lalaing, the *entrepreneur*, and Jacques d'Avanchy presenting themselves for the second time, each of them from his own side. Messire Jacques presented himself before the judge dressed in a long robe of crimson cloth of gold lined with marten fur that was comparable in style and colour to the violet shield that the aforesaid squire had touched. He, for his part, presented himself dressed in a long robe before withdrawing to his pavilion. Shortly afterwards, the marshal of the lists bestirred himself to bring over the swords to be used in the combat and he informed the *entrepreneur* that the squire had requested eleven strokes with sharpened weapons; these were to be dealt by stepping forward and back for only three paces, in accordance with the content of the chapters of arms. These swords were supplied and taken over to the squire, who took his pick of them. The announcements were made, the ceremonies performed, and the two men emerged from their pavilions. I will speak first about Jacques d'Avanchy who came out of his pavilion in full harness with his coat armour and his sword, known as an *estoc* d'armes*, in his hand. He had turned his left hand round so that it was covered by the rondel* of the sword. On his head he wore an armet in the Italian style, with a large wrapper attached. From the other side the *entrepreneur* came out of his pavilion; it was like a small tent made of vermilion silk and strewn with blue tears. He was armed in full harness and, over his armour, he wore a paltock with sleeves of vermilion silk covered in tears, as above; thus did he link his outfits to the particular type of (189) combat that he was to undertake, according to what was stipulated by the shields of his *emprise*. On his head he wore a basinet with a great visor which he had down, this being the only time that Messire Jacques had fought with his face covered. This is because the weapons to be used, *estocs*, which are sharpened and unrebated, require a high level of protection from the harness, as anyone who knows about the noble pursuit of arms would immediately understand. When Messire Jacques de Lalaing took hold of his *estoc* in his hand, he looked to me like one of the most handsome and proud-looking men-at-arms that I ever beheld, one whose beauty was without compare to that of anyone else I ever saw. They strode up to each other and, as Jacques d'Avanchy approached, he stopped when he was six paces away from his companion and took up a fixed stance in the sand, his left foot forward and the tip of his sword pointed towards his man. He made it clear that he wished to perform his duty well and to stand up to his opponent's strength. Messire Jacques strode boldly forward and, with a very heavy stroke, hit the squire between the left shoulder and the edge of the wrapper on his armet whilst the squire struck Messire Jacques on his left hip. The appointed guards then came between them and they had to step back three paces, as the chapters of arms required. For a second time, Messire Jacques advanced on his companion but he just held the same stance as before and pointed forward with the tip of his *estoc* to take the blow. On this second attack, the knight dealt a hard blow very close to where the first one had landed but the squire withstood it coolly and calmly, and did not retreat. The knight, who was very confident in these matters, did not continue his pursuit (190) but rather stepped back the regulation three paces before launching a third attack. To keep my story short, the knight maintained this rhythm of attack and ordered retreat until

[125] That is, Wednesday 16 September 1450.

the eleven strokes with the sword had been accomplished, with him dealing all the blows and the squire receiving them in the same way as he had done the first time, since he did not once shift from the original position that he had taken up. The judge then had them separated and each man went back to his pavilion. This was so that the two champions could take off their armour and put on new harnesses in order to perform the feat of arms on horseback that they had agreed to undertake. The day assigned for this joust was the Monday, as noted above. Whilst they were making themselves ready, some people went off to eat as it was getting late, so the knight and squire lost no time in arming and mounting up. Jacques d'Avanchy was the first one to present himself before the judge, and his horse was emblazoned in his coat of arms. From the other side the knight-*entrepreneur* came over to present himself; his horse wore a trapper of black velvet strewn with blue tears; his pavilion that he had quickly had put up was also black with blue tears, thus maintaining the link between his outfits and the stipulations [of the shields]. Toison d'or was the judge for the two men who presented themselves to him for the third time in order to undertake the agreed combats between them, as had been requested when d'Avanchy had touched the three shields. After this, each man went over to his end of the lists. The announcements were made, the ceremonies performed and the lances given out to them. On the first run, they failed to strike each other. On the second, (191) their lances crossed each other with some force. On the third, Messire Jacques de Lalaing broke his lance on his companion's pauldron-reinforce. On the fourth, they each struck home and damaged the tips of their lances. On the fifth, they both missed. On the sixth, the squire broke his lance at the butt and struck the knight on his plackart*. On the seventh, it was the knight only who struck home. On the eighth, both of them missed. On the ninth and final run in this combat, the knight struck the edge of the cross* of the squire's armet and the attaint was so great that the helmet* skull was caved in as far as the head. Had the blow been any lower and better placed than on the spot where it had struck, it would certainly have injured the squire's head. However, the point of the lance skated over the top and the squire was not harmed at all, but his armet was so badly damaged that he was advised not to carry on fighting or to try and finish the combat. Although the twenty-five courses had not been completed, the judge nonetheless regarded the fight as having been accomplished to the satisfaction of both men and so they were taken over to be presented to him. They then touched hands, since their fight was now over, and each man exited by the way in which he had come.

The following Friday,[126] the *entrepreneur* once more made his appearance before the judge, this for the sixth time that month, whilst from the other side came a squire from Burgundy, one named Guillaume Basam. He had had (192) the black shield touched, as was explained above, on the first Saturday of that present month. I think that this Basam was mounted on a horse that was decked out in his coat of arms. From the other side, the *entrepreneur* came out of his black tent, his horse likewise draped in black, thus continuing to match his outfits to the first type of combat. The announcements were made, the ceremonies performed, and the lances given out to them. The knight and the squire let their horses run at each other and, on this first course, each man made a very clean attaint even though neither lance was broken or dropped. After that, they ran four consecutive courses that all missed. On the sixth run, Messire Jacques broke his lance in a strike that

[126] That is, Friday 18 September 1450.

hit his companion between the four points. On the seventh, the squire snapped more than an inch off his lance-tip. On the eighth, ninth and tenth runs, they both missed. On the eleventh, they crossed lances with some force but failed to strike home. On the twelfth run, the *entrepreneur* broke his lance at the butt. They missed again on the thirteenth, fourteenth and fifteenth runs. On the sixteenth, the squire hit the *entrepreneur*, causing him to lose his couter-reinforce* but he soon put this piece back on. On the seventeenth run, they both missed again. On the eighteenth, Messire Jacques de Lalaing struck the squire's plackart on the left-hand side. The lance, which was a good strong one, had a fine, sharpened tip that wedged in the plackart and damaged it right down to the breastplate; indeed, if the lance had not broken from this blow, I fear that the squire (193) would have been badly injured as the breastplate would not have been able to withstand the force of the blow that had already penetrated and damaged the plackart, even though it was a strong and thick one. Thus went this eighteenth run and the squire's friends wanted him to stop fighting, fearing that another lance might hit him in the same place. However, the squire, who was a man of honour and great courage, said that he would persevere with God's help, and so they ran the nineteenth, twentieth and twenty-first courses all without striking each other. On the twenty-second run, both men hit home and then the remaining courses of the twenty-five were completed with nothing more being achieved. No more jousting was due to take place at the *Pas* and so they were taken over to Toison d'or, their judge, where they touched hands and each man went off at his leisure.

The following day,[127] the *entrepreneur* appeared before the judge and from the other side came a squire from the county of Burgundy named Jean de Villeneuve, known as Pasquoy; he was a good fighter with a tall and powerful physique. He was accompanied by the lord of Champdivers[128] and various other noblemen from that land. The squire withdrew to his pavilion to put his harness on whilst the marshal of the lists had the pollaxes brought over to him so that he could make his choice. He then took the other one to the *entrepreneur*, informing him that his (194) companion had requested sixty-one blows with this weapon. Once the announcements were made and the ceremonies performed, the two men came out of their pavilions and, as I recall, the *entrepreneur* was armed and dressed as on all those other occasions when he had fought a combat with pollaxes at this *pas*, except for the fact that he wore no armour on the whole of his right leg;[129] I was later told that he chose to do this so as to have more freedom of movement if his opponent went in close against him. As for the squire, he wore a harness with a coat armour and on his head he had a sallet used for war with a hounskull. The two of them strode confidently up to one another and, when they were about ten or twelve paces apart, Messire Jacques quickened his step and ran at the squire, striving to use the lower part of his weapon to strike his face. However, the squire parried the blow very coolly and the knight had to gather himself for another stroke. This the squire parried again and, with this move, he thought to be able to hit his companion's left arm with the hammer of his pollaxe. The knight deflected this blow nonetheless and

[127] Logically, this should be Saturday 19 September 1450.

[128] Guillaume de Champdivers was one of the defenders at the *Arbre Charlemagne* (1443) (OdLM, vol. 1, pp. 313–14); he fought for Philip the Good in the Ghent war where he was knighted before the battle of Gavere (1453). Alphonse Rousset, *Dictionnaire géographique, historique et statistique des communes de la Franche-Comté et des hameaux qui en dépendent, classés par département. Tome premier, département du Jura* (Besançon: Bintot Imprimeur-Libraire, 1853), p. 438.

[129] On Lalaing's gradual removal of pieces of his armour, see above, n. 124.

thrust the tail of his weapon [at him], using the spike to catch the squire on the hounskull's aventail* and pushing him away. They then came together once more with great vigour and ferocity, and in this move the knight struck Pasquoy on his coat armour with the underside-spike of his weapon. The squire, for his part, sustained this heavy blow and struck back whenever he could see his advantage; thus did their fight continue until the sixty-one blows with (195) the pollaxe had been exchanged. At this point, the judge threw down his baton and they were stopped in mid-fight before being taken over to him to touch hands.

The following Monday,[130] the *entrepreneur* appeared for the eighth time that month and from the other side came Gaspart de Dourtan, a squire from the county of Burgundy who was a renowned and powerful fighter. After the two men had put on their armour in their pavilions and the marshal of the lists had distributed the pollaxes, the *entrepreneur* was told that the squire had requested seventy-five blows with this weapon. The announcements were made and the ceremonies performed. The two champions came together with their pollaxes in their hands. I remember that Messire Jacques was armed in his usual manner, except for the fact that he had no greave* on his right leg, whereas the squire wore his harness with a coat armour and a basinet on his head with the visor down. They met up in front of the judge and a very fierce and hard battle commenced between the two of them. Each of them attacked his companion as if they were mortal enemies and it so happened that Messire Jacques dealt several dangerous blows to the squire's visor, aiming to pierce it with the underside-spike of his pollaxe. However, the squire, who was very strong, parried these blows, defending himself against his companion's manoeuvres and, with a downward stroke, (196) breaking the spike on Messire Jacques's pollaxe. On seeing that the knight's weapon was damaged, the squire attacked him with great vigour and so Messire Jacques, who was very self-assured in all his movements, went in against his companion and beat down his attack from so close up that he managed to stop him from landing blows with either end of his pollaxe. After several parries, Messire Jacques threw off the broken end of his weapon and struck home on the neck plate of the squire's basinet. Yet the squire did not back off and instead the fight between them carried on as hard and as fierce as before: whilst they fought in the lists, each man sought to hold his position and to get the advantage from the sun; I really could not say with any authority that either of them gained a foot of the lists against the other. Finally, after a very long battle, Messire Jacques de Lalaing threw out his right hand towards the squire's pollaxe and grabbed it by the shaft between his opponent's left hand and the underside-spike. The judge lost no time in throwing down his baton, whereupon the two men were taken and led over to him. Messire Jacques spoke to him in a very measured tone, offering to finish the combat if any fault had been found with it. Likewise, the squire lifted up his visor and he was found to be as fresh as he had been when he first pulled it down; he too spoke very confidently to the judge and it was evident from his speech that he was by no means out of breath. They touched hands and became good friends from that moment on; in fact, Gaspart was there with Messire Jacques in the Ghent war, and the knight had only good things to say about this squire, as can be seen later on in my account.[131] In honour of this squire, I can add

[130] Logically, this should be Monday 21 September 1450.

[131] According to La Marche, Jacques de Lalaing later told him that Gaspart de Dourtan was one of the three men who helped him rescue his brother, Philippe de Lalaing, during a raid outside Lokeren in May 1452 as part of Philip the Good's Ghent war. OdLM, vol. 2, p. 249.

what Messire Jacques told me several times, which is that (197) he definitely found Gaspart de Dourtan to have been the most formidable opponent with whom he ever did combat.

The following Wednesday, which was the fourteenth day of September,[132] Messire Jacques de Lalaing presented himself for the ninth time that month. This was the last combat of the month and of the whole *Pas*, and I don't remember Messire Jacques ever again fighting in closed lists. From the other side came a squire from the duchy of Burgundy, one Jean Pitois. Each man armed himself in his pavilion and the pollaxes were presented [to them] since the squire had had the white shield touched and had requested fifty-two blows with this weapon. The announcements were made and the ceremonies performed, whereupon the *entrepreneur* emerged from his pavilion, armed and decked out in the colours corresponding to the shield that had been touched, as was his habit; he wore no armour on his right leg. From the other side came Jean Pitois, armed as the case required, with his coat armour on and a sallet (198) with a hounskull on his head, more or less the same as that of the *entrepreneur.* It is true to say that the squire walked out in very good form and the two champions were fairly well matched in size. They came together fiercely, with the squire thinking to hit the knight with the underside-spike of his pollaxe. However, the knight parried the blow and used the squire's approach to hit him back. Yet, the squire stepped away after deflecting the stroke and so the two of them pursued one another, giving and receiving blows on each side; they grew greatly heated in this fierce combat as they used every ounce of their strength. After about thirty blows had been exchanged, Messire Jacques de Lalaing took one hand off his weapon and grabbed that of his companion, holding onto it so tightly that the squire could no longer wield it in his defence. Messire Jacques held his own weapon in his right hand near to the hammer head and used the topside-spike to land several blows on his companion's face. The squire parried some of these strokes by using his right fist wrapped in his gauntlet; he fought off the knight's attack with great vigour, hitting his face. The knight, for his part, deflected each blow using the side of his body and the arm with which he had seized his companion's weapon. Their battle went on so long in this manner that the squire's face was bloodied by the spike of the pollaxe. After the fight had continued for a great length of time, the two men were taken and separated by the guards, and Messire Jacques said to the squire: 'It's not good (199) fighting technique to use the fist, like women do!' to which the squire replied: 'If you had not taken hold of my pollaxe, I would have used that weapon to beat you off; men's hands are made for both attacking and defending.' Their exchange of words was cut short and they went up before the judge. Messire de Lalaing, as he presented himself, spoke very eloquently, saying that he came before him for the last time having — with God's help — performed and completed his *emprise*; he also offered to do more if [the judge] felt that it was necessary and he thanked Toison d'or for his supervision and excellent judgements. Because there were still fifteen or sixteen days left to run in that month of September and he did not know if anyone else would come to give their assistance to the Lady of Tears, he would carry on staying in the town until the

[132] This date does not tally with the previous ones that La Marche gives for this series of combats in the last month of the *Pas*, since Wednesdays in that month in 1450 fell on 2, 9, 16, 23 and 30 September; however, there was a Wednesday 14 October that year, hence La Marche's possible confusion. The Lalaing biography dates this final combat against Jean Pitois to Thursday 15 October, which is a correct date.

end of the month; he entreated the judge to do likewise, which he agreed to do. For his part, the squire also presented himself and they then embraced. The squire went off still in full harness to the Carmelite church of Notre-Dame[133] whilst Messire Jacques went to take off his armour in his pavilion. Once there, he sent a long robe of cloth of gold lined with fine sable fur over to Toison d'or, who had been his judge, as a reward (200) for his work; Messire Jacques then went back [to his lodgings] in his usual fashion.

The following Sunday, Messire Jacques de Lalaing organised a fine dinner in the manner of a banquet at the bishop's palace.[134] There was a great gathering of nobles and knights present, a huge quantity of wine and food, and many varied and dainty dishes. I recall that there was a very gracious *entremets** in the middle of a long table that was in the form of closed lists.[135] On one side, lined up next to each other, were represented all those who had fought against the *entrepreneur* at the *Pas*, each of them mounted and dressed exactly as he had been when he undertook his combat; facing them was a representation of (201) the *entrepreneur* dressed and armed with his pollaxe in his hand, as this is the weapon with which he had fought on the most occasions. Placed at his feet was a short text in verse, the substance of which was that he thanked his companions for the honour each of them had done him and he offered to serve them, as his brothers and friends, for as long as he should live, in both body and goods. The dinner was served with great pomp and, once the tables had been removed and grace said, the prizes were distributed according to the report made by Messire Jacques, the *entrepreneur*. First, the golden pollaxe was awarded to Gérard de Roussillon for having dealt the best blow with this weapon against Messire Jacques; the blow in question was a parry using the tail of his pollaxe with which Gérard had struck Messire Jacques on the edge of his sallet and then down his left shoulder, as was described in greater detail above in the account of these combats. The prize for the bout with the sword was awarded to Jacques d'Avanchy; for this no other explanation was asked of the *entrepreneur* since d'Avanchy was the only competitor who had chosen to fight with this weapon. As for the prize for the courses with the lance, this was awarded to Jean de Boniface, who had certainly ridden and fought extremely well, as has been recounted (202) above. That evening, Messire Jacques had to make peace between Tristan de Toulongeon and Gérard de Roussillon who, being youths, had come to blows in a heated debate. Indeed, Messire Jacques was so loved and esteemed by everyone that his counsel was always accepted.

Thus did the banquet end, as did the spectacle of this *pas*. On the last day that the pavilion was still standing, and when midday had come and gone, which is when the pavilion was usually taken down, all the noblemen and servants of Messire Jacques's

---

133 [Nostre Dame des Carmes]. In giving this alternative version of the name of the Carmelite church in Chalon-sur-Saône, La Marche seems to be stressing here the profound Marian roots of the Carmelites, whose official title was the Order of the Brothers of the Blessed Virgin Mary of Mount Carmel; this also makes explicit the link between this church, where Lalaing stayed during the days when the *Pas* was happening, and his placing of the whole event under the protection of the Virgin Mary.

134 This was the residence of Jean Germain, bishop of Nevers (1430–36) and Chalon-sur-Saône (1436–61). He was confessor to Isabel of Portugal (1430), chancellor of the Order of the Golden Fleece (1431–61) and an influential adviser of Philip the Good. PCB no. 880.

135 On La Marche's brief treatment of the *entremets* compared with the much lengthier one in the Lalaing biography, see Gaucher, '*Le Livre des Fais*'; Szkilnik, 'Mise en mots'.

entourage came to join in with the officers of arms whose job it was to remove the components of the décor of the *Pas* for the last time; they were all wearing coat armours and conducted themselves in a most honourable fashion. First of all came Léal,[136] Messire Jacques de Lalaing's pursuivant, who was carrying the unicorn, the fountain and the three shields. After him came Toulongeon Herald, who was carrying the Lady of Tears, and after him came Charolais Herald, who was carrying the image of the Virgin Mary who had graced and guarded the pavilion for the entire year. In that order they made their way to the lodgings of the *entrepreneur*, who was waiting with some of his friends for this concluding moment of his *emprise*. He let the unicorn be carried past him but he took off his hat before the Lady of Tears and knelt down on the ground before the Virgin Mary, kissing her feet with great devotion. Afterwards, these representations were taken to the church of Notre-Dame in Boulogne,[137] where they can still be seen on display in the oratory of the duke of Burgundy. Not long after that, the lord of Créquy returned to Picardy, from which he had been absent a good while because (203) of his travels, as noted above. Messire Jacques, his nephew, stayed in Chalon where the lords of that place and their neighbours entertained him royally as best they knew how. As has been said above, his virtue, gentility and courtliness, as well as the skilful, confident way in which he had executed his *pas*, made them love and honour him to the highest possible degree. You can well believe that the ladies of the place made gracious speeches in praise of him, calling him the 'good knight' and referring to him as a 'new Ponthus'[138] by dint of his virtues, valour and renown. Thus did everyone speak of Messire Jacques de Lalaing, his reputation being elevated above that of any other man of his time. When the month of September was over, he went off to Rome and from there travelled to Naples with a very fine company; as he journeyed through the lands of Italy and Naples he wore his *emprise*,[139] which he had undertaken to carry through the majority of Christian kingdoms. Yet no one touched it, even though there were some at the court of the king of Naples who wanted to; King Alfonso,[140] who at that time was king of Aragon and Naples, would not allow it because of the love he bore Duke Philippe of Burgundy, who was his brother-in-arms.[141]

---

[136] Many noble families had pursuivants and heralds at their service; 'Loyalty' (*Léal* = Loyal) was one of the most desired characteristics of these officers of arms. No information is available about who served Lalaing in this role in 1450.

[137] The church of Notre-Dame in Boulogne-sur-Mer was a well-known place of pilgrimage that owned a miraculous image of the Virgin Mary; the dukes of Burgundy and their wives often went there to make their offerings. Vaughan, *Philip the Good*, pp. 128, 343. The depositing of the various props used in this *pas* after it had finished recalls a similar action at the *Arbre Charlemagne*, where the two shields set up for challengers to touch were later taken to the church of Notre-Dame in Dijon for safe-keeping. OdLM, vol. 1, p. 333.

[138] This reference is to the eponymous hero of the very popular chivalric romance *Ponthus et Sidoine* (written between 1390 and 1424), who organises an *emprise* that is a *pas d'armes* in all but name: see Source 1. On the significance of this parallel between Lalaing and Ponthus drawn by the ladies of Chalon-sur-Saône, see Essay 6.

[139] On Lalaing's *emprise*, which he wore during his travels around Europe, see above, n. 4.

[140] Alfonso V the Magnanimous (1396–1458) was king of Aragon, Sicily and Sardinia (1416–58) and of Naples (1442–58).

[141] Alfonso was the first king to become a member of the Order of the Golden Fleece; this was at the Ghent chapter (1445). As the king himself was not present in Ghent at the time, Guillebert de Lannoy, a Burgundian councillor-chamberlain of Philip the Good (PCB no. 318), brought him the collar of the

In Naples, Messire Jacques met up with the duke, Johann of Cleves,[142] (204) the duke of Burgundy's nephew; the duke of Cleves was the one who had brought Messire Jacques up with him.[143] He was on his way home from Jerusalem, where he had been made a knight,[144] along with various other lords from his land. You should know that the king of Aragon received and entertained him most honourably, as much for the love that he bore the house of Burgundy as for the honour that he wanted to show the duke of Cleves, he being a person who was among the wisest, most handsome and accomplished princes of his day. King Alfonso himself was an honourable, generous and prodigious prince. From there the duke of Cleves took his leave, taking Messire Jacques de Lalaing with him, and they made their way to see the duke of Burgundy who, at that time, was staying in the land of Brabant, where they were warmly welcomed and received. With that, my account of the *Pas* of the Lady of Tears comes to an end.

knightly order in November 1446. In exchange, Alfonso offered Philip the Good membership of the Order of the Jar, the royal order of the Crown of Aragon founded by his father; hence La Marche's allusion here to how close the bonds were between the two men. COTO no. 41.

[142] Johann I (1419–81), duke of Cleves (r. 1448–81), count of the Mark (1461–81) and lord of Ravenstein (1448–81), was the eldest son of Adolf, duke of Cleves, and Marie of Burgundy, sister of Philip the Good. From the age of nine, he was educated at Philip's court and became a member of the Order of the Golden Fleece, together with Jacques de Lalaing at the Mons chapter (1451); he made his vow at the Feast of the Pheasant (1454). PCB no. 384; VdF no. 40.

[143] LF, pp. 24–30, 53–62; CL, pp. 81–5, 93–7.

[144] He was dubbed in Jerusalem by Jean V de Créquy (1450). COTO no. 47.

Thanks are due to Mario Damen, Jacob Deacon and Ralph Moffat for their helpful comments on various aspects of this translation.

Mario Damen

Source 8

The *Paso de El Pardo* (*Paso* of El Pardo), 1459

This source consists of a translation of a narrative account of this event.

Author: Diego Enríquez del Castillo

Language: Medieval Castilian

Manuscript source: Madrid, Archivo Histórico de la Nobleza, BAENA, C.134, D.5 (fully digitised at <http://pares.mcu.es:80/ParesBusquedas20/catalogo/description/6165857> [accessed 8 June 2024])

Edition used: Aureliano Sánchez Martín, ed., *Crónica de Enrique IV, de Diego Enríquez del Castillo* (Valladolid: Universidad de Valladolid. Secretariado de Publicaciones, 1994), pp. 168–70 (= DEC)

Select bibliography:

Barber, Richard, and Juliet Barker, *Tournaments: Jousts, Chivalry and Pageants in the Middle Ages* (New York: Weidenfeld & Nicolson, 1989), p. 101

DBE, lemma 'Beltrán de la Cueva'

Nadot, Sébastien, *Le Spectacle des joutes: Sport et courtoisie à la fin du Moyen Âge* (Rennes: Presses Universitaires de Rennes, 2012), pp. 61, 154, 246, 301, 337

Pilar Carceller Cerviño, María del, 'Realidad y representación de la nobleza castellana en el siglo XV: el linaje de la Cueva y la casa ducal de Alburquerque' (unpublished PhD dissertation, Universidad Complutense de Madrid, 2006), pp. 112–14

Tate, Brian, and Jeremy Lawrance, eds., *Alfonso de Palencia, Gesta Hispaniensia ex annalibus suorum dierum collecta* (Madrid: Real Academia de la Historia, 1999), pp. 286, 315–16

Torres Fontes, Juan, *Estudio sobre la 'Cronica de Enrique IV' del Dr. Galindez de Carvajal* (Murcia: Seminario de Historia de la Universidad de Murcia, 1946), pp. 208–9

Introduction

This *paso* took place in 1459 near the royal hunting lodge of El Pardo that was situated in the mountainous woodlands north-west of Madrid. The *entrepreneur** of the event was Beltrán de la Cueva, who organised it to mark the occasion when ambassadors of François II, duke of Brittany, came to Castile to visit King Enrique IV; it was the culmination of four days of chivalric events staged in their honour. The political context of the *Paso de El Pardo* can be understood from both an international and a national perspective. On the one hand, François II, who was inaugurated as duke in 1458, may have been seeking to affirm his political support for Castile, since, like his predecessors, he was in a constant struggle for autonomy from the king of France. For their part, the Castilian commercial elites in the harbour towns of the Bay of Biscay were very eager to forge an ever stronger relationship with the new duke of Brittany.[1] On the other hand, when considered in the context of the internal dynamics of the Castilian court, the *Paso* can be seen as the moment at which the career of Beltrán de la Cueva, the new favourite of Enrique IV, really took off. This nobleman, from Úbeda in Andalucía, started his career in the king's household in 1456 as guard and page of the lance and was appointed as *mayordomo mayor* (*grand maître d'hôtel*) two years later. The organisation of the *Paso* and the other chivalric events in El Pardo thus attests to his rise at court.[2]

The narrative account of the *Paso de El Pardo* comes from a chronicle written by Diego Enríquez del Castillo (*c*.1431–*c*.1503). This nobleman from Segovia studied theology at the University of Salamanca and became chaplain of Enrique, when he was the crown prince, sometime in the early 1450s. In 1460, shortly after the events described here, Enrique, now king, appointed Enríquez del Castillo as his official chronicler. At the same time, he became one of the king's councillors and served as an intermediary between him and certain rebellious noblemen later in the 1460s.[3] In 1466, the chronicler produced a Spanish translation for the duke of Albuquerque of an Italian version of *De re militari*, a standard military manual originally written by the Roman author Vegetius (late fourth century AD). The fact that it was Beltrán de la Cueva, the *entrepreneur* of this *paso*, who commissioned this translation bespeaks the close connection that there must have been between the chronicler and the organiser of the event. However, the death of Enrique IV in 1474 meant the end of Enríquez del Castillo's career at the Castilian court. It was only in the 1480s that he started to compile his chronicle on the reign of his former patron, with final revisions being done as late as the 1490s. In this work, he painted a favourable portrait of the deceased king.[4] Like the two previous *pasos* that had been hosted in Castile — that is, the *Paso de la Fuerte Ventura* (1428) and the *Paso de Valladolid* (1440) — the *Paso de El Pardo* seems to have been commemorated exclusively in a royal chronicle; the exception to this rule is the later *Paso de Jaén* (1462), which is recorded in a chivalric biography.[5]

What the description of the *Paso de El Pardo* in Enríquez del Castillo's chronicle also has in common with the narrative accounts of these other Castilian *pasos* is that it is very concise, in that not even the names of the *entrepreneur* or his challengers are given. Yet, in spite of this, the main characteristics of a *pas d'armes* are clearly in evidence here: an

---

[1] Robert Omnès, 'La Bretagne et les Bretons dans les chroniques de Castille (XIVe–XVIe siècles)', *Annales de Bretagne et des pays de l'Ouest*, 88.4 (1981), 395–417 (pp. 405–6).

[2] In the 1460s, Enrique gave him the titles of duke of Albuquerque and count of Ledesma. DBE, lemma 'Beltrán de la Cueva'; María del Pilar Carceller Cerviño, 'Realidad y representación de la nobleza castellana en el siglo XV: el linaje de la Cueva y la casa ducal de Alburquerque' (unpublished PhD dissertation, Universidad Complutense de Madrid, 2006), pp. 112–14; Jaime de Salazar y Acha, *La Casa del Rey de Castilla y León en la Edad Media* (Madrid: Centro de Estudios Políticos y Constitucionales, 2000), p. 351.

[3] On the exact nature of this complex conflict, see DBE, lemmata 'Diego Enríquez del Castillo' and 'Enrique IV'.

[4] DEC, pp. 22–31; DBE, lemma 'Diego Enríquez del Castillo'; María del Pilar Carceller Cerviño, 'La imagen nobiliaria en la tratadística caballeresca: Beltrán de la Cueva y Diego Enríquez del Castillo', *En la España medieval*, 24 (2001), 259–83 (pp. 260–8).

[5] See Sources 2, 3 and 10, respectively.

entrepreneur defends a *paso* (passage) in the form of a gate that is literally situated between two places (El Pardo and Madrid), and invites challengers to compete against him in a dramatised setting, one that also involved Wild Men and was governed by a set of rules of which only a glimpse can be seen. The *Paso* takes place in a purpose-built wooden arena with a tilt* barrier and is witnessed by a high-ranking audience. Yet, it also differs from other Castilian *pasos* — and, indeed, from those *pas d'armes* that were held in other places where this tournament form was very popular, such as Anjou, France and the Burgundian lands — in that it is the only one known to have been commemorated by the founding of a monastery, in this instance by the *entrepreneur*'s own patron. The monastery in question belonged to the Order of St Jerome, an order that enjoyed particular favour from the late medieval kings of Castile, and was located near the site of the actual *paso* in El Pardo; to cement the connection with this event, it was referred to as 'San Jerónimo del Paso': that is, 'St Jerome of the *Paso*'. Whilst Enríquez del Castillo states that the king performed this act of commemoration specifically in honour of his favourite, Beltrán de la Cueva, another royal chronicler, Alfonso de Palencia (1423–92), who was writing in Latin rather than in the vernacular, affirms instead that the foundation was intended, more generally, to 'honour the site in perpetual memory'.[6] Palencia even mentions in this context that the king commanded that the town of Colmenares, which is located 140 km to the west of Madrid in the mountainous area of the Sierra de Gredos and was a fief of the king's former favourite, Álvaro de Luna, should be renamed Mombeltrán.[7] This order was indeed executed, albeit slightly later in September 1461, and the new name of the town has been retained right up to the present day.[8]

Although Enríquez del Castillo's chronicle mentions the founding of the monastery of St Jerome in El Pardo by Enrique IV in 1461, it does not give an exact date for the *Paso* itself. However, María del Pilar Carceller Cerviño has suggested that the *Paso* is most likely to have taken place in 1459, this being the same year that La Cueva was admitted to the knightly Order of Santiago.[9] This date is confirmed by the author of the lemma on La Cueva in the DBE, who even pinpoints it to the summer of that year.

In the translation that follows, page numbers in parentheses have been inserted for ease of reference to Sánchez Martín's edition.

Translation

[In the previous chapter, the chronicler describes how the king moved with his household from Escalona to the royal palace (Real Alcázar) in Madrid. There they passed the time by organising festivities, jousts, cane games and bull runs*.]*

---

[6] Brian Tate and Jeremy Lawrance, eds, *Alfonso de Palencia, Gesta Hispaniensia ex annalibus suorum dierum collecta* (Madrid: Real Academia de la Historia, 1999), p. 286: 'locum illum nobilitandum perpetua memoratione'.

[7] Mombeltrán is a contraction of *mon* (from *monte*, meaning 'mountain') and the first name of the *entrepreneur* Beltrán. Because in Castilian the letter *n* cannot precede the *b*, the *n* is changed into *m*, with Mombeltrán as the result. On Álvaro de Luna, see Essay 1 and Sources 2 and 3.

[8] Tate and Lawrance, *Alfonso*, pp. 286, 315.

[9] Carceller Cerviño, 'Realidad', pp. 13–14. Compare Sébastien Nadot, *Le Spectacle des joutes: Sport et courtoisie à la fin du Moyen Âge* (Rennes: Presses Universitaires de Rennes, 2012), pp. 246, 337, who mentions both 1458 and 1460 as dates for this *paso*, but not 1459.

(168) **Chapter 24: How the duke of Brittany sent an ambassador to the king,[10] concerning certain alliances and pacts made with him, and how the king ordered grand festivities to be organised for him**

When the king was thus accompanied by the grandees[11] and other nobles from his kingdom, who honoured his court by turning out in great numbers, the duke of Brittany[12] sent an embassy[13] led by the foremost knight of his household, asking the king for a pact and an alliance. The king was very pleased about this and received him in fine style. While he was making a decision regarding the ambassador's request, the king commanded that a lavish festivity be organised in order to demonstrate his power and his high estate. He wanted this event to take place at his hunting lodge called El Pardo, which is a very delightful and suitable place, because of both the wooded mountains in the immediate surroundings and the multitude of animals[14] in the area, and is located two leagues[15] away from Madrid. The festivity was very elaborately organised, featuring both sumptuous decorations and large cabinets displaying silver objects weighing more than 20,000 gilded marks.[16] Here the king demonstrated the extent of his nobility and royal magnificence. When he saw two squires in livery, who were affecting an official air, going over furtively to the cabinets to steal some silver objects, he pretended not to see them and allowed them to keep their stolen goods and take them away. When the household officers[17] discovered that some silverware was missing and notified the king, he replied: 'The thieves were persons who needed that silverware, so they took it out of necessity. It is better that they

---

[10] Enrique IV of Castile (1425–74), son of Juan II and María of Aragon, king of Castile (1454–74), was married first to Blanca II of Navarre (1424–64), but they divorced in 1453 on the grounds that the marriage had not been 'consummated'; in 1455, he married his cousin Joana of Portugal (1439–75). DBE, lemma 'Enrique IV'.

[11] The *grandes* formed the top layer of the nobility in Castile, which consisted of some sixty entitled nobles, half of whom were counts and the rest dukes, marquesses and viscounts. María Concepción Quintanilla Raso, 'Los grandes nobles', *Medievalismo: boletín de la Sociedad Española de Estudios Medievales*, 13 (2004), 127–42.

[12] François II (1435–88), son of Richard, count of Étampes, and Marguerite of Orléans (daughter of Louis I), was married to Marguerite of Brittany and became duke in 1458.

[13] The author of the lemma 'Beltrán de la Cueva' in the DBE gives their surnames as Bois, Onisilre and Godelin. The chronicler Alfonso de Palencia suggests that the visit of Jean V, count of Armagnac, in 1462 was the reason behind the organisation of the *paso*, but this does not tally with the suggested chronology here. Tate and Lawrance, *Alfonso*, p. 316. On this occasion in 1462, a joust was indeed organised, with the king paying for the services of the King of Arms and five minstrels belonging to the duke of Sidonia. Miguel Ángel Ladero Quesada, '1462: Un año en la vida de Enrique IV, rey de Castilla', *En la España medieval*, 14 (1991), 237–74 (p. 258).

[14] Bulls were bred in the grounds of the royal residence whereas wild boars populated the woods. Ladero Quesada, '1462', p. 254.

[15] A *legua castellana* (Castilian league) is normally 4190 metres. The royal residence of El Pardo was situated some 15 km to the north-west of the Real Alcázar (Royal Palace) of Madrid, but did have extensive grounds.

[16] The silver mark in late medieval Castile consisted of eight ounces, weighing approximately 230 grams.

[17] The term used is *reposteros*, household officers with the special task of guarding and monitoring the personal goods of the monarch kept in the cabinets, especially the cutlery and silverware. Salazar y Acha, *La casa del rey*, pp. 237–40.

appropriated my possessions rather than those of any other. I forgive them so there is no need for you to try to find them.'

(169) The festivities lasted for four days. On the first day, a joust was organised with twenty knights, each team consisting of ten men, all of them expensively dressed and equipped. The prizes were a piece of brocade and two pieces of crimson velvet for those who performed the best. On the second day, there was a bull run and after that there was a cane game in which a hundred knights participated in two teams of fifty [men], consisting of the foremost nobles and the sons of grandees of the household, all richly attired and their horses decked out in gilded trappers*. On the third day, there was an impressive hunt both on horseback and on foot, where they killed many wild and dangerous animals. For these festivities, the king gave out many gifts of money, brocade, silk, cloth and luxurious linings of marten, ermine, sable and grey squirrel, not only to the queen,[18] her ladies and the principals of her household, but also to her employees, servants and other noble knights in her entourage.

On the fourth day, it so happened that the king had at that time, as his *mayordomo*[19] a person from an ancient and excellent noble family from Úbeda who was so close to him that none of the king's past favourites enjoyed as much favour as he alone did, according to the will of the king, and not without reason: he certainly had so much virtue that he deserved all of the prosperity and good luck that came to him. He was an exemplary servant, being without malice towards the king, magnificent in his estates, courtly and gracious towards all: he was generous to those who asked for this help. He spent lavishly, knew how to make merry and bestowed great honour on the good; he was also a fine rider of the jennet*, a great hunter, an extravagant consumer of fashion, and an honourable and generous person. Since he already had the respect of a great lord,[20] and because he derived great pleasure from [doing so], he agreed to organise a *paso* in the middle of the road near the town[21] [in order] to celebrate the return to Madrid of the king, the queen, the ambassador and other lords. This was to be done in the following manner. There was a tilt barrier surrounded by lists made of wood with gates through which those who came from El Pardo had to enter: the gates were guarded by some Wild Men who only let knights and noblemen accompanied by noble ladies pass on the condition that they would promise to run six courses with the defender; if they did not want to joust, they had to leave their right gauntlet.[22] Next to the barrier, a

---

[18] Joana of Portugal (1439–75), daughter of Duarte I, king of Portugal and Leonor of Aragon, married Enrique IV in 1455 and gave birth in 1462 to a daughter called Juana. Some years later, various rebellious nobles accused Juana of being illegitimate, on the grounds that the king himself was impotent, and claimed that her real father was Beltrán de la Cueva, the organiser of the *paso*. DBE, lemmata 'Juana de Portugal' and 'Juana de Castilla'.

[19] In an older edition of this chronicle, it is made explicit that this refers to 'un caballero que se llamaba Beltran de la Cueva' (a knight called Beltrán de la Cueva). Josef Miguel de Flores, ed., *Crónica del rey don Enrique el Quarto de este nombre, por su capellán y cronista Diego Enriquez del Castillo* (Madrid: D. Antonio de Sancha, 1787), p. 40.

[20] At this point, he was not yet numbered among the grandees, as he received the corresponding titles of count and duke later on in his career.

[21] The author of the lemma 'Beltrán de la Cueva' in the DBE identifies this place as Puerta de Hierro, on the bank of the river Manzanares, which was the entrance to the royal estate of El Pardo.

[22] Compare this stipulation with the fifteenth article of the chapters of arms of the *Paso Honroso* (1434),

well-crafted wooden arch[23] was constructed to which many golden letters were attached. After having finished his courses, he who broke three lances could go over to the arch and pick the first letter of his lady's name. There were also three tall stands: one where the king, the queen, her ladies and the ambassador could eat and spectate; another one for the grandees; and the third one for the judges of the joust.[24] All were given a very sumptuous dinner where everything was served in great abundance and was very well organised and arranged. The festivity lasted from morning until night, when the king and the queen (170) retired to their palaces.[25] Because this *paso* was an exceptional event, the king wanted to honour his *mayordomo* and support his undertaking, and so he ordered that a monastery of the Order of St Jerome be founded, this monastery now being referred to as San Jerónimo del Paso.[26]

When the event came to an end and the ambassador, who had been treated with so much honour, completed his mission, the king showered him with great gifts of horses, mules, silver, money and pieces of brocade and silk. With this he took his leave, being very contented and full of praise for the magnificence of the king's estate.

---

which stated that any knight or gentleman who came by the passage could not leave without depositing either one of his arms or his right spur. PH, p. 403.

[23] This is the second Castilian *paso* to feature an arch as part of its dramatised setting, since one was also present at the *Paso de la Fuerte Ventura*, where it is dubbed the 'Arch of the Daunting Adventure': see Source 2, p. 60.

[24] Nadot, *Le Spectacle*, p. 246, incorrectly states that a special wooden tower was constructed as a décor for this *paso*: although there was a tower in El Pardo, it was built in 1458 and intended for hunting. Ladero Quesada, '1462', pp. 252–4.

[25] The king and queen therefore seem to have had a palace each at their disposal.

[26] The monastery was constructed on the bank of the Manzanares river near El Pardo in front of the hermitage of St Anthony. The editors of the Latin chronicle of Alfonso de Palencia, which mentions the 'monasterium … appelatio Transitus', translate the name of the convent as 'Santa María del Paso', by which name it was also known. Tate and Lawrance, *Alfonso*, p. 286. By contrast, Enríquez del Castillo remarks that it 'is *now* being referred to as San Jerónimo del Paso': that is, at the time of writing the chronicle in the 1480s. In the first decade of the sixteenth century, because of its humid and unsanitary riverside setting, the Catholic monarchs, Ferdinand and Isabella, decided to move the monastery to El Prado in Madrid, which was nearer to their own royal residence, where it was renamed San Jerónimo el Real. *Ibid.*, p. 316.

Thanks are due to Catherine Blunk and Rosalind Brown-Grant for their helpful comments on earlier versions of this translation.

Klaus Oschema

Source 9

The *Pas du Compagnon à la Larme Blanche* (*Pas* of the Companion of the White Teardrop), Le Quesnoy, 1458

This source consists of a translation of the complete narrative account of this event.

Author: Georges Chastelain

Language: Middle French

Edition used: Jean-Claude Delclos, ed., *Georges Chastellain: Chronique. Les fragments du livre IV révélées par l'Additional Manuscript 54156 de la British Library* (Geneva: Droz, 1991), pp. 127–32 (= GCC)

Select bibliography:

Ambühl, Rémy, *Le séjour du futur Louis XI dans les pays de Philippe le Bon (1456–1461)* (Stavelot: Cercle d'histoire et d'archéologie du pays de Genappe, 2002)

Bureaux, Guillaume, 'Union et désunion de la noblesse en parade. Le rôle des Pas d'armes dans l'entretien des rivalités chevaleresques entre cours princières occidentales, XVe–XVIe siècles (Anjou, Bourgogne, France, Saint-Empire)' (unpublished PhD dissertation, Normandie Université, 2018)

Hiltmann, Torsten, 'Un État de noblesse et de chevalerie sans pareilles? Tournois et hérauts d'armes à la cour des ducs de Bourgogne', in *La cour de Bourgogne et l'Europe: le rayonnement et les limites d'un modèle culturel; actes du colloque international tenu à Paris les 9, 10 et 11 octobre 2007*, ed. by Werner Paravicini, Torsten Hiltmann and Frank Viltart (Ostfildern: Jan Thorbecke Verlag, 2013), pp. 253–88

Mérindol, Christian de, *Les fêtes de chevalerie à la cour du roi René: Emblématique, art et histoire (les joutes de Nancy, le Pas de Saumur et le Pas de Tarascon)* (Paris: Éditions du CTHS, 1993)

Nadot, Sébastien, *Le Spectacle des joutes: Sport et courtoisie à la fin du Moyen Âge* (Rennes: Presses Universitaires de Rennes, 2012)

Introduction

The *Pas du Compagnon à la Larme Blanche* took place in October 1458 at Le Quesnoy[1] in the county of Hainaut, one of the most important principalities of Duke Philip the Good of Burgundy. The event combined features that are typical of Burgundian *pas d'armes* in this period with more unusual characteristics. The author of the only narrative source, the

[1] France, dép. Nord, 70 km south-east of Lille.

official Burgundian *indiciaire* (court chronicler) Georges Chastelain (1414/15–75), refrains from calling it a *pas d'armes*, depicting it repeatedly as mere *joutes* (jousts). Nevertheless, most of the key elements of a *pas* are present.[2] While the symbolic passage remains unclear (or absent), the *entrepreneur** Guillaume de Moullon fought as sole defender against all challengers according to the chapters he had published through a 'Moor' (about whom we know nothing more). Duke Philip was present as a spectator and supported Guillaume financially to the sum of 500 *écus*. The text mentions the courtly audience, but does not clarify whether the lists were set up in the town of Le Quesnoy or at the castle (one of the major residences of the Burgundian dukes in the county of Hainaut; little now remains of the medieval buildings). Finally, the event was characterised by elements drawn from fictional narratives, including the publication of the challenge and the chapters through the 'Moor' and the *entrepreneur* presenting himself as 'the Companion of the White Teardrop'.

The *entrepreneurs* of Burgundian *pas* were usually vassals of the duke, some of them even knights of the prestigious Order of the Golden Fleece (founded in 1430). Not so Guillaume de Moullon, who came from the Dauphiné in the south of France and arrived at the Burgundian court in 1456 as a member of the household of the Dauphin Louis, who had fled there because of a conflict with his father, King Charles VII of France. Guillaume's relations with the dauphin soon cooled off dramatically and Louis sent him back to the Dauphiné. In organising this *pas*, Guillaume clearly wanted to leave his mark on the Burgundian court. The sympathetic depiction of his career and of the event itself in Chastelain's *Chronique*, but also the financial support provided by Duke Philip, indicate that the event was indeed perceived as a sort of parting gift, to show Guillaume off in an honourable light. The organisation of the *pas* itself took place in two stages: in August or September 1458, Guillaume sent his 'Moor', accompanied by two heralds, to Duke Philip at Arras in order to publish the challenge and the chapters. Philip allowed the announcement to be made but interrupted the proceedings after twelve of his noblemen had touched the *emprise**: the rest of the ceremonies were to take place at Le Quesnoy in the presence of the ladies. The date was set for 1 October 1458.

The following translation gives Chastelain's description of the proceedings at Le Quesnoy. While the fictitious elements appear relatively prominent at the beginning, the remainder of the text focuses on the names of the participants, their rich appearance and the quality of the combats. The only exception is Antoine, the Great Bastard of Burgundy, who staged a more theatrical entrance, in which he appeared in a portable structure that resembled a chapel or hermitage. Chastelain narrates the actual fighting quite briefly (and repeatedly underlines his desire to keep his account short, since the event was 'only a joust' and not 'serious', in his view), ending his description with the luxurious banquet organised by Duke Philip and the gifts that Guillaume received. The author then turns to another episode concerning a challenge by a German knight (one Heinrich Sasse, who presented his own *emprise* without asking the duke for his permission, thereby nearly causing a scandal).[3] As for the fictitious setting, whilst an *emprise* often

---

[2] On these characteristics, see Essay 1.

[3] [Hanry Sasse]. Two German knights, two brothers, called Heinrich Sasse appear at the Burgundian court in this period. The elder (d. *c.*1459) is mentioned in the household accounts from 1432 onwards and became Duke Philip's chamberlain (1457). The younger Heinrich is mentioned in 1453 and was probably a member of the household of Adolf of Cleves, lord of Ravenstein. According to Chastelain, the knight in question was unfamiliar with the customs at the Burgundian court, which might point to

presents the *entrepreneur* as being in the service of a lady or her prisoner, there is no information about the presence of such a motif in this case. Rather, Chastelain deliberately abridges the content of the letters and chapters that were read first at Arras in the presence of Duke Philip and then at Le Quesnoy in front of his daughter-in-law, Isabelle of Bourbon. The elements of the framing narrative that can be gleaned from Chastelain's account remain quite superficial and generic. The *entrepreneur*'s choice of name, insisting on the motif of the white teardrop (which is also reflected in his outfit on the first day), may have been inspired by models from courtly literature. The episode of the *fontaine del pin* (the fountain of the pinetree) as described in the thirteenth-century Prose Lancelot, for example, mentions a knight who wears an 'escus noirs dargent goutes menuement'[4] (black shield strewn with silver drops [tears?]). However, this connection appears quite loose. In fact, the motif of teardrops was relatively widespread in the imagery of the *pas d'armes*, having been used both at the first such event that took place in the Burgundian lands, the *Pas de l'Arbre Charlemagne* (Marsannay-la-Côte, 1443), and the later *Pas de la Fontaine des Pleurs* (Chalon-sur-Saône, 1449–50).[5]

The description of the *pas* that follows was long considered to be lost, until its discovery and publication by Jean-Claude Delclos in 1991. Until quite recently, it has been argued that this *pas* had probably never taken place,[6] since the formerly known parts of Chastelain's *Chronique* described only the events at Arras, but not the actual *pas* at Le Quesnoy. For ease of reference, the Arabic numerals in parentheses in the translation give the page numbers of Delclos's edition, whilst the Roman numerals indicate the numbering of the chapters.

TRANSLATION

[Context: The following passage is preceded by Chastelain's comments on the duke of Alençon's condemnation by King Charles VII in 1458 and his description of an unsuccessful Burgundian embassy to the royal court in this context.[7] The author then changes subject quite abruptly. After the description of the pas*, Chastelain continues with a lengthy anecdote concerning a German knight, Heinrich Sasse (the Younger?), who presented his* emprise *at court without Duke Philip's permission.]*

---

the younger Heinrich Sasse: GCC, pp. 133–6; see Werner Paravicini, *Ehrenvolle Abwesenheit: Studien zum adligen Reisen im späteren Mittelalter. Gesammelte Aufsätze*, ed. by Jan Hirschbiegel and Harm von Seggern (Ostfildern: Thorbecke Verlag, 2017), pp. 268–70.

4 H. Oskar Sommer, ed., *The Vulgate Version of the Arthurian Romances. Volume III: Le Livre de Lancelot del Lac. Part 1* (Washington: The Carnegie Institution, 1910), p. 278; Rémy Ambühl, *Le séjour du futur Louis XI dans les pays de Philippe le Bon (1456–1461)* (Stavelot: Cercle d'histoire et d'archéologie du pays de Genappe, 2002), p. 53 n. 208, identifies this passage as Guillaume's inspiration.

5 See Sources 4 and 7, respectively.

6 Guillaume Bureaux, 'Union et désunion de la noblesse en parade. Le rôle des Pas d'armes dans l'entretien des rivalités chevaleresques entre cours princières occidentales, XVe–XVIe siècles (Anjou, Bourgogne, France, Saint-Empire)' (unpublished PhD dissertation, Normandie Université, 2018), p. 345.

7 Jean II of Alençon was convicted of treason and incarcerated: see Philippe Contamine, 'Le premier procès de Jean II, duc d'Alençon (1456–58): quels enjeux, quels enseignements politiques?', in *Power and Persuasion: Essays on the Art of State Building in Honour of W. P. Blockmans*, ed. by Peter C. M. Hoppenbrouwers, Antheun Janse and Robert Stein (Turnhout: Brepols, 2010), pp. 103–22.

(127) **III**

And I come to the jousts for which the duke had given permission[8] to Guillaume de Moullon[9] to hold them before the ladies at Le Quesnoy, the day of which drew closer. The duke himself, setting aside his other important business, had come to the said Le Quesnoy in favour of the said Guillaume, as he had promised. Also present were the count of Nevers[10] and the countess,[11] who was a very beautiful and radiant lady with a rich entourage. So it happened that Guillaume de Moullon, who called himself [the Companion] 'of the White Teardrop', sent his Moor once more to the castle of Le Quesnoy to the gathering of lords who were there together with the four princesses[12] and all the other ladies and (128) damsels in large numbers. The said Moor, dressed and accompanied by two officers of arms as he had been at Arras,[13] presented a humbly written letter to the countess of Charolais,[14] which does not need to be mentioned because of its length and because the affair merely concerned jousts. However, once this letter was read out loud in front of everyone, the countess allowed her knight, who had read it, to ask for the content of the chapters, which were given immediately. After they were read, the countess, with the consent of the duke,[15] who was close by, and by his order, allowed the Moor to display his *emprise* and gave permission for anyone who wanted to touch it to do so. A chair was prepared that was entirely covered with cloth of gold and decorated all over with rich tapestries on which, by order of the countess, the officers of arms led the Moor to sit. As he sat there, twelve or thirteen noblemen, both knights and squires, came to touch the *emprise*. Their names were the bastard of Comminges,[16] Jean

---

[8] The presentation of the *emprise* at Arras in August or September 1458 is described in GC, vol. 3, pp. 462–6.

[9] [Guillame de Moulon]. Guillaume de Moullon was a knight from the Dauphiné: see Sébastien Nadot, *Le Spectacle des joutes: Sport et courtoisie à la fin du Moyen Âge* (Rennes: Presses Universitaires de Rennes, 2012), pp. 89–90; Ambühl, *Le séjour*, pp. 51–4. Guillaume's name varies in the sources (Meuillon, Meyllon, Moillon): see *ibid.*, p. 51 n. 198. He had already fought at the *Pas de la Joyeuse Garde/ Pas de Saumur* in 1446: Christian de Mérindol, *Les fêtes de chevalerie à la cour du roi René: Emblématique, art et histoire (les joutes de Nancy, le Pas de Saumur et le Pas de Tarascon)* (Paris: Éditions du CTHS, 1993), p. 12 n. 36. On this event at Saumur, see Source 5 and Essays 2 and 7.

[10] Charles of Burgundy (*c.*1414–64), count of Nevers and Rethel, was the son of Philippe of Burgundy, youngest brother of Duke John the Fearless of Burgundy, and Bonne of Artois. PCB no. 533.

[11] Marie d'Albret (before 1441–85), countess of Nevers and Rethel, was the daughter of Charles II d'Albret and Anne d'Armagnac; she married Charles of Burgundy, count of Nevers, in 1456. PCB no. 1945.

[12] The four ladies are not clearly identified: Chastelain mentions explicitly Isabelle of Bourbon (see below, n. 14), countess of Charolais, and Marie d'Albret (see above, n. 11). It seems probable that Isabel of Portugal (1397–1471; PCB no. 429), wife of Philip the Good, was also present, as well as the infant Mary of Burgundy (1457–82; PCB no. 1891), the only child of Charles the Bold and Isabelle of Bourbon.

[13] See above, n. 8.

[14] [la contesse de Charolois]. Isabelle of Bourbon (1435–65), countess of Charolais, was the daughter of Charles I, duke of Bourbon, and Agnès of Burgundy; she married Charles of Charolais (later Duke Charles the Bold), son of Philip the Good, in 1454. Mother of Mary of Burgundy, Charles's only legitimate child. PCB no. 921.

[15] Philip the Good (1396–1467), duke of Burgundy. PCB no. 1.

[16] [le bastard de Comingnes]. Bernard de Comminges, chamberlain of Philip the Good. PCB no. 1794.

de Halluin,[17] Messire Tristan de Toulongeon,[18] Messire Othon de Marquettes,[19] Jean de Trazegnies,[20] Messire Ferry de Grancey,[21] Messire Jean de Swaef,[22] Pierre de Massy,[23] Jean de Massy,[24] Messire Évrard de Digoine,[25] Jean de Digoine,[26] Louis de Chevallart[27] and, finally, the last of these was Messire Antoine, bastard of Burgundy,[28] who wanted to be the final jouster and to close the *pas*, since Messire Adolf of Cleves[29] was to open it. All these noble knights and squires prepared themselves lavishly in order to put themselves

[17] [Jehan de Halwin]. Probably Jean (II) de Halluin/Jan (II) van Halewijn (*c.*1440?–73), lord of Halluin/Halewijn, was a chamberlain of Charles the Bold (1468–73); see Pieter Donche, 'Verhaspelde van Halewijns ontrafeld, Roeselare en Boezinge ca. 1460', in *Vlaamse Stam*, 48.3 (2012), 225–46. PCB no. 2483.

[18] [messire Tristan de Toulongon]. Tristan de Toulongeon, son of Antoine de Toulongeon (d. 1432), was a squire of the stables and chamberlain of Philip the Good and Charles the Bold (1453–75). PCB no. 1795.

[19] [messire Hoste de Marquetes]. Othon de Marquettes, a nobleman from Hainaut who served in the company of Jacques de Lalaing (*c.*1446–47), was knighted in 1465. CL, p. 142 n. 214. He was a cupbearer of Philip the Good (1451): see René Petitprez and Théodore Leuridan, 'Monographie de Marquette en Ostrevant', in *Bulletin de la Société d'Études de la province de Cambrai*, 25 (1925), 81–236 (p. 96).

[20] Jean III de Trazegnies (1439–1513), was a chamberlain of Charles the Bold (1472–76). PCB no. 3247; and MmM, p. 403 no. 243.

[21] Ferry de Grancey was in the service of Charles of Burgundy, count of Nevers and Rethel (see above, n. 10); after Charles's death in 1464 he became a chamberlain of his successor, Jean of Burgundy. He fought in the *Pas de la Joyeuse Garde/Pas de Saumur* on the side of the challengers: see Mérindol, *Les fêtes*, p. 159.

[22] [Jehan de Swaue]. Jean II de Swaef (d. before November 1497), lord of Ruisbroek, came from an important patrician family from Brussels. He participated, amongst others, in the jousts of the White Bear at Bruges (1451 and 1453): see Jean Antoine De Jonghe, ed., *Cronijcke van den lande ende graefscepe van Vlaenderen gemaect door Nicolaes Despars … van de jaeren 405 tot 1492*, 4 vols, 2nd edn (Bruges: De Jonghe, 1840), vol. 3, pp. 470, 516. GCC erroneously gives the name as 'Sivane'. Thanks are due to Janet Portman (British Library) for providing a digital reproduction of the manuscript and to Mario Damen for his help in identifying this knight.

[23] Pierre de Massy was a member of the guard of Charles the Bold (1476). PCB no. 4010.

[24] [Jehan de Massy]. Jean de Massy was a cupbearer at the court of Philip the Good (1462). PCB no. 2204.

[25] Évrard de Digoine (d. 1473), was a cupbearer (1452–58) and chamberlain (1458–60?) at the court of Philip the Good (1447–60); he fought in the *Pas du Chevalier au Cygne* (Lille, 1454). PCB no. 1329; VdF, pp. 264–5.

[26] [Jehan de Digoine]. The son of Évrard de Digoine (see above, n. 25), though there is a possible confusion here with Chrétien de Digoine (d. after 1504), who also fought in the *Chevalier au Cygne* and was active 1452–69. PCB no. 1755; VdF, p. 264.

[27] [Loÿs de Chevallart]. Louis de Chevallart fought in the *Chevalier au Cygne* and in the *Pas du Perron Fée* (Bruges, 1463); he was a cupbearer of Philip the Good and appears in the Burgundian salary lists in 1464 and 1468. PCB no. 2477; VdF, p. 253.

[28] [messire Anthoine, bastard de Bourgoingne]. Antoine of Burgundy (1421–1504) was the illegitimate son of Philip the Good; after the death of his older half-brother, Corneille (d. 1452), he became known as the 'Great Bastard'. He occupied important positions at court and in the ducal government, and had a distinguished career as a jouster and participant in *pas d'armes*, becoming a member of the Order of the Golden Fleece (1456). COTO no. 54; PCB no. 1958.

[29] [messire Adolf de Cleves]. Adolf of Cleves (1425–92), lord of Ravenstein, was the second son of Duke Adolf II of Cleves and nephew of Philip the Good. Brought up at and fully integrated into the Burgundian court, he had an illustrious career as a tournament fighter, including the *Chevalier au Cygne*,

on display and, in so doing, incurred large expenses because they knew that the man with whom they had to compete[30] was a person of high reputation who had seen and experienced a great deal. In fact, since they regarded him highly and he was a foreigner,[31] they made a special effort to honour him by appearing richly dressed. Thus, there was none so poor that he failed to come into the lists clad in silk cloth, and the powerful and great lords wore wealthy outfits made of cloth of gold and embroidered velvet as well as other riches that would have been sufficient for a king's wedding.

(129) **IV**

The total number of those who touched the Moor's *emprise* was twenty-five: twelve at Arras[32] and thirteen in front of the ladies. Because the count of Charolais[33] was not present, this reduced the number of those who touched it, since he had gone with most of the young men of his household to Zeeland[34] to hold the *Vierscare*[35]— which is like a Parliament according to the custom of the land and which no one other than the lord himself or his eldest son can hold.

Then, on a very beautiful and clear Sunday in October, Guillaume de Moullon, known as 'the Companion of the White Teardrop', made his way into the lists, very beautifully mounted and armed; [his horse] was richly clad in black satin, strewn with white teardrops, embroidered with silver-thread, and [he himself bore] a shield of similar design. Once the ladies had arrived at the place and gathered at the windows, he readied himself to do his duty against Messire Adolf of Cleves, a very fine and excellent jouster, who was handsomely dressed, as were his servants who accompanied him, for he was wearing crimson velvet with very rich gold embroideries; he donated this clothing to the heralds after he had broken his lances — everyone had to break six of these, and there was a prize for the one who was the first to break them against his opponent. Guillaume did very well and showed himself to be a man of virtue, great courage and worth, one who was well acquainted with the practice of arms. The said Messire Adolf also did well and fought very vigorously: he was so used to this that no one was better than he at these

---

where he featured as *entrepreneur*, and the *Pas de l'Arbre d'Or* (Bruges, 1468). He was a member of the Order of the Golden Fleece (1456). COTO no. 55; PCB no. 817.

30 That is, Guillaume de Moullon.

31 The *entrepreneurs* of Burgundian *pas d'armes* were usually vassals of the duke, some of them also members of the Order of the Golden Fleece: Jacques Paviot, 'Le rôle des ordres de chevalerie dans la ritualisation de la cour', in *Rituels et cérémonies de cour de l'Empire romain à l'âge baroque*, ed. by Delphine Carrangeot, Bruno Laurioux and Vincent Puech (Villeneuve-d'Ascq: Presses Universitaires du Septentrion, 2018), pp. 97–106 (p. 105).

32 See above, n. 8.

33 [le conte de Charolois]. Charles the Bold (1433–77), count of Charolais, was the only surviving legitimate son of Philip the Good and Isabel of Portugal; he succeeded his father as duke of Burgundy in 1467. PCB no. 612.

34 The county of Zeeland, formally part of the Holy Roman Empire, was acquired by Philip the Good in 1433 (together with the county of Holland): see Richard Vaughan, *Philip the Good: The Apogee of Burgundy* (London/New York: Longman 1970), pp. 49–53.

35 This was a regional assembly with judicial and seigneurial powers: see Marie Charlotte Le Bailly, *Recht voor de Raad: Rechtspraak voor het Hof van Holland, Zeeland en West-Friesland in het midden van de vijftiende eeuw* (Hilversum: Uitgeverij Verloren, 2001), pp. 38 and 42–7.

matters; indeed, he had already won a prize for jousting one hundred and twenty times, this being a marvellous thing for a knight aged 30 or 32.

It would be too long and too tiresome to recount the courses run and how the other knights, barons and noblemen presented themselves at this event (130) as valiant men of good reputation. They were all very ostentatiously clad in rich silk cloth of different colours and with different emblems. There wasn't one of them who didn't do this, except for the bastard of Comminges, a noble squire of some standing, who did the opposite of what the others had done, in order to make people laugh, and another knight from Brabant, called Messire Jean de Swaef, who was likewise not dressed in a particularly fine fashion. Nonetheless, considering the group in general and taking everyone according to their merits, all showed themselves to be worthy men of noble character, and they gladly put themselves on display for the ladies. Amongst them, those who performed best were Messire Adolf of Cleves, Messire Claude de Toulongeon,[36] a very tall and handsome knight, Messire Philippe, bastard of Brabant,[37] the lord of Mourcourt,[38] Messire Antoine, bastard of Brabant,[39] Jean de Massy, Louis de Chevallart and the bastard of Burgundy, who was the last one to joust. Because these jousts lasted eight whole days before Guillaume de Moullon could complete all twenty-five bouts against these jousters, he appeared each time decked out in new attire, gradually increasing the costliness of his outfits. Also, during each of the eight days, the duke gave a banquet with all the ladies in attendance, where Guillaume was seated in a very honourable position each time and was well served and highly praised.

The bastard of Burgundy, who was truly a knight of high courage and one of the fine figures of his time, being of marvellously rich appearance and high ambition, entered the lists in an unusual manner, because he made his way through the streets, mounted and armed in a cell that resembled a kind of chapel that could be carried with the arms from inside.[40] Once he had arrived in the presence of the ladies, where Guillaume was walking about, a hermit emerged from this hermitage. Nobly clad and mounted on a beautiful charger entirely covered in cloth of gold, he was carrying a letter in his hand that he came over to present to the princesses who were at the windows. As soon as the letter had been read, inspected (131) and responded to, the aforesaid hermit returned

---

[36] [messire Glaude de Thoulonjon]. Claude de Toulongeon (1421/22–1503), son of Antoine de Toulongeon (d. 1432), was a chamberlain of Philip the Good and Charles the Bold from 1453, when he was knighted at Gavere, together with his brother Tristan (see above, n. 18). He was a member of the Order of the Golden Fleece (1481). PCB no. 1795; COTO no. 93.

[37] [messire Philippe, bastard de Braibant]. Philippe de Brabant (d. 1478), lord of Kruibeke and La Ferté, was the illegitimate son of Philippe of Saint-Pol, duke of Brabant, and (half-?) brother of Antoine de Brabant. He jousted at the *Perron Fée* and was a pantler* and chamberlain of Philip the Good, Charles the Bold and Maximilian. PCB no. 1454; VdF, pp. 247–48.

[38] Louis Le Jeune (d. 1477, battle of Nancy), lord of Mourcourt and later lord of Contay, served first in the household of Duchess Isabel of Portugal, then as chamberlain of Charles the Bold (1474); he fought in the *Chevalier au Cygne* and the *Arbre d'or*. PCB no. 1232; VdF, p. 257.

[39] [messire Anthoine, bastard de Braibant]. Antoine de Brabant (d. 1498), lord of Kruibeke and Hemiksem, was the illegitimate son of Philippe of Saint-Pol, duke of Brabant, and (half-?) brother of Philippe de Brabant. He jousted at the *Perron Fée* and was a cupbearer and chamberlain of Philip the Good. PCB no. 1453; VdF, p. 247.

[40] This mobile construction is hard to visualise: while it could be carried from the inside, according to Chastelain, it must have been spacious enough to hold at least two persons and two horses.

to his hermitage and went inside, saying to the knight who was resting there that the ladies requested that he put aside his sorrow and perform in their honour by coming out and showing himself in the lists, where so many honourable people were gathered; his honour and his good fortune could only increase as a result. The said knight then did so, appearing mounted and armed on a very beautiful destrier, but the horse and the harness were covered with such a large grey *josselin** that one could only see the tips of its hooves. However, this attire was immediately removed by order of the ladies, and underneath he was found to be the best-armed knight, finer than the others: [the destrier* was] richly clad in a trapper* of green velvet, strewn with embroidered silver butterflies and with an embroidered edge with his emblem that was one and a half feet wide, with golden barbicans,[41] most richly made in raised embroidery. As he stood dressed in this way, a beautiful veil was brought over to him by the hand of a lady, which he attached to his helm*. To Guillaume de Moullon was also sent an expensive and embroidered veil from the countess of Charolais which was carried into the lists by two knights. This veil was so long and wide that it could have covered his entire body from head to toe. This gave him immense pleasure as he took it as a very high and singular honour indeed. The bastard of Burgundy and he then performed their jousts very well and with great vigour; they executed their duties so diligently that each of them received [much] honour. Once these jousts were over and their lances broken, they began to joust in a *mêlée* with fifteen or sixteen others, pitting themselves very fiercely against one another, all of them freshly clad in silk. There Messire Philippe de Lalaing[42] really excelled himself physically and chased all the others out of the lists, winning the prize of the day.

(132) **V**

I could give a very long account of this event, where the duke together with all the ladies made every effort to do honour and provide good cheer to the said Guillaume, since he was a foreigner and from the house of the dauphin.[43] Although he has now left it, it would not be fitting for me to dwell on this at length, because, as I said, it was nothing more than an amusement and not something that put honour greatly at stake. I can therefore put it to one side so as to turn all the sooner to the more important matter that awaits me and which demands very insistently that I treat it.[44] However, it should be known that, as far as jousts are concerned, rarely have so much solemnity and ceremony been shown as was the case here, this being done more out of favour to the aforesaid Guillaume than

---

[41] The barbican was one of Antoine's personal emblems (Fr. *devises*) <https://devise.saprat.fr/personne/antoine-de-bourgogne> [accessed 20 June 2024].

[42] Philippe de Lalaing (*c.*1430–65), the younger brother of the famous knight and jouster, Jacques de Lalaing (*c.*1421–53), was a chamberlain at the court of Philip the Good (1449–65). PCB no. 1732. In 1463, he organised the *Perron Fée* as *entrepreneur*: see Sources 11a and 11b, respectively, and Essay 3.

[43] Louis XI (1423–83), was the eldest son of King Charles VII of France, whom he succeeded in 1461; as heir to the throne, he was dauphin of the Viennois. He fled to the court of Philip the Good (where he stayed 1456–61) due to a conflict with his father: see Ambühl, *Le séjour.*

[44] It is not entirely clear what Chastelain is referring to here, since the description of this *pas* is followed by another anecdote concerning courtly life. Further on, he describes an illness that struck Charles the Bold.

out of duty, since he himself had drawn up the chapters. Indeed, the duke was present on four or five occasions, more richly clad than anyone had ever seen him before out of great love for Guillaume, whom he looked upon with a very favourable eye. He also gave him five hundred gold *écus d'or* when he departed,[45] together with very pleasing and friendly words that came from his heart, this being what gave the said Guillaume more satisfaction than anything else that he had ever before achieved in his life. The best of all these jousters, the one who broke his lances in the least number of courses, was Messire Louis de Contay, lord of Mourcourt, who won the prize for the event. The countess of Charolais also gave a very beautiful diamond, worth one hundred *nobles*,[46] to Guillaume for him to pass on to his wife. Marvellous things could be said about the favours bestowed and the honours shown to him as well as the great love and affection that were showered on him from all sides. It was a long time since one had seen so much fondness being expressed towards a man by all, and the reason was that he had so many virtues and gifts that he had received from God. And yet, he was still cast aside by his master out of envy — a fate that he bore with great patience and in a way that did him much honour, as the situation demanded.[47]

[45] This payment is confirmed by archival sources: see Torsten Hiltmann, 'Un État de noblesse et de chevalerie sans pareilles? Tournois et hérauts d'armes à la cour des ducs de Bourgogne', in *La cour de Bourgogne et l'Europe: Le rayonnement et les limites d'un modèle culturel; actes du colloque international tenu à Paris les 9, 10 et 11 octobre 2007*, ed. by Werner Paravicini, Torsten Hiltmann and Franck Viltart (Ostfildern: Jan Thorbecke Verlag, 2013), pp. 253–88 (p. 258 n. 20). VdN, p. 319, gives the text of Lille, ADN B 2030, fol. 331r, which confirms the payment of 500 *écus d'or* of a value of forty-nine *groats*, amounting to a total of 612lb. 10s.

[46] English gold coin, first introduced in the mid-fourteenth century: see Peter Spufford, *Money and its Use in Medieval Europe* (Cambridge: Cambridge University Press, 1988), p. 282.

[47] For the deteriorating relation between Guillaume and the Dauphin, see GC, vol. 3, p. 464; Ambühl, *Le séjour*, pp. 51–4, especially p. 52.

Mario Damen

Source 10

The *Paso de Jaén* (*Paso* of Jaén), 1461

This source consists of a translation of a narrative account of this event.

Author: Pedro de Escavias?

Language: Medieval Castilian

Manuscript source: Madrid, Biblioteca Nacional, 2092 (*Relación de los fechos del muy magnifico e mas virtuoso Señor ... don Miguel Lucas muy digno Condestable de Castilla*), fols 66v–67v

Edition used: Juan de Mata Carriazo y Arroquia, ed., *Hechos del Condestable don Miguel Lucas de Iranzo (crónica del siglo XV)* (Madrid: Espasa-Calpe, 1940), pp. 58–9 (= HCMLI)

Select bibliography:

Barber, Richard, and Juliet Barker, *Tournaments: Jousts, Chivalry and Pageants in the Middle Ages* (New York: Weidenfeld & Nicolson, 1989), pp. 102, 164

Clare, Lucien, 'Fêtes, jeux et divertissements à la cour du connétable de Castille, Miguel Lucas de Iranzo (1460–1470)', in *La fête et l'écriture: Théâtre de cour, cour-théâtre en Espagne et en Italie, 1450–1530* (Aix-en-Provence: Université de Provence, 1987), pp. 5–32

Devaney, Thomas, *Enemies in the Plaza: Urban Spectacle and the End of Spanish Frontier Culture, 1460–1492* (Philadelphia: University of Pennsylvania Press, 2015), pp. 75–6, 92

Nadot, Sébastien, *Le Spectacle des joutes: Sport et courtoisie à la fin du Moyen Âge* (Rennes: Presses Universitaires de Rennes, 2012), pp. 89, 115, 150, 155, 172, 246

Introduction

The *Paso de Jaén* took place on 15 February 1461 on the Plaza del Arrabal (now known as the Plaza de la Constitución), which is the main market square of Jaén, a frontier town in Andalucía, some 100 km to the north of Granada. The *entrepreneur** of the *Paso* was Fernán Mexía (1424–*c.*1500),[1] a nobleman from Jaén. Although he was not the author of the narrative account of this *paso*, he was a prolific writer of poetry and prose: around 1477–78, he wrote his best-known work, *Nobiliario Vero*, a treatise on nobility and heraldry.[2] He was in the service of Miguel Lucas de Iranzo, a man of humble Basque

[1] Sébastien Nadot, *Le Spectacle des joutes: Sport et courtoisie à la fin du Moyen Âge* (Rennes: Presses Universitaires de Rennes, 2012), p. 246, erroneously states that the *entrepreneur* was Miguel Lucas de Iranzo, but this person was in fact Fernán Mexía's patron.

[2] DBE, lemma 'Fernán Mexía'.

origin who became a powerful local nobleman in the 1450s. Iranzo belonged to the same group of young noblemen as Beltrán de la Cueva, the *entrepreneur* of the *Paso de El Pardo* (1459),[3] both of whom were in the service of Enrique IV of Castile when he was still a crown prince. In 1455, a year after Enrique had succeeded his father Juan II (1405–54) as king, he made Iranzo a knight and appointed him as *condestable* (constable, a military title) of Castile in 1458, as a successor to Álvaro de Luna, a favourite of Juan II.[4] In the 1460s, however, Iranzo retired from the royal court and established himself in Jaén, from where he led several military expeditions into the kingdom of Granada in the 1460s, at that time the last Muslim-ruled territory of the Iberian Peninsula. At the same time, he became embroiled in noble factional rivalries and was eventually killed when attending Mass on 21 March 1473.[5]

The reason why the *Paso de Jaén* was organised by Fernán de Mexía in the first place was the marriage of his patron Iranzo to Teresa de Torres, who belonged to an influential Andalucian family. In honour of this occasion, which was celebrated on Sunday 25 January 1461, a series of chivalric festivities was organised in the town of Jaén over a period of three weeks, the *Paso* being the concluding event on 15 February. According to the sole narrative account of this event (see below), these festivities started on Monday 26 January on the Plaza de Santa María with a bull run* and a cane game*. The next day, they were followed by a bull run at the Plaza de la Magdalena.[6] On Thursday 29 January, another cane game was held on the Plaza del Arrabal in the presence of Iranzo at which many knights were wounded.[7] Two days later, another bull run was organised, this time on the Plaza San Juan.[8] On Sunday 1 February, a joust with lances and swords featuring twenty pairs of knights pitted against each other was staged on the Plaza del Arrabal, the square where the *Paso* would later be held. This joust was witnessed by the bishop of Salamanca,[9] many noble lords and ladies, the administrators of the town and foreigners[10] who were all seated in the stands that the town administration had constructed in the square and which were decorated with French cloth and tapestries. In front of the stands, the judges were seated on a high wooden platform also covered with cloth.[11] Other people watched from the windows or the roofs of the surrounding houses. In the evening, the tourneyers continued their fight, this time on foot with pollaxes on the patio of the newly built Iranzo Palace in

---

3 See Source 8.

4 On this figure, see Essay 1 and Sources 2 and 3.

5 DBE, lemma, 'Miguel Lucas de Iranzo'. Interestingly, in 1468, when Iranzo had fallen out of favour with King Enrique IV, Mexía plotted with some other noblemen to kill his patron. This plan was foiled and Mexía was imprisoned for years in the Alcázar, the royal palace, of Jaén.

6 HCMLI, pp. 49–50.

7 *Ibid.*, p. 53.

8 *Ibid.*, p. 54.

9 Gonzalo López de Vivero (*c.*1418–80), bishop of Salamanca (1446–80), conducted the marriage ceremony of Iranzo and Teresa de Torres. DBE, lemma 'Gonzalo López de Vivero'.

10 It is not clear who these 'estrangeros' were and if they really came from outside Castile or were simply from outside Jaén. They are mentioned in the context of the retinue of the bishop of Salamanca when they were given leaving presents after the festivities had finished. HCMLI, pp. 42, 59–60.

11 As Thomas Devaney, *Enemies in the Plaza: Urban Spectacle and the End of Spanish Frontier Culture, 1460–1492* (Philadelphia: University of Pennsylvania Press, 2015), p. 76, puts it, these arrangements 'ensured that the *grandes* were comfortable and that they were part of the spectacle, as much on stage as the participants'.

the Calle Maestra; again, many participants were wounded in this event.[12] On Monday 2 February, there was another bull run in the Plaza del Arrabal, whereas in the evening Iranzo's brother[13] ordered an event involving 'correr la sortija' (running at the ring*) to take place in front of the bridegroom's residence.

Given that the *Paso* itself was held in the same space as the joust on 1 February, it is highly likely that it used the same stands and platforms as those that had been constructed for the earlier event. It was not uncommon for *pas d'armes* to repurpose an existing infrastructure, as can be seen at the Burgundian *Pas du Perron Fée* held in Bruges in 1463, which reused the lists and stands that had been set up for some earlier jousts organised by the urban authorities.[14] All the necessary elements required for classifying this particular festivity at Jaén as a *paso*[15] are present in the narrative account devoted to it: the *entrepreneur* is depicted as an enslaved knight, a common literary trope in chivalric literature and *pas d'armes*[16] with which Fernán Mexía, being a writer himself, may well have been acquainted; he defends a *paso*, a wooden bridge in this case — which may be an allusion to the *Paso Honroso* of 1434 when the 'real' Órbigo Bridge near León served as the eponymous 'passage'[17] — and invites challengers to compete under a set of rules that are explained in a letter, albeit this letter has not come down to us, unlike other Iberian letters of challenge.[18] Moreover, the whole event took place in a publicly accessible urban setting that attracted a high-ranking audience and made use of ephemeral architecture.

The actual account of the *Paso de Jaén* comes from a chivalric biography of Iranzo that was probably written around 1472–73. Works in this literary genre record the life of an important knight, in which his feats of arms and knightly virtues demonstrated on both the tournament field and in battle generally play an important role; the usual impetus to write such a biography comes from either the nobleman himself or one of his family members.[19] This form of historiographical text was popular amongst the late medieval nobility of England, France and the Burgundian lands, and the authors of Castilian chivalric biographies, such as those of Alonso Pérez de Guzmán (1265–1309), Pero Niño (1378–1453) and Rodrigo Ponce de León (1444–92), a contemporary of Iranzo who played an important military role in the conquest of Granada in 1492, may well have drawn on these earlier French and Burgundian examples.[20] The biography of Iranzo is preserved in

---

[12] HCMLI, pp. 54–6.

[13] Nicolás Lucas de Iranzo, commander of Montizón, as he is referred later in the text. *Ibid.*, pp. 57–8.

[14] For a discussion of this event, see Essay 3 and Sources 11a and 11b.

[15] For fuller discussion of these elements, see Essay 1.

[16] Nadot, *Le Spectacle*, pp. 170–2. For other examples of this literary trope, see Essay 6.

[17] PH, pp. 91, 400–20.

[18] Martín de Riquer, *Lletres de batalla: cartells de deseiximents i capítols de passos d'armes*, Els nostres clàssics, 3 vols (Barcelona: Barcino, 1963–68).

[19] William T. Cotton, 'Teaching the Motifs of Chivalric Biography', in *The Study of Chivalry: Resources and Approaches*, ed. by Howell D. Chickering and Thomas H. Seiler (Kalamazoo, MI: Medieval Institute Publications, 1988), pp. 583–609 (p. 589); see also CL, pp. 42–3.

[20] DBE, lemmata 'Alonso Pérez de Guzmán', 'Pero Niño Laso de la Vega' and 'Rodrigo Ponce de León'. For editions of their chivalric biographies that were written, respectively, in the 1430s, 1440s and 1490s, see Miguel Ángel Ladero Quesada, 'Una biografía caballeresca del siglo XV: *La Coronica del yllustre y muy magnifico cauallero don Alonso Perez de Guzman el Bueno*', *En la España Medieval*, 22 (1999), 247–83 (especially pp. 248–9, on the possible influence of 'Burgundian models' on the Castilian chivalric biography); Gutierre Díez de Games and Rafael Beltrán Llavador, eds, *El Victorial* (Salamanca:

four manuscripts, of which the oldest and most trustworthy dates from the late fifteenth century and is now kept in the Biblioteca Nacional in Madrid.

The account of Iranzo's life and deeds was probably compiled by Pedro de Escavias (*c.*1410–*c.*1485), a member of an eminent family from the town of Andújar, some 70 km to the north of Jaén. Escavias, who was a protégé of Iranzo's, not only supported his patron in his military campaigns against the Nazarí kingdom of Granada in the 1460s but also dedicated some *coplas* (poems of four stanzas of four lines) to him.[21] However, the attribution of this work to Escavias has not gone unchallenged in recent years. Although Juan de Mata Carriazo y Arroquia, who edited the biography in the 1940s, was firmly of the opinion that Escavias was the sole author, scholars nowadays believe that he is more likely to have been the overall compiler of the biography, which was based on various accounts of episodes from Iranzo's life that were probably composed by other writers linked to him.[22]

Somewhat frustratingly, Iranzo's biography goes into far less detail on the *Paso de Jaén* itself (two pages of the modern edition) than it does on the series of festivities celebrating his marriage that preceded it (ten pages). This relative brevity may well be explained by the fact that he was merely a spectator at this particular event that featured instead the deeds performed by his protégé, Fernán Mexía, whereas he did compete in the earlier ones.

In the translation of this account of the *Paso* that follows, page numbers in parentheses have been inserted for ease of reference to Carriazo y Arroquia's edition.

Translation

(58) Because so many different things happened during these festivities, it is not only very laborious but almost impossible for anyone to presume to put it all in writing, and [this] could cause anger and annoyance to readers and listeners. That is why I am refraining from explaining in detail all the other things that happened on all the other days until the festivities came to an end. Suffice it to say that they spent as much time as daylight permitted on many cane games and bull runs, one after the other.

When night fell, after everybody had received sufficient sustenance, there were many *momeries** featuring multiple characters brought to life in various inventive performances and stagings; so many different types of costume, adornments and harnesses were used in them that it was a wonder to behold. That is how they passed the time until Sunday 15 February of the said year,[23] three weeks after the wedding ceremony of the aforesaid lord constable[24] and the countess.[25]

Ediciones Universidad de Salamanca, 1996); Juan Luis Carriazo Rubio, ed., *Historia de los hechos del marqués de Cádiz* (Granada: Universidad de Granada, 2003).

[21] DBE, lemma 'Pedro de Escavias'.

[22] HCMLI, pp. xxv–xxxi; Juan Bautista Avalle-Arce, *El cronista Pedro de Escavias: una vida del siglo XV* (Chapel Hill: The University of North Carolina Press, 1972), pp. 107–36; Michel Garcia, 'A propos de la Chronique du Connétable Miguel Lucas de Iranzo', *Bulletin Hispanique*, 75 (1973), 5–39; DBE, lemma 'Pedro de Escavias'; Devaney, *Enemies in the Plaza*, p. 195.

[23] That is, 1461.

[24] Miguel Lucas de Iranzo: see above, p. 200.

[25] That is, Teresa de Torres, daughter of Pedro de Torres and Guiomar Carrillo, both of whom were from influential Andalucian families.

Fernán Mexía,[26] their servant and kinsman, in his desire to serve them and to bring these festivities to an honourable end, ordered closed lists[27] to be put up in the Plaza Mayor del Arrabal and a *paso* to be held on that Sunday or the following day. He had a bridge constructed that crossed the said square and issued a letter of challenge stipulating that all or any knights and noblemen who wanted to cross the said bridge could run a certain number of courses against him under certain conditions to be determined by the judges who were there to oversee [the event].

(59) He[28] then came out on a very gentle horse covered with a trapper* of fine blue cloth adorned with embroidered teardrops,[29] [and wearing] a jousting harness*. On the saddle, there was a kind of cage with an effigy of his person[30] with a sword impaling his breast and with his hands tied with a chain. Next, out rode twelve knights to challenge him, being equipped for war with various trappers and accoutrements. On the aforesaid Sunday and following Monday, they ran many skilful courses in which many lances were broken and many blows received. The lord constable, the lady countess, the ladies Doña Guiomar and Doña Juana,[31] the lord bishop of Salamanca, the archdeacon of Toledo,[32] and all the other knights, noblemen and noble ladies were present in the stands, all gathered to honour this wedding and the festivities that accompanied it.

---

[26] [Fernánd Mexía]. Fernán Mexía (1424–*c.*1500), a nobleman from Jaén, was the son of Gonzalo Mexía de la Cerda and Isabel de Narváez. DBE, lemma 'Fernán Mexía'.

[27] The word *rencle*, which is used here in the original text to describe these lists, also recurs later in the biography where it recounts another joust organised on the same square on 15 January 1462; it seems to refer there to an enclosed area in which twenty knights jousted. HCMLI, p. 73.

[28] That is, Fernán Mexía.

[29] Teardrops were a popular decorative element or emblem in Burgundian *pas d'armes*, as for example at the *Pas de la Fontaine des Pleurs* (Chalon-sur-Saône, 1449–50) and the *Pas du Compagnon à la Larme Blanche* (Le Quesnoy, 1458): see Sources 7 and 9, respectively. On the translation of 'lagrimas de Moysen' (literally meaning 'teardrops of Moses') as embroidered teardrops, see the review by René Cortrait of Juan Ruiz, *Libro de Buen Amor*, ed. by Nicasio Salvador Miguel (Madrid: Magisterio Español, 1972) in *Bulletin Hispanique*, 75 (1973), 439–41.

[30] That is, Fernán Mexía. Although the exact meaning of this passage is somewhat obscure, the explanation of it given in Nadot, *Le Spectacle*, p. 172, namely that the *entrepreneur* himself is locked up in the cage, seems unlikely.

[31] Juana Alvárez de Iranzo was the constable's step-sister. Tess Knighton, 'Spaces and Contexts for Listening in 15th-Century Castile: The Case of the Constable's Palace in Jaén', *Early Music*, 25 (1997), 661–77 (p. 669).

[32] Alonso de Iranzo, brother of Miguel Lucas, was archdeacon of Toledo.

Thanks are due to Catherine Blunk and Rosalind Brown-Grant for their comments on an earlier version of this translation.

Michelle Szkilnik

Source 11a

The *Pas du Perron Fée* (*Pas* of the Enchanted Column), Bruges, 1463

This source consists of a translation of selected extracts from various narrative accounts of this event.

Author: unknown

Language: Middle French

Edition used: Chloé Horn, Anne Rochebouet, and Michelle Szkilnik, eds, *Le Pas du Perron Fée (Édition des manuscrits Paris, BnF fr 5739 et Lille BU 104* (Paris: Champion, 2013) (= PPF). See also Félix Brassart, *Le Pas du Perron fée tenu à Bruges en 1463 par le chevalier Philippe de Lalaing* (Douai: L. Crépin, 1874); Godfrey Allen Lester, 'Sir John Paston's *Grete Boke*: A Descriptive Index of British Library MS Landsdowne 285' (unpublished PhD dissertation, University of Sheffield, 1982) (for the edited text of the *Perron Fée*, see pp. 427–79); and MT, pp. 131–60.

Select bibliography:

Beaune, Colette, 'Le Pas du Perron Fée', in *Splendeurs de la cour de Bourgogne: récits et chroniques*, ed. by Danielle Régnier-Bohler (Paris: Laffont, 1995), pp. 1164–92

Lecuppre-Desjardin, Élodie, *La ville des cérémonies: Essai sur la communication politique dans les anciens Pays-Bas bourguignons* (Turnhout: Brepols, 2004)

——, 'L'imaginaire chevaleresque à l'assaut des villes: représentation et organisation des pas d'armes en milieu urbain au XVe siècle', in *Le Romanesque aux XIVe et XVe siècles*, ed. by Danielle Bohler (Bordeaux: Presses Universitaires de Bordeaux, 2009), pp. 227–39

Szkilnik, Michelle, 'Que lisaient les chevaliers du XVe siècle? Le témoignage du *Pas du Perron Fée*', *Le Moyen Français*, 68 (2011), pp. 103–14

Van den Abeele, Andries, 'De Wapenpas van de Betoverde Burcht, voorbode van de machtsgreep door Karel de Stoute', *Handelingen van het Genootschap voor Geschiedenis te Brugge*, 146 (2009), pp. 93–139

Introduction

The *Pas du Perron Fée* took place in Bruges on 28 April–17 May 1463. It ran over twelve days with breaks totalling eight days: on 30 April because the knights of the count of Charolais, who participated in the event, were not ready; and on 1–4 May because of the civic procession of the Holy Blood that was being held in the city. On 7, 10 and 15 May as well no combat took place, but no explanation is provided for these breaks. The *Pas* was originally planned to start on 6 February 1463 and to take place in Brussels, but was moved to a later date and a different location to accommodate the duke of Burgundy's plans.[1] The *entrepreneur** of the event was Philippe de Lalaing, brother of the famous Jacques de Lalaing, who was a well-connected knight at the court of Burgundy in his own right. He faced a total of fifty-two challengers, some of whom competed several times. Many, but not all, were high-ranking nobles, such as Adolf of Cleves, Antoine, the Great Bastard of Burgundy, Jacques and Louis de Luxembourg, and Charles of Charolais, the soon-to-be duke of Burgundy. The scenario of the *Pas* was not particularly original: the *entrepreneur* had been taken prisoner by a fairy lady, the so-called Lady of the Enchanted Column, who kept him in her magical *perron** (column), a large edifice guarded by a dwarf. Philippe could secure his release only by fighting challengers willing to touch one, or several, of three shields hanging from the column.

Three prose accounts of Philippe's *pas* survive, written by two, or possibly three, different people who probably witnessed it at first hand. One account (A) is preserved in a single manuscript.[2] It is the shortest of the three and reads almost like notes jotted down at the time of the event. It briefly enumerates Philippe's challengers, mentioning for each combat the attire worn by his opponent, the number of courses with the lance and/or strokes exchanged with the sword, and the winner of the combat. The account concludes with Philippe's release, the awarding of various prizes and the mention of the final dances. It does not give any information on the fictional scenario on which this *pas* was based. The second account (B) is preserved in six manuscripts.[3] Whoever wrote it may have made use of account A, as the description of the jousts is almost identical in both reports. The third account (C) is preserved in four manuscripts.[4] Accounts B and C both give a very detailed description of the set-up of the *Pas* and of the various jousts, as well as depicting Philippe's release and the celebrations marking the end of the event (awarding of prizes, banquet and dances). Yet they differ in their presentation of the scenario, the image of the Lady of the Enchanted Column and therefore of the organiser of the event. The beginning of account C reads like a short Arthurian romance that explains how a nameless knight is lost on a moor at dusk and encounters an unwelcoming dwarf who challenges him to accept a fearsome adventure. Account B opens with a prologue, one that is missing from A and C and which lists the books that may have encouraged Philippe de Lalaing to hold his *pas*: these are not just Arthurian romances but also *chansons de geste* and chronicles. It does not recount the circumstances that led to the nameless knight becoming a prisoner. It only reports that a powerful lady, who possesses numerous castles and strongholds, is in the habit of retaining knights in her Enchanted Column. Philippe de Lalaing happens to be one of them. When he complains to her that he is wasting his youth and valour in her prison, she offers him the chance to regain his freedom by taking on a challenge consisting of doing battle with many knights. Accounts B and C both preserve the 'chapters of arms' of this *pas* — that is, the rules regulating the competition — but they present them somewhat differently. The actual combats are nonetheless reported in a similar

---

[1] It is unclear why Philip the Good decided to go to Bruges at this time, and what business might have caused him to move the date and the location of Philippe de Lalaing's *pas*.

[2] Cambrai, BM, 1114.

[3] Arras, BM, 915; Arras, BM, 168; Lille, BU, 104; London, BL, Lansdowne 285; London, BL, Harley 48; Leeds, Royal Armouries Library, I.35.

[4] Paris, BnF, fr. 5739; Brussels, KBR, II 1156; the other two are held in the private collection of the present-day Comte de Lalaing. See CL, p. 56.

way in all three accounts: they take pleasure in describing the challengers' appearance as they enter the lists; they mention more briefly the number of lances broken and sword strokes exchanged; and, finally, they outline the festivities that were held to celebrate the completion of the *Pas*, which included the awarding of prizes to the best challengers as well as the banquet and dances organised by order of the duke of Burgundy.

Most of the manuscripts of these different versions[5] also give the content of *brevets*, short poetic pieces consisting of four rhyming octosyllables (rhyming pattern: *abba*) that are presented to each of Philippe's challengers in order to commemorate their exploits. The C account manuscripts reproduce them in full after the end of the *Pas*; the B account manuscripts present them in three different places — that is, after describing in turn the three kinds of prize presented to the challengers in accordance with the shield that they had touched. As for the single manuscript of the A account, it notes in the margin the first words of the appropriate *brevet* when its future recipient enters the lists. Although each poem supposedly concerns only one challenger, the conventional praises it contains could apply to many of the other knights; the beneficiary of each poem is not therefore always the same from one manuscript to another. None of the names of the authors of these accounts have come down to us. They were probably written by heralds attending the event, one of whom may be Limbourg Herald, who was in the service of the dukes of Burgundy — even though in the fictional scenario he is at the service of the lady — but we do not know who held this office at the time when the *Pas* was held.[6]

The translation that follows relates to the events that precede the actual jousts and the post-combat episodes as recounted in the B and C accounts, as preserved in Lille, BU, 104 and Paris, BnF, fr. 5739, respectively.[7] In it, page numbers in parentheses have been provided for ease of reference to Horn, Rochebouet and Szkilnik's edition; the Roman numerals in bold signalling the various chapters of the text have been retained from this edition for clarity.

Translation (1): C account, in Paris, BnF, fr. 5739

(97) **I.**

On the first day of January 1462,[8] my lord Philippe, son of Guillaume de Lalaing, brother of the deceased good knight Jacques de Lalaing (may God receive his soul), moved by a high and noble courage, and eager to secure the acquaintance, familiarity and friendship of every great and noble man, decided to hold a *pas d'armes* in the city of Brussels on the following sixth day of February. Therefore, he went to see the most excellent and most powerful prince and most redoubtable lord, the duke of Burgundy, in order to be granted consent and permission from the duke to hold his *pas*. Philippe, having humbly submitted

[5] With the exception of London, BL, Lansdowne 285; London, BL, Harley 48; Leeds, Royal Armouries Library, I.35.

[6] For a fuller discussion of this issue, see Essay 3.

[7] The manuscripts belonging to the Comte de Lalaing have been used to correct the Paris manuscript where needed. The order of the accounts presented here follows that in the edition — that is, with the C account preceding the B account.

[8] The year 1462 is given in *modo gallico* (in which the year begins on Easter Sunday and not on 1 January), which is 1463 according to modern style.

his request and petition, my lord granted it with humility and agreed that the *Pas* be held in the city of Brussels on the following sixth day of February. However, because of the occupations of my lord the duke, the day was moved to the twenty-eighth day of April 1463 in the city of Bruges, as will be clearly stated hereafter.

First, the chapters devised for the *Pas* will be set out, then all the proceedings, ceremonies and miscellaneous arrangements will be described, and what was accomplished with lances and swords, as it all happened.

(98) **II.**

As human voices celebrate extraordinary and admirable events and describe them as wonders, thus, recently, [O] noble princes and knights, renowned barons and squires, a very strange adventure has occurred nearby in the lands of the most excellent and victorious duke of Burgundy: a poor knight, lost on the moors and not knowing where to obtain lodging, found himself at nightfall, when the sun had set, between two large, broad ponds full of water. Finding himself there and being wary of looking around to obtain lodging for the night and afraid of wandering about at night in an unknown place, he finally reached the opening of a narrow passage where, as a first line of defence blocking the way, he found an obstacle in the form of a column,[9] with no dwelling to enquire about his whereabouts. Attached to this column was simply a brass horn inscribed with letters stating that whoever by adventure, or other means, had found his way to this place could take the horn and sound it twice and, the third time, he would get an answer. The truth is that the knight, seeing that it was nighttime and being afraid of the dangers that the night might conceal if he didn't obtain shelter, and not knowing the meaning of the horn, who had placed it here, who dwelt and lived in the column,[10] brought the horn to his mouth. Simply wishing to be heard by someone, he sounded the horn, which echoed through the mountain and the valley; ready to accept whatever might happen, he sounded it a third time.

Then, as quickly as if he had emerged from the ground, a strangely shaped dwarf appeared. (99) His garments were made of cloth of gold, but he had a scowling expression on his face. He started to confront the knight, saying to him: 'What dire adventure brings you right here, Sir knight, to alarm us at this hour? In the name of God, I assure you that your sounding of the horn may turn out badly for you, if Fortune is as unkind to you as she has been to others. Get down from your horse, leave it here with your armour and go back; or, surrender to a person whom you don't know and face the fearsome adventure that awaits you: this is the choice I give you.'

At that, the knight, taken aback[11] not so much by the situation as by the dwarf's manner, answered: 'Sir dwarf, I thought that now I had arrived here, I was at my journey's end. Therefore, if I turned back, I would bring shame on myself. My friend, a cruel adventure brought me here and I believed that I could find a lodging at my request. However, since Fortune is such that I came here recklessly, regardless of the dangers that might arise, I will not leave in a cowardly fashion for fear of what may befall me. At the

---

[9] The French word is *perron*, which might be a large stone or, as is the case here, some sort of column.

[10] Paris ms: 'le personne', corrected with Comte de Lalaing's manuscripts: 'perron' (= column).

[11] Paris ms: 'pour plus', corrected with Comte de Lalaing's manuscripts: 'perplex'.

least, I shall find in you some humanity tonight, I hope, and you will accommodate and shelter me like a poor knight. Tomorrow, when you care to tell me more about the nature of this place, for my sake or otherwise, I will give you my answer.'

III.

Truth to tell, that night the knight was taken good care of, as is customary with captive knights, and he was shown the kind of honours due to a nobleman. At that time, he did not encounter any other person, except the dwarf whom he had first met, a fact that amazed him. (100) The night went by, the day came, and the dwarf, meeting the knight as he got out of bed, said to him: 'Sir knight, you are a prisoner without knowing whose; you have come so far that your going back can only be to your advantage. Here lives a lady of high renown, called the Lady of the Enchanted Column. Her whim and her vocation are such that she has the power of halting and retaining any knight who passes by until she has clearly ascertained his virtue and valour.' At this, the knight who had been taken prisoner, in his wish to know why he had been detained, addressed the dwarf and said: 'Good friend, I beg you to take pity on me and to point out to the lady of this place that by remaining here too long, my youth will go to waste; tell her that I offer to accomplish whatever she desires and orders, to the best of my abilities.'

All of a sudden, the dwarf was moved to compassion by the knight's great humility and he went to see his lady, to whom he described the piteous laments and fulsome offers of service made by this poor knight. On hearing the case put forward by the dwarf, as he himself asserted later, the Lady of the Enchanted Column consented to be merciful and instructed her dwarf to tell the knight that, in order to assess the truthfulness of his words, he had to put himself to the test, and that other knights of high renown had to prove their worth against him, in their case so as to enhance their fame. In order to fulfil her desire, since ladies request that knightly exploits be highly praised and extolled, she had settled here on the condition that whenever a knight or a squire came and set foot in her domain, he would never be allowed to leave unless he followed her ruling and directive, which is that he test and assess his worth, on horseback and fully armed, against any knight or squire in the manner and fashion described hereafter.

(101) [The dwarf said:] 'Therefore, if Fortune decides that you don't remain here as a recreant,[12] you can acquire honour and profit, and those who increase your fame will themselves be richly rewarded. This is the case as it stands and you have heard the reason for your being detained. One thing among others is needed, which is that, in the residence of the most powerful and victorious prince, the duke of Burgundy, you publicise your adventure to all the noble knights and valiant men, who are more numerous there than anywhere else, and that, in begging them to assist in liberating you, as stipulated in the lady's ruling, you exhort them to strive for their own fame, so that without delay — since you might have other affairs elsewhere to attend to — you can return to freedom. I assure you that all I have just said to you is with the approval of the lady of this place and she herself will confirm it through her deeds and actions when the event is concluded.'

[12] A recreant is a defeated and/or cowardly knight.

IV.

When the knight saw that he was being detained without the use of force, and that he had no control over his destiny other than by acting boldly and trusting the dwarf, in his eagerness to regain his freedom, he replied: 'My dear friend, I thank my lady for the mercy she has shown me by so swiftly explaining her wishes and her reason for my imprisonment, albeit this is a form of hardship for me. However, in order to obey her commands, I am ready to accomplish whatever she wants. In order that I might better understand the meaning of this place, I beg you to tell me what I have to do.'

At this, the dwarf, more moved to pity than he had ever been, said: 'I have orders from my lady to tell you, as the first point concerning this *pas*, (102) that three shields covered with silk veils trimmed with gold will be attached to this column known as the Enchanted Column, on the second Sunday of every month.[13] Each of these veils will have a knot positioned in the middle of each shield, so that one can neither see nor guess what lies beneath.

The first shield, hanging on the right-hand side, signifies that all those knights or squires willing to touch it on the second Sunday, from sunrise to sunset, will be obliged to fight you with rebated swords*, each one in turn, in the order in which they touch the shield. Moreover, let it be known that, on entering the lists, all those noblemen who wish to obtain victory in the test signified by the shield will be presented with a lance and a sword. They will be able to use the lance as they please until they break or drop it; thereafter, they will have to strike with their swords seventeen times (or some other number of times). Whoever reaches that number first will win out over his opponent.

Item, the lady lets it be known to you that the second shield hanging from the middle of the Column signifies that to all noble knights and squires who wish to touch it on the day mentioned above, you will be obliged, after having completed what is required by the first shield, to perform and accomplish nine courses with the lance, wearing a harness for war and armed with a helm*, not otherwise; you will also have to run at the tilt*[14] in the usual manner.

Item, the lady lets it be known that the third shield hanging on the left-hand side of the Column signifies that to all noble knights and squires who want to touch it on that day, you will be obliged, after having completed what is required by the previous two shields, to provide eleven courses with the lance,[15] using a saddle for war and wearing a jousting harness, and to run at the tilt with lances of equal size, equipped with grappers* and coronals*.

(103) Item, the lady forbids anyone to touch more than one shield without her consent; this she will only grant as she sees fit, up to a certain number. And the lady will provide and supply all the lances, coronals and lance-heads that the knights will need, as well as the swords with which they will have to fight, all of them of a similar and equivalent kind, the sturdiness of which can be tested by the knights as they wish.

---

[13] The stipulation about the days when the shields could be touched does not have any bearing on the way that this *pas* was actually run.

[14] The original text reads: 'courre a la trille'.

[15] Accounts B and C disagree on the number of courses to be run according to the stipulations of the third shield: C gives eleven whereas B gives twelve (see below, p. 224). Even within the manuscript tradition of the B account, this number is not stable: the codex edited in MT, p. 138, for instance, mentions seventeen courses for this shield.

Item, each of those who have touched one or more of the three shields will be obliged, on the following Sunday, the following sixteenth day of February,[16] to hang from the Column a shield emblazoned with his coat of arms, this to be under the shield that he has touched and in the order in which he has touched it. If someone wants to remain incognito, he may cover his shield as he sees fit.

Item, the lady wants you to be at the Column on the first Sunday of February, ready to start performing your *emprise**.

Item, if it should so happen — God forbid! — that, while carrying out the difficult and dangerous feats mentioned above, you are wounded or gravely injured to such an extent that afterwards you are not confident enough or able to bear arms, the lady demands, in her benevolence, that whoever has harmed or injured you in this way completes on your behalf whatever remains to be done. The same obligation [as yours] will apply to those responsible for the mishap,[17] and you will have to provide horses, harnesses and equipment so that your *emprise* can be carried to completion, unless, on some later day, you wish to resume your duties, in which case you may do so.

Item, since, inevitably, among so many knights and noblemen, one is deemed to be better than another, whoever, among all of them, is seen and recognised as having performed most brilliantly in achieving what the shields require in the three categories of the *Pas*, he and he alone will win a special prize. It will be given and awarded to him outside, in a place and manner decided by the lady, at the appropriate time.

(104) Item, to compensate for the trouble that all the knights and squires will have gone to in order to liberate you, it is my duty to tell you that the lady wishes to guarantee that each of them will receive a prize of equal value at an official ceremony which will be enjoyable and devoid of any feelings of envy. This will take place on the evening of the final day.

Item, my lady has instructed me to tell you that on the days when you perform what is required by the shields, there will be a stand where knights and officers of arms will judge the knights and squires who wish to participate in the *Pas*; you and the others will be obliged to accept whatever they may decree. In addition, they will give a report of everyone's exploits to the ladies,[18] so that the prize might be awarded to whoever deserves it.

Item, a horn will hang from the Column, and the lady orders that when a knight or squire has sounded it, you withdraw straightaway, for it will not be sounded before the completion of the [combat decreed by the] shield that he has touched.'

Item, after this speech, the knight thanked the lady again, as well as the dwarf, and in order to expedite his deliverance, decided to dictate this letter. I, who happened to be there, (105) found out about this adventure and took responsibility for bringing this letter and proclaiming to you the adventure of the Enchanted Column.[19]

---

[16] In 1463, Sundays fell on 6, 13, 20 and 27 February. It was in 1464 that Sunday fell on 16 February. There seems to be some confusion about the dates, which perhaps suggests that the account was written over a year after the actual event had taken place.

[17] The original text reads: 'Et en pareille obligacion seront cellui ou ceux a qui la semblable pourroit advenir'. The context suggests that the dwarf has in mind the knights who might injure the *entrepreneur.* However, another meaning: 'those who experienced the same mishap' (= 'those who were similarly injured') is possible, though less satisfactory.

[18] The officers' reports probably provided a base for the accounts written at a later date.

[19] The narrator, who refers to himself as 'I', remains unknown, even though this is likely to have been Limbourg Herald.

'Noble and honourable knights from all the surrounding lands[20] — I do not know the [exact] honours and titles appropriate to you, except that everyone of your rank elects to address you in writing as noble and powerful lords — knights and noblemen, please let it be known that a strange and unexpected adventure has befallen me, a poor nameless knight. I have been seized and detained in a place called the Enchanted Column, from which I can neither run away nor escape either by force or in any other way, except by complying with the dangerous and stringent conditions imposed on my person, and by fighting, clad in steel, with all those who do me the honour of coming to liberate me, in accordance with the content of the chapters given to me by this lady, even though this matter seems to me both arduous and difficult to accomplish, unless Fortune, more than valour, comes to my assistance. Nonetheless, having secured the permission and consent of the lady of this place to proclaim my adventure everywhere, and in order to inform those who do not know about this matter as it stands, the poor knight-prisoner begs and requests you all that, from … ,[21] you find it agreeable, in order to increase your fame and your good fortune, to come to the Column, and there, with the intention of following the rules here established that will be explained to you at that location, to release me from my subjection: this outcome, as signified by the three shields that are hanging there and which you will have to touch, is in the hands of Fortune. (106) I, the servant of the nobility, the lowliest of you all, no matter what may befall me, will be grateful for your assistance with the help of God, to whom I commend you. Written in the prison of the Enchanted Column on the day of … '.[22]

V. The *emprise* of the Enchanted Column which was due to take place in Brussels

We must now go back and explain how the *Pas* took place in the city of Bruges. The truth of the matter is that on the marketplace of this city barriers were erected that were made of wood in the manner of lists. At the end of these barriers there was a column between fourteen and fifteen feet high, one ingeniously and beautifully made that was painted in various colours: gold, silver, blue, black, red and so on. From this Column hung the three aforesaid shields, as well as the horn mentioned above. Near the Column stood the dwarf, cloaked in a robe made of a dark blue cloth of gold and wearing a black velvet beret on his head.

On both sides of the Column were four griffins artistically made to look as if they were alive. Hidden inside them were four men in charge of operating them mechanically, that is to say that each of these griffins was attached to the Column with a chain and, with their physical strength, they would open the Column; the knight would come out through this opening anytime that he intended to do battle with those who turned up at his *pas*. The knight would then go back inside, as he pleased or when ordered to do so by the dwarf. Once he was inside, the Column would close up again and remain shut until such time (107) as the knight had to carry out his duties. The griffins were made to function this way for the full duration of the *Pas*.

---

[20] Here starts the letter supposedly dictated by the nameless knight. The 'I' refers to him and not to the narrator mentioned above.

[21] The date is missing in the manuscript.

[22] The date is also missing here. Thus ends the fictional scenario.

In the middle of these lists was a beautiful tall stand that was finely decked out and arrayed with cushions of red velvet and with tapestries. In this stand were [seated] the lord of La Roche,[23] the lord of Moreuil[24] and Toison d'or,[25] all three of them being councillors of my lord of Burgundy and judges appointed to this *pas* in order to take care of everything required of someone acting in the capacity of judge in a *pas d'armes* or a joust *à plaisance**, such as measuring lances and swords and registering all the arrivals and departures of those participating in the *pas*. These judges were accompanied by several officers of arms. Among them were Messire Arnoul de Créquy,[26] lord of Ambremont and Ivergny, and two Kings of Arms, those of Flanders and Artois. This knight and the Kings of Arms were in the service of the Lady of the Enchanted Column, and it was on her behalf that they brought swords and lances to the judges to be inspected and measured, then carried them over to all the challengers to let them choose their weapons. When these choices had been made, it was they who would bring the other lances and swords back to the knight of the *Pas*. This is how it was organised right up to the end of the event.

The lists were guarded by archers from my lord the duke's company and no one could enter them unless given permission to do so by the judges. In order to keep track of the order in which the challengers had touched the shields, the knight[27] and the officers would ask them their names, so that everybody might perform according to the rules of the shield they had touched.

Item, inside the lists and next to the Column stood Limbourg Herald, as appointed by the lady. At the dwarf's command, he would remove and take down the shield of the one who had done battle with the knight, (108) bring it back to his lady and report that the knight-prisoner had accomplished the adventure of the shield as touched by his opponent.

Each time that the knight of the Enchanted Column did battle with the challengers assigned to him on that day, the dwarf would go up to him and would say these severe words to him: 'Knight, go back to your prison. My lady orders you to do so.' On saying these words, he would strike him harshly with a staff, seize him by his horse's bridle and take him back to the Column. Every day, right up to the very end, he would maintain this abrupt manner and way of speaking, for as long as the *Pas* itself lasted.

---

[23] Philippe Pot, lord of La Roche-Nolay and Châteauneuf (*c.*1428–93), made a vow at the Feast of the Pheasant in Lille in 1454 and became a member of the Order of the Golden Fleece in 1461; he was a councillor-chamberlain of Philip the Good and Charles the Bold from 1451. COTO no. 60; PCB no. 1484.

[24] [seigneur d'Anoreul]. Waleran de Soissons, lord of Moreuil (d. 1464?) was a chamberlain of Philip the Good in 1458. PCB no. 1483.

[25] Jean Lefèvre de Saint-Rémy (*c.*1396–1468) was King of Arms of the Golden Fleece (1431–68) and had already officiated as judge for much of Jacques de Lalaing's *Pas de la Fontaine des Pleurs* (1449–50). PCB no. 545.

[26] [Hernoul de Crequi]. Arnoul III de Créquy, lord of Rimboval, Les Granges and Marquais à l'eau, was the son of Louis de Créquy and Anne de La Barre. The most recent genealogical works on the Créquy family do not mention the lordships of Ambremont and Ivergny in the possession of Arnoul, as is stated in the text. It is, moreover, important to note that Arnoul did not have a formal office at the Burgundian court, in contrast to, for example, Jean V de Créquy (see below, n. 78). Victorien Leman and Maxence Watelle, 'De cire et d'histoire: les sceaux de la famille de Créquy (XIIe–XVIe siècles)', *Dossiers généalogiques du Comité d'histoire du Haut-Pays*, 25 (2009), 16–26; and René Lesage, 'Notes sur la généalogie des Créquy aux XIIIe et XIVe siècles', *Dossiers généalogiques du Comité d'histoire du Haut-Pays*, 25 (2009), 49–74.

[27] That is, the knight appointed by the lady, i.e. Arnoul de Créquy.

[Between these two sections of the text is a description of the combats as they took place over the twelve days of the Pas*]*

XVIII. The end of the jousts

(129) When my lord Adolf of Cleves[28] brought the *Pas* to a close, the dwarf escorted the knight [of the *Pas*] over to the judges and the knight asked them whether or not he had completed and fulfilled his *pas* according to the content of his chapters. They replied that he had indeed completed and fulfilled his *pas* very well and very honourably according to the content of his chapters. On receiving their reply, the dwarf took him back to the Enchanted Column, as was his usual ritual.

As soon as the knight was back inside the Column, three Moors dressed in the costume of their country arrived,[29] each of whom was wearing one of the colours of the shields that were hanging from the Column. Their horses' trappers* were also of the same colours: the first trapper was of black velvet, the second of violet satin and the third of grey velvet. In this manner, they went over to the dwarf and requested that the shields hanging there be given to them to take back to the lady. (130) The dwarf had the shields handed over to them by his officer of arms. Each of the Moors took the shield in the colour which he himself was wearing and straightaway went back to the lady, one after the other, in the appropriate order, with the shields around their necks, according to the sequence in which these deeds had been performed; they then presented them to the lady. Thereupon a damsel arrived at the Column, one who was in the service of the lady, accompanied by two Kings of Arms and two knights. The damsel was dressed in blue satin and was wearing a cowl of black velvet, the liripipe* of which was wrapped round her face. Around her neck she wore a gold chain. She rode a white hackney* trappered in a rich violet cloth and was followed by three pages dressed in black satin on top of a dagged* grey cloth. They wore hoods of violet velvet in the English fashion[30] and rode horses decked with trappers: the first of these was of violet satin heavily adorned with golden buttons,[31] the second was of a rich violet cloth of gold and the third was of violet velvet. The damsel had a horse brought in for the knight that was in the Column.[32] On that horse was a violet harness with wide dangling bands bordered with gold and white silk, one strip of which had knots and another had golden teardrops fringed with white and violet silk.

---

[28] [Adolf de Clevez]. Adolf of Cleves, lord of Ravenstein (1425–92), the younger son of Duke Adolf of Cleves and Marie of Burgundy, sister of Philip the Good, was a very high-ranking and well-connected knight; he was also a famous jouster and close friend of Jacques de Lalaing. PCB no. 817.

[29] These so-called 'Moors' may have been played at these festivities by actual Black or North African men and women at the Burgundian court or by courtiers wearing blackface.

[30] It is difficult to know whether it is the style of the hoods, their material or their colour that is said here to be in the English fashion. On English fashion in the second half of the fifteenth century, see Margaret Scott, *Medieval Dress and Fashion* (London: British Library, 2007), pp. 152–6. Velvet does indeed seem to have been very popular.

[31] The original reads: 'boullons d'or': i.e. ornamental buttons meant to enhance the beauty and richness of the garment. See *ibid.*, p. 108. On the use of buttons, see Barbara Bettoni, 'Fashion, Tradition, and Innovation in Button Manufacturing in Early Modern Italy', *Technology and Culture*, 55.3 (2014), 675–710.

[32] The text reads: 'Ladicte damoeselle faisoit mener ung cheval en main', which suggests that she was accompanied by a page or servant, who was actually holding the bridle.

When this damsel came over to the Column, as said earlier, she found the dwarf and asked him for the key with which to unlock the knight. At once, the dwarf knelt down in front of the damsel and showed her much reverence before giving her the key which was made of gold. The Column was opened with this key and the damsel went inside and found the prisoner whom she immediately released. She had him mount the horse that she had brought [for him]. The knight had no arms other than his legharness*, (131) and he wore an Italian sleeveless coat[33] made of a green cloth of gold; on his head, he had a beret of black velvet. The damsel brought him thus attired in front of the judges, then took him over to my lord the duke of Burgundy and the ladies before taking him back once more to the place where he had been staying.

XIX. The banquet

My lord of Burgundy[34] was the lady's *grand maître d'hôtel* and he organised a splendid banquet in the great hall of his residence which was attended by the duchess of Bourbon and her two daughters.[35] Even though the doors to the hall were well guarded, the press was such that no one could enter or exit. Also in attendance at this banquet were my lord of Burgundy, his son my lord of Charolais,[36] the duke of Cleves,[37] my lord Jacques, son of the duke of Bourbon,[38] my lord Adolf of Cleves, the counts of Saint-Pol and Marle, of Brienne and Roucy, my lord Jacques de Luxembourg,[39] one of the sons of the prince of Orange,[40] and several other great lords.

During this banquet, there was an *entremets** in the form of a ship armed and equipped with the arms of my lord the duke of Burgundy, on which stood a lady dressed in a blue cloth of gold who acted as the master of the ship.

Then came my lord Arnoul de Créquy, knight of the Lady of the Enchanted Column, who was leading a Moorish woman on a horse. She herself led a pack-horse by the bridle,

---

33 Philippe wears a *huque*, a short, loose jacket with no sleeves or collar, which may be a *giornea*: on this garment, see Scott, *Medieval Dress*, p. 123. On the spread of Italian fashion to French and Burgundian courts, see Françoise Piponnier, *Costume et vie sociale à la cour d'Anjou, XIVe–XVe siècles* (Paris: Mouton, 1970), p. 183.

34 This refers to Philip the Good himself, who acts as the lady's steward.

35 Agnès of Burgundy (*c.*1407–76), duchess of Bourbon and the sister of Philip the Good, was married (1425) to Charles I of Bourbon (PCB no. 1032) and had six sons and five daughters with him; she came to Brussels with two of her daughters and two of her sons, and attended the *Pas*. PCB no. 1033.

36 Charles of Charolais (1433–77), son of Philip the Good, was to become duke of Burgundy in 1467.

37 Johann I (1419–81), elder brother of Adolf, became duke of Cleves in 1448. PCB no. 384.

38 Jacques of Bourbon (*c.*1444–68), younger son of Charles of Bourbon and Agnès of Burgundy, was Philip the Good's nephew; he was a member of the Order of the Golden Fleece (1468). PCB nos 1032, 1033, 1946.

39 Louis de Luxembourg (1418–75) was count of Saint-Pol. The other counts were his sons: Jean de Luxembourg (*c.*1436–76) was the count of Marle; Antoine de Luxembourg (d. 1515) was the count of Brienne and Roucy. Jacques de Luxembourg (1420–87), lord of Richebourg, was Louis's younger brother. PCB nos 697, 2227, 2279, 2280. The Luxembourg family was very well represented at the *Pas*. See Andries Van den Abeele, 'De Wapenpas van de Betoverde Burcht, voorbode van de machtsgreep door Karel de Stoute', *Handelingen van het Genootschap voor Geschiedenis te Brugge*, 146 (2009), 93–139 (p. 115).

40 [prince d'Orenge]. Louis de Charlon-Arlay (*c.*1390–1463), prince of Orange, was the son of Jean III of Orange and Marie de Baux.

that was decked out in grey velvet and was carrying three chests made of cuir-bouilli* that contained the prizes for those who had fought against the knight of the *Pas* according to the chapters and the rules of the shields described above. My lord Arnoul asked permission from my lord of Burgundy, on behalf of the lady, to distribute the prizes, which were all equal and identical, to all those who had done her knight the honour of doing battle with him. My lord answered that the ladies and he himself willingly gave their consent.

(132) After my lord Arnoul had secured their permission, the prizes were awarded to all those who had done battle with the knight at the *Pas*. Those who had fought with swords received a miniature shield[41] of black velvet bordered with gold and black silk; in the middle was a tassel with a silk cord so that it could be worn that night and the following day for love of the lady. In the middle of the cord, underneath the little tassel, was a small scroll of gilded parchment inscribed with four lines; this was a present from the lady to all those who had done battle with her knight. Similarly, those who had fought in harnesses of war, according to the rules of that particular shield, received miniature shields of violet velvet fringed with gold and silk and [bearing] a small tassel, complete with cords and scrolls like the others. To those who had fought with jousting harnesses were given miniature shields of grey velvet trimmed and fitted like the others.

Once the prizes had been awarded, out came three damsels dressed in plain tunics of white satin laced up at the side and trimmed with black velvet that were embroidered with a large P.[42] Each of them wore a gold necklace and a belt made of embroidery from Bruges[43] that was richly adorned with gold and silver. The knight of the lady, who was leading the three damsels, requested permission from my lord of Burgundy and my lady the duchess of Bourbon to give out the three main prizes, and to ask my lady the duchess of Bourbon to mandate two damsels from her retinue, or others as it pleased her, to present and award the three prizes that the afore-mentioned damsels had brought out on behalf of the Lady [of the Enchanted Column].

This is how it was done: the count of Saint-Pol received the prize reserved for the one who had best fought and competed according to the rules of the first shield, which comprised running one course with the lance and doing battle with the sword up to seventeen strokes. The prize itself was a miniature shield decked out in black velvet and embroidered with a golden heart; (133) in the middle of the heart was a small cord from which hung a gold ring. The second prize was awarded to my lord Adolf for having best run the nine courses with the lance in harness and saddle of war. The prize was a

[41] The French word is *targe* (in account B, a *targette*, a small *targe*), i.e a kind of shield. In this case, it is clearly a small badge of honour to be displayed on the knight's chest or arm.

[42] The letter P is probably a reference to the *entrepreneur* of the *Pas*, Philippe, but could also refer to the duke of Burgundy.

[43] Accounts B and C both mention that the damsels wear belts 'de bourgoise ferré d'or et d'argent'. 'Bourgoise' seems to be a hapax, yet the manuscript tradition is consistent (no variant). The lesson 'of the town' is not satisfactory as the belts are extremely rich and precious. One possible meaning is 'in the fashion of Bruges', with 'Bourgoise' being an alteration of 'brugeoise'. Although embroidery from Bruges became famous in the sixteenth century — that is, at a later time than the *Pas* — there may already have been a tradition of it in the fifteenth century. For instance, a miniature from Valerius Maximus' *Memorable Deeds and Sayings of the Romans*, produced in Bruges *c.*1475–80, shows a lady with an embroidered gold belt. See Margaret Scott, *Fashion in the Middle Ages* (Los Angeles: The J. Paul Getty Museum, 2011), p. 48.

miniature shield decked out in violet velvet and embroidered with a golden chest framed with Roman letters; from this chest hung a cord and a gold ring. The third prize was awarded to my lord Jacques de Luxembourg, for being the one who had best run the eleven courses with the lance in jousting harness and saddle of war. His prize was a miniature shield decked out in grey velvet embroidered with a sun and golden letters like the others, from which hung a cord and a gold ring.

As soon as the prizes had been given out, the dancing began. The three damsels were led out onto the dance floor and were honourably welcomed and commended. This is what happened at the sumptuous banquet organised by my lord of Burgundy for love of the Lady of the Enchanted Column, who had imprisoned the afore-mentioned knight. This banquet was the most magnificent and the most successful in every respect, and it featured the most splendid attires and caparisons ever seen in living memory.

TRANSLATION (2): B ACCOUNT, IN LILLE, BU, 104

(155) **I. Prologue**

My lord Philippe de Lalaing, son and heir of the lord of Lalaing in the county of Hainaut, who in his time had a passion for history, had pondered the great deeds of arms undertaken and accomplished by those valiant men, the knights who came before us, and had read about them in many noteworthy books — an activity he favoured whenever he could so as to avoid idleness — such as the Bible, the books of the kings recounting the exploits of David, Judas Maccabeus and his brothers,[44] as well as other valiant Jews, and also the deeds and conquests of the great and powerful king Alexander of Macedonia. He had also read about the valiant Hector of Troy and his brothers, in addition to others who were present at the destruction of Troy, Thebes, Athens and Carthage, and about the Romans who, at that time, were pagans and had no fear of dying in their wish to expand and defend their lands with the public weal in mind, and who prospered as long as they behaved that way. He had likewise read about the Christians who came after, and who exalted Jesus Christ's faith and abolished the evil customs ruling those who did not observe Christian doctrine. Among the first ones who laboured towards this end were the noble kings Perceforest, Uther Pendragon, Arthur, King Ban of Benoic, Bagdemagus of Gore[45]

[44] The books of the kings ('les livres des rois') might be a reference to the Book of Kings in the Bible, notwithstanding the plural form. David, king of Israel, and Judas Maccabeus are two of the three Jewish Worthies (the third being Joshua), in the famous medieval list of the Nine Worthies, which also comprised three pagans (Hector, Alexander the Great and Julius Caesar) and three Christians (King Arthur, Charlemagne and Godfrey of Bouillon). Most of these figures are listed by name further on in the prologue. See Michelle Szkilnik, 'Que lisaient les chevaliers du XVe siècle? Le témoignage du *Pas du Perron Fée*', *Le Moyen Français*, 68 (2011), 103–14; and, on the tradition of the Nine Worthies, see Wim van Anrooij, 'Nine Worthies', in *Encyclopedia of the Medieval Chronicle online*, ed. by Graeme Dunphy and Cristian Bratu (Leiden: Brill, 2014, article first published online in 2016).

[45] According to the *Roman de Perceforest*, a fourteenth-century prose romance that was much altered in the fifteenth century, Perceforest is the king of Britain and Arthur's ancestor. This text was very popular at the court of the dukes of Burgundy: see Gilles Roussineau, ed., *Roman de Perceforest*, 14 vols (Geneva: Droz, 1987–2014). Uther Pendragon is King Arthur's father and Ban of Benoic is Lancelot's father. Badgemagus of Gore, the father of the evil knight Meleagant, rival of Lancelot, plays an important role as one of Arthur's counsellors in the Arthurian prose romances that were written in the thirteenth

and their descendants, all the knights of the Round Table and countless others, for in their time, devils, with God's permission (156) and not otherwise, had such power over humans because of their lack of faith and limited education in this matter — being taught only by hermits and simple virtuous people who did not enjoy much consideration[46] — that illusion and fantasy, magic and deception reigned on earth with an astonishing sway. Yet, thanks to the great exploits of these kings as well as those of Galahad, son of Lancelot of the Lake, most of these evil circumstances came to an end, as told in the books of Perceforest, Lancelot, Tristan of Cornwall, Guiron le Courtois[47] and many other volumes that are full of these stories. Philippe had also read about the great and all-powerful King Charlemagne of France, his kings, princes, barons and knights who strove so hard in Germany, Spain, Italy, Lombardy, Guyenne and elsewhere, in order to convert all these various places to the faith of Jesus Christ. He had read too about Godfrey of Bouillon,[48] who conquered Jerusalem and was crowned king of the city, and after him his brother Baudoin, the kings, princes and barons who accompanied him to conquer eastern lands from the Saracens, and the many exploits achieved on both sides. He had read as well about the twenty-six splendid and noble feats of arms accomplished by his elder brother, the good and handsome knight my lord Jacques de Lalaing, in Spain, Scotland, Burgundy and Flanders, always to his honour and praise.[49] I suppose that, after all these readings, this good knight of Lalaing envisioned himself following in these good knights' footsteps as best he could. Without presuming to be as worthy as the least of them, but rather in order that some memory of him might survive, he undertook, (157) with the permission and approval of the most excellent and most powerful prince, his lord and godfather, Philippe, duke of Burgundy and Brabant, to hold a *pas* based on a fairylike narrative, one involving a great and powerful lady who had dominion over several strongholds and castles. Among her possessions she ruled over a column that was located in a strange place and made of a beautiful rock which changed colours every now and then, as it pleased her. Because of the wonders it comprised both inside and out, it was named the Enchanted Column. And,

century but still very much read, loved and copied in the fifteenth century, especially at the court of Burgundy. See Alexandre Micha, ed., *Lancelot: roman en prose du XIIIe siècle*, Textes littéraires français, 9 vols (Geneva: Droz, 1978–83).

[46] The French text reads 'dont l'on ne tenoit gueres grant compte'.

[47] The prose romance of *Tristan*, written in the thirteenth century, combined the story of Tristan with that of Arthur's knights. It likewise enjoyed great popularity at the court of Burgundy: see Philippe Ménard *et al.*, eds, *Tristan en prose*, 9 vols (Geneva, Droz, 1987–97). *Guiron le Courtois*, also dating from the thirteenth century, tells the story of the great knights of the generation preceding Arthur, such as Meliadus, Tristan's father, Esclabor, Palamedes's father, and Guiron, a newcomer in the Arthurian saga: see Lino Leonardi and Richard Trachsler, eds, *Il ciclo di Guiron le Courtois, romanzi in prosa del secolo XIII*, 6 vols to date (Florence: Edizioni del Galluzzo, 2020–21).

[48] Godfrey of Bouillon, a Frankish knight who participated in the First Crusade and the conquest of Jerusalem (1099), was invited to become king of Jerusalem, but refused to be crowned; he died in the Holy Land (1100). His brother Baudoin was crowned king of Jerusalem on Christmas Day, 1100. A legend rapidly developed around Godfrey, who was said to be descended from the mythical Knight of the Swan and became a hero of *chansons de geste* (*cycle de la Croisade*). See Suzanne Duparc-Quioc, ed., *Le Cycle de la Croisade* (Paris: Champion, 1955). On the historical character of this figure, see Pierre Aubé, *Godefroy de Bouillon* (Paris: Fayard, 1985).

[49] On the exploits accomplished by Philippe's brother, Jacques, and how their total number is calculated, see CL, p. 281 n. 627.

notwithstanding all her other possessions, she retained only one title: the Supreme Lady of the Enchanted Column.[50] From now on, whenever we mention her, we will refer to her as the Lady of the Enchanted Column, nothing else. This great lady had imprisoned several noblemen of high worth in her Column, the key to which she alone kept. Among the other knights, as was the will of Fortune, by extraordinary adventure, this good knight of Lalaing was alone retained and kept in her prison for a while.

II. [The Lady of the Enchanted Column proposes that the knight undertake a *pas*]

Yet, since everything must come to an end in one way or another, it so happened that one day the lady paid a visit to this good knight and told him: 'Messire Philippe, as you know, you are my prisoner and you cannot leave this place without my consent.' He replied: 'My lady, so it is, but when it pleases you, in your greatness and graciousness, I humbly request that you will have mercy on me, for you can see full well that if there is any worth in me, I am of an age to appear at places frequented by other knights who, at present, are in the residence of my prince, master and lord, places where, because nothing at this time is preventing them, (158) they engage in such great and honourable entertainments, as are proclaimed all over the world, that their names are exalted. Because of my being detained, I can neither be there nor appear at these places, which is my only cause of displeasure, since, thanks be to both God and to you, all the time that I have been here, I have experienced only kindness in this place, for which I thank you most humbly.'

When the lady heard him speak so virtuously and graciously, she was moved to pity and, out of generosity and the wish to avoid being seen as cruel, she said to him: 'Messire Philippe, I am very familiar with your own reputation as a good knight, and that of those from whom you are descended. For this reason, I will offer you an alternative:[51] if you want to be freed from this prison, you must undertake for love of me a courtly *pas d'armes*, with no other motive but love, this to be in the form and the manner stipulated in the chapters I will bring you tomorrow which have been devised as I wish them to be accomplished. If you complete this *pas* to your honour, I pledge my faith that I will grant you a full release. If you refuse, you will remain my prisoner forever.'

When the good knight heard the lady's proposition, he was overcome with joy, for she was speaking of what he loved above all else, and he thanked her very humbly. He then said to her: 'My lady, do you think that I am good enough to undertake and accomplish your worthy goal? For, without looking to make excuses, if I can do something that is agreeable to you, I wish to strive for it with all the power that God and Nature have given me. (159) As it pleases you, have these chapters delivered to me and appoint the time when you wish me to fulfil them; this I will do, if God so wishes this to befall me.'

The lady said to him: 'Now that I have your word, I will return here tomorrow morning. I want you to know that, for the duration of your *pas*, you will be housed in this Column every night until you have fulfilled your *emprise*. When my dwarf sounds

[50] The French text reads 'la Toute Passe Dame du Perron Fée', a title probably inspired by the name of a character in the *Roman de Perceforest*: see Szkilnik, 'Que lisaient?'

[51] The lady offers Philippe a *jeu-parti*, i.e. a game with two alternatives.

the horn, you must go back in, with a knight whom I will have appointed to serve and accompany you, because I cannot attend in person. It will suffice that this knight and various officers of arms report to me every night on your affairs and circumstances, and that they describe to me the coats of arms of the noblemen who have done battle with you that day; things will proceed in the same way every day until you have fulfilled your *pas* in its entirety.

I assure you that everyone, for his efforts and goodwill, will receive from me a ring as a small keepsake. I will award three main prizes to the three knights or squires who have performed the best according to the content of the chapters and the rules stipulated by the shields. These prizes will be presented by ladies or damsels in the service of the most powerful duke of Burgundy or of my lady the duchess of Bourbon, his sister, to whom, when you see them, you will very humbly recommend me and request that they accept this task. On the day that I award the prizes, my appointed knight will, on my behalf, once again request permission from them [to make these awards]. If you want to know who this knight will be, I tell you that it will be Arnoul de Créquy, who is of your lineage, as I have been informed.[52] (160) This is why I have appointed him to [assist] you: he is fully willing to be at your service and I expressly requested that he do so. Think tonight about what I have told you and, tomorrow morning, I will be back here with the chapters and you will give me your answer on all points, so that I can provide you in good time with what you need for your undertaking.'

The good knight then replied: 'My lady, your offer is so noble and courteous that I cannot thank you enough; may God help me to deserve it.'

Thereupon, the Lady of the Column departed and left the good knight who, all night long, could think of nothing but what she had told him and of the answer that he needed to give her, the following day, in order to please her.

When the night was over and daylight had come, the lady, with a noble company, returned to the Column as she had promised the knight, holding in her hand the chapters that she had mentioned to him. She then gave them to the good knight who read them aloud in full so that those who were there heard and understood them perfectly. He then said: 'My lady, since it is your gracious pleasure that I fulfil the content of these chapters, I promise you as a noble knight that I will accomplish them to the best of my ability.'

The lady thanked him, saying: 'I assure you that I will provide you with everything you need to undertake your *pas*. In this very place everything will be prepared, horses, harnesses, weapons, as well as other things; everything will be set up as I wish it to be and you will be satisfied, have no doubt about it. (161) I hereby inform you that you must be ready in person to start on the first day of January 1462[53] in the city of Brussels in Brabant, in front of the most excellent and most powerful prince Philippe, duke of Burgundy and Brabant; he will be your judge or someone else will whom he wishes to appoint. This will be in the presence of the noble and high princesses, ladies and damsels from his court, where currently, as I hear, the duchesses of Bourbon and Guelders[54] and other daughters

---

[52] On Arnoul de Créquy, see above, n. 26. Philippe de Lalaing's mother was Jeanne de Créquy, the daughter of Jean IV de Créquy, a relative of Arnoul's, and Jeanne de Roye.

[53] See above, introduction, pp. 205–6, for the reasons why this original date and location were later changed because of the duke's itinerary.

[54] The duchess of Guelders is probably Catherine, Philip the Good's niece, one of the daughters of Charles 1 of Bourbon and Agnès of Burgundy, who attended the *Pas*. She was to marry Adolf of

of Bourbon, with a noble and fine company, are in residence,[55] a fact which fills me with joy on account of my love for you, unless the duke wishes to hold the *pas* somewhere else and at another date.'

At this, the good knight was astounded and said to the lady with much humility: 'My lady, your words fill me with great astonishment; do not be displeased by what I will now ask of you.' The lady replied: 'Messire Philippe, speak as you please, I entreat you.' He then said: 'My lady, I tell you that I do not know whether I am asleep or awake, what adventure brought me here, whether I am here in spirit or in person, where this prison is located or in which country, except that I perfectly understand your language, as well as that of the persons who are with you, from which I presume that I am in France. You told me that I must soon be in Brussels, yet all the while I am a prisoner in this very place. I cannot therefore conceive how this might be done and I beg your pardon for requesting an explanation from you in so rude a manner.'

At these words, the lady began to smile and told him, with much courtesy: 'Messire Philippe, have no doubts about anything that has happened to you or that might happen to you. (162) Think only about being cheerful and fulfilling your *pas*. My answer, I tell you, is that the adventures of the world are varied and extraordinary. God and Fortune assign some kinds to one person and another kind to another person. Fortune has willed it that you be my prisoner — for which I thank her — and that you be [kept] in this Column. This place is of such nature and my power and ability are such that, wherever I want this Column to be carried and moved, wherever I want it to be and to remain, it will be there in an instant and with you inside it having suffered no bodily harm. Also, it will take on whatever colours I wish. On the days when you will do battle, both to do you honour and to enhance your achievements, it will be richly decorated in gold, silver, green and red; it will remain that way, unchanged, until your *pas* is finished and completed. This should suffice, by way of explanation, so do not ask for more: in all that I have told you, I will not fail you. Conduct yourself in such a way as not to fail either, if you wish to be liberated from my prison.'

On hearing these words, the good knight did not know what to add and was afraid of angering the lady and of doing something that might displease her; he thus resolved simply to tell her that on all these points he threw himself upon her mercy. At this, the Lady of the Enchanted Column departed and, on taking leave of the good knight, she said to him: 'Messire Philippe, I pray to God He grant that you do so well that you might acquire praise and acclaim all over the world, as well as the good grace of all the ladies who will hear about you. I hereby inform you that you will not see me in this place again, until I see that you are free and I release you from your prison. (163) However, I will leave Limbourg Herald with you as well as my dwarf to serve you in all your needs. They know where I reside most of the time and, through them, I will be updated daily about you and in a position to attend to your needs as necessary. Farewell.'

When the good knight heard the lady speak so kindly and so admirably, he almost fainted with joy and could no longer see or hear her, much to his dismay. Yet, being a

---

Egmond, duke of Guelders, in December 1463, and would become duchess only in 1465. Van den Abeele, 'Wapenpas', pp. 103–4. PCB no. 663. On the duchess of Bourbon, see above, n. 35.

[55] Since the autumn of 1462, Agnès of Burgundy and her daughters had been residing in Brussels at the court of Philip the Good, where he organised magnificent festivities in their honour. See Essay 3.

righteous knight, he consoled himself by addressing Limbourg in this way: 'Limbourg, since you have permission from my lady to go wherever you please, I beg you to head off without delay to see my most powerful and sovereign lord, my lord the duke of Burgundy, and to beseech him very humbly on my behalf that, in his graciousness, he allow you to proclaim in his residence, or wherever he pleases, these chapters given to me in your presence by my Lady of the Enchanted Column, and that he assign whichever days he chooses for my *pas*. May he forgive me for not presenting myself to his lordship in person: since you know of my circumstances, apologise to him on my behalf.'

III. The chapters are presented by Limbourg Herald and the Column is set up

Limbourg was all ready to carry out the order and left the good knight at the Column in the sole company of the dwarf. He went to Brussels where the duke was residing at the time. He offered his humble greetings to the duke and described in detail the adventure and the imprisonment of this good knight, in front of the knights of the court, all of whom were astounded. (164) The duke then asked Limbourg where this Enchanted Column was located and in which land, adding that he had never heard, in his day, that fairy ladies had the power to rule and govern over his lands; he felt as if the good old days of King Arthur had returned. The other knights said the same thing. Limbourg replied: 'I don't know what to say, other than that the lady is full of graciousness and benevolence, and that she speaks French beautifully. Yet I would not be able to tell you very easily which land this Column is located in nor by what adventure it is placed there, for I just don't know. However, my master, the good knight of Lalaing, humbly begs you, by your grace, to allow me to proclaim those chapters that you see here, in your presence and before all the people at your court.' The duke responded, saying: 'Read out these chapters and I will give my decision.'

Limbourg read the chapters out loud from start to finish. They were so honourable that all the dukes, princes and lords declared as one: 'This lady possesses great honour and we can see that she wants to stimulate into action those amongst us who are sleepy and corrupted. Blessed be she, for she has chosen one from among those of our court who is able to fulfil and achieve this goal. May God grant him that this comes to pass!'

The duke's reply was: 'I consent that you proclaim the chapters here and wherever else he asked you to. To those who touch one, two or more of the three shields, (165) you can assign them a day on which they need to be ready and fully equipped to carry out the undertaking of this *pas* according to the chapters of the Lady of the Enchanted Column, here in our city of Brussels, on the first day of January 1462.[56] In case our obligations are such and so pressing that we are unable to oversee the event, you will inform her of this in my name as soon as possible, as well as those who have touched her shields. This is what you will tell her when you see her, on our behalf, after greeting her.' The herald humbly thanked the duke and took his leave of him.

Thereafter several knights and squires went over to Limbourg and asked him where this Column and those shields that were to be touched were located, so that they could go and touch them in good time. Limbourg's answer was: 'My lords, this I cannot tell you

---

[56] 1463 in modern style. See above, n. 8.

plainly before I have spoken to my lady who rules over it; but I will very soon return and will be able to let you know then.'

With that, he took his leave and went back to the lady to find out where she wished to have the Column and the shields set up so that he could report back to the noblemen who wished to participate. The lady told him: 'Limbourg, the Column will be in Brussels tomorrow morning with Messire Philippe inside it. It will be in the shape of a rock made of hard grey stone. The three shields will be black, violet and grey and will hang from the Column that my dwarf will be guarding. There will also be a hunting horn hanging there that those willing to touch the shields must blow before touching them; this is so as to notify the dwarf who will explain [the rules of the game].[57] Go tell Messire Philippe what you learnt at the court of the duke of Burgundy, and inform him of my wishes. Let him be merry, and greet him on my behalf.'

Limbourg found himself at the Column. The dwarf was outside and let him in straightaway. The herald greeted the good knight on behalf of the duke of Burgundy and my lords the princes of his court. (166) He conveyed to him brotherly salutations on behalf of the knights, squires, ladies and damsels who dearly wished for him to be set free and released from his adventure. Also on behalf of the lady, he let him know that the Column with him inside it would be in the city of Brussels without fail early the following morning and that from it three shields would be hanging: 'That is to say, one black, the second grey and the third violet, with a hunting horn to be sounded by all of those wishing to do battle with you according to the instructions of the shield that they will have touched. The lady's dwarf here will write down their names as they arrive, and, depending on the shield they have touched, he will explain what rules relate to that particular shield and what each man will have to do. My lady commands you thus. Sir dwarf, conduct yourself in such a way that you cannot be found fault with, on pain of being punished at her will.'

The dwarf answered in an arrogant tone: 'Limbourg, I have been entrusted with past missions far more difficult than this one and no fault was found with me [on those occasions]. I will play my part to the full.' On hearing these words, Messire Philippe was filled with joy, his only wish being to find himself [back] amongst those noblemen of his acquaintance and to do what the lady had enjoined him according to her promise.

They spent most of the night in merry conversation. The following day, Philippe found himself fully equipped in Brussels, inside his Column, just as the lady had told the herald he would be.

IV. The shields

When the princes, knights and squires at the duke's court heard that the Column was there, they all went to see it and were amazed. (167) On noticing the three shields and the horn hanging from the Column that the dwarf was guarding closely, each in turn asked what the shields and the horn were for. The dwarf answered their every query, saying: 'If you are valiant enough to touch them, let me know.' 'Indeed, dwarf,' they answered, 'Since you are in charge, you will tell us what the horn is for, and the shields as well,

[57] The text reads: 'pour advertir le nain de ce qu'il aura a dire'. This seems to refer to the explanations that the dwarf gives to each of the challengers according to the shield he touches. See below.

and then we will confer on what to do.' 'In the name of God', said the dwarf, 'In this company, there are a fair number [of people] who, even though they might want to touch the shields, would not be received by me.' 'And why is that?', several of them asked. The dwarf answered: 'The *pas* that is going to take place here against a knight-prisoner is so finely and honourably appointed by my lady and mistress that, in order to take part in it, one has to be a nobleman. That is the first point. Furthermore, the one who sounds the horn must touch one of the three shields. As I say, the one who touches the black shield, which is the first of them, will have to run a course with a sharp-headed lance of war, its point cut into a smooth curve. He will then have to do battle with rebated swords* with a ground point — this to be used by striking from the top, along and across, and not with the point, on pain of losing one's honour and the prize — right up until twenty-seven strokes have been dealt and performed by one of the combatants; they will be mounted and equipped with saddles, armour and harnesses of war, on whatever horses they please. As soon as I sound the horn, their combat will be deemed to have finished and each of them must stop fighting and retreat to his [original] place.

(168) Furthermore, the one who touches the violet shield will have to run nine courses with lances that are armed and equipped with coronals of courtesy, vamplates* and grappers that my lady will provide for all comers, at her expense. It does not matter if the lances are broken or not. The combatants will be mounted and armed with harnesses of war and not otherwise. After completing their courses, they must retreat to their [starting] place.

Likewise, the one who touches the grey shield will have to undertake and complete twelve courses with lances against the knight-prisoner; these lances will all be equipped like the ones mentioned above. The competitors will be mounted and armed with jousting harnesses and saddles of war; when finished, they must retreat as stipulated before.

Listen carefully to what I tell you so that you do not make any mistakes or errors for which you could be blamed. Moreover, those of you who touch the shields must pledge the faith you owe to God and to the ladies that, unless you have a genuine and rightful impediment, you will appear on the days assigned to you by Limbourg Herald and at the place that he will tell you about. Be content with what I explained to you. Those who want to touch the shields, let them do so, but they must be [of noble descent] as I mentioned earlier and not otherwise, for they now face dangers and adventures. Let none forget to give his name, so that I can report them all to my lady.'

The first one to touch the shields was a noble Burgundian squire named Henri de Chissey;[58] after him came eighty-six more. However, because of my lord the duke's affairs, namely that he sent to the king an important embassy led by my lord of Croÿ[59] and others

[58] [Herry de Sticé]. Henri de Chissey (Chissey-en-Morvan) was a squire from the duchy of Burgundy (1443–85?). See Léonard Dauphant, 'Les 700 pensionnaires de Louis XI et édition d'un rôle de 1481', *Annuaire-bulletin de la Société de l'Histoire de France* (2015), 21–77. Henri de Chissey is listed (n° 186) in the *rôle*, as lord of Buffard, nephew of Gui d'Usié and 'chevalier d'honneur du Parlement de Dijon pour la Franche-Comté' (*chevalier d'honneur* of the Parlement of Dijon for the Franche-Comté).

[59] Antoine de Croÿ (*c.*1402–75), son of Jean de Croÿ and Marguerite de Craon, count of Porcien and Guines, was lord of Croÿ; he was brought up with Philip the Good and was a close friend and councillor of his. He later lost the confidence of Charles the Bold when Charles became duke of Burgundy, causing Antoine to take refuge at the royal court of France. As a very powerful lord at the time of the *Pas*, he had been sent to the king of France, Louis XI, to discuss the possibility of France buying back several

who took with them a fair number of the challengers, and because my lord of Nevers[60] was away [from court] and had taken with him several noblemen who had touched the shields and could not attend, there were only sixty-one challengers, [comprising both] knights and squires. (169) Their names and exploits will be given hereafter, and their coats of arms and apparel will all be described.

The dwarf said to Henri de Chissey: 'Henri de Chissey, I tell you that, as soon as you have accomplished what you have promised against the knight-prisoner, the blazon of your coat of arms will be taken down by Limbourg and brought by me to my lady. She commanded me to inform you and the others on this matter — this should not displease you as she is only doing so in order to know exactly who you are — and your blazon will not be put in a place where you or others might incur dishonour; on the contrary, she intends to put them in a place where your names and your arms will be exalted forever. You can be certain of this.'

When Henri de Chissey and the others heard what the dwarf said and what the lady had ordered him to do, they were fully satisfied and contented. They promised the dwarf that they would be ready to accomplish all that they had committed to doing, to the best of their ability, in the places and on the days assigned to them. They asked the dwarf to say as much to the lady and to humbly recommend them to her. He was also asked to tell the knight that they very much wanted to meet him and to release him from his prison. They were praying to God that He might grant that he win back his freedom with honour. With these words, the dwarf departed and told them that he would give the lady a truthful report of what he had seen and heard, and he took with him all their names that he had written down.

V. The *Pas* is postponed and moved to Bruges

As the first day of January approached, my lord the duke had it proclaimed and declared far and wide that he could not attend the *Pas* that had been cried in Brussels, so he was postponing it to the sixth day of February in Brussels.[61] (170) Limbourg Herald informed the Lady of the Column, who notified the good knight-prisoner. Although this news left him rather despondent, his great virtue and valour helped him to bear it lightly. Again, my lord the duke's affairs prevented him from holding the *Pas* on the sixth day of February, so he had it postponed once more to the following twenty-eighth day of April in the year 1463;[62] as a place in which to hold it, he chose the city of Bruges. He had this proclaimed at his court and in many other places.

When the Lady of the Enchanted Column heard that the date had been put back and the venue moved to Bruges, she made it known to the good knight, her prisoner, sending him kind words of comfort and urging him to bear it, for the delay was not of her doing,

cities located on the river Somme that had been given to Burgundy by the treaty of Arras (1435). PCB no. 228.

60 Charles of Burgundy (*c.*1414–64), count of Nevers and Rethel, was a cousin of Philip the Good. PCB no. 533.

61 According to account B, the *Pas* was postponed twice. Account C mentions only one such postponement, that from February to April.

62 Thursday 28 April 1463: the date is the same in *modo gallico* and in modern style, as Easter came before this day in that year.

but rather was at the duke's pleasure. He should be assured that his task and undertaking would be performed even better in every way.

When this good knight heard the gracious words that she had sent him, he took heart and felt more joyful. He did not mind his prison anymore, only the waiting involved. However, because there was no way round it, he was satisfied and most humbly recommended himself to the lady's good grace, begging her that she might kindly remember him in all her doings and that his undertaking might be so well prepared in every respect that he could come out of it with honour, this being his chief concern.

'Be in no doubt in this matter', the lady's envoy responded. 'I assure you that she is most concerned about all the different aspects, that is where you do battle, who she has appointed to keep you company and serve you, (171) and all your needs, just as she promised you. Be in full readiness to do battle in person on the dates specified and assigned to you.'

During that time, my lord the duke left Brussels and arrived in Bruges where he had it announced to the lords and governors of the town that he wished the *pas* of my lord Philippe de Lalaing to take place there and that they should prepare their marketplace and stock up on everything that was needed for such an occasion.

The people of Bruges came to my lord the duke and thanked him very humbly. They promised him that they would do their best, as indeed they did, for they had a large part of the marketplace fenced in with high lists; to the sides, they erected large and beautiful wooden stands, one of which was for my lord the duke, if he wished to attend, or for the person whom he chose to delegate in his place. Everyone strove to do their utmost and to stock up in order to welcome those who came to attend the festivities.

You can imagine just how well managed everything was, for Bruges, of all the towns in the world, is the one where it is easiest to find everything needed for a grand occasion, that is goods and merchandise, because it is so well served by the sea, and because of the rich and eminent merchants who reside there and travel there from all over.

VI. The beginning of the *Pas*

On the twenty-eighth day of April, early in the morning, you would have seen on the north side of the marketplace the tall and marvellous Enchanted Column, (172) which was decorated in four colours as promised by the lady: namely gold, silver, red and green. The good knight was inside, hale and hearty. At the four corners were four griffins, each of which was attached by a large gold chain. In front of the Column was the lady's dwarf: he was seated up high and held in his hand a thick club; he was dressed in a rich blue cloth of gold and wore a black velvet beret.

From the Column hung the aforementioned three shields of black, violet and grey, as well as the hunting horn, which was of gold. In front of the Column, set up on high, were all the coats of arms of the noblemen who were due to compete. These were arranged in the order in which they had touched the shields and were to do battle, with no regard for status or prestige, for the duke, the princes and great lords of his court had so decreed it in order to avoid causing any envy or animosity to arise.

[Next follows a description of the combats as they took place over the twelve days of the Pas.*]*

XVIII. The end of the jousts

(197) When the lord of Ravenstein[63] had completed all his courses against the knight-prisoner, which marked the end of the *Pas*, the knight came over to the judges and asked them if he had fulfilled the terms of the event as stipulated in the chapters proclaimed by the Lady of the Enchanted Column. If they determined and judged that something was amiss, he was ready to achieve and complete it. The judges told him: 'Gentle knight, you have done so much that your lady and all others must be satisfied. As for us, appointed as your judges by our redoubtable lord of Burgundy, we state and declare that we deem your *pas* to have been well and valiantly accomplished. May God grant you good fortune.'

At these words, the dwarf came on foot to fetch the knight and took him back inside the Column, as was his custom, leading his horse by the bridle.

(198) Soon after came three Moors dressed and adorned in Turkish costumes which were in the colours of the three aforementioned shields, that is black, violet and grey. The same was true of their horses' trappers: the first was of black velvet, the second of violet damask satin and the third of grey velvet. They asked the dwarf to give them the three shields hanging from the Column, in order to carry them back to the Lady of the Column who had requested them. The dwarf took them down and gave each of the Moors the shield in the colour that matched what he was wearing. As soon as they took possession of them, they returned to the lady, one after the other, in the proper order, with the shields around their necks.

The Lady of the Enchanted Column[64] then came into the lists, accompanied by my lord of Boussu,[65] my lord Arnoul de Créquy, Flanders King of Arms and Artois King of Arms, along with three pageboys. She was leading a horse by hand and wore a well-fitted blue satin dress with a black velvet hood and liripipes that framed her face; around her neck she wore a heavy gold chain. She rode a tall hackney that was trappered with a rich crimson cloth of gold. The first of her pageboys was dressed in a robe that was made of satin above the girdle and, below it, of dagged grey woollen cloth; his hood of violet velvet was in the English style. The other two [pages] were similarly attired. The first page's trapper was of violet satin thickly strewn with gold ornamental buttons, that of the second was of crimson cloth of gold and the third was of crimson velvet. The horse that the lady led in by hand had a harness of violet satin with a wide dangling band bordered with gold and white silk, fashioned like English knots, with ribbons fringed with pieces of white and purple silk.

(199) When the lady arrived in front of the Column, the dwarf came out to meet her with much deference. He brought her a large golden key that she took and joined to the Column as if there were a lock made for the key; with it, she opened the Column up so wide in the middle that she, the knights, the Kings of Arms and the horses all entered with ease. They released the good knight who was waiting there for his lady to bestow her grace

---

63 That is, Adolf of Cleves. See above, n. 28.

64 In account C, the lady does not come in person but rather sends a damsel in her place.

65 Pierre de Hénin-Liétard (1433–90), lord of Boussu, was Philippe de Lalaing's brother-in-law, having married his sister Isabelle (1453). He was in the retinue of Isabelle of Bourbon, countess of Charolais and wife of the future Charles the Bold; like Philippe de Lalaing, he made his vow at the Feast of the Pheasant (1454). PCB no. 1908.

and mercy on him. Immediately, she made him put on an Italian robe[66] of a green cloth of gold and a black velvet beret on his head; she also had him put on his legharness and mount the horse that had been led in by hand. She said to him: 'Messire Philippe, I thank you for the trouble and effort that you have gone to on my behalf and at my command; you have done so much that, from this moment onwards, I release you fully from your prison. You will come with me to my residence where I will welcome you to the best of my ability. Later on, I will have the prizes and gifts that I promised delivered to you so that you can distribute them to the noblemen who did me the honour of doing battle with you according to the content of my chapters. I will have my men carry them tonight to the residence of the powerful duke of Burgundy for him to present and give them out. I request you to recommend me to him and to ask that he be content with this process being done in this fashion.' After saying these words, she gave him a kiss as a sign of great affection.

When she had finished speaking and he had felt the noble lady's sweet kiss, heard her gracious words and was released from his prison, do not ask if he was happy! With great confidence, he told her: 'My lady, you did me so much honour and good in so many ways that I cannot thank you enough. (200) May God grant me the grace to deserve your kindness in time. I will always feel indebted to you, for your benevolence and merit have amplified this little bit of worth that was in me. When it is your noble pleasure to request from me something that it is in my ability to do for you, you can count on me as your knight from this day forth.'

The lady answered him: 'Messire Philippe, for now I am fully satisfied with what you have done, and so must be all the other ladies. Now that I have your friendship, henceforth you will have fuller acquaintance of me than you did earlier. Let this satisfy you for now. Let us also leave this place for you have been here too long and rather more than I would have wished, although I shall be very sorry to see you go. However, I take comfort in the prospect of often receiving good and joyful news from you [in the future].'

'My lady', the good knight said, 'One thing makes me happy: to have regained my freedom. Yet another makes me sad: to be removed from your lordship. Nevertheless, wherever I may be, I consider myself your servant.'

With these words, they left the Column after he had given her another kiss; the lady was unable to say another word but, with her gentle eyes full of tears, she made no great show of it.

From there, they rode over to the duke and the ladies where the lady did them much reverence, as did the good knight and all his companions. They did the same to the judges, with the lady thanking them for the trouble they had taken on account of her knight. The judges were full of deference to her and offered to be at her service. They all then left together and the lady had them ride along beside her at the same level as herself until they reached her residence. On her arrival there, she found knights, squires, ladies and damsels (201) who welcomed her honourably; he on whom she bestowed a cheerful countenance was greatly honoured.[67]

When the lady and the good knight had dismounted, she led him by the hand to her chamber and had him disarmed of his legharness. After some conversation, she had wine and spices brought in, and then everyone took their leave to go wheresoever they pleased.

---

[66] See above, n. 33.

[67] That is, Philippe de Lalaing.

The lady withdrew to her room, as did the good knight to his place and the lodging that had been reserved for him.

XIX. The banquet and prizes

In the evening, at the church of St Donatian,[68] the lady sent the good knight a Moorish woman mounted on a horse. She was leading by hand another horse that was richly trappered with grey velvet and was carrying three chests made of cuir-bouilli that were handsomely fitted out and contained the prizes that the lady had promised to distribute to those who had done battle with her knight-prisoner. The Moorish woman carried the keys to the chests and presented them on behalf of her mistress to the good knight who received them with great joy and honour. He had her dismount and stay until the evening when it would be time to take the presents to the banquet that the duke was giving and which he had ordered to be held in the great hall of his residence in Bruges[69] where there were several tables filled with no one but princes, princesses, knights, squires, ladies and damsels.

As an *entremets*, there was a rich boat that was fully equipped; its captain was a lady dressed in blue. To adorn and enhance this boat, the coats of arms of all the duke's lands were arranged and set out where required; these were [depicted] on both banners and pennons. There was great noise and great cheer going on throughout the hall. Trumpets and minstrels with loud and low instruments[70] were performing great melodies. This noble company made a beautiful sight, for everyone had dressed up most elegantly in costly attire (202), the better to honour the lady and to celebrate the good knight's return from prison after he had been so honourably released and set free.

When the noise was at its height, in came the knight appointed by the lady,[71] dressed in black velvet and mounted on a hackney. He rode into the hall leading the Moorish woman who was richly arrayed. She was on horseback and led by hand a packhorse trappered in grey velvet that was carrying the locked chests of cuir-bouilli that contained the gifts and presents sent by the lady to those who had done battle with her knight, each respectively according to the particular colour of the three shields.

Next, the knight appointed by the lady dismounted and bowed with great humility to the duke and the ladies, saying to them: 'Most eminent, most powerful and most excellent prince and my redoubtable lord, my Supreme Lady of the Enchanted Column, my mistress, sends me to your lordship and requests you most humbly that you consent to do her the honour of giving me leave to present to all these princes, knights and squires some small presents that are contained in these chests of cuir-bouilli. Her sole reason for sending these gifts to them is that they might remember her [by them], and, if it is their honour and pleasure to do so, they might wear them in open display tonight and all day tomorrow, and no longer if they choose not to do so.'

---

[68] The church of St Donatian in Bruges was the place where the relics of St Basil were kept. They were moved to another reliquary a few days after the *Pas*.

[69] This is the Prinsenhof in Bruges, one of the favoured residences of the dukes of Burgundy when they were in the Low Countries.

[70] The expression 'haut et bas' defines the type of instruments here: 'hauts instruments' make a loud sound, whereas 'bas instruments' make a soft one.

[71] That is, Arnoul de Créquy.

(203) The duke answered the knight with great courtesy, saying: 'If the ladies here present are agreeable to this, so am I.' The ladies, in their reply, said: 'Yes, my lord, since it is your pleasure.'

On being given leave, the appointed knight went over to the Moorish woman who was holding the chests and the keys and asked her for them. She immediately handed them over to him and the knight opened the chests up. He first opened the one containing the black miniature shields which were decorated in black velvet and trimmed all around with thread of gold and black silk. They were pierced in the middle and threaded through the hole was a cord made of silk ribbon with a gold tassel. Below the cord was a scroll of gilded parchment with azure letters. Each scroll contained only four lines that were graciously limned in honour and praise of him to whom it was presented. All were couched in different words and with varied rhymes; none of them was exactly the same in order to account for the diversity and status of the challengers. All these black miniature shields were presented and given out to those who had done battle with swords and run courses with just the one lance. The knight appointed by his lady and mistress entreated them to wear them in open display both that night and all day long from morning onwards the next day. The recipients promised to do so and humbly thanked the lady.

[Next follow the brevets *of the first shield]*

(208) Those who had done battle with a harness of war received miniature shields decorated in violet velvet, trimmed all around with gold and silk. They were pierced in the middle with a ribbon with gold tassels and scrolls similar to the ones mentioned above, and were inscribed with four lines that were finely expressed. The recipients were requested to wear them all night long and all the following day for love of the lady. This they promised to do.

[Next follow the brevets *of the second shield]*

(213) Those who had done battle with the customary jousting harnesses were presented with miniature shields decorated in grey velvet, trimmed all around and arranged in the same manner as the other ones. They were taken out of the third chest of cuir-bouilli, whereas the violet ones were removed from the second one. The [recipients] were requested to wear them all night long and all the following day, just like the others. They readily agreed to do so and thanked the lady, humbly recommending themselves to her.

[Next follow the brevets *of the third shield]*

XXIII. Dances and prize-giving

(217) When dinner was over and the tables had been removed, my lord Adolf of Cleves, lord of Ravenstein, the duke's nephew, started the dancing by leading onto the floor Mademoiselle Marguerite,[72] his cousin (they were the children of two sisters, both daughters of

[72] Marguerite of Bourbon (1444–83), daughter of Charles 1, duke of Bourbon, and of Agnès of Burgundy, was Philip the Good's niece. She married Philippe II of Savoy (1472). PCB no. 2271.

Duke Jean of Burgundy).[73] They danced so well that it could not have been done better, for my lord of Ravenstein was deemed to be one of the best male dancers in the kingdom of France and Mademoiselle one of the best female dancers. Next, up came my lord of Saint-Pol, my lord Jacques of Bourbon, my lord of Richebourg,[74] my lord of Arguel[75] and several others who all danced wonderfully well.

While the dancing was going on, three damsels entered the hall, led by the knight appointed by the lady. They were similarly dressed in long plain tunics of white satin that were trimmed with black velvet at the top and laced up at the side. Each of them was wearing a gold necklace encrusted with precious stones and a belt made of embroidery from Bruges that was richly adorned with gold and silver. Each damsel was carrying a tall shield of war. The first one was decorated in black velvet with a heart trimmed in gold from the middle of which flowed tears of gold; all around the shield were large Roman letters. From this heart there also hung a thin and elegant gold chain that was rather long; from the lower end of it dangled a gold ring enamelled inside with the lady's motto.

The second damsel carried another shield of the same sort and size as the first one. It was decorated in violet velvet and embroidered with a half-opened golden chest from which hung a gold chain similar to the one mentioned above, on the end of which a gold ring was dangling in the same manner as the first one. Again, all around it were large Roman letters richly inscribed.

The third damsel carried another shield decorated in grey velvet and embroidered with a golden sun with long rays. A chain and a gold ring similar to the other ones were dangling from it, (219) and all around, once again, large Roman letters adorned and embellished the shield.

When the damsels, who were very attractive, entered the hall to the sound of many drums and by the light of many torches, they remained near to the entrance and did not leave until the knight appointed by the lady went up to my lady the duchess of Bourbon, the duke's sister. After he had bowed to her, he said to her: 'Most eminent and powerful princess: here are three damsels sent by my lady and my mistress, who commends herself most humbly to your noble grace. They bring on her behalf the three principal prizes of the *pas* that was held in this town in your noble presence and in that of all the other ladies here. This is in order that they may be given out to those who, according to your judgement, performed the best in the two types of joust and in the combat with swords. I beg you, with great humility, to agree to lend me two of your damsels to assist me in making enquiries as to who the three noblemen should be to whom the prizes should be awarded.'

My lady of Bourbon answered: 'Your request pleases me greatly and I thank my lady your mistress wholeheartedly. Choose as you please which two damsels will accompany the three others, and let them distribute the prizes to those who, according to their judgement, have deserved them the most.'

---

[73] Philip the Good's father, John the Fearless (r. 1404–19), was murdered in 1419. As Adolf was the son of Marie of Burgundy, Philip and Agnès's sister, Marguerite was indeed his cousin.

[74] See above, nn. 38 and 39.

[75] Guillaume de Chalon-Arlay (*c.*1415–76), lord of Arguel, was to become prince of Orange in December 1463. Account C mentions only that one of the sons of the then prince of Orange attended the final banquet. See above, n. 40.

The knight[76] picked Mademoiselle Isabelle de Cousans and Mademoiselle Marguerite de Francières,[77] who went with him to fetch the three damsels who were holding the prizes and waiting for his return. The damsels greeted each other most honourably and, to accompany them in their enquiries, they picked my lord of Créquy[78] and my lord Simon de Lalaing;[79] as officers of arms, they chose Toison d'or, (220) and Flanders and Artois Kings of Arms. They went before the duke who welcomed the three damsels of the Lady of the Enchanted Column with much honour and joyfulness. He kissed them and then gave them his opinion.

Next they went up to my lady of Bourbon, who did the same and agreed with the duke's opinion, before finally going up to all the other ladies, with the result that it was found with fair judgement and complete impartiality that my lord of Saint-Pol deserved the black shield with the gold heart for having fought the best with swords. Secondly, as the best jouster with saddle and harness of war, my lord of Ravenstein was judged to have deserved the violet shield with the gold chest. The grey chest with the golden sun was to be given to my lord Jacques de Luxembourg, lord of Richebourg, as the best competitor with saddle of war and jousting harness.

Once the enquiries had been completed, the five damsels, accompanied by the aforesaid knights and officers of arms, brought over the prizes to be presented to the three above-named lords, who received them with joy. Up went the cries 'Cleves, Cleves!' and 'Luxembourg, Luxembourg!', these being shouted out twice in honour of the two brothers who shared the same battle cry and had received two of the prizes. The lords kissed the damsels and thanked them as they well knew how to do, for these were not the first prizes that had ever been awarded and given to them. The damsels withdrew, each one to her place, and then wine and spices were brought out as is customary in these princes' residences. This *pas*, now finished, hereby comes to an end.

---

[76] The knight mentioned here is Arnoul de Créquy, not Philippe de Lalaing.

[77] [Ysabiau de Consans … Margueritte de Francieres]. Isabelle de Cousant and Marguerite de Francières were both ladies-in-waiting of the duchess of Bourbon. No further information is available about either of them.

[78] Jean V de Créquy (*c.*1400–72), lord of Créquy (1411), Fressin and Canaples, was a councillor-chamberlain of Philip the Good (1426–58), *chevalier d'honneur* of Isabel of Bourbon (1458), a member of the Order of the Golden Fleece (1430) and Philippe de Lalaing's uncle. He organised and defended the jousts in Saint-Omer (1439) on the occasion of the marriage of Charles of Charolais (i.e. the future Charles the Bold) to Catherine of France and made his vow at the Feast of the Pheasant (1454). He was also a high-ranking guest at Jacques de Lalaing's *Pas de la Fontaine des Pleurs* in its final month: see Source 7, pp. 175–83. PCB no. 392; VdF no. 47; COTO no. 23.

[79] Simon de Lalaing (*c.*1405–77), lord of Montigny, Philippe de Lalaing's uncle, was a famous and respected knight of the Lalaing family and a chamberlain of both Philip the Good (1426–45 and 1449–58) and Charles the Bold (1474). PCB no. 403.

Mario Damen

Source 11b

The *Pas du Perron Fée* (*Pas* of the Enchanted Column), Bruges, 1463

This source consists of an edition and a translation of selected extracts from two financial accounts, one urban and one ducal, for the year 1462–63.

Author:

(1) unknown; known treasurers in that year were Wouter Utenhove, Jacob Breydel, Willem Haer, Jacob de Wulf and Gerard Groote.

(2) unknown; the receiver-general in that year was Robert de la Bouverie.

Language:

(1) Middle Dutch

(2) Middle French

Archival sources:

(1) The original account is kept in Bruges, Stadsarchief, Stadsrekening 1462–63. These urban accounts, however, were made in two copies, one for the town and the other sent to the *Chambre des Comptes* (Audit Office) in Lille. This edition is based on the latter one, i.e. Brussels, AR 32515.

(2) Lille, ADN B 2048

Editions used:

(1) (partial) Louis Gilliodts-van Severen, *Inventaire des archives de la ville de Bruges. Section première: Inventaire des chartes. Première série: treizième au seizième siècle*, 9 vols (Bruges: Gailliard, 1871–85), vol. 5, pp. 533–5

(2) none available. For a description of this account, see Chrétien Dehaisnes, *Inventaire Sommaire des Archives Départementales antérieures à 1790, Nord. Archives Civiles, Série B. Chambre des Comptes nos. 1842 à 2398*, 8 vols (Lille: L. Danel, 1881), vol. 4, p. 246.

Select bibliography:

Brown, Andrew, 'Urban Jousts in the Later Middle Ages: The White Bear of Bruges', *Revue Belge de Philologie et d'Histoire*, 78 (2000), 315–30

Van den Abeele, Andries, 'De Wapenpas van de Betoverde Burcht, voorbode van de machtsgreep door Karel de Stoute', *Handelingen van het Genootschap voor Geschiedenis te Brugge*, 146 (2009), 93–139 (includes a transcription of some of the entries of the account on pp. 109–11)

——, 'Karel de Stoute en de Wapenpas van de Betoverde Burcht', *Vlaanderen. Kunsttijdschrift*, 58 (2009), 98–103

INTRODUCTION

Extracts from both urban and ducal financial accounts have been edited and translated here in order to show how a *pas d'armes* and its related festivities were financed in the case of the *Pas du Perron Fée*, which was organised by Philippe de Lalaing in Bruges in April/ May 1463.[1] Apart from outlining the financial details of a *pas*, these accounts show that the *Perron Fée* was embedded in a range of other events during these months which were not only chivalric but also civic and religious in character. Financial accounts in the later Middle Ages were produced in order to provide oversight of the financial management of an officer in the service of a prince, a town, a nobleman or any institution that needed to control its receipts and expenditure.

The first set of extracts is taken from the account made by the five treasurers of Bruges whose responsibility it was to oversee and implement the town's financial policies. In this account, a clerk has recorded the treasurers' receipts and expenses for the town administration of Bruges in the year running from 2 September 1462. The account consists of fifty-nine folios that are written on both sides and numbered in a recent hand. The money of account (i.e. the denomination of money used in reckoning accounts but not issued as actual coins) is the Flemish pound *gros* of 240 groats. The *gros* (groat) was the standard silver coinage that formed the basis of most of the accounts across the Burgundian composite state. The pound as a money of account consisted of 20 *sous* (shillings, abbreviated as s.) and every *sou* consisted of 12 *deniers* (pennies, abbreviated as d.).[2]

The edition and translation of the account given here are based on a copy of the treasurers' original account which was kept in the Audit Office in Lille (now kept in the Rijksarchief in Brussels), as indicated on the first page by the words 'pour la court' (for the court). On that page, in a marginal note, it also states that the treasurers delivered the account on 23 August 1464 to Duke Philip the Good's councillors and commissioners for Bruges: namely, Josse de Lalaing,[3] knight and chamberlain; Pieter Bladelin, *maître d'hôtel*; Master Antoine Mauret, chaplain; and Paul Deschamps/van Overtvelt, bailiff of Bruges.[4] These commissioners were responsible for renewing the town administration on an annual basis (i.e. appointing the new local officeholders for the following year) and for auditing the financial account of the previous accounting year.[5] Expenses for *pas d'armes* and other jousts organised in the town can be found in several chapters of the account which are listed in the edition below.

The second set of extracts edited and translated here is taken from the account drawn up under the responsibility of Robert de la Bouverie, the receiver-general of Duke Philip the Good, which deals with the year beginning 1 October 1462. The money of account

---

[1] For a full discussion of this event, see Essay 3 and Source 11a.

[2] Peter Spufford, 'Moneys of Account in the Burgundian Netherlands', in *Monnaies de compte et monnaies réelles: Pays-Bas méridionaux et principauté de Liège au Moyen Âge et aux Temps modernes*, ed. by Johan van Heesch, Jean-Marie Yante and Hannes Lowagie, Études numismatiques, 5 (Louvain-la-Neuve: Marcel Hoc, 2016), pp. 137–62.

[3] He had taken over this role from his father, Simon de Lalaing, lord of Montigny, who was present in the town in September 1462. AR 32515 fol. 50v. See COTO no. 26.

[4] See PCB nos 2095, 1216, 1008, 590.

[5] Jan Dumolyn, *Staatsvorming en vorstelijke ambtenaren in het graafschap Vlaanderen (1419–1477)* (Antwerp/ Apeldoorn: Garant, 2003), pp. 26–7, 43–6.

used is the pound of forty Flemish groats, which had only a sixth of the value of the above-mentioned Flemish pound *gros* of 240 groats.[6] This account is kept in the archives of the ducal Audit Office in Lille, which are now held in Lille in the Archives Départementales du Nord. La Bouverie occupied this highest-ranking office in the ducal financial administration from 1 October 1460 until 30 September 1464. Interestingly, in the ducal account no direct expenses can be found related to the *Perron Fée*. However, two entries in relation to jousting and other activities of several members of the Bourbon dynasty who played an important role during this *pas* both as spectators and as participants have been included in the edition and translation given here.

6 Spufford, 'Moneys of Account'.

TEXT (1): FINANCIAL ACCOUNT OF THE TOWN OF BRUGES, 1462–63

AR 32515

Huutgheven van rideghelde

(fol. 30v)

Item, 29 in maerte ghesonden Janne Moens, forestier, ende met hem Olivier de Haze te Kennot an minen here van Charrolois hem biddende dat hem zoude willen ghelieven te commene ten steicspele ende ooc ten ommeghange van deser stede. Ende waren ute te wetene de voors. forestier 7 daghen ende Olivier de Haze 6 daghen comt: 3lb. 5s.

Huutgheven van wercke ende stoffe

(fol. 36r)

Item, betaelt den zelven van wercke by hem ghedaen als boven omme tfayt van wapene twelke mijn heere Phelips de Lalaing dede up de Maerct van deser stede, te wetene: om eene aleye te makene daer de scilden van wapene an hijnghen met eene aleye bedect te commene ende te rijdene uut ziner herberghe duer zijn perron in de bane; beede de henden van der voorseider bane te slutene met scuvende bailgen, buten ende binnen; ende omme te makene een huus in de middele van der voorseider bane omtrent 34 voeten wijd ende 22 voeten lanc daer de jugen metten hyraulden up laghen; de lijsten te stellene ende wech te doene alst van noode was; ende ooc de zelve lijsten te hooghene ende al weder te slijtene ende wech te voerne. An al bij 9 meesters ende een handcnape voor haerluder werc ende dachueren 7lb. 4s. groten. Ende voor al de stoffe van houte verbezicht ende ghelevert ten voirn. wercken metten voerghelde 12lb. 2s. 9d. groten, comt al alst blijct bij quitancie: 19lb. 6s. 9d.

TRANSLATION (1): FINANCIAL ACCOUNT OF THE TOWN OF BRUGES, 1462–63

AR 32515

[Section on] expenses relating to travel

(fol. 30v)

Item, on 29 March[7] Jan Moens, forester,[8] and Olivier de Haze[9] were sent[10] to Le Quesnoy[11] to my lord of Charolais[12] to ask him whether it would please him to come to the joust and also to [attend] the procession to be held in the town. And the said forester was away for seven days and Olivier de Haze for six days; total: 3lb. 5s.

[Section on] expenses relating to works and materials

(fol. 36r)

Item, paid to the same [Master Antheunis Goossins, carpenter] for the work done by him in relation to the feat of arms which my lord Philippe de Lalaing[13] performed on the Markt[14] of this town, that is to make a covered alley where the shields with the coats of arms were hung, through which [alley he] could make his way from the inn[15] [where he was staying] to the *perron**[16] in the lists; to close off the ends of the alley with moving barriers, both inside and outside; to create a stand in the middle of the said alley *c.*14 feet wide and 22 feet long, where the judges with the heralds were accommodated; to erect the fences and to take them down again when necessary; and also to raise the fences and to take them all down; for all this work done by nine master [carpenters] and a servant, for all their work and hours [along] with the freight costs of 12lb. 2s. 9d. *groten*. Total, as it appears from his[17] receipt: 19lb. 6s. 9d.

---

[7] That is, in the year 1463.

[8] The organiser of the annual jousts in Bruges is named after the legendary ninth-century first count of Flanders, a forester, who is thought to have killed a white bear in a fight to the death.

[9] No further information is available on this person.

[10] That is, by the town administration.

[11] This place in the county of Hainaut is where an important residence of the Burgundian dukes was located.

[12] Charles of Charolais (1433–77), the later Charles the Bold, was duke of Burgundy and count of Flanders.

[13] Philippe de Lalaing (*c.*1430–65, battle of Montlhéry), son of Guillaume de Lalaing and Jeanne de Créquy, was a chamberlain of Philip the Good (1449–64). PCB no. 1732.

[14] This is the main market square of Bruges.

[15] This is in contrast to the narrative source of the event, where it is suggested that Lalaing was imprisoned in the *perron* the whole time: see Source 11a, p. 212.

[16] On the structure of the *perron*, which at times appears to be a column and at other times a massive rock, see Essay 3 and Source 11a.

[17] That is, Master Antheunis Goossins.

Huutgheven van onsen gheduchten heere

(fol. 40r)

Item, betaelt van wijnen ghepresenteirt onzen gheduchten here ende prince ende minen here van Charrolois, te wetene onzen voirs. gheduchten here zijdert den 22sten dach van sporcle int jaer 62 tote den 7ten dach van hoymaendt 63, twelk zijn 125 daghen te 24 kannen sdaechs. Ende minen here van Charolois ten diverschen stonden 16 daghen te 12 kannen sdaechs comt al te gader 3432 kannen maken 6864 stoopen te diversche prijsen, alst blijct bij den presentbouc die daer of es, bedraghen toter somme van 209lb. 1s. 10d.

Huutgheven van ghemeene zaken

(fol. 46r)

Item, betaelt Janne van den Vagheviere thulpen van den banckette ghegheven minen gheduchten heere ende mer vrauwen van Borbon buten in zijn huus ten Vagheviere: 2lb. 4s. 2d.

(fols 46v–47r)

Item, betaelt van costen ghedaen bij causen van den beere ende steicspele van meye dat hiernaer volcht. Eerst Beerkin den hyrault over zine moeyte ende costen als hij ute trac metter aventure 20s. groten; den zelven over zijn laken 8s. groten; item, den ghesellen die den stekers van buten den wijn thuus droughen int scepenen huus 6s. groten; item, Gheeraert de grave van der kelchiede te brekene ende weder te makene mids datter twee lijsten waren 25s. groten; item, van der huere van 33 thenin keersplatteelen 2s. 9d. groten; item, betaelt den 9 stekers over haerlieder houdchurijnghe 57lb. 5s. 6d. groten, mids dat men ne gheene stekers ghecrighen en conste, ende waren alle ghecleet met zijdene lakenen te vespereye zijden keerels ende snavonds zijden clocken al doble; item, betaelt van der huere van der huuse van Cranenbuerch daer mijn gheduchte heere

[Section on] expenses on behalf of our renowned lord

(fol. 40r)

Item, paid for the wines presented to our redoubtable lord[18] and prince and to my lord of Charolais, that is to our redoubtable lord from 22 February in the year [14]62[19] until 7 July [14]63,[20] over a period of 125 days, at 24 pitchers[21] a day, and to my lord of Charolais over sixteen days,[22] at 12 pitchers a day, all together 3432 pitchers *[...]*. Total cost: 209lb. 1s. 10d.

[Section on] expenses relating to sundry matters

(fol. 46r)

Item, paid to Jan van den Vagheviere to help him with the costs incurred for the banquet given to my redoubtable lord and my lady of Bourbon in his house Ten Vagheviere: 2lb. 4s. 2d.

(fol. 46v)

Item, costs paid in relation to the [White] Bear and jousts of May.[23] First, Beerkin, the herald,[24] for his efforts and costs when he went out to recount the story [of the White Bear], 20s. *groten*; to the same for his cloth, 8s. *groten*; item, the servants who brought wine to the jousters from outside* to their lodgings and into the town hall, 6s. 4d. *groten*; item, Gerard to break up the paved way and to restore it again afterwards because there were two lists made, 25s. *groten*; item, for the rent of 34 tin-plate torch holders, 2s. 9d.; item, paid to nine jousters[25] for their horse trappers* and clothes, 57lb. 5s. 6d. *groten* because one[26] could not get any jousters and during the procession on the evening before the jousts they were all dressed in cloth, robes and cloaks of silk, all double stitched; item, paid for the rent of Craenenburg house[27] where my redoubtable lord

---

18 That is, Philip the Good, duke of Burgundy and count of Flanders, in this latter capacity being the lord of the treasurers of Bruges.

19 Meaning 1463, since Easter style was used in Bruges. Throughout the Burgundian composite state, as well as in many other European countries, the Easter cycle determined the start of a new year in the later Middle Ages.

20 This tallies with the period when Philip the Good was actually staying in Bruges. See Herman Vander Linden, *Itinéraires de Philippe le Bon, duc de Bourgogne (1419–1467) et de Charles, comte de Charolais (1433–1467)* (Brussels: Commission royale d'Histoire, 1940), pp. 451–6.

21 A pitcher contains two *stoop* of wine (4.4 litres).

22 This period seems to include fewer days than Charles actually spent in Bruges, this being from 22 April until 25 May 1463. Vander Linden, *Itinéraires*, pp. 453–4.

23 The jousts of the White Bear were normally held on the third Monday after Easter, which fell on 25 April in 1463. On this event, see Andries Van den Abeele, *Het ridderlijk gezelschap van de Witte Beer: steekspelen in Brugge tijdens de late Middeleeuwen* (Bruges: Walleyn, 2000); and Andrew Brown, 'Urban Jousts in the Later Middle Ages: The White Bear of Bruges', *Revue Belge de Philologie et d'Histoire*, 78 (2000), 315–30.

24 This herald, who was in the service of the jousting society of the White Bear, went by the evocative name of 'Beerkin' (Little Bear).

25 That is, members of the White Bear jousting society.

26 It is not clear whether 'one' refers here to the town administration of Bruges or to the leading members of the jousting society of the White Bear. In any case, the town paid for their attire.

27 Craenenburg house was centrally located on the Markt in Bruges and was often rented out by the town administration for high-ranking visitors to watch spectacles performed on the square.

lach met mer vrauwen van Bourbon zijnder zustre 3lb. groten; item, van der huere van den huuse In de Mane [in superscript: daer de joncvrouwen waren] 30s. groten; item, betaelt van costen ghedaen in beede de voors. huusen ende int scepenenhuus 5lb. 4s. groten; item van der houdchurijnghe in scepenenhuus 15s. groten; item, betaelt van der huere van den lakenen van an te slane ende te nayene 12s. groten; item, van den menestruelen 2lb. groten; item, betaelt Ector van Oudenaerde van waslichte by hem ghelevert doe 2lb. 10s. 4d.; item, betaelt meester Antheunis Goossins van twee lijsten te makene 2lb. groten; item van costen ghedaen tot Oliviers sHazen snavonds upden dach van der vespereye 22s. 4d. groten; item, betaelt Janne de Leauwe van eenen hoorne ghestoffeirt die ghepresenteirt was den ruddre van buten best doende ende coste 35s. groten; item, betaelt den forrestier van costen tzijnent ghedaen tsondaechsavonde daer de steicers joncvrouwen haten 30s. groten, comt al: 82lb. 6s. 3d. groten.

(fol. 47r)
Item, betaelt Janne Moens als forestier over de reste van 41lb. 13s. 4d. van der eerster jaerschare van zinen forrestierscepe ende voor de vulle betalinghe 25lb. groten. Ende Jan de Brune filius Lodewijcx als nieu forestier 16lb. 13s. 4d. groten, comt al: 41lb. 13s. 4d.

(fol. 51r)
Item, betaelt van lievelicheden ghesonden onzen gheduchten heere, mijnen heere ende mer vrauwen van Charrolois ende andre zekeren heeren bij hem wezende, binnen desen jare: 53lb. 5s. 1d.

Huutgheven van extraordinaire zaken

(fol. 52v)
Item, ten bevelene van onzen voors. gheduchten heere waren ghedaen maken bij meester Antheunis Goossins twee lijsten up de Maerct omme al daerover te stekene tsondaechs naer groote vastenavonde costen 2lb. groten. Item, doe betaelt Jacop filius Lionnis van

was staying with my lady of Bourbon,[28] his sister, 3lb. *groten*; item, for the rent of Die Maene house[29] where the ladies were staying, 30s. *groten*; item, paid for costs incurred both in the said houses and in the town hall, 5lb. 4s. *groten*; item, for decorations in the town hall,[30] 15s. gr; item, paid for the rent of the cloth that was stitched and riveted to the windows, 12s. *groten*; item, for the minstrels, 2lb. *groten*; item, paid to Hector van Oudenaarde for the wax lights he delivered, 2lb. 10s. *groten*; item, paid to Master Antheunis Goossins for the construction of two lists, 2lb. *groten*; item, for costs incurred at the house of Olivier Haze on the evening of the procession, 22s. 4d. *groten*; item, paid to Jan de Leeuw for a decorated horn which was presented to the knight of the challengers[31] who gave the best performance, 35s. *groten*; item, paid to the forester for his costs incurred at his place on Sunday evening where the jousters' wives had dinner, 30s. *groten*. Total: 82lb. 6s. 3d. *groten*.

(fol. 47r)
Item, paid to Jan Moens as former forester for the remaining part of 41lb. 13s. 4d. *groten* for the first year when he was forester, and, for the full payment, 25lb. *groten*. And to Jan de Brune, son of Lodewijk, as the new forester, 16lb. 14s. 4d. *groten*. Total: 41lb. 13s. 4d.

(fol. 51r)
Item, paid for delicacies sent to our redoubtable lord, my lord and lady of Charolais[32] and to various other lords who were with him, in the course of this year: 53lb. 5s. 1d.

[Section on] expenses relating to extraordinary matters[33]

(fol. 52v)
Item, by order of our redoubtable lord, Master Antheunis Goossins constructed two fences on the Markt over which one could joust[34] on the Sunday after Shrove Tuesday, 2lb. *groten*. Item, paid at that time to Jacob, son of Lionnis, for delivering

---

[28] Agnès of Burgundy (d. 1476), sister of Duke Philip the Good, was the widow of Charles of Bourbon (1401–56) with whom she had eleven children. PCB no. 1033.

[29] This house, called 'Die Maene' (The Moon), situated right next to Craenenburg house, was centrally located on the Markt in Bruges and often rented out by the town administration for high-ranking visitors to watch spectacles performed on the square.

[30] This building was not located on the Markt but rather some 250 m away on the Burg, another important square in Bruges.

[31] This prize is normally given to one of the challengers who comes from *buten* (outside) Bruges — that is, one who is not on the 'inside* team'.

[32] Isabelle of Bourbon (d. 1465), daughter of Charles of Bourbon and Agnès of Burgundy, was married to Charles of Charolais in Lille (1454). This is the only time that she is mentioned in these accounts, as she appears to have remained at Le Quesnoy rather than going to Bruges, even though her mother and sisters were present at the ducal court on the occasion of the *Pas*.

[33] Whereas the costs for the annual jousting event of the White Bear were considered as 'normal expenses', the expenses incurred for the *Perron Fée* were seen as 'extraordinary'. The total amount of extraordinary expenditure for this year was 774lb. 7s. 10d. *groten*, of which some 580lb. were spent on the *Pas*. When the expenses of the master carpenter (given in another entry) are also included, the total amount comes to 600lb. Since the sum of all the expenses of the town in this year was some 9140lb., Bruges thus spent *c*.6.6 per cent of its budget on the *Pas*.

[34] Meaning that this is a tilt* barrier.

1000 stroos bij hem gelevert omme de bane te stroeyene 6s. 8d. Ende den moederaers van de voors. bane te messene 20s. groten, comt al: 3lb. 6s. 8d.

(fol. 53r)

Item doe betaelt Dyne van den Houvere van den huuse in Cranebuerch daer onze gheduchte heere met mer vrauwen zijnre zustre inne zach steken den tijd van den voors. steecspele gheduerende: 3lb. groten.

Item, betaelt insghelijcx Jacoppe van Maldgeheem van zinen huuse in Coelkerke daer de wet inne zach steken den voors. tijd ghedeurende: 2lb.

Item, doe betaelt van costen ghedane den voors. tijd van den steickspele ghedaen bij den voorn. van der wet in fruute ende wijne: 12s. 3d.

Item, betaelt van eenen banckette ghegeven in scepenenhuus upden 24sten dach van april onzen gheduchten heere mer vrauwen van Bourbon, mijn heere van Charrolois ende vele andre diversche heeren ende vrauwen daer, de wet, notabelen ende joncvrouwen van deser stede waren, coste: 46lb.

Item, betaelt van den costen ghedaen bij causen van den passe ofte fayte van wapene hier ghedaen opte Maerct bij mijn heere mer Phelipse de Lalaing, ruddre. Eerst zo was ghegeven onzen gheduchten heere over tconsenteren dat men tvoors. pas hier binnen der stede ter jeghenwoordicheit van hem, mer vrauwen van Bourbon, zijnre zustre, mijn heere van Charrolois ende van vele andre diversche heeren van zinen bloede ende lieden van staten hier doe wesende, de somme van: 400lb.

(fol. 53v)

Item, doe ghgegeven ende betaelt mer Phelipse de Lalaing thulpe van den costen ende lasten die hij hadde int voirs. pas: 88lb. groten.

Item, doe betaelt diversche carremans van deser stede van 2130 carren zands die ghehaelt ende ghevoert worden upde Maerct ter plaetsen daer tvors. pas ghedaen was te 6s. groten thondert comt 6lb. 7s. 9d. groten. Ende den dekens van den muederaers van tvoors. zand te spreedene ende te heffene 20s. groten. Comt al: 7lb. 7s. 9d.

Item, doe betaelt Victoor Prumboud met zinen ghesellen van den puten te delvene ende de staken te helpene in stellene daer de scilden van wapenen anne hijnghen, ende van diverschen andren ghedelven bij hem ghedaen ter plaetsen voors., voor al: 28s. 11d.

Item, doe betaelt Dyne van den Houvere ter causen van den huuse in Cranebuerch daer ons gheduchte heere ende mijn vrauwe van Bourbon inne laghen den tijd gheduerende van den voors. passe: 8lb.

Item doe betaelt Jacoppe van Maldegheem van eender camere daer de buerchmeesters joncvrauwen tvoors. pas zagen: 3lb.

Item, doe betaelt Mathijs wijf van Campen van twee ofte drie cameren in haer huus daer mijn heere van Charrolois, mijn heere van Doornicke ende andre diversche heere inne laghen den tijd van den vorn. passe gheduerende: 8lb.

a thousand bundles of straw to spread over the jousting surface, 6s. 8d. And to the street sweepers to spread dung over the jousting surface, 20s. *groten*. Total: 3lb. 6s. 8d.

(fol. 53r)

Item, paid to Dyne van den Houvere of Craenenburg house, from which our redoubtable lord and my lady, his sister, watched the jousting for the duration of the said event: 3lb. *groten*.

Item, paid for the same reason to Jacob van Maldeghem for his house, Koolkerke,[35] from which the town administrators watched the jousting during the said time: 2lb.

Item, paid for costs incurred for fruit and wine during the said time of the joust by the said town administrators: 12s. 3d.

Item, paid for a banquet given in the town hall on 24 April for our redoubtable lord, my lady of Bourbon, my lord of Charolais and many other lords and ladies in the presence of members of the town administration, notables and ladies of the town, at a cost of 46lb.

Item, paid in connection to the costs incurred for the *pas* or feat of arms organised here on the Markt by my lord *Mer*[36] Philippe de Lalaing, knight: first, given to our redoubtable lord for giving his consent to hold the *pas* here in the town in the presence of my lord, my lady of Bourbon, his sister, my lord of Charolais and many other lords of his blood and other notable people here present at the time, the sum of 400lb.

(fol. 53v)

Item, given and paid to *Mer* Philippe de Lalaing, to help him to bear his costs and to meet the expenditure which he incurred during the said *pas*: 88lb. *groten*.

Item, paid to several carters of the town for 2130 cartloads of sand which were brought and taken to the Markt to the place where the *pas* was held at 6s. *groten* per hundred, total: 6lb. 7s. 9d. *groten*. And to the head of the street sweepers to spread and take away the said sand: 20s. *groten*. Total: 7lb. 7s. 9d.

Item, paid to Victor Prumboud with his servants to dig out pits and to insert the stakes on which the shields with the coats of arms were hung, and for several other pits to be dug at the said place; for all costs: 28s. 11d.

Item, paid to Dyne van den Houvere in relation to Craenenburg house where our redoubtable lord and my lady of Bourbon were staying during the time of the said *pas*: 8lb.

Item, paid to Jacob van Maldeghem for a room from which the burgomasters' wives watched the said *pas*: 3lb.

Item, paid to the wife of Mathijs van Campen for two or three rooms in her house where my lord of Charolais, my lord of Tournai and several other gentlemen were lodged during the time of the said *pas*: 8lb.

---

35 This was another centrally located house on the Markt in Bruges.

36 This is the equivalent of *Messire* in Middle Dutch, meaning that the person had been made a knight. Philippe had indeed received the accolade after the battle of Oudenaarde on 26 April 1452 during the Ghent war. JdC, vol. 2, p. 24.

Item, doe betaelt Mahieu Rousseel, cuenijnc van wapenen van Artois, in de name van den andren cuenynghen van wapenen over trecht ende tlossen van den lijsten bij composeren: 20s.

Item, doe betaelt Antheunis Maes, castelein van den scepenen huuse, van costen ghedaen op de stallagien daer de wet metsgaders de notable van deser stede waren binnen den tijd van den voorn. passe in broode, wijne ende fruute: 4lb. 18s. groten.

Item, betaelt den zelven Antheunis van costen bij hem verleyt up den 12^en^ ende 29^en^ dach van wedemaendt metsgaders andre daghen dertusschen als men stac up de Maerct ende insghelijcx als men tzwijn sloech aldaer, in broode, wijne ende fruute: 16s. 2d.

Item, betaelt Olivier de Haze over tonghebruuc dat hij hadde van te mueghen loten de staigen te steicspeile, de welke hij mainteneirt hem toebehoorende by cause van zijnen officie mids dat de stede dat lyet bethemmeren ende ofluken den tijt van den voors. passe gheduerende ende hem daervooren toegheleyt: 4lb. groten.

TEXT (2): FINANCIAL ACCOUNT OF THE RECEIVER-GENERAL OF DUKE PHILIP THE GOOD, 1462–63

ADN B 2048

Escuierie, achact de chevaulx, voictures, poinctures et autres choses touchant l'escuierie

(fols 237r–v)

Ou mois d'avril

A Lancelot de Ghindertale, armurier demourant à Bruxelles, la somme de trente-six escus d'or de 48 gros monnaie de Flandres pièce, pour ung harnois de joustes garny de heaulme, de gardebras et de harnois de jambes, tout complet ainsi qu'il appertient que par le commandement et ordonnance de mon dit seigneur il a fait et delivré à mon seigneur Jaques de Bourbon pour don que icellui seigneur lui en a fait pour jouster au pas que ont nagueres fait et tenu audit lieu de Bruxelles, messires Adolf de Cleves et

Item, paid to Mahieu Rousseel, Artois King of Arms, in the name of other Kings of Arms,[37] for the rights and obligations relating to the lists,[38] as was agreed: 20s. *groten.*

Item, paid to Antheunis Maes, warden of the town hall, for costs incurred relating to the stands where the town administrators, together with the notable people of the town, were seated during the time of the *pas*, for bread, wine and fruit: 4lb. 18s. *groten.*

Item, paid to the same Antheunis for costs incurred by him for bread, wine and fruit on the twelfth and nineteenth of May and the days in between when the jousting was held on the Markt and also for when the pig was being slaughtered: 16s. 2d.

Item, paid to Olivier de Haze, since he could not put up for raffle the stands for the joust which he maintains belonged to him because of his office since the town had them boarded up and locked away during the time of the *pas*, therefore granted to him: 4lb. *groten.*

TRANSLATION (2): FINANCIAL ACCOUNT OF THE RECEIVER-GENERAL OF DUKE PHILIP THE GOOD, 1462–63

ADN B 2048

[Section on the expenses relating to the] stables, purchase of horses, carriages, repairs and other things concerning the stables

(fols 237r–v)

For the month of April

Paid to Lancelot de Gindertale, armourer in the town of Brussels, the sum of 36 golden *écus* of 48 groats apiece, for the making and delivery of a complete jousting harness*, equipped with helm*, pauldron* and legharness*, as is fitting, this being ordered by my said lord[39] and delivered to my lord Jacques of Bourbon[40] as a gift from the said lord to him to joust in the *pas* that was recently held and organised in the said place of Brussels[41] by Messires Adolf of Cleves,[42] and [Antoine, the Great] Bastard

---

[37] The implication here is that Rousseel was in charge of redistributing these moneys to the other Kings of Arms mentioned in this entry.

[38] It is not entirely clear which 'rights' are being referred to here. In King René's *Livre des tournois*, it was stipulated that 'all the knights and squires who have never tourneyed before must pay for their helms and their welcome to arms, to the king of arms, heralds or pursuivants, at their pleasure or by the order of the judges'. Justin Sturgeon, *Text and Image in René d'Anjou's* Livre des tournois*: Constructing Authority and Identity in Fifteenth-Century Court Culture*, 3 vols (Woodbridge: Boydell Press, 2022), vol. 1, p. 221. On similar rights paid to heralds at a *pas* organised by Antoine de Lalaing in Brussels in 1503, see Source 14, p. 297.

[39] That is, Philip the Good.

[40] Jacques of Bourbon (d. 1468), youngest son of Agnès of Burgundy and Charles of Bourbon, is mentioned as a guest in the household of Philip the Good from October 1458, and of Charles of Charolais in July 1463, just after the *Perron Fée*. In May 1468, Jacques died in Bruges shortly after being made a member of the Order of the Golden Fleece by Charles the Bold, and was buried there in the church of St Donatian. COTO no. 66; PCB no. 1946.

[41] On this particular *pas* held in Brussels, about which we have almost no corroborating information, see Essay 3.

[42] Adolf of Cleves (1425–92), lord of Ravenstein (from 1450 onwards passed to him by his elder

Bastard de Bourgogne, à l'encontre de tous venans, pour ce par quictance dudit Lancelot faicte le 20e jour dudit mois d'avril mil 463, aussi certiffiée dudit Hervé de Meriadec, premier escuier d'escuierie de mon dit seigneur, cy rendue, ladicte somme de 36 escus qui valent: 43lb. 4s.

(fol. 238r)

Au deffraiement et despenses de bouche de madamoiselle Katherine de Bourbon, niepce de mon dit seigneur tant en allant de la ville de Bruges accompaignée de l'archevesque de Lyon et de mon seigneur Jacques de Bourbon, ses freres, ensemble de leurs gens et serviteurs jusques ou pais de Zellande où ilz sont nagueres allez jouer et esbatre à l'ostel de messire Adrian de Borssele, seigneur de Brigdamme, comme en retournant par devers mon dit seigneur au dit lieu de Bruges, ouquel voyage ilz ont seiourné par cincq jours entiers, commencans le 16e et finissans le 20e jours dudit mois d'avril, lesdits jours inclux, dont des parties et la declaracion de la dicte despense montent ensemble à la somme de quarante deux livres quinze solz six deniers de 40 gros monnaie de Flandres la livre. Pour ce, par certifficacion de messire Michault de Chaugy, l'un des maistres d'ostel de mon dit seigneur, faicte le 22e jour dudit mois d'avril oudit an 63 après Pasques, cy rendue, laditte somme de: 42lb. 15s. 6d. de 40 gros.

of Burgundy against all comers, this [being] on the basis of the receipt of the said Lancelot drawn up on the twentieth of the said month of April 1463, also certified by the said Hervé de Mériadec,[43] first squire of the stables of my said lord, [and] herewith delivered, the said sum of 36 *écus* which amounts to 43lb. 4s.

(fol. 238r)

For the expenses and subsistence costs of my lady Catherine of Bourbon, niece of my said lord, both in going out from the town of Bruges and returning [thereto], accompanied by the archbishop of Lyon[44] and by my lord Jacques of Bourbon, her brothers, together with their followers and servants, to the land of Zeeland where they recently went to disport and amuse themselves in the residence of Messire Adriaan van Borssele,[45] lord of Brigdamme, on which journey they spent five whole days, starting on the sixteenth and finishing on the twentieth day of April, with both days included, when they then returned to my said lord in the said place of Bruges, the expenses of which come to a total amount of 42lb. 15s. 6d. of 40 groats in Flemish pounds. This sum was certified by Messire Michaut de Chaugy,[46] one of the *maîtres d'hotel* of my said lord, on the twenty-second day of April in the said year [14]63 after Easter, [and] delivered with this, the said sum of 42lb. 15s. 6d. of 40 groats.

brother, Johann), son of Adolf, duke of Cleves, and Marie of Burgundy, sister of Philip the Good, was married to 1. Beatriz of Coimbra, and 2. Anne of Burgundy, an illegitimate daughter of Philip the Good. He was a guest at the Burgundian court (1439–62) and a member of the Order of the Golden Fleece (1456). COTO no. 55; PCB no. 817; VdF no. 39.

[43] Hervé de Mériadec (d. 1478), of Breton origin, married in 1457 to Jeanne de Croix, daughter of Jean VI, was initially in the service of Arthur III of Brittany, earl of Richmond; he was a squire of the stables in the household of Philip the Good (1435–67) and held several offices and possessions in the county of Flanders. Werner Paravicini, 'Un tombeau en Flandre: Hervé de Mériadec', *Francia. Forschungen zur westeuropäischen Geschichte*, 34.1 (2007), 85–146; VdF no. 143; PCB no. 739.

[44] Charles of Bourbon, archbishop of Lyon, son of Agnès of Burgundy and Charles of Bourbon, was a guest in the household of Philip the Good (1459–62) and of Charles of Charolais (July 1463). PCB no. 2093.

[45] Adriaan van Borssele (d. 1468), lord of Brigdamme, was married to 1. Maria van Kats, and 2. Anne of Burgundy, an illegitimate daughter of Philip the Good, who would marry Adolf of Cleves after her first husband's death; he was a chamberlain of Philip the Good (from 1458). PCB no. 1754.

[46] Michaut de Chaugy was in the service of Philip the Good, first as a substitute *maître d'hôtel* (1452), then as a *maître d'hôtel* (1458) and later still as *grand maître d'hôtel* (1463). PCB no. 1489.

Thanks are due to Rosalind Brown-Grant for her helpful comments on these translations.

Ralph Moffat

Source 12

The *Pas de l'Arbre d'Or* (*Pas* of the Golden Tree), Bruges, 1468

This source consists of a translation of the declaration and chapters of arms for this event.

Author: Antoine, the Great Bastard of Burgundy, or a member of his entourage such as the Golden Tree Herald referred to in the chapters of arms in the translation below.

Language: Middle French

Edition used: Leeds, Royal Armouries Library, I.35, fols 7r–10r, transcribed in MT, pp. 106–12. The narrative account of this event is also written up in several other manuscripts: London, BL, Lansdowne 285, fols 26r–29r (a partial copy); London, BL, Harley 69, fols 12r–13v (a sixteenth- or seventeenth-century copy, probably made from the Royal Armouries manuscript; this has been published in Francis Henry Cripps-Day, *The History of the Tournament in England and France* (London: Quaritch, 1918), Appendix VI, pp. lv–lix); Valenciennes, Bibliothèque Municipale, 776, fols 10v–11r (an incomplete version); this is probably the text drawn on by Olivier de La Marche, as noted in Catherine Emerson, *Olivier de La Marche and the Rhetoric of Fifteenth-Century Historiography* (Woodbridge: Boydell, 2004), p. 194.

Select bibliography:

Barber, Richard, and Juliet Barker, *Tournaments: Jousts, Chivalry and Pageants in the Middle Ages* (New York: Weidenfeld & Nicolson, 1989)

Brown, Andrew, and Graeme Small, eds, *Court and Civic Society in the Burgundian Low Countries, c. 1420–1530* (Manchester: Manchester University Press, 2007), pp. 36–85

Bureaux, Guillaume, 'Union et désunion de la noblesse en parade. Le rôle des Pas d'armes dans l'entretien des rivalités chevaleresques entre cours princières occidentales, XVe–XVIe siècles (Anjou, Bourgogne, France, Saint-Empire)' (unpublished PhD dissertation, Normandie Université, 2018)

Janssens, Albert, 'De wapenpas van de Gouden Boom: feestvieren op zijn Bourgondisch', *Vlaanderen. Kunsttijdschrift*, 58 (2009), 104–7

Stanesco, Michel, *Jeux d'errance du chevalier médiéval: Aspects ludiques de la fonction guerrière dans la littérature du Moyen Âge flamboyant* (Leiden: Brill, 1988)

INTRODUCTION

The *Pas de l'Arbre d'or* took place in the marketplace in Bruges that, five years earlier, had served as the venue for the *Pas du Perron Fée* organised by Philippe de Lalaing.[1] The *entrepreneur** of this supremely lavish event was Antoine, the eldest surviving natural son of Philip the Good, duke of Burgundy, who was thus known from 1453 by his honorific title 'the Great Bastard of Burgundy'. It took place over ten days in 1468 as part of the festivities that included no fewer than six banquets held in Bruges to celebrate the marriage of Margaret of York, sister to Edward IV of England, to Antoine's half-brother, Charles the Bold. Antoine may well have played some part in arranging this match. King Edward had sent his brother-in-law Anthony, Lord Scales, to accompany the bride-to-be and, in June of the previous year, Scales and the Great Bastard had fought one-on-one in a feat of arms in which they were the only combatants at Smithfield and had become brothers-in-arms. This earlier event may therefore have served as a pretext for secretly forging the marriage alliance.[2]

There are four detailed eyewitness accounts of the nuptial festivities and the combats of the *Arbre d'or*. The most comprehensive of these, written in Middle French, is that of the Burgundian courtier and chronicler Olivier de La Marche (*c.*1425–1502).[3] The second, also in Middle French, is recorded in the *mémoires* of Jean de Haynin (1423–95).[4] The Bruges rhetorician Anthonis de Roovere (1420–82), writing in Middle Dutch, provides a third.[5] The fourth, written in English, survives in a manuscript in the British Library, and was probably noted down by an English herald.[6]

The Royal Armouries manuscript is the only source to preserve both the original declaration — that is, the literary scene-setting — and the *chapitres*, or chapters of arms — i.e. the rules of engagement set out by the defender of the *pas*, which are written in Middle French. The folios on which these two texts have been copied have been dated to the later fifteenth century and the hand is *not* of the type used in the Burgundian court.[7] Although the copyist does not name himself, he does address the Great Bastard of Burgundy as his lord. It is highly likely, therefore, that the declaration was composed by Antoine, the Great Bastard, or by a herald in his employ. In it, the Knight of the Golden Tree, speaking in the first-person voice, explains that he is the servant of a mysterious *Dame de l'Isle Celée* (Lady of the Secret Isle) and that everything is being done in her honour. This lady is a character from the *Roman de Florimont*, the eponymous hero of which is presented as the supposed grandfather of Alexander the Great.[8] A prose version of this romance is preserved in a manuscript now in

---

[1] See Sources 11a and 11b; on the significance of Bruges as a venue for *pas d'armes*, see Essay 3.

[2] Sydney Anglo, 'Anglo-Burgundian Feats of Arms: Smithfield, June 1467', *Guildhall Miscellany*, 2 (1965), 271–83.

[3] OdLM, vol. 2, pp. 95–144. For a translation of selected extracts from this account, see Andrew Brown and Graeme Small, eds, *Court and Civic Society in the Burgundian Low Countries, c. 1420–1530* (Manchester: Manchester University Press, 2007), pp. 58–85.

[4] Dieudonné Brouwers, ed., *Mémoires de Jean, Sire de Haynin et de Louvignies 1465–1477*, 2 vols (Liège: Société des Bibliophiles liégeois, 1905–06), vol. 2, pp. 18–62.

[5] HKB, pp. 17–66.

[6] London, BL, Cotton Nero C IX, fols 173v–177v, published in Samuel Bentley, *Excerpta Historica, or, Illustrations of English History* (London: Bentley, 1831), pp. 227–39.

[7] MT, p. 18.

[8] This verse romance, dating from 1188, is by Aimon de Varennes: for an edition, see Alfons Hilka, ed., *Florimont, ein altfranzösischer Abenteuerroman* (Göttingen: Niemeyer, 1932). See also Gordon Kipling,

the BnF in Paris that was once in the ducal library of Philip the Good, and it is likely that this is the version alluded to here in the chapters of arms.[9] The eponymous Golden Tree itself is thought to be a symbol of the supposed Trojan origins of the Burgundian nobility.[10] In the actual chapters of arms, the fact that the first-person narrative voice is then taken by someone else who refers to the Knight of the Golden Tree in the third person suggests that these parts may well have been put together by a herald, possibly the Golden Tree Herald mentioned in the source, writing at the *entrepreneur*'s command.

Date	Defender	Challenger
Sunday 3 July	Antoine, the Great Bastard of Burgundy	1. Adolf of Cleves, lord of Ravenstein
Monday 4 July	Antoine, the Great Bastard of Burgundy	2. Louis de Chalon, lord of Châtel-Guyon 3. Jacques de Luxembourg, lord of Fiennes 4. Charles de Visen
Tuesday 5 July	Antoine, the Great Bastard of Burgundy	5. Jean IV de Chalon, lord of Arguel, son of the Prince of Orange 6. Antoine de Halluin/Antoon van Halewijn 7. Antoine de Luxembourg, lord of Roussy
Wednesday 6 July	Antoine, the Great Bastard of Burgundy	8. Jean de Chassa, lord of Monnet 9. Jacques de Luxembourg, lord of Richebourg 10. Philippe de Poitiers, lord of La Ferté 11. Claude de Vaudrey
Thursday 7 July	Antoine, the Great Bastard of Burgundy	12. Jean de Reiferscheit, count of Salm 13. Baudouin, bastard of Burgundy 14. Philippe de Croÿ, lord of Renty
Friday 8 July	Adolf of Cleves, lord of Ravenstein	15. Anthony Woodville, Lord Scales
	Charles de Visen	16. Antoine de Luxembourg, lord of Roussy 17. Jean de Rochefay, known as 'Le Rosquin', squire
Saturday 9 July	Philippe de Poitiers, lord of la Ferté	18. Jean de Ligne, lord of Ligne 19. Jacques de Harchies 20. Philippe de Crèvecoeur, lord of Esquerdes 21. John Woodville 22. Charles de Ternant, lord of Ternant

The Triumph of Honour: Burgundian Origins of the Elizabethan Renaissance (Leiden: Leiden University Press, 1977), pp. 22 and 117; and Annette Lindner, 'L'influence du roman chevaleresque français sur le pas d'armes', *PCEEB*, 31 (1991), 67–78 (p. 73).

9 Paris, BnF, fr. 12566.

10 Carol Chattaway, 'The Heroes of Philip the Bold', *PCEEB*, 41 (2001), 27–37. On the symbolism of such objects in the *pas d'armes*, see also Michel Stanesco, *Jeux d'errance du chevalier medieval: Aspects ludiques de la fonction guerrière dans la littérature du Moyen Âge flamboyant* (Leiden: Brill, 1988), chapter 9; and Jean-Pierre Jourdan, 'Le thème du Pas et de l'Emprise. Espaces symboliques et rituels d'alliance en France à la fin du Moyen Âge', *Éthnologie française*, 22.2 (1992), 172–84.

Date	Defender	Challenger
Sunday 10 July	Philippe de Poitiers, lord of La Ferté	23. Pierre of Bourbon, lord of Carency 24. Louis Le Jeune, lord of Mourcourt, later lord of Contay
	Louis Le Jeune, lord of Mourcourt, later lord of Contay	25. Francesco d'Este, marquis of Ferrara
	Claude de Vaudrey	26. Louis Le Jeune, lord of Mourcourt, later lord of Contay
Monday 11 July	Adolf of Cleves, lord of Ravenstein	27. Charles the Bold, duke of Burgundy

The tournament opened with a series of jousts that are summarised in the Table. At this *pas d'armes*, the combats were fought in order of seniority as well as by jousting prowess. Seniority was not necessarily indicated by aristocratic rank but rather by social position within the court of Burgundy and its allies. The role of the defender, as the Knight of the Golden Tree, was primordial. Antoine, the Great Bastard of Burgundy, who took this role, was supposed to joust every day and to lead the tourney team. He was, however, kicked by a horse on 8 July and could not continue after this date. Before his injury, he jousted fourteen times. There was only one combat at which he never intended to joust and that was against Lord Scales, his 'brother-in-arms'.[11] Adolf of Cleves, lord of Ravenstein and first cousin to the duke, was the next most senior combatant. He jousted three times in the most important combats, was the first challenger of the *pas* and the last defender (against the duke himself, Charles the Bold, who had otherwise not participated in the jousting) and was also the designated defender against Lord Scales. Philippe de Poitiers, lord of La Ferté,[12] was the next most senior combatant. When Antoine, the Great Bastard, was injured and could no longer compete, the role of Knight of the Golden Tree (the defender) was taken by Charles de Visen.[13] The following day, Visen was replaced as the Knight of the Golden Tree by Philippe de Poitiers, lord of La Ferté, who would have continued to the end of the *pas* had he, too, not been injured. When this second injury occurred, Louis Le Jeune de Contay, lord of Mourcourt,[14] was in the field as challenger and was temporarily promoted to defender for the next combat but replaced for the following combat as he was clearly not considered to be senior enough to continue in the role. Claude de Vaudrey,[15] who was famous for his jousting skills, finally took over the role. As a consolation, seemingly, Louis Le Jeune de Contay was uniquely allowed a second course as a challenger. Philippe de Poitiers jousted eight times.

11 See MT, pp. 48–9; for evidence of this brotherhood.

12 Philippe de Poitiers, lord of La Ferté (d. 1503), was a cupbearer of Philip the Good (1458) and a chamberlain of Charles the Bold (1474). PCB no. 1499.

13 Charles de Visen (1454–75) was *garde de joyaux de corps* (keeper of the personal jewels) of Charles the Bold (1474). PCB no. 1768.

14 Louis Le Jeune de Contay (d. 1477, Nancy) was a chamberlain of Charles the Bold (1474). PCB no. 1232.

15 Claude de Vaudrey (1443–1518) was a cupbearer of Philip the Good (from 1465) and a chamberlain of Charles the Bold (1474); he was also a military commander in the service of both dukes. PCB

These jousts were then followed on the Monday by a second event. In the chapters of arms, the *entrepreneur* invites all those who have already jousted against him to join him to form a team to take on all comers in a tourney* (Fr. *tournoy*). This was to be a mounted combat commencing with a single charge with lances followed by a *mêlée** with rebated swords. In the continued absence of Antoine the Great Bastard, Charles the Bold led a team of twenty-six defenders comprising the named jousters of the previous days who had formerly fought as challengers; his opponent was the lord of Joigny,[16] who led a team of twenty-six others also drawn from the challengers. This extract from the Royal Armouries manuscript is unique in that it contains the only text of a separate set of chapters of arms specifically for a tourney in any *pas d'armes.*

In this translation of the declaration and chapters of arms of the *Arbre d'or,* page numbers in parentheses have been provided for ease of reference to Ralph Moffat's transcription (in MT).

TRANSLATION

(106) The Beginning of the Declaration of the *Pas d'armes* of the Golden Tree

In honour of God Almighty — and by His grace and goodness — I, a poor knight called the Knight of the Golden Tree, have travelled through various distant regions. After much strife and many dangerous adventures had befallen me, one adventure in particular in these last days not long passed has not failed to have been a cause of particular regard and of great rendition of praise to God in recognition of it. Concerning this adventure, without further superfluous repetition of the things said above, the most high and noble princess, the Lady of the Secret Isle — my mistress and my lady — has, by these present letters, informed and advised on my behalf the most excellent and powerful prince, the duke of Burgundy,[17] my redoubtable lord here present. These letters are set down word for word right here at the start of my present chapters of arms to declare in full all the causes and circumstances which can motivate — and have motivated me — to make my way here to this glorious house of Burgundy and to have prayed and asked for the grace and licence to have the amicable acquaintance of the house of Burgundy's noble chivalry with their gracious company and to test one's mettle in single combat. My *emprise** to which I am bound may be beyond my valour and abilities; it may be unwise but is certainly worthy [as an undertaking]. Let it be known to all high and noble princes, barons, knights and squires of this most noble and famous house of Burgundy that today, in all humility, all that follows is being done in accordance with certain requests made of me (107) by the most high and noble lady, the Lady of the Secret Isle, according to the ceremony of a precious Golden Tree that has been placed in my hands by her. On certain conditions, and in very difficult

no. 2285. A very fine complete harness for foot combat that was made for him in the 1480s can still be admired in the Kunsthistorisches Museum, Vienna.

16 Charles de Chalon, count of Joigny, was a councillor-chamberlain of Charles the Bold (1474). PCB no. 1446.

17 That is, Charles the Bold.

circumstances for me, I will have this Golden Tree — by the grace and with the humble consent of the most excellent prince, my lord the duke of Burgundy — planted and guarded in the middle of his town of Bruges in the marketplace; as part of the ceremonies [that are] written and contained in this [declaration] in accordance with the command imposed on me. Therefore, as stipulated by my chapters of arms which will be fully described hereafter, it will be publicly proclaimed so that everyone may be satisfied. The nature of this rich Golden Tree thus planted and curiously guarded stipulates that a feat of arms demanding knightly skill is to be performed by me not out of presumption but in order that, by humbling myself, I may augment and increase the honour of others through my modest *emprise.* In all humility, I beg all noble and high princes, barons, knights and squires of this glorious house that it please them, after hearing the contents of my chapters of arms, to show favour and acquiesce to my humble prayers. May they bestir themselves to demonstrate the [necessary] courage to ensure my deliverance and to [partake in] the mystery of my *emprise.* This [*emprise*] is inspired by true noble love and honour for nobility. As I know well about the depth of honour and virtues existing here with marvellous clarity, I am all the more confident and hopeful that I will soon be released by your noble hands, may God preserve [you].

Here follows the form that the *Pas d'armes* of the Golden Tree will take

The Knight of the Golden Tree makes it known to all princes, barons, knights and squires and generally to all those to whom this noble *pardon d'armes*[18] applies, that, in order to accomplish the desire and will of his beautiful lady, as far as it lies within his power, he has undertaken, by appropriate leave, to hold and organise a *pas d'armes* involving both joust* and tourney. This *pas d'armes* will begin with the joust and be completed by a combat with rebated swords* without points according to the chapters of arms and under the conditions outlined hereafter. This is in the hope of breaking one hundred and one lances or that one hundred and one lances will be broken in this *emprise.* By this, it is meant that (108) he either breaks one hundred and one lances (on his opponents) or that one hundred and one lances will be broken [by his opponents] on him.[19] The defending knight intends to make himself ready to run [these courses] for eight days in a row, beginning on Sunday, the third day of this present month of July in the year [14]68.[20] Because this Knight of the Golden Tree asks and desires with all his might to have the acquaintance, love and familiarity of the princes, knights and noblemen of this triumphant and renowned house and, in order to prove the chivalry and prowess of several [of them], he has, to this end, comprised and compiled his said *pas d'armes* and *emprise* in such a manner that he will run every day for half an hour [timed] by the hourglass against four noblemen, without counting in each half hour the complications, delays or other time lost as will be more fully explained hereafter.

[18] See MT, p. 51, which notes that this term, in use from 1390, suggests that 'in this context *pardon* could be interpreted as *indulgence* or *celebration* whilst the remainder of the term contains the component *d'armes* as a reminder that these events do still involve some martial ability'.

[19] Correctly breaking the lance — the attaint* — on one's opponent is essential to victory in a joust.

[20] Written in the original text as 'l'an lxviij'.

Here follow the chapters of arms

The first chapter of arms stipulates that the lists will be made ready as is appropriate, and a rich Golden Tree will be planted in the middle. There will be a giant chained to this tree and, nearby on a column, a dwarf will be sitting.[21] He will have a horn round his neck and an hourglass before him with sand that measures half an hour. This hourglass will be started when the first lance is couched. The giant and dwarf will guard the entrance to the Knight of the Golden Tree's list; he will be in a pavilion.

The second chapter of arms stipulates that any knight or squire who wishes to come to this *pas d'armes* will be obliged to present himself at the entrance to the lists at such hour as [the Knight of the] Golden Tree will say and signify, mounted and armed as is appropriate in such a case [and] accompanied by six men on horseback and four on foot and no more — except for pages on horseback if he has any —, who may enter for as long as the joust lasts. There will be an officer of arms[22] [processing] before the knight or squire who will carry a shield emblazoned with this knight or squire's coat of arms to hang on the Golden Tree.

The third chapter of arms stipulates that no one may lead more men into the lists than is permitted, except for princes who may lead in as many as they see fit.

The fourth chapter of arms stipulates that, at the entrance to the lists, the said challenger to the *Pas* will strike three times with a great wooden hammer which hangs from the barrier.[23] Then the Knight of the Golden Tree will come out of his pavilion and ask: 'Who is it?' Having heard the answer, he will return to the dwarf who will unchain the giant who will go to open up the barrier and lead the knight into the lists [in order] to present him to the ladies.

The fifth chapter of arms stipulates that when the knight has made a tour of the tilt* he will return to his end [of the lists].[24] Then the Knight of the Golden Tree will send two fully equipped lances of which the knight will take his choice. Then, when he is ready, the dwarf will blow his horn. (109) After this, the Knight of the Golden Tree will come to the other end through a gate where he will be given his lance. They will be obliged to run with these lances until they are broken; at this point, they will be given others and will run thus for the rest of the half hour.

The sixth chapter of arms stipulates that as soon as these knights begin to run, the dwarf will attend to them in case one of them is disarmed, in which case the knights will be held back from running. From now it will be done in this manner.

The seventh chapter of arms stipulates that should it happen — God forbid! — that one of the knights is injured or disarmed to the extent that he is unable to run any more for that day, if it be the case that this happens to the Knight of the Golden Tree, he may place another in his stead as he sees fit in order to fulfil his *pas*. However, if it be the case that it should happen to the challenging knight of the *pas*, he will be deemed to have accomplished all in person without doing anything more.

---

[21] In the *Roman de Florimont*, this giant is named Garganeus, whilst dwarfs are a very common feature in *pas d'armes*, as, for example, at the Angevin *Pas de la Joyeuse Garde/Pas de Saumur* (1446) and at the Burgundian *Perron Fée*. For a discussion of these non-chivalric figures, see Essay 7.

[22] This is probably a reference to Golden Tree Herald, who is mentioned explicitly by name below (pp. 255, 257); for the identity of the person holding this office, see n. 25.

[23] That is, the barrier to the lists.

[24] This means riding up one side of the lists along the tilt and then back down the other side of it.

The eighth chapter of arms stipulates that he who breaks the most lances on his companion* during the half hour in the manner described above will win a gold ring; that is to say, he who has had the lances broken upon him will be obliged to present his adversary with the ring before leaving the lists as both see fit.

The ninth chapter of arms stipulates that should it happen — God forbid! — that one of the two should be borne to the ground by an attaint of the lance, either with or without the horse also being brought down, he who has dealt this blow will win a ruby set in a gold ring that will similarly be presented to him in the lists.

The tenth chapter of arms stipulates that no lance will be considered broken if it is broken on the saddle, or by an attaint below the saddle; rather, it must be broken at a point between the coronal* and the grapper* at least.

The eleventh chapter of arms stipulates that the Knight of the Golden Tree will deliver all the lances equipped with coronals, grappers, and vamplates* with which this *pas* will be run, and no one may run with any other [lances]. The challenger will have the choice of these lances each time.

The twelfth chapter of arms stipulates that when the half hour has passed and the dwarf's hourglass has run out, he will then sound his horn and two *plançons** will be carried in by Golden Tree (Herald).[25] The knight from the outside team* will have the choice of these two *plançons*. They will be obliged to run one course with these *plançons*, and no more, for the love of the Lady of the Secret Isle, in order to [attempt to make] one attaint and no more.

The thirteenth chapter of arms stipulates that there will be two or three noblemen appointed by my lord [the duke] on a stand in the middle of the lists with four officers of arms who will judge the lance breaks and evaluate who has broken the most lances and broken them the best; they will also adjudicate all other debates that might arise during this *pas* in order to award the prize fairly and without favour to whomsoever has performed the best. This they will confirm by their oath.

(110) The fourteenth chapter of arms stipulates that he who has broken the most lances [jousting] against the Knight of the Golden Tree during the *pas* in his half hour in the manner described above will be awarded the prize of the trappered* destrier* on which the Knight of the Golden Tree has run for that day, together with the harness* that he wore. This trappered destrier and harness will be presented to him in the lists in front of the ladies.

The fifteenth and final chapter of arms stipulates that because the Knight of the Golden Tree is a foreigner[26] and sparsely accompanied by men and those who could counsel him, he requests in the name of his mistress, the Lady of the Secret Isle, in all humility, that all the knights, princes and noblemen who will have run at this *pas* — if it so pleases them — do him the honour and courtesy of accompanying him[27] the day after they have run against him; that is to say, four by four, just as they had done at the *pas*. Once more, he asks most humbly that [this boon] might be granted him provided, however, that no one changes his horse lest it jeopardise his chance of winning the prize.

---

[25] This office was held by Americk Esturq. Valérie Bessey, Véronique Flammang, Émilie Lebailly and Werner Paravicini, eds., *Comptes de l'argentier de Charles le Téméraire, duc de Bourgogne*, 5 vols (Paris: Académie des Inscriptions et Belles-Lettres, 2001–14), vol. 1, p. 128.

[26] Meaning he is from an exotic foreign land, which is part of the fiction of this *pas*; in the actual *Roman de Florimont*, the eponymous hero is the son of the duke of Albania.

[27] That is, to form a team to compete in the tourney.

Here follow the chapters of arms of the tourney

The first chapter of arms stipulates this: all noblemen who have run against the defending knight will be personally obliged to join this knight and to associate with him in order to fulfil the tourney at his side and to undertake the feats of the sword bouts against all those who wish to come. Like the knight himself, they will all wear the attire[28] and insignia of the Golden Tree in honour of the Lady of the Secret Isle.

The second chapter of arms stipulates that all those who wish to tourney at this noble *pas* will be obliged to present themselves to the most high and victorious prince, the duke of Burgundy etc.[29] at the day and hour which he will have appointed for them.

The third chapter of arms stipulates that they will be obliged to present their shields all at the same time at the hour that will be made known to them in order that they may be placed on the Golden Tree in the same manner as the shields of the joust were.

The fourth chapter of arms stipulates that no one may carry swords unless they are without points and rebated such as are appropriate for used in a noble and honourable tourney. These swords will be presented to the judges by the officers of arms for them to inspect. After this, the dwarf will carry in several lances. The captain of the challengers from the outside team and his companions may each choose one of these and the dwarf will carry the others [over] to the defending knight and his companions.

(111) The fifth chapter of arms stipulates that when both sides have been equipped with lances and swords, the dwarf will return to the foot of the Golden Tree and blow his horn. Each man will then immediately begin to run one course of the lance only — and all at the same time. Next, they will take their swords from the dwarf and strike with as much strength in their arms and for as long as the Knight of the Golden Tree's prowess allows him to, in fulfilment of his promise to the Lady of the Secret Isle, and for as long as it pleases the ladies to determine. The *mêlée* will only come to an end at the ladies' pleasure.

The sixth chapter of arms stipulates that as soon as the fight has ceased, the defending knight will ask the ladies and judges at this event who, of either side, has performed the best with his sword on this occasion. The Knight of the Golden Tree will present the winner with his trappered horse and his harness as the prize of this tourney before leaving the lists.

The seventh chapter of arms stipulates that in order that all things are fully understood and performed to the utmost during this noble *emprise*, both in the joust and in the tourney, my redoubtable sovereign lord will appoint noblemen who are knowledgeable about these matters and who will have power over everything as though they were my lord himself.[30]

---

[28] Middle French *parure* has quite a wide-ranging meaning: here it is used to indicate that all the participants form a team by dressing in a similar manner to that of the Knight of the Golden Tree.

[29] This refers to the fact that all his other noble titles have been omitted for the sake of brevity.

[30] The judges at this *pas* were: Thomas de Loraille, lord of Escoville, ambassador and servant of the duke of Normandy; Philippe Pot, lord of La Roche; Claude de Toulongeon, lord of La Bastie, lieutenant of the marshal of Burgundy; and Robert, lord of Miraumont. Also in attendance were Toison d'or, King of Arms of the Golden Fleece (an office held by Gilles Gobet in 1468), and the English royal herald, Garter King of Arms (an office held by John Smert).

The eighth and final chapter of arms stipulates this: after the prize of the tourney has been awarded by the defending knight, at such time he will send over Golden Tree Herald, the combatant knight, the great prisoner, and his soldiers.[31] He will then have them take his Golden Tree, embellished with the aforementioned noble [heraldic] blazons, to the Lady of the Secret Isle. Thus, and in this manner, the adventure of the Golden Tree will be completed. The defending knight, accompanied by all those who have jousted and tourneyed with him, will then accompany the ladies to their lodgings; there they will retire, bringing this *emprise* to an end.

The Knight of the Golden Tree, this party's defender, in this case prays and asks you in all humility, most excellent and victorious prince and redoubtable lord, the duke of Burgundy, that you deign to accede to this humble request to accomplish this *emprise* and that it should be your pleasure to give judgement in this matter. May you be willing to assign a location, as well as granting support and ceremony, in order for this to be done. Therefore, if God gives such blessing to this supplicant that you, who have so many times found yourself engaged in the exercise of arms, should personally condescend to participate in fulfilling the wish of the beautiful lady, this knight would take it as the greatest blessing that could befall him. He asks and begs all other princes, barons, knights and generally all noblemen that it be their wish to labour in this matter as if for themselves in order that he might be released [from his promise to fight for his lady]. He also most humbly requests all princesses, (112) ladies and damsels to take pains to watch the test of chivalric mettle that will be performed against him; may they also wish to encourage and exhort their friends and [courtly] servants[32] to fulfil the request of this supplicant who will beg the God of Love to grant you that which you most desire. Amen.

Here ends the *Pas d'armes* of the Golden Tree

[31] This is unclear as none of these people, other than the herald, are recorded in any other source for this event.

[32] This means their lovers according to the courtly ritual of serving one's lady, just as the Knight of the Golden Tree is doing for the Lady of the Secret Isle. In addition, 'friend' here has the connotation of lover, which links up with the exhortation to the God of Love referred to in the very last line of the text.

Rosalind Brown-Grant

Source 13

The *Pas des armes de Sandricourt* (*Pas* of Sandricourt), 1493

This source consists of a translation of the complete narrative account of this event.

Author: Orléans Herald

Language: Middle French

Edition used: Augustin Vayssière, ed., *Le Pas des armes de Sandricourt. Relation d'un Tournoi donné en 1493 au château de ce nom, publié d'après un manuscrit de la Bibliothèque de l'Arsenal et l'imprimé du temps* (Paris: Léon Willem, 1874) (= PSt)

Select bibliography:

Botto, René, *L'Isle-Adam et sa région. Au temps des tournois 1493 et 1519* (L'Isle-Adam: Les Amis de L'Isle-Adam, 2006)

Bureaux, Guillaume, 'Union et désunion de la noblesse en parade. Le rôle des Pas d'armes dans l'entretien des rivalités chevaleresques entre cours princières occidentales, XVe–XVIe siècles (Anjou, Bourgogne, France, Saint-Empire)' (unpublished PhD dissertation, Normandie Université, 2018)

Cifarelli, Paola, 'Exemplaires d'ouvrages publiés par Antoine Vérard dans les bibliothèques turinoises', *Le Moyen Français*, 69 (2011), 15–34

Macfarlane, John, *Antoine Vérard*, Illustrated Monographs, 7 (London: Bibliographical Society at the Chiswick Press, 1899 [1900]), p. 121, no. 275

Introduction

This *pas d'armes* took place at the castle of Sandricourt, situated *c.*50 km north of Paris, a site which is no longer extant but was located near the present-day commune of Amblainville.[1] The event took place over five days (16–20 September 1493) after having been publicised as *articles* (chapters of arms) a few weeks earlier around various French cities and towns; it was 'cried', for example, at Paris on 24 August. The chief *entrepreneur* of the *pas* was Louis de Hédouville, lord of Sandricourt, a trusted councillor and courtier of King Charles VIII of France; he defended it at the head of a team of ten knights that included his younger brother, Jean de Hédouville, lord of Frémécourt. The competitors, some forty in number, who accepted the Hédouvilles' challenge were mostly from the surrounding areas

[1] Dép. Oise, rég. Hauts-de-France.

of northern France, with a particularly large and important contingent from Normandy. The challengers were organised for the most part into three teams of ten men each; these were led, respectively, by Jacques de Coligny, lord of Châtillon and Andelot, André de Valois, and Antoine Martel, lord of Beaumont. Another eleven competitors were unaffiliated to a specific group.

The event comprised four different *emprises* which took place at different locations in the environs of Sandricourt that were given names highly evocative of Arthurian romance. The first *emprise* was a foot combat involving spears and swords that pitted the defenders against each of the teams of challengers in turn; it was held at the *barrière périlleuse* (Perilous Barrier) just outside the castle gatehouse. The second *emprise* was a *mêlée** (also termed in the text as a *combat à la foule*) on horseback involving lances and swords which likewise saw the defenders take on each of the teams of challengers one after the other; it was located at the *carrefour ténébreux* (Tenebrous Crossroads), situated slightly further outside the castle precinct where there was an enclosed space called the *clos/champ de l'épine* (Field of Thorn). The third *emprise* was a joust* in open field (also known as a tiltless joust) that comprised a series of single combats between defenders and challengers from different teams, each of which consisted of one course of the lance and thirteen strokes with the sword; this also took place in the Field of Thorn at the Tenebrous Crossroads. The fourth and final *emprise* was an innovative event in which competitors set out on an individual quest, in the manner of Arthurian knights-errant, in order to seek adventure against whomsoever they should encounter, be it on horseback or on foot, as they wandered through the *forêt dévoyable* (literally, Pathless Forest, but more evocatively translated here as the Labyrinthine Forest), which was well outside the castle. Permission to hold the *pas* had been sought by the *entrepreneur*, Louis de Hédouville, from Charles VIII, who also gave him some money towards his expenses. The event was indeed very costly to stage, given the large number of competitors who came to take part in it as well as the great retinues of gentlemen and ladies who attended as spectators.

Unlike the authors of other narrative accounts of *pas d'armes*, such as the *Pas du Perron Fée* (Bruges, 1463) and that at Carignano (1504), who were probably heralds even if they did not make this explicit, possibly out of modesty, the author of the *Pas des armes de Sandricourt* immediately identifies himself as Orléans Herald, an officer of arms in the employ of Louis, duke of Orléans, the later Louis XII.[2] This figure uses both the first-person voice to introduce himself as the author at the beginning of his narrative and to express his appreciation of the deeds that he witnessed and the third-person voice to refer to his own role in the organisation of the *pas*. Orléans Herald's account of the *Pas des armes de Sandricourt* is extant in several manuscripts but, most unusually, the earliest extant version of it was published shortly after the event itself, probably by Antoine Vérard, the famous Parisian printer and publisher.[3] One unillustrated paper copy of this edition survives,[4] as do two illustrated copies on vellum,[5] these costly and prestigious examples attesting to

[2] See Essay 4, p. 443, where it suggests that Orléans Herald is likely to have compiled his text from different sources written at different times; for example, the articles publicising the event that he incorporates into his narrative naturally preceded the tournament itself.

[3] For a fuller discussion of the manuscript and printed tradition of the narrative accounts of the *Pas des armes de Sandricourt*, see *ibid.*, pp. 439–44.

[4] Turin, Biblioteca Nazionale Universitaria, Ris. 24.26; in-folio, eleven fols.

[5] Paris, BnF, Vélins 1033 and Vélins 1034; in-folio, thirteen fols.

the probable involvement of Vérard. Each of these two copies has ten miniatures,[6] which were probably produced around the same time but by different artists; hence, there are some slight differences between the two cycles. The earliest surviving manuscript copy of Orléans Herald's account of the *pas* dates from around ten years later than the event itself.[7] Its account differs from that of the early printed edition in being fuller at the beginning but less detailed at the end. Its cycle of nine images[8] follows that of Vélins 1034 closely but for two modifications: the first image comes before rather than after the introduction to the text and it lacks the miniature of the scene where refreshments are offered to the knights taking part in the Labyrinthine Forest *emprise*.[9] More than twenty years later still, another manuscript copy was produced;[10] this is modelled on Arsenal 3958 for both its text and images except for the fact that it has only eight miniatures,[11] since it omits the one devoted to the competitors returning to the castle of Sandricourt after the end of their combats in the Labyrinthine Forest.[12]

Orléans Herald's narrative is in prose and recounts each *emprise* in detail, noting who gave of their best in the various encounters but without mentioning any prize-giving ceremonies. It lists all the members of the various teams as well as the officiating judges, with the early printed edition also listing some of the highest-ranking ladies who were amongst the spectators. Unusually for a narrative account of a *pas d'armes*, it goes into some detail on the practicalities involved, specifying the costs per day that the *entrepreneur* incurred, noting the names of various high-status non-competitors who helped with the organisation and logistics, mentioning the large number of craftsmen who were on hand to help with repairs to arms and armour and referring to the surgeons and apothecaries who were there to deal with any injuries. It ends, however, on an explicitly Arthurian note, comparing the exploits of the nearly fifty competitors at Sandricourt to those of the finest knights of the Round Table itself.

This translation is based on the 1874 edition by Augustin Vayssière, which mostly follows the text contained in Arsenal 3958 but supplements this with details from the early printed edition that are omitted in the manuscript version, especially towards the end. Although Vayssière's edition is problematic in failing to indicate which specific source he is using at any particular point in his text, it does offer the most complete account of the *pas* and is the version most accessible to the non-specialist reader, who would otherwise have to grapple with both the philological and palaeographical challenges of the Middle French text in the early printed and manuscript copies. Corrections have been made to Vayssière's edition in the translation where it is inaccurate or diverges notably from his sources and these are explained in the footnotes. Page numbers in parentheses have been provided for ease of reference to this edition, including those pages left blank.

---

6 Fols A2r, A5v, A6r, A6v, B1r, B3v, B4r, B4v, B5r, B5v.

7 Paris, BnF Arsenal, 3958 Réserve [hereafter Arsenal 3958]; vellum, nineteen fols.

8 Fols 1v, 7r, 8r, 8v, 9v, 11v, 14r, 15r, 16r.

9 Vélins 1034, fol. B4v.

10 Paris, BnF, fr. 1436; paper, fols 108r–125r.

11 Fols 107v, 113r, 114r, 114v, 115v, 117v, 121r, 122v.

12 Vélins 1034, fol. B5v; Arsenal 3958, fol. 16r.

TRANSLATION

(3) These are the deeds of arms and martial feats performed and accomplished at the castle of Sandricourt, near Pontoise, on the sixteenth day of September in the year 1493, as witnessed by me, Orléans, herald of my lord the duke of Orléans,[13] along with the officers of arms of the king,[14] our lord. They have been compiled and written up truthfully, as has been seen and clearly demonstrated to all, according to the content of the articles[15] and the accomplishment of the feats of arms fully detailed here below. What has most led me to want to take up my pen in order to describe and publish these feats of arms is the noble enterprise and praiseworthy prowess which I know to have so enriched the noble hearts of those Frenchmen whose wish it was to undertake and complete this event — with its many (4) fine and chivalrous deeds — that was held at the castle of Sandricourt. This was in order to benefit not only themselves but also others who might draw from their example, turning their backs on a life of idleness — this being the source of all vice — in the knowledge that idleness, the enemy of virtue, often feminises virile hearts and no worse plight can befall a kingdom than to let its nobles fritter away their time in frivolous pursuits, especially in this Most Christian[16] kingdom of France where chivalry has flowered so fully that its fame has spread to all seven climes[17] of the world. In order to accomplish these deeds of arms, ten young noblemen came together and put themselves forward at this place of Sandricourt: they, for the love of the ladies and in their desire to spread a high degree of honour through the wandering paths of glorious renown, have undertaken and brought to completion these feats of arms which are outlined and detailed here below.

(5) **Here follow the articles of the tournament at Sandricourt**

Because any heart desirous of praise which, in the name of honour, longs above all things to please the ladies and wishes to savour every last drop of the infinite treasures of good renown, must submit his will and seek to bring about the ladies' pleasure, like one at the fountain from which all perfection of valour springs and flows, so it is (6) that at the castle

---

[13] Orléans Herald: no information is available on the identity of the person holding this office in 1493. However, Pierre Le Liassier, who had previously been Coucy, pursuivant to Marie of Cleves, duchess of Orléans, did perform this role in 1484 and may possibly have still been the office-holder at the time of Sandricourt. Le Liassier is mentioned in a receipt of 16 September 1484 regarding the painting of a shield for Louis, duke of Orléans, who participated in Claude de Vaudrey's *Pas du Chevalier au Souci* that had taken place a few weeks earlier. J. B. A. G. Joursanvault, *Catalogue analytique des archives de M. le baron de Joursanvault, contenant une précieuse collection de manuscrits, chartes et documens* [sic] *originaux au nombre de plus de quatre-vingt mille …*, 2 vols (Paris: J. Techener, 1838), vol. 1, p. 105.

[14] Charles VIII (1470–98), son of Louis XI, was king of France from 1483 to 1498.

[15] See above, p. 258.

[16] This way of styling the French king and hence the kingdom as 'Très Chrétien' (Most Christian), from the Latin *Rex Christianissimus*, came from the view that, due to the long association of the Franks and the Catholic Church, the French king had a special role as protector of the Church; this became an hereditary and exclusive title from the late fourteenth century onwards. Graeme Small, *Late Medieval France* (Basingstoke: Palgrave Macmillan, 2009), pp. 8–19.

[17] The medieval idea of the world being divided into seven different zones on the basis of their climates was inherited from classical antiquity. D. A. Shcheglov, 'Ptolemy's System of Seven Climata and Eratosthenes' Geography', *Geographia Antiqua*, 13 (2004/6), 21–37.

of Sandricourt, near Pontoise, there were so many excellent and accomplished ladies that the very best of the finest and most beautiful were residing there. These ladies, wishing to lead and enable these men ennobled with virtuous habits to attain ever higher glory, like mothers and nursemaids of the flower of chivalry, gave birth some time ago to ten young knights who, from their youth, were given the safekeeping of the castle.[18] There they spent their time performing deeds of arms, as in the days of old in this very place did the knights-errant who, for all time, kept up this worthy custom which is that no one should pass close by this place without performing feats of arms and testing himself against them and that no one might enter this castle without first pitting his body and his skill at arms, as the extraordinary beauty and incomparable goodness of these ladies so requires, this being the sovereign good that the eye can behold or the tongue demand. These knights took up the defence of these ladies and, at their request, in order to profit from their upbringing and so increase their worth, with the help of God and as service to them, were (7) determined to perform and accomplish the articles that follow, point for point.

First of all:

These knights being in the castle of Sandricourt in order to keep guard over it undertook together to assemble at the Perilous Barrier of this place, as was the custom, where none might approach without risk. There they found themselves on the fifteenth day of September,[19] on foot and armed, as was only proper, or as each man thought for the best, his sharp-edged sword*[20] at his side, his spear* with sharpened tip in his hand, in order to defend this Perilous Barrier against the first ten knights or others who, for the purpose of combat, wished to present themselves at the [castle] entrance. The defenders were committed to providing spears and swords of the kinds mentioned above and would fight the ten gentlemen, each team on its own side of the barrier, for as long as it pleased the ladies and the judges who would then stop them.[21]

The following day, the defenders, mounted (8) and armed, would come out of the castle at the sound of a horn, their lances with sharpened tips on their thighs and their swords at their sides, in order to face the first ten competitors who wished to present themselves so as to respect the custom of the castle. There they would undertake to fight each other freely[22] at the Tenebrous Crossroads,[23] with this combat going on for as long as the ladies and the

[18] The opening sentences of this section are a somewhat awkward mix of the actual (the setting of Sandricourt) and the allegorical (the ladies as both inspiring and nurturing male chivalric prowess).

[19] Although the articles as preserved in both the early printed edition and Arsenal 3958 give the opening date of the event as 15 September, which PSt replicates here, the *pas* did not in fact start until the following day, as the text itself indicates elsewhere three times (see above, p. 261, and below, p. 269 (twice)).

[20] PSt frequently describes the swords used at Sandricourt as *espées tranchantes* (sharp-edged swords, simplified hereafter in the translation to just 'swords' for the sake of brevity), whereas the early printed edition also tends to specify that they were *sans estoc*, that is, without thrusting points.

[21] Note the particular insistence throughout this text on the ladies' instrumental role in assisting the judges.

[22] The rules of engagement allowed here for a *mêlée* but, in actual fact, the part with lances proved so dangerous for the horses after the defenders fought the first team of challengers that, for the subsequent bouts against the second and third teams of challengers, the competitors were made to joust with lances one-on-one and could only fight as a group with swords thereafter: see below, pp. 271–2.

[23] That is, in the Field of Thorn, the enclosed space at the Tenebrous Crossroads, as the text later makes clear: see below, p. 264.

judges would see fit, before making them stop. He who killed the horse of his companion* with his lance would be taken by the heralds out of the lists and would not be allowed to continue fighting on that day, unless the ladies permitted it. If, in the heat of battle, one of the competitors were to lose his sword, he would be obliged forthwith by the heralds to give a gold ring to the one who disarmed him, which was to be presented to his lady, this ring to be of the value of 100 *écus*[24] or more.

Item, for the two days following, the defenders would come out of the place at the sounding of a horn and would gather at the Field of Thorn in order to fight in single combat against all those who wished to attend for these two days and perform feats of arms. This single combat would consist of one course of the lance with sharpened (9) tips and thirteen strokes of the sword; in this way, the risk of injury to the horses would be reduced.

If it should so happen during this combat that one of the gentlemen, whichever side he might be on, should lose his sword or be disarmed of any other piece of his harness* such that he could not complete this number of strokes, he would be obliged, before he could rearm and continue to fight, to make a present — through the intermediary of a herald — of 1000 *écus*[25] or more to the one who had disarmed him.

Item, all those who came to fight, from the beginning to the end of the event, would be presented with a choice of spears, lances and swords from which to choose to do combat.

Item, after the emblazoned shields of the gentlemen of the inside* team had been hung up over the gatehouse of the place, all those who wished to fight would come, either on foot or on horseback, and be obliged, before they could begin fighting, to have a herald bring their emblazoned shields for hanging up there; if they failed to do this, they would not be allowed to fight.

(10) Item, after the four days had passed, the noblemen of the castle, by the commandment of their mistresses[26] whose wishes they were performing by their noble exercise of the pursuit of arms, would head towards the Labyrinthine Forest where they had been instructed to seek and find adventures, and would be armed and mounted ready to go off on their wanderings. All knights and squires who wished to undertake an adventurous quest in this forest would be obliged, before entering it, to take lances and swords from the green pine in front of the castle of Sandricourt which would be given out to them in the manner described above. This quest would only take place on the one day. The aforesaid gentlemen would then be obliged to make their way to the dinner held on the following day inside the castle of Sandricourt. There, in the presence of the ladies and the judges, they would recount in good faith and on their honour the truth of what they had found and done during their quest in order that they might submit everything to the will and judgement of the ladies in this matter, since it is to them that the praise for all titles of honour rightfully belongs.[27]

---

[24] In the 1490s, the French golden *écu au soleil* was worth 1lb. 16s. 3d. *livres tournois*, so this means that 100 *écus* are worth 181lb. 5s. *livres tournois*. Peter Spufford, *Handbook of Medieval Exchange* (London: Offices of the Royal Historical Society, 1986), p. 193.

[25] This is the equivalent of 1812lb. 10s. *livres tournois*. *Ibid.*

[26] The term *maistresse* (mistress) is to be understood here as meaning the particular lady to whom a knight is devoted in the manner of a courtly lover.

[27] Although this is not clearly indicated in either PSt or Arsenal 3958, the articles concerning the rules of the *pas* end here and the next paragraph signals the start of Orléans Herald's actual account of the event; this is more visible in the early printed edition, where his account begins with a painted capital letter (Vélins 1033/1034, fol. A3r).

In order to take up arms and organise (11) this tournament, the ten gentlemen of the castle, who did not wish to begin anything with which fault might be found, went to see the king at Bois-Malesherbes[28] in order to obtain his permission, making their supplication and request so that these feats of arms might be amplified and knighthood itself exalted through having obtained his approval to hold them.

This supplication made, the king, after lengthy consideration with his council, gave these ten gentlemen leave to organise the tournament according to their intentions and in the manner described above. Furthermore, the king allowed them to publicise the event around all the towns, cities and places of the kingdom of France and wherever else it pleased them to do so.

After this permission had been granted, the ten gentlemen went to Paris, capital of the kingdom of France. There, on the twenty-fourth day of the month of August 1493, they had a trumpet sound at all the crossroads of the city of Paris, in order to proclaim the tournament. They let it be known that, on behalf of the king, all knights, squires, gentlemen, captains and other military leaders who wished to present themselves at this event at (12) the castle of Sandricourt, where the ten gentlemen defending the *pas* would await all comers wishing to fight on both foot and horseback in the places and spaces detailed hereafter, would be honourably received and warmly welcomed. The tournament would begin on the fifteenth day of the following month of September and, in the meantime, those who wished or intended to perform deeds of arms and to attend this event should arm and equip themselves properly in the way that they saw fit. Their shields emblazoned with their coat of arms should be sent by a herald to be hung up on the gatehouse of the castle of Sandricourt, as those of the ten gentlemen defending the *pas* had already been.

This event was publicised in numerous other towns and places in the kingdom of France and announced so widely that, on the fifteenth day of that month of September, so many noblemen had arrived to fight at the castle of Sandricourt that never before was anywhere so enhanced by the presence of so many excellent knights for the purposes of a tournament. There were also a huge number of ladies and damsels possessed of such extraordinary beauty that the splendour of their faces (13) lit up the entire region. Judges were appointed at the event to assess the encounters, uphold everyone's rights and do justice to them according to their deserts.

The first location set up for fighting was the Perilous Barrier, which was situated in front of the castle of Sandricourt. The only type of combat permitted was on foot, with spears for thrusting hard and swords for cutting fiercely. The rule was that the fighting should keep going for as long as the ladies and the judges there present chose before making the contestants stop.

The second location set up for fighting, [this time] on horseback in a *mêlée*, was the Tenebrous Crossroads, where the Field of Thorn was fenced off, itself enclosed by great wooden stands that the gentlemen-defenders had had built. At the two ends of the field were pavilions and tents a-plenty comprising great halls, chambers, kitchens and stables

[28] [Boys-Malezerbes]. Bois-Malesherbes, in the Loiret, was built in the fourteenth century by Jean de Montagu and eventually came into the possession of the admiral of France, Louis Malet de Graville (1438–1516). Charles VIII's presence at this residence, termed 'Le Malesherbois', is attested for 1 August 1493: *Itinéraire de Charles: Les lieux de séjour du roi (1483–1498)*, Paris, Cour de France.fr, 2020, Données publiées par Boris Bove d'après l'itinéraire édité par E. Petit <https://cour-de-france.fr/article5776.html> [accessed 20 June 2024].

that provided everything the challengers and others would need. Each of the ten knights had his own pavilion and tent in which to arm and disarm himself and to mount his horse. All those who chose to make their way there were handsomely entertained. When it was time for the fighting to start, these knights (14) came out of their pavilions, mounted and armed in order to do combat against all comers at the Tenebrous Crossroads or any of the other authorised locations.

Item, in the middle of the Field of Thorn were two great stands that faced each other on opposite sides of the area. The judges were in one of the stands, along with a number of great lords and other captains and military leaders; this was to watch the contestants, adjudicate the rights of each one according to his merits and also separate them when it was time to do so. In the other stand were the ladies and damsels in such great numbers that never before that time in France had such a magnificent gathering been so embellished by the female sex. They were there to watch the *mêlée*[29] and to give their own opinion on it in due course.

The Field of Thorn was the third location set up for fighting on horseback, this time in single combat, and it was where the ten knights defending the *pas* would take on all comers from morning until evening.

The fourth and final location appointed for performing feats of arms was the Labyrinthine Forest. Gathered there were all those of the inside team in order to do combat (15) against all those comers from the outside*; this was in the manner of knights-errant seeking their adventures in the forest, just as the Knights of the Round Table had done in the past. Before they were allowed to enter the forest, all the knights had to go over to the green pine in order to pick up lances and swords that were all of the same size. Once this was done, they went off into the forest to fight on both foot and horseback, each to the best of his ability; there they could fight *à outrance** since there were no judges to separate them.

At this tournament was a gentleman named Robinet de Framezelle,[30] who was the duke of Orléans's lieutenant in charge of a hundred lances.[31] With the help of the officers of arms, he was responsible for handing out the lances and swords to the competitors; he acquitted himself of this task so well that he earned honour and praise for it. Another man, named Claude de Rabodanges, lord of Thun[32] and captain of the bridge

---

[29] Whilst PSt, p. 14, refers to this combat here as a 'tournoy' (tourney*), either as a generic term for 'tournament' (as it does below, p. 276) or as a synonym for *mêlée*, the early printed edition (Vélins 1033/1034, fol. A4r) is more precise in explaining that this refers to the fight 'a la foulle'; hence this has been followed in the translation here.

[30] [Robinet de Framezelles]. Robinet de Framezelle, lord of Framezelle and Frane, was a councillor-chamberlain of Louis of Orléans, his bailiff of Sézanne and captain of a hundred lances. René Botto, *L'Isle-Adam et sa région au temps des tournois, 1493 et 1519* (L'Isle-Adam: Les amis de l'Isle-Adam, 2007), p. 96; JdA, vol. 4, p. 473; Joël Blanchard, ed., *Mémoires de Philippe de Commynes*, 2 vols (Geneva: Droz, 2007), vol. 2, p. 1283.

[31] A military company in this period often comprised a hundred lances; a lance was the smallest organisational unit in a medieval army, consisting of six to nine men including a heavily armoured man-at-arms and a group of several others who saw to his needs; these could include a mounted page, an armed servant, up to three mounted archers, a crossbowman, a handgunner and a pikeman on foot. Malcolm Vale, *War and Chivalry: Warfare and Aristocratic Culture in England, France and Burgundy at the End of the Middle Ages* (London: Duckworth and Co., 1981), p. 124.

[32] [Glaude de Rabodanges] Claude de Rabodanges (d. 1514), lord of Thun, Vaux-la-Reine and Palaiseau, was a councillor-chamberlain of Charles VIII, a squire of the duchess of Orléans, Marie

of Meulan,[33] also conducted himself very well and took a great deal of trouble on behalf of those on both the inside and the outside teams. Notable services were also performed for those on the inside team by a gentleman named Bernard de Villeneuve,[34] a squire of the (16) stables of our lord, the king; amongst others, he gave particularly good service to the lord of Méry[35] at this event. Young Camican[36] was another who likewise went to great lengths, his role being to serve his brother[37] as well as the other knight-defenders of the *pas*.

On the twelfth day of September, in the above-mentioned year, the shields of the ten gentlemen whose names are listed hereafter were presented to Orléans Herald[38] to be hung up at the gatehouse of the castle of Sandricourt; he duly put them up on that same day. These gentlemen, members of the team led by the lord of Châtillon, were: Jacques de Coligny, lord of Châtillon and Andelot;[39] Gaspard de Coligny, his brother;[40] the lord of Monsures;[41] Jean de Saint-Amadour;[42] Claude de Massabeau;[43] Louis de Rochefort;[44]

---

of Cleves, and captain of the Château-de-l'Oeuf in the Italian wars in 1495. JdA, vol. 1, p. 259; PPR, p. 1057.

33 This was a very important medieval bridge over the River Seine that was destroyed in the Allied bombing of France in May 1944. PSt takes this detail about Rabodanges's role as captain of the bridge of Meulan from the early printed edition (Vélins 1033/1034, fol. A4v), as it is not in Arsenal 3958 (fol. 5v).

34 [Bernard de Villeneufve]. Bernard de Villeneuve was a squire of the stables (*écuyer d'écurie*, sometimes also translated as 'equerry'), *valet de chambre* (1496) and a chamberlain of Charles VIII; he was later a *valet de chambre* of Louis XII (1499–1512). CdF, nos 2742, 2889, 3103; Yvonne Labande-Mailfert, *Charles VIII et son milieu (1470–1498). La jeunesse au pouvoir* (Paris: Klincksieck, 1974), p. 615.

35 See below, n. 94.

36 [le jeune Camican]. Bernard de Cassaignet, lord of Camican, was a squire of the stables of Charles VIII (1484–98), governor of Armagnac and provost of the marshals. CdF no. 2752; JdA, vol. 4, p. 449.

37 See below, n. 93.

38 See above, introduction, on how the author refers to himself in his text in both the first- and the third-person voice.

39 [Jacques de Colligny, seigneur de Chastillon & d'Andelot]. Jacques de Coligny (b. after 1467–1512), lord of Châtillon and Andelot, was a chamberlain of Charles VIII and captain of a hundred men-at-arms (1494); he also led a company of thirty lances for Louis XII in the Italian wars and became provost of Paris (1509). DBF, vol. 9, p. 226; JdA, vol. 4, p. 457; PPR, p. 1227.

40 [Gaspar de Colligny]. Gaspard I de Coligny (*c.*1465/70–1522), known as lord of Fromentes in his youth, was lieutenant of the company of the duke of Nemours (1501), marshal of France (1516), a member of the Order of St Michael (1517), and very active in the Italian wars. DBF, vol. 9, p. 222; GDH, vol. 1, p. 935; HMF, vol. 7, pp. 143–4; JdA, vol. 4, p. 457.

41 [le seigneur de Mousseures]. The Monsures were an old family from Picardy; the lord of Monsures referred to here may be Raoulquin/Raoul de Monsures (d. 1505), squire and lord of Guémicourt, Valalet, Luzières, Bohavost, Sainte-Segrée and Le Quint de Monsures <http://racineshistoire.free.fr/LGN/PDF/Monsures.pdf> [accessed 20 June 2024]. However, it could also be Josse de Gourlay, lord of Monsures, married to Jeanne Mauchevalier (see below, n. 117) who, after Josse's death, took a second husband, Jean de Halluin, in 1506. HMF, vol. 3, p. 914, para. D. He had fought in the outside team at the tourney that followed the jousts in the *Pas de l'Arbre d'or* (Bruges, 1468).

42 [Jehan de Sainct-Amadour]. Jean de Saint-Amadour, lord of Touaré and La Ragotière and viscount of Guignen, was a *valet de chambre* of Charles VIII (1496), captain of the infantry of Languedoc, and a pensioner of the queen, Anne of Brittany. CdF no. 2893; JdA, vol. 4, p. 532.

43 No information is available about him.

44 This Louis de Rochefort (d. 1563), of an old family from the duchy of Burgundy, was the son of Guy de Rochefort (d. 1507), who was chancellor of France (1497–1507), and his wife, Marie Chambellan,

Jacques de Bloc;[45] Jacques de Chabannes;[46] (17) Jacques de Lay;[47] and Germain de La Roque, known as Le Boeuf.[48] These were the first competitors to fight at the Perilous Barrier against those from the inside defending the *pas*, whose names will be listed here below.

On that same day, the shields of another ten gentlemen, those belonging to the Valois[49] team, were presented to Orléans Herald. These were: Guyot du Bus;[50] Jacques de Silly;[51] Jacques de Yverlay;[52] François de Théligny;[53] Guillaume de Saulx;[54] Monseigneur du Val;[55]

---

daughter of Henri Chambellan, who was receiver-general of finance in Burgundy. Botto, *L'Isle-Adam*, p. 96; GDH, vol. 6, p. 544.

45 No information is available on Jacques de Bloc but a Catherine de Bloc, lady of Eure, who may have been a sister of his, was a *dame d'honneur* in the household of Anne of Brittany (1494). CdF no. 2.

46 Both the early printed edition and Arsenal 3958 give this figure's name here as 'Ja(c)ques de Chabanolles' and refer to him later on as just 'Chabanolles' when he fights in the seventeenth course at the Field of Thorn against the lord of Clermont (Vélins 1033/1034, fols A4v and B3r, respectively; Arsenal 3958, fols 6r and 13v, respectively). There is little information available about him other than that he was lord of Chabanolles and was born *c.*1460. PSt diverges from these two sources in giving the name here as 'Jacques de Chabannes', this being the much better-known Jacques II de Chabannes (*c.*1470–1525, battle of Pavia), lord of La Palice and Pacy, who was an *enfant d'honneur* in the household of Charles VIII (1484–98), accompanied him in his war with Brittany (1486) and was heavily involved in the Italian wars for both Charles and Louis XII, becoming *grand maître de France* (1511) and later marshal of France (1515). CdF no. 2758; DBF, vol. 8, pp. 1001–2; DN, vol. 4, pp. 948–9; GDH, vol. 1, p. 681. PSt (p. 44) does later follow the early printed and manuscript sources by referring to a 'Chabanolles' in the combat at the Field of Thorn, but as if this was a completely different person from the Jacques de Chabannes named earlier (see below, n. 103).

47 A Jacques de Laye, of an old family from the Beaujolais region of Franche-Comté, was the son of Amé de Laye, lord of Meximieux; a sister of his, Françoise, was married in 1527. DN, vol. 11, p. 817.

48 [Germain de la Rocque, dit Le Beuf]. Germain de La Roque: no information is available on him but this family was from the county of Armagnac; Armand de La Roque, lord of La Roque, a squire who, in 1469, received rent for life of 100 *livres tournois* from Jean, count of Armagnac, for twenty-five years of service, may have been his father. DN, vol. 17, p. 614.

49 See below, n. 56.

50 [Guy du Bus]. Guyot du Bus, lord of Tison, married Anne de Cullant, a *fille d'honneur* in the household of Anne of Brittany (1496–98), on 19 September 1508. CdF no. 199; HMF, vol. 7, p. 83, para. B.

51 Jacques de Silly (d. 1503), lord of Lonray, Vaux and Pacey, was bailiff of the castle of Caen (1491), *maître d'hôtel* (1493) and a councillor-chamberlain of Charles VIII (1495); he was also captain of fifty lances and master of the king's artillery at Capaua in 1501. Botto, *L'Isle-Adam*, p. 93; CdF no. 2624; JdA, vol. 4, p. 541.

52 Jacques de Yverlay: no information is available about him, but his name may be a mistranscription of Yversay (dép. Vienne, rég. Nouvelle-Aquitaine), or of Giverlay, a Jacques de Giverlay, lord of Villebrosse, being a cupbearer of Francis I. CdF, no. 4189.

53 François de Théligny (d. 1523), lord of Lierville, was a *valet tranchant* and councillor-chamberlain of Louis XII (1499–1512), a pantler* of Francis I, and seneschal of Rouergue (1505–22). CdF nos 3012, 4104.

54 This Guillaume de Saulx, a member of an old family from near Dijon in the duchy of Burgundy, may have been the son of Guyard de Saulx, lord of Arc-sur-Tille, and Ève de Ligneville; his uncle, Érard de Saulx (d. 1477) was married to Antoinette de Dinteville (d. 1516). GDH, vol. 6, p. 116.

55 [Monseigneur du Val]. A Jacques du Val, knight and lord of Le Val, Gonnonville en Auge, Salles and Verneuil, had a grandson, Jean du Val, who was still alive in 1575. DN, vol 19, p. 364.

André de Valois;[56] Thomas de May;[57] Champoullet;[58] and Salenove.[59] These men fought on the second day at the Perilous Barrier against those from the inside defending the *pas*.

(18) That same day came a herald of my lord the king, named Touraine,[60] who presented to the above-named Orléans Herald the shields of ten gentlemen of the team led by the lord of Beaumont, whose names are as follows: Antoine Martel, lord of Beaumont;[61] Louis de Biguars, lord of La Londe;[62] Jean de Feschal, lord of Le Grippon, known as Marboué;[63] Jean de Rouville;[64] the lord of Bonnetot;[65] Jean Picart, lord of Radeval;[66] René Parent, *vicomte* of Rouen;[67] Jean de Manneville, lord of that place;[68]

---

[56] [Andri de Valloys]. No information is available about him.

[57] No information is available about him, but his name may be a mistranscription of Moÿ or Mouy. This family, members of whom were lords of Mailleraye, now known as La Mailleraye-sur-Seine (dép. Seine-Maritime in Normandy), intermarried with other families represented at Sandricourt such as the Hangest and the Villiers. HMF, vol. 5, p. 609, para. D; vol. 6, p. 747, para. A; vol. 7, pp. 13, para. C, 62, para. D, 132, para. A.

[58] No information is available about him.

[59] See below, n. 97.

[60] [Thoraine]. Touraine Herald: no information is available on the identity of the person holding this office in 1493.

[61] [Anthoine Martel, seigneur de Beaumont]. Antoine Martel (d. 1518), lord of Anglesqueville and later also of Bacqueville, commanded a vessel under his uncle, the admiral Louis Malet de Graville, in 1496. GDH, vol. 4, p. 924; HMF, vol. 8, p. 211. Neither of these sources mentions that he was lord of Beaumont.

[62] [Louis de Biguars, seigneur de La Londe]. Louis de Bigars, lord of Commin and Tourville, who became lord of La Londe after his half-brother, Jacques de Bigars, died without heirs, was captain of 2000 infantry and fifty lances and governor of Aversa. DN, vol. 3, pp. 219–20; JdA, vol. 4, p. 438.

[63] [Jehan de Feschal, seigneur du Grippon, dit Ma(r)bone]. Jean de Feschal, named as lord of Le Grippon in a charter dated 1490 (Paris, BnF, fr. 4901, fols 149r–154r), was also lord of Poligné (1527), a councillor-chamberlain of Louis XII, and bailiff and governor of Caen (1503); he was married to Claude de Silly, daughter of Jacques de Silly, who was also present at Sandricourt (see above, n. 51). Jean's father, René de Feschal, was also lord of Marboué, hence Jean's alternative title as given here in the text. HMF, vol. 8, p. 170, para. C.

[64] [Jehan de Rouville]. Jean de Rouville inherited his title of lord of Léry from his brother, Pierre (d. 1508). HMF, vol. 8, p. 711, para. A.

[65] [seigneur de Bouvetot]. This may be Jacques d'Ossencourt/Ochencourt, lord of Bonnetot, who was captain of infantry for Louis XII. JdA, vol. 4, p. 514.

[66] [Jehan Picart, seigneur de Radeval]. Jean Picart (d. 1523), lord of Radeval and Neubosc, also known as Picart the bailiff (of Estellan), son of Guillaume Picart, lord of Estellan and grandmaster of artillery, was a councillor and *maître d'hôtel* of Francis I. Botto, *L'Isle-Adam*, p. 93; CdF no. 4009; JdA, vol. 4, p. 519.

[67] René Parent, knight, councillor and *maître d'hôtel* of Louis XII, was 'vicomte *de l'eau* de Rouen', responsible for overseeing trade along the part of the River Seine that flowed through this town. Guillaume Bureaux, 'Union et désunion de la noblesse en parade. Le rôle des Pas d'armes dans l'entretien des rivalités chevaleresques entre cours princières occidentales, XVe–XVIe siècles (Anjou, Bourgogne, France, Saint-Empire)' (unpublished PhD dissertation, Normandie Université, 2018), p. 379, n. 1063; François Farin and Ignace du Soullet, *Histoire de la ville de Rouen*, 3 vols (Rouen: Du Souillet, 1738), vol. 1, p. 127 (which lists Parent in this role for 1506).

[68] [Jehan de Maneville]. This may be Jean IV de Hautemer, lord of Le Fournet and Fervaques, living in 1470, who was the great-grandson of Gérard de Hautemer, lord of Le Fournet, Le Mesnil-Tison and Manneville, who had divided up his estate between his wife and three children in 1414. HMF, vol. 7, p. 394, para. C.

Christophe d'Ymerville;[69] and the bastard of Girême.[70] These men fought on the third day at the Perilous Barrier against the defenders.

Charles de Campanes[71] had his shield presented on that day to Orléans Herald, along with the others whose names are as follows: (19) François de Sassenage;[72] Adrien de Genlis, lord of Abecourt;[73] Jacques de Marcillac;[74] Méry de Thibuvillier, known as Montault;[75] Jean de Vignolles;[76] Claude, bastard of Lentilhac;[77] Gilles de Compincourt;[78] and Guillaume de Méry,[79] *maréchal des logis* of my lord of Orléans.[80] These men fought at the Field of Thorn and in the Labyrinthine Forest, as will be recounted hereafter.

On the Monday, the sixteenth day of the month, two shields were received but it was not known whose they were, as they had chosen not to say. (20 is blank)

(21) That day, on the sixteenth of September, as had been arranged, on the stroke of ten o'clock in the morning the first combat took place at the Perilous Barrier of the castle of Sandricourt. The ten knight-defenders of the *pas*, all armed with their spears in their hands

69 [Christofle d'Ymerville]. No information is available about him.

70 [le bastard de Giresme]. Two members of this family, Guyot de Girême, who married Jacquette du Plessis (1451), and Renaud de Girême, the second husband of Jeanne Quiéret (whose father, Jacques Quiéret, died in 1470) may have been the father or even grandfather of this illegitimate scion of Girême, about whom no other information is available. HMF, vol. 4, p. 367, para. A (Guyot); vol. 7, p. 747, para. B (Renaud).

71 No information is available about him.

72 François de Sassenage, lord du Pont, son of Jacques de Sassenage and Jeanne de Commiers, was from the Dauphiné and served with the famous Chevalier Bayard in the War of the League of Cambrai (February 1508–December 1516); both he and Bayard were taken to England as prisoners following the Battle of the Spurs/Second Battle of Guinegatte (16 August 1513) in which the French lost to the Anglo-German forces. GDH, vol. 6, p. 108.

73 [Adrian de Jenly, seigneur d'Abecourt]. Adrien de Hangest, lord of Genlis, was an *enfant d'honneur* in the household of Charles VIII, a councillor-chamberlain of his and then a cupbearer (1520) and *gentilhomme de chambre* (1529) of Francis I. Botto, *L'Isle-Adam*, p. 95; CdF nos 2756, 3926, 4187; DBF, vol. 17, p. 576. His father, Jean III de Hangest, lord of Genlis, Abecourt and Magny, was bailiff of Évreux and a councillor-chamberlain of Charles VII. HMF, vol. 6, pp. 746–7.

74 [Jaques de Marcyllac]. Jacques de Marcillac: no information is available about him, but the lordship of Marcillac passed into the La Rochefoucauld family in the fifteenth century. DN, vol. 13, p. 187. François I, count of La Rochefoucauld, was lord of Marcillac at the time of the *pas* at Sandricourt. DN, vol. 17, pp. 348–9.

75 [Mery de Thibuvillier, dit Montault]. No information is available about him, but his name may be a mistranscription of Thibouville (dép. Eure in Normandy); a genealogy of the Montault family reveals no connection with him. HMF, vol. 7, pp. 603–5.

76 [Jehan de Vignolles]. Jean de Vignolles was a councillor of Louis XI. PPR, p. 1282.

77 [Claude, bastard de Lentillac/Lantillac]. Claude de Lentilhac, illegitimate son of Déodat/Dieudonné II de Lentilhac, lord of Lentilhac, who married Catherine de Vigier, was a man-at-arms in a company of fifty lances under the orders of Charles VIII that was led by Jean de Polignac, lord of Beaumont, in 1489. AGHNF, vol. 8, pp. 28–9 of the dossier 'De Lentilhac'.

78 No information is available about him.

79 This may be the 'Guillaume de Merry' mentioned in a Parisian notarial document (dated 6 April 1499) as having reduced his debt of fifty *écus* owed to a certain Claude Hubert by twenty *écus* through part-payment of a ruby. Claire Béchu, Florence Greffe and Isabelle Pebay, eds, *Minutier central des notaires de Paris, Minutes du XVe siècle de l'étude XIX, inventaire analytique [5232 actes]* (Paris: Archives nationales, 1993), p. 501, notice no. 4226.

80 A *maréchal des logis* was an officer in charge of organising the quartering of troops. DMF.

and their swords at their sides, came out of the castle of Sandricourt to fight at the Perilous Barrier in front of the place. All together in good order and in a very confident manner, accompanied by a great number of ladies and damsels, trumpets and Swiss drums,[81] they marched boldly (22) up to the barrier. There stood the lord of Châtillon with those on his team, all armed and determined to attack the barrier with vigour. The fight then began on both sides with great thrusts of the spear and strokes of the sword which were so fierce that sparks flew off their harnesses with each blow. The lord of Châtillon and his men attacked the barrier with great ferocity, but it was so strenuously guarded by the defenders that no sooner did a man approach it to enter the castle than he was firmly rebuffed. Of those on the inside team defending the barrier were the lords of Saint-Vallier[82] and Clermont,[83] Georges de Sully, governor of Coucy,[84] and Jacques de Dinteville[85] who, with great strokes of the sword as were necessary, performed marvellous feats of arms. They truly needed to do this as they were up against opponents who were very determined. The combat lasted a long time as everyone was eager, at this first encounter, to honour the ladies by putting their weapons to full use. Jacques de Dinteville disarmed one of those on the outside team of his sword. They [all] dealt each other more and more blows, giving the impression that they were engaged in a battle to the death. (23) The ladies and the judges, seeing that they seemed to be heading towards fighting *à outrance*, said 'Stop!', but they were all so intent on exchanging blows that it was very difficult to get them to desist. Nonetheless, in the end, those whose responsibility it was to separate them managed to make them disengage.

(24 is blank)

(25) That same day, at around four o'clock in the afternoon, the second bout began at the Perilous Barrier. One named Valois[86] came up armed with his team to take on the defenders.

As they engaged battle, they made sparks fly on both sides and their blows resounded in the air such that it amazed the spectators. With spears thrusting and swords slashing, each man put himself to the test so skilfully that never before was such a fierce attack or such a strong defence ever seen. The fight went on for a long time (26), mostly with blows from the spear, which was quite something to witness. Among those on the inside team who proved themselves worthy of honour were the lords of Sandricourt,[87] Méry and

---

[81] Drums used by Swiss troops, which mainly consisted of dense formations of infantry armed with pikes and halberds, were renowned for setting a slower beat than those used by other armies. Oliver Landolt, 'Akustische Dimensionen in der Militärgeschichte der spätmittelalterlichen Eidgenossenschaft', *Das Mittelalter*, 27.1 (2022), 51–67 (p. 61).

[82] See below, n. 92.

[83] [seigneur de Cler(e)mont]. Bernardin de Clermont, lord of Clermont and viscount of Talart, was an *enfant d'honneur* (1484–98) and a squire of the stables (1496) of Charles VIII and then a councillor-chamberlain of Louis XII. CdF no. 2740; GDH, vol. 1, p. 905.

[84] [George(s) de Sully]. Georges de Sully (d. 1496), lord of Romefort and Cors, was governor of Coucy, bailiff of Mantes and Meulan, and governor of Taranto for Charles VIII (1495), as well as a cupbearer in his household (1496). CdF no. 2672.

[85] [Jacques de Tinteville]. Jacques de Dinteville, lord of Eschanetz, Commarien, Villiers and Maisey, was the *grand veneur* (grand huntsman) of Charles VIII in Burgundy and captain of Beaune. JdA, vol. 4, p. 464.

[86] See above, n. 56.

[87] [Louis/Loys/Louys de Hedouville]. Louis de Hédouville (*c.*1462?–1504), lord of Sandricourt, married to Françoise de Rouvroy-Saint-Simon (1475), was chief *entrepreneur* of this *pas* as well as captain

Camican;[88] of those on the outside team, the lord of Bus[89] was held in high esteem. If I wanted to give a full description of all the other competitors' fine deeds according to their merits, I would grow tired before I could reach the end. However, suffice to say that after a long fight they were made to disengage and, once this had been done, they stood around the barrier talking about various matters together.

(27) On Tuesday, the seventeenth day of the said month of September, around ten o'clock in the morning, the third combat was fought by the ten knight-defenders of the inside team at the Perilous Barrier against the lord of Beaumont with his team of gentlemen from Normandy. They made every effort to attack the Perilous Barrier and performed marvels, acting like those who are desirous of attaining honour. Nonetheless, they were met so well by those of the inside team that they were unable to cross it by force of arms. There René Parent was brought down to the ground but quickly got up again. (28) Jean de Hédouville, lord of Frémécourt,[90] of the inside team, did great deeds at this combat that were worthy of praise. Those on the outside team dealt blows in a great flurry of limbs and wasted not a single strike with either spear or sword. What more can be said, other than that, after a lengthy exchange of blows on both sides, they were separated with some difficulty by the judges and those appointed to this task!

That same day, between four and five o'clock in the afternoon, a *mêlée* was fought at the Tenebrous Crossroads between the defenders and the outside team led by the lord of Châtillon. When everyone was assembled there, the defenders came out of their tents, mounted and armed, and engaged with those of the outside team like a tempest, running at each other with such swiftness that it seemed as if the very earth were shaking under their horses' hooves. They encountered each other so fiercely that, at the moment when their lances struck home and came up against the momentum of the horses, almost all of the lances were broken and three horses fell to the ground. Indeed, one of them on the inside team was so powerfully hit and brought down that it never got up again but rather died there and then on the field. The (29) other two horses, which belonged to members of the outside team, were badly wounded. The lords of Sandricourt and Châtillon struck each other with such force that Châtillon and his horse were felled to the ground by the impact of his opponent's lance that broke against him. After this, the fight continued with swords and several of the competitors were disarmed of their weapons. Of Châtillon's team, only five were not either brought down to the ground or dispossessed of their swords. During this *mêlée*, the lords of Saint-Vallier, Clermont, Méry and Camican all performed deeds of arms that were worthy of praise. In sum, on both sides everyone displayed such feats of prowess that they have stayed firmly in the memory.

---

and bailiff of Blois, bailiff of Caux, captain of Arques, captain of a hundred lances, and a squire of the stables and *maître d'hôtel* of Charles VIII. He was also a councillor-chamberlain of Louis, duke of Orléans (1496) and took a very active part in the Italian campaigns for him when he became King Louis XII. He died at Quiers in Piedmont. CdF no. 2737; DBF, vol. 17, p. 832; JdA, vol. 4, p. 485; M. le marquis de Magny, 'De Hédouville, Ile-de-France, Picardie, Champagne', in *Troisième registre du Livre d'or de la noblesse* (Paris: Secrétariat général du collège héraldique, 1846), pp. 227–36 (especially p. 230); PSt, introduction, pp. viii–xxv.

[88] See below, n. 93.

[89] See above, n. 50.

[90] [Jehan de Hedouville, seigneur de Fremecourt]. Jean de Hédouville, lord of Frémécourt, married Charlotte de Dillon (1478). De Magny, 'De Hédouville', p. 231.

(30 is blank)

(31) On Wednesday, the eighteenth day of the same month of September, at ten o'clock in the morning, the second combat in the form of a *mêlée* took place at the Tenebrous Crossroads. However, the judges were mindful of all the dangers that might arise from this encounter — after having seen what had transpired the day before — whereby several horses might be killed or maimed and even some of the knights too, which would be an irrecoverable loss. Seeing that there were two more bouts to be fought in the *mêlée*, in which many fine and (32) determined knights would be fighting, the aforesaid lords and judges went up to Valois, leader of the first team due to compete, in order to ask and request him, with the aim of avoiding any danger, that he and his men be content not to run at each other with lances as a group but rather to proceed one against one; afterwards, they could fight with swords in a *mêlée* as had been stipulated. Valois and those on his team would not grant this request until the knights defending the *pas* had said that they were happy to abide by it. The latter were equally very unwilling to accede to this request and so Valois and his men, along with all the others who were due to fight as a group at the Tenebrous Crossroads, were eager to compete as the defenders had done against the lord of Châtillon and his team, as has been described above. Nonetheless, hearing the request and prayers of the ladies couched in many gentle words, all the knights of both the inside and the outside teams were content to run at each other with lances one against the other. Many lances were then broken and many chivalrous feats accomplished. On the last run, the lord (33) of Camican shattered his lance with great force against a certain Champoullet. Certain others did likewise, but I won't say anything about them as it would take me too long. They then fought with swords in a *mêlée* and, in this part of the fight, the lord of Bus, on the Valois team, performed particularly well. On the inside team, this was also true of the lords of Camican and Frémécourt and of Georges de Sully. This *mêlée* was fought at such a heated intensity that no competitor was spared from receiving so many blows that it was enough to exhaust them all. After such a tough fight and such a long group battle, it was a struggle at the end to separate them.

On that day when the third bout was due to be fought at the Tenebrous Crossroads, at the stroke of four o'clock in the afternoon, the lord of Beaumont found himself at the appointed place with his team of gentlemen from Normandy, all of whom were fully armed and ready for combat as they had been told to be. The knight-defenders of the *pas* were there mounted and armed, all covered in cloth of gold and *orfèvrerie**. In this manner they left their tents, each of them accompanied by his servant for the combat, to the sound of myriad trumpets and Swiss drums. They (34) rode out so proudly and observed such good order in their ranks as they advanced that, from their appearance, they truly did seem to be knights of high worth who were deserving of praise. Before beginning to fight they made a circuit of the field, accompanied by the gentlemen who were carrying their lances and were there to serve them. When the time came for battle to commence, they each let their horses run so fiercely against their particular opponent that many a lance was smashed to smithereens. On this first run, the lord of Camican was up against a certain Jean Picart, lord of Radeval, and he made such an attaint* on him that his lance flew into pieces. One of those on the inside team, named Jacques de Bloc, and, on the outside team, Jean de Rouville, also made an attaint on each other with such force that each man broke his lance from the impact. Several other fine blows with the lance were given and received there, about which I'll say nothing; rather, I will come back to the combat with swords that was conducted as a *mêlée* and was so fierce that it seemed as if the competitors had vowed to fight each other to the death. So many terrible blows were exchanged that sparks flew with each sword stroke on the harness. Each (35) man dealt such hits as he felt himself capable of. Amongst others, the lords of Saint-Vallier, Sandricourt and Clermont distinguished themselves as it seemed that they were twice as strong at the end of the fight as at the beginning. The bout went on for so long that the judges decided that it was time to call a halt, hence the competitors were separated.

On Thursday, the nineteenth day of that month of September, at nine o'clock in the morning, the single combats began with those of the defending team taking on all comers at the Field of Thorn, as will shortly be recounted. That day the defenders were even more splendidly armed and mounted and even more finely equipped than before. From nine o'clock in the morning to sunset, they remained there at the Field of Thorn, on horseback and in full harness, their only pleasure being to strike with the lance and to run with the horse; some there were who fought against ten or twelve opponents and would have taken on even more if there had been any comers.

On that morning, the lord of Beaumont and those of his team held a banquet inside their tent at the Field of Thorn which was (36) attended by the ladies of France, Normandy and other lands who were present; with them were also a great number of knights and gentlemen defending the *pas* as well as other challengers. They were all served so excellently that no one's appetite was unable to do justice to all the things brought out to satisfy them.

Here are the names of all those who defended the *pas* against all comers and who, for eight[91] whole days, saw with immense pleasure to the entire needs of everyone, be they lords, judges, knights, gentlemen, ladies, damsels or others who were there in great numbers.

First of all:

Jean de Poitiers, lord of Saint-Vallier;[92] Bernardin de Clermont, viscount of Talart; Louis de Hédouville, lord of Sandricourt; Jean, lord of Camican;[93] Georges de Sully, governor of Coucy; Jean de Hédouville, lord of Frémécourt; Pierre d'Orgemont, lord of Méry;[94] (37) Jacques de Dinteville, the *grand veneur* of my lord of Orléans; *Dan* Jean, military leader;[95] and Jean de Saint-Soudain, squire.[96]

(38 is blank)

---

[91] This mention of eight days rather than the five that the fights actually lasted for (16–20 September) may refer to the fact that heralds started to put up the challengers' shields on 12 September: see above, pp. 266–9.

[92] [Jehan de Poictiers, seigneur de Sain(c)t-Vallier]. Jean de Poitiers (1475–1539), lord of Saint-Vallier and viscount of Estoile, was an *enfant d'honneur* of Charles VIII (1489), lieutenant-general of the governor of Dauphiné (1512), grand seneschal of Provence (1514), a member of the Order of St Michael (1515) and father of Diane de Poitiers (d. 1566), the famous mistress of King Henry II. CdF no. 2774; HMF, vol. 2, pp. 205–6.

[93] [Jehan, seigneur de Camican]. Jean de Cassaignet, lord of Camican and Busta, took part in the conquest of Naples (1495) and was in command of thirty-five lances. Botto, *L'Isle-Adam*, p. 92; JdA, vol. 4, p. 449.

[94] Pierre d'Orgemont (d. 1510), lord of Méry, Serbonne and Champs-sur-Marne, was a councillor-chamberlain of Charles VIII and treasurer of France. GDH, vol. 5, p. 379.

[95] [Damp Jehan]. *Dan* Jean, military leader: no information is available about him. A *dan/dam/damp* was a title given to someone whose rank is lower than that of a count but higher than that of a baron. DMF.

[96] [Jehan de Sainct-Souldain]. No information is available about him.

(39) On the nineteenth day of that month of September, the following courses with the lance were run at the Field of Thorn.

First of all:

For the first run, Jean de Saint-Amadour presented himself as a replacement for someone from the inside team who had been wounded the day before at the Tenebrous Crossroads, since it was stipulated that when one of the defenders of the *pas* was hurt or wounded to the extent that he was unable to fight, his place would be (40) taken by someone else from the lord of Châtillon's team, to which Saint-Amadour belonged. During this first round, he faced one of the competitors from the outside team named Campanes. The two of them ran at each other with lances but without making an attaint; they then fought most valiantly with swords.

The second run featured the lord of Camican, of the inside team, and François de Sassenage, of the outside team. The lord of Camican was hit very hard on his pauldron-reinforce* and then the two men fought a long battle with swords until they were finally separated.

Jacques de Dinteville, for the inside team, and a certain Vignolles, for the outside team, ran the third course followed by the sword fight, with Vignolles breaking his lance on the ground.

The fourth run opposed the lord of Camican and Adrien de Genlis, for the outside team; Camican was struck above the tasset* before they took up their swords to fight.

On the fifth run, Jacques de Dinteville, for the inside team, came up against Louis de Salenove,[97] for the outside team.

(41) The lord of Clermont, for the defenders, and the lord of Châtillon, for the challengers, ran the sixth course, which was very brutal as the lord of Châtillon struck his lance straight on the lord of Clermont himself; afterwards, they exchanged many blows with the sword.

For the seventh course, the lord of Camican, for the inside team, and one named Guillaume Le Cointe,[98] for the outside team, came into the lists. They encountered each other so cleanly in this run that on impact the lord of Camican's lance hit Le Cointe and flew off into pieces; they then took turns with their swords until a good number of blows had been dealt.

The lord of Saint-Vallier, for the inside team, and one named Marcillac, for the outside team, came into the field for the eighth course. They ran at each other so hard that it looked as if they would knock each other out when they encountered. Indeed, they struck one another with such tremendous force that the lord of Saint-Vallier's lance was smashed to pieces as it hit Marcillac, putting him in great danger of falling to the ground as the attaint made was so powerful that the grapper* (42) of Saint-Vallier's lance was broken. Once this had occurred, they engaged in a long fight with swords.

---

[97] [Louys de Sallenove]. Louis de Salenove: no information is available about him, but this family was closely allied to the Hédouvilles. De Magny, 'De Hédouville', p. 227.

[98] A Guillaume Le Cointe, son of François Le Cointe and Agnès de la Ferté-Hussau, is mentioned as being married to Jeanne du Tot, lady of Héranville; no precise dates are available for him but his grandson, Jacques-David du Perron (1556–1618), was bishop of Évreux (1592), a cardinal (1604), archbishop of Sens (1606), and great almoner of France (1606). DN, vol. 6, p. 13. Arsenal 3958 (fol. 12v) gives his name as Guillaume Le Conte, but no information is available about him either.

On the ninth run, the lord of Saint-Vallier was once more up for the inside team, this time against Guillaume de Méry, *maréchal des logis* of the duke of Orléans. Méry entered the field, mounted and armed with his lance on his thigh; he was accompanied by a shepherdess[99] riding a hackney* who was beautifully decked out and was leading Méry's horse by its rein. The two knights let their horses run with such force that it seemed as if they were being swept along in a storm! As they encountered, the lord of Saint-Vallier struck such a clean and powerful blow on Méry right on the visor of his armet* that he made him bend right back over his horse's rump. This blow caused Saint-Vallier to break both the lance-rest* on his breastplate and the grapper of his lance. If this hadn't happened, Méry was in real danger of being thrown to the ground. The shepherdess was very unhappy at seeing her master so badly done by. Nevertheless, nothing more came of it, other than that they went on to exchange many fierce blows with the sword. The lord of Saint-Vallier fought no more on that day (43): he had sustained a wound to his hand even though he had given no sign of this during the combat with swords.

The tenth course was run between the lord of Méry, for the defenders, and François de Théligny, for the challengers. They made no attaints with their lances but fought very well with swords.

The lord of Clermont and Guillaume de Saulx ran the eleventh course followed by a sword fight.

For the twelfth course, my lord of Sandricourt presented himself on behalf of the defenders, against Thomas de May, on behalf of the challengers. They failed to encounter with their lances but performed very well in the sword combat.

The thirteenth course pitted *Dan* Jean, of the inside team, against the bastard of Girême, of the outside team.

The lord of Camican and Picart the bailiff[100] ran the fourteenth course; although they failed to make an attaint with their lances, they fought very well with swords.

For the fifteenth course, Georges de Sully presented himself as a replacement for one of the defenders, against a certain (44) Marboué for the challengers. They fought with both lances and swords and, in the latter fight, Marboué was disarmed of his sword by Georges de Sully. His weapon was given back to him, by order of the judges and according to the ladies' wishes, on his paying a gold ring of the above-mentioned value[101] to the man who had disarmed him; afterwards, they finished their bout.

The sixteenth course was fought by the lord of Méry, on behalf of the inside team, against Guillaume de Houdricourt,[102] on behalf of the outside team. They did not manage to make an attaint with their lances but fought very well with their swords.

The seventeenth course saw the lord of Clermont present himself, as one of the defenders, against one named Chabanolles,[103] on behalf of the challengers. They ran the courses with lances and then fought with swords.

---

99 This motif of a shepherdess (whose expensive appearance indicates that she was actually a high-ranking noblewoman in costume) recalls in part the elaborate scenario of the Angevin *Pas de la Bergère* (Tarascon, 1449): see Source 6.

100 See above, n. 66.

101 See above, p. 263, where it is stipulated that the gold ring was to be worth at least 100 *écus*.

102 No information is available about him, but his name may be a mistranscription of Haudricourt (dép. Seine-Maritime in Normandy).

103 See above, n. 46.

For the eighteenth course, Louis de Hédouville, lord of Sandricourt, came into the lists to face the bastard of Lentilhac. They ran at each other most fiercely with lances and, in the sword combat, the lord of Sandricourt was disarmed of his weapon.

The lord of Saint-Amadour, as replacement for Jean de Hédouville of the inside team who (45) had hurt his hand, and a certain Bonnetot, of the outside team, ran the nineteenth course before fighting with swords.

Right from the very start of the twentieth course the lord of Camican, for the defenders, and one named Massabeau, for the challengers, acquitted themselves very well in the combats.

The twenty-first course was run by the lord of Méry, on behalf of the inside team, and by the lord of Bus, on behalf of the outside team. They ran at each other with lances with great ferocity and, in the sword fight, assailed each other so fiercely that it was as if they were mortal enemies. The lord of Méry's blows were so hard that straightaway the lord of Bus was disarmed of his couter-reinforce* but he was able to finish the fight, thanks to the ladies, by paying a gold ring to Méry and hence was rearmed. Once this had been done, they recommenced raining such great blows down on each other that they even cut through their harnesses. In the course of the fight, the lord of Méry came close enough to his man to be able to grab hold of the arm in which he was holding his sword and to follow through so forcefully that, by (46) spurring his horse against him, he spun the lord of Bus right round and sent both man and horse to the ground.

For the twenty-second course and the ensuing fight with swords, the lord of Méry, for the inside team, presented himself once more, this time against Champoullet, for the outside team. Méry hit Champoullet with his lance so neatly that he broke his stirrup-leather; during the sword fight, Méry brought Champoullet down to the ground, both him and his mount.

For the twenty-third course, Hédouville[104] was pitted against the challenger, the lord of Monsures; they did not make an attaint with their lances but fought very well with their swords.

For the twenty-fourth course, little Châtillon[105] presented himself, for the inside team, against Rouville, for the outside team. They did not manage to encounter with their lances but performed very well in the sword fight.

Many other fine courses with the lance and fierce combats with the sword were seen on that day, for there were thirty fights in all on that occasion, each involving both weapons.[106] Many horses were brought (47) down to the ground, numerous lances broken and several knights disarmed. The tournament went on throughout the entire day without stopping, which must have really tested the competitors, particularly those on the inside team who were performing feats of arms against all comers, with some of the defenders having to

---

[104] Presumably this is Louis de Hédouville, as it is mentioned above that his brother, Jean, was wounded and could not fight in this particular part of the tournament.

[105] [le petit Chastillon]. This is presumably a reference to the lord of Châtillon being small in stature rather than to a younger relative of his (since the latter is not mentioned elsewhere in the text): compare with 'le jeune Camican' (the young Camican), Bernard de Cassaignet, who is designated like this to distinguish him from his elder brother, Jean de Camican. See above, nn. 36 and 93, respectively.

[106] Whilst PSt, pp. 46–7, follows Arsenal 3958 in omitting the remaining six combats in this third *emprise*, the early printed edition (Vélins 1033/1044, fols. B3v–B4r) does gives a short précis of each of them.

fight ten or twelve men apiece on that day. Georges de Sully, for the defenders, and the lord of La Londe, for the challengers, brought the *pas* to a close.

(48 is blank)

(49) The next day, which was the twentieth day of September, between seven and eight o'clock in the morning, the knight-defenders of the *pas*, all in full harness, rode out of the castle of Sandricourt in order to enter the Labyrinthine Forest and to seek adventure in the manner of knights-errant, accompanied by ladies and damsels in great numbers. These knights were so splendidly arrayed that they were a marvel to behold: throughout the entire event, they changed their accoutrements and bard covers* each and every day.

As they made their way out of the castle, the knights-errant rode along (50) two by two, some here and others there, through the fields and woods wherever they thought that they might come across some adventure. Likewise, on their entry into the forest, those from the outside teams split up in order to see what they might encounter. As they were on their quest, Louis de Hédouville, lord of Sandricourt, and Picart the bailiff, from the outside team, found themselves in the forest and so, with lances couched, they ran their horses at each other and struck so fiercely that it was as if a storm and a whirlwind were tearing through the trees. On impact, their lances were broken and the two men stayed upright, putting their hands to their swords and fighting for quite some time. In the end, however, Picart the bailiff was disarmed of his sword by the lord of Sandricourt. The lord of Clermont, riding through the forest that day, fought against three different knights on the outside team, acquitting himself with great vigour for he refused no one who made his way over to fight him. In various different places, whether in the fields or in the woods, these knights-errant encountered each other and fought there all day long without rest. They were in so many different places that, (51) as far as the eye could see, there were knights locked in combat with one another, displaying so many feats of arms that were deserving of praise. That day, the lord of Saint-Vallier did not take part because he had sustained a wound to his hand, but he acted as a servant to the lord of Clermont the whole time in the forest and was very unhappy at not being able to be present with his companions. On one side and on the other, many lances were broken and many fine deeds of arms were performed there, such that it would take a long time to recount if all of them were to be committed to memory. Each of the knights-errant had several gentlemen with him who carried his lances and served him with whatever he needed. That day, all you could see in the trees and fields were knights fighting against one another and in so many places at once that it was impossible to follow everything that was going on.

(52 is blank)

(53) Also present were François de Coignac, lord of Merle,[107] and Guillaume de Lisle, lord of Marivaux,[108] who was the former *maître d'hôtel* of my lord the cardinal of

---

[107] [seigneur de Nelle]. François I de Coignac (d. 1536), lord of Merle, Saint-Jean-Ligoure, Villefavard, Jumillac, Château-Chervix, Colacie (1518) and Saint-Julien-du-Bois, was son of Antoine de Coignac and Gasparde de Merle <https://gw.geneanet.org/dfallieres?lang=fr&n=de+coignac&oc=0&p=francois> [accessed 20 June 2024]. HMF, vol. 4, p. 787, para. A, mentions Gasparde but not Antoine as her husband.

[108] [seigneur de Marivaulx]. Guillaume de Lisle (d. 1511), lord of Marivaux, Mesnil-Terribus, Jagny, Ybouvilliers and Sérifontaine, was *maître d'hôtel* of the cardinal of Bourbon in 1484. HMF, vol. 8, p. 792, para. B.

Bourbon.[109] These two men, at the request of the knight-defenders of the *pas*, had taken on the task and responsibility of being their *maîtres d'hôtel* and were in charge of organising various others who had been given the role of serving everyone at the castle of Sandricourt. On the day of the Labyrinthine Forest event, these *maîtres d'hôtel* were there on the quest, following the knights and with (54) others running around after them, who were carrying white and pale hypocras[110] as well as juleps[111] and purple-coloured syrups, jellies and other spiced confections which they served to whomsoever wanted them. Wherever they came across any of these knights and their gentlemen, they offered them whatever they wished and as much as they liked, for there was a great abundance of everything. This was a most extraordinary thing and was a mark of great honour for the knight-defenders of the *pas* to have brought such a quantity of provisions into the fields and woods for everyone to partake of as they wished.

One named Jean de Saint-Amadour, of the inside team, and Jean de Rouville, of the outside team, came across each other in the forest. No sooner did they approach each other than they spurred their horses and broke their lances: in the attaint, Jean de Saint-Amadour smashed his lance on Rouville. They then proceeded to fight with swords and, after exchanging a good number of blows on each side, Jean de Rouville found himself disarmed of his weapon. Jacques de Dinteville, for the defenders, and the lord of Bonnetot, for the challengers, came across each other as they were on their quest through the forest (55) and so ran at each other very fiercely. As they struck one another, Bonnetot hit the lord of Dinteville with his lance at one end of the sight of his armet which then crumpled up against his forehead. If the blow had been a clean attaint, Dinteville would have been in grave danger; nevertheless, despite having been placed at such a disadvantage, he held himself very firm and soon laid his hand on his sword to put up a very hard fight against Bonnetot.

(56 is blank)

(57) Also in the forest was Thomas de May, a knight-errant who sent a herald out into the woods to see if there was any other knight wandering around, like himself, who wished to fight him on foot with five thrusts of the spear and thirteen strokes of the sword. For this reason, one Le Boeuf, who likewise was looking for an opponent against whom to fight on foot, was very pleased to accept his challenge. They met up in a meadow running the length of the wood and there performed their feats of arms. As they fought with spears, (58) Thomas de May cut through Le Boeuf's harness in three places;[112] Le Boeuf was also disarmed of his sword which fell to the ground, but he managed to pick it up again and complete the number of strokes. Almost all of the knights were present to watch this combat as they had returned from their own quests in the forest where they had been fighting each other at great length.

(59) As they made their way back, the knights all rode along together, which was a very fine sight to see. They were accompanied by ladies, damsels and gentlemen, all of

---

[109] Charles II (1433–88), duke of Bourbon, was archbishop of Lyon from an early age and a cardinal from 1476. GDH, vol. 1, p. 241; PPR, p. 1215.

[110] Hypocras is a kind of mulled wine. DMF.

[111] A julep is a syrup made from wine that has been reduced with sugar and spices. DMF.

[112] PSt, p. 58, which follows the early printed edition (Velins 1033/1034, fol. B5v), is unclear here, stating that Thomas de May dealt Le Boeuf 'trois coups de lance *à jour*'; this has been clarified here using the reading given in Arsenal 3958, fol. 15v: 'le harnois dudit Beuf fut en trois lieux *percé à jour*' (emphasis added).

whom were present in large numbers. As they came to dismount at the castle of Sandricourt, they were very honourably greeted by the lady of the place,[113] the mother of Louis and Jean de Hédouville who were among the defenders of the *pas*. She was overjoyed to welcome such a fine and noble company to her home at Sandricourt.

(60) A splendid and copious banquet was served with everything that one could wish for, especially the finest wines in the world. In order to accommodate such a huge number of knights, lords, gentlemen, ladies and damsels who were there, they took the tables out into the courtyard of the castle, which was very broad and spacious. As for the seated guests, there were one hundred and twelve gentlemen on one table, not counting the ladies and damsels. There were so many of them, some in the halls and chambers of the castle, and all had to be served with many different kinds of dishes; in particular, they did not stint on the hypocras or on the wine. A very large quantity of flaming torches and lanterns was needed, both in the courtyard of the castle and the towers as well as around the outside of the place. From as far away as a league in all directions it was possible to see one's way to the castle as easily as if it were day.

At the banquet were a large group of Swiss drums and other instruments which didn't stop playing for a minute. Also arriving for the banquet came many noblemen, ladies and damsels from the lands of France, Normandy[114] and other places who were there to see the assembled company (61); all of them were welcomed and entertained most honourably.

After the banquet, the heralds went up into a gallery above the courtyard and there it was announced by Provence, the king's herald,[115] that all those knights-errant who had spent the day in the Labyrinthine Forest should come before the judges and the ladies in order to recount, in good faith and having sworn an oath on their honour, the adventures that they had had in the forest whilst they were out on their quest. This they did, with the ten knight-defenders of the *pas* speaking first. Then it was the turn of all the other knights as they were called upon to make their reports in front of the judges and the ladies. After this, dances, *morescas** and farces[116] were held on each of the nights which lasted until two o'clock in the morning. As long as the tournament lasted, this was the case, whether in the evenings or after the lunches, until it was time to fight again.

---

[113] Huguette de Brillac, who married Philippe de Hédouville (1430), was a *dame d'honneur* of Marie of Cleves. JdA, vol. 4, p. 445; Magny, 'De Hédouville', p. 230.

[114] After 1469, Normandy became permanently united to the French crown by King Louis XI, but the honorific title of 'duke of Normandy' was still occasionally given to a junior member of the French royal family; hence, perhaps, the slightly ambiguous phrasing here in the text as if Normandy were a separate land from France. Robert J. Knecht, *The Valois Kings of France 1328–1589* (London/New York: Hambledon, 2004), p. 90.

[115] Provence Herald: no information is available about the identity of the person holding this office in 1493, but he is mentioned as being present at Charles VIII's campaign in Naples in 1494 and as previously having been known as 'Gentil Garçon' (when he was presumably a pursuivant). [Godefroy] *Histoire de Charles VIII. roy de France, par Guillaume de Jaligny, André de la Vigne, & autres historiens de ce temps-là. Où sont decrites les choses les plus memorables arrivées pendant ce regne, depuis 1483 jusques en 1498. Enrichie de plusieurs memoires, observations, contracts de mariage, traitez de paix, et autres titres & pieces historiques non encore imprimées. Le tout recueïlli par feu Monsieur Godefroy, conseiller & historiographe ordinaire du Roy* (Paris: Imprimerie Royale, 1684), p. 133. Thanks are due to Nils Bock for this reference.

[116] PSt, p. 61, omits the comma after 'dances' and so has been corrected here using the early printed edition (Vélins 1033/1034, fol. B6r) which lists three different types of entertainment, i.e. 'danses, morisques et farces'.

The lady of Sandricourt was overjoyed to see all the merriment that was going on in her house, as were the two lords, her sons. Equally pleased were the judges, ladies and damsels (62) who were all very well accommodated in her house since the chambers and halls were finely appointed and equipped. For his part, the lord of Châtillon and his team had been put up and entertained by the lady of Monsures,[117] she being delighted to have them.

In order to know the names of all my lords the judges at this *pas*, here they are written out below.

First of all:

Monseigneur de La Roche-Guyon;[118] Monseigneur de Montmorency;[119] my lord the bailiff of Gisors;[120] my lord the bailiff of Senlis;[121] Monseigneur du Bellay;[122] and Ambroise de Villiers, lord of Vallangoujard.[123]

These lord-judges conducted themselves most honourably; without failing to give each man his due, they upheld everyone's rights. They took great trouble and effort each day to render (63) service to the gentlemen defending the *pas*, each of them according to what they could see was needed. Thanks to their excellent conduct during the event, there was not a single dispute or debate about any member of this company, which is quite something considering how many gentlemen and people of all different sorts were there. The highest possible honour is due both to the knights-defenders of the *pas* and those gentlemen who came as challengers. All of these men, whether on the inside or the outside teams, are beholden to God for the great worth that accrued to them.

Here follow the names of the ladies and damsels, whether those of France, Normandy or other countries.

---

[117] [madame de Mousseures]. This lady is possibly Marie (also known as Jeanne) de Caulaincourt, who married Raoulquin/Raoul de Monsures (1462); but it could also be Jeanne Mauchevalier, whose first husband was Josse de Gourlay (see above, n. 41).

[118] Bertin de Silly (*c.*1425–1506), lord of Lonray, La Houlette, L'Épinay-sur-Odon, Rochefort (-en-Yvelines) and Roncheville, who became lord of Roche-Guyon through his marriage to Marie de La Roche-Guyon (1476), was a councillor-chamberlain of Charles VIII and bailiff of Cotentin. GDH, vol. 5, p. 554; HMF, vol. 3, p. 30.

[119] [Monseigneur de Mommorency]. Guillaume de Montmorency (1453–1531) was a councillor-chamberlain of Charles VIII, Louis XII and Francis I and took part in the Italian wars for Louis XII. Botto, *L'Isle-Adam*, pp. 95–6; HMF, vol. 3, pp. 602–3.

[120] [Monseigneur le bailly de Gisors]. Jean de la Viefville/Vieuville, lord of Vestrechon-Bérincourt, was a councillor-chamberlain of Louis XII and bailiff of the castle and town of Gisors; he founded a chapel (1497) in the church of Gisors where he and his wife, Marguerite de Barlemont, were later buried. Victor Patte, *Histoire de Gisors* (Gisors: Ch. Lapierre Imprimeur-éditeur, 1896), pp. 256–8.

[121] [Monseigneur le bailly de Senlis]. Waleran de Sains (b. 1458), lord of Marigny and Montgérain, was a councillor-chamberlain of Charles VIII, as well as bailiff, captain and governor of Senlis (1484–1511); he was married to Jacqueline de Rouvroy de Saint-Simon, who may have been the sister of Louis de Hédouville's wife, Françoise. JdA, vol. 4, p. 532.

[122] [Monseigneur du Bellé]. René du Bellay (d. before 1532), lord of Bellay and Plessis-Macé, was captain of Charles VIII's troops in Brittany. GDH, vol 1, p. 44 (where he is named Bellai).

[123] [Ambroise de Viliers, seigneur de Vallerengoujart]. Ambroise de Villiers (d. 1503), son of Jacques de Villiers de l'Isle-Adam (d. 1471), was lord of Vallangoujard and captain of Pontoise under Louis XII. Botto, *L'Isle-Adam*, p. 94; HMF, vol. 7, p. 13, para. C.

First of all, from France:

Madame de Montmorency;[124] Mademoiselle de Fosseux;[125] Madame de Sandricourt;[126] Madame de Monsures;[127] Mademoiselle du Bellay;[128] (64) Mademoiselle de Frouville;[129] Mademoiselle de Thun;[130] and Mademoiselle de Saint-Cyr.[131]

Next follow the names of the ladies and damsels of Normandy.

First of all:

Madame du Home;[132] Madame de Tellan;[133] Madame d'Annebaut;[134] Mademoiselle de Montérolier;[135] Mademoiselle de Mésy;[136] and Mademoiselle de Bonnetot.[137]

---

[124] [Madame de Mommorancy]. This may be Anne Pot (d. 1510), who married Guillaume de Montmorency (1484), one of the judges at this *pas* (see above, n. 119); she was the eldest daughter of Guy, count of Saint-Pol and lord of Daimville, and Marie de Villiers de L'Isle-Adam. HMF, vol. 2, p. 118, para. E; vol. 3, p. 603, para. A.

[125] [Mademoiselle de Fousseux]. This is likely to have been a niece of Guillaume de Montmorency whose brother, Louis, was lord of Fosseux (d. 1490). DN, vol. 6, p. 560.

[126] See above, n. 113.

[127] On the possible identity of this person, see above, nn. 41 (Jeanne Mauchevalier) and 117 (Marie/Jeanne de Caulaincourt).

[128] [Mademoiselle du Bellé]. This is likely to have been a daughter or a niece of René du Bellay, one of the judges. René's brother Jacques had two daughters: Catherine, married to Jacques Turpin, lord of Crissé, and Jeanne, who was betrothed first to Tristan de Châtillon, lord of Argenton, and then to N. du Bouchet, lord of Puigressier. GDH, vol. 1, p. 44.

[129] [Mademoiselle de Froville]. This may be a daughter of Pierre de Frouville, lord of Serainville, who married Marguerite des Hayes; her brother, Guillaume II des Hayes, lord of Boisgueroust, was married in 1451. HMF, vol. 7, p. 472, para. D.

[130] [Mademoiselle de Thun]. This is likely to have been a daughter of Claude de Rabodanges, lord of Thun.

[131] [Mademoiselle de Saint-Cire]. This may be the daughter of Jean du Monceau, lord of Avon, Saint-Cyr, Pontserré and Argeville; in 1509 she was widowed on the death of her husband, Jean de Brichanteau, squire and lord of St-Martin de Nigelles (1503, after a legal dispute with his sister, the lady of Espernon) and captain of the castle of Espernon (1508). HMF, vol. 7, p. 902, para. C.

[132] This family from Normandy, whose name was spelt in many different ways, consisted of two branches, the elder based in England and the younger in Normandy; this Madame du Home may be Catherine Josel, wife of Guillaume II du Homméel, who was a pantler (1490) of Anne of France, King Louis XI's eldest daughter, and then lieutenant of the captaincy of Pont-Douve (1503). DN, vol. 10, pp. 693–8.

[133] [Madame de Tellan]. No information is available about her.

[134] [Madame d'Ennebost]. This could refer to either Marie Blosset or Péronne de Jeucourt, the first and second wives, respectively, of Jean II d'Annebaut, lord of Annebaut, Brestot and Appeville, who was hereditary constable of Normandy. GDH, vol. 1, p. 475; HMF, vol. 7, pp. 178–9.

[135] [Mademoiselle de Monterollier]. No information is available about her, but Montérolier (dép. Seine-Maritime) is in Normandy.

[136] [Mademoiselle de Mesy]. No information is available about her, but her name may be a mistranscription of Messy; this family had links in the mid-fifteenth century with the Orgemont family (they did homage to Pierre II d'Orgemont (d. 1492) for the lordship of Messy) and were linked by marriage to the Mouÿ (May?) family (see above, n. 57), both of whom were also represented at Sandricourt. GDH, vol. 5, p. 378; HMF, vol. 6, pp. 259, para. D.

[137] [Mademoiselle de Bouvetot]. This is likely to have been a daughter of Jacques d'Ossencourt/Ochencourt, lord of Bonnetot (see above, n. 65).

These ladies and damsels were all so honourably and richly dressed that every noble man present should take courage and find pleasure in doing something for love of them.

Also present at the castle of Sandricourt were doctors, surgeons and apothecaries who were there to provide assistance to those in need of it, all at the expense of the knight-defenders of the *pas*.

There were also armourers, saddlemakers, milliners, (65) tailors and all kinds of craftsmen, all of whom ate and drank at the castle of Sandricourt.[138] During the whole eight days, there were typically between 1800 and 2000 people eating and drinking either inside or outside the castle of Sandricourt,[139] whether they were defenders or challengers; everyone's costs were met, no matter where they came from. From morning until midnight, the tables did not stop being laden with all kinds of delicious dishes in twenty-five or thirty different parts of the castle. At any hour, if anyone so wished, they could have white or pale hypocras, as well as jellies of any kind that they could think of. The judges and the ladies had their own chambers set aside for them, where they were served with everything that they could wish for, all their costs being met by the knight-defenders of the *pas*. The expenses for each day amounted to between 400 and 500 *francs*.[140] For this reason, considering all that was done to organise this *pas* described herewith on the part of the knights and squires who undertook the feats of arms recounted above, it seems to me that it is hugely to their honour to have performed all these deeds over this period, this against forty noblemen (66) who, in turn, bestowed this honour on the knights who defended the *pas*, their names being given above.

In my view, since the time of King Arthur, whose memory is still alive and who founded the Round Table which included so many noble knights whose names have and always will be remembered, such as Messire Lancelot du Lac, Messire Gauvain, Messire Tristan de Lyonnais and Messire Palamèdes, all at one time members of the Round Table,[141] I can truly say that never has one read or seen in any history book since that time any jousts, tourneys or *béhourds** performed for the love of ladies that came anywhere close to the undertaking of martial deeds that was done at the *pas* of Sandricourt, nor which resemble so nearly those of the Knights of the Round Table. It is my opinion that all noblemen full of virtue, whether from the kingdom of France or from other countries and kingdoms of Christendom, must be saddened and dismayed at not having witnessed

---

[138] All these people would have come from nearby towns and would have been lodged in the castle or its environs for the duration of the event; they too would have formed part of the audience for this *pas*.

[139] These numbers may well not be exaggerated: eighty-one people are referred to by name or function in the text (fifty-one competitors, six judges, six helpers, three heralds, fifteen women) and many others are referred to as only a generic group (artisans, tailors, armourers, etc.). If each competitor, judge, helper or notable audience member had an entourage with him or her, of say, fifteen people (including servants), this would soon amount to over 1200 attendees.

[140] See Essay 4, pp. 438–9, where it is noted that the sums spent per day by Louis de Hédouville were enormous, particularly if compared to the annual wages given at the time by the French king to one of his best armourers, i.e. 240 *livres tournois*, where one *livre tournois* equates to one *franc*. See Eric Reppel, 'Minorités et circulations techniques: la confection des armures à Tours (XVe–XVIe siècles)', *Documents pour l'histoire des techniques*, 15 (2008), 24–31 (p. 31); and Spufford, *Handbook*, pp. 191–2.

[141] These are probably the most famous knights associated with the Round Table: see Alan Lupack, *Oxford Guide to Arthurian Literature and Legend* (Oxford: Oxford University Press, 2005), pp. 455–6 (Lancelot), 445–6 (Gawain), 471–2 (Tristan), 464 (Palamedes).

these feats of arms that took place at the castle of Sandricourt. I can safely say that they are quite right to do so since the knight-defenders of this *pas* fought against those challengers from the outside team at the (67) Perilous Barrier on foot three times, which they were not obliged to do, according to the articles, which stipulated that they were to fight there only once.[142] Yet, because they had such nobility of heart, they could not have refused any knight, no matter where they knew he had come from. Likewise, these knights defending the *pas* fought at the Tenebrous Crossroads three times in a *mêlée*, which they were also not obliged to do according to the articles.[143] From there, they went to the Field of Thorn, mounted and armed, their lances in their hands and their swords at their sides. There the knight-defenders of the *pas* engaged in single combat against all those who came from outside, as has been recounted in fuller detail above.

On the last day, these knights-errant went into the Labyrinthine Forest and there fought every knight who had come to seek adventure, all in pursuit of performing deeds of arms. They were told to take up lances and swords at the green pine, in front of the castle of Sandricourt, which is where, in the past, other noblemen had come looking for adventure. (68) And one can say that the Knights of the Round Table likewise came there searching for their own adventures too. May God grant, by His grace, that all noblemen gain from Him both the courage and the will to demonstrate forever the high and lofty intention that must find its home in any noble heart.

[142] The articles for this and the second *emprise* (see next note) clearly did not foresee the possibility that the ten knight-defenders would have to fight three different teams of ten challengers apiece.

[143] See previous note.

Thanks are due to Marina Viallon for her comments and suggestions on the translation of this source and its scholarly apparatus, and to Elizabeth L'Estrange and Kathleen Wilson-Chevalier for their suggestions on resources for researching late fifteenth-century historical figures at the French court.

Mario Damen

Source 14

The *Pas* of Brussels, 1503

This source consists of a translation of selected extracts from the narrative account concerning the circumstances preceding this *pas* and from the financial account of the town of Brussels.

Author:

(1) Antoine de Lalaing, lord of Montigny
(2) unknown; known treasurers in that year were Peter van der Noot, Amelrik Was, Jacob de Ruwe and Jan Anderlecht.[1]

Language:

(1) Middle French
(2) Middle Dutch

Archival source used:

(1) The manuscripts used for Louis Prosper Gachard's edition (see below) are Brussels, KBR, 7382, and The Hague, Koninklijke Bibliotheek, 131 B 9.
(2) The original account was kept in the city archive of Brussels but is no longer extant. These urban accounts, however, were made in two copies, one for the town and the other sent to the Audit Office. The edition given here is based on the latter copy: Brussels, AR 30949.

Edition used:

(1) Louis Prosper Gachard, ed., *Collection des voyages des souverains des Pays-Bas*, 4 vols (Brussels: F. Hayez, 1876), vol. 1, pp. 335–40 (= CdV)
(2) none available

Select bibliography:

Born, Robert, *Les Lalaing: une grande 'mesnie' hennuyère, de l'aventure d'Outrée au siècle des gueux (1096–1600)* (Brussels: Éditeurs d'art associés, 1986), p. 210

Damen, Mario, 'The Town as a Stage? Urban Space and Tournaments in Late Medieval Brussels', *Urban History*, 43.1 (2016), 47–71

[1] See Brussels, AR 30949 fol. 10r. The inventory wrongly names Wencelijn t'Serclaes, Philip van den Heetvelde and Bertelmeeus van Cattenbroeck as receivers.

INTRODUCTION

This event, organised by Antoine de Lalaing, took place on the main market square in Brussels, now known as the Grote Markt/Grand Place, over several days in the week before Christmas 1503: that is, from 17 to 23 December. It formed part of a series of chivalric entertainments (variously termed *emprise**, joust and *pas*) put on in the town to celebrate the return of the Habsburg prince, Archduke Philip the Fair (1478–1506), to the Netherlands after a two-year journey to Spain, Savoy and Austria, on which Lalaing had accompanied him in his capacity as chamberlain.

The original stimulus for the *Pas* seems to have occurred in September 1503 during Philip the Fair's visit to his father, Emperor Maximilian (1459–1519), in Innsbruck. Then Apolone of Innsbruck, a member of the household of Maximilian's second wife, Bianca Sforza (1472–1510), who was about to marry the count of Lodron, offered a 'crancelin', probably a garland of trefoil leaves, as the heraldic charge of the same name suggests, to four noblemen: the archduke; Ruprecht of the Palatinate, the count palatine; Floris van Egmond, lord of IJsselstein; and Antoine de Lalaing.[2] The recipients all put their garlands around their necks. On doing so, they were told by a courtier that if they wore their garlands uncovered, they would have to accept the challenge to fight against all those who touched them. Philip and the others accepted this condition and immediately had to proclaim how they would engage with their challengers if their *emprise* was touched. Philip, however, decided that this would take place when they returned to the Netherlands later that year.[3]

Desirous of providing entertainment during this festive period, particularly for the ladies, Philip held a one-day event on Sunday 15 December to perform his joust/*emprise*/*pas*, as did Ruprecht of the Palatinate, probably on Monday 16 December.[4] By contrast, and in spite of his much lower ranking at court, Antoine de Lalaing made the fulfilment of his *emprise* into a much bigger event that lasted over several days. On his behalf, on the feast of St Martin (11 November 1503), it was proclaimed at the court in Mechelen, where Philip's retinue had arrived after passing through Aachen, Maastricht, Sint-Truiden and Leuven, that a *pas d'armes* would take place in Brussels.[5] The day after, when Antoine wore his *emprise* around his neck it was touched by some thirty-five noblemen.[6] The town account of Brussels explains that his 'pas ende tfait van wapenen' (*pas* and feat of arms) finally took place from 17 to 23 December on the Grote Markt.[7]

All of these events attracted an illustrious audience of nobles, both male and female, as can be seen in the fact that two ladies of particularly high standing were present at it: Louise-Françoise of Savoy and her mother, Marie de Luxembourg, a powerful noblewoman who had survived her two princely husbands (Jacques of Savoy, lord of Romont, and François

---

[2] CdV, p. 309.

[3] *Ibid.*, pp. 321–3.

[4] For Philip's event see below, p. 291. The town administration of Brussels offered Ruprecht 4.5 *gelten* (11.7 litres) of Rhenish wine 'als hij hem wapende in den Hoeren opte Merc' (when he armed himself in the Hoorn on the Markt). AR 30949 fol. 179r.

[5] CdV, p. 337.

[6] Robert Born, *Les Lalaing: une grande 'mesnie' hennuyère, de l'aventure d'Outrée au siècle des gueux (1096–1600)* (Brussels: Éditeurs d'art associés, 1986), p. 210, mistakenly mentions this date, 12 November, as the day of Antoine's tournament in Brussels.

[7] AR 30949 fols 184v–185r.

of Bourbon, count of Vendôme). The presence of these ladies at the *Pas* is specifically mentioned in both sources, as translated here.[8] This had to do with the recent marriage of Louise-Françoise with the nobleman and courtier Hendrik III van Nassau.[9] Hendrik was the heir apparent of his uncle, the childless Count Engelbrecht II van Nassau, one of Philip the Fair's most important fiefholders in the Netherlands and his stadholder general.[10]

The motivation for Antoine de Lalaing, a younger brother of Charles, lord of Lalaing, to turn his *emprise* into a bigger event may have been that, although he was only a squire at the time,[11] he was the scion of a lineage whose earlier members had included famous jousters such as Jacques de Lalaing (*c.*1421–53) and Philippe de Lalaing (*c.*1430–65). Each of them had organised an important *pas d'armes* in the Burgundian lands under the Valois dukes: the *Pas de la Fontaine des Pleurs* (Chalon-sur-Saône, 1449–50) in the case of the former and the *Pas du Perron Fée* (Bruges, 1463) in the case of the latter, both of which were memorialised in numerous manuscript copies.[12] Antoine may therefore have been seeking to emulate the exploits of his first cousins once removed,[13] of nearly fifty years earlier, which he might have read about in his youth in the various manuscripts owned by his family that contained both the chivalric biography known as the *Livre des faits de messire Jacques de Lalaing*, which recorded Jacques's *pas*, and an account of the *Perron Fée*.[14] Unlike theirs, however, Antoine's *pas* was not widely commemorated in its day and, as a consequence, has largely escaped the notice of modern scholars. That his *pas* was at the time already considered as part of a family tradition is illustrated by the fact that on the day he wore his *emprise* in Mechelen, he was accompanied by five men belonging to the wider Lalaing lineage, including three illegitimate sons of two of Jacques and Philippe de Lalaing's brothers (Jean and Antoine).[15]

Two sources make explicit mention of Antoine's feat of arms, albeit in tantalisingly fragmentary form as part of a much larger festive programme. The first of these is a

---

[8] See below, pp. 291, 297–8.

[9] The marriage was celebrated during Philip's trip on 5 June 1503 to the Benedictine abbey of Ainay near Lyon, in the presence of the archduke and his entourage, the king of France and his wife. CdV, p. 292.

[10] On this figure, see COTO no. 77; MmM, no. 189; and below, n. 45.

[11] It is not clear when Antoine was knighted, but it is possible that the organisation of this *pas* in Brussels contributed to his obtaining the accolade. In the court ordinance of 1501 that was made for Philip the Fair's travels, he is listed among the category of *autres chambellans* (other chamberlains), which was below the category of 'normal' *chambellans* such as Floris van Egmond, who received a higher wage than Antoine. OHDB, p. 324. Antoine was definitely a knight when he entered the household of the future Charles V in 1510, being named as his second chamberlain in 1513. MmM, no. 135.

[12] See Sources 7 (*Fontaine des Pleurs*), 11a and 11b (*Perron Fée*); see also Essays 3 and 6.

[13] Their common ancestor was Othon de Lalaing, Jacques and Philippe's grandfather and Antoine's great-grandfather. CL, p. 10.

[14] See Essay 3; and Anne-Marie Legaré, '*Les Faits de Jacques de Lalaing* enluminés par le Maître d'Antoine Rolin', in *'Als ich can'. Liber amicorum in Memory of Professor Dr. Maurits Smeyers*, ed. by Bert Cardon, Jan Van der Stock and Dominique Vanwijnsberghe, 2 vols (Leuven/Dudley, MA: Peeters, 2002), vol. 2, pp. 773–93. Antoine may have been the patron of the illustrated copy of the *Livre des faits de Jacques de Lalaing*, dated *c.*1530, now in the J. Paul Getty Museum in Los Angeles: Wim Blockmans, 'Jacques de Lalaing: The Vitality of the Chivalric Ideal in the Burgundian Netherlands', in *A Knight for the Ages: Jacques de Lalaing and the Art of Chivalry*, ed. by Elizabeth Morrison (Los Angeles: The J. Paul Getty Museum, 2018), pp. 53–64 (p. 62).

[15] See below, p. 289.

narrative account of Philip the Fair's travels written up by Antoine himself, which is quite unusual for a *pas*, and the second is a financial account of the town of Brussels. In the first, Antoine mentions his *pas* as only one of a series of festivities that he recounts as being held to celebrate Philip's return to Brussels after his two years away. Most of the information given in this narrative is, therefore, about the courtly context in which it took place and the focus is understandably on Philip, rather than on Antoine himself. Lalaing identifies himself in the prologue of the manuscript as 'signeur de Montigny, filz de sire Josse de Lalaing, chevalier' (lord of Montigny, son of Messire Josse de Lalaing, knight). He claims that because of his 'amour de mon naturel signeur Philippe d'Austrice' (love of my natural lord, Philip of Austria) he has commemorated in writing what happened during his journey to Spain.[16] His account has been preserved in six manuscripts, none of them identified as autographs.[17] Unfortunately, Lalaing's account seems to be unfinished or incomplete, as it ends on 16 December with the preparation of his own *pas* and gives only a few details about the *emprise/pas* of Philip the Fair.

Similarly, in the second source, the administrative account for the town of Brussels, the heading of the section concerning the costs involved in setting up these events seems to indicate that it is about Philip's combat.[18] However, Lalaing is explicitly mentioned in this section as proclaiming his own *pas*, spread over five days from Tuesday 17 December onwards, which then utilised the infrastructure that Philip had had set up for his *emprise/pas* as it was quite common at late medieval chivalric tournaments for the same venue to be used for multiple events.[19] The total costs for the town were 111lb. Brabantine, of which the *entrepreneur** Antoine de Lalaing received a gift of 50lb. — that is, 45 per cent of the total amount allocated. The other costs mainly concerned the dinners given for the participants and guests in the town hall and the material expenses for setting up the *pas*. The total expenses of the town administration for that year were *c.*16,430lb.,[20] meaning that the costs for the *pas* were not even 0.7 per cent of the total budget.[21]

The financial account was drawn up by the three treasurers of Brussels whose responsibility it was to oversee and implement the town's financial policies. In this account, a clerk has recorded the treasurers' receipts and expenses for the town administration of Brussels in the year running from 24 June 1503. The account consists of 210 folios written on both sides, and the particular expenses related to the *pas* are grouped in the same section of

---

[16] CdV, p. 123. Despite this explicit mention of the author in the prologue, Daniel Coenen, 'De Lalaing, Antoine', in *Nouvelle biographie nationale*, 15 vols (Brussels: Palais des Académies, 2003), vol. 7, pp. 104–11 (p. 105), does not believe that Lalaing was the actual author because the structure and style of the account are more in line with those of the official chroniclers of the court; in his view, these unknown chroniclers put Lalaing's recollections down on paper, after which the nobleman inserted his name in the prologue. However, the fact that the narrative is recounted in the third-person voice does not necessarily mean that it was not written by Lalaing; rather, this may be a kind of humility device whereby the author avoids drawing attention to himself by using the first-person voice.

[17] CdV, pp. xiv–xv.

[18] See below, p. 293.

[19] This was the case, for example, in Bruges in April and May 1463, where the infrastructure on the main square, the Markt, was used for both the jousts of the White Bear and the *Pas du Perron Fée*. See Source 11b and Essay 3.

[20] AR 30949 fol. 203v.

[21] Compare this with the percentage of 6.6 per cent of the annual budget spent by the town administration of Bruges on the *Pas du Perron Fée* in 1463. See Source 11b, p. 241 n. 33.

the account. The money of account (i.e. the denomination of money used in reckoning accounts but not issued as actual coins or paper money) is the Brabantine pound of 160 groats. The account used for this translation is a copy of the treasurers' original account, which was kept in the Audit Office (Chambre des Comptes) in Brussels (now kept in the Rijksarchief in Brussels), as indicated on the first folio by the words 'om thof' (for the court).[22] On that folio, in a marginal note, it is also stated that the treasurers delivered the account to the Audit Office on 5 January 1505.

In the translation of the narrative account of Lalaing's *pas* that follows, page numbers in parentheses have been inserted for ease of reference to Gachard's edition.

TRANSLATION (1): NARRATIVE ACCOUNT BY ANTOINE DE LALAING

(335) This thirty-eighth chapter speaks about /.../ how my lord[23] was received in Maastricht, Sint-Truiden, Leuven and Mechelen; about the proclamation of a *pas d'armes* by my lord of Montigny[24] and how my lord went to Brussels; and about the death of my lady the Great[25] and her memorial service

/.../ (337) On the feast of St Martin,[26] a *pas d'armes* was proclaimed by Antoine de Lalaing, lord of Montigny, which was accomplished in Brussels in the manner described hereafter.

On Sunday 12 November, the said Antoine de Lalaing carried his *emprise* around his neck. This was the small garland which was given to him in Innsbruck by the bride of the count of Lodron, as recounted above.[27] On leaving his lodgings, the said Antoine was accompanied by the lord of Lalaing,[28] his brother, the lord of Brederode,[29] the lord

[22] AR 30949 fol. 10r.

[23] Philip the Fair (1478–1506), son of Maximilian of Austria and Mary of Burgundy, was married to Juana of Castile, daughter of Isabella I of Castile and Ferdinand II of Aragon, which eventually led to a personal union of the Low Countries, Franche-Comté and the Spanish kingdoms.

[24] [monseur de Montigny/Anthoine de Lalaing]. Antoine de Lalaing (1480–1540), lord of Montigny, Hoogstraten (count from 1518 onwards), and Culemborg, the second son of Josse de Lalaing and Bonne de Viefville, was married to Elisabeth van Culemborg (1509). He formed part of Philip the Fair's entourage as a chamberlain on this prince's journey to Spain (1501–03) and was second chamberlain of Charles V (from 1513), holding many administrative and military offices in the Habsburg state apparatus from that period on: he was head of the Financial Council (from 1515), a member of the Order of the Golden Fleece and of the Privy Council (from 1516), stadholder of Holland and Zeeland (1522–40), and stadholder of Utrecht (1529–40). MmM, no. 137; CdV, pp. vi–xiv.

[25] This refers to Margaret of York (1446–1503), the widow of Duke Charles the Bold (r. 1433–77), grandfather of Philip the Fair.

[26] That is, 11 November 1503.

[27] [conte de Lodron]. See CdV, pp. 321–3.

[28] Charles I de Lalaing (1466–1525), lord of Lalaing, the eldest son of Josse de Lalaing and Bonne de Viefvielle, was married to Jacqueline de Luxembourg (daughter of Jacques I); he was a councillor-chamberlain of Philip the Fair (from 1497) and a member of the Order of the Golden Fleece (1505). MmM, no. 139.

[29] Walraven II van Brederode (1462–1531), lord of Brederode, Vianen and Ameide, son of Reinoud II van Brederode and Yolande de Lalaing, was married to Margareta van Borssele; he was knighted by Maximilian I after his coronation (1486) and was a chamberlain of Philip the Fair (from 1495). MmM, no. 38; OHDB, pp. 170.

of Bugnicourt,[30] the lord of Wandonne,[31] his brother, captain Rodrigue de Lalaing[32] and by other lords and noblemen who were either related, allied or loyal to him. He went in this manner to attend my lord's Mass. The number of grandmasters[33] and nobles who touched his *emprise* was about thirty-five or thirty-six, as will be explained further below.[34]

A few days later, to pass the time with the ladies, Charles de Lannoy, lord of Senzeille,[35] undertook a combat *à la coutte*[36] against all comers which comprised one exchange with sharp-headed lances and one with sharpened swords; after he had accepted all their challenges, [he fought them] one after the other. He took on eight or ten gentlemen in this combat.

The next day, my lord left Mechelen and went to Brussels (338) where he made an honourable entry and his return was joyfully celebrated; my lord was cheerful that he had returned to the place from whence he had departed.

[....]

This thirty-ninth chapter deals with the manner in which my lord Hendrik van Nassau[37] went to Bohain[38] to find his wife and the ladies

---

[30] [seigneur de Buignicourt]. Ponthus de Lalaing, lord of Bugnicourt and Villers-au-Tertre, was an illegitimate son of Jean de Lalaing (brother of Jacques and Philippe) and married to Bonne van Wassenaar; he was a pantler* of Philip the Fair (1497). Félix Brassart, *Le blason de Lalaing. Notes généalogiques et héraldiques sur une ancienne et illustre maison* (Douai: L. Crépin, 1879), pp. 47–50; OHDB, p. 173.

[31] [seigneur de Vendomme]. Hercule de Lalaing (d. 1539), lord of Wandonne and Coupelles in Artois, was an illegitimate son of Jean de Lalaing and married to Jeanne du Mont, lady of Bernenchon. Félix Brassart, *Histoire et généalogie des comtes de Lalaing*, 2nd revised edition (Douai: Adam d'Aubers, 1854), pp. 30–1.

[32] [Rodicq de Lalaing]. Rodrigue de Lalaing, an illegitimate son of Antoine de Lalaing (i.e. the brother of Jacques and Philippe), was a member of the household of Philip the Fair, serving as a squire (1495), as captain of the archers (1497) and as *maître d'hotel* (1506). He accompanied Philip the Fair to Spain as a captain but was temporarily removed from office for having had a dispute with daggers and swords with another member of the household named Jean de Martigny in Ocaña, near Toledo (September 1502). OHDB, pp. 175, 230, 351, 371. He participated in the *Pas* of Mechelen (1491). Born, *Les Lalaing*, p. 194. Shortly before the *pas*, on 2 December 1503, Philip the Fair awarded him a gift of 80lb. to help him with his necessities since he had been ill just prior to it. ADN B fols 112v–113r.

[33] This term might refer to the *maîtres d'hotel* of Philip the Fair's household. In 1501, the *grand maître d'hotel* was Philippe of Burgundy, the youngest illegitimate son of Duke Philip the Good, (b. *c.*1465). OHDB, p. 325; MmM, no. 28.

[34] Unfortunately, these names are not in fact given below. However, it is a reasonable assumption that many of the noblemen mentioned in Lalaing's narrative did take part in the *Pas*.

[35] [seigneur de Saintzelles]. Charles de Lannoy (d. 1527), lord of Senzeille, son of Jean de Lannoy, lord of Mingoval, and Philipotte de Lalaing, was a councillor of Charles V (from 1515) and a member of the Order of the Golden Fleece (1516). MmM, no. 146.

[36] The meaning of this expression is obscure and so has been left untranslated here; it is not even clear whether the combat was on foot or on horseback.

[37] [Henry de Nassou]. Hendrik III van Nassau, son of Jan V van Nassau and Elisabeth van Hessen-Katzenelnbogen, was married to 1. Louise-Françoise of Savoy, 2. Claudia de Chalon, 3. Mencía de Mendoza. He inherited the possessions of his uncle, Engelbrecht II van Nassau, in the Netherlands upon his death (1504); he was a member of the Order of the Golden Fleece (1505), stadholder of Holland and Zeeland (1515–21) and a member of the Secret Council (1515–30) of Charles V. MmM, no. 190.

[38] [Bouhain]. Bohain, a castle and lordship in Picardy owned by the bride's mother, Marie de Luxembourg, was situated some 125 km away from Brussels.

who accompanied her, the great reception and triumph organised for them on their entry into Brussels, the *pas d'armes* that my lord performed, and other things

[The text then recounts how Hendrik and his wife, Louise-Françoise of Savoy, travelling via Le Quesnoy, Mons and Soignies, eventually arrived in Brussels. His wife's entourage consisted of her mother, Marie de Luxembourg,[39] *and many other high-ranking noble ladies of whom seven are mentioned by name.*[40]*]*

(339) The next day,[41] they[42] came to Brussels where my very redoubtable lord,[43] accompanied by the count palatine,[44] the count of Nassau,[45] the prince of Chimay[46] and many other grandmasters had arrived before them. My lord of Nassau[47] then took them to ...[48] where the ladies of Fiennes[49] and Lalaing[50] and many others had come at the request of

---

[39] Marie de Luxembourg (*c.*1470–1547), eldest daughter of Pierre II de Luxembourg, count of Saint-Pol, and Marguerite of Savoy, married first her uncle Jacques of Savoy, lord of Romont (1483) and then, after his death (1487), François of Bourbon, count of Vendôme (d. 1495). Because their son Charles was still a minor, she governed the Vendôme as his regent, enjoying its usufruct until her death. She owned twenty-five medieval manuscripts, among them copies of René of Anjou's *Livre des tournois* and Antoine de La Sale's *Jean de Saintré*. Anne S. Korteweg, 'La collection de livres d'une femme indépendante: Marie de Luxembourg (v. 1470–1547)', in *Livres et lectures de femmes en Europe entre Moyen Âge et Renaissance*, ed. by Anne-Marie Legaré and Bertrand Schnerb (Turnhout: Brepols, 2007), pp. 221–32; David Potter, 'The Luxembourg Inheritance. The House of Bourbon and its Lands in Northern France during the Sixteenth Century', *French History*, 6 (1992), 24–62 (pp. 28–9).

[40] Whilst the names of four of these seven ladies (Madame de Ravenstein, Madame de Porcien, Madame de Roeulx and Mademoiselle d'Antoing) are clear enough, those of 'Madame de Viege' (Viège/Vergy?), 'Mademoiselle de Vaelle' (Laval?) and 'Mademoiselle de Jeux' (Joux/Jauche?) are much less easy to identify.

[41] No exact date is indicated here but this must have been around the end of November; Philip the Fair, with Nassau in his entourage, was welcomed in Brussels on 18 November 1503.

[42] This refers to Hendrik III van Nassau, his wife and mother-in-law.

[43] That is, Philip the Fair.

[44] In his account, where Lalaing sometimes refers to the 'comte palatin' (count palatine) and on other occasions to the 'josne comte palatin' (the young count palatine), the same person is probably being identified, i.e. Ruprecht of the Palatinate (1481–1504).

[45] Engelbrecht II van Nassau (1451–1504), count of Nassau, lord of Breda, son of Jan IV van Nassau and Maria van Loon-Heinsberg, was a member of the Order of the Golden Fleece (1473), a councillor-chamberlain of Mary of Burgundy (1477) and first councillor-chamberlain of Maximilian of Austria (1482), as well as a councillor and keeper of the seal of Philip the Fair (1495) and a stadholder-general of the Netherlands (1496–98, 1501–03). COTO no. 77; MmM, no. 189; OHDB, p. 178.

[46] Charles I de Croÿ (*c.*1450–1527), prince of Chimay, son of Philippe de Croÿ and Walburge de Meurs, was married to Louise d'Albret and was first chamberlain of Maximilian (1482), who promoted his county of Chimay in Hainaut to a principality (1486). He was a member of the Order of the Golden Fleece (1491), a *chevalier d'honneur* of Juana of Castile (1498), a chamberlain of Philip the Fair (1494) and first chamberlain of Charles V, who was also his godson (1506). COTO no. 245; MmM, no. 65.

[47] Hendrik III van Nassau is meant here, as opposed to the count of Nassau, Engelbrecht II.

[48] Some words are missing here, but this probably refers to the palace of the Nassaus near the ducal Coudenberg Palace.

[49] Margareta van Brugge-Gruuthuse, daughter of Jan V van Brugge. COTO no. 107.

[50] This must refer to the wife of the lord of Lalaing, Charles I — that is, Jacqueline de Luxembourg, daughter of Jacques I. MmM, no. 139.

my lord[51] and of my lord of Nassau, in order to receive and welcome them. All the ladies were lodged there where they were treated in the best possible way, for my lord of Nassau held open court and one could see full tables which lacked for nothing from morning until night. The said lord[52] did everything in his power to make everybody feel welcome. Even my lord himself[53] thought only of things with which to entertain them, what with dancing, holding combats in the halls[54] in their presence and taking them out to hunt; indeed, they were treated so well and in such fine style that they said in all their lives they had never known such enjoyable festivities. Furthermore, in order to entertain them, my lord wanted to have the four *emprises* that had been planned in Innsbruck[55] performed in their presence,[56] but this was not possible because time was short and they[57] could not be held until the *entrepreneurs* were ready. Nonetheless, my lord insisted that they[58] stay on and, in the end, they agreed to remain there for another ten or twelve days, during which time my lord could accomplish his *pas*.

Sunday 15 December began in the following way: at two o'clock in the afternoon, my lord[59] was in the lists ready to accomplish what he was obliged to as regards competing against all the noblemen who had touched his *emprise*. All the said ladies were in the town hall,[60] with the stands where the lord judges were accommodated in front of them. All one could see were ladies at the windows around the whole of the Markt which was crowded with people. My lord wore a *sayon* made of cloth of gold and cloth of silver with stripes of crimson velvet, as was [his horse's] trapper*, both of which looked very fine; he also wore an ornament with white feathers laden with *orfèvrerie**.[61] (340) He was served by my lord the count palatin, the count of Nassau, my lord the prince of Chimay, my lord of Fiennes,[62] my lord of Ville,[63]

---

51 That is, Philip the Fair.

52 That is, Hendrik III van Nassau.

53 That is, Philip the Fair.

54 See also below, p. 295. Some of the hundreds of cartloads of sand for the *Pas* at the Grote Markt were delivered to the Coudenberg Palace for a jousting event in December.

55 This refers to Philip the Fair's visit to his father Maximilian in September 1503. See above, p. 285; and CdV, pp. 321–3.

56 That is, the ladies.

57 This refers to the different *emprises*.

58 That is, the ladies.

59 That is, Philip the Fair.

60 This suggests that they were watching the spectacle from the galleries of the town hall. On these galleries, see Mario Damen, 'The Town as a Stage? Urban Space and Tournaments in Late Medieval Brussels', *Urban History*, 43.1 (2016), 47–71 (p. 64).

61 A *sayon* is a man's outer garment with a fitted waist and a skirt with many gores (panels) that were cut so as to flare out towards the hem. In this example, the gores of the skirt probably alternated between the cloth of gold and the cloth of silver; the crimson velvet stripes may have been used to edge the skirt rather than serving as a third kind of gore. The reference to the feathered ornament probably refers to a crest to be worn on the top of the lord's helm. Thanks are due to Margaret Scott for her help in deciphering and translating these details.

62 Jacques II de Luxembourg (1443–1517), lord of Fiennes, son of Jacques I de Luxembourg, was married to Margareta van Brugge-Gruuthuse. He was a councillor-chamberlain of Maximilian of Austria and, from 1494 onwards, of Philip the Fair; he was a member of the Order of the Golden Fleece (1491) and stadholder of Flanders (1504–17). COTO no. 107; MmM, no. 163.

63 Jean de Luxembourg (*c.*1477–1508), lord of Ville, third son of Jacques I de Luxembourg, lord of Fiennes, and Marie de Berlaymont, lady of Ville, was married to Elisabeth van Culemborg, who, after

my lord of Chièvres,[64] the grand squire[65] and various others, and six noblemen on foot. All these grandmasters and noblemen were dressed in satin or in yellow, red and white damask, all made in the same fabric as the trappers. The trumpeters[66] and valets were similarly dressed, as they all had yellow caps with a yellow ribbon and a white feather. My lord entered the lists in this manner and, for the first course run against him … .[67]

TEXT (2): FINANCIAL ACCOUNT OF THE TOWN OF BRUSSELS, 1503–04

(fol. 184r)

Andere uutgeven gedaen ten steecspele dat onse genadigee heere gehouden heeft opte Merct des sondaechs 17 decembri

Ierst, meesteren Janne Vrancx, meester tymmerman deser stadt, die den rentmeesteren op zijnen eedt overbracht heeft dat diverse tymmerlieden die baillen, lijsten, huysen ende andere wercken gemaect hebben daer onse genedige heere over gesteken heeft; daer die jugen ende hieraulten opsaten, doen joncker Anthon van Lalang tpas ende tfait van wapenen beroepen hadde ende de verweerders inne gewapent ende gelogieert zijn geweest; de tafelen ende scragen ten banckette opter stadhuys gestelt hebben ende wederom afgebroken, daerover zij tsamen zijn geweest 121 dagen, te 4 stuvers sdaegs, valent: 6lb. 1s. groten.

Den selven meester Janne Vrancx van 17,5 dagen lanck tvoirs. werck te begaene, sdaegs 4 stuvers, valent: 17s. 6d. groten.

Den selven van vier vloerhouten, elc 10 voeten lanck, totter tonnen daer de helmen van den heeren die tvoirs. pas deden opgesteken waeren, ende ten heerden daer tvier in de huyskens van den selven op gemaect was, gelevert coste den voet een plac, 6 miten, valent: 4s. 2d. groten.

Diericke van Beerssel van 6412 voeten abeelen berts, coste elc hondert 12 stuvers, totten baillen, lijsten, huysen opte Merct ten voirs. steecspele gelevert, valent: 9lb. 12s. 4,5d. groten.

Jan Huyssegem met 4 gesellen, elc 27 dagen, compt tsamen op 135 dachueren elck te 2 stuvers, ende hebben gemaect de putten opte Merct om de stijlen, baillen, huysen in

---

his death, married Antoine de Lalaing. He was a chamberlain of Philip the Fair (from 1497), his second chamberlain (1501) and, after the death of Engelbrecht II van Nassau, became his first chamberlain; he was a member of the Order of the Golden Fleece (1501). MmM, no. 166.

64 Guillaume de Croÿ (1458–1521), lord of Chièvres, second son of Philippe de Croÿ and Jacqueline de Luxembourg, was married to Marie de Hamal. He was knighted by Maximilian of Austria on the day of his coronation (1486) and was a member of the Order of the Golden Fleece (1491); he was also a councillor-chamberlain of Philip the Fair (1494), grand-bailiff of Hainaut (1497–1503), and was appointed on 14 December 1503 (at the time of the *Pas*) as governor and grand-bailiff of Namur. COTO, no. 105; MmM, no. 68.

65 Claude Bonnard was a squire of the stables of Philip the Fair (1495) and later his grand and first squire of the stables (1501). CdV, p. 351; OHDB, pp. 176, 328.

66 Nine trumpeters are mentioned by name in Philip's court ordinance for his journey to Spain from November 1501. OHDB, p. 350.

67 This is where the manuscript ends, omitting all detail about the challengers and the *pas* held by Antoine de Lalaing from 17 December onwards.

TRANSLATION (2): FINANCIAL ACCOUNT OF THE TOWN OF BRUSSELS, 1503–04

(fol. 184r)

Other expenses incurred for the joust that our gracious lord[68] held on the Markt[69] on Sunday 17 December

First, paid to Master Jan Franks,[70] master carpenter of this town, who swore on his oath to the receiver that several carpenters had made the lists, the fences, the pavilions[71] and other structures used by our gracious lord to joust; [those structures] where the judges and heralds were seated when the squire[72] Antoine de Lalaing announced his *pas* and feat of arms, and [those structures] where the defenders were armed and lodged; for putting up and pulling down again the tables and trestles for the banquet in the town hall, for which they all worked a total of 121 days at a daily wage of 4 *stuivers*,[73] total: 6lb. 1s. *groten*.

Paid to the same Master Jan Franks for 17.5 days executing the said work, at a rate of 4 *stuivers* a day, total: 17s. 6d. *groten*.

Paid to the same for four boards, each of them 10 feet long,[74] for the barrels on which were placed the helms* of the lords who competed in the said *pas*[75] and for the hearths in which fires were made in the small pavilions, delivered at a cost of one *plak*[76] six *mijten*[77] per feet, total: 4s. 2d. *groten*.

Dirk van Beersel for 6412 feet[78] of poplar boards, at a cost of 12 *stuivers* per hundred, used for the lists, fences and pavilions constructed on the Markt: 9lb. 12s. 4.5d. *groten*.

Jan Huissegem with four workmen for 27 days each, totalling 135 days, at a rate of 2 *stuivers* a day, for making the pits on the Markt for the posts, fences and pavilions; to

---

68 That is, Philip the Fair.

69 Now the Grote Markt/Grand Place in Brussels.

70 No further information is available about him or any of the other craftsmen mentioned in this account.

71 Three small pavilions were set up, one for the judges, one for Lalaing as the defender of the *pas* and another one for the challengers. See below, p. 297.

72 The term *joncker* (French: *damoiseau*) used here refers to a nobleman of high birth who has not been knighted (yet). Antheun Janse, *Ridderschap in Holland. Portret van een adellijke elite in de late middeleeuwen* (Hilversum: Verloren, 2001), p. 89. On the exact date when he was knighted, see above, n. 11.

73 One *stuiver* equates here to 3d. *groten* Brabantine. One pound Brabantine (the money of account used here) is therefore the equivalent of eighty *stuivers*.

74 In Brussels, a foot measured 27.6 cm.

75 That is, the *pas* of Antoine de Lalaing.

76 One *plak* equals here 1d. *groten* Brabantine; one *stuiver* thus consists of three *plakken*.

77 One *plak* consists of twenty-four *mijten*.

78 That is, *c.*1768 m.

te settene; den savel gespreyt; de voyen van der stadhuys behangen; de huysen daer de steeckers inne gelogieert zijn geweest mit heren ende tinten te overspannene; den savel wederom op te scuppene, te vergaderene ende opte kerren te ladene; de huysen, baillen ende lijsten wederom af te doene ende ander diversch hantwerck te doene, betaelt: 3lb. 7s. 6d. groten.

Betaelt diverse kerrelieden van 633 kerren savels van aen de wintmoelen aen den Wollendriesch te halene ende opt hof in de groote sale, aldaer onse genedige heere stack, te vuerene ende oick op de Merct te brengene om de selve te savelen in weder zijden van den lijsten. Van elcker kerren betaelt van der vracht een plac, valent tsamen: 2lb. 12s. 9d. groten.

Diericke Wageman van 633 kerren savele uyten putte opten Haerdriesch te laten halene, van elcken kerren 12 mijten: 27s. 9d. groten.

(fol. 184v)

Janne van den Vekene van eender kerren cleemps, van 3 kerren gewerddden calck in de Cancelrie van Brabant opgesedt te halene ende ten huyse opte Merct gemaect te bringene: 1s. 2d. groten.

Baltasar van Somergem van 11 dage lanck de voirs vracht te kervene, sdaegs 2 stuvers: 5s. 6d. groten.

Willeme Lissen, meester metsere deser stadt, heeft op zijnen eede overbracht te wetene dat een metsere gewracht heeft 4,5 dagen, te 4 stuvers sdaegs, ende eenen oppercnape 4,5 dagen, sdaegs 2,5 stuvers, aen de schouwen in de berddderen huysen opten Merct daer de heeren ende steeckeren inne gelogieert waeren, te metsene, betaelt: 7s. 3d. groten.

Den selven van drie dagen tvoirs. werck te begaene, sdaegs 4 stuvers, valent: 3s. groten.

Janne de Ketele van 32 voederen, berddderen, sperren, staken, steen ende andere stoffe int Huys in de munte, in de Bleyckerije ende Rantsvoirtspoyen, int Southuys, aende Lakenspoye,

spread the sand; to drape the galleries of the town hall; to cover the pavilion where the jousters were lodged with curtains; to shovel up and collect the sand and put it on the carts; to dismantle the pavilions, the lists and fences; and to perform other manual services, paid to them: 3lb. 7s. 6d. *groten.*

Paid to several carters for 633 cartloads of sand taken from the windmill at the Wollendries[79] to bring it to the great hall in the palace[80] where our gracious lord[81] jousted. Also, to bring it to the Markt for depositing sand on both sides of the lists. Paid for every cartload one *plak*, total: 2lb. 12s. 9d. *groten.*

Dirk Wageman for 633 cartloads of sand which he took from the pit at the Haardries,[82] for every cartload 12 *mijten*: 27s. 9d. *groten.*

(fol. 184v)

Jan van den Vekene for bringing one cartload of clay and three cartloads of slaked lime from the Chancery of Brabant[83] to the pavilions on the Markt: 1s. 2d. *groten.*

Baltasar van Somergem for eleven days of cutting the [contents of the] said cartload[84] at a rate of 2 *stuivers* a day, total: 5s. 6d. *groten.*

Willem Lissen, master mason of this town, has sworn upon his oath that a master bricklayer worked 4.5 days at a daily rate of 4 *stuivers*, as well as one carrier for 4.5 days at a daily rate of 2.5 *stuivers*, [in order] to build the fireplaces in the wooden pavilions on the Markt where the jousters were lodged; paid to him: 7s. 3d. *groten.*

Paid to the same to execute the said work for three days, 4 *stuivers* a day, total: 3s. *groten.*

Jan de Ketel for 32 cartloads of planks, poles, stakes, stones and other materials from the Minthouse[85] in the Blekerij,[86] the Ransvoordspui,[87] in the Zouthuis,[88] in the Lakenspui[89]

---

[79] These are various fields just inside the town walls of Brussels, nowadays situated around the Poelaertplein. Bram Vannieuwenhuyze, 'Brussel, de ontwikkeling van een middeleeuwse stedelijke ruimte' (unpublished PhD dissertation, Universiteit Gent, 2008), p. 1209.

[80] This is the Aula Magna or Great Hall of the Coudenberg Palace, constructed by Philip the Good in the 1450s. It measured 150 × 60 feet (41.4 × 16.5 m) and was apparently big enough for jousting. The Aula was situated on the *piano nobile* and could be reached only via a monumental landing with two flights of stairs, which for trained horses would not have been difficult to manage. Vincent Heymans, Laetitia Cnockaert and Frédérique Honoré, eds., *Het Coudenbergpaleis te Brussel van middeleeuws kasteel tot archeologische site* (Ghent: Uitgeverij Snoeck, 2014), pp. 88–9, 96–103.

[81] That is, Philip the Fair.

[82] Is it not clear where this location is. It may refer to the 'dries' (common open space) in the village of Haren, to the north-west of Brussels.

[83] Built in 1496, the Chancery was located in the Kanselarijstraat which, today, is near the main railway station.

[84] That is, the clay and lime.

[85] There was a mint in Brussels from 1073 onwards. The Minthouse was one of the locations used by the town administration to store rye in order to secure a steady supply of this essential foodstuff and a stable price for it. Vannieuwenhuyze, 'Brussel', pp. 234, 1015.

[86] This is the district of the bleachers, situated nowadays around the Huidenvettersstraat. *Ibid.*, pp. 821–2.

[87] Nowadays, this is the Ninoofseplein. *Ibid.*, p. 1080.

[88] This is probably the Zouthuis, a saltery in the Zoutstraat, nowadays the Boterstraat. *Ibid.*, p. 1221.

[89] This is the lock (*spui*) that formed part of the Buitenste Lakenpoort. The attic of this lockhouse was used by the town administration for storing salt. *Ibid.*, pp. 390, 985.

ende in de Herberge van Haffligem te halene met zijnen wagene ende peerden ten lijsten ende baillen opte Merct ten voirs steecspelen te vuerene, te halen ende te bringene. Ende van 29 voedere stoffen aldaer afgebroken wederom in de munte te vuerene, zijn tsamen 61 voederen betaelt van den voedere 2 stuvers daeraf de rentmeester met hem overcomen zijn, om: 30s. 6d. groten.

Cornelijse Schermer van 15,5 ellen canevets, coste delle 4 plac, valent 5s. 3d. groten, van 14 ellen roede sayen fringen, coste delle 2 placken 6 mijten valent 2s. 7,5d. groten totten pavilloenen aen der jugen huys gelevert; van den selven te nayene 6 placken; van den selven pavilloene ende de tonne daer de helmen opstaken root ende wit te schilderene, daerop eenen houten appel staende met ons genedichs heeren wapene in beyden zijden te schilderen 10s. groten; ende van den huysen daer de heeren, die 't fait van den wapene inne deden, inne vertrocken, al wit te verwene 8s. groten, tsamen: 26s. 1,5d. groten.

Joncheeren Anthoon van Lalaing, raid ende camerlinck ons genedichs heeren, die tpas ende tfait van wapene alhier opte Merct opgesedt ende gedaen heeft 5 dagen lanck duerende, bij ordinancien ende bevele des selfs ons genedichs heeren hem gegeven ende gesconken 200 rijnsgulden, te 5s. groten Brabants: 50lb. groten.

Den hieraulten ons genedichs heeren voere trecht dat zij pretendeerden te hebbene aen de lijsten, huyskens daer de jugen opsaten, daer de voirs. joncker Anthoon als verweerdere hem inne wapene, opte Merct gemaect, ende de lijsten daer men over stack, tpas ende tfait van wapene dede betaelt 2lb. groten; voere de helmen ende scilden verwapent 3lb. groten tsamen: 5lb. groten.

(fol. 185r)

Baltasar van Somergem, Jacoppe van den Broecke, Ghijsbrecht van Lede ende Aerde van Callenberge van der poirten van den stadhuys achter ende voere acht dagen lanck te

and in the house of the abbey of Affligem,[90] to collect this with his cart and take it to the Markt for the lists and fences for the said joust. And [for another] 29 cartloads of dismantled material there, to take it to the mint again. Paid all together for 61 cartloads, as the receiver had agreed with him, at a rate of 2 *stuivers* per cartload: 30s. 6d. *groten*.

Cornelis Schermer [was] paid for 15.5 *el*[91] [of] tarpaulin at a cost of 4 *plak* per *el*, total 5s. 3d. *groten*; for 14 *el*[92] [of] red woollen fringes, at a cost of 2 *plakken*, 6 *mijten* per *el*, total 2s. 7.5d. *groten*, delivered for the pavilion of the judges, and to sew the said fabrics 6 *plakken*; to paint the same pavilion and the barrels on which the helms were placed in red and white, and to paint the coat of arms of our gracious lord on both sides of a wooden orb placed on it [i.e. on the pavilion] 10s. *groten*; and to paint all in white the pavilion where the lords stayed and from where they left to perform the feat of arms, 8s. *groten*. Total: 26s. 1.5d. *groten*.

Given and donated to the squire Antoine de Lalaing, councillor-chamberlain of our gracious lord, who organised and staged the *pas* and feat of arms here on the Markt over five days[93] by order and command of our gracious lord, the sum of 200 *rijnsgulden*, at a rate of 5s. *groten* Brabantine: 50lb. *groten*.[94]

Paid to the heralds[95] of our gracious lord for the rights they claimed to have to the lists, the small pavilions where the judges were seated and where the said squire Antoine as defender armed himself, and the barrier used for the joust and the *pas* and feat of arms, 2lb. *groten*; for painting the crests and coats of arms, 3lb. *groten*. Total: 5lb. *groten*.

(fol. 185r)

To Baltasar van Somergem, Jacob van den Broeke, Gijsbrecht van Lede and Aart van Callenberg for keeping watch over the gates of the town hall, both at the front and at the back, for eight days when my gracious lord jousted and performed his *pas* on the

---

[90] This is a Benedictine abbey some 20 km to the north-west of Brussels. Many abbeys in the Low Countries had houses, known as *refugia*, in nearby towns where they could shelter in case of danger.

[91] One *el* in Brabant measured 69.2 cm; here it therefore equates to *c.*10.73 m.

[92] That is, *c.*9.7 m.

[93] It can thus be concluded that Antoine de Lalaing's *pas* took place on 19, 20, 21, 22 and 23 December (see below, in the final entry, p. 299), whereas the joust and feat of arms of Philip the Fair took place on 17 December only, as suggested in the title of this section of the account.

[94] On 12 January 1504, Antoine received a gift from Philip the Fair of 220lb. (of forty *gros*) for services performed which do not explicitly mention the *pas*. However, the timing of this gift, which was 10 per cent more than the town's payment (the equivalent of 200lb. of forty *gros*), does suggest that the archduke regarded this chivalric event in a positive way. ADN B 2185 fol. 167r.

[95] It is not clear which heralds performed these activities at this *pas d'armes*. It is highly likely that Toison d'or King of Arms, Thomas Isaac at that time, was of their number, as he is mentioned as being one of the recipients of a winegift of three *gelten* of Rhenish wine (7.8 litres) from the town administration after the entry of Philip the Fair into Brussels on 18 November 1503. AR 30949 fol. 179v. In René of Anjou's *Livre des tournois*, it was stipulated that 'all the knights and squires who have never tourneyed before must pay for their helms and their welcome to arms, to the king of arms, heralds or pursuivants, at their pleasure or by the order of the judges'. Justin Sturgeon, *Text and Image in René d'Anjou's* Livre des tournois*: Constructing Authority and Identity in Fifteenth-Century Court Culture*, 3 vols (Woodbridge: Boydell Press, 2022), vol. 1, p. 221. However, the payment here seems to relate rather to the painting of the coats of arms of all participants on the ephemeral architecture. See also Source 11b.

bewarene, als onse genedige heere opte Merct gesteken ende tpas gedaen heeft, daeraf Baltasar ende Jacop van den Broecke elcken sdaegs 1s. 8d., ende de 2 dieneren elcken sdaegs 10d. groten, valent: 2lb. groten.

Thomase van der Hameyden van 4 scotelen nagelen, cost elck scotele 4,5 stuver totten voirs. lijsten gelevert, valent: 4s. 6d. groten.

Meester Janne Lemers van 6 paer strecleden coste 12 stuvers; 5 grindels 5 stuvers; ende van vier grindel sloten, tstuc 5 stuvers, totten berdderen huyskens opte Merct gelevert, betaelt: 4s. 6d. groten.

Betaelt aen den cost gedaen opter stadhuys met onsen genedigen heeren, den ertshertoge, mitter vrouwen van Vendome, mitter jonffrouwe van Nassouwen, ende anderen heeren ende vrouwen als men opte Merct gestoken heeft ende tpas van wapene gedaen 17, 19, 20, 21, 22 ende 23 dage in decembri anno 1500 drie, gedragene na uutwijsen van den partijen: 25lb. 15s. 1d. groten.

Somme 111lb. 5s. 6,5d. groten.

Markt.[96] Paid to both Baltasar and Jacob van den Broeke 1s. 8d. a day and to each of the two servants 10d. *groten* a day. Total: 2lb. *groten.*

Paid to Thomas van der Hameide for four packets of nails used for the lists, costing 4.5 *stuivers* per packet. Total: 4s. 6d. *groten.*

Paid to Master Jan Lemers who, for the small wooden pavilions on the Markt, delivered six pairs of hinges at a cost of 12 *stuivers*; five bolts for 5 *stuivers*; and four bolt locks, at 5 *stuivers* a piece: 4s. 6d. *groten.*

Paid for the dinners held in the town hall with our gracious lord the archduke,[97] my lady of Vendôme,[98] the lady of Nassau[99] and other lords and ladies, after finishing the jousting and the *pas d'armes* on the Markt on 17, 19, 20, 21, 22 and 23 December in the year 1503, as is clearly attested in the individual declarations: 25lb. 15s. 1d. *groten.*

Grand total: 111lb. 5s. 6.5d. *groten.*

---

[96] The number of days mentioned here is ambiguous, as that given below is six. However, we know from the narrative source (see above, p. 291) that Philip the Fair had his *emprise* on Sunday 15 December, which probably extended into Monday 16 December, when apparently no dinner was held in the town hall. This would make up the number of eight days, although they were definitely not all used solely for Philip's joust.

[97] Philip the Fair was also archduke of Austria.

[98] That is, Marie de Luxembourg. See above, n. 39.

[99] As Cimburga of Baden, wife of the then count of Nassau, Engelbrecht II, had already died in 1503, this probably refers to the new wife of Hendrik III van Nassau, Louise-Françoise of Savoy. See above, n. 37.

Thanks are due to Josephine van den Bent, Rosalind Brown-Grant, Ralph Moffat and Bram Vannieuwenhuyze for their helpful comments on these translations.

Thalia Brero and Rosalind Brown-Grant

Source 15

The *Pas* of Carignano, 1504

This source consists of a translation of selected extracts from a narrative account of this event and a financial document relating to it.

Author:

(1) of the narrative account: unknown, but likely to have been a herald
(2) of the financial document: unknown

Language: Middle French for both the narrative account and the financial document

Editions used:

(1) for the narrative account: 'Tournoi fait à Carignan par le duc Philibert le Beau', in Samuel Guichenon, *Histoire généalogique de la royale Maison de Savoie*, 2nd edition, 5 vols (Turin: J. M. Briolo, 1778), vol. 4/2, pp. 469–77 (= PC)
2) for the financial document: Max Bruchet, *Marguerite d'Autriche, duchesse de Savoie* (Lille: impr. Danel, 1927), pp. 323–4

Select bibliography:

Brero, Thalia, *Rituels dynastiques et mises en scène du pouvoir: Le cérémonial princier à la cour de Savoie* (Florence: SISMEL Edizioni del Galluzzo, 2017), pp. 81–3

——, 'Soirées festives et vie nocturne à la cour de Savoie', in *Le Banquet: manger, boire et parler ensemble (XIIe–XVIIe siècles)*, ed. by Bruno Laurioux, Agostino Paravicini Bagliani and Eva Pibiri, Micrologus Library, 91 (Firenze: SISMEL Edizioni del Galluzzo, 2018), pp. 229–60

Gentile, Luisa, *Riti ed emblemi: Processi di rappresentazione del potere principesco in area subalpina (XIII–XVI secc.)* (Turin: Silvio Zamorani Editore, 2008), p. 65

Introduction

This narrative account records a *pas d'armes* organised by Philibert II, duke of Savoy, in the Piedmontese town of Carignano in February 1504. It was held to celebrate the marriage of Laurent de Gorrevod, one of his favourites and his grand squire, to Philippa de La Palu, a noblewoman from Bresse. The marriage contract was signed at the castle of Carignano on Sunday 18 February 1504, the same day as the beginning of the *pas d'armes*; this date also coincides with the period of *Caresmeprenant*, the period of carnival festivities before the beginning of Lent, on Ash Wednesday, which fell on 21 February that year. The *Pas* of Carignano can therefore be seen as a

Shrovetide tournament.[1] The first part of the text reports on the combats that took place on 18–20 February 1504, as well as a contest that involved running at the ring* that took place on 25 February. The second part is devoted to the nocturnal activities of this assembly, mainly dances and *momeries**.

The original manuscript of this account is missing; the text has come down to us only thanks to the transcription made by the official historiographer of the court of Savoy, Samuel Guichenon (1607–64), whose *Histoire généalogique de la maison de Savoie* dates from the middle of the seventeenth century. At the end of this work, Guichenon published two volumes of *Preuves* as an appendix: these were copies of archival documents that he considered to be important for the history of the Savoyard ducal dynasty. Among them is a document entitled *Tournoi fait à Carignan par le duc Philibert le Beau*, extracts of which are translated here. The author of this text is unknown, but likely to have been a herald. Given that he twice mentions receiving instructions to write it, he was probably commissioned to do so, most likely by Duke Philibert II himself. The participants in the event are all named and their combats are described in great detail: the combatants' outfits and significant events are reported (broken swords, the duke's left pauldron-reinforce* being pierced by a lance, a horse falling to the ground, a broken helmet visor causing the judges to separate the combatants for safety reasons, etc.).

The narrative starts with a proclamation by a herald, reported in direct speech, which seems to give an antique, allegorical setting to the *pas*: Cupid, Juno, Pallas and Venus are thus mentioned as presiding over the event. The rules of engagement are then outlined: the duke of Savoy, Philibert II himself, and a gentleman named Sibuet de La Balme are to hold the *pas* as *tenans** (defenders) against all *venans** (challengers). Combat will take place at the barrier on foot: first with spears and then, when these are broken, with swords, until the judges separate the combatants and bring the bout to a close.

On the first day, Sunday 18 February, the two defenders fought as a pair against five pairs of challengers; among them were the brother of the duke of Savoy (the future duke Charles II), the bridegroom (Laurent de Gorrevod), various Savoyard gentlemen and a Burgundian squire. The following day, 19 February, seven pairs of challengers came to compete against the duke and his right-hand man; when they tired from their exertions after four consecutive combats, they were replaced by two other defenders for the last three combats. The participants, whether on the defending or the attacking side, were essentially Savoyard noblemen. In the evening, the prizes for these two days of fighting were awarded by the ladies and the judges to two of the challengers. The best fighters with spears and swords respectively were rewarded, but the ladies requested that two special prizes be awarded, one for the duke and one for his brother, Charles.

On the third day, 20 February, the rules of engagement were changed: this time the combatants were on horseback, wearing war harness, and they fought exclusively with their swords, two against two. The defenders were four Savoyard noblemen who fought two bouts each; they faced four teams of two challengers (eight knights in all). In the evening, prizes were awarded. The part of the account devoted to the jousts ends by mentioning a contest involving running at the ring that was organised a few days later,

[1] Shrovetide was a typical period for tournaments and feasting in general. Richard Barber and Juliet Barker, *Tournaments: Jousts, Chivalry and Pageants in the Middle Ages* (Woodbridge: Boydell Press, 1989), pp. 173, 176.

on 25 February. The second part of the account, devoted to the evening entertainments, then begins. The text retrospectively relates the '*momerie* by combat' of the evening of 18 February, the *momerie* of the Amazons of 19 February and that of the Slave-Knights of 20 February.

The translation that follows renders the preamble of this narrative account, in which a herald explains what gave rise to this *pas* and outlines its rules of engagement, as well as the most original passages of the text, namely those concerning the evening festivities. Not only are they described in particular detail but they seem to be an extension of the combats that took place during the day, as if a common scenario governed both the daytime jousts and the evening dances. Moreover, women play an especially prominent role during these entertainments: as formidable warriors in the all-female *momerie* of the Amazons and as mistresses holding valiant fighters in chains in that of the Slave-Knights. The duchess of Savoy, Margaret of Austria, probably played an important part in the conception of this event since she was highly influential at the Savoyard court.

Indeed, the second set of extracts translated here — a roll of expenses used as a *quittance* (receipt) in her household account — reveal that Margaret financed part of the expenses incurred in the organisation of the nightly festivities at the *Pas* of Carignano. Thus, a month and a half after the event, on 28 April 1504, her keeper of the wardrobe, Diego Flores, wrote a roll of some expenses incurred for the *momeries* that were organised in Carignano to entertain the Savoyard court during the evenings of the *pas*.[2] He handed this roll to a treasurer who subsequently ordered payment to him of the sum he had outlined; Diego Flores then declared on the back of the document that he had received this sum from the treasurer. This *quittance*, which is translated below, was used as a piece of evidence added to the account of the treasurer to justify these expenses. It shows that the materials used for some of the disguises and the costs involved in making them up were all paid for by Margaret, which thus confirms the impression that the *entrepreneurs* of this *pas d'armes* were both the duke and the duchess of Savoy, he being responsible for the daytime combats and she for the nighttime entertainments.[3]

In the translations that follow, page numbers in parentheses have been inserted for ease of reference to Guichenon's edition for the narrative account and to Bruchet's edition for the financial document.

TRANSLATION (1): NARRATIVE ACCOUNT

(469) The renown of the noble and the valiant in both deed and courage endures forever, and high and noble feats of arms should always be remembered so as to inspire nobles of the present day and to encourage those of the future to undertake the pursuit of arms. For there is nothing that corrupts nobility more — as Valerius Maximus says in the

[2] Most of these expenses relate to costumes used in the *momerie* of the Amazons that was performed on the second day of the *pas*, but it is possible that some items were bought for the other *momeries*, or even reused over several days.

[3] This hypothesis could be verified by looking into the duke's expenses in the Archivio di Stato in Turin.

second book of his work on the discipline of chivalry[4] — than being idle and failing to perform some noble endeavour. I have been ordered[5] to commit to writing some fine and glorious deeds of arms that were recently accomplished during Shrovetide in the town of Carignano at its castle, these deeds being on both foot and horseback. This is for the most high and redoubtable person of my most high and redoubtable lord, Monseigneur the duke of Savoy, Philibert II of this name,[6] who was present with my most high and redoubtable lady, Madame Marguerite of Austria, duchess of Savoy,[7] my redoutable lady Madame Blanche de Montferrat, dowager duchess of Savoy,[8] and several other lovely ladies and young damsels, whose names and surnames it would take too long to recount. These feats of arms were organised and performed as much out of noble conduct as of love for the ladies; it was also to honour the festivities in celebration of the marriage of the grand squire, my lord Laurent de Gorrevod,[9] who took as his bride the daughter[10] of the late Messire Hugues de La Palu, count of Varax, who was in his time marshal of Savoy.[11]

---

[4] Valerius Maximus was a Roman author of the first century AD. His *Facta et dicta mirabilia* (*Memorable Deeds and Sayings*) was one of the most copied Latin works in the Middle Ages. In this collection of historical anecdotes, the *exempla* on the Roman army and military discipline inspired medieval writings on chivalry. Anne Dubois, *Valère Maxime en français à la fin du Moyen Âge: Images et tradition* (Turnhout: Brepols, 2016).

[5] The name of the author of the text has not come down to us, but he was probably a herald in the service of the duke of Savoy. The use of the first-person voice underlines that his account is that of a trustworthy eyewitness.

[6] Philibert II of Savoy (1480–1504), son of Philippe II, duke of Savoy, and Marguerite of Bourbon, succeeded his father in 1497, at the age of seventeen. He married his first cousin Yolande-Louise of Savoy (1487–99), then, on her death, Margaret of Austria. Philibert II was succeeded on his death at the age of twenty-four by his brother, Charles II of Savoy, as he had produced no heirs. DBI, vol. 47, pp. 652–4.

[7] Margaret of Austria (1480–1530) was the daughter of the Holy Roman Emperor Maximilian I and Mary of Burgundy. She was married to 1. Charles VIII of France (1483), 2. Juan of Castile (1497) and 3. Philibert II of Savoy (1501): none of these unions produced an heir. After becoming the widow of Philibert II (1504), Margaret returned to Flanders to become regent of the Netherlands on behalf of her nephew, Charles V (1507–15, 1518–30). Max Bruchet, *Marguerite d'Autriche, duchesse de Savoie* (Lille: impr. Danel, 1927).

[8] [Blanche de Montferra, douaigiere de Savoie]. Blanche of Montferrat (1472–1519), daughter of William VIII Palaeologus, marquis of Montferrat, and Elisabetta Sforza, married Duke Charles I of Savoy in 1485. They had two children: Yolande-Louise and Charles-Jean-Amédée of Savoy. When her husband died in 1490, she acted as regent for their son until his death at the age of six in 1496. She then retired to the castle of Carignano, which was part of her dower, until her death in 1519. DBI, vol. 10, pp. 16–18.

[9] [Laurens de Gorrevod]. Laurent de Gorrevod (*c.*1470–1529), count of Pont-de-Vaux and viscount of Salins, son of Jean III de Gorrevod and Jeanne de Loriol-Challes, was grand squire to Philibert II of Savoy (1497) and governor of Bresse (1504). When the duke died, he followed his widow, Margaret of Austria, to the Netherlands in 1506 and, from then on, had a career at the Habsburg court and later at the Spanish court of Charles V. He was married twice, 1. to Philippa de La Palu (1504) and 2. to Claude de Rivoire (1509), but was succeeded by his cousin, Jean de Gorrevod, as he left no legitimate heirs. Florence Beaume, 'Les Gorrevod, de la Bresse à l'Empire', in *La noblesse des marches, de Bourgogne et d'ailleurs au temps de Marguerite d'Autriche (XVe–XVIe siècle): Annales de Bourgogne*, 89.3/4 (2017), 19–32.

[10] Philippa (or Philiberte) de La Palu was the daughter of Hugues de La Palu (see below, n. 11), and Antoinette de Polignac. HBB, p. 300.

[11] [Hugue de La Palu]. Hugues de La Palu, count of Varax and viscount of Salins, was the son of Guy de La Palu and Marguerite de Savigny. He was a member of the Order of the Collar of Savoy,

Of these events, the first to be held was a *pas* fought on foot over a barrier by my aforesaid lord[12] and Sibuet de La Baulme,[13] in the form described here below and the chapters of which follow hereafter:

'Now hear ye, hear ye, hear ye! Let it be known to you that, by his wish, Cupid's court has been in session, with a large number of his subjects in attendance. After several days, it has been proclaimed and announced by official decree in the presence of Juno, goddess of marriage, and of Pallas, from whom all good things flow, by Lady Venus who has voiced her decision that, in this matter, on the eighteenth day of February, which is the Sunday of *Caresmeprenant*,[14] a contract of marriage will be made between a nymph and her bridegroom at the castle of Carignano.

In this regard, Lady Fame herself[15] has brought this matter to the attention of two knights who, in order to honour the occasion, have undertaken to hold a *pas* in the following form for all comers: fighting two against two, these knights will take up their positions in the courtyard of the castle in front of the said town of Carignano next to a barrier in order to do combat on foot; they will be armed in the manner which is required in such cases.

The challengers will be allowed to take their pick of the spears* with sharpened tips which are to be used for thrusting until the competitors are ordered by my lords, the appointed judges, to desist.

Also presented to those from the outside* will be two-handed swords, for both cutting and (470) thrusting, and there [the competitors] will deal as many strokes against each other [as they can] until they are told to stop, as noted above.

The one from the outside who performs best with the spear will receive the prize of a rich jewel worth up to 500 *écus*.[16]

The one from the outside who performs best with the sword will receive a ring worth up to 1000 *écus*, etc.

---

lieutenant-general for King Charles VIII of France in Dauphiné, and marshal of Savoy (1494). He had two daughters by his first wife, Gilberte de Varax (who brought him his comital title), and a son and two daughters by his second wife, Antoinette de Polignac. These latter two daughters were Philippa (see above, n. 10) and Claudine, who was the first wife of Claude de Vaudrey, the renowned Burgundian jouster (his second wife, Marie de Challant, whom he married in 1510, was also a noblewoman at the court of Savoy). HBB, pp. 74, 300.

[12] That is, Philibert II of Savoy.

[13] [Siboet de La Balme]. Sibuet de La Baulme, lord of Ramasse, l'Asne and Charantonnay, son of Claude de La Baulme and Jeanne de Benier (who married in 1470), was the husband of Claudine, lady of Charantonnay, in 1530; they had six children. DN, vol. 2, p. 90.

[14] The Sunday before Shrove Tuesday and Ash Wednesday, so this is the period of carnival festivities before Lent.

[15] The text says that Fama was here 'sans son secretaire' (without her secretary), which can be read as meaning 'Lady Fame was there in person'. In Roman mythology, Fama, the 'public voice', is the personification of popular rumour, whom Virgil describes as having many eyes and mouths. In the medieval context, Fama was an allegory of fame and renown. Claude Gauvard, 'Fama', in *Dictionnaire du Moyen Âge*, ed. by Claude Gauvard, Alain de Libera and Michel Zink (Paris: Presses Universitaires de France, 2002), p. 515.

[16] In the 1490s (no figures are available for 1504), the French golden *écu au soleil* was worth 1lb. 16s. 3d. *livres tournois*, meaning that 500 *écus* were worth 906lb. 5s. *livres tournois*. Peter Spufford, *Handbook of Medieval Exchange* (London: Offices of the Royal Historical Society, 1986), p. 193.

Moreover, it is not to be thought that the ladies are so lacking in gratitude as to fail to bestow a fine and handsome gift on those from the inside* who perform the best with either the spear or the sword — as the judges decide — this being so as to encourage them to continue to do their utmost.

And if it should so happen — God forbid! — that either of the two defenders should be inconvenienced such that he is unable to carry on fighting, it will be at the discretion of the judges, if they please, to provide him with some assistance.

[A description follows of the combats at the barrier, first with spears then with swords, that took place on 18 and 19 February, and of those fought on horseback with swords that were held on 20 February.]

(475) In the evening, after dinner and dancing, by order of the ladies and on the advice of the judges, the prize and honour of the event for the defender who had performed the best was given to Gramont[17] by a fair and gentle damsel who entreated him, on behalf of the ladies, to seek always to do better and better.

The prize and honour of the event for the challenger who had performed the best, according to the ladies and by order of the judges, was given and awarded by another lovely young damsel who granted a gracious kiss to Messire Gauvain, lord of Candie.[18] He had been the most deserving of the challengers and the one who had fought most boldly and energetically, in the ladies' eyes, even though all the others had undoubtedly acquitted themselves well of their duty.

On the following Sunday,[19] the ladies donated a costly ring for running at the ring and ordered it to be attached to a column by a herald: three courses were to be run at this ring by each of the above-named men, by the ladies' command. The first of these was my most high and most redoubtable lord, his aforesaid grand squire,[20] the lord of Balleyson,[21] the knight and lord of Châteaufort and Hauteville,[22] Messire Sibuet de La Baulme, lord of

---

[17] This is likely to be Hugues de Meyria, lord of Gramont, Rosy, Sellias and Longmont, who was married to Marguerite de Grolée with whom he had two sons, Jean (who was knighted by Charles V at the battle of Pavia, in 1525) and Claude de Meyria. HBB, p. 127.

[18] [messire Gaulvent, sieur de Candie]. Gauvain de Candie (d. 1536), lord of Berruyre, son of Maurice de Candie, was a squire of Duke Charles II of Savoy and captain of the town of Chambéry in 1531. One of his younger brothers (Jean or Hugonin) also participated in this *pas d'armes* and is referred to in the narrative account as 'le jeune Candie' (young Candie). HBB, p. 90; ANADS, vol. 1, pp. 300–1.

[19] 25 February 1504, i.e. Invocavit, the first Sunday in Lent.

[20] That is, Laurent de Gorrevod: see above, n. 9.

[21] Claude de Balleyson (d. before 1541), baron of Hermance, Saint-Germain and Avanchy, son of Antoine de Balleyson, was a councillor and chamberlain to Duke Philibert II of Savoy and his successor, Duke Charles II. As ambassador, he went to the Netherlands to negotiate the hand of Margaret of Austria for Philibert II, and to Naples (1511) and to Lisbon (1521) for marriage projects for Charles II. He married Claudine-Antoinette, the lady of Avanchy, and had no children. Thalia Brero, *Rituels dynastiques et mises en scène du pouvoir: Le cérémonial princier à la cour de Savoie (1450–1550)* (Florence: SISMEL Edizioni del Galluzzo, 2017), pp. 575–6.

[22] [le chevallier et sieur de Chasteau-fort et d'Auteville]. This may be Alexandre de Montluel, lord of Châteaufort, Creste, Hauteville and Châtillon, son of Jean de Montluel and Guigonne de Luyrieu, who married Pernette de Viry; alternatively, it could be his son Nicolas, lord of Châteaufort and Hauteville, who married Françoise de Luyrieu. ANADS, vol. 4, p. 141.

Ramasse,[23] Messire Gauvain de Candie, Loriol,[24] Croque-Mouche,[25] Feillans,[26] Exchesq[27] and several others whom it would take too long to name. All of them were well armed, well mounted and richly equipped, with some even more finely decked out than others. At the end of the three courses, none of them had succeeding in taking the ring, which is why the ladies, by their grace, granted all of the competitors another three courses to run at it. Of these three courses, it was during the second one that the ring was taken by the lord of Balleyson and by Croque-Mouche. It was therefore recognised and agreed that, since they were the two who had succeeded in taking it, each of them would receive the value of the ring, with the request that they both continually make every effort to do better and better.

(476) Because some people like to see and hear about new things, I have been ordered to describe some of the delightful and elegant entertainments that took place [each day] once the above-mentioned combats had finished. Among the various entertainments that were organised on the first night of these wedding celebrations, was a *momerie* that involved a kind of fight between six gentlemen who, dancing into the room where all the nobles were gathered for the festivities, were fully armed with their weapons. Their harnesses* were covered in white and red silk with great stripes across [them], and they wore bourrelets* on their heads with crests representing damsels. After having danced twice round the room, they began to fight each other with polished swords, dealing each other great blows that were very impressive to watch. Having paid their respects where they were due, they withdrew, and further entertainments took place, both *momeries* and other kinds which I will refrain from describing.

The following evening, lots of entertainments likewise took place, including one involving my aforesaid most redoubtable lord,[28] accompanied by Messire François de Luxembourg, viscount of Martigues,[29] and three other knights of unknown identity who

---

[23] [messire Siboed de la Balme, sieur de Romasses]. See above, n. 13.

[24] Jean de Loriol, lord of Challes and Corgenon, was the son of Jacques de Loriol and Marie de Virieu. His sister was Jeanne de Loriol, mother of Laurent de Gorrevod; he was therefore the uncle of the groom whose wedding was celebrated at the *Pas* of Carignano. As tutor of Philibert II of Savoy, he was in charge of his education and accompanied him on his travels in France, Flanders and Italy. When Philibert became duke, he appointed Loriol councillor, chamberlain and *grand maître d'hôtel*, and made him governor of Bresse and of the city of Turin. He died childless and bequeathed his property to his nephews, Jean-Philibert de Challes and Laurent de Gorrevod. HBB, p. 227; Mario Zucchi, *I governatori dei principi reali di Savoia* (Turin: Tipografia del Collegio degli Artigianelli, 1925), pp. 27–8.

[25] No information is available about this person.

[26] Louis de Feillans, lord of Vologna, Chanay and Crèvecoeur, son of Antoine de Feillans and Claudine de Colombier, was governor of Verceil (1523). HBB, p. 174.

[27] This is perhaps a member of the Echaquet family, an old family of Annecy. ANADS, vol. 2, pp. 298–301.

[28] That is, Philibert II of Savoy.

[29] [messire Francois de Luxembourg, visconte de Martigue]. François I de Luxembourg-Martigues (*c.*1445–*c.*1511), son of Thibaud de Luxembourg and Philippine de Melun, came from a collateral branch of the house of Luxembourg which had inherited the viscounty of Martigues in Provence in 1481. Following his marriage to Louise of Savoy in 1487, he received various lordships in the duchy of Savoy and was succeeded by his son, François II de Luxembourg (*c.*1492–1553). Olivier Dessemontet, 'Les Luxembourg-Martigues, seigneurs au Pays de Vaud. 1487–1558', *Revue suisse d'histoire*, 4.1 (1954), 88–123.

were disguised and dressed like hermits in grey damask, each of them wearing the same kind of fine mask and carrying a large rosary as they pretended to be reciting their Hours.[30]

Once they took their seats, in came my most redoubtable lady, Madame Marguerite of Austria, duchess of Savoy, accompanied by Madame Louise of Savoy, viscountess of Martigues,[31] as well as two damsels dressed like Amazons, all of them dancing as they made their entrance in the following form and manner.

First of all came an elderly damsel dressed in a smock of fine linen worked with gold and silk in the fashion of a Saraceness. Underneath this smock she wore a yellow satin *cotte** with a coat armour* over it of yellow satin that was divided into black velvet quarters, each of which was adorned with a large cross of St Andrew made of cloth of silver.[32] On her head she wore a green[33] headcovering over a coif* of crimson satin covered with gold, and a fine white hat with a liripipe* made of tan-coloured taffeta. This damsel, who was performing the role of a herald, gave a fine and elegant speech, the substance of which is as follows:

Because of the good name and fine renown
That have now spread to many a land
Of the best duke who ever lived,
Seeing that he keeps his people in a state of peace
In his lands of Piedmont and Savoy,
Herewith, sent to him
By the wise lady, queen of the Amazons,
Are some of her ladies — lovely, virtuous,
And expert in the pursuit of arms —
Who have wasted little time in making their way here
Swiftly, and not without some difficulty and travail,
To this castle of Carignano
Where they had heard
That he wished today to disport himself
In the noble pursuit of arms,
The better to keep his subjects practised in the arts of war.
He himself would personally undertake —
With just one other gentleman —
To defend the *pas* at a barrier

[30] This practice refers to reciting prayers at given times of day, these prayers being outlined in a personal Book of Hours.

[31] [Madame Loyse de Savoie viscontesse de Martigues]. Louise of Savoy (1467–1520), daughter of Janus of Savoy and Hélène de Luxembourg, first married her cousin Jacques-Louis of Savoy, marquis of Gex. After his death, in 1487 she married François I de Luxembourg-Martigues (see above, n. 29). Louise of Savoy was the cousin of Duke Philibert II of Savoy. Dessemontet, 'Les Luxembourg-Martigues'.

[32] The cross of St Andrew was a Burgundian emblem and thus clearly relates to Margaret of Austria's family. D'Arcy Jonathan Dacre Boulton, 'The Order of the Golden Fleece and the Creation of Burgundian National Identity', in *The Ideology of Burgundy: The Promotion of National Consciousness, 1364–1565*, ed. by D'Arcy Jonathan Dacre Boulton and Jan Veenstra (Leiden: Brill, 2006), pp. 21–97.

[33] Guichenon's transcription has 'sinople' (green), but this may be a misreading of *linomple* (a type of very fine linen).

By thrusting at and repelling
Those knights who wished to see
If they could try and win [the barrier] from him on that day.
And seeing that it is said, in many places,
(477) That in this land there are some good knights
Who take pleasure in performing deeds of arms —
Whether in war or for love of the ladies —
These Amazons have now arrived here,
As you can see, equipped and ready,
To help him if he is brought down
And to come to his aid, if needed,
[Being] determined to defend this *pas*
On his behalf and not to fail him.
There is one,[34] in particular, whether she be close by or far away,
Who will always ready herself to come to his assistance
And who wishes word to spread far and wide
Of all he personally accomplishes and all his deeds;
For this is what she came into this world to do
And this good intention is what has brought her here.
Though she may be of the highest nobility
Known between here and Carthage,
And of a most chivalrous stock,
She could not be happier
And she thanks God wholeheartedly
For having destined her for such a person
As he who has upheld the *pas* this day,
With the help of God, and come out on top.
Furthermore, she desires to make common cause
With you, Madame Blanche,[35]
For these ladies have been told
That one of your damsels
Is due to take a husband tonight;
And, if her heart falters,
Let it be known that they are ready
To come fully equipped
And to bring her their loyal assistance,
Whether this be at a stroll, a trot or a run.[36]

---

[34] The poem is obviously referring to Margaret of Austria here, and alludes to the fact that she was of higher rank than her husband. See also Essay 6.

[35] Blanche of Montferrat, dowager duchess of Savoy: see above, n. 8. The poem implies that the bride, Philippa de La Palu, was in her service as a lady-in-waiting, but there is no other documentary evidence attesting to this fact.

[36] The last line of the elderly damsel-herald's speech seems to be making an elegant but unmistakeably suggestive allusion to the idea that the Amazons have come to boost the morale of the bride in her forthcoming nuptial 'joust' with her bridegroom, at whatever 'pace' the newly weds may take it. This mixture of courtliness and suggestiveness is a staple of Burgundian literary culture with which Margaret

Having announced the arrival of the said ladies to my most redoubtable lord, together with Madame Blanche de Montferrat, the dowager duchess of Savoy, and other people present, she left the room. On her return, once she had finishing delivering her message and had received a response, in came two black damsels[37] sounding trumpets. They were dressed in the same fashion as the elderly damsel except for the fact that, instead of coat armours, they wore long cloaks that fell to the floor, and their headcoverings were in the Turkish style. They played a fanfare in the manner of a *branle*,[38] to which those taking part in the *momerie* all danced.

Next, in order, came Mademoiselle of Savoy,[39] accompanied by three other lovely young damsels, who made their entrance in pairs and were dressed in the following manner. First of all, each of them wore a crimson satin coif that was very richly edged and wrapped up their hair like a man's hairstyle;[40] [on top they wore] fine white bonnets with tan-coloured ribbons that each had a costly balas ruby holding an aigrette of small feathers.[41] They wore long cloaks of an expensive cloth of gold quartered with black velvet — each piece of velvet having a cross of St Andrew sewn on it in silver —, with long outer sleeves of net fabric that fell to the floor and were laden with *orfèvrerie**, as well as inner sleeves made of richly embroidered cloth of silver. [They also wore] white belts with little

of Austria would have been very familiar, as seen in the fact that she owned a printed copy of Antoine Vérard's 1498 second edition of the late fifteenth-century scabrous story collection known as the *Cent Nouvelles nouvelles*. Marguerite Debae, *La bibliothèque de Marguerite d'Autriche: Essai de reconstruction d'après l'inventaire de 1523–24* (Louvain/Paris: Éditions Peeters, 1995), pp. 431–3.

[37] As there is no evidence of black people at the court of Savoy at this time, these damsels were probably ladies-in-waiting wearing blackface. Dressing up as a 'Moor' was not uncommon in courtly entertainment at the time, especially when it came to dancing *morescas**, which were very popular in fifteenth-century courts. The black damsels are wearing Turkish-style headcoverings: such *turqueries* were also fashionable at the time, reflecting the West's fascination with the Ottoman Empire since the fall of Constantinople in 1453. Margaret McGowan, *La danse à la Renaissance: Sources livresques et albums d'images* (Paris: Bibliothèque nationale de France, 2012), pp. 39–45; Alison Rosie, 'Morisques and Momeryes: Aspects of Court Entertainment at the Court of Savoy in the Fifteenth Century', in *Power, Culture and Religion in France c.1350–c.1550*, ed. by Christopher Allmand (Woodbridge: Boydell Press, 1989), pp. 57–74 (pp. 59–60, 69–71).

[38] A *branle* is a kind of dance that was very popular in Renaissance courts of France and England, where the dancers formed a circle or a line, usually holding hands, and moved to the left and to the right with single and double steps and kicks. Margaret McGowan, *Dance in the Renaissance. European Fashion, French Obsession* (New Haven, CT: Yale University Press, 2008), p. 95.

[39] Claude or Claudine of Savoy (d. 1528), an illegitimate daughter of Duke Philippe II of Savoy and Bonne de Romagnano, was Duke Philibert II's half-sister. She was brought up in the entourage of Margaret of Austria, and she accompanied her when Margaret left Savoy for Mechelen in 1506. Margaret had Claude legitimised by the emperor in 1510 and bequeathed her the sum of 10,000 *livres tournois*; she also organised Claude's marriage to Count Jacques III de Hornes, a knight of the Order of the Golden Fleece, in 1514, and paid the dowry herself. Bruchet, *Marguerite d'Autriche*, pp. 84–7.

[40] As can be seen in the portrait bust of Philibert of Savoy (Figure 6) reproduced in Essay 1, p. 337, there seems to have been a fashion for men at the court of Savoy of tucking their hair under caps that look a little like hairnets; a similar male hairstyle can be seen in various miniatures in Emperor Maximilian I's tournament book known as the *Freydal*: see Stefan Krause, ed., *Freydal. Medieval Games. The Book of Tournaments of Emperor Maximilian I* (Cologne: Taschen, 2019).

[41] An aigrette is a decorative headpiece consisting of a bunch of long (originally egret) feathers or a spray of gems imitating them; a balas ruby is a variety of this type of gemstone that was sourced from the eastern Mediterranean.

daggers at their sides with richly gilded hilts and white sheathes. In their left hands, they each bore a flaming torch of sculpted white wax and, in their right hands, they carried the armet* of one of the four above-mentioned ladies on top of a baton. From their belts hung the gauntlets of the four Amazons. These damsels, who were playing the role of pages, were all laden with long and heavy gold chains that were remarkably costly.

(478) Then came the elderly damsel described before, acting the part of officer of arms on behalf of my most redoubtable lady, and the others who were accompanying her; she was carrying a white baton in her hand. Next, my most redoutable lady and her company made their entrance, dancing in the manner of a *branle* to the sound of the trumpets as mentioned before; they were dressed and equipped as you will see, that is to say their bodies were clothed in the same way as the four above-mentioned damsels, except that the cloth of gold was finer and the bodices of their clothing were cut away where the cuirasses* of their harness made of fine silver could be seen, and the vambraces* the same. Over the top of these vambraces they wore long sleeves of net fabric that fell to the floor, belts with straps of wrought silver and the sheaths of their swords in the same material, the naked swords themselves being held in their hands ready for striking. On their heads, they wore their hair inside rich crimson coifs laden with precious stones; hanging out behind from under the coifs were two thick plaits of gold thread [that were] made to look like hair which reached right down to their calves. On top they wore fine white hats with liripipes of tan-coloured taffeta that were worn like masks; the hats themselves each had feather trimmings made of costly balas rubies holding tall egret plumes. I will leave aside the large, expensive jewellery that they wore, whether the gemstones or the other fineries, the value of which was estimated at over 60,000 *écus*.

The following evening, further elegant and delightful entertainments were organised, as is customary in such a house and on such an important occasion. One of these entertainments featured my lord, accompanied by his grand squire, the lord of Balleyson and Messire Sibuet de La Balme, lord of Romasses, who danced as they made their entrance into the room where the festivities were being held; they were fully armed with their weapons and accompanied by four fair ladies who led them in on long, thick chains of gold as if they were slaves. They were dressed in costly cloth of gold, on top of which they wore dagged* chemises of white satin. The costly nature of the ladies' clothing was a very fine thing [to see]. As they danced their way into the room, from the four corners came four other knights, each of whom was preceded by a trumpeter playing his instrument; they were all well armed and their harnesses were covered with green satin. Their aim was to steal the ladies away from the knights being held on chains. No sooner did the ladies catch sight of them and realise the danger they were in than they released the knights who were their prisoners from their chains and handed each of them a fine sword. The ladies had been carrying these naked swords in their hands and using them to the rhythm of the *branle* to beat their prisoners. Once these knights were free of their chains and had grabbed their swords, they ran at the four men who had come to steal the ladies away from them. A fierce battle then ensued, with the four interlopers putting up a good fight, but none of them was a match for my said lord who, with one stroke of his sword, brought down one of the opposing knights as well as another with a second stroke that ended up dislocating this man's shoulder. Such fine feats of arms were accomplished that it would take too long to recount them all, the same being the case if I had to describe all the other joyous festivities that took place as well!

TRANSLATION (2): FINANCIAL DOCUMENT RELATED TO THE *PAS*

(323) The items that Diego Flores,[42] keeper of the wardrobe of my most redoubtable lady, Madame the duchess of Savoy, has delivered and paid for by order of my aforesaid lady for the *momerie* that she organised during *Caresmeprenant* at Carignano in the year 1504.

First of all, for two wooden legs, including the metalwork and ropes and fashioning of the said legs: fourteen *sous* and six *deniers*: 14s. 6d.

Item, for a face mask: fifteen *sous*: 15*s*.

Item, for four other face masks bought by my lord *Maître* Carenchon,[43] who was reimbursed by the said Diego: six *florins* and 2 *gros*: 6fl. 2gr.

Item, in addition, for three yellow hats that Noe[44] bought: four *florins* and three *sous*: 4fl. 3g.

Item, for six other white hats: seven *florins*: 7fl.

Item, for six pieces[45] of yellow and black taffeta for a robe for Lordant[46] sent to him by order of my aforesaid lady, at 19 *sous* a piece: nine *florins* and six *sous*: 9fl. 6gr.

Item, for four pieces of tan-coloured taffeta for the sleeves of the pages in the said *momerie*: 6 *florins*: 6fl.

Item, for a piece and two-thirds of white taffeta for the sheaths of the swords in the said *momerie*: two *florins*, nine and three quarter *sous*: 33¾s.

Item, for three pieces of another tan-coloured taffeta for the liripipes of the white hats: five *florins*: 5fl.

Item, for crêpe cloth: one *florin* and nine *gros*: 1fl. 9gr.

Item, for laces in the said *momerie*: ten *sous* and six *deniers*: 10½gr.

Item, for four white bonnets at 20 *sous* a piece: eight *florins* and four *sous*: 8fl. 4gr.[47]

Item, for having the taffeta liripipes attached to the said bonnets: 4 *sous*: 4gr.

Item, for lashes and batons to make scourges[48] in the said *momerie*: 3½ *gros*: 3½gr.

Item, to a man and woman for sewing the aforesaid garments: two *testons*: 21gr.

Item, for a *teston* lost on a piece of taffeta bought from Cermanycle:[49] 10½ *gros*: 10½gr.

---

[42] Diego Flores was in the service of Margaret of Austria during her stay at the Spanish court (1497–99) following her marriage to Juan of Castile. When she became a widow, he followed her to Savoy (1500), where he was keeper of the wardrobe and of her jewels, and then to Flanders (1507), where he was her treasurer general until 1515, when he was discharged for his bad management of her finances. Nonetheless, he remained in charge of her wardrobe and jewels until 1523, then moved back to Spain to serve Charles V. He died between 1535 and 1540. Daniel Coenen, 'Florès, Diégo', in *Nouvelle biographie nationale*, 15 vols (Brussels: Palais des Académies, 2010), vol. 10, pp. 187–9.

[43] No information is available about him.

[44] No information is available about him.

[45] The word used in the original text is *rax*; its translation is uncertain.

[46] No information is available about this person, who was probably a dressmaker.

[47] In this document, *gros* and *sous* are at times used interchangeably.

[48] Even if they are not described in the narrative text, these scourges were probably used by the hermits at the beginning of the relevant *momerie*. *Battuti* — that is, confraternities of flagellants who mortified themselves to expiate their sins — were quite common in northern Italy in this period. Gavin Hammel, 'Revolutionary Flagellants? Clerical Perceptions of Flagellant Brotherhoods in Late Medieval Flanders and Italy', in *Faith's Boundaries: Laity and Clergy in Early Modern Confraternities*, ed. by Nicholas Terpstra, Adriano Prosperi and Stefania Pastore (Turnhout: Brepols, 2012), pp. 303–30.

[49] No information is available about him.

Item, for black ribbons: one *florin* four *gros*: 1fl. 4gr.
Item, for a key to the damsels' chamber: 1 *gros*.
Total amount: 58 *florins* 9¾ *gros*.

(324) The duchess of Savoy.
Louis Vionnet,[50] our treasurer, has paid and delivered to Diego Flores, keeper of our wardrobe, the sum of 58 *florins* 9¾ *gros* in Piedmontese currency that we owe him for the reasons outlined on the present roll written above and as notified here in this document signed by my hand; together with the receipt of the said Diego Flores, we wish, order and command the said sum of 58 *florins* 9¾ *gros*, for the reasons stated above to be logged, entered and registered into the first account [for the coming financial year] by the auditors appointed to this task, without raising any difficulty. Executed in Turin, the twenty-eighth day of April, 1504.
(Signed) Margaret
(Written on the back): I, Diego Flores, keeper of Madame's wardrobe, declare that I have received and obtained from Louis Vionnet, Madame's treasurer, the sum of 58 *florins* 9¾ *sous*, which was owed to me by my aforesaid lady, as can be seen from her letters and the above written roll; of this sum of 58 *florins* 9¾ *gros*, I acquit the treasurer and all others. Executed in Turin, the twelfth day of the month of June, in the year 1504.

[50] [Louis Vionet]. At this time, Louis Vionnet was assisting Jean-Louis de Piossasque, general treasurer of Margaret of Austria, duchess of Savoy. When she left Savoy for Mechelen, Vionnet became the treasurer of her Savoy dower. Bruchet, *Marguerite d'Autriche*, pp. 43, 59.

Thanks are due to Margaret Scott for her help in deciphering, translating and documenting some of the references to clothing in the narrative account of this event.

Alan V. Murray and Rosalind Brown-Grant

Source 16

The *Emprise of the Wild Knight of the Black Lady*, Edinburgh, 1507

This source consists of a translation of the *Articles* (chapters of arms) for this event.

Author: Marchmont Herald (William Cumming of Inverallochy)

Language: Middle French

Edition used: 'Les Articles de l'emprinsc [*sic*] du Chevalier Sauvage à la Dame Noire', in Marc de Vulson [given as Wlson] de la Colombière, *La Science heroique, traitant de la noblesse, de l'origine des armes de leurs blasons, & symboles, des tymbres, bourlets, couronnes, cimiers, lambrequins, supports, & tenans, & autres ornements de l'escu; de la deuise, & du cry de guerre, de l'escu pendant & des pas & emprises des anciens cheualiers, des formes differentes de leurs tombeaux; et des marques exterieures de l'escu de nos roys, des reynes, & enfans de France, & des officiers de la couronne, et de la maison du roy*, 2nd edition (Paris: Sebastien Mabre-Cramoisy, 1669), pp. 491–5 (= SH)

Select bibliography:

Edington, Carol, 'The Tournament in Medieval Scotland', in *Armies, Chivalry and Warfare in Medieval Britain and France: Proceedings of the 1995 Harlaxton Symposium*, ed. by Matthew J. Strickland (Stamford: Paul Watkins, 1998), pp. 46–62

Fradenburg, Louise Olga, *City, Marriage, Tournament: Arts of Rule in Late Medieval Scotland* (Madison, University of Wisconsin Press, 1991), pp. 192–243

Innes of Learney, Sir Thomas, 'Sir William Cumming of Inverallochy, Lord Lyon King of Arms, 1512–1519', *The Juridical Review*, 55 (1943), 24–38

Stevenson, Katie, *Chivalry and Knighthood in Scotland, 1424–1513* (Woodbridge: Boydell Press, 2006), pp. 72–99

——, 'Jurisdiction, Authority and Professionalisation: The Officers of Arms in Late Medieval Scotland', in *The Herald in Late Medieval Europe*, ed. by Katie Stevenson (Woodbridge: Boydell, 2006), pp. 41–66

Introduction

This text consists of a series of *Articles* dating from January 1507 that set out the details of a tournament to be held in Edinburgh in the summer of that year. It begins by describing a fictional scenario in which an unknown 'Wild Knight of the Black Lady', having received permission from King James IV of Scotland (1473–1513), has undertaken to perform feats of arms for the duration of five weeks against all comers who are 'Gentilshommes de nom & d'armes' (gentlemen in both name and deed).[1] It then goes on to set out the physical setting for the tournament, the various types of combat that will be offered and the rules and prizes associated with each, concluding with an invitation to participate that is addressed to all gentlemen and foreigners who wish to come to the kingdom of Scotland. These *Articles* can thus be seen to correspond closely to the typical *chapitres* (chapters of arms) proclaimed by the *entrepreneurs* of *pas d'armes* known from the continent.

'Les Articles de l'emprise du Chevalier Sauvage à la Dame Noire' (as the text is entitled in full) is preserved in a work by the French antiquarian and genealogist Marc de Vulson, Sieur de la Colombière (d. 1658). Vulson, who seems to have enjoyed the patronage of King Henry IV of France (1553–1610), published works on diverse subjects, but his main interest was the history of heraldry. *La Science heroique* deals with the origins of heraldry, the character of a wide range of armorial devices, the office of heralds and the principles of blazonry (heraldic description). By way of supporting material, Vulson included a large number of illustrations and independent texts, mostly reproduced with little explanation or analysis, but which nevertheless seem to have been discovered in the course of his own researches. The *Articles de l'emprise* are reproduced in Chapter XLIII of his work, which deals with the theme of *l'Escu pendant* (literally, 'the pendant shield'): that is, the practice of displaying shields by hanging them from trees (whether natural or artificial), pillars, columns or other artefacts during tournaments. This form of display was one of the principal features of *pas d'armes*, in which the hanging shields would often be struck by a knight who wished to challenge the bearer of the arms in question, and so Vulson gave descriptions of some of these events, such as the *Pas des armes de Sandricourt* of 1493.[2]

The text dealing with the *Wild Knight of the Black Lady* is dated to 22 January 1507.[3] It is signed in the name 'Marchmont Herald', the title of one of the Scottish officers of arms, which was a poetic name form relating to the castle of Roxburgh, situated on the border (marches) with England.[4] At the time the document was drawn up, the incumbent of this office was William Cumming of Inverallochy (d. 1519). He was knighted at some point during 1507; since it is known that the heralds were in charge of organising the tournament, it is possible that his knighthood was conferred in recognition of his services at the event. Cumming became the senior Scottish herald when he succeeded to the office of Lord Lyon King of Arms in 1512.[5]

Although Scots was the language of the royal court, the text preserved by Vulson is written in Middle French. Since it anticipates participants coming to the tournament not only from Scotland but also parts of the continent, it is likely that the invitation was

---

[1] SH, p. 491.

[2] On this event, see Essay 4 and Source 13.

[3] The text gives the date of its composition as '22. jour de Ianvier mil cinq cens six' (p. 493). In Scotland, until 1600 the year was reckoned as beginning on the feast of the Annunciation (25 March) rather than 1 January, so the date as given in the text relates to 1507, according to modern reckoning. See Hermann Grotefend, *Taschenbuch der Zeitrechnung des deutschen Mittelalters und der Neuzeit*, 13th edition (Hanover: Hahnsche Buchhandlung, 1991), p. 13.

[4] John H. Stevenson, *Heraldry in Scotland*, 2 vols (Glasgow: James Maclehose and Sons, 1914), vol. 1, p. 48.

[5] Sir Thomas Innes of Learney, 'Sir William Cumming of Inverallochy, Lord Lyon King of Arms, 1512–1519', *The Juridical Review*, 55 (1943), 24–38.

disseminated in multiple copies in both languages. The royal Miscellaneous Accounts (*Bursa Regis*) record a payment of forty-two shillings to Sir John Ramsay for the writing of the articles that the 'Franch knycht hed in France for the justing' (French knight had in France for the jousting).[6] This was a considerable sum, and more than would be justified for a piece of simple scribal work. A probable explanation is that Ramsay was paid to produce a French translation of a text first formulated in Scots by Marchmont Herald. The accounts also record payments for gold leaf to 'illummyn the articles send in France for the justing of the wild knycht for the blak lady' (illuminate the articles sent to France for the jousting of the Wild Knight for the Black Lady).[7] A richly decorated format for the articles would explain why at least one copy was preserved somewhere in France long enough for Vulson to discover it in the course of his researches in heraldry and genealogy.

Although the *Articles* proclaimed that the event would be held in August 1507, many items of expenditure recorded in the different accounts administered by the Lord Treasurer indicate that the jousting and other spectacles in fact took place in May and June of that year.[8] King James is documented as being resident in Edinburgh between April and June, but at the beginning of July he left on a journey taking in Perth, Stirling and Paisley, returning only at the end of the month, which would have left him little time to oversee preparations for a tournament due to take place in August.[9] It would seem, therefore, that despite his original intentions, James decided to have the event brought forward by several weeks.

It should be stressed that the *Articles* are very much a prescriptive text, which sets out a series of different *faits* (feats or combats) on both horse and foot. The first two were jousts, one with a tilt* barrier between each pair of combatants and one without, the latter requiring the combatants to wear full armour in order to give protection from head to foot. The text then states that some potential competitors might prefer to fight on foot, and sets out three different types of combat involving demi-lances, swords, pollaxes and short daggers. Whether all the elements described actually featured in the event is difficult to establish, although many of the other details mentioned can be confirmed from the different surviving accounts of payments recorded in the King's Wardrobe Accounts and Miscellaneous Accounts for the first half of 1507.

The text maintains the fiction that the Wild Knight, who can be regarded as the *entrepreneur*, was an unknown nobleman. In fact this role was taken by the king himself, as stated in the account of the tournament given by John Leslie, bishop of Ross.[10] The meaning of some of the French phrasing is not entirely clear at several points; this may well be the consequence of the fact that it was probably composed by a Scot whose

---

[6] TA, vol. 3, pp. 365, 372. The Ramsay mentioned here may be John Ramsay, 1st Lord Bothwell (d. 1513). His lands were declared forfeit in 1488 because of his intrigues with the English and he took refuge in England. He returned to Scotland in 1496 and was subsequently pardoned but not restored to the peerage. Nevertheless, he gradually returned to royal favour and by 1507 was serving in the royal household, although he continued his treacherous dealings with the English. See Norman Macdougall, *James IV* (Edinburgh: John Donald, 2015), pp. 17–19, 55–6, 62, 127–30.

[7] TA, vol. 3, p. 365.

[8] *Ibid.*, vol. 3, pp. 258–60, 385, 393–4.

[9] James Balfour Paul, ed., *The Register of the Great Seal of Scotland, A.D. 1424–1513* (Edinburgh: Scottish Text Society, 1882), pp. 659–67.

[10] JLBS, vol. 2, p. 128.

knowledge of French was good but by no means perfect. Nevertheless, the *Articles* do give a clear indication of a fictional scenario, represented by a Tree of Esperance and other allegorical infrastructure, as well as a literary theme featuring a Wild Knight in the service of a Black Lady. In this translation, page numbers have been provided in parentheses for ease of reference to Vulson's edition.

TRANSLATION

(491) God Eternal created and ordered all things to His blessed glory and did nothing in vain; likewise, His Son commanded His Apostles to guard against the vice of idleness. Thus, each person, according to his vocation — whether this be in the spiritual or the temporal realm — is beholden to praise, thank and serve Him, each according to his estate and the gifts that he has received from Him. Knowing that the most high, most excellent and ancient pursuit of arms — which is the mother and nursemaid of virtues and enemy of the vices — first took form in the heavens themselves, as is shown in both the Old and the New Testaments through Michael, David and Maccabeus,[11] it is for this reason all the more laudable a pursuit for knights, being principally in the service of God against the infidels where it is not just permitted, but meritorious. Moreover, since perfect knowledge of the noble art of chivalry cannot be attained without great familiarity and continual practice, this is why — also in praise of God and His most glorious and holy Mother, St Michael, St Andrew and St George[12] — a Wild Knight of the Black Lady has bestirred himself, together with two knights as his helpers,[13] and made his way to this kingdom whose reputation for practising the art of single combat he has heard about, it being his wish and intention to visit various countries and parts of the world, and to spend some of his time there in this pursuit, his chief aim being to augment our Faith through his efforts. Mindful of the fact that such a thing cannot be undertaken without the possibility of incurring grave risks or dishonour if he should fail in this endeavour, his goal is to offer an example to all men of high and noble courage to attain greater familiarity with it, so as to develop their skills which, in the future, they might choose to go and employ against the said infidels, for which they would be remembered forever. The said Wild Knight of the Black Lady, together with his two knights, has obtained the

[11] St Michael the Archangel was regarded in medieval theology as leader of the angelic army of God. King David was famous in the Old Testament for having defeated the Philistines, enemies of the Israelites, and later established a united kingdom of Israel with its capital at Jerusalem. Judas Maccabeus was the leader of a Jewish revolt in 167–160 BCE against the Macedonian Seleucid dynasty, which ruled much of the Near East. In the Middle Ages, both King David and Judas Maccabeus were considered as two of the Nine Worthies, a group of chivalric heroes consisting of three Jews, three pagans and three Christians, who were often celebrated in painting and literary texts. See Ruth Mazo Karras, 'Perfect Men? The Nine Worthies and Medieval Masculinities', *Collegium Medievale*, 33 (2020), 5–22.

[12] In the New Testament, St Andrew the Apostle was one of the first disciples of Jesus Christ. He was regarded as the patron saint of Scotland after some of his relics were brought there in the eighth century. St George of Lydda was a Roman soldier who was martyred for his Christian beliefs (traditionally in the year 303). In the Middle Ages, he was especially venerated as a patron of knights and chivalry.

[13] The King's Wardrobe Accounts for 1507 record payments for rich clothing to be made for John Dunlop and Alexander MacCulloch 'allocayis to the wild knycht' (allocated to the Wild Knight) (TA, vol. 3, p. 258). MacCulloch was a member of the king's household, and it is likely that Dunlop held a similar position. Macdougall, *James IV*, pp. 300, 312.

gracious permission of the most high, most excellent and most powerful prince, the king of Scots, to take up arms and undertake the feats of arms described hereafter according to his *emprises* for the duration of five weeks against all comers who are gentlemen in both name and deed.

These feats of arms will take place in this kingdom, in the town of Edinburgh on the Field of Memory which will be situated between the castle known as that of the Maidens and the Secret Pavilion, and in this Field will be the Tree of Esperance, which grows in the Garden of Patience and bears (492) leaves of Pleasure, flowers of Nobility and fruits of Honour.[14] At the foot of the tree will be attached five shields of different colours, one for each of the five weeks: the first of these will be white, the second grey, the third black, the fourth purple and the fifth gold. On each of these shields will be a golden letter crowned with the name of the Wild Knight and his Lady, together with his aforesaid companions and their own ladies, this letter being set out above as a signature.

First of all, these feats of arms will begin on horseback in plain armour* with at least six courses of the lance in the lists[15] — the lances to have sharp, tempered and pointed tips — and any more if it so pleases and accords with the wishes of the judges and the ladies; in addition to these courses there will also be another for the lady of him who requests it. And if he who requests this extra course should fail to break his lance on his opponent, he will be obliged to send a gold ring to the lady of the one to whom this did not happen, and to accept graciously the mishap that has befallen him.

Item, there will be other mounted combats with no barriers, in war harness* of plain armour from head to foot, without the combatants being secured, restrained or attached to the saddle, for at least as many courses with lances with sharp, tempered and pointed tips as result in their being struck, broken or dropped, and any more as it pleases and accords with the wishes of the judges and ladies, as stated above, and with an extra course for the lady of him who requests it.[16] If he who requests it should fail to break his lance on his opponent during this course, he will be obliged to send a gold ring, as stipulated above. Once these courses are over, they will take up[17] swords* sharpened for cutting

---

[14] Edinburgh Castle was often referred to in medieval literary texts as the Castle of the Maidens (Lat. *Castrum Puellarum*, Fr. *Château des Pucelles*), a name that evidently derived from obscure legends. See *An Inventory of the Ancient and Historical Monuments of the City of Edinburgh with the Thirteenth Report of the Commission* (Edinburgh: His Majesty's Stationery Office, 1951), pp. 34–7. The designations of the other locations seem to have been devised specifically for this occasion and do not relate to names current in Edinburgh at the time. The Miscellaneous Accounts for 1507 confirm the existence of a Tree of Esperance, which was decorated with apples, pears and leaves made of metal and fixed to its branches with wire (TA, vol. 3, pp. 385, 394).

[15] The mention of lists indicates that there was to be a wooden barrier between each pair of jousters, which reduced the body area that could be struck with the lance.

[16] In contrast to the previous item, this combat was to be fought without a tilt barrier; as the combatants' legs were exposed, a full harness of steel armour from head to foot was required to give complete protection. The saddle had no cantle or other fixings, so that a knight receiving a powerful strike would be unhorsed cleanly. On different types of saddle for the tournament, see Marina Viallon, 'The Tournament Saddle', in *The Medieval Tournament as Spectacle: Tourneys, Jousts and Pas d'Armes, 1100–1600*, ed. by Alan V. Murray and Karen Watts (Woodbridge: Boydell Press, 2020), pp. 98–119.

[17] The text gives the first person plural verbs *mettrons* and *combattrons*, which do not fit the preceding syntax. It is likely that these forms are editorial misreadings for the third person plural forms *mettront* and *combattront*.

and thrusting with which they will fight, using both blade and point, for at least nine strokes and any more as it pleases and accords with the wishes of the judges and ladies, plus another three strokes for the lady of him who requests it. And if it should so happen that he who requests this should drop his sword, during either the aforesaid nine strokes or those to be completed at the will of the judges and ladies, or has his blood drawn or falls off his horse to the ground, he will not be allowed to fight the three extra strokes requested by the lady.

Item, the horses are to be protected against both lances and swords; he who kills or wounds a horse will not complete the full bout and will be required to leave the field.

Item, because some may come who prefer to undertake this exercise in arms on foot rather than on horseback, the said Knight of the Black Lady, together with his two aforementioned companions, is willing to accommodate the wishes of all those men of worth who wish to compete in these feats, which will be conducted in three different ways.

(493) The first feat will be in plain armour with a shield around the neck or on the arm, and will involve each man throwing a spear* with a sharp point in the style of a demi-lance* and having a sword sharpened for cutting with the blade and thrusting with the tip. Once the spears have been thrown, the [men] will take up the aforesaid swords to defend themselves as required for at least seven strokes and any more as it pleases and accords with the wishes of the judges and ladies, plus another three strokes for the lady of him who requests it. And if he who requests it should drop his sword during either the aforesaid five strokes or those to be completed at the pleasure and will of the judges and ladies, or if he has his blood drawn or falls to the ground, he may not fight the extra strokes for his lady.

The second feat, also on foot in plain armour, will involve each man throwing a spear with a sharpened point in the style of a demi-lance, and also having a short dagger and a two-handed sword sharpened for cutting with the blade and thrusting with the point. Once the spears have been thrown, they will take up their swords to defend themselves as needed for at least five strokes and any more as it pleases and accords with the wishes of the judges and ladies, plus another three strokes for the lady of him who requests it. And if he who requests it should drop his sword during either the aforesaid five strokes or those to be completed at the pleasure and will of the judges and ladies, or if he has his blood drawn or falls to the ground, he may not fight the extra strokes for his lady.

Item, likewise on foot, in steel armour, with a pollaxe* in the hand and a spear for throwing, as well as a short dagger for defending onself if needed: once the spears have been thrown, they will fight with the said pollaxe for at least five strokes and any more as it pleases and accords with the wishes of the judges and ladies, plus another three strokes for the lady of him who requests it. And if he who requests it should drop his pollaxe during either the aforesaid five strokes or those to be completed at the pleasure and will of the judges and ladies, or if he has his blood drawn or falls to the ground, he may not fight the extra strokes for his lady.

Item, these aforesaid gentlemen, whether on foot or on horseback, must enter the field in full armour, with their visors down and their lances, swords, pollaxes and short daggers all in the proper form and manner that they have chosen to perform these feats of arms. No man may enter the field with them other than those intending to fight in the lists, who will each have a gentleman with him to serve his needs.

Item, all comers will be obliged to go up to the said Tree on the first day of August, which is when the combats will begin, and to touch the said white shield guarded by the

Black Lady who will be accompanied by (494) Wild Men, trumpets and other instruments.[18] There with the said Lady will be Kings of Arms and heralds, whose role will be to receive them as they declare with which weapons they wish to fight and hand over their shields emblazoned with their coat of arms and their device together with their names and surnames, all so that they can each be received according to their rank.

Item, if it so happens that one of these weapons should break, be it a lance, spear, sword, pollaxe or short dagger, another will be immediately offered by an officer of arms, who will be appointed to this task.

Item, if those who request these combats with lances, spears, pollaxes, swords and short daggers should drop one of these weapons, or have their blood drawn or fall to the ground, they will be immediately obliged to go into the above-named garden and present themselves to the Black Lady and offer her a golden heart.

Item, the lances and demi-lances which will have sharp, tempered and pointed tips, as well as the swords and daggers which will be sharpened for cutting with the blade and thrusting with the tip, will be provided by the said Knight of the Black Lady. The challengers will have their choice of these, together with the pollaxes; all these weapons will be sent to the judges and presented to them by an officer of arms.[19]

Item, all of the said gentlemen and foreigners who make their way to this kingdom in order to undertake these feats of arms will be allowed to fight in any or all of the aforesaid *emprises* as they wish, provided that, when they touch the shield, they let the officer of arms know. They must not drop[20] any of their weapons, or have their blood drawn, or fall to the ground, as stipulated above. These feats of arms will take place over five weeks, with the exception of feast days and Fridays.

If any gentleman present is of the opinion that these feats of arms, once completed, have not been properly conducted and says so to the aforementioned officers of arms, the Wild Knight, together with his two companions, will make every effort to meet his wishes.

Once these feats have been accomplished, prizes will be given to both those from the outside* [team] and those from the inside* [team] in each of the five different combats as appropriate; this will be adjudicated and decided entirely by the judges and the ladies.

Item, and if it so happened that some people were busy serving their princes and lords so that they were unable to make their way to this kingdom in the month of August, the Wild Knight accompanied by his two companions, as stated above, will still be happy to satisfy all gentlemen (495) who wish to compete at this event of five *emprises* and will fight with them whenever and however many times they wish in the following year and a day.

Item, the said Knight, together with his two knights, has submitted these articles to the said prince who, in answer to their great prayers, supplications and requests has granted him leave to perform the contents of these articles in his kingdom. All gentlemen in both name and deed who wish to come may make their way there, along with their harnesses and horses, without requiring further permission from him and will be warmly welcomed. In attestation of the truthfulness of the aforesaid articles, the Knight has

---

[18] The Miscellaneous Accounts for June 1507 record expenditure for clothing and goat skins worn by 'Wild Men', as well as payments for trumpeters and players of the shawm (a reeded instrument). See TA, vol. 3, pp. 393–4.

[19] This clause implies that the judges were to check that all weapons were of permitted length and quality, as is quite typical of continental *pas d'armes*.

[20] The sense is 'must not lose', but the text has the misprint *pendent* (hang) for *perdent* (lose).

signed them with a *lettre couronnée* bearing his name, together with those of his two knights and their ladies.[21]

Today, the twenty-second day of January 1506,[22] I, Marchmont, herald to the most high, most excellent and most powerful prince, the king of Scots, certify that I have been approached by a nobleman unknown to me who goes by the name of the 'Wild Knight of the Black Lady', accompanied by two knights, his helpers. He has shown and given me in writing the present aforesaid articles for which permission was granted by my said sovereign lord the king, these articles being signed with a *lettre couronnée* bearing his name, together with those of his two knights and their ladies. He has most insistently begged and entreated me, as an officer of arms, to sign them; in them are contained and outlined the *emprises* that they intend to undertake and perform with and against all those men who are noble in both name and deed and who wish to accomplish these feats that will take place in the town of Edinburgh from the first day of August in the year 1507 following. In order that even greater faith be placed in them, I have signed these articles with my hand at the command of the king, my sovereign lord, on the aforesaid day in the aforesaid year. MARCHMONT HERALD.[23]

[21] The meaning of the *lettre couronnée* (crowned letter) is not clear. It may be that the articles were headed by some form of monogram or rebus alluding to the Wild Knight and his companions.

[22] 22 January 1507, according to modern reckoning.

[23] The signature is given in capitals in the edition.

Thanks are due to Michelle Szkilnik and Karen Watts for their suggestions concerning parts of the translation of this text.

Part II: Essays

Thalia Brero, Mario Damen and Klaus Oschema

The *Pas d'armes* in Europe (Fifteenth–Sixteenth Centuries): the Transfer and Transformation of a Chivalric Event

Antoine de Lalaing (*c*.1480–1540) wrote a fascinating report on his travels to Iberia and different parts of the Habsburg territories in 1501–03 as a member of the household and retinue of Archduke Philip the Fair (1478–1506).[1] In it, Lalaing, who came from a line of renowned jousters, describes how the itinerant court was involved in different types of tournament. Between January and October 1502, he watched twenty-one cane games* (Figure 5) and bull runs* in Castile. On 13 June, he observed *joustes royales* (royal jousts), which were 'cried' in the town, on the main market square of Toledo (now Plaza de Zocodover) with the participation of fifteen *courreurs* (runners or jousters) both from Castile and the Low Countries.[2] On 23 and 24 April 1503, he witnessed an *armes* and a *pas* in the town of Bourg (the present Bourg-en-Bresse), in Savoy, when Philip visited his sister Margaret of Austria (1480–1530) and her husband Philibert II of Savoy (1480–1504). In September 1503, the archduke was in Innsbruck to visit his father, Emperor Maximilian (1459–1519).[3] Here both the princes and Lalaing became involved in a so-called *emprise**, a chivalric ritual whereby a knight wore a scarf, a cuff or a shackle on part of his armour that challengers touched as a prelude to undertaking combat with him. Apolone of Innsbruck, a member of the household of Maximilian's second wife, Bianca Sforza (1472–1510), who was going to marry the count of Lodron, sent to Maximilian, Philip the Fair, Lalaing and some other noblemen of the household 'ung cransselin de ses coleurs, faict de fil d'or et de fil de soye blance et de soye cramoisy' (a heraldic charge indicating a band of trefoil leaves in his colours, made of gold and white and crimson silk thread).[4] On 3 October, the day after the wedding, Philip the Fair and three noblemen put their *cransselin* around their necks. On doing so, they were told by a courtier that if they wore their *cransselin* uncovered 'à la fachon d'Allemaigne' (in the German style) they would have to accept the challenge to fight against all who touched it. Philip and the nobles accepted that condition and immediately had to proclaim how they would engage with their challengers if they touched their *emprise*. The archduke, however, decided that this would take place when they had returned to their northern lands. That very day, there was jousting 'à la mode d'Allemaigne' (in the German fashion).[5] On their return, Lalaing kept his promise and, on the feast of St Martin (11 November 1503), it was proclaimed on his behalf at the court in Mechelen that a *pas d'armes* would take place in Brussels. The day after, Antoine carried his 'emprise à son col' (around his neck) which, after Mass,

[1] CdV; see also Source 14.
[2] CdV, p. 184.
[3] *Ibid.*, p. 309.
[4] *Ibid.*, p. 321.
[5] *Ibid.*, pp. 322–3.

Figure 5. *Juego de cañas* (cane game) in Valladolid, on the occasion of Philip the Fair's visit to Castile. Unknown artist, first half of the sixteenth century. Brussels, Koninklijk Instituut voor het Kunstpatrimonium (KIK) — Institut royal du Patrimoine artistique (IRPA), no. 1015445 (cliché B184488). Photo: KIK-IRPA.

was indeed touched by some thirty-five nobles. Finally, the court moved to Brussels in December. On 16 December 1503, at two o'clock in the afternoon, Philip, who was also eager to complete his *pas*, was on the Grote Markt in Brussels prepared to take on all challengers who had touched his *emprise*. Lalaing's report ends here and mentions neither the actual combats nor his own *pas d'armes*. From the town accounts of Brussels we know that, from 17 to 23 December, Antoine did indeed hold his 'pas ende tfait van wapenen' (*pas* and feat of arms) on the Grote Markt, for which the town administration paid him 200 pounds (of forty groats) and organised several banquets afterwards in the town hall at a cost of 100 pounds.[6]

Lalaing's testimony is telling in several respects. First, we see how a court on the move created opportunities for jousting and other tournament forms in the towns it passed through, involving local elites as it went. Secondly, members of Philip the Fair's household seem to have been able to participate in whatever feats of arms they pleased in places as diverse as Toledo, Bourg, Innsbruck and Brussels, meaning that they were trained and equipped to take part in these events. Thirdly, although these feats of arms are named in a way that was perfectly clear to Lalaing and his contemporaries, we now have to reconstruct the precise differences between royal jousts, German jousts, feats of arms and *pas d'armes*. Nevertheless, we can recognise here certain features of jousting that existed for a very long time, such as the *emprise* and the *pas d'armes*, but which undoubtedly underwent many changes over the years.

In this essay, we focus on the *pas d'armes*, a type of chivalric event that was transferred and transformed from one court to another between *c.*1420 and *c.*1520. We analyse the *pas d'armes* as both a product and a platform of socio-cultural interaction, using the perspective

---

6 AR 30949 fols 184v–185r.

of cultural transfer.[7] This essay is thus interested in the transformation of specific features over time and in their spatial dissemination, thereby identifying moments and processes of contact, exchange, transformation and development. Indeed, Lalaing's report of 1503 shows that *pas d'armes* were at one and the same time chivalric events, at which knights from different geographical areas could meet, and spaces in which chivalric play, rules, norms and behaviour were defined and exchanged. The specific characteristics of these events were shaped or at least heavily influenced not only by travelling princes, nobles and knights, but also by the circulation of 'chapters of arms' (referred to as *chapitres* or *articles*) — which stipulated how and with what arms the combats were to be conducted — and of accounts describing *pas d'armes* amongst the courts of late medieval Europe. These will, therefore, merit special attention.

Our analysis follows the creation and reception (or reinterpretation) of *pas d'armes* in different kingdoms and principalities of fifteenth- to early sixteenth-century Europe. We consider that the different geographical contexts represent relatively specific cultural units that were in constant contact of varying intensity. At the same time, we are conscious of the fact that these units were not immutable and that the exchange worked both ways.[8] In fact, a detailed analysis of different *pas d'armes* can reveal to what extent this type of event belonged to a shared chivalric culture and how the particularities of each geographical sphere found their expression in the lists.[9] It goes without saying that over the timespan of almost a century, the character and nature of the event changed.[10] Hence this essay seeks to compare and contrast examples of effective and successful cultural transfer with a case where such a transfer did not take place, despite intensive contact and exchange.

It is our hypothesis that, overall, three interdependent factors could establish a milieu in which chivalric events such as *pas d'armes* could flourish. The first of these was the existence of a strong institutional environment in terms of courtly organisation/household and chivalric orders, focused on the prince and his closest relatives. Second was a well-developed chivalric spirit (influenced by political circumstances, crusading ideals and/or the role of women at the court as reflected in literary traditions) together with

7 See, for example, Matthias Middell, 'Kulturtransfer, Transferts culturels', *Docupedia-Zeitgeschichte: Begriffe, Methoden und Debatten der zeithistorischen Forschung* (online), (2016) <https://docupedia.de/zg/Kulturtransfer> [accessed 21 June 2024]; Michael Werner and Bénédicte Zimmermann, 'Beyond Comparison: *Histoire Croisée* and the Challenge of Reflexivity', *History and Theory*, 45.1 (2006), 30–50.

8 These *caveats* have been underlined by studies on transculturality and hybridity: see Laila Abu-Er-Rub *et al.*, eds, *Engaging Transculturality: Concepts, Key Terms, Case Studies*, (London/New York: Routledge, 2021); Georg Christ *et al.*, *Transkulturelle Verflechtungen: Mediävistische Perspektiven* (Göttingen: Universitätsverlag Göttingen, 2016); Wolfram Drews and Christian Scholl, eds, *Transkulturelle Verflechtungsprozesse in der Vormoderne* (Berlin: De Gruyter, 2016); Michael Borgolte and Bernd Schneidmüller, eds, *Hybride Kulturen im mittelalterlichen Europa/Hybrid Cultures in Medieval Europe* (Berlin: Akademie-Verlag, 2010).

9 Werner Paravicini, 'Gab es eine einheitliche Adelskultur Europas im späten Mittelalter?', in *Europa im späten Mittelalter. Politik – Gesellschaft – Kultur*, ed. by Rainer C. Schwinges, Christian Hesse and Peter Moraw (Munich: R. Oldenbourg Verlag, 2006), pp. 401–34, identifies shared characteristics of noble culture while underlining that they were not homogeneous on a 'European' level. The practice of tournaments seems to have been by and large specific to Latin Europe and played only a minor role in Byzantium: see Peter Schreiner, 'Turnier. D. Byzanz', *Lexikon des Mittelalters*, 8 (1997), col. 1118; and *idem*, 'Ritterspiele in Byzanz', *Jahrbuch der österreichischen Byzantinistik*, 46 (1996), 227–41.

10 On the varying and changing character of the *pas d'armes* across Europe, see Essays 4 and 5.

a class consciousness amongst the nobles that inspired them to undertake performances that allowed them to distinguish themselves either from 'newcomers' — that is, from the urban elites — or from other nobles who were competing for princely jobs or favours. The final factor was the availability of a suitable stage where this chivalric competition could take place and where noble values could be displayed, these often being supplied by urban environments where princely residences were located. Towns were not only able to meet all the competitors' needs (horses, arms, armour, luxurious clothes, jewellery, etc.), but were also willing to collaborate in the construction of ephemeral architecture in their most emblematic public spaces where a large audience could witness the events, this being essential for the construction of social distinction of the nobility. We will use these three factors as a test case for the institutional context of the transfer of the *pas* from one geographical area to another and for a possible explanation of why, on occasion, these transfers failed to occur. Furthermore, to distinguish the *pas* from other chivalric events we have defined five characteristic features: (1) a knight, the organiser (*entrepreneur**), who alone or together with other knights (2) defends either a passage (such as a bridge or a gate) or a symbolic object (such as a fountain or a column) against all challengers, thereby including a serial element, (3) this defence sometimes involving theatrical production and a fictional scenario and/or being organised according to a fixed set of rules known as chapters of arms, (4) and being witnessed by an audience (noble and non-noble, including women) (5) in a publicly accessible setting (often urban, but also near castles) and making use of ephemeral architecture.[11] Many of these features could also be present in the context of other chivalric events, but together they form a cluster that appears highly specific to the *pas d'armes*.

In the first section of this essay, we discuss the earliest traces of the *pas* that can be identified on the Iberian Peninsula, more precisely in Castile (*Paso de la Fuerte Ventura*, Valladolid, 1428) and in León (*Paso Honroso*, 1434), from where it spread to France and the Burgundian lands (see Map, p. 22). This transfer, on which we elaborate in a second section, did not take on the form of a simple, monodirectional dissemination, as the approaches, practices and attitudes changed during this process: when Burgundian knights took part in a *pas d'armes* in the 1440s, they seem to have had something different in mind from their Iberian predecessors a few decades earlier, whose events were more violent and embedded in factional rivalries within the royal household.[12] The history of the *pas d'armes* reached its apogee in the Burgundian lands and Anjou between *c.*1440 and *c.*1470, and numerous noblemen from elsewhere either witnessed or participated in examples of this particular feat of arms. In a third section, we analyse how, around 1500, this specific chivalric event was emulated in the duchy of Savoy, a French- and Italian-speaking part of the Holy Roman Empire, not least due to a long tradition of close kinship relations between the Burgundian-Habsburg and Savoyard ruling dynasties. However, while comparable ties also existed between the dynasties of Burgundy and Cleves, an analogous transfer did not occur in that part of the Empire, as our fourth section demonstrates.

---

[11] On the issue of the actual term *pas d'armes*, see Catherine Blunk, 'Faux Pas in the Chronicles: What is a *Pas d'Armes*?', in *The Medieval Chronicle 11*, ed. by Erik Kooper and Sjoerd Levelt (Turnhout: Brepols, 2018), pp. 87–107 (pp. 88, 91–2). What we present here is more a grid of possible defining characteristics than a strict definition.

[12] On the role of animosity in the Castilian *pas d'armes* compared to Burgundian ones, see Essay 6.

The *Paso de la Fuerte Ventura*, the first *pas d'armes*?

One of the first *pas d'armes* that we know of is described in four different chronicles and was celebrated on the Plaza Mayor of Valladolid on Tuesday 18 May 1428 under the aegis of the court of King Juan II of Castile (1405–54). The first and most extensive report of this event was written by Juan's falconer, Pedro Carrillo de Huete (*c.*1380–*c.*1448), who was knighted in 1407 and held office at the Castilian court until 1455.[13] The narrative forms part of his chronicle on the Castilian court under Juan II between 1420 and 1450. The transmission of the text, however, is somewhat complicated.[14]

The organiser of the *Paso de la Fuerte Ventura* was the Infante Enrique of Aragon (1400–45), third son of King Fernando I of Aragon (1380–1416), who had acted as regent of Castile in the years 1406–15 and made his young son *maestre* (grandmaster) of the Order of Santiago in 1409.[15] Enrique became one of the most prominent noblemen of Castile when he inherited the Castilian possessions of his father in 1416. The Aragonese had a heavy presence at the Castilian court in general and, in May 1428, in Valladolid in particular. Enrique's elder sister María (1396–1445), for example, was married to King Juan II of Castile, whereas his younger sister, the Infanta Leonor of Aragon (1402–45), was in Valladolid on her way from the Aragonese court to Lisbon, where she would marry the crown prince Infante Duarte I of Portugal (1391–1438). Also present in Valladolid was Enrique's elder brother, Juan II the Great of Aragon (1398–1479); he was the acting king of Navarre because of his marriage to Blanca I of Navarre (1385–1441). The only absentee was their elder brother, Alfonso V the Magnanimous (1396–1458), king of Aragon who, thanks to all these family ties, could pull many strings in the neighbouring kingdoms.

Enrique's main opponent at the Castilian court was Álvaro de Luna. The 1420s were characterised by political strife between them as leaders of competing factions of Castilian nobles in the late 1420s, so it is safe to say that the *Paso* took place in an atmosphere of intense rivalry.[16] The influence of Enrique and Juan II the Great on their brother-in-law, Juan II of Castile, had been so heavy that they managed to bring about the removal of Álvaro de Luna from court in August 1427. However, this triumph was short-lived because, in February 1428, the king restored the constable to office. The festivities of Valladolid may therefore have sought to re-establish the peace between the two rival factions at the Castilian court.[17]

The competitive spirit of the court is evident since the *Paso* was embedded in a series of chivalric events during the months of May and June that were organised by the main political protagonists of the Castilian court, each of whom did so in turn.[18] The festivities started on 2 May, when Álvaro de Luna jousted with seven knights (up to forty or fifty,

---

[13] See Source 2.

[14] For a fuller discussion of this issue, see the introduction to Source 2, p. 59.

[15] Angus MacKay, 'Enrique, Infante of Aragón', in *Medieval Iberia. An Encyclopedia*, ed. by Edmund Michael Gerli (New York: Routledge, 2003), pp. 306–7; DBE, lemma 'Enrique de Aragon'.

[16] Sébastien Nadot, *Le Spectacle des joutes: Sport et courtoisie à la fin du Moyen Âge* (Rennes: Presses Universitaires de Rennes, 2012), p. 284; Teofilo F. Ruiz, *A King Travels: Festive Traditions in Late Medieval and Early Modern Spain* (Princeton, NJ: Princeton University Press, 2012), pp. 231–2.

[17] DBE, lemma 'Álvaro de Luna'.

[18] For this and what follows see, in particular, PCH, pp. 19–27; LB, pp. 59–66; and the summary and analysis by Ruiz, *A King Travels*, pp. 226–34, 335–8.

according to Álvar García de Santa María) in 'arnés real' (royal harness*) against Juan II and his two brothers-in-law, Juan the Great and Enrique of Aragon. The second event was the actual *pas* of Enrique of Aragon on 18 May, celebrated on the main square of Valladolid. Most chroniclers relate this as a one-day event, although García de Santa María mentions that the feast lasted for six days, during which Enrique was 'faciendo sus justas é otras caballerías de cade dia' (performing either jousts or other chivalric feats every day).[19] This would make sense, as the next 'fiesta', that organised by Juan II the Great of Aragon, king of Navarre, with five knights, took place on 24 May in the same square.[20] Their opponents were Juan II of Castile accompanied by ten knights, all dressed as hunters and carrying horns and javelins, preceded by a lion and a bear guarded by barking hunting dogs, and Don Enrique, who appeared with five knights armed with lances. On 6 June, Juan II of Castile, dressed as God the father, organised yet another royal joust on the main square with twelve knights, who were dressed as twelve saints, like the Apostles, each with the symbol of his martyrdom in his hands. This time, the opponents were Enrique together with twelve knights, Juan II the Great — who appeared within a rock on a horse with a man holding a banner on top of it — with fifty knights, and the count of Castro with another twenty knights. The fifth and final event consisted of an *emprise* worn by the Aragonese knight Luis de Falces, which was touched by the Castilian nobleman Gonzalo de Guzmán, lord of Torija. On 8 June, these two men subsequently jousted in the garden of the palace of San Pablo in Valladolid in the presence of all the royals.[21]

When we consider the five characteristic features of *pas d'armes*, it becomes clear that all these events had individual organisers who are identified as *mantenedores* (defenders). Although this element alone is not distinctive enough to define them all as *pas*, for the event organised by Enrique a obvious passage — a second feature — *is* described: this was an arch between two towers with a banner reading: 'Este es el arco del pasaje peligroso de la fuerte ventura' (This is the Arch of the Dangerous Passage of the Daunting Adventure). On top of the two towers, two men with horns were placed as if they were gatekeepers.[22] A lady on horseback was accompanied by a herald who would ask the challengers entering the lists through the arch which adventure had attracted them to come to this dangerous passage and remind them that they couldn't pass by it without jousting. This was definitely part of the fictional scenario — a third feature — of the *Paso*, although the different accounts do not spell out its meaning in detail. Even if chapters of arms are not specifically mentioned, some jousting rules do seem to have been in place. The description of an 'entremés' (borrowing the French term *entremets**, meaning 'interlude', in the Spanish original),[23] one involving eight damsels on horses with a cart pulled by two horses and twenty footsoldiers on which a unspecified 'goddess' and another twelve damsels were singing accompanied by minstrels, confirms the impression that there was much more

---

19 AGSM, p. 16. On this chronicler, see Source 2, p. 59.

20 PCH, p. 23. Compare LB, p. 62, who incorrectly dates the event to 24 March.

21 This *emprise* is specifically mentioned by Cervantes in his *El ingenioso hidalgo don Quijote de la Mancha* of 1605. Martín de Riquer, *Vida caballeresca en la España del siglo XV* (Madrid: Gráficas Marina, 1965), pp. 67–8. Diego de Guzmán, brother of Gonzalo, would later touch the *emprise* of Jacques de Lalaing, which would lead to a foot combat on the nearby Plaza de San Pablo in February 1448. CL, pp. 171–6.

22 PCH, p. 21.

23 *Ibid.*, p. 21; LB, p. 60.

to see than jousting alone. Indeed, the accounts of the events organised by the kings of Navarre and Castile also indicate that there were disguises and role-playing. However, the ephemeral architecture, another characteristic feature, seems far less fully developed than in Enrique's *Paso.*

García de Santa María explicitly underlines that Enrique ordered the construction of the wooden buildings. He says it was estimated that it cost him more than 15,000 *florines*, and that most of this was spent on horses, horse equipment, silk and cloth of gold, as well as gowns with *argentaría**[24] for the members of his retinue. At the junction of the square with the Calle de Santiago, a Lombard from Enrique's entourage constructed a castle (alternatively called 'fortaleza' and 'Alcázar') that was made of wood and textiles but painted as if it was made of brick, thus alluding to royal power in general and (the coat of arms of) Castile in particular.[25] Next to the castle, a large gilded 'rueda de la aventura' (Wheel of Fortune) was placed with a richly adorned seat right in front of it, where a goddess would be seated. A 'tela de cañas' (tilt* made of canes) connected the castle with the arch mentioned above, hence mirroring the city gate of the Puerta del Campo at the end of the Calle de Santiago.[26] The largest tower of the ephemeral castle had not only four turrets but also a typical urban element, the belfry, on which a pillar was placed with a gilded griffin on top that held a large standard coloured white and red.[27] The griffin was the symbol of the Aragonese Order of the Jar, founded by Enrique's father, Fernando, in 1403. Although not explicitly mentioned by the Castilian chroniclers, this seems to imply that the *Paso* was performed under the aegis of this knightly order and not under that of the Order of the Band of King Juan II.[28] The belfry had varying functions according to the different chroniclers: Pérez de Guzmán says that the challengers rang it to indicate the number of jousts in which they wanted to engage, whereas in those reports derived from Carrillo de Huete, the bell functioned as a wake-up call for a lady, who would then interrogate the challengers, as noted above.[29]

In short, this ephemeral architecture was based on building traditions from princely, noble and urban environments, which brings us to the final features of the *pas*, namely the audience and the setting of the event. Valladolid is considered to be the centre of courtly and political activity during the reign of Juan II as most of the meetings of the Cortes (the

---

[24] This term probably has the same meaning as *orfèvrerie** in French.

[25] Nadot, *Le Spectacle*, p. 195. Although Nadot assumes that the castle was a heraldic representation of Juan II of Castile, in reality the coat of arms of Castile contains a castle with three towers, with the middle one being a little bigger than the other two, whereas here only one tower was constructed.

[26] PCH, p. 21.

[27] A white mantle and stole were worn by members of the Order of Jar: see D'Arcy Jonathan Dacre Boulton, *The Knights of the Crown: the Monarchical Orders of Knighthood in Later Medieval Europe 1325–1520* (Woodbridge: Boydell Press, 1987), p. 335. These colours of white and red may allude to St George, the patron saint of knighthood in general, or more specifically to the Enterprise or Order of St George, another knightly order founded in the 1370s by King Pere of Aragon, but no longer active in the 1420s as it was more or less replaced by the Order of the Jar. *Ibid.*, pp. 279–88. On the belfry as an urban symbol of autonomy, see Essay 3.

[28] Boulton, *Knights*, p. 330. A griffin was attached to the collar of the Order. Although Nadot, *Le Spectacle*, p. 196, states that the griffin was the symbol of Fernando, then appropriated by his son Enrique, the crest of the kings of Aragon was in fact a dragon rather than a griffin, even if it is often hard to distinguish between these two heraldic animals.

[29] FPG, p. 250; PCH, p. 22; LB, p. 61.

representatives of the three Estates) were held there.[30] The *Paso* was celebrated in the main square of Valladolid, now the Plaza Mayor. Being the most important marketplace of the town, with several guild houses, it also had religious significance, with the convent of San Francisco occupying the greater part of its southern side. The king also used the square to exercise and display his jurisdictional powers: for example, just before the jousts took place, he had a man called Juan García de Guadalajara, a member of the knightly Order of the Band, beheaded on the square.[31] The public square of Valladolid was deliberately chosen for this event and not the more 'royal' square of San Pablo, where the king's residence was situated, let alone the more secluded gardens of that residence, where the *emprise* of 8 June was held. The public square was large enough to construct the ephemeral architecture, to enable the participants to perform a full-scale joust and to host a considerable number of spectators. The town administration was clearly happy to collaborate with the king and his relatives and to temporarily close off its most important square. Unfortunately, because of the lack of urban financial accounts, it is impossible to know if the town also helped to finance the building of this impressive ephemeral architecture, but local craftsmen were doubtless involved in its preparation.

The *Paso de la Fuerte Ventura* was thus definitely a spectacular event that should be considered as one of the first *pas d'armes* ever held. Yet, we should be wary of declaring this event to be the birth of the *pas*. We are simply well informed about it, as it constituted an important moment in the reign of Juan II with Álvaro de Luna back in charge, one that would lead to the forced exit from the Castilian court of both Enrique and Juan later in June 1428. There is no doubt that other events preceded the *Paso*, but received much less coverage in the narrative sources. Archival evidence, for example, suggests that Enrique's eldest brother, Alfonso V the Magnanimous, organised several tournaments between 1426 and 1428 on the square of the Mercat in Valencia, when he resided in the town for a prolonged period. These events were not described in detail in chronicles, but the costs were mentioned in the urban financial accounts. Hence, we know that they did include some *grans entremeses* (extensive interludes) built on three carts with crowned Roman goddesses, the construction of a wooden structure with five towers called the castle of the *Fada Morgana* (Morgan le Fay) — financed by the town administration — that was defended by the king and high-ranking courtiers against assailants, and the appearance of twelve Wild Men dressed in hemp and with big cardboard heads.[32] For the Valladolid festivities of 1428, Enrique must have been inspired in some respects by Alfonso's impressive chivalric undertakings.[33] This demon-

---

[30] Francisco de Paula Cañas Gálvez, *El itinerario de la corte de Juan II de Castilla (1418–1454)* (Madrid: Silex Ediciones, 2007), pp. 71, 76.

[31] This man confessed, after being tortured, that he had falsified the name and seal of the constable of Castile when issuing several letters. FPG, p. 214; Ruiz, *A King Travels*, p. 336.

[32] Juan Vicente García Marsilla, 'El impacto de la Corte en la ciudad: Alfonso el Magnánimo en Valencia (1425–1428)', in *El Alimento del Estado y la salud de la Res Publica: Orígenes, estructura y desarrollo del gasto público en Europa*, ed. by Angel Galán Sánchez and Juan Manuel Carretero Zamora (Madrid: Instituto de Estudios Fiscales, 2013), pp. 291–308 (pp. 296–7).

[33] Juan Vicente García Marsilla, 'El poder visible: demanda y funciones del arte en la corte de Alfonso el Magnánimo', *Ars longa: cuadernos de arte*, 7–8 (1996), 33–47 (pp. 37–9); Álvaro Fernández de Córdova Miralles, 'L'impact de la Bourgogne sur la cour castillane des Trastamare', in *La cour de Bourgogne et l'Europe: le rayonnement et les limites d'un modèle culturel*, ed. by Werner Paravicini, Torsten Hiltmann and Frank Viltart (Ostfildern: Jan Thorbecke Verlag, 2013), pp. 593–630 (p. 608 n. 75).

strates that several characteristics of later *pas d'armes* were already present in Iberia in the 1420s. In most Iberian kingdoms, but especially in Castile and Aragon, the three factors that could establish a milieu favourable to this particular type of chivalric event — powerful princely institutions, a competitive *esprit de corps* amongst the nobles and a receptive urban environment — were in place. The question, then, is how the actual transfer and dissemination of this cultural form occurred from Iberia to north-western Europe.

From Iberia to Burgundy

Sébastien Nadot has already suggested that the immediate occasion of the *Paso de la Fuerte Ventura*, the subsequent marriage of the Infanta Leonor with the Portuguese crown prince Duarte, can be seen as a possible link between the Iberian realms and Burgundy, since a large Burgundian embassy was present in Lisbon in the spring of 1429 when this marriage was celebrated.[34] Among them were high-ranking nobles, such as Jean de Roubaix, Baudoin de Lannoy, André de Toulongeon, Pierre de Vaudrey, some heraldic officers and the court painter, Jan van Eyck, who had been commissioned to produce a portrait of Isabel of Portugal for her prospective future spouse, Duke Philip the Good.[35] In July, the marriage treaty was concluded and the ambassadors waited patiently for Isabel to travel with them by ship to the Burgundian lands. As part of this occasion, there were of course entertainments provided at the court, of which jousts and tourneys were an important part. Hence, marriages between royal and princely dynasties were essential in forging and cementing new forms of chivalric display. Nevertheless, it would be another fifteen years before the first Burgundian *pas d'armes* took place in 1443. We therefore have to consider other possible means of communication and transfer between the courts and nobilities of Europe.

The first point to make is that the Iberian Peninsula had long been an attractive destination for nobles from the Low Countries, either to fight in the so-called *Reconquista* and/or to undertake a pilgrimage to the shrine of St James in Santiago de Compostela in north-western Galicia.[36] For example, in June 1402, the seneschal of Hainaut, Jean de Werchin (1374–1415), wrote an *emprise* challenging all 'chevaliers, escuiers et gentilz hommes de nom et d'armes, sans reprouche' (knights, squires and noblemen in name and in arms, who are without reproach) between the towns of Coucy and Santiago de Compostela to take up arms against him while he completed his pilgrimage.[37] On his

---

[34] Nadot, *Le Spectacle*, pp. 19, 134.

[35] Louis-Prosper Gachard, ed., *Collection de documens* [sic] *inédits concernant l'histoire de la Belgique*, 3 vols (Brussels: Louis Hauman, 1834), vol. 2, pp. 64, 69.

[36] Werner Paravicini, 'Nobles Hennuyers sur les chemins du monde: Jean de Werchin et ses amis autour de 1400', in *idem*, *Noblesse: Studien zum adeligen Leben im spätmittelalterlichen Europa. Gesammelte Aufsätze*, ed. by Ulf-Christian Ewert, Andreas Ranft and Stephan Selzer (Ostfildern: Thorbecke Verlag, 2012), pp. 273–320 (pp. 283–6). For a discussion of the problematic ideological charges of the notion 'Reconquista', see Nikolas Jaspert, '"Reconquista". Interdependenzen und Tragfähigkeit eines wertekategorialen Deutungsmusters', in *Christlicher Norden – Muslimischer Süden. Ansprüche und Wirklichkeiten von Christen, Juden und Muslimen auf der Iberischen Halbinsel im Hoch- und Spätmittelalter*, ed. by Matthias M. Tischler and Alexander Fidora (Münster: Aschendorff Verlag, 2011), pp. 445–65.

[37] EdM, vol. 1, pp. 39–43; Werner Paravicini, 'Jean de Werchin, sénéchal de Hainaut, chevalier errant', in *idem*, *Noblesse: Studien zum adeligen Leben im spätmittelalterlichen Europa. Gesammelte Aufsätze*, ed. by Ewert, Ranft and Selzer, pp. 251–72; Martín de Riquer, *Caballeros andantes españoles* (Barcelona: Ariel, 2019), p. 118.

return, since he planned to pass through Portugal, Aragon, Valencia and Catalonia, it was clearly his intention to fight against Iberian knights. According to the Burgundian chronicler Enguerrand de Monstrelet (*c.*1390–1453), nobody showed up at Jean's place of departure, the court of the duke of Orléans, although the seneschal did indeed perform deeds of arms in seven different places on his way to Santiago, and at least once in Valencia,[38] and 'tous les princes qui estoient juges d'icelles armes furent contens de sa personne' (all the princes who were judges of these feats of arms were happy with his conduct).[39] The letter of the *emprise* was distributed in advance by his personal herald in all the territories and towns on his itinerary and it specified in detail the arms and armour to be used as well as some rules of engagement. It was not in fact Jean's first time in Iberia, nor his last: together with other Hainaut noblemen, he had already taken part in a tournament in Cardona (Catalonia) in 1399 and, in 1407, he took part in a feat of arms pitting four against four at the court of King Martín I (1356–1410) in Valencia.[40]

Jean de Werchin was definitely an example for the famous Burgundian knight Jacques de Lalaing (*c.*1421–53) during his own travels and chivalric exploits in Iberia in the 1440s and is indeed explicitly mentioned in the prologue of the latter's chivalric biography.[41] Jean's chivalric exploits therefore show that we should not simply focus on the axis Iberia–Burgundy *per se*, but rather consider that contacts took place in both directions and that earlier chivalric exchanges may have already influenced practices in Iberia beforehand.[42] Nadot may be right in suggesting that the Castilian chivalric tradition is key to understanding the spread of *emprises* and *pas d'armes* across Europe, but this tradition was not autonomous and must have been inspired and shaped in its turn by others, including Moorish ones.[43] The afore-mentioned cane games, a mock battle in which the participants were dressed as 'Moors' and threw spears made of canes at each other, is a good example in this respect. This game was practised widely by elites in Castile and Portugal, but also

---

[38] This was on 7 April 1403 against Lluis d'Abella. See Paravicini, 'Jean de Werchin', based on Martín de Riquer, *Lletres de batalla: cartells de deseiximents i capítols de passos d'armes*, Els nostres clàssics, 3 vols (Barcelona: Barcino, 1963–68), vol. 1, pp. 63 n. 17, 68.

[39] EdM, vol. 1, p. 43.

[40] Paravicini, 'Jean de Werchin', pp. 130–1.

[41] CL, p. 76. In fact, Jacques's first diplomatic journey was to Iberia in the company of his friend and master, Johann, duke of Cleves, who escorted his sister, Agnes, to Olite in the kingdom of Navarre where she would marry Carlos, the successor to the crown. This costly expedition, from July 1439 until March 1440, was led by Jacques's father, Guillaume de Lalaing. As a prolongation of this journey, part of the company also went on pilgrimage to Santiago de Compostela. Monique Sommé, 'De Flandre en Navarre: le voyage d'Agnès de Clèves, nièce de Philippe le Bon et princesse de Navarre, en 1439', in *L'itinéraire des seigneurs (XIVe–XVIe siècles): actes du colloque international de Lausanne et Romainmôtier, 29 novembre–1er décembre 2001*, ed. by Agostini Paravicini Bagliani and Eva Pibiri (Lausanne: Cahiers lausannois d'histoire médiévale, 2003), pp. 173–92 (pp. 180–2); Werner Paravicini, 'Un tombeau en Flandre: Hervé de Mériadec', *Francia: Forschungen zur westeuropäischen Geschichte*, 34.1 (2007), 85–146 (p. 100).

[42] This important point has been made already by Fernández de Córdova Miralles, 'L'impact', pp. 608–9; and Eric Bousmar, 'Pasos de armas, justas y torneos en la corte de Borgoña (siglo XV y principios del XVI). Imaginario caballeresco, rituales e implicaciones socio-políticas', in *El legado de Borgoña: fiesta y ceremonia cortesana en la Europa de los Austrias (1454–1648)*, ed. by Krista De Jonge, Bernardo José García García and Alicia Esteban Estríngana (Madrid: Fundación Carlos de Amberes, 2010), pp. 561–606 (p. 571).

[43] Nadot, *Le Spectacle*, p. 135.

in Northern Africa, from the late fourteenth until well into the seventeenth century. Thus, it became part of a shared culture and its presence in the Christian context was more than merely an act of appropriation by the Castilian nobility. Cane games were often held during courtly festivities and Joyous Entries in Castile and, for the participants, dressing and fighting like 'Moors' served as a means of showing that they really belonged to the aristocracy, although not all participants had the necessary equestrian skills or the appropriate equipment.[44] The *pas d'armes* was thus not unique in being an equestrian event that was used as a distinctive feature of how to display a noble lifestyle.

Apart from the knightly traffic going from north to south, that from the Iberian to the Burgundian sphere should also be taken into account. Martín de Riquer, Teofilo Ruiz, Nadot and others have already listed in detail the names and feats of arms of the knights who travelled from Iberia to the north in the 1430s and 1440s, these being mainly from Castile but also some from Aragon: examples include Juan de Merlo, Pedro Vásquez de Saavedra, Gutierre Quijada, Diego de Valera, François L'Aragonais, Felip Boyl and Jean de Boniface.[45] Yet, the question remains as to how the actual transfer took place. We can discern three factors in this process of acculturation. The first is the detailed accounts made by Burgundian chroniclers such as Jean Lefèvre de Saint-Rémy (*c.*1396–1468) and Enguerrand de Monstrelet of the chivalric *emprises* undertaken by Iberian noblemen. For example, both chroniclers dedicate many pages to the feat of arms between Juan de Merlo and Pierre de Bauffremont during the Congress of Arras on 11–12 August 1435, after Bauffremont had touched Merlo's *emprise.*[46] The authors focus in particular on the creation of a level playing field, meaning that both competitors had to use the same kind of weapons.[47] The fact that Merlo — one of Álvaro de Luna's men[48] — was present at this highly political Congress that sought to conclude a peace between Burgundy and France, testifies to Juan II's attempts to reach beyond Iberia in his policies. Merlo continued his journey to Basel, where his *emprise* was touched by another knight, which also fits into this pattern of Iberian knights reaching out to their noble counterparts elsewhere in Europe.[49]

Of course, the event in Arras was an *emprise* rather than a *pas d'armes*, meaning that it did not necessarily involve a passage or symbolic object, a theatrical scenario or ephemeral architecture. Nevertheless, it shows how the duke (as a judge), his courtiers (as aides), the

---

[44] Javier Irigoyen-Garcia, *Moors Dressed as Moors: Clothing, Social Distinction and Ethnicity in Early Modern Iberia* (Toronto: University of Toronto Press, 2018), pp. 28–39, especially p. 38: 'Moorish clothing for the game of canes was costly enough to be a sign of distinction and social status, but affordable enough to accommodate all sorts of local elites and not only titled nobles.' See also Noel Fallows, *Jousting in Medieval and Renaissance Iberia* (Woodbridge: Boydell Press, 2010), pp. 283–4.

[45] On the complex Aragonese origins of Jean de Boniface, see CL, p. 122.

[46] At least according to this chronicle: 'Fuele tocada su enpresa por … Pierres de Brecemont, señor de Charni' (his *emprise* was touched by Pierre de Bauffremont, lord of Charny): see FPG, p. 338. Monstrelet, by contrast, describes Merlo as an 'appellant' (challenger) 'sans querelle diffamatoire, pour acquérir honneur' (without a dishonourable dispute, so as to acquire honour): EdM, vol. 5, p. 139. Lefèvre de Saint-Rémy, for his part, simply calls this event 'armes' without identifying the challenger: JLdSR, vol. 2, pp. 313–21; see also Richard Vaughan, *Philip the Good: The Apogee of Burgundy* (London/New York: Longman, 1970), p. 146; and Riquer, *Vida*, p. 37.

[47] JLdSR, vol. 2, pp. 313–21; EdM, vol. 5, pp. 138–43.

[48] Fernández de Córdova Miralles, 'L'impact', p. 608.

[49] FPG, p. 338; Riquer, *Vida*, p. 40.

competitors (with their appropriate arms and armour) and the high-ranking spectators all gave shape to this highly formalised feat of arms on the town's main market square. It also demonstrates how the chroniclers (and in the case of Lefèvre de Saint-Rémy, Toison d'or King of Arms, the highest-ranking officer of arms in the Burgundian lands) recorded the event, with its as yet unwritten rules, for posterity. These accounts were read or heard by courtly audiences in the following years and so it comes as no surprise that many of these rules would later appear in the chapters of arms of Burgundian *pas d'armes* of the 1440s. The fact that both Lefèvre de Saint-Rémy and Monstrelet signal that Merlo had his visor raised during the combat on foot may even have inspired Jacques de Lalaing to do the same during many of his own feats of arms.[50]

The recruiting policy of the Burgundian dukes is a third factor of importance which may help explain the process of chivalric exchange. The Burgundian household was a melting pot that integrated different political, linguistic and cultural traditions. Pedro Vásquez de Saavedra is an interesting case with which to illustrate this point. His origins are uncertain, but Olivier de La Marche (*c.*1425–1502), a Burgundian courtier and historiographer, describes him as a knight from Castile. Vásquez's military track record and participation in (as well as his organisation of) several *pas d'armes* is impressive. Together with Diego de Valera, he was one of the two Castilian knights who took part in the *Pas de l'Arbre Charlemagne* of 1443, fighting with a raised visor against the *entrepreneur* Pierre de Bauffremont, lord of Charny.[51] The announcement of the event (i.e. through its chapters of arms) by a herald at the Castilian court — although Vásquez heard about it when he was in London — can be interpreted as yet another form of rapprochement between Castile and Burgundy. According to La Marche, the Castilian nobleman was at that time already known to members of the duke's household, who had seen him participating in a feat of arms in Cologne and who regarded him as an 'homme renommé' (man of renown); he would in fact go on to become a chamberlain of Philip the Good in that same year, at the instigation of Bauffremont.[52] The following year he took part in a naval expedition to Constantinople and the Black Sea, directed against the Ottoman Turks, that was under the command of Waleran de Wavrin.[53] In 1449–50, he participated in Jacques de Lalaing's *Pas de la Fontaine des Pleurs* as his aide.[54] In 1452–53, he fought in the Ghent war and, a year later, he made his vow at the Feast of the Pheasant in Lille, where he took part in the *Pas du Chevalier au Cygne*.[55] Together with Antoine of Burgundy, also known as the Great Bastard of Burgundy, and Philippe de Crèvecœur, Vásquez started to organise the *Pas de la Dame Inconnue* in Bruges in February 1463, but this event never actually took place as

50 CL, pp. 131, 201–2, 239.

51 See Source 4, p. 73.

52 OdlM, vol. 1, pp. 296, 305; Riquer, *Caballeros*, p. 155; PCB no. 1056.

53 Riquer, *Caballeros*, pp. 156–9. Waleran de Wavrin (also known as Waleran de Berlettes) was a nobleman from Walloon Flanders, a chamberlain of Philip the Good and the leader of a naval expedition from 1444 to 1446 against the Ottoman Turks. PCB no. 662.

54 CL, pp. 223–4.

55 Torsten Hiltmann, 'Un État de noblesse et de chevalerie sans pareilles? Tournois et hérauts d'armes à la cour des ducs de Bourgogne', in *La cour de Bourgogne et l'Europe: Le rayonnement et les limites d'un modèle culturel; actes du colloque international tenu à Paris les 9, 10 et 11 octobre 2007*, ed. by Werner Paravicini, Torsten Hiltmann and Franck Viltart (Ostfildern: Jan Thorbecke Verlag, 2013), pp. 253–88 (p. 265); Nadot, *Le Spectacle*, p. 136; MdE, vol. 2, p. 129; VdF, pp. 146, 344–5.

no challengers showed up.[56] In 1468, however, he did participate in the *Pas de l'Arbre d'or* at Bruges. Thus, what started as a one-off participation in a *pas d'armes* evolved into a far more permanent relationship between Vásquez and the Burgundian duke, his household and the chivalric endeavours of the Burgundian court over several decades. In this sense, it is questionable whether Vásquez and other Castilian knights were really exploring other European battle and tournament fields in their own right. It is more probable that he himself was influenced by chivalric practices at the Burgundian court, rather than merely bringing novelty into a fairly well-established princely and noble environment.

A fourth factor that underpins the cultural transfer of the *pas d'armes* concerns the widespread circulation of chapters of arms. We know that heralds were expressly sent by *entrepreneurs* to courts elsewhere in Europe, and that they played a fundamental role in the dissemination of these written documents. For example, Burgundian heralds travelled with these texts to the courts of Castile and Aragon to announce the *pas d'armes* organised by Pierre de Bauffremont in August 1443 near Dijon, as well as the feats of arms that Jacques de Lalaing was going to undertake in Castile in 1447–48. Bauffremont's chapters of arms were even translated into Catalan to make it easier for the knights in Aragon to understand what was expected of them.[57] Likewise, the chapters of arms that the Aragonese knight Felip Boyl used for his *emprise* were translated into English when he came to the court of King Henry VI (1421–71) in 1444–45.[58]

We also know that Burgundian knights sent challenges around Europe calling upon members of royal entourages to participate in *pas d'armes*. However, the exact intention of these challenges was not always clear and so noblemen from distant countries were not always inclined to travel a long way to attend them. For example, the Burgundian chronicler Georges Chastelain (*c.*1414/5–75) reports how Antoine of Burgundy, Philippe de Crèvecœur and the above-mentioned Pedro Vásquez de Saavedra sent letters of challenge carried by Charolais Herald to 'tous roys et royaumes chrestiens' (all Christian kings and realms) concerning a *pas d'armes* to be held in the lands of the duke 'pour la querelle et instance d'une dame' (for the dispute and at the request of a lady). According to Chastelain, Christian I, king of Denmark, Norway and Sweden, sent a squire named Henry to tell the duke in August/September 1463 at the court in Hesdin that the king and his knights would always be prepared to defend women and the oppressed, but that he really needed to know more about the 'secret de cestuy pas, de la nature et condition de la dame et de sa querelle, et de la manière et condition de la bataille qui se devoit faire pour elle, et en quel lieu' (secret of this *pas*, of the nature and condition of the lady and her quarrel, of the conditions of the battle that had to be fought on her behalf and in what place). Clearly, other foreign knights had some doubts about this *pas*, better

[56] For more detail, see Essay 3. See also Hiltmann, 'Un État', pp. 258–9, for further bibliographical references.

[57] Riquer, *Caballeros*, p. 154; and the translation in *idem*, *Lletres*, vol. 3, pp. 10–18. The chapters of arms of the *Paso Honroso* were also translated from Castilian into Catalan. See *ibid.*, vol. 2, pp. 137–45. For the visit of the herald Châteaubelin to the court of Juan II to announce the *Pas de l'Arbre Charlemagne*, see Source 3, p. 69. La Marche (OdLM, vol. 1, p. 322) specifically mentions that the Savoyard nobleman Martin Ballart, when presented before the duke during Bauffremont's *pas*, spoke 'en son piemontois' (in his Piedmontese). Jacques de Lalaing repeatedly needed a French-speaking courtier to communicate with the rulers of Iberia during his travels there. CL, pp. 179–80, 185.

[58] Riquer, *Caballeros*, p. 149; and the translation in *idem*, *Lletres*, vol. 3, pp. 25–6.

known as the *Pas de la Dame Inconnue*, because in the end nobody showed up, according to Chastelain, although Antoine himself maintained that this was because of the crusade that he had to lead in the duke's stead.[59] In short, challenges and chapters of arms circulated widely, from Portugal to Norway, informing knights of different princely and royal courts of the nature of the *pas d'armes*, but only to a certain extent. In these cases, the Burgundian court appears to have functioned as a chivalric centre that attracted foreign knights, although in others it worked also as an exporter of chivalric games, as we will see in the following section.

FROM BURGUNDY TO SAVOY

Although Savoy is not one of the territories that typically appear in historical analyses of the *pas d'armes*, events of this type were indeed organised in the Alpine duchy. Between 1498 and 1522, five potential *pas d'armes* can be identified — potential, because the sources leave certain points in the dark, and none of these feats of arms clearly combines all of the five characteristics of the *pas d'armes* established at the beginning of this essay. However, the overall impression is that, fifty years after France, Anjou and the Burgundian lands had adopted and transformed this specific type of chivalric event, Savoy was in turn influenced by the *pas d'armes* phenomenon.

Savoy was situated south of Burgundy and occupied, just like the latter, large territories on the margins between the kingdom of France and the Holy Roman Empire. In the fifteenth and sixteenth centuries, the dukes of Savoy ruled over an area that extended from Lake Geneva to the port of Nice on the Mediterranean, and from the gates of Lyon to eastern Piedmont. Despite its large size, however, Savoy remained a secondary power on the European chessboard and had far fewer financial resources than, for example, the Burgundian composite state. It had enjoyed something of a golden age from 1391 to 1439 under the reign of Amédée VIII (1383–1451), a count of Savoy who had been elevated to the rank of duke by Emperor Sigismund in 1416. After his reign, the duchy entered a long phase of political decline. During the second half of the fifteenth century, no fewer than seven dukes (some of them mere children) succeeded each other on the throne of Savoy, thus considerably weakening ducal power both politically and financially.[60]

Yet, from the end of the fifteenth century to 1522, several feats of arms were organised at the Savoyard court. This chivalric vogue spanned the reign of two dukes in particular: Philibert II (Figure 6), from 1497 to 1504, and Charles II of Savoy, from 1504 to 1553. Meanwhile, the Italian Wars (1494–1559), during which France and the Empire were fighting against each other for possession of territories in Italy, gave the weakened Savoyard state more and more strategic importance. Indeed, most of the Alpine passes granting access to the Italian peninsula from the north were located on Savoyard territory; the authorisation of the duke of Savoy was therefore necessary for anyone wanting to send armies to Italy. Moreover, the marriages contracted by these two dukes were both above their

[59] GC, vol. 4, pp. 311, 370–2. For the detailed description of Duke Philip the Good's authorisation and the chapters, see JDI, pp. 474–82. According to a letter written in 1466 by a squire of Antoine of Burgundy, this *pas* could not take place because of Pope Pius II's crusade plans: see MT, pp. 81, 335.

[60] For the political context, see Thalia Brero, *Rituels dynastiques et mises en scène du pouvoir: Le cérémonial princier à la cour de Savoie* (Florence: SISMEL Edizioni del Galuzzo, 2017), pp. 3–22.

Figure 6. Duke Philibert II of Savoy (1480–1504). Portrait bust (walnut wood) made by Conrad Meit, Mechelen, *c.*1518. 12.5 × 29 × 10.8 cm. London, British Museum, Waddesdon Bequest, WB 261. Photo: The Trustees of the British Museum.

rank and clearly illustrate Savoy's sudden political ascension: in 1501, Philibert II married Margaret of Austria (1480–1530), daughter of Emperor Maximilian I and the duchess Mary of Burgundy; in 1523, his younger brother and successor, Charles II, married Beatriz of Portugal (1504–38), daughter of King Manuel I of Portugal and María of Aragon.

Like the Burgundian composite state, Savoy was multilingual and brought together several distinct geographical and cultural areas. Bisected by the Alps, the Savoyard duchy encompassed a French-speaking area in the north (the 'Savoie propre' (actual Savoy) from which the ruling family originated) and an Italian-speaking area in the south. Originally, the Savoyard rulers had dominion only north of the Alps and their first capital was Chambéry. However, by the end of the fifteenth century, the centre of gravity of the duchy began to shift southwards towards Piedmont.[61]

When *pas d'armes* were organised in Savoy at the turn of the sixteenth century, the duke's household was still predominantly French-speaking and composed mainly of aristocrats from north of the Alps. However, the process of Italianisation had already begun. Piedmontese nobles were multiplying in the duke's entourage and an ever-increasing proportion of members of the household came from Italian-speaking territories, as the court resided more and more in the south, particularly around Turin, which was to become the capital of the duchy in the second half of the sixteenth century.

---

[61] Lino Marini, *Savoiardi e piemontesi nello Stato sabaudo (1418–1601)* (Rome: Istituto storico italiano per l'Età Moderna e Contemporanea, 1962).

The ruling family of Savoy had demonstrated a strong dynastic identity and chivalric consciousness as early as the fourteenth century. For example, it was among the first ruling dynasties in Europe to create an order of chivalry, the Order of the Collar (1364), it adopted an elaborate funeral ceremony[62] and it used sophisticated emblems as insignia of its power.[63] Yet, a century later, the situation was quite different. Far from being a centre of innovation, the Savoyard court conformed in almost every respect to Franco-Burgundian custom, both in the organisation of the household and in the way that ceremonies were conducted. This may suggest a deliberate strategy on the part of the Savoyard dukes to assert their place in international politics by imitating prestigious models that were recognised throughout Europe.

Thus, despite their increasing orientation towards their southern possessions, the dukes of Savoy continued to follow the cultural influence provided by their neighbours in the north-west. They were speaking French, they married mostly princesses from the French sphere, and cultural life at court was mainly inspired by Francophone courts, even if they were princes of the Empire. Yet, even more than from the kings of France, they seem to have drawn inspiration from the dukes of Burgundy, with whom they had established close ties. In 1393 already, Amédée VIII of Savoy had married Marie of Burgundy, daughter of Duke Philip the Bold. It is therefore probably no coincidence that, a century later, Savoy would undergo some kind of chivalric revival precisely at the time of the wedding between the descendants of these two dynasties, when Philibert II of Savoy married Margaret of Austria, the only daughter of Mary of Burgundy and Maximilian I — who was himself known for his passion for tournaments and chivalric culture.[64]

Indeed, in the first decades of the sixteenth century, most Savoyard court events were directly inspired by Burgundian examples. For instance, the chivalric Order of the Collar, which had fallen into oblivion, was revived in 1518 by Charles II. He renamed it the Order of the Annunciation and provided new statutes that were practically identical to those of the Burgundian Order of the Golden Fleece that had been created by Duke Philip the Good in Bruges in 1430. The rituals of the Savoyard court also seem to have come under Burgundian influence: in 1534, the funeral of a Savoyard prince, Philippe, count of Genevois, was modelled entirely on that of Philip the Fair in Mechelen, as described by Jean Lemaire de Belges in 1507.[65]

The festivities and splendour of the Burgundian court were very well known in Savoy, thanks to accounts written by the people who had attended them. Savoyard contingents were, for example, present at some Burgundian *pas d'armes*, especially the

---

[62] Counts Amédée VI (d. 1383) and Amédée VII (d. 1391) both had double funerals: during the first, their bodies were buried quite simply in the Savoyard necropolis, Hautecombe; during the second, magnificent funeral ceremonies took place, with a knightly offering whereby weapons, horses and banners were presented to the church: see Nadia Pollini, *La mort du prince: Rituels funéraires de la Maison de Savoie (1343–1451)* (Lausanne: Cahiers lausannois d'histoire médiévale, 1994) pp. 71–5.

[63] Luisa Gentile, *Riti ed emblemi: Processi di rappresentazione del potere principesco in area subalpina (XIII–XVI secc.)* (Turin: Silvio Zamorani Editore, 2008), pp. 139, 262.

[64] See below, pp. 358–61.

[65] Thalia Brero, 'La fête de l'ordre de l'Annonciade. Une innovation cérémonielle du duc Charles II de Savoie', in *Mémoires de cours: Études offertes à Agostino Paravicini Bagliani par ses collègues et élèves de l'Université de Lausanne*, ed. by Bernard Andenmatten *et al.* (Lausanne: Cahiers lausannois d'histoire médiévale, 2008), pp. 303–33; *eadem*, *Rituels dynastiques*, pp. 489–90.

two that were closest to the Savoyard borders. At the first of these, in 1443, Duke Louis of Savoy attended the *Pas de l'Arbre Charlemagne* near Dijon with his wife Anne of Cyprus, his brother Philippe, count of Geneva, the herald Savoy and several noblemen from the duchy. Two of them, his favourite Jean de Compeys and Jacques de Challant, distinguished themselves during combat, although a Piedmontese called Martin Ballart made a very bad impression by being ridiculously boastful, at least according to Olivier de La Marche.[66] At the second event, held seven years later in 1450, Jacques d'Avanchy, a Savoyard nobleman who belonged to the household of Louis of Savoy, took up Jacques de Lalaing's challenge at the *Pas de la Fontaine des Pleurs* in Chalon-sur-Saône, through the intermediary of Piedmont, herald of the duke of Savoy, who, on his behalf, touched the shields that had been set up for all comers so as to indicate their acceptance of Lalaing's challenge.[67] A number of knights-errant also passed through Savoy: for example, the Aragonese Jean de Boniface came to challenge Jean de Compeys in Savoy in 1447, and, two years later, Duke Louis presided over the joust that took place between the two of them on the castle square of Turin.[68]

This circulation of men and women between Savoy and Burgundy — it being important not to overlook the significance of foreign brides and their retinues in the cultural transfers between courts — went hand in hand with that of written testimonies and reports of chivalric undertakings. Shortly after the wedding of Charles the Bold and Margaret of York in Bruges (1468), a *Traictié des noces de monseigneur le duc de Bourgoigne et de Brabant* reached the Savoyard court.[69] This narrative (a variant of Olivier de La Marche's account of the same event) includes a description of the *Pas de l'Arbre d'or* organised as part of the wedding celebrations by Antoine, the Great Bastard of Burgundy.[70] Two years later, La Marche's account of the *Pas de la Dame Sauvage*, that was staged in Ghent in 1470 by the Burgundian nobleman Claude de Vaudrey,[71] was addressed to Philippe of Savoy (1438–97), count of Bresse and Bugey, who became duke of Savoy towards the end of his life, in 1496.

Of course, Savoy had its own tradition of tournaments; they are documented from the reign of Count Amédée VI (1334–83) onwards, he being known as the 'Green Count' because he was particularly renowned for wearing this colour during jousts.[72] Between

---

66 OdLM, vol. 1, pp. 266, 295–6, 302, 309–10, 320–3; Pierre du Bois, 'Chronique de la Maison de Challant', ed. by Orphée Zanolli, *Archivium Augustanum*, 4 (1970), 63–7. On the Ballart incident, see also Essay 6. On Challant, see Source 4, pp. 76–7; for a short poem by an unknown author on his extracurricular fight against Diego de Valera as part of the latter's *emprise*, see CPM.

67 CL, pp. 232, 240–3, 249. Jacques d'Avanchy turned out to be one of the three prize winners of the *Pas* and was rewarded with a golden sword by Lalaing.

68 Gentile, *Riti ed emblemi*, p. 63.

69 Auguste Dufour and François Rabut, eds, 'Description inédite des fêtes célébrées à Bruges en 1468 à l'occasion du mariage du duc Charles le Téméraire avec Marguerite d'York', *Mémoires de la Commission des antiquités de la Côte-d'Or*, 9 (1877), 311–53.

70 OdLM, vol. 3, pp. 101–200; on the dissemination of these wedding narratives, see Werner Paravicini, 'The Court of the Dukes of Burgundy. A Model for Europe?', in *Princes, Patronage and the Nobility: The Court at the Beginning of the Modern Age (c. 1450–1650)*, ed. by Ronald G. Asch and Adolf M. Birke (Oxford: Oxford University Press, 1991), pp. 69–102.

71 Bernard Prost, ed., *Traicté de la forme et devis comme on faict les tournois par Olivier de la Marche, Hardouin de la Jaille, Anthoine de la Sale, etc.* (Paris: A. Barraud, 1878), pp. 55–6.

72 Eugene L. Cox, *The Green Count of Savoy: Amadeus VI and Transalpine Savoy in the Fourteenth Century* (Princeton, NJ: Princeton University Press, 1967), pp. 92–8.

1347 and 1356, at least nine tournaments were organised in the Savoyard territories north of the Alps; some chronicles (in particular the one written by Jean d'Orville, known as Cabaret) give detailed descriptions of these events.[73] During the first decades of the fifteenth century, which correspond to Amédée VIII's reign, the financial accounts of the court mention a dozen jousts; these were often organised in connection with courtly celebrations but not in any systematic fashion. For instance, in 1433, Jean Lefèvre de Saint-Rémy, in his capacity as Toison d'or, accompanied Philip the Good to Chambéry for the sumptuous wedding between Louis of Savoy and Anne of Cyprus. The King of Arms and chronicler noted with surprise that 'fust la feste sans tournoy et jouste' (there was no tournament or joust accompanying this celebration).[74]

From the 1440s onwards, in parallel with the political and economic decline of the duchy, the practice of jousting clearly diminished at the Savoyard court and ceremonies became more modest. Of course, chivalric activities did not disappear completely, thanks to noblemen such as Jean de Compeys, as noted above. Indeed, some sources indicate that derivatives of *pas d'armes* were practised in Savoy.[75] However, it is not until the very end of the fifteenth century that *pas d'armes* do seem to have been organised on a larger scale. The sources mention five such events.

The first took place in Geneva. On 19 March 1498, a 'faict d'armes' (feat of arms) that seems to have had the structure of a *pas d'armes* was organised in the city. This event is known thanks to a list that summarises the names and coats of arms of the four defenders (Philibert de Challant, Bertrand de Lucinge, 'Ferriez' and Ognas) and the forty-four challengers (among whom were the duke himself and his half-brother, René, the Great Bastard of Savoy), but does not specify who the *entrepreneur* was.[76] This laconic document says nothing about a fictional plot or setting, but it does suggest an event of some magnitude, given the fact that almost fifty combatants participated in it. This feat of arms was possibly linked to the Joyous Entry of Philibert II into the town that had taken place three weeks earlier, on 24 February 1498.[77]

The second event also happened in Geneva, but three years later, in 1501. When Duke Philibert II married Margaret of Austria in Romainmôtier on 1 December 1501, the couple left almost immediately for Geneva, where the new duchess of Savoy made her Joyous Entry on 8 December. A few days later, 'grosses joustes de .VI. qui receurent tous venans' (great jousts where six [defenders] received all challengers) were organised in the same town in a very elaborate setting. We know of the event thanks to the description of

---

[73] On tournaments at the Savoyard court, see Gentile, *Riti ed emblemi*, pp. 57–60.

[74] JLdSR, vol. 2, p. 297.

[75] In 1445, on Shrove Tuesday, the crown prince, the future Amédée IX of Savoy, is said to have fought 'contre tous vennans' (against all comers) but, as he was only ten years old at the time, the combats must have had a playful rather than a martial dimension: see Gentile, *Riti ed emblemi*, p. 61. In February 1466, the duchess Yolande of France organised a tournament in Chambéry at which four gentlemen appeared to be defending a *pas*: see Elio Colombo, *Iolanda, duchessa di Savoia (1465–1478)* (Turin: Paravia, 1893), p. 11.

[76] TG, pp. 373–7. A. Fourtier, who edited this document in the nineteenth century, found it among the original manuscripts collected in the seventeenth century by Samuel Guichenon, who summarises it in his *Histoire généalogique de la royale Maison de Savoie*, 5 vols (Turin: J. M. Briolo, 1778–80), vol. 2, p. 183.

[77] François Bonivard, *Chroniques de Genève*, ed. by Micheline Tripet, 3 vols (Geneva: Droz, 2001–14), vol. 1, p. 235.

the Burgundian chronicler Jean Molinet (1435–1507), who was in the service of Archduke Philip the Fair, Margaret's brother.[78]

The third of these events was organised in Bourg, the main town of Bresse, in April 1503, when the ducal couple held a reception here for Philip the Fair, who, on his way back from a trip to Spain, stopped in Savoy to visit his sister Margaret. A *pas* had been prepared to entertain the visitor, but both princes fell ill and the combat was postponed. However, it took place a few days later in a simplified version. The events are reported in Antoine de Lalaing's account of Philip the Fair's first voyage to Spain, as mentioned in the introduction of this essay.[79]

The fourth *pas* was organised in Carignano, in Piedmont, where the court of Savoy gathered from 18 to 20 February 1504 to attend the wedding of Laurent de Gorrevod, grand squire of Duke Philibert II and one of his favourites, and Philippa de La Palu.[80] This event served as a pretext for the duke to organise a 'pas à la barriere à pied' (a *pas* on foot at a barrier), which lasted three days and brought together twenty-six competitors. This event is recounted in the only Savoyard account specifically dedicated to recording a feat of arms. Although the original is lost, the text has come down to us through a trustworthy seventeenth-century edition.[81]

The fifth event took place eighteen years later, in 1522, in Ivrea. Duke Philibert II had died a few months after the *Pas* of Carignano. He was succeeded by his brother, Charles II, who seems to have been less enthusiastic about tournaments: it was only on the occasion of the christening of his first child, Adrien, in December 1522, that a feat of arms of some magnitude was organised once again in Savoy. This chivalric event is reported in a very long account of the baptism written in Italian.[82] The festivities lasted for four days; the second and third days were devoted to jousting. Hence, the account of the combats is part of a larger text describing other celebrations as well.

The evidence we have for each of these five events is very uneven. The first three feats of arms were organised north of the Alps and their existence is known only through relatively brief passages of documents that are not specifically dedicated to the events themselves, namely a list of participants and passages taken from two Burgundian chronicles. The other two events, those organised in Piedmont, are reported in accounts that were explicitly written to commemorate them and which devote dozens of pages to the jousts. It should also be noted that these five feats of arms were all organised as entertainments in the context of courtly ceremonies: Joyous Entries (Geneva, 1498 and 1501), the reception of a foreign prince (Bourg, 1503), a wedding (Carignano, 1504) and a baptism (Ivrea, 1522).

To what extent can these events really be characterised as *pas d'armes*? In order to determine this, let us analyse them in the light of the five essential characteristics outlined at the beginning of this essay. The first key element is the *entrepreneur* at the origin of the *pas d'armes*. The Savoyard sources are rarely explicit on this matter, but there is one exception:

78 JM, vol. 2, pp. 495–6.

79 CdV, pp. 287–9.

80 Philippa de La Palu was daughter of Hugues de La Palu, count of Varax. Her sister married Claude de Vaudrey, who is mentioned below in the context of his combat against Maximilian: see HBB, p. 300.

81 PC, pp. 469–77; see also Source 15.

82 ARCT, pp. 251–437.

Antoine de Lalaing clearly indicates that the *entrepreneur* of the *pas d'armes* in Bourg (1503) was the 'baron de Chevron': 'il fist publier une tres-belles armes' (he had a very fine feat of arms proclaimed).[83] This was probably François de Chevron-Villette, who was a councillor and chamberlain of Philibert II.

The texts documenting the other four events point to the duke of Savoy himself as the *entrepreneur.* In Geneva in 1498, it was decided to 'faire faict d'armes pour le bon plaisir et commandement de notre très redoubté seigneur monseigneur le duc de Savoye' (organise a feat of arms by order of, and for the pleasure of, our lord, the duke of Savoy).[84] Six years later, at the *Pas* of Carignano in 1504, two knights having supposedly been told by 'la deesse Fame' (Fama, goddess of Fame) of the forthcoming wedding of the grand squire Laurent de Gorrevod, 'pour honnor[er] la feste ont entreprins tenir ung pas' (held a *pas* to celebrate the occasion).[85] The two men are not named but, since the defenders of the *pas* were Duke Philibert II himself and a nobleman called Sibuet de La Balme, we can probably assume that they were also the *entrepreneurs.* In the Savoyard context, where feats of arms were generally part of larger courtly festivities, it is not surprising that the *entrepreneur* was often the duke himself.

The second key characteristic of a *pas d'armes* is that the *entrepreneurs* defend a passage or a symbolic object against challengers, alone or with the help of other defenders. It is clear that *tenans** and *venans** (defenders and challengers) are both present in the five feats of arms of our corpus. This is also indirectly confirmed by a decorative element: an artificial tree, from which the defenders' shields were hung, was present at three of the events in question. In Geneva in 1498, four combatants were 'attendant contre tous venants', who put 'leurs escus à l'arbrose pour faire faict d'armes' (waiting for challengers to come who would hang their shields on the tree in order to proceed to undertake a feat of arms).[86] In Bourg in 1503, a pine tree from which hung three plain shields (one grey, one yellow and one red) as well as the arms of seven 'deffendans' was put on a platform. These defenders undertook to fight all challengers who presented themselves, the nature of the combat depending on which shield they touched, a recurring feature of many *pas d'armes.*[87] Finally, in Ivrea in 1522, the defenders' shields were arranged on an artificial tree, where a 'nymph' hung a red shield that the challengers had to strike in order to ask for permission to do combat.[88]

While there is no doubt about the presence of defenders and challengers, the sources do not always indicate what exactly they had to defend. In several cases, the only element to be guarded seems to have been a barrier, protected by some defenders as they sought to prevent challengers from crossing it. For instance, Molinet states that in Geneva, in 1501, knights 'deffendirent une barrière contre tous venans' (defended a barrier against all challengers),[89] though they did not succeed very well in performing this task, since the structure ended up in pieces. At Carignano, in 1504, the defenders were once again two knights (including the duke), who had 'entreprins tenir ung pas … à tous venans deux à

[83] CdV, p. 287.
[84] TG, p. 373.
[85] PC, p. 469.
[86] TG, p. 373.
[87] CdV, p. 287.
[88] ARCT, p. 329.
[89] JM, vol. 2, p. 497.

deux' (held a *pas* against all challengers, two by two). The first two days were dedicated to a 'pas à la barrière à pied' (*pas* at the barrier on foot), followed by jousting on horseback with swords on the third day; in addition, individual jousts and running at the ring* were also part of the festivities.[90] The first day of the 1522 feat of arms at Ivrea was likewise dedicated to 'il corere a l'annello' (running at the ring) and to jousting, with the second day being devoted to a 'fiera pugna alla barriera' (fierce combat at the barrier).[91] In Savoy, a *pas d'armes* could thus involve many different types of combat.

There is, then, no doubt about the noblemen involved in the Savoyard *pas*, the actual role they played and the diverse combat forms that they practised. As for the staging of the event and the remaining three characteristics of a *pas d'armes* — namely, the fictional setting, the audience and the location — these merit further attention. Let us deal first with the latter two, as the question of the theatrical production and the fictional scenario will be treated more extensively later. The two earliest *pas* in our corpus (1498 and 1501) took place in Geneva, which was then, together with Turin, the largest town in the duchy of Savoy: both cities had a population of just over 10,000 at that time.[92] The third *pas* took place in 1503 in Bourg, which was the largest town in Bresse, but probably had no more than 3000 or 4000 inhabitants. The last two events took place in Carignano (1504) and Ivrea (1522), respectively 20 km south and 50 km north of Turin. Both were relatively small towns, but they hosted castles where the Savoyard household regularly took up residence. While the Carignano *pas d'armes*, which was held in the courtyard of the castle, was a fairly select event attended mainly by courtiers, the Ivrea *pas* was also accessible to an urban audience.

Nevertheless, it is difficult to get a grasp of the actual impact of the *pas* on the Savoyard nobility and, more widely, on the subjects of the duke. The texts refer to the audience in a largely indirect way, mentioning the ladies, the judges and the heralds only in passing to confirm that they were present. Yet, it is typical of these accounts to emphasise the presence of noble ladies and not to mention any urban audience: the authors apparently wanted to avoid bothering their intended readership with details about the spectators that would have transformed the *pas* into an urban event. Only the account of the *pas* of Ivrea in 1522 repeatedly mentions the public, referring to an urban audience as well as spectators from the nobility. For example, it describes the installation of stands in the square next to Ivrea castle, including a platform leaning against the castle for 'una innumere turba de damicelle, nobille et citadine' (an innumerable crowd of damsels from the nobility and the town alike).[93] This account mentions that the crowd flocked to watch the combats in the square, but, furthermore, that people were also watching the spectacle from the windows and the rooftops.[94] Of particular interest are the emotions of the audience described in the narrative: the ladies turn pale during particularly violent exchanges and the audience is saddened when two Piedmontese knights suffer such a severe blow that one almost dies and the other is carried off with a broken leg.[95]

---

[90] PC, p. 469.

[91] ARCT, p. 349.

[92] Rinaldo Comba, ed., *Storia di Torino, vol. 2: Il basso Medioevo e la prima età moderna (1280–1536)* (Turin: Einaudi, 1997), pp. 431–2; DHS, lemma 'Genève (canton)'.

[93] ARCT, p. 350.

[94] *Ibid.*, pp. 326, 332–3, 349.

[95] *Ibid.*, pp. 356–8.

Further evidence of audience involvement in the spectacle at Ivrea is that burlesque interludes took place between two combats specifically to amuse the spectators: for example, a hideous nun mingled with the audience with firecrackers and rockets that exploded under her skirts. To avoid her, the spectators moved away and fell over, which caused general hilarity. Later, firecrackers attached to the tail of a mule, ridden by a mock-priest, made everyone laugh.[96] There is little doubt that this large audience included more than just the Savoyard court and the bourgeoisie of Ivrea. Indeed, the text itself mentions 'l'inepta et fremente plebe' (the uninitiated and excitable people) — that is, commoners — who were apparently so numerous that one could not see the ground anymore.[97] People had probably come from further afield to see this courtly festivity, at least from as far away as Turin.

To come back to the third characteristic associated with the *pas d'armes*, that of the presence of a fictional/theatrical scenario, it is true to say that the Savoyard sources focus on the names of the participants, their clothing and their performances rather than on a narrative framework that highlights a passage in the form of a bridge, a crossing or other construction that had to be defended. Indeed, these elements are given very little prominence in our texts. However, the presence of ephemeral architecture does provide us with valuable clues about a fictional scenario underpinning the organisation of the event, as we saw above in the case of the *Paso de la Fuerte Ventura*.[98] In Geneva in 1501 and in Bourg in 1503, the settings of the feats of arms recall the ephemeral architecture built for Joyous Entries.[99] In Geneva, for instance, the jousting took place close to an artificial castle decorated with the head of an enormous lion (possibly a reference to Margaret of Austria's coat of arms, which included such an heraldic device); nearby was the 'jardin d'Austrice' (garden of Austria), decorated with daisies (*marguerites* in French). The combats were started off by six fire-breathing dragons that flew from the highest tower of the castle and bore the arms of the six jousters.[100] The simultaneously personal and dynastic dimension of these settings suggests that some elements from the Joyous Entry that Margaret of Austria had received in this city a few days earlier had been reused for the joust itself.

Similarly, Antoine de Lalaing reports that in Bourg in 1503, next to the tree bearing the shields, was 'l'ymage d'une pucelle bien accoustrée, pareille à l'entrepreneur, jettante par ses mamelles eaue en une fontaine, et emprès elle quatre homes saulvages bien faicts' (the representation of a well-dressed maiden, dressed in a similar fashion to the *entrepreneur*, whose breasts spouted forth water, and near her were four very convincing Wild Men).[101] This fountain had in fact been presented to Margaret of Austria at her Joyous Entry into Bourg in the previous year, so it was an effective recycling of an attraction that had worked well on that occasion.[102] This was probably also the case with the Wild Men, these being symbols of fertility and essential figures in the entries offered to young brides, who were expected to produce offspring for the dynasty that they were joining. In any case, a new

---

[96] *Ibid.*, pp. 358–9, 362–3.

[97] *Ibid.*, p. 344. The same topos is also used by chroniclers to describe the audience at tournaments in Brussels. See Mario Damen, 'The Town as a Stage? Urban Space and Tournaments in Late Medieval Brussels', *Urban History*, 43.1 (2016), 47–71 (pp. 59–61).

[98] See above, pp. 327–30.

[99] Brero, *Rituels dynastiques*, pp. 291–305.

[100] JM, vol. 2, pp. 495–6.

[101] CdV, p. 288.

[102] Jules Baux, *Histoire de l'Église de Brou* (Lyon: impr. de A. Vingtrinier, 1854), pp. 27–8.

life was given to these artefacts, which, transposed to the context of the joust, were put at the service of creating a fiction. The fact that the giant maiden of the fountain was dressed like the *entrepreneur* (i.e. in matching colours) could well be an indication of this; when he changed his clothes, she also changed hers, probably following a narrative of some kind.[103]

In addition to the use of ephemeral architecture itself, the descriptions of the fights allow us to hypothesise about some of the details of a probable fictional scenario underpinning these chivalric events. In Geneva in 1501, a Piedmontese knight arrived in the lists led by a ten-year-old girl wearing a splendid dress 'à lettres d'or' (with golden letters), who held him prisoner by a white silk belt to which he was tied.[104] The motif of the knight imprisoned by a lady was recurrent in many *pas d'armes*, such as the *Pas du Perron Fée* (Bruges, 1463), where, in order to regain his freedom, the prisoner had to agree to challenge other knights in different kinds of combat.[105] The figure of the 'Slave-Knight' had also appeared in the *Pas de l'Arbre d'or*, an account of which circulated in Savoy.[106] Apart from references to well-known motifs familiar from Burgundian *pas*, the scenarios of the Savoyard *pas* would also seem to have come under other influences. At Carignano in 1504, for example, the herald's proclamation opening the *pas* evokes images from classical antiquity: he announces that Cupid has gathered his subjects and that in the presence of Juno, Pallas and Venus, the marriage of 'a nymph' and her future husband (i.e. Philippa de La Palu and Laurent de Gorrevod) was agreed upon.[107] This kind of role-playing indicates that the intended courtly audience had at least some familiarity with the characters and stories of Roman mythology.

In the Savoyard corpus, if the descriptions of the combats themselves do not provide extensive information about possible fictional/theatrical/narrative scenarios, the nocturnal entertainments and post-combat parties do give us some valuable clues. Indeed, the dances that took place during all of the evening entertainments at the Carignano *pas* could well have been intended to be a continuation of the narrative of the jousts, since their choreography mimed a combat.[108] A 'momerie par mode de combats' (*momerie** in a fighting mode), and others featuring Amazons and Slave-Knights respectively entertained the participants during the three evenings of the *pas*. These dramatised dances were performed by members of the Savoyard court, including the duke and duchess themselves.[109]

The second evening of the Carignano *pas*, 19 February 1504, is particularly interesting. The entertainment began with the arrival of the duke and three other noblemen disguised as hermits. Next, a herald-damsel dressed in a coat of arms adorned with the cross of St Andrew[110] made her entrance. She proclaimed that the queen of the Amazons, having

[103] CdV, p. 288.

[104] JM, vol. 2, pp. 495–6.

[105] On the *Perron Fée*, see Essay 3 and Source 11a.

[106] OdLM, vol. 3, pp. 164, 168. On the figure of the Slave-Knight, the knight imprisoned by a lady or the prisoner of love in the *pas d'armes*, see Nadot, *Le Spectacle*, pp. 171–5, 184.

[107] PC, p. 469.

[108] *Ibid.*, pp. 476–8.

[109] Margaret McGowan, *La danse à la Renaissance: Sources livresques et albums d'images* (Paris: Bibliothèque nationale de France, 2012), pp. 39–45; Alison Rosie, 'Morisques and Momeryes: Aspects of Court Entertainment at the Court of Savoy in the Fifteenth Century', in *Power, Culture and Religion in France c.1350–c.1550*, ed. by Christopher Allmand (Woodbridge: Boydell Press, 1989), pp. 57–74 (pp. 59–60, 69–71).

[110] St Andrew was the patron saint of the dukes of Burgundy, Margaret of Austria's ancestors.

Figure 7. Amazons. *Le secret de l'histoire naturelle contenant les merveilles et choses mémorables du monde* (France, *c.*1480–85). Paris, BnF, fr. 22971, fol. 2r. Photo: BnF.

heard of the *pas d'armes* held by the duke of Savoy, had sent troops to Carignano to assist him. Two female trumpeters then announced their arrival, and four Amazons (including Margaret of Austria herself) and their pages (including Claude of Savoy, illegitimate daughter of the duke's father), all dressed in extravagant warrior costumes, came into the room, then danced a *moresca** (Figure 7).[111]

[111] PC, p. 476. See also the reading of this episode in Essay 6.

The following evening, a *momerie* based on the theme of the Slave-Knight was presented. Four gentlemen dressed in white satin shirts danced into the room, accompanied by four ladies, 'qui les emmenoient encheinés de grosses et longues cheines d'or comme esclaves' (who led them in on long, thick chains of gold as if they were slaves).[112] These dancers were the two defenders of the *pas d'armes*, Duke Philibert II of Savoy and Sibuet de La Balme, Laurent de Gorrevod, the bridegroom whose wedding was being celebrated by the *pas*, and Claude de Balleyson, one of the duke's favourites. Suddenly, four other knights appeared, seemingly intent on kidnapping the ladies. As the women untied their prisoners, a combat ensued in which Philibert particularly distinguished himself: 'n'en y eust nul qui se peut comparer à mondit seigneur, car d'un coup d'espée abattit un sien chevallier adversaire, et d'un aultre coup d'espée un aultre, de sorte qu'il lui rompit une espaule' (none of them was a match for my said lord who, with one stroke of his sword, brought down one of the opposing knights as well as another with a second stroke that ended up dislocating this man's shoulder).[113] The evenings at Carignano were thus perhaps the extension of a narrative that had begun during the day's jousts, but which employed a different register — dancing instead of fighting — and gave the ladies an active part in the scenario.

It should also be noted that, unlike most Burgundian *pas d'armes*, the main plot of the *Pas* of Carignano was based not on chivalric romances but rather on classical mythology. Of course, elements from antiquity were not absent from fifteenth-century feats of arms. We may recall, for example, the goddesses who appeared in the decorations of the Castilian feats of arms of the 1420s, the *entremets* based on the theme of the 'Twelve Labours of Hercules' in the *Pas de l'Arbre d'or*, or Mars and Pallas dictating to Claude de Vaudrey the chapters of his duel with Maximilian in Worms in 1495.[114] Nevertheless, this fictional setting evoking classical antiquity seems to be a novel feature for a *pas d'armes*, one that underwent considerable development towards the turn of the sixteenth century. It should also come as no surprise that this synthesis between a form of chivalric entertainment from the French-speaking world and a theme very much in vogue in the Italian peninsula took place precisely in a principality that straddled the Alps.

The tournament organised in Ivrea in 1522 for the baptism of Adrian of Savoy likewise probably employed a classical context. Beginning with a pyrotechnical show,[115] it entertained the audience with an artificial storm composed of smoke, thunder and lightning, which, when it dissipated, revealed a ruined tower on top of which a naked and crowned little boy stood, holding a sword in his right hand and a sceptre in his left. At his feet, the golden letters 'Petite pluie abat grand van' (A small rain can drive away a strong wind) were written: a clear reference to the newborn who was destined to rule Savoy.[116] This representation, with its classical overtones, coupled with the 'nymph' who hung the combatants' shields on the tree, also suggests a Greco-Roman context. Similar allusions can also be observed during the prize-giving ceremony in the evening, which

[112] PC, p. 478.

[113] *Ibid.*

[114] See below, p. 359.

[115] On the use of a similar device in what may well be a Scottish example of a *pas d'armes*, see Essay 5.

[116] ARCT, pp. 333–4. *Le livre des faits de messire Jacques de Lalaing* reports that at the time of the *Pas de Nancy*, the expression 'pou de pluie abat grant vent' (a little rain can drive away a great wind) was used by the duchess of Calabria, Marie of Bourbon, to predict the success of Jacques de Lalaing, who was then only a young squire. LF, p. 94; CL, p. 113.

was probably scripted. The same scene was repeated several times: one of the duchess's ladies-in-waiting awarded that day's winner a piece of jewellery, while giving a speech full of classical references that was certainly not improvised. With an equally elaborate reply, the winner, out of modesty, refused the prize and gallantly offered it in return to the lady. Thanks to these dramatic twists and turns, the fictional atmosphere of the *pas* can be seen to have continued outside the lists.[117] As at Carignano, the evening festivities at Ivrea are described in detail in the sources, and one may well wonder whether the *pas* was in fact just one of several components of a festive scenario that linked together ceremony, jousting, banqueting and night-time entertainment.

At the beginning of this essay, we postulated three conditions characterising cultural contexts in which the *pas* can develop, which we can now apply to the case of Savoy. First, an elaborate courtly infrastructure was definitely in place in this duchy, which, despite certain difficult periods, was still one of the most important ducal houses in western Europe. The second condition, a lively spirit of chivalry, is more difficult to discern. Although the crusading ideal was in decline around the turn of the sixteenth century, Duke Philibert still attempted to embody the chivalric ideals of the past. The Savoyard *pas d'armes* had a brief golden age under his reign, when he organised four of them (out of the five we know of) over a period of six years. Born in 1480, Philibert was seventeen years old when he came to power and only twenty-four when he died. Although traditional historiography presents him as being more interested in hunting than in ruling, one could also add jousting to his list of passions, as he was expected to take part in all of the above-mentioned feats of arms.[118] Illness prevented him from being one of the defenders in Bourg in 1503, but he fought alongside his half-brother René, the Great Bastard of Savoy, in Geneva in 1498 and in 1501, and was the star of the *pas d'armes* of Carignano in 1504. As organiser of this *pas*, he was also one of its two defenders, receiving a prize from the ladies and distinguishing himself in the nocturnal dance performances. His youth and his temperament were clearly related to the frequency of feats of arms that took place during his reign. His wife, Margaret of Austria, was herself present at three of the four feats of arms in which he took part. Moreover, she actively participated in the last one since she helped to sponsor it, as is demonstrated by her financial accounts in which the costumes for the dances performed at Carignano appear on her expenses.[119]

Yet, there is another explanation for the duke's endeavours to revive the *pas d'armes*: the fact that the Savoyard dynasty, after many difficult decades, was trying to return to the forefront of the European political scene. This was spurred on by the Italian Wars, which, as we have seen, suddenly gave the duchy an unprecedented importance. As part of its efforts, the court of Savoy began a process of staging power through ceremonies, taking inspiration from the great Burgundian courtly celebrations of the time of Philip the Good and Charles the Bold, which remained an important point of reference in terms

---

[117] Thalia Brero, 'Soirées festives et vie nocturne à la cour de Savoie', in *Le Banquet: manger, boire et parler ensemble (XIIe–XVIIe siècles)*, ed. by Bruno Laurioux, Agostino Paravicini Bagliani and Eva Pibiri, Micrologus Library, 91 (Florence: SISMEL Edizioni del Galluzzo, 2018), pp. 229–60 (pp. 238–40).

[118] On the subject of the princes participating in tournaments, see Torsten Hiltmann, 'Ideal und Physis. Der spätmittelalterliche Fürst in Turnier und Zweikampf', in *Die Performanz der Mächtigen: Rangordnung und Idoneität in höfischen Gesellschaften des Mittelalters*, ed. by Klaus Oschema *et al.* (Ostfildern: Jan Thorbecke Verlag, 2015), pp. 121–49.

[119] See Source 15, pp. 311–12.

of magnificence. There was, of course, one important difference between the Savoyard and the Burgundian contexts: in Savoy, chivalric events that can be seen as *pas d'armes* were organised by the duke himself, whereas those held in the Burgundian lands were staged by noblemen, albeit with the consent and sponsorship of the duke, which were indispensable.

The third condition fostering the development of the *pas* is the urban setting that allowed such events to be staged and watched by a large audience. Although Savoy was far less urban than the central principalities of the Burgundian composite state, it was characterised by two fairly densely populated regions (the possessions north of the Alps and Piedmont), which were separated by a cultural desert, the Alps.

It is true, however, that the Savoyard *pas d'armes* were, above all, internal events in the duchy, without a real international dimension. With a few exceptions, such as the 'chevaliers franchois' (French knights) who showed up in Bourg in 1503 to challenge the defenders, or the noblemen who came from the Low Countries in the retinue of Margaret of Austria, the combatants were almost all from the Savoyard territories north of the Alps. The feat of arms at Ivrea in 1522 was innovative, as Piedmontese courtiers of more recent extraction also took part in the combats, which clearly indicates a desire to integrate all the nobility of Savoy.[120] It was also the last feat of arms that was organised in Savoy for a period of some sixty-five years; the duchy had fallen on hard times, particularly between 1536 and 1559, after the invasion by Bern and France, which led to its being dismantled. In 1587, the duke of Savoy, Charles-Emmanuel I, organised jousts in the great hall of the castle of Turin to celebrate the baptism of his first-born son, Philip-Emmanuel. The pattern of the *pas* was preserved: two defenders, the 'Dédaigné' and the 'Désespéré' (the Scorned and the Desperate), prevented the challengers from entering the 'Temple de la Félicité amoureuse' (Temple of the Joy of Love). In very elaborate settings, the charge was led by the duke himself and other members of the court in what were probably choreographed combats.[121]

Finally, let us return to the varied means by which the actual narratives of Savoyard *pas d'armes* have come to our knowledge. Two of them (Geneva, 1501 and Bourg, 1503) are by Burgundian writers, Jean Molinet and Antoine de Lalaing; two others (Carignano, 1504 and Ivrea, 1522) were written by Savoyards, but they have come down to us thanks to later printed versions, the original manuscripts having been lost. How many others might have escaped our notice? For example, Gaspar Correia, a Portuguese chronicler, indicates that following the wedding of Charles II of Savoy and Beatriz of Portugal, which took place in Nice in 1523, a tournament was held; the chronicler does not give any details except that the audience was struck by a woman leading two knights who were held captive by

---

[120] Gentile, *Riti ed emblemi*, pp. 65–6. On the question of the integration of the nobility, see also Essay 6.

[121] Gualterio Rizzi, ed., *Repertorio di feste alla corte di Savoie (1346–1669). Raccolto dai trattati di C. F. Ménestrier* (Turin: Centro Studi Piemontesi, 1973), pp. 5–6; Domenico Filiberto Bucci, *Il Solenne Battesimo del Serenissimo Prencipe di Piemonte Filippo Emanuelle [...]* (Turin: Bevilacqua, 1588), pp. 18–46, 55–60. On early modern tournaments, see Helen Watanabe O'Kelly, *Triumphal Shews: Tournaments at German-Speaking Courts in their European Context, 1560–1730* (Berlin: Gebr. Mann Verlag, 1992); Marina Viallon, 'Never-Ending Chivalry: Tournaments in Renaissance France from Charles VIII to Louis XIII', in *Tournaments: A Thousand Years of Chivalry*, ed. by Stefan Krause (London: Thomas del Mar, 2022), pp. 101–15.

golden chains.[122] This pattern, which is found in the Burgundian *Pas de l'Arbre d'or*, in the Savoyard *pas* of Geneva in 1501 and that of Carignano in 1504, may well suggest that a *pas*, of which nothing else is known, was organised on this occasion. In short, the Savoyard *pas d'armes* — essentially internal events that were usually linked to other celebrations — were far less 'mediatised' than their Burgundian counterparts, but they attest clearly to the fact that the cultural transfer of *pas d'armes* occurred in a wider geographical and chronological framework than scholars have hitherto thought.

THOU SHALT NOT *PAS*? THE LIMITS OF CULTURAL TRANSFER

While the *pas d'armes* spread from the Iberian realms to France, Burgundy and probably even Savoy, a closer look at the regions further east reveals the limits of this transfer. Several territories and their ruling dynasties developed very close ties to the Burgundian dukes, who became princes of the Empire themselves as a result of the expansion of their rule during the fifteenth century.[123] However, the *pas d'armes* did not spread into the German-speaking parts of the Empire. The duchy of Cleves and the case of Emperor Maximilian I furnish two particularly telling examples of its failure to do so.

Starting in the later fourteenth century, the counts and dukes (as of 1417)[124] of Cleves became tightly integrated into the Burgundian sphere.[125] Adolf of the Mark (1332/33–94), the first count who ruled over Cleves and the Mark, struck an alliance with the French king Charles VI (1368–1422). Because of the latter's illness, which effectively prevented him from ruling during prolonged periods, a regency council was established in which the Burgundian duke Philip the Bold (1363–1404) played a central role.[126] Adolf's son, Adolf II of Cleves (1373–1448), intensified this Burgundian orientation: he became the vassal of Duke John the Fearless (1371–1419) and even married John's daughter, Marie, in 1406.[127]

[122] José Pereira da Costa, ed., *Gaspar Correia, Crónicas de D. Manuel e de D. João III (até 1533)* (Lisbon: Academia das Ciências, 1992), p. 155.

[123] Robert Stein, *Magnanimous Dukes and Rising States: The Unification of the Burgundian Netherlands, 1380–1480* (Oxford: Oxford University Press, 2017), pp. 19, 35–48.

[124] See Manuel Hagemann and Hiram Kümper, *1417: Kleve wird Herzogtum. Mit der Erhebungsurkunde vom 28. April 1417 in Transkription, Übersetzung und Kommentar* (Cleves: Klevischer Verein für Kultur und Geschichte, 2017).

[125] Abraham Glezerman and Michael Harsgor, *Cleve – ein unerfülltes Schicksal: Aufstieg, Rückzug und Zerfall eines Territorialstaates* (Berlin: Duncker & Humblot, 1985); *Land im Mittelpunkt der Mächte: Die Herzogtümer Jülich, Kleve, Berg* (Cleves: Boss, 1984). For relations with Burgundy, see Gregor Hövelmann, 'Die Anfänge der Beziehungen zwischen Kleve und den Herzögen von Burgund', *Annalen des Historischen Vereins für den Niederrhein*, 161 (1959), 232–43; Petra Ehm, *Burgund und das Reich: Spätmittelalterliche Außenpolitik am Beispiel der Regierung Karls des Kühnen (1465–1477)* (Munich: R. Oldenbourg Verlag, 2002), pp. 28–35, 37–43.

[126] Hiram Kümper, 'Adolf III. von Kleve-Mark (*1332/33–†1394): Zweimal (fast) Bischof und Begründer der Union mit Kleve', in *Die Grafen von der Mark: Ein biographisches Handbuch*, ed. by Dietrich Thier and Stefan Pätzold (Witten: Bergischer Verlag, 2021), pp. 251–86 (pp. 253–56). On Charles VI and Philip the Bold, see Bernard Guenée, *La folie de Charles VI, roi bien-aimé* (Paris: Perrin, 2004); Richard Vaughan, *Philip the Bold: The Formation of the Burgundian State* (London/New York: Longman, 1962), pp. 44, 56.

[127] The marriage was consummated in 1415 (Marie was born in 1394): see Jens Lieven, 'Adolf IV./II. (1394–1448) und Johann I. von Kleve-Mark (1448–1481)', in *Die Grafen von der Mark: Ein biographisches Handbuch*, ed. by Dietrich Thier and Stefan Pätzold (Witten: Bergischer Verlag, 2021), pp. 303–28

At least four of Adolf and Marie's children received their education at the Burgundian court.[128] The couple's first son (and Adolf's successor) Johann (1419–81) is thought to have arrived in the Burgundian lands as early as 1428; in 1430, his retinue became part of the household of the duchess, Isabel of Portugal (1397–1471).[129] Johann was present at the peace Congress at Arras (1435),[130] received gifts from his uncle Philip the Good and appeared regularly in the 'écroes de gages' (salary lists) from January 1436 onwards.[131] Contemporaries were well aware of this: the Cleves chronicler Gert van der Schuren mentions that Johann was called 'dat kynt van Ghent' (the child of Ghent), because he attended school there, and that he became well acquainted with the 'Ruterwerk' (business of knighthood).[132] Present at several key moments of Burgundian history,[133] Johann also chose a Burgundian alliance when he married his wife Élisabeth in 1455: her parents were Jean of Burgundy, count of Nevers and Rethel, and Jacqueline d'Ailly. In 1451, Johann was finally elected as a knight of the Order of the Golden Fleece.[134]

Several other members of the Cleves dynasty were equally drawn into the Burgundian sphere, not least by way of marriages that Philip the Good arranged for his nieces.[135] Johann's younger brother, Adolf of Cleves (1425–92), who married Beatriz of Coimbra in 1453, also became a knight of the Order of the Golden Fleece (1456).[136] He was undoubtedly the most 'Burgundian' member of his family, with the strongest record of engagement in tournaments. As lord of Ravenstein, he held an important lordship and castle in fief in the northern part of the duchy of Brabant and continued to play a key part in Burgundian politics well after the demise of Charles the Bold (1433–77).

Adolf II of Cleves and his descendants were thus literally part of the Burgundian family and well acquainted with the court's culture, including feasts, banquets and tournaments, during which they repeatedly played major roles. This situation provided ample

---

(pp. 307–8); Bertrand Schnerb, *Jean sans Peur: Le prince meurtrier* (Paris: Éditions Payot & Rivages, 2005), pp. 183, 185–6.

128 Holger Kruse, *Hof, Amt und Gagen: Die täglichen Gagenlisten des burgundischen Hofes (1430–1467) und der erste Hofstaat Karls des Kühnen* (Bonn: Bouvier, 1996), pp. 152–3.

129 Holger Kruse and Werner Paravicini, eds, *Die Hofordnungen der Herzöge von Burgund. Band 1: Herzog Philipp der Gute 1407–1467*, Instrumenta, 15 (Ostfildern: Jan Thorbecke Verlag, 2005), pp. 97–8.

130 André Bossuat, ed., *Antoine de la Taverne, Journal de la Paix d'Arras (1435)* (Arras: L'Avenir, 1936), pp. 33–4, 53, 56 and *passim*. GvdS, p. 146; Dieter Scheler, 'Köln oder Brüssel: die heimlichen Hauptstädte von Kleve-Mark', in *Dieter Scheler: Stadt und Kirche, Land und Herrschaft am Niederrhein in Mittelalter und anbrechender Neuzeit. Gesammelte Studien*, ed. by Hiram Kümper and Andrea Berlin (Münster/New York: Waxmann, 2019), pp. 27–41 (p. 29).

131 Jacques Paviot, ed., *Portugal et Bourgogne au XVe siècle (1384–1482): Recueil de documents extraits des archives bourguignonnes* (Lisbon/Paris: Centre Culturel Calouste Gulbenkian/Commission nationale pour les commémorations des découvertes portugaises, 1995), p. 259; Scheler, 'Köln oder Brüssel', p. 29; Kruse and Paravicini, *Die Hofordnungen*, p. 97. Earlier appearances of Johann in the *écroes* first concern his father's retinue, then remain sporadic: PCB no. 0384.

132 GvdS, p. 146; Lieven, 'Adolf IV./II.', p. 319. See also Joël Blanchard, ed., *Mémoires de Philippe de Commynes*, 2 vols (Geneva: Droz, 2007), vol. 1, p. 390.

133 Scheler, 'Köln oder Brüssel', pp. 28–36; Lieven, 'Adolf IV./II.', p. 319.

134 COTO, pp. 109–12.

135 Adolf's daughters, Katharina and Maria, were an essential part of Philip the Good's marriage politics: see Vaughan, *Philip the Good*, p. 124; C. A. J. Armstrong, 'La politique matrimoniale des ducs de Bourgogne de la maison de Valois', *Annales de Bourgogne*, 40 (1968), 5–58, 89–139 (p. 19).

136 COTO, pp. 131–4.

opportunity for cultural transfer[137] and pertinent examples can be found in several contexts, although it remains difficult to establish whether individual objects or practices definitively reflect strictly Burgundian influence. The dukes of Cleves were, for example, amongst the first princes in the Holy Roman Empire to produce 'ordinances' (i.e. normative texts that regulated the structure of the household) for their court.[138] Their funerary tradition was also probably inspired by Burgundian examples: the sepulchral monuments in Cleves share similarities with the tombs at Champmol, where the dukes of Burgundy were buried, and Adolf II's foundation of a Carthusian monastery at Wesel as a new dynastic burial place may equally have followed this model.[139] As for more chivalric traditions, Adolf II founded an Order of St Anthony that may have been inspired by the Golden Fleece,[140] although it remained rather short-lived, disappearing from the sources in 1483, and could not compete with its more exclusive and prestigious model.

Most importantly, however, members of the house of Cleves repeatedly participated in tournaments in the Burgundian lands and beyond, including *pas d'armes*. Johann I, for example, jousted at Dijon (or Besançon) and Brussels.[141] In Lille, he organised one of the feasts that paved the way for the famous Feast of the Pheasant in 1454, during which his brother Adolf announced his *Pas du Chevalier au Cygne*;[142] the famous tournament champion Jacques de Lalaing was described as his *mignon* (protégé).[143] How deeply Johann was imbued with Burgundian culture is expressed in one quite spectacular episode: in the summer of 1448, he challenged the archbishop Dietrich of Cologne to a single combat in order to avoid more military bloodshed during the Soest Feud![144] Nothing came of this initiative,

---

[137] On the influence in the arts, see Hans Peter Hilger, 'Kleve und Burgund', in *Land im Mittelpunkt der Mächte: Die Herzogtümer Jülich, Kleve, Berg* (Cleves: Boss-Verlag, 1985), pp. 209–33. For a recent attempt to collect and analyse pertinent material, see Marian Bornemann, 'Vorbild Burgund? Die Hoforganisation und Hofkultur der Herzöge von Kleve im 15. Jahrhundert' (unpublished MA dissertation, Ruhr-Universität Bochum, 2022).

[138] Klaus Flink and Bert Thissen, eds, *Die klevischen Hofordnungen* (Cologne/Weimar/Vienna: Böhlau, 1997). In this respect, Paravicini, 'Court of the Dukes', pp. 90–1, has to be slightly modified, since these texts were not available to him at the time of publication.

[139] Lieven, 'Adolf IV./II.', p. 318; Hilger, 'Kleve und Burgund', pp. 225–7; for Champmol, see Renate Prochno, *Die Kartause von Champmol: Grablege der burgundischen Herzöge 1364–1477* (Berlin: Akademie-Verlag, 2002).

[140] Leo Peters, 'Der jülichsche Hubertus- und klevische Antonius-Ritterorden', in *Land im Mittelpunkt der Mächte: Die Herzogtümer Jülich, Kleve, Berg* (Cleves: Boss-Verlag, 1985), pp. 125–32 (pp. 128–30). The foundation 'before 1435' allows for Burgundian influence, but it might have taken place as early as 1420 (the charter is lost). Adolf I had already established at least two — albeit rather short-lived — chivalric societies.

[141] OdLM, vol. 1, p. 267 (Dijon or Besançon, 1442), vol. 2, pp. 52–3 (Brussels, 1444). On the author's penchant for waxing lyrical about those whom he considered to be chivalric heroes, see Jean Devaux, 'Le culte du héros chevaleresque dans les *Mémoires* d'Olivier de la Marche', *PCEEB*, 41 (2001), 53–66; see also Catherine Emerson, *Olivier de la Marche and the Rhetoric of Fifteenth Century Historiography* (Woodbridge: Boydell Press, 2004).

[142] OdLM, vol. 2, pp. 333, 346 (Johann at Lille); MdE, vol. 2, p. 114; VdF, pp. 31–2, 109–13.

[143] OdLM, vol. 1, p. 268; see also Klaus Oschema, *Freundschaft und Nähe im spätmittelalterlichen Burgund: Studien zum Spannungsfeld von Emotion und Institution* (Cologne/Weimar/Vienna: Böhlau, 2006), p. 373; and CL, introduction, pp. 17–18.

[144] Joseph Hansen, ed., *Westfalen und Rheinland im 15. Jahrhundert. Vol. 1: Die Soester Fehde* (Leipzig: Hirzel, 1888), pp. 356–7, 360–2. In the early 1440s, the city of Soest sought to liberate itself from its

as was the case in virtually all of such challenges that we know of (not to mention the singularity of challenging a cleric), but Johann's attempt strongly resembles a comparable proposition by Philip the Good, who had challenged Duke Humphrey of Gloucester in 1425 in order to settle the conflict over the territories of Jacqueline of Bavaria.[145]

Johann's brother Adolf of Cleves had an even more illustrious chivalric career, distinguishing himself in jousts at Dijon, Lille and elsewhere.[146] Georges Chastelain mentions his participation, amongst other occasions, in a tournament organised by Charles, count of Charolais, at Lille in August 1458.[147] On this occasion, Adolf, Philippe Pot and Pedro Vásquez de Saavedra publicly wore an *emprise* and proposed to organise a more fully fledged event that might have become a *pas d'armes*. They didn't succeed, however: although they sent their chapters to England, owing to the political situation the English noblemen did not receive their king's permission to leave and take up the three men's challenge.[148]

In the same year, Adolf was one of the noblemen who accepted a challenge organised by Guillaume de Meuillon (or Moullon) that was carried by a 'Moor' to the Burgundian court: Chastelain recounts that Duke Philip allowed twelve members of his court to touch the *emprise*, but insisted that the rest of the proceedings were to take place in a setting where the ladies could be present.[149] This *Pas du Compagnon à la Larme Blanche*, referred to by the name chosen for himself by Guillaume in his fictional framework, finally took place in October 1458 at Le Quesnoy.[150] It was unusual in the series of Burgundian *pas d'armes* in that its *entrepreneur* was neither a vassal of Duke Philip nor a member of the Golden Fleece.[151] Chastelain explicitly refrained from describing it in more detail 'pour ce que ne furent que joustes' (because the affair merely concerned jousts)[152] and never calls it a *pas d'armes*. Still, his narrative highlights two participants: Adolf of Cleves and Antoine of Burgundy, the Great Bastard.[153] Exactly a decade later, in 1468, these two were once again the central protagonists during the *Pas de l'Arbre d'or* in Bruges on the occasion of Charles the Bold's

---

lord, the archbishop of Cologne, and offered its allegiance to Duke Adolf II of Cleves. The conflict had wide repercussions and lasted from 1444 to 1449: see Heinz-Dieter Heimann, 'Die Soester Fehde', in *Soest. Geschichte der Stadt. Bd. 2: Die Welt der Bürger. Politik, Gesellschaft und Kultur im spätmittelalterlichen Soest*, ed. by Heinz-Dieter Heimann, Wilfried Ehbrecht and Gerhard Köhn (Soest: Mocker & Jahn, 1996), pp. 173–260 (pp. 236–7).

[145] Vaughan, *Philip the Good*, pp. 38–9; on princely combats, see also Élodie Lecuppre-Desjardin, 'Le duel judiciaire dans les villes des anciens Pays-Bas bourguignons: privilège urbain ou acte de rébellion?', in *Agon und Distinktion: Soziale Räume des Zweikampfs zwischen Mittelalter und Neuzeit*, ed. by Uwe Israel and Christian Jaser (Berlin: LIT-Verlag, 2016), pp. 181–97 (pp. 184–5).

[146] OdLM, vol. 1, p. 286 (Dijon, 1443?); vol. 2, pp. 379 (Lille, 1454), 401 (Lille, 1454).

[147] GC, vol. 3, p. 452.

[148] *Ibid.*, vol. 3, pp. 454–5. In 1455, the conflicts between York and Lancaster that led to the Wars of the Roses had erupted.

[149] *Ibid.*, vol. 3, pp. 463–4.

[150] GCC, pp. 127–32: see Source 9. See also Nadot, *Le Spectacle*, p. 131 (Nadot terms it the *Pas du Quesnoy*: see *ibid.*, pp. 89, 266, and dates the event to 1456).

[151] See Jacques Paviot, 'Le rôle des ordres de chevalerie dans la ritualisation de la cour', in *Rituels et cérémonies de cour de l'Empire romain à l'âge baroque*, ed. by Delphine Carrangeot, Bruno Laurioux and Vincent Puech (Villeneuve-d'Ascq: Presses Universitaires du Septentrion, 2018), pp. 97–106 (p. 105).

[152] GCC, p. 128.

[153] GC, vol. 3, p. 466; GCC, pp. 127–8; for the terminology, see also Blunk, 'Faux Pas'. On Antoine, see COTO, pp. 129–31.

marriage to Margaret of York.[154] While Antoine acted as its *entrepreneur* and defender, Adolf was the first challenger and their combat opened the event. The large depiction of this scene in a manuscript of the *Excellente Cronike van Vlaenderen* thus shows the coat of arms of Cleves and the Mark prominently alongside the Burgundian arms and those of Antoine (Figure 8).

Adolf participated on many occasions in Burgundian jousting events. In the *Pas du Perron Fée* in 1463, he was accompanied by his brother Johann and others, including Philip the Good, Charles of Charolais (i.e. the future Charles the Bold) and Louis de Luxembourg, count of Saint-Pol.[155] Although he was usually addressed (and thus perceived) as lord of Ravenstein, Adolf's self-presentation clearly played on his paternal traditions. At the *Pas du Chevalier au Cygne*, for example, the arms of Cleves and accompanying motifs figured even more prominently than at the *Arbre d'or*: on the day of the Feast of the Pheasant (17 February 1454), Adolf impersonated the 'Swan Knight', the mythical founding figure of the house of Cleves.[156] Although Duke Philip may himself have been more interested in the related story of Godfrey of Bouillon when he acquired a series of three tapestries that depicted the story of the 'Swan Knight' in 1462,[157] the setting in 1454 clearly underlined the tradition of Cleves.[158]

Members of the Cleves family thus played prominent and active roles in Burgundian tournament culture and were keen participants in chivalric and courtly life. In 1450, for example, Johann I of Cleves travelled to Jerusalem, and he repeatedly carried out diplomatic tasks for his Burgundian uncle.[159] The significance of such activities was not lost on their subjects. The chronicler Gerd van der Schuren, for example, mentioned not only the

---

[154] OdLM, vol. 3, pp. 123–33; see also Werner Paravicini, 'Die zwölf "Magnificences" Karls des Kühnen', in *Formen und Funktionen öffentlicher Kommunikation im Mittelalter*, ed. by Gerd Althoff (Stuttgart: Jan Thorbecke Verlag, 2001), pp. 319–95 (pp. 331–9); and Eric Bousmar, 'Jousting at the Court of Burgundy. The "Pas d'armes": Shifts in Scenario, Location and Recruitment', in *Staging the Court of Burgundy: Proceedings of the Conference 'The Splendour of Burgundy'*, ed. by Wim Blockmans *et al.* (Turnhout/London: Brepols/Harvey Miller, 2013), pp. 75–84.

[155] PPF, pp. 118–19 (Paris, BnF, fr. 5739), 186–7 (Lille, BU, 104). See also Andries Van den Abeele, 'De Wapenpas van de Betoverde Burcht, voorbode van de machtsgreep door Karel de Stoute', *Handelingen van het Genootschap voor Geschiedenis te Brugge*, 146 (2009), 93–139.

[156] OdLM, vol. 2, p. 345. See, for example, 'Clevisches Wappenbüchlein um 1475', in *150 Jahre Landkreis Kleve: Beiträge zu der geschichtlichen Entwicklung* (Cleves: Boss, 1966) [no page numbers]; on the legend and its role in the construction of family identity in Cleves, see Jens Lieven, *Adel, Herrschaft und Memoria: Studien zur Erinnerungskultur der Grafen von Kleve und Geldern im Hochmittelalter (1020–1250)* (Bielefeld: Verlag für Regionalgeschichte, 2008), pp. 148–78. For the Brabantine dimension of the motif, see Jan Frans Willems, ed., *De Brabantsche Yeesten, of rymkronyk van Braband, door Jan De Klerk, van Antwerpen* (Brussels: Hayez, 1839), pp. 1–2; Sjoerd Bijker, 'The Functions of the Late Medieval Brabantine Legend of Brabon', in *Networks, Regions and Nations: Shaping Identities in the Low Countries, 1300–1650*, ed. by Robert Stein and Judith Pollmann (Leiden/Boston, MA: Brill, 2010), pp. 91–109.

[157] Two surviving fragments are preserved at Vienna and Krakow: see Anna Rapp Buri and Monica Stucky-Schürer, *Burgundische Tapisserien* (Munich: Hirmer, 2001), pp. 280–9, who suggest that this series was not inspired by Adolf's appearance in 1454 (p. 286). This seems to be corroborated by Romina Westphal, 'Tapestry and Gender: On the Hero and Heroine Motifs and the Construction of Burgundian Identity' (unpublished PhD dissertation, University of Leeds, 2019), pp. 147–79, who mentions Adolf's appearance in 1454 but not the Cleves dimension of the motif (p. 175).

[158] MdE, vol. 2, p. 120; OdLM, vol. 2, p. 342; VdF, p. 110.

[159] Kathrin Kelzenberg, *Heiliglandfrömmigkeit im Nordwesten des Reiches: die Herzogtümer Brabant, Geldern, Jülich und Kleve im späten Mittelalter* (Heidelberg: Universitätsverlag Winter, 2022), pp. 99–141; on the

Figure 8. The two opponents of the first combat of the *Pas de l'Arbre d'Or*, Antoine of Burgundy and Adolf of Cleves. The shields in the tree display the coats of arms of Antoine (left), Charles the Bold (centre) and Cleves-Mark (right). *Excellente Cronike van Vlaenderen* (*c*.1490–1500). Douai, BM, 1110, fol. 268v. Photo: IRHT-CNRS.

tournaments that took place in the counties of the Mark and Cleves in his chronicle, but also the counts' and dukes' pilgrimages and their *reissen* (crusading journeys) to Prussia.[160] According to him, Duke Adolf I had spent no less than 100,000 'schylde' (*écus*, gold coins) on travels, tournaments and social activities in places such as Granada, Heidelberg and Paris, but also Brussels as well as other places in Brabant.[161] Concerning the tournaments, however, Van der Schuren does not refer to the splendid Burgundian *pas d'armes*, but rather to regional events at Cologne, Mainz and Andernach.[162]

The general awareness of the need for chivalric display is equally evident in the work of Arnold Heymerick, a cleric at Xanten and a humanist, especially in his panegyric on Johann II of Cleves (1458–1521), who received a Golden Rose (a symbolic gift awarded to exemplary Christian princes) from Pope Innocent VIII in 1489. Heymerick praised his duke in the highest terms, depicting him and his court as chivalric and splendid: when the procession that brought the rose arrived at the city of Cleves, the duke, as he waited, was surrounded by his most distinguished noblemen, who all carried collars and were accompanied by knights in sumptuous attire: 'Dux vero triumphator cum proceribus nobilibus et torquatis, equestrisque ordinis viris miranda preciositate amictis' (But the triumphant duke [waited] with the most distinguished noblemen, who were wearing collars, and marvellously well-clad knights).[163]

Yet, while courtly splendour was visibly appreciated in Cleves, neither Heymerick nor other sources contain any indication that *pas d'armes* were organised there. Based on the criteria we identified at the beginning of this essay — an institutionalised court culture, the presence of a strong chivalric spirit amongst a class-conscious nobility and the availability of a suitable stage — we have to assume that the court and nobility in Cleves did not reach the critical mass that would have allowed for the organisation of such an elaborate event. Not only did staging a *pas d'armes* imply a significant financial burden, but the event's success was dependent on the presence of a sufficient number of stakeholders, participants and onlookers.

Concerning the potential stage, the urban centres available to the dukes of Cleves were hardly promising settings in which to host a major chivalric event: towns such as Cleves, Wesel or Kalkar[164] could not compete in size and wealth with Bruges or Ghent, and the

---

stay at Naples, see *ibid.*, pp. 105, 113, 119–21. In 1459, Johann was part of a Burgundian embassy to see Pope Pius II at Mantua: see MdE, vol. 2, pp. 377–93.

160 GvdS, p. 29: Count Engelbert I of the Mark travelled to Prussia in 1261–62; see Gerhard E. Sollbach, 'Engelbert I. Graf von der Mark (*vor 1249–†1277)', in *Die Grafen von der Mark: Ein biographisches Handbuch*, ed. by Dietrich Thier and Stefan Pätzold (Witten: Bergischer Verlag, 2021), pp. 69–84 (pp. 82–3). On these late medieval crusades in Prussia, see Werner Paravicini, *Die Preußenreisen des europäischen Adels*, Beihefte der Francia, vol. 17. 1–2, 2 vols (Sigmaringen: Jan Thorbecke Verlag, 1989–95); *idem*, *Adlig leben im 14. Jahrhundert. Weshalb sie fuhren: Die Preußenreisen des europäischen Adels. Teil 3* (Göttingen: V&R unipress, 2020) ; *idem*, *Verlust und Dauer. Weshalb sie nicht mehr fuhren und was an die Stelle trat: Die Preußenreisen des europäischen Adels. Teil 4* (Göttingen: V&R unipress, 2024).

161 GvdS, p. 138.

162 *Ibid.*

163 Dieter Scheler, ed., *Die Goldene Rose des Herzogs Johann von Kleve: Der Bericht Arnold Heymericks von der Überreichung der Goldenen Rose im Jahr 1489* (Cleves: Stadtarchiv Kleve, 1992), p. 74.

164 Around 1550, Cleves had *c.*2200 inhabitants, Wesel *c.*6750, Kalkar *c.*1700: see Klaus Flink, 'Die klevischen Herzöge und ihre Städte, 1394–1592', in *Land im Mittelpunkt der Mächte: Die Herzogtümer Jülich, Kleve, Berg* (Cleves: Boss-Verlag, 1985), pp. 75–98 (p. 83).

contrast is even stronger in the case of Hamm, Iserlohn or Unna in the county of the Mark. Other, more promising urban centres in the area were not at the dukes' disposal. The imperial city of Dortmund, for example, had traditionally strained relations with the counts of the Mark[165] and Soest became available only towards the late 1440s, when the dukes of Cleves forcefully acquired it from the archbishop of Cologne.[166] The dukes' own cities visibly failed to provide a propitious setting for the staging of representative tournaments — in contrast to what Gerard Nijsten described for late medieval Arnhem in the nearby duchy of Guelders.[167] While Guelders functioned as an effective transmission belt for cultural features and courtly practices between Burgundy and the Empire,[168] Cleves illustrates the limits of transfer, at least as far as the *pas d'armes* are concerned, even though the decisive reasons remain somewhat elusive.

This is all the more remarkable given that some of the towns in the region around Cleves and the Mark *did* have a tournament culture. In addition to the tournaments at Cologne, Mainz and Andernach, in which Duke Adolf II took part, according to Van der Schuren, we can identify further events at Dortmund (1442, 1445, 1484?), Mainz (1480, 1481?) and Cologne (1481, 1486).[169] Eberhard, a son of Count Adolf I of the Mark, even met an untimely end during a tournament at Neuss in 1241, one that was still remembered in late medieval chronicles.[170] For 1347, Van der Schuren describes a 'heerliken hoff' (magnificent court) and a 'steeckspeel' (joust) organised by the young count, Engelbert III, at Hamm.[171] While this long-standing tournament tradition continued into the fifteenth century, none of the later events show the influence of *pas d'armes* that the dukes of Cleves witnessed in the Burgundian lands.

Besides the characteristics of the urban network and culture in Cleves, the structure and orientation of the regional nobility probably also played an important role in the apparent failure of cultural transfer. *Vivre noblement* (living a noble lifestyle) came with a hefty price tag and nobles in Cleves and in the Mark had relatively modest financial

---

[165] See Thomas Schilp, 'Die Reichsstadt (1250–1802)', in *Geschichte der Stadt Dortmund*, ed. by Stadtarchiv Dortmund (Dortmund: Harenberg, 1994), pp. 69–211 (pp. 80–92). Gerhard of the Mark organised a tournament in Dortmund in 1442: see Johannes Franck and Joseph Hansen, eds, 'Chronik des Johann Kerkhörde von 1405–1463', in *Die Chroniken der deutschen Städte vom 14. bis ins 16. Jahrhundert*, vol. 20: *Dortmund. Neuss* (Leipzig: Hirzel, 1887), pp. 1–145 (pp. 64–5), but the description underlines that this was an unusual event which the inhabitants of the city had not expected.

[166] Heimann, 'Die Soester Fehde'; Ehm, *Burgund und das Reich*, pp. 37–43.

[167] Gerard J. M. Nijsten, *In the Shadow of Burgundy: The Court of Guelders in the Late Middle Ages*, Cambridge Studies in Medieval Life and Thought, 4th ser., 58 (Cambridge: Cambridge University Press, 2004), p. 399.

[168] Gerard J. M. Nijsten, 'Hof und Kultur. Charakteristik eines mittelgroßen Fürstenhofes am Niederrhein', in *Gelre – Geldern – Gelderland. Geschichte und Kultur des Herzogtums Geldern*, ed. by Johannes Stinner and Karl-Heinz Tekath (Guelders: Verlag des Historischen Vereins für Geldern und Umgegend, 2001), pp. 373–82 (p. 377).

[169] See the list in Hans H. Pöschko, 'Turniere in Mittel- und Süddeutschland von 1400 bis 1550. Katalog der Kampfspiele und der Teilnehmer' (unpublished PhD dissertation, Universität Stuttgart, 1987).

[170] GvdS, p. 11; see also Fritz Zschaeck, ed., *Die Chronik der Grafen von der Mark von Levold von Northof (Levoldi de Northof Chronica comitum de Marka)* (Berlin: Weidmannsche Buchhandlung, 1929), p. 34.

[171] GvdS, p. 28; and see *ibid.*, p. 83, for a tournament at Heidelberg (in 1400) on the occasion of Adolf II's marriage to Agnes, a daughter of the Roman-German king Ruprecht.

means: few (if any) noblemen and knights could have afforded to become the *entrepreneur* of a *pas d'armes*,[172] and the number of challengers they might have hoped to attract in the region was equally limited for the same reason. In addition, the court of Cleves itself could not compete in size with Burgundy or even Guelders.[173] The ducal family of Cleves might thus have preferred to invest in their participation in Burgundian *pas*, where they could be seen by a vast crowd. Finally, one should not underestimate the role and importance of regional traditions and preferences. Even though German noblemen shared the Burgundian predilection for knightly prowess, tournaments in the Empire were often more collective endeavours, organised by chivalric societies of the regional nobility, although individual princes or nobles were also active in this field.[174]

A similar mixture of contact, interest and yet lack of transfer can be observed in the case of Emperor Maximilian I. After his marriage to Mary of Burgundy in 1477, which led to the integration of large parts of the Burgundian inheritance into the Habsburg dominions,[175] Maximilian engaged wholeheartedly in the chivalric culture that he encountered in his new territories and enjoyed participating in jousts and tournaments.[176] In addition, his self-representation as an ideal chivalric hero dominates the autobiographical works that are part of his *gedechtnus*-project through which he sought to ensure his lasting memory:[177] the *Freydal*, the *Weisskunig* and the *Theuerdank*. The first of these texts focuses

[172] For the costs involved for the *entrepreneur*, the challengers, the host and the town in question, see Essay 3; see also CL, pp. 28–33.

[173] A systematic study is a desideratum: Flink and Thissen, eds, *Die klevischen Hofordnungen*, p. xxi, estimate an average size of 250 persons for Cleves; Nijsten, *Hof und Kultur*, p. 373, speaks of 300 to 600 for Guelders. The court of Charles the Bold grew to over 300 noblemen, not including its numerous non-noble members: see Valérie Bessey, Sonja Dünnebeil and Werner Paravicini, eds, *Die Hofordnungen Herzog Karls des Kühnen 1467–1477* (Berlin: Peter Lang, 2021), p. 14.

[174] Peter Jezler, Peter Niederhäuser and Elke Jezler, eds, *Ritterturnier. Geschichte einer Festkultur* (Lucerne: Quaternio Verlag, 2014); Werner Meyer, 'Turniergesellschaften: Bemerkungen zur sozialgeschichtlichen Bedeutung der Turniere im Spätmittelalter', in *Das ritterliche Turnier im Mittelalter. Beiträge zu einer vergleichenden Formen- und Verhaltensgeschichte des Rittertums*, ed. by Josef Fleckenstein (Göttingen: Vandenhoeck & Ruprecht, 1986), pp. 500–12 (pp. 501–2).

[175] See Klaus Oschema, 'Wege des Hauses Habsburg in den Westen Europas 1477 bis 1519', in *König Rudolf I. und der Aufstieg des Hauses Habsburg im Mittelalter*, ed. by Bernd Schneidmüller (Darmstadt: WBG, 2019), pp. 410–38; Jan Hirschbiegel, 'Mary and Maximilian – Burgundy and Habsburg: The Rise of an Empire', in *Unions and Divisions: New Forms of Rule in Medieval and Renaissance Europe*, ed. by Paul Srodecki, Norbert Kersken and Rimvydas Petrauskas (Abingdon: Routledge, 2023), pp. 210–23.

[176] On Maximilian, see Hermann Wiesflecker, *Kaiser Maximilian I. Das Reich, Österreich und Europa an der Wende zu Neuzeit*, 5 vols (Munich: Oldenbourg, 1971–86); on the Burgundian influence, see Malte Prietzel, 'Imitation, Inspiration und Desinteresse. Die Auseinandersetzung Maximilians I. mit den politischen Traditionen Burgunds', in *'Das kommt mir spanisch vor'. Eigenes und Fremdes in den deutsch-spanischen Beziehungen des späten Mittelalters*, ed. by Klaus Herbers and Nikolas Jaspert (Münster: Lit-Verlag, 2004), pp. 87–106. On Maximilian's penchant for chivalry, see, for example, Pierre Terjanian, ed., *The Last Knight: The Art, Armor, and Ambition of Maximilian I* (New York: The Metropolitan Museum of Art, 2019); Dirk H. Breiding, 'Rennen, Stechen und Turnier zur Zeit Maximilians I.', in *'Vor Halbtausend Jahren…': Festschrift zur Erinnerung an den Besuch des Kaisers Maximilian I. in St. Wendel*, ed. by Cornelieke Lagerwaard (St. Wendel: Stiftung Dr. Walter Bruch, 2012), pp. 53–84.

[177] Jan-Dirk Müller, *Gedechtnus. Literatur u. Hofgesellschaft um Maximilian I* (Munich: Fink, 1982); Larry Silver, *Marketing Maximilian. The Visual Ideology of a Holy Roman Emperor* (Princeton, NJ: Princeton University Press, 2008).

almost entirely on tournament scenes, but the other two equally feature such events in both text and image.[178] Nevertheless, there is no indication that Maximilian either participated in or organised a fully fledged *pas d'armes*.

The closest he seems to have come to such an event is his famous joust and sword-fight with the Burgundian nobleman Claude de Vaudrey at Worms in September 1495.[179] Vaudrey, who came from a line of renowned jousters, already had quite a reputation as a knight, having not only participated in numerous tournaments but also organised two *pas d'armes* of his own,[180] when he chose to present a challenge written in a stylised literary fashion to his lord Maximilian: according to Molinet, the successor of Chastelain as the official chronicler at the Burgundian court, he contacted Maximilian in 1494 in Antwerp through Toison d'or King of Arms (a role held at that time by Thomas Isaac), who presented his request to the ruler. Vaudrey introduced himself as the 'chevalier esclave, serviteur à la belle geande à la blonde perrucque' (enslaved knight, servant to the Beautiful Giantess in the Blond Wig), asking the king to touch his *emprise*.[181] Maximilian graciously did so and Vaudrey presented the detailed chapters to him. He explained how the god Mars, accompanied by Pallas, had appeared to him in a series of dreams and declared that he should not sit at a table, kiss a lady, go to war or swear an oath to a lord before he had fought against the most valiant and virtuous knight in the world.[182]

Maximilian must have been flattered to be identified as this ideal knight and accepted the challenge. However, the two adversaries might have had different things in mind: whilst Vaudrey was probably thinking along the lines of a highly stylised chivalric *emprise*,[183] Maximilian's perspective was more pragmatic. The fact that the fight, which was scheduled to take place in 1495 at Worms, where Maximilian had announced an imperial diet, was repeatedly postponed[184] is quite telling: Vaudrey doubtless sought a magnificent

---

[178] Stefan Krause, ed., *Freydal: Medieval Games, The Book of Tournaments of Emperor Maximilian I* (Cologne: Taschen, 2019); Stephan Füssel, ed., *Die Abenteuer des Ritters Theuerdank: Kolorierter Nachdruck der Gesamtausgabe von 1517* (Cologne: Taschen, 2003); Heinrich T. Musper, ed., *Weisskunig*, 2 vols (Stuttgart: Kohlhammer, 1956).

[179] Malte Prietzel, '"Letzter Ritter" und "Vater der Landsknechte". Fürstliche Gewaltausübung als Praxis und Inszenierung', in *Maximilians Welt: Kaiser Maximilian I. im Spannungsfeld zwischen Innovation und Tradition*, ed. by Johannes Helmrath, Ursula Kocher and Andrea Sieber, Berliner Mittelalter- und Frühneuzeitforschung, 22 (Göttingen: V & R unipress, 2018), pp. 209–24 (pp. 210–17); Hiltmann, 'Ideal und Physis', pp. 142–3. On Claude de Vaudrey, see Georges Bischoff, 'Claude de Vaudrey, le meilleur chevalier du monde', *PCEEB*, 58 (2018), 251–73.

[180] In addition to the *Pas de la Dame Sauvage*, Claude was also the *entrepreneur* of the *Pas du Chevalier au Souci*, which was held as part of the celebrations in Paris in 1484 following the coronation of King Charles VIII of France. CRC, paragraphs 82–126. For a translation of the narrative account of this event, see Supplementary Source 2, Liverpool University Press Digital Collaboration Hub <https://liverpooluniversitypress.manifoldapp.org/projects/pas-d-armes-casebook> [accessed 1 November 2024].

[181] JM, vol. 2, pp. 400–1. In the *Chevalier au Souci*, Claude presents himself as being bound in a more abstract way (i.e. by a burden of sorrow), but the narrative account of that event likewise emphasises the idea of fighting in order to be liberated from a constraint: CRC, paragraphs 89, 92.

[182] JM, vol. 2, p. 402.

[183] *Ibid.*, vol. 2, p. 399, explicitly uses the term *pas d'armes*. The account of the *Chevalier au Souci* repeatedly refers to the event as an *emprise*, but also makes it clear that Claude's intention as *entrepreneur* was to open and defend a *pas*. CRC, paragraphs 89, 93, 95.

[184] Evidence for the actual date is contradictory. Our most reliable source, the correspondence of Zaccaria Contarini and Benedetto Trevisano, the Venetian ambassadors at Worms, mentions that

Figure 9. One of the sixty-four tournament scenes in the *Freydal* depicts the fight between Claude de Vaudrey ('Claude Badre') and Freydal (i.e. Maximilian) in a relatively abstract setting. *Freydal.* Vienna, Kunsthistorisches Museum, KK 5073, fol. 39r. Photo: KHM-Museumsverband.

stage for this feat of arms, whereas Maximilian clearly had other things on his mind. In the end, the fight took place on 3 September (Figure 9). According to Ludwig of Eyb (1450–1521), a nobleman and humanist from Franconia, who witnessed the scene and described it in his biography of the Franconian nobleman Wilwolt of Schaumburg (*c.*1450–1510), the combat was staged in an impressive setting:[185] there were stands for the spectators, two tents for the protagonists and lavish decorations with cloth of gold and tapestries. Ludwig also mentions a number of noble men and women in the audience (including Queen Bianca Sforza), princes who served as judges, their aides and the heralds. When the fight

the fight had been scheduled for 31 August, but was postponed until 3 September: see Hermann Wiesflecker *et al.*, eds, *Ausgewählte Regesten des Kaiserreiches unter Maximilian I. 1493–1519. Vol. 1: 1493–1495* (Vienna/Cologne: Böhlau, 1990), pp. 295–6, no. 2401. On 16 August, they explained that Maximilian had repeatedly postponed the date and that Claude de Vaudrey practically badgered him on this matter: see *ibid.*, p. 281, no. 2299.

185 See Helgard Ulmschneider, ed., *Ludwig von Eyb der Jüngere: Geschichten und Taten Wilwolts von Schaumburg* (Münster/New York: Waxmann, 2018), pp. 271–4; Prietzel, '"Letzter Ritter"', pp. 211–13.

was about to begin, a herald ordered the audience to remain silent and not to distract the competitors. This detailed description of setting and context contrasts with the brevity of the actual fight itself: the opponents jousted once with lances and continued fighting on foot with swords. Apparently, Maximilian rapidly overcame his older adversary, who lost his sword and had to surrender. At that point, Count Rudolf of Anhalt-Zerbst, who officiated as the judge, broke his staff in order to indicate the end of the combat.[186] Afterwards, a *mêlée* was organised, in which an unknown number of noblemen and knights participated who are not identified in the sources, before the evening festivities began. As the winner of the joust, Maximilian received a gold chain with a gold ring, which he immediately passed on to Claude de Vaudrey, who gave it, in turn, to Queen Bianca.[187]

While the ruler's fight with Vaudrey certainly captured their contemporaries' attention, it was only one element of the festivities that accompanied the imperial diet, during which Maximilian fought on several occasions.[188] Ludwig of Eyb also mentions that Maximilian and many of the princes and knights in attendance organised a kind of Arthurian Round Table, calling each other by Arthurian names, as they fought and feasted.[189] No such literary motifs appear in the context of the fight with Claude de Vaudrey, however: either they were absent from this combat or the spectators didn't deem them worth mentioning. Even an author as deeply imbued with Burgundian chivalric culture as Olivier de La Marche described the event merely as 'armes en lices closes' (arms in closed lists), although he did mention the *emprise*.[190]

Was, then, the event at Worms a *pas d'armes*?[191] When we apply the five characteristics mentioned in our introduction, the answer has to be negative: the actual fight was not organised by a clearly identifiably *entrepreneur* who defended a passage against all challengers and the fictional scenario that Claude de Vaudrey had tried to propose with his challenge at Antwerp did not play any discernible role at Worms. In fact, our sources illustrate instead the limits of the dissemination of the model of the *pas*: while Molinet's description underlines the fictional scenario, the setting at Worms and its descriptions express something different, perhaps even a mutual lack of understanding. The knights and princes of the Empire were willing to follow chivalric models and to demonstrate their prowess, virtue and manliness through fighting, yet they did so in a more down-to-earth manner. This did not preclude luxurious settings, but they lacked the intricate arrangements and framing narratives that made the *pas d'armes* so special. Accordingly, the events mentioned by recent studies that seek to detect the presence of *pas d'armes* 'in the Empire' actually happened in places that were under immediate Burgundian rule.[192] The limits of transfer concerning this type of

---

[186] Ulmschneider, *Ludwig von Eyb*, p. 274.

[187] Ludwig of Eyb omits this detail; see, however, Heinrich Boos, 'Tagebuch des Reinhard Noltz, Bürgermeisters der Stadt Worms 1493–1509, mit Berücksichtigung der offiziellen Acta Wormatiensa 1487–1501', in *Quellen zur Geschichte der Stadt Worms. III. Teil: Chroniken*, ed. by Heinrich Boos (Berlin: Weidmannsche Buchhandlung, 1893), pp. 371–584 (p. 397).

[188] See Prietzel, '"Letzter Ritter"', pp. 214–15, for Maximilian's fights with Wilwolt of Schaumburg and Friedrich of Saxony.

[189] Ulmschneider, *Ludwig von Eyb*, p. 274; Prietzel, '"Letzter Ritter"', p. 214.

[190] OdLM, vol. 3, p. 309; Hiltmann, 'Ideal und Physis', p. 142.

[191] Bischoff, 'Claude de Vaudrey', p. 258, does however classify the event as a *pas*.

[192] Guillaume Bureaux, 'Union et désunion de la noblesse en parade. Le rôle des Pas d'armes dans l'entretien des rivalités chevaleresques entre cours princières occidentales, XVe–XVIe siècles (Anjou,

chivalric event did not therefore simply coincide with either the 'political' border between France and the Empire or the linguistic divide between a Francophone and a Germanophone sphere. Realities on the ground were far more complex than these categories would suggest, and our analysis effectively highlights the importance of the Burgundian courtly institutions and literary culture for the spread of the *pas d'armes*.

CONCLUSION

European chivalric culture took on many forms and, as we have aimed to show, the particular phenomenon of the *pas d'armes* was shaped by cross-cultural exchange informed by letters, normative and narrative texts that were generated and transferred by travelling princes, noblemen and heralds. While the transmission of the *pas d'armes* can be traced from the Iberian Peninsula to Burgundy (but also to France and Anjou), it seems to have found its limits at the borders of the Holy Roman Empire — at least in its German-speaking territories that were not part of the Burgundian sphere. Even a dynasty such as that of the dukes of Cleves, which was effectively part of the Burgundian family, did not seek to emulate this practice in its own territories — and even a chivalric enthusiast such as Emperor Maximilian I did not import this specific feature of the Burgundian tradition. The reasons behind this limitation still remain unclear: they might have to do with the more modest development of the urban setting in many of the German-speaking regions of the Empire, but also with the specific character of its tournament culture, which was heavily reliant on horizontally structured chivalric societies organised by the regional nobility. In any case, our observations demonstrate that we should not hastily characterise the *pas d'armes* as a 'European' phenomenon.

With the exception of the first Castilian *pas d'armes*, all the fifteenth-century events we know of as yet were intimately connected to the French language: they were mainly reported in French narratives and they took place in French- (and sometimes Dutch-) speaking territories. Only in the early sixteenth century does the *pas* spread to other geographical areas: Piedmont (Carignano, 1504 and Ivrea, 1522) or Scotland (the *Wild Knight of the Black Lady*, 1507–08).[193] In spite of its success in the Burgundian lands (but also in France and Anjou) and in spite of Burgundy's reputation and role as a cultural model, the only court that effectively seized upon this practice was that of the (mainly) French-speaking duchy of Savoy, where the motifs from classical mythology employed can be seen to anticipate the transformation towards Renaissance forms of chivalric fighting and festivities and an Italian influence.

The apparent link between the transmission of the *pas d'armes* and the French language is intimately related to the nature of the sources through which they are known to us:

Bourgogne, France, Saint-Empire)' (unpublished PhD dissertation, Normandie Université, 2018), p. 64, lists Mechelen (1491), Vincelles (1512), Nozeroy (1519) and Binche (1549), in addition to Worms (1495). The important princely residences of Mechelen and Binche were situated in Brabant and Hainaut, respectively, and formed part of the Habsburg territories in the North. Nozeroy and Vincelles were located in the Franche-Comté: while formally belonging to the Empire, they were primarily part of the Burgundian sphere. See also *ibid.*, pp. 194–5, for the distinction between 'French' and 'Imperial' *pas d'armes*. The sixteenth-century events follow a different logic from that of their fifteenth-century forerunners: see *ibid.*, p. 57, and above, n. 121. See also Essay 4.

[193] See above, pp. 336–50, and Essay 5.

until now, historians have studied them almost exclusively through the narrative texts that relate these events. The exploration of other sources, such as courtly and urban financial accounts, may yet modify our picture.[194] In addition, the Savoyard examples indicate that numerous *pas d'armes* may have gone unnoticed, since descriptions of courtly celebrations sometimes contain only traces of pertinent events without going into details — not every *pas* received such detailed literary coverage as did the *Perron Fée*, for example. The description of the baptism of Francis I's son, Francis of France, at Fontainebleau in 1518, for instance, ends with a *pas d'armes* that was organised to close the celebration.[195] Further research is thus necessary to establish whether there were other *pas d'armes* like this, hitherto unidentified as such, and to explore the extent to which this particular type of chivalric event was adapted and transformed in later sixteenth-century courtly environments.[196]

[194] See Essay 3.

[195] Théodore Godefroy and Denis Godefroy, eds, *Le Cérémonial françois*, 2 vols (Paris: Sébastien Cramoisy, 1649), vol. 2, pp. 142–3.

[196] See Essay 4; Watanabe O'Kelly, *Triumphal Shews*; and Mario Damen, 'Tournaments and the Integration of the Nobility in the Habsburg Composite State', *Renaissance Quarterly*, 76.2 (2023), 497–541.

Thanks are due to Rosalind Brown-Grant for her stimulating comments on earlier versions of this essay.

Anne D. Hedeman and Justin Sturgeon

The *Relation du Pas de Saumur*: Text, Image and Heraldic Context

The *Relation du Pas de Saumur* (St Petersburg, National Library of Russia, fr. F. p. XIV, 4) is a densely illuminated account in verse of this *pas d'armes*, also known as the *Pas de la Joyeuse Garde*, that took place at Saumur between June 26 and August 7 1446 under the aegis of the Angevin court with René of Anjou as *entrepreneur**.[1] This manuscript, dating from the 1470s, is a unique version of the lost original verse chronicle written shortly after the event. As such, it offers a rare opportunity to explore the description and visualisation of this particular tournament type. It is possible that this lost original may have been owned by Isabelle of Lorraine, René's first wife, who died in 1453 and whose arms are visible beneath those repainted on the presentation page (Figure 10).[2] However, as we will argue later in this study, the particular form given to Isabelle's arms suggests that this version postdates her death and might be an indicator less of ownership than of familial affiliation and commemoration. We analyse the manuscript of the *Relation* within the contexts of its fabrication and reception in the 1470s in order to understand how its organisation and illustration were indeed intended to serve as both a record of the event and a construction of a memorial for descendants of René, even if it may not have been an exact copy.

René of Anjou (1409–80), the *entrepreneur* of the *Joyeuse Garde*, was the second son of Louis II of Anjou (1377–1417), king of Naples and duke of Anjou, and his wife Yolanda of Aragon (1384–1442), queen of Aragon, duchess of Anjou and countess of Provence.[3]

---

[1] On the role of the *entrepreneur* in organising a *pas d'armes* and for a flexible definition of this type of tournament, see Essay 1. For discussion of the literary genre of the *pas*, see Catherine Blunk, 'Between Sport and Theatre: How Spectacular was the *Pas d'armes*?', in *The Medieval Tournament as Spectacle: Tourneys, Jousts and Pas d'Armes, 1100–1600*, ed. by Alan V. Murray and Karen Watts (Woodbridge: Boydell Press, 2020), pp. 120–38. Here we use *Pas de la Joyeuse Garde* (abbreviated hereafter to *Joyeuse Garde*) as the formal title of the event and *Relation du Pas de Saumur* (abbreviated hereafter to *Relation*) when referring to the edition of the text preserved in the manuscript (= PSr); see also Source 5.

[2] The manuscript has been dated to the 1470s on the bases of costume, the use of René's heraldic colours of black and red, and watermarks. For the suggestion that the costume seems to date to the 1470s and for the earliest identification of the original, now overpainted coat of arms on fol. 2r as belonging to René's first wife Isabelle of Lorraine, see Nicole Reynaud, 'Barthélemy d'Eyck avant 1450', *Revue de l'art*, 84 (1989), 22–43 (p. 38). For discussion of watermarks, see below under 'Codicology' (pp. 371–4).

[3] For this and the following, see Théodore de Quatrebarbes, *Histoire de René d'Anjou* (Angers: Cosnier et Lachèse, 1853); Albert Lecoy de la Marche, *Le roi René, sa vie, son administration, ses travaux littéraires et artistiques*, 2 vols (Paris: Librairie de Firmin-Didot frères, fils et cie, 1875); Margaret L. Kekewich, *The Good King: René of Anjou and Fifteenth Century Europe* (Basingstoke: Palgrave Macmillan, 2008); Jean Favier, *Le roi René* (Paris: Fayard, 2008); and Justin Sturgeon, *Text and Image in René d'Anjou's* Livre des tournois*: Constructing Authority and Identity in Fifteenth-Century Court Culture*, 3 vols (Woodbridge: Boydell Press, 2022), vol. 1, pp. 5–12.

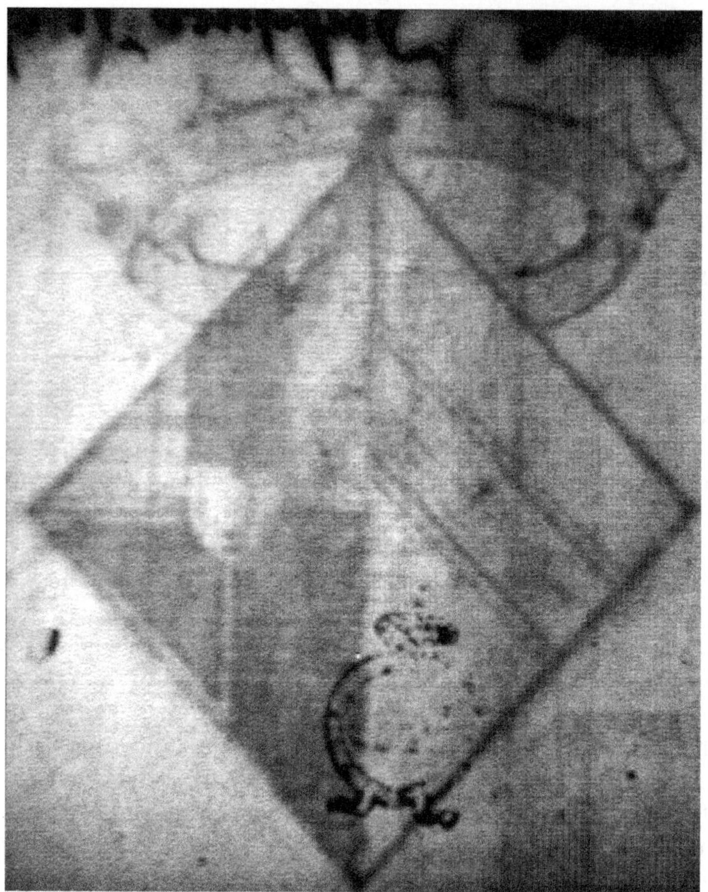

Figure 10. Underpainting showing the coat of arms of Isabelle of Lorraine. *Relation du Pas de Saumur.* St Petersburg, NLR, fr. F. p. XIV, 4, fol. 2r. Photo: NLR.

In 1420, René married Isabelle of Lorraine (1400–53), who was daughter and heiress of Charles II (1364–1431), duke of Lorraine. As part of the terms of their marriage treaty, René was placed under the guardianship of his father-in-law and of Louis I, duke of Bar (1370/75–1430). When his guardians died in 1430 and 1431, René inherited claims to both the duchy of Lorraine and Bar, but he continued to recognise Isabelle's pre-eminence in Lorraine, because he gave that duchy to their son, Jean, when Isabelle died.[4]

Count Antoine de Vaudémont (*c.*1400–58), lord of Joinville, contested René's claim to Lorraine. In July 1431, when René and Antoine met in battle, René was defeated, captured and imprisoned until 1437 by Philip the Good, duke of Burgundy (1396–1467),

[4] For an analysis of events that consider the different roles of René's wives, especially Isabelle's role in governing René's territories while he was imprisoned by Philip the Good, see Marion Chaigne-Legouy, 'Reine "ordinaire", reine "extraordinaire": la place de Jeanne de Laval et d'Isabelle de Lorraine dans le gouvernement de René d'Anjou', in *René d'Anjou (1409–1480): Pouvoirs et gouvernement*, ed. by Noël-Yves Tonnerre and Jean-Michel Matz (Rennes: Presses Universitaires de Rennes, 2011) pp. 77–103.

who had supported Antoine's claim.[5] During this time, René's older brother, Louis III (1403–34) died and René became duke of Anjou and count of Maine and Provence. In addition, Johanna II, queen of Naples (1373–1435) adopted René as her heir, as she had his brother Louis before him. When the duke of Burgundy released René in 1437, he toured his territories, establishing regencies in Bar and Lorraine and travelling to Naples in 1438 to join his wife Isabelle, who had held the lieutenancy of René's realm during his imprisonment and worked to keep King Alfonso V of Aragon (1396–1458), a claimant to the throne of Naples, in check.[6] René continued to combat Alfonso, but was forced to concede the kingdom in 1442.

After losing Naples, René sought to establish diplomatic ties with European leaders, building and solidifying relationships through the marriages of his children. René was already brother-in-law of King Charles VII of France (1403–61), who had married his sister Marie of Anjou (1404–63) in 1422.[7] In 1444, René's son and heir, Jean II of Anjou (1424–70), married Philip the Good's niece, Marie of Bourbon (1428–48), and, in 1445, his elder daughter, Yolande of Anjou (1428–83), married Ferry II de Vaudémont-Lorraine whilst his younger daughter, Margaret of Anjou (1430–82), married King Henry VI of England (1421–71).[8] Through these marriages René smoothed the conflicts in which he had been embroiled with the duke of Burgundy and the count of Vaudémont and solidified relations with the kings of France and England. In 1454, a year after René's wife Isabelle died, he married Jeanne de Laval (1433–98).[9]

Once René's political situation stabilised he became more involved in cultural pursuits, participating in and sponsoring tournaments in the 1440s, reviving the Order of the Crescent in 1448 and, after his marriage to Jeanne de Laval, patronising artists, including among others the artist Barthélemy d'Eyck, who illustrated René's writings, such as *Le mortification de vaine plaisance* (1455), the *Livre du Coeur d'Amour épris* (1457) and the *Traité de la forme et devis comme on peut faire les tournois* (*c.*1460–65).[10]

---

[5] Bertrand Schnerb, *Bulgnéville (1431): L'état bourguignon prend pied en Lorraine* (Paris: Economica, 1993); and Kekewich, *The Good King*, pp. 27–32.

[6] Kekewich, *The Good King*, pp. 45–79.

[7] Bernard Chevalier, 'Marie d'Anjou, une reine sans gloire, 1404–1463', in *Autour de Marguerite d'Écosse: Reines, princesses et dames du XVe siècle*, ed. by Geneviève and Philippe Contamine (Paris: Honoré Champion, 1999), pp. 81–98.

[8] Bonita Marie Cron, 'The Duke of Suffolk, the Angevin Marriage, and the Ceding of Maine, 1445', *Journal of Medieval History*, 20 (1994), 77–99; and Kekewich, *The Good King*, pp. 80 102.

[9] Pierre Le Roy, *La reine Jeanne, Jeanne de Laval, seconde épouse du roi René, 1433–1498* (Mayenne: Éditions régionales de l'Ouest, 1996).

[10] For discussion of these and for further bibliography, see Lecoy de la Marche, *Le roi René*; Françoise Piponnier, *Costume et vie sociale: La cour d'Anjou XIVe–XVe siècle* (Paris: Mouton, 1970); Françoise Robin, *La cour d'Anjou-Provence: La vie artistique sous le règne de René* (Paris: Éditions A. et J. Picard, 1985); Michael T. Reynolds, 'René of Anjou, King of Sicily, and the Order of the Croissant', *Journal of Medieval History*, 19 (1993), 125–61; Christian de Mérindol, 'L'ordre du Croissant: mises au point et perspectives', in *La noblesse dans les territoires Angevins à la fin du moyen âge*, ed. by Noël Coulet and Jean-Michel Matz, Collection de l'École française de Rome, 275 (Rome: École française de Rome, 2000), pp. 499–509; Gabriel Bianciotto, 'Passion du livre et des lettres à la cour de René d'Anjou', in *Splendeur de l'enluminure: le roi René et les livres*, ed. by Marc-Édouard Gautier and François Avril (Angers: Ville d'Angers, 2009), pp. 85–103; Rose-Marie Ferré, *Réne d'Anjou et les arts: Le jeu des mots et des images* (Turnhout: Brepols, 2012); and Sturgeon, *Text and Image*.

THE *RELATION DU PAS DE SAUMUR*

In René's Angevin territories, Saumur was the second city to Angers, which was the primary residence and seat of administration of the dukes of Anjou.[11] René had spent much of his youth in and around Saumur and followed his mother's practice in maintaining the infrastructure of Saumur as he refurbished castles, houses and ecclesiastical foundations in the cities of Anjou.[12] The castle of Saumur, situated overlooking the Loire, was one of the most beautiful in his domain, and it was sufficiently famous that it was one of twelve castles belonging to diverse members of the royal house selected for inclusion in the calendar pages of Duke Jean of Berry's *Très riches heures* (Chantilly, Musée Condê, 65) as painted by the Limbourg brothers (Figure 11).[13] The castle of Saumur had been left to René's mother, Yolanda of Aragon, as part of her dower when Louis II of Anjou died in 1417. A few weeks after his mother's death, René gave the city of Saumur along with other holdings in Anjou and Provence to his wife, Isabelle of Lorraine.[14] When she died and René married Jeanne de Laval, he gave Jeanne the city and castle of Saumur, along with several other properties.[15] According to René's itinerary, which is based on surviving and dated official acts, he travelled widely in his lands and visited Saumur regularly until he left for Provence in 1471, where he stayed until his death in 1480.[16] Once Jeanne de Laval's inheritance was confirmed by René's successor, she returned from Provence to Anjou and resided at Saumur and Beaufort until her death in 1498.

---

[11] François Comte, 'Les lieux du pouvoir ducal à Angers au XVe siècle', in *René d'Anjou (1409–1480). Pouvoirs et gouvernement*, ed. by Jean-Michel Matz and Noël-Yves Tonnerre (Rennes: Presses Universitaires de Rennes, 2011), pp. 163–94.

[12] For René's architectural and artistic patronage in Angers, Saumur and other sites in Anjou and Provence, see Lecoy de la Marche, *Le roi René*, vol. 2, pp. 3–132; Hubert Landais, 'La construction d'une grande demeure de la fin du moyen âge. Le château de Saumur, résidence des ducs d'Anjou aux XIVe et XVe siècles', in *La noblesse dans les territoires Angevins à la fin du moyen âge*, ed. by Noël Coulet and Jean-Michel Matz, Collection de l'École française de Rome, 275 (Rome: École française de Rome, 2000), pp. 189–203; Mary Whiteley, 'The Château of the Dukes of Anjou at Saumur, 1360–1480', in *Anjou: Medieval Art, Architecture and Archaeology*, ed. by John McNeill and Daniel Prigent (Leeds: Maney, 2003), pp. 247–58; Mary Whiteley and Jacqueline Mongellaz, 'Le faste d'une résidence princière à la fin du XIVe et au tout début du XVe siècle', in *Le château et la citadelle de Saumur: architecture du pouvoir*, ed. by Emmanuel Litoux and Éric Cron (Paris: Société française d'archéologie, 2010), pp. 91–107.

[13] The illuminations of the calendar were begun by the Limbourgs around 1413–16 and completed *c.*1446 by Barthélemy d'Eyck and *c.*1485–89 by Jean Colombe. In this visual 'collection', Saumur takes its place alongside castles, palaces and fortresses at Lusignan, Dourdan, Étampes, Vincennes, Poitiers and Paris that belonged to Duke Jean of Berry and other members of the royal family. See Millard Meiss, *French Painting in the Time of Jean de Berry: The Limbourgs and their Contemporaries*, 2 vols (New York: G. Braziller, 1974), vol. 1, pp. 201–6; and Emmanuel Litoux, 'Le château de Saumur et son portrait dans les *Très riches heures du duc de Berry*', in *Le château et l'art, à la croisée des sources, t. 1, Mehun-sur-Yèvre* (Mehun-sur-Yèvre: Groupe historique et archéologique de la région de Mehun-sur-Yère, 2011), pp. 53–83.

[14] These were the first among many gifts to Isabelle that Lecoy de la Marche, *Le roi René*, vol. 1, p. 263, cites: the cities of Saumur, Brignoles, Barjols and Saint-Remi de Provence in 1442, the county of Beaufort in 1444, the manors of Launay and Palis in 1446, among others.

[15] Jeanne also received a third of the revenues of the duchy of Anjou, half the revenues of the duchy of Bar and the salt tax from Provence, among other castles and revenue streams in Anjou and Provence; in 1461, René signed an act stipulating that she would retain the contents of her dower after his death. *Ibid.*, pp. 304–5.

[16] *Ibid.*, vol. 2, pp. 437–96.

Figure 11. Activity for the month of September and the castle of Saumur. *Très riches heures*. Chantilly, Musée Condé, 65, fol. 10v. Photo: Musée Condé.

The manuscript of the *Relation* provides unique insight into the importance and legacy of René of Anjou's *pas d'armes.*[17] Until now, scholarly study of this densely illuminated manuscript commemorating the *Joyeuse Garde* has considered it to be a textual and visual replica of a lost original made shortly after 1446 at René's request. Scholars have used it as a surrogate through which to study both the actual events of René's *pas* in 1446 and the illustrations of the lost original, which they attribute to his favourite artist, Barthélemy d'Eyck.[18] Natalia Elagina and Jane Taylor have complicated this approach, but still concentrated on the lost original and on René: in the volume accompanying the facsimile of the manuscript, Elagina speculated that the *Relation* could have been commissioned by René as a copy of the original manuscript, while Taylor has analysed the lost original as a conscious commemoration designed to shape historical memory.[19]

Our analysis echoes some of the themes that interest Taylor, who emphasises the importance attached to performance at fourteenth- and fifteenth-century courts and the vogue for luxurious manuscripts to commemorate these performances, but we question the implicit and problematic assumption by scholars that the manuscript reflects a lost 'original'.[20] Instead, our consideration of the manuscript's codicology, of relations between text and image, of artistic context and provenance, and of heraldic emblems and their historic owners aims to reveal the expanded memorial function of the manuscript in St Petersburg, which served to cement the status of the owners of the manuscript in the 1470s by linking them explicitly to the historic event.

---

[17] For the numerous *pas* sponsored by René of Anjou, see Christian de Mérindol, *Les fêtes de chevalerie à la cour du roi René: Emblématique, art et histoire (Les joutes de Nancy, le Pas de Saumur et le Pas de Tarascon)* (Paris: Éditions du CTHS, 1993); *idem*, 'Les joutes de Nancy, le Pas de Saumur et le Pas de Tarascon, fêtes de chevalerie à la cour du roi René (1445–1449)', *PCEEB*, 34 (1994), 187–202; and Guillaume Bureaux, 'Union et désunion de la noblesse en parade. Le rôle des Pas d'armes dans l'entretien des rivalités chevaleresques entre cours princières occidentales, XVe–XVIe siècles (Anjou, Bourgogne, France, Saint-Empire)' (unpublished PhD dissertation, Normandie Université, 2018), pp. 36–47, 360–72.

[18] See, among others, Christian de Mérindol, 'Le Livre des tournois du roi René. Nouvelles lectures', *Bulletin de la Société nationale des Antiquaires de France* (1992) [1994], 177–90; *idem*, *Les fêtes*; Gabriel Bianciotto, 'Le pas d'armes de Saumur (1446) et la vie chevaleresque à la cour de René d'Anjou', in *Le Roi René: René, duc d'Anjou, de Bar et de Lorraine, roi de Sicile et de Jerusalem, roi d'Aragon, comte de Provence, 1409–1480: actes du colloque international, Avignon, 13, 14, 15 juin 1981*, ed. by Gabriel Bianciotto ([Avignon]: Annales Universitaires d'Avignon, 1986), pp. 1–16; Reynaud, 'Barthélemy d'Eyck', pp. 22–43; Marc-Édouard Gautier and François Avril, eds, *Splendeur de l'enluminure: Le Roi René et les livres* (Angers: Ville d'Angers, 2009), pp. 88–91 and cat. 12, pp. 244–7; Bianciotto, 'Passion du livre', pp. 88–91.

[19] See Natalia Elagina, 'Le "pas de Saumur". Eine französische Handschrift des 15. Jahrhunderts aus der Sammlung der Russischen Nationalbibliothek (Fr. F. XIV. Nr. 4)', in PSr, pp. 27–42, especially pp. 36–40; and Jane H. M. Taylor, 'La fête comme performance, le livre comme document: Le pas de Saumur', in *Les arts et les lettres en Provence au temps du roi René*, ed. by Chantal Connochie-Bourgne and Valérie Gontero-Lauze (Aix-en-Provence: Presses Universitaires de Provence, 2013), pp. 233–41.

[20] Comparison between this version and a shorter prose account giving a different order of jousts and listing some different jousters as contained in the recently rediscovered manuscript of Guillaume Leseur, *Histoire de Gaston IV, comte de Foix* (Berlin, Staatsbibliothek, Preußischer Kulturbesitz, Ham. 606, fols 76r– 96v) supports our approach to the *Relation* manuscript that considers how it might have functioned in the 1470s. For a translation of Leseur's narrative account of this event, see Supplementary Source 1, Liverpool University Press Digital Collaboration Hub <https://liverpooluniversitypress.manifoldapp.org/projects/pas-d-armes-casebook> [accessed 1 November 2024].

We consider here a series of fundamental questions that help us move from analysis of the construction of the manuscript to its reception. First, a codicological analysis of the manuscript that considers its fabrication by scribes and artists will offer a better understanding of the relationship between this manuscript and its lost model. Second, we will demonstrate that the illustrations of the text were innovative in the way that they avoided a repetitive listing of jousts and of the events that precede and follow them in order to guide readers to the moments that the manuscript's makers wished them to focus on as being the most important. Third, we will show that the manipulation of heraldry offers insight into both the events of 1446 and political concerns in the 1470s. Finally, we will consider the possibility that the manuscript's memorial function made it an appropriate gift for René's heirs.

CODICOLOGY

The *Relation* was transcribed by a single scribe on paper ruled in two columns and arranged in four quires, each made up of six bifolia. The two distinct watermarks on its paper are characteristic of paper originating in Piedmont *c.*1474–77 and Genoa *c.*1472 and 1475–79, thus supporting a date for the manuscript in the 1470s.[21] It is densely illustrated with miniatures of different sizes: thirty-six pictures are two columns wide, one fills one and a half columns, and fifty-three are a single column wide. Eighty of these miniatures show jousts in which actual historical figures can be identified through a combination of textual description and painted heraldic and emblematic details.

It is difficult to separate the artistic hands that painted the manuscript, because multiple artists with generic relationships to each other collaborated on it.[22] They worked on unbound bifolia: the first artist did the front and back of the first bifolium (fols 2r–v and 13r–v) and the front of the second (fols 12v and 13r), while a second artist did the back of the second bifolium in the first quire (fols 3v and 12r) and the front and backs of the third, fourth and sixth bifolios (fols 4r–v, 5r–v, 10r–v and 11r–v) with the assistance of a third artist who did the fifth bifolio (fols 6r–v and 9r–v). Another artist, closely related to the first, did the second quire (fols 14r–25v). Multiple artists collaborated on the rest of the illuminations, filling the third and fourth quires (fols 25r–48v), and it is striking that this is where most of the unfinished illuminations or illuminations that had to be corrected appear.[23] Throughout, whilst artists varied aspects of composition ranging

---

[21] For these codicological observations, see Elagina, 'Le "pas de Saumur"', pp. 30–1; and Denis Zypkin, 'Der Codex *Le pas de Samur* (Fr. F. XIV,4): Zur kodikologischen Erforsching des Papiers', in PSr, pp. 43–51.

[22] What follows builds on Elagina, 'Le "pas de Saumur"', pp. 34–5. She observes that several artists collaborated on the manuscript and makes specific reference to differences between the drawings of the first quire (fols 2r–12r) and later quires. To suggest the roles of different hands, she analyses the different renditions of the crest of Jean (Giovanni) Cossa, as well as noting the difficulties created for text/image relationships when the illuminations are one column wide.

[23] Some of the errors and corrections provide evidence about the origins of the visual models for the illuminations. For instance, fol. 25v originally showed the arms that belonged on fol. 26r. Because the opening at fols 25v–26r is not a bifolium, the artist must have been looking at either a bound book or a series of models presented in the correct order. In addition, Elagina, 'Le "pas de Saumur"', pp. 36–9 and n. 47, observes that because some descriptions of the crest and the horse's equipment are not provided by the text, the pictures are often the only source for that information. She cites the representations

from landscape setting to colour of costume, they nonetheless strove to preserve accurate heraldic markings.

Despite the participation of multiple artists, each of them employs a basic compositional model consistently, one that varies only slightly in detail between one-column and larger two-column representations. In each representation, defenders wear their own helms and ride in from the left on the near side of the list on horses covered by the team's trapper*. The challengers always approach from the right on the other side of the list. Their horses wear personalised trappers, and the challengers carry their own shields and wear their own helms. A team of their *parens/parans* — i.e. members of the family or household who usually wear a version of the knights' colours — accompany jousters from each team.[24] When the scene of jousting is two columns rather than one column wide, the artists expand their model in all but one case by filling the empty middle ground with a representation of the lady and the dwarf mounted on horses as they watch the joust.[25]

These visual components of the manuscript serve two functions. The eighty images of jousting identify individuals by accurately representing their coats of arms and emblems, sometimes even clarifying confusing information in the text. For instance, Christian de Mérindol shows that the painter must have worked independently of the author; he observes that the artist represented the lord of Brion on the attacking team on folios 13r and 13v with a helm that correctly represented a bear, while the author equivocated, describing it as '… ung lyon/Tymbré ou estoit ung hourson' ([it had] a crest with a lion or a bear).[26] Indeed, the accuracy of the visual representations is so striking that Mérindol speculated that the artist of the lost model must have actually attended the jousts to make sketches or notes about the participants, and he assumes unquestioningly that the artist of the surviving manuscript copied such details exactly.[27]

The few cases where jousts described in the text are not illustrated or texts and images appear in margins make clear that the scribe laying out the book had trouble keeping a tight relationship between the placement of images of jousts and the texts describing them when the balance between the text and images shifted. As will become clear, this raises questions about the relationship between the manuscript in St Petersburg and its putative lost model.

At the very least, the book's makers experimented with multiple solutions to the problem of keeping the text and images synchronised. The first solution occurs on fol. 12r (Figure 12), where a stanza penned by a second scribe was added in the bottom margin to describe the illumination of the joust that fills two columns just above it. It seems that

---

of Guerry de Charno, Guillaume de Chevigny, Jean Cossa, Guillaume Desbans, Philibert de La Jaille, Guillaume de Moullon and Spinola as falling into this category. Further, she suggests that the manuscript was not copied page for page, but rather was made as an 'expanded edition' of the old codex that resulted in some infelicities. For instance, many of the helms in the latter half of the manuscript are incomplete, suggesting that there may have been a rush to complete them or that the artists did not have access to visual models for them.

24 For discussion of the role of these figures, see Essay 7.

25 The only exception is fol. 12r, perhaps because it is part of an expansive cycle painted on fols 2r–12r by a distinctive hand. In this two-column joust scene, the lady is the only spectator. For further discussion of the lady and the dwarf, see *ibid.*

26 Mérindol, *Les fêtes*, p. 9; for the text, *Relation*, PSr, stanza 67, p. 79.

27 Mérindol, *Les fêtes*, pp. 10–11.

Figure 12. The lady leads Jean (Giovanni) Cossa from castle to tournament site; joust between Cossa and Jean V, lord of Bueil. *Relation du Pas de Saumur.* St Petersburg, NLR, fr. F. p. XIV, 4, fols 11v–12r. Photo: NLR.

the scribe recognised that the challenge of keeping images of jousts near the stanzas that describe them was only going to get worse; by folio 14v, as he continued transcribing, he began adjusting the image's scale, introducing occasional spaces for single-column images so that the connection between text and image would continue to be tight. Eventually the textual description of individual jousts became shorter — typically one or two stanzas — and this solution no longer worked. This problem first becomes visible on fols 32v–33r (Figure 13), where the image of the joust between Godefroy de Jupeleu and Jean III Le Meingre, known as Boucicaut, is painted in the lower left margin directly below stanza 158, which it illustrates. However, that did not solve the problem. The facing folio of this opening contains stanzas 160–1 and is illustrated by two images that illustrate jousts described in stanzas 160–2. The scribe and artist caught up with the problem of texts and images on the subsequent folio 33v. They included the account of two subsequent jousts described in stanzas 162–4, but they illustrated them with only one image, skipping the illustration that could have shown Jean Cossa and Gobert des Massues (stanzas 162–3) and choosing to illustrate instead the combat between Jean Crespin and Jean Blosset (stanza 164). Might this be because Jean Cossa had already been painted in the previous illumination on fol. 33r?

The second place where selected jousts were not illustrated is in the fourth and final quire (fols 37r–48r) of the manuscript. It seems that the scribe was trying to complete the manuscript within this quire and, in doing so, faced problems with layout for a second time.

Figure 13. Godefroy de Jupeleu jousts with Jean III Le Meingre, known as Boucicaut; Guillaume de Chevigny jousts with Jean de Mesnil-Simon; Guillaume Desbans jousts with Charles Blosset. *Relation du Pas de Saumur.* St Petersburg, NLR, fr. F. p. XIV, 4, fols 32v–33r. Photo: NLR.

This led to the omission of illuminations showing the jousts between Jean de Fénétrange and Antoine d'Aubusson (stanzas 186–8), Antoine de Prie and Messire Auvregnays (stanza 200) and Jean Cossa and Méry de Melay (stanzas 202–3). The omission of illustrations of three jousts permitted one folio in the quire to be left blank in order to be cut, but it was not excised. Folio 43r, the bifolio at the centre of the quire, still preserves a note to the binder: 'vacat car il ny fault [rien] Reliez on le poura cou[per]' (skip, because [nothing] is lacking. [When] you bind, you can cut it). Folios 44r–48r contain the unillustrated text that terminates the manuscript.

TEXT AND IMAGE

Examination of the relationship between text and image in the *Relation* reveals that its images serve as visual markers that draw special attention to key moments of the historic event and to specific passages within the textual account. The manuscript is exceptional among those describing contemporary *pas d'armes* with which René was involved; for instance, the account of the *Pas de la Bergère,* which took place in 1449 in Tarascon with René in attendance, appears in a manuscript with just one illumination.[28] Descriptions of

[28] See Source 6, where this manuscript, Paris, BnF, fr. 1974, is described and the miniature reproduced (Figure 4).

contemporary *pas* in French or Burgundian territories are also less densely illustrated than the *Relation*. For comparison, the description of the *Pas de la Fontaine des Pleurs*, as organised by Jacques de Lalaing at Chalon-sur-Saône in 1449–50, gets three illuminations apiece in each of the three illustrated copies of the *Livre des faits de messire Jacques de Lalaing*,[29] whilst the programme of miniatures in the four illustrated versions of the *Pas des armes de Sandricourt*, which took place in 1493, varies between eight and ten images.[30]

As was typical of manuscripts describing *pas d'armes*, texts at the beginning and ending of the *Relation* place René's actions in a broader historical context by framing this contemporary history in reference to both Arthurian tradition and the medieval motif of the Nine Worthies. Mérindol was the first to note that the opening lines of the *Relation* mention Lancelot changing the name of the *Doloureuse Garde* to *Joyeuse Garde*, and thus evoke the Arthurian past and the source of the title for the *pas* staged at Saumur.[31] Mérindol showed further that the choice of Saumur as the site for René's *pas* reinforced Arthurian comparisons. Its location on the Loire near a city and forest parallels site descriptions in a text by Jacques d'Armagnac, *La forme des tournois au temps du Roi Uter et du Roy Artus, suivie de l'armorial des chevaliers de la Table ronde*, written *c.*1465–70; this work not only mentions René explicitly but describes an ideal site that evokes Saumur.[32]

The ending of the *Relation*, by contrast, situates René's chivalric achievements within the tradition of the Nine Worthies. Not only does it imply that René deserved a place

[29] On the *Pas de la Fontaine des Pleurs*, see CL, pp. 211–51. For the illustrated copies of this text, see Paris, BnF, fr. 16830, early 1470s, fols 124r, 134v, 142r; Comte de Lalaing, private collection, no shelfmark, dated 1518, fols 108v, 118r, 124v; and Los Angeles, J. Paul Getty Museum, 114, dated *c.*1530, fols 113r, 123r, 129v. On the latest of these three manuscripts, see also Elisabeth Morrison, ed., *A Knight for the Ages: Jacques de Lalaing and the Art of Chivalry* (Los Angeles: The J. Paul Getty Museum, 2018), pp. 34–9, plates 11–13.

[30] For a full description of the miniatures in the different versions of this text (in both early printed book and manuscript form), see Source 13 and Essay 4. For the suggestion that the visual representations of the *Relation* and the *Pas des armes de Sandricourt* are exceptions because of the number of their illuminations, see Bureaux, 'Union et désunion', pp. 66–76; and *idem*, 'Pas d'armes et vide iconographique: quand le texte doit remplacer l'image (XVe siècle)', *Perspectives Médiévales* <http://journals.openedition.org/peme/12792> [accessed 21 June 2024].

[31] See Essay 7, pp. 509–10, for a translation of this part of the text. For an elaboration of the connections between Lancelot, the duchy of Anjou, and René, see Mérindol, *Les fêtes*, pp. 18–19; Armand Strubel, 'Les pas d'armes: le tournoi entre le romanesque et le théâtral', in *Théâtre et spectacles hier et aujourd'hui. Moyen Âge et Renaissance: Actes du 115e congrès national des sociétés savants (Avignon 1990), section d'histoire médiévale et de philologie* (Paris: Éditions du CTHS, 1991), pp. 273–84 (p. 280); and Marco Nievergelt, 'The Quest for Chivalry in the Waning Middle Ages: The Wanderings of René d'Anjou and Olivier de la Marche', *Fifteenth Century Studies*, 36 (2011), pp. 137–67 (p. 140).

[32] *La forme des tournois au temps du Roi Uter et du Roy Artus* exists in at least twenty known manuscripts, one of which also included Rene of Anjou's *Livre des tournois*. See Edouard Sandoz, 'Tourneys in the Arthurian Tradition', *Speculum*, 19 (1944), 389–420; and Lisa Jefferson, 'Tournaments, Heraldry and the Knights of the Round Table', in *Arthurian Literature XIV*, ed. by James P. Carley and Felicity Riddy (Woodbridge: D. S. Brewer, 1996), pp. 69–157. However, Gabriel Bianciotto, 'René d'Anjou et les chevaliers d'Arthur', in *Le tournoi au moyen âge, actes du Colloque des 25 et 26 janvier 2002*, ed. by Nicole Gonthier, Cahiers du Centre d'Histoire Médiévale, 3 (Lyon: Université Jean Moulin, 2003), pp. 113–33, cautions that the Arthurian theme could be seen as subservient to René's more fundamental desire to exalt chivalry and to promote his own position in relation to the French king and nobility.

among these illustrious figures, as had happened earlier to Bertrand du Guesclin,[33] but it also suggests that the *Joyeuse Garde* surpassed all prior chivalric displays:

Certes es hystoires de Gresse,
D'Albion, Troie et Lutesse,
N'en livre d'armes n'en Vegesse,
N'ay rien leu de tele enterprise.

(Certainly [neither] in the history of Greece,/Of Albion, Troy and Lutece,/Nor in any book of arms or in Vegetius,/Has anyone read about such an undertaking).[34]

The unknown author explains, furthermore, that he had written his history precisely because the achievements of René are equal to those of noteworthy knights of the past, including the Nine Worthies and other historical heroes:

Aussi peu voy ploie guerie,
Si lame ou espee ne varie,
Comme du temps de l'escuerie
De Hector le preus et d'Achilles
Dont la memoire n'est perie.
René regnant en seigneurie
A esté noblesse merye
De maints hardiez et vaillans faiz.

Alixandre qui conquist plus,
Aussi Julius Gayus,
Josué et Machabeus,
Ces trois juifs et deux paiens;
David, Remus et Romulus,
Charlemaigne, le roy Artus,
Goddeffroy qui feit le surplus
Moult a l'onneur des crestiens,
Julius Cesar et les siens,
Pompee, Cartaige et Priens
Qui tant conquisdrent de biens,
Comme il est durable memoire,
Savez que s'ilz neussent fait riens
Ne fussent d'onneur es liens?

---

[33] On the Nine Worthies, see Craig Taylor, *Chivalry and the Ideals of Knighthood in France during the Hundred Years War* (Cambridge: Cambridge University Press, 2013), p. 10. It was common for parallels to be drawn between contemporary figures and the Nine Worthies: see, for example, the eulogisation of Bertrand du Guesclin by Eustache Deschamps and others, *ibid.*, p. 118. For visual depictions of the Nine Worthies and of Bertrand du Guesclin's promotion as one of them, see Elizabeth Morrison and Anne D. Hedeman, *Imagining the Past in France: History in Manuscript Painting 1250–1500* (Los Angeles: The J. Paul Getty Museum, 2010), pp. 260–1, cat. nos 65–68 reproduced on pp. 305–17.

[34] *Relation*, PSr, stanza 227, p. 110.

Les livres en sont faiz enciens
Et pourtraite mainte histoire.

(I cannot foresee this wound being healed,/If neither sword nor blade are tempered,/As in the time of the squires/Of Hector the worthy and of Achilles/ Whose memory is still alive. During the reign of René,/The nobility has benefited/ From many bold and valiant exploits.

Alexander who conquered much,/Also Gaius Julius [Caesar],/Joshua and Maccabeus,/These three Jews and two pagans;/David, Remus and Romulus,/ Charlemagne, King Arthur,/Godfrey who did the rest,/Much to the honour of Christians,/Julius Caesar and his [men],/Pompey, Carthaginians [?], and [Priam?]/Who conquered so much,/Of whom memory still remains./Do you know that if they had done nothing,/There would be no honour in [feudal] bonds?/ Many ancient books are full of it/And many a history [of that] is portrayed).[35]

Between the introductory Arthurian and broader concluding historical context, the *Relation* also links René's *Pas* with one that took place immediately before his. René had won the *Pas de la Gueule du Dragon* (also known as the *Pas du Rocher Périlleux*), held between Chinon and Razilly in May 1446, and agreed to host the next competition, beginning in June 1446.[36] That competition, the *Joyeuse Garde*, pitted René's camp against that of the French king, Charles VII. The emblems of the defenders, who included René, members of prominent French noble families tied to René and many officers of his court, were pansies scattered on a vermilion field. The challengers, who included representatives of the king of France, members of the royal council, several princes and members of other prominent families, wore diverse emblems on their horses' trappers. Knights on both sides wore helms with individualised torses (i.e. decorated twisted trims) and crests.

The opening of the *Relation* describes a procession that took place the night before the *pas* began, leaving the castle of Saumur to wind its way to the field where the competition would take place, about seventy-five yards to the south-east of the castle of Saumur: 'Du cousté de devers Loudun,/Assez plus pres de moitié d'un/Demy trait d'arc de l'ediffice' (On the side towards Loudon,/And half as close again as/Half a bowshot from this castle).[37]

---

[35] We would like to thank Christine Bourgeois, Catherine Blunk and Michelle Szkilnik for their advice on translating this passage. See *Relation*, PSr, stanzas 235–6, p. 111; and Bianciotto, 'René d'Anjou et les chevaliers d'Arthur'.

[36] See the account of this tournament in Leseur: HGF, vol. 1, pp. 194–5; HGFMO; and Berlin, Ham. 606 (fols 98v–129v); for a translation of this account, see Supplementary Source 1, Liverpool University Press Digital Collaboration Hub <https://liverpooluniversitypress.manifoldapp.org/projects/pas-d-armes-casebook> [accessed 1 November 2024]. See also Mérindol, *Les fêtes*; *idem*, 'Le livre des tournois', p. 177; Bianciotto, 'Le pas d'armes de Saumur (1446)', p. 6; Robin, *La Cour d'Anjou-Provence*, pp. 49–53; and Rose-Marie Ferré, 'Culture théâtrale et enluminure à la cour du roi René', in *Splendeur de l'enluminure: le roi René et les livres*, ed. by Marc-Édouard Gautier and François Avril (Angers: Ville d'Angers, 2009), pp. 179–89 (p. 181). Given the limited details provided about this event in the *Relation*, we have opted to refer to it as a *pas d'armes* rather than an *emprise*. For more on the specific use and meaning of terms such as *pas* and *emprise*, see Introduction and Essay 1.

[37] *Relation*, PSr, stanza 31, p. 72. The analysis by James Fergusson, 'A Pair of Butts', *Scottish Historical Review*, 34.117, part 1 (1955), 19–25, of distances between practice butts for archery suggests that the

Figure 14. Procession from the castle of Saumur to the field of competition. *Relation du Pas de Saumur.* St Petersburg, NLR, fr. F. p. XIV, 4, fol. 6r. Photo: NLR.

René's artist, Barthélemy d'Eyck, evoked the placement of the field of competition in proximity to the castle when he completed the lower portion of the Limbourg brothers' painting of September in the *Très riches heures* sometime after 1446. He added a list and *perron** (a term that can designate a stone, pillar or column, and which here is the third of these) in the landscape in the foreground (see Figure 11).[38] The largest illumination in the *Relation* (Figure 14) illustrates faithfully the description of the procession from the castle to this site of competition. The procession begins with two elderly 'Saracens' leading angry lions, who are followed by a mounted squire bearing a large standard covered with pansies, heralds wearing coat armours*, two mounted clerks of the judges holding scrolls with the order of the jousts, four mounted judges in long red robes holding white batons, mounted musicians with trumpets, a dwarf holding a mace and wearing a turban, like a 'Moor', mounted on a horse in a trapper of pansies on a red ground, and a beautiful maiden led on a horse, holding before her a shield with pansies. Men follow, pouring out of the castle to watch the spectacle. As the text's description continues, it evokes what is not represented in the illuminations to this portion of the manuscript: when the procession arrived at the tournament site, the shield was attached to a large marble column and the dwarf was left to guard it. The lions were attached to the column under the care of the Saracens. Then the lady and the nobles returned to Saumur to feast before the *pas* began the next day.

The rest of the text concentrates on the jousts, which lasted until August. From folio 9 onwards, the poem almost always specifies who fought, what helms and crests were worn, how horses were trappered and who was victorious, because 'escripre fait longe souvenir' (writing makes memory last).[39] Each time there was a new joust, the challenger would strike the shield on the column and the maiden and dwarf would escort the defender to the list where he would joust under the watchful eyes of the judges and their clerks. Once six lances had been broken, the jousts were over, leaving the judges to deliberate and select the winner.

Although the scenes of jousting are the most repetitive and heraldically significant scenes in the manuscript, other images work selectively to emphasise the setting and ritual for the *Joyeuse Garde* and to provide periodic visual reminders of repeated actions that precede and follow each joust. For instance, after showing the procession to the tournament field with all its participants (see Figure 14), the initial series of images centres on the first joust of the first day between Ferry II de Vaudémont-Lorraine and Guillaume d'Harcourt, count of Tancarville, and illustrates the events that happened for each joust but were rarely represented subsequently in the manuscript. First (Figure 15), Guillaume d'Harcourt strikes the shield hanging on the column guarded by lions in the presence of the dwarf. Then (Figure 16) the dwarf rides to the castle of Saumur and sounds his horn

---

upper limit for a bow shot was 300 yards. Thus, in considering the location described in the *Relation*, it is likely that the *pas* took place about seventy-five yards south-east of the castle. For an earlier discussion of the distance, see Bianciotti, 'Le pas d'armes de Saumur (1446)'. We would like to thank Ralph Moffat and Catherine Blunk for their advice on this question. For a discussion of evidence suggesting that René's manor house at Launay may have housed one team for the *Joyeuse Garde*, see Bureaux, 'Union et désunion', pp. 103–4, 157, and 360–72.

[38] For discussion of this addition, see Patricia Stirnemann, 'Barthélemy d'Eyck et les *Très riches heures*', in *Dans l'atelier de Michel Pastoureau*, ed. by Claudia Rabel, François Jacquesson and Laurent Hablot (Tours: Presses Universitaires François-Rabelais, 2021), pp. 290–3; and for discussion of the Arthurian associations of the *perron* in the *Pas du Perron Fée* (Bruges, 1463), see Essay 3.

[39] *Relation*, PSr, stanza 50, p. 76.

Figure 15. Guillaume d'Harcourt, count of Tancarville, calls for the 'Defender' to fight. *Relation du Pas de Saumur.* St Petersburg, NLR, fr. F. p. XIV, 4, fol. 9r. Photo: NLR.

Figure 16. The dwarf blows his horn in front of the Saumur castle gate; Ferry II de Vaudémont-Lorraine rides from the castle to the tournament site. *Relation du Pas de Saumur.* St Petersburg, NLR, fr. F. p. XIV, 4, fols 9v–10r. Photo: NLR.

to signal that there is a challenge, and the lady who had borne the shield to the list leads Ferry II de Vaudémont-Lorraine, the first combatant on René of Anjou's team, out of the castle to follow the dwarf to the field of combat. At the field (Figure 17), Ferry jousts against Guillaume in front of the lady and dwarf who watch from horseback, while the judges and their clerks watch from a stand built to give them a good view of the action.

This level of visual detail is rare in the manuscript. While the judges are mentioned at several intervals in the text, the picture in Figure 17 is the only scene that shows them on the field, although they are included amongst the people shown in the image of the initial procession in Figure 14. Similarly, despite the fact that the lady always leads the combatant to the field and back and the challenger always strikes the shield, these scenes are also rarely represented in the manuscript; illuminations show the lady leading the combatant to the field only three additional times and the challenger striking the shield on the column only five additional times.[40] Clearly it is the individual jousts that are the primary visual focus in the manuscript in St Petersburg.

[40] In total, the lady leads Ferry II de Vaudémont-Lorraine, Jean Cossa, Ferry again, and René of Anjou to the field on fols 10r, 11v, 15r and 24r, and the combatants Guillaume d'Harcourt, count of Tancarville, Charles of Burgundy, count of Nevers, Jean Poton de Saintrailles, Charles d'Artois, count of Eu, Jean II, duke of Alençon, and Antoine de Chabannes, count of Dammartin, strike the shield on fols 9r, 15r, 18r, 22r, 23v and 41v, respectively.

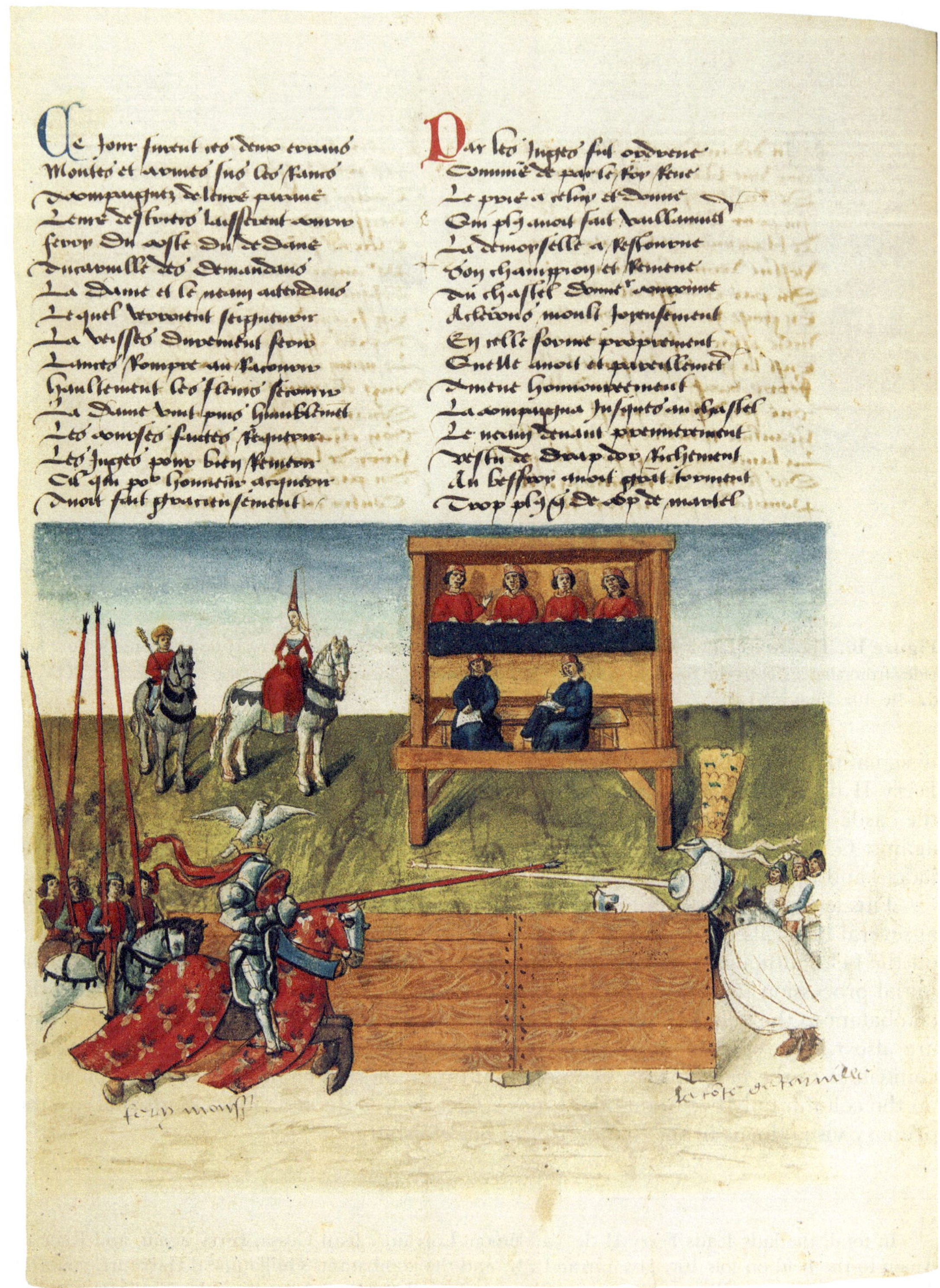

Figure 17. Ferry II de Vaudémont-Lorraine jousts with Guillaume d'Harcourt, count of Tancarville. *Relation du Pas de Saumur.* St Petersburg, NLR, fr. F. p. XIV, 4, fol. 10v. Photo: NLR.

However, the images also manipulate the cycle in order to draw special attention to René of Anjou and his son-in law, Ferry II de Vaudémont-Lorraine, who ultimately won the competition. As the first jouster on the first day, Ferry receives an expanded visual cycle that introduces readers to how each joust unfolds, but also celebrates him. His joust against Charles of Burgundy, count of Nevers, on the seventh day also receives three scenes on fols 15r–15v, as does Réne's joust with Jean II, duke of Alençon, on fols 24r–24v. These sequences amplify the actions of Ferry and René visually, thus signalling their special roles in this particular manuscript as the winner and the *entrepreneur* of the *Pas*, respectively.

The special attention paid to both Ferry and René in the *Joyeuse Garde* may be a feature of this manuscript. The problems faced by the book's designer with the layout of images and texts, as seen in Figures 12 and 13, are evidence that he was, at the very least, adapting a visual model that might have been larger in scale. This is something that also happened with later copies of René's *Traité de la forme et devis comme on peut faire les tournois* made *c.*1460–1510. For example, in the manuscript copy of this work commissioned around 1488 by Louis de Bruges, lord of Gruuthuse, additional images were added in the form of a prologue that adapted the image cycle of the source. This addition functioned to memorialise a tournament that Louis's ancestors had hosted while simultaneously affirming his own status as a knight of renown.[41] Therefore, while we cannot assume that the volume in St Petersburg is an exact replica of René's original manuscript, we can assume that specific decisions were made as it was fabricated in order to particularise its visual programme for its patron.

Heraldic representation

The heraldic programme contained within the cycle of text and illuminations of the *Relation* accomplishes much more than just offering an accurate record of the identities of the participants. This programme is primarily made up of three elements: the heraldic crests and torses that the individual combatants wear on their helms, their mounts' trappers, and the coats of arms and colours found on the work's opening folios. A holistic approach, one that considers the interaction of the three heraldic elements as important signs deployed systematically in this manuscript, reinforces the likelihood that alterations were made to the image cycle and further strengthens the conclusion that this manuscript was produced as a specific act of remembrance. At its heart, the *Relation* is certainly concerned with the memorialisation of the event hosted by René in 1446. However, a consideration of the manuscript — the physical object that embodies the *Relation* — within the context of its production suggests that its heraldry was linked both to remembrance *and* to Angevin identity at a critical time in the dynasty's history. To reveal the extent of this dual function of heraldry, it is essential to consider its role in contemporary depictions of individual and group identities.

At the time of the *Joyeuse Garde*, heraldic display had long been an integral part of tournaments. Participants and organisers spent enormous sums of money on ensuring that both the event and their own heraldic identities were a spectacle to behold.[42] Authors and illuminators went to great lengths to include accurate descriptions and visualisations of the

---

[41] See Sturgeon, *Text and Image*, vol. 1, pp. 262–77.

[42] See, for instance, the case study of a tournament held in Brussels in 1439 by Mario Damen, 'The Town, the Duke, his Courtiers, and their Tournament. A Spectacle in Brussels, 4–7 May 1439', in *Staging the Court of Burgundy: Proceedings of the Conference 'The Splendour of Burgundy'*, ed. by Wim Blockmans *et al.* (Turnhout/London: Brepols/Harvey Miller, 2013), pp. 85–95.

coats of arms of participants in chivalric romances and chronicles. René was certainly well versed in this visual language of display and identity.[43] For instance, at the tournament held at Nancy in 1445, he took to the field bedecked in heraldry that specifically evoked both his royal (if only titular) status and the ancestry of his family.[44] Given that this event was staged, at least in part, to provide a spectacle that celebrated the betrothal of his daughter to the king of England, it was crucial that René equated the legacy and standing of his family to that of his royal English guests.

However, René was also keenly aware of the power that heraldic language had for conveying symbolic meaning. In the representation of him in the *Relation* attending the *Gueule du Dragon/Rocher Périlleux*, held between Chinon and Razilly just prior to the event at Saumur (Figure 18), René is painted as though he had assumed a more allegorical heraldic identity, wearing a black coat armour, dressing his mount in a black trapper and carrying a black shield, all of which were painted with tears. A team of his *parens* follow him in the illumination, and they wear silver tunics with silver tears as well as red and black hose and hats. The textual description of René in the *Relation* does not include these details, simply describing him as 'Armé tout noir obscurement/Fut, de housseure paraillement' (He was armed mysteriously, all in black,/As was his horse's trapper).[45] The image contains additional information, and yet is independent of all known textual descriptions.[46] At no point in the text does the author offer a single definitive explanation for René's heraldic trappings. In fact, ambiguity and multi-layered meanings may well have been the whole point of this illustration of him.

Scholars have interpreted this highly symbolic display variously as an act of mourning of the recent death of his son, Louis, or as René's sorrow after having his advances rebuffed by a lady.[47] However, tears were also used para-heraldically. For example, there were golden tears on Philippe de Lalaing's black robe when he jousted in the *Pas du Chevalier au Cygne* in 1454 and earlier, on the white, violet and black shields that challengers touched, and on the

---

[43] Sturgeon, *Text and Image*, vol. 1, pp. 65–7.

[44] Mérindol, 'Les joutes de Nancy', p. 189.

[45] *Relation*, PSr, stanza 13, p. 69.

[46] Gaston du Fresne de Beaucourt, ed., *Histoire de Charles VII*, 6 vols (Paris: Librairie de la Société Bibliographique, 1881–91), vol. 4, p. 184, describes René in the same way as did Lecoy de la Marche, *Le roi René*, vol. 2, p. 146. Both wrote that he wore black armour, held a black lance, rode a horse trappered in black and bore a black shield covered with tears, their mutual source being VT, p. 82. In his analysis of the *Relation*, Bianciotto, 'Le pas d'armes de Saumur (1446)', p. 4, noted that Marc de Vulson de la Colombière, the editor of this source, often amplified his account by combining material taken from the text with description based on details in the manuscript's illustrations. That is also the case here. By contrast, the descriptions of René and his *parens* at Chinon/Razilly in Leseur's account in Berlin, Ham. 606 (fol. 104v) emphasise his wearing cloth of gold and the colours blue and white.

[47] Biancotti summarises these speculative points of view and concludes that the most logical explanation recorded in the *Relation* is that a lady whose colours René offered to defend had refused him, as the *Relation* describes. See Bianciotto, 'Le pas d'armes de Saumur (1446)', p. 7; and *Relation*, PSr, stanza 12, p. 69. Nonetheless, it is also possible, as Mario Damen has suggested in a private communication to us, that René's wearing of black may have been in emulation of Philip the Good. René had ample opportunity to study Philip's sartorial splendour when he was imprisoned by him in 1431–37. See also Sophie Jolivet, 'La construction d'une image: Philippe le Bon et le noir (1419–1467)', in *Se vêtir à la cour en Europe, 1400–1815*, ed. by Isabelle Paresys and Natacha Coquery (Villeneuve d'Ascq: Institut de recherches historiques du Septentrion, 2011), pp. 27–42.

Figure 18. René of Anjou processes at the *Pas de la Gueule du Dragon. Relation du Pas de Saumur.* St Petersburg, NLR, fr. F. p. XIV, 4, fol. 3r. Photo: NLR.

robes of the lady who guards them and of the knight-defender at the *Pas de la Fontaine des Pleurs* organised by Philippe's brother, Jacques de Lalaing.[48] Indeed, René himself paid for comparable ensembles as recorded in an account from 1451: 'quatre harnois de brodeure … faiz a larmes de fil d'or dont le champ est de damas gris … une jacquette de brodeure … pareille lesd. harnois' (four embroidered ensembles … made with tears in gold thread on a grey damask field … an embroidered padded doublet … like the ensemble) and '7 jacquettes pareilles' (seven similar padded doublets) for '6 paiges et le varlet de pied' (for six pages and the messenger).[49] These examples may demonstrate that René was not only versed in the important role heraldry played in tournament settings but was also aware of the potential role of heraldry to serve as a tool for communicating diverse messages.

It is undisputed that the careful attention given by the artists responsible for the *Relation* to rendering the heraldic identities of individual participants reflects a pervasive cultural concern with the memorialisation of individual knightly prowess and reputation gained through participation in the tournament.[50] The author reinforces this interpretation when he writes that his main purpose in composing the work is to provide a record of the deeds of the knights for future generations, 'Affin qu'il en soit longuement/En tres hault honneur souvenance' (So that it will long be remembered/In the very highest honour).[51]

In each of the eighty illuminations of the *Relation* that depict jousts between paired combatants, the individuals can be identified by a combination of their heraldic crests and the textual description that accompanies the image. The combined effect of the textual description and accurate depiction of the heraldic identities of the participants is to firmly anchor the identities of the participants in the mind of readers and viewers. In the case of any authorial confusion or uncertainty about a specific individual's heraldic crest or the colour of their mount's trapper, this is always expressed within the illumination.[52]

Furthermore, images or written descriptions may have served as a record of the encounters that the author referenced when writing his original account.[53] He himself admits that he did not arrive until the last week of the *Pas*.[54] Therefore, for much of his work he must have relied on others' accounts of the events, whether given in written, oral or visual form. The presence of clerks in one of the earliest images from the visual cycle (see above, Figure 17) raises the possibility that some written accounts were composed at the time of the event itself. This image shows two individuals, each holding a sheet of parchment and a writing implement, seated in the lower level of the viewing stand below the tournament's judges. In addition, the author's confusion over specific crests suggests at least partial reliance on visual images.[55] For example, the representation of the lord of Brion's crest, which the author had described as 'a lion or a bear', suggests that, in this instance, he relied on an image to describe the crest. Comparison of the crest of the lord of Brion (Figure 19) with the one of the later artist's depictions of the lions chained to the

---

[48] See Essay 3; and also CL, pp. 213, 219, 223, 228, 231, 234 and 241.

[49] Piponnier, *Costume et vie sociale*, p. 244.

[50] For example, see Jurii P. Malinin, 'Das Werk "Le pas de Saumur von 1446" und sein Autor', in PSr, pp. 11–26, 17.

[51] *Relation*, PSr, stanza 8, p. 68.

[52] PSr, p. 16. See also above, n. 23.

[53] Elagina, 'Le "pas de Saumur"', pp. 37–8.

[54] Malinin, 'Das Werk', p. 15.

[55] Elagina, 'Le "pas de Saumur"', pp. 34–8.

Figure 19. Louis de Beauvau jousts with Louis de Brion. *Relation du Pas de Saumur.* St Petersburg, NLR, fr. F. p. XIV, 4, fol. 13r. Photo: NLR.

Figure 20. The count of Nevers calls for the 'Defender' to fight and Ferry II de Vaudémont-Lorraine rides to the field. *Relation du Pas de Saumur.* St Petersburg, NLR, fr. F. p. XIV, 4, fol. 15r. Photo: NLR.

perron (Figure 20) reveals that confusion is understandable; this particular artist renders the faces of bears and lions so that they are hardly distinguishable from one another.

However, it would be going too far to conclude that the author had access to images depicting every single encounter or to speculate that he relied solely on images. In certain instances, the author apologises for not providing a description of a particular individual's crest or trapper, stating that he did not have access to it, but rather would ask for and include the details later. For instance, in the passage that recounts the encounter between Jean Cossa and René Chauderier, the lord of La Poussonierre, the author excuses his lack of knowledge about the latter's crest by stating he was not at the event when the joust took place.[56] Similarly, in the description of the joust between Ferry II de Vaudémont-Lorraine and Guillaume d'Harcourt, count of Tancarville, the author begs the reader's indulgence for his ignorance about the defender's trapper when he writes:

> Mais dire ne puis vrayement
> Quelle coulleur, car proprement
> N'ay peu savoir, mes briefvement
> M'en enquerray plus plainement
> Aprés en feray mencion.
>
> (The colour of which I cannot state/For indeed, I could not find out, but before long/I will make enquiries to do so,/And will supply this information later).[57]

Yet, the manuscript contains images that accurately record the heraldic identities of certain participants that the author stated he could not describe. What are we to make, then, of this discrepancy? While this copy of the *Relation* was based on a lost exemplar, there is evidence that the visual cycle may have been altered with a specific intent. The inclusion of images with accurate heraldic identities for the jousters in cases where the text does not describe those elements suggests two hypothetical scenarios. The first is that the author did not have access to either an image or any written account that may have existed at the time he was writing shortly after the *Pas* took place in 1446. The second possibility is that the image may have been added during the process of fabricating the later copy in the 1470s. In this latter scenario, the artists of the manuscript in St Petersburg would have learned the heraldic elements through another means and may have composed additional images, following the layout and style of the originals. The alteration of visual programmes in later copies of a given work through the addition or alteration of images to support political or dynastic concerns was common in secular books, particularly histories.[58] It may well be that this is also the case for the manuscript in St Petersburg.

The visual depiction of heraldry in the *Relation* serves to advance the narrative element within the manuscript. Heraldic devices functioned as tags for the subjects of a narrative

---

[56] Malinin, 'Das Werk', p. 16.

[57] *Relation*, PSr, stanza 51, p. 76.

[58] For examples, see Sturgeon, *Text and Image*, vol. 1, pp. 262–78; and Anne D. Hedeman, *The Royal Image: Illustrations of the Grandes chroniques de France, 1274–1422* (Berkeley: University of California Press, 1991).

throughout chivalric literature, including within chronicles, romances, chivalric biographies and didactic manuals.[59] Sequences of images, such as the encounter between Ferry II de Vaudémont-Lorraine and Guillaume d'Harcourt, show the full encounter staged across four different images representing the challenge, the call to arms, the procession from the castle and the joust (see above, Figures 15–17). The four illuminations are linked together through the heraldic identities of the knights and supported by the textual account. While this is the only sequence to be so extensive in scope, its placement as a visual depiction of the first encounter sets the stage for the rest of the image cycle, encouraging readers to flesh out subsequent competitions with comparable details in their imagination.

Because it is tied directly to both a family's and an individual's identity, heraldry also functioned as an effective way to augment a person's reputation. René himself acknowledged the central role that heraldry played in tournament rituals in the *Livre des tournois* (*c.*1460–65) when he wrote about the acquisition of fame and honour being linked to an individual's heraldic identity. In a speech given by the King of Arms to the judges in the *Traité de la forme et devis comme on peut faire les tournois*, this heraldic officer outlined four reasons why the judges should participate in the tournament. In both the first reason and his concluding statement, he emphasised both their role in identifying competitors in the tournament and the importance to the competitors of winning honour and spreading fame:

> Et tout premierement, en pourra on mieulx congnoistre lesquelx sont d'ancienne noblesse venuz et extraiz, par le port de leurs armes et levement de timbres … [L]a chose sorte a effet, et par facon que renommee et bruit par tout puiesse aller de maintenir noblesse et d'acroistre honneur, ad ce que, au plaisir Dieu, chacun gentil homme doresenavant puisse estre desireux de continuer plus souvant l'exercise d'armes.
>
> (And first, all may know which men are come of ancient nobility by the way they bear arms and crests … (T)he tourney will take place in such a way that fame and widespread word will go out to sustain nobility and increase honour, so that, if it pleases God, every gentleman will wish from thenceforward to practise the exercise of arms more often).[60]

During the fifteenth century, heralds' responsibilities included not only knowing the coats of arms of numerous individuals but also recording and reporting on their deeds, thereby providing essential documentation to help spread their fame.[61] Following the

---

[59] See Florence Bouchet, 'Rhétorique de l'héraldique dans le roman arthurien tardif: Le "Meliador" de Froissart et le "Livre du Cuer d'Amours espris" de René d'Anjou', *Romania*, 116 (1989), 239–55 (pp. 240, 243–4, 250–1); Mark Cruse, 'Costuming the Past: Heraldry in Illustrations of the *Roman d'Alexandre* (Oxford, Bodleian Library, MS Bodley 264)', *Gesta*, 45.1 (2006), 43–59; Christian Freigang, 'Le tournoi idéal: la création du bon chevalier et la politique courtoise de René d'Anjou', in *René d'Anjou, écrivain et mécène (1409–1480)*, ed. by Florence Bouchet (Turnhout: Brepols, 2011), pp. 179–96 (p. 183); and Sturgeon, *Text and Image*, vol. 1, pp. 78–83.

[60] Sturgeon, *Text and Image*, vol. 1, p. 126 and vol. 2, pp. 34–7. Online translation by Elizabeth Bennett, René of Anjou, 'King René's Tournament Book' (1998) <https://www.princeton.edu/~ezb/rene/renebook.html> [accessed 21 June 2024].

[61] Sylvie Lefèvre, *Antoine de la Sale: La fabrique de l'œuvre et de l'écrivain. Suivi de l'édition critique du Traité*

Joyeuse Garde, René created a position within his court for a new heraldic officer. Jean de Maslin was invested in this role in 1447 and granted the heraldic title of *Fleur de Pensée Pursuivant*, in an obvious reference to the field of pansies motif that was pervasive throughout the event at Saumur.[62] The emphasis on the heraldic identity of the participants in the *Relation* reflects contemporary practice and thus bolstered the renown of the individual participants by linking their individual deeds to the spectacle and reputation of the event.

In addition to the memorialisation of individuals, the visual heraldic programme of the *Relation* functions to reinforce the group identity of both the knightly participants and, most notably, the defenders. At the centre of the *Joyeuse Garde* is a series of rituals that makes up the event. While the preponderance of images focuses on the jousts between paired mounted combatants, those that do not serve a vital function in expanding the reader's understanding of the event. With the exception of the single isolated picture of the dwarf on horseback outside Saumur, the reader always sees a readily identifiable jouster in the illuminations illustrating the *Relation*. Indeed, even that isolated picture is part of an opening in which it faces an image on the opposite page that includes the knight Ferry II de Vaudémont-Lorraine (see above, Figure 16). The distinguishing features that mark these participants in the *pas* as knights are their armour, which is an obvious reference to their martial endeavours, and their heraldic display. The crests, torses, trappers and shields mark them as members of an elite social class whose identity is partially defined through their participation in this tournament. They constitute a subgroup that is distinct from the other participants and actors within the tournament, such as noble ladies, men-at-arms, heralds and even the judges.[63]

That said, when taken in the aggregate, the images emphasise the unity of the defenders. Every member of the defending party rides a mount trappered in the symbolic device associated with the tournament itself: pansies scattered on a vermilion field. Each defender also carries a shield emblazoned with the same motif and nearly every defender wears a torse in matching colours on their helm. This, of course, ties them more closely to the visual theme of the event emblazoned on the heraldic tabards, pennons, shield carried by the maiden (which was later hung from the column) and other trappers represented in the image of the opening procession in Figure 14. The visual unity of the defenders is accentuated by their contrast with the challengers, who carry shields decorated in their personal motifs that match the trappers worn by their horses.

Furthermore, the images of the jousts are arranged to highlight the defenders rather than the challengers. In every image of combat, the defender is placed in the foreground of the image, to the viewer's side of the jousting barrier, and moving from left to right (as in Figure 21; and above, Figures 12, 13, 17 and 19). This consistent choice on the part of the artists serves to further enhance the presence of the defenders, who, because of their placement in the foreground, display heraldic emblems in their entirety. This contrasts with the depictions of the challengers, who are, to varying degrees, obscured by the barrier.

---

des anciens et des nouveaux tournois (Geneva: Librairie Droz, 2006), pp. 302, 311; Sturgeon, *Text and Image*, vol. 1, pp. 122–8.

[62] Lecoy de la Marche, *Le roi René*, vol. 1, p. 257; Christian de Mérindol, 'Rois d'armes et poursuivants à la cour d'Anjou au temps du roi René', *Revue du Nord*, 88 (2006), 617–30 (p. 619).

[63] For discussion of other participants at this event, see Essay 7.

Figure 21. Ferry II de Vaudémont-Lorraine jousts with the count of Nevers. *Relation du Pas de Saumur.* St Petersburg, NLR, fr. F. p. XIV, 4, fol. 15v. Photo: NLR.

The result of the arrangement is even more acutely apparent in the single-column images, where, because of spatial constraints, the artists were able to show a smaller portion of the challengers and their mounts than, for instance, in the combats in Figure 13.

The deliberate choice to compose the images in this way is further suggested by the various images of the challengers striking the shield attached to the column and the placement of the viewing stands in an early image (see above, Figure 17). The artists did not demonstrate as consistent a point of view when they designed the challenge images as they had in the jousting images. Challengers are shown striking the shield from both the left and right without any discernible reason behind the change (compare instances in Figures 15 and 20). Furthermore, even when a challenger strikes the shield from the left, in the jousting images that immediately follow the challenge he will be shown coming from the right and placed opposite the barrier from the viewer's perspective (Figure 21).

The final element of the visual heraldic programme that merits consideration is the work's frontispiece, which contains three emblems (Figure 22). The first, the coat of arms in the upper portion of the image, is an unidentified later addition that offers no insight into the original owner of the manuscript.[64] However, the second, the crowned lozenge-shaped coat of arms in the lower half of the page, repeats the coat of arms in a later addition painted over the original coat of arms of Isabelle of Lorraine, René's first wife, as shown in Figure 10.[65] The third emblem that bears consideration is the black and red livery colours that fill the background and that are also worn by René's *parens* in the representation of the *Gueule du Dragon/Rocher Périlleux* in Figure 18, discussed above. René adopted a variety of livery colours for his household during his lifetime; at various times these were black, white and grey; white and purple; and finally, during the last decade of his life, black and red.[66] He spent a great deal of effort on organising and dressing his household officers in various colours so as to denote their rank and position, although this effort tailed off in his later years. Livery and the most fashionable dress were reserved for the highest members of the household as a means to distinguish the royal family from everyone else. The black and red combination was used widely in the 1470s by René to identify his family,[67] as for instance on the inner wings of The Burning Bush Triptych painted by Nicolas Fromont in 1475–76 (Figure 23). In summation, the painted arms of Isabelle and the black and red livery colours in the scene of presentation and that of René at Chinon/Razilly (compare Figures 18 and 22) function to anchor the work and the event it commemorates firmly within the Angevin sphere after the death of Isabelle.

Indeed, the overall effect of the heraldic programme is to reinforce the position and unity of the defending party in the mind of the reader while simultaneously emphasising the chivalric exploits of both the defenders and the challengers. Given that the defenders all had direct ties to René as members of his family or household, or as prominent officers,

---

64 Elagina, 'Le "pas de Saumur"', p. 40.

65 Reynaud, 'Barthélemy d'Eyck', p. 38.

66 Piponnier, *Costume et vie sociale*, pp. 243–59.

67 For this and the following, see Reynaud, 'Barthélemy d'Eyck', p. 38; Elagina, 'Le "pas de Saumur"', p. 39 and fig. 3; and Gautier and Avril, *Splendeur de l'enluminure*, pp. 153–5 and 244–7. Christian de Mérindol, *Le roi René et la seconde maison d'Anjou: Emblématique, art, histoire* (Paris: Le Léopard d'or, 1987), pp. 127–30 and 162–5, categorises the colours of black and red as being widely used in the 1470s and he clarifies that René assumed the arms after his son Jean was given the duchy of Lorraine in 1453.

Figure 22. Presentation of the book to René of Anjou; repainted arms covering those of Isabelle of Lorraine. *Relation du Pas de Saumur.* St Petersburg, NLR, ms. fr. F. p. XIV, 4, fol. 2r. Photo: NLR.

Figure 23. The Burning Bush Triptych by Nicolas Fromont. Aix-en-Provence, Cathédrale St Sauveur. Photo: Bridgeman Images.

the image cycle expands on the textual content by visually anchoring the event and the Angevin dynasty in the mind of the reader as a paragon of chivalric endeavour, one worthy of remembrance, and as being on an equal footing with the Arthurian, biblical and historical heroes that the culture of the time celebrated and sought to emulate.

Provenance and remembrance

The localisation of the paper on which the *Relation* is written to Italy in the 1470s and both the original heraldic charge on its presentation page and the inclusion of René's colours of black and red raise important questions about the circumstances of creation of the manuscript copy in St Petersburg and its original ownership.[68] While the presentation of the book to René (Figure 22) takes place in a space decorated with the colours of black and red that René used widely in the 1470s, Isabelle's coat of arms impales her arms of Lorraine with the version of René's arms that he began to use in 1453 after her death. Thus, although the model for the manuscript in St Petersburg could possibly have been made for Isabelle of Lorraine, the manuscript made in the 1470s, roughly thirty years after the event it commemorates, could not. Its evocation of Rene's first wife and representation

[68] See Reynaud, 'Barthélemy d'Eyck', p. 38; Elagina, 'Le "pas de Saumur"', p. 39 and fig. 3; and Gautier and Avril, *Splendeur de l'enluminure*, pp. 153–5 and 244–7.

Figure 24. Drawing of Isabelle of Lorraine in prayer, detail of a lost window from the Chapel of St Bernadin in the church of the Cordeliers at Angers. Recueil Gaignières — Modes — Maisons étrangères — 1ère Partie: Maison d'Anjou-Sicile. Paris, BnF, Estampes, Réserve OB-10-FOL, fol. 15r. Photo: BnF.

Figure 25. Drawing of Yolande of Anjou in prayer, detail of a lost window from the Chapel of St Bernadin in the church of the Cordeliers at Angers. Recueil Gaignières — Modes — Maisons étrangères — 1ère Partie: Maison d'Anjou-Sicile. Paris, BnF, Estampes, Réserve OB-10-FOL, fol. 15r. Photo: BnF.

of an historic chivalric event certainly has a memorial quality. Might it therefore have been made as a sort of dynastic celebration for one of René and Isabelle's children?

The couple had four children: Jean (d. 1470), Louis (d. 1444), Yolande (d. 1483) and Marguerite (d. 1482). Only the daughters were alive when this manuscript was made, and Yolande seems the more likely of the two to have been its owner. Not only was she married to Ferry II, count of Vaudémont-Lorraine (d. 1470), who jousts first and wins the *Joyeuse Garde*, but her arms were almost identical to her mother's, albeit in reverse, so it is possible that this might encourage an association of their arms. Isabelle of Lorraine's arms in the *Relation* are equivalent to those in her portrait (Figure 24) from the window of the chapel that René founded in 1453 to house the funerary monument for his heart; they are also almost the mirror image of Yolande of Anjou's (Figure 25) in the same window, with the exception of a sixth part of Lorraine on the sinister side. The large window in the chapel had scenes from the life of St Bernadin and dynastic representations of René, depicted with both of his wives and his then living children: namely, Jean II, Jeanne de Laval, René, Isabelle of Lorraine, Yolande of Anjou, duchess of Lorraine, and Margaret of Anjou.[69] Might the inclusion of a coat of arms for Isabelle of Lorraine in the frontispiece — a coat of arms that we know only from monuments made after her death — class this armorial representation of her as commemorative and therefore suggest that Yolande may have been its designated owner or even its patron?

Yolande of Anjou does indeed seem the most likely candidate as the manuscript's patron. By commissioning this single manuscript she would have been able to commemorate a number of important personages: her parents, represented through the arms of her mother and the painted depiction of her father on the presentation page; her husband, Ferry II, count of Vaudémont-Lorraine; and perhaps even herself, if the association were being made between her arms and those of her mother. In particular, this manuscript of the *Relation* would have been a highly appropriate present for Yolande and Ferry's son, René II, who had grown up at the court of his grandfather. He would doubtless have seen in the manuscript a memorial to the chivalric exploits of his father and grandfather, a more subtle celebration of his grandmother and, possibly, even a reminder of his mother.

Conclusion

Consideration of the manuscript of the *Relation* within the contexts of its fabrication and reception expands our understanding of the potential reception of this work in the 1470s, when it was far and away the mostly densely illustrated manuscript commemorating a *pas d'armes*. The codicology of the manuscript and the relationship between its text and illustration encourage us to see its function as that of a memorial. The ninety illuminations of the *Relation* demand attention and they guide viewers in subtle ways to understand the steps each knight went through — the challenge, the call to arms, the procession from the castle and the joust. To avoid repetition, they represent the full set of steps only once. Presumably they assumed that readers would imagine the steps as they read about the other knights' exploits.

---

[69] The full set of Gaignière's drawings of René's family from the window are available online at the website Collecta <https://www.collecta.fr> [accessed 21 June 2024], when searching 'Couvent de Cordeliers d'Angers'. On the chapel, see also Lecoy de la Marche, *Le roi René*, vol. 2, pp. 25–7.

Paradoxically, the images also allowed viewers from the 1470s to see into both the past and their present. They could watch the historical jousters from 1446 identified by their heraldic display as, simultaneously, a second view grounded in the 1470s was constructed by the subjects and compositions of the illuminations. There is much that would appeal to the primary audience that we have imagined in the 1470s: René II, the son of Yolande of Anjou and of Ferry II de Vaudémont-Lorraine and the grandson of René of Anjou, the *entrepreneur* of the *pas*, and of his first wife, Isabelle of Lorraine. The extended visual attention given to René II's father and grandfather in the *Relation* is notable, since their images are the ones that most fully illustrate the stages of the competition in sixteen of the manuscript's ninety illuminations. The visual prominence given to the defenders, most of whom came from the Angevin courtly milieu, would doubtless also have appealed to a younger member of the Angevin line. Finally, the inclusion of the arms of his grandmother in the book unites both past and present; it combines Isabelle of Lorraine's arms impaled with the arms that René of Anjou began using in 1453 at the bottom of the page on which René is seen enthroned before a wall decorated with his heraldic colours from the 1470s, thus referencing the queen who died in 1453 and the king who was very much alive in the 1470s. The celebration of Yolande of Anjou's father, mother and husband would doubtless have pleased René II's mother, Yolande herself, who may well have presented the illuminated *Relation* to her son as a gift intended to function both as a family history and as a model for noble behaviour.

Mario Damen and Michelle Szkilnik

The Social and Literary Environment of a Chivalric Event: the Case of the *Pas du Perron Fée*, Bruges, 1463

From 28 April to 17 May, on the Markt, the main market square in the Flemish town of Bruges, a grandiose jousting event took place that drew a crowd of knights, noble men and ladies, and, presumably, town citizens, eager to admire impressive deeds of arms and sumptuous garments. The organiser of this *pas d'armes*, known as the *Pas du Perron Fée*, was Philippe de Lalaing (*c.*1430–65), one of the knights in the service of the Burgundian duke Philip the Good (1396–1467), who demonstrated his prowess on both the battle and tournament fields and belonged, moreover, to the select circle of knights who not only took a vow at the famous Feast of the Pheasant in 1454 to join their lord on a crusade, but also fulfilled that promise. He was to die on 16 July 1465 in the battle of Montlhéry, which pitted the troops of King Louis XI of France (1423–81) against those of the so-called League of the Public Weal, led by Charles of Charolais (the future Charles the Bold, 1433–77), and was buried there. Of him the chronicler Philippe de Commynes rightfully wrote that 'il étoit d'une rasse dont peu s'en est trouvé qui n'ayent estéz vaillans et courageux et presque tous morts en servant leurs seigneurs en guerre' (He was of a stock of which very few turned out to be less valiant and courageous [than him] and almost all of whom died in war serving their lords).[1]

As an attentive reader of romances and *chansons de geste*, Philippe devised for his *pas d'armes* a scenario of Arthurian inspiration. In one of the accounts of the *Pas*,[2] the narrator recounts what reads like a short romance: an anonymous knight, looking for lodging at sunset, rides on a moor, along a narrow path, between ponds, when he encounters a great stone (a *perron**) blocking his way. A metal horn hangs from the stone and letters inscribed on it invite the passerby to sound the horn three times and face the consequences. The knight having complied, a frowning dwarf suddenly appears and presents the knight with a choice between two alternatives (a *jeu-parti*[3]): he can either relinquish his horse and arms, and leave, or turn himself in, waiting for a 'sauvage aventure' (fearsome adventure). The knight chooses to be hosted for the night. The next morning, the dwarf explains that the knight is the prisoner of the 'Dame du Perron Fée' (Lady of the Enchanted Column), who imprisons all the knights riding by. In order to obtain his freedom, he must agree

---

[1] Philippe de Commynes, *Mémoires*, ed. by Joël Blanchard (Paris: Librairie Générale Française, 2001), p. 104. Also cited in Andries Van den Abeele, 'De Wapenpas van de Betoverde Burcht, voorbode van de machtsgreep door Karel de Stoute', *Handelingen van het Genootschap voor Geschiedenis te Brugge*, 146 (2009), 93–139 (p. 101).

[2] See Source 11a.

[3] A *jeu-parti* was originally a lyrical debate based on a dilemma question such as 'which is better, the love of a cleric or the love of a knight?' Each poet defended his position in turn in alternating stanzas. The term *jeu-parti* later comes to mean a game with two alternatives.

to challenge other knights to various kinds of fight duly outlined by the dwarf. The knight then dictates a letter stating the conditions set out by the dwarf and hands it to an anonymous narrator, who, fortuitously, happens to be in the area. The narrator, whose name is never disclosed, delivers the letter, presumably to the court of Burgundy. This brief summary testifies to the attraction of literature: real-life knights aspired to rival their literary counterparts, such as the heroes of *Perceforest*, a romance twice mentioned in the prologue of the *Perron Fée*.[4] Whether Philippe alone came up with the scenario of his *pas* or had the help of heralds, he certainly endorsed its Arthurian spirit.

The principal aim of this essay is to show that this particular *pas d'armes* was firmly built on both socio-political and literary traditions. Therefore, we analyse Philippe's personal motivations and the social and literary context in which he devised his undertaking, using both administrative and narrative sources. We will address the problems and opportunities these sources provide when scholars attempt to reconstruct a late medieval *pas d'armes*. Although both types of source offer complementary information concerning organisers, participants and sponsors, they also present many contradictions and problems that cannot easily be resolved. Thus, for example, the town accounts of Bruges supply many details concerning the material realisation of the *Perron Fée*, but they neither always tally with the descriptions in the narrative sources, nor reveal the motives of the parties involved. The different narrative accounts of this *pas* likewise raise questions of authorship, audiences and the reception of the text. Examining the various manuscript contexts, patrons and owners thus allows us to offer some answers as to why this event enjoyed such lasting fame, in comparison to other similar spectacles.

We know of eleven manuscripts that describe this chivalric event in detail.[5] If we apply the recently calculated survival rate of medieval literary works and documents in Middle French of 53.5 per cent, this means that some ten manuscripts must have been lost.[6] Although they all deal with the same historical occasion, they do not give the exact same account because they derive from at least two witnesses, or possibly even three. One account (A), preserved in a single manuscript, is very short. The other two, accounts B and C, give a much more detailed description of the setup of the *Pas* and of the celebrations marking the end of the event. Yet they offer a different presentation of the scenario: as we shall see, C insists on the magical dimension of the *Pas*, whereas B underlines its courtly aspect.

To understand Philippe de Lalaing's motives in organising his *pas* in Bruges, we sketch in a first section his biography, highlighting in particular both the relationship with his famous brother Jacques (*c.*1421–53), and his career within the household of Philip the Good. In historiography, Philippe's elder brother has always dominated. This is, of course, due to Jacques's chivalric life and untimely death at the siege of Poeke in July 1453, and his subsequent commemoration in the *Livre des faits de messire Jacques de Lalaing*, compiled in the early 1470s, of which many copies circulated amongst members of the Lalaing dynasty. Hence, Philippe was somewhat eclipsed by his more illustrious brother and has, as a result, received far less attention from scholars. In the second section, the

---

4 In the B account: see below.

5 For a description of the manuscripts and their links, see PPF, pp. 44–68.

6 Mike Kestemont, Folgert Karsdorp *et al.*, 'Forgotten Books: The Application of Unseen Species Models to the Survival of Culture', *Science*, 375.6582 (2022), 765–69 (p. 769).

focus is on the social and political framework of the *Perron Fée*. The narrative sources easily lend themselves to the conclusion that this *pas* was a strictly courtly event. Moreover, they tend to marginalise the urban context in which it took place. We will therefore unravel the urban embedding of this event that was held on the main market square of Bruges, one of the most important economic hubs of the late medieval Low Countries. We will situate this event within the context of the jousting tradition in the Flemish town as well as noting the very busy calendar of events that took place in April and May 1463. Furthermore, we will examine the relationship between the town administration, the duke and his son Charles of Charolais; the initiative taken by nobles themselves in staging these events; and the eagerness of the towns to collaborate and co-organise them (just as modern-day cities compete to host the Olympic Games). For the literary framework, treated in the third section, we pay particular attention to the prologues describing the scenario, as well as to the concluding festivities, including the awarding of *brevets* (short commemorative verses)[7] in order to assess the importance of literary models on the *pas d'armes*. This event was popular enough to motivate three independent reports, informed, as we shall see, by different agendas.[8] At a time when towns were staging *mystères* and *miracles*, there is no doubt that these aristocratic spectacles, hosted and performed in towns, held special significance for the organisers and competitors as well as for the people of the town, albeit not of exactly the same kind.

The Lalaing family and the pursuit of chivalric glory

Philippe de Lalaing, probably born around 1430, was the third son of Guillaume de Lalaing and Jeanne de Créquy.[9] Lalaing and Créquy were high-ranking noble families from the county of Hainaut. Philippe is specifically mentioned in the chivalric biography of his brother at the moment when Jacques leaves his family home, the castle of Lalaing, to join the duke of Cleves, who takes him to the court of his uncle, Philip the Good, duke of Burgundy. As the only brother present, he hears his father instruct Jacques on how to avoid the Seven Deadly Sins 'pour acquerir gloire et bonne renommee … il vous convient suyvir ceulx lesquelz vous verrez y estre de bonnes meurs' (to follow the example of those whose habits you deem virtuous in order to win glory and fine renown). This was around 1441, when Jacques was about twenty years old and Philippe is said to be 'moult … jenne' (very young).[10]

On Jacques de Lalaing's death, his biographer makes this intriguing remark on Philippe's position within the family:

> A sa mort perdirent moult ses amis, en especial un sien frere qu'il amoit moult chierement pour ce qu'il vëoit estre en lui grant apparence et beau commencement.

---

[7] See below, p. 425.

[8] On the possible link between A and B, see the introduction to the edition in PPF, pp. 25–6.

[9] Félix Brassart, *Le blason de Lalaing: Notes généalogiques et héraldiques sur une ancienne et illustre maison* (Douai: L. Crépin, 1879), p. 41, estimates that Philippe was born around 1430 but does not give any evidence for this. Since Philip the Good was probably his godfather, this could have happened any time after 1427, when he took control of Hainaut with the help of the brothers Guillaume and Simon de Lalaing in diverse administrative and military matters.

[10] LF, pp. 32, 34; CL, pp. 85–6.

Car tous ses fais, dis et meurs tournoient tous a vaillance et bonnes vertus. Et doncques pour la belle apparense que vëoit messire Jacque de Lalain en son frere Phelippe, il avoit du tout conclut en soy que, les guerres de Flandres achievees, pour la grant amour qu'il avoit a icelui Phelippe, son frere, lui donner tout tel droit et action qu'il lui povoit escheoir aprez le trespas du seigneur de Lalain, son pere, c'est assavoir la seignourye de Lalain.

(His death was a huge loss to his friends, especially his brother Philippe whom Messire Jacques loved dearly, seeing the great potential he had in making a fine start to his career and how his deeds, words and habits were all dedicated to the pursuit of valour and virtue. Because of the excellent qualities that Messire Jacques saw in his brother Philippe, he had decided that, once the wars in Flanders were over, out of the great love he bore him he would grant him all the rights and dues that would accrue to him on the death of the lord of Lalaing, his father, that is the lordship of Lalaing itself).[11]

Jacques himself planned to go on crusade, according to his biographer, and, as he probably did not expect to return from this military expedition, he would have arranged the inheritance of the eponymous lordship of Lalaing. Philippe became second in the line of succession because his elder brother, Jean, had an ecclesiastical career with prestigious offices as provost of Saint-Amé in Douai (from 1437) and of Saint-Lambert in Liège (from 1443).

Already on 17 July 1453, exactly two weeks after Jacques's demise, Philippe was appointed as chamberlain in the household of Philip the Good as substitute for his deceased brother.[12] He was able to take on this role, which was reserved for knights, as he had received the accolade after the battle of Oudenaarde on 26 April 1452 during the Ghent war. Philippe's knighthood was conferred on him by Jean of Burgundy, count of Étampes and a close relative of Philip the Good,[13] together with other noblemen such as Antoine of Burgundy, also known as the Great Bastard, Antoine Rolin, Philippe de Horn, Georges de Rosimbos, Guillaume and Antoine de Vaudrey and many others.[14] Interestingly, Philippe

[11] LF, pp. 551–2; CL, p. 328.

[12] Holger Kruse and Werner Paravicini, eds., *Die Hofordnungen der Herzöge von Burgund. Band 1: Herzog Philipp der Gute 1407–1467*, Instrumenta, 15 (Ostfildern: Jan Thorbecke Verlag, 2005), p. 268 (no. 44b). In the court ordinance of 1458, he is still mentioned as belonging to this category of officers. See *ibid.*, p. 374 (no. 64). Concerning his presence in Bruges at the time of the *Pas*, Philippe is mentioned in the daily paylists of the Burgundian household from 3 May 1463 until 1 July 1463 as being in Bruges and, later that month, he was also paid for being with the duke in Lille. PCB no. 1732.

[13] He was a son of Philippe of Burgundy (third son of Philip the Bold) and Bonne d'Artois who would later marry Philip the Good after the death of her first husband, Philippe de Nevers, who died at the battle of Agincourt in 1415. Before Jean could confer knighthood on others, he had to be knighted himself, which he asked either Louis de Luxembourg, count of Saint-Pol (according to Jacques du Clercq), or Jean de Luxembourg, bastard of Saint-Pol, lord of Haubourdin (according to Olivier de La Marche) to do. JdC, vol. 2, p. 23; OdLM, vol. 2, p. 237.

[14] Werner Paravicini, 'Soziale Schichtung und soziale Mobilität am Hof der Herzöge von Burgund', in *Menschen am Hof der Herzöge von Burgund: Gesammelte Aufsätze*, ed. by Holger Kruse, Werner Paravicini and Andreas Ranft (Stuttgart: Thorbecke, 2002), pp. 371–426 (pp. 409–10). Lalaing is only mentioned by the chronicler Jacques du Clercq: JdC, vol. 2, p. 24.

was not knighted by his brother, Jacques, even though we know that he did knight at least two men in his own entourage.[15]

For the Lalaings, the Ghent war became, in a sense, a family affair, as Jacques and Philippe were both active participants in it. They succeeded in liberating not only the town of Oudenaarde from the siege of the Ghenters, but also their beloved uncle, Simon, who had been installed there as captain by Philip the Good in order to cut off the supplies coming from the south over the River Scheldt to Ghent.[16] Both Philippe and his other uncle, Sanche de Lalaing, acted as knights in the company and under the command of Jacques as *chevalier banneret*, knight banneret, a high-ranking noble commander in the Burgundian army, thus showing the internal hierarchy within the family.[17] Philippe proved himself to be a brave knight, even though his brother had to rescue him more than once.[18] Was this bravery or simply recklessness on his part? In any case, this suggests some kind of rashness that is also perceptible in the accounts of the *Perron Fée*. Philippe and his uncle, Simon, were compensated by the duke for losing a horse, each to the value of 60lb., a clear sign that the members of the Lalaing family frequently fought side by side and were not afraid to commit themselves on the battlefield, their actions being positively viewed by the duke.[19]

Was Philippe's aspiration therefore to become a member of the Burgundian chivalric Order of the Golden Fleece and was the organisation of a *pas* a means to this end? The title of knight was, in any case, needed to become a member of this prestigious Order which, since its foundation by Philip the Good in 1430, was a select circle of high-ranking nobles drawn mainly from the different Burgundian lands and of foreign princes who had taken an oath of loyalty to the duke. Whereas Philippe's uncle, Simon, was admitted to the Order during its second chapter in December 1431, which was celebrated in Lille, his

---

[15] LF, p. 443; CL, p. 274. Jean of Burgundy was the leader of the Burgundian army sent to relieve Oudenaarde, so this may be the reason why it was he and not Jacques who conferred knighthood upon Philippe.

[16] Richard Vaughan, *Philip the Good: The Apogee of Burgundian Power* (London/New York: Longman, 1970), p. 317.

[17] Bert Verwerft, 'De goede ridder onder de loep genomen. Een detailanalyse van de militaire compagnie van Jacques de Lalaing ten tijde van de Gentse opstand (1453)', *Handelingen van de Maatschappij voor Geschiedenis en Oudheidkunde te Gent*, 75 (2022), 3–76. Two other Hainaut knights from this company, Waleran de Landas and Othon de Marquette, and three squires had already accompanied Jacques de Lalaing on his trip to the Iberian Peninsula in 1446–47 when he was performing an *emprise*, a sign that these knights and their families maintained long-standing relationships with each other.

[18] On 18 May 1452, Philippe and two other members of Jacques's company had become stuck in the mud near the town of Lokeren and Jacques rescued them before the Ghenters could attack them. LF, pp. 455–8; and CL, pp. 279–80; see also Jean Antoine De Jonghe, ed., *Cronijcke van den lande ende graefscepe van Vlaenderen … van de jaeren 405 tot 1492*, 4 vols (Bruges: Uytgever in de Noordzandstraet, 1837–40), vol. 3, pp. 488–9. On 6 December 1452, after setting fire to the village of Merelbeke, Philippe came too close to Ghent and had to flee to Ename, where he was eventually saved by his brother and his garrison from Oudenaarde. This is not mentioned in the *Livre des faits* but in the Flemish chronicle: *ibid.*, pp. 506–7.

[19] ADN B 2012 fol. 283v. This compensation possibly had to do with the fact that Simon de Lalaing escorted the Burgundian duchess, Isabel of Portugal, from Lille to Bruges in March 1453, in which operation he lost not only a horse but also several men-at-arms and archers in an ambush by the Ghenters. JdC, vol. 2, p. 95. On this incident, see also OdLM, vol. 2, pp. 296–7.

father was never invited to enter this circle of ducal confidants. Moreover, Guillaume was also overlooked in favour of his eldest son, Jacques, who was elected during the chapter in Mons in May 1451 together with his patron, Johann of Cleves, Philip the Good's nephew, as members of this exclusive knightly order.[20]

Up to 1463, there were two possible occasions when Philippe could have become a Fleece knight: the chapter of May 1456 celebrated in The Hague and that of Saint-Omer in May 1461. When we consider the names of the ten knights elected at these chapters, it becomes understandable why Philippe had not (yet) reached the required rank: one king, two princes, three close relatives of the duke (Jean of Burgundy, Antoine of Burgundy and Adolf of Cleves, lord of Ravenstein) and four nobles who were either more active on the diplomatic and military fronts or higher placed in the hierarchy of the Burgundian court (Thibaud IX de Neuchâtel, Philippe Pot, Guy de Roye, Louis de Bruges).[21]

Since promotion within the household or other Burgundian institutions was seemingly blocked, the only way for Philippe to distinguish himself was on the battle and tournament fields. It thus comes as no surprise that he made his vow of the Pheasant in February 1454 in Lille to go with the duke to Turkey to fight the infidels together with his brother-in-law, Pierre de Hénin-Liétard, lord of Boussu.[22] The phrasing of their vow recalls the tourneying spirit with which they wanted to engage in battle; not only did they wear an *emprise** but they also stated that they wanted to fight together against two adversaries or even three, if it was the will of God.[23] This boasting, and the fact that Philippe chose to wear an *emprise* (of unspecified form), is consistent with the image projected by the *Perron Fée*: that of a dashing young knight eager to take part in any adventure in a flamboyant manner, perhaps inspired by his reading of romances.

The Feast of the Pheasant was heavily imbued with a chivalric spirit. Philippe is specifically mentioned as one of the twelve nobles (including Charles of Charolais and the duke of Cleves) who participated in the first *momerie* and dance after which Charles was elected as the best jouster during the *Pas du Chevalier au Cygne*.[24] In this *pas*, organised by Adolf of Cleves, brother to the duke of Cleves, Philippe was one of the challengers.[25] During his

---

[20] COTO nos 47, 51.

[21] *Ibid.*, nos 53–62.

[22] He was the son of Jean de Hénin-Liétard and Catherine de Béthune. PCB no. 1908; COTO no. 89; VdF, no. 96.

[23] OdLM, vol. 2, p. 392; and VdF, pp. 140–1. They were not the only nobles who vowed to sport an *emprise*: Claude de Toulongeon also swore to wear one to engage in arms on foot or on horseback against the Turks, whereas Chrétien de Digoine stated that he would wear an *emprise* in case he returned from the crusade, passing through three Christian realms in order to engage in combat on foot or on horseback. OdLM, vol. 2, pp. 392–4; VdF, pp. 142, 145.

[24] OdLM, vol. 2, p. 378. In another manuscript of La Marche's text, Philippe de Lannoy is mentioned instead of Philippe de Lalaing. VdF, p. 131.

[25] OdLM, vol. 2, pp. 345–8; and VdF, pp. 112–13, mention as challengers by name Gérard de Roussillon, Jean de Montfort, Louis de Luxembourg, count of Saint-Pol, Thibaud de Luxembourg, lord of Fiennes, Charles, count of Charolais, Antoine of Burgundy, Louis de Bruges, Louis Le Jeune de Contay, lord of Mourcourt, Chrétien de Digoine, Évrard de Digoine, Jean de Ghistelles, Philippe de Lalaing and Louis de Chevallart, but there were 'plusieurs aultres jousteurs' (several other jousters). Mathieu d'Escouchy mentions some of these others: Claude de Rochebaron, Pedro Vásquez de Saavedra, Jean de Brevette, Jean de Chassau (also known as Beneton) and Jean de Masilles. MdE, vol. 2, pp. 129–30. On the issue of theatricality, see JdC, vol. 2, p. 196.

joust he was dressed in a black velvet gown adorned with golden tears and on the back of the caparison was a cross of St Andrew, this being not only one of the duke's favourite patron saints, whose emblem was frequently worn during military expeditions, but also the patron saint of the Order of the Golden Fleece.[26] This might refer to Philippe's outright ambitions to become a member of this prestigious knightly order. The tears may likewise have made subtle reference to the heraldic decoration of his brother Jacques, who wore a white tunic strewn with blue tears at the *Pas de la Fontaine des Pleurs* organised in the town of Chalon-sur-Saône in 1449–50.[27] Whatever his reasons, this choice of garment shows that Philippe was good at exploiting emblematic signs that might ingratiate him with the duke and win him some favour.

Even so, Philippe took his vow seriously: he did indeed participate in an expedition to the Eastern Mediterranean with Antoine of Burgundy. On 29 June 1463, a Burgundian embassy, consisting of Simon de Lalaing and Jean de Wavrin, amongst others, left Bruges for Rome to discuss with the pope the Burgundian participation in the crusade against the Turks. They returned around mid-December. In the end, Philip the Good decided not to go in person but rather sent his bastard son Antoine in his place. The plan was to sail to Marseille with some fifteen ships, where the expedition would be joined by another twelve ships, mainly Italian galleys. Simon de Lalaing was Antoine's lieutenant-general and captain of one of the galleys, as was Pedro Vásquez de Saavedra, a knight from Castile in the service of Philip the Good and one of Jacques de Lalaing's helpers at the *Fontaine des Pleurs*. The chronicler Georges Chastelain mentions 'messire Philippe de Lalaing' as one of the other noble participants, along with Pedro Vásquez de Saavedra, the 'bastards de Brabant', Philippe and Antoine, sons of the last duke of Brabant, Philippe of Saint-Pol (1404–30), two challengers at the *Perron Fée*; the combination of jousting and crusading was thus not an exclusive feature of the Lalaing family. Finally, the expedition left the harbour of Sluis on 21 May 1464, a year after the conclusion of the *Pas*. Travelling via Galicia, where they visited the shrine of St James in Santiago de Compostela, and Ceuta, they arrived in Marseille in September.[28] There the plague broke out on board one of the ships and, according to Chastelain, some 500 'nobles … et belles gens d'armes' (nobles and good men-at-arms), amongst them 'deux beaux escuyers' (two fine squires), Philippe and François de Lalaing, sons of Simon, died of the disease.[29] Our Philippe de Lalaing survived and probably travelled overland with his uncle, Simon, and Antoine of Burgundy back to the Burgundian lands in January 1465. Therefore, after ten years, both Simon and Philippe had fulfilled their vow of the Pheasant and had made an attempt to go on crusade, something which could not be said of the majority of the noblemen present at the Feast of the Pheasant in 1454.

The prologue of the B account of the *Perron Fée* suggests that Philippe's extensive reading of pseudo-historical texts and *chansons de geste*, amongst them the stories of Godfrey of Bouillon, king of Jerusalem, had inspired him to fight against the 'infidels'. Yet he also drew his inspiration from Arthurian romances, such as *Perceforest* and the

---

26 MdE, vol. 2, p. 129; VdF, pp. 111–12. On St Andrew, see Vaughan, *Philip the Good*, pp. 39, 329, 389.

27 LF, p. 339; CL, p. 223.

28 Jacques Paviot, *La politique navale des ducs de Bourgogne, 1384–1482* (Lille: Presses Universitaires de Lille, 1995), pp. 127–33.

29 GC, vol. 5, pp. 46–7; Brassart, *Le blason*, pp. 59–60.

Lancelot cycle.[30] The wide array of readings that are said to have influenced him nuances the image that we have of Philippe: was his participation in the crusade motivated by piety or did he see it as the culmination of the ideal career according to Antoine de La Sale's romance, *Jean de Saintré*?[31] Both motivations were probably present. The deeds of arms on the battlefield of the crusade were the continuation of those accomplished within the lists. Philippe wanted to follow in the footsteps of those knights from the past, which also included his brother: although he did not claim to be as good as the least of these knights, he still wanted some memory of himself to survive — a good example of the humility topos. Indeed, the prologue says that he was inspired by the twenty-six feats of arms performed by his elder brother, which brought him great honour.[32] Jacques de Lalaing had certainly set a standard that was difficult to meet, not only for his brother but also for other ambitious knights. Chastelain reports, for example, that Antoine of Burgundy wanted to organise a *pas* in 1463, in clear competition with Lalaing, with which he wished to 'surpasser tous autres chevaliers de devant luy, par plus hautement et plus amplement que nul oncques, là où messire Jacques de Lalaing jusq'à ce jour avoit et tenoit la gloire sur tous les devant passés' (outshine all the knights before him, more highly and grandly than anyone else, where Jacques de Lalaing to this day obtained glory compared to all prior knights).[33]

In short, the organisation of the *Perron Fée* in Bruges fitted neatly into Philippe's career, which was geared towards high-level chivalric performances with the aim of eventually leading to promotion within the household and/or membership of the Order of the Golden Fleece. But, of course, nobles like Philippe de Lalaing also had concerns other than just pleasing their master. Both Jacques and, after his death, Philippe, as eldest sons, had the task of ensuring the continuity of the house and the lineage of Lalaing. However, neither of them managed to find a suitable marriage partner during their lives. Was each man too preoccupied with his chivalric endeavours on the battle and tournament fields to find a noblewoman from a prestigious noble family? It was not entirely unusual for noblemen to marry at a later age; for example, Jean de Ligne married Jacqueline de Croÿ aged thirty-eight, their uncle Simon de Lalaing married at the age of thirty-six, as did Jacques's patron Johann of Cleves, but Antoine of Burgundy married at

[30] On Lalaing's reading habits, see Michelle Szkilnik, 'Que lisaient les chevaliers du XVe siècle? Le témoignage du *Pas du Perron Fée*', *Le Moyen Français*, 68 (2011), 103–14. On the Arthurian framing of the Angevin *Pas de la Joyeuse Garde/Pas de Saumur* (1446), see Essays 2 and 7.

[31] Michelle Szkilnik, *Jean de Saintré: une carrière chevaleresque au XVe siècle* (Geneva: Droz, 2003). *Jean de Saintré* was composed in 1456 by Antoine de La Sale, who was also a herald. See Antoine de la Sale, *Jehan de Saintré*, ed. and trans. by Joël Blanchard and Michel Quereuil (Paris: Livre de Poche, 1995); and *idem*, *Jean de Saintré: A Late Medieval Education in Love and Chivalry*, trans. by Roberta L. Krueger and Jane H. M. Taylor (Philadelphia: University of Pennsylvania Press, 2014). Parts of the romance were included in the biography of Jacques de Lalaing, specifically the long lecture on the Seven Deadly Sins that Jacques's father gives his son prior to his departure and which, as we have seen, Philippe is also said to have witnessed. Geoffroy de Charny's *Livre de chevalerie* (*c.*1352), another very influential book (albeit absent from the list of Philippe's supposed reading matter) was also insistent that a knight's ideal progression was from jousting to warfare and, finally, to crusade.

[32] PPF, p. 156.

[33] GC, vol. 4, p. 371. For an edition of the letters of challenge and chapters of arms for this event, see JDI, pp. 474–82.

the age of eighteen, Jean de Croÿ at twenty-five and Louis de Bruges at twenty-eight.[34] Jacques died a bachelor at the age of thirty-two, as did Philippe at thirty-five! It is possible that they were waiting to mature and earn a little more social prestige that would enable them to marry higher-ranking noblewomen, from the Cleves dynasty, for example, in the case of Jacques,[35] or the Luxembourg dynasty (five challengers in the *Pas*), in the case of Philippe, or even from the ducal family itself.[36] The social environment of the *Perron Fée*, with its banquets and festivities, would not seem, however, to have created the right opportunities for Philippe to find a suitable partner, even though tournaments had, since time immemorial, provided an excellent opportunity for marriage arrangements between noble families to be concluded.[37]

In Jacques's case, his devotion to the Virgin Mary and the crusading ideal may have inspired him to remain unmarried, witness the last passage in the *Livre des faits* stating that:

> tout son vouloir sy estoit de s'en aller user sa vye et exposer son corps au service de Nostre Seigneur et de soy tenir en frontiere sur les marces des Infideles sans jamais plus retourner par deça, en retenant certaine pension d'argent, pour son estat entretenir
>
> (his only wish was to go and spend the rest of his life dedicating himself to the service of Our Lord by defending the frontier of the lands occupied by the Infidel, never more to return to these parts. He would keep a simple money pension in order to maintain his estate).[38]

This does not sound as if he was planning to marry and have a family, although of course it represents the point of view of the biographer, who may have wanted to add a saintly air to the deceased hero. Did a similar degree of piety also play a role in Philippe's life? This hypothesis is more difficult to support in view of the fact that he begat several illegitimate children despite his remaining unmarried: these were two daughters and a son who sported the knightly name of Méliador.[39] Nevertheless, just like the *Fontaine des*

---

[34] See their respective biographies in COTO nos 22, 26, 47, 54, 61, 87.

[35] Colette Beaune suggests that Jacques aspired to marry Marie of Cleves: Colette Beaune, '*Le Livre des faits du bon chevalier messire Jacques de Lalaing*', in *Splendeurs de la cour de Bourgogne: récits et chroniques*, ed. by Danielle Régnier-Bohler (Paris: Laffont, 1995), pp. 1193–410 (p. 1198). On Marie's role in Jacques's life, see CL, pp. 17, 106.

[36] For example, at the age of fifty Pierre de Bauffremont, the organiser of the *Pas de l'Arbre Charlemagne*, made a final marriage to Marie of Burgundy, an illegitimate daughter of Philip the Good, after the death of his two previous wives. COTO no. 20.

[37] Antheun Janse, 'Tourneyers and Spectators: The Shrovetide Tournament at The Hague, 1391', in *The Court as a Stage: England and the Low Countries in the Later Middle Ages*, ed. by Antheun Janse and Steven Gunn (Woodbridge: Boydell Press, 2006), pp. 39–52 (p. 41); Andrew Brown and Graeme Small, *Court and Civic Society in the Burgundian Low Countries c.1420–1530* (Manchester: Manchester University Press, 2007), pp. 23–5.

[38] LF, p. 552; CL, p. 328.

[39] Brassart, *Le blason*, pp. 89–92. Méliador is the name of the main character in Jean Froissart's *Roman de Meliador* (*c.*1380), the last Arthurian verse romance written in French.

Pleurs, Philippe's chivalric event in Bruges definitely had a religious side to it (albeit less pronounced), as we will see in the next section.

The *Perron Fée*: courtly or urban event?

All the accounts of the *Perron Fée* describe at length the sumptuous attire and clothing of the defender and his challengers, suggesting the authors' fascination with courtly life, whereas they mention the urban setting of the *Pas* only in passing. From this fragmentary information as well as from different administrative documents, it is nonetheless possible to assess the crucial role of the city in the staging of this event. In this section, our aim is to situate the *Pas* in a cycle of events that took place in Bruges in the spring of 1463, and to reveal its urban embedding. In the B account of the *Perron Fée*, it is stated that Limbourg Herald informed the duke in Brussels about Philippe's plans for his *pas*. The event was supposed to take place on 1 January 1463, but was then postponed by the duke to 7 February of the same year, much to Lalaing's displeasure.[40] Indeed, the itinerary of the duke shows that he spent almost the entire year of 1462 and the month of January 1463 in Brussels. However, on 11 February he left the town and, after a trip of twelve days through Brabant, Flanders and Zeeland, made his entry into Bruges on 22 February, which was Shrove Tuesday, accompanied by his sister Agnès of Burgundy, the widow of Charles of Bourbon (1401–56).[41] The Bourbon dynasty was closely connected to that of Burgundy since, in 1454, Philip's son Charles had married Isabelle (1437–65), she being in fact a full niece of Charles. The marriage of Catherine of Bourbon, also present at the *Perron Fée*, with the future duke of Guelders, Adolf of Egmond, later in 1463 is further evidence that the Bourbons had become, just like the Cleves before them, a client dynasty of the Burgundian dukes.[42] The chronicler Jacques du Clercq recounts how the duchess Agnès had already been staying at the Burgundian court in Brussels since November 1462 with 'deux de ses filles a marier avecq elle' (with two of her daughters who were ready for marriage), probably Catherine and Jeanne, as well as four of her sons. On their arrival, 'plusieurs joustes et esbattements' (several jousts and amusements) were organised in honour of the three ladies and in the presence of Charles of Charolais, Johann and Adolf of Cleves, Adolf of Egmond, son of the duke of Guelders, Jean of Burgundy, count of Étampes, Louis de Luxembourg, count of Saint-Pol, and Antoine of Burgundy.[43] It was probably this event — described as a *pas* in the ducal financial account — for which Philip the Good offered Jacques of Bourbon, Agnès's youngest son, a jousting harness.[44] Indeed, a Brabantine chronicle records as a

---

[40] PPF, pp. 165–6, 169–70.

[41] Herman Vander Linden, *Itinéraires de Philippe le Bon, duc de Bourgogne (1419–1467) et de Charles, comte de Charolais (1433–1467)* (Brussels: Commission royale d'Histoire, 1940), pp. 450–1.

[42] C. A. J. Armstrong, 'La politique matrimoniale des ducs de Bourgogne de la Maison de Valois', *Annales de Bourgogne*, 40 (1968), 5–58, 89–139 (pp. 7, 15, 95); Vaughan, *Philip the Good*, pp. 163, 289–92. On Egmond, see COTO no. 58.

[43] Jacques du Clercq (JdC, vol. 3, p. 233) mentions their arrival 'environ' (around) St Catherine's day (25 November) whereas, according to Philip's itinerary (Vander Linden, *Itinéraires*, p. 447), they arrived on 14 November. On the presence of 'mesdamoiselles de Bourbon' as guests at the Burgundian court in 1462–3, see PCB no. 2234.

[44] 'pour ung harnois de joustes … pour jouster au pas que ont nagueres fait et tenu audit lieu de Bruxelles, messires Adolf de Cleves et Bastard de Bourgogne, à l'encontre de tous venans' (for a jousting

'groot steecspel' (grand joust) an extraordinary event in 1462 that shows characteristics of a *pas*, including defenders magnificently attired and accompanied by floats, one with a large boat, another with lions, monkeys and other animals on top of a mountain, and a third with an elephant carrying a castle with armed men.[45]

Apart from the Bourbon family and their entourage, there were other guests at the Burgundian court who followed the duke on this particular occasion: Master Pieter Knorre and the squire Rudolf Schenk, lord of Tautenburg, acting in the capacity of ambassadors to Wilhelm III, duke of Saxony, and his wife, Anna of Bohemia. They had already been at the court since September 1462, where they were involved in negotiating with the duke the sums to be paid to their master since he had revived his claims on the duchy of Luxembourg on the grounds of his wife's hereditary rights. They spent another three months in Bruges, until 22 May, and must therefore have witnessed the *Pas*.[46] This also becomes clear from a report they sent to their masters in January 1463. Herein they state how they were impressed by all sorts of banquets, dances and jousting that occurred at the court, and 'nemlich ein furnemen ritterspils, vormals ungehoret' (above all by a noble knightly game, never heard of before) which could not even be described in words, possibly referring to the *pas* of November 1462 staged in Brussels.[47] Hence, the *Perron Fée* was clearly embedded in a range of spectacles intended in the first instance for a princely and noble audience, in the context of making international diplomatic alliances.

Philip the Good, his sister Agnès and their entourages arrived by boat from Ghent. The town administration prepared a Joyous Entry for them with seven 'personaigen' (*tableaux vivants*), staged by the guilds, amongst them one on the riverside with the Seven Virtues (unspecified), another with the goddess Venus and 'vele schoone maechden' (many beautiful maidens) on a castle built on boats in the River Reie, and another also staged on boats with the figures of Paris, Venus, Juno and Pallas.[48] Interestingly, the *entremets** performed at the closing banquet of the *Pas* seems to mirror these urban *tableaux vivants*:

> une riche galee de tout bien appointee, dont estoit le patron une dame vestue de drap bleu. Et pour parer et enrichier ladite galee, les armes des paÿs du duc estoient mises et assises ou il appartenoit, tant en banieres que en estandart

harness … to joust in the *pas* that was recently held and organised in the said place of Brussels by Messires Adolf of Cleves, and [Antoine, the Great] Bastard of Burgundy against all comers). ADN B 2048 fols 237r–237v, registered on 20 April 1463: see Source 11b. On Jacques, see COTO no. 66; PCB no. 1946. In May 1468, Jacques would die in Bruges shortly after being made a member of the Order of the Golden Fleece by Charles the Bold, where he was buried in the church of St Donatian.

[45] Charles Piot, ed., 'Brabandsche Kronijk, 1288 tot 1469', in *Chroniques de Brabant et de Flandre* (Brussels: Hayez, 1879), pp. 48–62 (p. 60).

[46] ADN B 2048 fol. 225r. The duke gave them 300 pounds (of forty groats) for the expenses they incurred for themselves and their fourteen servants.

[47] Adolf Bachmann, ed., *Urkundliche Nachträge zur Österreichisch-Deutschen Geschichte im Zeitalter Kaiser Friedrich III* (Vienna: Tempsky, 1892), p. 15.

[48] AR 32515 fol. 52v (published in Louis Gilliodts-van Severen, *Inventaire des archives de la ville de Bruges. Section première: Inventaire des chartes. Première série: treizième au seizième siècle*, 9 vols (Bruges: Gailliard, 1871–85), vol. 5, pp. 532–3. The guild of the fishmongers won two silver plates in the competition for the prize of the most beautifully executed performance.

(a rich boat was fully equipped; its captain was a lady dressed in blue. To adorn and enhance this boat, the coats of arms of all the duke's lands were arranged and set out where required; these were [depicted] on both banners and pennons).[49]

The galley reflects both the importance of Bruges as an international harbour and the composite character of the Burgundian lands through this display of coats of arms. All members of the household and challengers in the *Pas*, who originated from Holland to Picardy, and from Luxembourg to Burgundy, could feel themselves properly represented in it.

After the duke had installed himself in the princely residence of the Prinsenhof, he immediately ordered the town administration to set up a jousting field on the Markt covered with a thousand bundles of straw and dung where the jousts were held on the following Sunday (27 February).[50] The town would then seem to have wanted to make use of the momentum provided by the duke's presence: on 29 March, the *forestier* (Forester) of that year, Jan Moens, went to the ducal castle in Le Quesnoy where Charles and his wife, Isabelle of Bourbon, were residing, to invite him 'te commene ten steicspele ende ooc ten ommeghange van deser stede' (to come and attend the joust and the procession of this town), referring to the annual joust of the White Bear and the procession of the relic of the Holy Blood.[51] Eventually, Charles left Le Quesnoy on 20 April and, travelling via Ath and Ghent, arrived in Bruges on 22 April, exactly two months after his father. Remarkably enough, his wife stayed in Le Quesnoy and so did not join her mother and sisters in Bruges.[52]

This highlights several aspects concerning the interplay of the ducal court, the nobility and the towns in the Burgundian lands. First, it shows that the collaboration of the town was crucial for staging these kinds of event.[53] The urban economy could provide the court and the participants at a *pas* with all necessities; indeed, it is explicitly stated in account B of the *Perron Fée* that Bruges could provide the 'feste' (festivity) with all kinds of merchandise, and that the citizens were thankful for having the *Pas* in their town and ready to deliver whatever was needed.[54] Moreover, the town administration was willing to offer its most emblematic commercial and political space, the Markt, for the event. This square was dominated by the belfry, a powerful symbol of urban autonomy,[55] with the Old Hall and

[49] PPF, p. 201.

[50] AR 32515 fol. 52v.

[51] AR 32515 fol. 30v. Note that the account does not mention the *Pas* here; Charles was invited to attend the urban events.

[52] Vander Linden, *Itinéraires*, pp. 453–4. On 24 April, on the eve of the White Bear, the town administration organised a banquet for the duke, his sister and his son and 'vele andre diversche heeren ende vrauwen' (many other lords and ladies) at a cost of 276lb. (of forty groats). AR 32515 fol. 53r.

[53] Mario Damen, 'The Town as a Stage? Urban Space and Tournaments in Late Medieval Brussels', *Urban History*, 43.1 (2016), 47–71.

[54] 'ceulx de Bruges vindrent devers Monseigneur le duc et le merchierent tres humblement, et luy promirrent qu'il se efforceroient de faire tout le mieulx qu'ilz porroient' (the people of Bruges came to my lord the duke and thanked him very humbly. They promised him that they would do their best). PPF, p. 171.

[55] Only the town administration was entitled to order the bell to be rung, e.g., in the event of danger such as a fire or military troops approaching, as a call to arms for urban militias, a call to attend civic meetings, etc. The belfry was, moreover, essential for the day-to-day organisation of the social and economic life of the town. Raymond Van Uytven, 'Flämische Belfriede und sudniederländische

the impressive New or Water Hall covering the canal of the Kraanreie and offering space for loading and selling goods.[56] Both the narrative and financial sources show how the square was partly closed off, and how the lists, stands and ephemeral architecture were constructed by a master carpenter at the town's expense.[57]

Secondly, town administrations, which expected to derive economic and political benefits from the presence of the duke and his household in the town, were very eager to stage these events.[58] Contemporary writers versed in tournaments, such as Antoine de La Sale, were well aware of this aspect: 'Et sont maintes bonnes villes qui leur offrent les deffrais à nombre de chevaulx et le bancquet, pour avoir le prouffit des survenans' (there are many good cities that provide horses and cover the price of the banquet to benefit from those flooding in).[59] For example, in May 1448, the town of Saint-Omer was in competition with Lille and Arras, who had offered 'grans sommes de deniers' (large sums of money) to Jean de Luxembourg, lord of Haubourdin, to organise a *pas* there. Apparently, the bid of 1600 *écus* (of forty-eight groats) by the councillors of Saint-Omer was enough to convince this high-ranking nobleman and councillor-chamberlain of Duke Philip the Good to organise this event, now known as the *Pas de la Belle Pèlerine*, which was held near the capital of Artois in July–August 1449 — that is, more than a year later. In spite of these and other costs, the town expected that 'par l'assemblée des seigneurs et autres qui à ceste cause se feroit en ceste dite ville, le peuple dicelle et corps dicelle y peust avoir prouffit' (the people and the administration of the town would benefit from the assembly of the lords and others that would take place in this town).[60] In 1461, the town administration of Lille was equally confident that the sum of 400 pounds (of twenty groats) granted to Antoine of Burgundy for his costs in organising a *pas* on the Place du Marché was well spent, as he could advance and protect the interests not just of the town but also those of the castellany and the administrative and juridical districts surrounding the town.[61] In Bruges in 1463, something similar may have been at stake. The duke had not been in the town since April 1461 and the Coudenberg Palace in Brussels had become his favourite residence.[62] The shifting of the *Perron Fée* from Brussels to Bruges in 1463 was

---

Bauwerke im Mittelalter: Symbol und Mythos', in *Information, Kommunikation und Selbstdarstellung in Mittelalterlichen Gemeinden*, ed. by Alfred Haverkamp and Elisabeth Müller-Luckner (Munich: Oldenbourg Verlag, 1998), pp. 125–60.

[56] Andrew Brown and Jan Dumolyn, *Medieval Bruges, c. 850–1550* (Cambridge: Cambridge University Press, 2018), pp. 161–4.

[57] See Source 11b.

[58] Mario Damen, 'The Town, the Duke, his Courtiers and their Tournament. A Spectacle in Brussels, 4–7 May 1439', in *Staging the Court of Burgundy: Proceedings of the Conference 'The Splendour of Burgundy'*, ed. by Wim Blockmans *et al.* (Turnhout/London: Brepols/Harvey Miller, 2013), pp. 85–95. See also Sébastien Nadot, *Le Spectacle des joutes: Sport et courtoisie à la fin du Moyen Âge* (Rennes: Presses Universitaires de Rennes, 2012), p. 130.

[59] Sylvie Lefèvre, *Antoine de la Sale: la fabrique de l'œuvre et de l'écrivain. Suivi de l'édition critique du Traité des anciens et des nouveaux tournois* (Geneva: Droz, 2006), p. 307.

[60] Pagart d'Hermansart, *Les frais du pas d'armes de la Croix pèlerine, 1449* (Saint-Omer: H. D'Homont, 1892), pp. 4–5, 7. See also Richard Barber and Juliet Barker, *Tournaments, Jousts, Chivalry, and Pageants in the Middle Ages* (New York: Weidenfeld & Nicolson, 1989), p. 118; and VdN, pp. 176–7, which gives an incorrect figure for the value of the *écus*.

[61] VdN, pp. 138–9, 320–1.

[62] Vander Linden, *Itinéraires*, p. 426.

probably facilitated by a payment of 2400lb. (of forty groats) made by the town administration to the duke for allowing the *Pas* to be held in the town in his presence, whereas the organiser, Philippe de Lalaing, had to content himself with 528lb. as compensation for his costs from the same source. Although this is far less than the sum given to the duke, for Lalaing it was a substantial amount, worth almost five times his annual wages in the ducal household; as far as we know, the duke did not provide any gifts or allowances to Lalaing or others as compensation for their costs of participating in the event.[63]

The financial involvement of the urban administration thus serves as a good indicator of the interaction between the *entrepreneur** and the host town. That Bruges was definitely at that time very keen to help nobles stage feats of arms becomes even clearer from the following entry in the town accounts of Bruges of 1463–64:

> Item, ghegheven mijn heren Antheunis den bastaert van Bourgongen, de welke annam hier binnen der stede van Brugghe zijn fait van wapene te doene, daer hij zekeren tijt gheduerende verbeyt heift omme tvoirs. fayt te vulcommene jeghens alle maniere van hedelen mannen ende daeromme ghedaen grooten cost thulpe van zijnen voirs costen 445lb. 11s. 6d.
>
> (Item, given to my lord Antoine, bastard of Burgundy who had taken the initiative to organise his feat of arms here in the town for which he spent some time to fulfil the said feat against all kinds of noblemen and for this he had incurred great costs, therefore to help him for the said costs, 445lb. 11s. 6d.)[64]

This *pas*, better known as the *Pas de la Dame Inconnue*, would seem to be the one mentioned by Chastelain, who reveals that the Great Bastard sent Charolais Herald to all Christian realms challenging nobles to take up arms against him and his two fellow *entrepreneurs*, the knights and chamberlains Philippe de Crèvecoeur and Pedro Vásquez de Saavedra. It was planned for the beginning of February 1463, when Philip the Good was still in Brussels, the chapters of arms being sealed and issued by the three knights on 26 February, when the court had already moved to Bruges. It was stipulated in the chapters that, in order to give foreign knights the opportunity to come to the Low Countries, the *pas* would start on 1 October 1463 and would, if necessary, start up again in April 1464 if some could not arrive in time. The Great Bastard was staying at the Benedictine abbey of Sint-Andries,

---

[63] AR 32515 fols 53r–53v; Van den Abeele, 'De Wapenpas', pp. 110–11. The sum mentioned in the account of Bruges is 88lb. Flemish (of 240 groats), which is the equivalent of 528lb. (of forty groats). As a chamberlain, Philippe was entitled to serve three months a year in the ducal household with four horses, meaning that he had three servants. He could therefore expect a daily wage of 24s., meaning a maximum wage of *c.*36lb. (of forty groats) a month, for three months a year, adding up to *c.*110lb. a year.

[64] The amount mentioned in the account is 74lb. 5s. 3d., but is recalculated here to pounds of forty groats. AR 32516 fol. 50v. See also Andrew Brown, *Civic Ceremony and Religion in Medieval Bruges c. 1300–1520* (Cambridge: Cambridge University Press, 2011), pp. 259–60, for a reference to the minutes of the town administration of 1464 that confirm that nobody showed up at Antoine's feat of arms. The relationship between Antoine and the town seems to have been a close one: in the same year of 1463, he was elected king of the shooting guild of St George, whose annual archery contests he attended regularly. *Ibid.*, p. 254. In these years, Antoine received an annual pension of 4840lb. (of forty groats) from Duke Philip the Good, which puts the money he received from the town of Bruges into perspective. ADN B 2048 fol. 121v.

some 3 km to the west of Bruges, whereas the other two nobles were in nearby houses, waiting for challengers, but 'nul ne comparut' (nobody showed up).[65] This particular case demonstrates that the success of a *pas* depended not only on the willingness of a town to collaborate with the *entrepreneur* on its organisation but also on the availability of eligible opponents. It is perhaps for this reason that *entrepreneurs* such as Philippe de Lalaing sought to tie their *pas* into other festivities when the court and possible foreign visitors would be present. Audiences for these festivities were thus already in place and so organisers could maximise their chances of running a successful event.

In the specific case of Bruges, we should also take into account that the idea of setting up a *pas d'armes* fell onto fertile ground because the town had a long-standing jousting tradition. The presence of a prosperous and organised elite possessing horses and armour was a great stimulus for the staging of chivalric activities here. There is evidence that the count of Flanders and his entourage also participated in jousts organised in the town, at least from the 1330s onwards. However, the founding of a jousting society, known as the White Bear, cannot be confirmed until more than half a century later.[66] Around 1400, the society even obtained its own building, the so-called Poortersloge (burghers' lodge), built in the commercial district of the town and mostly financed by the town administration, which was dominated by international merchants and hostellers. This lodge, which was similar to the English guildhall or the Italian *loggia*, became a vibrant social, political and cultural centre of the town in the fifteenth century where the urban elite, the Flemish nobility and members of the Burgundian household (and even the duke himself)[67] could meet on an informal basis and where banquets, balls and table games were organised.[68] The jousts of the White Bear were normally held on the third Monday after Easter, and were set up by the *forestier*, who was so-called after the legendary first count of Flanders in the ninth century, who is supposed to have killed a white bear in a fight to the death.[69]

The date that the White Bear fell on in 1463 was 25 April. A herald in the service of the town would cry the 'aventure' (adventure) in advance in other towns, such as Lille, Valenciennes and Douai, as well as in noble and princely residences.[70] Normally, at least the organiser ('roi' or king) accompanied by one or two fellow-jousters of a similar annual jousting event in Lille would come, as well as high-ranking guests from the ducal household. In 1457, Philip the Good, together with the Dauphin Louis (the

---

[65] GC, vol. 4, p. 311; JDI, pp. 471, 481–2. Interestingly, three years later, Antoine would claim that he could not undertake this *pas* because of the crusade expedition (see above, p. 407). MT, pp. 81, 335. On this issue, see also GC, vol. 4, p. 372.

[66] Andries Van den Abeele, *Het ridderlijk gezelschap van de Witte Beer: steekspelen in Brugge tijdens de late Middeleeuwen* (Bruges: Walleyn, 2000), pp. 9–14; Andrew Brown, 'Urban Jousts in the Later Middle Ages: The White Bear of Bruges', *Revue Belge de Philologie et d'Histoire*, 78 (2000), 315–30 (pp. 316–18). Although in Lille there was no formal jousting society, there was a similar annual jousting event called 'L'Épinette': VdN, pp. 178–86.

[67] In April 1447, for example, the burgomasters and 'andere notablen van der stede' (other notable people of the town) had a banquet in the lodge with the duke, Johann of Cleves, and 'andere edele van den hove' (other nobles of the household) at a cost of more than 50lb. (of forty groats). AR 32499 fol. 57r.

[68] Frederik Buylaert, Jan Dumolyn and Jelle De Rock, 'La Loge des Bourgeois de Bruges: les stratégies de distinction d'une élite commerçante cosmopolite', *Revue du Nord*, 98 (2016), 37–69.

[69] Van den Abeele, *Het ridderlijk gezelschap*, pp. 10–12.

[70] AR 32515 fol. 32v.

future Louis XI of France) and many illustrious courtiers and their wives, had witnessed his son Charles participating in this event with at least six noblemen from his retinue.[71] It comes as no surprise, then, that Charles participated again in the jousts of the White Bear in 1463 and that Charles de Visen, a member of his household and challenger in the *Perron Fée*, won the so-called prize of the bear — there is debate about whether this was a wooden image of a bear or a real animal — which was normally given to somebody from outside the town.[72] The town accounts show that part of the infrastructure (two lists constructed on the Markt) that were built for the jousts of the White Bear were reused for Lalaing's event, which started on 28 April. Moreover, the town paid nine jousters — probably members of the White Bear — for the silk gowns of the jousters and their horses' trappers* worn during their procession through the town to the Markt.[73] This shows how, in these urban chivalric events, 'court' and 'town' were intermingled in multiple ways.

In addition to this civic event and Philippe's own *pas*, there was even more going on in the town at that time. The third of May was the day on which the procession of the Holy Blood relic took place, this being the most important annual religious feast of the town. This relic, supposedly the true blood of Christ, was said to have been brought to Bruges by Count Thierry of Alsace after the Second Crusade in 1150, but was more probably stolen in Constantinople during the Fourth Crusade in 1204.[74] Moreover, the feast day was the start of the annual fair of Bruges, which attracted many merchants and buyers. This multiplicity of near-simultaneous events may therefore explain the long interval between 29 April and 5 May when no jousting at the *Pas* took place, as is explicitly mentioned in all three accounts of the *Perron Fée*.[75] Indeed, the jousts of the White Bear and those of the *Pas* took place in an atmosphere of vibrant economic, social and religious activity in the town. At the same time, we might even read the *Pas* as deliberately encompassing the urban and liturgical procession of the Holy Blood, which was a celebration not only of civic order and peace, with the participation of the

---

[71] Brown and Small, *Court*, pp. 225–6. Charles spent most of his money on clothing for himself and his jousters (six noblemen) as well as on jewellery given to several noblewomen, amongst them Margaretha van Borssele, wife of Louis de Bruges.

[72] See ADN B 7662 no. 157113, a sixteenth-century copy of a board with the names of the prize-winners that was placed in the building of the fraternity, the Poortersloge. This contradicts what Nicolas Despars, the contemporary chronicler, says in his account of the event, since he does not mention Charolais but rather names Antoine of Burgundy as a prominent participant and Jean de Quiévrain as the prize winner. De Jonghe, *Cronijcke*, vol. 3, p. 558. On the prize of the bear, see Van den Abeele, *Het ridderlijk gezelschap*, pp. 40–2.

[73] AR 32515 fol. 46v.

[74] Noël Geirnaert, 'De oudste sporen van het Heilig Bloed in Brugge (1255–1310)', *Handelingen van het Genootschap voor Geschiedenis*, 147.2 (2010), 247–55; Brown, *Civic Ceremony*, p. 8.

[75] On 30 April, no jousting occurred 'pour ce que les gens de monseigneur de Charolois n'estoient point pretz' (because the retinue of my lord of Charolais was not ready). Jousting resumed on 5 May. B: 'Et le prumier jour de may fu le pas continué jusques au jeudy enssievant, V[e] jour dudit mois, pour la solemnité de la procession de Bruge et aultre chose' ([on] the first day of May the *Pas* was put on hold until the following Thursday, fifth day of the month, because of the solemn procession of Bruges and other reasons). PPF, p. 180. *Continuer* here means 'postpone'. A gives the same text as B, whereas C reads: 'Le III[e] jour dudit pas se fist le V[e] jour de may' ('the third day of the *Pas* fell on the fifth day of May'), *ibid.*, p. 112. See n. VIII.I in *ibid.*, pp. 230–1.

majority of the guilds and religious associations, but also of the crusading endeavours of the counts of Flanders in the past.[76] It is telling in this respect that two weeks after the end of the *Pas*, on 30 May, the relics of St Basil, normally kept in the church of St Donatian — which were brought to Bruges by Robert II of Jerusalem, count of Flanders, after the First Crusade — were moved to a new reliquary made of gold and silver in the presence of the duke, Charles of Charolais, a range of household officers, prelates and a large number of citizens.[77] Furthermore, it is probably no coincidence that on the evening of the closure of the *Pas*, after having shared wine and spices with the Lady of the Enchanted Column, Philippe is said to have withdrawn to the same church of St Donatian, according to account B. That evening, the Lady sends him at the 'logis qui luy estoit apointiet' (lodging that had been reserved for him) a 'Moorish' woman bringing a horse loaded with three chests containing the gifts to be awarded as prizes.[78] Here, again, we see how the religious, courtly and urban aspects of this *pas* are interwoven in a complex manner.

The town went to great efforts to make the *Pas* a success. For the event, 2130 cartloads of sand were spread on the pavement of the Markt. A stage richly decorated with velvet cushions and tapestries was erected to accommodate the three judges and the heralds of the event.[79] The lists were guarded by the duke's archers. Philip delegated his role of judging to Toison d'or King of Arms (Jean Lefèvre de Saint-Rémy) and two nobles so that he could watch the *Pas* together with his sister from the house known as Craenenburg; this was well situated on the Markt with a balcony and was therefore often rented out by the town administration to host high-ranking visitors.[80] This is confirmed by account B of the *Pas*, which stipulates that the house was situated exactly opposite the stage with the three judges 'pour les mieulx veoir, et tous les faisans, a son aise' (in order to see them better as well as all the participants, at his leisure).[81]

In this context, we should also devote some attention to the eponymous object of the *Pas* in Bruges: the *perron*. In medieval romances, a *perron* was a large stone used by knights to get on and off their horses, or a stone on which one could sit or lie. It often sported an inscription intended to give information to passersby. Two famous literary examples of a *perron* are the one supporting an anvil with a sword embedded in it that was destined to be pulled out by the future King Arthur in the *Roman de Merlin* (*c.*1200–10) and the floating *perron* from which Galahad would successfully remove another sword in the *Queste del Saint Graal* (*c.*1220–25). We also find *perrons* as simple columns in late

[76] Andrew Brown, 'Civic Ritual: Bruges and the Counts of Flanders in the Later Middle Ages', *The English Historical Review*, 112.446 (1997), 277–99 (pp. 292, 298).

[77] Brown, *Civic Ceremony*, pp. 121, 251. Since Charles left the town the day after (31 May), it is possible that he stayed in Bruges only in order to attend this specific ceremony.

[78] 'A Saint Donas au soir envoia la dame une More montee a cheval au bon chevalier, qui menoit ung cheval en main richement houchiet d'un velours gris sur quoy avoit trois coffres … ' (In the evening, at the church of St Donatian, the lady sent the good knight a Moorish woman mounted on a horse. She was leading by hand another horse that was richly trappered with grey velvet and was carrying three chests). PPF, p. 201.

[79] AR 32515 fol. 53v; Van den Abeele, 'De Wapenpas', p. 109. See also Source 11b, p. 243.

[80] The cost of the rent was 48lb. (of forty groats). AR 32515 fol. 53r. Charles of Charolais was lodged in another house at the Markt that was rented for a similar price.

[81] PPF, pp. 172–3.

medieval noble landscapes, as, for instance, in the September miniature of the castle of Saumur in the *Très Riches Heures du Duc de Berry*, where the *perron* is placed next to the tilting yard.[82] Nonetheless, it was not an exclusive symbol of noble or princely justice as some authors have suggested.[83] In cities such as Namur, Dinant, Huy and especially Liège, it was the symbol of local juridical authority. In November 1467, after Charles the Bold had defeated the rebellious Liégeois, the duke decided to remove the town's *perron* and send it to Bruges, where it was placed on the Beursplein, the square of the famous inn known as Van der Buerse.[84]

In the Arthurian-inspired tale of the *Perron Fée*, the *perron* encountered by the knight on the narrow path appears at first to be a simple stone from which a horn is hanging: 'un obstacle fait en maniere d'un perron … au dit perron pendoit un cor d'araing' (an obstacle in the form of a column … attached to this column was simply a brass horn).[85] It also sports an inscription. Later, the text suggests that someone might live in the *perron*.[86] Nonetheless, this first *perron* looks different from the magic one that holds Philippe prisoner, this latter being much more like an edifice. The B account describes it as being placed in the town of Brussels and that it was 'en forme de une roche de pierre dure et grise, et les trois escus noir, violet et gris pendans au perron' (in the shape of a rock made of hard grey stone. The three shields will be black, violet and grey); these were to be touched by Philippe's challengers.[87] It therefore had a practical function, just like trees had in other *pas*, with the difference here that Philippe was hidden inside it.[88] The account does not specify where the *perron* stood, so it could equally have been placed in the gardens of the Coudenberg Palace, the ducal residence, or in one of the more public spaces of the town, such as the Grote Markt. What was finally set up on the Markt in Bruges was indeed larger than the first description tells us. It was built on the north side of the Markt — that is, in front of and mirroring the belfry, which was situated on the south side — and painted in vivid colours. This large edifice, fourteen to fifteen feet

---

[82] For a reproduction of this miniature see Essay 2, p. 369, fig. 11.

[83] Jean-Pierre Jourdan, 'Le perron de chevalerie à la fin du Moyen Âge: aspects d'un symbole', in *Seigneurs et seigneuries au Moyen Âge*, Congrès national des sociétés historiques et scientifiques, 1992, Clermont-Ferrand, 117 (Paris: Éditions du CTHS, 1993), pp. 581–98; Élodie Lecuppre-Desjardin, *La ville des cérémonies: Essai sur la communication politique dans les anciens Pays-Bas bourguignons* (Turnhout: Brepols, 2004), pp. 208–9.

[84] Pierre François Xavier de Ram, ed., *Documents relatifs aux troubles du pays de Liège, sous les princes-évêques Louis de Bourbon et Jean de Horne, 1455–1505* (Brussels: Hayez, 1844), p. 366. Sydney Anglo, 'L'Arbre de chevalerie et le perron dans les tournois', in *Les fêtes de la Renaissance 3. Quinzième Colloque International d'études humanistes Tours, 10–22 Juillet 1972*, ed. by Jean Jacquot and Elie Konigson (Paris: Éditions du CNRS, 1975), pp. 283–98 (p. 298), mentions this but situates the removed Liège *perron* wrongly on the Markt. See also Marc Boone, 'Destroying and Reconstructing the City: The Inculcation and Arrogation of Princely Power in the Burgundian-Habsburg Netherlands (14th–16th Centuries)', in *The Propagation of Power in the Medieval West: Selected Proceedings of the International Conference. Groningen, 20–23 November 1997*, ed. by Martin Gosman, Arjo Vanderjagt and Jan Veenstra, Mediaevalia Groningana, 23 (Groningen: Forsten, 1996), pp. 1–33 (pp. 22–3).

[85] PPF, p. 98 (account C).

[86] See Source 11a, p. 208.

[87] PPF, p. 165.

[88] *Ibid.*, pp. 165–6 (account B). On the similar function of trees and *perrons*, see Anglo, 'L'Arbre'.

high, had a gate through which the *entrepreneur* could enter and leave the lists.[89] The town accounts reveal more about its ingenious construction:

> Item, betaelt den zelven … om eene aleye te makene daer de scilden van wapene an hijnghen met eene aleye bede te commene ende te rijdene uut ziner herberghe duer zijn perron in de bane; beede de henden van der voorseider bane te slutene met scuvende bailgen, buten ende binnen
>
> (Item, paid to the same [Master Anthonis Goossins, carpenter] … to make a covered alley where the shields with the coats of arms were hung, through which [alley he] could make his way from the inn [where he was staying] to the *perron* in the lists; to close off the ends of the alley with moving barriers, both inside and outside).[90]

Philippe could thereby access the *perron* without being seen by the audience. The narrative source informs us that the *perron* could open and close to the jousting area thanks to four griffins chained to its four corners which were operated by men concealed inside these artificial animals. This fictitious prison was securely closed: at the end of the *Pas*, a damsel (C) or the Lady herself (B) uses a golden key to open the *perron* and free the knight.[91] Next to three shields, coloured black, grey and violet, a horn was appended to the *perron* and the dwarf would blow it in order to bring the combat to an end. Thus, the *perron* could appeal to both noble and urban audiences, as the different meanings of the term made it possible for this Arthurian object to be adapted to an urban setting. For a medieval audience, the *perron* called to mind both romance episodes and urban and noble reality, hence fusing the imaginary and actual worlds.

Whilst all this may be true, the question remains as to whether this *pas* was, ultimately, a predominantly courtly event. Indeed, it could be organised only because of the presence of the duke, his high-ranking (international) guests and his household in the town; what is more, the move from Brussels to Bruges was caused by the itinerary of the duke and his court. The town seems to be nothing more than a stage on which Philippe de Lalaing and all the other challengers imposed their noble signature, and which, according to some historians, even served to settle a long-standing power dispute at the Burgundian court, namely that between adherents of Charles of Charolais and the clan of the Croÿ.[92] Significantly, the narrative sources stress the courtly character of the event, saying that 'il y ot plusieurs tables plaines de princes, princesses, chevaliers et escuiers, dames et damoiselles et non autres gens' (there were several tables filled with no one but princes, princesses, knights, squires, ladies and damsels).[93] They therefore give the impression that non-noble people were not present, hence downplaying the urban setting of the event and representing the *Pas* to their audience as an exclusively noble occasion.

Interestingly, the ducal financial accounts do not indicate that serious money was spent on this *pas*, such as in providing the *entrepreneur* with lavish gifts and household

---

[89] PPF, p. 106 (account C).

[90] AR 32515 fol. 36r; Van den Abeele, 'De Wapenpas', p. 109. See also Source 11b, p. 237.

[91] PPF p. 130 (account C), p. 199 (account B).

[92] Lecuppre-Desjardin, *La ville*, p. 205; see also Van den Abeele, 'De Wapenpas', pp. 114–15.

[93] PPF, p. 201 (account B).

officers with arms, armour or special gowns, as was the case for other chivalric events.[94] Moreover, when we analyse the social and professional background of the challengers who came to fight him, the *Pas* was far from being a pure courtly event. In May 1463, some 250 courtiers are mentioned on the paylists of the household as being present in Bruges.[95] We find only four jousters of the *Perron Fée* in these paylists: Philippe of Bourbon,[96] Antoine de Croÿ,[97] Philippe de Glimes and Thibaud de Luxembourg, lord of Fiennes, with Antoine of Burgundy, the Great Bastard, being notably absent. When we scrutinise the list of the challengers more broadly, we find another thirty courtiers who do not appear in the wage lists of May 1463, as most household officers were only paid for three months a year. Nonetheless, ten of them would acquire a position in the household after May 1463.[98] This means that only twenty-four of the fifty-two challengers — not even half of them — were attached to any of the princely households (Philip the Good, Charles of Charolais, Isabel of Portugal, Isabelle of Bourbon) at the time of the *Pas*.[99] Of these men, only three belonged to the select circle of thirty members of the Order of the Golden Fleece,[100] meaning that the *Pas* was a platform more for knights of lesser rank than for high-ranking noblemen. This suggests that a wider circle of nobles than just Fleece knights or household officers participated on this occasion. It also means that the *Pas* was set up as a rather open event, as is confirmed by the narrative sources, which state that, after the duke had fixed the new date and location of the *Pas*, 'il le fist publier en son hostel et par tous aultrez lieux' (he had this proclaimed at his court and in many other places).[101]

The participation of three local Flemish noblemen in the *Pas* — Willem van Stavele, viscount of Veurne, Daniël van Moerkerke and Josse Bonin/Joost Boonem — illustrates

---

94 See CL, pp. 28–9, for an analysis of the gifts bestowed on Jacques de Lalaing for the organisation of his feats of arms; and Damen, 'The Town, the Duke', for the duke's expenditure on a tournament in Brussels in May 1439.

95 PCB écrou no. 14196 (based on ADN B 3428 no. 117868), paylist of 4 May 1463. See also the paylist of 18 May (PCB écrou no. 14201), which is not very different from it.

96 PCB no. 4342. Not to be confused with Philippe of Bourbon, lord of Beaujeu (PCB no. 881). In 1474, he is mentioned as a chamberlain of Charles the Bold, meaning that he had been knighted. In 1463, however, he was still a squire.

97 He is mentioned as 'Antoine de Croÿ, seigneur de Sainpi' (PPF, p. 112). Van den Abeele, 'De Wapenpas', p. 120, suggests that this person should be identified as Philippe de Croÿ, the eldest son of Antoine's brother Jean, who would indeed inherit the lordship of Sempy from his father. However, in the paylist of 4 May 1463, Philippe is mentioned separately from the 'sire de Sempy', who is identified as Antoine de Croÿ in PCB no. 228. The presence of 'mijn heere van Croy' (my lord of Croÿ) in Bruges is also attested during the Holy Blood procession for the rent of a room from which he could see the event. AR 32515 fol. 51r. In short, the participation of Antoine, more than sixty years old at the time of the *Pas*, should not be ruled out.

98 The men in question are: Jean of Burgundy, son of Corneille, bastard of Burgundy (PCB no. 2473), Louis Chevallart (no. 2477), Charles de Courcelles (no. 2051), Dreux de Humières (no. 2615), Jean de Ligne (no. 2815), Jean de Rebreviette (no. 5003), Guillaume de Stavele (no. 2628), Jean de Trazegnies (no. 3247), Jean de Velu (no. 2831) and Joost van Wassenaar (no. 2488).

99 Compare Van den Abeele, 'De Wapenpas', p. 129, who counts nineteen courtiers including Henry de Chissey and Guillaume de Reichecourt, who, however, cannot be traced in the PCB database.

100 Charles of Charolais, Adolf of Cleves and Antoine de Croÿ.

101 PPF, p. 170 (account B).

both the open character of this event and the broader connections of the jousters. None of them had a household function at the time of the *Pas* and only Van Stavele would later be on the paylists of Charles the Bold in 1468–69.[102] Boonem was the only nobleman with local roots in Bruges, although his exact identity cannot be established: the authors may have been confused about his first name since it concerned not Joost/Josse but Joris (George) Bonin, who later won the prize of the lance at the feast of the White Bear in 1474, which made him the *forestier* for the feast of the following year.[103] In any case, Joost or Joris belonged to one of the wealthiest merchant and hosteller families of Bruges, who occupied important administrative functions in the administration of both the town and the Franc of Bruges and were active members of the jousting society of the White Bear.[104] Interestingly, it is not Joost or Joris, but rather his relatives Jan, Karel and Dirk Boonem, who are all mentioned in the household lists of Charles of Charolais and later Charles the Bold, testifying also to their close contacts with the ducal court.[105]

The importance of the *Pas* to the court is further demonstrated by the fact that seven of the challengers were high-ranking nobles of princely descent who are mentioned only as guests in the different households: these include Adolf of Cleves, lord of Ravenstein, Jacques of Bourbon and no fewer than five members of the Luxembourg dynasty, the three brothers Louis, Thibaud and Jacques, and two sons of Louis's, namely Antoine and Jean. The Luxembourgs had to navigate carefully between the interests of the Burgundian duke and the French king, their lands being spread over both their territories. During the years 1458–63, when Charles of Charolais was slowly advancing towards political and military leadership, the Luxembourgs showed their allegiance towards the future duke in both martial and cultural ways.[106] In the *Pas*, they sported black and violet, the

102 Frederik Buylaert, *Repertorium van de Vlaamse adel (ca. 1350–ca. 1500)* (Ghent: Academia Press, 2011), pp. 104–5, 645, 572–3; and PCB no. 2628 (Van Stavele). The absence of the renowned local nobleman Louis de Bruges, lord of Gruuthuse, is striking. Although he was the duke's stadholder, the duke's first representative in all his affairs, of the counties of Holland and Zeeland in The Hague from November 1462 onwards, he travelled to Bruges on 28 April 1463 and stayed in the duke's household for an entire month, handling some 'secret affairs', meaning that he was present during the whole of the *Pas*. ADN B 2058 fol. 161r.

103 ADN 7662 no. 157113.

104 Jean Jacques Gailliard, *Bruges et le Franc ou leur magistrature et leur noblesse, avec des données historiques et généalogiques sur chaque famille*, 6 vols (Bruges: Gaillard, 1857–64), vol. 6, pp. 298–305. See also Van den Abeele, 'De Wapenpas', p. 127. The Franc of Bruges (Dutch: Brugse Vrije) was one of the castellanies of the county of Flanders, consisting of the countryside around Bruges.

105 Jan (Jean) is mentioned as *échanson* (cupbearer) of Charles from 1457 onwards, but for the year 1463 he served only from July onwards. PCB no. 1916. For Karel (Charles) and Dirk (Thierry), see PCB nos 2286 and 3263.

106 In the *Cent Nouvelles nouvelles*, a collection of tales that is presented as being narrated at Philip the Good's court in 1458–59, the Luxembourgs figure prominently alongside some of their servants and clients, such as Antoine de La Sale and Jean V de Créquy, Philippe de Lalaing's uncle. Graeme Small, 'Tales from the Chamber. The *Cent Nouvelles nouvelles* between Burgundy and Luxembourg', in *The Cent Nouvelles nouvelles (Burgundy-Luxembourg-France, 1458–c. 1550): Text and Paratext, Codex and Context*, ed. by Graeme Small, Texte, Codex & Contexte, 23 (Turnhout: Brepols, 2023), pp. 267–90 (pp. 282–7). Since various members of the Créquy family played an important part in supporting Philippe de Lalaing during his *pas* (PPF, pp. 107, 131, 159, 173, 174, 198, 219), it is likely that there were also links of patronage, kinship and/or service between the Luxembourgs and Lalaings. On this point, see also CL, p. 140 n. 206.

colours of Charles of Charolais, testifying to their loyalty.[107] The embedding of the event within the Burgundian household was additionally strengthened by the involvement of a number of other household officers: three judges, three heraldic officers, one knight who acted as servant of the Lady of the Enchanted Column, and several nobles (including the duke himself) whose only task was to accompany either the *entrepreneur* or the challengers into the lists.

In short, staging the *Pas* in the urban setting of Bruges meant that both non-courtly audiences and participants other than just nobles attached to the court played a significant part in the event. Nonetheless, the presence and participation of the duke, his son, high-ranking guests from other princely families and household officers who played crucial roles, implies that the court put a significant stamp on the actual performance of the *Pas*.

THE TEXTUAL EVIDENCE OF THE *PAS DU PERRON FÉE*

Yet, despite the importance of the urban setting as revealed in the administrative sources discussed above, the literary sources say far less about it, as was typical of most *pas d'armes* narratives. Instead, they stress how Philippe conforms to models inherited from literature and vies to emulate romance characters such as Cleriadus, the hero of *Cleriadus et Meliadice*, a romance whose author's name has not come down to us, which was written in the 1440s and which expounds on the ideal career for a young knight (tournaments, *emprises*, crusade, marriage into a royal family). In this romance, Cleriadus organises an *emprise* that is a *pas d'armes* in all but name, in which he adopts the disguise of the 'Green Knight'.[108] An earlier romance, which was probably a model for *Cleriadus et Meliadice*, provides a similar scenario: in the anonymous *Ponthus et Sidoine*, written at the end of the fourteenth century, the main character, Ponthus, also sets up an *emprise* for the love of his lady, Sidoine.[109] In account C of the *Perron Fée*,[110] the setting (time of day, moor, ponds, *perron* and horn), the anonymity of the knight, the characters (the dwarf, the Lady) and the scenario (a *jeu-parti*) remind the readers, and presumably the medieval audience, of numerous Arthurian episodes. Arthurian romances were avidly read, copied and rewritten at the court of Burgundy. For instance, David Aubert, a learned scribe and writer working for Philip the Good, copied the lengthy *Roman de Perceforest* in 1459–60. In this romance, which purports to recount the prehistory of Arthur's kingdom, fifteenth-century knights could find all the requisite Arthurian paraphernalia. Account B opens with a prologue (absent from C) listing texts that might have encouraged Philippe de Lalaing to hold his *Pas*. *Perceforest* is mentioned twice in this list and, moreover, at the end of the prologue, the Lady is named 'la Toute Passe Dame du Perron Fée' (the Supreme Lady of the Enchanted Column), which recalls the name that one of the heroes of *Perceforest* gives to his lady: 'la Toutepasse' (the Supreme One), because her beauty and virtues surpass those of all other women in the kingdom of Great Britain. Since this *senhal* (code name) is not a common one, there is a good chance that it was borrowed from *Perceforest*.

---

107 Van den Abeele, 'De Wapenpas', p. 124.

108 On *Cleriadus et Meliadice*, see Michelle Szkilnik, 'Vraies et fausses réminiscences arthuriennes dans *Clériadus et Méliadice*', in *Arthur après Arthur: La matière arthurienne tardive en dehors du roman arthurien*, ed. by Christine Ferlampin-Acher (Rennes: Presses Universitaires de Rennes, 2017), pp. 27–40.

109 See Source 1.

110 See above, p. 402.

Indeed, the whole scenario is reminiscent of an episode from the beginning of *Perceforest*: Flavora, queen of the Royde Montagne, sends, thanks to her magic art, a *perron* to celebrate Perceforest's coronation. The stone is inscribed with letters announcing 'grandes merveilles' (wondrous events) and later on a mysterious knight ties two flying dragons to the *perron*. As suggested by Jean-Pierre Jourdan, who comments on this episode of *Perceforest* in his article on *perrons de chevalerie*, dragons or griffins play the same role and add to the mystery of the scene.[111]

Account B does not retell as precisely as C the circumstances that led to the anonymous knight becoming the prisoner of the Lady. While not drawing on Arthurian material as much as C does, B develops more fully a courtly situation: Philippe undertakes his *pas* for the love of the lady: 'il fault que faictes pour l'amour de moy ung pas d'armes courtoises sans nulle querelle aultre que d'amours' (you must undertake for love of me a courtly *pas d'armes*, with no other motive but love).[112] At the end of the *Pas*, the Lady herself releases Philippe, happy that he did so well and yet sad that they will have to part. Philippe shares her feelings and assures her that he will remain her knight forever. They exchange two kisses while tears come to their eyes. Later, when he is sent back to the court, Philippe refers to the lady as 'la Toute Passe du Perron faé, ma maistresse' (the Supreme Lady of the Enchanted Column, my lady).[113] In account C, the knight will never meet the lady whose prisoner he is, as he deals only with her messenger, the dwarf.[114] At the end, the damsel who frees him from his prison is not the Lady of the Enchanted Column, but rather her envoy. Conversely, in account B, Philippe and the lady meet several times; she comforts him when the *Pas* is moved to a later date, reassures him about his ability to make his way to where the challenge will take place (the *perron* and its prisoner can be magically transported at will), promises him a warm welcome at her court and, indeed, takes him to her chambers after his release, where they share wine and spices before retreating to separate rooms. Thus ends the amorous affair!

Although Philippe presumably devised the scenario himself,[115] its textual representation differs markedly from one account to the other: C is more magical whilst B is more courtly, which suggests that the authors of the different versions also had a distinct take on the event. Could the two accounts have been intended for different audiences? In B, the court of Burgundy plays a much larger role, as can be seen in a number of ways. First, the Lady appears to be acquainted with the duke and his visitors. She is aware of the presence of the duchesses of Bourbon (Agnès of Burgundy) and Guelders (Catherine of Bourbon) 'et aultres filles de Bourbon' (and other daughters of Bourbon)[116] at the time when Philippe will hold his *pas*, which seems to hint at the duke's endeavours to contract marriages for the sisters of his daughter-in-law, Isabelle of Bourbon.[117] Secondly, Limbourg Herald, who

---

[111] Jourdan, 'Le perron', p. 584.

[112] PPF, p. 158.

[113] *Ibid.*, p. 202.

[114] On the role of dwarfs in *pas d'armes*, see Essay 7.

[115] '… il conchupt en son entendement qu'il voulroit selon sa puissance ensievir en aulcunes fachons les bons chevalier dessusditz … il entreprist … de faire ung pas sur une fiction de faerie' ([he] envisioned himself following in these good knights' footsteps as best he could … he undertook … to hold a *pas* based on a fairylike narrative). PPF, pp. 156–7.

[116] *Ibid.*, p. 161.

[117] Strictly speaking, Catherine of Bourbon was not yet duchess of Guelders, as she would marry

is dispatched to court to announce Lalaing's challenge, interacts with noblemen and with the duke himself, who shows his surprise on hearing about the lady: 'Il ne ouÿ jamais parler que en son tamps les dames faees eussent puissance de regner ne seignourir en ses paÿs, et qu'il pensoit que l'ancien tamps revenoit comme il faisoit du temps du roy Artus' ([He] had never heard, in his day, that fairy ladies had the power to rule and govern over his lands; he felt as if the good old days of King Arthur had returned).[118] Although we don't know the identity of Limbourg Herald in 1463, we do know from the daily lists of wages of the household that he was present in Bruges in May together with Artois and Brabant Kings of Arms and Bourgogne Herald.[119] In 1449, Limbourg Herald touched the white shield of the defender Jacques de Lalaing at the *Fontaine des Pleurs* in the name of a nobleman called Jean de Villeneuve. At that time, Tristan Lombin occupied the office of Limbourg Herald. In 1468, it was Jacques Liefkens who held this office.[120] In the Royal Armouries Library manuscript (I.35), which preserves a copy of the B account of the *Perron Fée*, a Limbourg Herald is mentioned alongside Toison d'Or in the account of the joust that pitted Antoine of Burgundy against Anthony Woodville at Smithfield in England in June 1467. Whoever held that office in 1463 was therefore invested with an important function.

Thirdly, at the closure of the *Pas*, the Lady rides by the stands where the duke and his company are seated and greets them, before returning to her abode. Both accounts mention that the final banquet is hosted by the duke in the great hall of his residence in Bruges,[121] yet the image that each report gives of Philippe is quite different. In C, he is a victim of Fortune: 'puis que Fortune ainsi veult que adveuglement venu y soye, non obstant quelque dangier qui en peult ensuir …' (since Fortune is such that I came here recklessly, regardless of the dangers that might arise),[122] which puts him in the power of the Lady of the Enchanted Column, a Morgan-type fairy woman with whom no romantic involvement is possible, or even desirable. Thanks to his valour and virtue, Philippe manages to regain his freedom. As noted above, a damsel is sent by the Lady of the Enchanted Column to set him free after his last combat, yet there is no indication of Philippe's feelings or, for that matter, of hers. Curiously, the only 'amour' mentioned is the one that the duke of Burgundy himself displays towards the Lady when hosting the final banquet ('[le] beau banquet que mondit seigneur de Bourgoingne fist pour l'amour de laditte Dame du Perron Faé' (the sumptuous banquet organised by my lord

---

Adolf of Egmond, the future duke of Guelders, on 23 December 1463 in Bruges, and would become duchess only in 1465. Van den Abeele, 'De Wapenpas', pp. 103–4. It is therefore possible that Katharina of Cleves, the actual duchess of Guelders, is being referred to here. See also note II.9 in PPF, p. 226. The administrative sources attest only to the presence of 'madamoiselle Katherine de Bourbon, niepce de mon dit seigneur' (my lady Catherine of Bourbon, niece of the said lord), ADN B 2048 fol. 238r, and 'mijn vrauwen van Bourbon, zijnre zustre' (my lady of Bourbon, his sister), AR 32515 fol. 53r.

118 PPF, p. 164.

119 PCB écrou no. 14196 (based on ADN B 3428 no. 117868). Of these officers of arms, only Artois King of Arms, Mahieu Roussel, is paid 6lb. (of forty groats) by the town administration 'in de name van den andren cuenynghen van wapenen over trecht ende tlossen van den lijsten' (in the name of other Kings of Arms, for the rights and obligations of the lists). AR 32515 fol. 53v. On Roussel, see PCB no. 709.

120 PCB no. 5063; CL, p. 232.

121 PPF, p. 131 (account C); p. 201 (account B).

122 *Ibid.*, p. 99.

of Burgundy for love of the Lady of the Enchanted Column).[123] Moreover, *amour* here merely means 'regard' or, at the most, 'friendliness'. In B, in contrast, the Lady seems amorous and Philippe, as we have seen, does fight for love of her. Although the fiction of a love affair is curtailed, Philippe comes across as a Lancelot-type character, whose value increases through his love for his lady.[124] In short, the two accounts offer a different image of the Lady and of her relationship to both Philippe and the court of Burgundy: whereas in C she is mysterious and somewhat threatening, in B she appears as a much more benevolent figure, being eager to uphold the interests of the court of Burgundy. This image may have been more agreeable to the duke.

The *brevets* presented to Philippe's challengers at the banquet tend to minimise this difference between the two accounts. While account B mentions the awarding of the brevets but does not specify how they came to be written, account C states that the Lady had them specially composed for each of Philippe's challengers in order to reflect his specific qualities.[125] That she is the one who sponsored the writing of these little poetic pieces modifies her image somewhat. Although distant and seemingly forbidding, she is nonetheless willing to celebrate courtly values. The *brevets* were very probably produced by a herald, the one supposedly in the service of the Lady, perhaps Limbourg,[126] and may have circulated independently. In the end, however, all the accounts had to mention them, praise the event and the participants.

Of the four manuscripts preserving the C account, three are dedicated to celebrating the Lalaing family and this is unlikely to be coincidental. Of the two now in a private collection, that of the present-day Comte de Lalaing, one is dated after 1507, the other from 1518.[127] They contain *Les Faits de Jacques de Lalaing*, Jacques de Lalaing's epitaph, the *Pas du Perron Fée*, *Sepultures d'aulcuns de la maison de Lalaing*,[128] *Epitaphe de Simon de Lalaing*, *Epitaphe de Josse de Lalaing*, *Blason des Armes de Lalaing* and *Epitaphes en prose de Simon, Josse et Charles II de Lalaing*.[129] Anne-Marie Legaré, in her study of these two codices, has convincingly shown that they were intended to preserve the memory of the Lalaing family. At that time, all the children of Guillaume de Lalaing and Jeanne de Créquy, representing the elder branch of the family, had died. The second branch, descended from Simon de Lalaing, had acquired the lordship of Lalaing. The first manuscript was owned by either Charles I de Lalaing, eldest son of Josse de Lalaing, or his younger brother Antoine, who, possibly inspired by these books, organised his own *pas* in Brussels in 1503.[130] The second one, a private commission from Charles I, was compiled to 'perpétuer la mémoire de son ancêtre Jacques' (perpetuate the memory of his ancestor Jacques). Legaré concludes that the book is a 'véritable réceptacle

---

[123] *Ibid.*, p. 133.

[124] On the agency of women in *pas d'armes*, see especially Essay 6.

[125] See the introduction to Source 11a, p. 207.

[126] On the *brevets*, see PPF, pp. 31–4.

[127] CL, pp. 55–6.

[128] See Anne-Marie Legaré, '*Les Faits de Jacques de Lalaing* enluminés par le Maître d'Antoine Rolin', in '*Als ich can*': *Liber amicorum in Memory of Professor Dr. Maurits Smeyers*, ed. by Bert Cardon, Jan Van der Stock and Dominique Vanwijnsberghe, 2 vols (Leuven/Dudley, MA: Peeters, 2002), vol. 2, pp. 773–93, who omits this text in her list of contents, no doubt because it was copied by a different scribe.

[129] The manuscripts preserve basically the same texts, but in a different order: see *ibid.*, pp. 778, 780.

[130] On this *pas*, see Essay 1 and Source 14.

de la mémoire d'une famille' (an authentic repository of the memory of a family).[131] As for manuscript Brussels, KBR, II 1156, dating from about 1560, it is, in its first half, a mirror copy of the 1507 manuscript: it contains the same texts, in the same order and with the same errors.[132] Contrary to what Claude Thiry, who described the codex in a 1973 article, has suggested,[133] the unique copyist of the Brussels manuscript was not compiling items from different codices — at least for the first half of his book — and neither is he responsible for the numerous mistakes that Thiry deplored.[134] Thiry does not give any information on who the sixteenth-century owners of KBR, II 1156 might have been. Yet, whoever compiled this substantial manuscript was likewise intent on consciously preserving the memory of the Lalaing family, since he retained all the texts given by his model.

If the aim of these three collections was to celebrate the Lalaing dynasty as devout and religious, account C was a better choice than account B. Although B does stress family connections, naming two sons of Simon de Lalaing who accompanied Philippe de Lalaing into the lists, and mentioning explicitly the lord of Boussu as Philippe's brother-in-law,[135] these connections are essentially mundane and confirm Philippe's image as a knight well ensconced in a courtly setting. Jacques de Lalaing, Philippe's brother, is consistently presented as a pious knight and a fervent devotee of the Virgin Mary. As we have already noted, Jacques never married and we have no knowledge of any amorous affair that he might have had, whereas Philippe must have had some romance because he fathered children, albeit illegitimate ones, and it is impossible to know if Philippe's children even had the same mother. The love scenario, described in account B as Philippe's very own invention, sounds consistent with his free and easy attitude towards women and sexuality. Yet it conflicted with his brother's upright behaviour. Account C, which makes Philippe the victim of a predatory woman, but one able to extricate himself from a dangerous situation, offered a model that was closer to that of his brother Jacques. Although terming the lady in account C 'predatory' may seem a little strong, she nonetheless remains mysterious and distant, her domain being a dangerous place that is guarded by hostile characters, such as the haughty dwarf and the four griffins. Philippe is not defending a besieged lady who requires help; rather, he is trying to escape her and, like Lancelot when made prisoner by Morgain,[136] he is forced to accept the dire conditions that the lady imposes on him. Of course, in B Philippe is also a prisoner, but, as seen above, the lady is much more amenable, since she sounds almost sorry to have to retain Philippe and love seems to be her motivation. If, as suggested by Hanno Wijsman, Guillaume de Lalaing may

---

[131] Legaré, '*Les Faits*', pp. 785, 788.

[132] These are: *Les Faits de Jacques de Lalaing* (fols 1r–226r) his epitaph (fols 226r–227r), *Le Pas du Perron Fée* (fols 227r–259r), *Sepultures d'aulcuns de la maison de Lalaing* (fol. 260r), *Epitaphe de feu messire Simon de Lalaing* (fols 260v–261v), *Epitaphe de monseigneur Josse de Lalaing* (fols 262r–264r), *Le Blason des Armes de Lalaing* (fols 264v–267v), *Epitaphes en prose de Simon, Josse et Charles II de Lalaing* (fols 268r–269r). The texts that follow these are unrelated to the Lalaing family. Legaré, '*Les Faits*', p. 774 n. 11, mentions that the Brussels manuscript is related to Valenciennes, BM, 665, at least for the copy of the *Faits de Jacques de Lalaing*.

[133] Claude Thiry, 'Un inédit de Jean Molinet: l'épitaphe de Josse de Lalaing, sire de Montigny (1483)', *Bulletin de la Commission royale d'Histoire*, 139.1 (1973), 29–66.

[134] *Ibid.*, p. 57.

[135] PPF, p. 174.

[136] Alexandre Micha, ed., *Lancelot: roman en prose du XIIIe siècle*, Textes littéraires français, 9 vols (Geneva: Droz, 1978), vol. 5.

have commissioned the *Livre des faits* because of his regret at 'his lack of male offspring in general and his famous son's death in particular',[137] might he also have been responsible for account C and the less amorous image of Philippe that this version promotes? In this case, C would be later than B, and would have been written as a mean of correcting Philippe's image in this earlier version.

The six manuscripts preserving account B consist mainly of texts that deal with jousting and chivalrous celebrations. For one of these, London, BL, Lansdowne 285, we have valuable information: this manuscript is a miscellany largely copied around 1469 by William Ebesham for Sir John Paston II, although the account of the *Perron Fée* seems to have been written in another hand and probably at a slightly later date.[138] It comprises texts written in English, in French and even in Latin, showing Paston's fascination with courtly rituals: celebrations, jousts, descriptions of feasts and banquets, privileges granted to heralds and Kings of Arms, and so on. The *Perron Fée* fits perfectly into this textual environment. We know that, in 1468, John Paston II attended Margaret of York's marriage to Charles the Bold in Bruges.[139] The memory of Philippe's *Pas* was surely still vivid at that date and it could be then that John Paston obtained a copy of the *Perron Fée*. In any case, the memory of Philippe's brother Jacques was still very much alive, as it is shortly after this time that his father Guillaume probably commissioned his biography.

As for the other manuscripts, we know that some were owned by heralds or Kings of Arms.[140] The fact that Limbourg Herald plays a prominent role in the first part of account B may explain why it was preferred to account C by these owners, presuming again that both versions circulated widely enough so that copyists and/or their patrons could make an informed choice between them. As we have seen, in C the dwarf is the knight's only interlocutor and mediator with the lady. He takes the knight over to the judges at the end of the jousts and back to the *perron*.[141] There is no mention of a herald, as we do not know either the identity or the status of the narrator bringing the letter of arms to the court. In B, by contrast, Limbourg Herald is as important as the dwarf. He not only takes the letter to the court of Burgundy, reads it publicly and gives details about the knight's whereabouts, but also brings back the duke's answer and confers with the lady before reporting to the knight and the dwarf, even admonishing the latter to act accordingly, a remark that elicits a haughty response from the dwarf. Limbourg is also in charge of taking down the shields that the would-be challengers have appended to the *perron* before the event. Whereas C does mention that the knights have left their shields beforehand, nothing is said about their circumstances afterwards.[142] Limbourg's significant role in account B is consistent with the importance of heralds in organising,

---

137 Hanno Wijsman, 'The Visual Tradition of the *Book of the Deeds of Jacques de Lalaing*', in *A Knight for the Ages: Jacques de Lalaing and the Art of Chivalry*, ed. by Elizabeth Morrison (Los Angeles: The J. Paul Getty Museum, 2018), pp. 107–20 (p. 107).

138 Five hands can be discerned in it. See PPF, p. 53 n. 102. On this manuscript, see Godfrey Allen Lester, *Sir John Paston's Grete Boke: A Descriptive Index with an Introduction of British Library MS. Lansdowne 285* (Woodbridge: Boydell & Brewer, 1984).

139 *Ibid.*, p. 132.

140 For instance, Lille, Royal Armouries, Harley.

141 PPF, p. 129.

142 *Ibid.*, p. 103.

staging and reporting on *pas d'armes* and tournaments. It is indeed surprising that C seems to ignore the likely presence of one of them in the event. Félix Brassart, who edited the Paris manuscript, has suggested that the anonymous narrator, who claims to have brought Philippe de Lalaing's letter of arms to the court of Burgundy, might be Limbourg, who did indeed do this, according to account B.[143] If Limbourg was therefore the author of C, he downplayed his own part to the extent of literally erasing his character, an act of modesty fairly common on the part of heralds. For example, Gilles Gobet, the successor of Jean Lefèvre de Saint-Rémy as Toison d'or King of Arms and the possible author of the *Livre des faits*, likewise downplays his role in Jacques de Lalaing's biography.[144] Gobet might have been one of the subordinates mentioned in the *Perron Fée*.[145] This would not only strengthen the connection between the *Livre des faits* and the accounts of the *Perron Fée*, but also highlight the family's role in acquiring manuscripts about their sons' deeds. Conversely, it is much more difficult to suggest who might have written accounts A and B. It could have been Jean Lefèvre de Saint-Rémy, who held the office of Toison d'or in 1463, or one of his subordinates, who were in charge of reporting on the deeds of arms performed by knights of the Order of the Golden Fleece. Strikingly, only three (albeit high-ranking) members of this Order acted as challengers in the *Pas*, whereas four others (Jacques of Bourbon, Jean de Ligne, Jean and Jacques de Luxembourg) would become members of it at a later stage.

According to an inventory taken in 1471 at his castle in Angers, René of Anjou owned a manuscript of the *Pas*. We do not know which account of the event it preserved. The title in the inventory does, however, provide a clue: 'un cayer en papier rollé du pas fait à Brucelles par messir Phelipe de Lalain' (a rolled quire [containing] the *pas* held in Brussels by Messire Philippe de Lalaing).[146] Whilst it is impossible to match this short description with any of the remaining manuscripts with any certainty, the fact that the *pas d'armes* is wrongly located in Brussels suggests that the *cayer* preserved the B version of the text. As we have seen, C quickly establishes that the *Pas* took place in Bruges whereas the B account only specifies the location much later. The person responsible for the inventory may have read only the beginning of the account and believed that the *Pas* had indeed taken place in Brussels. It is impossible to ascertain whether René of Anjou chose account B rather than C on purpose. On the one hand, the C account, with its Arthurian trappings, might have appealed to a writer who was himself fascinated by the Arthurian world; on the other hand, René might have enjoyed the humour and lightheartedness of account B.[147]

The conclusions one can draw from the manuscript tradition thus remain fragmentary and tentative as there is so much that is unknown: who wrote the various accounts of the *Pas*, and for whom? Although it is tempting to hypothesise that Guillaume de Lalaing was responsible for account C, this must remain a supposition. For some codices, the history of their transmission undoubtedly provides information on the way the *Perron Fée* was read at the time when the manuscripts were composed or later on. Yet, as we have cautiously

---

143 Brassart, *Le blason*, p. 18.

144 CL, pp. 53–4.

145 See, for instance, PPF, pp. 107, 172–4.

146 Mentioned by Brassart, *Le Pas*, p. 15. See also ECMR, p. 262.

147 On René and his taste for *pas d'armes* and jousting, see Essays 2 and 7 on the *Pas de la Joyeuse Garde*/ *Pas de Saumur* and Source 5.

underlined here, it is difficult, perhaps impossible, to assert that retaining one account over another was an informed and conscious choice on any particular patron or reader's part.

CONCLUSION

According to Richard Vaughan, the modern biographer of the Burgundian dukes, the battle of Montlhéry on 16 July 1465 'was bloody but indecisive'.[148] Philippe de Lalaing was one of the few of the 300–400 men who lost their lives there to be remembered by name by various chroniclers. Philippe de Commynes thinks he died in the battle 'pour estre mal armé' (because he was poorly equipped), whereas Jean de Haynin indicates that Philippe was buried in Montlhéry on 18 July with the assistance of his brother Antoine and his uncle Jean V de Créquy, who also formed part of the army of Charles of Charolais.[149] His being remembered at all in this fashion cannot be due solely to his link to his more famous brother, but rather should be ascribed to Philippe's own deeds of arms on the battle and tournament fields and the fulfilment of his vow of the Pheasant, even though he never reached Constantinople.

As we have argued here, Philippe's motives for organising the *Pas* are not entirely clear. If he did so in a spirit of emulation, as stated in the prologue of the B account, it was not in imitation of his brother's *pas d'armes* in Chalon-sur-Saône (which was different both in setup and context, with the court virtually absent), but could rather be interpreted as his bid to become a member of the Order of the Golden Fleece. Although he did not ultimately achieve this aim because of his untimely death, the organisation of the *Perron Fée* and his own performance in it certainly contributed to his fame.

The different accounts of the *Perron Fée* do mention the urban setting of the *Pas* but they do not go into detail about this aspect; it is likely that the viewpoint of the authors was that the noble audience of these manuscripts would not be interested in reading too many details of that sort because these would reduce the *Pas* to an urban occasion. Yet, the *Perron Fée* was clearly embedded in a busy cycle of urban events that even resulted in a pause in the jousting in the first week of May. Bruges was eager to receive the duke and his son Charles, the crown prince, and went to great efforts to make the event a success, providing financial, material and logistical support where needed. The town was used to organising annual jousting festivities and the urban population was accustomed to attending and 'interpreting' them. At the same time, the *perron* as an object was not strictly either 'urban' or 'noble', as it appealed to a variety of audiences. The interplay of town, duke and nobles — either attached to the ducal household or aspiring to be so — is fundamental to understanding the success of this particular event. Yet the narratives — and for most *pas d'armes* this is the only document that survives — tend to downplay the role of urban institutions and stress instead the agency of the *entrepreneur*, a decision that makes perfect sense given that *pas d'armes* were chivalric accomplishments geared towards celebrating courtly life and values.

The simple fact that the *Perron Fée* is recorded in three different versions, of which eleven manuscripts have survived, attests clearly to its popularity. Three of these codices preserve texts celebrating the Lalaing dynasty, the first one being invariably the *Livre des*

[148] Vaughan, *Philip the Good*, pp. 385–7.
[149] Blanchard, ed., *Mémoires*, p. 112; JDH, vol. 1, pp. 42–3.

faits de messire Jacques de Lalaing. Undoubtedly, whoever commissioned and/or compiled these collections made a conscious effort to promote a glorious image of the best-known members of the elder branch of the family. Although the second branch is represented, with the epitaphs of Simon de Lalaing and his son Josse, it is noteworthy that the first two texts are devoted to the glorious deeds of the two brothers, as if to underline that, although this branch was on the brink of extinction — since, by 1470, three of the four Lalaing brothers, Jacques, Philippe and Antoine, had died without legal issue[150] — the memory of it was still very much alive and needed to be kept as such. Yet, it is also significant that the *Perron Fée* mostly circulated independently of the biography of Jacques, and it is striking that the account that was the most widely disseminated of all retains what we have termed the 'courtly scenario'. Paradoxically, then, if the Lalaing family were intent on preserving an image of the two brothers as austere knights devoted to their prince and to lofty ideals, this did not succeed very well in the case of Philippe.

[150] Guillaume de Lalaing and Jeanne de Créquy's only living son, Jean, was a cleric and could not formally inherit his father's lordships. According to Brassart, *Le blason*, pp. 95–8, he did not lead a particularly exemplary life, having had a relationship with the daughter of the Lalaing miller, with whom he had five children, later legitimised when he married their mother. In order to prevent the Lalaing lordships from falling to his sister Yolande's children and therefore the name of the family from becoming extinct, Jean sold the Lalaing lordships to his cousin, Josse. CL, pp. 37–42.

Thanks are due to Rosalind Brown-Grant and Jan Dumolyn for their insightful comments on earlier versions of this essay.

Marina Viallon

'In the Way of the Knights-Errant': the Sixteenth-Century Legacy of a Roleplay Game from the *Pas des armes de Sandricourt* (1493)

At the beginning of the French Renaissance period, starting around 1500, chivalry was still an essential part of the everyday life of the nobility, with tournaments being its most spectacular and lavish public manifestation. Most French Renaissance tournaments followed the form of the *pas d'armes*, to the extent that by the end of the fifteenth century the terms 'tournament' and '*pas* (*d'armes*)' had become synonymous and were used interchangeably. From then on, in France, a tournament was called a *pas* whenever it adopted the structure of a group of *tenans** (defenders) challenging a group of *venans** (attackers) to fight in one or more *emprises*, meaning the different types of combat proposed at the event.[1] Whilst keeping this basic framework, these sixteenth-century French '*pas d'armes*' evolved in many varied forms, with some remaining very close to the fifteenth-century tradition, being almost like 're-enactments'. Indeed, if some of them could take the form of complex scenarios with settings and costumes, many had no theme at all, but their form itself already referred to traditional chivalric literature, as this pattern was inspired by the literary trope of the knight-errant seeking adventure and encountering adversaries on his way or defending a place, an idea or a person against external challengers. When they did have a particular theme, French Renaissance tournaments could refer to contemporary warfare, oriental figures, chivalric literature or classical culture, or to a mixture of all of these.[2] The term *pas* (*d'armes*) is found in the publication of many tournament regulations in sixteenth-century France, and even in the official name of some of them,[3] such as the *Pas des armes de l'Arc Triomphal*, the title given to the great tournament held in Paris in November 1514 to celebrate the Royal Entry of Queen Mary Tudor, Louis XII's new wife.[4]

In the Renaissance, the form of the *pas d'armes* was often linked to the idea of dividing the competitors into teams called *bandes*. The *bande* referred to a military company and comprised a group of knights led by a captain. The captain's name was then used to

[1] In late medieval and Renaissance tournaments held in France, each different type of combat constituting a *pas d'armes* was referred to as an *emprise*.

[2] See Marina Viallon, 'Never-Ending Chivalry: Tournaments in Renaissance France from Charles VIII to Louis XIII', in *Tournament: A Thousand Years of Chivalry*, ed. by Stefan Krause (Vienna: Kunsthistorisches Museum/London: Thomas del Mar, 2022), pp. 101–15. See also Marina Viallon, 'Les tournois à la cour de France à la Renaissance' (unpublished PhD dissertation, École Pratique des Hautes Études, Paris, 2023).

[3] *L'ordre et les articles du tournoy, entrepris pour la selennité du tresheureux couronnement et triumphante entrée du treschrestien Roy Henry, second de ce nom, nostre souverain Seigneur, et de la Royne son espouse, nostre souveraine Dame* (Paris: Jean André, 1549), n.p.

[4] See GCM.

designate the *bande* and, even when the combats were in fact individual, as in the case of jousts, it was always noted which team a knight belonged to. Symbolically, the captain was the main *venan* responding to the challenge and members of his *bande* were his *aides* (helpers), with the latter usually wearing their leader's colours. During collective combats, such as *mêlées*, the whole *bande* would fight together; for individual combats, all members of the same team would make their entry, then fight one after another against the *tenans* before the next team did the same. *Bandes*, however, were not the exact equivalent of today's sports teams because, except for group fighting, their number could vary within the same event and no prizes were given to the whole group but only to individuals. Sometimes, various *venans* would even come unaffiliated to a *bande*, whether alone or in a small group without a captain. Most of the time, these unaffiliated knights presented themselves under pseudonyms taken from medieval romance or as knights-errant coming from faraway lands.[5] The term knight-errant originates from the French *chevalier errant* (wandering knight) and was very prominent among the chivalric themes used in French Renaissance tournaments. The knight-errant was an ideal straight from the pages of chivalric romance, that of a lonely figure wandering the land, seeking adventure and opportunities to undertake deeds of arms that were important enough to be remembered. If this theme was usually illustrated in France by the names adopted by the participants, the settings or the costumed characters, it also inspired a very original and specific style of *pas d'armes* that brought the embodiment of the theme to a whole other level, this being usually referred to at the time as tournaments 'in the way of the knights-errant'.

This chapter discusses the first documented occurrence of this unusual form of tournament event in the context of the *Pas des armes de Sandricourt* (1493) and reveals how the detailed narrative account produced of it, which was also the first independent tournament account to appear in early printed form, influenced other *pas d'armes* organised later in the sixteenth century, each of which adapted this form to the circumstances of the specific event into which it was inserted.

THE *PAS* AT SANDRICOURT

This 'quest of the knights-errant' was first documented during one of the most famous late medieval French tournaments: the *Pas des armes de Sandricourt*, or *Pas de Sandricourt*, held on 16–20 September 1493. Sandricourt, located about 50 km north of Paris, consisted at the time of a small piece of land with farms clustered around a castle that no longer exists. The tournament was organised by the chief *entrepreneur*, Louis de Hédouville, lord of Sandricourt, who obtained permission from King Charles VIII (1470–98) for it to be held and for its *articles*[6] or chapters of arms — the set of rules and all information related to the event — to be proclaimed in Paris and other cities in the kingdom in the hope of attracting participants from all over France. The memory of this tournament survives

[5] For example, at the tournament held in Paris in June 1549 for the Royal Entry of King Henry II and Queen Catherine de' Medici, six 'knights-errant from Ferrara' and an 'adventurer from Cyprus' showed up alongside the traditional *bandes*. See the report of this event by the ambassador of Mantua in Riccardo Truffi, *Giostre e cantori de giostre* (Rocca S. Casciano: L. Capelli, 1945), pp. 221–2.

[6] In late fifteenth-century France, the term *articles* replaced the term *chapitres*, but the two terms are synonymous.

Figure 26. Foot combat at the barrier with spears. Orléans Herald, *Le pas des armes de Sandricourt* (Paris: A. Vérard, 1493). Paris, BnF, Vélins 1034, fol. A5v. Photo: BnF.

mostly thanks to an official account composed by Orléans Herald and printed shortly after the event.[7]

The *pas*, originally planned to start on 15 September, was indeed first officially announced on 24 August in Paris before being proclaimed elsewhere in France, although the names of these other 'villes, citez et places' (towns, cities and places) remain unknown.[8] The tournament proposed four *emprises* set in three different locations around the castle of Sandricourt, all of which were referred to by names inspired by courtly romance. The first of these was a foot combat with spear and sword at the *barrière périlleuse* (Perilous Barrier) situated in front of the castle gate (Figure 26). The second event consisted of several *mêlées*, or mock battles on horseback, fought with lances and then swords, at the *carrefour ténébreux* (Tenebrous Crossroads), at which a fenced arena with stands, called the *champ de l'épine* (Field of Thorn), had been built. The third *emprise*, individual jousts* in the open field, first with the lance and then with the sword, was then set in this latter location (Figure 27).

---

[7] Orléans (Herald), *Le pas des armes de Sandricourt* (Paris: A. Vérard, 1493). For a transcription of this printed version, see VT, pp. 147–70. For a transcription (in modernised French) of the 1500–10 version of the narrative account from Paris, BnF Arsenal, 3958 Réserve ([hereafter Arsenal 3958], see René Botto, *L'Isle-Adam et sa région au temps des tournois, 1493 et 1519* (L'Isle-Adam: Les amis de L'Isle-Adam, 2007), pp. 20–54. For an edition that amalgamates these two versions, see Louis-Augustin Vayssière, ed. *Le Pas des armes de Sandricourt: Relation d'un tournoi donné en 1493 au château de ce nom, publiée d'après un manuscrit de la Bibliothèque de l'Arsenal et l'imprimé du temps* (Paris: L. Willem, 1874) (= PSt); see also Source 13, page references to which have also been supplied here for ease of cross-referencing.

[8] Orléans (Herald), *Le pas des armes*, fol. A3r; VT, p. 150; PSt, p. 11.

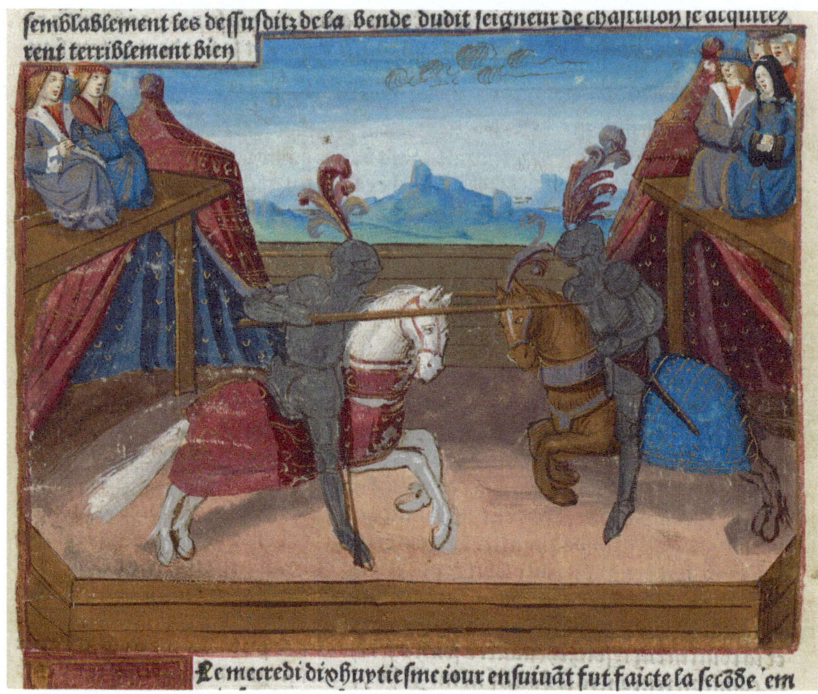

Figure 27. Joust in open field. Orléans Herald, *Le pas des armes de Sandricourt* (Paris: A. Vérard, 1493). Paris, BnF, Vélins 1034, fol. B1r. Photo: BnF.

The final event, which took place on the last day, the 'knights-errant challenge', was held in the nearby wood dubbed the *forêt dévoyable* (Labyrinthine Forest) for the occasion.

The tournament of Sandricourt finally began on Monday 16 September. Among the ten *tenans* were Louis de Hédouville and his brother Jean, lord of Frémécourt, with other knights drawn from among their friends and relatives, such as Jacques de Dinteville, who was in the service of the duke of Orléans, as were the Hédouvilles, and Pierre d'Orgemont, lord of Méry, a place located near to Sandricourt, who was also at that time a member of the royal household, as was Louis de Hédouville. Forty-one *venans* responded to the challenge, these being organised in three *bandes* of ten knights that were led, respectively, by Jacques de Coligny, lord of Châtillon, André de Valois, and Antoine Martel, lord of Beaumont. The remaining eleven challengers were unaffiliated to any group and participated only in the jousts and the knights-errant challenge. In order to be admitted to the combats, participants were invited beforehand to register with heralds and to hang their heraldic shields at the castle gate. On the first day, at ten o'clock in the morning, the first combat at the barriers saw the *tenans* facing Châtillon's *bande*; the second, at four o'clock in the afternoon, was against that of Valois. The following morning, Beaumont's *bande* fought the last foot combat; in the afternoon between four and five o'clock, the second *emprise*, the *mêlées*, started, with Châtillon's *bande* squaring up to the ten *tenans* (Figure 28). The initial charge with the lance, however, was so violent that not only were many horses frightened, wounded or even killed, but some riders were also injured. This caused the judges to request the participants in the two remaining *mêlées* to fight individually with their lances and only to fight all together for the combat with swords. The *venans* were initially unhappy with this change of plan,

Figure 28. *Mêlée* at the *pas*. Orléans Herald, *Le pas des armes de Sandricourt* (Paris: A. Vérard, 1493). Paris, BnF, Vélins 1034, fol. B3v. Photo: BnF.

claiming that it was unfair to make them engage in a less dangerous — and thus less honourable — form of combat than that which the first *bande* had done. Thanks to the intercession of the ladies, however, they eventually accepted the new rule and, on Wednesday 18 September, the Valois and Beaumont *bandes* continued the second *emprise*. On the following day, from nine o'clock in the morning until dusk, the *tenans* (substituted by some members of Châtillon's *bande* when they needed to rest),[9] jousted in the open field against 'tous venans' (all comers),[10] running one course with sharpened lances and exchanging thirteen strokes with sharp-edged swords without thrusting points. Here the *venans* were no longer fighting as *bandes*, and thirty of these combats are recorded as having taken place on that day.

If these three types of combat were very fashionable in France at that time, the fourth and final one of Sandricourt's *emprises*, that held on 20 September, was more original and unusual. For the 'quête (quest)[11] of the *forêt dévoyable*, as described in the chapters of arms, the *tenans* left the castle in the morning in order to wander at random, two by two, in the nearby forest and its surrounding fields, 'querans leurs advantures, comme faisoient jadis les seigneurs de la Table Ronde' (looking for adventure as the lords of the Round Table

[9] It was common practice during long jousting contests for *tenans* to have substitutes, called *aides* (helpers), who often belonged to the teams of *venans* but who fought as *tenans* on a specific day. This is particularly prevalent, for example, in later important royal tournaments such as the *Pas des armes de l'Arc Triumphal* or the Field of Cloth of Gold in 1520. See Viallon, 'Les tournois', p. 24.

[10] Orléans (Herald), *Le pas des armes*, fol. A3v; VT, p. 151; PSt, p. 35.

[11] Orléans (Herald), *Le pas des armes*, fol. A3r; VT, p. 150; PSt, p. 10.

Figure 29. Participants entering the *forêt dévoyable*. Orléans Herald, *Le pas des armes de Sandricourt* (Paris: A. Vérard, 1493). Paris, BnF, Vélins 1033, fol. B4r. Photo: BnF.

used to do) (Figure 29).[12] Shortly after they left, all the *venans* did the same. Participants rode around the forest for the whole day, engaging in combat whenever a *tenan* came across a *venan*. Spectators of the tournament, including the ladies, also rode about at random in the same area, watching the combats that they encountered by chance or by following one particular knight. Throughout the day gentlemen and servants, based somewhere near the forest, offered food and beverages to the audience and to participants who needed to rest (Figure 30).

Whilst most of the knights fought on horseback with lances and swords, some, exceptionally, chose to fight on foot. For example, Thomas de May, one of the *venans*, sent a herald round towards the end of the day to find out if any of the knights-errant would fight on foot against him with five thrusts of the spear and thirteen strokes with the sword. Another *venan*, Germain de La Roque, nicknamed 'Le Bœuf' (The Ox), took up the challenge, and both men met in a field along the edge of the forest, watched by most of the audience and other knights returning from their own quests. The combat, as described in the official account of the tournament, was long and intense, and Le Bœuf's armour ended up being pierced three times by his opponent's spear (Figure 31). If it seems strange that a combat between two *venans*, as opposed to one between a *tenan* and a *venan*, was deemed admissible, we should remember that Thomas de May challenged his opponent in character — that is, whilst he was acting as the knight-errant of a story setting up an *emprise d'armes*. In other words, this final form of challenge was effectively a kind of tournament

[12] Orléans (Herald), *Le pas des armes*, fol. A4r; VT, p. 152; PSt, p. 15.

Figure 30. Refreshments given to the participants and spectators of the knights-errant challenge in the *forêt dévoyable*. Orléans Herald, *Le pas des armes de Sandricourt* (Paris: A. Vérard, 1493). Paris, BnF, Vélins 1034, fol. B4v. Photo: BnF.

Figure 31. Foot combat between Thomas de May and Germain de La Roque in the *forêt dévoyable*. Orléans Herald, *Le pas des armes de Sandricourt* (Paris: A. Vérard, 1493). Paris, BnF, Vélins 1034, fol. B5r. Photo: BnF.

within a tournament. As all the competitors were randomly scattered around the area, the judges and heralds, just like the rest of the audience, could not attend and supervise every fight, which thereby increased the risk of injury, as no one would be around to stop a combat if it became too violent or life-threatening. During a supervised tournament, when such a thing happened, the marshals — acting on either their own initiative or at the command of judges — would separate the fighters with the help of batons or spears. When everyone was back at the castle of Sandricourt for the night and gathered together for the final banquet, the contestants were, one by one, expected to tell the judges and ladies all about their adventures that day, starting with the *tenans*, swearing on their honour to stick to the truth. If no prizes were either promised or awarded for this particular challenge or indeed for the whole tournament, there is no doubt that the storytelling talents of each of the knights would have been just as important in the evaluation of everyone's skills and reputation as were the fights themselves. Such an atypical challenge, as close as it could be to the quests described in imaginative literature, but also in a way resembling the first unsupervised tournaments held during the twelfth century, seemed to have filled the participants and spectators at Sandricourt with enthusiasm, giving them a live experience that was redolent of both the real and the legendary past of chivalry.

For the whole duration of the tournament at Sandricourt, banquets, music, dances, *momeries** and other festivities were organised for the entertainment of the guests at each lunch and dinner, which explains why fights in the afternoon would usually resume as late as four o'clock. For eight days, in addition to the competitors, the small castle of Sandricourt and its surroundings welcomed hundreds of noble guests, their servants and all kinds of people and craftsmen necessary for such an event to take place. Listed in the written account, they included physicians, surgeons, apothecaries, armourers, saddlers and tailors, who had, for the most part, probably come from large cities and towns, perhaps alongside the participants themselves, and were gathered at Sandricourt only for the duration of the tournament.[13] Everything happening at the castle was supervised by Huguette de Brillac, lady of Sandricourt, Louis de Hédouville's mother, who acted as the main hostess of the event. The author of the account estimated the total number of people present for the occasion at between 1800 and 2000.[14] Although only the names of the participants, the judges and the most important ladies and damsels are cited, the rest of the audience was probably essentially composed of noble men and women coming from their social circles, as well as from the royal and Orléans ducal courts, followed by their own retinues. Except for the ladies and judges, who had their own chambers, any space in the castle was fully packed out, and tables were set in every available room, even outside in the courtyard, for serving food and drink all day to all those present. Many people probably had to stay outside the castle of Sandricourt, in nearby castles, villages and manors,[15] or even in tents put up for the occasion. All the provisions and entertainments were paid for and supplied by Louis de Hédouville and the other *tenans*, who are said by the author to have spent between 400 and 500 *francs* (equivalent to 400–500 *livres tournois*) for each of the five days

[13] Orléans (Herald), *Le pas des armes*, fol. B6v; VT, p. 168; PSt, pp. 65–6.

[14] Orléans (Herald), *Le pas des armes*, fol. B6v; VT, p. 168; PSt, p. 66.

[15] We know, for example, that the lord of Châtillon and his *bande* were hosted in a house owned by the lady of Monsures, the exact location of which is unknown: Orléans (Herald), *Le pas des armes*, fol. B6r; VT, p. 166; PSt, p. 62.

of the tournament, not including all that had already been spent on the preparations before it even started.[16] This was a huge amount of money, as can be seen, for example, by comparing it with the annual wages given at the time by the king to one of his best armourers, which were 240 *livres tournois*.[17]

COMMEMORATING THE *PAS* AT SANDRICOURT

This expensive *pas d'armes* and its extraordinary knights-errant challenge, set far from any large city, could have fallen into complete historical oblivion if it had not been recorded in detail by Orléans, herald of Duke Louis II of Orléans, and printed shortly after the event under the title of *Le pas des armes de Sandricourt*. This book, published by Antoine Vérard in Paris, is the earliest known independent printed record of a tournament. The standard version was unillustrated and printed on paper,[18] but luxury versions were also printed on vellum and illuminated by hand. Today, only two of these vellum versions, illustrated by two different artists, are extant, both preserved at the BnF in Paris (Vélins 1033 and Vélins 1034) (Figures 32 and 33). Whilst the cheaper paper books were probably aimed at a larger audience, these vellum copies were likely to have been commissioned for important figures or patrons linked to the tournament, such as the chief *entrepreneur*, Louis de Hédouville, the duke of Orléans or the king of France himself. The content is the work of Orléans Herald, who presents himself in the introduction and tells the reader to trust his writing as he was a direct witness of the tournament, alongside his colleagues involved in its organisation, all of whom were heralds of the king of France. The author sees his record of the event as being a duty that he performed in order to inspire noblemen to exert themselves and perform deeds of arms, so as to prevent idleness spoiling the proud and honourable knighthood of France.[19] This introduction, giving us the dates and location of the event, is immediately followed by the *articles* of the tournament, as they were orally proclaimed in Paris and elsewhere in France, and perhaps thereafter spread through manuscript copies among the nobility.

Following the *articles*, the author describes the different locations of the challenges with their courtly names and briefly recounts some of the events that took place at each of them. He then makes a rapid mention of the shield-hanging ceremony at the castle

---

[16] Informing the reader how much money was spent during a tournament, spectacle or festivity was a way of giving them a sense of the richness and magnificence involved in it. Most of the time, however, such amounts, also circulating as rumours among the people attending the event, were even more exaggerated than the real expenditure. For example, during the festivities held at Châtellerault in 1541 for the wedding of Jeanne of Navarre and the duke of Cleves, an ambassador reported that the knights-errant tournament challenge held in the nearby forest was said to have cost about 40,000 *écus* in total (about 120,000 *livres tournois*), which seems rather too expensive for this event alone, given what we know from accounts of similar tournaments, and was therefore probably a rumour rather than an established fact. Archivio di Stato di Mantova, A.G. 639, letter from Gio Battista da Gambara to the duchess of Mantua, Châtellerault, 15 June 1541.

[17] Eric Reppel, 'Minorités et circulations techniques: la confection des armures à Tours (XVe–XVIe siècles)', *Documents pour l'histoire des techniques*, 15 (2008), 24–31 (p. 31).

[18] The only preserved paper version known to us is kept in the library of the University of Turin, Ris. 24.26. See Paola Cifarelli, 'Exemplaires d'ouvrages publiés par Antoine Vérard dans les bibliothèques turinoises', *Le Moyen Français*, 69 (2011), 15–34 (p. 18).

[19] Orléans (Herald), *Le pas des armes*, fol. A1v; VT, p. 147; PSt, p. 4.

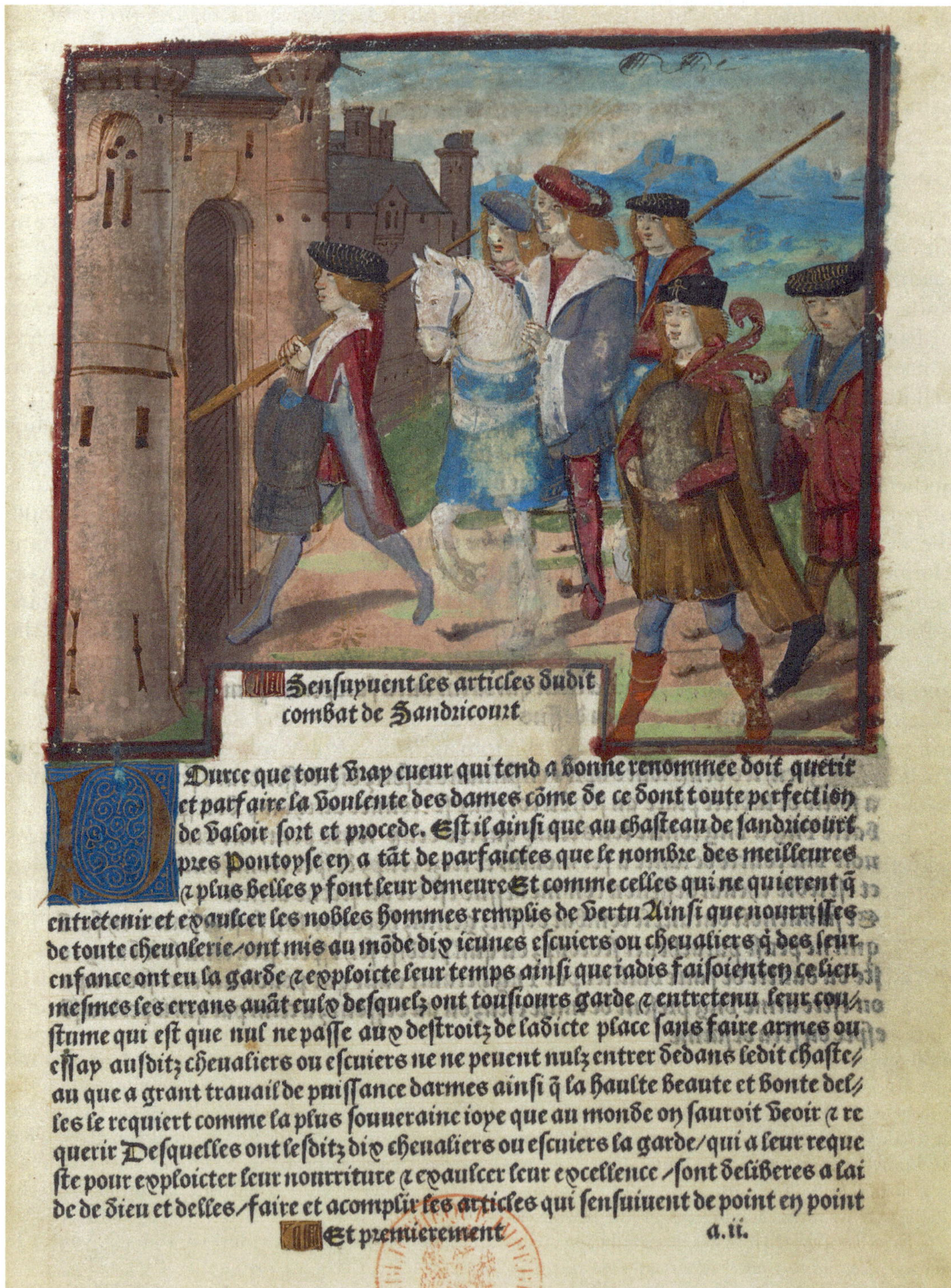

Sensuyuent les articles dudit
combat de Sandricourt

Pource que tout vray cueur qui tend a bonne renommee doit querir
et parfaire la voulente des dames cõme de ce dont toute perfection
de valoir sort et procede. Est il ainsi que au chasteau de sandricourt
pres Pontoyse en a tãt de parfaictes que le nombre des meilleures
⁊ plus belles y font leur demeure Et comme celles qui ne quierent q̄
entretenir et exaulcer les nobles hommes remplis de vertu Ainsi que nourrisses
de toute chevalerie / ont mis au mõde dix ieunes escuiers ou chevaliers q̄ des leur
enfance ont eu la garde ⁊ exploicte leur temps ainsi que iadis faisoient en ce lieu
mesmes les errans avãt eulx desquelz ont tousiours garde ⁊ entretenu leur cou/
stume qui est que nul ne passe aux destroitz de ladicte place sans faire armes ou
essay ausditz chevaliers ou escuiers ne ne peuent nulz entrer dedans ledit chaste/
au que a grant travail de puissance darmes ainsi q̄ la haulte beaute et bonte del/
les le requiert comme la plus souveraine ioye que au monde on sauroit veoir ⁊ re
querir Desquelles ont lesditz dix chevaliers ou escuiers la garde / qui a leur reque
ste pour exploicter leur nourriture ⁊ exaulcer leur excellence / sont deliberes a lai
de de dieu et delles / faire et acomplir les articles qui sensuivent de point en point
Et premierement a.ii.

Figure 32. Page showing the arrival of the tournament participants at the castle of Sandricourt and the beginning of the tournament's *articles*. Orléans Herald, *Le pas des armes de Sandricourt* (Paris: A. Vérard, 1493). Paris, BnF, Vélins 1034, fol. A2r. Photo: BnF.

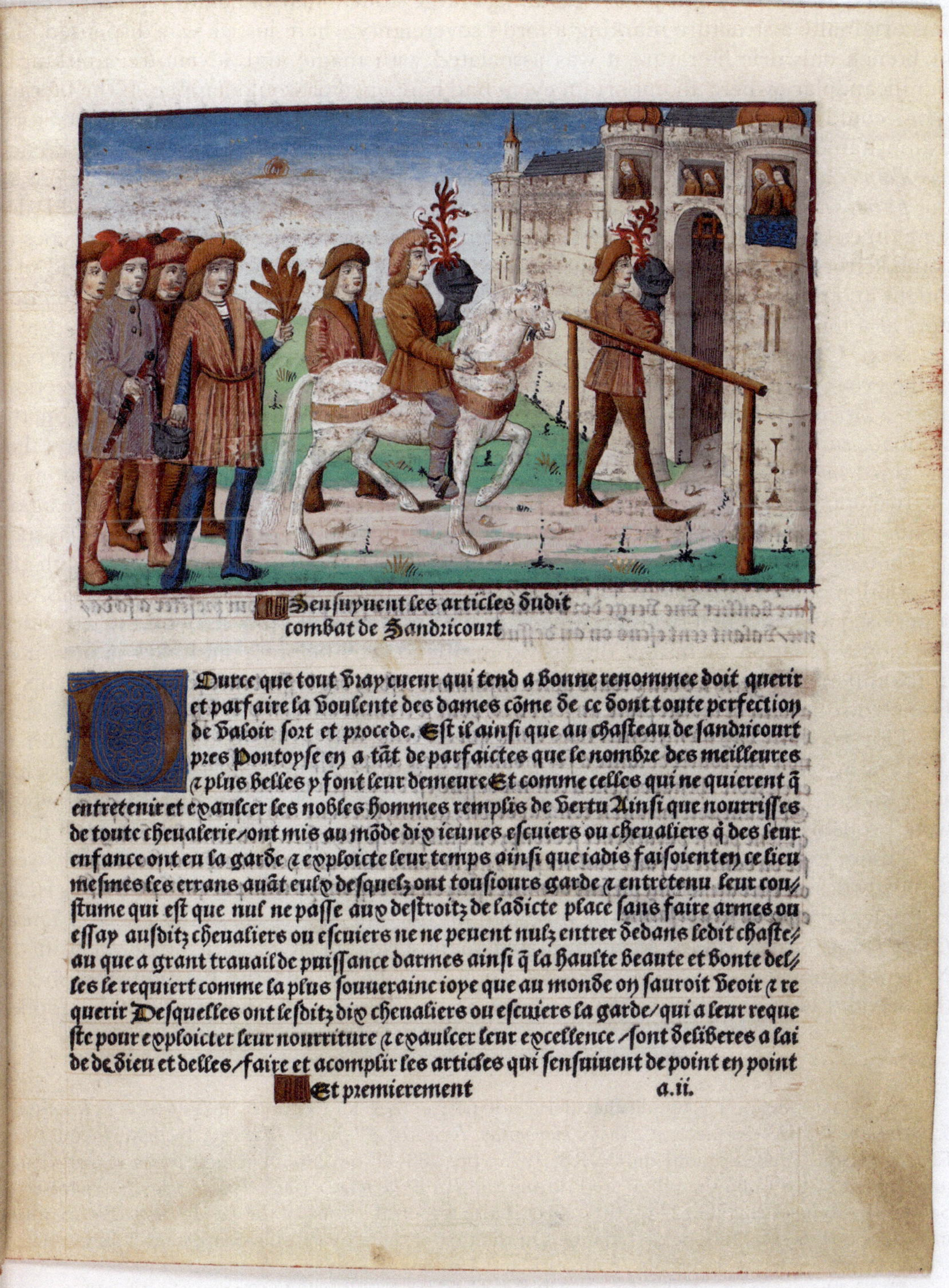

Sensuyvent les articles dudit
combat de Sandricourt

Pource que tout vray cueur qui tend a bonne renommee doit querir
et parfaire la voulente des dames cõme de ce dont toute perfection
de valoir sort et procede. Est il ainsi que au chasteau de sandricourt
pres Pontoyse en a tãt de parfaictes que le nombre des meilleures
& plus belles y font leur demeure Et comme celles qui ne quierent q̃
entretenir et exaulcer les nobles hommes remplis de vertu Ainsi que nourrisses
de toute chevalerie/ont mis au mõde dix ieunes escuiers ou chevaliers q̇ des leur
enfance ont eu la garde & exploicte leur temps ainsi que iadis faisoient en ce lieu
mesmes les errans avãt eulx desquelz ont tousiours garde & entretenu leur cou/
stume qui est que nul ne passe aux destroitz de ladicte place sans faire armes ou
essay ausditz chevaliers ou escuiers ne ne peuent nulz entrer dedans ledit chaste/
au que a grant travail de puissance darmes ainsi q̃ la haulte beaute et bonte del/
les le requiert comme la plus souveraine ioye que au monde on sauroit veoir & re
querir Desquelles ont lesditz dix chevaliers ou escuiers la garde/qui a leur reque
ste pour exploicter leur nourriture & exaulcer leur excellence/sont deliberes a lai
de de dieu et delles/faire et acomplir les articles qui sensuivent de point en point

Et premierement a.ii.

Figure 33. Page showing the arrival of the tournament participants at the castle of Sandricourt and the beginning of the tournament's *articles*. Orléans Herald, *Le pas des armes de Sandricourt* (Paris: A. Vérard, 1493). Paris, BnF, Vélins 1033, fol. A2r. Photo: BnF.

gate, used as a *perron**. The *perron*, meaning a large stone, pillar or column in Old French, was originally a structure marking a lord's sovereignty where justice was dispensed, but in French chivalric literature it was associated with magic and adventure, marking a significant place where an important event had happened or would happen. If the literary *perron* could embody a wide range of symbols serving the moral purpose of the story, its tournament version also had a more concrete function. *Perrons* first appear in French *pas d'armes* around the middle of the fifteenth century.[20] One of the main functions of the *perron* was to serve as a place for the participants' shields to be hung; it could also sometimes be used by the *entrepreneur* to put up shields symbolising the different types of combat from which the participants had to choose.[21] Hanging the heraldic shield of a knight and touching the shields of *emprise* was the official way of registering the competitors at a tournament.

Next, Orléans Herald gives us the whole list of participants before the actual account of the event, starting on 16 September with the foot combat at the barrier. In this section, after a brief description of the ceremonial entry, the author essentially focuses on the combats, summarising the most notable feats of arms that he observed on those days. For the third *emprise*, each of the thirty jousts is listed, describing the names and actions of the two opponents involved. For the knights-errant challenge, Orléans Herald once again recalls the most important actions performed and the names of their protagonists, such as Thomas de May's improvised *emprise d'armes*. The account of the event ends with the description of the final banquet, followed by lists of names of all the judges and ladies who supervised and attended the tournament, as well as a general account of all the festivities, the money spent on them and the crowd in attendance, before a summary is presented of the different challenges fought during the week and the degree to which the knights of France distinguished themselves.

This account, despite the novelty of being produced through the new medium of the printing press, still follows the tradition of fifteenth-century tournament manuscripts such as the various narrative accounts of the *Pas du Perron Fée* (Bruges, 1463), which were probably written up by officers of arms in the service of Philip the Good. This is even more evident in the vellum versions of the *Pas des armes de Sandricourt*, which were explicitly designed to look like illuminated manuscripts. The layout of these versions is, for example, very close to what can be observed for the official account of the *Pas de la Joyeuse Garde/Pas de Saumur* (1446), an illuminated manuscript surviving in a single copy in the National Library of Russia in St Petersburg.[22] Antoine Vérard, the Parisian publisher of the account who was close to the circles of power, is, moreover, known to have supplied

---

[20] See Sydney Anglo, 'L'arbre de chevalerie et le perron dans les tournois', in *Les fêtes de la Renaissance 3: Quinzième Colloque International d'études humanistes Tours, 10–22 Juillet 1972*, ed. by Jean Jacquot and Elie Konigson (Paris: Éditions du CNRS, 1975), pp. 283–98 (p. 296). The first *perron* recorded in a tournament seems to be the pillar used during the *Pas de la Joyeuse Garde/Pas de Saumur*, organised at Saumur by René of Anjou in 1446; this object is also a central feature of the *Pas du Perron Fée* organised in Bruges in 1463 by Philippe de Lalaing. On the first of these two events, see Essays 2 and 7; on the second event, see Essay 3. See also Sources 5 and 11a, respectively.

[21] This is the case at both the Angevin *Pas de la Bergère* (Tarascon, 1449) organised by Philippe de Lenoncourt and Philibert de Laigue, and the Burgundian *Pas de la Fontaine des Pleurs* (Chalon-sur-Saône, 1449–50) organised by Jacques de Lalaing: see Sources 6 and 7, respectively.

[22] St Petersburg, NLR, fr. F. p. XIV, 4.

King Charles VIII and his entourage with several printed versions of chivalric romances that the young king and his court particularly enjoyed.[23]

The text of the *pas* at Sandricourt itself is also in direct line with medieval practice: this is a herald's report, focused on combats and individual prowess, with attention paid to the ritualised and ceremonial aspect of the event,[24] whereas later French Renaissance official tournament accounts, especially after 1530, had a more literary approach and were written by intellectuals or poets with less interest in the descriptions of combats: examples include the account of the tournament of Châtellerault (1541), described later in this chapter. The discontinuity and repetitions in the text as a whole suggest that it was composed by assembling several texts that were originally written separately, whether before (such as the *articles*), during or immediately after the event, with the addition of an introduction and a conclusion to give the account more coherence.

The compilation of various texts from different origins (Orléans may in fact not be the original author of the whole text) is a phenomenon commonly seen in festivity accounts up to the seventeenth century.[25] This was especially common for tournaments and carousels,[26] as some of the reported texts, like the *articles* proclaimed in advance, were written at different moments of the event. The herald nonetheless tries to give his text the appearance of a timeless tale, with descriptions echoing in their formulation traditional chivalric stories, as if he were reporting deeds of arms from Arthurian times. Explicit reference to the knights of the Round Table is indeed made several times in the account, such as in the conclusion of the text, where the author says that, since the time of Arthur and his knights, no combats had more closely resembled those of the heroes of the Round Table than those performed at the *Pas* of Sandricourt.[27]

Interestingly, about ten years later, an illustrated manuscript copy of this text, now also preserved at the BnF in Paris (Arsenal 3958), was produced for an unknown patron,

---

[23] Benjamin Deruelle, *De papier, de fer et de sang: chevaliers et chevalerie à l'épreuve de la modernité (ca 1460–ca 1620)* (Paris: Publications de la Sorbonne, 2015), pp. 67, 85.

[24] Philippe Contamine, 'Office d'armes et noblesse dans la France de la fin du Moyen Âge', *Bulletin de la Société Nationale des Antiquaires de France* (1994) [1996], 310–22 (p. 314).

[25] Benoît Bolduc, *La fête imprimée: Spectacles et cérémonies politiques (1549–1662)* (Paris: Classiques Garnier, 2016), p. 167.

[26] For a definition of this type of event, see below, n. 44.

[27] 'Et me semble depuis le temps du roi Artus dont est encore à present mémoire, qui fut commanceur de la Table Ronde, dont il y avoit de si nobles chevaliers, dont est mémoire à present, et sera à tousjours; comme Messire Lancelot du Lac, Messire Gauvain, Messire Tristan de Leonnois, Messire Palamedes, qui tous jadis estoient de la Table Ronde. Puis bien dire qu'on n'a point veu ne leu en Histoire quelconque, que depuis ce temps-là se soit fait pour l'amour des Dames, pas, joustes, tournois, ne behours, qui se doivent tant approchier de l'exercice d'armes que fait le Pas de Sandricourt, ne au plus prés des faits desdits Chevaliers de la Table Ronde' (In my view, since the time of King Arthur, whose memory is still alive and who founded the Round Table which included so many noble knights whose names have and always will be remembered, such as Messire Lancelot du Lac, Messire Gauvain, Messire Tristan de Lyonnais and Messire Palamèdes, all at one time members of the Round Table, I can truly say that never has one read or seen in any history book since that time any *pas*, jousts, tourneys or *béhourds* performed for the love of ladies that came anywhere close to the undertaking of martial deeds that was done at the *Pas* of Sandricourt, nor which resemble so nearly those of the Knights of the Round Table). Orléans (Herald), *Le pas des armes*, fol. B7; VT, p. 169; PSt, p. 66; translated in Source 13, p. 282.

someone probably connected to the event (Figure 34). The illuminations in this manuscript version are cruder copies of those from BnF, Vélins 1034, the vellum printed version possibly made for Louis de Hédouville, and costumes have been slightly updated to match the fashion of the years 1500–10.[28] More significantly, the text itself is slightly different: typographical errors have been corrected, some sentences have been made clearer and elements have been added when others were removed, perhaps because they were deemed to be no longer relevant a decade later. In other words, the account has been updated here, probably by someone who attended the tournament, as it provides clarifications that only a former spectator could give. This person may even have been the author of the first text, Orléans Herald himself, wanting to give a better version for posterity. The fact that it was copied from the version possibly made for Hédouville also reveals that it was produced in the circle of the lord of Sandricourt, probably for himself or for someone to whom he was closely linked.

TABLE COMPARING THE EXISTING COPIES OF THE ILLUSTRATED NARRATIVE ACCOUNTS OF THE *PAS DES ARMES DE SANDRICOURT*

Shelfmark	**BnF, Vélins 1033**	**BnF, Vélins 1034**	**BnF Arsenal, 3958 Réserve**	**BnF, fr. 1436**
Type of document	Printed vellum	Printed vellum	Manuscript on vellum	Manuscript on paper (in collection of texts, fols 104r–125r)
Date	1493	1493	1500–10	*c.*1527–45
Version of text (1493 original or 1500–10 modified)	Original	Original	Modified	Modified (with additional text)
Number of illuminations	10	10	9 (copied from BnF Vélins 1034)	8 (copied from BnF Arsenal 3958)
Probable original ownership	Charles VIII or Duke Louis of Orléans	Louis de Hédouville, lord of Sandricourt	?	Patron from the Sandricourt area

Despite its romantic allusions, however, the original production of this text was far from being an innocent courtly gesture, and the commemoration of this tournament had to be as important as the *pas d'armes* itself. Even if Charles VIII approved of it and allowed it to be proclaimed, the *Pas* of Sandricourt seems, above all, to have been an event sponsored and supported by his cousin, Louis, duke of Orléans (1462–1515). Louis de Hédouville himself was chosen as an *écuyer d'écurie* (equerry) of the king in 1492, but came from a family

[28] The eighth illustration of Paris, BnF, Vélins 1034 (fol. B4v), which represents the refreshments given to the participants, has been omitted in the later manuscript copy.

Figure 34. Arrival of the tournament participants at the castle of Sandricourt. *Le pas des armes de Sandricourt.* Manuscript on vellum, *c.*1500–10. Paris, BnF Arsenal, 3958 Réserve, fol. 1v. Photo: BnF Arsenal.

that had long served the Orléans branch of the royal family, and was previously one of the duke's personal advisers.[29] Many of the other participants had more or less direct and obvious connections with the duke, as in the case of one of the *venans*, Guillaume de Méry, who was his *maréchal des logis* (officer in charge of organising the quartering of troops), or the *tenan* Jacques de Dinteville, his *grand veneur* (grand huntsman). Moreover, the duke sent his own herald, Orléans, not only as one of the tournament's officers of arms but as the person who would eventually write up the official narrative account of it. We also know that Louis of Orléans gave Hédouville 100 gold *écus* (equivalent to 300 *livres tournois*) to help him cover the tournament's expenses.[30]

Indeed, this tournament can be seen to be directly implicated in French high politics of the early 1490s. The duke of Orléans, who was one of the leaders of the so-called *Guerre Folle* (Mad War), an aristocratic rebellion against the king that took place between 1485 and 1488, had spent three years in prison before Charles VIII decided to pardon and release him in 1491. Louis of Orléans subsequently remained an official supporter of Charles until his cousin's sudden death in 1498 brought him to the French throne as King Louis XII. In 1493, however, Charles VIII, who had recently taken up the reins of the kingdom after the regency of his sister, Anne de Beaujeu (1483–91), was already planning to conquer the kingdom of Naples, to which he was an official heir,[31] whilst Louis had hereditary designs on the duchy of Milan. Yet, for such an undertaking the young king needed the support of a majority of his military nobility, and his cousin had many useful connections amongst them. We do not know, unfortunately, whose idea it was to stage the *Pas* of Sandricourt: the original initiative could have come from Louis de Hédouville, Louis of Orléans or Charles VIII himself. Yet, whoever was behind the decision to hold this event in the first place, it became a means of serving Charles VIII's policy by using Louis of Orléans's influence over the French nobility.

Although they were represented by their heralds, neither the king nor his cousin actually attended the event at Sandricourt, perhaps to keep the tournament at a lower level of magnificence, as their presence would have meant that the organiser incurred far greater expense in order to accommodate them and their retinues. However, by attracting some of the greatest knights of the kingdom to a *pas d'armes* that celebrated the ideals of chivalry and involved the participants in a knight-errant roleplay, Charles VIII and Louis of Orléans were mentally preparing them for the Italian 'quest' they were planning, which was presented almost as a crusade, as Charles VIII considered himself to be heir to the kingdoms of both Naples and Jerusalem; thus, helping him to seize Naples would be the first step towards the liberation of the Holy Land.

Such tournaments as that at Sandricourt also helped to foster useful connections between the French rulers' already faithful courtiers and other French (and even some Flemish) knights.[32] Apart from one whole *bande* from Normandy,[33] these knights from all

---

[29] Botto, *L'Isle-Adam*, p. 14.

[30] *Ibid.*, p. 15.

[31] As a descendant of Yolanda of Aragon (1381–1442), duchess of Anjou (his great-grandmother), and the great-nephew of King René (1409–80), Charles VIII laid claim to the house of Anjou's rights over the kingdom of Naples and Jerusalem.

[32] Nicolas Le Roux, *Le crépuscule de la chevalerie: Noblesse et guerre au siècle de la Renaissance* (Ceyzérieu: Champ Vallon, 2015), p. 171.

[33] That of Antoine Martel, lord of Beaumont.

over the country were mixed together in their teams, creating early opportunities to fight together. The use of chivalric culture for gathering and winning the loyalty of supporters, especially prior to a military campaign, was common practice in Europe. For example, it had been used by other princes such as the dukes of Burgundy at, for example, the *Pas du Chevalier au Cygne* (Lille, 1454), which was linked to Duke Philip the Good's project of launching a new crusade.[34] When assembling his army in Lyon in the spring of 1494 before launching his first Italian campaign, Charles VIII organised several other tournaments for the same purpose of winning his knights' loyalty, including a *pas* planned by the gentlemen of his household,[35] thus resulting in many of them truly experiencing the French invasion of Italy as their own knight-errant quest.[36] Re-enacting the deeds of legendary knights of the past alongside other members of their kind would revive the chivalric imagination of these men-at-arms and inspire them to follow their king and captains on a real campaign, where they could hope to emulate the feats of arms of their heroes. Beside the combats themselves, all the social events taking place during the tournament, such as dances and banquets, also served as opportunities to create or reinforce social bonds between individuals, many of whom were about to fight side by side in Italy.

The printed publication of the *Pas des armes de Sandricourt* is therefore also likely to have played a part in Charles's political plans. The paper version may have been disseminated rapidly among the nobility who could not attend the event itself, with the aim of awakening their chivalric sense through reading about the tales of other French knights' deeds of arms, making them even more ready to respond affirmatively when the king called on their assistance for his Italian campaign. This text, through all the names cited in it, was also a celebration of the nobility who were present at the event, the lords and ladies of northern Île-de-France in particular, to which Hédouville and many other participants belonged.[37] Indeed, many of the Sandricourt tourneyers became important figures in the following years, not only by distinguishing themselves through their actions during the Italian wars but also thanks to Louis of Orléans becoming King Louis XII in 1498: for example, Louis de Hédouville later became Louis XII's chamberlain and governor of the royal castle of Blois and Gaspard I de Coligny eventually became marshal of France in 1516. Moreover, many of the Sandricourt names are the continuators of a large number of French Renaissance aristocratic lines, they and their relatives being found in the highest spheres of the royal court: this is the case of the Coligny, Dinteville, Montmorency and Poitiers families.

The text of the 1493 tournament at Sandricourt, through both its original version and later copies, remained an important repository of memory for these people, particularly the lords of Sandricourt and their relatives. We can see this in the manuscript version of *c.*1500–10 (Arsenal 3958) or even later, in another manuscript based on this earlier

---

[34] Guillaume Bureaux, 'Union et désunion de la noblesse en parade. Le rôle des Pas d'armes dans l'entretien des rivalités chevaleresques entre cours princières occidentales, XVe–XVIe siècles (Anjou, Bourgogne, France, Saint-Empire)' (unpublished PhD dissertation, Normandie Université, 2018), p. 206.

[35] BnF, Collection of copies of documents on French History, known as the *Portefeuilles Fontanieu*, arranged by Gaspard-Moyse de Fontanieu in 1767, naf. 7644 vols 149–150, Charles VIII (1494–98), fols 52–54.

[36] Deruelle, *De papier*, p. 38.

[37] Guillaume Bureaux, 'Le jeu entre politique, romanesque et théâtral. Le pas d'armes de Sandricourt (1493)', *Histilien* (2019) <https://histilien.hypotheses.org/28> [accessed 22 June 2024].

Figure 35. Arrival of the tournament participants at the castle of Sandricourt. 'Le pas des armes de Sandricourt', in *Armoriaux de la Table Ronde*. Manuscript on paper, *c.*1525–45. Paris, BnF, fr. 1436, fol. 107v. Photo: BnF.

one made around 1525–45 (BnF, fr. 1436), which combined its account of the event with copies of armorials of the knights of the Round Table and the illustrated account of the 1519 tournament of Chambly and Bailleul, an event organised in the same area in direct reference to the 1493 *pas d'armes*, as we shall see later in this study (Figure 35).[38] This other version of Orléans Herald's account is identical to that of Arsenal 3958, with the notable addition of a 'description du lieu et chasteau de Sandricourt' (description of the place and castle of Sandricourt),[39] in which we learn that, in the chapel of the castle, one could still see the shields of all the participants hanging on the walls, thus preserving the 'perdurable mémoire' (enduring memory) of their deeds for posterity.[40]

Furthermore, the memory of the *Pas* of Sandricourt was still alive in the early seventeenth century owing to the illustrated versions of the text that recounts it. The Musée du Louvre preserves a magnificent series of eight drawings made by the Parisian artist Nicolas Baullery in around 1610, illustrating the main events of the famous 1493 tournament in chronological order (Figures 36 and 37).[41] The first drawing shows the participants' arrival at the castle, while the last shows the final banquet.[42] Between these two images, a pair of others depict the foot combat at the barrier, another pair the mounted combats (*mêlées* and jousts), and a further pair the knights-errant challenge in the forest. We do not know the purpose of these drawings, but their format and their organisation by pairs indicate a likely project for a series of tapestries or murals. This may have been a commission for his castle by the lord of Sandricourt himself, who, at that time, was Louis de Rouvroy de St-Simon (*c.*1575–after 1608). Indeed, Baullery's drawings are chiefly inspired by the illustrations of the printed vellum copy Vélins 1034 — the same as the one used for the manuscript copy, possibly owned by Hédouville — which Rouvroy de St-Simon would have inherited from his ancestor,[43] and the representations of the castle of Sandricourt seen in the background of some of them have been made from direct observation of the building. The early seventeenth-century lord of Sandricourt may well have given Baullery access to all the necessary sources for him to represent an accurate depiction of the famous event, using the original text and its images, inspiration from other late medieval artworks such as tapestries, and access to the castle and its surroundings. In early seventeenth-century France, as tournaments were slowly going out of fashion at court to be replaced by running at the ring*, quintain or carousels,[44] the provincial nobility was still very much attached to this tradition and, above all, the symbolism attached to these types of festivity.[45] Tournaments and

[38] Paris, BnF, fr. 1436: see fols 104r–125r for the narrative account of the *Pas des armes de Sandricourt*.

[39] *Ibid.*, fols 105r–107r. Botto, *L'Isle-Adam*, pp. 55–9; PSt, pp. 71–6.

[40] BnF, fr. 1436, fol. 106r. Botto, *L'Isle-Adam*, p. 57; PSt, p. 74.

[41] Musée du Louvre, département des arts graphiques, inv. 23703–23710.

[42] Mislabelled in the eighteenth century as being number 7 in the series ('Coming back from the *forêt dévoyable*'), inv. 23709 is in fact the first of the series, representing the arrival at the castle on the first day of the tournament.

[43] It is possible that Baullery had access to the other printed vellum copy, Vélins 1033, which was kept in the royal collection, but its influence on his drawings is less easy to confirm.

[44] Quintain was a military game and training exercise in which a rider had to hit special points on a fixed or rotating dummy; carousel was the name given to military games of Islamic origin in which two or more squadrons of riders simulated a battle by executing elaborate and rehearsed manoeuvres, using fake weapons or harmless projectiles such as terracotta balls. Viallon, 'Les tournois', pp. 29 and 45.

[45] Marine Roussillon, *Don Quichotte à Versailles: L'imaginaire médiéval du Grand Siècle* (Ceyzérieu: Champ Vallon, 2022), pp. 99–100.

Figure 36. Foot combat at the barrier at the *Pas des armes de Sandricourt* in 1493. Drawing (ink and gouache on paper) by Nicolas Baullery, *c.*1600–10, 31.8 × 52 cm. Paris, Musée du Louvre, inv. 23703. Photo: Musée du Louvre.

Figure 37. Joust in open field at the *Pas des armes de Sandricourt* in 1493. Drawing (ink and gouache on paper) by Nicolas Baullery, *c.*1600–10, 33.8 × 52 cm. Paris, Musée du Louvre, inv. 23705. Photo: Musée du Louvre.

chivalric culture were still seen by the nobility as a celebration of their importance and role in society, even as they were facing the increasing centralisation of royal power in France, since kings, especially from the reigns of Louis XI and Charles VIII onwards, progressively abrogated to themselves the power that they had once shared more widely with the high nobility.[46] Through the memory of Sandricourt, Baullery's project was perhaps a way for his patron to celebrate the knightly prowess of his ancestors and their companions, and thus served as a means of putting his illustrious origins on public display.

Yet, despite their artistic qualities, the final tapestries or murals produced from Baullery's drawings would only have fully made sense to someone who was familiar with the original text and so we might imagine the lord of Sandricourt recounting the story of his ancestor's tournament to his guests while showing the pictures, or allowing them to be enjoyed by other visiting local lords who shared the same memory. The original text is therefore responsible for the long-term memory and fame of the 1493 *pas d'armes*, but this was particularly the case of its most original challenge, that of the knights-errant, which was to inspire later French tournaments directly, as we shall now see.

The knights-errant challenge: from Sandricourt to the royal court

The most documented tournament directly inspired by the 1493 *pas d'armes* is the event organised during the month of July 1519 at the castles of Chambly, Bailleul, Esches, Montagny, L'Isle-Adam and Méry,[47] all of which are in the wider vicinity of Sandricourt and which involved mainly the local nobility. Several of the named participants and organisers were even directly related to those who attended the *Pas* of Sandricourt, such as Méry d'Orgemont, lord of Méry, whose father Pierre was a *tenan* in 1493. Rather than comprising a single discrete event like that at Sandricourt, this later occasion consisted of a series of tournaments involving the same group of people moving from one castle to another during a whole month. Before the first combats, the *tenans*, led by Tanguy de La Motte, lord of Chambly, went to several castles in the area, starting with Bailleul, where the various *bandes* of *venans* where staying, in order to launch an official challenge to them for the first event of the series. This event started at the beginning of July with running at the ring and a *mêlée* with lances and swords at Chambly, followed by running at the ring, a *mêlée* with lances and swords and a bastion (siege-tournament)[48] at Bailleul, and then by another bastion at Esches. The party then moved on to Montagny for more running at the ring as well as a *mêlée* with swords and a bastion, before staying at L'Isle-Adam in order to attend lavish banquets and other festivities. After 25 July, they moved to the surroundings of the castle of Méry, where another running at the ring was followed by a knights-errant challenge, which we will discuss here. The only extant narrative source for this series of tournaments is an illustrated text copied from a lost original alongside armorials of the Round Table and a copy of *Le pas des armes de Sandricourt* in the above-mentioned manuscript of *c.*1527–45.[49]

[46] Deruelle, *De papier*, p. 562.

[47] Now Méry-sur-Oise.

[48] The bastion, invented by the French in the early sixteenth century, was a type of tournament that simulated a siege: this involved a group defending a more or less elaborate fortification against one or several other teams, sometimes using tactics similar to those of real siege warfare. Viallon, 'Never-Ending Chivalry', p. 102.

[49] BnF, fr. 1436: for the tournaments of Chambly, Bailleul, etc., see fols 126r–137r.

Figure 38. Knights-errant challenge in the *forêt dévoyée*, near the castle of Méry, in 1519. 'Description des tournois faits en l'an 1519 à Chambly et Bailleul', in *Armoriaux de la Table Ronde*. Manuscript on paper, *c.*1525–45. Paris, BnF, fr. 1436, fol. 135r. Photo: BnF.

The final tournament at Méry was directly inspired by Sandricourt's final challenge, as can be seen in the very similar name derived from chivalric romance that they gave to the forest in which it was set: the *forêt dévoyée* (Figure 38). As at Sandricourt, both *venans* and *tenans* put themselves to the test by riding in and around a forest or wood close to Méry castle, while spectators, ladies and judges followed them on horseback. In the middle of the tournament area were installed great tents, pavilions and loggias (*galeries*) made of branches and leaves where food and refreshments were on offer, allowing all the participants and guests to rest and enjoy their time at their leisure during the day.

The written account of this event goes into less detail about the knights' individual feats of arms than the Sandricourt text, but it nonetheless reports the anecdote of King Francis I (1494–1547) himself supposedly hearing about the knights-errant challenge and wanting to take part in it incognito with some of his friends. For this purpose, he even secretly sent their harnesses to a nearby farm. However, Louise of Savoy (1476–1531), the king's mother, heard about his plans and forbade her son to do any such thing, arguing that it would be hazardous to enter such a challenge without the opponent knowing that he was fighting against the king, and reminding him how dangerous it was because of the lack of supervision.[50] In the case of Francis, any accident happening to the king would also be embarrassing for the opponent and might even have caused diplomatic issues. Listening to his mother's advice, the king eventually attended the event only as a spectator. This anecdote, whilst being a little implausible, nonetheless shows the personal interest that the

[50] Botto, *L'Isle-Adam*, p. 82.

French king took in the knights-errant tournament in particular. Having grown up at the court of Louis XII alongside several of the former *tenans* and *venans* of Sandricourt, Francis was probably aware of what had occurred at the 1493 *pas d'armes* and wanted to seize the opportunity to experience for himself this extraordinary type of event, which seemed as close as possible to what the life of a true knight-errant from chivalric romance would have been. Unfortunately for the king, as his mother reminded him, this form of tournament was not very compatible with royal and courtly etiquette and so, in order to be taken up at the king's own court, the knights-errant challenge had to be adapted.

A good example of just such a courtly version of this type of event was held as part of the tournaments organised in June 1541 at the castle of Châtellerault in Poitou in order to celebrate the wedding of Francis I's niece, Princess Jeanne of Navarre (1528–72), to Duke Wilhelm V of Cleves (1516–92). The festivities, organised by the king, were attended by the whole of the French court. Whilst most of the jousts and entertainments took place at the castle itself, on 17 June everyone moved to the nearby forest for a *pas d'armes* 'à l'imitation des chevaliers errants' (in the way of the knights-errant),[51] or, as the ambassador of Mantua put it, 'per immitar gli cavalieri dalla tavola rotonda' (in the way of the knights of the Round Table).[52] The original version of the challenge as invented at Sandricourt in 1493 was not possible in the context of such a courtly event, because the audience here at Châtellerault was much more numerous and illustrious and there were strict protocols to be observed in terms of how the royal personages were to present themselves in public. Thus, instead of having participants and spectators riding randomly through the woods, the *pas d'armes* was organised around four stations built in the forest and spaced about 400 metres apart. At each location was built a large, fenced arena surrounded by ephemeral architecture such as pavilions, galleries and huts made of branches and leaves, as well as wine fountains, all intended for the comfort of the courtiers attending the combats. Each of the stations was guarded by a *tenan* defending his mistress's honour, helped by members of his *bande*, with *venans* and spectators moving in sequence from one location to another.

The official printed account of this *pas d'armes*, as edited by the Parisian publisher Denis Janot in 1541, details the event's proceedings. The first station was guarded by the Dauphin Henri, the king's eldest son. Along the path leading to the lists, the courtiers arriving from the town of Châtellerault could see several tents and huts in which various knights-errant were waiting with their arms ready for anyone to take up their challenge. When the audience was installed around the first arena, the knights-errant came out one by one to challenge the Dauphin Henri alone, with jousts in the open field using lances and swords. These first combats, however, seem to have been staged, as Henri was very conveniently the victor of them all, as well as presenting very dramatic situations embellished by a *mise en scène*, such as one of the knights-errant being spectacularly unhorsed by Henri and then taken off the field in a light litter adorned with leafy branches that was carried by servants wearing the dauphin's colours.[53] In fact, these knights-errant, whose

---

[51] *Recueil des triumphes faictz en la ville de Chastellerauld aux nopces de tresillustre et magnanime prince le duc de Cleves et de Julliers, etc., et de la tresillustre princesse de Navarre fille unicque des Roy et Royne de Navarre* (Paris: D. Janot, 1541), fol. A1r.

[52] Archivio di Stato di Mantova, A.G. 639.

[53] *Recueil des triumphes*, fol. C1r.

names, whether real or fictional, are not given, were not genuine opponents but rather generic characters from chivalric romance and thus formed part of the general *mise en scène*. The story of this *pas* followed the literary trope of a group of knights-errant travelling in the woods and encountering adventure on the way in the form of other knights-errant, hermits and their monkey riding on an ass, and the *tenans* defending their place where *perrons* were also erected.

After this first phase, the real *venans*, whose correct names *are* given, came forward, led by the French king. They arrived in a lavish procession involving ladies, musicians and rich chariots, and paraded around the field. These challengers then fought individual combats with lances in the open field with the dauphin and the members of his *bande*, before assembling all together for a *mêlée* with swords. After this, everybody moved on to the next station. Along the way, they came across similar huts and pavilions inhabited by other anonymous knights-errant, who gave immediate challenge to the newcomers with lances and swords on horseback as soon as they saw them on the path. After these jousts, which were less obviously choreographed than those that had opened the event, the group of *venans* arrived at the station guarded by Charles of Orléans (1522–45), the king's younger son. Next to it was a hermitage with two hermits, whom the knights asked for directions, a common scene found in chivalric romances such as Chrétien de Troyes's late twelfth-century work *Perceval* (*Le conte du Graal*). At this station, the *venans* fought against the duke of Orléans and his *bande*, first individually with lances, then once again all together in a *mêlée* with swords. Everyone then moved on to the third station, guarded by the duke of Nevers,[54] and then to the fourth, guarded by the count of Aumale,[55] where the same succession of combats took place.

Even if the organisers of and participants at this event at Châtellerault kept to the spirit of the original challenge of Sandricourt, they nonetheless turned it into a more supervised, complex and spectacular form, one that was more appropriate for a high-ranking courtly audience and more aligned with the standards of magnificence of the French court, especially for a princely wedding, where festivities and ceremonials were among the most elaborate and lavish of their time.[56] Moreover, the scenario of the *pas d'armes* also had to meet the standards of royal etiquette and political protocol. Thus, the choice of the four guardians and the order in which they were stationed were carefully calculated: first one would encounter the heir to the throne, then the king's second son. The staged individual jousts that the Dauphin Henri fought at the beginning against the knights-errant were thus a theatrical means by which to showcase the military and chivalric prowess of the future king. The following stations were also guarded by two important princes: Nevers and Aumale. These two lords were not only close companions of the king but also military leaders and rulers involved in the defence of the north-eastern border of France with the German Empire. In fact, the marriage of the king's niece to the duke of Cleves, a German prince from this area, was above all a political alliance that served to reinforce Francis I's influence in this region.

At Châtellerault, then, the knights-errant challenge, whilst kept as a very original type of *pas d'armes*, was nonetheless adapted to the concerns and issues typical of French royal

---

[54] François I of Cleves, count then duke of Nevers (1516–62).

[55] Claude of Lorraine-Guise, count then duke of Aumale (1526–73).

[56] Viallon, 'Never-Ending Chivalry', p. 101.

tournaments of the time. Indeed, at the French Renaissance court where, as an Mantuan ambassador reported, 'non si attende ad altro che darsi bon tempo tutto il di in giostre, feste con belissime mascarate sempre diverse' (they spend every day enjoying themselves with jousts and feasts and gorgeous masques that were constantly changing),[57] the *pas d'armes* in all its new forms and variations was still an important tool of power, one used by the French kings for staging their social and political representation, such as that organised at Argentan in October 1517, for example, where the scenario, as written by Francis I's sister Margaret of Angoulême, celebrated the king's conquests in Italy under the guise of a story filled with hermits and knights-errant.[58]

CONCLUSION

The tournament 'in the way of the knights-errant' was invented for the first time as one of the challenges of the *pas d'armes* of Sandricourt in 1493 as a 'real' experience of the ideal romance figure of the knight-errant, an ultimate chivalric fantasy for these French knights. Inspired by imaginative literature, it was a way for the participants to create their own adventures, not only through the combats that they undertook in the forest, but also through the tales of their deeds of arms that they were asked to recount at the final banquet. Some of these stories made it into the official printed account, which became an inspiration for many French chivalric tournaments up to the early seventeenth century. Yet, behind this apparently innocent and playful celebration of chivalric culture, the *pas d'armes* of Sandricourt and its publication were calculated political moves on the part of both Charles VIII and Louis of Orléans, principally as a means of preparing for the king's first Italian campaign of 1494. Perhaps because this *pas d'armes* was not linked to any particular occasion (such as a wedding, coronation or victory) and its political aspect could be understood only in its immediate context, the official account would seem to have been timeless enough for it to become a model for other, later tournaments that were likewise inspired by the ever-popular chivalric romances, whether the old Arthurian and Charlemagne cycles translated into Middle French or the new stories such as Garci Rodríguez de Montalvo's *Amadís de Gaula* (1508) and Ludovico Ariosto's *Orlando Furioso* (1516).[59] Because it is specific and unique, and therefore readily traceable, the knight-errant challenge is therefore a very good case study of how tournaments and other spectacles influenced each other over time and how they were frequently modified and augmented in order to adapt them to new and different contexts.

[57] Archivio di Stato di Mantova, A.G. 639.

[58] Archivio di Stato di Mantova, A.G. 634, letter from Anastasio Turrioni to Federico Gonzaga, Argentan, 3 October 1517.

[59] Deruelle, *De papier*, pp. 50–1.

Alan V. Murray

The *Pas d'armes* in Scotland: King James IV and the Tournaments of the *Wild Knight of the Black Lady* (1507–08)

The *pas d'armes* seems to have been relatively restricted in its geographical range, which marked a notable difference from both earlier and other contemporary tournament forms. The mass tourney, originating in northern France and the southern Low Countries in the late eleventh and early twelfth centuries, rapidly spread throughout Western Europe, as did many forms of jousting between the thirteenth and sixteenth centuries. However, the specific type of jousting event that historians have categorised as the *pas d'armes* had a much more uneven distribution. The earliest such contests seem to have originated in Castile and Aragon and spread to the northern and eastern parts of the kingdom of France, above all the territories of the Valois dukes of Burgundy, as well as in Anjou, Lorraine and Savoy.[1] By contrast, evidence for the *pas d'armes* in other parts of France and elsewhere in Europe is either sketchy or non-existent. This restriction to certain areas is puzzling if we consider the evident enthusiasm for diverse tournament forms found elsewhere. Despite the proximity of many German principalities to Lorraine and the possessions of the dukes of Burgundy, one searches in vain for *pas d'armes* in the German-speaking countries. The many dedicated tournament societies (*Turniergesellschaften*) that were established throughout the empire either knew nothing of the *pas d'armes* or did not regard the form as worth cultivating; even King and Emperor Maximilian, despite his links to Burgundy through marriage and inheritance, showed no enthusiasm for it among the many and sometimes exotic tournament forms that he encouraged.[2]

Situated on the periphery of north-western Europe, with a largely subsistence economy, the kingdom of Scotland might at first sight seem like unfavourable ground for the flourishing of the elaborate and expensive entertainment that constituted the *pas d'armes.* Yet, by the end of the fifteenth century, the country's secular elite considered itself to be part of an international chivalric culture, especially in its Francophone form. The Auld Alliance,

[1] See Eric Bousmar, 'Jousting at the Court of Burgundy. The "Pas d'armes": Shifts in Scenario, Location and Recruitment', in *Staging the Court of Burgundy: Proceedings of the Conference 'The Splendour of Burgundy'*, ed. by Wim Blockmans *et al.* (Turnhout/London: Brepols/Harvey Miller, 2013), pp. 75–84; Catherine Blunk, '*Faux pas* in the Chronicles: What is a *Pas d'armes*?', in *The Medieval Chronicle 11*, ed. by Erik Kooper and Sjoerd Levelt (Leiden: Brill, 2018), pp. 87–107; and *eadem*, 'Between Sport and Theatre: How Spectacular was the *Pas d'armes*?', in *The Medieval Tournament as Spectacle: Tourneys, Jousts and Pas d'Armes, 1100–1600*, ed. by Alan V. Murray and Karen Watts (Woodbridge: Boydell Press, 2020), pp. 120–38.

[2] Andreas Ranft, *Adelsgesellschaften: Gruppenbildung und Genossenschaft im spätmittelalterlichen Reich* (Sigmaringen: Thorbecke, 1994); Sabine Haag, Alfried Wieczorek, Matthias Pfaffenbichler and Hans-Jürgen Buderer, eds, *Kaiser Maximilian I: Der letzte Ritter und das höfische Turnier* (Regensburg: Schnell & Steiner, 2014); Natalie Anderson, 'Power and Pageantry: The Tournament at the Court of Maximilian I', in *The Medieval Tournament as Spectacle: Tourneys, Jousts and Pas d'Armes, 1100–1600*, ed. by Alan V. Murray and Karen Watts (Woodbridge: Boydell Press, 2020), pp. 185–207; and, especially, Essay 1.

originally concluded with France in 1295, remained a cornerstone of Scotland's attempts to maintain its independence against the more powerful kingdom of England, and by 1400 it was France that exercised the main political and cultural influences on the country. Bonds between the two allies intensified during the Hundred Years War, when numerous Scottish nobles served France as soldiers, in many cases settling there.[3]

Scotland was relatively poor and could not support large numbers of knights, nor did it breed the heavy horses favoured for warfare and tournaments. These circumstances meant that it could not bring together hundreds of competitors in mass tourneys as was common in northern France or the Low Countries. There were several recorded cases of jousting between English and Scottish knights (which involved far fewer participants than tourneys) in the period after 1330, but these seem to have had the character of feats of arms rather than formal chivalric events; most of them took place in the context of warfare between the kingdoms in the Border counties or sieges further inland. It is only in the fifteenth century that we see clearer evidence for the emergence of a tournament culture in Scotland. In some cases the tournaments involved participants from the kingdom of France or the Burgundian state, as on the occasion when the famous jouster Jacques de Lalaing and two of his companions fought against three knights from the affinity of the Douglas family at Stirling during Shrovetide 1449.[4] The fullest flowering of tournaments in Scotland occurred during the reign of James IV, who came to the throne as a young man in 1488 and died, still in the prime of manhood, in battle against his English enemies in 1513.

The only substantial research on Scottish tournaments has been undertaken by Carol Edington, Louise Olga Fradenburg and Katie Stevenson, who, despite the often scanty source material, have identified a considerable number of tournaments and discussed how they were employed as an instrument of royal rulership. Edington describes some (but not all) of James IV's tournaments as *pas d'armes*, but does not go into detail about her reasons for applying this terminology to them. Fradenburg is aware of continental events such as the Burgundian *Pas de l'Arbre d'or* held in Bruges in 1468, but does not draw any significant parallels with the Scottish tournaments. Stevenson offers an excellent analysis of the development of tournaments in Scotland, but does not use the term *pas d'armes* at all. None of these three historians attempts to establish clear criteria that would allow or disallow any identification of any Scottish tournaments with the continental forms.[5] The aim of this essay, then, is to establish the fundamental characteristics of two thematically related tournaments held by James IV in Edinburgh in 1507 and 1508 in order to

---

[3] Philippe Contamine, 'Scottish Soldiers in France in the Second Half of the Fifteenth Century: Mercenaries, Immigrants or Frenchmen in the Making?', in *The Scottish Soldier Abroad, 1247–1967*, ed. by Grant G. Simpson (Edinburgh: John Donald, 1992), pp. 19–30; Michel Ducein, 'L'Écosse dans la guerre de Cent Ans', in *Finances, pouvoirs et mémoire: Mélanges offerts à Jean Favier*, ed. by Jean Kerhervé and Albert Rigaudière (Brest: Fayard, 1999), pp. 297–91; Elizabeth Bonner, 'Scotland's "Auld Alliance" with France, 1295–1560', *History*, 84 (1999), 5–30; James Laidlaw, ed., *The Auld Alliance: France and Scotland over 700 Years* (Edinburgh: Edinburgh University Press, 1999).

[4] See CL, pp. 191–204.

[5] Carol Edington, 'The Tournament in Medieval Scotland', in *Armies, Chivalry and Warfare in Medieval Britain and France: Proceedings of the 1995 Harlaxton Symposium*, ed. by Matthew J. Strickland (Stamford: Paul Watkins, 1998), pp. 46–62; Louise Olga Fradenburg, *City, Marriage, Tournament: Arts of Rule in Late Medieval Scotland* (Madison: University of Wisconsin Press, 1991), pp. 192–243; Katie Stevenson, *Chivalry and Knighthood in Scotland, 1424–1513* (Woodbridge: Boydell Press, 2006), pp. 72–99.

determine whether these events can be categorised as forms of the *pas d'armes* known from similar tournaments held in the Burgundian state, Anjou and elsewhere.

Tournament culture under James IV

King James IV came to the throne at the age of fifteen as a result of a coup d'état mounted by a significant section of the Scottish nobility, during which his father James III was killed. For several years the young king remained under the tutelage of this baronial party, and it was not until 1495 that he took full control of government. He was determined to avoid any further uprisings like the one that had dethroned his father and was thus keenly aware of the importance of cultivating and maintaining ties to the chief men of the realm. The young king was imbued with ideas of chivalry and loved music, song and all manner of entertainments. He was physically active, especially enjoying archery, gunnery, hunting and falconry.[6] He hoped to make a pilgrimage to the Holy Land, an aspiration which later developed into a desire to lead a crusade to recover Jerusalem.[7]

James was determined to bind the Scottish nobility to him in a manner that his father had conspicuously failed to do, and tournaments were one of the means that he decided to employ to achieve this end. According to the chronicler Robert Lindsay of Pitscottie, James began to stage tournaments soon after he came of age, stating that:

> This prince … sindrie tymes wald gar mak proclematiouns out throw his realme to all and sindrie his lordis, earleis and barrouns quhilk was abill for iusting or tornament to come to Edinburgh to him and thair to exerceis them selffis for his plesour as they war best accustomit, sum to rin witht speir, sum to fight witht the battell axe and harnis, sum to feight witht the tuo handit suord, sum to schut the hand bow, corsebow and collvering.
>
> (on several occasions … this prince would have proclamations made throughout his realm to all and sundry of his lords, earls and barons who were able to take part in jousting or tournaments, to come to Edinburgh and to disport themselves there for his pleasure as they were best able to do, some to joust with the lance, some to fight with the battleaxe in armour, some to fight with the two-handed sword, and some to shoot the handbow, crossbow and culverin).[8]

These events allowed the nobility to participate in prestigious events at the royal court in the company of the king and their peers. The competitor judged to have performed best

---

[6] On James IV and his reign, see Robert L. Mackie, *King James IV of Scotland: A Brief Survey of his Life and Times* (Edinburgh: Oliver and Boyd, 1958); Ranald Nicholson, *Scotland: The Later Middle Ages* (Edinburgh: Oliver and Boyd, 1974), pp. 530–606; Norman Macdougall, *James IV* (Edinburgh: John Donald, 1989); Roger Mason, 'Renaissance Monarchy? Stewart Kingship (1469–1542)', in *Scottish Kingship, 1306–1542: Essays in Honour of Norman Macdougall*, ed. by Michael Brown and Roland Tanner (Edinburgh: John Donald, 2008), pp. 255–78.

[7] Alan Macquarrie, *Scotland and the Crusades, 1095–1560* (Edinburgh: John Donald, 1997), pp. 107–13; Macdougall, *James IV*, pp. 199–208.

[8] HCS, vol. 1, pp. 231–2. This edition uses the original spelling of Lindesay for the author's name, but Lindsay is now preferred by historians.

in each event was presented by the king with a prize appropriate to the form of combat in which he had distinguished himself, in the form of a weapon richly ornamented with gold. These prizes were not only valuable items in their own right, but tangible marks of honour that could be preserved and displayed by the noble families in question in memory of the distinction they had attained in the royal presence.[9] The tournaments also burnished the king's reputation — and, by implication, that of his noble subjects — on the international stage. Pitscottie concluded that:

> Be this way and meane the king brocht his realme to great manheid and honouris, that the tyme of his iusting and tornamentis sprang throw all Europe quhilk caussit money forand knychtis to come out of strange contrieis to Scottland to seik iusting because they hard the nobill fame and knychtlie game of the prince of Scottland and of his lordis and barrouns and gentillmen.
>
> (By these ways and means the king brought his realm to a state of great manhood and honour, so that the reputation of his jousting and tournaments spread throughout Europe, which caused many knights from abroad to come from foreign countries to Scotland to seek jousting, because they heard of the noble fame and knightly pursuits of the prince of Scotland and of his lords and barons and gentlemen.)[10]

James held tournaments at midsummer 1504 and at Shrovetide in 1503, 1505 and 1506, and also promoted both jousting and foot combat as part of the celebrations to accompany special occasions. In 1496, he gave refuge to the Flemish impostor Perkin Warbeck, who claimed to be Richard, duke of York, younger son of the late King Edward IV of England (1442–83). James saw the pretender as a useful weapon against his more powerful neighbour, Henry VII (1457–1509) of England, and arranged a marriage for him with his own cousin, Lady Catherine Gordon, which was celebrated with a series of jousts in which the king took part and was wounded in the hand. However, after an abortive invasion of northern England James decided to abandon his support for Warbeck and eventually sought peace with Henry VII.[11] After long negotiations, the two parties concluded a treaty in 1503, which was cemented by a marriage between James and Henry's eldest daughter, Margaret Tudor (1489–1541). In the same year as the treaty was signed, the future queen was welcomed in Edinburgh with a pageant that included a joust between Sir Patrick Hamilton of Kincavil and the squire Patrick Sinclair; this was ostensibly a duel fought over the love of a lady, although, as Stevenson argues, it was probably a 'stylised performance' in keeping with the joyous occasion. The wedding of James and Margaret in Edinburgh on 8 August 1503 was accompanied by a series of elaborate and costly feasts and entertainments, which included three days of jousting and foot combat.[12] James's love of tournaments can also be seen in a gift to his new wife, a prayer book written and illustrated in Flanders (probably by an artist in Ghent). One of the marginal illustrations shows a most unreligious jousting scene (Figure 39).

---

9 *Ibid.*, vol. 1, p. 231.

10 *Ibid.*, vol. 1, pp. 231–2.

11 Macdougall, *James IV*, pp. 117–23; Stevenson, *Chivalry and Knighthood*, p. 84.

12 HCS, vol. 1, pp. 239–40; Stevenson, *Chivalry and Knighthood*, pp. 89–93.

Figure 39. Jousting scene in margin of the Prayerbook of James IV of Scotland. Vienna, Österreichische Nationalbibliothek, Cod. 1897, fol. 38r. Photo: ÖNB.

The king not only organised and presided over tournaments but also, as in the festivities for Perkin Warbeck in 1496, took part in jousting himself. The personal participation of ruling monarchs in tournaments was still a relatively new phenomenon. In the twelfth century, European kings tended to stand aloof from tourneys, probably suspicious of the potential for disorder or conspiracy when numbers of noblemen with large armed retinues gathered together. In the thirteenth and the fourteenth centuries, rulers took a greater interest in jousting events, which involved smaller numbers of contestants than the earlier tourneys and were thus easier to control. However, they tended to act primarily as patrons and presiders rather than participants, and it was only in the fifteenth century that monarchs took part in tournaments personally. This activity was only possible because of significant developments in technology, which helped to resolve one of the fundamental dilemmas of Western kingship. On the one hand, monarchs were expected to embody martial virtues, and could earn the respect of their subjects by demonstrating these in battle or tournaments. On the other hand, there was a reasonable expectation (especially on the part of their counsellors) that they should not needlessly risk life and limb, since injury or death of a ruler would have serious consequences for the stability and security of a realm. The development of plate armour with fully articulated joints covering the arms and legs and helmets giving all-round protection to the head, made it far easier for rulers to indulge in tournaments — above all jousting and foot combat — with a greatly reduced risk of serious injury. Nevertheless, the personal involvement of monarchs as combatants was a gradual process. In his youth Philip the Good (1396–1467), then count of Charolais, took part in various tournaments, but gave up this activity on succeeding his father as duke of Burgundy in 1419. Philip's son, Charles the Bold (1433–77), first took part in tournaments at the age of sixteen, having trained with the famous Jacques de Lalaing, and gained a reputation as a strong and competent jouster, but largely desisted after becoming duke, with some (mostly formal) exceptions such as the occasion of his marriage to Margaret of York. It was thus a quite new development that James IV of Scotland and his contemporaries Maximilian (1459–1519), Henry VIII of England (1491–1547) and Francis I of France (1494–1547) continued to fight in tournaments of various kinds well after succeeding their fathers.[13]

James took a particular interest in all forms of technology (ranging from artillery to dentistry), and undoubtedly wished to have the best possible jousting equipment for himself. While Scottish workshops produced metal weapons, helmets and pieces of armour for use in war, the country did not have the skilled manufacturing capacity to create the sophisticated full harnesses of plate that offered the maximum protection to jousters, and it is likely that the king had much of his jousting equipment made abroad, probably in France or Flanders, although the final fitting was done in Scotland.[14] The Treasurer's accounts

[13] Torsten Hiltmann, 'Ideal und Physis. Der spätmittelalterliche Fürst in Turnier und Zweikampf', in *Die Performanz der Mächtigen. Rangordnung und Idoneität in höfischen Gesellschaften des späten Mittelalters*, ed. by Klaus Oschema *et al.* (Ostfildern: Jan Thorbecke Verlag, 2015), pp. 121–50.

[14] In June 1508, the king's treasurer made a payment of 35s. to the cutler William Rae for 'persing of holes in the Kingis harnes … translating of the Kingis harnes, cutting and persing in divers partis' (TA, vol. 4, p. 121). In this context, *translating* must have meant a final fitting of the harness (i.e. the full suit of armour) to the wearer's body, which was done by drilling holes in the armour so that individual pieces could be tied to the arming doublet worn under the complete harness, while *cutting* probably referred to trimming the edges of some pieces. However, piercing had to be kept to a minimum, as any holes

also reveal that the king had a 'gret hors' (great horse), which was in the keeping of a Frenchman named Jacques and shod by a French blacksmith. It is likely that this animal was a warhorse (which was larger than the native breeds) imported from the continent, along with specialist personnel to look after it.[15]

The *Tournaments of the Wild Knight of the Black Lady*

By late 1506, James was evidently thinking of staging a tournament that would be more novel and elaborate than those he had organised previously. The Treasurer's Accounts for February and March 1507 record payments for the writing and illumination of articles sent to France for the 'justing of the wild knycht for the blak lady' (jousting of the Wild Knight for the Black Lady), which must have been formulated some time previously.[16] Remarkably, a French text entitled *Articles de l'emprise du Chevalier Sauvage à la Dame Noire* survives in a work on heraldry compiled by the French antiquarian Marc de Vulson de la Colombière (d. 1658) and first published in 1639.[17] The *Articles* are dated 22 January 1507 and written in the name of Marchmont Herald, one of the Scottish officers of arms. They state that a personage called the 'Wild Knight of the Black Lady', together with two companions, would undertake *faits d'armes* (feats of arms) against all comers who were gentlemen in name and deed, with permission of the king of Scotland, in August 1507. These *Articles* are analogous to the *chapitres* or chapters of arms that were normally sent out to announce the framework, conditions and rules determined for a specific *pas d'armes*, and it is likely that multiple versions were produced in order to cover the different realms to which they were sent. Letters written by Sir John Ramsay were passed to a French knight who presumably took them abroad, and it is possible that other copies were taken by heralds, who were often sent on missions abroad as they were regarded as having diplomatic immunity. It is surely no coincidence that in March 1507, Rothesay Herald, newly promoted from the rank of Bluemantle Pursuivant, was sent to France, Portugal and Spain on the king's errands.[18]

Although the French *Articles* announce August 1507 as the date of the tournament, the payments recorded in the Lord Treasurer's Accounts make clear that the jousting and other events were already taking place in May and June, and it would seem that, for whatever reason, James brought forward the tournament by several weeks.[19] The *Articles* recognise that some potential participants might be unable to come to Scotland

---

would weaken the metal. It would therefore seem that James's armour was supplied by its (presumably continental) manufacturer without holes, which were drilled by his own armourer in Scotland to ensure the closest possible fit.

[15] *Ibid.*, vol. 3, pp. 366, 371, 381, 382–3, 389–91, 404. The great horse was evidently powerful enough to break the leg of a man named Johnson, who was paid compensation of five French crowns (*ibid.*, vol. 3, p. 383), while an anonymous man received 15s. for injuries done by 'the Kingis hors' (king's horse) (*ibid.*, vol. 3, p. 372).

[16] *Ibid.*, vol. 3, pp. 365, 372.

[17] SH, pp. 491–5; see also Source 16.

[18] TA, vol. 3, pp. 365–6. On Marchmont and the other heralds, see Katie Stevenson, 'Jurisdiction, Authority and Professionalisation: The Officers of Arms in Late Medieval Scotland', in *The Herald in Late Medieval Europe*, ed. by Katie Stevenson (Woodbridge: Boydell Press, 2006), pp. 41–66.

[19] SH, pp. 494–5.

in August, and thus state that the Wild Knight and his two companions would be willing to satisfy any gentlemen in the course of the following year and a day. The existence of this undertaking, together with the circumstance that the tournament was held earlier than originally planned, may have been the reason why James decided to hold another event, with the same thematic framework, a year after the original one. Certainly the Treasurer's accounts show payments for another tournament in May and June 1508, and the allegorical framework and much of the infrastructure were the same as those of the previous year.[20]

It is this second tournament that is described in the histories of John Leslie, bishop of Ross, and Robert Lindsay of Pitscottie.[21] Their chronology is somewhat confused, but both place it in the same year as the arrival of a French embassy led by Bernard Stewart (known in French as Bérault Stuart), lord of Aubigny and count of Beaumont-le-Roger, the descendant of a Scottish family that had settled in France and risen high in royal service during the Hundred Years War. Stewart acted as judge at the tournament, but died at Corstorphine, a village west of Edinburgh, on 12 June 1508, which provides a *terminus ad quem* for the event.[22]

The allegorical framework and infrastructure of both tournaments must have been decided well in advance of the events, since they were mentioned in the announcements sent abroad to maximise the participation of foreign knights. Pitscottie emphasises that James wanted the tournament in 1508 to be well publicised in France, England and Denmark, which suited his international ambitions. Scotland had long-standing political and cultural ties with France, while the peace treaty of 1503 meant that English knights were also welcome at Scottish tournaments. Participation of knights from Denmark might seem less obvious, but it should be remembered that the king's mother Margaret (1456–86) was the daughter of Christian I of Denmark (1426–81), and even after her death James maintained close relations and correspondence with his uncle Hans (1455–1513), king of Denmark, Norway and Sweden.[23]

The tournaments of 1507 and 1508 were both set in the same fictional framework, whose key characteristics were derived from imaginative literature. The French *Articles* maintain the fiction of a mysterious and anonymous Wild Knight who has received permission from the king of Scots to joust with all challengers, but it must have been an open secret that this personage was played by King James himself. As Bishop Leslie wrote, 'This wyld knycht was the king himself, quha wes vaileyant in armeis, and could very weill exerce the same' (this Wild Knight was the king himself, who was valiant in arms, and knew very well how to exercise with them).[24] Leslie further explains the king's choice of a fictional identity:

---

20 TA, vol. 4, pp. 13–27, 117–29.

21 Respectively, JLBS, vol. 2, p. 128; and HCS, vol. 1, pp. 242–4.

22 Philippe Contamine, 'Entre France et Écosse: Bérault Stuart, seigneur d'Aubigny (vers 1452–1508), chef de guerre, diplomate, écrivain militaire', in *The Auld Alliance: France and Scotland over 700 Years*, ed. by James Laidlaw (Edinburgh: Edinburgh University Press, 1999), pp. 59–76; Bryony Coombs, 'Identity and Agency in the Patronage of Bérault Stuart d'Aubigny: The Political Self-Fashioning of a Franco-Scottish Soldier and Diplomat', *Medieval Journal*, 7 (2017), 89–143.

23 HCS, vol. 1, pp. 242–3.

24 JLBS, vol. 2, p. 128.

> He was of sik corage, that quhom evir he hard maist commendet in vertuous and valȝeant actes, he intendit and kaist, him ay to follow, bot heiring of not ane in ancient antiquitie amang al his predecessours, to quhom he wald be sa conforme as to King Arthur; remembreng of King Arthuris Knychts, and thair forme desyreng to follow quha war knychtes of the round table, that tyme he wald be called a knycht of King Arthuris brocht up in the wodis.
>
> (He was of such courage that whoever he heard most commended in virtuous and valiant acts, he intended and chose to follow him always, but hearing of no one in antiquity among all his predecessors to whom he wished to conform as much as to King Arthur, that, remembering King Arthur's knights, and thus desiring to follow those who were knights of the Round Table, on this occasion he wished to be known as a knight of King Arthur who had been brought up in the woods).[25]

The story of a child of noble birth who is brought up far from courtly life in a desolate landscape, but eventually attains the accolade of knighthood, is one of the principal themes of Arthurian literature, notably in the romances of Perceval by the late twelfth-century romancer Chrétien de Troyes and his continuators. Whether James or his counsellors were conversant with these works is perhaps doubtful, given that they had been written around three centuries previously. However, Arthurian literature remained popular and vital in Scotland, where the late fifteenth century saw the composition of two new romances, *Golagros and Gawain* and *Lancelot of the Laik.* Parts of both were derived from French originals, suggesting that some French-language Arthurian works were in circulation in Scotland at the time of their composition.[26] It has been recently argued that the production of a printed edition of *Golagros and Gawain* in 1508 came about because of King James's growing interest in leading a crusade against the Turks.[27]

In contrast to the other accounts, Pitscottie names the protagonist as the 'Black Knight', rather than the 'Wild Knight'. This might simply be a faulty memory, but there may be a rational explanation for his evident confusion. He relates that some of the foreign challengers in 1508 wore white clothing, explaining that King James wore black in order to contrast with them. By the late Middle Ages, black clothing was popular in elite circles, especially at the court of the dukes of Burgundy, and it seems to have been regarded as signalling high status. The King's Wardrobe Accounts show that James made numerous purchases of black cloth from manufactures in the Burgundian state; they are recorded as *Rislis blak,* which was produced in Lille (known in Flemish as Rijsel) and seems to have been of higher quality and thus more expensive than the homemade equivalent, *Scottis blak.* So it is entirely possible that James appeared in costly black clothing (possibly worn

---

[25] *Ibid.*

[26] Nicola Royan, '"Na les vailyeant than ony uthir princis of Britane". Representations of Arthur in Scotland 1480–1540', *Scottish Studies Review*, 3 (2002), 9–20; Elizabeth Archibald, '*Lancelot of the Laik*', in *The Scots and Medieval Arthurian Legend*, ed. by Rhiannon Purdie and Nicola Royan (Woodbridge: Boydell Press, 2005), pp. 71–82; Rhiannon Purdie, 'The Search for Scottishness in *Golagros and Gawane*', in *The Scots and Medieval Arthurian Legend*, ed. by Rhiannon Purdie and Nicola Royan (Woodbridge: Boydell Press, 2005), pp. 95–108.

[27] Kristin Bovaird-Abbo, '"Reirdit on ane riche roche beside ane riveir": Martial Landscape and James IV of Scotland in *The Knightly Tale of Golagros and Gawane*', *Neophilologus*, 98 (2014), 675–88.

over his armour when jousting), and that this colour was also further used as part of the wider allegorical framework.[28]

The adoption of a fictional persona by an *entrepreneur** was one of the central features of recorded *pas d'armes*, and the staging of such events often involved the provision of objects imbued with allegorical significance as well as associated theatrical elements. Thus the Burgundian *Pas du Perron Fée* (Bruges, 1463) and *Pas de la Dame Sauvage* (Ghent, 1470) featured a *perron** from which shields were hung, to be struck by challengers.[29]

Early sixteenth-century Edinburgh and the adjoining (but administratively separate) burgh of Canongate were built on a long slope that fell away from the castle rock, extending as far as the Palace of Holyroodhouse approximately two miles to the east. The tournaments must have taken place on level ground near the palace. The French *Articles* state that the feats of arms shall take place:

> en cedit royaume & ville d'Edimbourg dedans le Camp de Souvenir, lequel sera entre le chasteau nommé des Pucelles, et le Pavillon Secret, & dedans ledit Camp sera l'arbre d'Esperance, lequel croist au jardin de Patience, portant feuilles de plaisance, la fleur de noblesse, et le fruit d'honneur.
>
> (in this kingdom in the town of Edinburgh on the Field of Memory, which will be situated between the castle known as that of the Maidens and the Secret Pavilion, and in this Field will be the Tree of Esperance, which grows in the Garden of Patience and bears leaves of Pleasure, flowers of Nobility, and fruits of Honour).[30]

The 'Castle of the Maidens' was a traditional literary designation for Edinburgh Castle, but the other allegorical names given for venues seem to have been devised specifically for this occasion. In both 1507 and 1508, a richly decorated 'great pavilion' was constructed from canvas stretched over an iron frame. It was occupied by the Wild Knight and his retinue, while there was a smaller pavilion for the Black Lady and her attendants. The central feature of the scenery was a Tree of Esperance. Whether this was an actual plant or an artificial construction is difficult to ascertain, but it was richly decorated with objects illustrating its symbolism. The tree erected in 1507 was covered with eighteen dozen leaves, six dozen flowers and thirty-seven pears, all of them made from metal and fastened to the tree with wire and nails; the pears cost two shillings each. It is possible that the metal leaves, flowers and pears were given out as prizes or souvenirs, since another tree was set up and similarly decorated in 1508, with new expenditure being recorded for the decoration on this occasion, although some elements seem to have been reused, as payments were

---

[28] HCS, vol. 1, p. 243; Françoise Piponnier and Perrine Mane, *Dress in the Middle Ages* (New Haven, CT: Yale University Press, 1997), pp. 14–18: John H. A. Munro, 'The Anti-Red Shift – To the Dark Side: Colour Changes in Flemish Luxury Woollens, 1300–1550', in *Medieval Clothing and Textiles, vol. 3*, ed. by Robin Netherton and Gale R. Owen-Crocker (Woodbridge: Boydell Press, 2007), pp. 55–95; Sophie Jolivet, 'La construction d'une image: Philippe le Bon et le noir (1419–1467)', in *Se vêtir à la cour en Europe, 1400–1815*, ed. by Isabelle Paresys and Natacha Coquery (Villeneuve d'Ascq: Institut de recherches historiques du Septentrion, 2011), pp. 27–42. For examples of *Rislis blak* and *Scottis blak*, see TA, vol. 3, pp. 38, 47, 99, 100, 253; vol. 4, pp. 19–20, 24, 25.

[29] Blunk, 'Between Sport and Theatre', pp. 124–5.

[30] SH, pp. 491–2.

made for the mending of leaves in 1508. In addition to this rich decoration, the French text foresaw that the tree would be hung with the shields of competing knights.[31] The Tree of Esperance thus seems to have been envisaged as the central, programmatic focus of the tournaments, and is reminiscent of similar trees that featured in *pas d'armes* held in France, such as the *Pas de l'Arbre Charlemagne*, held at Marsannay-la-Côte near Dijon in 1443, or the *Pas de l'Arbre d'or*, organised in Bruges by Antoine, the Great Bastard of Burgundy, in 1468.[32]

James's tournaments went further than some earlier *pas d'armes* in featuring the actual personification of a character other than the fictional protagonist. In the *chapitres* for the *Arbre d'or*, Antoine of Burgundy presented himself as a poor 'Knight of the Golden Tree' acting in the service of the 'Lady of the Secret Isle'. Yet, while the staging of that event was to feature a giant and a dwarf stationed by a symbolic golden tree, the Lady seems to have remained as a purely hypothetical personage, who did not actually appear in the proceedings.[33] Similarly, in the *Dame Sauvage*, the eponymous Wild Lady was not personified, but rather depicted on a shield that would be awarded as a prize.[34] During the two tournaments in Edinburgh, in contrast, the Black Lady was personified by a real woman;[35] the Treasurer's accounts reveal several payments for fine clothing for herself, her attendants and two squires who accompanied her, William Ogilvy and Alexander Elphinstone.[36]

The identity of the personage who played the part of the Black Lady is problematic. Recent research has revealed the presence at the Scottish court of several 'Moors', a term that could have referred either to Africans or to Moriscos from the Iberian peninsula. Scotland was not directly involved in the slave trade, but such individuals may have been captured along with Spanish or Portuguese vessels seized by Scottish privateers operating in the Atlantic.[37] Some commentators have identified the Black Lady with an African woman apostrophised by the poet William Dunbar, who gives a grotesque and unflattering description of her physical features. However, Dunbar's subject was only one of several 'Moors' at the Scottish court, and there is no direct evidence to connect her with the Black Lady. Indeed, as Fradenburg points out, it is impossible to say whether the

---

31 TA, vol. 3, pp. 258–60, 365–94; vol. 4, pp. 120–9; SH, pp. 491–2. The Treasurer's accounts also mention apples made for the tournament, although it is unclear whether these were hung on the Tree (TA, vol. 3, p. 385).

32 See Sources 4 and 12, respectively.

33 Leeds, Royal Armouries Library, I.35, fols 7r–10r; see also Source 12.

34 Blunk, 'Between Sport and Theatre', p. 123. In the narrative accounts of the Burgundian *Perron Fée*, the degree of involvement of the 'Lady of the Enchanted Column' in the dramatised action varies greatly from version to version: see Essay 3 and Source 11a.

35 In this respect, this Scottish tournament would seem to be closer to those organised in the Angevin sphere. For example, at the *Pas de la Bergère* (Tarascon, 1449) the eponymous Shepherdess in whose honour the event is being organised does appear as an actual character, being played by Isabelle de Lenoncourt, probably a sister or daughter of one of the *entrepreneurs*, Philippe de Lenoncourt: see Source 6. Similarly, at the *Pas de la Joyeuse Garde/Pas de Saumur* (1446) organised by René of Anjou, the unnamed lady featured in the chapters of arms was played by different ladies of the Angevin court on different days: on this event, see Essays 2 and 7 and Source 5.

36 TA, vol. 3, pp. 258, 259, 260; vol. 4, p. 119.

37 Sue Niebrzydowski, 'The Sultana and Her Sisters: Black Women in the British Isles before 1530', *Women's History Review*, 10 (2001), 187–210.

character was actually played by a black woman at all, or whether she may have been a white woman dressed in black or even wearing blackface, given that the accounts record payments for black sleeves, gloves and other items, and that the king had a predilection for this colour in his own clothing.[38] There was also a long tradition of knights in literary tournaments wearing plain colours rather than their own proper armorial emblems or devices when they wished to appear incognito.[39] Although modern historians have tended to refer to the 'tournaments of the Wild Knight *and* the Black Lady', it should be noted that the French articles use the designation *Le Chevalier Sauvage à la Dame Noire*, using the preposition *à* (rather than the conjunction *et*), meaning 'of' or 'for' the Black Lady, probably as an indication that the Wild Knight was considered to be either in the Lady's service or fighting to gain her as a prize. Irrespective of the Black Lady's ethnicity, the addition of a second fictional character with a physical presence alongside the Wild Knight lent the proceedings greater variety and exoticism.[40]

The French *Articles* envisage a large number of jousts with lances, as well as foot combats with lances, demi-lances*, swords, pollaxes and daggers, but, given that the timing of the first tournament (and possibly other arrangements) was changed, it is impossible to say whether in the event all of these were held in the manner originally proposed; frustratingly, the Scots narratives say little about the actual contests. The Treasurer's accounts for both years show payments for a great deal of weaponry, armour, horses and horse equipment, which was much more than was required for the king's own use. Pitscottie explains that the lords and barons 'war commandit to mak thame reddie againe the said day apoincted for to enarme thame selffis in thair best arrey and in the same armur and waponis that thay thocht thame selffis best to fecht into' (were commanded to make themselves ready for the appointed day by arming themselves in their best array and in the same armour and weapons that they thought themselves best able to fight in), but it would seem that the king was supplying equipment to at least some of those Scots who did not have gear of the requisite standard.[41] He also made gifts of money or equipment to various French knights and paid an armourer for seventeen days to attend to them. Other detail concerning the allegorical framework can be glimpsed in the accounts. The sum of £5 12s. 6d. was paid to one Piers the Painter to cut out 'letteres for cotis and bardis for hors hosouris' (letters for coats and bards* for horse trappers*), using 2½ ells of velvet. This formulation probably refers to letters spelling out mottoes or rebuses that were displayed on coat armours* and horse trappings, suggesting that participants other than the king may have reflected allegorical themes in their own clothing and equipment.[42]

---

[38] Priscilla Bawcutt, ed., *The Poems of William Dunbar*, 2 vols (Glasgow: Association for Scottish Literary Studies, 1998), vol. 1, p. 113; vol. 2, pp. 350–2; Victor Sherb, 'The Tournament of Power: Public Combat and Social Inferiority in Late Medieval England', *Studies in Medieval and Renaissance History*, n.s. 12 (1991), 105–28; Stevenson, *Chivalry and Knighthood*, pp. 72–99; Fradenburg, *City, Marriage, Tournament*, pp. 254–60.

[39] Gerard J. Brault, *Early Blazon: Heraldic Description in the Twelfth and Thirteenth Centuries with Special Reference to Arthurian Heraldry*, 2nd edition (Cambridge: Boydell, 1997), pp. 31–5.

[40] The Treasurer's accounts for February 1507 refer to a 'Wild Knycht *for* the Blak Lady', which seems to correspond to the French expression (TA, vol. 3, p. 365).

[41] *Ibid.*, vol. 3, pp. 396–7; HCS, vol. 1, p. 242.

[42] TA, vol. 4, p. 22. Examples of such mottoes and rebuses can be seen in the illustrations in the tournament book of Emperor Frederick III and Emperor Maximilian I (Munich, Bayerische Staatsbibliothek, Cod. Icon. 398).

The events were supervised by Lyon Herald and the other Scottish officers of arms, who received additional payments in recognition of their services, and they had a particular role in the judging of the combats.[43] In 1508, the king appointed Bernard Stewart as presider and judge, although he was evidently assisted by the heralds. The high-quality equipment available to King James meant that he could take a central part in these events, and he jousted and fought on foot in the guise of the Wild Knight.[44] The king was (unsurprisingly) adjudged to be the best competitor overall, and symbolically carried off the Black Lady as his prize. There were also prizes for the best performer in each category of combat, who received a weapon ornamented with gold or silver appropriate to the discipline in which he had performed. The judges decided that the best archer was James Hamilton, earl of Arran (d. 1529), a first cousin of the king. Cuthbert Cunningham, earl of Glencairn (d. 1540/1541), was 'the best riner of the speir' (literally, 'runner of the spear'). This phrase might refer to jousting, but since the Wild Knight was judged to be the best overall competitor, in which jousting was the main event, it might more readily relate to a combat in which the competitors began by throwing spears and then continued fighting with swords, as specified in the French *Articles* transmitted by Vulson. Andrew Lord Gray (d. 1514) was 'the best fechtar with the battellaix' (best fighter with the battleaxe). The best fighter with the 'twa handit sword' (two-handed sword) was Sir Patrick Hamilton; this was probably Sir Patrick Hamilton of Kincavel (d. 1520), younger brother of the earl of Arran. As reported for tournaments held earlier in the reign, each of these barons was rewarded with presentation weapons decorated with gold or silver to keep in memory of their deeds.[45] The Treasurer's accounts for 1507 record payments for gilt weapons, including swords, battleaxes, daggers and maces; these were clearly too valuable to be used in combat, and must have been bestowed as prizes.[46] Members of the king's household were given prominent roles as squires to the Wild Knight and the Black Lady.

The significance of the Arthurian character adopted by the king was reinforced by performative displays that took place outwith the combats, as well as indoor entertainments. In addition to his two squires, the Wild Knight was accompanied by an entourage whose members were dressed in 'wildmen cotis' — that is, coats of Wild Men.[47] The French *Articles* also specify that the Tree of Esperance was to be guarded by the Black Lady along with Wild Men as well as heralds and musicians.[48] In an essay on Scottish court entertainments, Lesley Mickel has argued that these men were intended to represent Scottish Highlanders, who were often seen as wild, liminal and uncouth, but it is not evident how they would have fitted into an Arthurian theme.[49] As the king spoke Gaelic himself,[50] it would have been possible for him to persuade some of his Highland vassals to provide suitably clad attendants if he had wanted them. In fact, the garb of the Wild Men

---

43 TA, vol. 4, p. 117.

44 JLBS, vol. 2, p. 128; HCS, vol. 1, pp. 242–4.

45 HCS, vol. 1, pp. 242–4; SH, p. 493.

46 TA, vol. 3, p. 396.

47 *Ibid.*, vol. 3, p. 385.

48 SH, pp. 493–4.

49 Lesley Mickel, 'Our Hielandmen: Scots in Court Entertainments at Home and Abroad, 1507–1616', *Renaissance Studies*, 33 (2019), 185–203.

50 On the king's knowledge of Gaelic and other languages, see Mackie, *King James IV of Scotland*, pp. 118–19.

Figure 40. Wild Men in the margins of the Prayerbook of James IV of Scotland. Vienna, Österreichische Nationalbibliothek, Cod. 1897, fol. 49v. Photo: ÖNB.

suggests a much more exotic significance. The Lord Treasurer's accounts reveal that their costumes involved 'hert hornes and gayt skinnis' (deer horns and goatskins). Goats, both domesticated and feral, were plentiful in Scotland; their hides provided the main elements of the Wild Men's clothing, which was completed by antlers sourced from Tullibardine in Perthshire.[51] Wild Men, usually depicted as hairy, and either naked or with minimal clothing, were a popular theme in the art and heraldry of the later Middle Ages and were also known to have been played by costumed actors or musicians in continental *pas d'armes* such as the *Dame Sauvage*.[52] They were evidently also a particular interest of James's. One of the leaves of the prayer book he had illustrated in Flanders shows several hairy Wild Men, one of them sitting on the back of an oversized seabird and fighting against an armoured sea monster (Figure 40). This theme may have been developed in a more theatrical manner here at the tournament. The miscellaneous royal accounts record a rather puzzling payment of 5s. for bringing 'the tame hert fra Strivelin quhilk wes slayn in the barres' (the tame deer from Stirling which was slain at the barriers), which was probably brought from the king's park there.[53] The reference to slaying suggests that the Wild Men were not just passive attendants but may have acted out hunting scenes, presumably during the intervals between combat. In courtly literature a hunt, particularly when it involved an impressive stag, often provided the prelude or framework for a narrative in which a knight responded to a challenge or otherwise set out in search of adventure, before returning to court to receive the recognition of his peers.[54] The costuming of the king's attendants and their performances thus drew attention to the character played by the king while also linking to a wider international chivalric culture.

Further performative elements were built around the Black Lady and her attendants. At the end of May 1508, she was carried in a 'Chair Triumphale', presumably a form of litter, by fourteen men from the castle to the *barres* — that is, the lists — and from there to the abbey, which was situated close to the palace of Holyroodhouse. This procession was an important element, since it provided a spectacle for a greater number of the urban population than would have been able to see the jousting and other martial competitions. It should be remembered, moreover, that the city's economy received a massive boost through the multifarious payments to armourers, cutlers, painters, drapers, tailors, victuallers, labourers and other diverse artisans.[55]

The proceedings also involved specialists in theatre. The culmination of the tournament of 1508 was a series of banquets held in the palace over three days, in which feasting was interspersed with farces and other plays and entertainments organised by Andrew Forman, bishop of Moray. They concluded with an impressive dramatic performance. At the final banquet on the third day, 'thair come ane clwdd out of the rwffe of the hall as appeirit to men and opnit and cleikkit vp the blak lady in presence of thame all that scho was no moir seine' (it seemed to those present that a cloud descended from the roof of the hall,

---

[51] TA, vol. 3, pp. 385–6, 393; Catherine Smith, 'The "Poor Man's Mart": History and Archaeology of Goats in Scotland', *Tayside and Fife Archaeological Journal*, 28 (2022), 81–99.

[52] Blunk, 'Between Sport and Theatre', p. 123.

[53] TA, vol. 4, p. 128.

[54] Julia Weitbrecht, 'In der *Forest aventureuse*: Jagd, Initiation und Aventiure in erzählhistorischer Perspektive', in *Aventiure: Ereignis und Erzählung*, ed. by Michael Schwarzbach-Dobson and Franziska Wenzel (Berlin: Erich Schmidt Verlag, 2022), pp. 109–25.

[55] TA, vol. 4, p. 119.

then opened and snatched up the Black Lady in the presence of everyone, so that she could no longer be seen). Pitscottie reports that some of those present thought that this action was done by 'igramancie' (necromancy).[56] This sounds like the reaction of impressionable spectators who did not fully comprehend what they were seeing. Andrew Forman had spent most of his career in royal service, serving as an apostolic protonotary before being appointed to his bishopric; he later became archbishop of St Andrews and vice-regent for King James V. He was undoubtedly trusted by the king and had access to considerable resources, and the sudden disappearance of the Black Lady was most likely to have been the product of some very slick staging effects.[57] By the early sixteenth century, dramatic performances often called for players to be lowered to the stage from above or lifted up from it; for example, angels were shown descending to the earth or biblical characters were carried up to Heaven. Those responsible for the staging of drama had worked out the technology that enabled such spectacular effects to be carried out, using ropes, windlasses or pulleys to lower and hoist players in and out of sight, which were often combined with pyrotechnic effects. The cloud that enveloped the Black Lady was probably simply smoke, which not only added to the drama but would serve to obscure any mechanical devices being employed.[58] King James could certainly congratulate himself on a spectacular end to a successful event that must have impressed his own barons and foreign visitors alike.

Conclusion

How far can the tournaments of the *Wild Knight of the Black Lady* be considered as *pas d'armes*? The central component on both occasions was a series of jousts, with additional foot combats involving spears, swords, pollaxes, maces and daggers. The format of the tournaments was evidently conceived by the king, who also participated in them, and the organisation, conduct and judging of most of the events were overseen by the royal heralds. In these respects, the contests were not fundamentally different from other forms of tournament held previously in Scotland. Nor does terminology assist us; the French *Articles* refer to *faits d'armes* (feats of arms), while the sources in Scots speak only of tournaments and jousting. Nevertheless, it is possible to identify at least five key features that correspond to characteristics of *pas d'armes* as they had been conceived and enacted on the continent up to that time.[59] The first of these is a fictional scenario, embodied by the characters of the Wild Knight, adopted by the protagonist James IV (whom we should consider to be the *entrepreneur*), and the Black Lady. The second feature is the existence of an *emprise* inviting participation in the tournament, corresponding to the *chapitres* often featuring in continental *pas d'armes*, which was announced several months in advance by means of written and illuminated articles and conveyed to foreign countries by heralds

---

[56] HCS, vol. 1, p. 244.

[57] C. A. McGladdery, 'Andrew Forman (c.1465–1521)', in *Oxford Dictionary of National Biography* <https://doi.org/10.1093/ref:odnb/9883> [accessed 22 June 2024].

[58] Philip Butterworth and Peter Harrop, 'The Providers of Pyrotechnics in Plays and Celebrations', in *Material Culture and Early Drama*, ed. by Clifford Davidson (Kalamazoo, MI: Medieval Institute Publications, 1999), pp. 59–74; Philip Butterworth, *Staging Conventions in Medieval English Theatre* (Cambridge: Cambridge University Press, 2014), pp. 148–52.

[59] On key characteristics of *pas d'armes* and the circumstances needed at a court for this type of chivalric entertainment to flourish, see Essay 1.

and specially commissioned knights. The third is the erection of a central programmatic object, the Tree of Esperance, decorated with ornaments that were proclaimed as having symbolic meanings relating to chivalric virtues (pleasure, nobility and honour). The fourth is the adoption of distinctive, allegorical costumes by the Wild Knight, the Black Lady, attendants clad as Wild Men and (perhaps) jousters bearing mottoes and emblematic devices on their clothing and caparisons. The fifth and final feature is performative elements taking place outwith the combats, comprising farces and other entertainments, but also dramatic appearances by the Wild Men and the procession and theatrical disappearance of the Black Lady.

The tournaments of the *Wild Knight of the Black Lady* are the first such event held in Scotland within an allegorical framework that determined the characters, staging and performances that featured in it. These elements did not have a particularly strong degree of literary coherence, but the same could be said of several of the *pas d'armes* staged on the continent; one thinks, for example, of the rather vaguely defined characteristics of the Knight of the Golden Tree and the Lady of the Secret Isle in the *pas* organised by Antoine, the Great Bastard of Burgundy, in 1468.[60] The analysis given here of the events presented in 1507 and 1508 thus suggests that James IV was aware of the principal features of the continental *pas d'armes* and was keen to instrumentalise this tournament form as a means of conciliating his nobility and demonstrating his own prowess and largesse to an international audience. James could also congratulate himself on having stolen a march on his wealthier and more powerful southern neighbour: indeed, it is remarkable that the tournaments of the *Wild Knight of the Black Lady* took place several years before the first allegorically themed jousting event to be promoted by James's brother-in-law, Henry VIII of England, at Westminster in 1511.[61] One can well imagine that the success of his tournaments might have prompted James to envisage further festivities on a similar pattern. However, the king's untimely death at the battle of Flodden in 1513 after the resumption of hostilities with England deprived Scotland of its energetic and popular monarch. The ensuing regency and renewed war with England were not conducive to the holding of lavish courtly spectacles and, as far as the current state of research can establish, James IV's tournaments of 1507 and 1508 remain the only examples of the *pas d'armes* to have been held in Scotland.

---

[60] For example, the figure of the Lady of the Secret Isle is only very loosely based on a character in Aimon de Varennes' late twelfth-century *Roman de Florimont*: see Source 12, p. 249; see also Annette Lindner, 'L'influence du roman chevaleresque français sur le pas d'armes', *PCEEB*, 31 (1991), 67–78.

[61] The Westminster Tournament was held in February 1511 to celebrate the birth of a son to Henry's wife Catherine of Aragon the previous month, and involved allegorical staging and decoration. It was commemorated in a magnificent vellum roll now kept in the College of Arms, London. For description and analysis, see Sydney Anglo, *The Great Tournament Roll of Westminster* (Oxford: Clarendon Press, 1968).

Rosalind Brown-Grant

Pas d'armes and the Construction of Chivalric Masculinity: Ethics and Erotics of Knightly Combat

Compared with the earliest tournament forms, such as the tourney* or *mêlée**, in which competitors ranged across a wide, unenclosed area, the *pas d'armes*, a form of chivalric combat involving individuals or teams of competitors in closed lists, ostensibly to defend or attack a specific location (e.g. a bridge, fountain or column, whether real or constructed for the purpose), was highly ritualised and tightly regulated. This made it the ideal arena for the demonstration of individual feats of martial prowess that played an important part in the construction of chivalric masculinity in late medieval Europe.[1] The chivalric biographies, chronicles, heralds' reports, memoirs and standalone narrative accounts that celebrate the deeds accomplished by knights and squires at these events allow us to examine the contemporary formation of chivalric masculine identity since they were not only commemorative in preserving a record of the competitors' exploits for posterity but also prescriptive in teaching the tenets of knighthood to a noble audience through the martial contests they recounted. As Olivier de La Marche (*c.*1425–1502), whose *Mémoires* are a major source for chivalric combats that took place in the Burgundian composite state, puts it in his account of the *Pas de l'Arbre Charlemagne* (Marsannay-la-Côte, near Dijon, 1443), the first *pas* that he himself witnessed, his aim was to:

> *ramentevoir* la chevallerie monstrée de tous les partiz, et aussi *par maniere d'escolle et de doctrine* aux nobles hommes qui viendront cy après, qui, peult estre, desireront de eulx monstrer et faire congnoistre en leur advenir comme leurs devanchiers
>
> (*commit to memory* the chivalric deeds that were performed by those present and [offer] *a form of teaching and instruction* to all noble men who will come hereafter and who may wish to demonstrate [their prowess] and make a name for themselves in the future as their predecessors did before them).[2]

In her standard work on the formation of medieval masculinity, which includes an important chapter on chivalry, Ruth Mazo Karras argues that a core feature of masculine identity in this period was 'the need to prove oneself in competition with other men and to dominate others'.[3] Chivalric events, including *pas d'armes*, provided a forum

[1] See Richard Barber and Juliet Barker, *Tournaments: Jousts, Chivalry and Pageants in the Middle Ages* (New York: Weidenfeld & Nicolson, 1989); Sébastien Nadot, *Le Spectacle des joutes: Sport et courtoisie à la fin du Moyen Âge* (Rennes: Presses Universitaires de Rennes, 2012).

[2] OdLM, vol. 1, p. 290, emphasis added. See also Catherine Emerson, *Olivier de La Marche and the Rhetoric of Fifteenth-Century Historiography* (Woodbridge: Boydell Press, 2004).

[3] Ruth Mazo Karras, *From Boys to Men: Formations of Masculinity in Late Medieval Europe* (Philadelphia: University of Pennsylvania Press, 2003), p. 10.

for the demonstration of superiority over other men with individual male dominance being achieved 'through violence and through control of women'.[4] In this perspective, even the men's seeming submission to the ladies who supposedly inspired or ordered them to undertake these deeds — according, at least, to the fictional scenarios that often accompany the 'chapters of arms' that publicised the *pas* — was really just another way of impressing other males. As Karras argues: 'The woman was only an object over which the battles of the men were fought, even when she was placed in a position of ostensible superiority.'[5] Whilst women formed part of the audience at *pas d'armes* and men might claim to be jousting to win their love, such chivalric display was essentially 'for other men, and it was other men who ultimately evaluated the young man and ruled him a full man'.[6]

Yet, the emphasis in many narrative accounts of *pas d'armes* was not simply on relating the actual combats themselves (the number of blows exchanged, lances broken, wounds inflicted, etc.) in order to judge which contestant had emerged dominant over all the others. Of just as much interest to those who recorded these occasions was the display of wealth and noble status by the elaborately robed and accoutred defenders and challengers of the combats as they entered the lists flanked by an entourage of illustrious friends and relatives. Equally important to these writers was the courteous spirit in which the competitors conducted themselves towards each other, towards those officiating at the bouts and towards the spectators who had come to see them demonstrate their skills in pursuit of their sport, whether on the field itself or during the post-combat festivities that usually followed them.

It would seem, then, that chivalric masculinity as constructed in accounts of *pas d'armes* should not principally be defined in terms of how high-status men exerted their physical dominance over each other. After all, whilst Karras states that those knights 'whose chivalric deeds were most admired were those who were most successful at violence', she herself also emphasises that masculine honour was achieved through courtliness and gentility: chivalric masculinity involved both competition and brotherhood in which knights rejoiced in each other's victories, declared their love for each other and celebrated together after having fought each other.[7] We might therefore question whether *pas d'armes* were simply a means for competitors to prove their own superiority or whether they also provided a context in which they could affirm their fellows' noble identity in their mutual aspiration to demonstrate their membership of a chivalric elite. Similarly, whilst *pas d'armes* were indisputably homosocial occasions, it is also a matter of some debate as to whether women's involvement was merely that of a currency, as 'tokens in a game of masculine competition' by which a knight's success was measured, as Karras puts it,[8] or if they could exercise genuine agency of their own in determining how the male competitors' actions were to be interpreted, particularly if they themselves were involved in the organisation and financing of these exhibitions of male prowess and could thus affect the shaping of masculine identity within them. Ultimately, too, it remains to be seen if these different facets of the *pas d'armes* could co-exist within the same event or if

4 *Ibid.*
5 *Ibid.*, p. 55.
6 *Ibid.*, p. 65.
7 *Ibid.*, pp. 21, 25, 31, 44–7, 62.
8 *Ibid.*, p. 51. For examples of scholars who would dispute Karras's views here, see below, n. 77.

some were more characterised by one aspect than another, depending on the particular cultural or political context in which each was staged.

In seeking to answer these questions, this study will focus on two issues that are central to understanding how chivalric masculinity was presented by the writers who commemorated the *pas d'armes*. The first is the *ethics* of these combats, ethics here being used in the Aristotelian sense of demonstrating virtuous conduct through the individual's mastery of himself, an idea employed in works as wide-ranging as mirrors for princes such as Giles of Rome's highly influential *De regimine principum* (1277–80) and chivalric biographies such as Jean de Bueil's immensely popular *Jouvencel* (*c.*1466).[9] In a tournament context, this notion of ethics translates into how a man's honour was exhibited and upheld through the correctness of his speech and appearance and in his observance of the rules of engagement created for a particular *pas d'armes*. It was these rules that allowed the male competitors' desire to achieve dominance over one another to be reconciled with the ethical imperative to display magnanimity in the face of either victory or defeat. The second issue to be discussed here is the *erotics* of these events: that is, how the homosocial bonds between men were mediated through the power relations between the male contestants and the female figures who often supposedly inspired or ordered them to undertake a *pas d'armes*, and the ways in which women were able to put their own stamp on the meanings conveyed by these chivalric displays of male prowess.

The narrative sources on which this study will draw are those recounting a range of *pas d'armes* that took place in the Burgundian lands during the reigns of Duke Philip the Good (1419–67) and his son Charles the Bold (1467–77), these events being particularly well documented: principally, the *Pas de l'Arbre Charlemagne*, the *Pas de la Fontaine des Pleurs* (Chalon-sur-Saône, 1449–50) and the *Pas de l'Arbre d'or* (Bruges, 1468), as well as others such as the *Pas du Perron Fée* (Bruges, 1463) and the *Pas de la Dame Sauvage* (Ghent, 1470). Although La Marche, in both his *Mémoires* and other accounts that circulated independently, is by far the most prolific commentator on these Burgundian *pas*,[10] other sources for them include the chivalric biography known as the *Livre des faits de messire Jacques de Lalaing* (early 1470s) for the *Fontaine des Pleurs*[11] and the various different standalone narrative accounts of the *Perron Fée*, which was organised by Jacques de Lalaing's younger brother, Philippe.[12] Comparison will also be made between these Burgundian sources and those commemorating

[9] Following Aristotle, these works argue that the individual must strive for virtue in his 'monostic' life (i.e. his personal ethics), his economic life (i.e. as head of a household or a military unit) and his political life (i.e. as head of a realm or lordship). See Matthew Kempshall, *The Common Good in Late Medieval Political Thought* (Oxford: Clarendon Press, 1999); and S. H. Rigby, *Wisdom and Chivalry: Chaucer's* Knight's Tale *and Medieval Political Theory* (Leiden/Boston, MA: Brill, 2009).

[10] OdLM, vol. 1, pp. 283–7, 290–324, 324–35 (*Arbre Charlemagne*); *ibid.*, vol. 2, pp. 141–69, 173–205 (*Fontaine des Pleurs*); *ibid.*, vol. 3, pp. 123–201 (*Arbre d'or*); 'Traicté d'un tournoy tenu a Gand par Claude de Vauldray, seigneur de l'Aigle, l'an 1469 (vieux style)', in Bernard Prost, ed., *Traicté de la forme et devis comme on faict les tournois par Olivier de la Marche, Hardouin de la Jaille, Anthoine de la Sale, etc.* (Paris: A. Barraud, 1878), pp. 55–95 (*Dame Sauvage*).

[11] The biographer, who compiled the text from a range of sources including romances, chronicles and heralds' reports, is unknown but is likely to have been one of the heralds who either witnessed many of the hero's exploits at firsthand or had access to reliable eyewitness accounts of them: see CL, introduction, pp. 47–54.

[12] The identities of the authors of the three different accounts of this *pas* have not come down to us but they were probably heralds who may or may not have been present at the event itself.

similar events that were staged in two other courts, Castile and Savoy, which had extensive cultural, economic and political links with Burgundy.[13] These are, respectively, the *Paso Honroso* (Órbigo Bridge, near León, 1434)[14] and the eponymous *Pas* of Carignano (1504);[15] in the latter case, a financial document relating to the post-combat entertainments has also been consulted as it offers unusual evidence of women's involvement in the organisation of one of these events.[16]

ETHICS OF THE *PAS D'ARMES*: RULE-MAKERS AND RULE-BREAKERS

Whilst, in the context of war, knights were accustomed to see the ends as justifying the means and so to accept few rules that limited their actions in the pursuit of victory once a conflict had been properly declared,[17] this was far from being the case in the less bellicose context of tournaments such as *pas d'armes*. Here rules were desirable given that the passions inevitably involved in any form of armed combat between two noblemen always potentially ran the risk of degenerating into a private quarrel that could then embroil whole families in a feud.[18] In order to avoid such conflicts arising in the *pas d'armes*, detailed *chapitres* (chapters of arms), which subjected such events to tight regulation, were composed in advance by, or at least at the behest of, the *entrepreneur* (the event's organiser and chief defender) and were circulated by heralds at courts where knights and squires would hear of them. With their quasi-legal language, in setting out the rules of encounter that all those accepting the challenge of the joust were expected to observe,[19] these chapters have much in common with late medieval ordinances regulating the conduct of judicial duels and were similarly intended to preserve the honour of each man who participated in them.[20] The

---

[13] For the links between these various courts see Essay 1; on Castile and Burgundy in particular, see Álvaro Fernández de Córdova Miralles, 'L'impact de la Bourgogne et la cour castillane des Trastamare', in *La cour de Bourgogne et l'Europe: Le rayonnement et les limites d'un modèle culturel; actes du colloque international tenu à Paris les 9, 10 et 11 octobre 2007*, ed. by Werner Paravicini, Torsten Hiltmann and Franck Viltart (Ostfildern: Jan Thorbecke Verlag, 2013), pp. 593–630.

[14] Pero Rodríguez de Lena (active first half of fifteenth century), the author who wrote up this *pas* organised by the Castilian knight Suero de Quiñones (*c.*1409–56), was a chronicler who also witnessed it at firsthand. Órbigo, a village situated some 30 km from León, was on the pilgrimage route to Santiago de Compostela and was the site of a hospital of the Order of the Knights Hospitaller.

[15] The organiser of this event was the duke of Savoy, Philibert II (1480–1504); the author of the narrative account is unknown but was probably a herald commissioned by the duke himself: see Source 15.

[16] The financial document relating to expenses paid on behalf of Philibert's wife, Margaret of Austria (1480–1530), is published in Max Bruchet, *Marguerite d'Autriche, duchesse de Savoie* (Lille: impr. Danel, 1927), pp. 323–4: see Source 15.

[17] See Rigby, *Wisdom and Chivalry*, pp. 217–18.

[18] Article 13 of the chapters of arms of the *Paso Honroso* explicitly seeks to pre-empt this eventuality: 'que si acaesciere, assí de los cavalleros come de los gentileshomes, [en] las armas que fizieren, llevar ventaja o ferir a mí o a alguno de los cavalleros que conmigo serán, *que nunca les será demandado por nosotros, ni parientes ni amigos nuestros*' (if it should come to pass, either to the knights or the gentlemen, in the deeds of arms that they shall perform, that they take the advantage or wound me or any of the knights who shall be with me, *they shall never be sued by us, nor by relatives or friends of ours*) (PH, p. 403, emphasis added).

[19] Michelle Szkilnik, *Jean de Saintré: une carrière chevaleresque au XVe siècle* (Geneva: Droz, 2003), p. 74.

[20] See BP.

need to establish ethical fair play and equity between opponents is thus central to these chapters, which typically stipulate: the need to prove one's noble lineage (usually on both the maternal and the paternal side) so as to be allowed to compete; which weapons were to be used in any particular event (either sharpened or rebated, and generally supplied by the *entrepreneur* with the challenger having first choice of them); how many blows with sword or pollaxe were to be exchanged or courses with lances run (either decreed by the *entrepreneur* or left up to the challenger to decide); what types of harness* (single or double) or saddles (those used for war or those for jousting) were permitted; what forfeits were to be imposed in the event of one competitor gaining a particular advantage over another (through unhorsing him or causing him to lose his weapon and/or fall to the ground); whether or not it was permissible for a challenger to watch the *entrepreneur* fight before his own bout was due, and so on.

The enforcement of these rules was the responsibility of judges, who were princes such as the duke of Burgundy himself, many of whom delegated this task to high-ranking heralds such as the Burgundian King of Arms, Toison d'or (an office most famously held by Jean Lefèvre de Saint-Rémy) or to knights with many years of jousting experience behind them, such as the Castilian Pedro Vásquez de Saavedra, who had fought in the *Arbre Charlemagne*, been an aide to Jacques de Lalaing at the *Fontaine des Pleurs* and was one of the *entrepreneurs* at the *Pas de la Dame Inconnue* (Bruges, 1463 or 1464)[21] before becoming a judge at the *Dame Sauvage*. The judges were often assisted in their deliberations by other officials such as Kings of Arms and heralds who recorded the event. Likewise, marshals of the lists were in charge of men of lesser rank tasked with keeping the spectators apart from those fighting, separating the combatants when the stipulated number of blows had been exchanged or courses with lances run and stopping a fight if it was becoming too uneven or if one of the competitors risked suffering a serious injury. As a means of formally signalling the end of 'hostilities' between the two champions, the judge(s) would often explicitly instruct them to be good friends and require them to make a gesture of reconciliation by touching hands; they would then either exit the lists together, sometimes with their arms around each other, or depart in an agreed order that upheld each man's honour (the *entrepreneur* usually being the one who left the field last, as it was his to defend) and the challenger would frequently organise a dinner for his opponent.[22]

Contemporary accounts of *pas d'armes*, many of which were written by direct witnesses of them, generally show these rules being scrupulously observed.[23] It is therefore those moments when an individual *fails* to respect them that are particularly telling in what

---

[21] See JDI.

[22] See Klaus Oschema, 'Toucher et être touché: gestes de conciliation et émotions dans les duels judiciaires', *Médiévales*, 61 (2011), 142–61.

[23] Lack of space here precludes extensive comparative analysis of *pas d'armes* staged at courts in Anjou and France that also had close political and cultural ties with Burgundy, but there is little to no evidence of rule-breaking by the male competitors at these events. For example, see Source 6 (stanza 47, ll. 553–64), on the Angevin *Pas de la Bergère* (Tarascon, 1449), where the only divergence from the rules is that Ferry II de Vaudémont-Lorraine breaks four lances instead of three and is not only praised by the author, Louis de Beauvau, for this feat but also receives the prize for the best performance by a challenger. See also Source 13, p. 280, on the northern French *Pas des armes de Sandricourt* (1493), where the author, Orléans Herald, specifically says that there were no disputes among any of the competitors because the whole event was so well adjudicated by the judges.

they reveal about attitudes towards the ethical component of chivalric masculinity as displayed through these events and how this is linked to the male competitors' quest for dominance in the lists. As we shall see, the narrative of the *Paso Honroso* by Castilian chronicler Pero Rodríguez de Lena recounts an uncharacteristically high number of instances of rule-breaking by both the challengers and defenders of the joust in their eagerness to make their mark, but offers little direct commentary on them, whereas La Marche and the biographer of Jacques de Lalaing deal with the far fewer lapses of ethical conduct in the Burgundian *pas d'armes* in a very different manner.

What is particularly striking about Rodríguez de Lena's account of the *Paso Honroso*, which was held some nine years before the earliest of the Burgundian jousts, the *Arbre Charlemagne*, is its ambiguity in depicting those champions — including even the *entrepreneur*, Suero de Quiñones himself — whose desire to emerge as victors led them to engage in unethical conduct during their combats. The rule governing the *Paso Honroso* was that competitors should run courses with lances until three weapons were broken (Article 3),[24] and so the chronicler dutifully records the results of each encounter and notes whether or not a lance was shattered. Whilst Rodríguez de Lena offers his own occasional interpretation of the results on the basis of equivalents (e.g. a wound received from a lance gives points to the man doing the wounding, as when challenger Rodrigo Quijada draws blood from defender Diego de Bazán),[25] he generally notes the consensus view of who was deemed to *llevar lo mejor/la vantaja* (take the advantage) or explicitly states his own opinion regarding to whom he would *dar lo mejor/la vantaja* (give the advantage).[26] The precise question of who was adjudged victorious in these individual encounters was therefore assumed to be important both to those participating in it and to those subsequently reading the narrative account of it.

Yet, in spite of the clear-cut nature of the outcomes of the combats at this Castilian event, Rodríguez de Lena consistently repeats the euphemistic phrase *tomar revés* (to suffer a reversal of fortune) in order to explain why a particular person lost on a particular day, rather than attributing their defeat to lesser ability. Similarly, he offers his personal judgement of someone's poor skill only on technical rather than ethical grounds, such as when a competitor misses his opponent and strikes his horse instead, which he describes pejoratively as an 'encuentro feo' (ugly encounter), as in the case of challenger Alfonso Cabeda against defender Sancho de Rabanal's horse.[27] Furthermore, as we shall see below, even when recounting the most blatant transgressions of the rules of the *pas*, Rodríguez de Lena tends simply to repeat the judges' responses to these infractions and explicitly refrains from either adding his own gloss on these responses or judging who had the *mejor/vantaja* in the compromised bout itself. He thus leaves it up to the reader to decide whether these incidents are to be viewed as either audacious or reprehensible and so how to interpret the masculine conduct they demonstrate.

The first and least serious type of infraction that the chronicler identifies is when a competitor, out of eagerness to finish a bout and to maintain a certain momentum in

[24] PH, p. 401.

[25] *Ibid.*, p. 441.

[26] For examples of the former expression, see *ibid.*, pp. 408, 417, 431, 450, 461, 463, 465, 468, 475, 489, 492; of the latter, pp. 411, 424, 433, 436, 439, 441, 472, 478.

[27] *Ibid.*, p. 451.

his jousting, refuses to obey the judges' command to leave the field. Defender Gómez de Villacorta, for example, twice declines to exit the lists, the first time against challenger Diego de Sanromán, when they both flout the judges' instruction to break for lunch, and the second time against challenger Lope de Ferrara.[28] In both cases, Rodríguez de Lena merely states that the competitors eventually had to do the judges' bidding.

A second, more serious type of infraction involves 'unsporting' conduct, as when challenger Gonzalo de Castañeda omits to pull up his lance after the horse ridden by his opponent, the *entrepreneur* Suero de Quiñones, has stopped in mid-run, a fault commented on by the author in only the mildest fashion with, as he puts it, Castañeda 'non qurando de cortesía que deviera guardar' (not thinking of the courtesy which he should observe).[29] Similarly, in the case of defender Sancho de Rabanal, who complains to the judges when they rule that the remainder of his fight with challenger Gonzalo de León should be postponed since the latter had started to feel ill from the effects of having drunk unclean water the night before, Rodríguez de Lena observes laconically that he will refrain from saying anymore about it as the sick man was the one who was winning after having broken two lances. Hence the narrator simply leaves it up to the reader to infer Rabanal's frustration at being told to stop fighting before he could try to give a better account of himself.[30]

The third type of infraction is that of out-and-out cheating involving the use of an improper piece of equipment, such as a saddle of a kind proscribed by the chapters of arms, which would give the cheat a distinct advantage over his opponent. For instance, when challenger Diego Zapata's fight against defender Pedro de Nava is finished, with the former having broken one lance to the latter's two, Zapata is found to have been riding unfairly tied to his saddle, leading the judges to reprimand his team captain, Gutierre Quijada, for allowing this to happen and threaten to order from the field anyone else guilty of the same offence.[31] Rodríguez de Lena, for his part, simply observes that the wronged competitor clearly had the advantage over his opponent anyway, thus implying that the cheat's ruse was to no avail.[32] A similar case is that of challenger Juan de Villalobos against defender Lope de Stúñiga, when the former's saddle is deemed by the judges not to conform to the war saddles stipulated in the chapters of arms (Article 1) by being too high at the front and back, and so holding him too firmly in place.[33] Interestingly, whilst Villalobos then compounds the felony by refusing to change his saddle, Stúñiga doubles down on his opponent's attempt to gain an unfair advantage by begging the judges *not* to make him switch; indeed, he claims

---

[28] *Ibid.*, pp. 474, 491.

[29] *Ibid.*, p. 430.

[30] *Ibid.*, p. 468.

[31] *Ibid.*, p. 449.

[32] *Ibid.*, p. 450.

[33] Whilst the Article itself insists somewhat generically on the use of 'arneses de guerra' (war harnesses*) (*ibid.*, p. 400), the narrator later explains that this specifically includes war saddles: 'aquella silla, que non era de guerra, e en los capítolos de Suero se contenía que las armas se fiziessen en arnés de guerra, e sin vantaja ninguna' (it was not a war saddle, and in Suero's Articles it was stated that the deeds of arms be performed in war harness, and without any advantage) (*ibid.*, p. 426). See also Marina Viallon, 'The Tournament Saddle', in *The Medieval Tournament as Spectacle: Tourneys, Jousts and Pas d'Armes, 1100–1600*, ed. by Alan V. Murray and Karen Watts (Woodbridge: Boydell Press, 2020), pp. 99–119.

that even if Villalobos were to use a hundred sturdier saddles, he would still take him on. When the author, Rodríguez de Lena, concludes by noting that the judges eventually give in to Stúñiga's 'voluntad' (pertinacity)[34] and allow the fight to continue, although banning the use of all such saddles for the rest of the event, he leaves it open as to how to read the wronged man's attitude, which can be seen as a kind of extravagant one-upmanship in allowing himself to be put at such a disadvantage by his opponent.

Indeed, this extravagance shown by Stúñiga towards another's infraction of the rules is mirrored in a final type of ethical transgression at the *Paso Honroso*, that of removing pieces of one's harness after entering the lists but without the judges' express permission to do so, which the chronicler nonetheless still refrains from condemning outright. Whilst Suero de Quiñones makes it clear in his chapters of arms that such a procedure needs to be agreed in advance (Article 10)[35] — presumably since running courses with lances was very dangerous compared with foot combat with swords or pollaxes because of the far greater impact involved — various knights, including Suero himself, proceed to flout this rule quite spectacularly, eliciting little comment from Rodríguez de Lena. For instance, challenger Bueso de Solís removes his right pauldron* (i.e. shoulder defence) part-way through his fight against defender Gómez de Villacorta, causing the latter to do the same so as to respect parity, much to the annoyance of the judges, not least because the two knights are thereby breaking the oath they swore on entering the lists to observe the written rules. Moreover, the two competitors then not only remonstrate with the judges but also boast that they would gladly compete in their jupons* (i.e. their padded arming doublets) if they could, with the author adding solely that the two are eventually obliged to obey the judges and put their armour back on and noting that Solís tries to save face by claiming to be unaware of the ruling in the first place.[36] When the *entrepreneur* himself breaks his own rule by removing no fewer than three of the most protective pieces of harness — that is, his visor, his left pauldron and his plackart* (which protects the stomach area) — he makes a vainglorious speech about his being the equivalent of three different knights, each with one piece of armour missing, whose arrival in the lists he had told the king's own herald, Monreal, to announce.[37] The judges respond to Suero's rule-breaking by refusing to allow the fight to continue on the grounds that it would be too dangerous, ordering him to be imprisoned in his own pavilion and commanding his musicians to stop playing as he is escorted away.[38] Whilst Rodríguez de Lena recounts the 'gran saña' (great umbrage) of the judges at being placed in this position and their being 'enojados' (vexed) to the extent that they stop anyone else from competing on that day, he nonetheless pointedly omits to pass direct judgement on the transgressive *entrepreneur* himself.[39]

The chronicler of the *Paso Honroso* thus persists in presenting in a largely neutral and objective manner these various episodes of infraction in which competitors demonstrate

---

[34] PH, p. 426.

[35] *Ibid.*, p. 402.

[36] *Ibid.*, pp. 434–5.

[37] *Ibid.*, pp. 442–3.

[38] *Ibid.*, pp. 444–6. According to Noel Fallows, *Jousting in Medieval and Renaissance Iberia* (Woodbridge: Boydell Press, 2010), p. 178, Suero may have made a secret pact with his opponent not to strike him properly whilst wearing so little protection and may have been seeking to pass off his foolhardiness as being motivated by extreme lovesickness.

[39] PH, p. 446.

their willingness to cheat in more or less flagrant ways in their desire to showcase their superiority over others, whether by actually physically beating their opponent in the lists or by demonstrating one-upmanship through vaingloriously putting themselves at a perilous disadvantage. It may well be that the concern with determining clear winners and losers and who predominates at the *Paso Honroso* is one factor explaining why there were so many of these infractions, which is in fact very out of line with most other *pas d'armes*. Another factor might be the high political stakes involved, as not only were the challengers from Catalonia, Aragon and Navarre, which, at that time, were in various forms of dispute with Castile, which is where the defenders were from, but there were also two different political factions then vying for power within the Castilian court itself.[40] Hence this event seems to have functioned more like earlier forms of tournament, where competitors were effectively practising for actual warfare against political or military opponents and creating bonds between the members of each factional group.[41] A further possible explanation is that competitors at the *Paso Honroso* wanted to stand out and were therefore driven to bend and break the rules with the principal aim of making the event 'more "war-like" and less artificial', as Grant Gearhart puts it, the better to show off their valour.[42] Yet, whatever the specific motivation behind these infractions, Rodríguez de Lena's commemoration of this important Castilian event would certainly seem to place far more stress on demonstrating — and even implicitly showcasing as examples of extreme chivalric bravura and machismo — the audacious and spectacular lengths to which some were prepared to go as they jockeyed for their place in this markedly fractious chivalric pecking order than on showing how the different competitors affirmed one another's chivalric identity as members of a law-abiding elite brotherhood.

Karras's characterisation of chivalric masculinity as being driven by a desire to dominate other men would certainly seem to be borne out in the example of this particular Castilian event, where cheating appears to have been rife as a means of achieving such superiority. However, the same cannot be said of the later Burgundian *pas d'armes*, where the attitude of those who recorded them towards rule-breakers and rule-breaking is very different, conforming more closely to Karras's contrasting emphasis on the importance of honour and brotherhood in these combats. The accounts of Jacques de Lalaing's year-long *Fontaine des Pleurs* by La Marche and by the anonymous author of the *Livre des faits* are especially instructive in this regard, as they each relate two instances of infraction

---

[40] See Nadot, *Le Spectacle*, p. 116: the Castilian group under the command of Gutierre Quijada belonged to a different faction at the royal court from that of the *entrepreneur*, Suero de Quiñones: whilst the former was close to the so-called Infantes of Aragon (i.e. the sons of King Fernando I of Aragon who were trying to wrest power from their cousin, King Juan II of Castile), the latter was linked to Juan's sometime favourite, Álvaro de Luna, constable of Castile. On this contemporary power struggle, see Nicholas Round, *The Greatest Man Uncrowned: A Study of the Fall of Don Alvaro de Luna* (London: Tamesis Books, 1986), pp. 6–10; Fernández de Córdova, 'L'impact', pp. 606–8. On the role played by Álvaro de Luna in relation to various other Castilian *pas d'armes* such as the *Paso de la Fuerte Ventura* (Valladolid, 1428), the *Paso de Valladolid* (1440) and the *Paso de El Pardo* (1459), see Sources 2, 3 and 8, respectively.

[41] On the tensions between the Aragonese and Castilian competitors in particular, see Nadot, *Le Spectacle*, p. 85. On Castilian chivalric culture in general, see Samuel A. Claussen, *Chivalry and Violence in Late Medieval Castile*, Warfare in History (Woodbridge: Boydell Press, 2020).

[42] Grant Gearhart, 'The Knight and War: Alternative Displays of Masculinity in *El Passo Honroso de Suero de Quiñones, El Victorial*, and the *Historia de los Hechos del Marquéz de Cádiz*' (unpublished PhD dissertation, University of North Carolina at Chapel Hill, 2015), pp. 55, 149.

of the rules by the challengers, and the *entrepreneur*'s response to them, in a manner that reveals the ethical viewpoints of the two authors and of Lalaing himself on questions of honour and proper masculine conduct. In contrast to the chronicler of the *Paso Honroso*, whose neutral and objective narration leads him to avoid passing judgement on even the most egregious cases of cheating, these Burgundian authors, whilst displaying extreme discretion in discussing those instances where a competitor fails to abide by the rules of the *pas* so as to avoid tarnishing a nobleman's reputation for posterity in their texts, nonetheless make it absolutely clear when they do or do not condone his actual behaviour. As La Marche says, when writing about a particularly delicate incident at the *Arbre Charlemagne* concerning a certain Martin Ballart (to which we shall shortly return): 'tout noble est tenu de garder l'honneur d'ung aultre, et principalement en escriptures, où sont couchées et empreintes les memoires des hommes bonnes ou mauvaises' (all nobles are obliged to uphold the honour of another, principally in their writings, where the memory of men, whether good or bad, is laid down and inscribed).[43]

The first, and less serious, instance of rule-breaking in Jacques de Lalaing's *pas* that concerns us here is that by the lord of Espiry, Aimé de Rabutin, who was one of the few knights attending this event to adopt chivalric incognito, calling himself the 'Chevalier Mescongneu' (Unknown Knight) for reasons that are left unexplained in the Lalaing biography but are examined in some detail by La Marche, who provides an intriguing gloss on the whole episode.[44] According to La Marche, the lord of Espiry masks his identity because he was aware that he had gone against the chapters of arms of this *pas*, which forbade competitors from watching Lalaing prior to their own appointed bouts;[45] he thus wanted to minimise his potential dishonour if the *entrepreneur* refused to fight him when his turn came.[46] La Marche then manages to transform the whole problem of the lord of Espiry's potentially gaining an unfair advantage over Lalaing into a very different issue, one which actually redounds to the honour of both challenger and *entrepreneur*. Claiming that the lord of Espiry wrote 'unes gracieuses lettres' (some gracious letters) to Lalaing to ask for his permission to compete in spite of his confessed infraction, La Marche explains that it was observing the *entrepreneur*'s 'chevaleureuse contenance et avec tant d'adresse, de force et de vertu de chevalier' (chivalrous conduct, skill, strength and knightly virtue) that 'enluminoit et eslevoit si haut la renommée dudit pas' (had so greatly exalted and enhanced the renown of the said *pas*)[47] which inspired the lord of Espiry to become one of the challengers whose aim in competing was to bring comfort to the 'dame de Plours' (the Lady of Tears), the allegorical figure of the Church in whose honour and defence the whole event had been organised.[48] Though doubtless designed to flatter Lalaing, the lord of Espiry's letters, in La Marche's interpretation, show the

---

[43] OdLM, vol. 1, p. 322.

[44] LF, pp. 354, 363; CL, pp. 232, 236.

[45] La Marche does not include the actual chapters of arms in his account so, for this particular stipulation, see LF, pp. 315–16; CL, pp. 212–13.

[46] OdLM, vol. 2, p. 174.

[47] *Ibid.*, p. 175. See also Source 7.

[48] LF, p. 313; CL, pp. 211–12. On the symbolism of this *pas*, see Élisabeth Gaucher, '*Le Livre des Fais de Jacques de Lalain*: Texte et image', *Le Moyen Âge*, 95 (1989), 503–18; and Michelle Szkilnik, 'Mise en mots, mise en images: *Le Livre des Faits du bon chevalier Jacques de Lalain*', *Ateliers (Cahiers de la Maison de Recherche, Université Charles de Gaulle–Lille 3)*, 30 (2003), 75–87.

positive influence of the *entrepreneur*'s *pas* on other men in stimulating them to join him in expressing their devotion to the Church. La Marche reinforces this point about the challenger's piety by describing how, prior to the actual combat, he says prayers in his pavilion and makes the sign of the cross with a 'bannerolle de devotion' (banderole of devotion) as he steps outside it.[49] Far from seeing the lord of Espiry as an unethical rule-breaker attempting to exert dominance over the defender of the *pas*, La Marche presents him as a particularly impressive figure,[50] one whose pious response to the event mirrors that of the *entrepreneur* himself, who, every day before engaging combat, hears Mass at the Carmelite church of Chalon-sur-Saône.[51]

The more serious infraction of the rules that occurs in Lalaing's *pas* is committed by Claude Pitois, lord of Saint-Bonnet, who refuses to accept the judge's ruling that the *entrepreneur* had brought him down to the ground during his fight with the pollaxe and that he should thus wear a golden bracelet with a padlock from which only a lady could release him, as was stipulated in the fourth chapter of arms. This episode provides a marked contrast to the earlier one of Jean de Boniface who, on being defeated in a similar manner by Lalaing in his fight with the pollaxe, accepts the forfeit of the golden bracelet and padlock 'moult agreablement et le portoit, *comme raison estoit*' (with great pleasure and put it on, *as was only right*).[52] In other words, the difference between Boniface as a gracious loser and Pitois as a poor loser exemplifies the ethical imperative of magnanimity in combat that is clearly demonstrated by the eponymous hero of the very popular chivalric romance *Ponthus et Sidoine* (written between 1390 and 1424), of whom it is said that he was 'aussi joyeux … quant il perdoit comme quant il gaengnoit' (he was just as joyful … about losing as he was about winning), this text being one which, as we shall see below, was to have an influence on later fictional and historical *pas d'armes*.[53]

The Pitois incident is dealt with at greater length in the *Livre des faits* than in La Marche, but the critical tone of the two accounts is unmistakeable, even though they focus on slightly different aspects of it. La Marche anticipates Pitois's intransigence concerning the *dénouement* of the bout by explaining how, prior to stepping into the lists, he twice refuses to respect the terms of engagement set out in the chapters of arms whereby he should specify how many blows with the pollaxe he wished to exchange with Lalaing. According to La Marche, Pitois is explicitly criticised even by his own friends and relatives for saying only that they should fight until one of them is brought down to the ground or loses his weapon and for his arrogance in failing to do as all the other competitors before him had done; implicitly, he is also presented as being vainglorious in trying to go one better than

---

49 OdLM, vol. 2, pp. 182–3.

50 The lord of Espiry is a clear favourite with La Marche, who states: 'pour ce que sa maniere de faire me sembla honneste et de bon exemple pour les escoutans, j'ay bien voulu escripre au long son cas et son faict' (because the way he conducted himself appears to me to offer a good and honourable example for those listening, it has been my wish to describe him and his actions in some detail) (*ibid.*, vol. 2, p. 181). See also Jean Devaux, 'Le culte du héros chevaleresque dans les *Mémoires* d'Olivier de la Marche', *PCEEB*, 41 (2001), 53–66.

51 See CL, introduction, pp. 25–6. The religious underpinning of the event is also reinforced by Lalaing's having organised it during a Jubilee year when pardons were taking place in Rome and at a location through which many noblemen would be travelling on their way to see the pope.

52 LF, p. 348; CL, p. 229; emphasis added.

53 PS, p. 15. See below, p. 496.

everybody else, including the *entrepreneur* himself, by making the fight more difficult.[54] Then, at the end of their combat, Pitois, who is formally adjudged to have been defeated by the defender, twice refuses to accept the forfeit of the bracelet that Lalaing wishes to impose on him, claiming that both champions were on the ground and so he should be no more liable to a forfeit than the *entrepreneur* himself.[55] The Lalaing biographer, for his part, recounts how Pitois's friends try to de-escalate matters by persuading the *entrepreneur* not to insist on imposing the forfeit, on the grounds that 'ilz estoyent tous deux a un prince et que il devoyent tous deux garder l'onneur l'un de l'autre' (both of them were loyal to the same prince [i.e. Duke Philip the Good] and that each man needed to uphold the other one's honour).[56] It is eventually agreed that Pitois will publicly pronounce to Lalaing a form of words set out in a letter requesting the *entrepreneur* to forego sending the bracelet and reassuring him that any words that Pitois is said to have spoken about him were not intended to diminish his honour.[57] By these means, peace is finally restored between the two men — and face saved all round — when Lalaing is convinced by Pitois of his readiness to pronounce the agreed form of words and thus not only absolves him of having to do so but also acquits him of having to accept the bracelet itself.[58]

As the *Livre des faits* suggests, Lalaing's magnanimous response to Pitois's unethical refusal to accept the judge's ruling on the outcome of the combat and his failure to respect the chapters of arms shows that the *entrepreneur*'s priority was not to be declared the victor and thereby demonstrate his dominance over his opponent. Rather, it was to restore good relations between two men who were of similar standing at the same court in the sense that they were both vassals of the duke of Burgundy, from whom they held fiefs and lordships, albeit Lalaing was of higher rank than Pitois, being a knight and a chamberlain in the ducal household, whereas Pitois was only a squire and had no official function at the court. Both La Marche and the *Livre des faits* underline this need for re-establishing fraternal amity by stating that the two champions were reconciled and thereafter become good friends[59] and, indeed, 'sy bons amis que apaines porroit on dire de deux freres' (such good friends that one might have taken them for brothers).[60]

Whilst these two instances of a competitor's unethical infraction of the *written* rules of the *Fontaine des Pleurs* are handled with great diplomacy by both the author of the *Livre des faits* and La Marche, another case of the egregious infraction of an *un*written but cardinal rule governing all forms of chivalric combat, including the *pas d'armes*, is dealt with by La Marche without mincing his words. In his account of the *Arbre Charlemagne*, La Marche relates how a member of a Savoyard contingent of knights and squires, one Martin Ballart, boasts vaingloriously of being able to take on three or four of the best of the defending

54 OdLM, vol. 2, p. 178.

55 Lalaing uses a wrestling move known as the *cornemuse* (i.e. locking his opponent's head under his armpit as a bagpipe player does with his instrument to draw air into it) to throw Pitois onto the ground on his back and pin him down beneath him. Technically, then, the latter has his back and limbs in contact with the ground, whereas the former's trunk is held off it since he is in fact lying on top of his man, hence the judge's ruling that Pitois alone had incurred the forfeit.

56 LF, p. 361; CL, p. 235.

57 *Ibid.*

58 LF, p. 363; CL, p. 236.

59 OdLM, vol. 2, p. 181.

60 LF, p. 363; CL, p. 236.

team in foot combat, much to the apparent amusement of Philip the Good, the judge at this *pas d'armes*.[61] Unlike the chronicler of the *Paso Honroso*, who, as we noted above, simply records without comment such instances of vainglorious behaviour as those demonstrated by both challengers and defenders at the Castilian tournament, La Marche presents this boasting as an unforgivable lapse in chivalric etiquette and proceeds to disparage Ballart in every possible way. He describes his unprepossessing physical appearance as that of 'ung grand homme maigre … de condicion grant parlier et fort grant vanteur, et apparent de petite vertu' (a tall thin man … by nature a big mouth and a tremendous boaster, and with an appearance of little worth); explains that his noble origins take some vouching for in order for him to be even reluctantly accepted as an opponent by the defending team; recounts how Ballart makes his excuses to the judge, Philip the Good, as he enters the lists, complaining that he is very poorly equipped; states that he runs all eleven of the stipulated courses with the lance badly, neither striking his man (Jean de Chaumergy) nor putting himself in the correct position to be struck; and tells how Ballart is finally dumbfounded when, at the end of the fight on horseback, Chaumergy sarcastically (rather than vaingloriously) offers to perform the desired foot combat with him and to take off four pieces of his harness so as to give him an advantage.[62] La Marche's reluctance even to relate this unfortunate episode is palpable, as we saw above, but he justifies his failure to have 'gardé, glosé ou palié l'honneur dudit Martin' (upheld, glossed or defended the said Martin's honour) on the grounds that his bad example needs to be shown to other young men in order that 'ilz se gardent d'estre vanteulx ne golias en parolles, car souvent et communement le lyon en parolles est la brebis en oeuvres' (they avoid being boastful or too free with their tongues, for it is often generally the case that the one who appears to be a lion through his speech is revealed as a sheep through his actions).[63] In departing so markedly from his usual practice in retelling this unpleasant and unethical incident in detail, La Marche portrays Ballart as a clear antitype of chivalric masculinity, one whose extreme behaviour incites his opponents to depart in turn from their own normal courteous practice as they resort to one-upmanship, humiliate him in public and close the ranks of chivalric brotherhood against him.

These accounts of Burgundian *pas d'armes* by La Marche and the author of the *Livre des faits* thus demonstrate how competitors in these events were expected to uphold the rules of engagement and what the likely consequences were for their standing in the chivalric community when they failed to do so. We can discount the possibility that Ballart and Pitois were singled out for criticism by these two authors, both of whom were avid champions of Burgundian knighthood, on the grounds that neither of them belonged to the innermost circles of the duke's chivalric elite. All of the challengers at the *Arbre Charlemagne* were from 'outside', since knights and squires from France and the Burgundian lands were explicitly excluded from competing in it.[64] Conversely, at the *Fontaine des Pleurs*, Lalaing deliberately wanted to include Burgundian knights and most of the challengers at this event were indeed connected to the ducal court in some way.[65] Neither Ballart nor Pitois

---

[61] OdLM, vol. 1, p. 321.

[62] *Ibid.*, pp. 321, 322, 323.

[63] *Ibid.*, p. 323.

[64] The chapters of arms of the *Arbre Charlemagne*, in which this exclusion is spelt out, are preserved only by the chronicler Enguerrand de Monstrelet: see EdM, vol. 6, pp. 68–73 (p. 69) and Source 4.

[65] See OdLM, vol. 2, pp. 42–3, for this explanation, which is not given in the *Livre des faits*.

was therefore more of an outsider than any of the other challengers at these two events, which implies that they were criticised by La Marche and the author of the *Livre des faits* precisely because they did break the rules whereas others didn't.

In contrast, then, to the chronicler of the *Paso Honroso*, commentators on Burgundian *pas d'armes*, as we have seen, couch their critiques of rule-breakers in careful but trenchant language so as to leave the reader in no doubt about the ethical behaviour expected of a knight or squire whose desire to dominate his opponent must nonetheless be tempered by adherence to the protocols of the contest. The clear divergence between these Castilian and Burgundian masculine chivalric norms is perhaps best encapsulated by their two most illustrious *entrepreneurs* in their respective attitudes towards removing parts of their harness. On the one hand, in the *Paso Honroso*, Suero de Quiñones breaks his own written rules in order to put himself at extreme risk of injury in the highly dangerous form of combat on horseback. On the other hand, in the *Fontaine des Pleurs*, Jacques de Lalaing obeys his own rules about not needing a judge's prior permission in order to test his valour but without putting himself in too much danger; this he does in the much safer form of foot combat with pollaxes, removing only his right leg protection in his bouts against Jean de Villeneuve, Jean Pitois and Jacques d'Avanchy, and also taking off his right gauntlet against the last of these three. These notable differences of emphasis between the Iberian and Burgundian tournament cultures may be due to the fact that, unlike in the Castilian *pas d'armes*, there was far less political instability and factional rivalry between nobles bubbling under the surface of the events held in the Burgundian lands since, even though they often involved participants hailing from different parts of the duke's realm, they had all sworn allegiance to the same prince.[66] Similarly, whereas the *Paso Honroso* is deeply concerned with establishing who the victors of the bouts were, *pas d'armes* such as the *Fontaine des Pleurs* seem to be much more interested in allowing each man to give of his best and to conduct himself in such a way as to redound to his own and his friends' and family's honour, thus adding to the total sum of chivalric renown at the Burgundian court.[67]

Erotics of the *Pas d'Armes*; or, What Does Woman Want?

Having looked at what the *ethics* of the *pas d'armes* can tell us about the construction of chivalric masculinity in the Castilian and Burgundian spheres, let us turn now to examining the *erotics* of this type of tournament: that is, the part played by heterosexual relations between men and women in shaping the identities of those who competed at these events. There is a wealth of evidence of women's involvement at the *pas d'armes* in various different roles, primarily as chivalric muses but also as participants in the

[66] As Éric Bousmar, 'Jousting at the Court of Burgundy. The "Pas d'armes": Shifts in Scenario, Location and Recruitment', in *Staging the Court of Burgundy: Proceedings of the Conference 'The Splendour of Burgundy'*, ed. by Wim Blockmans *et al.* (Turnhout/London: Brepols/Harvey Miller, 2013), pp. 75–84, puts it concerning the *Fontaine des Pleurs*: 'Certainly, this *pas* can have contributed to a better integration of the various elements of the nobility within the ducal state' (p. 78).

[67] Even in accounts of the *Perron Fée*, where a set number of courses with lances is stipulated for each bout and the number of lances broken by each competitor is recorded, the emphasis is much more on the clothes worn by the jousters and the members of their entourages as they enter the lists than on the scores.

staging of the festivities either pre- or post-combat, as spectators and as advisers to the judges in determining prize-winners. Yet, as we shall see, scholars are nonetheless in disagreement about the extent and significance of this involvement, with some arguing that women did exert a genuine influence on masculinity whilst others deny that this was the case.

As is well known, the chapters of arms related to *pas d'armes*, particularly in the Burgundian context, are generally preceded by a letter outlining a fictional scenario in which a lady commands a knight to organise such an event in her honour or entreats him to do so in her defence,[68] with many of these *pas* now being referred to by the name — or, more accurately, the *senhal* (code name) — of the lady in question: for example, the *Bergère* (Shepherdess) (Tarascon, 1449), the *Belle Pèlerine* (Beautiful Pilgrim) (Saint-Omer, 1449), the *Dame Inconnue* (Unknown Lady) and the *Dame Sauvage* (Wild Lady). Other events, such as the *Fontaine des Pleurs*, the *Perron Fée* and the *Arbre d'or*, also allude to a similar figure in their fictional scenarios: respectively, the 'Dame des Pleurs' (Lady of Tears), the 'Dame du Perron Fée' (Lady of the Enchanted Column) and the 'Dame de l'Isle Celée' (Lady of the Secret Isle). Although it is not always clear from the narrative accounts whether these female characters were played by actual women as part of the dramatic staging of the event[69] or were represented in the form of statues or paintings — perhaps to add to the atmosphere of the *mistere* (mystery), as these theatrical elements are commonly termed — they do sometimes feature prominently in the dramatic *entremets** that follow the combats,[70] as well as in the illumination cycles of the manuscripts preserving the event, as in the case of the 'Dame des Pleurs' (along with the Virgin Mary), for example, in the *Livre des faits* (Figure 41).[71]

---

[68] See Annette Lindner, 'L'influence du roman chevaleresque français sur le pas d'armes', *PCEEB*, 31 (1991), 67–78; Jean-Pierre Jourdan, 'Le thème du Pas et de l'Emprise. Espaces symboliques et rituels d'alliance en France à la fin du Moyen Âge', *Éthnologie française*, 22:2 (1992), 172–84; and *idem*, 'Le thème du pas d'armes dans le royaume de France (Bourgogne, Anjou) à la fin du Moyen Âge: aspects d'un théâtre de chevalerie', in *Théâtre et spectacles hier et aujourd'hui. Moyen âge et renaissance: actes du 115e congrès national des Sociétés savantes (Avignon, 1990), Section d'histoire médiévale et de philologie* (Paris: Éditions du CTHS, 1991), pp. 285–304.

[69] At the *Pas de la Bergère*, the eponymous Shepherdess in whose honour the event is being organised does appear as an actual character throughout, being played by Isabelle de Lenoncourt, probably a sister or daughter of one of the *entrepreneurs*, Philippe de Lenoncourt: see Source 6. Similarly, at the *Pas de la Joyeuse Garde/Pas de Saumur* (1446) organised by René of Anjou, the unnamed lady featured in the chapters of arms who leads the defenders into the lists was played by different ladies of the Angevin court on different days: on this event, see Essays 2 and 7 and Source 5.

[70] On these images and the ambiguity of the *mistere*, see Gaucher, '*Le Livre des Fais*'; and Szkilnik, 'Mise en mots'. See also Christina Normore, *A Feast for the Eyes: Art, Performance and the Late Medieval Banquet* (Chicago, IL: University of Chicago Press, 2015), pp. 138–47.

[71] The same scene is illustrated in the two other illustrated manuscripts of the Lalaing biography: Paris, BnF, fr. 16830, fol. 124r; and Comte de Lalaing, private collection, no shelfmark, dated 1518, fol. 108v (reproduced in Elizabeth Morrison, 'Creating the Ideal Knight through Illumination: The Artists of the Getty Lalaing', in *A Knight for the Ages: Jacques de Lalaing and the Art of Chivalry*, ed. by Elizabeth Morrison (Los Angeles: The J. Paul Getty Museum, 2018), pp. 90–105 (p. 97, fig. 22). See also Essays 2 and 7 on the representation of women in St Petersburg, NLR, fr. F. p. XIV, 4, the spectacular manuscript preserving the narrative account of the *Joyeuse Garde/Saumur*; see also Source 6, pp. 114–17, for a discussion of the miniature depicting the eponymous Shepherdess (Figure 4) in the unique manuscript containing the poem of the *Bergère*.

Figure 41. The knight-defender's pavilion at the *Pas de la Fontaine des Pleurs*, showing the 'Dame des Pleurs' (left), Charolais Herald holding a sword and a pollaxe (right), and the Madonna and Child (top centre); the town of Chalon-sur-Saône is visible in the background (top left). *Livre des faits de messire Jacques de Lalaing*. Los Angeles, J. Paul Getty Museum, 114, fol. 113r. Photo: Getty.

Furthermore, male competitors at these *pas d'armes* often explicitly declare that their motivation to compete in the lists comes from their love for a particular lady whom they wish to serve and many of them seem to have worn letters or emblems on their coat armours* and horses' trappers* that referred to that lady's name in an encoded form that is now largely impenetrable to us.[72] This is particularly true of the *Perron Fée*, the contemporary accounts of which abound in the description of such items, such as Jean de

[72] Nadot, *Le Spectacle*, pp. 203–6; and Denis Hüe, 'La Bergère et le tournoyeur, coutumes et costumes des parades amoureuses à la cour d'Anjou-Provence', in *Les arts et les lettres en Provence au temps du Roi René*, ed. by Chantal Connochie-Bourgne and Valérie Gontero-Lauze (Aix-en-Provence: Presses

Saint-Marcel's display of various letters including Y and A, and Jacques de Luxembourg's use of the letters D, K and A, the meaning of which is now impossible to know.[73] This same event also celebrates love as a key motivating factor in many of the four-line verse *brevets*, one per competitor, that are appended at the end of the narrative, particularly in the case of the younger men such as Guyot de Songny:

> Se haulte amour volés acquerre,
> Soyez d'honneur songneux tousjour,
> Car a honneur ne fault amour
> Non plus que la pluie a la terre.
>
> (If noble love you wish to attain,
> Be ever mindful of honour,
> For honour cannot do without love
> Any more than the earth can do without rain).[74]

Other contestants, although by no means the majority, openly parade their amorous intentions, as, for instance, when Jean de Boniface is described as entering the field at the *Fontaine des Pleurs* with a banner that assertively declares: 'Qui a belle donne, garde le bien' (He who possesses a beautiful lady should guard her well).[75] The Burgundian knight Jean de Chassa, lord of Monnet, makes a particularly elaborate entrance at the *Arbre d'or* in his punning guise as the 'Chevalier esclave' (Slave-Knight). Announcing in a long letter that his lady has finally taken pity on him and told him to attempt to earn her love by competing in an important joust, the knight is accompanied by a damsel of hers who will later relate his adventures to her mistress; also in his retinue are four extravagantly dressed and bearded men holding feathered spears. As Olivier de La Marche remarks, this was a most pleasing spectacle to behold but, unfortunately and somewhat bathetically, the lovesick and well-intentioned 'Chevalier esclave' is then deemed to be wearing an ill-fitting helm which prevents him from seeing an opponent or aiming his blows properly and so has to be excused from competing![76]

Scholars such as Éric Bousmar, Sébastien Nadot and Audrey Pennel have taken these indicators of women's involvement in the inspiring, planning, staging and spectating of *pas d'armes*, as well as in other historical accounts of tournaments and in imaginative texts such as romances, as clear evidence of women's influence on the construction of knightly identity even at these fundamentally homosocial events.[77] Others, however, such

---

Universitaires de Provence, 2013), pp. 243–59. For an example of a coded name from the *Bergère* that is unusually easy to decipher from the initial letter displayed, see Source 6, p. 132 n. 47.

[73] PPF, pp. 111, 125.

[74] *Ibid.*, p. 205. Significantly, the *brevets* attributed to older, higher-ranking competitors such as Adolf of Cleves, lord of Ravenstein (*ibid.*, p. 209), are much more likely to refer to their pursuit of glory and renown than of love.

[75] LF, p. 343; CL, p. 226.

[76] OdLM, vol. 3, pp. 154–9.

[77] Éric Bousmar, 'La place des hommes et des femmes dans les fêtes de cour bourguignonnes (Philippe le Bon - Charles le Hardi)', *PCEEB*, 34 (1994), 123–43; Nadot, *Le Spectacle*, pp. 179–87; and Audrey Pennel, 'Des hourds aux lices: la place des dames dans les enluminures des tournois et Pas d'armes aux XIVe et XVe siècle', *Francia. Forschungen zur westeuropäischen Geschichte*, 46 (2019), 431–42.

as Jean-Pierre Jourdan, have tended to see the fictional lady in whose name the *entrepreneur* organises his *pas* as being a stand-in for the prince, with the knight's professed loyalty and obedience to the lady simultaneously serving to show his worthiness as a courtier and man-at-arms to the actual lord at whose court he seeks promotion.[78] Karras, as we noted above, has gone even further than Jourdan in deeming women's role at these homosocial events to be symbolic at best. In her view, the fictional scenarios of male obedience in the *pas d'armes* are largely fantasy compensations for men's actual domination of women in medieval aristocratic society.[79]

This scholarly debate on the erotics of the *pas d'armes* thus raises the following questions: what different forms could the homosocial relations of these events take, what functions could they serve and did they simply constitute a means whereby men sought pre-eminence over both their male peers and women? Furthermore, do the narrative accounts of these events reveal how women could make themselves heard as desiring subjects who were in dialogue with, or even resistant to, the homosocial concerns that characterised the *pas d'armes*? Finally, when looking at the material considerations involved in staging these costly events, do we have any evidence of women who occupied real positions of political power or who held the financial purse strings being able to put their own stamp on these contests in more than just a tokenistic fashion?

By way of entering into this debate, if we compare two examples of events performed in the Burgundian lands whose undeniably homosocial focus would seem, at first sight, to confirm Karras's view of women's insignificance to these events with one from Savoy where female figures are described as featuring much more prominently in the post-combat festivities, we can glimpse something of the different strategies by which women could attempt to write themselves into the script of a particular tournament and so put their own interpretation on the meaning of the chivalric feats performed by the male contestants.

The accounts of the *Arbre Charlemagne* and the *Fontaine des Pleurs* by La Marche and the anonymous author of the *Livre des faits* reveal an overwhelming emphasis on homosocial rather than heterosexual relations, but in ways that are by no means simply about the assertion of male dominance, whether over other men or over women. La Marche says almost nothing about the role of ladies in judging who is to be awarded the prizes at either of these events or about female spectatorship at the actual combats of the *Arbre Charlemagne*. He notes only in passing that the duke and duchess of Orléans visit Jacques de Lalaing's *Fontaine des Pleurs*,[80] but his allusion to the duchess, Marie of Cleves, makes no reference to her being the lady to whom Lalaing was perhaps secretly devoted, as some modern commentators on the *Livre des faits*, where she appears as an admiring spectator at the hero's first joust at Nancy, have speculated.[81] The Lalaing biographer, for his part, does acknowledge the presence of the ladies of the town of Chalon-sur-Saône at the *Fontaine des Pleurs* when he relates how Lalaing organises a banquet in their

---

[78] Jean-Pierre Jourdan, 'Le langage amoureux dans le combat de chevalerie à la fin du Moyen Âge (France, Bourgogne, Anjou)', *Le Moyen Âge*, 99 (1993), 83–106.

[79] Karras, *From Boys to Men*, p. 25.

[80] OdLM, vol. 2, p. 173.

[81] See CL, introduction, p. 45; at the moment of explaining how Lalaing died, the narrator asserts that the lady who inspired the hero to adopt his chivalric motto of 'La Nonpareille' (She Who is Without Equal) was none other than the Virgin Mary, a disclosure that further enhances Lalaing's reputation for piety that is an important feature of his biography.

honour at the end of the *pas* and sends them a letter purportedly written by the 'Dame des Pleurs' asking for the ladies' indulgence towards the *entrepreneur* who had served her so faithfully and presenting him as their 'serf d'armes et serviteur' (serf-at-arms and servant).[82] Yet, the *Livre des faits* also makes it absolutely clear that the ladies have no part to play in the judging of the *Fontaine des Pleurs*, as it is Lalaing alone who decides which of his opponents has won the prize for the best blows struck with the pollaxe (Gérard de Roussillon), the sword (Jacques d'Avanchy) and the lance (Jean de Boniface).[83] This lack of textual emphasis on the role of actual women — as opposed to the figurative 'Dame des Pleurs' and the Virgin Mary — at the *Fontaine des Pleurs* is matched by a similar lack of visual emphasis on them in illuminated manuscripts of the *Livre des faits*. Of the cycle of two images devoted to Lalaing's combats at this event against, respectively, the lord of Espiry and Jean Pitois that are featured in each of the three illustrated codices of this work, only one has a single female spectator present (the Espiry bout),[84] whereas the other two manuscripts show either no spectators at all at either of them[85] or depict an entirely male audience at both of them (Figure 42).[86]

Developing the symbolism of the *Arbre Charlemagne*, which involves tears, a fountain and a dedication to the Virgin Mary, this being its only reference to a female inspirer of male prowess, the later *Fontaine des Pleurs* adds to its fictional scenario a 'Dame des Pleurs', as we noted above, but her role is that of an allegorical stimulus to crusade, being a symbol of the beset Church, rather than that of a romantic muse to a lovelorn knight. This is underscored in the descriptions of the *entremets* following the end of the combats that are offered by both La Marche and the *Livre des faits*. For La Marche, who discusses these festivities only very briefly, what is primarily of interest is how Lalaing has the representations of both the 'Dame' and the Virgin Mary taken to his lodgings, where he kisses the feet of the latter in veneration, before they are removed to the church of Notre-Dame in Boulogne.[87] The *Livre des faits* devotes far more space to these post-combat celebrations but its description similarly

[82] LF, p. 403; CL, p. 250.

[83] LF, pp. 399–400; CL, p. 249. Compared to some *pas d'armes*, such as the *Perron Fée*, where the prizes appear to have been given to the highest-ranking competitors — Adolf of Cleves, Louis de Luxembourg and Jacques de Luxembourg, these latter two being linked to the Bourbon dynasty that was present in large numbers at this event — these prizes do seem to tally with the author's account of which were the most exciting bouts, even if there may also have been a diplomatic dimension to two of them being awarded to non-Burgundians, i.e. Jean de Boniface (referred to throughout as 'the Sicilian knight') and Jacques d'Avanchy (a Savoyard squire); in the latter case, he was the only challenger who chose to fight Lalaing with swords. See also Nadot, *Le Spectacle*, pp. 113–14, on the politics behind prize-giving at the *pas d'armes*.

[84] Comte de Lalaing, private collection, no shelfmark, dated 1518, fol. 118r, reproduced in Hanno Wijsman, 'The Visual Tradition of the Book of the Deeds of Jacques de Lalaing', in *A Knight for the Ages: Jacques de Lalaing and the Art of Chivalry*, ed. by Elizabeth Morrison (Los Angeles: The J. Paul Getty Museum, 2018), pp. 107–19 (p. 113, fig. 13). For women's presence as spectators in *Livre des faits* miniatures depicting Lalaing's combats at tournaments *other* than his *pas d'armes* see below, n. 102.

[85] Paris, BnF, fr. 16830, fols 134v and 142r.

[86] See also Los Angeles, J. Paul Getty Museum, 114, fol. 129v, for the Pitois bout, reproduced in CL, introduction, p. 64, fig. 4.

[87] OdLM, vol. 2, p. 202. According to La Marche, *ibid.*, vol. 1, p. 333, the same thing was done with the two shields set up for competitors to strike at the *Arbre Charlemagne*, which were taken to the church of Notre-Dame in Dijon for safe-keeping.

Figure 42. Jacques de Lalaing in combat with the lord of Espiry, watched by a group of exclusively male spectators. *Livre des faits de messire Jacques de Lalaing.* Los Angeles, J. Paul Getty Museum, 114, fol. 123r. Photo: Getty.

serves to highlight Lalaing's piety, as he offers up various prayers of thanks and supplication to both the 'Dame' and the Virgin.[88]

If the accounts of both the *Arbre Charlemagne* and the *Fontaine des Pleurs* thus present the inspiration for the competitors' desire to participate in the *pas* as being essentially religious instead of amorous, focused as they are on honouring the Virgin Mary rather than any earthly lady, this combination of piety and chivalry also serves the knights at these events in another, but distinctly homosocial, way: that of showcasing their talents both to their male peers and, even more importantly, to their male superior, the Burgundian duke, Philip the Good.[89] In La Marche's retelling of the *Arbre Charlemagne*, for example, much is made of

---

[88] LF, pp. 390–8; CL, pp. 246–8.

[89] For Nadot, *Le Spectacle*, p. 186, the competitor at a *pas d'armes* is courting his lord and prince as much as he is a particular lady.

how the first challenger to fight the *entrepreneur* in the lists, the Castilian Pedro Vásquez de Saavedra, cuts such an impressive figure in terms of his speech, manner, appearance and prowess that his opponent, Pierre de Bauffremont, lord of Charny, subsequently sponsors his appointment at the Burgundian court as a chamberlain in the ducal household.[90] Likewise, at this same event, La Marche emphasises how another Castilian knight, Diego de Valera (who was also a chronicler and author of various treatises, including one on the nature of 'true' nobility) is perceived by all to be 'gracieulx et courtois, et fort aggreable a chascun' (gracious and courteous, and highly agreeable to everyone).[91]

This homosocial focus on male sociability and attractiveness to other men, rather than on women's involvement in these two events, is taken even further in La Marche's representation of Lalaing at the *Fontaine des Pleurs*, where the *entrepreneur*'s sheer charisma is seen to captivate all those knights and squires who come into contact with him as either competitors or spectators: 'à l'occasion de ses vertuz, l'avoient prins en telle amour et extime, que tous le queroient, aimoient et prisoient' (because of his virtues, they had conceived such affection and esteem for him that they all sought him out, loved and prized him).[92] Indeed, La Marche goes on to say that Lalaing exerts such a fascination over the people of Chalon-sur-Saône and its environs — an area with which he had no prior connection, being from Hainaut rather than from the duchy of Burgundy — that the local male notables flock to form part of his entourage as he enters the lists, leaving some of his opponents struggling to keep their own closest relatives and friends in their company.[93] That Lalaing's demonstration of his personality and talents at this *pas d'armes* served him well not only with his male peers but also with his superiors is seen in his election soon afterwards as a member of the Order of the Golden Fleece at its chapter in Mons in May 1451.[94]

In addition to remarking on the competitors' personal and social agreeableness to other men at these two *pas d'armes*, La Marche also frequently passes comment on their physical appearance and how this bespeaks their chivalric prowess, thereby casting over them a homosocial gaze of a more aestheticising kind. In the *Arbre Charlemagne*, for example, he mentions a 'volet bien delié' (very delicate veil) worn by the *entrepreneur* on his helm, but, rather than this being glossed as a love token from a putative lady worn in her honour, he suggests that this may in fact have been a means by which the rather pale-faced Bauffremont could give his complexion a little more colour, presumably so as to make himself appear more full-blooded and vigorous in his opponents' eyes.[95] In relation

[90] OdLM, vol. 2, p. 156.

[91] *Ibid.*, vol. 1, p. 305. See also Florence Serrano, 'La ficcionalización de Diego de Valera en la literatura borgoñona', in *Mosén Diego de Valera: Entre las armas y las letras*, ed. by Cristina Moya García (Woodbridge: Tamesis, 2014), pp. 53–62; and CPM, which is an edition of a short poem written about this *pas* by an unknown author that recounts how Valera brought his own *emprise* to it and was permitted to joust against one of the Burgundian defenders, Jacques de Challant.

[92] OdLM, vol. 2, p. 156.

[93] *Ibid.*, vol. 2, p. 185.

[94] For a discussion of how Philippe de Lalaing's *pas* was perhaps a bid for his own election to the Golden Fleece in emulation of his more illustrious elder brother, see Essay 3, pp. 405–6.

[95] OdLM, vol. 1, p. 298. La Marche also says that others there present understood this veil to be a means by which the *entrepreneur* made it difficult to see where the holes (presumably for breathing) were located in his visor.

to the *Fontaine des Pleurs*, La Marche crowns his depiction of Lalaing as pious and charismatic with a glowing appreciation of his looks, describing him as 'l'ung des beaulx et fiers hommes d'armes que oncques je veisse, et plus beau, sans comparaison, que jamais ne l'avoye veu' (one of the most handsome and proud-looking men-at-arms that I ever beheld, one whose beauty was without compare to that of anyone else I ever saw).[96]

Yet it was not only La Marche who was struck by Lalaing's extraordinary physical beauty at this most homosocial of *pas d'armes*: he himself notes the admiring female gaze that was also cast on the young knight by the ladies of Chalon-sur-Saône — even if their presence at the actual combats is not mentioned in his narrative — which led them to dub Lalaing a 'nouvel Pontus' (new Ponthus).[97] This explicit parallel with the romance of *Ponthus et Sidoine* alludes to its eponymous hero in his guise as the 'Chevalier Noir Dolent aux Armes Blanches' (Sorrowing Black Knight of the White Arms) who organises his own fictional *emprise* — one that anticipates many of the features of actual historical *pas d'armes* — in the forest of Broceliande and sends his defeated challengers to the most beautiful lady in Brittany, who is, of course, none other than his great love, Sidoine.[98]

Although this reference to Lalaing as the embodiment of Ponthus has led some modern commentators to assume mistakenly that the *entrepreneur* himself consciously modelled his *pas d'armes* on his romance counterpart's *emprise*,[99] this was not actually the case.[100] However, the analogy drawn between Lalaing and Ponthus does point up the divergence between the interpretations of this particular chivalric *entrepreneur* made by the male and the female figures who come into contact with him at this event. Thus, whilst La Marche shows how the aestheticising homosocial gaze of the men constructs him as a pious and inspirational embodiment of male chivalric prowess, even if this too is not entirely untinged by the erotic,[101] the courtly but nonetheless amorous heterosexual gaze of the ladies constructs him as a male object of desire by projecting onto him the qualities of the romance hero fighting for love of his lady. This juxtaposition of

---

[96] *Ibid.*, vol. 2, p. 189.

[97] *Ibid.*, vol. 2, p. 203. Perhaps because of the lasting renown that Lalaing acquired at this *pas d'armes* and the link made here with Ponthus, this romance hero's name was given to both a son and a grandson of Jacques's younger brother, Jean de Lalaing (d. 1498): see Robert Born, *Les Lalaing: une grande 'mesnie' hennuyère, de l'aventure d'Outrée au siècle des gueux (1096–1600)* (Brussels: Éditeurs d'art associés, 1986), p. 3; see also Source 14, p. 289 n. 30.

[98] On Ponthus's role as a model of chivalric magnanimity see above, n. 53; see also Source 1.

[99] See, for example, Lindner, 'L'influence'; and Éric Bousmar, 'Pasos de armas, justas y torneos en la corte de Borgoña (siglo XV y principios del XVI). Imaginario caballeresco, rituales e implicaciones socio-políticas', in *El legado de Borgoña: Fiesta y ceremonia cortesana en la Europa de los Austrias (1454–1648)*, ed. by Krista De Jonge, Bernardo J. García García and Alicia Esteban Estríngana (Madrid: Fundación Carlos de Amberes/Marcial Pons Ediciones de Historia, 2010), pp. 561–605 (p. 568).

[100] What they do have in common is that each features a fountain and is due to last a full year; however, the personnel of Ponthus's *pas* are a dwarf, an elderly damsel and a hermit, whereas those of the *Fontaine des Pleurs* are Charolais Herald, a unicorn and the 'Dame des Pleurs'.

[101] On the potentially homoerotic dimension of knightly homosociality, see Richard E. Zeikowitz, *Homoeroticism and Chivalry: Discourses of Male Same-Sex Desire in the Fourteenth Century* (New York/Basingstoke: Palgrave Macmillan, 2003), p. 83, who notes: 'While authors might not consciously invite male readers to form homoerotic identifications this is a potential combined effect of vivid descriptions, an apparent cultural mode of visualizing what one reads, and the fervor some male readers have for chivalry.'

homosocial aesthetics and heterosexual erotics is even more marked in the *Livre des faits* where, at numerous chivalric contests, albeit not the *Fontaine des Pleurs* itself, the beauty of Lalaing's physique is similarly lauded by the narrator whilst the looks cast on him by women as he rides through the streets on his way to the lists are unequivocally amorous, if not downright lustful, as in this example where he is watched as he travels through Pamplona on his way to fight Diego de Guzmán as part of an *emprise* that he undertook in the Iberian Peninsula: 'de dames et de damoiselles fut voulentiers veu, et asséz est a croire que aucunes en y avoit qui bien euissent volut avoir changiet a leur mari pour l'avoir, se ainsi se eust peut faire' (the ladies and damsels in particular gazed longingly at him, and it is safe to say that there were those who would have gladly exchanged their husbands for him, if they could have done so).[102] Whilst, admittedly, we only have access to these female voices through the filter of the male narrators of these works, this consistent eroticising appreciation of knights such as Lalaing would seem to be indicative of women's agency in asserting their own response to men's displays as chivalric performers, even when their participation as inspirational figures, prize-givers or spectators is given far less attention in narratives dominated by the depiction of relations between chivalric males.

The other and even more compelling example of a *pas d'armes* at which women put their own interpretation on events is the Savoyard *Pas* of Carignano. This tournament, which consisted principally of successive pairs of men fighting on foot, first with spears* and then with swords over a barrier, took place on 18–25 February 1504. It was organised by the duke of Savoy, Philibert II, as part of the celebrations attached to the wedding of one of his courtiers, Laurent de Gorrevod, to Philippa de La Palu, daughter of another eminent Savoyard family. Significantly, Philibert's wife, the duchess Margaret of Austria, a woman who was steeped in the courtly entertainments and values of the Burgundian court, being the only daughter of Mary of Burgundy and her husband, Maximilian of Austria,[103] seems to have played a major part in the post-combat festivities, which took the form of various *momeries** (dramatised dances) held over three consecutive evenings (18, 19 and 20 February 1504).[104] Although the narrative retelling of this event — which was probably written by a herald who witnessed it, presumably at the instigation of either Duke Philibert or Laurent de Gorrevod, whose marriage it celebrated[105] — survives only as a seventeenth-century antiquarian's transcription of an earlier manuscript,[106] the financial

[102] LF, p. 176; CL, p. 151. Lalaing's entry into Ghent for his joust with Jean de Boniface has a similar impact on the ladies of the town, which suggests that this is something of a topos in this text: LF, pp. 139–40; CL, p. 134. On Lalaing's physical beauty more generally, see LF, pp. 107, 109 and especially 195; CL, pp. 117, 118 and especially 160. Significantly, ladies *are* depicted as spectators at both the Boniface and Guzmán jousts in all images of these events in the three illustrated manuscripts of the *Livre des faits*: Paris, BnF, fr. 16830, fols 47r and 81v; Comte de Lalaing, private collection, no shelfmark, dated 1518, fols 41v and 70v; Los Angeles, J. Paul Getty Museum, 114, fols 48v and 76r.

[103] See Dagmar Eichberger, ed., *Women of Distinction: Margaret of York, Margaret of Austria* (Turnhout: Brepols, 2005).

[104] Thalia Brero, 'Soirées festives et vie nocturne à la cour de Savoie', in *Le Banquet: manger, boire et parler ensemble (XIIe–XVIIe siècles)*, ed. by Bruno Laurioux, Agostino Paravicini Bagliani and Eva Pibiri, Micrologus Library, 91 (Florence: SISMEL Edizioni del Galluzzo, 2018), pp. 229–60, especially 244–6, 256–7

[105] See PC, pp. 469, 476, for the two references made by the narrator to the commission he was given to write up the event.

[106] This antiquarian was Samuel Guichenon (1607–64).

account of Margaret of Austria, which outlines the different items used in the *entremets* for which she herself paid, is extant. It thus constitutes a very important and unusual piece of evidence attesting to the shaping of a *pas d'armes* by an actual woman, in contrast to the more usual male *entrepreneur*'s deployment of a fictional female figure.

The most interesting of these festivities for our purposes is the *momerie* organised on the second evening (19 February), which represents the arrival in Carignano of a delegation of Amazons dressed in sumptuous gowns over which they wear breastplates and carry swords and shields, a group of which Margaret of Austria herself formed a part. The arrival in a castle hall of armed female warriors was not, in itself, a wholly unusual dramatic theme to be enacted on a chivalric occasion, since there was a similar episode at the *Arbre d'or*, which was likewise held to celebrate a marriage, that of Margaret of York and Charles the Bold in 1468. During this particular Burgundian event, celebrated in Bruges, at which the bride and new duchess was the guest of honour but played no active role, a whole series of lavishly staged *entremets* was organised around the theme of the Twelve Labours of Hercules, including one where he and Theseus fight against two Amazons. Yet the meaning attached to the Amazons' appearance at Carignano, as revealed through a lengthy speech delivered by an elderly but richly dressed damsel who serves as their herald, is very different from that given to their appearance at the *Arbre d'or*, and it is this interpretation that reveals Margaret of Austria's agency as both a notable participant in a chivalric event and a shaper of chivalric masculinity.

At the earlier Burgundian *pas d'armes*, as recounted by La Marche, the heavily armed and bellicose Amazons enter the hall on horseback and proceed to fight Hercules and Theseus with spears and swords.[107] The author diplomatically refuses to say whether it was the men or the women who won the actual combat, but the accompanying *brevet* explains that the significance of this dramatic interlude for those knights watching is that they should never underestimate an opponent even if they appear to have 'feminins corps' (women's bodies), a compliment which becomes even more backhanded when this deceptive appearance is comically extended to all those whose bodies are weak, missing a limb or even twisted in some way.[108]

By contrast, at the *Pas* of Carignano the Amazons' *momerie* is the only one to feature a group made up entirely of women and it is described in the narrative in far more detail than either of the other two that bookend it on different nights. These were a choreographed combat between six 'gentilshommes' (gentlemen) that featured the duke and five other men dressed as hermits (18 February) and an 'ebattemen' (entertainment) involving four 'Slave-Knights' dancing with four ladies who hold them prisoner on long golden chains and release them only when four other knights enter the room and try to 'attack' the ladies (20 February).[109] The gloss provided on the Amazons' *momerie* by their elderly damsel-herald is that they have come to bring their loving aid and assistance to the ducal *entrepreneur* by taking his place in the lists if he should be brought down and find himself unable to continue to defend the field, this being a contingency for which any

---

[107] Normore, *A Feast for the Eyes*, p. 174, states that these festivities in 1468 took place in 'temporary halls erected for the large crowds'.

[108] OdLM, vol. 3, pp. 168–9.

[109] This last entertainment becomes quite physical as the ladies beat their prisoners with their swords to encourage them to fight and the duke, one of the prisoners, even goes so far as to dislocate the shoulder of his opponent by accident!

pas d'armes had to plan.[110] The damsel-herald's speech then becomes a thinly disguised paean to a wife's loving devotion to her husband — and thus more obviously relevant to the wedding that was being celebrated at this event — as one Amazon in particular, that clearly incarnated by Margaret herself, is said to be especially ready to leap to his aid in order to help publicise his great renown as defender of his *pas*. Moreover, being of '[le] plus haut parentaige' (the highest nobility) and coming from 'lignee ... chevallereuse' (chivalrous stock) herself, this Amazon happily embraces her God-given duty towards him. Preceded by various damsels carrying their armets* and gauntlets, the actual 'Amazons' then enter the hall, gorgeously dressed and with silver breastplates and sword belts, dancing elegantly but showing their readiness for combat by brandishing their unsheathed swords in their hands.

Far, then, from these Amazons being presented as knights' antagonists whose supposed physical inferiority should not be underestimated, as was the lesson supplied by the interlude at the *Arbre d'or*, the female warriors here at Carignano are depicted as men's loving helpmeets. This distinctly companionate interpretation of the Amazons would seem to be down to Margaret of Austria herself. Not only was she famed for being deeply devoted to Philibert, her second husband, but also, as the financial account reveals, it was she who paid for the cost of various 'faulx visaiges' (masks), white hats and tan-coloured taffeta used for the liripipes* to hang off them, and for the white taffeta used for the sheaths of the swords, all of which items are also mentioned in the narrative itself as being worn by the ladies playing the Amazons.[111] Yet, such an unusual depiction of the heterosexual relations underpinning the *Pas* of Carignano through this particular dramatic episode should not necessarily surprise us. It is, after all, heavily indebted to the positive representation of the Amazons and, in particular, their queen, Penthesilea, who came lovingly (if too late) to the aid of Hector in the Trojan War, as formulated by Christine de Pizan (1364–*c.*1430) in her pro-feminine catalogue of famous women, the *Livre de la Cité des Dames* (1404–05).[112] This text was extremely popular at the Burgundian court, with Margaret herself owning at least one manuscript copy as well as a set of tapestries based upon it.[113] A similarly appreciative view of the Amazons was promoted in the *Neuf Preuses* (Nine Female Worthies) motif that was produced as a complement to the *Neuf Preux* (Nine [Male] Worthies), a theme that was also immortalised at the Burgundian court in a series

---

[110] For example, at the *Arbre d'or*, the *entrepreneur*, Antoine, the Great Bastard of Burgundy, Charles the Bold's half-brother, is injured part-way through the event and has to be substituted: see OdLM, vol. 3, pp. 173, 188.

[111] See Bruchet, *Marguerite d'Autriche*, p. 323; PC, pp. 476–8.

[112] I.19: *La Città delle Dame*, ed. by Earl Jeffrey Richards and trans. by Patrizia Caraffi (Milan: Luni Editrice, 1998), pp. 123–31; and *The Book of the City of Ladies*, trans. by Rosalind Brown-Grant (Harmondsworth: Penguin Classics, 1999), pp. 43–6. On medieval views of the Amazons, which ranged from the monstrous to the illustrious, see Danièle James-Raoul, 'Les Amazones au Moyen Âge', in *En quête d'utopies*, ed. by Claude Thomasset and Danièle James-Raoul (Paris: Presses de l'Université Paris-Sorbonne, 2005), pp. 195–230.

[113] Brussels, KBR, 9235–37. On Margaret of Austria as bibliophile, see Marguerite Debae, *La bibliothèque de Marguerite d'Autriche: essai de reconstitution d'après l'inventaire de 1523–1524* (Louvain/Paris: Éditions Peeters, 1995); and Hanno Wijsman, *Luxury Bound: Illustrated Manuscript Production and Noble and Princely Book Ownership in the Burgundian Netherlands (1400–1550)* (Turnhout: Brepols, 2010), pp. 201–7. On Margaret's tapestry of the *Cité des Dames*, see Susan Groag Bell, *The Lost Tapestries of Christine de Pizan* (Berkeley: University of California Press, 2004), p. 43.

of tapestries that included Penthesilea and which may have been closely modelled on those of Christine's *Cité des Dames*.[114]

The marked contrast between the Amazons' *momerie* at Carignano and that of the four ladies holding the Slave-Knights on golden chains that took place on the following evening thus underscores the very different view of heterosexual relations in the chivalric context that Margaret of Austria, as a powerful, high-status woman with her own independent financial means, was able to promote. Its presentation of the bond between the male *entrepreneur* and his armed female helpmeet as one based on the love borne by one chivalric peer for another, one which has much in common with the ideal of loving brothers-in-arms,[115] could not be more different from the usual *pas d'armes* fictional scenario of the female chivalric muse holding sway over the knight-*entrepreneur* where the question of who really holds power in the relationship is moot.

Conclusion

This analysis of the ethics and erotics of the *pas d'armes* as seen in a range of examples from the Burgundian lands, Castile and Savoy has aimed to show that the construction of chivalric masculinity through events of this kind is not only more complex than simply that of knights proving their dominance over each other and over women, but could also vary significantly depending on the specific cultural and political milieu in which any given *pas* was staged. Chivalry as demonstrated through these ritualised combats was not a zero-sum game whereby the winner took all and proved his superiority to other men. Rather, as we have seen, and as Karras herself recognised, these fights also allowed a competitor to express his sense of belonging to an elite brotherhood of knights whose ethical observance of the rules of the game ideally brought honour to both himself and his opponents.[116] When such observance was missing at a *pas d'armes*, for instance because of cheating or boasting, this had to be handled with extreme care by those recording these events in their efforts to avoid either taking sides in a political conflict or harming a man's reputation unduly. On the one hand, in the politically fractious and somewhat bellicose, not to say macho, Castilian context of the *Paso Honroso*, this meant leaving it up to the reader to draw their own conclusions about whether such divergent, even extravagant, behaviour was to be admired or condemned. On the other hand, in the Burgundian context, *pas d'armes* could serve to attract foreign knights to the ducal court, to integrate nobles from different parts of the Burgundian lands into a single fighting corps and even to drum up support for crusade. Hence this meant showing with great diplomacy how to prevent the serious tensions between contestants that could arise from such behaviour either diminishing a man's renown or endangering the cohesion of the chivalric community and polity to which the competitors belonged or aspired to belong. Nor was women's role in the formation of masculine identity at these homosocial events

---

[114] See Romina Westphal, 'Tapestry and Gender: On the Hero and Heroine Motifs and the Construction of Burgundian Identity' (unpublished PhD dissertation, University of Leeds, 2019), p. 21.

[115] See Marianne J. Ailes, 'The Medieval Male Couple and the Language of Homosociality', in *Masculinity in Medieval Europe*, ed. by Dawn M. Hadley (Harlow: Routledge, 1999), pp. 214–37; and Paul Dingman, 'Ethics and Emotions: A Cultural History of Chivalric Friendship in Medieval/Early Modern Times' (unpublished PhD dissertation, University of Rochester, New York, 2012).

[116] Karras, *From Boys to Men*, pp. 38–9.

restricted to playing the largely symbolic part of the imperious but aloof *domna* imposed on them by male *entrepreneurs* and competitors alike. The responses of at least two sets of ladies, albeit of different status — the townswomen at Chalon-sur-Saône and the Savoyard duchess and her female companions at Carignano — to the *pas* which they respectively witnessed show their resistance to being marginalised in the narrative accounts of these events. Whilst the former voiced their own erotic fantasy about the *entrepreneur* himself at a *pas d'armes* which had a distinctly pious underpinning, the latter shifted its paradigm of love and heterosexual power relations to that of affection and respect between chivalric equals, as befits a court culture presided over by a forceful and amorous duchess. In terms, then, of the competing agendas of masculinity, namely homosociality and heterosexuality, the *pas d'armes* would seem not to have had a single essence but rather a variety of different and sometimes conflicting potentials, these being given a precise shape at a particular time and in a particular place according to the aims of those authors who either elected or were commissioned to record them for posterity.

I am grateful to S. H. Rigby for his comments on successive drafts of this essay.

Christina Normore

 Exceptional bodies in the *Relation du Pas de Saumur*

From 26 June to 5 August 1446, the area surrounding the castle of Saumur witnessed a vision drawn straight from Arthurian romance. A dwarf and two lions stood guard over a marble column, on which hung a vermilion shield covered with pansies. A series of fantastically garbed challengers rode up to the shield and hit it with their lances, signalling their intent to test their prowess in a joust with one of the team of knights and squires who waited in a nearby castle. Summoned by the dwarf, these defenders were led by beautiful ladies to the lists, where they and the challengers would clash before the adjudicating eyes of their followers, the ladies, the dwarf and experienced military men and heralds appointed as official judges. While the victors were gifted with jewels, their true reward was meant to be the high regard they might win from their peers and audience through their display of physical excellence.

The forty days of jousts and festivities known as the *Pas de la Joyeuse Garde* (also known as the *Pas de Saumur*) were the culmination of a string of tournaments held in the Loire valley in the summer of 1446.[1] The participation of many members of the French chivalric elite during the summer months (a time traditionally used for military campaigns) was made possible by a recently negotiated truce in the Hundred Years War (1337–1453), a decades-long Anglo-French conflict that had briefly halted following the Treaty of Tours (1444) and the marriage of King Henry IV of England to Margaret of Anjou (1445). While the Loire valley was a regular summer retreat for the French court, the location of the month-long festivities at the castle and town of Saumur strengthens the claims of other sources that the *Joyeuse Garde* was conducted under the aegis of the king's ally and close relative René, duke of Anjou and titular king of Sicily and Jerusalem (1409–80). René had purchased the Manoir de Launay in 1444 and, after extensive renovations, gifted it to his wife, Isabelle, duchess of Lorraine (1400–53) in 1446, the same year that the *Joyeuse Garde* was staged nearby.[2]

Like many such events, this *pas d'armes* mixed sportive combat with chivalric romance. On one side was a team of defenders — all members of René's court who wore their duke's favoured emblem of pansies. On the other side was a series of challengers associated with the court of King Charles VII of France (1403–61). All the combatants were noblemen, but they were accompanied and observed by a far greater mix of individuals: noblewomen, who led the men to the lists and hosted them at nightly feasting; trained performers such as the dwarf, who were tasked with helping to foster a chivalric ambiance; lower-ranking

[1] For a more extended discussion of the historical background to this event, see Essay 2.

[2] Christian de Mérindol, 'Les demeures du roi René en Anjou et leur decoration peinte', *Bulletin de la Société Nationale des Antiquaires de France* (1978–79) [1982], 180–93 (p. 186).

courtiers and the townspeople from Saumur, who went unmentioned in surviving sources but are known to have made up the audiences of other such events and were presumably present here as well.

The *Joyeuse Garde* is known today mainly through two narrative accounts: a short prose description by Mathieu d'Escouchy (1420–82), a chronicler associated with the French royal court, and a poem preserved in a manuscript produced a generation after the event now in St Petersburg, NLR, fr. F. p. XIV, 4 (hereafter *Relation du Pas de Saumur*, abbreviated to *Relation*), which is closely linked to the Angevin court.[3] As Anne D. Hedeman and Justin Sturgeon discuss in Essay 2 of the present volume, the *Relation* manuscript is especially notable as one of the few surviving examples of a verbal description of a tournament accompanied by an extended cycle of illuminations, executed by a small group of artists working within what appears to be a carefully planned programme. The differing interests and biases of d'Escouchy's text and the text and images of the *Relation* complicate a reconstruction of the precise details of the *Joyeuse Garde*'s organisation and patronage.

The *Joyeuse Garde* is generally accepted today as a prime example of a class of tournament scholars call *pas d'armes*. This characterisation rests in part on the *Relation* poet's reference to it as a 'pas'[4] and in part on the competition's formal qualities. *Pas d'armes* are usually defined as tournaments in which an individual or team defended a location against all comers (or at least all comers deemed sufficiently noble), a task that distantly echoes the real military practice of guarding a passage (*pas*). Yet, as even the brief description of the *Joyeuse Garde* above makes clear, rule-governed physical competition was only one of its defining elements. Equally important was its contribution to what Michel Stanesco has termed the *enromancement* (romanticisation) of the later Middle Ages, a practice of not only deliberately inserting fictive elements into reality in the pursuit of a more literary way of being but also attempting to harness chivalric literature as a means of renovating the quotidian world.[5] Although they disagree in other elements of their interpretation of the *pas*, the multiple memorialisations of the *Joyeuse Garde* in prose, poem and image alike make clear that its charm for its early audiences lay in its ability to bring the romanticised Arthurian past into their fifteenth-century present.

The combination of what would now be termed sport and theatre was such a frequent feature of fifteenth-century *pas d'armes* that modern scholars debate whether narrative frames should be considered a defining feature of this type of tournament.[6] Was the *pas d'armes* either a form of theatre or physical instantiation of a chivalric romance, and thus

---

[3] A third account of the *Joyeuse Garde*, which is shorter than the *Relation* and written in prose, is contained in Guillaume Leseur, *Histoire de Gaston IV, comte de Foix*: see HGF, vol. 1, pp. 194–5; HGFMO; and, especially, a recently rediscovered manuscript of this text (Berlin, Staatsbibliothek, Preußischer Kulturbesitz, Ham. 606, fols 76r– 96v). The version in this manuscript gives a different order of jousts and lists some different jousters at the event. For a translation of Leseur's narrative account of this event, see Supplementary Source 1, Liverpool University Press Digital Collaboration Hub <https://liverpool-universitypress.manifoldapp.org/projects/pas-d-armes-casebook> [accessed 1 November 2024].

[4] PSr, 67.

[5] Michel Stanesco, *Jeux d'errance du chevalier medieval: Aspects ludiques de la fonction guerrière dans la littérature du Moyen Âge flamboyant* (Leiden: Brill, 1988), esp. pp. 17–26.

[6] As Catherine Blunk, 'Between Sport and Theatre: How Spectacular was the *Pas d'armes*?', in *The Medieval Tournament as Spectacle*, ed. by Alan V. Murray and Karen Watts (Woodbridge: Boydell Press, 2020), pp. 120–38, has noted, disagreement about the definition of the term has surrounded *pas d'armes* since it first emerged in the fifteenth century and continues to the present day.

required fictional elements? Or was it instead fundamentally defined by the conditions of combat, and thus might easily shed narrative elements in favour of either military training or sport?[7] Without firmly deciding this issue for all cases, in what follows I want to redirect the discussion to consider how the logics of the competitive and fictive elements in *pas d'armes* worked together in cases where the two were indeed combined. My question here is not whether all *pas d'armes* require a fictional frame but, rather, why combine the two? How might a joust and a theatrical performance logically and productively inform each other?

To understand both what occurred at the *Joyeuse Garde* and what elements were considered particularly noteworthy, I will first outline the various discrepancies and alignments between the two main surviving accounts. While differing in some important respects, d'Escouchy's account and the *Relation* both insist on framing the event in relation to the Arthurian models and on the importance of what I shall term 'exceptional bodies' in creating an atmosphere of historical romance. In this respect, the *Joyeuse Garde* was quite typical of its genre. Whether one looks to the fighters' displaying exceptional physical skill in the lists or to the beautiful women and exoticised people and animals who brought life to the fictive frame, *pas d'armes* are often populated by bodies that are marked as outside of the everyday. While scholars working within disability and gender studies have explored parallel phenomena in modern sport and medieval and modern performance arts, the case of the *Joyeuse Garde* suggests that modern theories of the stare and gaze can only partially account for the activities and memorialisation of the late medieval *pas d'armes*. In particular, the evidence of the *Joyeuse Garde* calls into question two common assumptions in modern scholarship: that power lies in seeing rather than being observed, and that ideal and normative bodies are universally synonymous. An examination of the visual and textual treatment of the three types of human bodies that framed the combat in the *Relation* — the fighters' male attendants, women and the dwarf — reveals the centrality of the exceptional (rather than normative) body in this *pas d'armes* and, by extension, the larger chivalric complex of which it was part. The mobilisation of these seemingly extraneous bodies, and the juxtapositions staged between them and with the combatants, simultaneously enact and question the acts of observation and display that were crucial to the fighters' performances of martial prowess. The exceptional bodies of the *Joyeuse Garde* and their reception thus serve as useful reminders of the cultural relativity of the acts of observing and being observed, complicating modern beliefs about the ways in which both acts intersect, interpret and control human bodies.

[7] Research on sport is strongly modernist in focus, and frequently either assumes sport as a category to be a purely modern phenomenon or alternatively makes overly simplified delineations between 'traditional' sports and 'modern' sport (this distinction is further complicated by the equation of modern sport with European origins). Despite the differences between the fifteenth-century and modern phenomena (which exist in most spheres of cultural expression), considering tournament in terms of sport helps to highlight its combination of public, rule-based, intentionally non-lethal competition with its goal of achieving both personal excellence and public acclaim through display of physical ability. For the historiography on sport and modernity, see Douglas Booth, 'Constructing Knowledge: Histories of Modern Sport', in *A Companion to Sport*, ed. by David L. Andrews and Ben Carrington (Hoboken, NJ: Blackwell Publishing, 2013), pp. 23–40. For a summary of recent critiques of this construct, see Samuel M. Clevenger, 'Sport History, Modernity and the Logic of Coloniality: A Case for Decoloniality', *Rethinking History*, 21 (2017), 586–605.

The accounts

Current reconstructions of the events at the *Joyeuse Garde* are based primarily on the short prose description in the chronicle of Mathieu d'Escouchy and the more elaborated visual and poetic account in the *Relation* manuscript now housed in St Petersburg. This manuscript dates to the end of the fifteenth century, nearly thirty years after the events it recounts: as Anne D. Hedeman and Justin Sturgeon argue in their essay in this volume, it must be treated as a complex act of memorialisation rather than a neutral source. The text is a long poem by an unknown author, who claims to have been an eyewitness at many parts of the *pas* and to have gathered evidence from others concerning sections that he missed. In addition to the poem, the *Relation* manuscript unusually includes an extensive illumination cycle. This image cycle offers a complementary but alternative account of the events in 1446, forming what Christian de Mérindol has termed 'un double témoignage' (a double testimony): nowhere is this interplay more apparent than in the ways that the two media position human figures as spectators and spectacles for the reader and viewer's gaze.[8]

It is worth noting at the outset that a full reconstruction of the lived experience of the *Joyeuse Garde* will always remain elusive. While it is unusually well-documented for an event of its type, the details chosen for attention and exclusion by the authors and artists at times differ in ways that clearly indicate the selective nature of the surviving evidence. Even a brief comparison of the d'Escouchy and *Relation* accounts reveals discrepancies that point to the divergent goals of the two authors.

D'Escouchy's account is relatively brief and, in many respects, vague: he gives a general date of 1446 for the 'pluseurs joustes … et aussy aultres esbatemens de grans coustaiges et despens' (many jousts … and other costly and expensive entertainments) held at the French court that year.[9] According to d'Escouchy, the primary motivation for all these entertainments was the need to amuse and maintain the martial skills of the male members of the French nobility, who were experiencing a lull in the hostilities of the Hundred Years War. Summer — traditionally a prime time for staging military campaigns — thus found the courtiers somewhat at a loose end.

Among the many entertainments staged in this unusual time of peace, d'Escouchy singles out the events at Saumur. He presents the *Joyeuse Garde* as a joint project between Charles VII of France and René of Anjou. In attempting to define the form of this tournament, d'Escouchy does not use the term *pas d'armes* but does describe the event as analogous to the Arthurian practice of guarding a passage against all noble comers. For d'Escouchy, the *Joyeuse Garde* was an impressive, but also troubled, event:

> par male fortune, à l'une de ces journées, fu tué d'un coup de lanche ung gentil chevallier, qui estoit au Roy de Secile, nommé messire Auvregnas Champron; dont toutte la compaignie fut troublée; et sy en y eut diverses fois pluseurs de blechiez assez rudement. Et pour ces causes, les Roys et seigneurs dessusdis commencèrent à tenner; et par ainsy se deslaissèrent iceulx esbastemens assez brief ensievant

[8] Christian de Mérindol, *Les fêtes de chevalerie à la cour du roi René: Emblématique, art et histoire (les joutes de Nancy, le Pas de Saumur et le Pas de Tarascon)* (Paris: Éditions du CTHS, 1993), p. 8.

[9] MdE, vol. 1, p. 107.

(by ill fortune, on one of these days, a lance-strike killed a gentle knight, who was a follower of the king of Sicily, named Messire Auvregnas Champron; thus, the entire company was troubled, and there were brutal enough injuries here and there on several occasions. And for these reasons, the kings and their lords began to tire; and so they quit these entertainments not long afterwards).[10]

Despite the short length of d'Escouchy's chronicle passage, it nevertheless manages to disagree with the far longer *Relation* on multiple fronts. The two agree as to the general political and temporal moment of the *pas*. However, the *Relation* downplays the role of the French king, instead framing the *Joyeuse Garde* as an Angevin event. Textually, this is done both by directly claiming René of Anjou as the event's sole *entrepreneur** (organiser or patron) and by situating the *Joyeuse Garde* within a sequence of Angevin, rather than royal French, tournaments. Visually it is accomplished by devoting the first two miniatures to images of René, who appears as the recipient of the author's account on folio 2r and as the Black Knight on folio 3r. It remains unclear which account's presentation is more accurate as, unfortunately, no archival documentation indicating the funding sources for the *pas* are known to have survived. However, regardless of reality, this muddling of the question of patronage and appropriate court context speaks to the political purposes of the two authors: whilst d'Escouchy favours the royal cause,[11] the *Relation* is visually and textually framed as an account intended for the Angevin court.[12]

Other differences between the two accounts indicate that the *Relation* author and illuminators — while not expressly lying — were willing to bend the truth in pursuit of a more celebratory account than d'Escouchy provided. Perhaps the most notable difference between the two accounts is that the *Relation* glosses over the death that dominated d'Escouchy's memory of the event: the fatal combat between Auvregnas Champron and the French courtier Antoine de Prie is unillustrated and the death unmentioned, the poet summarising the joust by stating simply: 'Je suis contant que plus n'en die/De ce qui fut fait et commis' (I am content to say no more/Of what happened and was done).[13] Other injuries are likewise downplayed, and the *pas* as a whole concludes not with disappointment and ennui but instead with a procession: 'Toute estoit semee la voye/De toute plaisance et de joye' (The whole way was strewn/With all pleasantness and joy).[14] Indeed, the author concludes, this was an event equal to any in the history of ancient Greece, Britain or France.[15]

[10] *Ibid.*, vol. 1, p. 108.

[11] The question of d'Escouchy's political affiliations is complex given his defection from the Burgundian cause to Louis XI in the 1460s, the time when the editor of his chronicle, Gaston du Fresne de Beaucourt, speculated that he began to write his continuation of Monstrelet's chronicle (MdE, 'Introduction', vol. 1, p. xxxix). As d'Escouchy was not a member or known supporter of the Angevin court, however, it is unsurprising that he would choose to elevate Charles VII over René of Anjou in this case.

[12] As Hedeman and Sturgeon argue elsewhere in this volume, while the precise intended recipient is unclear, their Angevin affiliation is evident from the dedication page and coat of arms included in the manuscript.

[13] *Relation*, PSr, stanza 200, p. 104. This was the sole combat for both contestants at the *Joyeuse Garde.* Auvregnas Champron is currently unattested outside of this incident; Antoine de Prie was the younger brother of Jean V, lord of Prie, a councillor at the French royal court. *Ibid.*, p. 143.

[14] *Ibid.*, stanza 226, p. 109.

[15] *Ibid.*, stanza 227, p. 110.

The differences between the surviving accounts of the *Joyeuse Garde* highlight several points for consideration. One is that they tend to differ in terms not of fact but of emphasis and interpretation. Both agree, for instance, that this event took place between courtiers attached to Charles VII and René of Anjou, that the general location was near the castle of Saumur, and that the lull in Anglo-French hostilities allowed time and energy for the enterprise. They differ, however, in terms of how they choose to present these facts, and ultimately in how they judge the success of the *pas*. Ultimately, d'Escouchy considers it a tragic event in the history of the French court. Several manuscripts of his text follow his account of the *Joyeuse Garde* with the tale of another joust gone wrong in the following year that resulted in the death of one of the *Joyeuse Garde*'s French participants, namely Louis de Bueil, the dauphin's chamberlain. While d'Escouchy does not condemn the nobility's desire to stage and take part in tournaments, his chapter stresses the dangers more than the pleasures of such competitions. In contrast, the *Relation* author attempts to elevate the *Joyeuse Garde* to the level of great historical events and celebrates its participants' prowess. The differences between the two accounts are in large part the result of the divergent interests of the two authors, but they should also alert us to the multiple opinions that probably existed among other participants and spectators at the time. As with all performances, the organisers might try to communicate their intent through a *pas d'armes* but the vagaries of actual performance and the disposition of observers could easily lead to quite different messages being received by those participating in the event, its later recorders and their eventual readers.

THE ARTHURIAN FRAME

Given their disagreements, it is notable that the one point upon which d'Escouchy and the unknown author of the *Relation* emphatically agree is the importance of the connection between the *Joyeuse Garde* and the world of chivalric, particularly Arthurian, romance. Rather than referring to this event as a *pas d'armes*, d'Escouchy explains its purpose through an extended description based in the romance tradition:

> dont par les aucuns pooit sambler qu'ilz voulsissent ensievyr et tenir les termes que jadis les chevalliers de la Table Ronde, que mist sus en son temps ce très puissant prince lequel on trouve ès anciennes histoires avoir regné sy haultement, c'est assavoir le Roy Artus. Et la raison pour quoy: car on faisoit publier par officiers d'armes en pluseurs lieux, qu'il y avoit certain nombre de chevalliers ou nobles à garder ung pas, qui estoit desnommé par propre nom, contre tous iceulx qui aler ou passer y vorroient: ouqel pas y avoit aucuns lyons, tigres, licornes, ou bestes samblables. Y avoit aussy pluseurs aultres devises et declaracions très honnourables et moult haultaines. Et pour vray, en faisant et continuant les besoingnes dessusdictes, y fut fait moult belles armes et de notables assamblées et joyeux esbastemens.
>
> (For by these various acts, it seemed that they wished to follow and hold to the terms as once did the knights of the Round Table, which was founded in his time by the most powerful prince, whom one finds in the ancient histories ruled so nobly, that is to say, King Arthur. And the reason for this is that they had officers of arms announce in many places that there would be a certain number of knights or nobles guarding a passage, which was denoted by its proper name, against all those

who would come or wished to pass by there: this passage had various lions, tigers, unicorns, or similar beasts. There were as well many other very honourable and most noble devices and declarations. And in truth, in performing and continuing the good deeds described above, there were many fine feats of arms displayed as well as important gatherings and joyful entertainments).[16]

The *Relation* author likewise expressly connects the form of the *Joyeuse Garde* with the Arthurian tradition, and particularly with the legacy of the most noble knight ever born, Lancelot:

Et pour bailler par inventoire,
Affin de durable memoire,
Honneur a tenir consistoire
En son hault et royal manoir,
Chastel pompeux assis sur Loire,
La ordrene ung repertoire
Pour estre tous temps meritoire
A ceulx qui armes vouldroient voir
Prouesse, vaillance et savoir.
Si Noblesse fait son debvoir,
Clerement peut appercevoir
Que le plus vaillant qui soit né
A cecy voulu concepvoir
Et par tous lieux fait assavoir,
Affin des nobles esmouvoir
Pour avoir le pris coronné.

Et pour ce qu'on trouve en escript
Es anciens romans, ou on lit
Qu'avoit jadis mal et delit
Lors en la Doloureuse Garde,
Quant Lancelot le gean prit,
Son escu tumba par despit
Devant le nain qui le reprit,
Commis au paveillon pour garde,
Puis la nomma Joieuse Garde.
Ainsi est, qui bien le regarde,
Ce pas comprins

(In order to give an account of it/So that it is preserved in memory,/Honour, holding assembly/In his high and royal domain —/A glorious castle situated on the Loire —,/Ordered it to be set up as a place/That would be worthy for all time/For those who would like to see/Exploits, bravery, and skill./If Nobility does her duty/It will clearly be seen/That the bravest who was ever born/Has wished

16 MdE, vol. 1, pp. 107–8.

this to be executed/And to let it be known far and wide/So that noblemen will be moved/To aspire to being crowned with the prize.

And because one finds it written/In ancient tales, where one reads/That pain and pleasure were to be had/When, at the Dolorous Guard,/Lancelot overcame the giant/But, out of annoyance, dropped his shield/In front of the dwarf, who picked it up/And placed it in the pavilion for safe keeping,/Then named it the Joyous Guard,/So this is also the case, for whoever looks carefully,/Of this *pas*).[17]

As elsewhere in their texts, there are differences here in emphasis and interpretation. On the one hand, d'Escouchy's recounting of the narrative frame focuses on the group activities of the knights, which he links to those undertaken in the time of the noble king Arthur. In assimilating the French jousters of his own day with the knights of the Round Table, d'Escouchy thus subtly manages, in passing, to praise their royal leader, Charles VII. The *Relation* author's Arthurian world, on the other hand, is centred on Lancelot. In part, this may be connected to his general valorisation of René of Anjou, who had already appeared in the text in the guise of the Black Knight, a probable reference to Lancelot's early career, when he travels under various forms of chivalric incognito, referring to himself variously as the White Knight, Red Knight, and so on.[18] But it also speaks to a larger difference between the two authors' understandings of the *Joyeuse Garde. Pas d'armes* were highly conflicted cultural sites. They were communal events intended to form relationships between members of the chivalric community and to teach future generations of warriors. Yet they were also fraught locations where combatants hoped to prove their personal skill and bravery; this desire for individual victory created a competitive pressure so intense that at times it drove participants to behaviours that contradicted both the rules and commonsense.[19] These competing forces within the *pas d'armes* are evident in the accounts of the *Joyeuse Garde.* Where d'Escouchy sees the event as largely a group effort, with individual names arising only in the case of death, the *Relation* author presents it as a celebration of individual, rather than group, brilliance. As 'le plus vaillant qui soit né' (the bravest who was ever born), the exceptional Lancelot stands apart from all his fellows. For the *Relation* author, this exceptional status makes him an ideal towards whom any true noble should aspire. Where d'Escouchy presents the participants as wishing to bond together in following an honourable and ancient lifestyle, the *Relation* author sees the impulse to take part in such an event as being driven by individual psychology. The mutually supporting desires for personal growth and fame should lead men to wish to be crowned with the prize.

In both accounts the Arthurian frame is not simply a matter of knightly behaviour. D'Escouchy and the *Relation* author agree on the importance of what might at first seem to be extraneous additional actors. In d'Escouchy's account these are led by 'various lions, tigers, unicorns, or similar beasts'. Such animal attractions were a common feature of festival staging at various Francophone courts at this time, but are a phenomenon that has yet to receive focused study. In some cases, exotic animals were pressed into service: lions

---

17 *Relation*, PSr, stanzas 3–4, p. 67; see also Source 5.

18 On René's interest in Lancelot, see Mérindol, *Les fêtes*, pp. 18–19.

19 On the more personal aspirations behind a *pas d'armes*, see Essay 3; on rule-bending and rule-breaking, see Essay 6.

from court menageries were often subjected to the indignity of chained presence, as when a real lion was chained to a fountain at the Burgundian Feast of the Pheasant (1454). Other animals, such as unicorns, might have appeared as sculptures or been enacted by humans or animals in costume; the artificiality of this approach opened up a complex space in which contemporary viewers might either enjoy or question the illusion.[20] For instance, while some accounts of the later *Pas du Perron Fée* (Bruges, 1463) claim that there were four griffins chained to the titular *perron* (column),[21] others make clear that these were only 'griffons bien et gentement fais a fachon de griffons' (griffins artistically made to look like they were alive) and were in fact controlled by men inside the statues/costumes.[22] However exotic cats and unicorns might have been actualised at the *Joyeuse Garde*, d'Escouchy seems in this case to have favoured suspending disbelief, accepting the presence of such creatures as signs of the historical setting and romance of the competition; indeed, they clearly registered more strongly than the other 'devices and very honourable and most noble declarations', which he mentions in only vague terms. For d'Escouchy, then, the physical presence of exceptional animals was key to producing the sense of a return to the days of King Arthur's court.

Although the *Relation* poet mentions that two lions guarded the shields at the *Joyeuse Garde*, his introduction and the following account instead highlight the presence of exceptional humans as links to a chivalric past. Among the hundreds, if not thousands, of battles recounted in Arthurian romances, the *Relation* author chose to link the events at Saumur with the final showdown at the Dolorous Guard. This is an important moment in Lancelot's early career, recounted most canonically in the early thirteenth-century Prose Lancelot.[23] Early scenes in this sequence recall the classic form of the *pas d'armes*: in order to free prisoners held in the castle of the Dolorous Guard, the challenger Lancelot fights alone against defending groups of knights; with the aid of magical shields, he defeats them and wins initial access to the castle. After numerous intervening episodes, Lancelot finally returns to lift the enchantments that curse the castle and become its true lord, transforming the Dolorous Guard into his stronghold of Joyous Guard. Despite his pose of referencing

---

[20] For a longer discussion of the play between the artificial and the real in creating wondrous effects, see Christina Normore, *A Feast for the Eyes: Art, Performance and the Late Medieval Banquet* (Chicago, IL: University of Chicago Press, 2015), especially chapters 1 and 5.

[21] E.g. the account in Lille, BU, 104 (PPF, p. 172).

[22] *Ibid.*, p. 106; see also Source 11a.

[23] The Prose Lancelot remained popular in the fifteenth century and continued to circulate among the French and Angevin elites, contributing to the legibility of this reference both at the time of the joust and the making of the manuscript one generation later. For example, a surviving copy, Dijon, BM, 527, was made for René's nephew and heir Charles around 1450; interestingly, around the time of the creation of the *Relation* manuscript two decades later, Charles became the son-in-law of Ferry II de Vaudémont-Lorraine, one of the most prominent jousters at the *Joyeuse Garde*. Discussion of the combats in the Dolorous Guard have primarily centred on the question of the character and role of the supernatural and the possible ways in which these encounters foreshadow later events in the Arthurian world: see Elspeth M. Kennedy, 'The Role of the Supernatural in the First Part of the Old French Prose Lancelot', in *Studies in Medieval Literature and Languages in Memory of Frederick Whitehead*, ed. by William Rothwell *et al.* (Manchester: Manchester University Press, 1973), pp. 172–84; Daniel Poirion, 'La Douloureuse Garde', in *Approches du Lancelot en prose*, ed. by Jean Dufournet (Geneva: Slatkine, 1984), pp. 25–48; Lisa Jefferson, 'The Keys to the Enchantments of Dolorous Guard', *Medium Aevum*, 58.1 (1989), 59–79; Christine Ferlampin-Acher, 'La Douloureuse Garde du Lancelot en prose: les clefs du désenchantement', in *Les clefs des textes médiévaux*, ed. by Fabienne Pomel (Rennes: Presses Universitaires de Rennes, 2006), pp. 157–73.

a well-known tale, the version provided by the *Relation* author differs markedly from that found in the Prose Lancelot. The climax of the Prose Lancelot's account of the changing of the name of Dolorous Guard takes place in a cavern and features battles between Lancelot and a series of marvellous beings both mechanical and diabolical. The *Relation* author offers a rather different account of events, instead imagining Lancelot in an outdoor setting defeating a giant. The giant's shield is then taken away as booty by a watching dwarf, who guards it within a tent. The *Relation*'s account of Lancelot's experience clearly offers a narrative that is far easier to link to the narrative of the *Joyeuse Garde* itself. Likewise set above ground, the rules of this event required each challenger to declare his intention to fight by striking a shield mounted on a column in front of the watchful eyes of an exotically clothed dwarf seated in a tent. While the poet never states it directly, he strongly implies that the reader should understand the fifteenth-century shield and dwarf as being echoes of or perhaps identical with the shield and dwarf in his Lancelot tale.

While scholars may legitimately debate the necessity of a narrative component for *pas d'armes*, all the surviving evidence suggests that it was a defining element in the *Joyeuse Garde*. Despite their many disagreements on other points, d'Escouchy and the *Relation* author present Arthurian romance as both the primary inspiration and a key reference point for the design of the event. The disagreements between the two authors expose the multi-faceted nature of such attempts to live out the ideals of romance and the contradictory ways in which the values and proper actions of even a seemingly shared Arthurian model were understood by individual members of fifteenth-century courts. Joined in their desire to literally embody the Arthurian past described in romances, the recorders and probably the participants might nevertheless have had quite different expectations about the details of the ideal that they hoped to bring forth in the process.

Discrepancies between the two authors also complicate more prosaic attempts at fixing meaning, making it difficult to definitively state what or who was deployed to give this Arthurian fantasy physical form at the *Joyeuse Garde*. D'Escouchy focused his attention on unusual animals and does not mention the dwarf; the *Relation* author instead elevates the figure of the dwarf as the site of exotic chivalry and mentions the lions only in passing. What can, however, be broadly stated is that d'Escouchy and the *Relation* poet both ultimately agree that living, unusual bodies were crucial in creating the feel of romance and necessary to transform a modern competition into an event worthy of the Round Table.

TO SEE AND BE SEEN

Up to this point, I have concentrated my discussion on the textual record, yet there is also much to be gleaned from a close examination of the extensive image cycle in the *Relation*. Like the textual accounts discussed above, the *Relation*'s illuminations should be considered a valuable source for understanding the fifteenth-century reception and interpretation of the *Joyeuse Garde*, rather than a neutral record for reconstructing the event. Mérindol has argued that the veristic details of the illuminations signal that they are drawn from sketches done on site during the tournament, and probably by the planner of the visual programme.[24] Despite the great strengths of Mérindol's treatment

---

24 Mérindol, *Les fêtes*, p. 9.

of the manuscript in other respects, this conclusion confuses the visual rhetoric of realism with the actuality of direct observation. Realism and attention to minute detail are common elements in the paintings and sculptures commissioned by the Angevin and other Francophone courts of this period and were used equally to depict both recent events and those from antiquity or even fictional romance. As with modern film special effects that simulate both historical and completely fictitious battles with astonishing detail, the presence of a veristic style and even of the artists' corrections of the author's errors regarding heraldry in a fifteenth-century context cannot be taken to register more than a shared desire among many elite patrons for vivid depictions that could create an illusion of real experience. Despite the marked role of the visual in vivifying textual descriptions of the *pas d'armes*, there is currently no solid evidence that the combat portions of fifteenth-century *pas d'armes* were ever sketched on site; *pas d'armes* accounts are not often illustrated.[25] Rather than relying on direct observation of the bouts, the rare miniaturists depicting *pas d'armes* creatively synthesised multiple sources such as stock compositions, the accompanying textual account and/or other verbal recountings and heraldic representations of coats of arms and crests. This general remove is exacerbated by the late date of the *Relation* manuscript, which was made decades after the *Joyeuse Garde.* Even if the illuminations closely follow an earlier lost prototype, the images we see now are at best a tertiary record, a copy of an earlier artist or artists' imagining of events. As Jane H. M. Taylor has argued, the veristic style of these illuminations is best seen as being analogous to the pose of eyewitness in the accompanying text, a rhetorical gesture meant to aid in the memorialisation of the *Joyeuse Garde.*[26] But, precisely because they cannot be taken as direct reportage, the miniatures are a vital source for understanding how an event such as this one was interpreted, remembered and memorialised. Given the lack of a defined tradition for depicting *pas d'armes*, the artists' choices offer a welcome window into how the team of painters assembled to depict the *Joyeuse Garde* believed such an event should be run and what elements they considered most likely to convince posterity of the value of a *pas d'armes.*[27]

Among the most noticeable features of the illumination cycle is its emphasis on human bodies both looking and being observed. The *Relation* manuscript is heavily illuminated, with eighty-six miniatures spread out among its first forty-two folios. Of these, eighty-four images are devoted to the *pas* itself, with seventy-five scenes of combat and the remaining nine showing related activities such as a challenger striking a shield or processions from the castle by the defenders and their allies. An astonishing eighty-three of the eighty-six miniatures include images of onlookers: the act of observation outstrips even the act of combat as a defining feature of the *Joyeuse Garde.*

This emphasis on looking can in part be explained by the more general importance of observation and display within tournament culture. Both literary and historical

---

[25] Guillaume Bureaux, 'Pas d'armes et vide iconographique: quand le texte doit remplacer l'image (XVe siècle)', *Perspectives médiévales*, 38 (2017) <https://journals.openedition.org/peme/12792> [accessed 22 June 2024].

[26] Jane H. M. Taylor, 'La fête comme performance, le livre comme document: le Pas de Saumur', in *Les arts et les lettres en Provence au temps du roi René*, ed. by Chantal Connochie-Bourgne and Valérie Gontero-Lauze (Presses Universitaires de Provence, 2013), pp. 233–41 (p. 239).

[27] For a discussion of the different hands in the illumination cycle and a broader framing of the visual programme, see Essay 2.

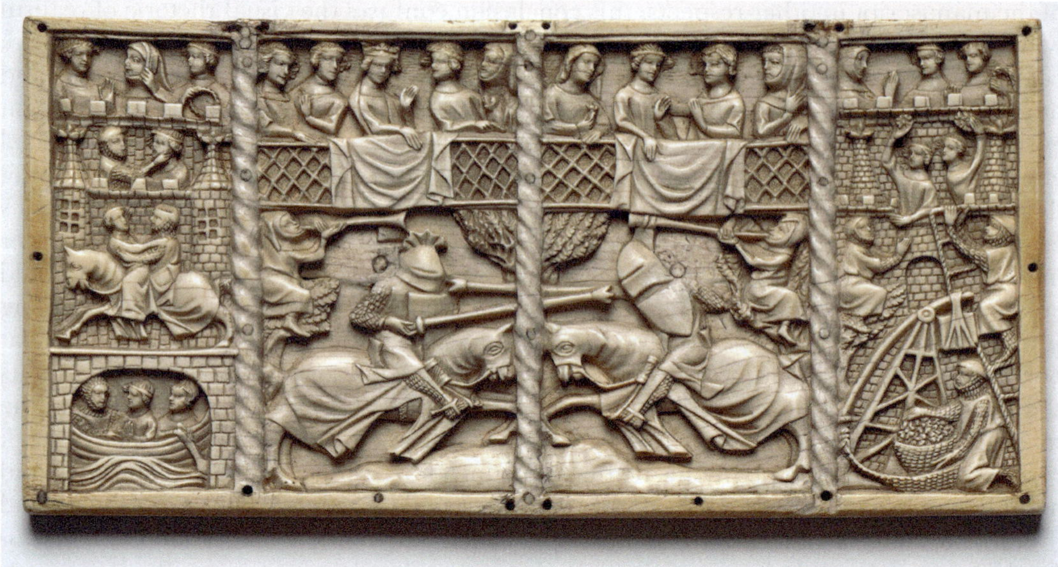

Figure 43. Panel from an ivory casket, fourteenth century. France, Lorraine? Cleveland Museum of Art, 1978.39a. Photo: Cleveland Museum of Art, licensed under CC0 1.0.

tournaments regularly included space for observers, and the admiring gazes of both female and male equals and superiors were particularly sought after by late medieval tournament participants intent on increasing their fame and honour through their displays of skill.[28] This emphasis on tournaments as a hypervisible performance of martial ability is perhaps most clearly manifested in the iconographic shorthand developed to indicate a tournament. Across multiple media, fourteenth- and fifteenth-century artists regularly depicted a tournament by showing a joust (or occasionally *mêlée*) in the central foreground, watched from above by an audience placed on a balcony or a free-standing raised enclosure.[29] This formula was so ubiquitous that it could even communicate its general courtly meaning without any precise literary reference. An utterly generic example on an ivory casket lid now in Cleveland, for example, shows two knights charging towards each other at high speed at the centre, flanked by trumpet blowers (Figure 43).

[28] While often remarked upon, the actual ways in which looking functioned and was structured within tournament settings is usually not explored in great depth and has been heavily dominated by discussion of the role of women in these events. For examples of studies that engage in more detail with the issue of vision or related aspects of tournament, see Mary Arlene Santina, *The Tournament and Literature: Literary Representations of the Medieval Tournament in Old French Works, 1150–1236* (New York: Peter Lang, 1999), especially pp. 91–108; Elizabeth L'Estrange, 'Gazing at Gawain: Reconsidering Tournaments, Courtly Love, and the Lady Who Looks', *Medieval Feminist Forum*, 44.2 (2008), 74–96; Cornelia Logemann, 'Reenactment: Tournaments, Chronicles and Visual History', *Iran*, 57.1 (2019), 31–48; James Titterton, '*Por pris et por enor*: Ideas of Honour as Reflected in the Medieval Tournament', in *The Medieval Tournament as Spectacle: Tourneys, Jousts and Pas d'Armes, 1100–1600*, ed. by Alan V. Murray and Karen Watts (Woodbridge: Boydell Press, 2020), pp. 44–61.

[29] Depictions of tournament are rare before the end of the thirteenth century, then increase dramatically in number: see Logemann, 'Reenactment', p. 35.

Above them, safely enclosed on a raised platform, a noble audience of ladies and unarmed, well-dressed young men looks down on the knights and raises their hands in speaking gestures, suggesting that they are discussing the merits of the performers below. Related iconographic formulae were employed in multiple manuscripts to depict everything from general discussions of the tournament form, as in the copies of René of Anjou's tournament book (1460s),[30] to representations of historical events, as, for instance, in the *c.*1445 depiction of a tournament between the duke of Brabant and king of England in the *Brabantsche Yeesten.*[31]

One of the more curious features of the *Relation* is its artists' decision to avoid this familiar iconographic formula almost entirely. This choice was not forced by the realities of the *Joyeuse Garde* itself, as described by the accompanying text. As it makes clear, at least one viewing platform was erected at this event: after listing the seven judges, the poet notes that: 'Tous sept estoient au chauffault/Ensemble logez au plus hault/Pour veoir le bien et le default/Affin d'en juger en raison' (All seven were in the stand,/Seated together at the very top,/So as to see what was good and what less so,/And to judge it all fairly).[32]

At least one of the artists was aware of this centrally positioned platform, and of the conventions for depicting tournaments. The first representation of a joust in the manuscript on folio 10v shows the French challenger, Guillaume d'Harcourt, count of Tancarville, and the Angevin defender, Ferry II de Vaudémont-Lorraine, crossing lances in the foreground (Figure 44). Their combat is viewed by a group of men who are either drawn at a smaller scale or meant to represent children or young adults on ponies. Their presence is signalled by the text, which states that each man was accompanied by his *parans* (entourage). Behind the lists in the middle ground are two additional groups of onlookers. To the left are a mounted dwarf and lady. While tournament images do not usually include figures from the tournament's dramatic frame, these two figures are mentioned in the text, where a series of scene-setting rhymes ending in *-ans* concludes by noting 'La dame et le neain actendans' (The lady and the dwarf waited).[33] To the centre right is a large platform on two levels. Below sit two scribes dressed in blue, who appear to be busily taking notes. Above them sit four men dressed in red clothing, which the text indicates was worn by the judges. The judges' bodies are generally frontal, suggesting that they are watching the joust from their privileged vantage point. But they also engage with each other: the man at the far left raises his hand in a speaking gesture as he converses with his companion while the pair at the right slightly turn their bodies towards each other. Their mix of observation and conversation lacks the amorous connotations of the Cleveland box lid but still demonstrates the illuminator's knowledge of the typical iconographic formula for depicting tournaments.

Given the ubiquity of the standard tournament iconography in late medieval elite visual culture and the high degree of compositional repetition in the *Relation*'s illuminations, it is surprising to find that this miniature offers the sole representation of the judges' box in the entire manuscript. The artists instead repeatedly deploy two set compositions

---

[30] Paris, BnF, fr. 2696.

[31] Brussels, KBR, IV 684, fols 43v–44r. See Mario Damen, 'The Town as a Stage: Urban Space and Tournaments in Late Medieval Brussels', *Urban History*, 43.1 (2016), 47–71 (pp. 57–60). I would like to thank Mario Damen for alerting me to this example.

[32] *Relation*, PSr, stanza 28, p. 72.

[33] *Ibid.*, stanza 57, p. 77.

Figure 44. Ferry II de Vaudémont-Lorraine jousts with Guillaume d'Harcourt, count of Tancarville. *Relation du Pas de Saumur.* St Petersburg, NLR, fr. F. p. XIV, 4, fol. 10v. Photo: NLR.

Figure 45. Godefroy de Jupeleu jousts with Jean III Le Meingre, known as Boucicaut; Guillaume de Chevigny jousts with Jean de Mesnil-Simon; Guillaume Desbans jousts with Charles Blosset. *Relation du Pas de Saumur.* St Petersburg, NLR, fr. F. p. XIV, 4, fols 32v–33r. Photo: NLR.

for the dozens of jousting images that follow, one for single-column miniatures and the other for double-column miniatures. The single-column miniatures are understandably more compressed (e.g. Figure 45, fols 32v–33r). They heavily foreground the combatants at centre and eliminate middle-ground figures to show instead a distant background skyline.

Such images still highlight the importance of the audience, but displace the act of observation to the *parans*. The active nature of the *parans*' viewing is signalled by the turning of their heads and bodies to simultaneously indicate attention to the joust and discussion with their fellows, poses that echo tournament images where the audience is placed on a balustrade above the action. That these groups of watchful men are meant to be the *parans* of the two combatants rather than a more stable general audience is implied by the ways that the groups vary across the miniature cycle. The most notable sign of their affiliation with their principal is the use of dress, with each group wearing the colours of the knights they accompany. That they are meant to be seen as assistants as well as followers is suggested by the prominent lances that each group holds, which similarly often align with the colour schemes of the combatants.

The variation in numbers of lances that the *parans* carry may be intended to mark differences in the number of courses run, providing a supplement to the poem, which is largely silent about this key detail of the competition. If so, the artists must have relied on a lost source that not only supplemented but also disagreed with the *Relation* text. The clearest evidence of this divergence is on folio 13r (Figure 46), which depicts the scene after the combat between the lords of Brion and Beauvau. Here, the text unusually relates that during the bout:

> Maintes lances ce jour casserent.
> Plus de six courses trespasserent,
> Esgaulx en armes se trouverent.
> La septiesme courir laisserent,
> Faicte fut tres joyeusement.
> Celle course faicte, cesserent
>
> (Many lances were broken that day./More than six courses took place,/They found themselves to be equals in arms./The seventh course left,/Was done very joyfully./ With this course completed, they stopped).[34]

In the accompanying image, the *parans* on each side carry four lances; even if the additional lance of the combatant is counted, the resulting five falls short of the seven courses mentioned by the poem.

As assistants and onlookers, the *parans* bookend even the most cramped scenes of combat in the manuscript, suggesting that the artists felt that their role was integral to conveying the experience of the *Joyeuse Garde.* In this respect, the visual programme deviates from the text, which rarely mentions the *parans* after the first joust. Their repeated presence aligns instead with larger cultural understandings of the importance of such followers in tournaments. Textual accounts of other *pas d'armes* do name and describe the combatant's entourage, and René of Anjou repeatedly insists on the importance of a large (and ideally well-dressed) set of male followers as a necessity for jousters in his prescriptive *Traité de la forme et devis comme on peut faire les tournois.*[35] As with the corrections of coats of arms noted by Mérindol, and perhaps the varying numbers of lances, the artists' attention to the *parans* can be seen as a means by which the visual programme supplemented and refined the account provided by the accompanying poem.

In the *Relation*, the ubiquitous *parans* underscore the importance that the artists placed on the observability of the chivalric performance. Since Leon Battista Alberti, the early fifteenth-century Florentine aesthetic theorist, first advised painters to include a pointing figure in their compositions who would direct the viewer's gaze and indicate how one should interpret the rest of the scene, art historians and critics have regularly asserted that the images of audience figures serve as a surrogate or model for the actual viewer of the artwork in which they appear.[36] This line of argument has been pursued by art historians examining tournament images, who have likewise singled out pictured viewers as doubles and as sites for self-reflection for those real viewers who might encounter such images, whether on the cover of an ivory mirror or as they turned the pages of a manuscript.[37] The

---

[34] *Ibid.*, stanza 69, p. 80.

[35] René d'Anjou, *Traité de la forme et devis d'un tournoi* (Paris: Éditions de la Revue Verve, 1946), p. 52.

[36] Leon Battista Alberti, *On Painting*, trans. by John Spencer (New Haven, CT: Yale University Press, 1966), p. 78.

[37] See, for example, L'Estrange, 'Gazing at Gawain', pp. 83–7; and Logemann, 'Reenactment', p. 32.

Figure 46. Louis de Beauvau jousts with Louis de Brion. *Relation du Pas de Saumur.* St Petersburg, NLR, fr. F. p. XIV, 4, fol. 13r. Photo: NLR.

substitution of the *parans* for the more typically distanced audience of tournament imagery offers a distinctive model for the ideal audience. Across the many miniatures in which they appear, the role of the *parans* is consistently two-fold: they look and they accompany their fighting principal. These two acts of observing and supporting thus become conflated in the *Relation*. While typical tournament iconography presents viewing as the prerogative of those who will judge the knights, the *Relation* instead offers up a vision of viewing as an act of companionship between noblemen. The *parans* act as admiring bookends to the martial display that they frame, ceding the spotlight both through their marginal placement and their smaller size. The movement of their bodies and gazes towards each miniature's centre directs the viewer's attention to the knights and models viewing and remembering the jousts as a form of friendship or kinship with those who sought the glory of their peers' recognition. Viewing here, then, is a communal activity, undertaken by groups of men as a way of literally and figuratively recognising the skill of their fellows.

THE LADIES AND THE DWARF

While this model of companionate viewing numerically dominates the visual representations in the *Relation*, the *parans* are in fact only one of several types of non-combatant depicted observing the performances of the fighters. In many miniatures, far greater pictorial emphasis is given to the ladies and the dwarf than to the *parans* themselves. The repeated depiction of these two types of non-combatant not only highlights their importance within the specific context of the *Joyeuse Garde* but also offers a window into the complex roles that tournaments and bodies might play in the performative construction of gender and power relationships in late medieval courts.

If the *parans* are assistants and viewers, the activities ascribed to the ladies and the dwarf in both the text and miniatures construct them instead as simultaneously spectators and spectacles. Mounted on horseback, the lady and dwarf are prominently placed in each of the double-column miniatures of combat (e.g. Figure 46).[38] They are located near the centre along the horizontal axis. On the vertical axis, they break the horizon line near the crossing of the lances, which consistently meet either just below them or form an X across their bodies. The pair thus marks the moment of martial engagement between the combatants. The well-dressed and fair-skinned lady looks directly forward at the joust with her hands demurely clasped in her lap. Although the text indicates that different women accompanied the combatants to the field at different jousts, the pictured women are largely indistinguishable from each other: even the changes in the colour of their dresses appear to be the result of changes in artistic hand rather than an indication of the identity of the individual depicted.[39] The dwarf sits astride his horse, with a ceremonial mace resting on his right shoulder. He wears a turban, red robe and brown leggings or boots: his clothing speaks to his role as a guardian of the combatants belonging to the side of the defenders.

This pair of observers differs from the *parans* groups in several respects. Where the *parans* vary in details of pose and number across miniatures, the lady and dwarf are largely static. In all but one example, the lady is placed at left, the dwarf at right. The two figures

---

[38] A lady appears once alone (fol. 12r); the remaining twenty miniatures pair the lady and dwarf.

[39] My thanks to Anne D. Hedeman for pointing out this alignment to me: on the hands involved, see Essay 2.

are shown at various distances from each other, but never look towards each other or otherwise seem to acknowledge the other's presence: unlike the lively *parans*, the attention of the lady and dwarf pair is fully fixed on the combatants below. Where the bodies of the *parans* bookend and direct attention to the combatants, the lady's and dwarf's prominent placement distracts the viewer's attention away from the joust, complicating any simple story about who or what is meant to be the primary object of contemplation here.

The *Relation* also depicts each member of this pair taking part in events outside the field of combat, performing roles that add texture to their appearance during the jousts. Women receive greater emphasis in the text of the *Relation* than in the accompanying imagery. They play three basic roles in the poem: they are the organisers of and main actors at the feasting and other activities that take place outside the actual combat; they are participants in the tournament's diegesis who lead the defenders to the field, act as the staged spectators for the combatants and are the purported recipients of the rewards given to the men for individual matches; and they are one of several groups of judges for the contest. The first of these roles probably offered the greatest space for individual female agency and prestige in reality. As noted above, René's wife Isabelle of Lorraine became the owner of the castle of Saumur in 1446; the *Relation* poet does not mention this but does praise her as the hostess of the first night of feasting held for the jousts.[40] This area of female control and self-assertion, however, was eliminated from the visual programme. The *Relation* artists depicted the women only in the context of the combats and processions.

In contrast to their role as hosts for the feasting — where the poet repeatedly draws attention to the presence of named noblewomen — the women's performance as companions and audiences for the fighters regularly blurred the boundaries between scripted character and reality. In the text and image alike, many of the individual women who performed this role are treated as interchangeable, referred to simply as *la dame* (the lady) in the text and shown as generic beauties in the illuminations. This general pattern, however, is sometimes interrupted: some of the women who perform these roles are named, praised or even given short speeches within the text. These three methods of indicating individuality are not universally linked. Not surprisingly, the ladies named are often either themselves courtiers or relatives of established members of René of Anjou's court: thus, for example, Jeanne de Marley, the heiress of René's chamberlain Colart de Marley, led Louis de Beauvau to his match against the lord of Brion.[41] But even unnamed ladies could draw the author's attention. For example, the lady accompanying Jean (Giovanni) Cossa (an Italian in the service of René of Anjou) is claimed to have urged her principal to fight bravely, saying:

> '... Pour moy vous retien
> Et vous commande comme au mien.
> Secourés ces fleurs de pancees,
> Escuier de tres bel maintien!
> Faictes au jourduy quelque bien
> Et tant que par vostre moyen,
> Elles soient d'onneur exaucees.'

---

[40] *Relation*, PSr, stanza 41, p. 74.
[41] *Ibid.*, stanza 68, p. 79.

('For me you are retained/And I will order you as my own./Protect these pansies,/ Squire of such fine bearing!/Today do some good,/As much as you are able,/Such that their honour is thereby increased').[42]

The lady's speech thus blended praise of Cossa's physical beauty with attention to the event's narrative frame, in which the defenders were meant to uphold the honour of René's favoured pansy emblem.

Such admonitions and, indeed, all the roles ascribed to women in the *Relation* are closely aligned with the stereotypical behaviours of ladies in courtly literary romance. Romances are replete with ladies who admire and admonish knights as the unnamed lady does Cossa, as well as with women performing the various roles of hostess, audience, muse and judge. Equally generic are the terms in which the female participants are depicted, as the poet describes them as possessing '... tant de doulceur/De savance et de baudeur,/De beaulté en corps, en coulleur/Plus que oieil ne cueur n'en devise' (... such sweetness,/Cleverness, joy,/Beauty and radiance,/More than either eye or heart could tell).[43] Similarly, the ladies shown by the artists share the oval faces, light skin and elaborate dress generally used to denote aristocratic beauty in Western European paintings of the period.[44]

For a modern audience, it might at first sight seem self-evident that such depictions of women as hyper-visible spectacles are at their core disempowering.[45] The repetitive comments about the ladies' beauty, elegant bearing and noble birth mark their bodies as ones worthy of attention for both their aesthetic qualities and their suitability for marriage, qualities that we might assume would be of greatest interest to elite men taking part in the joust and reading about the event. The fact that this is a beauty that distracts from the action of the joust might also seem to divorce the women from the dynamic role given to their aristocratic male counterparts. Both the poised stillness of the women pictured observing the jousts and the poetic digressions on the topic of the ladies' attractiveness literally pause the unfolding narrative. Parallel narrative and visual strategies are often associated with female objectification in modern film criticism, as in Laura Mulvey's influential study of the mechanisms by which culturally idealised female bodies were fetishised in classic Hollywood cinema.[46]

However, modern hierarchies that connect the ability to view with power and conversely conflate being viewed with being controlled can obscure the complexities of fifteenth-century European norms as revealed by attending to the female spectator-spectacles of the *Joyeuse Garde*. Several generations of film scholarship have nuanced early theories of the gaze such as Mulvey's, probing the ways in which the diversity of film audiences complicate any simple understanding of how and why viewers identify with cinematic images, or alternatively critique or refuse identification with them.[47] Similarly, historical scholarship

[42] *Ibid.*, stanza 62, p. 78.

[43] *Ibid.*, stanza 5, p. 67.

[44] For other examples of this physical type executed by a range of artists, see the depictions of women in the images discussed in Sources 1 and 6 (Figures 1–3, and 4, respectively).

[45] Such critiques are now ubiquitous, but their popularisation is often traced in part to John Berger's succinct formulation 'Men look at women. Women look at themselves being looked at' in the second episode of the 1972 BBC series *Ways of Seeing*.

[46] Laura Mulvey, 'Visual Pleasure and Narrative Cinema', *Screen*, 16 (1975), 6–18.

[47] The literature is vast: for examples of influential work on forms of female cinematic gaze that

on the medieval period has attempted to recoup a potential for female empowerment by stressing the power implicit in their role as observers and judges of such events.[48] While this attention to the role of women as viewers is an important line of research, it is only a part of the story. Equally important is a reconsideration of the modern assumption that being the admired subject of a gaze is a universally disempowering position. In the *Joyeuse Garde* accounts, the attention paid to female beauty is arguably the strongest point of convergence between them and their male counterparts. As the lady's speech to Cossa cited above makes clear, beauty is a quality attached to the appearance of male jousters, not just their female companions. The elaborate costumes worn by the male participants in this event and the attention paid to recording them in both the text and images speak to the premium men placed on presenting a luxurious and eye-catching appearance in this setting. Indeed, such displays were part of a larger chivalric culture that celebrated elite physical beauty as a quality possessed by ideal men such as Lancelot, and which at times used identical terms to describe desirable male and female bodies.[49] The supposed passivity of beauty is likewise complicated in this setting. In both the *Relation* and d'Escouchy's account, beauty of body and dress is inextricably linked to the performance of martial ability. As in many other late medieval descriptions of tournament and mortal combat alike, *bel/belle* (beautiful) is the term most frequently used to denote a well-performed joust in the *Joyeuse Garde*; it is also used to praise the entire event, as when d'Escouchy comments that 'y fut fait moult belles armes' (there were many beautiful feats of arms).[50] Such overlaps suggest that there may be more than a coincidental connection between the crossing of the lances and the ladies who are positioned behind them in the *Relation* miniatures: both martial skill and physical attraction are united by a shared understanding of beauty not as the norm, as it is at times presented today, but rather as the aesthetic of exceptional excellence. Within this cultural frame, the literary praise and images in the *Relation* that purported to describe the historical reality of the noblewomen at the *Joyeuse Garde* in terms that so closely recall the roles of ladies in romance may speak less to a desire to control or devalue them than to the women's engagement in the same processes of *enromancement* outlined by Stanesco that both d'Escouchy and the *Relation* poet noted as a primary motivation for their male counterparts' participation in the *pas d'armes*. If an early manuscript of the *Relation* was indeed owned by Duchess Isabelle of Lorraine, as recent scholarship suggests, then the text's direct references to her and other female members of her court might be seen as enacting a particularly complicated set of movements in which literary models are embodied only then to be reinscribed into text and images for readers/viewers' contemplation of their own acts of observing.[51]

---

complicate Mulvey, see bell hooks, 'The Oppositional Gaze: Black Female Spectators', in *Black Looks: Race and Representation* (Boston, MA: South End Press, 1992), pp. 115–31; Mary Anne Doane, 'Film and the Masquerade: Theorising the Female Spectator', *Screen*, 23 (1982), 74–87.

[48] See, for example, Essay 6. On the gaze *per se*, see L'Estrange, 'Gazing at Gawain'.

[49] See, for example, E. Jane Burns, 'Courtly Love: Who Needs It? Recent Feminist Work in the Medieval French Tradition', *Signs*, 27 (2001), 23–57, especially pp. 47–8; *eadem*, *Courtly Love Undressed: Reading Through Clothes in Medieval French Culture* (Philadelphia: University of Pennsylvania Press, 2002); and Jane Gilbert, 'Boys will be … What? Gender, Sexuality, and Childhood in *Floire et Blancheflor* and *Floris et Lyriope*', *Exemplaria*, 9 (1997), 39–61.

[50] MdE, vol. 1, p. 108.

[51] On the ownership of the possible original, see Essay 2.

The acts of seeing and being seen, as well as role-playing and *enromancement*, are further complicated by the single most pictured individual in the *Relation* image cycle: the dwarf. Hovering between a character and an actor, the dwarf's performance and memorialisation alike manifest the centrality of exceptional humans in this event. Unfortunately, it is not currently possible to identify the actor who played this pivotal part. The *Relation* poet simply refers to him as *le nain* (the dwarf) and no archival or descriptive source identifying him more fully seems to have survived.[52] This lack of documentation is far from unusual; the equation of actors of all sizes with their roles is a frequent feature of literary descriptions of various types of festival at this time.[53] But it is especially problematic because of the vexed relationship between reality and fantasy that haunts the biographies and scholarly treatment of humans of notably small stature, who have frequently suffered from their equation with the mythological beings also referred to as dwarfs.[54] Without further information, attempts to parse more fully what is a performance of the Arthurian dwarf character and what should be attributed to the quotidian social identity of the performer must here remain highly speculative.

It is quite probable that the performer of this role was an adult male displaying characteristics typical of documented cases of dwarfism. The illuminations depict him not simply as small, but more precisely with features of skeletal dysplasia, which here resulted in a head and trunk similar in size to those of the other figures, but legs and arms of notably shorter length (e.g. Figure 44). Mounted on a horse, the man's torso and head size make him at first glance appear comparable in height to the woman at his side. The difference that would be clear in a standing figure is here more subtly signalled by the fact that the man's feet and stirrups rest at his mount's shoulder rather than extending below its chest, as do the legs of the other figures riding similarly sized horses in the same miniatures. Of course, the accurate depiction of typical features of skeletal dyplasia cannot in and of itself be taken as proof of the actor's physical appearance; as discussed above, the verism of the miniatures is more a matter of period style than actual observation of real events or individuals. However, the attention the artists paid to the physical traits typical of a common type of dwarfism indicates both that the details that marked dwarf bodies as exceptional were known to the artists and their intended viewers and that these traits were the ones that the artists felt should be remembered as those of the real performer.

Further support for the possibility that the dwarf character was enacted by a man with dwarfism can be found in the documented presence of men and women of exceptional size at several Francophone courts during this period.[55] The dukes and duchesses of Burgundy, for instance, had multiple retainers who were described as giants and dwarfs and who

[52] René of Anjou's financial records are extremely patchy for this period and non-existent for the year 1446, rendering it impossible to determine not only if any individual was paid for this performance directly, but also which, if any, of the many dwarfs known to have worked at his court in subsequent years might have been already employed at court, and thus potentially available for this position.

[53] For a discussion of the range of ways individuals were and were not identified with their roles, see Normore, *Feast for the Eyes*, chapter 2.

[54] On the social contingency of the definition of dwarfism and the problems raised by the frequent equation of short humans with a mythical dwarven race, see Betty M. Adelson, *The Lives of Dwarfs: Their Journey from Public Curiosity toward Social Liberation* (New Brunswick, NJ: Rutgers University Press, 2005), pp. xv–xx, 87–135.

[55] Maurice Lever, *Le sceptre et la marotte* (Paris: Fayard, 1996), pp. 121–31.

regularly performed in their court entertainments. Extant archival records also suggest that René of Anjou had a special interest in dwarf courtiers, dozens of whom appear to have served him in entertainment capacities.[56] The most famous of these was the man known only as Triboulet, who combined notable acrobatic, acting and literary skills.[57] Triboulet's status at René's court is evident from his memorialisation in a bronze medal by Francesco Laurana, a court artist who also cast medals of René, his second wife Jeanne de Laval and several of the jousters from the *Joyeuse Garde*.[58] Triboulet is first documented as René's retainer in 1447, but, even if he did not play the part of the dwarf in this case, his storied career suggests the larger value placed on dwarf entertainers within this milieu.

While his precise identity remains unclear, the extensive nature of the dwarf's performance at the *Joyeuse Garde* suggests that a skilled, trusted and well-informed performer would have been required for the role, probably a permanent member of the Angevin ducal household. The dwarf was integral to the multi-week festivities and required to be present throughout their entirety. Indeed, given that both the ladies and fighters changed regularly between bouts, the dwarf's part radically outstripped that of any other individual and provided a point of continuity throughout the sprawling event. Fortunately, this role was to a certain extent repetitive: day after day he waited in his silk tent beside the shield on a column. When a challenger hit the shield he would make a great noise, then ride to the castle to call for the defenders to come to the lists. He then observed the joust and (fictionally) provided the prizes for the winner of the bouts. However, even if repetition provided a stable frame for the actor, all of his actions were crucial to the *pas*, providing the links between the three elements of challenge, joust and recognition. Because of this, the dwarf was well placed to add excitement and variety to what might otherwise become somewhat repetitive events. According to the *Relation* poet, the dwarf regularly performed speeches as the guardian of the shield. Thus, for example, at the first joust he reportedly spoke at length with the lady at the castle gate:

Pour la dame humblement requerre
De son escu brief revancher
Qu'elle avoit fait atacher
Au perron; et ja trebucher
L'avoit ung estrangier de guerre,
Abatu du tout, mis a terre,
...
Grant honneur luy fera conquerre
Ou dyamant pour le debvoir.

(To humbly request that the lady/Quickly avenge the shield/That she had attached to the column./A strange warrior had knocked it/Right down to the ground/ ... Great honour could be won/Or a diamond, for the trouble).[59]

---

[56] *Ibid.*, pp. 126–9.

[57] Bruno Roy, 'Triboulet, Josseaume et Pathelin à la cour de René d'Anjou', *Le Moyen Âge*, 7 (1980), 7–56; Lever, *Sceptre*, pp. 126–8.

[58] These include Jean (Giovanni) Cossa (1466), Jean of Anjou and Ferry II de Vaudémont-Lorraine (1464). The medallion for Triboulet was cast in 1461, the same year as that made for Jeanne.

[59] *Relation*, PSr, stanza 53, pp. 76–7.

A few days later, the poet recounts an entirely different speech given on a similar occasion, when the dwarf chides the defenders for their lack of speed in volunteering to face the French challenger Jean de Bueil: his demand whether the reluctant defenders are 'de Tours ou d'Angiers' (from Tours or Angers) makes probable reference to Jean de Bueil's military captaincies.[60] In order to tailor as well as to deliver these speeches whenever necessary in order to keep the event lively over the month of festivities, the dwarf performer must have had familiarity with the biographies of the various participants and possessed the improvisational skills to connect these details to the current situation in amusing or interesting ways.

Unlike the ladies or knights, whose real-world identities often remained at play in the reception of their performance, the unknown dwarf actor seems to have been intentionally subsumed into the role of 'the dwarf'. As such, his body was on display much as were those of the ladies he frequently accompanied, but to somewhat different effect. Where the ladies were presented primarily as figures of beauty and desire, the dwarf seems to have been insistently framed as a figure of what Christine de Pizan notably termed *estrangeté* or strangeness, an aesthetic quality that combined exoticism, ingenuity and novelty and which was much prized at fourteenth- and fifteenth-century Francophone courts.[61] According to both the text and images of the *Relation*, the visible difference of the dwarf's bodily proportions was heightened by the use of 'Eastern' costume including an elaborate turban, an ensemble that the text describes as being 'comme ung Mor' (like a Moor).[62]

Together, body and clothing functioned to set the dwarf apart from the larger chivalric community. His scripted behaviour, on the other hand, cast him rather as a trusted and trustworthy servant of the shield. Despite their seeming contradiction, these elements were probably seen as entirely logically consistent at the time. The character of the dwarf at the *Joyeuse Garde* neatly aligns with recent discussions of Arthurian dwarfs by Anne Martineau and Christine Marie Neufeld.[63] As Martineau notes, the role of dwarfs in high and late medieval French texts differs in several respects from that found in other European literary traditions. French authors usually present dwarfs as humans of uncommon stature who might serve magicians or fairies but were not themselves magical beings.[64] They are overwhelmingly male, and usually have shortened limbs with larger heads and trunks. Although a small number of individuals are named, the vast majority are, like the dwarf in the *Relation*, simply referred to as 'the dwarf'. While the authors of Arthurian romances sometimes make negative aesthetic judgements about dwarfs' size and proportions, the French Arthurian dwarfs are most often trusted servants to noble men and women rather than antagonists. At the same time, as Neufeld outlines, Arthurian dwarfs are regularly marked as different from their masters and mistresses, particularly in terms of their relationship to sexuality and desire, and can serve as foils that highlight the purportedly superior masculinity of their larger male counterparts.[65]

---

[60] *Ibid.*, stanza 61, p. 78.

[61] On this quality, see Normore, *Feast for the Eyes*, chapter 5.

[62] *Relation*, PSr, stanza 36, p. 73.

[63] Anne Martineau, *Le nain et le chevalier: Essai sur les nains français du Moyen Âge* (Paris: Presses de l'Université de Paris-Sorbonne, 2003); Christine Marie Neufeld, 'A Dwarf in King Arthur's Court: Perceiving Disability in Arthurian Romance', *Arthuriana*, 25 (2015), 25–35.

[64] The glaring exception to this is Tristan's servant Tronc, who is revealed to be the fairy king Oberon. Such figures, however, are very few and far between.

[65] Neufeld, 'A Dwarf', pp. 29–30.

Dwarf actors performed similar roles in other tournaments and court performances. At the wedding banquet for the marriage of Charles the Bold of Burgundy and Margaret of York (1468), for example, Madame de Beaugrand — a dwarf in the service of Charles's daughter, Mary — rode into the dining hall on a lion and welcomed the duchess on behalf of her new stepdaughter and subjects, according to the account given of the event by the Burgundian historiographer Olivier de La Marche.[66] An unnamed dwarf also appeared prominently as the servant of the mysterious fairy who purportedly imprisoned the *entrepreneur* in the titular *perron* at the *Pas du Perron Fée*. Whether assisting real ladies or fairies, riding exotic beasts or explaining magical powers, these roles combined the role of trusted confidant and representative with elements of wonder in a manner similar to the dwarf at the *Joyeuse Garde*; the repetitive appearance of dwarfs in such scenarios suggests that one of the purposes of the appearance of the dwarf at this event was, indeed, precisely to create the impression that the unfolding events lay at the boundary between the real and the imaginary worlds.

Less clear is how such performances were seen by the actors themselves. For the combatants and ladies alike, embodying romance offered numerous rewards both in terms of personal pleasure and social capital. The dearth of information regarding the lived experiences of dwarfs during this period makes it far more tenuous to speculate about how they perceived their engagement with the phenomenon of *enromancement*. Did romance — with its presentation of dwarfs as the loyal confidants of great heroes and heroines — offer the same type of space to reimagine reality for them as it did for the nobility they served? Or did their roles, which often exoticised their bodies, separate them from their fellow courtiers?

This second possibility gains some strength from a more extensive examination of the miniatures in the *Relation*. If these images and the accompanying text suggest that the beauty of the ladies is intended to resonate with the beauty of the male knight's display of costume and athleticism alike, the male dwarf instead allows for a comparison of two types of masculine body. Clothing plays an important role in this. The dwarf's turban and robes are not only exotic but also civilian in nature; while he holds a golden mace, this is probably meant to be seen as a symbol of office rather than a functional weapon. His placement alongside the lady further reinforces his role as a non-combatant. Yet the physical differences between the bodies of the knights and that of the dwarf are also at play. The images regularly highlight the strength and dynamism of the combatants' leg muscles through strong diagonals reinforced by the pointed boots preferred in the period, presenting the martial body as one that is clearly distinguishable from the shortened limbs of the dwarf. Similar contrasts are created in the miniatures depicting challengers striking the shield. On folio 9r, for example (Figure 47), the dwarf appears seated at the miniature's centre, his static position contrasting sharply with that of the jouster and horse, who gallop forward to impale the shield. The strong diagonal of the shaft of the lance passes just above the dwarf's head, linking him to the action even as it highlights the fact that the dwarf's own weapon remains at rest. The passive dwarf and the active combatant are thus presented as each other's opposites.

It is important, however, to distinguish between the ways in which this display of difference was understood in the fifteenth century and the ways in which similar spectacles

---

[66] OdLM, vol. 3, p. 136.

Figure 47. Guillaume d'Harcourt, count of Tancarville, calls for the 'Defender' to fight. *Relation du Pas de Saumur.* St Petersburg, NLR, fr. F. p. XIV, 4, fol. 9r. Photo: NLR.

might be understood today. It is common for scholars to interpret the display of dwarfs' bodies across multiple time periods within the frame of the modern freakshow or what Rosemarie Garland-Thomson theorised as the stare, a type of looking that marks the observed body as disabled and disempowered.[67] As with modern theories regarding the gendered gaze, discussions of the stare often valorise the act of returning the look, or staring back, as a strategy for empowerment and resistance.[68] In the case of the *Joyeuse Garde*, however, it is unlikely that such a strategy could have had its intended effect. Looking is a key feature of the dwarf's activities, yet at times this act itself seems to be coded as one of disempowerment. For instance, the dwarf repeatedly observes the fall of the shield that he is pledged to protect. Instead of directly intervening in its defence, however, he must repeatedly solicit the aid of other men, whose bodies are implicitly promoted as physically superior to his own. During the jousts he observes these men's prowess, following which he honours them by offering his admiration and wealth. Looking is here coded as a sign of passivity; being seen becomes elevated as the space of power. In contrast to modern regimes in which viewing is privileged over being viewed, being on display was not in and of itself a problem in the minds of the fifteenth-century participants in the *Joyeuse Garde* and their descendants. Ultimately, the most exceptional bodies at the event are those of elite fighters, who are framed as spectacles not only through their repeated description and representation but also by the range of viewers — *parans*, ladies, dwarf and reader — whose attention they command.

Attending to the dwarf and the ladies thus begins to unravel the connections between looking and power at work in the *Joyeuse Garde*. As in better-studied modern forms of performance, this event, and perhaps the *pas d'armes* in general, could function as synecdoches for a larger system in which acts of bodily display and observation intertwined with the perpetuation of social hierarchies. Yet the *Joyeuse Garde* also complicates modern discussions of spectacle by revealing the historical contingency of relationships between power and vision. In contrast to modern scholarly models that code viewing as active and being viewed as passive, the insistent display of elite masculine prowess at this event emphasises that dominance can be expressed through commanding the gaze of others, that there is a power in being seen. While they might at first seem extraneous to the combat that was the supposed core of the *pas d'armes*, the women, dwarf and attendants thus reveal the complexity of chivalric display, which combines beauty, spectacle and power in ways that run counter to modern models that are often generalised as universal patterns of human behaviour.

Conclusion

Like many forms of fifteenth-century elite cultural production, participation in the *pas d'armes* offered both rewards and dangers. In a society that equated chivalric worth with peer recognition of prowess and honour, it was imperative that squires and knights not only be, but be seen to be, exceptional: as other contributors to this volume make clear, the combats of the *pas d'armes* offered a stage on which elite men hoped to gain such recognition. The accompanying fictive frames, however, often introduce other figures who

[67] Rosemarie Garland-Thomson, *Staring: How We Look* (Oxford: Oxford University Press, 2009).

[68] Eli Clare, 'Gawking, Gaping, Staring', *GLQ: A Journal of Lesbian and Gay Studies*, 9 (2003), 257–61.

serve as at once appreciative audiences and alternative centres of visual attention. In the case of the *Joyeuse Garde*, the Arthurian frame provides two such figures — the lady and the dwarf — whose equally exceptional bodies and steady gazes nuance a simple reading of chivalric display and its observation. Their performances as viewers and viewed alike force us to question our own implicit assumptions about what each of these roles entails and how each is embedded within culturally specific understandings of sight and power. Future research into the many other exceptional beings who accompany the combatants in other *pas d'armes* — from Wild Women to pilgrims — will no doubt problematise the model proposed here, but investigating such figures promises to further illuminate the ever-changing relationship between vision and power, and the ways in which the twin spectacles of sport and theatre complement and complicate each other in practice.

Ralph Moffat

Glossary

À outrance: literally 'to the extreme' (*outrance*) — a term used to categorise combat that has almost all the dangers of fighting in war. Even if a competitor were to be killed, no blame would be allocated.

À plaisance: literally 'of pleasure' (*plaisance*), as opposed to *à outrance* — a combat in which the chances of injury are greatly reduced by the use of such safety features as blunted weapons; sometimes also referred to as fighting with *armes courtoises* (literally, with arms of courtesy), as at the *Joyeuse Garde/Saumur*.

Argentaría: see ***Orfèvrerie***.

Armet (Fr. ***armet***, ***eaumet***, Cast. ***elmete***): a close-fitting helmet that protects the head by means of deep, hinged cheekpieces that are secured to one another beneath the chin; the **cross** of an armet refers to this T-shaped face opening (*Fontaine des Pleurs*). Additional facial defence is provided by a visor and a reinforcing front plate, now known as a **wrapper**, that can be strapped on over the whole. The French word *bevor*, when paired with this helmet, probably refers to this wrapper (*Fontaine des Pleurs*).

Armour, plain (Fr. ***harnois blanc***): see under **Harness**.

Arms of courtesy (Fr. ***armes courtoises***): see under ***À plaisance***.

Arnés: see **Harness**.

Attaint (Fr. ***attainte***): the attaint is a correct strike in mounted lance combat, especially the joust (*Arbre Charlemagne*, Sandricourt). It must be on target. The 'four points' mentioned in the *Fontaine des Pleurs* are the four quarters of the upper body's target area. Furthermore, the lance-shaft must be shattered with such force that, had it been in battle, it would have seriously injured or killed an opponent. It is for this reason that an attaint to the head is considered to be one of the best. Judges can inspect the broken lance-shaft to ensure the attaint was true. For example, it is stipulated in the rules of the *Arbre d'or* that the lance must be broken at a point between these lance-fittings: the **coronal** and **grapper**. Likewise, at the *Arbre Charlemagne*, the breakage point must be between the lance-head and the grapper.

Aventail (Fr. ***camail***): see under **Hounskull**.

Barbuta: a mail neck and chin defence, not to be confused with the helmet known as the barbute.

Bard cover (Fr. ***couverture de barde***): fabric covers for the bard, which is solid horse armour made of either steel plates or **cuir-bouilli**.

Barrier/Cloth barrier: see under **Tilt**.

Basinet (Fr. ***bacinet***, ***bachinet***): for use in foot combat, by the period of the *pas*, this helmet was the type now known as a 'great basinet'. It is a large helmet that encompasses the head. The helmet skull (mail bowl) is egg- or acorn-shaped and extends down over the back of the neck and top of the shoulders. It has a large visor (often of a bulbous shape) with chin- and neck-plates to provide even more protection.

Bec de faucon: see under **Pollaxe**.

Béhourd: a combat of the type held in an enclosed space, which is a simplified form of tourney, fought with either swords or lances.

Bevor (Fr. ***bevor***, ***bavière***): a plate chin and throat defence most commonly borne with the **sallet**. See also **Armet**.

Bourrelet: a crown made of padding used as a base for a woman's headdress or a man's hood.

Bourrelet-chaperon: a type of hat with a hood worn over a bourrelet.

Bow, Turkish (Fr. ***arc turquois***): this weapon is probably of the sort used by the mounted archers many crusaders had faced in the Holy Land.

Breathing holes/Breaths, of a helm (Fr. ***ventaille***): see under **Helm**.

Bull run: an ancient tradition in the Iberian Peninsula that was normally part of a wider range of festivities such as Joyous Entries, royal weddings, jousts and cane games; groups of nobles on horseback and on foot engaged in the killing of the bulls with spears and daggers.

Cane game (Fr. ***jeu des cannes***; Cast. ***juego de cañas***): a typical Iberian/North-African tourney fought with spears made of canes.

Coat armour (Fr. ***cotte d'armes***): a fabric over-garment for the body worn over armour that displays a heraldic blazon referred to as a man's 'arms', hence 'coat of arms'; sometimes incorrectly referred to as a surcoat. Usually tailored from a sumptuous textile; there is no evidence that it had any defensive properties.

Coif: a close-fitting cap made of fabric for civilian use (as worn by the ladies dressed as Amazons at Carignano) or of mail for use in combat (*Ponthus et Sidoine*).

Companion (Fr. ***compaignon***): a term that can be applied to a fellow combatant either on one's own team *or* on an opposing one. It stresses that fact that such fighting men were of a similar elite status.

Coronal (Fr. ***rochet***): a type of lance-head used in jousts, particularly those *à plaisance*, that literally means 'little crown'. It has small prongs designed to catch on an opponent's harness causing the lance to shatter (see **Attaint**) whilst reducing the chance of serious injury. That it sometimes carries the adjective *courtois* in Fr. further emphasises the fact that it is for use in friendly contests (*Bergère*, *Perron Fée*). See also **Lance**, under fittings.

Cotte: a long-sleeved tunic fitted at the top and a little wider from the hips to the knees or the ankles.

Courser: a horse bred for speed and lighter than a destrier, intended as much for hunting and jousting as for war.

Couter: a form of plate elbow defence.

Couter-reinforce: see under **Pauldron**.

Cross: see under **Armet**.

Cuirass: the combined steel breastplate and backplate providing the protection to the torso as a key component of a complete harness. Those worn by the ladies at Carignano are made of fine silver.

Cuir-bouilli: hardened animal hide.

Dagged [clothing]: a decorative technique that involves cutting fabric into thick strips.

Demi-lance: a spear half the length of a lance used in jousting. In the events where this weapon was specified (*Wild Knight*), it was envisaged that the competitors would commence combat by throwing their demi-lances at their opponents and then continue at close quarters with swords or staff weapons.

Destrier: a fast and powerfully built horse used for both jousting and war; sometimes also referred to as a charger.

Double harness: see under **Harness**.

Emprise: confusingly, this term has a number of different meanings that are often dependent on context. It is frequently used in a general sense to mean any kind of chivalric undertaking (by an ***entrepreneur***) and can be employed as a synonym for a *pas d'armes* itself. It also has a more specific meaning of a chivalric ritual whereby a knight wears a token such as a scarf, a cuff or a shackle on part of his armour that challengers touch as a prelude to undertaking combat with him; at some *pas d'armes*, challengers came to the event wearing just such an *emprise* and had to seek permission from the judge or lord who was presiding over it to allow his token to be touched and a combat to take place (Diego de Valera at the *Arbre Charlemagne*). Finally, the actual token itself can be referred to as an *emprise*.

Entremets (Cast. ***entremés***): originally meaning dishes served between courses at a banquet, accompanied by some form of entertainment, these grew ever more lavish over time, becoming dramatised interludes that often featured allegorical or classical figures (*Arbre d'or*, Carignano) or tableaux vivants representing the *entrepreneur* and competitors at a particular event (*Fontaine des Pleurs*).

Entrepreneur: literally, the one who undertakes (from Fr. *entreprendre*), meaning the person who organises a chivalric event such as an ***emprise***, *pas* or **tourney**) and is usually its chief defender. An *entrepreneur* at a *pas* can fight either on his own (*Fontaine des Pleurs*, *Perron Fée*, *Arbre d'or*), with one other nobleman (*Bergère*, Carignano) or as the captain of a team (*Arbre Charlemagne*, Sandricourt); the *entrepreneur* either signs his actual name to a declaration of challenge or chapters of arms of an event so as to put his imprimatur on it or adopts chivalric incognito, albeit it was usually left very easy to work out who the real person was behind this disguise (*Fontaine des Pleurs*, *Perron Fée*, *Arbre d'or*).

Estoc: a type of sword with a thick square-sectioned blade and sharp thrusting point or tip that can be wielded in one or two hands. That it is described as an 'arming' *estoc* (*estoc d'armes*) in the *Fontaine des Pleurs* is evidence for its being the same size as the arming sword, i.e. the medium-length sword-type habitually borne at the warrior's hip.

Fletching (Fr. ***empennee***): flight feathers (usually goose) fitted to an arrow to ensure its true flight.

Four points: see under **Attaint**.

Gaignepain: a type of specialised gauntlet for the right hand for use in the tourney and joust.

Gentle (Fr. ***gent/gentil***): this epithet means that the knight or squire it qualifies is from the upper classes, the term being derived from the Latin *gens/gentilis*, meaning someone who was a man, not a serf, i.e. a member of the lower classes; it is also sometimes applied to someone's 'birth' (*Arbre Charlemagne*) or their 'heart' (*Ponthus et Sidoine*, *Bergère*) but is most often found as part of the noun 'gentleman' (Sandricourt, *Wild Knight*).

Gorget, of mail (Fr. ***gorgerin***): a mail neck defence.

Grapper (Fr. ***agrappe*** or ***arrêt de lance***): a section fitted to the rear of the lance-shaft designed to catch in the lance-rest on impact (see **Lance-rest**).

Greaves: see under **Legharness**.

Hackney (Fr. ***haquenee***): a small horse or a mare with an ambling gait, intended to be ridden especially, though not solely, by women.

Harness (Fr. ***harnois***, Cast. ***arnés***): a complete plate armour. Plain or 'white' armour (*harnois blanc*) or being *armé à blanc* means that the harness worn is of polished steel (*Wild Knight*). That 'for war' (Fr. *de guerre*, Cast. *de guerra*) is the type of armour commonly borne on the battlefield (*Bergère*, *Perron Fée*, *Paso Honroso*, *Wild Knight*). The designations 'double' and 'single' (*Arbre Charlemagne*) refer to the use of reinforcing plates (see **Pauldron**). The Cast. *arnés de correr* (*Valladolid*) is a harness for running courses with the lance, i.e. in mounted combat such as jousting. The royal harness (*arnés real*) referred to in Castilian sources probably refers to the finery of the harness borne in the presence of royalty. See also **Legharness**.

Harness, for a horse: see **Horse-harness**.

Helm (Fr. ***heaume***): these are of two types: 1) the **great helm**, i.e. a large helmet that encloses the entire head, with 'sights' (Fr. *vue*) and 'breaths' (Fr. *ventaille*) being apertures that allow for vision and easier breathing, respectively (*Ponthus et Sidoine*); and 2) the **jousting helm** (as used at all the other *pas*), which had been developed by armourers specifically for jousting *à plaisance*; firmly affixed to the torso defences at the front and back, its thick, prow-shaped front greatly reduces the chances of injury.

Helmet skull: the main bowl of a helmet. Olivier de La Marche employs the word *coiffe* (*Fontaine des Pleurs*) which, in this case, refers to the helmet skull.

Horse-harness: the complete practical leather and fabric fittings for a horse. Mainly consisting of straps and buckles, it does not completely cover the animal in the way a trapper does. See also **Trapper** and **Bard cover**.

Hounskull (Fr. ***houscolle***): a mail head and neck defence of unknown form. One part of it is referred to as a *camail* (*Fontaine des Pleurs*), known in Eng. as the **aventail**, i.e. the circular-cone-shaped mail neck defence affixed to the basinet helmet type in common use in the fourteenth century.

Inside: This means the person or the team defending the *pas* from the inside (Fr. *ceux de dedans*) as opposed to the challenger(s) from outside (Fr. *ceux de dehors*). See also ***Tenans***.

Jennet (Cast. ***gineta***): a small, smooth-gaited Spanish horse for light riding.

Jeu des cannes: see **Cane game**.

Josselin: a type of strong cloth made in the town of Josselin in Brittany.

Joust (Fr. ***joute***, Cast. ***justa***): a type of mounted combat with lances. To win, one must shatter a lance on an opponent (see **Attaint**), but in some cases unseating an opponent or driving both man and horse to the ground are considered best. The joust can be run with or without a **tilt** barrier separating the horses: in the latter instance, when fighting one-on-one, it is often termed in French sources a *joute en champ ouvert* (joust in open field) or a *joute hors-lice* (tiltless joust); this is what takes place at Sandricourt in the third *emprise* at the Field of Thorn, where the competitors fight in *combats singuliers* involving one course of the lance and then thirteen strokes with swords. The difference between the joust ***à plaisance*** and the joust ***à outrance*** lies in the equipment used: specialised pieces had been developed to reduce the chance of injury in the former (see **Coronal**, **Harness**, **Helm** and **Vamplate**); in the latter, the equipment did not differ greatly from that used on the battlefield. A joust royal (Cast. *justa real*, Fr. *jouste royale*) took place in the presence — or even with the participation — of royalty.

Juego de cañas: see **Cane game.**

Jupon: the French and Castilian word for arming doublet, i.e. the padded fabric foundation garment to which body armour is laced.

Lance: this weapon consists of a solid wooden shaft ranging in length from roughly nine to fourteen feet. Parity of type and length is ensured in many of the *pas* (*Arbre Charlemagne*, *Bergère*, *Arbre d'or*, *Perron Fée*). For its fittings, see **Coronal**, **Grapper**, **Lance-rest** and **Vamplate**. The Eng. word spear is used interchangeably with lance: see **Spear**.

Lance-rest (Fr. ***arrêt de cuirasse***): for mounted combat with lances, it is a metal section fitted to the top right-hand side of the breastplate, usually attached by means of a pin and staple so that it can be removed and the breastplate worn for foot combat. Otherwise, it is riveted on with a hinged joint so that it can be folded back when a sword is being used. When the lance is couched under the arm, the **grapper** on the lance-shaft catches on it on impact with an opponent. This prevents the lance shooting back and damaging the arm or hand. Furthermore, the full force of man and mount is channelled through the lance-head to shatter on, or unhorse, his opponent. Indeed, it is noted at the *Fontaine des Pleurs* that, 'if his lance-rest had not broken when he dealt this blow, the tip would have gone into the knight's body'. Confusingly, the Fr. word *arrêt/arrete* is sometimes used both for this and the grapper and it is only from the context that the two can be differentiated (*Arbre Charlemagne*).

Languet: see **Pollaxe**.

Legharness (Fr. ***harnois de jambes***): the complete assemblage of plate defences for the leg, i.e. thighs (cuisses), knees (poleyns) and lower legs (**greaves**). It might also be fitted with plate foot defences (sabatons).

Liripipe (Fr. ***cornette***): a strip of cloth hanging from the hood or the hat that can be wrapped around the head or neck.

Mantenedores: see ***Tenans***.

Mêlée: literally meaning 'mixed' or 'mingled', this term can be used in the context of both war and *pas d'armes* combats in the sense that there are multiple combatants who may strike each other at will. It is not a specific *type* of combat in and of itself. Sometimes also termed *combat à la foule* (from Fr. *foule*: crowd), as at Sandricourt, to indicate that there are multiple participants and no barriers between them during fighting with lances and then swords.

Momerie: a kind of dramatised dance in which the participants, dressed in disguise, embodied various mythical, historical or chivalric characters.

Moresca (Fr. ***morisque***): a lively form of dance that supposedly originated in Moorish Spain; it involved contortions and acrobatics made to rhythmic music and was performed in disguise.

Orfèvrerie (Cast. ***argentaría***): motifs made of precious metals and/or jewels in the form of letters or pendants that were worn on a gown but were either stitched or pinned on so that they could achieve their effect immediately, without the expense of the longer-term commitment of using valuable metal threads to make a textile; the effect could be transferred to another garment by the simple expedient of snipping a few threads or removing pins.

Outside: this means the person or the team (Fr. *ceux de dehors*) challenging the person or those defending the *pas* from the inside (Fr. *ceux de dedans*). See also ***venans***.

Paltock (Fr. ***paletot***): a loose jacket with sleeves.

Pantler (Fr. ***panetier***): an officer in charge of the bread or the pantry in a noble household.

Pauldron (Fr. ***gardebras***): a plate defence for the shoulder and upper arm consisting of articulated steel plates (lames). A secondary plate, the **pauldron-reinforce** (Fr. *grand gardebras*), can be affixed at the front by means of a pin and staple to offer extra protection, especially in mounted combat. At Carignano, there is mention of a pauldron-reinforce for the left pauldron (*grand gardebras gauche*). The *petit gardebras* (*Fontaine des Pleurs*) is a **couter-reinforce**, i.e. a plate placed over the couter.

Pauldron-reinforce: see under **Pauldron**.

Perron: a large upright stone, pillar or column often imbued with magical or symbolic significance in imaginative literature of the period, with the exact object it refers to in a *pas d'armes* account being dependent on the particular context. It was frequently used to hang the shields signifying the challenge of the event that those wishing to compete had to touch or have touched by a herald (*Joyeuse Garde/Saumur, Perron Fée*); the shields of those challengers accepted for combat would also often be hung up on it. At other *pas d'armes*, a tree (*Arbre Charlemagne, Bergère, Arbre d'or*) or even a gatehouse (Sandricourt) serves this same purpose.

Plackart (Fr. ***placart***): the lower front plate of a two-part breastplate; overlapping up over the upper breastplate, it offers extra protection to the abdomen.

Plançon: a type of heavy lance wielded in the joust (*Arbre d'or*), its exact form being unknown as there are no surviving examples; not be confused with the spiked club of the same name.

Pollaxe (Fr. ***hache***): taking its name from the Eng. poll (head), it is a medium-length staff weapon. Its components are a wooden shaft, the tail (Fr. *que*), a spike at the other end of the shaft and a cuboidal head. This head usually has a thrusting spike at the front. It can be fitted with different types of spike on the other sides. These include the *bec de faucon*, a curved spike in the shape of a falcon's beak; and a hammer head (*mail*, *maillet*) with a face rather like a meat tenderiser. The languets (*Fontaine des Pleurs*) are strips of metal by which the metal head is riveted to the wooden shaft.

Rondel (Fr. ***rondelle***): a disc-shaped hand guard affixed to a sword or, more commonly, a dagger. An *estoc* fitted with a rondel is wielded at the *Fontaine des Pleurs*. Confusingly, the word *rondelle* is also used for vamplate in Fr.

Royal harness (Cast. ***arnés real***): see under **Harness**.

Running at the ring: a military game and a traditional tournament exercise that consisted of a rider trying to carry off a suspended ring on the tip of his lance (Carignano, *Jaén*).

Saddle (Fr. ***selle***): these are of two types: 1) the war saddle provides the warrior with more manoeuvrability as it has a lower cantle and pommel, which means that he is more likely to be unhorsed on impact with a lance, and there is also little protection for the legs; 2) the jousting saddle holds the jouster up higher from the horse's back with legs fully extended in the stirrups; it has a high, enclosing cantle and pommel and often descends low over the front of the jouster's legs.

Sallet (Fr. ***salade***): the most common helmet-type borne by the fifteenth-century fighting man. Usually of a single piece, it provides protection to the back of the head and neck by means of its protruding 'tail', whilst the forehead and face are protected either by the **helmet skull** (main bowl) being extended over the face with chiselled-out aperture or apertures (now known as 'sights') or by fitting a visor. It is usually paired with the **bevor**, a plate defence for the chin and throat.

Shaffron (Fr. ***chanfrein***): a plate head defence for a horse.

Sharp-edged sword: see under **Sword**.

Shield, of horn: this refers to small pieces of stag-antler glued onto the shield's front (*Bergère*).

Sight (of a helm) (Fr. ***vue***): see under **Helm**.

Single harness: see under **Harness**.

Spear: the differentiation of the word 'lance' for mounted combat from 'spear' for foot combat is not a contemporary one. Spears used in foot combat at the barriers are either thrust (Carignano, Sandricourt) or thrown (*Wild Knight*).

Sword: unless otherwise stated in the chapters of arms of a *pas*, the sword is of exactly the same type as that wielded in war. These can be used for fighting at the barrier on foot and in mounted combat (Carignano). There are, however, sometimes modifications. For example, in *Ponthus et Sidoine* it is stated that 'after the joust, he will fight *à outrance* with a sharp-edged sword (i.e. *bran d'acier*) without a thrusting point'; similar swords were also wielded at Sandricourt. The use of fully blunted (rebated) swords is stipulated at the *Perron Fée*; those borne in the tourney at the *Arbre d'or* are also of this sort. See also ***Estoc***.

Tail (Fr. ***que***): see under **Pollaxe**.

Tasset (Fr. ***tassete***): a shovel-head-shaped plate for the defence of the upper thigh. Tassets come as pairs and are strapped and buckled to the lower edge of the lower-torso plate defences.

Tenans (Cast. ***mantenedores***): in the sense of 'those who hold', i.e. the defenders of a *pas* against challengers or ***venans***. See also **Inside**.

Tilt: a wooden barrier separating the combatants in a joust or similar mounted combat that is derived from the French *toile* (cloth), since this structure was often covered with fabric. Whilst some *pas d'armes* refer to this as a *toille* or cloth barrier (*Fontaine des Pleurs*), others, such as Carignano, employ the word *barriere*, possibly because there were matching structures for both the mounted and foot combats. This Iberian invention was first introduced into Burgundian chivalric culture at Bruges in 1430 on the occasion of Philip the Good's marriage to Isabel of Portugal.

Tourney (Fr. **tournoi/tournoy**): sometimes used loosely as a synonym for 'tournament' or even *mêlée* (Sandricourt), this term also has the more specific meaning of a two-part combat that begins with a charge with lances and then becomes a fight with swords and is fought in pairs or teams. The only *pas d'armes* to have actual chapters of arms for a tourney in this latter sense is the *Arbre d'or*. See also ***Béhourd***.

Trapper (Fr. ***couverture***, ***housse***, ***houssure***): a fabric horse-cover usually made of fine textiles. See also **Bard cover** and **Horse-harness**.

Vambrace (Fr. ***avantbras***): a solid plate defence for the forearm; those borne by the ladies at Carignano are made of fine silver.

Vamplate (Fr. ***rondelle***): a circular-cone-shaped steel plate affixed to a lance to protect the hand and arm. It is most commonly used in mounted combat, especially the joust.

Venans (Cast. ***aventureros***): in the sense of 'those who come', i.e. challengers to the defenders of the *pas* or *tenans*. See also **Outside**.

Wrapper: a reinforcing plate strapped over the front of the armet (see under **Armet**). In French sources (*Fontaine des Pleurs*), the word *bevor* is used for this plate. This should not be confused with the English **bevor**.

Bibliography

Archival sources, manuscripts and incunabulae

Arras

Bibliothèque Municipale, 168 (*Pas du Perron Fée*)

Bibliothèque Municipale, 915 (*Pas du Perron Fée*)

Berlin, Staatsbibliothek, Preußischer Kulturbesitz, Ham. 606 (Guillaume Leseur, *Histoire de Gaston IV, comte de Foix*)

Brussels

Algemeen Rijksarchief, Archieven van de Rekenkamers, Registers

Koninklijke Bibliotheek/Bibliothèque royale, 7382 (*Relation du voyage de Philippe le Beau en Espagne*)

Koninklijke Bibliotheek/Bibliothèque royale, 9235–37 (Christine de Pizan, *Livre de la Cité des Dames*)

Koninklijke Bibliotheek/Bibliothèque royale, 9547 (*Jean de Saintré*)

Koninklijke Bibliotheek/Bibliothèque royale, II 1156 (*Livre des faits de messire Jacques de Lalaing*; *Pas du Perron Fée*)

Koniniklijke Bibliotheek/Bibliothèque royale, IV 684 (*Brabantsche Yeesten*)

Cambrai, Bibliothèque Municipale, 1114 (*Pas du Perron Fée*)

Cambridge, Cambridge University Library, Hh.3.16 (*Ponthus et Sidoine*)

Chantilly, Musée Condé, 65 (*Très riches heures*)

Comte de Lalaing, private collection, no shelfmark, dated 1518 (*Livre des faits de messire Jacques de Lalaing*)

Douai, Bibliothèque Municipale, 1110 (*Excellente Cronike van Vlaenderen*)

El Escorial

Real Biblioteca del Monasterio de San Lorenzo, e-IV-5 (*Coronación del rey Carlos VIII de Francia y fiestas que se hicieron (1484)*)

Real Biblioteca del Monasterio de San Lorenzo, X-II-2 (*Crónica de Juan II*)

Real Biblioteca del Monasterio de San Lorenzo, X-II-13 (*Crónica de Juan II*)

The Hague, Koninklijke Bibliotheek, 131 B 9 (*Les deux voyages faiz en Espaing par Phelippe archiduc d'Austrice*)

Leeds, Royal Armouries Library, I.35 (Three Tournament Manuscripts)

Lille

Archives départementales du Nord, Série B, Chambre des Comptes

Bibliothèque Universitaire, 104 (*Pas du Perron Fée*)

London

British Library, Cotton Nero C IX (A miscellany containing an obituary of a benefactor to Christ Church Canterbury, compiled c.1100, a cartulary of the Knights of St John in England begun in 1442, and a narrative of the Marriage of Margaret of York to Charles the Bold)

British Library, Cotton Nero D IX, fols 2r–108r (*Jean de Saintré*)

British Library, Egerton 1070 (René of Anjou's Book of Hours)

British Library, Harley 69 (A large collection of tracts, letters, and notes in English and French concerning court affairs and entertainment, jousting and the bearing of coats of arms, known as 'The booke of certaine triumphes', 1575–1625)

British Library, Harley 48 (*Pas du Perron Fée*)

British Library, Harley 4379–4380 (*Chroniques de Jean Froissart*)

British Library, Lansdowne 285 (A book of chivalric texts composed for Sir John Paston, including the *Pas du Perron Fée*)

British Library, Royal 15 E VI, known as the Shrewsbury Book, fols 207r–226v (*Ponthus et Sidoine*)

British Library, Royal 20 C II, fols 1r–209r (*Cleriadus et Meliadice*)

Los Angeles, J. Paul Getty Museum, 114 (*Livre des faits de messire Jacques de Lalaing*)

Madrid

Archivo Histórico de la Nobleza, BAENA, C.134, D.5 (*Crónica de Enrique IV, rey de Castilla y de León*)

Biblioteca Nacional, 2092, fols 66v–67v (*Relación de los fechos del muy magnifico e mas virtuoso Señor ... don Miguel Lucas muy digno Condestable de Castilla*)

Biblioteca Nacional, 9945 (*Crónica de Don Juan II o Crónica del Halconero*)

Mantua

Archivio di Stato di Mantova, A.G. 634 (letter from Anastasio Turrioni to Federico Gonzaga, Argentan, 3 October 1517)

Archivio di Stato di Mantova, A.G. 639 (letter from Gio Battista da Gambara to the duchess of Mantua, Châtellerault, 15 June 1541)

Munich, Bayerische Staatsbibliothek, Cod. Icon. 398 (Tournament Book of Emperor Frederick III and Emperor Maximilian I)

Paris

Archives nationales de France, P//1334/14 (administrative accounts of René of Anjou)

Bibliothèque nationale de France, Bibliothèque de l'Arsenal, 3958 Réserve (*Le pas des armes de Sandricourt*)

Bibliothèque nationale de France, fr. 1436 (*Armoriaux de la Table Ronde*, including 'Le Pas des armes de Sandricourt' and 'Description des tournois faits l'an 1519 à Chambly et Bailleul')

Bibliothèque nationale de France, fr. 1974 (*Pas de la Bergère*)

Bibliothèque nationale de France, fr. 2696 (René of Anjou, *Livre des tournois*)

Bibliothèque nationale de France, fr. 5739 (*Pas du Perron Fée*)

Bibliothèque nationale de France, fr. 12566 (*Roman de Florimont*)

Bibliothèque nationale de France, fr. 12572, fols 1r–123r (*Jehan d'Avennes*)

Bibliothèque nationale de France, fr. 16830 (*Livre des faits de messire Jacques de Lalaing*)

Bibliothèque nationale de France, naf. 10169 (*Ponthus et Sidoine*)

Bibliothèque nationale de France, Vélins 1033 (*Le pas des armes de Sandricourt*)

Bibliothèque nationale de France, Vélins 1034 (*Le pas des armes de Sandricourt*)

Musée du Louvre, département des arts graphiques, inv. 23703–23710 (Nicolas Baullery, drawings of the *Pas des armes de Sandricourt*)

St Petersburg, National Library of Russia, fr. F. p. XIV, 4 (*Relation du Pas de Saumur*)

Turin, Biblioteca Nazionale Universitaria, Ris. 24.26 (*Le pas des armes de Sandricourt*)

Valenciennes, Bibliothèque Municipale, 776 (Olivier de La Marche, *Mémoires*)

Vienna, Österreichische Nationalbibliothek, Cod. 1897 (Prayerbook of King James IV of Scotland)

Printed primary sources

Alberti, Leon Battista, *On Painting*, trans. by John Spencer (New Haven, CT: Yale University Press, 1966)

Anglo, Sydney, *The Great Tournament Roll of Westminster* (Oxford: Clarendon Press, 1968)

An Inventory of the Ancient and Historical Monuments of the City of Edinburgh with the Thirteenth Report of the Commission (Edinburgh: His Majesty's Stationery Office, 1951)

Anjou, René of, *Traité de la forme et devis d'un tournoi* (Paris: Éditions de la Revue Verve, 1946)

——, 'King René's Tournament Book', trans. Elizabeth Bennett (1998) <https://www.princeton.edu/~ezb/rene/renehome.html>

Annunziata, Anthony, 'Teaching the *pas d'armes*', in *The Study of Chivalry: Resources and Approaches*, ed. by Howell Chickering and Thomas H. Seiler (Kalamazoo, MI: Medieval Institute Publications, 1988), pp. 556–82

Arroyo Ilera, Fernando, and Juan de Pineda, eds, *Libro del Passo Honroso defendido por el excelente caballero Suero de Quiñones*, Textos Medievales, 38 (Valencia: Editorial Anubar, 1970)

Bachmann, Adolf, ed., *Urkundliche Nachträge zur Österreichisch-Deutschen Geschichte im Zeitalter Kaiser Friedrich III* (Vienna: Tempsky, 1892)

Bawcutt, Priscilla, ed., *The Poems of William Dunbar*, 2 vols (Glasgow: Association for Scottish Literary Studies, 1998)

Beaune, Colette, trans., '*Le Livre des faits du bon chevalier messire Jacques de Lalaing*', in *Splendeurs de la cour de Bourgogne: récits et chroniques*, ed. by Danielle Régnier-Bohler (Paris: Laffont, 1995), pp. 1193–410

Beaune, Henri, and Jules d'Arbaumont, eds, *Mémoires d'Olivier de La Marche, maître d'hôtel et capitaine des gardes de Charles le Téméraire*, 4 vols (Paris: Librairie Renouard, 1883–84)

Bentley, Samuel, *Excerpta Historica, or, Illustrations of English History* (London: Bentley, 1831)

Bessey, Valérie, Jean-Marie Cauchies and Werner Paravicini, eds, *Les ordonnances de l'hôtel des ducs de Bourgogne, vol. 3: Marie de Bourgogne, Maximilien d'Autriche et Philippe le Beau 1477–1506* (Berlin: Peter Lang, 2019)

——, Sonja Dünnebeil and Werner Paravicini, eds, *Die Hofordnungen Herzog Karls des Kühnen 1467–1477* (Berlin: Peter Lang, 2021)

——, Véronique Flammang, Émilie Lebailly and Werner Paravicini, eds., *Comptes de l'argentier de Charles le Téméraire, duc de Bourgogne*, 5 vols (Paris: Académie des Inscriptions et Belles-Lettres, 2001–14)

Bianciotto, Gabriel, *Le Roman de Troyle*, 2 vols (Rouen: Publications de l'Université de Rouen, 1994)

Blanchard, Joël, ed., *Mémoires de Philippe de Commynes* (Paris: Libraire Générale Française, 2001)

——, ed., *Mémoires de Philippe de Commynes*, 2 vols (Geneva: Droz, 2007)

Bois, Pierre du, 'Chronique de la Maison de Challant', ed. by Orphée Zanolli, *Archivum Augustanum*, 4 (1970), 1–136

Bonivard, François, *Chroniques de Genève*, ed. by Micheline Tripet, 3 vols (Geneva: Droz, 2001–14)

Boos, Heinrich, 'Tagebuch des Reinhard Noltz, Bürgermeisters der Stadt Worms 1493–1509, mit Berücksichtigung der offiziellen Acta Wormatiensa 1487–1501', in *Quellen zur Geschichte der Stadt Worms. III. Teil: Chroniken*, ed. by Heinrich Boos (Berlin: Weidmannsche Buchhandlung, 1893), pp. 371–584

Bossuat, André, ed., *Antoine de la Taverne, Journal de la Paix d'Arras (1435)* (Arras: L'Avenir, 1936)

Botto, René, *L'Isle-Adam et sa région au temps des tournois, 1493 et 1519* (L'Isle-Adam: Les amis de l'Isle-Adam, 2007)

Brassart, Félix, ed., *Le Pas du Perron Fée, tenu à Bruges, en 1463, par le chevalier Philippe de Lalaing* (Douai: L. Crépin, 1874)

Brero, Thalia, 'Pas d'armes organisé par le duc Philibert II de Savoie à Carignan (1504)', in *Fêtes, cérémonies et rites dans la cour de Savoie médiévale: Une anthologie de sources* (forthcoming)

Brouwers, Dieudonné, ed., *Mémoires de Jean, Sire de Haynin et de Louvignies 1465–1477*, 2 vols (Liège: Société des Bibliophiles liégeois, 1905–06)

Brown, Andrew, and Graeme Small, eds, *Court and Civic Society in the Burgundian Low Countries, c. 1420–1530* (Manchester: Manchester University Press, 2007)

Brown-Grant, Rosalind, and Mario Damen, trans., *A Chivalric Life: The Book of the Deeds of Messire Jacques de Lalaing* (Woodbridge: Boydell Press, 2022)

Bruchet, Max, *Marguerite d'Autriche, duchesse de Savoie* (Lille: impr. Danel, 1927)

Bryant, Nigel, trans., *The Tournaments at Le Hem and Chauvency: Sarrasin, The Romance of Le Hem, Jacques Bretel, The Tournament at Chauvency* (Woodbridge: Boydell Press, 2020)

Bucci, Domenico Filiberto, *Il Solenne Battesimo del Serenissimo Prencipe di Piemonte Filippo Emanuelle …* (Turin: Bevilacqua, 1588)

Buylaert, Frederik, *Repertorium van de Vlaamse adel (ca. 1350–ca. 1500)* (Ghent: Academia Press, 2011)

Caron, Marie-Thérèse, *Les vœux du Faisan, noblesse en fête, esprit de croisade: Le manuscrit français 11594 de la Bibliothèque nationale de France* (Turnhout: Brepols, 2003)

Carriazo Arroquia, Juan de Mata, ed., *Hechos del Condestable don Miguel Lucas de Iranzo (crónica del siglo XV)* (Madrid: Espasa-Calpe, 1940)

——, ed., *Crónica del halconero de Juan II, Pedro Carrillo de Huete (hasta ahora inédita)*, Colección de crónicas españolas, 8 (Madrid: Espasa-Calpe, 1946)

——, ed., *Refundición de la crónica del halconero por el obispo Don Lope Barrientos (hasta ahora inédita)*, Colección de crónicas españolas, 9 (Madrid: Espasa-Calpe, 1946)

Carriazo Rubio, Juan Luis, ed., *Historia de los hechos del marqués de Cádiz* (Granada: Universidad de Granada, 2003)

Chalon, R. H. G., ed., *Les mémoires de Messire Jean, seigneur de Haynin et de Louvegnies, chevalier (1465–1477)*, 2 vols (Mons: Em. Hoyois, 1842)

Chanveau, Gilbert (Montjoie King of arms), *L'ordre des joustes faictes à Paris à l'entrée de la royne* (Paris: no known publisher, 1514)

'Clevisches Wappenbüchlein um 1475', in *150 Jahre Landkreis Kleve: Beiträge zu der geschichtlichen Entwicklung* (Cleves: Boss, 1966)

Courteault, Henri, ed., *Histoire de Gaston IV de Foix, par Guillaume Leseur: Chronique française inédite du XVe siècle*, 2 vols (Paris: H. Laurens, 1893–96)

——, 'Le manuscrit original de l'*Histoire de Gaston IV comte de Foix*, par Guillaume Leseur. Additions et corrections à l'édition de cette chronique', *Annuaire-bulletin de la Société de l'Histoire de France*, 43 (1906), 180–212

——, Léonce Cellier and Marie-Henriette Jullien, eds, *Les chroniques du roi Charles VII par Gilles le Bouvier dit le Héraut Berry* (Paris: C. Klincksieck, 1979)

Crapelet, Georges Adrien, ed., *Le pas d'armes de la bergère maintenu au tournoi de Tarascon* (Paris: Crapelet, 1828)

De Crécy, Marie-Claude, ed., *Le Roman de Ponthus et Sidoine* (Geneva: Droz, 1997)

De Jonghe, Jean Antoine ed., *Cronijcke van den lande ende graefscepe van Vlaenderen … van de jaeren 405 tot 1492*, 4 vols, 2nd edn (Bruges: Uytgever in de Noordzandstraet, 1837–40)

Delclos, Jean-Claude, ed., *Georges Chastellain, Chronique: les fragments du livre IV révélés par l'Additional Manuscript 54156 de la British Library* (Geneva: Droz, 1991)

Dickson, T., and James Balfour Paul, eds, *Accounts of the Lord High Treasurer of Scotland*, 12 vols (Edinburgh: Scottish Text Society, 1877–1916)

Díez de Games, Gutierre, and Rafael Beltrán Llavador, eds, *El Victorial* (Salamanca: Ediciones Universidad de Salamanca, 1996)

Douët-d'Arcq, Louis Claude, ed., *La chronique d'Enguerran de Monstrelet en deux livres avec pièces justificatives, 1440–1444*, Société de l'Histoire de France, 6 vols (Paris: Jules Renouard, 1857–62)

Doutrepont, Georges, and Omer Jodogne, eds, *Chroniques de Jean Molinet*, Collection des anciens auteurs belges, 3 vols (Brussels: Palais des Académies, 1935)

Dufour, Auguste, ed., 'Adrianeo: récit des cérémonies, tournois et autres réjouissances qui ont eu lieu à Ivrée à l'occasion du baptême du prince Adrien de Savoie (1522)', *Mémoires et documents publiés par la Société savoisienne d'histoire et d'archéologie*, 9 (1865), 251–437

——, and François Rabut, 'Description inédite des fêtes célébrées à Bruges en 1468 à l'occasion du mariage du duc Charles le Téméraire avec Marguerite d'York', *Mémoires de la Commission des antiquités de la Côte-d'Or*, 9 (1877), 311–53

Duparc-Quioc, Suzanne, ed., *Le Cycle de la Croisade* (Paris: Champion, 1955)

Elagina, Natalia, *et al.*, eds, *Das Turnierbuch für René d'Anjou (Le Pas de Saumur): Vollständige Faksimile-Ausgabe im Originalformat der Handschrift Codex Fr. F. XIV Nr. 4 der Russischen Nationalbibliothek in St. Petersburg* (Graz: Akademische Druck und Verlagsanstalt, 1998)

Flink, Klaus, and Bert Thissen, eds, *Die klevischen Hofordnungen* (Cologne/Weimar/Vienna: Böhlau, 1997)

Flores, Josef Miguel de, ed., *Crónica del rey don Enrique el Quarto de este nombre, por su capellán y cronista Diego Enriquez del Castillo* (Madrid: D. Antonio de Sancha, 1787)

Fourtier, A., 'Un tournoi à Genève en 1498', *Revue nobiliaire, héraldique et biographique*, 8 (1873), 373–7

Franck, Johannes, and Joseph Hansen, eds, 'Chronik des Johann Kerkhörde von 1405–1463', in *Die Chroniken der deutschen Städte vom 14. bis ins 16. Jahrhundert, vol. 20: Dortmund. Neuss* (Leipzig: Hirzel, 1887), pp. 1–145

Fresne de Beaucourt, Gaston du, ed., *Chronique de Mathieu d'Escouchy*, Société de l'Histoire de France, 3 vols (Paris: Mme Veuve Jules Renouard, 1863–64)

Füssel, Stephan, ed., *Die Abenteuer des Ritters Theuerdank: Kolorierter Nachdruck der Gesamtausgabe von 1517* (Cologne: Taschen, 2003)

Gachard, Louis Prosper, ed., *Collection de documens* [sic] *inédits concernant l'histoire de la Belgique*, 3 vols (Brussels: Louis Hauman, 1834), vol. 2

——, *Collection des voyages des souverains des Pays-Bas*, 4 vols (Brussels: F. Hayez, 1876), vol. 1

Gailliard, Jean Jacques, *Bruges et le Franc ou leur magistrature et leur noblesse, avec des données historiques et généalogiques sur chaque famille*, 6 vols (Bruges: Gaillard, 1857–64), vol. 6

Galindez de Carvajal, Lorenzo, ed., *Crónica del serenísimo rey don Juan el segundo* (Logroño: Arnaldo Guillén de Brocar, 1517)

——, ed., *Crónica del señor rey Don Juan II compilado por Fernando Pérez de Guzmán* (Valencia: Monfort, 1779)

Gilliodts-van Severen, Louis, *Inventaire des archives de la ville de Bruges. Section première: Inventaire des chartes. Première série: treizième au seizième siècle*, 9 vols (Bruges: Gailliard, 1871–85), vol. 5

Godefroy, Théodore, and Denis Godefroy, eds, *Le Cérémonial françois*, 2 vols (Paris: Sébastien Cramoisy, 1649)

Guichenon, Samuel, *Histoire de Bresse et de Bugey, justifiée par chartes, titres, chroniques …* (Lyon: Huguenon et Ravaud, 1650)

——, *Histoire généalogique de la royale Maison de Savoie*, 2nd edition, 5 vols (Turin: J. M. Briolo, 1778), vol. 4/2

Guiffrey, Jules, ed., *Inventaires de Jean duc de Berry (1401–1416)*, 2 vols (Paris: Ernest Leroux, 1894)

Hansen, Joseph, ed., *Westfalen und Rheinland im 15. Jahrhundert. Vol. 1: Die Soester Fehde* (Leipzig: Hirzel, 1888)

Hermansart, Pagart d', *Les frais du pas d'armes de la Croix pèlerine, 1449* (Saint-Omer: H. D'Homont, 1892)

Hilka, Alfons, ed., *Florimont, ein altfranzösischer Abenteuerroman* (Göttingen: Niemeyer, 1932)

Horn, Chloé, Anne Rochebouet, and Michelle Szkilnik, eds, *Le Pas du Perron Fée (Édition des manuscrits Paris, BnF fr 5739 et Lille BU 104* (Paris: Champion, 2013)

Izquierdo, Marta López, and Lola Pons Rodríguez, eds, *Coronación del rey Carlos VIII de Francia y fiestas que se hicieron (1484): Edición del ms. e-IV-5 de la Biblioteca de San Lorenzo de El Escorial*, nouvelle édition [en ligne] (Paris: e-Spania Books, 2015) <http://books.openedition.org/esb/887>

Joursanvault, J. B. A. G., *Catalogue analytique des archives de M. le baron de Joursanvault, contenant une précieuse collection de manuscrits, chartes et documens* [sic] *originaux au nombre de plus de quatre-vingt mille …* , 2 vols (Paris: J. Techener, 1838)

Kalbfleisch, Julia, ed., *Le Triumphe des Dames von Olivier de La Marche: Ausgabe nach den Handschriften* (Rostock: Adlers Erben, 1901)

Kervyn de Lettenhove, M. le baron J. B. M. C., ed., *Oeuvres de Georges Chastellain*, 8 vols (Brussels: F. Heussner, 1863–66)

——, 'II. La joute de la Dame Inconnue à Bruxelles. – La joute du sire de Commines et du sire de Jonvelle à Bruges', *Compte-rendu des séances de la Commission royale d'Histoire*, 2me Série 11 (1878), 473–86

Krause, Stefan, ed., *Freydal: Medieval Games, The Book of Tournaments of Emperor Maximilian I* (Cologne: Taschen, 2019)

Kruse, Holger, and Werner Paravicini, eds, *Die Hofordnungen der Herzöge von Burgund. Band 1: Herzog Philipp der Gute 1407–1467*, Instrumenta, 15 (Ostfildern: Jan Thorbecke Verlag, 2005)

Ladero Quesada, Miguel Ángel, '1462: Un año en la vida de Enrique IV, rey de Castilla', *En la España medieval*, 14 (1991), 237–74

——, 'Una biografía caballeresca del siglo XV: *La Coronica del yllustre y muy magnifico cauallero don Alonso Perez de Guzman el Bueno*', *En la España Medieval*, 22 (1999), 247–83

La Marche, Olivier de, 'Traicté d'un tournoy tenu a Gand par Claude de Vauldray, seigneur de l'Aigle, l'an 1469 (vieux style)', in Bernard Prost, ed., *Traicté de la forme et devis comme on faict les tournois par Olivier de la Marche, Hardouin de la Jaille, Anthoine de la Sale, etc.* (Paris: A. Barraud, 1878), pp. 55–95

La Sale, Antoine de, *Jehan de Saintré*, ed. by Joël Blanchard and trans. by Michel Quereuil (Paris: Livre de Poche, 1995)

——, *Jean de Saintré: A Late Medieval Education in Love and Chivalry*, trans. by Roberta Krueger and Jane H. M. Taylor (Philadelphia: University of Pennsylvania Press, 2014)

Lecoy de la Marche, Albert, ed., *Extraits des comptes et mémoriaux du roi René, pour servir à l'histoire des arts au XVe siècle, publiés d'après les originaux des Archives nationales* (Paris: Société de l'École des Chartes, 1873)

Lefèvre, Sylvie, *Antoine de la Sale: la fabrique de l'œuvre et de l'écrivain. Suivi de l'édition critique du Traité des anciens et des nouveaux tournois* (Geneva: Droz, 2006)

Leonardi, Lino, and Richard Trachsler, eds, *Il ciclo di Guiron le Courtois, romanzi in prosa del secolo XIII*, 6 vols to date (Florence: Edizioni del Galluzzo, 2020–21)

Leslie, John, *The Historie of Scotland Written … by Jhone Leslie Bishop of Rosse*, ed. by E. G. Cody, 2 vols (Edinburgh: Scottish Text Society, 1888–95)

Lester, Godfrey Allen, *Sir John Paston's Grete Boke: A Descriptive Index with an Introduction of British Library MS. Lansdowne 285* (Woodbridge: Boydell & Brewer, 1984)

Lindsay of Pitscottie, Robert, *The History and Chronicles of Scotland Written and Collected by Robert Lindesay of Pitscottie*, ed. by Æneas J. G. Mackay, 3 vols (Edinburgh: Scottish Text Society, 1899–1911), vol. 1, pp. 231–2

L'ordre et les articles du tournoy, entrepris pour la selennité du tresheureux couronnement et triumphante entrée du treschrestien Roy Henry, second de ce nom, nostre souverain Seigneur, et de la Royne son espouse, nostre souveraine Dame (Paris: Jean André, 1549)

Maulde La Clavière, René de, ed., *Procédures politiques du règne de Louis XII* (Paris: Imprimerie nationale, 1885)

——, ed., *Chroniques de Louis XII par Jean d'Auton*, 4 vols (Paris: Librairie Renouard, 1889–95)

Ménard, Philippe, *et al.*, eds, *Tristan en prose*, 9 vols (Geneva, Droz, 1987–97)

Micha, Alexandre, ed., *Lancelot: roman en prose du XIIIe siècle*, Textes littéraires français, 9 vols (Geneva: Droz, 1978–83)

Moffat, Ralph, *Medieval Arms and Armour: A Sourcebook. Volume I: The Fourteenth Century* (Woodbridge: Boydell Press, 2022)

Morand, François, ed., *Chronique de Jean le Fèvre, seigneur de Saint-Remy*, 2 vols (Paris: Renouard, 1876)

——, ed., 'Épître de Jean le Fèvre, seigneur de Saint-Remy', *Annuaire-bulletin de la Société de l'Histoire de France*, 21 (1884), 177–240

Musper, Heinrich T., ed., *Weisskunig*, 2 vols (Stuttgart: Kohlhammer, 1956)

Orléans (Herald), *Le pas des armes de Sandricourt* (Paris: A. Vérard, 1493)

Pasquier, Félix, and Henri Courteault, eds, *Chroniques romanes des comtes de Foix* (Foix: Gadrat Ainé, 1895)

Paul, James Balfour, ed., *The Register of the Great Seal of Scotland, A.D. 1424–1513* (Edinburgh: Scottish Text Society, 1882)

Paviot, Jacques, ed., *Portugal et Bourgogne au XVe siècle (1384–1482): Recueil de documents extraits des archives bourguignonnes* (Lisbon/Paris: Centre Culturel Calouste Gulbenkian/Commission nationale pour les commémorations des découvertes portugaises, 1995)

Pereira da Costa, José, ed., *Gaspar Correia, Crónicas de D. Manuel e de D. João III (até 1533)* (Lisbon: Academia das Ciências, 1992)

Piot, Charles, ed., 'Brabandsche Kronijk, 1288 tot 1469', in *Chroniques de Brabant et de Flandre* (Brussels: Hayez, 1879), pp. 48–62

Pizan, Christine de, *La Città delle Dame*, ed. by Earl Jeffrey Richards and trans. by Patrizia Caraffi (Milan: Luni Editrice, 1998)

——, *The Book of the City of Ladies*, trans. by Rosalind Brown-Grant (Harmondsworth: Penguin Classics, 1999)

Prost, Bernard, ed., *Traités du duel judiciaire: relations de pas d'armes et tournois* (Paris: L. Willem, 1872)

——, *Traicté de la forme et devis comme on faict les tournois par Olivier de la Marche, Hardouin de la Jaille, Anthoine de la Sale, etc.* (Paris: A. Barraud, 1878)

Quéruel, Danielle, ed., *L'istoire de tres vaillans princez monseigneur Jehan d'Avennes* (Villeneuve d'Ascq: Presses Universitaires du Septentrion, 1997)

Ram, Pierre François Xavier de, ed., *Documents relatifs aux troubles du pays de Liège, sous les princes-évêques Louis de Bourbon et Jean de Horne, 1455–1505* (Brussels: Hayez, 1844)

Rámirez de Arellano, Feliciano, José Sancho Rayón and Francisco de Zabálburu, eds, 'Crónica de Don Juan II de Castilla por Álvar Garcia de Santa Maria (1420–1434) Conclusion (1428 a 1434)', in *Colección de documentos inéditos para la historia de España*, 100 (Madrid: R. Marco y Viñas, 1891), pp. 3–410

Recueil des triumphes faictz en la ville de Chastellerauld aux nopces de tresillustre et magnanime prince le duc de Cleves et de Julliers, etc., et de la tresillustre princesse de Navarre fille unicque des Roy et Royne de Navarre (Paris: D. Janot, 1541)

Reiffenberg, Frédéric baron de, ed., *Mémoires de J. du Clercq*, 4 vols (Brussels: Arnold Lacrosse, 1823)

Rizzi, Gualterio, ed., *Repertorio di feste alla corte di Savoie (1346–1669): Raccolto dai trattati di C. F. Ménestrier* (Turin: Centro Studi Piemontesi, 1973)

Rodríguez de Lena, Pero, *El Passo Honroso de Suero de Quiñones (1434)* (selected passages), in *Jousting in Medieval and Renaissance Iberia*, Noel Fallows (Woodbridge: Boydell Press, 2010), pp. 399–501

Roussineau, Gilles, ed. and trans., *Regnault et Jeanneton*, Textes littéraires français, 610 (Geneva: Droz, 2012)

Roussineau, Gilles, ed., *Roman de Perceforest*, 14 vols (Geneva: Droz, 1987–2014)

Sánchez Martín, Aureliano, ed., *Crónica de Enrique IV, de Diego Enríquez del Castillo* (Valladolid: Universidad de Valladolid. Secretariado de Publicaciones, 1994)

Scheler, Dieter, ed., *Die Goldene Rose des Herzogs Johann von Kleve: Der Bericht Arnold Heymericks von der Überreichung der Goldenen Rose im Jahr 1489* (Cleves: Stadtarchiv Kleve, 1992)

Scholten, Robert, ed., *Clevische Chronik nach der Originalhandschrift des Gert van der Schuren nebst Vorgeschichte und Zusätzen von Turck* (Cleves: Boss, 1884)

Sommer, H. Oskar, ed., *The Vulgate Version of the Arthurian Romances. Volume III: Le Livre de Lancelot del Lac. Part 1* (Washington DC: The Carnegie Institution, 1910)

Springer, Emmy, '*Les Fais de Messire Jacques de Lalain* de Jean Lefèvre de Saint-Rémy' (unpublished PhD dissertation, Université de Paris III – Sorbonne Nouvelle, 1982)

Stein, Henri, '*Chanson du Pas de Marsannay* (1443)', *Bibliothèque de l'École des Chartes*, 82 (1921), 330–7

Tate, Brian, and Jeremy Lawrance, eds, *Alfonso de Palencia, Gesta Hispaniensia ex annalibus suorum dierum collecta* (Madrid: Real Academia de la Historia, 1999)

Thiry, Claude, 'Un inédit de Jean Molinet: l'épitaphe de Josse de Lalaing, sire de Montigny (1483)', *Bulletin de la Commission royale d'Histoire*, 139.1 (1973), 29–66

Ulmschneider, Helgard, ed., *Ludwig von Eyb der Jüngere: Geschichten und Taten Wilwolts von Schaumburg*, Studien und Text zum Mittelalter und der frühen Neuzeit, 21 (Münster/New York: Waxmann, 2018)

Vayssière, Augustin, ed., *Le Pas des armes de Sandricourt: Relation d'un Tournoi donné en 1493 au château de ce nom, publié d'après un manuscrit de la Bibliothèque de l'Arsenal et l'imprimé du temps* (Paris: Léon Willem, 1874)

'VII. Canton de Mortagne. Emprunt par le seigneur de la Mallièvre du roman de Julius César, en 1458', *Société de l'émulation de la Vendée pour le développment de l'agriculture, des sciences, lettres et arts: Annuaire départemental*, quatrième année (1857), 237–9

Vulson [given as Wlson] de la Colombière, Marc de, *La Science heroique, traitant de la noblesse, de l'origine des armes de leurs blasons, & symboles, des tymbres, bourlets, couronnes, cimiers, lambrequins, supports, & tenans, & autres ornements de l'escu; de la deuise, & du cry de guerre, de l'escu pendant & des pas & emprises des anciens cheualiers, des formes differentes de leurs tombeaux; et des marques exterieures de l'escu de nos roys, des reynes, & enfans de France, & des officiers de la couronne, et de la maison du roy*, 2nd edition (Paris: Sebastien Mabre-Cramoisy, 1669)

——, *Le vray theatre de l'honneur de la chevalerie, ou le Miroir de la noblesse, contenant les combats ou jeux sacrez des Grecs et des Romains, les triomphes, les tournois, les joustes, les pas, les emprises ou entreprises, les armes, les combats à la barriere, les carrosels, les courses de bague et de la quintaine, les machines, les chariots de triomphe, les cartels, les devises, les prix, les voeux, les sermens, les ceremonies, les statuts, les ordres et autres magnificences et exercices des anciens nobles durant la paix* (Paris: A. Courbé, 1648)

Wiesflecker, Hermann, *et al.*, eds, *Ausgewählte Regesten des Kaiserreiches unter Maximilian I. 1493–1519. Vol. 1: 1493–1495* (Vienna/Cologne: Böhlau, 1990)

Willems, Jan Frans, ed., *De Brabantsche Yeesten, of rymkronyk van Braband, door Jan De Klerk, van Antwerpen* (Brussels: Hayez, 1839)

Williams, Harry F., '*Le Pas de la Bergère*. A Critical Edition', *Fifteenth Century Studies*, 17 (1990), 485–513

Zink, Gaston, ed., *Cleriadus et Meliadice: roman en prose du XVe siècle* (Geneva: Droz, 1984)

Zschaeck, Fritz, ed., *Die Chronik der Grafen von der Mark von Levold von Northof (Levoldi de Northof Chronica comitum de Marka)* (Berlin: Weidmannsche Buchhandlung, 1929)

Secondary sources

Abu-Er-Rub, Laila, *et al.*, eds, *Engaging Transculturality: Concepts, Key Terms, Case Studies* (London/New York: Routledge, 2021)

Adelson, Betty M., *The Lives of Dwarfs: Their Journey from Public Curiosity toward Social Liberation* (New Brunswick, NJ: Rutgers University Press, 2005)

Ailes, Marianne J., 'The Medieval Male Couple and the Language of Homosociality', in *Masculinity in Medieval Europe*, ed. by Dawn M. Hadley (Harlow: Routledge, 1999), pp. 214–37

Ambühl, Rémy, *Le séjour du futur Louis XI dans les pays de Philippe le Bon (1456–1461)* (Stavelot: Cercle d'histoire et d'archéologie du pays de Genappe, 2002)

Anderson, Natalie, 'Power and Pageantry: The Tournament at the Court of Maximilian I', in *The Medieval Tournament as Spectacle: Tourneys, Jousts and Pas d'Armes, 1100–1600*, ed. by Alan V. Murray and Karen Watts (Woodbridge: Boydell Press, 2020), pp. 185–20

Anglo, Sydney, 'Anglo-Burgundian Feats of Arms: Smithfield, June 1467', *Guildhall Miscellany*, 2 (1965), 271–83

——, 'L'Arbre de chevalerie et le perron dans les tournois', in *Les fêtes de la Renaissance 3: Quinzième Colloque International d'études humanistes Tours, 10–22 Juillet 1972*, ed. by Jean Jacquot and Elie Konigson (Paris: Éditions du CNRS, 1975), pp. 283–98

——, 'The Tournament at Binche', in *Charles V, Prince Philip, and the Politics of Succession: Imperial Festivities in Mons and Hainault, 1549*, ed. by Margaret McGowan and Margaret Shewring (Turnhout: Brepols, 2020), pp. 223–41

Anselme de Sainte-Marie, Le Père, *Histoire généalogique et chronologique de la maison royale de France et … des grands officiers de la Couronne*, 9 vols (Paris: La Compagnie des Libraires, 1726–30)

Archibald, Elizabeth, '*Lancelot of the Laik*', in *The Scots and Medieval Arthurian Legend*, ed. by Rhiannon Purdie and Nicola Royan (Woodbridge: D. S. Brewer, 2005), pp. 71–82

Armstrong, C. A. J., 'La politique matrimoniale des ducs de Bourgogne de la Maison de Valois', *Annales de Bourgogne*, 40 (1968), 5–58, 89–139

Aubé, Pierre, *Godefroy de Bouillon* (Paris: Fayard, 1985)

Avalle-Arce, Juan Bautista, *El cronista Pedro de Escavias: una vida del siglo XV* (Chapel Hill: The University of North Carolina Press, 1972)

Avril, François, and Nicole Reynaud, eds, *Les manuscrits à peintures en France 1440–1520* (Paris: Bibliothèque nationale, 1993)

Balteau, J., *et al.*, *Dictionnaire de biographie française* (Paris: Letouzey et Ané, 1933)

Barber, Richard, 'Chivalry in the Tournament and *Pas d'Armes*', in *A Companion to Chivalry*, ed. by Robert W. Jones and Peter Coss (Woodbridge: Boydell Press, 2019), pp. 119–37

——, and Juliet Barker, *Tournaments: Jousts, Chivalry and Pageants in the Middle Ages* (New York: Weidenfeld & Nicolson, 1989)

Barker, Juliet, *The Tournament in England, 1100–1400* (Woodbridge: Boydell and Brewer, 1986)

Baumgaertner, William E., *Squires, Knights, Barons, Kings: War and Politics in Fifteenth Century England* (Bloomington, IN: Trafford Publishing, 2010)

Bautista, Francisco, 'La segunda parte de la *Crónica de Juan II*: borradores y texto definitivo', *Cahiers d'études hispaniques médiévales*, 37.1 (2014), 105–38

Baux, Jules, *Histoire de l'Église de Brou* (Lyon: Imp. de A. Vingtrinier, 1854)

Beaucourt, Gaston du Fresne, marquis de, *Histoire de Charles VII*, 6 vols (Paris: Librairie de la Société Bibliographique, 1881–91)

Beaume, Florence, 'Les Gorrevod, de la Bresse à l'Empire', *La noblesse des marches, de Bourgogne et d'ailleurs au temps de Marguerite d'Autriche (XVe–XVIe siècle). Annales de Bourgogne*, 89.3/4 (2017), 19–32

Beaune, Henri, and Jules d'Arbaumont, eds, *La noblesse aux états de Bourgogne, de 1350 à 1789* (Dijon: Lamarche Libraire-Éditeur, 1864)

Béchu, Claire, Florence Greffe and Isabelle Pebay, eds, *Minutier central des notaires de Paris, Minutes du XVe siècle de l'étude XIX, inventaire analytique [5232 actes]* (Paris: Archives nationales, 1993)

Bettoni, Barbara, 'Fashion, Tradition, and Innovation in Button Manufacturing in Early Modern Italy', *Technology and Culture*, 55.3 (2014), 675–710

Bianciotto, Gabriel, 'Le pas d'armes de Saumur (1446) et la vie chevaleresque à la cour de René d'Anjou', in *Le Roi René: René, duc d'Anjou, de Bar et de Lorraine, roi de Sicile et de Jerusalem, roi d'Aragon, comte de Provence, 1409–1480: actes du colloque international, Avignon, 13, 14, 15 juin 1981*, ed. by Gabriel Bianciotto ([Avignon]: Annales Universitaires d'Avignon, 1986), pp. 1–16

——, 'René d'Anjou et les chevaliers d'Arthur', in *Le tournoi au moyen âge, actes du Colloque des 25 et 26 janvier 2002*, ed. by Nicole Gonthier, Cahiers du Centre d'Histoire Médiévale, 3 (Lyon: Université Jean Moulin, 2003), pp. 113–33

——, 'Passion du livre et des lettres à la cour du roi René', in *Splendeur de l'enluminure: le roi René et les livres*, ed. by Marc-Édouard Gautier and François Avril (Angers: Ville d'Angers, 2009), pp. 85–103

Bijker, Sjoerd, 'The Functions of the Late Medieval Brabantine Legend of Brabon', in *Networks, Regions and Nations: Shaping Identities in the Low Countries, 1300–1650*, ed. by Robert Stein and Judith Pollmann (Leiden/Boston, MA: Brill, 2010), pp. 91–109

Bischoff, Georges, 'Claude de Vaudrey, le meilleur chevalier du monde', *PCEEB*, 58 (2018), 251–73

Blair, Claude, *European Armour, c. 1066–c. 1700* (London: Batsford, 1958)

——, *European and American Arms, c. 1100–1850* (London: Batsford, 1962)

Blanchard, Joël, *La pastorale en France aux XIVe et XVe siècles: Recherches sur les structures de l'imaginaire médiéval* (Paris: Honoré Champion, 1983)

Blockmans, Wim, 'Jacques de Lalaing: The Vitality of the Chivalric Ideal in the Burgundian Netherlands', in *A Knight for the Ages: Jacques de Lalaing and the Art of Chivalry*, ed. by Elizabeth Morrison (Los Angeles: The J. Paul Getty Museum, 2018), pp. 53–64

Blunk, Catherine, 'La vois des hiraus: the Poetics of Tournament in Late Medieval Chronicle and Romance' (unpublished PhD dissertation, University of Wisconsin-Madison, 2008)

——, 'Je cuidoie avoir bien fait: Saintré and the Rules of the Game', *Medieval Feminist Forum: A Journal of Gender and Sexuality*, 52.2 (2017), 102–50

——, 'Faux pas in the Chronicles: What is a *pas d'armes*?', in *The Medieval Chronicle 11*, ed. by Erik Kooper and Sjoerd Levelt (Turnhout: Brepols, 2018), pp. 87–107

——, 'Between Sport and Theatre: How Spectacular was the *Pas d'armes*?', in *The Medieval Tournament as Spectacle: Tourneys, Jousts and Pas d'Armes, 1100–1600*, ed. by Alan V. Murray and Karen Watts (Woodbridge: Boydell Press, 2020), pp. 120–38

Bolduc, Benoît, *La fête imprimée: Spectacles et cérémonies politiques (1549–1662)* (Paris: Classiques Garnier, 2016)

Bonner, Elizabeth, 'Scotland's "Auld Alliance" with France, 1295–1560', *History*, 84 (1999), 5–30

Boone, Marc, 'Destroying and Reconstructing the City: The Inculcation and Arrogation of Princely Power in the Burgundian-Habsburg Netherlands (14th–16th Centuries)', in *The Propagation of Power in the Medieval West: Selected Proceedings of the International Conference, Groningen, 20–23 November 1997*, ed. by Martin Gosman, Arjo Vanderjagt and Jan Veenstra, Mediaevalia Groningana, 23 (Groningen: Forsten, 1996), pp. 1–33

Booth, Douglas, 'Constructing Knowledge: Histories of Modern Sport', in *A Companion to Sport*, ed. by David L. Andrews and Ben Carrington (Hoboken, NJ: Blackwell Publishing, 2013), pp. 23–40

Borgolte, Michael, and Bernd Schneidmüller, eds, *Hybride Kulturen im mittelalterlichen Europa/Hybride Cultures in Medieval Europe*, Europa im Mittelalter, 16 (Berlin: Akademie-Verlag, 2010)

Born, Robert, *Les Lalaing: une grande 'mesnie' hennuyère, de l'aventure d'Outrée au siècle des gueux (1096–1600)* (Brussels: Éditeurs d'art associés, 1986)

Bornemann, Marian, 'Vorbild Burgund? Die Hoforganisation und Hofkultur der Herzöge von Kleve im 15. Jahrhundert' (unpublished MA dissertation, Ruhr-University Bochum, 2022)

Bouchet, Florence, 'Rhétorique de l'héraldique dans le roman arthurien tardif: Le "Meliador" de Froissart et le "Livre du Cuer d'Amours espris" de René d'Anjou', *Romania*, 116 (1989), 239–55

——, ed., *René d'Anjou, écrivain et mécène (1409–1480)* (Turnhout: Brepols, 2011)

Boulton, D'Arcy Jonathan Dacre, *The Knights of the Crown: The Monarchical Orders of Knighthood in Later Medieval Europe, 1325–1520* (Woodbridge: Boydell Press, 1987)

——, 'The Order of the Golden Fleece and the Creation of Burgundian National Identity', in *The Ideology of Burgundy: The Promotion of National Consciousness, 1364–1565*, ed. by D'Arcy Jonathan Dacre Boulton and Jan Veenstra (Leiden: Brill, 2006), pp. 21–97

Bousmar, Éric, 'La place des hommes et des femmes dans les fêtes de cour bourguignonnes (Philippe le Bon–Charles le Hardi)', *PCEEB*, 34 (1994), 123–43

——, 'Pasos de armas, justas y torneos en la corte de Borgoña (siglo XV y principios del XVI). Imaginario caballeresco, rituales e implicaciones socio-políticas', in *El legado de Borgoña: Fiesta y ceremonia cortesana en la Europa de los Austrias (1454–1648)*, ed. by Krista De Jonge, Bernardo J. García García and Alicia Esteban Estríngana (Madrid: Fundación Carlos de Amberes/Marcial Pons Ediciones de Historia, 2010), pp. 561–605

——, 'Jousting at the Court of Burgundy. The "Pas d'armes": Shifts in Scenario, Location and Recruitment', in *Staging the Court of Burgundy: Proceedings of the Conference 'The Splendour of Burgundy'*, ed. by Wim Blockmans *et al.* (Turnhout/London: Brepols/Harvey Miller, 2013), pp. 75–84

Bovaird-Abbo, Kristin, '"Reirdit on ane riche roche beside ane riveir": Martial Landscape and James IV of Scotland in *The Knightly Tale of Golagros and Gawane*', *Neophilologus*, 98 (2014), 675–88

Brassart, Félix, *Histoire et généalogie des comtes de Lalaing*, 2nd revised edition (Douai: Adam d'Aubers, 1854)

——, *Le blason de Lalaing: Notes généalogiques et héraldiques sur une ancienne et illustre maison* (Douai: L. Crépin, 1879)

Brault, Gerard J., *Early Blazon: Heraldic Description in the Twelfth and Thirteenth Centuries with Special Reference to Arthurian Heraldry*, 2nd edition (Cambridge: Boydell Press, 1997)

Breiding, Dirk H., 'Rennen, Stechen und Turnier zur Zeit Maximilians I.', in *'Vor Halbtausend Jahren …': Festschrift zur Erinnerung an den Besuch des Kaisers Maximilian I. in St. Wendel*, ed. by Cornelieke Lagerwaard (St. Wendel: Stiftung Dr. Walter Bruch, 2012), pp. 53–84

Brero, Thalia, 'La fête de l'ordre de l'Annonciade. Une innovation cérémonielle du duc Charles II de Savoie', in *Mémoires de cours: Études offertes à Agostino Paravicini Bagliani par ses collègues et élèves de l'Université de Lausanne*, ed. by Bernard Andenmatten *et al.* (Lausanne: Cahiers lausannois d'histoire médiévale, 2008), pp. 303–33

——, *Rituels dynastiques et mises en scène du pouvoir: Le cérémonial princier à la cour de Savoie (1450–1550)* (Florence: SISMEL Edizioni del Galluzzo, 2017)

——, 'Soirées festives et vie nocturne à la cour de Savoie', in *Le Banquet: manger, boire et parler ensemble (XIIe–XVIIe siècles)*, ed. by Bruno Laurioux, Agostino Paravicini Bagliani and Eva Pibiri, Micrologus Library, 91 (Florence: SISMEL Edizioni del Galluzzo, 2018), pp. 229–60

Brown, Andrew, 'Civic Ritual: Bruges and the Counts of Flanders in the Later Middle Ages', *The English Historical Review*, 112.446 (1997), 277–99

——, 'Urban Jousts in the Later Middle Ages: The White Bear of Bruges', *Revue Belge de Philologie et d'Histoire*, 78 (2000), 315–30

——, *Civic Ceremony and Religion in Medieval Bruges c. 1300–1520* (Cambridge: Cambridge University Press, 2011)

——, and Jan Dumolyn, *Medieval Bruges, c. 850–1550* (Cambridge: Cambridge University Press, 2018)

——, 'Huizinga's Autumn: The Burgundian Court at Play', in *Rereading Huizinga: Autumn of the Middle Ages, a Century Later*, ed. by Peter Arnade, Martha C. Howell and Anton van der Lem (Amsterdam: Amsterdam University Press, 2019), pp. 25–40

Brown-Grant, Rosalind, *French Romance of the Later Middle Ages: Gender, Morality, and Desire* (Oxford: Oxford University Press, 2008)

——, 'Narrative Style in Burgundian Chronicles of the Later Middle Ages', *Viator*, 42.2 (2011), 233–82

——, 'Art Imitating Life Imitating Art? Representations of the *Pas d'armes* in Burgundian Prose Romance: The Case of *Jehan d'Avennes*', in *The Medieval Tournament as Spectacle: Tourneys, Jousts and Pas d'Armes, 1100–1600*, ed. by Alan V. Murray and Karen Watts (Woodbridge: Boydell Press, 2020), pp. 139–54

Bureaux, Guillaume, 'Pas d'armes et vide iconographique: quand le texte doit remplacer l'image (XVe siècle)', *Perspectives médiévales*, 38 (2017) <https://journals.openedition.org/peme/12792>

——, 'Union et désunion de la noblesse en parade: Le rôle des Pas d'armes dans l'entretien des rivalités chevaleresques entre cours princières occidentales, XVe–XVIe siècles (Anjou, Bourgogne, France, Saint-Empire)' (unpublished PhD dissertation, Normandie Université, 2018)

——, 'Le jeu entre politique, romanesque et théâtral: Le pas d'armes de Sandricourt (1493)', *Histilien* (2019) <https://histilien.hypotheses.org/28>

Burns, E. Jane, 'Courtly Love: Who Needs It? Recent Feminist Work in the Medieval French Tradition', *Signs*, 27 (2001), 23–57

——, *Courtly Love Undressed: Reading Through Clothes in Medieval French Culture* (Philadelphia: University of Pennsylvania Press, 2002)

Butterworth, Philip, *Staging Conventions in Medieval English Theatre* (Cambridge: Cambridge University Press, 2014)

——, and Peter Harrop, 'The Providers of Pyrotechnics in Plays and Celebrations', in *Material Culture and Early Drama*, ed. by Clifford Davidson (Kalamazoo, MI: Medieval Institute Publications, 1999), pp. 59–74

Buylaert, Frederik, Jan Dumolyn and Jelle De Rock, 'La Loge des Bourgeois de Bruges: les stratégies de distinction d'une élite commerçante cosmopolite', *Revue du Nord*, 98 (2016), 37–69

Capre, François, *Catalogue des chevaliers de l'Ordre du Collier de Savoye* (Turin: Barthélémy Zavatte, 1654)

Capwell, Tobias, 'Armor, Weapons, and Combat in the Getty Lalaing', in *A Knight for the Ages: Jacques de Lalaing and the Art of Chivalry*, ed. by Elizabeth Morrison (Los Angeles: The J. Paul Getty Museum, 2018), pp. 151–64

——, *Arms and Armour of the Medieval Joust* (Leeds: Royal Armouries Museum, 2018)

Carceller Cerviño, María del Pilar, 'La imagen nobiliaria en la tratadística caballeresca: Beltrán de la Cueva y Diego Enríquez del Castillo', *En la España medieval*, 24 (2001), 259–83

——, 'Realidad y representación de la nobleza castellana en el siglo XV: el linaje de la Cueva y la casa ducal de Alburquerque' (unpublished PhD dissertation, Universidad Complutense de Madrid, 2006)

Caron, Marie-Thérèse, *La noblesse dans le Duché de Bourgogne 1315–1477* (Lille: Presses Universitaires de Lille, 1987)

Castelnuovo, Guido, 'Le veneur d'Espagne: Noblesse seigneuriale et cour princière en Savoie au XVe siècle', in *Mémoires de cours: Études offertes à Agostino Paravicini Bagliani par ses collègues et élèves de l'Université de Lausanne*, ed. by Bernard Andenmatten *et al.* (Lausanne: Cahiers lausannois d'histoire médiévale, 2008), pp. 257–74

Chaigne-Legouy, Marion, 'Reine "ordinaire", reine "extraordinaire": la place de Jeanne de Laval et d'Isabelle de Lorraine dans le gouvernement de René d'Anjou', in *René d'Anjou (1409–1480): Pouvoirs et gouvernement*, ed. by Noël-Yves Tonnerre and Jean-Michel Matz (Rennes: Presses Universitaires de Rennes, 2011), pp. 77–103

Chas Aguión, Antonio, 'Gonzalo de Quadros. Hidalgo, justador y poeta de cancionero', *Revista de poética medieval*, 28 (2014), 35–55

Chattaway, Carol, 'The Heroes of Philip the Bold', *PCEEB*, 41 (2001), 27–37

Chevalier, Bernard, 'Marie d'Anjou, une reine sans gloire, 1404–1463', in *Autour de Marguerite d'Écosse: Reines, princesses et dames du XVe siècle*, ed. by Geneviève and Philippe Contamine (Paris: Honoré Champion, 1999), pp. 81–98

Christ, Georg, *et al.*, *Transkulturelle Verflechtungen: mediävistische Perspektiven* (Göttingen: Universitätsverlag Göttingen, 2016)

Cifarelli, Paola, 'Exemplaires d'ouvrages publiés par Antoine Vérard dans les bibliothèques turinoises', *Le Moyen Français*, 69 (2011), 15–34

Clare, Eli, 'Gawking, Gaping, Staring', *GLQ: A Journal of Lesbian and Gay Studies*, 9 (2003), 257–61

Clare, Lucien, 'Fêtes, jeux et divertissements à la cour du connétable de Castille, Miguel Lucas de Iranzo (1460–1470)', in *La fête et l'écriture: Théâtre de cour, cour-théâtre en Espagne et en Italie, 1450–1530* (Aix-en-Provence: Université de Provence, 1987), pp. 5–32

Claussen, Samuel A., *Chivalry and Violence in Late Medieval Castile*, Warfare in History (Woodbridge: Boydell Press, 2020)

Clevenger, Samuel M., 'Sport History, Modernity and the Logic of Coloniality: A Case for Decoloniality', *Rethinking History*, 21 (2017), 586–605

Coenen, Daniel, 'De Lalaing, Antoine', in *Nouvelle biographie nationale*, 15 vols (Brussels: Palais des Académies, 2003), vol. 7, pp. 104–11

——, 'Florès, Diégo', in *Nouvelle biographie nationale*, 15 vols (Brussels: Palais des Académies, 2010), vol. 10, pp. 187–9

Colombo, Elio, *Iolanda, duchessa di Savoia (1465–1478)* (Turin: Paravia, 1893)

Comba, Rinaldo, ed., *Storia di Torino. Vol. 2: Il basso Medioevo e la prima età moderna (1280–1536)* (Turin: Einaudi, 1997)

Comte, François, 'Les lieux du pouvoir ducal à Angers au XVe siècle', in *René d'Anjou (1409–1480): Pouvoirs et gouvernement*, ed. by Jean-Michel Matz and Noël-Yves Tonnerre (Rennes: Presses Universitaires de Rennes, 2011), pp. 163–94

Contamine, Philippe, 'Les tournois en France à la fin du moyen âge', in *Das ritterliche Turnier im Mittelalter: Beiträge zu einer vergleichenden Formen und Verhaltensgeschichte des Ritterturms*, ed. by Josef Fleckenstein (Göttingen: Vandenhoeck and Ruprecht, 1985), pp. 425–49

——, 'Scottish Soldiers in France in the Second Half of the Fifteenth Century: Mercenaries, Immigrants or Frenchmen in the Making?', in *The Scottish Soldier Abroad, 1247–1967*, ed. by Grant G. Simpson (Edinburgh: John Donald, 1992), pp. 19–30

——, 'Office d'armes et noblesse dans la France de la fin du Moyen Âge', *Bulletin de la Société Nationale des Antiquaires de France* (1994) [1996], 310–22

——, 'Entre France et Écosse: Bérault Stuart, seigneur d'Aubigny (vers 1452–1508), chef de guerre, diplomate, écrivain militaire', in *The Auld Alliance: France and Scotland over 700 Years*, ed. by James Laidlaw (Edinburgh: Edinburgh University Press, 1999), pp. 59–76

——, 'Le premier procès de Jean II, duc d'Alençon (1456–1458): quels enjeux, quels enseignements politiques?', in *Power and Persuasion: Essays on the Art of State Building in Honour of W. P. Blockmans*, ed. by Peter C. M. Hoppenbrouwers, Antheun Janse and Robert Stein (Turnhout: Brepols, 2010), pp. 103–22

Contenson, Louis de, 'Le château de Sercy', *Bulletin Monumental*, 73 (1909), 98–126

Cools, Hans, *Mannen met macht: edellieden en de modern staat in de Bourgondisch-Habsburgse landen (1475–1530)* (Zutphen: Walburg, 2001)

Coombs, Bryony, 'Identity and Agency in the Patronage of Bérault Stuart d'Aubigny: The Political Self-Fashioning of a Franco-Scottish Soldier and Diplomat', *Medieval Journal*, 7 (2017), 89–143

Cortrait, René, Review of Juan Ruiz, *Libro de Buen Amor*, ed. by Nicasio Salvador Miguel (Madrid: Magisterio Español, 1972) in *Bulletin Hispanique*, 75 (1973), 439–41

Cotton, William T., 'Teaching the Motifs of Chivalric Biography', in *The Study of Chivalry: Resources and Approaches*, ed. by Howell D. Chickering and Thomas H. Seiler (Kalamazoo, MI: Medieval Institute Publications, 1988), pp. 583–609

Cox, Eugene L., *The Green Count of Savoy: Amedeus VI and Transalpine Savoy in the Fourteenth Century* (Princeton, NJ: Princeton University Press, 1967)

Crane, Susan, *Performance of the Self* (Philadelphia: University of Pennsylvania Press, 2002)

Cripps-Day, Francis Henry, *The History of the Tournament in England and France* (London: Quaritch, 1918)

Cron, Bonita Marie, 'The Duke of Suffolk, the Angevin Marriage, and the Ceding of Maine, 1445', *Journal of Medieval History*, 20 (1994), 77–99

Crouch, David, *Tournament* (London: Hambledon, 2006)

Cruse, Mark, 'Costuming the Past: Heraldry in Illustrations of the "Roman d'Alexandre" (Oxford, Bodleian Library, MS Bodley 264)', *Gesta*, 45.1 (2006), 43–59

Damen, Mario, 'The Town, the Duke, his Courtiers and their Tournament: A Spectacle in Brussels, 4–7 May 1439', in *Staging the Court of Burgundy: Proceedings of the Conference 'The Splendour of Burgundy'*, ed. by Wim Blockmans *et al.* (Turnhout/London: Brepols/Harvey Miller, 2013), pp. 85–95

——, 'The Town as a Stage? Urban Space and Tournaments in Late Medieval Brussels', *Urban History*, 43.1 (2016), 47–71

——, 'Tournaments and the Integration of the Nobility in the Habsburg Composite State', *Renaissance Quarterly*, 76.2 (2023), 497–541

Dauphant, Léonard, 'Les 700 pensionnaires de Louis XI et édition d'un rôle de 1481', *Annuaire-bulletin de la Société de l'Histoire de France* (2011), 21–77

Debae, Marguerite, *La bibliothèque de Marguerite d'Autriche: essai de reconstitution d'après l'inventaire de 1523–1524* (Louvain/Paris: Éditions Peeters, 1995)

Dehaisnes, Chrétien, *Inventaire Sommaire des Archives Départementales antérieures à 1790, Nord. Archives Civiles, Série B. Chambre des Comptes nos. 1842 à 2398*, 8 vols (Lille: L. Danel, 1881)

Deruelle, Benjamin, *De papier, de fer et de sang: Chevaliers et chevalerie à l'épreuve de la modernité (ca 1460–ca 1620)* (Paris: Publications de la Sorbonne, 2015)

De Smedt, Raphaël, ed., *Les chevaliers de l'Ordre de la Toison d'or au XVe siècle: Notices bio-bibliographiques*, 2nd revised edition (Frankfurt am Main: Peter Lang, 2000)

Dessemontet, Olivier, 'Les Luxembourg-Martigues, seigneurs au Pays de Vaud. 1487–1558', *Revue suisse d'histoire*, 4.1 (1954), 88–123

Devaney, Thomas, *Enemies in the Plaza: Urban Spectacle and the End of Spanish Frontier Culture, 1460–1492* (Philadelphia: University of Pennsylvania Press, 2015)

Devaux, Jean, 'Le culte du héros chevaleresque dans les *Mémoires* d'Olivier de la Marche', *PCEEB*, 41 (2001), 53–66

Dingman, Paul, 'Ethics and Emotions: A Cultural History of Chivalric Friendship in Medieval/Early Modern Times' (unpublished PhD dissertation, University of Rochester, New York, 2012)

Dizionario biografico degli Italiani (Rome: Istituto della Enciclopedia Italiana, 1960–)

Doane, Mary Anne, 'Film and the Masquerade: Theorising the Female Spectator', *Screen*, 23 (1982), 74–87

Donche, Pieter, 'Verhaspelde van Halewijns ontrafeld, Roeselare en Boezinge ca. 1460', *Vlaamse Stam*, 48.3 (2012), 225–46

Drews, Wolfram, and Christian Scholl, eds, *Transkulturelle Verflechtungsprozesse in der Vormoderne* (Berlin: De Gruyter, 2016)

Dubois, Anne, *Valère Maxime en français à la fin du Moyen Âge: Images et tradition* (Turnhout: Brepols, 2016)

Ducein, Michel, 'L'Écosse dans la guerre de Cent Ans', in *Finances, pouvoirs et mémoire: Mélanges offerts à Jean Favier*, ed. by Jean Kerhervé and Albert Rigaudière (Brest: Fayard, 1999), pp. 297–91

Dumolyn, Jan, *Staatsvorming en vorstelijke ambtenaren in het graafschap Vlaanderen (1419–1477)* (Antwerp/Apeldoorn: Garant, 2003)

Edington, Carol, 'The Tournament in Medieval Scotland', in *Armies, Chivalry and Warfare in Medieval Britain and France: Proceedings of the 1995 Harlaxton Symposium*, ed. by Matthew J. Strickland (Stamford: Paul Watkins, 1998), pp. 46–62

Ehm, Petra, *Burgund und das Reich: Spätmittelalterliche Außenpolitik am Beispiel der Regierung Karls des Kühnen (1465–1477)* (Munich: R. Oldenbourg Verlag, 2002)

Eichberger, Dagmar, ed., *Women of Distinction: Margaret of York, Margaret of Austria* (Turnhout: Brepols, 2005)

Elagina, Natalia, 'Le "pas de Saumur". Eine französische Handschrift des 15. Jahrhunderts aus der Sammlung der Russischen Nationalbibliothek (Fr. F. XIV. Nr. 4)', in *Das Turnierbuch für René d'Anjou (Le Pas de Saumur): Vollständige Faksimile-Ausgabe im Originalformat der Handschrift Codex Fr. F. XIV Nr. 4 der Russischen Nationalbibliothek in St. Petersburg*, ed. by Natalia Elagina *et al.* (Graz: Akademische Druck und Verlagsanstalt, 1998), pp. 27–42

Emerson, Catherine, '"Tel estat que peust faire le filz aisné légitime de Bourgoingne": Antoine, Great Bastard of Burgundy and Olivier de La Marche', *PCEEB*, 41 (2001), 77–87

——, *Olivier de la Marche and the Rhetoric of Fifteenth-Century Historiography* (Woodbridge: Boydell Press, 2004)

Enschede, Adriaan Justus, ed., 'Huwelijksplechtigheden van Karel van Bourgondië en Margaretha van York', in *Kronijk van het Historisch Genootschap gevestigd te Utrecht*, 22 (1866), 17–71

Espin, Elsa, 'Résolution d'une énigme héraldique: Honorat de Berre et l'Adoration de l'Enfant', *Revue française d'héraldique et de sigillographie – Études en ligne* (2020) <http://sfhs-rfhs.fr/wp-content/PDF/articles/RFHS_W_2020_001.pdf>

Fallows, Noel, *Jousting in Medieval and Renaissance Iberia* (Woodbridge: Boydell Press, 2010)

——, 'Introduction', in *A Cultural History of Sport in the Medieval Age*, ed. by Noel Fallows (London: Bloomsbury, 2022), pp. 1–34

——, 'Rules and Order', in *A Cultural History of Sport in the Medieval Age*, ed. by Noel Fallows (London: Bloomsbury, 2022), pp. 113–40

Farin, François, and Ignace du Soullet, *Histoire de la ville de Rouen*, 3 vols (Rouen: Du Souillet, 1738)

Favier, Jean, *Le roi René* (Paris: Fayard, 2008)

Fergusson, James, 'A Pair of Butts', *Scottish Historical Review*, 34.117, part 1 (1955), 19–25

Ferlampin-Acher, Christine, 'La Douloureuse Garde du Lancelot en prose: les clefs du désenchantement', in *Les clefs des textes médiévaux*, ed. by Fabienne Pomel (Rennes: Presses Universitaires de Rennes, 2006), pp. 157–73

Fernández de Córdova Miralles, Álvaro, 'L'impact de la Bourgogne et la cour castillane des Trastamare', in *La cour de Bourgogne et l'Europe: Le rayonnement et les limites d'un modèle culturel; actes du colloque international tenu à Paris les 9, 10 et 11 octobre 2007*, ed. by Werner Paravicini, Torsten Hiltmann and Franck Viltart (Ostfildern: Jan Thorbecke Verlag, 2013), pp. 593–630

Ferré, Rose-Marie, 'Les ecclésiastiques et les fêtes profanes à la cour de René d'Anjou: l'exemple du Pas de Saumur', in *L'artiste et le clerc: Commandes artistiques des grands ecclésiastiques à la fin du Moyen Âge (XIVe–XVIe siècles)*, ed. by Fabienne Joubert, Cultures et civilisations médiévales, 35 (Paris: Presses de l'Université de Paris-Sorbonne, 2006), pp. 351–70

——, 'Culture théâtrale et enluminure à la cour du roi René', in *Splendeur de l'enluminure: le roi René et les livres*, ed. by Marc-Édouard Gautier and François Avril (Angers: Ville d'Angers, 2009), pp. 179–89

——, *Réne d'Anjou et les arts: Le jeu des mots et des images* (Turnhout: Brepols, 2012)

Finoli, Anna Maria, '*Le Pas Saladin*: de Jaffa aux côtes de l'Angleterre', in *Quant l'ung amy pour l'autre veille: Mélanges de moyen français offerts à Claude Thiry*, ed. by Tania Van Hemelryck and Maria Colombo Timelli (Turnhout: Brepols, 2008), pp. 113–21

Flink, Klaus, 'Die klevischen Herzöge und ihre Städte, 1394–1592', in *Land im Mittelpunkt der Mächte: Die Herzogtümer Jülich, Kleve, Berg* (Cleves: Boss-Verlag, 1985), pp. 75–98

Foras, Éloi-Amédée de, *Armorial et nobiliaire de l'ancien duché de Savoie*, 5 vols (Grenoble: Edouard Allier, 1863–1938)

Forster, Loïs, 'Les pas d'armes et emprises d'armes dans la formation chevaleresque au XVe siècle: L'exemple de Jacques de Lalaing', in *La construction du militaire, Volume 2: Cultures et identités combattantes en Europe de la guerre de Cent Ans à l'entre-deux guerres*, ed. by Benjamin Deruelle and Arnaud Guinier (Paris: Éditions de la Sorbonne, 2017), pp. 93–116

——, 'Chevaliers et hommes d'armes dans l'espace bourguignon au XVe siècle' (unpublished PhD dissertation, Université de Lille, 2018)

Fradenburg, Louise Olga, *City, Marriage, Tournament: Arts of Rule in Late Medieval Scotland* (Madison: University of Wisconsin Press, 1991)

Freigang, Christian, 'Le tournoi idéal: la création du bon chevalier et la politique courtoise de René d'Anjou', in *René d'Anjou, écrivain et mécène (1409–1480)*, ed. by Florence Bouchet (Turnhout: Brepols, 2011), pp. 179–96

Fresco, Karen, 'Christine de Pizan's *Livre des fais d'armes et de chevalerie* and the Coherence of BL Ms. Royal 15 E. vi', in *Collections in Context: The Organization of Knowledge and Community in Europe*, ed. by Karen Fresco and Anne D. Hedeman (Columbus: The Ohio State University Press, 2020), pp. 151–88

Fresco, Karen and Anne D. Hedeman, eds, *Collections in Context: The Organization of Knowledge and Community in Europe* (Columbus: The Ohio State University Press, 2020)

Gaier, Claude, 'Technique des combats singuliers d'après les auteurs "bourguignons" du XVe siècle', *Le Moyen Âge*, 91 (1985), 415–57, and *Le Moyen Âge*, 92 (1986), 5–40

Garcia, Michel, 'A propos de la Chronique du Connétable Miguel Lucas de Iranzo', *Bulletin Hispanique*, 75 (1973), 5–39

García Marsilla, Juan Vicente, 'El poder visible: demanda y funciones del arte en la corte de Alfonso el Magnánimo', *Ars longa: cuadernos de arte*, 7–8 (1996), 33–47

——, 'El impacto de la Corte en la ciudad: Alfonso el Magnánimo en Valencia (1425–1428)', in *El Alimento del Estado y la salud de la Res Publica: Orígenes, estructura y desarrollo del gasto público en Europa*, ed. by Angel Galán Sánchez and Juan Manuel Carretero Zamora (Madrid: Instituto de Estudios Fiscales, 2013), pp. 291–308

Garland-Thomson, Rosemarie, *Staring: How We Look* (Oxford: Oxford University Press, 2009)

Gaucher, Élisabeth, '*Le Livre des Fais de Jacques de Lalain*: Texte et image', *Le Moyen Âge*, 95 (1989), 503–18

——, 'Les joutes de Saint-Inglevert: perception et écriture d'un événement historique pendant la Guerre de Cent Ans', *Le Moyen Âge*, 102 (1996), 229–43

Gautier, Marc-Édouard, and François Avril, eds, *Splendeur de l'enluminure: le roi René et les livres* (Angers: Ville d'Angers, 2009)

Gauvard, Claude, 'Fama', in *Dictionnaire du Moyen Âge*, ed. by Claude Gauvard, Alain de Libera and Michel Zink (Paris: Presses Universitaires de France, 2002), p. 515

Gay, Victor, *Glossaire archéologique du Moyen Âge et de la Renaissance*, 2 vols (Paris: Librairie de la Société Bibliographique, 1887)

Gearhart, Grant, 'The Knight and War: Alternative Displays of Masculinity in *El Passo Honroso de Suero de Quiñones*, *El Victorial*, and the *Historia de los Hechos del Marquéz de Cádiz*' (unpublished PhD dissertation, University of North Carolina at Chapel Hill, 2015)

Geirnaert, Noël, 'De oudste sporen van het Heilig Bloed in Brugge (1255–1310)', *Handelingen van het Genootschap voor Geschiedenis*, 147.2 (2010), 247–55

Gentile, Luisa, *Riti ed emblemi: Processi di rappresentazione del potere principesco in area subalpina (XIII–XVI secc.)* (Turin: Silvio Zamorani Editore, 2008)

Gilbert, Jane, 'Boys will be … What? Gender, Sexuality, and Childhood in *Floire et Blancheflor* and *Floris et Lyriope*', *Exemplaria*, 9 (1997), 39–61

Glezerman, Abraham, and Michael Harsgor, *Cleve – ein unerfülltes Schicksal: Aufstieg, Rückzug und Verfall eines Territorialstaates* (Berlin: Duncker & Humblot, 1985)

[Godefroy] *Histoire de Charles VIII. roy de France, par Guillaume de Jaligny, André de la Vigne, & autres historiens de ce temps-là. Où sont decrites les choses les plus memorables arrivées pendant ce regne, depuis 1483 jusques en 1498. Enrichie de plusieurs memoires, observations, contracts de mariage, traitez de paix, et autres titres & pieces historiques non encore imprimées. Le tout recueïlli par feu Monsieur Godefroy, conseiller & historiographe ordinaire du Roy* (Paris: Imprimerie Royale, 1684)

Groag Bell, Susan, *The Lost Tapestries of Christine de Pizan* (Berkeley: University of California Press, 2004)

Grollimund, Florian, 'Un puissant seigneur bourguignon au château de Couches: Claude de Montagu', in *Chastels et maisons fortes en Bourgogne, IV: Actes des journées de castellologie de Bourgogne, 2010–2012*, ed. by Hervé Mouillebouche and Brigitte Colas (Chagny: Centre de Castellologie de Bourgogne, 2014), pp. 273–88

Grosjean, Alexandre, *Toison d'or et sa plume: La Chronique de Jean Lefèvre de Saint-Rémy*, Burgundica, 25 (Turnhout: Brepols, 2017)

Grotefend, Hermann, *Taschenbuch der Zeitrechnung des deutschen Mittelalters und der Neuzeit*, 13th edition (Hanover: Hahnsche Buchhandlung, 1991)

Guenée, Bernard, *La folie de Charles VI: roi bien-aimé* (Paris: Perrin, 2004)

Haag, Sabine, Alfried Wieczorek, Matthias Pfaffenbichler and Hans-Jürgen Buderer, eds, *Kaiser Maximilian I: Der letzte Ritter und das höfische Turnier* (Regensburg: Schnell & Steiner, 2014)

Hagemann, Manuel, and Hiram Kümper, *1417: Kleve wird Herzogtum: Mit der Erhebungsurkunde vom 28. April 1417 in Transkription, Übersetzung und Kommentar* (Cleves: Klevischer Verein für Kultur und Geschichte/Freunde der Schwanenburg e.V, 2017)

Hammel, Gavin, 'Revolutionary Flagellants? Clerical Perceptions of Flagellant Brotherhoods in Late Medieval Flanders and Italy', in *Faith's Boundaries: Laity and Clergy in Early Modern Confraternities*, ed. by Nicholas Terpstra, Adriano Prosperi and Stefania Pastore (Turnhout: Brepols, 2012), pp. 303–30

Hamon, Étienne, *Un chantier flamboyant et son rayonnement: Gisors et les églises du Vexin français* (Besançon: Presses Universitaires de Franche-Comté/Société des Antiquaires de Normandie, 2008)

Hedeman, Anne D., *The Royal Image: Illustrations of the Grandes chroniques de France, 1274–1422* (Berkeley: University of California Press, 1991)

——, 'Collecting Images: The Role of the Visual in the Shrewsbury Book (BL Ms. Royal 15 E. vi)', in *Collections in Context: The Organization of Knowledge and Community in Europe*, ed. by Karen Fresco and Anne D. Hedeman (Columbus: The Ohio State University Press, 2020), pp. 99–104

Heimann, Heinz-Dieter, 'Die Soester Fehde', in *Soest. Geschichte der Stadt. Bd. 2: Die Welt der Bürger. Politik, Gesellschaft und Kultur im spätmittelalterlichen Soest*, ed. by Heinz-Dieter Heimann, Wilfried Ehbrecht and Gerhard Köhn (Soest: Mocker & Jahn, 1996), pp. 173–260

Heymans, Vincent, Laetitia Cnockaert and Frédérique Honoré, eds, *Het Coudenbergpaleis te Brussel van middeleeuws kasteel tot archeologische site* (Ghent: Uitgeverij Snoeck, 2014)

Hilger, Hans Peter, 'Kleve und Burgund', in *Land im Mittelpunkt der Mächte: Die Herzogtümer Jülich, Kleve, Berg* (Cleves: Boss-Verlag, 1985), pp. 209–33

Hiltmann, Torsten, 'Un État de noblesse et de chevalerie sans pareilles? Tournois et hérauts d'armes à la cour des ducs de Bourgogne', in *La cour de Bourgogne et l'Europe: Le rayonnement et les limites d'un modèle culturel; actes du colloque international tenu à Paris les 9, 10 et 11 octobre 2007*, ed. by Werner Paravicini, Torsten Hiltmann and Franck Viltart (Ostfildern: Jan Thorbecke Verlag, 2013), pp. 253–88

——, 'Ideal und Physis. Der spätmittelalterliche Fürst in Turnier und Zweikampf', in *Die Performanz der Mächtigen: Rangordnung und Idoneität in höfischen Gesellschaften des Mittelalters*, ed. by Klaus Oschema *et al.* (Ostfildern: Jan Thorbecke Verlag, 2015), pp. 121–49

Hirschbiegel, Jan, 'Mary and Maximilian – Burgundy and Habsburg: The Rise of an Empire', in *Unions and Divisions: New Forms of Rule in Medieval and Renaissance Europe*, ed. by Paul Srodecki, Norbert Kersken and Rimvydas Petrauskas (Abingdon: Routledge, 2023), pp. 210–23

hooks, bell, 'The Oppositional Gaze: Black Female Spectators', in *Black Looks: Race and Representation* (Boston, MA: South End Press, 1992), pp. 115–31

Hövelmann, Gregor, 'Die Anfänge der Beziehungen zwischen Kleve und den Herzögen von Burgund', *Annalen des Historischen Vereins für den Niederrhein*, 161 (1959), 232–43

Hozier de Sérigny, Antoine Marie d', *Armorial général ou registres de la noblesse de France*, 3 vols (Paris: Pierre Prault, 1752)

Hüe, Denis, 'La Bergère et le tournoyeur, coutumes et costumes des parades amoureuses à la cour d'Anjou-Provence', in *Les arts et les lettres en Provence au temps du Roi René*, ed. by Chantal Connochie-Bourgne and Valérie Gontero-Lauze (Aix-en-Provence: Presses Universitaires de Provence, 2013), pp. 243–59

Huizinga, Johan, *Herfsttij der middeleeuwen: Studie over levens- en gedachtenvormen der veertiende en vijftiende eeuw in Frankrijk en de Nederlanden* (Haarlem: H. D. Tjeenk Willink & Zoon, 1919)

——, *Homo ludens: A Study of the Play-Element in Culture* (Boston, MA: Beacon Press, 1955)

——, *Autumntide of the Middle Ages: A Study of Forms of Life and Thought of the Fourteenth and Fifteenth Centuries in France and the Low Countries*, ed. by Anton van der Lem and Graeme Small, trans. by Diane Webb (Leiden: Leiden University Press, 2020)

Innes of Learney, Sir Thomas, 'Sir William Cumming of Inverallochy, Lord Lyon King of Arms, 1512–1519', *The Juridical Review*, 55 (1943), 24–38

Irigoyen-Garcia, Javier, *Moors Dressed as Moors: Clothing, Social Distinction and Ethnicity in Early Modern Iberia* (Toronto: University of Toronto Press, 2018)

Jackson, William Henry, 'The Tournament and Chivalry in German Tournament Books of the Sixteenth Century and in the Literary Works of Emperor Maximilian I', in *The Ideals and Practice of Medieval Knighthood*, ed. by Ruth Harvey and Christopher Harper-Bill (Woodbridge: Boydell Press, 1986), pp. 49–73

James, Montague Rhodes, 'Unpublished Description by M. R. James of Cambridge, University Library, MS Hh.3.16 (*Ponthus et Sidoine*)' <https://doi.org/10.17863/CAM.67883>

James-Raoul, Danièle, 'Les Amazones au Moyen Âge', in *En quête d'utopies*, ed. by Claude Thomasset and Danièle James-Raoul (Paris: Presses de l'Université Paris-Sorbonne, 2005), pp. 195–230

Janse, Antheun, *Ridderschap in Holland: Portret van een adellijke elite in de late middeleeuwen* (Hilversum: Verloren, 2001)

——, 'Tourneyers and Spectators: The Shrovetide Tournament at The Hague, 1391', in *The Court as a Stage: England and the Low Countries in the Later Middle Ages*, ed. by Antheun Janse and Steven Gunn (Woodbridge: Boydell Press, 2006), pp. 39–52

Janssens, Albert, 'De wapenpas van de Gouden Boom: feestvieren op zijn Bourgondisch', *Vlaanderen. Kunsttijdschrift*, 58 (2009), 104–7

Jaspert, Nikolas, '"Reconquista". Interdependenzen und Tragfähigkeit eines wertekategorialen Deutungsmusters', in *Christlicher Norden – Muslimischer Süden: Ansprüche und Wirklichkeiten von Christen, Juden und Muslimen auf der Iberischen Halbinsel im Hoch- und Spätmittelalter*, ed. by Matthias M. Tischler and Alexander Fidora (Münster: Aschendorff Verlag, 2011), pp. 445–65

Jefferson, Lisa, 'The Keys to the Enchantments of Dolorous Guard', *Medium Aevum*, 58.1 (1989), 59–79

——, 'Tournaments, Heraldry and the Knights of the Round Table', in *Arthurian Literature XIV*, ed. by James P. Carley and Felicity Riddy (Woodbridge: D. S. Brewer, 1996), 69–157

Jezler, Peter, Peter Niederhäuser and Elke Jezler, eds, *Ritterturnier: Geschichte einer Festkultur* (Lucerne: Quaternio Verlag, 2014)

Jolivet, Sophie, 'La construction d'une image: Philippe le Bon et le noir (1419–1467)', in *Se vêtir à la cour en Europe, 1400–1815*, ed. by Isabelle Paresys and Natacha Coquery (Villeneuve d'Ascq: Institut de recherches historiques du Septentrion, 2011), pp. 27–42

Jones, Leslie C., and Jonathan J. G. Alexander, 'The Annunciation to the Shepherdess', *Studies in Iconography*, 24 (2003), 165–98

Jones, Robert, *Knight: The Warrior and World of Chivalry* (Oxford: Osprey, 2011)

Jourdan, Jean-Pierre, 'Le thème du pas d'armes dans le royaume de France (Bourgogne, Anjou) à la fin du Moyen Âge: aspects d'un théâtre de chevalerie', in *Théâtre et spectacles hier et aujourd'hui: Moyen âge et Renaissance. Actes du 115e Congrès National des Sociétés Savantes (Avignon, 1990). Section d'histoire médiévale et de philologie* (Paris: Éditions du CTHS, 1991), pp. 285–304

——, 'Le symbolisme politique du pas dans le royaume de France (Bourgogne et Anjou) à la fin du moyen âge', *Journal of Medieval History*, 18 (1992), 161–81

——, 'Le thème du Pas et de l'Emprise: Espaces symboliques et rituels d'alliance en France à la fin du Moyen Âge', *Éthnologie française*, 22.2 (1992), 172–84

——, 'Le langage amoureux dans le combat de chevalerie à la fin du Moyen Âge (France, Bourgogne, Anjou)', *Le Moyen Âge*, 99 (1993), 83–106

——, 'Le perron de chevalerie à la fin du Moyen Âge: aspects d'un symbole', in *Seigneurs et seigneuries au Moyen Âge*, Congrès national des sociétés historiques et scientifiques, 1992, Clermont-Ferrand, 117 (Paris: Éditions du CTHS, 1993), pp. 581–98

Karras, Ruth Mazo, *From Boys to Men: Formations of Masculinity in Late Medieval Europe* (Philadelphia: University of Pennsylvania Press, 2003)

——, 'Perfect Men? The Nine Worthies and Medieval Masculinities', *Collegium Medievale*, 33 (2020), 5–22

Kekewich, Margaret L., *The Good King: René of Anjou and Fifteenth Century Europe* (Basingstoke: Palgrave Macmillan, 2008)

Kelzenberg, Kathrin, *Heiliglandfrömmigkeit im Nordwesten des Reiches: die Herzogtümer Brabant, Geldern, Jülich und Kleve im späten Mittelalter* (Heidelberg: Universitätsverlag Winter, 2022)

Kempshall, Matthew, *The Common Good in Late Medieval Political Thought* (Oxford: Clarendon Press, 1999)

Kennedy, Elspeth M., 'The Role of the Supernatural in the First Part of the Old French Prose Lancelot', in *Studies in Medieval Literature and Languages in Memory of Frederick Whitehead*, ed. by William Rothwell *et al.* (Manchester: Manchester University Press, 1973), pp. 172–84

Kestemont, Mike, Folgert Karsdorp, *et al.*, 'Forgotten Books: The Application of Unseen Species Models to the Survival of Culture', *Science*, 375.6582 (2022), 765–69

Kipling, Gordon, *The Triumph of Honour: Burgundian Origins of the Elizabethan Renaissance* (Leiden: Leiden University Press, 1977)

Knecht, Robert J., *The Valois Kings of France 1328–1589* (London/New York: Hambledon, 2004)

Knighton, Tess, 'Spaces and Contexts for Listening in 15th-Century Castile: The Case of the Constable's Palace in Jaén', *Early Music*, 25 (1997), 661–77

Korteweg, Anne S. 'La collection de livres d'une femme indépendante: Marie de Luxembourg (v. 1470–1547)', in *Livres et lectures de femmes en Europe entre Moyen Âge et Renaissance*, ed. by Anne-Marie Legaré and Bertrand Schnerb (Turnhout: Brepols, 2007), pp. 221–32

Kruse, Holger, *Hof, Amt und Gagen: Die täglichen Gagenlisten des burgundischen Hofes (1430–1467) und der erste Hofstaat Karls des Kühnen (1456)* (Bonn: Bouvier Verlag, 1996)

Kümper, Hiram, 'Adolf III. von Kleve-Mark (*1332/33–†1394): Zweimal (fast) Bischof und Begründer der Union mit Kleve', in *Die Grafen von der Mark: Ein biographisches Handbuch*, ed. by Dietrich Thier and Stefan Pätzold (Witten: Bergischer Verlag, 2021), pp. 251–86

Labande-Mailfert, Yvonne, *Charles VIII et son milieu (1470–1498): La jeunesse au pouvoir* (Paris: Klincksieck, 1974)

La Chenaye-Desbois, François-Alexandre Aubert de, *Dictionnaire de la noblesse* … , 3rd edition, 19 vols (Paris: Schlesinger, 1866–76)

Laidlaw, James, ed., *The Auld Alliance: France and Scotland over 700 Years* (Edinburgh: Edinburgh University Press, 1999)

Lainé, P. Louis, *Archives généalogiques et historiques de la noblesse de France* … , 11 vols (Paris: Chez l'auteur, 1828–50)

Landais, Hubert, 'La construction d'une grande demeure de la fin du moyen âge. Le château de Saumur, résidence des ducs d'Anjou aux XIVe et XVe siècles', in *La noblesse dans les territoires*

Angevins à la fin du moyen âge, ed. by Noël Coulet and Jean-Michel Matz, Collection de l'École française de Rome, 275 (Rome: École française de Rome, 2000), pp. 189–203

Land im Mittelpunkt der Mächte: Die Herzogtümer Jülich, Kleve, Berg (Cleves: Boss, 1984)

Landolt, Oliver, 'Akustische Dimensionen in der Militärgeschichte der spätmittelalterlichen Eidgenossenschaft', *Das Mittelalter*, 27.1 (2022), 51–67

Launet, Charles de, 'Un curieux tournoi: le pas d'armes de la Bergère tenu au tournoi de Tarascon', *Hidalguia*, 35 (1987), 193–203

Le Bailly, Marie Charlotte, *Recht voor de Raad: Rechtspraak voor het Hof van Holland, Zeeland en West-Friesland in het midden van de vijftiende eeuw* (Hilversum: Uitgeverij Verloren, 2001)

Lecoy de la Marche, Albert, *Le roi René, sa vie, son administration, ses travaux littéraires et artistiques*, 2 vols (Paris: Librairie de Firmin-Didot frères, fils et cie, 1875)

Lecuppre-Desjardin, Élodie, *La ville des cérémonies: Essai sur la communication politique dans les anciens Pays-Bas bourguignons* (Turnhout: Brepols, 2004)

——, 'Le duel judiciaire dans les villes des anciens Pays-Bas bourguignons: privilège urbain ou acte de rébellion?', in *Agon und Distinktion: Soziale Räume des Zweikampfs zwischen Mittelalter und Neuzeit*, ed. by Uwe Israel and Christian Jaser (Berlin: LIT-Verlag, 2016), pp. 181–97

Legaré, Anne-Marie, '*Les Faits de Jacques de Lalaing* enluminés par le Maître d'Antoine Rolin', in *'Als ich can': Liber amicorum in Memory of Professor Dr. Maurits Smeyers*, ed. by Bert Cardon, Jan Van der Stock and Dominique Vanwijnsberghe, 2 vols (Leuven/Dudley, MA: Peeters, 2002), vol. 2, pp. 773–93

Leman, Victorien, and Maxence Watelle, 'De cire et d'histoire: les sceaux de la famille de Créquy (XIIe–XVIe siècles)', *Dossiers généalogiques du Comité d'histoire du Haut-Pays*, 25 (2009), 16–26

Le Roux, Nicolas, *Le crépuscule de la chevalerie: Noblesse et guerre au siècle de la Renaissance* (Ceyzérieu: Champ Vallon, 2015)

Le Roy, Pierre, *La reine Jeanne, Jeanne de Laval, seconde épouse du roi René, 1433–1498* (Mayenne: Éditions régionales de l'Ouest, 1996)

Lesage, René, 'Notes sur la généalogie des Créquy aux XIIIe et XIVe siècles', *Dossiers généalogiques du Comité d'histoire du Haut-Pays*, 25 (2009), 49–74

L'Estrange, Elizabeth, 'Gazing at Gawain: Reconsidering Tournaments, Courtly Love, and the Lady Who Looks', *Medieval Feminist Forum*, 44.2 (2008), 74–96

Lever, Maurice, *Le sceptre et la marotte* (Paris: Fayard, 1996)

Lieven, Jens, *Adel, Herrschaft und Memoria: Studien zur Erinnerungskultur der Grafen von Kleve und Geldern im Hochmittelalter (1020–1250)* (Bielefeld: Verlag für Regionalgeschichte, 2008)

——, 'Adolf IV./II. (1394–1448) und Johann I. von Kleve-Mark (1448–1481)', in *Die Grafen von der Mark: Ein biographisches Handbuch*, ed. by Dietrich Thier and Stefan Pätzold (Witten: Bergischer Verlag, 2021), pp. 303–38

Lindner, Annette, 'L'influence du roman chevaleresque français sur le pas d'armes', *PCEEB*, 31 (1991), 67–78

Litoux, Emmanuel, 'Le château de Saumur et son portrait dans les *Très riches heures du duc de Berry*', in *Le château et l'art, à la croisée des sources, t. 1, Mehun-sur-Yèvre* (Mehun-sur-Yèvre: Groupe historique et archéologique de la région de Mehun-sur-Yère, 2011), pp. 53–83

Logemann, Cornelia, 'Reenactment: Tournaments, Chronicles and Visual History', *Iran*, 57.1 (2019), 31–48

Loomis, Laura Hibbard, 'Arthur's Round Table', *Proceedings of the Modern Language Association*, 41.4 (1926), 771–84

Lupack, Alan, *Oxford Guide to Arthurian Literature and Legend* (Oxford: Oxford University Press, 2005)

Macdougall, Norman, *James IV* (Edinburgh: John Donald, 1989)

Macfarlane, John, *Antoine Vérard*, Illustrated Monographs, 7 (London: Bibliographical Society at the Chiswick Press, 1899 [1900])

McGladdery, C. A., 'Andrew Forman (c. 1465–1520)', *Oxford Dictionary of National Biography* <https://doi.org/10.1093/ref:odnb/9883>

McGowan, Margaret, *Dance in the Renaissance: European Fashion, French Obsession* (New Haven, CT: Yale University Press, 2008)

——, *La danse à la Renaissance: Sources livresques et albums d'images* (Paris: Bibliothèque nationale de France, 2012)

MacKay, Angus, 'Enrique, Infante of Aragón', in *Medieval Iberia: An Encyclopedia*, ed. by Edmund Michael Gerli (New York: Routledge, 2003), pp. 306–7

Mackie, Robert L., *King James IV of Scotland: A Brief Survey of His Life and Times* (Edinburgh: Oliver and Boyd, 1958)

McLean, Will, 'Outrance and Plaisance', *Journal of Medieval Military History*, 8 (2010), 155–70

Macquarrie, Alan, *Scotland and the Crusades, 1095–1560* (Edinburgh: John Donald, 1997)

Magny, M. le marquis de, 'De Hédouville, Ile-de-France, Picardie, Champagne', in *Troisième registre du Livre d'or de la noblesse* (Paris: Secrétariat général du collège héraldique, 1846), pp. 227–36

Malinin, Jurii P., 'Das Werk "Le pas de Saumur von 1446" und sein Autor', in *Das Turnierbuch für René d'Anjou (Le Pas de Saumur): Vollständige Faksimile-Ausgabe im Originalformat der Handschrift Codex Fr. F. XIV Nr. 4 der Russischen Nationalbibliothek in St. Petersburg*, ed. by Natalia Elagina *et al.* (Graz: Akademische Druck und Verlagsanstalt, 1998), pp. 11–26

Marini, Lino, *Savoiardi e piemontesi nello Stato sabaudo: (1418–1601)* (Rome: Istituto storico italiano per l'Età Moderna e Contemporanea, 1962)

Martín, José-Luis, *Enrique IV de Castilla: Rey de Navarra, Príncipe de Cataluña* (Hondarribia: Nerea, 2003)

Martineau, Anne, *Le nain et le chevalier: Essai sur les nains français du Moyen Âge* (Paris: Presses de l'Université de Paris-Sorbonne, 2003)

Mason, Roger, 'Renaissance Monarchy? Stewart Kingship (1469–1542)', in *Scottish Kingship, 1306–1542: Essays in Honour of Norman Macdougall*, ed. by Michael Brown and Roland Tanner (Edinburgh: John Donald, 2008), pp. 255–78

Matile, Georges-Auguste, *Histoire de la seigneurie de Valangin jusqu'à sa réunion à la Directe en 1592* (Neuchâtel: Imprimerie de James Attinger, 1852)

Matthieu, Ernest, 'La reconnaissance par les États de Hainaut de Charles le Téméraire comme héritier du comté en 1465', *Bulletin de la Commission royale d'Histoire*, 55.13 (1886), 225–42

Meiss, Millard, *French Painting in the Time of Jean de Berry: The Limbourgs and their Contemporaries*, 2 vols (New York: G. Braziller, 1974)

Melville, Gert, 'Der Held in Szene gesetzt: einige Bilder und Gedanken zu Jacques de Lalaing und seinem Pas d'armes de la Fontaine des Pleurs', in *'Aufführung' und 'Schrift' in Mittelalter und früher Neuzeit*, ed. by Jan-Dirk Müller (Stuttgart: Metzler, 1996), pp. 253–86

Mérindol, Christian de, 'Les demeures du roi René en Anjou et leur décoration peinte', *Bulletin de la Société Nationale des Antiquaires de France* (1978–79) [1982], 180–93

——, *Le roi René et la seconde maison d'Anjou: Emblématique, art, histoire* (Paris: Léopard d'or, 1987)

——, 'Le Livre des tournois du roi René. Nouvelles lectures', *Bulletin de la Société Nationale des Antiquaires de France* (1992) [1994], 177–90

——, *Les fêtes de chevalerie à la cour du roi René: Emblématique, art et histoire (les joutes de Nancy, le Pas de Saumur et le Pas de Tarascon)* (Paris: Éditions du CTHS, 1993)

——, 'Les joutes de Nancy, le Pas de Saumur et le Pas de Tarascon, fêtes de chevalerie à la cour du roi René (1445–1449)', *PCEEB*, 34 (1994), 187–202

——, 'L'ordre du Croissant: Mises au point et perspectives', in *La noblesse dans les territoires angevins à la fin du moyen âge: Actes du colloque international organisé par l'Université d'Angers, Angers-Saumur, 3–6 juin 1998*, ed. by Noël Coulet and Jean-Michel Matz, Collection de l'École française de Rome, 275 (Rome: École Française de Rome, 2000), 499–509

——, 'Rois d'armes et poursuivants à la cour d'Anjou au temps du roi René', *Revue du Nord*, 88 (2006), 617–30

Meyer, Werner, 'Turniergesellschaften: Bemerkungen zur sozialgeschichtlichen Bedeutung der Turniere im Spätmittelalter', in *Das ritterliche Turnier im Mittelalter: Beiträge zu einer vergleichenden Formen- und Verhaltensgeschichte des Rittertums*, ed. by Josef Fleckenstein (Göttingen: Vandenhoeck & Ruprecht, 1986), pp. 500–12

Mickel, Lesley, 'Our Hielandmen: Scots in Court Entertainments at Home and Abroad, 1507–1616', *Renaissance Studies*, 33 (2019), 185–203

Middell, Matthias, 'Kulturtransfer, Transferts culturels', *Docupedia-Zeitgeschichte: Begriffe, Methoden und Debatten der zeithistorischen Forschung* (28 January 2016) <https://docupedia.de/zg/Kulturtransfer>

Militzer, Klaus, 'Turniere in Köln', *Jahrbuch des Kölnischen Geschichtsvereins*, 64.1 (2015), 37–60

Millar, Alistair, 'Olivier de La Marche and the Court of Burgundy, *c.*1425–1502' (unpublished PhD dissertation, University of Edinburgh, 1996) <https://era.ed.ac.uk/handle/1842/1540>

Moffat, Ralph, 'The Medieval Tournament: Chivalry, Heraldry and Reality. An Edition and Analysis of Three Fifteenth-Century Tournament Manuscripts' (unpublished PhD dissertation, University of Leeds, 2010)

——, '*Alle myne harneys for the justes*: Documents as a Source for Medieval Jousting Armour', in *The Medieval Tournament as Spectacle: Tourneys, Jousts and Pas d'Armes, 1100–1600*, ed. by Alan V. Murray and Karen Watts (Woodbridge: Boydell Press, 2020), pp. 77–97

Moréri, Louis, *Le Grand Dictionnaire historique …* , 10 vols (Paris: Jacques Vincent, 1759)

Morrison, Elizabeth, ed., *A Knight for the Ages: Jacques de Lalaing and the Art of Chivalry* (Los Angeles: The J. Paul Getty Museum, 2018)

——, 'Creating the Ideal Knight through Illumination: The Artists of the Getty Lalaing', in *A Knight for the Ages: Jacques de Lalaing and the Art of Chivalry*, ed. by Elizabeth Morrison (Los Angeles: The J. Paul Getty Museum, 2018), pp. 90–105

——, and Anne D. Hedeman, *Imagining the Past in France: History in Manuscript Painting 1250–1500* (Los Angeles: The J. Paul Getty Museum, 2010)

Muhlberger, Steven, *Deeds of Arms: Formal Combats in the Late Fourteenth Century* (Highland Village, TX: Chivalry Bookshelf, 2005)

Müller, Jan-Dirk, *Gedechtnus: Literatur und Hofgesellschaft um Maximilian I* (Munich: Fink, 1982)

Mulvey, Laura, 'Visual Pleasure and Narrative Cinema', *Screen*, 16 (1975), 6–18

Munro, John H. A., 'The Anti-Red Shift – To the Dark Side: Colour Changes in Flemish Luxury Woollens, 1300–1550', in *Medieval Clothing and Textiles, vol. 3*, ed. by Robin Netherton and Gale R. Owen-Crocker (Woodbridge: Boydell Press, 2007), pp. 55–95

Nadot, Sébastien, *Rompez les lances! Chevaliers et tournois au Moyen Âge* (Paris: Autrement, 2010)

——, *Le Spectacle des joutes: Sport et courtoisie à la fin du Moyen Âge* (Rennes: Presses Universitaires de Rennes, 2012)

Neufeld, Christine Marie, 'A Dwarf in King Arthur's Court: Perceiving Disability in Arthurian Romance', *Arthuriana*, 25 (2015), 25–35

Nicholson, Ranald, *Scotland: The Later Middle Ages* (Edinburgh: Oliver and Boyd, 1974)

Niebrzydowski, Sue, 'The Sultana and Her Sisters: Black Women in the British Isles before 1530', *Women's History Review*, 10 (2001), 187–210

Nievergelt, Marco, 'The Quest for Chivalry in the Waning Middle Ages: The Wanderings of René d'Anjou and Olivier de la Marche', *Fifteenth Century Studies*, 36 (2011), 137–67

Nijsten, Gerard J. M., 'Hof und Kultur: Charakteristik eines mittelgroßen Fürstenhofes am Niederrhein', in *Gelre – Geldern – Gelderland: Geschichte und Kultur des Herzogtums Geldern*, ed. by Johannes Stinner and Karl-Heinz Tekath (Guelders: Verlag des Historischen Vereins für Geldern und Umgegend, 2001), pp. 373–82

——, *In the Shadow of Burgundy: The Court of Guelders in the Late Middle Ages*, Cambridge Studies in Medieval Life and Thought, 4th ser., 58 (Cambridge: Cambridge University Press, 2004)

Normore, Christina, *A Feast for the Eyes: Art, Performance and the Late Medieval Banquet* (Chicago, IL: University of Chicago Press, 2015)

Omnès, Robert, 'La Bretagne et les Bretons dans les chroniques de Castille (XIVe–XVIe siècles)', *Annales de Bretagne et des pays de l'Ouest*, 88.4 (1981), 395–417

Ortega Gato, Esteban, 'Los Enríquez, almirantes de Castilla', *Publicaciones de la Institución Tello Téllez de Meneses*, 70 (1999), 23–65

Oschema, Klaus, *Freundschaft und Nähe im spätmittelalterlichen Burgund: Studien zum Spannungsfeld von Emotion und Institution* (Cologne/Weimar/Vienna: Böhlau, 2006)

——, 'Toucher et être touché: gestes de conciliation et émotions dans les duels judiciaires', *Médiévales*, 61 (2011), 142–61

——, 'Wege des Hauses Habsburg in den Westen Europas 1477 bis 1519', in *König Rudolf I. und der Aufstieg des Hauses Habsburg im Mittelalter*, ed. by Bernd Schneidmüller (Darmstadt: WBG, 2019), pp. 410–38

Owen-Crocker, Gale, Elizabeth Coatsworth and Maria Hayward, eds, *Encyclopedia of Medieval Dress and Textiles of the British Isles c. 450–1450* (Leiden: Brill, 2012)

Paden, William D., *The Medieval Pastourelle* (New York: Garland, 1987)

Paravicini, Werner, *Die Preußenreisen des europäischen Adels*, Beihefte der Francia, vol. 17. 1–2, 2 vols (Sigmaringen: Jan Thorbecke Verlag, 1989)

——, 'The Court of the Dukes of Burgundy. A Model for Europe?', in *Princes, Patronage and the Nobility: The Court at the Beginning of the Modern Age (c. 1450–1650)*, ed. by Ronald G. Asch and Adolf M. Birke (Oxford: Oxford University Press, 1991), pp. 69–102

——, 'Die zwölf "Magnificences" Karls des Kühnen', in *Formen und Funktionen öffentlicher Kommunikation im Mittelalter*, ed. by Gerd Althoff (Stuttgart: Jan Thorbecke Verlag, 2001), pp. 319–95

——, 'Soziale Schichtung und soziale Mobilität am Hof der Herzöge von Burgund', in *Menschen am Hof der Herzöge von Burgund: Gesammelte Aufsätze*, ed. by Holger Kruse, Werner Paravicini and Andreas Ranft (Stuttgart: Thorbecke, 2002), pp. 371–426

——, 'Gab es eine einheitliche Adelskultur Europas im späten Mittelalter?', in *Europa im späten Mittelalter: Politik – Gesellschaft – Kultur*, ed. by Rainer Christoph Schwinges, Peter Moraw and Christian Hesse (Munich: Oldenbourg Verlag, 2006), pp. 401–34

——, 'Un tombeau en Flandre: Hervé de Mériadec', *Francia: Forschungen zur westeuropäischen Geschichte*, 34.1 (2007), 85–146

——, 'Jean de Werchin, sénéchal de Hainaut, chevalier errant', in *idem*, *Noblesse: Studien zum adeligen Leben im spätmittelalterlichen Europa. Gesammelte Aufsätze*, ed. by Ulf-Christian Ewert, Andreas Ranft and Stephan Selzer (Ostfildern: Thorbecke Verlag, 2012), pp. 251–72

——, 'Nobles Hennuyers sur les chemins du monde: Jean de Werchin et ses amis autour de 1400', in *idem*, *Noblesse: Studien zum adeligen Leben im spätmittelalterlichen Europa. Gesammelte Aufsätze*, ed. by Ulf-Christian Ewert, Andreas Ranft and Stephan Selzer (Ostfildern: Thorbecke Verlag, 2012), pp. 273–320

——, *Ehrenvolle Abwesenheit: Studien zum adligen Reisen im späteren Mittelalter. Gesammelte Aufsätze*, ed. by Jan Hirschbiegel and Harm von Seggern (Ostfildern: Thorbecke Verlag, 2017)

——, *Adlig leben im 14. Jahrhundert. Weshalb sie fuhren: Die Preussenreisen des europäischen Adels. Teil 3* (Göttingen: V&R unipress, 2020)

——, Verlust und Dauer. *Weshalb sie nicht mehr fuhren und was an die Stelle trat: Die Preußenreisen des europäischen Adels. Teil 4* (Göttingen: V&R unipress, 2024)

Passier, Henri, 'Dictionnaire de la noblesse de Franche-Comté de Bourgogne', *Revue historique nobiliaire et biographique*, nouvelle série, 6 (1870–71), 75–89

Pastoureau, Michel, *Les armoiries* (Turnhout: Brepols, 1976)

Patte, Victor, *Histoire de Gisors* (Gisors: Ch. Lapierre Imprimeur-éditeur, 1896)

Paula Cañas Gálvez, Francisco de, *El itinerario de la corte de Juan II de Castilla (1418–1454)* (Madrid: Silex Ediciones, 2007)

Paviot, Jacques, *La politique navale des ducs de Bourgogne, 1384–1482* (Lille: Presses Universitaires de Lille, 1995)

——, 'Le rôle des ordres de chevalerie dans la ritualisation de la cour', in *Rituels et cérémonies de cour de l'Empire romain à l'âge baroque*, ed. by Delphine Carrangeot, Bruno Laurioux and Vincent Puech (Villeneuve d'Ascq: Presses Universitaires du Septentrion, 2018), pp. 97–106

Pennel, Audrey, 'Des hourds aux lices: la place des dames dans les enluminures des tournois et Pas d'armes aux XIVe et XVe siècle', *Francia: Forschungen zur westeuropäischen Geschichte*, 46 (2019), 431–42

Peters, Leo, 'Der jülichsche Hubertus- und klevische Antonius-Ritterorden', in *Land im Mittelpunkt der Mächte: Die Herzogtümer Jülich, Kleve, Berg* (Cleves: Boss-Verlag, 1985), pp. 125–32

Petitprez, René, and Théodore Leuridan, 'Monographie de Marquette en Ostrevant', in *Bulletin de la Société d'Études de la province de Cambrai*, 25 (1925), 81–236

Piponnier, Françoise, *Costume et vie sociale: La cour d'Anjou XIVe–XVe siècle* (Paris: Mouton, 1970)

——, and Perrine Mane, *Dress in the Middle Ages* (New Haven, CT: Yale University Press, 1997)

Planche, Alice, 'Du tournoi au théâtre en Bourgogne: Le Pas de la Fontaine des Pleurs à Chalon-sur-Saône, 1449–1450', *Le Moyen Âge*, 81 (1975), 97–128

Poirion, Daniel, 'La Douloureuse Garde', in *Approches du Lancelot en prose*, ed. by Jean Dufournet (Geneva: Slatkine, 1984), pp. 25–48

Pollini, Nadia, *La mort du prince: Rituels funéraires de la Maison de Savoie (1343–1451)* (Lausanne: Cahiers lausannois d'histoire médiévale, 1994)

Pöschko, Hans H., 'Turniere in Mittel- und Süddeutschland von 1400 bis 1550: Katalog der Kampfspiele und der Teilnehmer' (unpublished PhD dissertation, Universität Stuttgart, 1987)

Potter, David, 'The Luxembourg Inheritance: The House of Bourbon and its Lands in Northern France during the Sixteenth Century', *French History*, 6 (1992), 24–62

Prietzel, Malte, 'Imitation, Inspiration und Desinteresse: Die Auseinandersetzung Maximilians I. mit den politischen Traditionen Burgunds', in *'Das kommt mir spanisch vor': Eigenes und Fremdes in den deutsch-spanischen Beziehungen des späten Mittelalters*, ed. by Klaus Herbers and Nikolas Jaspert (Münster: LIT-Verlag, 2004), pp. 87–106

——, '"Letzter Ritter" und "Vater der Landsknechte": Fürstliche Gewaltausübung als Praxis und Inszenierung', in *Maximilians Welt. Kaiser Maximilian I. im Spannungsfeld zwischen Innovation und Tradition*, ed. by Johannes Helmrath, Ursula Kocher and Andrea Sieber, Berliner Mittelalter- und Frühneuzeitforschung, 22 (Göttingen: V & R unipress, 2018), pp. 209–24

Prochno, Renate, *Die Kartause von Champmol: Grablege der burgundischen Herzöge 1364–1477* (Berlin: Akademie-Verlag, 2002)

Purdie, Rhiannon, 'The Search for Scottishness in *Golagros and Gawane*', in *The Scots and Medieval Arthurian Legend*, ed. by Rhiannon Purdie and Nicola Royan (Woodbridge: Boydell Press, 2005), pp. 95–108

Quatrebarbes, Théodore de, *Histoire de René d'Anjou* (Angers: Cosnier et Lachèse, 1853)

Quintanilla Raso, María Concepción, 'Los grandes nobles', *Medievalismo: boletín de la Sociedad Española de Estudios Medievales*, 13 (2004), 127–42

Ranft, Andreas, *Adelsgesellschaften: Gruppenbildung und Genossenschaft im spätmittelalterlichen Reich* (Sigmaringen: Thorbecke, 1994)

Rapp Buri, Anna, and Monica Stucky-Schürer, *Burgundische Tapisserien* (Munich: Hirmer, 2001)

Reppel, Eric, 'Minorités et circulations techniques: la confection des armures à Tours (XVe–XVIe siècles)', *Documents pour l'histoire des techniques*, 15 (2008), 24–31

Reynaud, Nicole, 'Barthélemy d'Eyck avant 1450', *Revue de l'art*, 84 (1989), 22–43

Reynolds, Catherine, 'The Shrewsbury Book, British Library, Royal MS 15 E.VI', in *Medieval Art, Architecture and Archaeology at Rouen*, ed. by Jenny Stratford (Leeds: The British Archaeological Association, 1993), pp. 109–16

Reynolds, Michael T., 'René of Anjou, King of Sicily, and the Order of the Croissant', *Journal of Medieval History*, 19 (1993), 125–61

Rigby, S. H., *Wisdom and Chivalry: Chaucer's* Knight's Tale *and Medieval Political Theory* (Leiden/ Boston, MA: Brill, 2009)

Riquer, Martín de, *Lletres de batalla: cartells de deseiximents i capítols de passos d'armes*, Els nostres clàssics, 3 vols (Barcelona: Barcino, 1963–68)

——, *Vida caballeresca en la España del siglo XV* (Madrid: Gráficas Marina, 1965)

——, *Caballeros andantes españoles* (Barcelona: Ariel, 2019)

Robin, Françoise. *La cour d'Anjou-Provence: La vie artistique sous le règne de René* (Paris: Éditions A. et J. Picard, 1985)

Rosie, Alison, 'Morisques and Momeryes: Aspects of Court Entertainment at the Court of Savoy in the Fifteenth Century', in *Power, Culture and Religion in France c.1350–c.1550*, ed. by Christopher Allmand (Woodbridge: Boydell Press, 1989), pp. 57–74

Round, Nicholas, *The Greatest Man Uncrowned: A Study of the Fall of Don Alvaro de Luna* (London: Tamesis Books, 1986)

Rousset, Alphonse, *Dictionnaire géographique, historique et statistique des communes de la Franche-Comté et des hameaux qui en dépendent, classés par département: Tome premier, département du Jura* (Besançon: Bintot Imprimeur-Libraire, 1853)

Roussillon, Marine, *Don Quichotte à Versailles: L'imaginaire médiéval du Grand Siècle* (Ceyzérieu: Champ Vallon, 2022)

Roy, Bruno, 'Triboulet, Josseaume et Pathelin à la cour de René d'Anjou', *Le Moyen Âge*, 7 (1980), 7–56

Royan, Nicola, '"Na les vailyeant than ony uthir princis of Britane": Representations of Arthur in Scotland 1480–1540', *Scottish Studies Review*, 3 (2002), 9–20

Rucquoi, Adeline, 'La Péninsule Ibérique et la cour de Bourgogne', in *La cour de Bourgogne et l'Europe: le rayonnement et les limites d'un modèle culturel; actes du colloque international tenu à Paris les 9, 10 et 11 octobre 2007*, ed. by Werner Paravicini, Torsten Hiltmann and Frank Viltart (Ostfildern: Jan Thorbecke Verlag, 2013), pp. 581–91

Ruiz, Teofilo F., *A King Travels: Festive Traditions in Late Medieval and Early Modern Spain* (Princeton, NJ: Princeton University Press, 2012)

Salazar y Acha, Jaime de, *La Casa del Rey de Castilla y León en la Edad Media* (Madrid: Centro de Estudios Políticos y Constitucionales, 2000)

Salazar y Castro, Luis de, *Historia genealogica de la casa de Lara* (Madrid: Llanos y Guzman, 1696)

Sandoz, Edouard, 'Tourneys in the Arthurian Tradition', *Speculum*, 19 (1944), 389–420

Santina, Mary Arlene, *The Tournament and Literature: Literary Representations of the Medieval Tournament in Old French Works, 1150–1236* (New York: Peter Lang, 1999)

Scheler, Dieter, 'Köln oder Brüssel: die heimlichen Hauptstädte von Kleve-Mark', in *Dieter Scheler: Stadt und Kirche, Land und Herrschaft am Niederrhein in Mittelalter und anbrechender Neuzeit. Gesammelte Studien*, ed. by Hiram Kümper and Andrea Berlin (Münster/New York: Waxmann, 2019), pp. 27–41

Schilp, Thomas, 'Die Reichsstadt (1250–1802)', in *Geschichte der Stadt Dortmund*, ed. by Stadtarchiv Dortmund (Dortmund: Harenberg, 1994), pp. 69–211

Schnerb, Bertrand, *Bulgnéville (1431): L'état bourguignon prend pied en Lorraine* (Paris: Economica, 1993)

——, *Jean sans Peur: Le prince meurtrier* (Paris: Payot, 2005)

——, *L'État bourguignon: 1363–1477* (Paris: Perrin, 2006)

Schreiner, Peter, 'Ritterspiele in Byzanz', *Jahrbuch der österreichischen Byzantinistik*, 46 (1996), 227–41

——, 'Turnier. D. Byzanz', *Lexikon des Mittelalters*, 8 (1997), col. 1118

Schrijver, H. de, *De oude landmaten in Vlaanderen* (Brussels: Simon Stevin, 1968)

Scott, Margaret, *Medieval Dress and Fashion* (London: British Library, 2007)

——, *Fashion in the Middle Ages* (Los Angeles: The J. Paul Getty Museum, 2011)

Serrano, Florence, 'La ficcionalizacion de Diego de Valera en la literature borgoñona', in *Mosén Diego de Valera: Entre las armas y las letras*, ed. by Cristina Moya García (Woodbridge: Tamesis, 2014), pp. 53–62

Seyffert, Oskar, *The Dictionary of Classical Mythology, Religion, Literature and Art* (New York: Gramercy Books, 1995)

Shcheglov, D. A., 'Ptolemy's System of Seven Climata and Eratosthenes' Geography', *Geographia Antiqua*, 13 (2004/6), 21–37

Sherb, Victor, 'The Tournament of Power: Public Combat and Social Inferiority in Late Medieval England', *Studies in Medieval and Renaissance History*, n.s. 12 (1991), 105–28

Silver, Larry, *Marketing Maximilian: The Visual Ideology of a Holy Roman Emperor* (Princeton, NJ: Princeton University Press, 2008)

Small, Graeme, *Late Medieval France* (Basingstoke: Palgrave Macmillan, 2009)

——, 'Tales from the Chamber: The *Cent Nouvelles nouvelles* between Burgundy and Luxembourg', in *The Cent Nouvelles nouvelles (Burgundy-Luxembourg-France, 1458–c. 1550): Text and Paratext, Codex and Context*, ed. by Graeme Small, Texte, Codex & Contexte, 23 (Turnhout: Brepols, 2023), pp. 267–90

Smith, Catherine, 'The "Poor Man's Mart": History and Archaeology of Goats in Scotland', *Tayside and Fife Archaeological Journal*, 28 (2022), 81–99

Smith, Geri L., *The Medieval French Pastourelle Tradition: Poetic Motivations and Generic Transformations* (Gainesville: University Press of Florida, 2009)

Sollbach, Gerhard E., 'Engelbert I. Graf von der Mark (*vor 1249–†1277)', in *Die Grafen von der Mark: Ein biographisches Handbuch*, ed. by Dietrich Thier and Stefan Pätzold (Witten: Bergischer Verlag, 2021), pp. 69–84

Sommé, Monique, *Isabelle de Portugal, duchesse de Bourgogne: une femme au pouvoir au XVe siècle*, Histoire et civilisations (Villeneuve d'Ascq: Presses Universitaires du Septentrion, 1998)

——, 'De Flandre en Navarre: le voyage d'Agnès de Clèves, nièce de Philippe le Bon et princesse de Navarre, en 1439', in *L'itinéraire des seigneurs (XIVe–XVIe siècles): actes du colloque international de Lausanne et Romainmôtier, 29 novembre–1er décembre 2001*, ed. by Agostino Paravicini Bagliani and Eva Pibiri (Lausanne: Cahiers lausannois d'histoire médiévale, 2003), pp. 173–92

Spufford, Peter, *Handbook of Medieval Exchange* (London: Offices of the Royal Historical Society, 1986)

——, *Money and its Use in Medieval Europe* (Cambridge: Cambridge University Press, 1988)

——, 'Moneys of Account in the Burgundian Netherlands', in *Monnaies de compte et monnaies réelles: Pays-Bas méridionaux et principauté de Liège au Moyen Âge et aux Temps modernes*, ed. by Johan van Heesch, Jean-Marie Yante and Hannes Lowagie, Études numismatiques, 5 (Louvain-la-Neuve: Marcel Hoc, 2016), pp. 137–62

Stanesco, Michel, *Jeux d'errance du chevalier medieval: Aspects ludiques de la fonction guerrière dans la littérature du Moyen Âge flamboyant* (Leiden: Brill, 1988)

Stein, Robert, 'An Urban Network in the Medieval Low Countries. A Cultural Approach', in *Networks, Regions and Nations: Shaping Identities in the Low Countries, 1300–1650*, ed. by Robert Stein and Judith Pollmann (Leiden: Brill, 2010), pp. 43–71

——, *Magnanimous Dukes and Rising States: The Unification of the Burgundian Netherlands, 1380–1480* (Oxford: Oxford University Press, 2017)

Stevenson, John H., *Heraldry in Scotland*, 2 vols (Glasgow: James Maclehose and Sons, 1914)

Stevenson, Katie, *Chivalry and Knighthood in Scotland, 1424–1513* (Woodbridge: Boydell Press, 2006)

——, 'Jurisdiction, Authority and Professionalisation: The Officers of Arms in Late Medieval Scotland', in *The Herald in Late Medieval Europe*, ed. by Katie Stevenson (Woodbridge: Boydell Press, 2006), pp. 41–66

Stirnemann, Patricia, 'Barthélemy d'Eyck et les *Très Riches Heures*', in *Dans l'atelier de Michel Pastoureau*, ed. by Claudia Rabel, François Jacquesson and Laurent Hablot (Tours: Presses Universitaires François-Rabelais, 2021), pp. 290–3

Strubel, Armand, 'Les pas d'armes: le tournoi entre le romanesque et le théâtral', in *Théâtre et spectacles hier et aujourd'hui: Moyen âge et Renaissance. Actes du 115e Congrès National des Sociétés Savantes (Avignon, 1990). Section d'histoire médiévale et de philologie* (Paris: Éditions du CTHS, 1991), pp. 273–84

Sturgeon, Justin, *Text and Image in René d'Anjou's* Livre des tournois*: Constructing Authority and Identity in Fifteenth-Century Court Culture*, 3 vols (Woodbridge: Boydell Press, 2022)

Szkilnik, Michelle, *Jean de Saintré: une carrière chevaleresque au XVe siècle* (Geneva: Droz, 2003)

——, 'Mise en mots, mise en images: *Le Livre des Faits du bon chevalier Jacques de Lalain*', *Ateliers (Cahiers de la Maison de Recherche, Université Charles de Gaulle–Lille 3)*, 30 (2003), 75–87

——, 'Que lisaient les chevaliers du XVe siècle? Le témoignage du *Pas du Perron Fée*', *Le Moyen Français*, 68 (2011), 103–14

——, 'Vraies et fausses réminiscences arthuriennes dans *Clériadus et Méliadice*', in *Arthur après Arthur: La matière arthurienne tardive en dehors du roman arthurien*, ed. by Christine Ferlampin-Acher (Rennes: Presses Universitaires de Rennes, 2017), pp. 27–40

Taylor, Craig, *Chivalry and the Ideals of Knighthood in France during the Hundred Years War* (Cambridge: Cambridge University Press, 2013)

Taylor, Jane H. M., 'Image as Reception: Antoine de la Sale's *Le petit Jehan de Saintré*', in *Literary Aspects of Courtly Culture*, ed. by Donald Maddox and Sara Sturm-Maddox (Cambridge: D. S. Brewer, 1994), pp. 265–79

——, '"Une gente pastourelle": René d'Anjou, Louis de Beauvau et le Pas d'armes de la bergère', in *René d'Anjou, écrivain et mécène (1409–1480)*, ed. by Florence Bouchet (Turnhout: Brepols, 2011), pp. 197–208

——, 'La fête comme performance, le livre comme document: le Pas de Saumur', in *Les arts et les lettres en Provence au temps du roi René*, ed. by Chantal Connochie-Bourgne and Valérie Gontero-Lauze (Aix-en-Provence: Presses Universitaires de Provence, 2013), pp. 233–41

Terjanian, Pierre, ed., *The Last Knight: The Art, Armor, and Ambition of Maximilian I* (New York: The Metropolitan Museum of Art, 2019)

Titterton, James, '*Por pris et por enor*: Ideas of Honour as Reflected in the Medieval Tournament', in *The Medieval Tournament as Spectacle: Tourneys, Jousts and Pas d'Armes, 1100–1600*, ed. by Alan V. Murray and Karen Watts (Woodbridge: Boydell Press, 2020), pp. 44–61

Torre y Franco-Romero, Lucas de, 'Mosén Diego de Valera. Su vida y sus obras', *Boletín de la Real Academia de Historia*, 64 (1914), 50–83

Torres Fontes, Juan, *Estudio sobre la 'Cronica de Enrique IV' del Dr. Galindez de Carvajal* (Murcia: Seminario de Historia de la Universidad de Murcia, 1946)

Truffi, Riccardo, *Giostre e cantori de giostre* (Rocca S. Casciano: L. Capelli, 1945)

Vale, Juliet, *Edward III and Chivalry: Chivalric Society and its Context, 1270–1350* (Woodbridge: Boydell Press, 1982)

Vale, Malcolm, *War and Chivalry: Warfare and Aristocratic Culture in England, France and Burgundy* (London: Duckworth and Co., 1981)

——, 'Le tournoi dans la France du Nord, l'Angleterre et les Pays-Bas (1280–1440)', in *Théâtre et spectacles hier et aujourd'hui: Moyen âge et Renaissance. Actes du 115e Congrès National des Sociétés Savantes (Avignon, 1990). Section d'histoire médiévale et de philologie* (Paris: Éditions du CTHS, 1991), pp. 263–71

Van Anrooij, Wim, 'Nine Worthies', in *Encyclopedia of the Medieval Chronicle online*, ed. by Graeme Dunphy and Cristian Bratu (Leiden: Brill, 2014, article first published online in 2016)

Van Buren, Anne, and Roger Wieck, *Illuminating Fashion: Dress in the Art of Medieval France and the Netherlands, 1325–1515* (London: GILES, 2011)

Van den Abeele, Andries, *Het ridderlijk gezelschap van de Witte Beer: Steekspelen in Brugge tijdens de late Middeleeuwen* (Bruges: Walleyn, 2000)

——, 'De Wapenpas van de Betoverde Burcht, voorbode van de machtsgreep door Karel de Stoute', *Handelingen van het Genootschap voor Geschiedenis te Brugge*, 146 (2009), 93–139

——, 'Karel de Stoute en de Wapenpas van de Betoverde Burcht', *Vlaanderen: Kunsttijdschrift*, 58 (2009), 98–103

Van den Neste, Évelyne, *Tournois, joutes, pas d'armes dans les villes de Flandre à la fin du Moyen Âge (1300–1486)* (Paris: École des Chartes, 1996)

Vander Linden, Herman, *Itinéraires de Philippe le Bon, duc de Bourgogne (1419–1467) et de Charles, comte de Charolais (1433–1467)* (Brussels: Commission Royale d'Histoire, 1940)

Vannieuwenhuyze, Bram, 'Brussel, de ontwikkeling van een middeleeuwse stedelijke ruimte' (unpublished PhD dissertation, Universiteit Gent, 2008)

Van Uytven, Raymond, 'Flämische Belfriede und sudniederländische Bauwerke im Mittelalter: Symbol und Mythos', in *Information, Kommunikation und Selbstdarstellung in Mittelalterlichen Gemeinden*, ed. by Alfred Haverkamp and Elisabeth Müller-Luckner (Munich: Oldenbourg Verlag, 1998), pp. 125–60

Vaughan, Richard, *Philip the Bold: The Formation of the Burgundian State* (London/New York: Longman, 1962)

——, *Philip the Good: The Apogee of Burgundy* (London/New York: Longman, 1970)

——, *Charles the Bold: The Last Valois Duke of Burgundy* (London/New York: Longman, 1973)

Verwerft, Bert, 'De goede ridder onder de loep genomen: Een detailanalyse van de militaire compagnie van Jacques de Lalaing ten tijde van de Gentse opstand (1453)', *Handelingen van de Maatschappij voor Geschiedenis en Oudheidkunde te Gent*, 75 (2022), 3–76

Viallon, Marina, 'The Tournament Saddle', in *The Medieval Tournament as Spectacle: Tourneys, Jousts and Pas d'Armes, 1100–1600*, ed. by Alan V. Murray and Karen Watts (Woodbridge: Boydell Press, 2020), pp. 99–119

——, 'Never-Ending Chivalry: Tournaments in Renaissance France from Charles VIII to Louis XIII', in *Tournaments: A Thousand Years of Chivalry*, ed. by Stefan Krause (London: Thomas del Mar, 2022), pp. 101–15

——, 'Les tournois à la cour de France à la Renaissance' (unpublished PhD dissertation, École Pratique des Hautes Études, Paris, 2023)

Watanabe O'Kelly, Helen, 'Tournaments and their Relevance for Warfare in the Early Modern Period', *European History Quarterly*, 20 (1990), 451–63

——, *Triumphal Shews: Tournaments at German-Speaking Courts in Their European Context, 1560–1730* (Berlin: Gebr. Mann Verlag, 1992)

Weitbrecht, Julia, 'In der *Forest aventureuse*: Jagd, Initiation und Aventiure in erzählhistorischer Perspektive', in *Aventiure: Ereignis und Erzählung*, ed. by Michael Schwarzbach-Dobson and Franziska Wenzel (Berlin: Erich Schmidt Verlag, 2022), pp. 109–25

Werner, Matthias, and Bénédicte Zimmermann, 'Beyond Comparison: *Histoire Croisée* and the Challenge of Reflexivity', *History and Theory*, 45.1 (2006), 30–50

Westphal, Romina, 'Tapestry and Gender: On the Hero and Heroine Motifs and the Construction of Burgundian Identity' (unpublished PhD dissertation, University of Leeds, 2019)

Whitbread, Rachael E., 'Tournaments, Jousts and Duels: Formal Combats in England and France, circa 1380–1440' (unpublished PhD dissertation, University of York, 2013)

Whiteley, Mary, 'The Château of the Dukes of Anjou at Saumur, 1360–1480', in *Anjou: Medieval Art, Architecture and Archaeology*, ed. by John McNeill and Daniel Prigent (Leeds: Maney, 2003), pp. 247–58

——, and Jacqueline Mongellaz, 'Le faste d'une résidence princière à la fin du XIVe et au tout début du XVe siècle', in *Le château et la citadelle de Saumur: architecture du pouvoir*, ed. by Emmanuel Litoux and Éric Cron (Paris: Société française d'archéologie, 2010), pp. 91–107

Wiesflecker, Hermann, *Kaiser Maximilian I: Das Reich, Österreich und Europa an der Wende zu Neuzeit*, 5 vols (Munich: Oldenbourg, 1971–86)

Wijsman, Hanno, *Luxury Bound: Illustrated Manuscript Production and Noble and Princely Book Ownership in the Burgundian Netherlands (1400–1550)* (Turnhout: Brepols, 2010)

——, 'The Visual Tradition of the *Book of the Deeds of Jacques de Lalaing*', in *A Knight for the Ages: Jacques de Lalaing and the Art of Chivalry*, ed. by Elizabeth Morrison (Los Angeles: The J. Paul Getty Museum, 2018), pp. 107–20

Zeikowitz, Richard E., *Homoeroticism and Chivalry: Discourses of Male Same-Sex Desire in the Fourteenth Century* (New York/Basingstoke: Palgrave Macmillan, 2003)

Zotz, Thomas, 'Adel, Bürgertum und Turniere in Deutschen Städten', in *Das ritterliche Turnier im Mittelalter: Beiträge zu einer vergleichenden Formen- und Verhaltensgeschichte des Rittertums*, ed. by Josef Fleckenstein (Göttingen: Vandenhoeck & Ruprecht, 1985), pp. 450–99

Zucchi, Mario, *I governatori dei principi reali di Savoia* (Turin: Tipografia del Collegio degli Artigianelli, 1925)

Zypkin, Denis, 'Der Codex *Le pas de Samur* (Fr. F. XIV,4): Zur kodikologischen Erforsching des Papiers', in *Das Turnierbuch für René d'Anjou (Le Pas de Saumur): Vollständige Faksimile-Ausgabe im Originalformat der Handschrift Codex Fr. F. XIV Nr. 4 der Russischen Nationalbibliothek in St. Petersburg*, ed. by Natalia Elagina *et al.* (Graz: Akademische Druck und Verlagsanstalt, 1998), pp. 43–51

Web-based sources

Collecta <https://www.collecta.fr>

Cour de France <https://cour-de-france.fr/>

Diccionario biográfico electrónico of the Real Academia de la Historia <https://dbe.rah.es>

Dictionnaire du Moyen Français (1330–1500) <http://zeus.atilf.fr/dmf/>

Dictionnaire historique de la Suisse <https://hls-dhs-dss.ch>

Itinéraire de Charles. Les lieux de séjour du roi (1483–1498), Paris, Cour de France.fr, 2020. Données publiées par Boris Bove d'après l'itinéraire édité par E. Petit <https://cour-de-france.fr/article5776.html>

The Online Froissart, version 1.5, ed. by Peter Ainsworth and Godfried Croenen (Sheffield: HRIOnline, 2013) <http://www.dhi.ac.uk/onlinefroissart>

Oxford Dictionary of National Biography <https://www.oxforddnb.com/>

Prosopographia Curiae Burgundicae <http://www.prosopographia-burgundica.org/>

Index

This index lists both subject matter and names. Concerning the former, all concepts and broad topics mentioned in the text have been listed and, where needed, subdivided into sub-entries or even sub-sub-entries. As for the latter, all the names of people, places, institutions, *pas d'armes* and other chivalric events, battles/wars and literary/historiographical works mentioned in the Sources and Essays have been included, except for those that are mentioned in the bibliography. Names of modern scholars and of persons and places mentioned only in the footnotes to the texts of the Sources have not been listed in this index. Names of fictional characters are listed under the entry for the text in which they appear and alphabetised by their first name. All kings, queens, princes and princesses are also alphabetised under their first name; all other individuals are listed under their surname. Titles, dignitics and lordships are indicated when they are mentioned in the text. When a person is referred to in the text only by his or her title (e.g. the duke of Cleves), rather than by his or her name, this has been cross-referenced in the index to the name (e.g. Johann of Cleves). Where, despite every effort made to identify as many persons as possible, no name can be supplied for them, they have been referred to by their title, dignity, lordship or function as mentioned in the sources (e.g. Tellan, Madame de, and Carenchon, *Maître*).